| Business Insights | Companies in Assignments |
|---|---|
| **Business Insight:** Accounting Quality<br>**Business Insight:** Warren Buffett on MD&A<br>**Business Insight:** Warren Buffett on Audit Committees | Abercrombie & Fitch, Apple, Briggs & Stratton, Cisco, Colgate-Palmolive, Dell, Disney, DuPont, Enron, Ford, General Mills, General Motors, Hewlett-Packard, Intel, JetBlue, Kimberly-Clark, Kraft Foods, McDonald's, Merck, Motorola, Nokia, Nordstrom, Procter & Gamble, Staples, Starbucks, 3M, TJX Companies |
| **Business Insight:** How Much Debt is Reasonable?<br>**Business Insight:** Apple's Market-to-Book Values<br>**Business Insight:** Insights into Apple's Statement of Cash Flows | Abercrombie & Fitch, Apple, Comcast, Dell, Harley-Davdison, Home Depot, Johnson & Johnson, Nike, Procter & Gamble, Staples, Starbucks, Target, 3M, TJX Companies, Verizon, Wal-Mart |
| **Business Insight:** Accounting Scandals and Improper Adjustments | Allstate Insurance, Coldwater Creek, Costco, Foot Locker, Harley-Davdison, Lowe's |
| **Business Insight:** Home Depot's ROE and RNOA<br>**Business Insight:** Tax Shield<br>**Business Insight:** Tax Rates for Computing NOPAT<br>**Business Insight:** Home Depot's NOPM<br>**Business Insight:** Home Depot's NOAT | Abercrombie & Fitch, Albertsons, Caterpillar, Comcast, CVS, The Gap, General Electric, Home Depot, Intel, Intuit, Lockheed Martin, Lowe's, McDonald's, Merck, Procter & Gamble, Southwest Airlines, Staples, Target, 3M, TJX Companies, UPS, Valero Energy, Verizon, Walgreen, Wal-Mart |
| **Business Insight:** Ratios Across Industries<br>**Business Insight:** Cisco's Revenue Recognition<br>**Business Insight:** Disney's Revenue Recognition<br>**Business Insight:** Pfizer's R&D<br>**Business Insight:** Pfizer's Restructuring<br>**Business Insight:** Pro Forma Income and Managerial Motives | Abercrombie & Fitch, Advanced Micro Devices, Albertsons, Altria, Amazon.Com, Bank of America, Barnes & Noble, Benihana, Boeing, Bristol-Myers Squibb, Centex, Cisco, Dow Chemical, Dow Jones, FedEx, The Gap, General Electric, Intel, Intuit, John Deere, Johnson Controls, The Limited, Lucent, Merck, MTV, Oracle, Pfizer, RealMoney.Com, Target, TheStreet.Com, Time-Warner, Xerox |
| **Business Insight:** Sears' Cookie Jar<br>**Business Insight:** WorldCom and Improper Cost Capitalization | Abbott Laboratories, Abercrombie & Fitch, Best Buy, Carnival, Caterpillar, Colgate-Palmolive, Deere & Co., Dow Chemical, General Electric, Harley-Davidson, Hewlett-Packard, Intel, Intuit, Kaiser Aluminum, Kraft, Microsoft, Oracle, Procter & Gamble, Rohm and Haas, Sharper Image, Texas Instruments, 3M, TJ Maxx, W.W. Grainger |
| **Business Insight:** Pitfalls of Acquired Growth<br>**Business Insight:** Determining the Parent Company in an Acquisition | Abbott Laboratories, American Express, Amgen, AT&T, Berkshire Hathaway, CNA Financial, Caterpillar, Coca Cola, DuPont, General Mills, Hewlett-Packard, Merck, MetLife, Pfizer, Procter & Gamble, Wells Fargo |
| **Business Insight:** Verizon's Zero Coupon Debt | Boston Scientific, Bristol-Myers Squibb, Comcast, CVS, Deere & Co., Ford, General Mills, Pepsi Bottling Group, Southwest Airlines |
| | Abercrombie & Fitch, Altria, AT&T, Best Buy, Bristol-Myers Squibb, Cisco, Caterpillar, Fortune Brands, IMS Health, JetBlue, Lucent Technologies, Merck, Procter & Gamble, Viacom |
| **Business Insight:** Why GM's Bonds Were Rated Junk | Abercrombie & Fitch, American Express, Best Buy, Continental Airlines, Dow Chemical, DuPont, FedEx, Ford, Fortune Brands, Harley-Davidson, Nike, Nordstrom, Staples, Verizon, Xerox, YUM! Brands |
| **Business Insight:** What is eBay's Operating Cash Flow?<br>**Business Insight:** Tyco Buys Operating Cash Flow | Abbott Laboratories, Abercrombie & Fitch, Best Buy, CBS, General Mills, Harley-Davidson, Intel, Intuit, Nike, Oracle, Pfizer, Southwest Airlines, TAP Pharmaceutical Products, Whole Foods Market, Xerox |
| **Business Insight:** Analysts' Earnings Forecasts | Abbott Laboratories, Abercrombie & Fitch, CVS, Harley-Davidson, Intel, Oracle, PepsiCo, Starbucks, 3M |
| **Business Insights** | **Companies in Assignments** |

Third Edition

# Financial Accounting for MBAs

PETER D. EASTON

JOHN J. WILD

ROBERT F. HALSEY

MARY LEA McANALLY

Cambridge
BUSINESS PUBLISHERS

To my daughters, Joanne and Stacey
   —PDE

To my wife Gail and children, Kimberly, Jonathan, Stephanie, and Trevor;
and my parents, Leonard and Mary
   —JJW

To my wife Ellie and children, Grace and Christian
   —RFH

To my husband Brittan, my children Loic, Maclean, Quinn and Kay, and my
understanding co-authors LK and CW.
   —MLM

## Cambridge Business Publishers

FINANCIAL ACCOUNTING FOR MBAs, Third Edition, by Peter D. Easton,
John J. Wild, Robert F. Halsey, and Mary Lea McAnally.

**ISBN 0-9787279-3-2**

**Bookstores & Faculty:** to order this book, contact the company via email
**customerservice@cambridgepub.com** or call 800-619-6473.

**Retail Customers & Students:** to order this book, please visit the book's website and order
directly online.

**For permission** to use material from this text, contact the company via email
**permissions@cambridgepub.com.**

Printed in the United States of America.
10 9 8 7 6 5 4 3 2 1

The combined skills and expertise of Easton, Wild, Halsey, and McAnally create the ideal team to author the first new financial accounting textbook for MBAs in more than a generation. Their collective experience in award-winning teaching, consulting, and research in the area of financial accounting and analysis provides a powerful foundation for this innovative textbook.

**PETER D. EASTON** is an expert in accounting and valuation and holds the Notre Dame Alumni Chair in Accountancy in the Mendoza College of Business. Professor Easton's expertise is widely recognized by the academic research community and by the legal community. Professor Easton is a Principal in Chicago Partners LLC, where he serves as a consultant on accounting and valuation issues.

Professor Easton holds undergraduate degrees from the University of Adelaide and the University of South Australia. He holds a graduate degree from the University of New England and a PhD in Business Administration (majoring in accounting and finance) from the University of California, Berkeley.

Professor Easton's research on corporate valuation has been published in the *Journal of Accounting and Economics, Journal of Accounting Research, The Accounting Review, Contemporary Accounting Research, Review of Accounting Studies,* and *Journal of Business Finance and Accounting.* Professor Easton has served as an associate editor for 11 leading accounting journals and he is currently an associate editor for the *Journal of Accounting Research, Contemporary Accounting Research, Journal of Business Finance and Accounting,* and *Journal of Accounting, Auditing, and Finance.* He is an editor of the *Review of Accounting Studies.*

Professor Easton has held appointments at the University of Chicago, the University of California at Berkeley, Ohio State University, Macquarie University, the Australian Graduate School of Management, the University of Melbourne, and Nyenrode University. He is the recipient of numerous awards for excellence in teaching and in research. Professor Easton regularly teaches accounting analysis and security valuation to MBAs. In addition, Professor Easton has taught managerial accounting at the graduate level.

**JOHN J. WILD** is professor of accounting and the Robert and Monica Beyer Distinguished Professor at the University of Wisconsin at Madison. He previously held appointments at Michigan State University and the University of Manchester in England. He received his BBA, MS, and PhD from the University of Wisconsin.

Professor Wild teaches courses in accounting and analysis at both the undergraduate and graduate levels. He has received the Mabel W. Chipman Excellence-in-Teaching Award, the departmental Excellence-in-Teaching Award, and the MBA Teaching Excellence Award from the 2003 and 2005 graduation class at the University of Wisconsin. He also received the Beta Alpha Psi and Salmonson Excellence-in-Teaching Award from Michigan State University. Professor Wild is a past KPMG Peat Marwick National Fellow and is a prior recipient of fellowships from the American Accounting Association and the Ernst & Young Foundation.

Professor Wild is an active member of the American Accounting Association and its sections. He has served on several committees of these organizations, including the Outstanding Accounting Educator Award, Wildman Award, National Program Advisory, Publications, and Research Committees. Professor Wild is author of several best-selling books. His research articles on financial accounting and analysis appear in *The Accounting Review, Journal of Accounting Research, Journal of Accounting and Economics, Contemporary Accounting Research, Journal of Accounting, Auditing & Finance, Journal of Accounting and Public Policy, Journal of Business Finance and Accounting, Auditing: A Journal of Theory and Practice,* and other accounting and business journals. He is past associate editor of *Contemporary Accounting Research* and has served on editorial boards of several respected journals, including *The Accounting Review* and the *Journal of Accounting and Public Policy.*

**ROBERT F. HALSEY** is an associate professor at Babson College. He received his MBA and PhD from the University of Wisconsin. Prior to obtaining his PhD he worked as the chief financial officer (CFO) of a privately held retailing and manufacturing company and as the vice president and manager of the commercial lending division of a large bank.

Professor Halsey teaches courses in financial and managerial accounting at both the graduate and undergraduate levels, including a popular course in financial statement analysis for second year MBA students. He has also taught numerous executive education courses for large multinational companies through Babson's School of Executive Education as well as for a number of stock brokerage firms in the Boston area. He is regarded as an innovative teacher and has been recognized for outstanding teaching at both the University of Wisconsin and Babson College. He is the recipient of an Ernst & Young Fellowship and is a member of the Beta Gamma Sigma and Phi Eta Sigma honor societies.

Professor Halsey's research interests are in the area of financial reporting, including firm valuation, financial statement analysis, and disclosure issues. He is the coauthor of *Financial Statement Analysis,* published by McGraw-Hill/Irwin, and has publications in *Advances in Quantitative Analysis of Finance and Accounting, The Journal of the American Taxation Association, Issues in Accounting Education, The Portable MBA in Finance and Accounting* (3rd ed.), the *CPA Journal, AICPA Professor/Practitioner Case Development Program,* and in other accounting and analysis journals. He has also developed exam preparation materials for the CFA examination and administers numerous CFA review courses in the Northeast.

**MARY LEA McANALLY** is an associate professor and Mays Research Fellow at Texas A&M University. Professor McAnally teaches financial accounting and reporting in the MBA and Executive programs. Her casebook (co-authored with D. Eric Hirst), "Cases in Financial Reporting" is published by Prentice Hall. She has received several faculty-determined teaching awards including the Beazley Award and the Trammell/CBA Foundation Award. She has also received numerous student-initiated awards including the MBA Teaching Award at UT (1995, 2000, 2001, 2002), the MBA Association Distinguished Faculty Award at A&M (2003 and 2004) and the Class of 1997 Award for Outstanding and Memorable Faculty Member (2002). In 2006, the A&M Association of Former Students granted Professor McAnally the Distinguished Achievement Award.

Professor McAnally's research interests include accounting and disclosure of stock options, and accounting for risk. She has published articles in the leading academic journals including *Journal of Accounting and Economics, Journal of Accounting Research, The Accounting Review, Contemporary Accounting Research,* and *Journal of Accounting Auditing and Finance.* In 2005, Professor McAnally received the Mays Business School Research Achievement Award. She works closely with doctoral students and has served on numerous doctoral committees. She was the director of A&M's doctoral program until 2007.

Professor McAnally is active in the American Accounting Association and its FARS section and has been involved with the New Faculty Consortium, the FASB conference, several doctoral consortia and the KPMG PhD project.

Professor McAnally holds an undergraduate degree from the University of Alberta and a PhD from Stanford University. She is a Chartered Accountant (Canada) and Certified Internal Auditor. Prior to arriving at A&M in 2002, Professor McAnally held positions at University of Texas at Austin, University of Calgary, University of Alberta, Canadian National Railways, and Dunwoody and Company Chartered Accountants.

**W**elcome to the Third Edition of *Financial Accounting for MBAs*. Our main goal in writing this book was to satisfy the needs of today's business manager by providing the most contemporary, engaging, and user-oriented textbook available. This book is the product of extensive market research including focus groups, market surveys, class tests, manuscript reviews, and interviews with faculty from across the country. We are grateful to students and faculty who used the First and Second Editions and whose feedback greatly benefited this Third Edition.

## TARGET AUDIENCE

*Financial Accounting for MBAs* is intended for use in full-time, part-time, executive, and evening MBA programs that include a financial accounting course as part of the curriculum, and one in which managerial decision making and analysis are emphasized. This book easily accommodates mini-courses lasting several days as well as extended courses lasting a full semester.

## INNOVATIVE APPROACH

*Financial Accounting for MBAs* is managerially oriented and focuses on the most salient aspects of accounting. It teaches MBA students how to read, analyze, and interpret financial accounting data to make informed business decisions. This textbook makes financial accounting **engaging, relevant,** and **contemporary.** To that end, it consistently incorporates **real company data,** both in the body of each module and throughout assignment material.

## FLEXIBLE STRUCTURE

The MBA curricula, instructor preferences, and course lengths vary across colleges. Accordingly and to the extent possible, the 13 modules that make up *Financial Accounting for MBAs* were designed independently of one another. This modular presentation enables each college and instructor to "customize" the book to best fit the needs of their students. Our introduction and discussion of financial statements constitute Modules 1, 2, and 3. Module 4 presents the analysis of financial statements with an emphasis on analysis of operating profitability. Modules 5 through 10 highlight major financial accounting topics including assets, liabilities, equity, and off-balance-sheet financing. Module 11 explains adjusting and forecasting financial statements. Module 12 introduces simple valuation models. Module 13 concludes with a comprehensive case on Kimberly-Clark and acts as a capstone for the course.

### Transaction Analysis and Statement Preparation

Instructors differ in their coverage of accounting mechanics. Some focus on the effects of transactions on financial statements using the balance sheet equation format. Others include coverage of journal entries and T-accounts. We accommodate both teaching styles in this Third Edition. Specifically, Module 2 provides an expanded discussion of the effects of transactions using our innovative financial statement effects template. Emphasis is on the analysis of Apple's summary transactions, which concludes with the preparation of its financial statements. Module 3, which is entirely optional, allows an instructor to drill down and focus on accounting mechanics: journal entries and T-accounts. It illustrates accounting for numerous transactions, including those involving accounting adjustments. It concludes with the preparation of a trial balance and the four financial statements, again using Apple. This detailed transaction analysis uses the same financial statement effects template, with journal entries and T-accounts highlighted in the margin. Thus, these two modules accommodate the spectrum of teaching styles—instructors can elect to use either or both modules to suit their preferences, and their students are not deprived of any information as a result of that selection.

## Flexibility for Courses of Varying Lengths

Many instructors have approached us to ask about suggested class structures based on courses of varying length. To that end, we provide the following table of possible course designs:

| | 15 Week Semester-Course | 10 Week Quarter-Course | 6 Week Mini-Course | 1 Week Intensive-Course |
|---|---|---|---|---|
| **MODULE 1** Financial Accounting for MBAs | Week 1 | Week 1 | Week 1 | Day 1 (Module 1 and either Module 2 or Module 3) |
| **MODULE 2** Introducing Financial Statements and Transaction Analysis | Week 2 | Week 2 | Week 2 | |
| **MODULE 3** Constructing Financial Statements and Analyzing Transactions | Week 2 (optional) | Week 2 (optional) | Week 2 (optional) | |
| **MODULE 4** Constructing and Reporting Financial Statements | Weeks 3 and 4 | Week 3 | Week 3 | Day 2 |
| **MODULE 5** Reporting and Analyzing Operating Income | Week 5 | Week 4 | Skim | Skim |
| **MODULE 6** Reporting and Analyzing Operating Assets | Week 6 | Week 5 | Week 4 | Day 3 |
| **MODULE 7** Reporting and Analyzing Intercorporate Investments | Week 7 | Optional | Optional | Optional |
| **MODULE 8** Reporting and Analyzing Nonowner Financing | Week 8 | Week 6 | Week 5 | Day 4 |
| **MODULE 9** Reporting and Analyzing Owner Financing | Week 9 | Week 7 | Week 6 | Day 5 |
| **MODULE 10** Reporting and Analyzing Off-Balance-Sheet Financing | Weeks 10 and 11 | Week 8 | Optional | Optional |
| **MODULE 11** Adjusting and Forecasting Financial Statements | Week 12 | Week 9 | Optional | Optional |
| **MODULE 12** Analyzing and Valuing Equity Securities | Week 13 | Week 10 | Optional | Optional |
| **MODULE 13** Comprehensive Case | Week 14 | Optional | Optional | Optional |

# MANAGERIAL EMPHASIS

As MBA instructors, we recognize that the core MBA financial accounting course is not directed toward accounting majors. *Financial Accounting for MBAs* embraces this reality. This book highlights **financial reporting, analysis, interpretation,** and **decision making.** We incorporate the following **financial statement effects template** to train MBA students in understanding the economic ramifications of transactions and their impacts on all key financial statements. This analytical tool is a great resource for

MBA students in learning accounting and applying it to their future courses and careers. Each transaction is identified in the "Transaction" column. Then, the dollar amounts (positive or negative) of the financial statement effects are recorded in the appropriate balance sheet or income statement columns. The template also reflects the statement of cash flow effects (via the cash column) and the statement of stockholders' equity effects (via the contributed capital and earned capital columns). The earned capital account is immediately updated to reflect any income or loss arising from each transaction (denoted by the arrow line from net income to earned capital). This template is instructive as it reveals the financial impacts of transactions, and it provides insights into the effects of accounting choices.

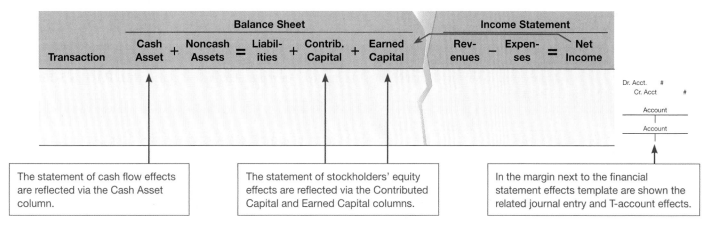

Tomorrow's MBA graduates must be skilled in using financial statements to make business decisions. These skills often require application of ratio analyses, benchmarking, forecasting, valuation, and other aspects of financial statement analysis to decision making. Furthermore, tomorrow's MBA graduates must have the skills to go beyond basic financial statements and to interpret and apply nonfinancial statement disclosures, such as footnotes and supplementary reports. This book, therefore, emphasizes real company data, including detailed footnote and other management disclosures, and shows how to use this information to make managerial inferences and decisions. This approach makes financial accounting interesting and relevant for all MBA students.

# INNOVATIVE PEDAGOGY

*Financial Accounting for MBAs* includes special features specifically designed for the MBA student.

## Focus Companies for Each Module

Each module's content is explained through the accounting and reporting activities of real companies. To that end, each module incorporates a "focus company" for special emphasis and demonstration. The enhanced instructional value of focus companies comes from the way they engage MBA students in real analysis and interpretation. Focus companies were selected based on the industries that MBA students typically enter upon graduation.

## Focus Company by Module

| MODULE 1 | Berkshire Hathaway | MODULE 8 | Verizon |
|---|---|---|---|
| MODULE 2 | Apple | MODULE 9 | Accenture |
| MODULE 3 | Apple | MODULE 10 | Southwest Airlines |
| MODULE 4 | Home Depot | MODULE 11 | Procter & Gamble |
| MODULE 5 | Pfizer | MODULE 12 | Johnson & Johnson |
| MODULE 6 | Cisco | MODULE 13 | Kimberly-Clark |
| MODULE 7 | Google | APPENDIX B | Starbucks |

## Real Company Data Throughout

Market research and reviewer feedback tell us that one of instructors' greatest frustrations with other MBA textbooks is their lack of real company data. We have gone to great lengths to incorporate real company data throughout each module to reinforce important concepts and engage MBA students. We engage nonaccounting MBA students specializing in finance, marketing, management, real estate, operations, and so forth, with companies and scenarios that are relevant to them. For representative examples, **SEE PAGES 4-5; 5-5; 6-11.**

## Managerial and Decision Making Orientation

One primary goal of a MBA financial accounting course is to teach students the skills needed to apply their accounting knowledge to solving real business problems and making informed business decisions. With that goal in mind, Managerial Decision boxes in each module encourage students to apply the material presented to solving actual business scenarios. For representative examples, **SEE PAGES 5-15; 6-12; 8-23.**

## Research Insights for MBAs

Academic research plays an important role in the way business is conducted, accounting is performed, and students are taught. It is important for students to recognize how modern research and modern business practice interact. Therefore, we periodically incorporate relevant research to help students understand the important relation between research and modern business. For representative examples, **SEE PAGES 4-18; 5-26; 11-7.**

## Mid-Module and Module-End Reviews

Financial accounting can be challenging—especially for MBA students lacking business experience or previous exposure to business courses. To reinforce concepts presented in each module and to ensure student comprehension, we include mid-module and module-end reviews that require students to recall and apply the financial accounting techniques and concepts described in each module. For representative examples, **SEE PAGES 4-14; 8-6; 11-9.**

## Excellent, Class-Tested Assignment Materials

Excellent assignment material is a must-have component of any successful textbook (and class). We went to great lengths to create the best assignments possible from contemporary financial statements. In keeping with the rest of the book, we used real company data extensively. We also ensured that assignments reflect our belief that MBA students should be trained in analyzing accounting information to make business decisions, as opposed to working on mechanical bookkeeping tasks. Assignments encourage students to analyze accounting information, interpret it, and apply the knowledge gained to a business decision. There are five categories of assignments: **Discussion Questions**, **Mini Exercises**, **Exercises**, **Problems**, and **Cases**. For representative examples, **SEE PAGES 4-34; 6-45; 10-31.**

# THIRD EDITION CHANGES

Based on classroom use and reviewer feedback, a number of substantive changes have been made in the third edition to further enhance the MBA students' experiences:

### General Revisions Made to Each Module

- All Focus Company financial statements are new or have been updated to reflect each company's latest available filings
- All assignments using real company data are new or have been updated to reflect each company's latest available filings
- New Case section added to the end of each module's assignments
- Expanded financial statement effects template to include T-accounts and journal entries in margin
- Revised financial statement effects template makes the relation between the Income Statement and Balance Sheet more transparent to students

▥ Added many new assignments requiring comparisons across competing companies and industries

▥ Appendix B on the statement of cash flows is now included in the book

## Module 1—Financial Accounting for MBAs

▥ Updated focus company—Berkshire Hathaway

▥ Reorganized module

- Moved the demand and supply of information section to the beginning of the module
- Moved planning, financing, investing and operating activities discussions to the relevant financial statement sections
- Simplified ROE and RNOA disaggregation section
- Streamlined competitive analysis/environment section

▥ Provided motivation to financial reporting issues with probing questions

▥ Simplified financial statements and linkages by removing advanced accounts

▥ Added new appendix on accessing financial information using EDGAR

## Module 2—Introducing Financial Statements and Transaction Analysis

▥ New focus company—Apple

▥ Expanded statement of cash flows discussion to include intuition for adjustments

▥ Expanded the financial statement effects template discussion with additional transactions

▥ Linked the financial statement effects template to financial statement preparation

▥ Added new section on non-financial sources of information, including 10-K and analyst reports

▥ New assignments address cash flow issues, including comparisons across competitors

## Module 3—Constructing Financial Statements and Analyzing Transactions

▥ New focus company (links with Module 2)—Apple

▥ New, OPTIONAL module covers journalizing transactions, accounting adjustments and the accounting cycle

▥ Added illustrations using the template for the following range of transactions:

- capital contributions
- purchase and sale of inventories
- capital distributions
- accounting adjustments

- dividend payments
- depreciation
- revenue recognition
- closing process

▥ Additional assignments include those requiring journal entries and adjustments

## Module 4—Analyzing and Interpreting Financial Statements

▥ New focus company—Home Depot

▥ Streamlined module and simplified layout

- ROE disaggregation focuses on RNOA; details of the nonoperating return moved to Appendix 4A
- Tied liquidity and solvency analysis to an intuitive explanation of leverage

▥ Analyzed Lowes in the module reviews to offer competitive comparisons

▥ New Appendix 4B has in-depth discussion of nonoperating return, including computations

## Module 5—Reporting and Analyzing Operating Income

▥ New focus company—Pfizer

▥ Revised layout to systematically walk-through Pfizer's income statement and to frame the discussion

▥ New focus on operating and nonoperating components

▥ Streamlined foreign exchange discussion to focus on income statement effects; explanation of balance sheet effects moved to Module 9

▥ Expanded discussion and illustration of income taxes

▥ Added new explanation and example for unearned revenues

▥ Moved EPS explanation to the body of the text

### Module 6—Reporting and Analyzing Operating Assets

- New focus company—Cisco Systems
- Expanded sections on analysis implications for receivables, inventories and PPE
- Added expanded ratio analysis and interpretation of operating assets
- New mid-module reviews using Cisco's competitors: Lucent, Avaya, and Hewlett-Packard

### Module 7—Reporting and Analyzing Intercorporate Investments

- New focus company—Google
- Streamlined explanation of equity method investments using Abbott Labs investment in TAP Pharmaceuticals
- New mid-module reviews using Google's competitor: Yahoo!
- Revised subsidiary IPO section
- Added new section on discontinued operations
- Revised derivative discussion (in Appendix 7C) using Southwest Airlines

### Module 8—Reporting and Analyzing Nonowner Financing

- Updated focus company—Verizon Communications
- Added new discussion on accounts payable and warranties
- Added new illustration and explanation on Verizon's redemption of MCI debt
- Revised discussions on credit ratings and cost of debt sections

### Module 9—Reporting and Analyzing Owner Financing

- New focus company—Accenture
- Added new comprehensive income section, including foreign currency translations
- Added new section on restricted stock compensation
- Revised stock option discussion to reflect new accounting standards
- Revised section on equity carve-outs and convertible securities

### Module 10—Reporting and Analyzing Off-Balance-Sheet Financing

- New focus company—Southwest Airlines
- Revised sections on both leasing and pensions
- New section on special purpose entities (SPEs) and the consolidation of those entities under FIN 46(R)

### Module 11—Adjusting and Forecasting Financial Statements

- Updated focus company—Procter & Gamble
- Revised presentation of parsimonious forecasting and added new illustration

### Module 12—Analyzing and Valuing Equity Securities

- Updated focus company—Johnson & Johnson
- Revised mid-module reviews and explanations

### Module 13—Comprehensive Case

- Updated focus company—Kimberly-Clark
- Revised all illustrations using current data and companies
- Expanded several analyses and interpretations to enhance its use as a 'capstone' module

## SUPPLEMENT PACKAGE

### For Instructors

**Electronic Solutions Manual:** Created by the authors, the *Solutions Manual* contains complete solutions to all the assignment material in the text.

**PowerPoint:** The PowerPoint slides outline key elements of each module.

**Electronic Test Bank:** Written by the authors, the test bank includes multiple-choice items, matching questions, short essay questions, and problems.

**Website:** All instructor materials are accessible via the book's Website (password protected) along with other useful links and information. www.cambridgepub.com

## For Students

**Student Solutions Manual:** Created by the authors, the student solutions manual contains all solutions to the even-numbered assignment materials in the textbook. This is a restricted item that is only available to students after their instructor has authorized its purchase. ISBN 0-9787279-4-0

**Website:** Useful links are available to students free of charge on the book's website. www.cambridgepub.com

# ACKNOWLEDGMENTS

All three editions of this book benefited greatly from the valuable feedback of focus group attendees, reviewers, students, and colleagues. We are extremely grateful to them for their help in making this project a success.

Ashiq Ali, *University of Texas—Dallas*
Steve Baginski, *University of Georgia*
Eli Bartov, *New York University*
Dan Bens, *University of Arizona*
Denny Beresford, *University of Georgia*
Mark Bradshaw, *Harvard University*
John Briginshaw, *Pepperdine University*
Mary Ellen Carter, *University of Pennsylvania*
Agnes Cheng, *University of Houston*
Carol Dee, *University of Colorado—Denver*
Elizabeth Demers, *INSEAD*
Vicki Dickinson, *University of Florida*
Jeffrey Doyle, *University of Utah*
Thomas Dyckman, *Cornell University*
James Edwards, *University of South Carolina*
John Eichenseher, *University of Wisconsin*
Gerard Engeholm, *Pace University*
Mark Finn, *Northwestern University*
Richard Frankel, *Washington University*
Julia Grant, *Case Western Reserve University*
Karl Hackenbrack, *Vanderbilt University*
Michelle Hanlon, *University of Michigan*
Al Hartgraves, *Emory University*
Carla Hayn, *University of California—Los Angeles*
Frank Heflin, *Florida State University*
Clayton Hock, *Miami University*
Judith Hora, *University of San Diego*
Court Huber, *University of Texas—Austin*
Richard Hurley, *University of Connecticut*
Ross Jennings, *University of Texas—Austin*
Sanjay Kallapur, *Purdue University*
Saleha Khumawala, *University of Houston*
Ron King, *Washington University*
Krishna Kumar, *George Washington University*
Lisa Kutcher, *University of Oregon*
Brian Leventhal, *University of Illinois—Chicago*
Joshua Livnat, *New York University*
Barbara Lougee, *University of California—Irvine*
Luann Lynch, *University of Virginia—Darden*

Greg Miller, *Harvard University*
Melanie Mogg, *University of Minnesota*
Steve Monahan, *INSEAD*
Dennis Murray, *University of Colorado—Denver*
Sandeep Nabar, *Oklahoma State University*
Doron Nissim, *Columbia University*
Susan Parker, *Santa Clara University*
Stephen Penman, *Columbia University*
Mark Penno, *University of Iowa*
Kathy Petroni, *Michigan State University*
Christine Petrovits, *New York University*
Kirk Philipich, *University of Michigan—Dearborn*
Morton Pincus, *University of California—Irvine*
Grace Pownall, *Emory University*
Ram Ramanan, *University of Notre Dame*
Susan Riffe, *Southern Methodist University*
Andrew Schmidt, *Columbia University*
Chandra Seethamraju, *Washington University*
Stephen Sefcik, *University of Washington*
Kenneth Shaw, *University of Missouri*
Paul Simko, *University of Virginia—Darden*
Pam Smith, *Northern Illinois University*
Sri Sridharan, *Northwestern University*
Charles Stanley, *Baylor University*
Jens Stephan, *University of Cincinnati*
Phillip Stocken, *Dartmouth College*
K.R. Subramanyam, *University of Southern California*
Gary Taylor, *University of Alabama*
Sam Tiras, *University of Buffalo*
Mark Vargus, *University of Texas—Dallas*
James Wallace, *Claremont Graduate School*
Charles Wasley, *University of Rochester*
Greg Waymire, *Emory University*
Edward Werner, *Drexel University*
Jeffrey Williams, *University of Michigan*
David Wright, *University of Michigan*
Michelle Yetman, *University of California—Davis*
Tzachi Zack, *Washington University*
Xiao-Jun Zhang, *University of California—Berkeley*

In addition, we are extremely grateful to George Werthman and the entire team at Cambridge Business Publishers for their encouragement, enthusiasm, and guidance. Their market research, editorial development, and promotional efforts surpassed our expectations. We have had a very positive textbook authoring experience with each edition of this book thanks, in large part, to our publisher.

*Peter*          *John*          *Bob*          *Mary Lea*

March 2007

# BRIEF CONTENTS

# CONTENTS

## MODULE **Eight**

# Reporting and Analyzing Nonowner Financing 8-1

## MODULE **Nine**

# Reporting and Analyzing Owner Financing 9-1

## MODULE **Ten**

# Reporting and Analyzing Off-Balance-Sheet Financing 10-1

# Financial Accounting for MBAs

## LEARNING OBJECTIVES

**LO1** Identify and discuss the users and suppliers of financial information. (p. 1-5)

**LO2** Identify and explain the four financial statements, and define the accounting equation. (p. 1-8)

**LO3** Explain the basics of profitability analysis. (p. 1-16)

**LO4** Describe business analysis within the context of a competitive environment. (p. 1-18)

**LO5** Describe the accounting principles that guide preparation of financial statements. (p. 1-23)

## BERKSHIRE HATHAWAY

Berkshire Hathaway is a holding company. It owns numerous businesses that pursue diverse activities. In 2005, Berkshire Hathaway reported total assets of $198 billion, stockholders' equity of $92 billion, sales of $82 billion, net profit of $8.5 billion, operating cash flow of $9.5 billion, and employed 192,000 workers.[1]

The legendary Warren Buffett, the 'Sage of Omaha,' who studied under the renowned Benjamin Graham (a founder of modern value-investing), manages Berkshire Hathaway. Buffett's investment philosophy is to acquire and hold companies over the long run. His acquisition criteria, taken from Berkshire Hathaway's annual report, follow:

1. Large purchases (at least $75 million of pretax earnings).
2. Demonstrated consistent earning power (future projections are of *no* interest to us, nor are 'turnaround' situations).
3. Businesses earning good returns on equity while employing little or no debt.
4. Management in place (we can't supply it).
5. Simple businesses (if there's lots of technology, we won't understand it).
6. An offering price (we don't want to waste our time or that of the seller by talking, even preliminarily, about a transaction when price is unknown).

At least three of Buffett's six criteria relate to financial performance. First, he seeks businesses with large and consistent earning power. Buffett is

---

[1] Berkshire Hathaway's 2005 balance sheet includes an atypical third column of numbers labeled "pro forma" (which means "as if") that reflect a stock transaction that happened after the year end. Berkshire Hathaway provides the pro forma numbers so that financial statement readers can see the effect of the transaction and make apples-to-apples comparisons in the future. The balance sheet numbers we discuss in this module are the 2005 numbers that reflect only events that happened in 2005.

Getty Images

not only looking for consistent earnings, but earnings that are measured according to accounting policies that closely mirror the underlying economic performance of the business.

Second, Buffett focuses on "businesses earning good returns on equity," defined as net income divided by average stockholders' equity: "Our preference would be to reach our goal by directly owning a diversified group of businesses that generate cash and consistently earn above-average returns" (Berkshire Hathaway annual report). For management to earn a good return on equity, it must focus on both net income (financial performance) and equity (financial condition).

Third, Buffett values companies based on their ability to generate consistent earnings and cash. He focuses on *intrinsic value,* which he defines in each annual report as follows:

> Intrinsic value is an all-important concept that offers the only logical approach to evaluating the relative attractiveness of investments and businesses. Intrinsic value can be defined simply: It is the discounted value of the cash that can be taken out of a business during its remaining life.

The discounted value Buffett describes is the present (today's) value of the cash flows the company expects to generate in the future. Cash is generated when companies are well managed and operate profitably and efficiently.

Warren Buffett provides some especially useful investment guidance in his Chairman's letter from the Berkshire Hathaway annual report:

> Three suggestions for investors: First, beware of companies displaying weak accounting. If a company still does not expense options, or if its pension assumptions are fanciful, watch out. When managements take the low road in aspects that are visible, it is likely they are following a similar path behind the scenes. There is seldom just one cockroach in the kitchen.

> Second, unintelligible footnotes usually indicate untrustworthy management. If you can't understand a footnote or other managerial explanation, it's usually because the CEO doesn't want you to. Enron's descriptions of certain transactions still baffle me.

*(Continued on next page)*

*(Continued from previous page)*

Finally, be suspicious of companies that trumpet earnings projections and growth expectations. Businesses seldom operate in a tranquil, no-surprise environment, and earnings simply don't advance smoothly (except, of course, in the offering books of investment bankers).

This book will explain Buffett's references to stock option accounting and pension assumptions as well as a host of other accounting issues that affect interpretation and valuation of companies' financial performance. We will analyze and interpret the footnotes, which Buffett views as crucial to quality financial reporting and analysis. Our philosophy is simple: we must understand the intricacies and nuances of financial reporting to become critical readers and users of financial reports for company analysis and valuation. Financial statements tell a story, a business story. The task is to understand that story, to analyze and interpret it in the context of competing stories, and to apply the knowledge gleaned to business decisions.

Sources: Berkshire Hathaway *2005 10-K Report*, Berkshire Hathaway *2001–2005 Annual Reports*.

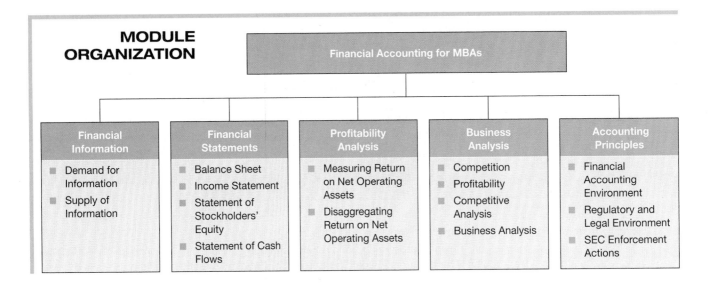

# REPORTING ON BUSINESS ACTIVITIES

To effectively manage a company or infer whether it is well managed, we must understand the company's fundamental business activities. The information system called *financial accounting* helps us understand these business activities. This system reports on a company's performance and financial condition, and conveys executive management's privileged information and insights.

As managers, financial accounting information helps us to evaluate potential future strategies and ascertain the effectiveness of present and past strategies. It improves the soundness of our investment decisions, such as how to allocate resources across alternative investment projects and whether to invest additional resources in existing product lines or divisions. As managers, we also use financial accounting information to prepare client proposals, analyze the effectiveness of production processes, and evaluate the performance of management teams.

As investors, financial accounting information helps us determine which companies' stock to purchase or sell. Yet, before it is used to make decisions, the financial accounting information must be scrutinized and sometimes adjusted. This is accomplished, in part, by analyzing information contained in footnotes to companies' financial reports to determine the quality of reported figures and to make any necessary adjustments.

More generally, financial accounting satisfies the needs of different groups of users. Within firms, the *functioning* of this information system involves application of accounting standards to produce financial reports. Effectively using this information system involves making judgments, assumptions, and estimates based on data contained in the financial reports. The greatest value we derive from this system as users of financial information is the insight we gain into the business activities of the company under analysis.

To effectively analyze and use accounting information, we must consider the business context in which the information is created—see Exhibit 1.1. Without exception, all companies *plan* business activities, *finance* those activities, *invest* in those activities, and then engage in *operating* activities. Firms conduct all these activities while confronting *business forces*, including market constraints and competitive pressures. Financial accounting provides crucial input in advance of strategic planning. It also provides information about the relative success of those plans, which can be used to take corrective action or make new operating, investing, and financing decisions.

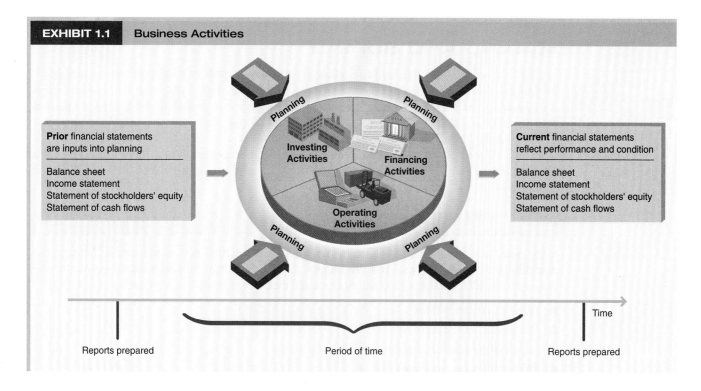

**EXHIBIT 1.1     Business Activities**

Prior financial statements are inputs into planning

Balance sheet
Income statement
Statement of stockholders' equity
Statement of cash flows

Investing Activities
Financing Activities
Operating Activities
Planning

Current financial statements reflect performance and condition

Balance sheet
Income statement
Statement of stockholders' equity
Statement of cash flows

Reports prepared          Period of time          Reports prepared          Time

Exhibit 1.1 depicts the business activities for a typical company. The outer (green) ring is the planning process that reflects the overarching goals and objectives of the company within which strategic decisions are made. Those strategic decisions involve company financing, asset management, and daily operations. Apple, Inc., the focus company in Modules 2 and 3, provides the following description of its business strategy in its annual report:

> **Business Strategy**   The Company is committed to bringing the best personal computing and music experience to students, educators, creative professionals, businesses, government agencies, and consumers through its innovative hardware, software, peripherals, services, and Internet offerings. The Company's business strategy leverages its unique ability, through the design and development of its own operating system, hardware, and many software applications and technologies, to bring to its customers new products and solutions with superior ease-of-use, seamless integration, and innovative industrial design. The Company believes continual investment in research and development is critical to facilitate innovation of new and improved products and technologies. Besides updates to its existing line of personal computers and related software, services, peripherals, and networking solutions, the Company continues to capitalize on the convergence of digital consumer electronics and the computer by creating innovations like the iPod and iTunes Music Store. The Company's strategy also includes expanding its distribution network to effectively reach more of its targeted customers and provide them a high-quality sales and after-sales support experience.

A company's *strategic* (or *business*) *plan* reflects how it plans to achieve its goals and objectives. A plan's success depends on an effective analysis of market demand and supply. Specifically, a company must assess demand for its products and services, and assess the supply of its inputs (both labor and capital). The plan must also include competitive analyses, opportunity assessments, and consideration of business threats.

Historical financial statements provide valuable insight into the success of a company's strategic plan, and are an important input to the planning process. Financial statements highlight those portions of the strategic plan that proved to be effective and, thus, warrant additional capital investment. They also reveal areas that are less effective, and provide valuable information that aids in development of remedial action.

Once strategic adjustments are planned and implemented, the resulting financial statements provide input into the planning process for the following year; and this process recycles. Understanding a company's strategic plan helps focus our analysis of financial statements by placing them in proper context.

# FINANCIAL ACCOUNTING INFORMATION: DEMAND AND SUPPLY

**LO1** Identify and discuss the users and suppliers of financial information.

Financial accounting information facilitates economic transactions and promotes efficient resource allocations. Demand for financial reporting has existed for centuries as a means to facilitate efficient contracting and risk-sharing. Decision makers and other stakeholders demand information on a company's past and prospective returns and risks. Companies are encouraged to supply such information to lower their costs of financing and to lower some less obvious costs such as political, contracting, and labor costs.

As with all goods, the supply of information depends on companies weighing the costs of disclosure against the benefits of disclosure. Regulatory agencies intervene in this process with various disclosure requirements that establish a minimum supply of information.

---

**BUSINESS INSIGHT** | **Accounting Quality**

In the bear market that followed the bursting of the dot.com bubble, and amid a series of corporate scandals such as Enron, Tyco, and WorldCom, Congress passed the *Sarbanes-Oxley Act,* often referred to as *SOX*. SOX sought to rectify perceived problems in accounting, including:

- Weak audit committees
- Non-independent auditors
- Limited management responsibility for accounting
- Deficient internal controls

Increased scrutiny of financial reporting and internal controls has had some success. A report by Glass, Lewis and Co., a corporate-governance research firm, shows that the number of financial restatements by publicly traded companies surged to a record 1,295 in 2005—which is one restatement for each 12 public companies, and more than triple the 2002 total, the year SOX passed. The Glass, Lewis and Co. report concluded that "when so many companies produce inaccurate financial statements, it seriously calls into question the quality of information that investors relied upon to make capital-allocation decisions" (**CFO.Com**, 2006). Bottom line: we must be critical readers of financial reports.

---

## Demand for Information

Demand for financial accounting information extends to numerous users that include:

- Managers and employees
- Investment analysts and information intermediaries
- Creditors and suppliers
- Shareholders and directors
- Customers and strategic partners
- Regulators and tax agencies
- Voters and their representatives

### Managers and Employees

For their own well-being and future earnings potential, managers and employees demand accounting information on the financial condition, profitability, and prospects of their companies. Managers and employees also demand comparative financial information on competing companies and other business opportunities. This permits them to conduct comparative analyses to benchmark company performance and condition.

Managers and employees also demand financial accounting information for use in compensation and bonus contracts that are tied to such numbers. The popularity of employee profit sharing and stock ownership plans has further increased demand for financial information. Other sources of demand include union contracts that link wage negotiations to accounting numbers and pension and benefit plans whose solvency depends on company performance.

### Investment Analysts and Information Intermediaries

Investment analysts and other information intermediaries such as financial press writers and business commentators are interested in predicting companies' future performance. Expectations about future profitability and the ability to generate cash impact the price of securities and a company's ability to borrow money at favorable terms. Financial reports reflect information about past performance and current resources available to companies. These reports also provide information on claims on those resources, including suppliers, creditors, lenders, and shareholders. This information allows analysts to make informed assessments about future financial performance and condition so they can provide stock recommendations or write commentaries.

### Creditors and Suppliers

Banks and other lenders demand financial accounting information to help determine loan terms, loan amounts, interest rates, and required collateral. Loan agreements often include contractual requirements, called **covenants**, that restrict the borrower's behavior in some fashion. For example, loan covenants might require the loan recipient to maintain minimum levels of working capital, retained earnings, interest coverage, and so forth to safeguard lenders. Covenant violations can yield technical default, enabling the creditor to demand early payment or other compensation.

Suppliers similarly demand financial information to establish credit sales terms and to determine their long-term commitment to supply-chain relations. Both creditors and suppliers use financial information to monitor and adjust their contracts and commitments with a debtor company.

### Shareholders and Directors

Shareholders and directors demand financial accounting information to assess the profitability and risks of companies, and to monitor the performance of their managers. Shareholders and others (including investment analysts, brokers, potential investors, etc.) look for information useful in their investment decisions. **Fundamental analysis** uses financial information to estimate company value and to form buy-sell stock strategies.

Both directors and shareholders use accounting information to evaluate managerial performance. Managers similarly use such information to request an increase in compensation and managerial power from directors. Outside directors are crucial to determining who runs the company, and these directors use accounting information to help make leadership decisions.

### Customers and Strategic Partners

Customers (both current and potential) demand accounting information to assess a company's ability to provide products or services as agreed and to assess the company's staying power and reliability. Strategic partners wish to estimate the company's profitability to assess the fairness of returns on mutual transactions and strategic alliances.

### Regulators and Tax Agencies

Regulators (such as the SEC, the Federal Trade Commission, and the Federal Reserve Bank) and tax agencies demand accounting information for tax policies, antitrust assessments, public protection, price setting, import-export analyses, and various other uses. Timely and reliable information is crucial to effective regulatory policy. Moreover, accounting information is often central to social and economic policy. For example, governments often grant monopoly rights to electric and gas companies serving specific areas in exchange for regulation over prices charged to consumers. These prices are mainly determined from accounting measures.

### Voters and their Representatives

Voters and their representatives to national, state, and local governments demand accounting information for policy decisions. The decisions can involve economic, social, taxation, and other initiatives. Voters and their representatives also use accounting information to monitor government spending. We have all heard of the $1,000 hammer type stories that government watchdog groups uncover while sifting through accounting data. Contributors to nonprofit organizations also demand accounting information to assess the impact of their donations.

## Supply of Information

In general, the quantity and quality of accounting information that firms provide are determined by managers' assessment of the benefits and costs of disclosure. Management releases information provided the benefits of disclosing that information outweigh the costs of doing so. Both *regulation* and *bargaining power* affect disclosure costs and benefits and thus play roles in determining the supply of accounting information.

Most areas of the world regulate the minimum levels of accounting disclosures. In the United States, publicly traded firms must file financial accounting information with the Securities Exchange Commission (SEC). The two main compulsory SEC filings are:

- Form **10-K**: the audited annual report that includes the four financial statements, discussed below, together with explanatory notes and the management's discussion and analysis of financial results.

- Form **10-Q**: the unaudited quarterly report that includes summary versions of the four financial statements and limited additional disclosures.

Forms 10-K and 10-Q are available electronically from the SEC Website (see Appendix 1A).

The minimum, regulated level of information is not the standard. Both the quantity and quality of information differ across companies and over time. We need only look at several annual reports to see considerable variance in the amount and type of accounting information supplied. For example, differences abound on disclosures for segment operations, product performance reports, and financing activities. Further, some stakeholders possess ample bargaining power to obtain accounting information for themselves. These typically include private lenders and major suppliers and customers.

### Benefits of Disclosure

The benefits of supplying accounting information extend to a company's capital, labor, input, and output markets. Companies must compete in these markets. For example, capital markets provide debt and equity financing; the better a company's prospects, the lower is its cost of capital (as reflected in lower interest rates or higher stock prices). The same holds for a company's recruiting efforts in labor markets and its ability to establish superior supplier-customer relations in the input and output markets.

A company's performance in these markets depends on success with its business activities *and* the market's awareness of that success. Companies reap the benefits of disclosure with good news information about their products, processes, management, and so forth. That is, there are real economic incentives for companies to disclose reliable (audited) accounting information enabling them to better compete in capital, labor, input, and output markets.

What inhibits companies from providing false or misleading good news? There are several constraints. An important constraint imposed by stakeholders is that of audit requirements and legal repercussions associated with inaccurate accounting information. Another relates to reputation effects from disclosures as subsequent events either support or refute earlier news.

### Costs of Disclosure

The costs of supplying accounting information include its preparation and dissemination, competitive disadvantages, litigation potential, and political costs. Preparation and dissemination costs can be substantial, but much of this cost is already borne by inside managers who need the same information for their own business decisions. The potential for information to yield competitive disadvantages is high. Companies are concerned that disclosures of their activities such as product or segment successes, strategic alliances or pursuits, technological or system innovations, and product or process quality improvements will harm their competitive advantages. Also, companies are frequently sued when disclosures create expectations that are not met. Highly visible companies often face political and public pressure, which creates "political costs." These companies often try to appear as if they do not generate excess profits. For example, government defense contractors, large software conglomerates, and oil companies are favorite targets of public scrutiny. Disclosure costs are higher for companies facing political costs.

A recent rule increased the cost of voluntary financial disclosures for all publicly traded companies. In August 2000, the SEC adopted Regulation FD, or Reg FD for short, to curb the practice of selective disclosure by public companies (called issuers by the SEC) to certain shareholders and financial analysts. In the past, many companies disclosed important information in meetings and conference calls that excluded individual shareholders. The goal of this rule is to even the playing field for all investors. Reg FD reads as follows: "Whenever an issuer discloses any material nonpublic information regarding that issuer, the issuer shall make public disclosure of that information . . . simultaneously, in the case of an intentional disclosure; and . . . promptly, in the case of a non-intentional disclosure." Reg FD increased disclosure costs and led some companies to curtail the supply of financial information to all users.

# FINANCIAL STATEMENTS

Companies use four financial statements to periodically report on business activities. These statements are the: balance sheet, income statement, statement of stockholders' equity, and statement of cash flows.

Exhibit 1.2 shows how these statements are linked across time. A balance sheet reports on a company's financial position at a *point in time*. The income statement, statement of stockholders' equity, and the statement of cash flows report on performance over a *period of time*. The three statements in the middle of Exhibit 1.2 (period-of-time statements) link the balance sheet from the beginning to the end of a period.

A one-year, or annual, reporting period is common and is called the *accounting, or fiscal, year.* Of course, firms prepare financial statements more frequently; semi-annual, quarterly, and monthly financial statements are common. *Calendar-year* companies have reporting periods beginning on January 1 and ending on December

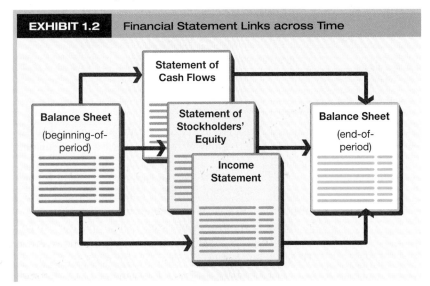

| EXHIBIT 1.2 | Financial Statement Links across Time |

31. Berkshire Hathaway is a calendar-year company. Some companies choose a fiscal year ending on a date other than December 31, such as when sales and inventory are low. For example, Best Buy's fiscal year-end is always near February 1, after the busy holiday season.

## Balance Sheet

A balance sheet reports a company's financial position at a point in time. The balance sheet reports the company's *resources* (*assets*), namely what the company owns. The balance sheet also reports the *sources* of asset financing. There are two ways a company can finance its assets. It can raise money from shareholders; this is *owner financing*. It can also raise money from banks or other creditors and suppliers; this is *nonowner financing*. This means that both owners and nonowners hold claims on company assets. Owner claims on assets are referred to as *equity* and nonowner claims are referred to as *liabilities* (or debt). Since all financing must be invested in something, we obtain the following basic relation: *investing equals financing*. This equality is called the **accounting equation,** which follows:

**LO2** Identify and explain the four financial statements, and define the accounting equation.

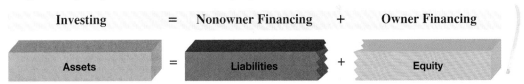

| **Investing** | = | **Nonowner Financing** | + | **Owner Financing** |
| Assets | = | Liabilities | + | Equity |

The accounting equation works for all companies at all points in time.

The balance sheet for **Berkshire Hathaway** is in Exhibit 1.3 (condensed). Refer to this balance sheet to verify the following amounts: assets = \$198,325 million, liabilities = \$106,025 million, and equity = \$92,300 million. Assets equal liabilities plus equity, which reflects the accounting equation: investing equals financing.

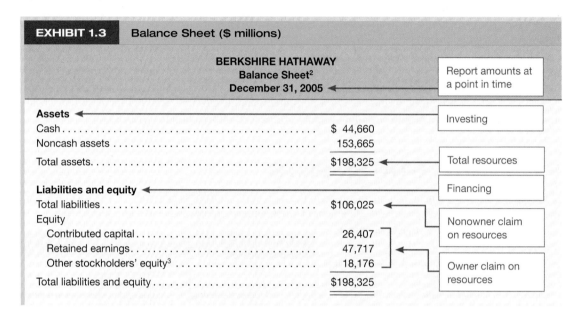

| **EXHIBIT 1.3** | Balance Sheet (\$ millions) | |
|---|---|---|
| **BERKSHIRE HATHAWAY** Balance Sheet[2] December 31, 2005 | | Report amounts at a point in time |
| **Assets** | | Investing |
| Cash | \$ 44,660 | |
| Noncash assets | 153,665 | |
| Total assets | \$198,325 | Total resources |
| **Liabilities and equity** | | Financing |
| Total liabilities | \$106,025 | Nonowner claim on resources |
| Equity | | |
| Contributed capital | 26,407 | |
| Retained earnings | 47,717 | |
| Other stockholders' equity[3] | 18,176 | Owner claim on resources |
| Total liabilities and equity | \$198,325 | |

## Investing Activities

Balance sheets are organized like the accounting equation. Investing activities are represented by company assets. These assets are financed by a combination of nonowner financing (liabilities) and owner financing (equity).

For simplicity, Berkshire Hathaway's balance sheet in Exhibit 1.3 categorizes assets into cash and noncash assets. Noncash assets consist of several asset categories (Module 2 explains the composition of noncash assets). These categories are listed in order of their nearness to cash. For example, companies own a category of assets called inventories. These are goods that the company intends to sell to its customers. Inventories are converted into cash when they are sold within a short period of time. Hence, they are classified as short-term assets. Companies also report a category called property, plant and equipment. This category includes a company's office buildings or manufacturing facilities. Property, plant and equipment assets will be held for an extended period of time and are, therefore, generally classified as long-term assets.

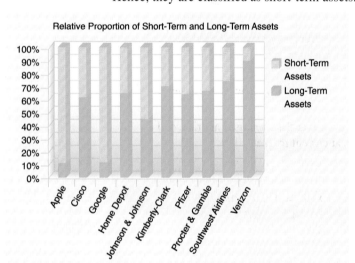

Relative Proportion of Short-Term and Long-Term Assets

Short-Term Assets

Long-Term Assets

The relative proportion of short-term and long-term assets is largely determined by a company's business model. This is evident in the graph to the left that depicts the relative proportion of short and long-term assets for several companies that we feature in this book. Companies such as Apple and Google require little investment in long-term assets. On the other hand, Verizon and Southwest Airlines require a large investment in long-term assets. Although managers can influence the relative amounts and proportion of assets, their flexibility is somewhat limited by the nature of their industries.

---

[2] Financial statement titles often begin with the word *consolidated*. This means that the financial statement includes a parent company and one or more subsidiaries, companies that the parent company owns. We discuss consolidation in Module 7.

[3] For Berkshire Hathaway, other stockholders' equity includes accumulated other comprehensive income and minority interests. These and other components of stockholders' equity are discussed in Modules 7 and 9.

## Financing Activities

Assets must be paid for, and funding is provided by a combination of owner and nonowner financing. Owner (or equity) financing includes resources contributed to the company by its owners along with any profit retained by the company. Nonowner (creditor or debt) financing is borrowed money. We distinguish financing sources for an important reason: borrowed money entails a legal obligation to repay amounts owed, and failure to repay amounts borrowed can result in severe consequences for the borrower. Equity financing entails no such legal obligation for repayment.

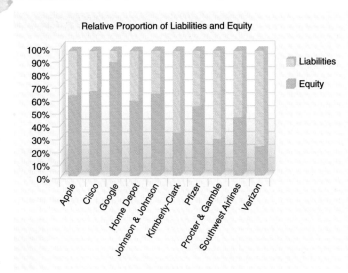

The relative proportion of nonowner (liabilities) and owner (equity) financing is largely determined by a company's business model. This is evident in the graph to the right; again citing many of the companies we feature as focus companies in this book.

Google is a relatively new company that is expanding into new markets. Its business model is, therefore, more risky than that of a more established company operating in relatively stable markets. Google, therefore, cannot afford to take on additional risk of higher nonowner financing levels. On the other hand, Proctor and Gamble competes in consumer goods markets that are largely predictable and stable. It can, therefore, operate with more nonowner financing.

Our discussion of investing and financing activities uses many terms and concepts that we explain later in the book. Our desire here is to provide a sneak preview into the interplay among financial statements, manager behavior, and economics. Some questions that we might have at this early stage regarding the balance sheet follow:

- Berkshire Hathaway reports $44.7 billion of cash on its 2005 balance sheet, which is 23% of total assets. Many investment-type companies such as Berkshire Hathaway and high-tech companies such as Cisco Systems carry high levels of cash. Why is that? Is there a cost to holding too much cash? Is it costly to carry too little cash?

- The relative proportion of short-term and long-term assets is largely dictated by companies' business models. Why is this the case? Why is the composition of assets on balance sheets for companies in the same industry similar? By what degree can a company's asset composition safely deviate from industry norms?

- What are the trade-offs in financing a company by owner versus nonowner financing? If nonowner financing is less costly, why don't we see companies financed entirely with borrowed money?

- How do shareholders influence the strategic direction of a company? How can long-term creditors influence strategic direction?

- Most assets and liabilities are reported on the balance sheet at their acquisition price, called *historical cost*. Would reporting assets and liabilities at current market values be more informative? What problems might reporting balance sheets using current market value cause?

Review the Berkshire Hathaway balance sheet summarized in Exhibit 1.3 and think about these questions. We provide answers for each of these questions as we progress through the book.

## Income Statement

An **income statement** reports on a company's performance over a period of time and lists amounts for revenues (also called sales) and expenses. Revenues less expenses yield the bottom-line net income amount.

**Berkshire Hathaway**'s income statement is in Exhibit 1.4. Refer to its income statement to verify the following: revenues = $81,663 million, expenses = $73,135 million, and net income = $8,528 million. Net income reflects the profit (also called earnings) to owners for that specific period.

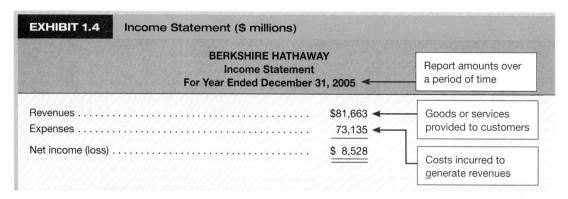

| EXHIBIT 1.4 | Income Statement ($ millions) |
|---|---|

**BERKSHIRE HATHAWAY**
**Income Statement**
**For Year Ended December 31, 2005** ← Report amounts over a period of time

| | |
|---|---|
| Revenues . . . . . . . . . . . . . . . . . . . . . . . . . . . . . . . . . . . . . . . . . | $81,663 ← Goods or services provided to customers |
| Expenses . . . . . . . . . . . . . . . . . . . . . . . . . . . . . . . . . . . . . . . . . . | 73,135 ← |
| Net income (loss) . . . . . . . . . . . . . . . . . . . . . . . . . . . . . . . . . . . | $ 8,528 ← Costs incurred to generate revenues |

Manufacturing and merchandising companies typically disclose the cost of goods sold (also called cost of sales) in the income statement. This measure is reported following revenues. It is also common to report the gross profit subtotal, which is revenues less the cost of goods sold. The company's remaining expenses are then reported below gross profit. This income statement layout follows:

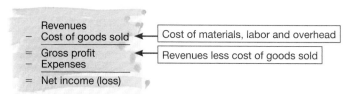

```
   Revenues
 − Cost of goods sold  ← Cost of materials, labor and overhead
 = Gross profit        ← Revenues less cost of goods sold
 − Expenses
 = Net income (loss)
```

## Operating Activities

Operating activities use company resources to produce, promote, and sell its products and services. These activities extend from input markets involving suppliers of materials and labor to a company's output markets involving customers of products and services. Input markets generate most *expenses* (or *costs*) such as inventory, salaries, materials, and logistics. Output markets generate *revenues* (or *sales*) to customers. Output markets also generate some expenses such as marketing and distributing products and services to customers. Net income arises when revenues exceed expenses. A loss occurs when expenses exceed revenues.

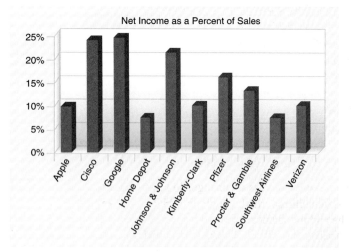

Net Income as a Percent of Sales

Differences exist in the relative profitability of companies across industries. Although effective management can increase the profitability of a company, business models play a large part in determining company profitability within an industry. These differences are highlighted in the graph (to the left) of net income as a percentage of sales for several companies we highlight in this book.

Home Depot operates in a mature industry with little ability to differentiate its products from those of its competitors. Hence, its net income as a percentage of sales is low. Southwest Airlines faces a different kind of problem: having competitors that are desperate and trying to survive. Profitability will not return to the transportation industry until weaker competitors are no longer protected by bankruptcy courts. At the other end of the spectrum are Cisco and Google. Both are dominant in their industries with products protected by patent laws. Their profitability levels are more akin to that of monopolists.

As a sneak preview, we might consider the following questions regarding the income statement:

- Assume that a company sells a product to a customer who promises to pay in 30 days. Should the seller recognize the sale when it is made or when cash is collected?

- When a company purchases a long-term asset such as a building, its cost is reported on the balance sheet as an asset. Should a company, instead, record the cost of that building as an expense when it is acquired? If not, how should a company report the cost of that asset over the course of its useful life?

▨ Manufacturers and merchandisers report the cost of a product as an expense when the product sale is recorded. How might we measure the costs of a product that is sold by a merchandiser? By a manufacturer?

▨ If an asset, such as a building, increases in value, that increase in value is not reported as income until the building is sold, if ever. What concerns arise if we record increases in asset values as part of income, when measurement of that increase is based on appraised values?

▨ Employees commonly earn wages that are yet to be paid at the end of a particular period. Should their wages be recognized as an expense in the period that the work is performed, or when the wages are paid?

▨ Companies are not allowed to report profit on transactions relating to their own stock. That is, they don't report income when stock is sold, nor do they report an expense when dividends are paid to shareholders. Why is this the case?

Review the Berkshire Hathaway income statement summarized in Exhibit 1.4 and think about these questions. We provide answers for each of these questions as we progress through the book.

---

**RESEARCH INSIGHT**    **Are Earnings Important?**

A recent study asked top finance executives of publicly traded companies to *rank the three most important measures to report to outsiders.* The study reports that:

> "[More than 50% of] CFOs state that earnings are the most important financial metric to external constituents . . . this finding could reflect superior informational content in earnings over the other metrics. Alternatively, it could reflect myopic managerial concern about earnings. The emphasis on earnings is noteworthy because cash flows continue to be the measure emphasized in the academic finance literature."

The study also reports that CFOs view year-over-year earnings to be of critical importance to outsiders. Why is that? The study provides the following insights.

> "CFOs note that the first item in a press release is often a comparison of current quarter earnings with four quarters lagged quarterly earnings . . . CFOs also mention that while analysts' forecasts can be guided by management, last year's quarterly earnings number is a benchmark that is harder, if not impossible, to manage after the 10-Q has been filed with the SEC . . . Several executives mention that comparison to seasonally lagged earnings numbers provides a measure of earnings momentum and growth, and therefore is a useful gauge of corporate performance."

Thus, are earnings important? To the majority of finance chiefs surveyed, the answer is a resounding yes. (Source: Graham, et al., *Journal of Accounting and Economics,* 2005)

---

## Statement of Stockholders' Equity

The **statement of stockholders' equity**, or simply *statement of equity,* reports on changes in key types of equity over a period of time. For each type of equity the statement reports the beginning balance, a summary of the activity in the account during the year, and the ending balance. Berkshire Hathaway's statement of stockholders' equity is in Exhibit 1.5. During the recent period, its equity changed due to share issuances and income reinvestment. Berkshire Hathaway classifies these changes into three categories:

▨ Contributed capital from stockholders' net contributions to the company

▨ Retained earnings over the life of the company minus all dividends ever paid

▨ Other (see footnote 3)

Contributed capital represents the cash the company received from the sale of stock to stockholders (also called shareholders), less any funds expended for the repurchase of stock. Retained earnings (also called *earned capital* or *reinvested capital*) represent the cumulative total amount of income that the company has earned and that has been retained in the business and not distributed to shareholders in the form of dividends. The change in retained earnings links consecutive balance sheets via the income statement.

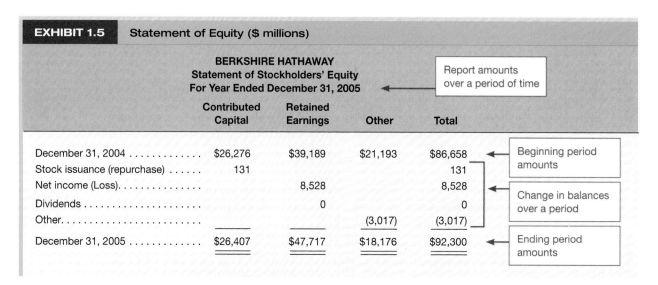

**EXHIBIT 1.5**  Statement of Equity ($ millions)

**BERKSHIRE HATHAWAY**
**Statement of Stockholders' Equity**
**For Year Ended December 31, 2005**

Report amounts over a period of time

| | Contributed Capital | Retained Earnings | Other | Total | |
|---|---|---|---|---|---|
| December 31, 2004 . . . . . . . . . . . . . | $26,276 | $39,189 | $21,193 | $86,658 | Beginning period amounts |
| Stock issuance (repurchase) . . . . . . | 131 | | | 131 | |
| Net income (Loss). . . . . . . . . . . . . . | | 8,528 | | 8,528 | Change in balances over a period |
| Dividends . . . . . . . . . . . . . . . . . . . . | | 0 | | 0 | |
| Other. . . . . . . . . . . . . . . . . . . . . . . | | | (3,017) | (3,017) | |
| December 31, 2005 . . . . . . . . . . . . | $26,407 | $47,717 | $18,176 | $92,300 | Ending period amounts |

For Berkshire Hathaway, its recent year's retained earnings increases from $39,189 million to $47,717 million. This increase of $8,528 million is explained by net income of $8,528 million and no payment of dividends. (Ending retained earnings = Beginning retained earnings + Net income − Dividends; we discuss this relation further in Module 2).

## Statement of Cash Flows

The **statement of cash flows** reports the change (either an increase or a decrease) in a company's cash balance over a period of time. The statement reports on cash inflows and outflows from operating, investing, and financing activities over a period of time. Berkshire Hathaway's statement of cash flows is in Exhibit 1.6. Its cash balance increased by $1,233 million in the recent period. Of this increase in cash, operating activities generated an $9,446 million cash inflow, investing activities reduced cash by $13,841 million, and financing activities yielded a cash inflow of $5,628 million.

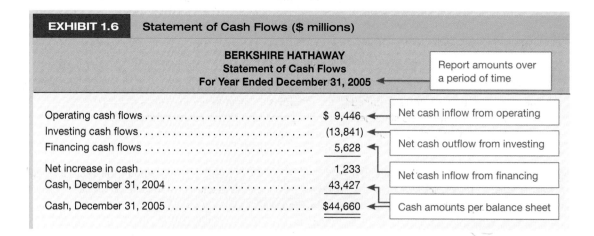

**EXHIBIT 1.6**  Statement of Cash Flows ($ millions)

**BERKSHIRE HATHAWAY**
**Statement of Cash Flows**
**For Year Ended December 31, 2005**

Report amounts over a period of time

| | | |
|---|---|---|
| Operating cash flows . . . . . . . . . . . . . . . . . . . . . . . . . . . . . | $ 9,446 | Net cash inflow from operating |
| Investing cash flows. . . . . . . . . . . . . . . . . . . . . . . . . . . . . . | (13,841) | Net cash outflow from investing |
| Financing cash flows . . . . . . . . . . . . . . . . . . . . . . . . . . . . . | 5,628 | Net cash inflow from financing |
| Net increase in cash. . . . . . . . . . . . . . . . . . . . . . . . . | 1,233 | |
| Cash, December 31, 2004 . . . . . . . . . . . . . . . . . . . . . . . | 43,427 | |
| Cash, December 31, 2005 . . . . . . . . . . . . . . . . . . . . . . . | $44,660 | Cash amounts per balance sheet |

Berkshire Hathaway's operating cash flow of $9,446 million does not equal its $8,528 million net income. Generally, a company's net cash flow for a period does *not* equal its net income for the period. This is due to timing differences between when revenue and expense items are recognized on the income statement and when cash is received and paid. (We discuss this concept further in subsequent modules.)

Both cash flow and net income numbers are important for business decisions. Each is used in security valuation models, and both help users of accounting reports understand and assess a company's past, present, and future business activities.

As a sneak preview, we might consider the following questions regarding the statement of cash flows:

- What is the usefulness of companies providing the statement of cash flows? Do the balance sheet and income statement provide sufficient cash flow information?

- What types of information are disclosed in the statement of cash flows and why are they important?

- What kinds of activities are reported in each of the operating, investing and financing sections of the statement of cash flows? How is this information useful?

- Is it important for a company to report net cash inflows (positive amounts) relating to operating activities over the longer term? What are the implications if operating cash flows are negative for an extended period of time?

- Why is it important to know the composition of a company's investment activities? What kind of information might we look for? Are positive investing cash flows favorable?

- Is it important to know the sources of a company's financing activities? What questions might that information help us answer?

- How might the composition of operating, investing and financing cash flows change over a company's life cycle?

- Is the bottom line increase in cash flow the key number? Why or why not?

Review the Berkshire Hathaway statement of cash flows summarized in Exhibit 1.6 and think about these questions. We provide answers for each of these questions as we progress through the book.

## Financial Statement Linkages

The four financial statements are linked within and across periods—see Exhibit 1.2.

- The income statement and the balance sheet are linked via retained earnings. For Berkshire Hathaway, the $8,528 million increase in retained earnings (reported on the balance sheet) equals its net income (reported on the income statement). Berkshire Hathaway did not pay dividends this year.

- Retained earnings, contributed capital, and other equity balances appear both on the statement of stockholders' equity and the balance sheet.

- The statement of cash flows is linked to the income statement as net income is a component of operating cash flow. The statement of cash flows is also linked to the balance sheet as the change in the balance sheet cash account reflects the net of cash inflows and outflows for the period.

Items that impact one financial statement ripple through the others. Linkages among the four financial statements are an important feature of the accounting system. We discuss this concept further and present a numerical example illustrating these linkages in Module 2.

| BUSINESS INSIGHT | Warren Buffett on Financial Reports |

"When Charlie and I read reports, we have no interest in pictures of personnel, plants or products. References to EBITDA [earnings before interest, taxes, depreciation and amortization] make us shudder—does management think the tooth fairy pays for capital expenditures? We're very suspicious of accounting methodology that is vague or unclear, since too often that means management wishes to hide something. And we don't want to read messages that a public relations department or consultant has turned out. Instead, we expect a company's CEO to explain in his or her own words what's happening." —Berkshire Hathaway **annual report**

# Information Beyond Financial Statements

Important financial information about a company is communicated to various decision makers through reports other than the four financial statements. These reports include the following:

- Management Discussion and Analysis (MD&A)
- Independent Auditor Report
- Financial statement footnotes
- Regulatory filings, including proxy statements and other SEC filings

We describe and explain the usefulness of these additional information sources throughout the book.

---

**MANAGERIAL DECISION**   **You Are the Product Manager**

There is often friction between investors' need for information and a company's desire to safeguard competitive advantages. Assume that you are a key-product manager at your company. Your department has test-marketed a potentially lucrative new product, which it plans to further finance. You are asked for advice on the extent of information to disclose about the new product in the MD&A section of the company's upcoming annual report. What advice do you provide and why? [Answer, p. 1-30]

---

## MID-MODULE REVIEW

The following financial information is from Allstate Corporation, a competitor of Berkshire Hathaway's GEICO Insurance, for the year ended December 31, 2005 ($ millions).

| | |
|---|---:|
| Cash, ending year | $ 313 |
| Cash flows from operations | 5,605 |
| Revenues | 35,383 |
| Stockholders' equity | 20,186 |
| Cash flows from financing | (555) |
| Total liabilities | 135,886 |
| Expenses | 33,618 |
| Noncash assets | 155,759 |
| Cash flows from investing | (5,151) |
| Net income | 1,765 |
| Cash, beginning year | 414 |

### Required

1. Prepare an income statement, balance sheet, and statement of cash flows for Allstate at December 31, 2005.
2. Compare the balance sheet and income statement of Allstate to those of Berkshire Hathaway in Exhibits 1.3 and 1.4. What differences are observed?

### Solution

1.

**ALLSTATE CORPORATION**
**Income Statement**
**For Year Ended December 31, 2005**

| | |
|---|---:|
| Revenues | $35,383 |
| Expenses | 33,618 |
| Net income | $ 1,765 |

| ALLSTATE CORPORATION Balance Sheet December 31, 2005 | | | |
|---|---|---|---|
| Cash asset . . . . . . . . . | $ 313 | Total liabilities . . . . . . . . . . | $135,886 |
| Noncash assets . . . . . | 155,759 | Stockholders' equity . . . . . | 20,186 |
| Total assets. . . . . . . . | $156,072 | Total liabilities and equity . . | $156,072 |

| ALLSTATE CORPORATION Statement of Cash Flows For Year Ended December 31, 2005 | |
|---|---|
| Cash flows from operations . . . . . . . . . . . . . . . . . . . . . . . . . . . . . . . . . | $5,605 |
| Cash flows from investing . . . . . . . . . . . . . . . . . . . . . . . . . . . . . . . . . | (5,151) |
| Cash flows from financing . . . . . . . . . . . . . . . . . . . . . . . . . . . . . . . . . | (555) |
| Net increase (decrease) in cash . . . . . . . . . . . . . . . . . . . . . . . . . . . . | (101) |
| Cash, beginning year . . . . . . . . . . . . . . . . . . . . . . . . . . . . . . . . . . . . | 414 |
| Cash, ending year . . . . . . . . . . . . . . . . . . . . . . . . . . . . . . . . . . . . . . | $ 313 |

2.  Berkshire Hathaway is a larger company; its total assets are $198,325 million compared to Allstate's assets of $156,072 million. In percentage terms, Berkshire Hathaway is 27% larger. The income statements of the two companies are markedly different. Berkshire Hathaway reports more than twice as much revenue ($81,663 million compared to $35,383 million). The difference in net income is even more drastic; Berkshire Hathaway earned $8,528 million whereas Allstate reported net income of only $1,765 million. This is nearly five times more net income! The two companies are not direct competitors in that Berkshire Hathaway has a wide array of companies in its consolidated group, whereas Allstate is mainly a property and casualty insurer.

# PROFITABILITY ANALYSIS

This section previews the analysis framework of this book. This framework is used extensively by market professionals who analyze financial reports to evaluate company management and value the company's debt and equity securities. Analysis of financial performance is crucial in assessing prior strategic decisions and evaluating strategic alternatives.

**LO3** Explain the basics of profitability analysis.

## Return on Net Operating Assets

Suppose we learn that a company reports an operating profit of $10 million. Is this company performing well? Knowing that a company reports a profit is certainly positive as it indicates that customers value its goods or services and that its revenues exceed expenses. However, we cannot assess how well it is performing. To explain, suppose we learn that this company has $500 million in operating assets. We now assess the $10 million in operating profit as low. This is because relative to the size of its asset investment, the company earned a paltry 2% return, computed as $10 million divided by $500 million. A 2% return is what a much lower-risk savings account might yield. The important point is that a company's profitability must be assessed with respect to the size of its investment. The metric we used here is known as the *return on net operating assets* (RNOA)—defined as net operating profit after tax for that period, divided by the average net operating assets for that period.

## Components of Return on Net Operating Assets

We can separate return on net operating assets into two components: profitability and productivity. Profitability relates net operating profit after tax to sales, called the *net operating profit margin* (NOPM), and reflects the profit earned on each sales dollar. Management wants to earn as much profit as possible from sales.

Productivity relates sales to net operating assets. This component, called the *net operating asset turnover* (NOAT), reflects sales generated by each dollar of operating assets. Management wants to maximize asset productivity, that is, to achieve the highest possible sales level for a given level of operating assets (or to achieve a given level of sales with the smallest level of operating assets).

Exhibit 1.7 depicts the disaggregation of return on net operating assets into these two components. Profitability (NOPM) and productivity (NOAT) are multiplied to yield the return on net operating assets (RNOA).

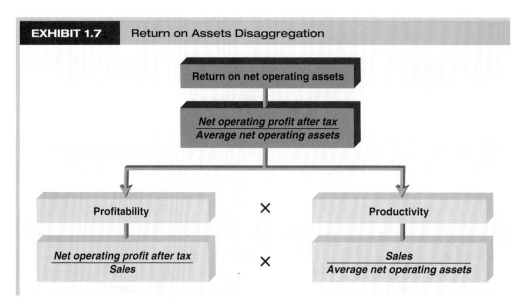

There are an infinite number of combinations of net operating profit margin and net operating asset turnover that yield the same return on net operating assets. To illustrate, Exhibit 1.8 graphs actual combinations of these two components for many industries over the past 15 years. The solid line represents those profitability and productivity combinations that yield a 10.3% return on net operating assets, which is the median return for all publicly traded companies. Industries such as restaurants and retailers have low profit margins but very high asset turnovers. Asset intensive industries, such as coal and pharmaceuticals, earn a high profit margin but do not turn their assets over as frequently.

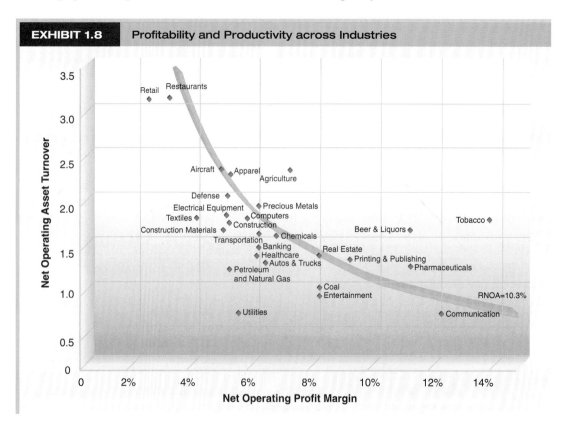

## Return on Equity

Another important analysis measure is return on equity (ROE), which compares net income to average stockholders' equity. In this case, company earnings are compared to the level of stockholder (not total) investment. We further discuss ROE, RNOA, and their disaggregation in Module 4.

---

**MANAGERIAL DECISION**    **You Are the Chief Financial Officer**

You are reviewing your company's financial performance for the first six months of the year and are unsatisfied with the results. How can you use return on net operating assets disaggregation to identify areas for improvement? [Answer, p. 1-30]

---

## Financial Accounting and Business Analysis

Analysis and interpretation of financial statements must consider the broader business context in which a company operates. This section describes how to systematically consider those broader business forces to enhance our analytical and interpretive skills. We can then better extract insights from financial statements and better estimate future performance and company value.

**LO4** Describe business analysis within the context of a competitive environment.

### Analyzing the Competitive Environment

Financial statements are influenced by five important forces that confront the company and determine its competitive intensity: (A) industry competition, (B) buyer power, (C) supplier power, (D) product substitutes, and (E) threat of entry (for further discussion, see *Porter, Competitive Strategy: Techniques for Analyzing Industries and Competitors,* 1980 and 1998). These five forces are depicted graphically in Exhibit 1.9.

**EXHIBIT 1.9    Competitive Forces within the Broader Business Environment**

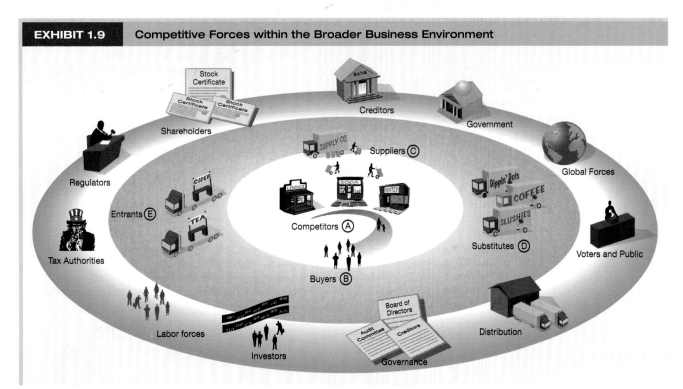

The five forces depicted in Exhibit 1.9 are key determinants of profitability.

(A) **Industry competition** Competition and rivalry raises the cost of doing business as companies must hire and train competitive workers, advertise products, research and develop products, and other related activities.

(B) **Bargaining power of buyers** Buyers with strong bargaining power can extract price concessions and demand a higher level of service and delayed payment terms; this force reduces both profits from sales and the operating cash flows to sellers.

Ⓒ **Bargaining power of suppliers** Suppliers with strong bargaining power can demand higher prices and earlier payments, yielding adverse effects on profits and cash flows to buyers.

Ⓓ **Threat of substitution** As the number of product substitutes increases, sellers have less power to raise prices and/or pass on costs to buyers; accordingly, threat of substitution places downward pressure on profits of sellers.

Ⓔ **Threat of entry** New market entrants increase competition; to mitigate that threat, companies expend monies on activities such as new technologies, promotion, and human development to erect *barriers to entry* and to create *economies of scale.*

This broader business environment affects the level of profitability that a company can expect to earn. Global economic forces and the quality and cost of labor affect the macroeconomy in which the company operates. Government regulation, borrowing agreements exacted by creditors, and internal governance procedures also affect the range of operating activities in which a company can engage. In addition, strategic plans are influenced by the oversight of equity markets, and investors are loathe to allow companies the freedom to manage for the longer term. Each of these external forces affects a company's strategic planning and expected level of profitability.

The relative strength of companies within their industries, and vis-à-vis suppliers and customers, is an important determinant of both their profitability and the structure of their balance sheets. As competition intensifies, profitability likely declines, and the amount of assets companies need to carry on their balance sheet likely increases. These changes in the income statement and the balance sheet can adversely impact operating performance.

## Effect on RNOA and Its Components

Exhibit 1.8 plots operating profit margin (NOPM) and asset turnover (NOAT) for many industries. This graph reveals differences that exist across industries and how those differences are reflected in financial performance metrics.

Individual companies *within* an industry can be plotted in a similar manner. Generally, companies that effectively mitigate competitive forces are able to move toward the upper right area of the graph. That is, they are able to earn greater profit margins, or produce a higher turnover of operating assets, or both. The net result is that they are able to earn a higher RNOA than their peers.

## Applying Competitive Analysis

We apply the competitive analysis framework to help interpret the financial results of McLane Company. McLane is a subsidiary of Berkshire Hathaway and was acquired in 2003 as explained in the following note to the Berkshire Hathaway annual report:

> On May 23, 2003, Berkshire acquired McLane Company, Inc., ("McLane") a distributor of grocery and food products to retailers, convenience stores and restaurants. Results of McLane's business operations are included in Berkshire's consolidated results beginning on that date. McLane's revenues in 2005 totaled $24.1 billion compared to $23.4 billion in 2004 and approximately $22.0 billion for the full year of 2003. Sales of grocery products increased about 5% in 2005 and were partially offset by lower sales to foodservice customers. McLane's business is marked by high sales volume and very low profit margins. Pretax earnings in 2005 of $217 million declined $11 million versus 2004. The gross margin percentage was relatively unchanged between years. However, the resulting increased gross profit was more than offset by higher payroll, fuel and insurance expenses. Approximately 33% of McLane's annual revenues currently derive from sales to Wal-Mart. Loss or curtailment of purchasing by Wal-Mart could have a material adverse impact on revenues and pre-tax earnings of McLane.

McLane is a wholesaler of food products; it purchases food products in finished and semifinished form from agricultural and food-related businesses and resells them to grocery and convenience food stores. The extensive distribution network required in this business entails considerable investment.

***Industry Analysis*** Our business analysis of McLane's financial results includes the following observations:

▪ **Industry competitors** McLane has many competitors with food products that are difficult to differentiate.

- **Bargaining power of buyers** The note above reveals that 33% of McLane's sales are to Wal-Mart, which has considerable buying power that limits seller profits; also, the food industry is characterized by high turnover and low profit margins, which implies that cost control is key to success.

- **Bargaining power of suppliers** McLane is large ($24 billion in annual sales), which implies its suppliers are unlikely to exert forces to increase its cost of sales.

- **Threat of substitution** Grocery items are usually not well differentiated; this means the threat of substitution is high, which inhibits its ability to raise selling prices.

- **Threat of entry** High investment costs, such as warehousing and logistics, are a barrier to entry in McLane's business; this means the threat of entry is relatively low.

Our analysis reveals that McLane is a high-volume, low-margin company. Its ability to control costs is crucial to its financial performance, including its ability to fully utilize its assets. Evaluation of McLane's financial statements should focus on that dimension.

**Business Analysis** Quality analysis depends on an effective business analysis. Before we analyze a single accounting number, we must ask questions about a company's business environment such as the following:

- *Life cycle* At what stage in its life is this company? Is it a startup, experiencing growing pains? Is it strong and mature, reaping the benefits of competitive advantages? Is it nearing the end of its life, trying to milk what it can from stagnant product lines?

- *Outputs* What products does it sell? Are its products new, established, or dated? Do its products have substitutes? How complicated are its products to produce?

- *Buyers* Who are its buyers? Are buyers in good financial condition? Do buyers have substantial purchasing power? Can the seller dictate sales terms to buyers?

- *Inputs* Who are its suppliers? Are there many supply sources? Does the company depend on a few supply sources with potential for high input costs?

- *Competition* In what kind of markets does it operate? Are markets open? Is the market competitive? Does the company have competitive advantages? Can it protect itself from new entrants? At what cost? How must it compete to survive?

- *Financing* Must it seek financing from public markets? Is it going public? Is it seeking to use its stock to acquire another company? Is it in danger of defaulting on debt covenants? Are there incentives to tell an overly optimistic story to attract lower cost financing or to avoid default on debt?

- *Labor* Who are its managers? What are their backgrounds? Can they be trusted? Are they competent? What is the state of employee relations? Is labor unionized?

- *Governance* How effective is its corporate governance? Does it have a strong and independent board of directors? Does a strong audit committee of the board exist, and is it populated with outsiders? Does management have a large portion of its wealth tied to the company's stock?

- *Risk* Is it subject to lawsuits from competitors or shareholders? Is it under investigation by regulators? Has it changed auditors? If so, why? Are its auditors independent? Does it face environmental and/or political risks?

We must assess the broader business context in which a company operates as we read and interpret its financial statements. A review of financial statements, which reflect business activities, cannot be undertaken in a vacuum. It is contextual and can only be effectively undertaken within the framework of a thorough understanding of the broader forces that impact company performance. We should view the above questions as a sneak preview of the types we will ask and answer throughout this book when we read and interpret financial statements.

## MODULE-END REVIEW

Following are selected data from Progressive Corporation's 2005 10-K.

| $ millions | 2005 |
| --- | --- |
| Sales. . . . . . . . . . . . . . . . . . . . . . . . . . . . . | $14,303 |
| Net operating profit after tax . . . . . . . . . . . . | 1,450 |
| Net income. . . . . . . . . . . . . . . . . . . . . . . . . | 1,394 |
| Average net operating assets. . . . . . . . . . . . | 6,916 |
| Average stockholders' equity. . . . . . . . . . . . | 5,631 |

### Required

a. Compute Progressive's return on net operating assets. Disaggregate the RNOA into its profitability and productivity components.

b. Compute Progressive's return on equity (ROE).

c. Consider Exhibit 1.8 that plots industries' RNOA components. Where does Progressive fit on the graph? How does Progressive's profitability and productivity compare to other industries?

### Solution

a. RNOA = net operating profit after tax / average net operating assets = $1,450 / $6,916 = 21.0%. The profitability component is net operating profit after tax / sales = $1,450 / $14,303 = 10.1%, and the productivity component is sales / average net operating assets = $14,303 / $6,916 = 2.07. Notice that 10.1% × 2.07 = 20.9%. Thus, the two components, when multiplied yield RNOA (with a minor rounding difference).

b. ROE = net income / average stockholders' equity = $1,394 / $5,631 = 24.8%.

c. Progressive has a very high RNOA. Net operating asset turnover is 2, which is not unusual (most of the industries have turnovers between 1.5 and 2). However, with a 10.1% NOPM, Progressive is more profitable than most industries with the exception of Tobacco, Pharmaceuticals, Communications and Liquor. Thus, Progressive's high RNOA derives from its high profitability and its solid asset productivity.

# APPENDIX 1A: Accessing SEC Filings using EDGAR

All publicly traded companies are required to file various reports with the SEC, two of which are the 10-Q (quarterly financial statements) and the 10-K (annual financial statements). The SEC archives these reports in a system called EDGAR, an acronym for electronic data gathering and retrieval. Following is a brief tutorial to access these electronic filings. The SEC's web site is **http://www.sec.gov**.

1. Following is the opening screen. Click on Search for Company Filings (highlighted below)

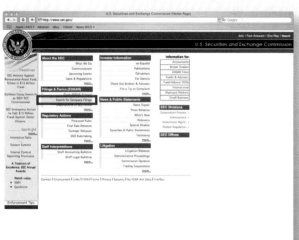

2. Then, click on Companies & Other Filers

3. In **Company name**, type in the name of the company you are looking for. In this case, we are searching for Berkshire Hathaway. Then click on 'Find Companies.'

4. Several references to Berkshire appear. Click on the **CIK** (the SEC's numbering system) next to Berkshire Hathaway, Inc.

5. Find the form you want to access. In this case we are looking for its 10-K. Click on the **html** link because it's easier to read than the text file.

6. The various exhibits relating to Berkshire Hathaway's 10-K appear. Click on the **10-K** line.

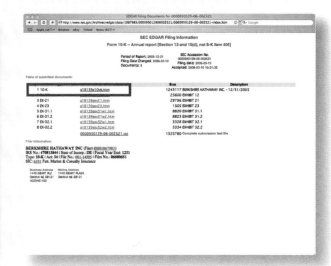

7. The Berkshire Hathaway 10-K will open up. The file is searchable.

# APPENDIX 1B: Accounting Principles and Governance

## Financial Accounting Environment

**LO5** Describe the accounting principles that guide preparation of financial statements.

Information in financial statements is crucial to valuing a company's debt and equity securities. Financial statements information can affect the price the market is willing to pay for the company's equity securities and interest rates attached to its debt securities.

The importance of financial statements means that their reliability is paramount. This includes the crucial role of ethics. To the extent that financial performance and condition are accurately communicated to business decision makers, debt and equity securities are more accurately priced. When securities are mis-priced, resources can be inefficiently allocated both within and across economies. Accurate, reliable financial statements are also important for the effective functioning of many other markets such as labor, input, and output markets.

To illustrate, recall the consequences of a breakdown in the integrity of the financial accounting system at Enron. Once it became clear that Enron had not faithfully and accurately reported its financial condition and performance, the market became unwilling to purchase Enron's securities. The value of its debt and equity securities dropped precipitously and the company was unable to obtain cash needed for operating activities. Within months of the disclosure of its financial accounting irregularities, Enron, with revenues of over $100 billion and total company value of over $60 billion, the fifth largest U.S. company, was bankrupt!

Further historical evidence of the importance of financial accounting is provided by the Great Depression of the 20th century. This depression was caused, in large part, by the failure of companies to faithfully report their financial condition and performance.

### Oversight of Financial Accounting

The stock market crash of 1929 and the ensuing Great Depression led Congress to pass the 1933 Securities Act. This act had two main objectives: (1) to require disclosure of financial and other information about securities being offered for public sale; and (2) to prohibit deceit, misrepresentations, and other fraud in the sale of securities. This act also required that companies register all securities proposed for public sale and disclose information about the securities being offered, including information about company financial condition and performance. This act became and remains a foundation for contemporary financial reporting.

Congress also passed the 1934 Securities Exchange Act, which created the **Securities and Exchange Commission** (SEC) and gave it broad powers to regulate the issuance and trading of securities. The act also provided that companies with more than $10 million in assets and whose securities are held by more than 500 owners must file annual and other periodic reports, including financial statements that are available for download from the SEC's **EDGAR** database (**www.sec.gov**).

The SEC has ultimate authority over U.S. financial reporting, including setting accounting standards for preparing financial statements. Since 1939, however, the SEC has looked to the private sector to set accounting standards—the SEC retains the right to overrule or revise standards with which it disagrees. One such private sector organization is the American Institute of Certified Public Accountants (AICPA), whose two committees, the Committee on Accounting Procedure (1939–59) and the Accounting Principles Board (1959–73), authored the initial body of accounting standards.

Currently, the **Financial Accounting Standards Board (FASB)** sets U.S. financial accounting standards. The FASB is an independent body overseen by a foundation, whose members include public accounting firms, investment managers, academics, and corporate managers. The FASB has published over 150 accounting standards governing the preparation of financial reports. This is in addition to over 40 standards that were written by predecessor organizations to the FASB, numerous bulletins and interpretations, Emerging Issues Task Force (EITF) statements, AICPA statements of position (SOP), and direct SEC guidance, along with speeches made by high-ranking SEC personnel, all of which form the body of accounting standards governing financial statements. Collectively, these pronouncements, rules and guidance create what is called **Generally Accepted Accounting Principles (GAAP).**

The standard-setting process is arduous, often lasting up to a decade and involving extensive comment by the public, public officials, accountants, academics, investors, analysts, and corporate preparers of financial reports. To influence the standard-setting process, special interest groups often lobby members of Congress to pressure the SEC and, ultimately, the FASB, on issues about which constituents feel strongly. The reason for this involved process is that amendments to existing standards or the creation of new standards affect the reported financial performance and condition of companies. Consequently, given the widespread impact of financial accounting, there are considerable economic consequences as a result of accounting changes.

## International Accounting Standards and Convergence

A single set of international accounting standards that is accepted in all capital markets throughout the world does not exist. In the U.S., public firms must file financial reports using U.S. generally accepted accounting principles (GAAP). Foreign firms filing with the SEC can use U.S. GAAP, their home country GAAP, or international standards—although if they use their home country GAAP or international standards, foreign issuers must reconcile their numbers to U.S. GAAP.

The International Accounting Standards Board (IASB) oversees development of international accounting standards. In 2002, the FASB and the IASB announced their commitment to minimize differences between U.S. and international accounting standards. Although the two rule-making bodies have achieved consensus on broad philosophical issues, agreement on the detailed wording of standards is more difficult to achieve.

Differences between U.S. and international accounting standards remain. One major advance, however, is that beginning in 2005, European Union companies must use IASB standards rather than their home-country GAAP. Summaries of differences between U.S. and international GAAP are available on the web. One source is the large international public accounting firms (for example, see **PWC.com** and search IFRS and GAAP).

## Choices in Financial Accounting

Some people mistakenly assume that financial accounting is an exact discipline—that is, companies select the one proper accounting method to account for a transaction, and then follow the rules. The reality is that GAAP allows companies choices in preparing financial statements. The choice of methods often yields financial statements that are markedly different from one another in terms of reported income, assets, liabilities, and equity amounts.

People often are surprised that financial statements comprise numerous estimates. For example, companies must estimate the amounts that will eventually be collected from customers, the length of time that buildings and equipment will be productive, the value impairments of assets, the future costs of warranty claims, and the eventual payouts on pension plans.

| Recent Accounting Scandals | |
| --- | --- |
| **Company** | **Allegations** |
| Adelphia Communications (ADELQ) | Founding Rigas family collected $3.1 billion in off-balance-sheet loans backed by Adelphia; overstated results by inflating capital expenses and hiding debt. |
| TWX Time Warner (TWX) | As the ad market faltered and AOL's purchase of Time Warner loomed, AOL inflated sales by booking revenue for barter deals and ads it sold for third parties. These questionable revenues boosted growth rates and sealed the deal. AOL also boosted sales via "round-trip" deals with advertisers and suppliers. |
| Bristol-Myers Squibb (BMY) | Inflated its 2001 revenue by $1.5 billion by "channel stuffing," or forcing wholesalers to accept more inventory than they could sell to get inventory off Bristol-Myers' books. |
| Enron | Created profits and hid debt totaling over $1 billion by improperly using off-the-books partnerships; manipulated the Texas power market; bribed foreign governments to win contracts abroad; manipulated California energy market. |
| Global Crossing | Engaged in network capacity "swaps" with other carriers to inflate revenue; shredded documents related to accounting practices. |
| Halliburton (HAL) | Improperly booked $100 million in annual construction-cost overruns before customers agreed to pay for them. |
| Qwest Communications International (Q) | Inflated revenue using network capacity "swaps" and improper accounting for long-term deals. |
| Tyco (TYC) | Ex-CEO L. Dennis Kozlowski indicted for tax evasion; Kozlowski and former CFO Mark H. Swartz, convicted of taking unauthorized loans from the company. |
| WorldCom | Overstated cash flow by booking $11 billion in operating expenses as capital costs; loaned founder Bernard Ebbers $400 million off-the-books. |
| Xerox (XRX) | Falsified financial results for five years, over-reported income by $1.5 billion. |

Accounting standard setters walk a fine line regarding choice in accounting. On one hand, they are concerned that choice in preparing financial statements will lead to abuse by those seeking to gain by influencing decisions of financial statement users. On the other hand, standard setters are concerned that companies are too diverse for a "one size fits all" financial accounting system.

For example, Enron exemplifies the problems that accompany rigid accounting standards. A set of accounting standards relating to special purpose entities (SPEs) provided preparers with guidelines under which those entities were or were not to be consolidated. Unfortunately, once the SPE guidelines were set, some people worked diligently to structure SPE transactions so as to just miss the consolidation requirements and achieve *off-balance-sheet* financing. This is just one example of how, with rigid standards, companies can adhere to the letter of the rule, but not its intent. In such situations, the financial statements are not fairly presented.

For most of its existence, the FASB has promulgated standards that were quite complicated and replete with guidelines. This invited abuse of the type embodied by the Enron scandal. In recent years, the pendulum has begun to swing away from such rigidity. Now, once financial statements are prepared, company management is required to step back from the details and make a judgment on whether the statements taken as a whole 'fairly present' the financial condition of the company.

Moreover, since the enactment of the **Sarbanes-Oxley Act,** the SEC requires the chief executive officer (CEO) of the company and its chief financial officer (CFO) to personally sign a statement attesting to the accuracy and completeness of the financial statements. This requirement is an important step in restoring confidence in the integrity of financial accounting. The statements signed by both the CEO and CFO contain the following statements:

- Both the CEO and CFO have personally reviewed the annual report
- There are no untrue statements of a material fact that would make the statements misleading
- Financial statements fairly present in all material respects the financial condition of the company
- All material facts are disclosed to the company's auditors and board of directors
- No changes to its system of internal controls are made unless properly communicated

The Sarbanes-Oxley Act also imposed fines and potential jail time for executives. Presumably, the prospect of personal losses is designed to make these executives more vigilant in monitoring the financial accounting system.

# Regulatory and Legal Environment

Even though key executives must personally attest to the completeness and accuracy of company financial statements, markets demand further assurances from outside parties to achieve the level of confidence necessary to warrant investment, credit, and other business decisions. The regulatory and legal environment provides further assurance that financial statements are complete and accurate.

## Audit Committee

Law requires each publicly traded company to have a board of directors, where stockholders elect each director. This board represents the company owners and oversees management. The board also hires the company's executive management and regularly reviews company operations.

The board of directors usually establishes several subcommittees to focus on particular governance tasks such as compensation, strategic plans, and financial management. Exhibit 1.10 illustrates a typical organization of a company's governance structure. Corporate governance refers to the checks and balances that monitor company and manager activities. Governance committees are commonplace. One of these, the audit committee, oversees the financial accounting system.

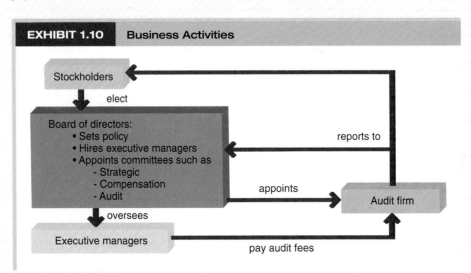

**EXHIBIT 1.10**   **Business Activities**

The audit committee must consist solely of outside directors, and cannot include the CEO. As part of its over-sight of the financial accounting system, the audit committee focuses on **internal controls**, which are the policies and procedures used to protect assets, ensure reliable accounting, promote efficient operations, and urge adherence to company policies.

## Statement of Management Responsibility

Following passage of the Sarbanes-Oxley Act, the SEC issued a ruling requiring companies "to include in their an-nual reports a report of management on the company's internal control over financial reporting." Many companies incorporate the rule's requirements by reference in their disclosures. Others, like Home Depot in Exhibit 1.11 make explicit reference to the rule's provisions.

---

**EXHIBIT 1.11     Responsibility for Financial Reporting**

**Management's Responsibility Financial Statements**

The financial statements presented in this Annual Report have been prepared with integrity and objectivity and are the responsibility of the management of The Home Depot, Inc. These financial statements have been prepared in conformity with U.S. generally accepted accounting principles and properly reflect certain estimates and judgments based upon the best available information.

The financial statements of the Company have been audited by KPMG LLP, an independent registered public accounting firm. Their accompanying report is based upon an audit conducted in accordance with the standards of the Public Company Accounting Oversight Board (United States).

The Audit Committee of the Board of Directors, consisting solely of outside directors, meets five times a year with the independent registered public accounting firm, the internal auditors and representatives of management to discuss auditing and financial reporting matters. In addition, a telephonic meeting is held prior to each quarterly earnings release. The Audit Committee retains the independent registered public accounting firm and regularly reviews the internal accounting controls, the activities of the independent registered public accounting firm and internal auditors and the financial condition of the Company. Both the Company's independent registered public accounting firm and the internal auditors have free access to the Audit Committee.

**Management's Report on Internal Control over Financial Reporting**

Our management is responsible for establishing and maintaining adequate internal control over financial reporting, as such term is defined in Exchange Act Rules 13a–15(f). Under the supervision and with the participation of our management, including our principal executive officer and principal financial officer, we conducted an evaluation of the effectiveness of our internal control over financial reporting based on the framework in *Internal Control—Integrated Framework* issued by the Committee of Sponsoring Organizations of the Treadway Commission (COSO). Based on our evaluation, our management concluded that our internal control over financial reporting was effective as of January 30, 2005. Our management's assessment of the effectiveness of our internal control over financial reporting as of January 30, 2005 has been audited by KPMG LLP, an independent registered public accounting firm, as stated in its report which is included herein.

Robert L. Nardelli
Chairman, President &
Chief Executive Officer

Carol B. Tomé
Executive Vice President &
Chief Financial Officer

Kelly H. Barrett
Vice Presient
Corporate Controller

---

The statement of responsibility contains several assertions by management:

1. Financial statements are prepared by management, which assumes responsibility for them
2. Financial statements are prepared in conformity with GAAP
3. Financial statements are audited by an external auditing firm
4. Board of directors has an audit committee to oversee the financial accounting system and the system of internal controls
5. Management is responsible for establishing and maintaining adequate internal control over financial reporting.

It is important to remember that management prepares financial statements—not the auditors who are hired to express an opinion on those statements. Moreover, remember that management's interests may or may not be aligned with those of other stakeholders.

## Audit Report

Financial statements for each publicly traded company must be audited by an independent audit firm. There are four large, international auditing firms that are authorized by the SEC to provide auditing services for companies that issue securities to the public:

1. **Deloitte & Touche LLP**
2. **Ernst & Young LLP**
3. **KPMG LLP**
4. **PricewaterhouseCoopers LLP**

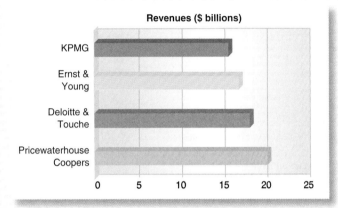

**Revenues ($ billions)**

These four firms provide opinions for the majority of financial statements filed by publicly traded U.S. companies. There also are a number of regional accounting firms that provide audit services to both publicly traded and nontraded private companies.

A company's Board of Directors hires the auditors to review and express an opinion on its financial statements. The audit opinion expressed by Deloitte & Touche, LLP on the financial statements of **Berkshire Hathaway** is reproduced in Exhibit 1.12.

---

**EXHIBIT 1.12**    **Audit Report for Berkshire Hathaway**

To the Board of Directors and Shareholders, Berkshire Hathaway Inc.

We have audited the accompanying consolidated balance sheets of Berkshire Hathaway Inc. and subsidiaries (the "Company") as of December 31, 2005 and 2004, and the related consolidated statements of earnings, cash flows and changes in shareholders' equity and comprehensive income for each of the three years in the period ended December 31, 2005. These financial statements are the responsibility of the Company's management. Our responsibility is to express an opinion on these financial statements based on our audits.

We conducted our audits in accordance with the standards of the Public Company Accounting Oversight Board (United States). Those standards require that we plan and perform the audit to obtain reasonable assurance about whether the financial statements are free of material misstatement. An audit includes examining, on a test basis, evidence supporting the amounts and disclosures in the financial statements. An audit also includes assessing the accounting principles used and significant estimates made by management, as well as evaluating the overall financial statement presentation. We believe that our audits provide a reasonable basis for our opinion.

In our opinion, such consolidated financial statements present fairly, in all material respects, the financial position of Berkshire Hathaway Inc. and subsidiaries as of December 31, 2005 and 2004, and the results of their operations and their cash flows for each of the three years in the period ended December 31, 2005, in conformity with accounting principles generally accepted in the United States of America.

We have also audited, in accordance with the standards of the Public Company Accounting Oversight Board (United States), the effectiveness of the Company's internal control over financial reporting as of December 31, 2005, based on the criteria established in *Internal Control—Integrated Framework* issued by the Committee of Sponsoring Organizations of the Treadway Commission and our report dated March 2, 2006 expressed an unqualified opinion on management's assessment of the effectiveness of the Company's internal control over financial reporting and an unqualified opinion on the effectiveness of the Company's internal control over financial reporting.

DELOITTE & TOUCHE LLP

Omaha, Nebraska

March 2, 2006

The basic 'clean' audit report is consistent across companies and includes these assertions:

- Financial statements *present fairly, in all material respects* a company's financial condition, in conformity with GAAP.
- Financial statements are management's responsibility. Auditor responsibility is to express an opinion on those statements.
- Auditing involves a sampling of transactions, not investigation of each transaction.
- Audit opinion provides *reasonable assurance* that the statements are free of *material* misstatements, not a guarantee.
- Auditors review accounting policies used by management and the estimates used in preparing the statements.

Unless all of these conditions are met, the auditor cannot issue a clean opinion. Instead, the auditor issues a "qualified" opinion and states the reasons a clean opinion cannot be issued. Financial report readers should scrutinize with care both the qualified audit opinion and the financial statements themselves.

The audit opinion is not based on a test of each transaction. Auditors usually develop statistical samples and infer test results to other transactions. The audit report is not a guarantee that no misstatements exist. Auditors only provide reasonable assurance that the statements are free of material misstatements. Their use of the word reasonable is deliberate, as they do not want to be held to an absolute standard should problems be subsequently uncovered. The word material is used in the sense that an item must be of sufficient magnitude to change the perceptions or decisions of the financial statement user (such as a decision to purchase stock or extend credit).

The requirement of auditor independence is the cornerstone of effective auditing and is subject to debate because the company pays the auditor's fees. Regulators have questioned the perceived lack of independence of auditing firms and the degree to which declining independence compromises the ability of auditing firms to challenge a client's dubious accounting.

The Sarbanes-Oxley Act contained several provisions designed to encourage auditor independence:

1. It established the Public Company Accounting Oversight Board to oversee the development of audit standards and to monitor the effectiveness of auditors,
2. It prohibits auditors from offering certain types of consulting services, and requires audit partners to rotate clients every five years, and
3. It requires audit committees to consist of independent members.

---

**BUSINESS INSIGHT    Warren Buffett on Audit Committees**

"Audit committees can't audit. Only a company's outside auditor can determine whether the earnings that a management purports to have made are suspect. Reforms that ignore this reality and that instead focus on the structure and charter of the audit committee will accomplish little.

As we've discussed, far too many managers have fudged their company's numbers in recent years, using both accounting and operational techniques that are typically legal but that nevertheless materially mislead investors. Frequently, auditors knew about these deceptions. Too often, however, they remained silent. The key job of the audit committee is simply to get the auditors to divulge what they know.

To do this job, the committee must make sure that the auditors worry more about misleading its members than about offending management. In recent years auditors have not felt that way. They have instead generally viewed the CEO, rather than the shareholders or directors, as their client. That has been a natural result of day-to-day working relationships and also of the auditors' understanding that, no matter what the board says, the CEO and CFO pay their fees and determine whether they are retained for both auditing and other work. The rules that have been recently instituted won't materially change this reality. What will break this cozy relationship is audit committees unequivocally putting auditors on the spot, making them understand they will become liable for major monetary penalties if they don't come forth with what they know or suspect."—Warren Buffett, Berkshire Hathaway annual report

---

# SEC Enforcement Actions

Companies whose securities are issued to the public must file reports with the SEC (see **www.sec.gov**). One of these reports is the 10-K, which includes the annual financial statements (quarterly statements are filed under report 10-Q). The 10-K report provides more information than the company's glossy annual report, which is partly a marketing document (although the basic financial statements are identical). You should use the 10-K because of its additional information.

The SEC has ultimate authority to accept or reject financial statements that companies submit. Should the SEC reject a company's financial statements, the company must restate and refile them. Restatements are time-consuming, publicly known, and restating companies typically see their stock market value slide. For example, in 2006, the SEC required Fannie Mae to restate its financial statements. The SEC commenced litigation, and the following excerpts come from the criminal complaint:

> The Federal National Mortgage Association engaged in a financial fraud involving multiple violations of Generally Accepted Accounting Principles ("GAAP") in connection with the preparation of its annual and quarterly financial statements. These violations had the effect, among other things, of falsely portraying stable earnings growth and reduced income statement volatility and, for year-ended 1998, of maximizing bonuses and achieving forecasted earnings. Between 1998 and 2004, Fannie Mae, a shareholder-owned government sponsored enterprise, misstated its results of operations and issued materially false and misleading financial statements in various reports and in filings with the Commission.
>
> The Company's accounting was inconsistent with GAAP. Additionally, the Company's reported financial results were smoothed through misapplications of GAAP. These practices were not disclosed to investors.
>
> As a direct result of these violations, and other errors, Fannie Mae expects to restate its historical financial statements for the years ended December 31, 2003 and 2002, and for the quarters ended June 30, 2004 and March 31, 2004. This restatement will result in at least a $1.1 billion reduction of previously reported net income.

The Commission's investigation uncovered numerous transactions over several years by which Fannie Mae management intentionally smoothed out gyrations in its earnings to show investors it was a low-risk company. In addition, the SEC charged that the company's accounting policies were created to shape the company's books in a way that made it appear that the company had reached earnings targets, thus triggering the maximum possible bonus payout for executives.

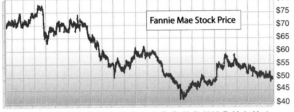

Following litigation of the above-referenced complaint, Fannie Mae fired its senior management team, including its CEO and CFO. It also agreed to pay a $400 million penalty, restate its previously issued financial reports, reform its accounting policies, and institute stricter internal controls over its accounting procedures. Fannie Mae's stock (FNM) lost a third of its market value during the proceedings—see margin graph. The SEC's power to require restatement, with its consequent damage to company reputation and company stock price, is a major deterrent to those desiring to bias their financial accounts to achieve a particular goal.

## Courts

Courts provide remedies to individuals or companies that suffer damages as a result of material misstatements in financial statements. Typical court actions involve shareholders who sue the company and its auditors, alleging that the company disclosed, and the auditors attested to, false and misleading financial statements. The number of such shareholder suits has declined in the past few years. Nonetheless, shareholder suits are chronically in the news. Stanford Law School's Securities Class Action Clearinghouse commented that "Two factors are likely responsible for the decline. First, lawsuits arising from the dramatic boom and bust of U.S. equities in the late 1990s and early 2000s are now largely behind us. Second, improved governance in the wake of the Enron and WorldCom frauds likely reduced the actual incidence of fraud." The SEC and the New York District Attorney successfully brought suit against Adelphia Communications Corporation and its owners on behalf of the U.S. Government and numerous investors, creditors, employees and others affiliated with the company. The press release announcing the settlement read, in part:

> *Washington, D.C., April 25, 2005*—The Securities and Exchange Commission today announced that it and the United States Attorney's Office for the Southern District of New York (USAO) reached an agreement to settle a civil enforcement action and resolve criminal charges against Adelphia Communications Corporation, its founder John J. Rigas, and his three sons, Timothy J. Rigas, Michael J. Rigas and James P. Rigas, in one of the most extensive financial frauds ever to take place at a public company.
>
> In its complaint, the Commission charged that Adelphia, at the direction of the individual defendants: (1) fraudulently excluded billions of dollars in liabilities from its consolidated financial statements by hiding them on the books of off-balance sheet affiliates; (2) falsified operating statistics and inflated earnings to meet Wall Street estimates; and (3) concealed rampant self-dealing by the Rigas family, including the undisclosed use of corporate funds for purchases of Adelphia stock and luxury condominiums.
>
> Mark K. Schonfeld, Director of the SEC's Northeast Regional Office, said, "This settlement agreement presents a strong, coordinated approach by the SEC and the U.S. Attorney's Office to resolving one of the most complicated and egregious financial frauds committed at a public company. The

settlement provides an expedient and effective way to provide victims of Adelphia's fraud with a substantial recovery while at the same time enabling Adelphia to emerge from Chapter 11 bankruptcy."

The settlement terms of this action, and related criminal actions against the Rigas family, resulted in the following:

- Rigas family members forfeited in excess of $1.5 billion in assets derived from the fraud; the funds were used, in part, to establish a fund for the fraud victims.
- Rigas family members were barred from acting as officers or directors of a public company.
- John Rigas, the 80-year-old founder of Adelphia Communications, was sentenced to 15 years in prison.
- Timothy Rigas, the ex-finance chief, was sentenced to 20 years.

# GUIDANCE ANSWERS

### MANAGERIAL DECISION    You Are the Product Manager

As a manager, you must balance two conflicting objectives—namely, mandatory disclosure requirements and your company's need to protect its competitive advantages. You must comply with all minimum required disclosure rules. The extent to which you offer additional disclosures depends on the sensitivity of the information; that is, how beneficial it is to your existing and potential competitors. Another consideration is how the information disclosed will impact your existing and potential investors. Disclosures such as this can be beneficial in that they inform investors and others about your company's successful investments. Still, there are many stakeholders impacted by your disclosure decision and each must be given due consideration.

### MANAGERIAL DECISION    You Are the Chief Financial Officer

Financial performance is typically measured by return on net operating assets, which can be disaggregated into the net operating profit margin (net operating profit after tax/sales) and the net operating asset turnover (sales/ average net operating assets). This disaggregation might lead you to review factors affecting profitability (gross margins and expense control) and to assess how effectively your company is utilizing its assets (the turnover rates). Finding ways to increase profitability for a given level of investment or to reduce the amount of invested capital while not adversely impacting profitability contributes to improved financial performance.

Superscript <sup>A(B)</sup> denotes assignments based on Appendix 1A (1B).

# DISCUSSION QUESTIONS

**Q1-1.** A firm's planning activities motivate and shape three types of business activities. List the three activities. Describe how financial accounting reports can provide useful information for each activity. How can subsequent financial accounting reports be used to evaluate the success of each of the activities?

**Q1-2.** The accounting equation (Assets = Liabilities + Equity) is a fundamental business concept. Explain what this equation reveals about a company's sources and uses of funds and the claims on company resources.

**Q1-3.** Companies prepare four primary financial statements. What are those financial statements and what information is typically conveyed in each?

**Q1-4.** Does a balance sheet report on a period of time or at a point in time? Explain the information conveyed in the balance sheet.

**Q1-5.** Does an income statement report on a period of time or at a point in time? Explain the information conveyed in the income statement.

**Q1-6.** Does a statement of cash flows report on a period of time or at a point in time? Explain the information and activities conveyed in the statement of cash flows.

**Q1-7.** Explain how a company's four primary financial statements are linked.

**Q1-8.** Financial statements are used by several interested stakeholders. List three or more potential external users of financial statements. Explain how each constituent on your list might use financial statement information in their decision making process.

**Q1-9.** What ethical issues might managers face in dealing with confidential information?

**Q1-10.<sup>A</sup>** Access the 2006 10-K for Procter & Gamble at the SEC's EDGAR database of financial reports (**www.sec.gov**). Who is P&G's auditor? What specific language does the auditor use in expressing its opinion and what responsibilities does it assume?

Procter & Gamble (PG)

**Q1-11.**ᴮ Business decision makers external to the company increasingly demand more financial information from companies. Discuss the reasons why companies have traditionally opposed the efforts of regulatory agencies like the SEC to require more disclosure.

**Q1-12.**ᴮ What are generally accepted accounting principles and what organizations presently establish them?

**Q1-13.**ᴮ Corporate governance has received considerable attention since the collapse of Enron and other accounting-related scandals. What is meant by corporate governance? What are the primary means by which sound corporate governance is achieved?

Enron

**Q1-14.**ᴮ What is the primary function of the auditor? In your own words, describe what an audit opinion says.

**Q1-15.** Describe a decision that requires financial accounting information, other than a stock investment decision. How is financial accounting information useful in making this decision?

**Q1-16.** Users of financial information are vitally concerned with the company's strategic direction. Despite their understanding of this need for information, companies are reluctant to supply it. Why? In particular, what costs are companies concerned about?

**Q1-17.** One of Warren Buffett's acquisition criteria is to invest in businesses "earning good return on equity." The return on equity (ROE) formula uses both net income and stockholders' equity. Why is it important to relate net income to stockholders' equity? Why isn't it sufficient to merely concentrate on companies with the highest net income?

**Q1-18.** One of Warren Buffett's acquisition criteria is to invest in businesses "earning good return on equity, while employing little or no debt." Why is Buffett concerned about debt?

# MINI EXERCISES

**M1-19. Relating Financing and Investing Activities (LO2)**
In a recent year, the total assets of Dell, Inc. equal $15,470 million and its equity is $4,873 million. What is the amount of its liabilities? Does Dell receive more financing from its owners or nonowners? What percentage of financing is provided by Dell's owners?

Dell, Inc. (DELL)

**M1-20. Relating Financing and Investing Activities (LO2)**
In a recent year, the total assets of Ford Motor Company equal $315,920 million and its liabilities equal $304,269 million. What is the amount of Ford's equity? Does Ford receive more financing from its owners or nonowners. What percentage of financing is provided by its owners?

Ford Motor Company (F)

**M1-21. Applying the Accounting Equation and Computing Financing Proportions (LO2)**
Use the accounting equation to compute the missing financial amounts (a), (b), and (c). Which of these companies is more owner-financed? Which of these companies is more nonowner-financed? Discuss why the proportion of owner financing might differ across these three businesses.

| ($ millions) | Assets | = | Liabilities | + | Equity |
|---|---|---|---|---|---|
| Hewlett-Packard........ | $74,708 | | $ 36,962 | | $ (a) |
| General Mills........... | $18,227 | | $ (b) | | $4,175 |
| General Motors........ | $ (c) | | $365,057 | | $6,814 |

Hewlett-Packard (HPQ)
General Mills (GIS)
General Motors (GM)

**M1-22.**ᴬ **Identifying Key Numbers from Financial Statements (LO2)**
Access the October 2006 10-K for Starbucks Corporation at the SEC's EDGAR database for financial reports (**www.sec.gov**). What did Starbucks report for total assets, liabilities, and equity at October 1, 2006? Confirm that the accounting equation holds. What percent of Starbucks' assets is financed by nonowners?

Starbucks (SBUX)

**M1-23.**ᴬ **Verifying Linkages Between Financial Statements (LO2)**
Access the 2005 10-K for DuPont at the SEC's EDGAR database of financial reports (**www.sec.gov**). Using its December 31, 2005, consolidated statement of stockholders' equity, prepare a table to reconcile the opening and ending balances of its retained (reinvested) earnings for 2005 by showing the activity in the account during the year.

E. I. DuPont de Nemours (DD)

**M1-24. Identifying Financial Statement Line Items and Accounts (LO2)**
Several line items and account titles are listed below. For each, indicate in which of the following financial statement(s) we would likely find the item or account: income statement (IS), balance sheet (BS), statement of stockholders' equity (SE), or statement of cash flows (SCF).

a. Cash asset
b. Expenses
c. Noncash assets
d. Contributed capital
e. Cash outflow for capital expenditures
f. Retained earnings
g. Cash inflow for stock issued
h. Cash outflow for dividends
i. Net income

**M1-25.**  **Identifying Ethical Issues and Accounting Choices**  (LO5)

Assume that you are a technology services provider and you must decide on whether to record revenue from the installation of computer software for one of your clients. Your contract calls for acceptance of the software by the client within six months of installation. According to the contract, you will be paid only when the client "accepts" the installation. Although you have not yet received your client's formal acceptance, you are confident that it is forthcoming. Failure to record these revenues will cause your company to miss Wall Street's earnings estimates. What stakeholders will be affected by your decision and how might they be affected?

**M1-26.**[B]  **Understanding Internal Controls and their Importance**  (LO5)

The **Sarbanes-Oxley Act** legislation requires companies to report on the effectiveness of their internal controls. The SEC administers the Sarbanes-Oxley Act, and defines internal controls as follows:

> "A process designed by, or under the supervision of, the registrant's principal executive and principal financial officers . . . to provide reasonable assurance regarding the reliability of financial reporting and the preparation of financial statements for external purposes in accordance with generally accepted accounting principles."

Why do you think Congress believes internal controls are such an important area to monitor and report on?

# EXERCISES

**E1-27.**  **Applying the Accounting Equation and Assessing Financing Contributions**  (LO2)

Determine the missing amounts on lines (a), (b), and (c) below. Which of these companies is more owner-financed? Which of these companies is more nonowner-financed?

| ($ millions) | Assets | = | Liabilities | + | Equity | |
|---|---|---|---|---|---|---|
| a. Motorola, Inc.......... | $31,152 | = | $    ? | | $11,239 | Motorola, Inc. (MOT) |
| b. Kraft Foods ......... | $    ? | = | $31,268 | | $25,832 | Kraft Foods (KFT) |
| c. Merck & Co......... | $47,561 | = | $29,361 | | $    ? | Merck & Co. (MRK) |

**E1-28.**  **Applying the Accounting Equation and Assessing Financial Statement Linkages**  (LO2)

Answer the following questions. (*Hint*: Apply the accounting equation.)

a.  Intel had assets equal to $44,224 million and liabilities equal to $8,756 million for a recent year-end. What was Intel's total equity at year-end?    Intel (INTC)

b.  At the beginning of a recent year, JetBlue's assets were $1,378 million and its equity was $415 million. During the year, assets increased $70 million and liabilities increased $30 million. What was JetBlue's equity at the end of the year?    JetBlue (JBLU)

c.  At the beginning of a recent year, The Walt Disney Company's liabilities equaled $26,197 million. During the year, assets increased by $400 million, and year-end assets equaled $50,388 million. Liabilities decreased $100 million during the year. What were beginning and ending amounts for Walt Disney's equity?    The Walt Disney Company (DIS)

**E1-29.**  **Specifying Financial Information Users and Uses**  (LO1)

Financial statements have a wide audience of interested stakeholders. Identify two or more financial statement users that are external to the company. For each user on your list, specify two questions that could be addressed with financial statement information.

**E1-30.**  **Applying Financial Statement Relations to Compute Dividends**  (LO2)

Colgate-Palmolive reports the following dollar balances in its retained earnings account.    Colgate-Palmolive (CL)

| ($ millions) | 2005 | 2004 |
|---|---|---|
| Retained earnings  . . . . . . . . | 8,968.1 | 8,223.9 |

During 2005, Colgate-Palmolive reported net income of $1,351.4 million. What amount of dividends, if any, did Colgate-Palmolive pay to its shareholders in 2005? What percent of its net income did Colgate-Palmolive pay out in 2005?

**E1-31.** **Computing and Interpreting Financial Statement Ratios**  (LO3)

Briggs & Stratton
(BGG)

Following are selected ratios of Briggs & Stratton (manufacturer of engines) for 2005 and 2004.

| RNOA Component | 2005 | 2004 |
| --- | --- | --- |
| Profitability (Net operating profit after tax / Sales) . . . . . . . | 4.67% | 7.82% |
| Productivity (Sales / Average net operating assets). . . . . . | 2.08 | 1.77 |

a.    Was the company profitable in 2005? What evidence do you have of this?

b.    Is the change in productivity (net operating asset turnover) a positive development? Explain.

c.    Compute the company's return on net operating assets (RNOA) for 2005 (show computations).

**E1-32.** **Computing Return on Net Operating Assets and Applying the Accounting Equation**  (LO3)

Nordstrom, Inc.
(JWN)

Nordstrom, Inc., reports net operating profit after tax of $477.2 million for its fiscal year ended January 2006. At the beginning of that fiscal year, Nordstrom had $2,777.3 million in net operating assets. By fiscal year-end 2006, total net operating assets had grown to $2,973.1 million. What is Nordstrom's return on net operating assets (RNOA)?

**E1-33.** **Discussing Accounting in Society**  (LO1)

Financial accounting plays an important role in modern society and business.

a.    Identify two or more external stakeholders that are interested in a company's financial statements and what their particular interests are.

b.    What are *generally accepted accounting principles*? What organizations have primary responsibility for the formulation of GAAP?

c.    What role does financial accounting play in the allocation of society's financial resources?

d.    What are three aspects of the accounting environment that can create ethical pressure on management?

**E1-34.** **Computing Return on Equity**  (LO3)

Starbucks (SBUX)

Starbucks reports net income for 2006 of $564 million. Its stockholders' equity is $2,229 million and $2,090 million for 2006 and 2005, respectively.

a.    Compute its return on equity for 2006.

b.    Starbucks repurchased over $850 million of its common stock in 2006. How did this repurchase affect Starbucks' ROE?

c.    Why do you think a company like Starbucks repurchases its own stock?

# PROBLEMS

**P1-35.** **Computing Return on Equity and Return on Net Operating Assets**  (LO3)

Staples (SPLS)

The following table contains financial statement information for Staples, Inc.

| ($ millions) | 2006 | 2005 | 2004 | 2003 |
| --- | --- | --- | --- | --- |
| Net operating profit after tax . . . . . . . . | $ 853,632 | $ 731,817 | $ 518,887 | $ 443,737 |
| Net income. . . . . . . . . . . . . . . . . . . . | 834,409 | 708,388 | 490,211 | 446,000 |
| Net operating assets . . . . . . . . . . . . . | 4,367,221 | 4,202,136 | 3,486,208 | 3,618,429 |
| Stockholders' equity . . . . . . . . . . . . . | 4,425,471 | 4,115,196 | 3,662,900 | 2,658,892 |

**Required**

a.    Compute the return on equity (ROE) for 2004 through 2006. What trend is observed? How does Staples' ROE compare with the approximately 12% average ROE for publicly traded companies?

b.    Compute the return on net operating assets (RNOA) for 2004 through 2006. What trends are observed? How does Staples' RNOA compare with the approximate 10% average RNOA for publicly traded companies?

c.    What factors might allow a company like Staples to reap above-average returns?

**P1-36.** **Formulating Financial Statements from Raw Data**  (LO2)

General Mills, Inc.
(GIS)

Following is selected financial information from General Mills, Inc., for its fiscal year ended May 30, 2004 ($ millions).

| | | |
|---|---|---|
| Cash and cash equivalents ... _asset_ ......... | $ 751 | BS |
| Net cash provided by operating activities .. _Flow var_ 1,461 | | SCF |
| Net sales.................... | 11,070 | IS |
| Stockholders' equity ................ | 5,547 | BS |
| Cost of sales.................. | 6,584 | IS |
| Net cash used by financing activities.......... | (943) | SCF |
| Total liabilities.................... | 12,901 | BS |
| Total expenses .. _Other expenses_ ......... | 3,431 | IS |
| Noncash assets .................... | 17,697 | BS |
| Net cash used by investing activities.......... | (470) | SCF |
| Net income..................... | 1,055 | IS |
| Cash and cash equivalents beginning year ....... | 703 | SCF |

**Required**

_1055    18448    48_

Prepare the income statement, balance sheet, and statement of cash flows for General Mills, Inc.

**P1-37.** **Formulating Financial Statements from Raw Data** **(LO2)**

Following is selected financial information from Abercrombie & Fitch for its fiscal year ended January 31, 2005 ($ millions).

Abercrombie & Fitch (ANF)

| | |
|---|---|
| Cash and equivalents........................ | $ 350 |
| Cash provided by operating activities ........... | 426 |
| Sales..................................... | 2,021 |
| Stockholders' equity ....................... | 669 |
| Cost of goods sold......................... | 1,111 |
| Cash used for financing activities .............. | (412) |
| Total liabilities............................. | 679 |
| Expenses ................................. | 694 |
| Noncash assets ............................ | 998 |
| Cash provided by investing activities............ | 280 |
| Net income................................ | 216 |
| Cash and cash equivalents beginning year ........ | 56 |

**Required**

Prepare the income statement, balance sheet, and statement of cash flows for Abercrombie & Fitch.

**P1-38.** **Formulating Financial Statements from Raw Data** **(LO2)**

Following is selected financial information from Cisco Systems, Inc., for the year ended July 30, 2005 ($ millions).

Cisco Systems, Inc. (CSCO)

| | |
|---|---|
| Cash and cash equivalents .................... | $ 4,742 |
| Cash provided by operating activities ........... | 7,568 |
| Sales..................................... | 24,801 |
| Stockholders' equity ....................... | 23,184 |
| Cost of goods sold......................... | 8,130 |
| Cash used in financing activities ................ | (9,162) |
| Total liabilities............................. | 10,699 |
| Expenses ................................. | 10,930 |
| Noncash assets ............................ | 29,141 |
| Cash provided by investing activities............ | 2,614 |
| Net income................................ | 5,741 |
| Cash and cash equivalents beginning year ........ | 3,722 |

**Required**

Prepare the income statement, balance sheet, and statement of cash flows for Cisco Systems, Inc.

**P1-39.** **Formulating a Statement of Stockholders' Equity from Raw Data** **(LO2)**

Crocker Corporation began calendar-year 2005 with stockholders' equity of $100,000, consisting of contributed capital of $70,000 and retained earnings of $30,000. During 2005, it issued additional stock for total cash proceeds of $30,000. It also reported $50,000 of net income, and paid $25,000 as a cash dividend to shareholders.

**Required**

Prepare the 2005 statement of stockholders' equity for Crocker Corporation.

**P1-40. Formulating a Statement of Stockholders' Equity from Raw Data (LO2)**

EA Systems, Inc., reports the following selected information at December 31, 2005 ($ millions).

| | |
|---|---|
| Contributed capital, December 31, 2004 and 2005.... | $ 550 |
| Retained earnings, December 31, 2004............. | 2,437 |
| Cash dividends, 2005........................... | 281 |
| Net income, 2005.............................. | 859 |

**Required**

Use this information to prepare the statement of stockholders' equity for EA Systems, Inc., for 2005.

**P1-41. Computing, Analyzing, and Interpreting Return on Equity (LO3)**

Kimberly-Clark (KMB)

Procter & Gamble (PG)

Following are summary financial statement data for both Kimberly-Clark and Procter & Gamble (industry competitors) for 2004 and 2005.

| Kimberly-Clark Corporation (KMB) | | |
|---|---|---|
| ($ millions) | Stockholders' Equity | Net Income |
| 2004.................. | $6,630 | $1,800 |
| 2005.................. | 5,558 | 1,568 |

| Procter & Gamble Company (PG) | | |
|---|---|---|
| ($ millions) | Stockholders' Equity | Net Income |
| 2004.................. | $18,190 | $6,156 |
| 2005.................. | 18,475 | 6,923 |

**Required**

a. Compute the return on equity (net income/average stockholders' equity) for 2005.
b. Which company reports a higher return on equity for 2005? Both companies used cash to repurchase large amounts of common stock in 2005. How do these repurchases affect return on equity? Why might a company wish to repurchase its own common stock?

**P1-42. Conducting Business Analysis (LO4)**

Procter & Gamble (PG)

Refer to the information in P1-41 to answer the following requirements.

**Required**

a. Discuss the possible reasons for Procter & Gamble's higher ROE in terms of its relative position in the competitive environment. (*Hint:* Review Porter's five forces analysis.)
b. Drawing on the analysis of part *a*, assess the competitive strength of Procter & Gamble.

**P1-43. Computing, Analyzing, and Interpreting Return on Equity (LO3)**

Nokia (NOK)

Nokia manufactures, markets, and sells phones and other electronics. Total stockholders' equity for Nokia is €14,576 in 2005 and €14,871 in 2004. In 2005, Nokia reported net income of €3,582 on sales of €34,191.

**Required**

a. What is Nokia's return on equity for 2005?
b. What are total expenses for Nokia in 2005?
c. Nokia used cash to repurchase a large amount of its common stock in 2004. What motivations might Nokia have for repurchasing its common stock?

**P1-44. Comparing Abercrombie & Fitch and TJX Companies (LO3)**

Abercrombie & Fitch (ANF) and TJX Companies (TJX)

Following are selected financial statement data from Abercrombie & Fitch (ANF—upscale clothing retailer) and TJX Companies (TJX—value priced clothing retailer including TJ Maxx)—both dated the end of January 2006.

| ($ millions) | ANF | TJX |
|---|---|---|
| Sales. . . . . . . . . . . . . . . . . . . . . . . . . . . . | $2,784.7 | $16,057.9 |
| Net operating profit after tax . . . . . . . . . . . | 352.8 | 675.3 |
| Net operating assets—2006. . . . . . . . . . . . | 584.0 | 2,548.2 |
| Net operating assets—2005. . . . . . . . . . . . | 669.3 | 2,321.2 |

#### Required

a. Compute the return on net operating assets for both companies for the year end January 2006.

b. Disaggregate the RNOAs for both companies into the net operating profit margin and the net operating asset turnover.

c. What differences are observed? Evaluate these differences in light of the two companies' business models. Which company has better financial performance?

**P1-45. Computing, Analyzing, and Interpreting Return on Net Operating Assets and its Components** (LO3)

McDonald's Corporation (MCD) reported 2005 net operating profit after tax of $2,614 million on net sales of $20,460 million. The December 31, 2005, balance sheet of MCD reports the following.

*McDonald's Corporation (MCD)*

| ($ millions) | 2005 | 2004 |
|---|---|---|
| Net operating assets . . . . . . . . . | $23,497 | $22,083 |

#### Required

a. What is MCD's return on net operating assets? Given that the average RNOA for fast-food restaurants is about 5.5%, how does MCD compare on RNOA? Explain why MCD's RNOA might be so different from the average fast-food restaurant.

b. Decompose MCD's RNOA into its net operating profit margin and its net operating asset turnover.

c. Suggest specific actions that McDonald's might take to improve (1) its net operating profit margin, and (2) its net operating asset turnover.

**P1-46. Disaggregating Return on Net Operating Assets Over Time** (LO3)

Following are selected financial statement data from 3M Company for 2002 through 2005.

*3M Company (MMM)*

| ($ millions) | 2005 | 2004 | 2003 | 2002 |
|---|---|---|---|---|
| Net sales. . . . . . . . . . . . . . . . . . . . . . | $21,167 | $20,011 | $18,232 | $16,332 |
| Net operating profit after tax . . . . . . . | 3,256 | 2,976 | 2,413 | 1,980 |
| Net operating assets . . . . . . . . . . . . | 12,209 | 12,972 | 10,604 | 9,132 |

#### Required

a. Compute 3M Company's return on net operating assets for 2003 through 2005. What trends are observed?

b. Disaggregate 3M's RNOA into the net operating profit margin and the net operating asset turnover for 2003 through 2005.

c. Which RNOA component appears to be driving the trend observed in part a? Explain.

**P1-47.[A] Reading and Interpreting Audit Opinions** (LO5)

Apple, Inc.'s 2005 financial statements include the following audit report from KPMG LLP

*Apple, Inc. (AAPL)*

REPORT OF INDEPENDENT REGISTERED PUBLIC ACCOUNTING FIRM

The Board of Directors and Shareholders
Apple, Inc.:

We have audited the accompanying consolidated balance sheets of Apple, Inc. and subsidiaries (the Company) as of September 24, 2005 and September 25, 2004, and the related consolidated statements of operations, shareholders' equity and cash flows for each of the years in the three-year period ended September 24, 2005. These consolidated financial statements are the responsibility of the Company's management. Our responsibility is to express an opinion on these consolidated financial statements based on our audits.

*Continued*

We conducted our audits in accordance with the standards of the Public Company Accounting Oversight Board (United States). Those standards require that we plan and perform the audit to obtain reasonable assurance about whether the consolidated financial statements are free of material misstatement An audit includes examining, on a test basis, evidence supporting the amounts and disclosures in the consolidated financial statements. An audit also includes assessing the accounting principles used and significant estimates made by management, as well as evaluating the overall financial statement presentation. We believe that our audits provide a reasonable basis for our opinion.

In our opinion, the consolidated financial statements referred to above present fairly, in all material respects, the financial position of the Company as of September 24, 2005 and September 25, 2004, and the results of their operations and their cash flows for each of the years in the three-year period ended September 24, 2005, in conformity with U.S. generally accepted accounting principles.

We also have audited, in accordance with the standards of the Public Company Accounting Oversight Board (United States), the effectiveness of the Company's internal control over financial reporting as of September 24, 2005, based on criteria established in *Internal Control-Integrated Framework* issued by the Committee of Sponsoring Organizations of the Treadway Commission (COSO), and our report dated November 29, 2005 expressed an unqualified opinion on management's assessment of and the effective operation of internal control over financial reporting.

As discussed in Note 1 to the consolidated financial statements, the Company changed its method of accounting for asset retirement obligations and for financial instruments with characteristics of both liabilities and equity in 2003.

fs/ KPMG LLP

Mountain View, California
November 29, 2005

### Required

a. To whom is the report addressed? Why?

b. In your own words, briefly describe the audit process. What steps do auditors take to determine whether a company's financial statements are free from material misstatement?

c. What is the nature of KPMG's opinion? What do you believe the word *fairly* means? Is KPMG providing a guarantee to Apple's financial statement users?

d. What other opinion is KPMG rendering? Why is this opinion important?

e. What do you believe is the purpose of the last paragraph of KPMG's audit report?

**P1-48. Reading and Interpreting CEO Certifications (LO5)**

Apple, Inc. (AAPL)

Following is the CEO Certification required by the Sarbanes-Oxley Act and signed by Apple CEO Steve Jobs. Apple's Chief Financial Officer signed a similar form.

CERTIFICATIONS

I, Steven P. Jobs, certify that:

1. I have reviewed this annual report on Form 10-K of Apple, Inc.;

2. Based on my knowledge, this report does not contain any untrue statement of a material fact or omit to state a material fact necessary to make the statements made, in light of the circumstances under which such statements were made, not misleading with respect to the period covered by this report;

3. Based on my knowledge, the financial statements, and other financial information included in this report, fairly present in all material respects the financial condition, results of operations and cash flows of the registrant as of, and for, the periods presented in this report;

4. The registrant's other certifying officer(s) and I are responsible for establishing and maintaining disclosure controls and procedures (as defined in Exchange Act Rules 13a-15(e) and 15d-15(e)) and internal control over financial reporting (as defined in Exchange Act Rules 13a-15(f) and 15d-15(f) for the registrant) and have:

   (a) Designed such disclosure controls and procedures, or caused such disclosure controls and procedures to be designed under our supervision, to ensure that material information relating to the registrant, including its consolidated subsidiaries, is made known to us by others within those entities, particularly during the period in which this report is being prepared;

   (b) Designed such internal control over financial reporting, or caused such internal control over financial reporting to be designed under our supervision, to provide reasonable assurance regarding the reliability of financial reporting and the preparation of financial statements for external purposes in accordance with generally accepted accounting principles;

   (c) Evaluated the effectiveness of the registrant's disclosure controls and procedures and presented in this report our conclusions about the effectiveness of the disclosure controls and procedures, as of the end of the period covered by this report based on such evaluation; and

   (d) Disclosed in this report any change in the registrant's internal control over financial reporting that occurred during the registrant's most recent fiscal quarter (the registrant's fourth fiscal quarter in the case of an annual report) that has materially affected, or is reasonably likely to materially affect, the registrant's internal control over financial reporting; and

*Continued*

5.  The registrant's other certifying officer(s) and I have disclosed, based on our most recent evaluation of internal control over financial reporting, to the registrant's auditors and the audit committee of the registrant's board of directors (or persons performing the equivalent functions):

    (a)  All significant deficiencies and material weaknesses in the design or operation of internal control over financial reporting which are reasonably likely to adversely affect the registrant's ability to record, process, summarize, and report financial information; and

    (b)  Any fraud, whether or not material, that involves management or other employees who have a significant role in the registrant's internal control over financial reporting.

Date: November 29, 2005

By: _____/s/ STEVEN P. JOBS_____

Steven P. Jobs

Chief Executive Officer

**Required**

*a.*  Summarize the assertions that Steve Jobs made in this certification.

*b.*  Why did Congress feel it important that CEOs and CFOs sign such certifications?

*c.*  What potential liability do you believe the CEO and CFO are assuming by signing such certifications?

**P1-49.  Assessing Corporate Governance   (LO5)**

Review the corporate governance section of General Electric's Website (**GE.com/en/company/investor/ corp_governance.htm**). By some accounts, GE has established one of the best corporate governance structures in the world.

General Electric (GE)

**Required**

*a.*  In your words, briefly describe GE's governance structure.

*b.*  What is the main purpose of this governance structure?

# CASES

**C1-50.  Management Application: Strategic Financing   (LO2)**

You and your management team are working to develop the strategic direction of your company for the next three years. One issue you are discussing is how to finance the projected increases in operating assets. Your options are to rely more heavily on operating creditors, borrow the funds, or to sell additional stock in your company. Discuss the pros and cons of each source of financing.

**C1-51.  Management Application: Statement Analysis   (LO3)**

You are evaluating your company's recent operating performance and are trying to decide on the relative weights you should put on the income statement, the balance sheet, and the statement of cash flows. Discuss the information each of these statements provides and its role in evaluating operating performance.

**C1-52.  Management Application: Analyst Relations   (LO2)**

Your investor relations department reports to you that stockholders and financial analysts evaluate the quality of a company's financial reports based on their "transparency," namely the clarity and completeness of the company's financial disclosures. Discuss the trade-offs of providing more or less transparent financial reports.

**C1-53.  Ethics and Governance: Management Communications   (LO5)**

The Business Insight box on page 1-14 quotes Warren Buffett on the use of accounting jargon. Many companies publicly describe their performance using terms such as "EBITDA" or "earnings purged of various expenses" because they believe these terms more effectively reflect their companies' performance than GAAP-defined terms such as net income. What ethical issues might arise from the use of such terms and what challenges does their use present for the governance of the company by shareholders and directors?

**C1-54.[B]  Ethics and Governance: Auditor Independence   (LO5)**

The SEC has been concerned with the "independence" of external auditing firms. It is especially concerned about how large non-audit (such as consulting) fees might impact how aggressively auditing firms pursue accounting issues they uncover in their audits. Congress recently passed legislation that prohibits accounting firms from providing both consulting and auditing services to the same client. How might consulting fees affect auditor independence? What other conflicts of interest might exist for auditors? How do these conflicts impact the governance process?

# Introducing Financial Statements and Transaction Analysis

## LEARNING OBJECTIVES

**LO1** Describe information conveyed by the financial statements. (p. 2-5)

**LO2** Explain and illustrate linkages among the four financial statements. (p. 2-21)

**LO3** Illustrate use of the financial statement effects template to summarize accounting transactions. (p. 2-23)

## APPLE

In 1985, the board of directors of Apple along with the new CEO John Sculley, dismissed Steve Jobs, Apple's co-founder. Fast forward 12 years—Apple is struggling to survive. After a series of crippling financial losses, the company's stock price is at an all-time low. In a complete about face, the board asks Steve Jobs to return as interim CEO to begin a critical restructuring of the company's product line. True to form, Jobs shows up at his first meeting with Apple senior executives wearing shorts, sneakers, and a few days' beard growth. Sitting in a swivel chair and spinning slowly, Jobs begins quizzing the executives. "O.K., tell me what's wrong with this place," asks Jobs. Mumbled replies and embarrassed looks ensue. Jobs cuts them short and jumps up: "It's the products! So what's wrong with the products?" Again, more weak answers and again Jobs cut them off. "The products SUCK!" he roars. "There's no sex in them anymore!"

Jobs was right—Apple was mired in a sea of problems, many stemming from a weak product line. The company's decision to design proprietary software that was often incompatible with Windows had relegated Apple to a niche player in the highly competitive, low-margin PC business. Years before, Microsoft had replicated the Mac operating system and licensed the software to PC manufacturers such as Dell. Now, the Mac clung to a 3% market share. Apple reported a net loss in 2001, and its cumulative profit from 2001-2003 amounted to an anemic $109 million. Apple's prospects were dim.

That was then. This is now. Apple's 2005 iPod sales surpassed $4.5 billion, growing at over 250% per year since 2003. iPods now account for nearly three-quarters of all MP3 players sold in the U.S. In the past two years, iPods made up more than half of Apple's total sales growth, and operating profits have increased to $1.65 billion. Accompanying the meteoric rise of its music player, Apple recently announced that its iTunes Music Store had sold its two-billionth song.

Getty Images

Apple's shares (ticker: AAPL) now trade above $60, a staggering 15 times the $4 they fetched ten years ago when the Jobs came back on board. Indeed, Apple's stock has increased six-fold in the past two years, as the following price chart illustrates. The total stock market value of Apple stock (called the market capitalization or market cap) exceeds $50 billion.

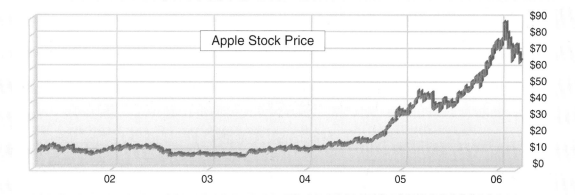

This module explains each financial statement: the balance sheet, the income statement, the statement of cash flows, and the statement of stockholders' equity. Let's begin with a sneak preview of Apple's financial statements.

Apple's balance sheet is very liquid (many of its assets can be readily converted to cash), with over 70% of its assets in cash and marketable securities. Liquidity is important for companies like Apple that must react quickly to opportunities and changing market conditions. Like other high-techs, much of Apple's production is subcontracted. Consequently, Apple's property, plant and equipment make up only 7% of its assets.

On the financing side of its balance sheet, nearly two-thirds of Apple's resources come from owner financing: from common stock sold to shareholders and from past profits reinvested in the business. Technology companies such as Apple, which have uncertain product life-cycles and highly volatile cash flows, avoid

*(Continued on next page)*

*(Continued from previous page)*

high debt levels that might cause financial problems in a business downturn. Apple's nonowner financing consists of low-cost credit from suppliers (accounts payable) and unpaid overhead expenses (accrued liabilities).

Consider Apple's income statement: driven by the popularity and high profit margins of iPods, Apple recently reported over $1.6 billion of operating income. This is impressive given that Apple spends four cents of every sales dollar on research and development and runs expensive advertising campaigns.

Yet companies cannot live by profits alone. It is cash that pays bills. Profits and cash flow are two different concepts, each providing a different perspective on company performance. Apple generated over $2.5 billion of cash flow from operating activities, nearly twice its profit level. This is due to noncash expenses included on Apple's income statement and effective management of its balance sheet. We review Apple's cash flows in this module.

Apple pays no dividends and its newly issued common stock relates primarily to executive stock options. These capital transactions are reported in the statement of stockholders' equity.

While it is important to understand what is reported in each of the four financial statements, it is also important to know what is *not* reported. To illustrate, *Fortune* reported that "Jobs cut a deal with the Big Five record companies . . . to sell songs on iTunes, but they were afraid of Internet piracy. So Jobs promised to wrap their songs in Apple's *FairPlay*—the only copy-protection software that is iPod-compatible. Other digital music services such as Yahoo Music Unlimited and Napster reached similar deals with the big record labels. But Apple refused to license *FairPlay* to them. So those companies turned to Microsoft for copy protection. That means none of the songs sold by those services can be played on the wildly popular iPod. Instead, users of the services had to rely on inferior devices made by companies like Samsung and SanDisk that supported Microsoft's Windows Media format."

Apple's copy-protection software described above creates a barrier to competition that allows iPod to earn above-average profits. This represents a valuable resource to Apple, but it is not reported on Apple's balance sheet. Consider another example. Apple's software engineers write code and create software that will generate profits for Apple in the future. While this represents a valuable resource to Apple, it is not reported on the balance sheet because Apple expensed the software engineers' salaries when the code was written. We discuss these and other issues relating to asset recognition and measurement in this module.

Sources: Apple 2005 10-K; Apple 2005 Annual Report; *BusinessWeek*, 2006; *Fortune*, 2006.

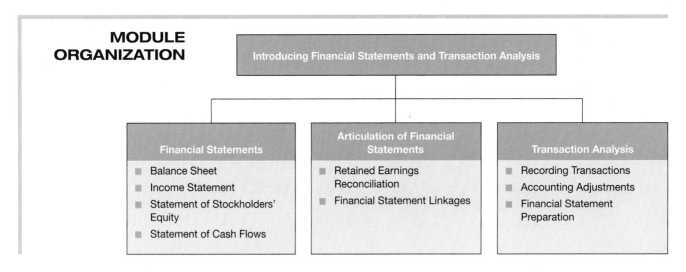

## INTRODUCTION

Prior to reviewing the four financial statements, we examine how costs flow through the financial accounting system. For this purpose, we look at the balance sheet (that lists what the company owns and what it owes at a *point* in time) and the income statement (that lists the company's revenues, expenses, and income for a *period* of time).

Companies incur costs to acquire resources that will be used in operations. Every cost creates either an immediate or a future economic benefit. Determining when the company will realize the benefit from a cost is paramount. When a cost creates an immediate benefit, such as gasoline used in delivery vehicles, the company records the cost in the income statement as an expense. When a cost creates a future economic benefit, such as inventory to be resold or equipment to be later used for manufacturing, the company records the cost on the balance sheet as an asset. The definition of an asset is "a future economic benefit." An asset remains on the company's balance sheet until it is used up. When an asset is used up, the company realizes the economic benefit from the asset; that is, there is no future economic benefit left so there is no asset left. Then, the asset's cost is transferred from the balance sheet to the income statement where it is labeled as an expense. This is why assets are sometimes referred to as prepaid or deferred expenses.

Companies expense certain costs, such as research and development salaries, as they are incurred because even though the costs will likely bring future economic benefits, the related asset cannot be reliably measured. (We discuss the concept of measurement later in this module). Exhibit 2.1 illustrates how costs flow from the balance sheet to the income statement.

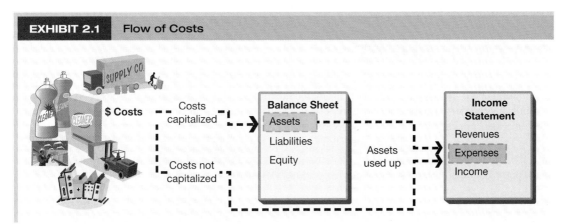

**EXHIBIT 2.1    Flow of Costs**

All costs are either held on the balance sheet or are transferred to the income statement. When costs are recorded on the balance sheet, assets are reported and expenses are deferred to a later period. Once the company receives benefits from the assets, the related costs are transferred from the balance sheet to the income statement. At that point, assets are reduced and expenses are recorded in the current period.

Tracking the flow of costs from the balance sheet to the income statement is an important part of accounting. If the cost transfer occurs more slowly than it should, current income is higher than it should be. If companies transfer costs too quickly, current income is lower than it should be. GAAP allows companies some flexibility in transferring costs. As such, there is potential for abuse, especially when managers confront pressures to achieve income targets.

Corporate scandals involving WorldCom and Enron regrettably illustrate improper cost transfers designed to achieve higher profit levels. Neither company transferred costs from the balance sheet to the income statement as quickly as they should have. This had the effect of overstating assets on the balance sheet and net income on the income statement. In subsequent litigation, the SEC and the Justice Department contended that these companies intentionally overstated net income to boost stock prices. A number of senior executives from both Enron and WorldCom were sentenced to lengthy jail terms as a result of their criminal actions.

The decision about whether and when to transfer costs impacts more than current period income. When costs are transferred too quickly, current period income is understated *and* future period income is overstated because once costs are removed from the balance sheet they do not impact future period income. Conversely, if costs are transferred too slowly from the balance sheet, current period income is overstated and future period income is understated. The improper transfer of costs, therefore, creates *income shifting:* increasing current period income and decreasing future period income, *or* depressing current period income and increasing future period income.

What does GAAP advise about the transfer of costs? Asset costs should transfer to the income statement when the asset no longer has any future economic benefit (i.e. it no longer meets the definition of an asset). For example, when inventories are purchased or manufactured, their cost is recorded on the balance sheet as an asset called *inventories*. When inventories are sold, they no longer have an economic benefit to the company and their cost is transferred to the income statement in an expense called *cost of goods sold*. Cost of goods sold represents the cost of inventories sold during that period. This expense is recognized in the same period as the revenue generated from the sale.

As another example, consider equipment costs. When a company acquires equipment, the cost of the equipment is recorded on the balance sheet in an asset called *equipment* (often included in the general category of property, plant, and equipment, or PPE). When equipment is used in operations, a portion of the acquisition cost is transferred to the income statement to match against the sales the equipment helped generate. To illustrate, if an asset costs $100,000, and 10% of it is used up this period in operating activities, then $10,000 of the asset's cost is transferred from the balance sheet to the income statement. This process is called *depreciation* and the expense related to this transfer of costs is called depreciation expense.

---

**MANAGERIAL DECISION**    **You Are the Securities Analyst**

You are analyzing the performance of a company that hired a new CEO during the current year. The current year's income statement includes an expense labeled "asset write-offs." Write-offs represent the accelerated transfer of costs from the balance sheet to the income statement. Are you concerned about the legitimacy of these expenses? Why or why not? [Answer, p. 2-32]

---

# BALANCE SHEET

**LO1** Describe information conveyed by the financial statements.

The balance sheet is divided into three sections: assets, liabilities, and stockholders' equity. It provides information about the resources available to management and the claims against those resources by creditors and shareholders. The balance sheet reports the assets, liabilities and equity at a *point* in time. Balance sheet accounts are called "permanent accounts" in that they carry over from period to period; that is, the ending balance from one period becomes the beginning balance for the next. (Income statement accounts are called "temporary accounts." They are zeroed out at the end of each accounting period so that subsequent periods show only the sales, expenses, and net income for that period.)

## Assets—Reflecting Investing Activities

Companies acquire assets to yield a return for their shareholders. Assets are expected to produce economic benefits in the form of revenues, either directly such as with inventory or indirectly such as with a manufacturing plant that produces inventories for sale. To create shareholder value, assets must yield income that is in excess of the cost of the invested and borrowed funds used to acquire the assets.

The asset section of the Apple balance sheet is shown in Exhibit 2.2. Apple reports $11,551 million of total assets as of September 24, 2005, its year-end. The amounts reported on the balance sheet are at a *point in time*—that is, the close of business on the day of the report. An asset must possess two characteristics to be reported on the balance sheet:

1. It must be owned (or controlled) by the company.
2. It must possess expected future economic benefits.

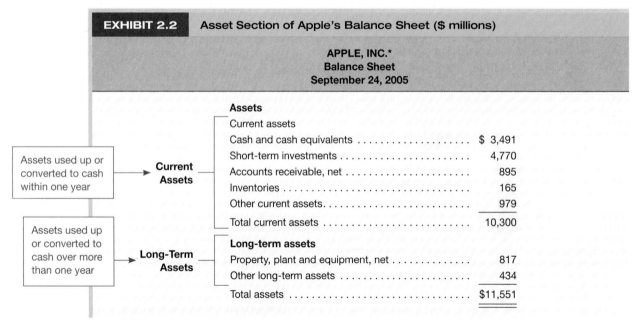

| EXHIBIT 2.2 | Asset Section of Apple's Balance Sheet ($ millions) |

**APPLE, INC.***
**Balance Sheet**
**September 24, 2005**

**Assets**

Current assets

Assets used up or converted to cash within one year → **Current Assets**

| | |
|---|---|
| Cash and cash equivalents | $ 3,491 |
| Short-term investments | 4,770 |
| Accounts receivable, net | 895 |
| Inventories | 165 |
| Other current assets | 979 |
| Total current assets | 10,300 |

Assets used up or converted to cash over more than one year → **Long-Term Assets**

**Long-term assets**

| | |
|---|---|
| Property, plant and equipment, net | 817 |
| Other long-term assets | 434 |
| Total assets | $11,551 |

* Apple restated its financial statements in 2006 to correct its accounting for employee stock options (see Appendix 1B for a discussion of restatements and Module 9 for a discussion of employee stock options). This restatement, required by the SEC, related to back-dating stock options and impacted many companies in that year. Thus, Apple's 2005 statements included in subsequent years' filings are slightly different from its 2005 statements here. To view its financial statements used in this module, search for Apple's 10-K with a filing date of "2005-12-01" on the SEC Website.

The first requirement, owning or controlling an asset, implies that a company has legal title to the asset, such as the title to property, or has the unrestricted right to use the asset, such as a lease on the property. The second requirement implies that a company expects to realize a benefit from the asset. Benefits can be cash inflows from the sale of an asset or from sales of products produced by the asset. Benefits also can refer to the receipt of other assets such as with an account receivable from a credit sale. Or, benefits can arise from future services the company will enjoy, such as prepaying for a year-long insurance policy.

## Current Assets

The balance sheet lists assets in order of decreasing **liquidity**, which refers to the ease of converting non-cash assets into cash. The most liquid assets are called **current assets** and they are listed first. A company expects to convert its current assets into cash or use those assets in operations within the coming fiscal year.[1] Typical examples of current assets follow:

**Cash**—currency, bank deposits, and investments with an original maturity of 90 days or less (called *cash equivalents*);

**Marketable securities**—short-term investments that can be quickly sold to raise cash;

**Accounts receivable, net**—amounts due to the company from customers arising from the sale of products on credit ("net" refers to uncollectible accounts explained in Module 6);

**Inventory**—goods purchased or produced for sale to customers;

**Prepaid expenses**—costs paid in advance for rent, insurance, advertising or other services.

Apple reports current assets of $10,300 million in 2005, which is 89% of its total assets. The amount of current assets is an important measure of liquidity. Companies require a degree of liquidity to operate effectively, as they must be able to respond to changing market conditions and take advantage of opportunities. However, current assets are expensive to hold (they must be stored, insured, monitored, financed, and so forth)—and they typically generate returns that are less than those from noncurrent assets. As a result, companies seek to maintain only just enough current assets to cover liquidity needs, but not so much so as to unnecessarily reduce income.

## Long-Term Assets

The second section of the balance sheet reports long-term (noncurrent) assets. Long-term assets include the following:

**Property, plant and equipment (PPE), net**—land, factory buildings, warehouses, office buildings, machinery, motor vehicles, office equipment and other items used in operating activities ("net" refers to subtraction of accumulated depreciation, the portion of the assets' cost that has been transferred from the balance sheet to the income statement, which is explained in Module 6);

**Long-term investments**—investments that the company does not intend to sell in the near future;

**Intangible and other assets**—assets without physical substance, including patents, trademarks, franchise rights, goodwill and other costs the company incurred that provide future benefits.

Long-term assets are not expected to be converted into cash for some time and are, therefore, listed after current assets.

## Measuring Assets

Assets are reported at their original acquisition costs, or **historical costs**, and not at their current market values. (Exceptions are marketable securities that are recorded on the balance sheet at current market values, and assets whose future economic benefits have become impaired and are written down on the balance sheet to fair market value.) The concept of historical costs is not without controversy. The controversy arises because of the trade-off between the **relevance** of current market values for many business decisions and the **reliability** of historical cost measures.

To illustrate, imagine we are financial analysts and want to determine the value of a company. The company's value equals the value of its assets less the value of its liabilities. Current market values of company

---

[1] Technically, current assets include those assets expected to be converted into cash within the upcoming year or the company's operating cycle (the cash-to-cash cycle), whichever is longer. Fortune Brands (manufacturer of Jim Beam Whiskey) provides an example of a current asset with a cash conversion cycle of longer than one year. Its inventory footnote reports: "In accordance with generally recognized trade practices, bulk whiskey inventories are classified as current assets, although the majority of such inventories, due to the duration of aging processes, ordinarily will not be sold within one year."

assets (and liabilities) are more informative and relevant to our analysis than are historic costs. But how can we determine market values? For some assets, like marketable securities, values are readily obtained from online quotes or from *The Wall Street Journal.* For other assets like property, plant, and equipment, market values are far more subjective and difficult to estimate. It would be easier for us, as analysts, if companies reported market values on their balance sheet. However, allowing companies to report estimates of asset market values would introduce potential *bias* into financial reporting. Consequently, companies continue to report historical costs because the loss in reliability from using subjective market values on the balance sheet is considered to be greater than the loss in relevance from using historical costs.

It is important to realize that balance sheets only include items that can be reliably measured. If a company cannot assign a monetary amount to an asset with relative certainty, it does not recognize an asset on the balance sheet. This means that there are, typically, considerable "assets" that are not reflected on a balance sheet. For example, the well-known apple image is absent from Apple's balance sheet. This image is called an "unrecognized intangible asset." Both requirements for an asset are met: Apple owns the brand and it expects to realize future benefits from the logo. The problem is reliably measuring the expected future benefits to be derived from the image. Intangible assets such as the Coke bottle silhouette, the iPod brand, and the Nike swoosh are not on their respective balance sheets. Companies only report intangible assets on the balance sheet when they are purchased. Any internally created intangible assets are not reported on a balance sheet. A sizable amount of resources is, therefore, potentially omitted from companies' balance sheets.

Excluded intangible assets often relate to *knowledge-based* (intellectual) assets, such as a strong management team, a well-designed supply chain, or superior technology. Although these intangible assets confer a competitive advantage to the company, and yield above-normal income (and clear economic benefits to those companies), they cannot be reliably measured. This is one reason why companies in knowledge-based industries are so difficult to analyze.

Excluded intangible assets are, however, presumably reflected in companies' market values. This can yield a large difference between the market value and the book value of a company's equity. This is illustrated in the following ratios of market value to book value: Apple is 7.6; Cisco is 5.3; IBM is 3.9; and Citigroup is 2.1. Market-to-book ratios are greater for companies with large knowledge-based assets, which are not reported on the balance sheet, but are reflected in company market value. Companies such as Citigroup have fewer of these assets. Hence, their balance sheets usually reflect a greater portion of company value.

## Liabilities and Equity—Reflecting Financing Activities

Liabilities and stockholders' equity represent the sources of capital the company uses to finance the acquisition of assets. In general, liabilities represent a company's future economic sacrifices. Liabilities are

---

**BUSINESS INSIGHT**    **How Much Debt Is Reasonable?**

Apple reports total assets of $11,551 million, liabilities of $4,085 million, and stockholders' equity of $7,466 million. This reveals that it finances 35% of its assets with borrowed funds and 65% with shareholder investment. This is a lower percentage of non-owner financing than other companies such as The Gap, Target, and Procter & Gamble (P&G), but about the same as Cisco Systems. Companies must monitor their financing sources and amounts. Too much reliance on equity capital is expensive. And, too much borrowing is risky. The level of debt that a company can effectively manage depends on the stability and reliability of its operating cash flows. Companies such as P&G, Target, and The Gap can manage relatively high debt levels because their cash flows are relatively stable. Apple and Cisco, on the other hand, operate in industries that change rapidly. They cannot afford to take on too much borrowing risk.

| ($ millions) | Assets | Liabilities | Liabilities to Assets ratio | Equity | Equity to Assets ratio |
|---|---|---|---|---|---|
| Cisco Systems, Inc. . . . . . . . | $33,883 | $10,709 | 32% | $23,174 | 68% |
| Apple, Inc. . . . . . . . . . . . . . . | 11,551 | 4,085 | 35% | 7,466 | 65% |
| Gap, Inc. . . . . . . . . . . . . . . . | 10,048 | 5,112 | 51% | 4,936 | 49% |
| Target Corporation . . . . . . . . | 32,293 | 19,264 | 60% | 13,029 | 40% |
| Procter & Gamble Co. . . . . . . | 61,527 | 44,050 | 72% | 17,477 | 28% |

borrowed funds such as accounts payable, accrued liabilities, and obligations to lenders or bond investors. They can be interest-bearing or non-interest-bearing.

Equity represents capital that has been invested by the shareholders, either directly via the purchase of stock (net of any company repurchases of stock from its shareholders, called *treasury stock*) or indirectly in the form of *retained earnings* that reflect earnings that are reinvested in the business and not paid out as dividends. We discuss liabilities and equity in this section.

The liabilities and stockholders' equity sections of the Apple balance sheet are reproduced in Exhibit 2.3. Apple reports $4,085 million of total liabilities and $7,466 million of stockholders' equity as of its 2005 year-end.

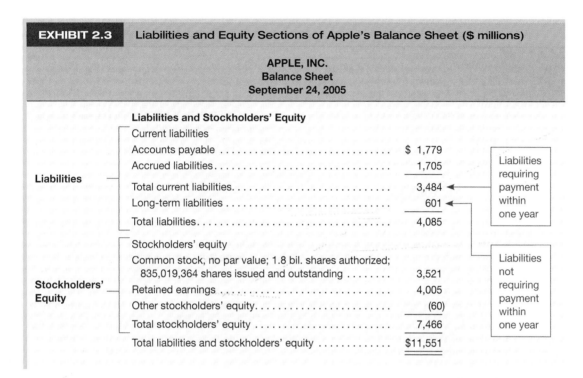

| EXHIBIT 2.3 | Liabilities and Equity Sections of Apple's Balance Sheet ($ millions) |

**APPLE, INC.**
**Balance Sheet**
**September 24, 2005**

**Liabilities and Stockholders' Equity**

| | | |
|---|---|---|
| | Current liabilities | |
| | Accounts payable | $ 1,779 |
| | Accrued liabilities | 1,705 |
| **Liabilities** | Total current liabilities | 3,484 |
| | Long-term liabilities | 601 |
| | Total liabilities | 4,085 |
| | Stockholders' equity | |
| | Common stock, no par value; 1.8 bil. shares authorized; 835,019,364 shares issued and outstanding | 3,521 |
| **Stockholders' Equity** | Retained earnings | 4,005 |
| | Other stockholders' equity | (60) |
| | Total stockholders' equity | 7,466 |
| | Total liabilities and stockholders' equity | $11,551 |

Liabilities requiring payment within one year

Liabilities not requiring payment within one year

Why would Apple obtain capital from both borrowed funds and shareholders? Why not just one or the other? The answer lies in their relative costs and the contractual agreements that Apple has with each.

Creditors have the first claim on the assets of the company. As a result, their position is not as risky and, accordingly, their expected return on investment is less than that required by shareholders (also, interest is tax deductible whereas dividends are not). This makes debt a less expensive source of capital than equity. So, then, why should a company not finance itself entirely with borrowed funds? The reason is that borrowed funds entail contractual obligations to repay the principal and interest on the debt. If a company cannot make these payments when they come due, creditors can force the company into bankruptcy and potentially put the company out of business. Shareholders, in contrast, cannot require repurchase of their stock, or even the payment of dividends. Thus, companies take on a level of debt that they can comfortably repay at reasonable interest costs. The remaining balance required to fund business activities is financed with more costly equity capital.

## Current Liabilities

The balance sheet lists liabilities in order of maturity. Obligations that are due within one year are called **current liabilities.** Examples of common current liabilities follow:

**Accounts payable**—amounts owed to suppliers for goods and services purchased on credit.

**Accrued liabilities**—obligations for expenses that have been incurred but not yet paid; examples are accrued wages payable (wages earned by employees but not yet paid), accrued interest payable (interest that is owing but has not been paid), and accrued income taxes (taxes due).

**Unearned revenues**—obligations created when the company accepts payment in advance for goods or services it will deliver in the future; also called advances from customers, customer deposits, or deferred revenues.

**Short-term notes payable**—short-term debt payable to banks or other creditors.

**Current maturities of long-term debt**—principal portion of long-term debt that is due to be paid within one year.

Apple reports current liabilities of $3,484 on its 2005 balance sheet.

Accounts payable arise when one company purchases goods or services from another company. Typically, sellers offer credit terms when selling to other companies, rather than expecting cash on delivery. The seller records an account receivable and the buyer records an account payable. Apple reports accounts payable of $1,779 million as of the balance sheet date. Liabilities that arise from transactions such as those making up its accounts payable are relatively uncomplicated. That is, a transaction occurs (inventory purchase), a bill is sent, and the amount owed is reported on the balance sheet as a liability.

Apple's accrued liabilities total $1,705 million. Accrued liabilities refer to incomplete transactions. For example, employees work and earn wages, but usually are not paid until later. They must be reported as expense in the period that employees earn them because those wages have been incurred by the company. Also, a liability (wages payable) must be set up on the balance sheet. This is an *accrual*. Other common accruals include the recording of liabilities such as rent and utilities payable, taxes payable, and interest payable on borrowings. All of these accruals involve recognition of expense in the income statement and a liability on the balance sheet. (We discuss accruals later in this module.)

**Net working capital**, or simply working capital, reflects the difference between current assets and current liabilities and is defined as follows:

$$\text{Net Working Capital} = \text{Current Assets} - \text{Current Liabilities}$$

We usually prefer to see more current assets than current liabilities to ensure that companies are liquid. That is, companies should have sufficient funds to pay their short-term debts as they mature. The net working capital required to conduct business depends on the company's **operating (or cash) cycle**, which is the time between paying cash for goods or employee services and receiving cash from customers—see Exhibit 2.4.

Companies, for example, use cash to purchase or manufacture inventories held for resale. Inventories are usually purchased on credit (accounts payable) from suppliers. This financing is called **trade credit**. Inventories are sold, either on credit (accounts receivable) or for cash. When receivables are ultimately collected, a portion of the cash received is used to repay accounts payable and the remainder goes to the cash account for the next operating cycle.

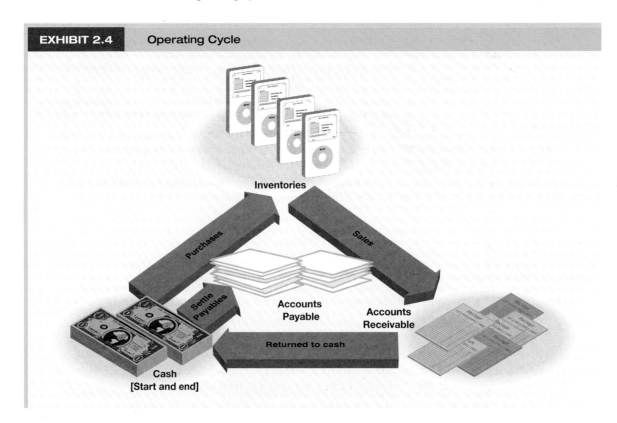

**EXHIBIT 2.4    Operating Cycle**

When cash is invested in inventory, the inventory can remain with the company for 30 to 90 days or more. Once inventory is sold, the resulting accounts receivable can remain with the company for another 30 to 90 days. Assets such as inventory and accounts receivable are costly to hold and, as such, companies strive to reduce operating cycles with various initiatives that aim to:

▪ Decrease accounts receivable by better collection procedures
▪ Reduce inventory levels by improved production systems and management
▪ Increase trade credit to minimize the cash invested in inventories

Analysts often use the "cash cycle" to evaluate company liquidity. The cash cycle is the number of days the company has its cash tied up in receivables and inventories, less the number of days of trade credit provided by company suppliers.

## Noncurrent Liabilities

**Noncurrent liabilities** are obligations due after one year. Examples of noncurrent liabilities follow:

**Long-term debt**—amounts borrowed from creditors that are scheduled to be repaid more than one year in the future; any portion of long-term debt that is due within one year is reclassified as a current liability called *current maturities of long-term debt*. Long-term debt includes bonds, mortgages, and other long-term loans.

**Other long-term liabilities**—various obligations, such as pension liabilities and long-term tax liabilities, that will be settled a year or more into the future. We discuss these items in later modules.

Apple reports $601 million of noncurrent liabilities. As is typical of high-tech companies, Apple has no long-term debt. Instead, all of its noncurrent liabilities relate to deferred revenue and deferred taxes.

Deferred (unearned) revenue arises when a company receives cash in advance of providing a good or service. When cash is received, the company records a liability (deferred or unearned revenue), which represents the company's obligation to provide the good or service in the future. When the company ultimately delivers the good or provides the service, the deferred revenue account is reduced and revenues are recorded in the income statement, thus increasing net income. Deferred taxes relate to future tax liabilities resulting from differences between the income reported to shareholders and that reported to tax authorities. We discuss deferred taxes in Module 5.

## Stockholders' Equity

**Stockholders' equity** reflects financing provided from company owners. Equity is often referred to as *residual interest*. That is, stockholders have a claim on any assets in excess of what is needed to meet company obligations to creditors. The following are examples of items typically included in equity:

**Common stock**—par value of stock received from the original sale of common stock to investors.

**Preferred stock**—value of stock received from the original sale of preferred stock to investors; preferred stock has fewer ownership rights compared to common stock.

**Additional paid-in capital**—amounts received from the original sale of stock to investors in addition to the par value of common and preferred stock.

**Treasury stock**—amount the company paid to reacquire its common stock from shareholders.

**Retained earnings**—accumulated net income (profit) that has not been distributed to stockholders as dividends.

**Accumulated other comprehensive income or loss**—accumulated changes in equity that are not reported in the income statement (explained in Module 9).

Contributed Capital

Earned Capital

The equity section of a balance sheet consists of two basic components: contributed capital and earned capital. **Contributed capital** is the net funding that a company has received from issuing and reacquiring its equity shares; that is, the funds received from issuing shares less any funds paid to repurchase such shares. Apple reports $7,466 million in total stockholders' equity. Its contributed capital is $3,521 million.

Apple's common stock is "no par." This means that Apple records all of its contributed capital in the common stock account and records no additional paid-in capital. Apple's stockholders (via its board of directors) have authorized it to issue up to 1.8 billion shares of common stock. To date, it has sold (issued) 835,019,364 shares for total proceeds of $3,521 million, or $4.22 per share, on average. Apple has repurchased no shares of stock to date. We explain these and other equity details in Module 9.

| BUSINESS INSIGHT | Apple's Market and Book Values |
|---|---|

Apple's market value has historically exceeded its book value of equity (see graph below). Much of Apple's market value derives from intangible assets such as brand equity that are not fully reflected on its balance sheet, and from favorable expectations of future financial performance (particularly in recent years). Apple has incurred many costs such as R&D, advertising, and promotion that will probably yield future economic benefits. However, Apple expensed these costs (did not capitalize them as assets) because their future benefits were uncertain and therefore could not be reliably measured. Companies capitalize intangible assets only when those assets are purchased, and not when they are internally developed. Consequently, Apple's balance sheet and the balance sheets of many knowledge-based companies are, arguably, less informative about company value.

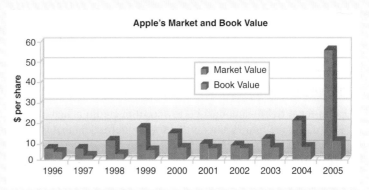

Apple's Market and Book Value

Earned capital is the cumulative net income (loss) that has been retained by the company (not paid out to shareholders as dividends). Apple's earned capital (titled Retained Earnings) totals $4,005 million as of its 2005 year-end.

## Retained Earnings

There is an important relation for retained earnings that reconciles its beginning and ending balances as follows:

$$
\begin{array}{l}
\text{Beginning retained earnings} \\
\pm \text{ Net income (loss)} \\
- \text{ Dividends} \\
\hline
= \text{ Ending retained earnings}
\end{array}
$$

This is a useful relation to remember. Apple's retained earnings increases (or decreases) each year by the amount of its reported net income (loss). If Apple paid dividends, its retained earnings would decrease further, but Apple currently pays no dividends. (There are other items that can impact retained earnings that we discuss in later modules.) After we explain the income statement, we will revisit this relation and show how retained earnings link the balance sheet and income statement.

**Book Value vs Market Value** Reported stockholders' equity is the "value" of the company determined by GAAP. Stockholders equity is commonly referred to as the company's **book value**. This value is different from a company's **market value** (market capitalization or market cap), which is computed by multiplying the number of outstanding common shares by the per share market value. Book value and market value can differ for several reasons, mostly related to the recognition of transactions and events in financial statements such as the following:

- GAAP generally reports assets and liabilities at historical costs, whereas the market attempts to estimate fair market values.

- GAAP excludes resources that cannot be reliably measured such as talented management, employee morale, recent innovations and successful marketing, whereas the market attempts to value these.

- GAAP does not consider market differences in which companies operate such as competitive conditions and expected changes, whereas the market attempts to factor in these differences in determining value.

▒ GAAP does not usually report expected future performance, whereas the market attempts to predict and value future performance.

Presently for U.S. companies, book value is, on average, about two-thirds of market value. This means that the market has drawn on information in addition to that provided in the balance sheet and income statement in valuing equity shares. A major part of this information is in financial statement notes, but not all.

It is important to understand that, eventually, all factors determining company market value are reflected in financial statements and book value. Assets are eventually sold and liabilities are settled. Moreover, talented management, employee morale, technological innovations, and successful marketing are all eventually recognized in reported profit. The difference between book value and market value is one of timing. To the extent that market value is accurate, the change in stockholders' equity usually represents the change in company market value with a lag.

# INCOME STATEMENT

The income statement reports revenues earned during a period, the expenses incurred to produce those revenues, and the resulting net income or loss. The general structure of the income statement follows:

|     | Revenues |
| --- | --- |
| −   | Cost of goods sold |
|     | Gross profit |
| −   | Operating expenses |
|     | Operating profit |
| −   | Nonoperating expenses (+ Nonoperating revenues) |
| −   | Tax expense |
|     | Income from continuing operations |
| +/− | Nonrecurring items, net of tax |
| =   | Net income |

Apple's income statement from its 2005 10-K is shown in Exhibit 2.5. Apple reports net income of $1,335 million on sales of $13,931 million. As is typical of many large companies, less than $0.10 of each dollar of sales is brought down to the bottom line (many companies report less than a nickel in profit for every dollar of sales)—for Apple, it is $0.096 of each dollar, computed as $1,335 million divided by $13,931 million. The remainder of each sales dollar, $0.904 (computed as $1 minus $0.096) relates to

| **EXHIBIT 2.5** | **Apple's Income Statement ($ millions)** |
| --- | --- |

**APPLE, INC.**
**Income Statement**
**For Year Ended September 24, 2005**

| | |
| --- | --- |
| Net sales. . . . . . . . . . . . . . . . . . . . . . . . . . . . . . . . . . . . | $13,931 |
| Cost of sales. . . . . . . . . . . . . . . . . . . . . . . . . . . . . . . . . | 9,888 |
| Gross margin . . . . . . . . . . . . . . . . . . . . . . . . . . . . . . . . . | 4,043 |
| Operating expenses | |
| Research and development . . . . . . . . . . . . . . . . . . . . . . . | 534 |
| Selling, general, and administrative . . . . . . . . . . . . . . . . . . | 1,859 |
| Total operating expenses . . . . . . . . . . . . . . . . . . . . . . . . | 2,393 |
| Operating profit . . . . . . . . . . . . . . . . . . . . . . . . . . . . . . . | 1,650 |
| Other revenue and expense | |
| Interest and other income, net . . . . . . . . . . . . . . . . . . . . . . | 165 |
| Income before provision for income taxes. . . . . . . . . . . . . . | 1,815 |
| Provision for income taxes. . . . . . . . . . . . . . . . . . . . . . . . | 480 |
| Net income . . . . . . . . . . . . . . . . . . . . . . . . . . . . . . . . . . | $ 1,335 |

costs incurred to generate sales, such as cost of sales, wages, advertising, interest, equipment costs, research and development expenses, and taxes.

To analyze an income statement we need to understand some terminology. **Revenues** (Sales) are increases in net assets (assets less liabilities) as a result of ordinary operating activities. **Expenses** are decreases in net assets used to generate revenues, including costs of sales, operating costs like wages and advertising (usually titled selling, general, and administrative expenses or SG&A), and nonoperating costs like interest on debt. The difference between revenues and expenses is **net income** when revenues exceed expenses, or **net loss** when expenses exceed revenues. The terms income, profit, and earnings are used interchangeably (as are revenues and sales, and expenses and costs).

**Operating expenses** are the usual and customary costs that a company incurs to support its operating activities. These include cost of goods sold, selling expenses, depreciation expense, and research and development expense. Not all of these expenses require a cash outlay; for example, depreciation expense is a noncash expense, as are accruals of liabilities such as wages payable, that recognize the expense in advance of cash payment. **Nonoperating expenses** relate to the company's financing and investing activities, and include interest expense and interest or dividend income. Business decision makers and analysts usually segregate operating and nonoperating activities as they offer different insights into company performance and condition.

## Revenue Recognition and Matching

An important consideration in preparing the income statement is *when* to recognize revenues and expenses. For many revenues and expenses, the decision is easy. When a customer purchases groceries, pays with a check, and walks out of the store with the groceries, we know that the sale is made and revenue should be recognized. Or, when companies receive and pay an electric bill with a check, they have clearly incurred an expense that should be recognized.

However, should Apple recognize revenue when it sells iPods to a retailer who does not have to pay Apple for 60 days? Should Apple recognize an expense for employees who work this week but will not be paid until the first of next month? The answer to both of these questions is yes.

Two fundamental principles guide recognition of revenues and expenses:

> **Revenue Recognition Principle**—recognize revenues when *earned*
>
> **Matching Principle**—recognize expenses when *incurred.*

These two principles are the foundation of **accrual accounting**, which is the accounting system used to prepare all GAAP-based financial statements. The general approach is this: first, recognize revenues in the time period they are earned; then, record all expenses *incurred* to generate those revenues during that same time period (this is called matching expenses to revenues). Net income is then correctly reported for that period.

Recognizing revenues when earned does not necessarily imply the receipt of cash. Revenue is e*arned* when the company has done everything that it is supposed to do. This means that a sale of goods on credit would qualify for recognition as long as the revenues are earned. Likewise, companies recognize an expense when it is *incurred*, even if no cash is paid. For example, companies recognize as expenses the wages earned by employees, even though they will not be paid until the next pay period. The company records an expense but pays no cash; instead, it records an accrued liability for the wages payable. (We discuss accrual accounting later in this module, and Modules 3 and 5 review accrual accounting in more detail.)

Accrual accounting requires estimates and assumptions. Examples include estimating how much revenue has been earned on a long-term contract, the amount of accounts receivable that will not be collected,

---

**MANAGERIAL DECISION**     **You Are the Operations Manager**

You are the operations manager on a new consumer product that was launched this period with very successful sales. The Chief Financial Officer (CFO) asks you to prepare an estimate of warranty costs to charge against those sales. Why does the CFO desire a warranty cost estimate? What hurdles must you address in arriving at such an estimate? [Answer, p.2-33]

the degree to which equipment has been "used up," the cleanup costs that a company must eventually pay for environmental liabilities, and numerous other estimates. All of these estimates and assumptions affect both reported net income and the balance sheet. Judgments affect all financial statements. This is an important by-product of accrual accounting. We discuss these estimates and assumptions, and their effects on financial statements, throughout the book.

## Reporting of Transitory Items

To this point, we have only considered income from continuing operations and its components. A more comprehensive income statement format is in Exhibit 2.6. The most noticeable difference involves two additional components of net income located at the bottom of the statement.

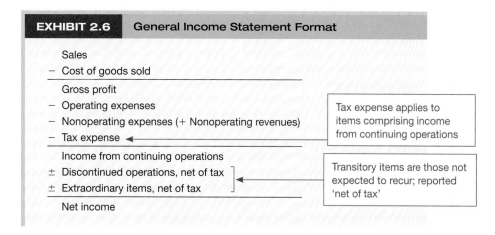

**EXHIBIT 2.6    General Income Statement Format**

These two components are specifically segregated from the "income from continuing operations" and are defined as follows (these items are further described in Module 5):[2]

1. **Discontinued operations**  Gains or losses (and net income or loss) from business segments that are being sold or have been sold in the current period.
2. **Extraordinary items**  Gains or losses from events that are both *unusual* and *infrequent* and are, therefore, excluded from income from continuing operations.

These two components are segregated because they represent **transitory items**, which reflect transactions or events that are unlikely to recur. Many readers of financial statements are interested in *future* company performance. They analyze current year financial statements to gain clues to better *predict* future performance. (Stock prices, for example, are based on a company's expected profits and cash flows.)

Transitory items, by definition, are unlikely to arise in future periods. Although transitory items can help us analyze past performance, they are largely irrelevant to predicting future performance. This means that investors and other users tend to focus on income from continuing operations because it is the level of profitability that is likely to **persist** (continue) into the future. Likewise, the financial press tends to focus on income from continuing operations when it discloses corporate earnings (often described as *earnings before one-time charges*).

# STATEMENT OF STOCKHOLDERS' EQUITY

The statement of stockholders' equity reconciles the beginning and ending balances of stockholders' equity accounts.

---

[2] Under current GAAP, **changes in accounting principles,** that once were included as transitory items, are applied retrospectively. That is, the company goes back and amends previous income statements to incorporate the effect of any new accounting principle. Under prior GAAP, the company made one, large cumulative adjustment to income in the period of the change. An exception to this relates to changes in depreciation methods, which are applied prospectively like a change in an estimate (retrospective adjustment is not made).

The statement of stockholders' equity for Apple is shown in Exhibit 2.7.

| EXHIBIT 2.7 | Apple's Statement of Stockholders' Equity | | | |
| --- | --- | --- | --- | --- |

**APPLE, INC.**
**Statement of Stockholders' Equity**
**For Year Ended September 24, 2005**

| ($ millions) | Common Stock | Retained Earnings | Other Stockholders' Equity | Total Stockholders' Equity |
| --- | --- | --- | --- | --- |
| Balance at September 25, 2004. . . . . . | $2,514 | $2,670 | $(108) | $5,076 |
| Common stock issued . . . . . . . . . . . . . . | 1,007 | | | 1,007 |
| Net income. . . . . . . . . . . . . . . . . . . . . . | | 1,335 | | 1,335 |
| Dividends . . . . . . . . . . . . . . . . . . . . . . . | | 0 | | 0 |
| Other. . . . . . . . . . . . . . . . . . . . . . . . . . | | | 48 | 48 |
| Balance at September 24, 2005. . . . . . | $3,521 | $4,005 | $ (60) | $7,466 |

Apple's first equity component is common stock. The balance in common stock at the beginning of the year is $2,514 million. During 2005, Apple issued $1,007 million worth of common stock to employees who exercised stock options. At the end of 2005, the common stock account reports a balance of $3,521 million.

Apple's second stockholders' equity component is retained earnings. It totals $2,670 million at the start of 2005. During the year, it increased by $1,335 million from net income. (Apple's retained earnings do not decrease for dividends because Apple pays no dividends.) The balance of retained earnings at year-end is $4,005 million.

In sum, total stockholders' equity begins the year at $5,076 million (including $108 million relating to miscellaneous accounts that reduce total stockholders' equity) and ends 2005 with a balance of $7,466 million (including $60 million relating to miscellaneous accounts that reduce total stockholders' equity) for a net increase of $2,390 million.

| RESEARCH INSIGHT | Market-to-Book Ratio |
| --- | --- |

The market-to-book ratio, also called price-to-book, refers to a company's market value divided by its book (equity) value—it is also computed as stock price per share divided by book value per share. Research shows that the market-to-book ratio exhibits considerable variability over time. Specifically, over the past few decades, the median (50th percentile) market-to-book ratio was less than 1.0 during the mid-1970s, over 2.0 during the mid-1990s, and often between 1.0 and 2.0 during the 1960s and 1980s.

# STATEMENT OF CASH FLOWS

The balance sheet and income statement are prepared using accrual accounting, in which revenues are recognized when earned and expenses when incurred. This means that companies can report income even though no cash is received. Cash shortages—due to unexpected cash outlays or when customers refuse to or cannot pay—can create economic hardships for companies and even cause their demise.

To assess cash flows, we must assess a company's cash management. Obligations to employees, creditors, and others are usually settled with cash. Illiquid companies (those lacking cash) are at risk of failure and typically reflect poor investing activities. Given the importance of cash management, the SEC and FASB require disclosure of the statement of cash flows in addition to the balance sheet, income statement, and statement of equity.

The income statement provides information about the economic viability of the company's products and services. It tells us whether the company can sell its products and services at prices that cover its costs and that also provide a reasonable return to lenders and stockholders. On the other hand, the statement of cash flows provides information about the company's ability to generate cash from those same transactions. It tells us from what sources the company has generated its cash (so we can evaluate whether those sources are persistent or transitory) and what it has done with the cash it generated.

## Statement Format and Data Sources

The statement of cash flows is formatted to report cash inflows and cash outflows by the three primary business activities:

- *Cash flows from operating activities*  Cash flows from the company's transactions and events that relate to its operations.
- *Cash flows from investing activities*  Cash flows from acquisitions and divestitures of investments and long-term assets.
- *Cash flows from financing activities*  Cash flows from issuances of and payments toward borrowings and equity.

The combined cash flows from these three sections yield the net change in cash for the period. Preparation of these three sections of the statement of cash flows draws generally on parts of both the income statement and the balance sheet, and those sections are highlighted in blue as follows:

| Cash flow section | Information from income statement | Information from balance sheet | |
|---|---|---|---|
| Net cash flows from operating activities. . . . | Revenues<br>− Expenses<br>= Net income | Current assets<br>Long-term assets | Current liabilities<br>Long-term liabilities<br>Equity |
| Net cash flows from investing activities . . . . | Revenues<br>− Expenses<br>= Net income | Current assets<br>Long-term assets | Current liabilities<br>Long-term liabilities<br>Equity |
| Net cash flows from financing activities . . . . | Revenues<br>− Expenses<br>= Net income | Current assets<br>Long-term assets | Current liabilities<br>Long-term liabilities<br>Equity |

Specifically, the three sections draw generally on the following information:

- **Net cash flows from operating activities** draws on the income statement and the current asset and current liabilities sections of the balance sheet.
- **Net cash flows from investing activities** uses the long-term assets section of the balance sheet.
- **Net cash flows from financing activities** draws on the long-term liabilities and stockholders' equity sections of the balance sheet.

These relations do not hold exactly, but they provide us a useful way to visualize the construction of the statement of cash flows.

In analyzing the statement of cash flows, you should not necessarily conclude that the company is better off if cash increases and worse off if cash decreases. It is not the change in cash that is most important, but the reasons behind the change. For example, what are the sources of cash inflows? Are these sources transitory? Are these sources mainly from operating activities? To what uses have cash inflows been put? Such questions and answers are key to properly using the statement of cash flows.

Exhibit 2.8 shows Apple's statement of cash flows. Apple reported $2,535 million in net cash inflows from operating activities in 2005. This is substantially greater than its net income of $1,335 million. The operating activities section of the statement of cash flows reconciles the difference between net income

| EXHIBIT 2.8 | Apple's Statement of Cash Flows ($ millions) |
|---|---|

**APPLE, INC.**
**Statement of Cash Flows**
**For Year Ended September 24, 2005**

| | |
|---|---:|
| **Operating Activities** | |
| Net income | $1,335 |
| Depreciation and amortization | 179 |
| Other noncash expenses, net | 556 |
| Increase in accounts receivable | (121) |
| Increase in inventories | (64) |
| Increases in other current assets | (211) |
| Increases in accounts payable | 328 |
| Increases in other liabilities | 533 |
| Cash generated by operating activities | 2,535 |
| **Investing Activities** | |
| Increase in short-term investments | (2,275) |
| Purchases of property, plant and equipment | (260) |
| Increase in other long-term assets | (21) |
| Cash used for investing activities | (2,556) |
| **Financing Activities** | |
| Proceeds from issuance of common stock | 543 |
| Cash generated by financing activities | 543 |
| Increase in cash and cash equivalents | $ 522 |
| Cash and cash equivalents, beginning of year | 2,969 |
| Cash and cash equivalents, end of year | $3,491 |

and operating cash flow. The difference is due to the add-back of depreciation, a noncash expense in the income statement, and other noncash expenses, together with changes in operating assets and liabilities. We discuss these changes, and how to interpret them, in more detail below.

Apple reports a net cash outflow of $2,556 million for investing activities, mainly for investments in marketable securities. Apple also generated $543 million from financing activities, mainly cash received when Apple issued shares to employees who exercised their options to purchase common stock (the remaining $464 million of the $1,007 million referenced as common stock issued in Exhibit 2.7 is included in net cash flow from operating activities; the reason for this classification is discussed in Appendix B).

Overall, Apple's cash flow picture is quite strong. It is generating cash from operating activities and the sale of stock to employees, and is investing excess cash in marketable securities to ensure future liquidity.

## Cash Flow Computations

It is sometimes difficult to understand why certain accounts are added to and subtracted from net income to yield net cash flows from operating activities. It often takes more than one pass through this section to grasp how this part of the cash flow statement is constructed.

A key to understanding these computations is to remember that under accrual accounting, revenues are recognized when earned and expenses when incurred. This recognition policy does not necessarily coincide with the receipt or payment of cash. The top line (net income) of the operating section of the statement of cash flows represents net (accrual) income under GAAP. The bottom line (net cash flows from operating activities) is the *cash profit* had the company constructed its income statement on a cash basis rather than an accrual basis. Computing net cash flows from operating activities begins with GAAP profit and adjusts it to compute cash profit using the following general approach:

| | Add (+) or Subtract (−) from Net Income |
|---|---|
| Net income. . . . . . . . . . . . . . . . . . . . . . . . | $  # |
| Add: depreciation. . . . . . . . . . . . . . . . . . . . | + |
| Adjust for changes in current assets | |
|   Subtract increases in current assets . . . . | − |
|   Add decreases in current assets . . . . . . . | + |
| Adjust for changes in current liabilities | |
|   Add increases in current liabilities . . . . . . | + |
|   Subtract decreases in current liabilities . . | − |
| Net cash flow from operating activities . . . . | $  # |

Typically, net income is first adjusted for noncash expenses such as depreciation, and is then adjusted for changes in current assets and current liabilities to yield net cash flow from operating activities, or cash profit. The depreciation adjustment merely zeros out depreciation expense, a noncash expense, which is

---

**BUSINESS INSIGHT**     **Insights into Apple's Statement of Cash Flows**

The following provides insights into the computation of some amounts in the operating section of Apple's statement of cash flows in Exhibit 2.8 ($ millions).

| Statement amount | Explanation of computation |
|---|---|
| Depreciation and amortization, $179 | When buildings and equipment are acquired, their cost is recorded on the balance sheet as an asset. Subsequently, as the assets are used up to generate revenues, a portion of their cost is transferred from the balance sheet to the income statement as an expense, called *depreciation*. Depreciation expense does not involve the payment of cash (that occurs when the asset is purchased). If we want to compute *cash profit*, we must add back depreciation expense to zero it out from income. The $179 in the second line of the statement of cash flows merely zeros out (undoes) the depreciation expense that was subtracted when Apple computed GAAP net income. Likewise, the third line (other noncash expenditures of $556) uses the same concept. |
| Increase in accounts receivable, $(121) | When a company sells goods *on credit*, it records revenue because it is earned, even though cash is not yet received. When Apple sold $121 of goods on credit, its revenues and net income increased by that amount, but no cash was received. Apple's cash profit is, thus, $121 less than net income. The $121 is subtracted from net income in computing net cash inflows from operations. |
| Increase in inventories, $(64) | When Apple purchases inventories, the purchase cost is reported on its balance sheet as a current asset. When inventories are sold, their cost is removed from the balance sheet and transferred to the income statement as an expense called cost of goods sold. If some inventories acquired are not yet sold, their cost is not yet reported in cost of goods sold and net income. The subtraction of $64 relates to the increase in inventories; it reflects the fact that cost of goods sold does not include all of the cash that was spent on inventories. That is, $64 cash was spent that is not yet reflected in cost of goods sold. Thus, the $64 is deducted from net income to compute *cash profit* for the period. |
| Increases in accounts payable, $328 | Apple purchases much of its inventories on credit. The $328 increase in accounts payable reflects inventories that have been purchased, but have not yet been paid for in cash. The add-back of this $328 to net income reflects the fact that *cash profit* is $328 higher because $328 of accounts payable are not yet paid. |

deducted in computing net income. The following table provides brief explanations of adjustments for receivables, inventories, and payables and accruals:

| | Change in account balance... | Means that... | Which requires this adjustment to net income to yield cash profit... |
|---|---|---|---|
| Receivables | Increase | Sales and net income increase, but cash is not yet received | Deduct increase in receivables from net income |
| | Decrease | More cash is received than is reported in sales and net income | Add decrease in receivables to net income |
| Inventories | Increase | Cash is paid for inventories that are not yet reflected in cost of goods sold | Deduct increase in inventories from net income |
| | Decrease | Cost of goods sold includes inventory costs that were paid for in a prior period | Add decrease in inventories to net income |
| Payables and accruals | Increase | More goods and services are acquired on credit, delaying cash payment | Add increase in payables and accruals to net income |
| | Decrease | More cash is paid than is reflected in cost of goods sold or operating expenses | Deduct decrease in payables and accruals from net income |

It is also helpful to use the following decision guide, involving changes in assets, liabilities, and equity, to understand increases and decreases in cash flows.

| | Cash flow increases from | Cash flow decreases from |
|---|---|---|
| Assets. . . . . . . . . . . . . . . | Account decreases | Account increases |
| Liabilities and equity. . . . . | Account increases | Account decreases |

The table above applies to all sections of the statement of cash flows. To determine if a change in each asset and liability account creates a cash inflow or outflow, examine the change and apply the decision rules from the table. For example, in the investing section, cash decreases when PPE assets increase. In the financing section, borrowing from a bank increases cash. Module 3 and Appendix B near the end of the book describe the preparation of the statement of cash flows in detail.

Sometimes the cash flow effect of an item reported in the statement of cash flows does not agree with the difference in the balance sheet accounts that we observe. This can be due to several factors. One common factor is when a company uses its own stock to acquire another entity. There is no cash effect from a stock acquisition and, hence, it is not reported in the statement of cash flows. Yet, the company does increase its assets and liabilities when it adds the acquired company's assets and liabilities to its balance sheet. (We cover acquisitions in Module 7.)

Knowledge of how companies record cash inflows and outflows helps us better understand the statement of cash flows. Determining how changes in asset and liability accounts affect cash provides an analytic tool *and* offers greater insight into managing a business. For instance, reducing the levels of receivables and inventories increases cash. Similarly, increasing the levels of accounts payable and accrued liabilities increases cash. Managing cash balances by managing other accounts is called *working capital management*, which is important for all companies.

## MID-MODULE REVIEW

Following are account balances ($ millions) for Dell, Inc. Using these data, prepare its income statement and statement of cash flows for the fiscal year ended February 3, 2006. Prepare its balance sheet dated February 3, 2006.

| | | | |
|---|---|---|---|
| Cash and cash equivalents | $ 7,042 | Inventories | $ 576 |
| Net cash used in financing activities and other | (6,422) | Accounts payable | 9,840 |
| Long-term debt | 504 | Other stockholders' equity | (18,157) |
| Property, plant and equipment, net | 2,005 | Long-term Investments | 2,691 |
| Other noncurrent assets | 707 | Other short-term assets | 2,620 |
| Accrued and other liabilities | 6,087 | Retained earnings | 12,746 |
| Other noncurrent liabilities | 2,549 | Receivables | 5,452 |
| Short-term investments | 2,016 | Selling, general and administrative expenses | 5,140 |
| Income tax expense | 1,002 | Research and development expenses | 463 |
| Net cash provided by operating activities | 4,839 | Cost of revenue | 45,958 |
| Paid-in capital | 9,540 | Net cash provided by investing activities | 3,878 |
| Cash and cash equivalents at beginning of period | 4,747 | Investment and other income, net | 227 |
| Net revenue | 55,908 | | |

## Solution

### DELL, INC.
### Balance Sheet
### February 3, 2006

| ASSETS | | LIABILITIES AND EQUITY | |
|---|---|---|---|
| Current assets | | Current liabilities | |
| Cash and cash equivalents | $ 7,042 | Accounts payable | $ 9,840 |
| Short-term investments | 2,016 | Accrued and other liabilities | 6,087 |
| Receivables | 5,452 | Total current liabilities | 15,927 |
| Inventories | 576 | Long-term debt | 504 |
| Other short-term assets | 2,620 | Other noncurrent liabilities | 2,549 |
| Total current assets | 17,706 | Total liabilities | 18,980 |
| Property, plant, and equipment, net | 2,005 | Stockholders' equity | |
| Long-term Investments | 2,691 | Paid-in capital | 9,540 |
| Other noncurrent assets | 707 | Retained earnings | 12,746 |
| | | Other stockholders' equity | (18,157) |
| Total assets | $23,109 | Total stockholders' equity | 4,129 |
| | | Total liabilities and stockholders' equity | $23,109 |

### DELL, INC.
### Income Statement
### For Fiscal Year Ended February 3, 2006

| | |
|---|---|
| Net revenue | $55,908 |
| Cost of revenue | 45,958 |
| Gross margin | 9,950 |
| Operating expenses | |
| Selling, general, and administrative | 5,140 |
| Research and development expenses | 463 |
| Total operating expenses | 5,603 |
| Operating income | 4,347 |
| Investment and other income, net | 227 |
| Income before income taxes | 4,574 |
| Income tax provision | 1,002 |
| Net income | $ 3,572 |

**DELL, INC.**
**Statement of Cash Flows**
**For Fiscal Year Ended February 3, 2006**

| | |
|---|---|
| Net cash provided by operating activities . . . . . . . . . . . . | $4,839 |
| Net cash provided by investing activities . . . . . . . . . . . . . | 3,878 |
| Net cash used in financing activities and other . . . . . . . . | (6,422) |
| Net increase in cash and cash equivalents . . . . . . . . . . . | 2,295 |
| Cash and cash equivalents at beginning of period . . . . . . | 4,747 |
| Cash and cash equivalents at end of period . . . . . . . . . . . | $7,042 |

# ARTICULATION OF FINANCIAL STATEMENTS

**LO2** Explain and illustrate linkages among the four financial statements.

The four financial statements are linked with each other and linked across time. This linkage is called **articulation**. This section demonstrates the articulation of financial statements using Apple.

## Retained Earnings Reconciliation

The balance sheet and income statement are linked via retained earnings. Recall that retained earnings is updated each period as follows:

Beginning retained earnings
± Net income (loss)
− Dividends
= Ending retained earnings

Retained earnings reflect cumulative income that has not yet been distributed to shareholders. Exhibit 2.9 shows Apple's retained earnings reconciliation for 2005.

**EXHIBIT 2.9** Apple's Retained Earnings Reconciliation

**APPLE, INC.**
**Retained Earnings Reconciliation ($ millions)**
**For Year Ended September 24, 2005**

| | |
|---|---|
| Retained earnings, September 25, 2004 . . . . . . . . . . . . . . . . . . | $2,670 |
| Add: Net income (loss) . . . . . . . . . . . . . . . . . . . . . . . . . . . . . | 1,335 |
| Less: Dividends . . . . . . . . . . . . . . . . . . . . . . . . . . . . . . . . . . | 0 |
| Retained earnings, September 24, 2005 . . . . . . . . . . . . . . . . . | $4,005 |

This reconciliation of retained earnings links the balance sheet and income statement.

In the absence of transactions with stockholders—such as stock issuances and repurchases, and dividend payments—the change in stockholders' equity equals income or loss for the period. The income statement, thus, measures the change in company value as measured by *GAAP*. This is not necessarily company value as measured by the *market*. Of course, all value-relevant items eventually find their way into the income statement. So, from a macro-perspective, the income statement does measure change in company value. This is why stock prices react to reported income and to analysts' expectations about future income.

# Financial Statement Linkages

Articulation of the four financial statements is shown in Exhibit 2.10. Apple begins 2005 with assets of $8,050 million, consisting of cash for $2,969 million and noncash assets for $5,081 million. These investments are financed with $2,974 million from nonowners and $5,076 million from shareholders. The owner financing consists of contributed capital of $2,514 million, retained earnings of $2,670 million, and other stockholders' equity of $(108) million.

**EXHIBIT 2.10** Articulation of Apple Financial Statements ($ millions)

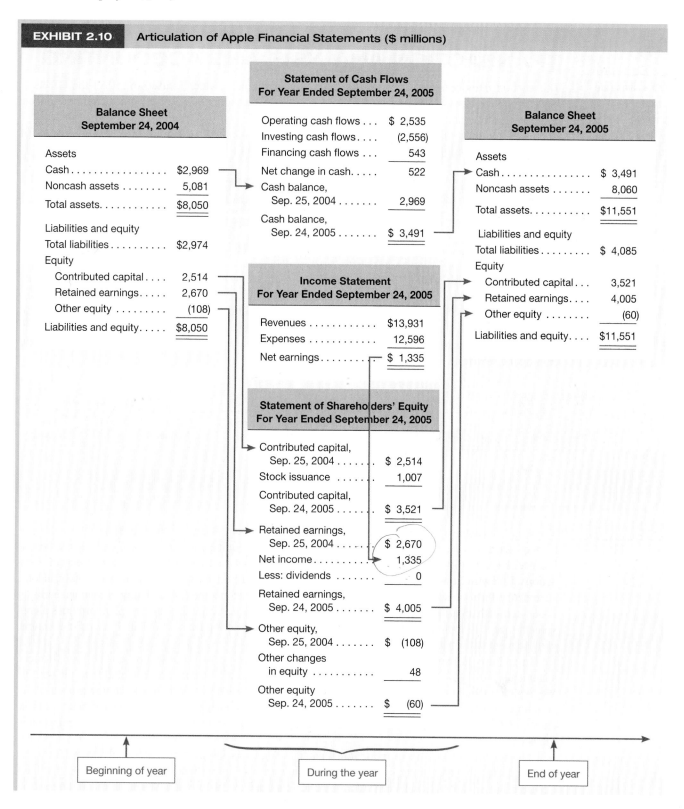

Exhibit 2.10 shows balance sheets at the beginning and end of the year on the left and right columns respectively. The middle column reflects operating activities for 2005. The statement of cash flows explains how operating, investing, and financing activities increase the cash balance by $522 million from $2,969 million at the beginning of the year to $3,491 million at year-end. The ending balance in cash is reported in the year-end balance sheet on the right.

Apple's $1,335 million net income reported on the income statement is also carried over to the statement of shareholders' equity. The net income explains the change in retained earnings reported in the statement of shareholders' equity since Apple paid no dividends in that year.

# TRANSACTION ANALYSIS AND ACCOUNTING

**LO3** Illustrate use of the financial statement effects template to summarize accounting transactions.

This section introduces our financial statement effects template, which is used to reflect the effects of transactions on financial statements. A more detailed explanation is in Module 3, but that module is not required to understand and apply the template.

Apple reports total assets of $11,551 million, total liabilities of $4,085 million, and equity of $7,466 million. The accounting equation for Apple follows ($ million):

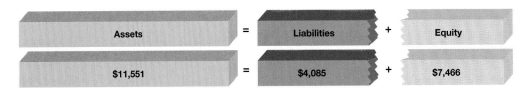

We often draw on this relation to assess the effects of transactions and events, different accounting methods, and choices that managers make in preparing financial statements. We are interested in knowing, for example, the effects of an asset write-off (removal of an impaired asset) on the balance sheet, income statement, and cash flow statement. Or, we might want to understand how the failure to recognize a liability would understate liabilities and overstate profits and equity. To perform these sorts of analyses, we employ the following *financial statement effects template*:

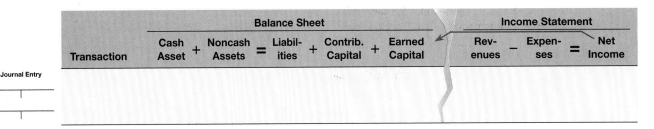

The template captures the transaction and its financial statement effects on the four financial statements: balance sheet, income statement, statement of stockholders' equity, and statement of cash flows. For the balance sheet, we differentiate between cash and noncash assets so as to identify the cash effects of transactions. Likewise, equity is separated into the contributed and earned capital components. Finally, income statement effects are separated into revenues, expenses, and net income (the updating of retained earnings is denoted with an arrow line running from net income to earned capital). This template provides a convenient means to represent relatively complex financial accounting transactions and events in a simple, concise manner for both analysis and interpretation.

In addition to using the template to show the dollar effects of a transaction on the four financial statements, we also include each transaction's *journal entry* and *T-account* representation in the margin. We explain journal entries and T-accounts in Module 3; these are part of the bookkeeping aspects of accounting. The margin entries can be ignored without any loss of insight gained from the template. (Journal entries and T-accounts use acronyms for account titles; a list of acronyms is in Appendix C near the end of the book.)

The process leading up to preparing financial statements involves two steps: (1) recording transactions during the accounting period, and (2) adjusting accounting records to reflect events that have occurred but are not yet evidenced by an external transaction. We provide a brief introduction to these two steps, followed by a comprehensive example that includes preparation of financial statements (a more detailed illustration of this process is in Module 3).

## Recording Transactions

All transactions affecting a company are recorded in its accounting records. For example, assume that a company paid $100 cash wages to employees. This is reflected in the following financial statement effects template.

| | Balance Sheet | | | | | | Income Statement | | |
|---|---|---|---|---|---|---|---|---|---|
| Transaction | Cash Asset | + Noncash Assets | = Liabilities | + Contrib. Capital | + Earned Capital | | Revenues | − Expenses | = Net Income |
| Pay $100 cash for wages | −100 Cash | | = | | −100 Retained Earnings | | | − +100 Wages Expense | = −100 |

WE 100
Cash 100
WE
100 |
Cash
| 100

Cash assets are reduced by $100, and wage expense of $100 is reflected in the income statement, which reduces income and retained earnings by that amount. All transactions incurred by the company during the accounting period are recorded similarly. We show several further examples in our comprehensive illustration later in this section.

## Adjusting Accounts

We must understand accounting adjustments (commonly called *accruals*) to fully analyze and interpret financial statements. In the transaction above, we record wage expense that has been earned by (and paid to) employees during the period. What if the employees were not paid for wages earned at period-end? Should the expense still be recorded? The answer is yes. The *matching principle* requires that all expenses incurred to generate, directly or indirectly, the revenues reported in the period must be recorded. This is the case even if those expenses are still unpaid at period-end. The reason is that failure to recognize wages expense would overstate net income for the period because wages have been earned and should be reported as expense in this period. Also, failure to record those wages at period-end would understate liabilities. Thus, neither the income statement nor the balance sheet would be accurate. Adjustments are, therefore, necessary to accurately portray financial condition and performance of a company.

There are four types of adjustments, which are illustrated in the following graphic.

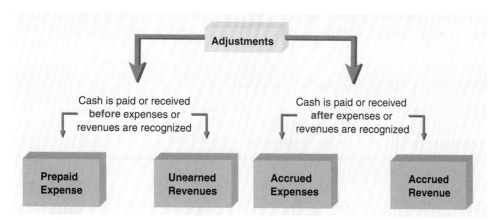

The first two adjustments (on the left) relate to the receipt or payment of cash before revenue or expense is recognized. The second two (on the right) relate to the receipt or payment of cash after revenue or expense is recognized.

Two types of adjustments arise when cash is received or paid *before* recognition of revenue or expense.

***Prepaid expenses*** Prepaid expenses reflect advance cash payments that will ultimately become expenses; an example is the payment of radio advertising that will not be aired until sometime in the future.

***Unearned revenues*** Unearned revenues reflect cash received from customers before any services or goods are provided; an example is cash received from patrons for tickets to an upcoming concert.

Similarly, two types of adjustments arise when cash is received or paid *after* recognition of revenue or expense.

***Accrued expenses*** Accrued expenses are expenses incurred and recognized on the income statement, even though they are not yet paid in cash; an example is wages owed to employees who performed work but who have not yet been paid.

***Accrued revenues*** Accrued revenues are revenues earned and recognized on the income statement, even though cash is not yet received; examples include accounts receivable and revenue earned under a long-term contract.

To illustrate the adjustment required with the wages example above, assume that the $100 of wages earned this period is paid the following period. The period-end adjustment, and subsequent payment the following period, are both reflected in the following template.

| | Balance Sheet | | | | | | Income Statement | | |
|---|---|---|---|---|---|---|---|---|---|
| Transaction | Cash Asset | + Noncash Assets | = Liabil- ities | + Contrib. Capital | + Earned Capital | | Rev- enues | − Expen- ses | = Net Income |
| Period 1: Accrue $100 wages expense and liability | | | = +100 Wages Payable | | −100 Retained Earnings | | | − +100 Wages Expense | = −100 |
| Period 2: Pay $100 cash for wages | −100 Cash | | = −100 Wages Payable | | | | | | |

| | |
|---|---|
| WE | 100 |
| WP | 100 |
| WE | |
| 100 | |
| WP | |
| | 100 |

| | |
|---|---|
| WP | 100 |
| Cash | 100 |
| WP | |
| 100 | |
| Cash | |
| | 100 |

Wages expense is recorded in period 1's income statement because it is incurred by the company and earned by employees in that period. Also, a liability is recorded in period 1 reflecting the company's obligation to make payment to employees. In period 2, the wages are paid, which means that both cash and the liability are reduced.

Companies make adjustments to better report their financial performance and condition. Each of these adjustments is made by company managers and accountants based on the review of financial statements and information suggesting that adjustments are necessary to properly reflect financial condition and performance.

## Preparing Financial Statements

Each of the four financial statements can be prepared directly from our financial statement effects template. The balance sheet and income statement accounts, and their respective balances, can be read off the bottom row that totals the transactions and adjustments recorded during the period. The statement of cash flows and statement of stockholders' equity are represented by the cash column and the contributed and earned capital columns, respectively.

### Illustration: Recording Transactions, Adjusting Accounts, and Preparing Statements

This section provides a comprehensive illustration that uses the financial statement effects template with a number of transactions related to Apple's 2005 financial statements shown earlier. These summary transactions are described in the far left column of the following template. Each column is summed to arrive at the balance sheet and income statement totals which tie to Apple's statements. Detailed explanations for each transaction are provided after the template. Then, we use the information in the template to construct Apple's financial statements.

| Transaction | Cash Asset | + | Noncash Assets | = | Liabil- ities | + | Contrib. Capital | + | Earned Capital | | Rev- enues | − | Expen- ses | = | Net Income |
|---|---|---|---|---|---|---|---|---|---|---|---|---|---|---|---|
| Balance Sept. 25, 2004 | 2,969 | | 5,081 | = | 2,974 | | 2,406 | | 2,670 | | | | | = | |
| 1. Issue common stock for $1,040 cash | +1,040 Cash | | | = | | | +1,040 Common stock | | | | | | | = | |
| 2. Purchase $289 of PPE, financed by $289 of long-term debt | | | +289 PPE, net | = | +289 Long-Term Debt | | | | | | | | | = | |
| 3. Purchase $9,952 of inventories on credit | | | +9,952 Inventories | = | +9,952 Accounts Payable | | | | | | | | | = | |
| 4. Sell inventories for $13,931 on credit; the cost of inventories is $9,888 | | | +13,931 Accounts Receivable | = | | | | | +13,931 Retained Earnings | | +13,931 Sales | | | = | +13,931 |
| | | | −9,888 Inventory | = | | | | | −9,888 Retained Earnings | | | − | +9,888 Cost of Goods Sold | = | −9,888 |
| 5. Receive $13,810 cash for accounts receivable; Pay $9,686 cash for accounts payable and other liabilities | +13,810 Cash | | −13,810 Accounts Receivable | = | | | | | | | | | | = | |
| | −9,686 Cash | | | = | −9,686 Accounts Payable | | | | | | | | | = | |
| 6. Pay $1,973 cash for R&D, SGA (excluding depreciation), interest, and taxes | −1,973 Cash | | | = | | | | | −1,973 Retained Earnings | | | − | +1,973 Operating Expenses | = | −1,973 |
| 7. Accrue expenses of $556 | | | | = | +556 Accrued Liabilities | | | | −556 Retained Earnings | | | − | +556 Operating Expenses | = | −556 |
| 8. Purchase noncash assets for $2,669 cash | −2,669 Cash | | +2,669 Investments in Securities | = | | | | | | | | | | = | |
| 9. Record depreciation of $179 | | | −179 PPE, net | = | | | | | −179 Retained Earnings | | | − | +179 Depreciation Expense | = | −179 |
| 10. Miscellaneous | | | +15 Other Assets | = | | | +15 Other Accum. Comp. Income | | | | | | | = | |
| Balance, Sept. 24, 2005 | 3,491 | + | 8,060 | = | 4,085 | + | 3,461 | + | 4,005 | | 13,931 | − | 12,596 | = | 1,335 |

***Transaction Explanation*** Apple begins fiscal year 2005 with $8,050 million in total assets, consisting of $2,969 million of cash and $5,081 million of noncash assets. It also reports $2,974 million of liabilities and $5,076 million of stockholders' equity ($2,406 million of contributed capital, which includes other equity for this exhibit, and $2,670 million of earned capital). During the year, ten summary transactions occur that are described below.

1. **Owner Financing.** Companies raise funds from two sources: investing from shareholders and borrowing from creditors. Transaction 1 reflects issuance of common stock for $1,040 million. Cash is increased by that amount, as is contributed capital. Stock issuance (as well as its repurchase and any dividends paid to shareholders) does not impact income. Companies cannot record profit by trading in their own stock.

2. **Purchase PPE financed by debt.** Apple acquires $289 million of property, plant and equipment (PPE), and it finances this acquisition with a $289 million loan. Noncash assets increase by the $289 million of PPE, and liabilities increase by $289 million of long-term debt. PPE is initially reported on the balance sheet. When plant and equipment are used, a portion of the purchase cost is transferred from the balance sheet to the income statement as an expense called depreciation. Accounting for depreciation is shown in Transaction 9. The borrowing of money does not yield income, and repaying the principal amount borrowed is not an expense. Paying interest *on* liabilities, however, is an expense.

3. **Purchase inventories on credit.** Companies commonly acquire inventories from suppliers *on credit*. The phrase "on credit" means that the purchase has not yet been paid for. A purchaser is typically allowed 30 days or more during which to make payment. When acquired in this manner, noncash assets (inventories) increase by the $9,952 million cost of the acquired inventory, and a liability (accounts payable) increases to reflect the amount owed to the supplier. Although inventories (iPods, for example) normally carry a retail selling price that is higher than its cost, this eventual profit is not recognized until inventories are sold.

4. **Sell inventories on credit.** Apple subsequently sells inventories that cost $9,888 million for a retail selling price of $13,931 million *on credit*. The phrase "on credit" means that Apple has not yet received cash for the selling price; cash receipt is expected in the future. The sale of inventories is recorded in two parts: the revenue part and the expense part. First, the sale is recorded by an increase in both revenues and noncash assets (accounts receivable). Revenues increase net income which, in turn, increases earned capital. Second, the cost of inventories sold is removed from the balance sheet (Apple no longer owns those assets), and is transferred to the income statement as an expense, called *cost of goods sold,* which decreases both net income and earned capital by $9,888.

5. **Collect receivables and settle payables.** Apple receives $13,810 million cash from the collection of its accounts receivable, thus reducing noncash assets (accounts receivable) by that amount. Apple uses these proceeds to pay off $9,686 of its liabilities (accounts payable and other liabilities). There is a net increase in cash of $4,124. Collecting accounts receivable does not yield revenue; instead, revenue is recognized when *earned* (see Transaction 4). Thus, recognizing revenue when earned does not necessarily yield an immediate cash increase.

6. **Pay cash for expenses.** Apple pays $1,973 million cash for expenses. This payment increases expenses, and reduces net income (and earned capital). Expenses are recognized when incurred, regardless of when they are paid. Expenses are both incurred and paid in this transaction. Transaction 7 is a case where expenses are recognized *before* being paid.

7. **Accrue expenses.** Accrued expenses relate to expenses that are incurred but not yet paid. For example, employees often work near the end of a period but are not paid until the next period. The company must record wages expense even though employees have not yet been paid in cash. The rationale is that expenses must be *matched* against current period revenues to report the correct income for the period. In this transaction, Apple accrues $556 million of expenses, which reduces net income (and earned capital). Apple simultaneously records a $556 million increase in liabilities for its obligation to make future payment. This transaction is an accounting adjustment, or accrual.

8. **Purchase noncash assets.** Apple uses $2,669 million of its excess cash to purchase marketable securities as an investment. Thus, noncash assets increase. This is a common use of excess cash, especially for high-tech companies that desire added liquidity to take advantage of opportunities in a rapidly changing industry.

9. **Record depreciation.** Transaction 9 is another accounting adjustment. In this case, Apple recognizes that a portion of its plant and equipment is "used up" while generating revenues. Thus, it matches a portion of the PPE cost as an expense against the revenues recognized during the period. In this case, $179 million of PPE cost is removed from the balance sheet and transferred to the income statement as depreciation expense. Net income (and earned capital) is reduced by $179 million.

10. **Miscellaneous.** The final transaction is a miscellaneous adjustment to noncash assets and contributed capital.

The column totals from the financial statement effects template can be used to prepare Apple's financial statements. Apple's 2005 balance sheet and income statement are derived from the template as follows.

| Balance Sheet | |
| --- | --- |
| Cash asset | $ 3,491 |
| Noncash assets | 8,060 |
| Total assets | $11,551 |
| Liabilities | $ 4,085 |
| Contributed capital | 3,461 |
| Earned capital | 4,005 |
| Total liabilities and equity | $11,551 |

| Income Statement | |
| --- | --- |
| Revenues | $13,931 |
| Expenses | 12,596 |
| Net income | $ 1,335 |

A summary of Apple's cash transactions can be constructed drawing on the cash column of the template. The cash column of the financial effects template reveals that cash increases by $522 million during the year from $2,969 million to $3,491 million. Items that contribute to this net increase are identified by the cash entries in that column. Preparation of the statement of cash flows is covered in Module 3 and Appendix B.

Apple's statement of stockholders' equity summarizes the transactions relating to its equity accounts. This statement follows and is organized into its contributed capital and earned capital categories of equity.

| Statement of Stockholders' Equity | Contributed Capital | Earned Capital | Total |
| --- | --- | --- | --- |
| Balance, September 25, 2004 | $2,406 | $2,670 | $5,076 |
| Issuance of common stock | 1,040 | | 1,040 |
| Net income | | 1,335 | 1,335 |
| Miscellaneous | 15 | | 15 |
| Balance, September 24, 2005 | $3,461 | $4,005 | $7,466 |

Apple's financial statements are abbreviated versions of those reproduced earlier in the module. We describe the preparation of financial statements and other accounting details at greater length in Module 3.

# MODULE-END REVIEW

**Part 1** At December 31, 2007, assume that the records of Hewlett-Packard show the following amounts. Use this information, as necessary, to prepare the company's 2007 income statement (ignore income taxes).

| | | | |
|---|---|---|---|
| Cash | $ 3,000 | Cash dividends | $ 1,000 |
| Accounts receivable | 12,000 | Revenues | 25,000 |
| Office equipment | 32,250 | Rent expense | 5,000 |
| Land | 36,000 | Wages expense | 8,000 |
| Accounts payable | 7,500 | Utilities expense | 2,000 |
| Common stock | 45,750 | Other expenses | 4,000 |

## Solution

**HEWLETT-PACKARD**
**Income Statement**
**For Year Ended December 31, 2007**

| | | |
|---|---|---|
| Revenues | | $25,000 |
| Expenses | | |
| Wages expense | $8,000 | |
| Rent expense | 5,000 | |
| Utilities expense | 2,000 | |
| Other expenses | 4,000 | |
| Total expenses | | 19,000 |
| Net income | | $ 6,000 |

**Part 2** Assume that the following is selected financial information for Hewlett-Packard for the year ended December 31, 2007.

| | | | |
|---|---|---|---|
| Retained earnings, Dec. 31, 2007 | $30,000 | Dividends | $1,000 |
| Net income | $6,000 | Retained earnings, Dec. 31, 2006 | $25,000 |

Reconcile its retained earnings for the 2007 fiscal year.

## Solution

**HEWLETT-PACKARD**
**Retained Earnings Reconciliation**
**For Year Ended December 31, 2005**

| | |
|---|---|
| Retained earnings, Dec. 31, 2006 | $25,000 |
| Add: Net income | 6,000 |
| Less: Dividends | (1,000) |
| Retained earnings, Dec. 31, 2007 | $30,000 |

**Part 3** Use the listing of accounts and figures reported in part 1 along with the ending retained earnings from part 2 to prepare the December 31, 2007 balance sheet for Hewlett-Packard.

## Solution

| HEWLETT-PACKARD<br>Balance Sheet<br>December 31, 2007 | | | |
|---|---|---|---|
| Cash . . . . . . . . . . . . . . . . | $ 3,000 | Accounts payable . . . . . . . . . . | $ 7,500 |
| Accounts receivable . . . . . | 12,000 | | |
| Office equipment . . . . . . . | 32,250 | Common stock . . . . . . . . . . . . | 45,750 |
| Land . . . . . . . . . . . . . . . . . | 36,000 | Retained earnings . . . . . . . . . | 30,000 |
| Total assets . . . . . . . . . . . | $83,250 | Total liabilities and equity . . . . . | $83,250 |

# APPENDIX 2A: Additional Information Sources

The four financial statements are only a part of the information available to financial statement users. Additional information, from a variety of sources, provides useful insight into company operating activities and future prospects. This section highlights additional information sources.

## Form 10-K

Companies with publicly traded securities must file a detailed annual report and discussion of their business activities in their Form 10-K with the SEC (quarterly reports are filed on form 10-Q). Many of the disclosures in the 10-K are mandated by law and include the following general categories: Item 1, *Business;* Item 1A. *Risk Factors;* Item 2, *Properties;* Item 3, *Legal Proceedings;* Item 4, *Submission of Matters to a Vote of Security Holders;* Item 5, *Market for Registrant's Common Equity and Related Stockholder Matters;* Item 6, *Selected Financial Data;* Item 7, *Management's Discussion and Analysis of Financial Condition and Results of Operations;* Item 7A, *Quantitative and Qualitative Disclosures About Market Risk;* Item 8, *Financial Statements and Supplementary Data;* Item 9, *Changes in and Disagreements With Accountants on Accounting and Financial Disclosure;* Item 9A, *Controls and Procedures.*

### Description of the Business (Item 1)

Companies must provide a general description of their business, including their principal products and services, the source and availability of required raw materials, all patents, trademarks, licenses, and important related agreements, seasonality of the business, any dependence upon a single customer, competitive conditions, including particular markets in which the company competes, the product offerings in those markets, and the status of its competitive environment. Companies must also provide a description of their overall strategy. Apple's partial disclosure follows:

> The Company's business strategy leverages its unique ability, through the design and development of its own operating system, hardware, and many software applications and technologies, to bring to its customers new products and solutions with superior ease-of-use, seamless integration, and innovative industrial design. The Company believes continual investment in research and development is critical to facilitate innovation of new and improved products and technologies. Besides updates to its existing line of personal computers and related software, services, peripherals, and networking solutions, the Company continues to capitalize on the convergence of digital consumer electronics and the computer by creating innovations like the iPod and iTunes Music Store. The Company's strategy also includes expanding its distribution network to effectively reach more of its targeted customers and provide them a high-quality sales and after-sales support experience.

### Management's Discussion and Analysis of Financial Condition and Results of Operations (Item 7)

The management discussion and analysis (MD&A) section of the 10-K contains valuable insight into the company's results of operations. In addition to an executive overview of company status and its recent operating results, the MD&A section includes information relating to its critical accounting policies and estimates used in preparing its financial statements, a detailed discussion of its sales activity, year-over-year comparisons of operating activities, analysis of gross margin, operating expenses, taxes, and off-balance-sheet and contractual obligations, assessment of factors that affect future results and financial condition. Item 7A reports quantitative and qualitative disclosures about market risk. For example, Apple makes the following disclosure relating to its Mac operating system and its iPods.

> The Company is currently the only maker of hardware using the Mac OS. The Mac OS has a minority market share in the personal computer market, which is dominated by makers of computers utilizing other competing operating systems, including Windows and Linux. The Company's future operating results and financial condition are substantially dependent on its ability to continue to develop improvements to the Macintosh platform in order to maintain perceived design and functional advantages over competing platforms. Additionally, if unauthorized copies of the Mac OS are used on other companies' hardware products and result in decreased demand for the Company's hardware products, the Company's results of operations may be adversely affected.
>
> The Company is currently focused on market opportunities related to digital music distribution and related consumer electronic devices, including iPods. The Company faces increasing competition from other companies promoting their own digital music products, including music enabled cell phones, distribution services, and free peer-to-peer music services. These competitors include both new entrants with different market approaches, such as subscription services models, and also larger companies that may have greater technical, marketing, distribution, and other resources than those of the Company, as well as established hardware, software, and digital content supplier relationships. Failure to effectively compete could negatively affect the Company's operating results and financial position. There can be no assurance that the Company will be able to continue to provide products and services that effectively compete in these markets or successfully distribute and sell digital music outside the U.S. The Company may also have to respond to price competition by lowering prices and/or increasing features which could adversely affect the Company's music product gross margins as well as overall Company gross margins.

## Form 8-K

Another useful report that is required by the SEC and is publicly available is the Form 8-K. This form must be filed within 4 business days of any of the following events:

- Entry into or termination of a material definitive agreement (including petition for bankruptcy)
- Exit from a line of business or impairment of assets
- Change in the company's certified public accounting firm
- Change in control of the company
- Departure of the company's executive officers
- Changes in the company's articles of incorporation or bylaws

Form 8-Ks are typically used by outsiders to monitor for material adverse changes in the company.

## Analyst Reports

Sell-side analysts provide their clients with objective analyses of company operating activities. Frequently, these reports include a discussion of the competitive environment for each of the company's principal product lines, strengths and weaknesses of the company, and an investment recommendation, including financial analysis and a stock price target. For example, Citigroup provides the following in its June 2006 report to clients on Apple:

**citigroup**

See page 5 for Analyst Certification and Important Disclosures

Target Price Change ☑
Estimate Change ☑

### Apple (AAPL)

**AAPL: Revising Estimates; Reiterate Buy**

| BUY (1) |
| --- |
| High Risk (H) |

Mkt Cap: **$50,610 mil.**

REITERATE BUY RATING, REVISED TARGET $75

Despite our estimate revisions, we maintain a Buy rating on Apple shares for two reasons. First, we believe that our 2Q06, FY07 and FY08 estimate revisions are already reflected in the valuation of the shares, which now trade at a reasonable 21X our revised operating EPS of 2.33 (excluding net cash). Second, we continue to expect a steady stream of new products between now and calendar year end, including a new iPod nano with larger storage capacity and lower price/GB, a new video iPod with larger storage capacity, Mac OS X 10.5 (Leopard), an Intel-based high-end desktop, Intel-based servers and storage arrays, and finally, a portable video player. We also see potential for other new, purely incremental products in 2007 and beyond, including cell phones and media hubs.

The analyst report often contains a balanced discussion of both positive and negative aspects of the company as illustrated in the following 2006 report from Bear Stearns regarding Apple.

---

## BEAR STEARNS

**IT HARDWARE**

**US Equity Research**

**June 15, 2006**

### Positives
- Strong brand name, fiercely loyal customer base, defensible installed base
- Innovative products and design strategies
- Incremental opportunities through "digital lifestyle" (iPod, iTunes, iDVD, iMovie, iPhoto)
- Ongoing efforts to monetize beyond-the-box revenue streams (e.g. software, paid subscription services, iTunes Store downloads) to help offset cyclicality of hardware business
- Excellent cash position and balance sheet—exited fiscal 2Q06 around $9.36 per diluted share in net cash
- Intel-based hardware and "Boot Camp" could spur upgrade cycle and new wave of demand
- Multiple growth drivers (e.g. Intel Macs, iPod nano, iPod video, iPod points of distribution)
- Ramp of flash-memory-based iPod could ignite new wave of growth for iPod business
- Improving consistency and execution (exceeded results in twelve consecutive quarters)

### Concerns
- Transition risk associated with shift to Intel architecture
- Growth rates appear to be peaking and are likely to slow which can hurt a stock's P/E multiple
- Ultimate size of the music/MP3 player market is unknown along with increasing competition from multiple vendors
- Historical inability to capture a wider customer base and grow market share without a more compelling product offering to attract new users and penetrate the Wintel world, although "halo" effect appears to be playing out
- "Hit-driven" nature of business model which can produce erratic results
- Could face difficulties reconciling channel conflicts between retail stores and resellers which Apple is prepared to face to have greater control of its customer relationship

---

## Credit Services

Several firms including Standard & Poor's (**StandardAndPoors.com**), Moody's Investors Service (**Moodys.com**), and Fitch Ratings (**FitchRatings.com**) provide credit analysis that assists potential lenders, investors, employees, and other users in evaluating a company's creditworthiness and future financial viability. Credit analysis is a specialized field of analysis, quite different from the equity analysis illustrated here. These firms issue credit ratings on publicly issued bonds as well as on firms' commercial paper.

## Data Services

A number of companies supply financial statement data in easy-to-download spreadsheet formats. Thomson Corporation (**Thomson.com**) provides a wealth of information to its database subscribers, including the widely quoted *First Call* summary of analysts' earnings forecasts. Standard & Poor's provides financial data for all publicly traded companies in its *Compustat* database. This database reports a plethora of individual data items for all publicly traded companies or for any specified subset of companies. These data are useful for performing statistical analysis and making comparisons across companies or within industries.

## GUIDANCE ANSWERS

**MANAGERIAL DECISION**     **You are the Securities Analyst**

Of special concern is the possibility that the new CEO is shifting costs to the current period in lieu of recording them in future periods. Evidence suggests that such behavior occurs when a new management team takes control. The reasoning is that the new management can blame poor current period performance on prior management and, at the same time, rid the balance sheet (and new management team) of costs that would normally be expensed in future periods.

| MANAGERIAL DECISION | You are the Operations Manager |
| --- | --- |

The CFO desires a warranty cost estimate that matches the sales generated from the new product. To arrive at such an estimate, you must estimate the number and types of deficiencies in your product and the costs associated with each per the warranty provisions. This is often a difficult task for product engineers because it forces them to focus on product failures and associated costs.

Superscript <sup>A</sup> denotes assignments based on Appendix 2A.

# DISCUSSION QUESTIONS

**Q2-1.** The balance sheet consists of assets, liabilities, and equity. Define each category and provide two examples of accounts reported within each category.

**Q2-2.** Two important concepts that guide income statement reporting are the revenue recognition principle and the matching principle. Define and explain each of these two guiding principles.

**Q2-3.** GAAP is based on the concept of accrual accounting. Define and describe accrual accounting.

**Q2-4.** Analysts attempt to identify transitory items in an income statement. Define transitory items. What is the purpose of identifying transitory items?

**Q2-5.** What is the statement of stockholders' equity? What useful information does it contain?

**Q2-6.** What is the statement of cash flows? What useful information does it contain?

**Q2-7.** Define and explain the concept of financial statement articulation. What insight comes from understanding articulation?

**Q2-8.** Describe the flow of costs for the purchase of a machine. At what point do such costs become expenses? Why is it necessary to record the expenses related to the machine in the same period as the revenues it produces?

**Q2-9.** What are the two essential characteristics of an asset?

**Q2-10.** What does the concept of liquidity refer to? Explain.

**Q2-11.** What does the term *current* denote when referring to assets?

**Q2-12.** Assets are recorded at historical costs even though current market values might, arguably, be more relevant to financial statement readers. Describe the reasoning behind historical cost usage.

**Q2-13.** Identify three intangible assets that are likely to be *excluded* from the balance sheet because they cannot be reliably measured.

**Q2-14.** Identify three intangible assets that are recorded on the balance sheet.

**Q2-15.** What are accrued liabilities? Provide an example.

**Q2-16.** Define net working capital. Explain how increasing the amount of trade credit can reduce the net working capital for a company.

**Q2-17.** What is the difference between company *book value* and *market value*? Explain why these two amounts differ.

**Q2-18.** The financial statement effects template includes an arrow line running from net income to earned capital. What does this arrow line denote?

# MINI EXERCISES

**M2-19. Identifying and Classifying Financial Statement Items (LO1)**
For each of the following items, indicate whether they would be reported in the balance sheet (B) or income statement (I).

| | | | | | |
| --- | --- | --- | --- | --- | --- |
| *a.* | Net income | *d.* | Accumulated depreciation | *g.* | Interest expense |
| *b.* | Retained earnings | *e.* | Wages expense | *h.* | Interest payable |
| *c.* | Depreciation expense | *f.* | Wages payable | *i.* | Sales |

**M2-20. Identifying and Classifying Financial Statement Items** **(LO1)**

For each of the following items, indicate whether they would be reported in the balance sheet (B) or income statement (I).

a.  Machinery
b.  Supplies expense
c.  Inventories
d.  Sales

e.  Common stock
f.  Factory buildings
g.  Receivables
h.  Taxes payable

i.  Taxes expense
j.  Cost of goods sold
k.  Long-term debt
l.  Treasury stock

**M2-21. Computing and Comparing Income and Cash Flow Measures** **(LO1)**

Healy Corporation recorded service revenues of $100,000 in 2007, of which $70,000 were on credit and $30,000 were for cash. Moreover, of the $70,000 credit sales for 2007, Healy collected $20,000 cash on those receivables before year-end 2007. The company also paid $25,000 cash for 2007 wages. Its employees also earned another $15,000 in wages for 2007, which were not yet paid at year-end 2007. (a) Compute the company's net income for 2007. (b) How much net cash inflow or outflow did the company generate in 2007? Explain why Healy's net income and net cash flow differ.

**M2-22. Assigning Accounts to Sections of the Balance Sheet** **(LO1)**

Identify each of the following accounts as a component of assets (A), liabilities (L), or equity (E).

a.  Cash and cash equivalents  _____
b.  Wages payable  _____
c.  Common stock  _____
d.  Equipment  _____

e.  Long-term debt  _____
f.  Retained earnings  _____
g.  Additional paid-in capital  _____
h.  Taxes payable  _____

**M2-23. Computing Performance Measures Using the Accounting Equation** **(LO1)**

Use your knowledge of accounting relations to complete the following table for Trenton Company.

|  | 2005 | 2006 |
|---|---|---|
| Beginning retained earnings..... | $89,089 | $    ? |
| Net income (loss) ............. | ? | 48,192 |
| Dividends.................. | 0 | 15,060 |
| Ending retained earnings ....... | 69,634 | ? |

**M2-24. Reconciling Retained Earnings** **(LO1)**

Following is financial information from Johnson & Johnson for the 2005 fiscal year ended January 1, 2006. Prepare the 2005 fiscal-year retained earnings reconciliation for Johnson & Johnson ($ millions).

Johnson & Johnson (JNJ)

| Retained earnings, Jan. 2, 2005......$35,223 | Dividends...................... | $3,793 |
|---|---|---|
| Net earnings.................... 10,411 | Retained earnings, Jan. 1, 2006 ..... | ? |
| Other retained earnings changes..... (370) | | |

**M2-25. Analyzing Transactions to Compute Net Income** **(LO1)**

Guay Corp., a start-up company, provided services that were acceptable to its customers and billed those customers for $350,000 in 2007. However, Guay collected only $280,000 cash in 2007, and the remaining $70,000 of 2007 revenues were collected in 2008. Guay employees earned $200,000 in 2007 wages that were not paid until the first week of 2008. How much net income does Guay report for 2007? For 2008 (assuming no new transactions)?

**M2-26. Analyzing Transactions using the Financial Statement Effects Template** **(LO3)**

Report the effects for each of the following independent transactions using the financial statement effects template.

a.  Issue stock for $1,000 cash.
b.  Purchase inventory for $500 cash.
c.  Sell inventory in transaction b for $2,000 on credit.
d.  Receive $2,000 cash toward transaction c receivable.

# EXERCISES

**E2-27.   Constructing Financial Statements from Account Data   (LO1)**

Barth Company reports the following year-end account balances at December 31, 2007. Prepare the 2007 income statement and the balance sheet as of December 31, 2007.

| | | | |
|---|---:|---|---:|
| Accounts payable............ | $ 16,000 | Inventory ................... | $ 36,000 |
| Accounts receivable.......... | 30,000 | Land....................... | 80,000 |
| Bonds payable, long-term ...... | 200,000 | Goodwill.................... | 8,000 |
| Buildings................... | 151,000 | Retained earnings ............ | 60,000 |
| Cash....................... | 48,000 | Sales revenue................ | 400,000 |
| Common stock............... | 150,000 | Supplies inventory ........... | 3,000 |
| Cost of goods sold............ | 180,000 | Supplies expense............. | 6,000 |
| Equipment ................. | 70,000 | Wages expense .............. | 40,000 |

**E2-28.   Constructing Financial Statements from Transaction Data   (LO1)**

Baiman Corporation commences operations at the beginning of January. It provides its services on credit and bills its customers $30,000 for January sales. Its employees also earn January wages of $12,000 that are not paid until the first of February. Complete the following statements for the month-end of January.

| Income Statement | |
|---|---|
| Sales.................. | $ |
| Wages expense .......... | |
| Net income (loss) ........ | $ |

| Balance Sheet | |
|---|---|
| Cash.................. | $ |
| Accounts receivable....... | |
| Total assets.............. | $ |
| | |
| Wages payable........... | $ |
| Retained earnings ........ | |
| Total liabilities and equity ... | $ |

**E2-29.   Analyzing and Reporting Financial Statement Effects of Transactions   (LO3)**

L. Demers launched a professional services firm on March 1. The firm will prepare financial statements at each month-end. In March (its first month), Demers executed the following transactions. Prepare an income statement for Demers Company for the month of March.

a.   Demers (owner) invested in the company, $100,000 cash and $20,000 in property and equipment. The company issued common stock to Demers.

b.   The company paid $3,200 cash for rent of office furnishings and facilities for March.

c.   The company performed services for clients and immediately received $4,000 cash earned.

d.   The company performed services for clients and sent a bill for $14,000 with payment due within 60 days.

e.   The company compensated an office employee with $4,800 cash as salary for March.

f.   The company received $10,000 cash as partial payment on the amount owed from clients in transaction d.

g.   The company paid $935 cash in dividends to Demers (owner).

**E2-30.   Analyzing Transactions Using the Financial Statement Effects Template   (LO3)**

Enter the effects of each of the transactions a through g from Exercise 2-29 using the financial statement effects template shown in the module.

**E2-31.** **Identifying and Classifying Balance Sheet and Income Statement Accounts** (LO1)

Following are selected accounts for Procter & Gamble. (*a*) Indicate the appropriate classification of each account as appearing in either its balance sheet (B) or its income statement (I). (*b*) Using the following data, compute total assets and total expenses. (*c*) Compute its net profit margin (net income/sales) and its total liabilities-to-equity ratio (total liabilities/stockholders' equity).

Procter & Gamble (PG)

| ($ millions) | Amount | Classification |
|---|---|---|
| Sales. | $43,373 | |
| Accumulated depreciation | 10,438 | |
| Depreciation expense. | 1,703 | |
| Retained earnings | 11,686 | |
| Net income. | 5,186 | |
| Property, plant & equipment, net | 13,104 | |
| Selling, general & administrative expense | 13,009 | |
| Accounts receivable. | 3,038 | |
| Total liabilities. | 27,520 | |
| Stockholders' equity | 16,186 | |

**E2-32.** **Identifying and Classifying Balance Sheet and Income Statement Accounts** (LO1)

Following are selected accounts for Target Corporation. (*a*) Indicate the appropriate classification of each account as appearing in either its balance sheet (B) or its income statement (I). (*b*) Using the following data, compute total assets and total expenses. (*c*) Compute its net profit margin (net income/sales) and its total liability-to-equity ratio (total liabilities/stockholders' equity).

Target Corporation (TGT)

| ($ millions) | Amount | Classification |
|---|---|---|
| Sales. | $48,163 | |
| Accumulated depreciation | 6,178 | |
| Depreciation expense. | 1,320 | |
| Retained earnings | 9,648 | |
| Net income. | 1,841 | |
| Property, plant & equipment, net | 16,969 | |
| Selling, general & administrative expense | 11,534 | |
| Accounts receivable. | 5,776 | |
| Total liabilities. | 20,327 | |
| Stockholders' equity | 11,065 | |

**E2-33.** **Comparing TJX and Abercrombie & Fitch** (LO1)

Following are selected income statement and balance sheet data from two retailers: Abercrombie & Fitch (clothing retailer in the high-end market) and TJX Companies (clothing retailer in the value-priced market).

Abercrombie & Fitch (ANF)

TJX Companies (TJX)

| Income Statement ($ millions) | ANF | TJX |
|---|---|---|
| Sales. | $2,021 | $14,913 |
| Cost of goods sold. | 680 | 11,399 |
| Gross profit. | 1,341 | 3,514 |
| Total expenses | 1,125 | 2,904 |
| Net income. | $ 216 | $ 610 |

| Balance Sheet ($ millions) | ANF | TJX |
|---|---|---|
| Current assets . . . . . . . . . . . . . . . | $ 672 | $ 2,905 |
| Long-term assets . . . . . . . . . . . . . | 715 | 2,170 |
| Total assets. . . . . . . . . . . . . . . . . | $1,387 | $ 5,075 |
| Current liabilities. . . . . . . . . . . . . . | $429 | $ 2,204 |
| Long-term liabilities . . . . . . . . . . . | 288 | 1,124 |
| Total liabilities . . . . . . . . . . . . . . . . | 717 | 3,328 |
| Stockholders' equity . . . . . . . . . . . | 670 | 1,747 |
| Total liabilities and equity . . . . . . . . | $1,387 | $ 5,075 |

a.   Express each income statement account as a percentage of sales. Comment on any differences observed between these two companies, especially as they relate to their respective business models.

b.   Express each balance sheet account as a percentage of total assets. Comment on any differences observed between these two companies, especially as they relate to their respective business models.

c.   Which company has a higher proportion of stockholders' equity (and a lower proportion of debt)? What do the ratios tell us about relative riskiness of the two companies?

**E2-34.    Comparing Apple and Dell    (LO1)**

Apple (AAPL)
Dell (DELL)

Following are selected income statement and balance sheet data from two computer competitors: Apple and Dell.

| Income Statement ($ millions) | Apple | Dell |
|---|---|---|
| Sales. . . . . . . . . . . . . . . . . . . . . . | $13,931 | $49,205 |
| Cost of goods sold. . . . . . . . . . . . | 9,888 | 40,190 |
| Gross profit. . . . . . . . . . . . . . . . . | 4,043 | 9,015 |
| Total expenses . . . . . . . . . . . . . . | 2,708 | 5,972 |
| Net income. . . . . . . . . . . . . . . . . | $ 1,335 | $ 3,043 |

| Balance Sheet ($ millions) | Apple | Dell |
|---|---|---|
| Current assets . . . . . . . . . . . . . . | $10,300 | $16,897 |
| Long-term assets . . . . . . . . . . . . . | 1,251 | 6,318 |
| Total assets. . . . . . . . . . . . . . . . | $11,551 | $23,215 |
| Current liabilities. . . . . . . . . . . . . | $ 3,484 | $14,136 |
| Long-term liabilities . . . . . . . . . . | 601 | 2,594 |
| Total liabilities . . . . . . . . . . . . . . . | 4,085 | 16,730 |
| Stockholders' equity . . . . . . . . . . | 7,466 | 6,485 |
| Total liabilities and equity . . . . . . . | $11,551 | $23,215 |

a.   Express each income statement account as a percentage of sales. Comment on any differences observed between the two companies, especially as they relate to their respective business models. (*Hint:* Apple's gross profit as a percentage of sales is considerably higher than Dell's. What aspect of Apple's business do we believe is driving its profitability?)

b.   Apple has chosen to structure itself with a higher proportion of equity (and a lower proportion of debt) than Dell. What implication does this capital structure decision have for an evaluation of the relative riskiness of these two companies?

**E2-35.** **Comparing Income Statements and Balance Sheets of Competitors**  (LO1)

Following are selected income statement and balance sheet data for two communications companies: Comcast and Verizon.

Comcast (CMCA)

Verizon (VZ)

| Income Statement ($ millions) | Comcast | Verizon |
|---|---|---|
| Sales. . . . . . . . . . . . . . . . . . . . . . . | $22,255 | $75,112 |
| Cost of goods sold. . . . . . . . . . . . | 7,969 | 25,469 |
| Gross profit. . . . . . . . . . . . . . . . . | 14,286 | 49,643 |
| Total expenses . . . . . . . . . . . . . . | 13,358 | 42,246 |
| Net income. . . . . . . . . . . . . . . . . | $   928 | $ 7,397 |

| Balance Sheet ($ millions) | Comcast | Verizon |
|---|---|---|
| Current assets . . . . . . . . . . . . . . | $   2,954 | $ 16,448 |
| Long-term assets . . . . . . . . . . . | 100,192 | 151,682 |
| Total assets. . . . . . . . . . . . . . . | $103,146 | $168,130 |
| Current liabilities. . . . . . . . . . . . | $   6,269 | $ 25,063 |
| Long-term liabilities . . . . . . . . . | 56,001 | 76,633 |
| Total liabilities . . . . . . . . . . . . . | 62,270 | 101,696 |
| Stockholders' equity . . . . . . . . | 40,876 | 66,434 |
| Total liabilities and equity . . . . . . | $103,146 | $168,130 |

a.  Express each income statement account as a percentage of sales. Comment on any differences observed between the two companies, especially as they relate to their respective business models.

b.  Express each balance sheet account as a percentage of total assets. Comment on any differences observed between the two companies, especially as they relate to their respective business models.

c.  Both Verizon and Comcast have chosen a capital structure with a higher proportion of liabilities than equity. What implications does this capital structure decision have for our evaluation of the riskiness of these two companies? Take into consideration the large level of capital expenditures that each must make to remain competitive.

**E2-36.** **Comparing Financial Information Across Industries**  (LO1)

Use the data and computations required in parts a and b of exercises E2-33 and E2-35 to compare TJX Companies and Verizon Communications.

TJX Companies (TJX)

Verizon Communications (VZ)

a.  Compare gross profit and net income as a percentage of sales for these two companies. How might differences in their respective business models explain the differences observed?

b.  Compare sales versus total assets. What do observed differences indicate about the relative capital intensity of these two industries?

c.  Which company has the highest percentage of total liabilities to stockholders' equity? What do differences in this percentage imply about the relative riskiness of these two companies?

d.  Verizon requires large annual expenditures on new equipment to remain competitive with other companies in the communications industry. What implications does its debt level have for its ability to fund those expenditures?

e.  Compare the ratio of net income to stockholders' equity for these two companies. Which business model appears to be yielding the highest returns on shareholder investment? Using answers to parts a through d above, identify the factors that appear to drive the ratio of net income to stockholders' equity.

E2-37. **Analyzing Transactions using the Financial Statement Effects Template** (LO3)

Record the effect of each of the following independent transactions using the financial statement effects template.

a. Wages of $500 are earned by employees but not yet paid.
b. $2,000 of inventory is purchased on credit.
c. Inventory purchased in transaction b is sold for $3,000 on credit.
d. Collected $3,000 cash from transaction c.
e. Equipment is acquired for $5,000 cash.
f. Recorded $1,000 depreciation expense on equipment from transaction e.
g. Paid $10,000 cash toward a note payable that came due.
h. Paid $2,000 cash for interest on borrowings.

# PROBLEMS

P2-38. **Constructing and Analyzing Balance Sheet Amounts from Incomplete Data** (LO1)

3M Company (MMM)

Selected balance sheet amounts for 3M Company, a manufacturer of consumer and business products, for five recent years follow.

| $ millions | Current Assets | Long-Term Assets | Total Assets | Current Liabilities | Long-Term Liabilities | Total Liabilities | Stockholders' Equity |
|---|---|---|---|---|---|---|---|
| 2001..... | $6,296 | $    ? | $14,606 | $4,509 | $    ? | $ 8,520 | $ 6,086 |
| 2002..... | ? | 9,270 | 15,329 | 4,457 | 4,879 | 9,336 | ? |
| 2003..... | 7,720 | 9,880 | ? | ? | 4,633 | 9,715 | 7,885 |
| 2004..... | 8,720 | 11,988 | ? | 6,071 | 4,259 | ? | 10,378 |
| 2005..... | ? | 13,398 | 20,513 | 5,238 | 5,175 | 10,413 | ? |

**Required**

a. Compute the missing balance sheet amounts for each of the five years shown.
b. What types of accounts would we expect to be included in current assets? In long-term assets?

P2-39. **Analyzing, Reconstructing and Interpreting Balance Sheet Data** (LO1)

Abercrombie & Fitch (ANF)

Selected balance sheet amounts for Abercrombie & Fitch, a retailer of name-brand apparel at premium prices, for five recent years follow.

| $ millions | Current Assets | Long-Term Assets | Total Assets | Current Liabilities | Long-Term Liabilities | Total Liabilities | Stockholders' Equity |
|---|---|---|---|---|---|---|---|
| 2002..... | $  ? | $365 | ? | $164 | $  ? | $175 | $595 |
| 2003..... | 601 | 394 | ? | 211 | 34 | 245 | ? |
| 2004..... | 753 | ? | 1,383 | ? | 214 | 525 | 858 |
| 2005..... | 671 | 716 | ? | 429 | ? | ? | 669 |
| 2006..... | 947 | ? | 1,790 | ? | 303 | 795 | ? |

**Required**

a. Compute the missing balance sheet amounts for each of the five years shown.
b. What asset category would we expect to constitute the majority of Abercrombie's current assets?
c. Does the company appear to be conservatively financed; that is, financed by a greater proportion of equity than of debt? Explain

**P2-40.** **Analyzing, Reconstructing and Interpreting Balance Sheet Data** (LO1)

Selected balance sheet amounts for Albertsons Inc., a grocery company, for five recent years follow.

Albertsons Inc.

| $ millions | Current Assets | Long-Term Assets | Total Assets | Current Liabilities | Long-Term Liabilities | Total Liabilities | Equity Stockholders' |
|---|---|---|---|---|---|---|---|
| 2002 ..... | $4,609 | $   ? | $15,967 | $3,582 | $   ? | $10,052 | $5,915 |
| 2003 ..... | 4,268 | 10,943 | ? | 3,448 | 6,566 | ? | ? |
| 2004 ..... | ? | 10,975 | 15,394 | 3,685 | 6,328 | 10,013 | ? |
| 2005 ..... | 4,295 | 14,016 | ? | 4,085 | ? | ? | 5,421 |
| 2006 ..... | 4,355 | ? | 17,871 | ? | 8,284 | 12,164 | 5,707 |

**Required**

a. Compute the missing balance sheet amounts for each of the five years shown.

b. What asset category would we expect to constitute the majority of Albertsons' current assets? Of its long-term assets?

c. Is the company conservatively financed; that is, is it financed by a greater proportion of equity than of debt? Explain.

**P2-41.** **Comparing Operating Characteristics Across Industries** (LO1)

Following are selected income statement and balance sheet data for companies in different industries.

| $ millions | Sales | Cost of Goods Sold | Gross Profit | Net income | Assets | Liabilities | Stockholders' Equity |
|---|---|---|---|---|---|---|---|
| Harley-Davidson.... | $ 5,342 | $ 3,302 | $ 2,040 | $ 960 | $ 5,255 | $ 2,171 | $ 3,084 |
| Nike, Inc........... | 13,740 | 7,624 | 6,116 | 1,212 | 8,794 | 3,149 | 5,645 |
| Starbucks Corp..... | 6,369 | 2,605 | 3,764 | 494 | 3,514 | 1,423 | 2,091 |
| Target Corp. ....... | 51,271 | 34,927 | 16,344 | 2,408 | 34,995 | 20,790 | 14,205 |

Harley-Davidson (HOG)
Nike (NKE)
Starbucks (SBUX)
Target (TGT)

**Required**

a. Compute the following ratios for each company.
1. Gross profit / Sales
2. Net income / Sales
3. Net income / Stockholders' equity
4. Liabilities / Stockholders' equity

b. Comment on any differences we observe among the companies' gross profit to sales ratios and net income as a percentage of sales. Do differences in the companies' business models explain the differences observed?

c. Which company reports the highest ratio of net income to equity? Suggest one or more reasons for this result.

d. Which company has financed itself with the highest percentage of liabilities to equity? Suggest one or more reasons why this company can take on such debt levels.

**P2-42.** **Comparing Cash Flows Across Retailers** (LO1)

Following are selected accounts from the income statement and the statement of cash flows for several retailers.

| $ millions | Sales | Net Income | Cash Flows from Operating | Cash Flows from Investing | Cash Flows from Financing |
|---|---|---|---|---|---|
| Federated Dept. Stores .... | $ 22,390 | $ 1,406 | $ 1,950 | $ (2,506) | $   (58) |
| Home Depot, Inc. ......... | 81,511 | 5,838 | 6,484 | (4,586) | (1,612) |
| Staples, Inc. ............. | 16,079 | 834 | 1,235 | (634) | (621) |
| Target Corp. ............. | 52,620 | 2,408 | 4,451 | (4,149) | (899) |
| Wal-Mart Stores .......... | 312,427 | 11,231 | 17,633 | (14,183) | (2,422) |

Federated (FD)
Home Depot (HD)
Staples (SPLS)
Target (TGT)
Wal-Mart (WMT)

**Required**

a.  Compute the ratio of net income to sales for each company. Rank the companies on the basis of this ratio. Do their respective business models give insight into these differences?

b.  Compute net cash flows from operating activities as a percentage of sales. Rank the companies on the basis of this ratio. Does this ranking coincide with the ratio rankings from part *a*? Suggest one or more reasons for any differences you observe.

c.  Compute net cash flows from investing activities as a percentage of sales. Rank the companies on the basis of the absolute value of this ratio. Does this ranking coincide with the ratio rankings from part *a*? Suggest one or more reasons for any differences you observe.

d.  Each of these companies report negative cash flows from financing activities. What does it mean for a company to have net cash *outflow* from financing?

**P2-43.** **Interpreting the Statement of Cash Flows** (LO1)

Wal-Mart (WMT)

Following is the statement of cash flows for Wal-Mart Stores, Inc.

| WAL-MART STORES, INC<br>Statement of Cash Flows ($ millions)<br>For Year Ended January 31, 2006 | |
| --- | --- |
| **Operating activities** | |
| Net income | $11,231 |
| Depreciation | 4,717 |
| Increase in accounts receivable | (456) |
| Increase in inventories | (1,733) |
| Increase in accounts payable | 2,390 |
| Increase in accrued liabilities | 993 |
| Other | 491 |
| Net cash flows from operating activities | 17,633 |
| **Investing activities** | |
| Purchase of property and equipment | (14,563) |
| Other | 380 |
| Net cash flows from investing activities | (14,183) |
| **Financing activities** | |
| Increase in debt | 3,916 |
| Purchase of company stock | (3,580) |
| Dividends paid | (2,511) |
| Other | (349) |
| Net cash flows from financing activities | (2,524) |
| Net increase in cash and cash equivalents | $    926 |
| Cash at beginning of year | 5,488 |
| Cash at end of year | $ 6,414 |

**Required**

a.  Why does Wal-Mart add back depreciation to compute net cash flows from operating activities?

b.  Wal-Mart reports a cash outflow of $1,733 million from an increase in inventories and a cash inflow of $2,390 million from an increase in accounts payable. How does Wal-Mart's relative bargaining power with its suppliers affect cash outflows for inventory purchases?

c.  Wal-Mart reports that it invested $14,563 million in property and equipment. Is this an appropriate amount for Wal-Mart to invest? Would our opinion change if the expenditure was to purchase another company rather than to purchase separate assets?

d.  Wal-Mart indicates that it paid $3,580 million to repurchase its common stock in 2005 and, in addition, paid dividends of $2,511 million. Thus, Wal-Mart paid $6,091 million of cash to its shareholders during the year. How do we evaluate that use of cash relative to other possible uses for Wal-Mart's cash?

e.  Provide an overall assessment of Wal-Mart's cash flows for 2005. In the analysis, consider the sources and uses of cash.

**P2-44.** **Interpreting the Statement of Cash Flows** (LO1)
Following is the statement of cash flows for Verizon.

Verizon (VZ)

| VERIZON<br>Statement of Cash Flows<br>For Year Ended December 31, 2005 ($ millions) | |
| --- | --- |
| **Operating activities** | |
| Net income | $ 7,397 |
| Depreciation | 14,047 |
| Increase in accounts receivable | (933) |
| Increase in inventories | (252) |
| Decrease in accounts payable and accrued liabilities | (1,034) |
| Other | 2,787 |
| Net cash flows from operating activities | 22,012 |
| **Investing activities** | |
| Purchase of property and equipment | (15,324) |
| Other | (3,168) |
| Net cash flows from investing activities | (18,492) |
| **Financing activities** | |
| Increase in debt | 3,616 |
| Repayment of debt | (3,919) |
| Purchase of company stock | (304) |
| Dividends paid | (4,427) |
| Net cash flows from financing activities | (5,034) |
| Net decrease in cash and cash equivalents | $ (1,514) |
| Cash at beginning of year | 2,290 |
| Cash at end of year | $ 776 |

**Required**
a. Why does Verizon add back depreciation to compute net cash flows from operating activities?
b. What does the size of the depreciation add-back indicate about the relative capital intensity of this industry?
c. Verizon reports that it invested $15,324 million in property and equipment. These expenditures are necessitated by market pressures as the company faces stiff competition from other communications companies, such as Comcast. Where in the 10-K might we find additional information about these capital expenditures to ascertain whether Verizon is addressing the company's most pressing needs?
d. Verizon's statement of cash flows indicates that the company paid $3,919 million in debt payments, financed, in part, by the additional borrowing of $3,616 million on short-term notes. Is this a good strategy?
e. During the year, Verizon paid dividends of $4,427 million but did not repay a sizeable portion of its debt. How should we assess the payment of dividends? Specifically, how do dividend payments differ from debt payments?
f. Provide an overall assessment of Verizon's cash flows for 2005. In the analysis, consider the sources and uses of cash.

**P2-45.** **Analyzing Transactions using the Financial Statement Effects Template** (LO3)
On March 1, S. Penman (owner) launched AniFoods, Inc., an organic foods retailing company. Following are the transactions for its first month of business.
a. S. Penman (owner) contributed $100,000 cash to the company in return for common stock. Penman also lent the company $55,000. This $55,000 note is due one year hence.
b. The company purchased equipment in the amount of $50,000, paying $10,000 cash and signing a note payable to the equipment manufacturer for the remaining balance.
c. The company purchased inventory for $80,000 cash in March.
d. The company had March sales of $100,000 of which $60,000 was for cash and $40,000 on credit. Total cost of goods sold for its March sales was $70,000.

> e.   The company purchased future advertising time from a local radio station for $10,000 cash.
>
> f.   During March, $7,500 worth of radio spots purchased in *e* are aired. The remaining spots will be aired in April.
>
> g.   Employee wages earned and paid during March total $15,000 cash.
>
> h.   Prior to disclosing the financial statements, the company recognized that employees had earned an additional $1,000 in wages that will be paid in the next period.
>
> i.   The company recorded $2,000 of depreciation for March relating to its equipment.

**Required**

Record the effect of each transaction using the financial statement effects template shown in the module.

**P2-46.    Preparing an Income Statement and Balance Sheet from Transaction Data    (LO1)**

Use the information in Problem 2-45 to complete the following requirement.

**Required**

Prepare a March income statement and a balance sheet as of the end of March, for AniFoods, Inc.

**P2-47.    Reconciling and Computing Operating Cash Flows from Net Income    (LO1)**

Petroni Company reports the following selected results for its calendar year 2005.

| | |
|---|---:|
| Net income.................. | $130,000 |
| Depreciation expense.......... | 25,000 |
| Accounts receivable increase.... | 10,000 |
| Accounts payable increase ..... | 6,000 |
| Prepaid expenses decrease..... | 3,000 |
| Wages payable decrease....... | 4,000 |

**Required**

a.   Prepare the operating section only of Petroni Company's statement of cash flows for 2005.

b.   Does the positive sign on depreciation expense indicate that the company is generating cash by recording depreciation? Explain.

c.   Explain why the increase in accounts receivable is a use of cash in the statement of cash flows.

d.   Explain why the decrease in prepaid expense is a source of cash in the statement of cash flows.

# CASES

**C2-48.** **Management Application: Understanding Company Operating Cycle and Management Strategy** (LO1)

Consider the operating cycle as depicted in Exhibit 2.4, to answer the following questions.

a. Why might a company want to reduce its cash cycle? (*Hint*: Consider the financial statement implications of reducing the cash cycle.)

b. How might a company reduce its cash cycle?

c. Examine and discuss the potential impacts on *customers* and *suppliers* of taking the actions identified in part *b*.

**C2-49.** **Ethics and Governance: Understanding Revenue Recognition and Expense Matching** (LO1)

Revenue should be recognized when it is earned and expense when incurred. Given some lack of specificity in these terms, companies have some latitude when applying GAAP to determine when to recognize revenues and expenses. A few companies use this latitude to manage reported earnings. Some have argued that it is not necessarily bad for companies to manage earnings in that, by doing so, management (1) can better provide investors and creditors with reported earnings that are closer to "core" earnings (that is, management purges earnings of components deemed irrelevant or distracting so that share prices better reflect company performance); and (2) presents the company in the best light, which benefits both shareholders and employees—a Machiavellian argument that 'the end justifies the means.'

a. Is it good that GAAP is written as broadly as it is? Explain. What are the pros and cons of defining accounting terms more strictly?

b. Assess (both pro and con) the Machiavellian argument above that defends managing earnings.

# Constructing Financial Statements and Analyzing Transactions

## LEARNING OBJECTIVES

**LO1** Analyze and record transactions using the financial statement effects template. (p. 3-4)

**LO2** Prepare and explain accounting adjustments and their financial statement effects. (p. 3-9)

**LO3** Explain and construct the trial balance. (p. 3-13)

**LO4** Construct financial statements from account balances. (p. 3-16)

**LO5** Describe the closing process. (p. 3-21)

## APPLE

In late 2001, Apple Computer launched the iPod, arguably the most important product in the company's history. A basic hard-drive-based player, the iPod was not a new concept. Yet, Apple created a durable, slim, and sexy package, paired it with ear buds, and made the iPod a fashion statement as well as a great music player. Marrying the hardware with the intuitive Apple-like software for navigation, the company had a winning combination. By the end of 2001, nearly 125,000 iPods had flown off the shelves.

The following March, Apple launched a 10 GB version of the iPod followed by a 20 GB version in July. Apple soon introduced its scroll wheel, similar to a touch pad with no moving parts. Apple sold 700,000 iPods in 2002.

The company announced even more innovations in early 2003: a 30 GB version, an improved connector that could use both FireWire and USB ports, and, the biggest coup: the iTunes music store. With that innovation, consumers could play songs on a PC, burn songs to a CD, or download them to their iPod. 2003 also witnessed the advent of the now-famous marketing campaign showcasing black silhouettes holding the blazing white iPod while dancing to its tunes. By mid-2003, Apple announced a new 40 GB version and unit sales soared to 939,000.

Apple soon introduced a smaller model, the iPod mini in five colors, and boasted more sophisticated ear buds to reduce background noise. But the major innovation was the advent of iPod video. The iPod was now a complete audio-visual phenomenon and well positioned to compete in the growing handheld communications market. 2004 unit sales were 4.4

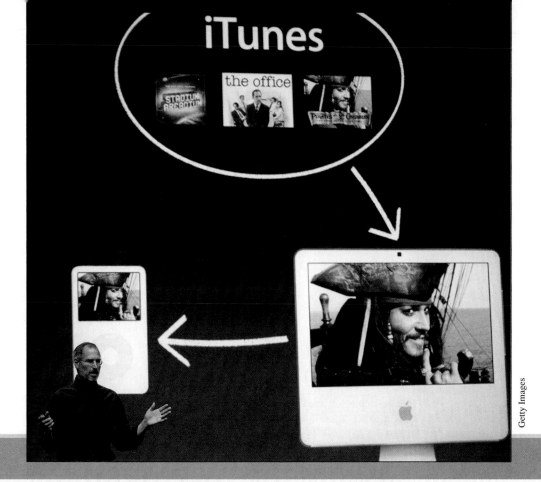

million, a 370% increase over the prior year! But the story wasn't over: in 2005, Apple sold a staggering 22 million iPods for a total of $4.5 billion. And in 2006, iTunes sold more than a billion songs.

To bring each iPod to market, Apple must purchase component parts, manufacture the iPods, hire sales personnel, pay advertisers, and distribute finished iPods. Each of these activities involves a transaction that Apple's accounting records must capture. The resulting financial statements tell the story of Apple's manufacturing and sales process in financial language.

This module explains how the accounting system captures business transactions, creates financial records, and aggregates the individual records to produce the financial reports that we read and interpret in company 10-Ks.

Sources: Apple 2005 Annual Report; osViews.com, May 03, 2005; Apple 2005 10-K; *Fortune*, January 2007.

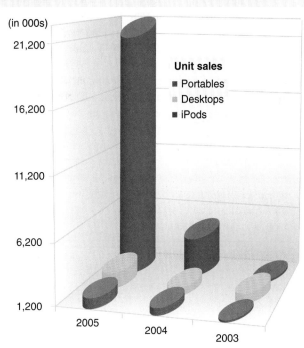

(in 000s)

**Unit sales**
- ■ Portables
- ▨ Desktops
- ■ iPods

21,200

16,200

11,200

6,200

1,200

2005　2004　2003

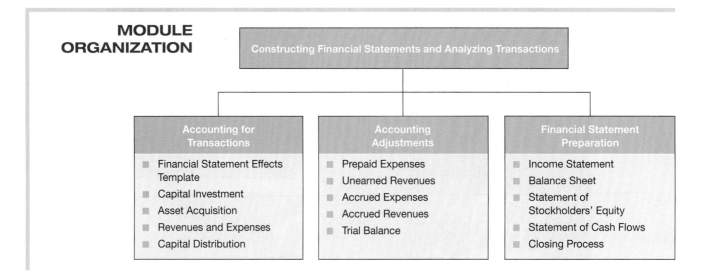

## MODULE ORGANIZATION

**Constructing Financial Statements and Analyzing Transactions**

| **Accounting for Transactions** | **Accounting Adjustments** | **Financial Statement Preparation** |
|---|---|---|
| ■ Financial Statement Effects Template | ■ Prepaid Expenses | ■ Income Statement |
| ■ Capital Investment | ■ Unearned Revenues | ■ Balance Sheet |
| ■ Asset Acquisition | ■ Accrued Expenses | ■ Statement of Stockholders' Equity |
| ■ Revenues and Expenses | ■ Accrued Revenues | ■ Statement of Cash Flows |
| ■ Capital Distribution | ■ Trial Balance | ■ Closing Process |

## INTRODUCTION

Financial statements report on the financial performance of a business using the language of accounting. To prepare these statements, companies translate day-to-day transactions into accounting records (called journals), and then record (post) them to individual accounts. At the end of an accounting period, each of these accounts is totaled, and the resulting balances are used to prepare financial statements. After the financial statements are prepared, the temporary (income statement) accounts are 'zeroed out' so that the next period can begin anew—akin to clearing a scoreboard for the next game. Permanent (balance sheet) accounts continue to reflect financial position and carry over from period to period—akin to keeping track of wins and losses even when a particular scoreboard is cleared.

The accounting cycle is illustrated in Exhibit 3.1. Transactions are first recorded in the accounting records. Each of these transactions is, generally, the result of an external transaction, such as recording a sale to a customer or the payment of wages to employees. Once all of the transactions have been recorded during the accounting period, the company adjusts the accounting records to recognize a number of events that have occurred, but which have not yet been recorded. These might include the recognition of wage expense and the related wages payable for those employees who have earned wages, but have not yet been paid, or the recognition of depreciation expense for buildings and equipment. These adjustments are made at the end of the accounting period to properly adjust the accounting records in preparation of financial statements. Once all adjustments are made, financial statements are prepared. Details of the accounting cycle are described in this module.

| **EXHIBIT 3.1** | **Accounting Cycle** |
|---|---|

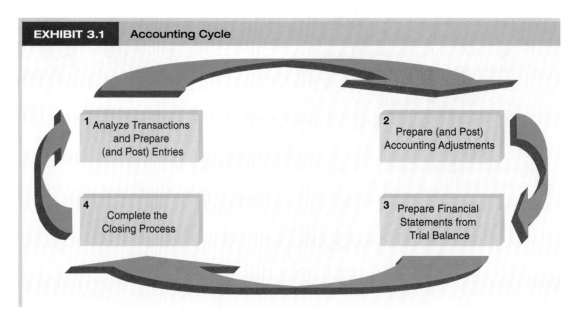

1 Analyze Transactions and Prepare (and Post) Entries

2 Prepare (and Post) Accounting Adjustments

3 Prepare Financial Statements from Trial Balance

4 Complete the Closing Process

Understanding the financial statement preparation process requires an understanding of the language used to record business transactions in accounting records. The recording and statement preparation processes are readily understood once we learn that language (of financial effects) and its mechanics (entries and posting). The goal of this module is to explain that language and those mechanics.

Even if we never journalize a transaction or prepare a financial statement, understanding the accounting process aids us in analyzing and interpreting accounting reports. Understanding the accounting language also aids communication with business professionals within a company and with members of the business community outside of a company.

# ACCOUNTING FOR TRANSACTIONS

This section explains how we account for and assess business transactions. We describe the financial statement effects template that we use throughout the book. We then illustrate its application to four main categories of business transactions.

**LO1** Analyze and record transactions using the financial statement effects template.

## Financial Statement Effects Template

Transaction analysis refers to the process of analyzing, identifying, and recording the financial statement effects of transactions. For this purpose, we use the following **financial statement effects template**.

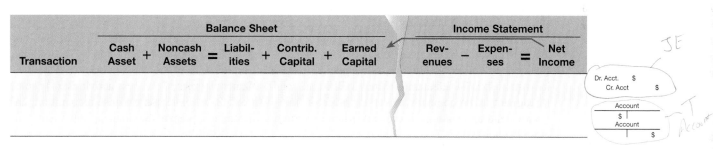

| | Balance Sheet | | | | | | Income Statement | | |
| Transaction | Cash Asset | + Noncash Assets | = Liabil- ities | + Contrib. Capital | + Earned Capital | | Rev- enues | − Expen- ses | = Net Income |

Each transaction is identified in the "Transaction" column. Then, the dollar amounts (positive or negative) of the financial statement effects are recorded in the appropriate balance sheet or income statement columns. The template also reflects the statement of cash flow effects (via the cash column) and the statement of stockholders' equity effects (via the contributed capital and earned capital columns). The retained earnings account, one of the accounts in earned capital, is immediately updated to reflect any income or loss arising from each transaction (denoted by the arrow line from net income to earned capital). This template is instructive as it reveals the financial impacts of transactions, and it provides insights into the effects of accounting choices.

## T-Accounts and Journal Entries

In the margin next to the financial statement effects template are shown the related journal entry and T-account effects. The **T-Accounts,** named for their likeness to a large 'T', are used to reflect increases and decreases to individual accounts. When a transaction occurs, it is recorded (*journalized*) in the accounting books (*general ledger*) of the company, and the affected accounts are increased or decreased. This process of continuously updating individual account balances from transactions is referred to as *posting* transactions to accounts. A T-account provides a simple illustration of the financial effects of each transaction.

Specifically, one side of the T-account is used for increases and the other for decreases. A convenient way to remember which side records increases is to recall the accounting equation: **Assets = Liabilities + Equity.** Assets are on the left side of the equation. So, the left side of an asset T-account records increases in the asset—the right side records decreases. Liabilities and equity are on the right side of the accounting equation. So, the right side of a liability and an equity T-account records increases and the left side records decreases. This relation is represented graphically as follows.

| Assets | = | Liabilities | + | Equity |
| + | − | | − | + | | − | + |
| Increases | Decreases | | Decreases | Increases | | Decreases | Increases |

Journal entries also capture the effects of transactions. Journal entries reflect increases and decreases to accounts using the language of debits and credits. Debits and credits are "directions" that simply refer to the left or right side of a T-account, respectively. We can superimpose the descriptors of debit and credit on a T-account as follows.

| Account Title | |
|---|---|
| Debit | Credit |
| (Left side) | (Right side) |

The left side of the T-account is the "debit" side and the right side is the "credit" side. This holds for all T-accounts. Thus, to record an increase in an asset, we enter an amount on the left or debit side of the T-account—that is, we *debit the account*. Decreases in assets are recorded with an entry on the opposite (credit) side. To record an increase in a liability or equity account, we enter an amount on the right or credit side of the T-account—we *credit the account*. Decreases in liability or equity accounts are recorded on the opposite (debit) side.

In the margin of our financial statement effects template, we show the journal entry first, followed by the related T-accounts. In accounting jargon, this sequence relates to *journalizing* the entry and *posting* it to the affected accounts. The T-accounts represent the financial impact of each transaction on the respective asset, liability or equity accounts.

## Introduction to Transaction Analysis

This section uses Apple, Inc., to illustrate the accounting for selected business transactions. The assumed time frame will be one quarter, as all public companies are required to prepare financial statements at least quarterly. We select transactions to illustrate four fundamental types of business activities: (1) capital investment in the company, (2) asset (inventory) acquisition, (3) revenue and expense recognition, and (4) dividend distribution. Next, we consider accounting adjustments, prepare the financial statements, and close the books.

## Capital Investment

Assume that Apple investors contribute $300 cash to the company in exchange for common stock. Apple's cash and common stock both increase. Recall that common stock is a component of contributed capital. The financial statement effects template reflects this transaction as follows.

| | | Balance Sheet | | | | | | Income Statement | | |
|---|---|---|---|---|---|---|---|---|---|---|
| Transaction | Cash Asset | + | Noncash Assets | = | Liabil- ities | + | Contrib. Capital | + Earned Capital | Rev- enues | − Expen- ses | = Net Income |
| Issued stock for $300 cash | +300 Cash | | | = | | | +300 Common Stock | | | = |

Margin notes:
Cash 300
CS 300
Cash
300 |
CS
| 300

### Journal Entry and T-Account

Although it is not our intent to refer to journal entries and T-accounts in this book, we will describe them for this first transaction. Specifically, the $300 debit equals the $300 credit in the journal entry: assets ($300 cash) = liabilities ($0) + equity ($300 common stock). This balance in transactions is the basis of *double-entry accounting*. For simplicity, we use acronyms (such as CS for common stock) in journal entries and T-accounts. (A listing of accounts and acronyms is located in Appendix C near the end of the book.) The journal entry for this transaction is

Cash. . . . . . . . . . . . . . . . . . . . . . . . . . . . . . . . . . . . . . . . . . . . .    300
    CS (Common Stock) . . . . . . . . . . . . . . . . . . . . . . . . . . . . . .         300

Convention dictates that debits are listed first, followed by credits—the latter are indented.[1] The total debit(s) must always equal the total credit(s) for each transaction. The T-account representation for this transaction follows:

| Cash | | CS | |
|---|---|---|---|
| 300 | | | 300 |

Cash is an asset; thus, a cash increase is recorded on the left or debit side of the T-account. Common stock is an equity account; thus, a common stock increase is recorded on the right or credit side.

## Asset (Inventory) Acquisition

Assume that Apple purchases $2,000 worth of iPods from its supplier (we keep this illustration simple by ignoring Apple's manufacturing activities). When one company buys from another, it is normal to give a period of time in which to pay the obligation due, usually 30 to 60 days, or more. This purchase "on credit" (also called *on account*) means that Apple owes its supplier $2,000 for the purchase. Apple records the cost of the purchased iPods as an asset called inventories, which are goods held for resale. This acquisition of iPods on credit is recorded as follows.

| | Balance Sheet | | | | | | Income Statement | | |
|---|---|---|---|---|---|---|---|---|---|
| Transaction | Cash Asset | + Noncash Assets | = Liabil- ities | + Contrib. Capital | + Earned Capital | | Rev- enues | − Expen- ses | = Net Income |
| Purchase iPods for $2,000 on credit | | +2,000 Inventories | +2,000 = Accounts Payable | | | | | | = |

| INV | | |
|---|---|---|
| | 2,000 | |

| AP | |
|---|---|
| | 2,000 |

| INV | |
|---|---|
| 2,000 | |

| AP | |
|---|---|
| | 2,000 |

## Revenue and Expense Recognition

Assume that Apple sells iPods that cost $600 to a retailer for $700 on credit. The sale *on credit* means that the customer has not yet paid and Apple has a $700 account receivable.

Can Apple record the $700 sale as revenue even though it has not collected any cash? The answer is yes. This decision reflects an important concept in accounting, called the **revenue recognition principle,** which is part of *accrual accounting*. The revenue recognition principle prescribes that a company can recognize revenues provided that two conditions are met:

1. Revenues are *earned*, and
2. Revenues are *realized* or *realizable*.

**Earned** means that the company has done whatever it is required to do. In this case, it means that Apple has delivered the iPods to its retail customer. **Realized** or **realizable** means that the seller has either received cash or will receive cash at some point in the future. That is, Apple can recognize revenue if it expects to collect the $700 account receivable in the future. (We explain revenue recognition in more detail in Module 5.)

Recording the $700 sale is only half the transaction. Apple must also record the decrease in iPod inventory of $600. When a company purchases inventory, it records the cost on the balance sheet as an asset. When inventory is sold, the "asset" is used up and its cost must be transferred from the balance sheet to the income statement as an expense. In particular, the expense associated with inventory is called cost of goods sold. Thus, the second part of Apple's revenue transaction is to remove the cost of the iPods from the balance sheet and recognize the cost of goods sold (an expense) in its income statement. This will match the cost of the inventory to the related revenue.

---

[1] There can be more than one debit and one credit for a transaction. To illustrate, assume that Apple raises $300 cash, with $200 from investors and $100 borrowed from a bank. The resulting journal entry is:

| Cash............................................. | 300 | |
|---|---|---|
| CS (common stock)................................. | | 200 |
| NP (note payable)................................. | | 100 |

Matching of expenses with revenues in this manner is evidence of the **matching principle.** Once revenues are recognized (using the revenue recognition principle), we must then match all related expenses incurred to generate those revenues *in the same period* that we recognize the revenue. This yields the proper measure of income for the period and is an application of accrual accounting.

The $700 sale of Apple iPods that cost $600 is recorded as follows.

| | Balance Sheet | | | | | | Income Statement | | |
|---|---|---|---|---|---|---|---|---|---|
| Transaction | Cash Asset | + Noncash Assets | = Liabil- ities | + Contrib. Capital | + Earned Capital | | Rev- enues | − Expen- ses | = Net Income |
| Sold $700 of iPods on credit | | +700 Accounts = Receivable | | | +700 Retained Earnings | | +700 Sales | | = +700 |
| Record $600 cost of the $700 iPod sale | | −600 Inventory = | | | −600 Retained Earnings | | | +600 − Cost of = Goods Sold | −600 |

AR    700
Sales    700
     AR
700
   Sales
          700

COGS  600
INV    600
   COGS
600
   INV
       600

The first part of this sales transaction records the $700 sale and the $700 increase in accounts receivable. Revenues are earned and therefore recognized even though no cash was received. The sale is reflected in the account receivable that will later be converted to cash. The increase in revenues increases income, which increases retained earnings.[2]

The second part of this sale transaction transfers the $600 in inventory on the balance sheet to the income statement as the cost of iPods sold. This entry increases expenses, and decreases both income and retained earnings. The transaction also reduces assets because Apple no longer owns the inventory; it is "used up."

## Capital Distributions

Assume that Apple decides to pay $50 to its shareholders in the form of a cash dividend. Dividends are treated as a return of shareholders' investment. All transactions between the company and its shareholders are considered financing transactions. This includes payment of dividends, the issuance of stock, and any subsequent stock repurchase. Financing transactions affect only the balance sheet; they do not affect the income statement. Dividends are distributions of income. They represent the portion of income that the company chooses to distribute to shareholders—the portion that will no longer be retained. Thus, dividends reduce retained earnings. It is important to distinguish dividends from expenses—dividends are NOT an expense, they do not reduce net income. They are a distribution of net income; they reduce retained earnings. Apple's $50 dividend payment is reflected in the following template. (Companies typically record dividends in a separate dividends account and then later, in the closing process, this account is transferred to retained earnings. The template depicts dividends as an immediate reduction of retained earnings, which is part of earned capital. The end result of both approaches is identical.)

| | Balance Sheet | | | | | | Income Statement | | |
|---|---|---|---|---|---|---|---|---|---|
| Transaction | Cash Asset | + Noncash Assets | = Liabil- ities | + Contrib. Capital | + Earned Capital | | Rev- enues | − Expen- ses | = Net Income |
| Paid $50 cash for dividends | −50 Cash | | = | | −50 Dividends | | | | = |

DIV    50
Cash    50
   DIV
50
   Cash
       50

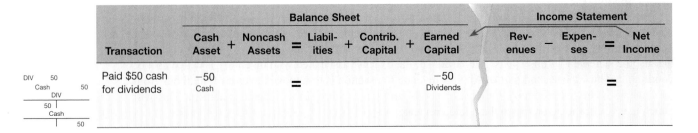

---

[2] The retained earnings account is not automatically updated in most accounting software programs as our financial effects template illustrates. Instead, accountants transfer income to retained earnings using a journal entry as part of the closing process. We briefly explain the closing process near the end of this module and more fully in Appendix 3A.

## MID-MODULE REVIEW 1

Assume that Symantec Corporation experienced the following six transactions relating to a capital investment, the purchase and sale of inventory, the collection of an account receivable, and the payment of an account payable.

1. Shareholders contribute $3,000 cash to Symantec in exchange for its common shares.
2. Symantec purchases $1,000 of inventory on credit.
3. Symantec sells $300 of inventory for $500 on credit.
4. Symantec collects $300 cash owed by customers from part 3.
5. Symantec pays $400 cash toward its accounts payable to suppliers.
6. Symantec pays $20 cash for dividends to its stockholders.

### Required

Record each transaction in the financial statement effects template. Include journal entries for each account in the margin and post those entries to T-accounts.

### Solution

| | Balance Sheet | | | | | | Income Statement | | |
|---|---|---|---|---|---|---|---|---|---|
| Transaction | Cash Asset | + Noncash Assets | = Liabil- ities | + Contrib. Capital | + Earned Capital | | Rev- enues | − Expen- ses | = Net Income |
| 1. Issue stock for $3,000 cash | +3,000 Cash | | = | +3,000 Common Stock | | | | | = |
| 2. Purchase $1,000 of inventory on credit | | +1,000 Inventory | = +1,000 Accounts Payable | | | | | | = |
| 3a. Sell inventory for $500 on credit | | +500 Accounts Receivable | = | | +500 Retained Earnings | | +500 Sales | | = +500 |
| 3b. Record $300 cost of inventory sold | | −300 Inventory | = | | −300 Retained Earnings | | | − +300 Cost of Goods Sold | = −300 |
| 4. Collect $300 cash owed by customers | +300 Cash | −300 Accounts Receivable | = | | | | | | = |
| 5. Pay $400 cash toward accounts payable | −400 Cash | | = −400 Accounts payable | | | | | | = |
| 6. Pay $20 cash for dividends | −20 Cash | | = | | −20 Dividends | | | | = |

T-accounts (margin):

```
Cash    3,000
     CS      3,000
        Cash
3,000 |
     CS
        |   3,000

INV     1,000
     AP      1,000
        INV
1,000 |
      AP
        |   1,000

AR      500
     Sales    500
        AR
500 |
     Sales
        |   500

COGS    300
     INV      300
       COGS
300 |
      INV
        |   300

Cash    300
     AR      300
       Cash
300 |
      AR
        |   300

AP      400
     Cash     400
        AP
400 |
      Cash
        |   400

DIV     20
     Cash     20
        DIV
20 |
      Cash
        |   20
```

# ACCOUNTING ADJUSTMENTS (ACCRUALS)

Recognizing revenue when earned (even if not received in cash), and matching expenses when incurred (even if not paid in cash), are cornerstones of **accrual accounting,** which is required under

**LO2** Prepare and explain accounting adjustments and their financial statement effects.

GAAP.[3] Understanding accounting adjustments, commonly called *accruals*, is crucial to effectively analyzing and interpreting financial statements. In this module's Apple illustration, we recorded inventory as a purchase even though no cash was paid, and we recognized the sale as revenue even though no cash was received. Both of these transactions reflect accrual accounting. Some accounting adjustments affect the balance sheet alone (as with purchasing inventory on account). Other adjustments affect the balance sheet *and* the income statement (as with selling inventory on account). Accounting adjustments can affect asset, liability or equity accounts, and can either increase or decrease net income.

Companies make adjustments to more accurately report their financial performance and condition. For example, employees might not have been paid for wages earned at the end of an accounting period. Failure to recognize this labor cost would understate the company's total liabilities (because wages payable would be too low), and would overstate net income for the period (because wages expense would be too low). Thus, neither the balance sheet nor the income statement would be accurate.

Accounting adjustments yield a more accurate presentation of the economic results of a company for a period. Despite their (generally) beneficial effects, adjustments can be misused. Managers can use adjustments to bias reported income, rendering it higher or lower than it really is. Adjustments, if misused, can adversely affect business and investment decisions. Many recent accounting scandals have resulted from improper use of adjustments. Although outsiders cannot directly observe companies' specific accounting entries, their impact can be detected as changes in balance sheet and income statement accounts. Those changes provide signals for financial statement analysis. Consequently, understanding the accrual process will help us know what to look for as we analyze companies' financial reports.

---

**BUSINESS INSIGHT**    Accounting Scandals and Improper Adjustments

Many accounting scandals involve the improper use of adjustments to manipulate income. The following table highlights three specific adjustment manipulations by companies. These accounting scandals underscore the important role of adjustments in financial accounting and the economic impact they can have on balance sheets and income statements. When used improperly, adjustments distort financial reports and can mislead investors and other financial statement users. (Source: "Corporate Scandal Sheet," Forbes 2002.)

| Company | Allegations | Accounting Adjustment |
|---|---|---|
| Halliburton (HAL) | Improperly booked $100 million in annual construction cost overruns before customers agreed to pay for them. | Halliburton recognized revenues before earned. Its accounting entry increased accounts receivable and revenue, thereby inflating net income. It later wrote off the receivables when customers refused to pay. |
| WorldCom (WCOEQ) | Improperly recorded $11 billion of operating expenses as capital costs (assets). | WorldCom recorded costs as assets on the balance sheet rather than as expenses in the income statement. This inflated both assets and income. It later wrote off the assets (and reduced income) when the transactions were uncovered. |
| Xerox (XRX) | Overstated net income by $1.5 billion over five years. | Customers purchased copiers and service contracts as one purchase. Xerox allocated most of the "sale" to hardware, thereby recognizing revenues before they were earned under service contracts. |

---

Exhibit 3.2 identifies four general types of accounting adjustments which are briefly described on the next page.

---

[3] **Cash accounting** recognizes revenues when cash is received and expenses when cash is paid. This is not acceptable accounting under GAAP. However, small businesses that do not prepare financial reports for public investors and creditors, sometimes use cash accounting.

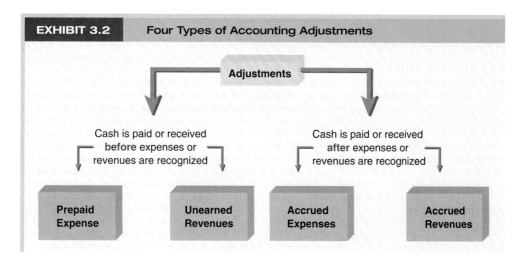

**EXHIBIT 3.2    Four Types of Accounting Adjustments**

*Prepaid expenses*  Prepaid expenses reflect advance cash payments that will ultimately become expenses. An example is the payment of radio advertising that will not be aired until sometime in the future.

*Unearned revenues*  Unearned revenues reflect cash received from customers before any services or goods are provided. An example is cash received from patrons for tickets to an upcoming concert.

*Accrued expenses*  Accrued expenses are expenses incurred and recognized on the income statement, even though they are not yet paid in cash. An example is wages owed to employees who performed work but who have not yet been paid.

*Accrued revenues*  Accrued revenues are revenues earned and recognized on the income statement, even though cash is not yet received. Examples include sales on credit and revenue earned under a long-term contract.

The remainder of this section illustrates how Apple's financial statements would reflect each of these four types of adjustments.

## RESEARCH INSIGHT    Accruals: Good or Bad?

Accounting accruals are used to study the effects of earnings management on financial accounting. Earnings management is broadly defined as the use of accounting discretion to distort reported earnings. Managers have incentives to manage earnings in many situations. For example, managers have tendencies to accelerate revenue recognition to increase stock prices prior to equity offerings. Also, management buyouts occur when management repurchases common stock and take the company "private." In this case, research shows that managers decelerate revenue recognition to depress stock prices prior to the management buyout. Research also shows that managers use discretion when reporting special items to either meet or beat analysts' forecasts of earnings and/or to avoid reporting a loss. Not all earnings management occurs for opportunistic reasons. Research shows that managers use accruals to communicate private information about future profitability to outsiders. For example, management might signal future profitability through use of income-decreasing accruals to show investors that it can afford to apply conservative accounting. This "signaling" through accruals is found to precede stock splits and dividend increases.

To examine the information conveyed in accruals, we must determine what portion of accruals is unexpected. These accruals are referred to as "discretionary accruals" and are estimated using regression models. Total accruals are defined as the difference between net income before extraordinary items and cash flows from operations. Total accruals can be decomposed into changes in working capital accounts (such as accounts receivable, inventory, accounts payable, and accrued liabilities) and noncash income statement accounts (such as depreciation and special items). Regression is used to determine the predicted (or expected) change in total accruals that should be generated from actual changes in sales and the level of fixed assets for each firm in each year. Actual total accruals are compared with predicted total accruals and the difference is considered to be the unexpected accruals (the discretionary portion). In sum, we must look at reported earnings in conjunction with other earnings quality signals (such as levels of disclosure, degree of corporate governance, and industry performance) to interpret information in accruals.

## Prepaid Expenses (Assets)

Assume that Apple pays $200 to purchase time on MTV for future iPod ads. Apple's cash account decreases by $200. Should the $200 advertising cost be recorded as an expense when Apple pays MTV, when MTV airs the ads, or at some other point? Under accrual accounting, Apple must record an expense when it is incurred. That means Apple should expense the ads when MTV airs them. When Apple pays for the advertisement, it records an asset; Apple "owns" TV time that will presumably provide future benefits when the ads air. In the interim, the cost of the ads is an asset on the balance sheet. Apple's financial statement effects template follows for this transaction. There is a decrease in cash and an increase in the advertising asset, titled prepaid advertising.

PPDA    200
  Cash            200
        PPDA
  200 |
    Cash
        |        200

| | Balance Sheet | | | | | | Income Statement | | |
|---|---|---|---|---|---|---|---|---|---|
| Transaction | Cash Asset | + Noncash Assets | = Liabil- ities | + Contrib. Capital | + Earned Capital | | Rev- enues | − Expen- ses | = Net Income |
| Pay $200 cash in advance for ad time | −200 Cash | +200 Prepaid Advertising | = | | | | | | = |

When an ad airs, the prepaid advertising asset is used up and the portion of the prepaid advertising account relating to the aired ad is reduced. The cost is transferred to the income statement as advertising expense.

## Unearned Revenues (Liabilities)

Assume that Apple receives $400 cash from a customer as advance payment on a multi-unit iPod sale to be delivered next month. Apple must record cash received on its balance sheet, but cannot recognize revenue from the order until earned, which is generally when iPods are delivered to the customer. Until then, Apple must recognize a liability called unearned or deferred revenue that represents Apple's obligation to fulfill the order at some future point. The financial statement effects template for this transaction follows.

Cash    400
  UR              400
        Cash
  400 |
    UR
        |        400

| | Balance Sheet | | | | | | Income Statement | | |
|---|---|---|---|---|---|---|---|---|---|
| Transaction | Cash Asset | + Noncash Assets | = Liabil- ities | + Contrib. Capital | + Earned Capital | | Rev- enues | − Expen- ses | = Net Income |
| Received $400 cash in advance for iPod sale | +400 Cash | | +400 = Unearned Revenue | | | | | | = |

Assume that Apple delivers the iPods a month later (but still within the fiscal quarter). Apple must recognize the $400 as revenue at delivery because it is now earned. Thus, net income increases by $400. The second part of this transaction is to record the cost of the iPods sold. Assuming the cost is $150, Apple reduces iPod inventory by $150 and records cost of goods sold by the same amount. These effects are reflected in the following template.

UR    400
  Sales          400
        UR
  400 |
    Sales
        |        400

COGS    150
  INV            150
        COGS
  150 |
    INV
        |        150

| | Balance Sheet | | | | | | Income Statement | | |
|---|---|---|---|---|---|---|---|---|---|
| Transaction | Cash Asset | + Noncash Assets | = Liabil- ities | + Contrib. Capital | + Earned Capital | | Rev- enues | − Expen- ses | = Net Income |
| Delivered $400 of iPods paid in advance | | | −400 = Unearned Revenues | | +400 Retained Earnings | | +400 Sales | | = +400 |
| Record $150 cost of the $400 iPod sale | | −150 Inventory = | | | −150 Retained Earnings | | | +150 − Cost of Goods Sold | = −150 |

## Accrued Expenses (Liabilities)

Assume that Apple's sales staff earns $100 of sales commissions this period that will not be paid until next period. The sales staff earned the wages as they made the sales. However, because Apple pays its employees twice a month, the related cash payment will not occur until the next pay period. Should Apple record the wages earned by its employees as an expense even though payment has not yet been made? The answer is yes. The matching principle requires Apple to recognize wages expense when it is *incurred*, even if not paid in cash. It must record wages expense incurred as a liability (wages payable).

| Transaction | Cash Asset | + | Noncash Assets | = | Liabil-ities | + | Contrib. Capital | + | Earned Capital | Rev-enues | − | Expen-ses | = | Net Income |
|---|---|---|---|---|---|---|---|---|---|---|---|---|---|---|
| Incurred $100 of wages not yet paid | | | | = | +100 Wages Payable | | | | −100 Retained Earnings | | − | +100 Wages Expense | = | −100 |

| WE | 100 | |
|---|---|---|
| WP | | 100 |
| | WE | |
| 100 | | |
| | WP | |
| | | 100 |

In the next period, when Apple pays the wages, it reduces both cash and wages payable. Net income is not affected by the cash payment; instead, net income decreased in the previous period when Apple accrued the wage expense.

Next assume that Apple rents office space and that it owes $25 in rent at period-end. Apple has incurred rent expense in the current period and that expense must be recorded this period. Failing to make this adjustment would mean that Apple's liabilities (rent payable) would be understated and its income would be overstated. The entry to record the accrual of rent expense for office space follows.

| Transaction | Cash Asset | + | Noncash Assets | = | Liabil-ities | + | Contrib. Capital | + | Earned Capital | Rev-enues | − | Expen-ses | = | Net Income |
|---|---|---|---|---|---|---|---|---|---|---|---|---|---|---|
| Incurred $25 of rent not yet paid | | | | = | +25 Rent Payable | | | | −25 Retained Earnings | | − | +25 Rent Expense | = | −25 |

| RNTE | 25 | |
|---|---|---|
| RNTP | | 25 |
| | RNTE | |
| 25 | | |
| | RNTP | |
| | | 25 |

## Accrued Revenues (Assets)

Assume that Apple delivers iPods to a customer in Germany who will pay next quarter. The sales price for those units is $500 and the cost is $400. Apple has completed its revenue earning process with this sale and must accrue revenue from the German customer even though Apple received no cash. Like all sales transactions, Apple must record two parts, the sales revenue and the cost of sales. The financial effects template for this two-part transaction follows.

| Transaction | Cash Asset | + | Noncash Assets | = | Liabil-ities | + | Contrib. Capital | + | Earned Capital | Rev-enues | − | Expen-ses | = | Net Income |
|---|---|---|---|---|---|---|---|---|---|---|---|---|---|---|
| Sold $500 of iPods on credit | | | +500 Accounts Receivable | = | | | | | +500 Retained Earnings | +500 Sales | | | = | +500 |
| Record $400 cost for $500 iPod sale | | | −400 Inventory | = | | | | | −400 Retained Earnings | | − | +400 Cost of Goods Sold | = | −400 |

| AR | 500 | |
|---|---|---|
| Sales | | 500 |
| | AR | |
| 500 | | |
| | Sales | |
| | | 500 |

| COGS | 400 | |
|---|---|---|
| INV | | 400 |
| | COGS | |
| 400 | | |
| | INV | |
| | | 400 |

## Summary of Accounting Adjustments

Adjustments are an important part of the accounting process and are crucial to accurate and informative financial accounting. It is through the accruals process that managers communicate information about future cash flows. For example, from accrual information, we know that Apple paid for a resource (advertising) that it has not yet used. We know that all cash advances from customers have been honored because there are no unearned revenues. We know that employees have earned wages but Apple won't pay them until a future period. We know that revenues have been earned but cash not yet received. Those accruals tell us about Apple's past performance and, perhaps more importantly, about Apple's future cash flows. When used correctly, accruals convey a wealth of information about the past and the future that is useful in our evaluation of company financial performance and condition. Thus, we can use accrual information to more precisely value companies' equity and debt securities.

Not all managers are honest; some misuse accounting accruals to improperly recognize revenues and expenses. Abuses include accruing revenue before it is earned; and accruing expenses in the wrong period or in the wrong amount. These actions are fraudulent as they deliberately overstate or understate revenues and expenses and, thus, reported net income is incorrect. Safeguards against this type of managerial behavior include corporate governance systems (internal controls, accounting policies and procedures, routine scrutiny of accounting reports, and audit committees) and external checks and balances (independent auditors, regulatory bodies, and the court system). Collectively, these safeguards aim to protect interests of companies' internal and external stakeholders. When managers abuse accounting systems, tough and swift sanctions remind others that corporate malfeasance is unacceptable. Videos of police officers leading corporate executives to jail in handcuffs (the infamous "perp walk") sends that message.

> **MANAGERIAL DECISION**    **You Are the CFO**
>
> The plant manager of your company informs you of the leakage of hazardous waste from your company's factory. It is estimated that cleanup will cost $10 million. Part 1: What effect will recording this accrual have on your company's balance sheet and its income statement? Part 2: Accounting rules require you to record the accrual if it is both probable and can be reliably estimated. Although the cleanup is relatively certain, the cost is a guess at this point. Consequently, you have some discretion whether to record the accrual. Discuss the parties that are likely affected by your decision on whether or not to record the liability and related expense, and the ethical issues involved.
> [Answer 3-25]

## Trial Balance Preparation and Use

**LO3** Explain and construct the trial balance.

After Apple records all of its transactions, it must prepare financial statements so it can assess its financial performance and condition for the quarter. The following template shows a summary of Apple's transactions thus far.

The first step in preparing financial statements is to prepare a **trial balance,** which is a listing of all accounts and their balances at a point in time. To prepare a trial balance we compile a listing of accounts, their balances, and we determine whether that balance is a debit or credit. Its purpose is to prove the mathematical equality of debits and credits, provide a useful tool to uncover any accounting errors, and help prepare the financial statements.

| Transaction | Cash Asset | + | Noncash Assets | = | Liabilities | + | Contrib. Capital | + | Earned Capital | | Revenues | − | Expenses | = | Net Income | |
|---|---|---|---|---|---|---|---|---|---|---|---|---|---|---|---|---|
| Issued stock for $300 cash | +300 Cash | | | = | | | +300 Common Stock | | | | | | | = | | Cash 300 / CS 300 — Cash 300 / CS 300 |
| Purchase $2,000 of iPods on credit | | | +2,000 Inventory | = | +2,000 Accounts Payable | | | | | | | | | = | | INV 2,000 / AP 2,000 — INV 2,000 / AP 2,000 |
| Sold $700 of iPods on credit | | | +700 Accounts Receivable | = | | | | | +700 Retained Earnings | | +700 Sales | | | = | +700 | AR 700 / Sales 700 — AR 700 / Sales 700 |
| Record $600 cost of $700 iPod sale | | | −600 Inventory | = | | | | | −600 Retained Earnings | | | − | +600 Cost of Goods Sold | = | −600 | COGS 600 / INV 600 — COGS 600 / INV 600 |
| Paid $50 cash for dividends | −50 Cash | | | = | | | | | −50 Dividends | | | | | = | | DIV 50 / Cash 50 — DIV 50 / Cash 50 |
| Pay $200 cash in advance for ad time | −200 Cash | | +200 Prepaid Advertising | = | | | | | | | | | | | = | | PPDA 200 / Cash 200 — PPDA 200 / Cash 200 |
| Received $400 cash in advance for iPod sale | +400 Cash | | | = | +400 Unearned Revenue | | | | | | | | | | = | | Cash 400 / UR 400 — Cash 400 / UR 400 |
| Delivered $400 of iPods paid in advance | | | | = | −400 Unearned Revenues | | | | +400 Retained Earnings | | +400 Sales | | | = | +400 | UR 400 / Sales 400 — UR 400 / Sales 400 |
| Record $150 cost of $400 iPod sale | | | −150 Inventory | = | | | | | −150 Retained Earnings | | | − | +150 Cost of Goods Sold | = | −150 | COGS 150 / INV 150 — COGS 150 / INV 150 |
| Incurred $100 of wages not yet paid | | | | = | +100 Wages Payable | | | | −100 Retained Earnings | | | − | +100 Wages Expense | = | −100 | WE 100 / WP 100 — WE 100 / WP 100 |
| Incurred $25 of rent not yet paid | | | | = | +25 Rent Payable | | | | −25 Retained Earnings | | | − | +25 Rent Expense | = | −25 | RNTE 25 / RNTP 25 — RNTE 25 / RNTP 25 |
| Sold $500 of iPods on credit | | | +500 Accounts Receivable | = | | | | | +500 Retained Earnings | | +500 Sales | | | = | +500 | AR 500 / Sales 500 — AR 500 / Sales 500 |
| Record $400 cost of $500 iPod sale | | | −400 Inventory | = | | | | | −400 Retained Earnings | | | − | +400 Cost of Goods Sold | = | −400 | COGS 400 / INV 400 — COGS 400 / INV 400 |
| **Total** | 450 | + | 2,250 | = | 2,125 | + | 300 | + | 275 | | 1,600 | − | 1,275 | = | 325 | |

The trial balance for Apple, which we assume to be as of December 31, 2007, follows.

| APPLE<br>Trial Balance<br>December 31, 2007 | Debit | Credit |
|---|---|---|
| Cash................... | $ 450 | |
| Accounts receivable......... | 1,200 | |
| Inventories ............... | 850 | |
| Prepaid advertising......... | 200 | |
| Accounts payable.......... | | $2,000 |
| Wages payable............ | | 100 |
| Rent payable ............. | | 25 |
| Unearned revenues ......... | | 0 |
| Common stock............ | | 300 |
| Dividends ................ | 50 | |
| Sales.................... | | 1,600 |
| Cost of goods sold.......... | 1,150 | |
| Wage expense ............ | 100 | |
| Rent expense............. | 25 | |
| Totals .................. | $4,025 | $4,025 |

The trial balance amounts consist of the ending balance for each of the accounts. For the Apple illustration, we total all transactions for each account listed in the template. To illustrate, cash has an ending balance of $450 ($300 − $50 − $200 + $400). Also, because cash is an asset (which is on the left hand side of the balance sheet), it normally has a debit balance (which is on the left hand side of the T-accounts). We can confirm the ending cash debit balance by totalling each of the cash T-account entries. Liabilities and equity accounts normally have credit balances (because they are on the right hand side of the balance sheet), and we can confirm these ending credit balances by referring to their respective T-accounts in the template.

The trial balance shows total debits equal $4,025, which also equals total credits. Accordingly, we know that all of the template transactions balance. We do not know, however, that all required journal entries have been properly included, or if Apple recorded entries that it should not have. (An *unadjusted trial balance* is one that is prepared prior to accounting adjustments; an *adjusted trial balance* is one prepared after accounting adjustments are entered.)

## MID-MODULE REVIEW 2

Refer to the transactions in Mid-Module Review 1. Assume that Symantec Corporation reports the following additional transactions.

1. Symantec pays $100 cash toward rent for the next period.
2. Symantec receives $200 cash in advance from a client for future consulting services.
3. Symantec employees earn $50 in wages that will not be paid until the next period.
4. Symantec provides $150 of services revenue and bills the client.

### Required
Record each of these additional transactions using the financial statement effects template. Also record the journal entry for each transaction in the margin and post each entry to T-accounts. Prepare a trial balance for Symantec reflecting these transactions together with those of Mid-Module Review 1.

## Solution

| | Balance Sheet | | | | | Income Statement | | |
|---|---|---|---|---|---|---|---|---|
| Transaction | Cash Asset + | Noncash Assets = | Liabil- ities + | Contrib. Capital + | Earned Capital | Rev- enues − | Expen- ses = | Net Income |
| Pays $100 cash for next period rent | −100 Cash | +100 Prepaid rent = | | | | | = | |
| Receives $200 cash advance for future services | +500 Cash | = | +500 Unearned revenues | | | | = | |
| Incurs $50 in wages to be paid next period | | = | +50 Wages payable | | −50 Retained Earnings | − | +50 Wage expense = | −50 |
| Provides $150 of services and bills client | | +150 Accounts receivable = | | | +150 Retained Earnings | +150 Sales | = | +150 |

PPRNT 100
Cash 100
PPRNT
100
Cash
100

Cash 500
UR 500
Cash
500
UR
500

WE 50
WP 50
WE
50
WP
50

AR 150
Sales 150
AR
150
Sales
150

| SYMANTEC Trial Balance | | |
|---|---|---|
| | Debit | Credit |
| Cash..................... | $3,280 | |
| Accounts receivable......... | 350 | |
| Inventories ............... | 700 | |
| Prepaid rent .............. | 100 | |
| Accounts payable........... | | $ 600 |
| Wages payable............. | | 50 |
| Unearned revenues ......... | | 500 |
| Common stock............. | | 3,000 |
| Dividends ................. | 20 | |
| Sales..................... | | 650 |
| Cost of goods sold.......... | 300 | |
| Wage expense ............. | 50 | |
| Totals ................... | $4,800 | $4,800 |

# FINANCIAL STATEMENT PREPARATION

Financial statement preparation involves working with the accounts in the adjusted trial balance to properly report them in financial statements. There is an order to financial statement preparation. First, a company prepares its income statement using the income statement accounts. It then uses the net income number and dividend information to update the retained earnings account. Second, it prepares the balance sheet using the updated retained earnings account along with the remaining balance sheet accounts from the trial balance. Third, it prepares the statement of stockholders' equity. Fourth, it prepares the statement of cash flows using information from the cash account (and other sources).

**LO4** Construct financial statements from the trial balance.

## Income Statement

Apple's income statement follows. Apple's trial balance reveals four income statement accounts. Those income statement accounts are called *temporary accounts* because they begin each accounting period with a zero balance. Apple's income statement also includes a line for gross profit because that subtotal is important to evaluate manufacturers' performance and profitability. Income for this quarterly period is $325 (we ignore taxes in this illustration).

| APPLE Income Statement For Quarter Ended December 31, 2007 | |
| --- | --- |
| Sales.................... | $1,600 |
| Cost of goods sold.......... | 1,150 |
| Gross profit............... | 450 |
| Wage expense ............. | 100 |
| Rent expense.............. | 25 |
| Net income................ | $ 325 |

## Retained Earnings Computation

Apple updates its retained earnings balance at period-end using income from the income statement and the dividends information from its trial balance. (For simplicity, we assume retained earnings is zero at the beginning of this period). This computation follows.

| APPLE Retained Earnings Computation For Quarter Ended December 31, 2007 | |
| --- | --- |
| Retained earnings, beginning of period......... | $ 0 |
| Add: Net income (loss)................... | 325 |
| Deduct: Dividends........................ | 50 |
| Retained earnings, end of period............. | $275 |

## Balance Sheet

Once Apple computes its ending balance in retained earnings, it can prepare its balance sheet, which follows. Balance sheet accounts are called *permanent accounts* because their respective balances carry over from one period to the next. For example, the cash balance at the end of the current accounting period (ended December 31, 2007) is $450, which will be the balance at the beginning of the next accounting period (beginning January 1, 2008).

| APPLE Balance Sheet December 31, 2007 | |
| --- | --- |
| **Assets** | |
| Cash.................................. | $ 450 |
| Accounts receivable..................... | 1,200 |
| Inventories ........................... | 850 |
| Prepaid advertising..................... | 200 |
| Total assets........................... | $2,700 |
| **Liabilities and Stockholders' Equity** | |
| Liabilities | |
| Accounts payable....................... | $2,000 |
| Wages payable......................... | 100 |
| Rent payable .......................... | 25 |
| Total liabilities........................ | 2,125 |
| Stockholders' equity | |
| Common stock......................... | 300 |
| Retained earnings ..................... | 275 |
| Total liabilities and stockholders' equity....... | $2,700 |

## Statement of Stockholders' Equity

Apple uses the information pertaining to its contributed capital and earned capital categories to prepare the statement of stockholders' equity, as follows.

| | Contributed Capital | Earned Capital | Total Stockholders' Equity |
|---|---|---|---|
| **APPLE** **Statement of Stockholders' Equity** **For Quarter Ended December 31, 2007** | | | |
| Beginning balance . . . . . . . . . . . . . . | $  0 | $  0 | $  0 |
| Stock issuance. . . . . . . . . . . . . . . . . | 300 | | 300 |
| Net income (loss) . . . . . . . . . . . . . . | | 325 | 325 |
| Dividends . . . . . . . . . . . . . . . . . . . . . | | (50) | (50) |
| Ending balance. . . . . . . . . . . . . . . . | $300 | $275 | $575 |

## Statement of Cash Flows

The statement of cash flows summarizes the cash-based transactions for the period and reports the sources and uses of cash. Each cash transaction represents an operating, investing, or financing activity. To prepare the statement, Apple uses the Cash column of the financial statement effects template, see above. The following cash flow statement for Apple is based on the *direct method* for reporting operating cash flows. The indirect method is an alternative presentation, which we discuss later. During the current period, Apple's cash increased by $450. Its increase in cash consists of a $200 net cash inflow from operating activities plus a $250 cash inflow from financing activities. There were no investing activities during this period.

| **APPLE** **Statement of Cash Flows (Direct Method)** **For Quarter Ended December 31, 2007** | |
|---|---|
| Operating activities | |
| Receipts from sales contracts . . . . . . . . . . . . . . | $400 |
| Payments for advertising . . . . . . . . . . . . . . . . . | (200) |
| Net cash flows from operating activities . . . . . . | 200 |
| Investing activities | |
| Net cash flows from investing activities. . . . . . . | 0 |
| Financing activities | |
| Issuance of common stock . . . . . . . . . . . . . . . . | 300 |
| Payment of cash dividends . . . . . . . . . . . . . . . | (50) |
| Net cash flows from financing activities. . . . . . . | 250 |
| Net change in cash . . . . . . . . . . . . . . . . . . . . . | $450 |
| Cash, beginning of period . . . . . . . . . . . . . . . . | 0 |
| Cash, end of period . . . . . . . . . . . . . . . . . . . . . | $450 |

In practice, preparing a statement of cash flows is more complicated. Companies can have millions of transactions in the cash account and the task of classifying each transaction as operating, investing or financing would be costly and time consuming. Instead, companies prepare the statement of cash flows using the current income statement and the balance sheets for the current and prior periods. The basic approach is to adjust net income to arrive at net cash flows from operating activities (the so-called *indirect method*) and then review changes in balance sheet accounts (by comparing the opening and ending balances) to arrive at net cash flows from investing and financing activities.

As mentioned, there are two methods to display net cash flows from operating activities: the direct method and the indirect method. Both methods report the same net operating cash flow, the only difference is in presentation. Companies can choose which method to follow. Apple's simplified statement of cash flows above, is an example of the direct method. However, the **indirect method** is, by far, the most widely used method in practice today (over 98% of public companies use it). The indirect method computes operating cash flows *indirectly* by adjusting net income using the following format.

| | Add (+) or Subtract (−) from Net Income |
|---|---|
| Net income . . . . . . . . . . . . . . . . . . . . . . . . . . | $ # |
| Add: depreciation expense . . . . . . . . . . . . . . . | + |
| Adjust for changes in current assets | |
|   Subtract increases in current assets . . . . . . . | − |
|   Add decreases in current assets . . . . . . . . . | + |
| Adjust for changes in current liabilities | |
|   Add increases in current liabilities . . . . . . . . . | + |
|   Subtract decreases in current liabilities . . . . . | − |
| Net cash flow from operating activities . . . . . . . | $ # |

Net income is first adjusted for noncash expenses such as depreciation and amortization, and is then adjusted for changes in current assets and current liabilities to yield net cash flow from operating activities, or *cash profit*. The depreciation adjustment merely zeros out (undoes the effect of) depreciation expense, a noncash expense, which is deducted in computing net income. The following table provides brief explanations of adjustments for receivables, inventories, and payables and accruals.

| | Change in account balance . . . | Means that . . . | Which requires this adjustment to net income to yield cash profit . . . |
|---|---|---|---|
| Receivables | Increase | Sales and net income increase, but cash is not yet received | Deduct increase in receivables from net income |
| | Decrease | More cash is received than is reported in sales and net income | Add decrease in receivables to net income |
| Inventories | Increase | Cash is paid for inventories that are not yet reflected in cost of goods sold | Deduct increase in inventories from net income |
| | Decrease | Cost of goods sold includes inventory costs that were paid for in a prior period | Add decrease in inventories to net income |
| Payables and accruals | Increase | More goods and services are acquired on credit, delaying cash payment | Add increase in payables and accruals to net income |
| | Decrease | More cash is paid than that reflected in cost of goods sold or operating expenses | Deduct decrease in payables and accruals from net income |

It is also helpful to use the following decision guide, involving changes in assets, liabilities, and equity, to understand increases and decreases in cash flows.

| | Cash flow increases from | Cash flow decreases from |
|---|---|---|
| Assets . . . . . . . . . . . . . . . . . . . . . . | Account decreases | Account increases |
| Liabilities and equity . . . . . . . . . . . | Account increases | Account decreases |

Using this decision guide we can determine the cash flow effects of the income statement and balance sheet information and categorize them into the following table for our Apple illustration.

| Financial Element | Change | Source or Use | Cash Flow Effect | Classification on SCF |
|---|---|---|---|---|
| Current assets | | | | |
| Accounts receivable . . . . . . . . | + $1,200 | Use | $(1,200) | Operating |
| Increase in inventories . . . . . . | + 850 | Use | (850) | Operating |
| Prepaid advertising. . . . . . . . . | + 200 | Use | (200) | Operating |
| Noncurrent assets | | | | |
| PPE. . . . . . . . . . . . . . . . . . . . | 0 | | 0 | Investing |
| Accumulated depreciation . . . | | Neither | 0* | Operating |
| Current liabilities | | | | |
| Accounts payable. . . . . . . . . . | + 2,000 | Source | 2,000 | Operating |
| Wages payable . . . . . . . . . . . . | + 100 | Source | 100 | Operating |
| Rent payable. . . . . . . . . . . . . | + 25 | Source | 25 | Operating |
| Long-term liabilities . . . . . . . . . | 0 | | 0 | Financing |
| Stockholders' equity | | | | |
| Common stock . . . . . . . . . . . . | + 300 | Source | 300 | Financing |
| Retained earnings | | | | |
| Net income . . . . . . . . . . . . . | + 325 | Source | 325 | Operating |
| Dividends . . . . . . . . . . . . . | + 50 | Use | (50) | Financing |
| Total (net cash flow) . . . . . . . . . | | | $   450 | |

*Depreciation, if present, is added to net income in computing cash flows from operating activities.

Increases in the three current assets reflect a use of cash, and are subtracted in the operating section of the statement of cash flows. Increases in noncurrent PPE assets are coded likewise, but are classified as an investing activity. An increase in accumulated depreciation reflects the recording of depreciation expense in the income statement, which is a noncash expense that must be zeroed out (with an addition to net income) to yield cash profit. Increases in the three current liabilities reflect sources of cash, and are recorded as positive amounts in the statement of cash flows.

Issuance of common stock is a source of cash, and the payment of dividends to shareholders is a use of cash. Both of these are reflected in the financing section of the statement of cash flows. The financing section also reflects any increases or decreases in borrowings as sources (uses), respectively. The increase in retained earnings, resulting from net income, is a source of cash, but it is reported as an operating activity. (Components of the change in retained earnings, net income less dividends, are reflected in the statement of cash flows and, consequently, the change in retained earnings is already recognized.)

The sum of these elements yields a net increase in cash of $450. This is the same result we obtained earlier using the direct method. Reporting these elements by operating, investing and financing activities yields the following familiar form of the statement of cash flows (statement shown to the right).

| APPLE Statement of Cash Flows (Indirect Method) For Quarter Ended December 31, 2007 | |
|---|---|
| Operating activities | |
| Net income. . . . . . . . . . . . . . . . . . . . . . . . . . . . . | $   325 |
| Depreciation and other noncash expenses . . . . . | 0 |
| Increase in accounts receivable . . . . . . . . . . . . . | (1,200) |
| Increase in inventories . . . . . . . . . . . . . . . . . . . | (850) |
| Increase in prepaid advertising. . . . . . . . . . . . . | (200) |
| Increase in accounts payable. . . . . . . . . . . . . . . | 2,000 |
| Increase in wages payable . . . . . . . . . . . . . . . . . | 100 |
| Increase in rent payable . . . . . . . . . . . . . . . . . . . | 25 |
| Net cash flows from operating activities . . . . . . . . | 200 |
| Investing activities | |
| Net cash flows from investing activities. . . . . . . . . | 0 |
| Financing activities | |
| Issuance of common stock . . . . . . . . . . . . . . . . . | 300 |
| Payment of cash dividends . . . . . . . . . . . . . . . . . | (50) |
| Net cash flows from financing activities. . . . . . . . . | 250 |
| Net change in cash. . . . . . . . . . . . . . . . . . . . . . . . | $   450 |
| Cash, beginning of period . . . . . . . . . . . . . . . . . . | 0 |
| Cash, end of period . . . . . . . . . . . . . . . . . . . . . . . | $   450 |

## Closing Process

**LO5** Describe the closing process.

The **closing process** refers to the 'zeroing out' of revenue and expense accounts (the temporary accounts) by transferring their ending balances to retained earnings. (Recall, income statement accounts—revenues and expenses—and the dividend account are temporary accounts because their balances are zero at the end of each accounting period; balance sheet accounts carry over from period to period and are called permanent accounts.) The closing process is typically carried out via a series of journal entries that successively zero out each revenue and expense account, transferring those balances to retained earnings. The result is that all income statement accounts begin the next period with zero balances. The balance sheet accounts do not need to be similarly adjusted because their balances carry over from period to period. Recall the scoreboard analogy.

Our financial statement effects template makes the closing process unnecessary because the template updates retained earnings with each revenue and expense entry. The arrow that runs from net income to retained earnings (part of earned capital) highlights the continual updating. To illustrate, recall the following entries that reflect Apple's initial sale of iPods on credit.

| | Balance Sheet | | | | | | | Income Statement | | | | | |
|---|---|---|---|---|---|---|---|---|---|---|---|---|---|
| Transaction | Cash Asset | + | Noncash Assets | = | Liabil-ities | + | Contrib. Capital | + | Earned Capital | | Rev-enues | − | Expen-ses | = | Net Income |
| Sold $700 of iPods on credit | | | +700 Accounts Receivable | = | | | | | +700 Retained Earnings | | +700 Sales | | | = | +700 |
| Record $600 cost of $700 iPod sale | | | −600 Inventory | = | | | | | −600 Retained Earnings | | | − | +600 Cost of Goods Sold | = | −600 |

T-accounts (left margin):

```
AR        700
  Sales        700
      AR
700 |
  Sales
      |  700

COGS  600
  INV        600
      COGS
600 |
  INV
      |  600
```

Sales of $700 increase net income by $700, which the template immediately transfers to retained earnings. Likewise, cost of goods sold reduces net income by $600, and this reduction is immediately carried to retained earnings. Consequently, the financial statement effects template always reports an updated retained earnings, making the closing process unnecessary.

It is important to distinguish our financial statement effects template from companies' accounting systems. The financial statement effects template and T-accounts are pedagogical tools that represent transactions' effects on the four financial statements. The template is highly stylized but its simplicity is instructive. In practice, managers use journal entries to record transactions and adjustments. The template captures these in summarized fashion. However, income statement transactions are not automatically transferred to retained earnings and retained earnings is not continuously updated. All companies perform the closing process—someone or some program must transfer the temporary account balances to retained earnings. Thus, it is important to understand the closing process and why companies "close" the books each period. We describe the mechanical details of the closing process in Appendix 3A.

The entire accounting process, from analysis of basic transactions to financial statement preparation to the closing process, is called the **accounting cycle.** As we discuss at the outset of this module and portray graphically in Exhibit 3.1, there are four basic processes in the accounting cycle. First, companies analyze transactions and prepare (and post) entries. Second, companies prepare (and post) adjusting entries. Third, financial statements are prepared from an adjusted trial balance. Fourth, companies perform the closing process. The analysis and posting of transactions is done regularly during each accounting period. However, the preparation of accounting adjustments and financial statements is only done at the end of an accounting period. At this point, we have explained and illustrated all aspects of the accounting cycle.

# MODULE-END REVIEW

Refer to the transactions in Mid-Module Reviews 1 and 2. From those transactions, assume that Symantec Corporation prepares the following trial balance. Also assume its transactions are for the quarter ended December 31, 2007.

| SYMANTEC Trial Balance December 31, 2007 | Debit | Credit |
|---|---|---|
| Cash . . . . . . . . . . . . . . . . . . . . . | $3,280 | |
| Accounts receivable . . . . . . . . . | 350 | |
| Inventories . . . . . . . . . . . . . . . | 700 | |
| Prepaid rent . . . . . . . . . . . . . . | 100 | |
| Accounts payable . . . . . . . . . . . | | $  600 |
| Wages payable . . . . . . . . . . . . . | | 50 |
| Unearned revenues . . . . . . . . . | | 500 |
| Common stock . . . . . . . . . . . . . | | 3,000 |
| Dividends . . . . . . . . . . . . . . . . . | 20 | |
| Sales . . . . . . . . . . . . . . . . . . . . | | 650 |
| Cost of goods sold . . . . . . . . . . | 300 | |
| Wage expense . . . . . . . . . . . . . | 50 | |
| Totals . . . . . . . . . . . . . . . . . . . | $4,800 | $4,800 |

## Required

Prepare Symantec's income statement, statement of stockholders' equity, balance sheet, and statement of cash flows.

## Solution

| SYMANTEC Income Statement For Quarter Ended December 31, 2007 | |
|---|---|
| Sales . . . . . . . . . . . . . . . . . . . . . . . . . . . . . . . . . . . . . . | $650 |
| Cost of goods sold . . . . . . . . . . . . . . . . . . . . . . . . . . . | 300 |
| Gross profit . . . . . . . . . . . . . . . . . . . . . . . . . . . . . . . . . | 350 |
| Wage expense . . . . . . . . . . . . . . . . . . . . . . . . . . . . . . | 50 |
| Net income . . . . . . . . . . . . . . . . . . . . . . . . . . . . . . . . . | $300 |

| SYMANTEC Retained Earnings Computation For Quarter Ended December 31, 2007 | |
|---|---|
| Retained earnings, beginning of period . . . . . . . . . . . . | $  0 |
| Add:    Net income (loss) . . . . . . . . . . . . . . . . . . . . . . | 300 |
| Deduct: Dividends . . . . . . . . . . . . . . . . . . . . . . . . . . . | (20) |
| Retained earnings, end of period . . . . . . . . . . . . . . . . | $280 |

**SYMANTEC**
**Balance Sheet**
**December 31, 2007**

**Assets**

| | |
|---|---:|
| Cash | $3,280 |
| Accounts receivable | 350 |
| Inventories | 700 |
| Prepaid rent | 100 |
| Total assets | $4,430 |

**Liabilities and Stockholders' Equity**

Liabilities

| | |
|---|---:|
| Accounts payable | $ 600 |
| Wages payable | 50 |
| Unearned revenues | 500 |
| Total liabilities | 1,150 |

Stockholders' equity

| | |
|---|---:|
| Common stock | 3,000 |
| Retained earnings | 280 |
| Total liabilities and stockholders' equity | $4,430 |

**SYMANTEC**
**Statement of Stockholders' Equity**
**For Quarter Ended December 31, 2007**

| | Contributed Capital | Earned Capital | Total Stockholders' Equity |
|---|---:|---:|---:|
| Beginning balance | $ 0 | $ 0 | $ 0 |
| Stock issuance | 3,000 | | 3,000 |
| Net income (loss) | | 300 | |
| Dividends | | (20) | (20) |
| Ending balance | $3,000 | $280 | $3,280 |

**SYMANTEC**
**Statement of Cash Flows**
**For Quarter Ended December 31, 2007**

Operating activities

| | |
|---|---:|
| Net income | $ 300 |
| Depreciation and other noncash expenses | 0 |
| Gains or losses on asset sales | 0 |
| Increase in accounts receivable | (350) |
| Increase in inventories | (700) |
| Increase in prepaid rent | (100) |
| Increase in accounts payable | 600 |
| Increase in wages payable | 50 |
| Increase in unearned revenues | 500 |
| Net cash flows from operating activities | 300 |

Investing activities

| | |
|---|---:|
| Net cash flows from investing activities | 0 |

Financing activities

| | |
|---|---:|
| Issuance of common stock | 3,000 |
| Payment of cash dividends | (20) |
| Net cash flows from financing activities | 2,980 |
| Net change in cash | $3,280 |
| Cash, beginning of period | 0 |
| Cash, end of period | $3,280 |

# APPENDIX 3A: Closing Process Using Journal Entries

The idea of the closing process is to close all temporary accounts—all the income statement accounts and any dividend account. The balance in each temporary account is transferred to retained earnings leaving the temporary accounts with zero balances. That way, the temporary accounts are ready to capture transaction data for the next period. The closing process brings the retained earnings account up to date so that it is accurate and so that the balance sheet can be prepared. To illustrate, let's return to Apple's income statement.

| APPLE Income Statement For Quarter Ended December 31, 2007 | |
| --- | --- |
| Sales. | $1,600 |
| Cost of goods sold. | 1,150 |
| Gross profit. | 450 |
| Wage expense | 100 |
| Rent expense | 25 |
| Net income. | $ 325 |

The closing process transfers the ending balances for each of these income statement accounts, to retained earnings. The dividend account is a temporary account and therefore, it also must be closed to retained earnings. The journal entries, and the related T-accounts, follow for this 3-step process.

1. Close all revenue accounts.

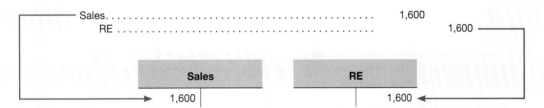

| Sales. | 1,600 |
| --- | --- |
| RE | 1,600 |

2. Close all expense accounts.

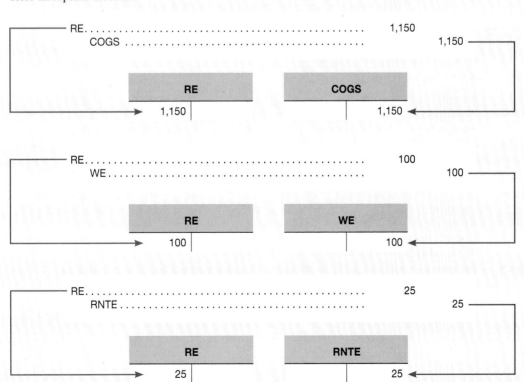

| RE. | 1,150 |
| --- | --- |
| COGS | 1,150 |

| RE. | 100 |
| --- | --- |
| WE. | 100 |

| RE. | 25 |
| --- | --- |
| RNTE. | 25 |

3. Close any dividend accounts.

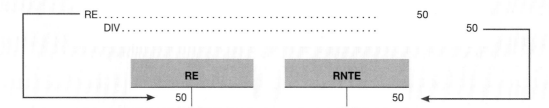

Apple must close one revenue account, three expense accounts, and a dividend account to retained earnings at the end of the period. The first closing entry transfers the $1,600 balance in the sales account to retained earnings. The closing entry debits sales for $1,600 (because the sales account has a $1,600 credit balance at period-end) and credits retained earnings. The second closing entry closes cost of good sold ($1,150), wages expense ($100), and rent expense ($25). The entry credits each of the expense accounts because their ending balances are debit balances. Third, the $50 dividend account balance is transferred to retained earnings. All the temporary accounts are now *closed*.

Retained earnings, which began the period with a zero balance, now reports a balance of $275, which equals net income for the period less the dividends paid to shareholders. This is the balance Apple reports in the stockholders' equity section of its balance sheet. Further, all of the income statement accounts (sales, cost of goods sold, wages expense, and rent expense) and the dividend account now show zero balances to begin the next period.

# GUIDANCE ANSWERS

MANAGERIAL DECISION      **You Are the CFO**

Part 1: Liabilities will increase by $10 million for the estimated amount of the cleanup, an expense in that amount will be recognized in the income statement, thus reducing both income and retained earnings (equity) by $10 million. Part 2: Stakeholders affected by recognition decisions of this type are often much broader than first realized. Management is directly involved in the decision. The accrual can affect the market value of the company, its relations with lenders and suppliers, its auditors, and many other stakeholders. Further, if recording the accrual is the right accounting decision, failure to do so can foster unethical behavior throughout the company, thus affecting additional company employees.

Superscript [A] denotes assignments based on Appendix 3A.

# DISCUSSION QUESTIONS

**Q3-1.** What does the term *fiscal year* mean?

**Q3-2.** What is the purpose of a general journal?

**Q3-3.** Explain the process of posting.

**Q3-4.** What four different types of adjustments are frequently necessary before financial statements are prepared at the end of an accounting period? Give at least one example of each type.

**Q3-5.** On January 1, Prepaid Insurance was debited for $1,872 related to the cost of a two-year premium, with coverage beginning immediately. How should this account be adjusted on January 31 before financial statements are prepared for the current month?

**Q3-6.** At the beginning of January, the first month of the accounting year, the Supplies account (asset) had a debit balance of $825. During January, purchases of $260 worth of supplies were debited to the account. At the end of January, $630 of supplies were still available. How should this account be adjusted? If no adjustment is made, describe the impact on (a) the income statement for January, and (b) the balance sheet prepared at January 31?

**Q3-7.** The publisher of *Accounting View*, a monthly magazine, received $9,720 cash on January 1 for new subscriptions covering the next 24 months, with service beginning immediately. (a) Use the financial statement effects template to record the receipt of the $9,720. (b) Use the template to show how the accounts should be adjusted at the end of January before financial statements are prepared for the current month.

**Q3-8.** Refer to Question Q3-7. Prepare journal entries for the receipt of cash and the delivery of the magazines.

**Q3-9.** Trombley Travel Agency pays an employee $475 in wages each Friday for the five-day work week ending on Friday. The last Friday of January falls on January 27. How should Trombley Travel Agency adjust wages expense on January 31, its fiscal year-end?

**Q3-10.** The Basu Company earns interest amounting to $360 per month on its investments. The company receives the interest revenue every six months, on December 31 and June 30. Monthly financial statements are prepared. Which accounts should Basu adjust on January 31?

**Q3-11.** [A] What types of accounts are closed at the end of the accounting year? What are the three major steps in the closing process?

# MINI EXERCISES

**M3-12. Assessing Financial Statement Effects of Transactions  (LO1)**

DeFond Services, a firm providing art services for advertisers, began business on June 1, 2007. The following accounts are needed to record the transactions for June: Cash; Accounts Receivable; Supplies; Office Equipment; Accounts Payable; Common Stock; Retained Earnings; Service Fees Earned; Rent Expense; Utilities Expense; and Salaries Expense. Record the following transactions for June using the financial statement effects template.

June  1   M. DeFond invested $12,000 cash to begin the business in exchange for common stock.
  2   Paid $950 cash for June rent.
  3   Purchased $6,400 of office equipment on credit.
  6   Purchased $3,800 of art materials and other supplies; the company paid $1,800 cash with the remainder due within 30 days.
  11   Billed clients $4,700 for services rendered.
  17   Collected $3,250 cash from clients on their accounts billed on June 11.
  19   Paid $3,000 cash toward the account for office equipment (see June 3).
  25   Paid $900 cash for dividends.
  30   Paid $350 cash for June utilities.
  30   Paid $2,500 cash for June salaries.

**M3-13. Preparing Journal Entries and Posting  (LO1)**

Refer to the information in M3-12. Prepare a journal entry for each transaction. Create a T-account for each account, and then post the journal entries to the T-accounts (use dates to reference each entry).

**M3-14. Assessing Financial Statement Effects of Transactions  (LO1)**

Verrecchia Company, a cleaning services firm, began business on April 1, 2007. The company created the following accounts to record the transactions for April: Cash; Accounts Receivable; Supplies; Prepaid Van Lease; Equipment; Notes Payable; Accounts Payable; Common Stock; Retained Earnings; Cleaning Fees Earned; Wages Expense; Advertising Expense; and Van Fuel Expense. Record the following transactions for April using the financial statement effects template.

April  1   R. Verrecchia invested $9,000 cash to begin the business in exchange for common stock.
  2   Paid $2,850 cash for six months' lease on van for the business.
  3   Borrowed $10,000 cash from bank and signed note payable agreeing to repay it in 1 year plus 10% interest.
  4   Purchased $5,500 of cleaning equipment; the company paid $2,500 cash with the remainder due within 30 days.
  5   Paid $4,300 cash for cleaning supplies.
  7   Paid $350 cash for advertisements to run in the area newspaper during April.
  21   Billed customers $3,500 for services performed.
  23   Paid $3,000 cash toward the account for cleaning equipment (see April 4).
  28   Collected $2,300 cash from customers on their accounts billed on April 21.
  29   Paid $1,000 cash for dividends.
  30   Paid $1,750 cash for April wages.
  30   Paid $995 cash for gasoline used during April.

**M3-15. Preparing Journal Entries and Posting  (LO1)**

Refer to the information in M3-14. Prepare a journal entry for each transaction. Create a T-account for each account, and then post the journal entries to the T-accounts (use dates to reference each entry).

**M3-16.** **Assessing Financial Statement Effects of Transactions and Adjustments**  (LO1, 2)

Schrand Services offers janitorial services on both a contract basis and an hourly basis. On January 1, 2006, Schrand collected $20,100 cash in advance on a six-month contract for work to be performed evenly during the next six months.

a.  Prepare the entry on January 1 to reflect the receipt of $20,100 cash for contract work; use the financial statements effect template.

b.  Adjust the appropriate accounts on January 31, 2006, for the contract work done during January; use the financial statements effect template.

c.  At January 31, a total of 30 hours of hourly rate janitor work was unbilled. The billing rate is $19 per hour. Prepare the accounting adjustment needed on January 31, 2006, using the financial statements effect template. (Note: The firm uses the account Fees Receivable to reflect amounts due but not yet billed.)

**M3-17.** **Preparing Accounting Adjustments**  (LO1, 2)

Refer to the information in M3-16. Prepare a journal entry for each of parts a, b, and c.

**M3-18.** **Assessing Financial Statement Effects of Transactions and Adjustments**  (LO2)

Selected accounts of Piotroski Properties, a real estate management firm, are shown below as of January 31, 2008, before any accounts have been adjusted.

|  | Debits | Credits |
|---|---|---|
| Prepaid Insurance . . . . . . . . . . . . . . . . . . | $6,660 | |
| Supplies . . . . . . . . . . . . . . . . . . . . . . . . | 1,930 | |
| Office Equipment . . . . . . . . . . . . . . . . . . | 5,952 | |
| Unearned Rent Revenue . . . . . . . . . . . . . | | $ 5,250 |
| Salaries Expense . . . . . . . . . . . . . . . . . . | 3,100 | |
| Rent Revenue. . . . . . . . . . . . . . . . . . . . . | | 15,000 |

Piotroski Properties prepares monthly financial statements. Using the following information, adjust the accounts as necessary on January 31 using the financial statements effect template.

a.  Prepaid Insurance represents a three-year premium paid on January 1, 2008.

b.  Supplies of $850 were still available on January 31.

c.  Office equipment is expected to last eight years (or 96 months).

d.  On January 1, 2006, Piotroski collected $5,250 for six months' rent in advance from a tenant renting space for $875 per month.

e.  Salaries of $490 have been earned by employees but yet not recorded as of January 31.

**M3-19.** **Preparing Accounting Adjustments**  (LO2)

Refer to the information in M3-18. Prepare journal entries for each of parts a through e.

**M3-20.** **Inferring Transactions from Financial Statements**  (LO1, 2)

Foot Locker, Inc. (FL)

Foot Locker, Inc., a retailer of athletic footwear and apparel, operates 3,921 stores in the United States, Canada, Europe and Asia Pacific. During its fiscal year ended in 2006, Foot Locker purchased merchandise inventory costing $4,047 ($ millions). Assume that Foot Locker makes all purchases on credit, and that its accounts payable is only used for inventory purchases. The following T-accounts reflect information contained in the company's fiscal 2005 and 2006 balance sheets ($ millions).

| Inventories | | | Accounts Payable | | |
|---|---|---|---|---|---|
| 2005 Bal. | 1,151 | | | 381 | 2005 Bal. |
| 2006 Bal. | 1,254 | | | 361 | 2006 Bal. |

a.  Use the financial statement effects template to record Foot Locker's 2006 purchases.

b.  What amount did Foot Locker pay in cash to its suppliers during fiscal year 2006? Explain.

c.  Use the financial statement effects template to record cost of goods sold for its fiscal years 2006.

**M3-21.** **Preparing Journal Entries and Posting**  (LO1, 2)

Foot Locker, Inc. (FL)

Refer to the information in M3-20. Prepare journal entries for each of parts a, b and c.

**M3-22. Preparing a Statement of Stockholders' Equity  (LO4)**

On December 31, 2005, the accounts of Leuz Architect Services showed credit balances in its Common Stock and Retained Earnings accounts of $30,000 and $18,000, respectively. The company's stock issuances for 2006 totaled $6,000, and it paid $9,700 cash dividends in 2006. During 2006, the company had net income of $29,900. Prepare a 2006 statement of stockholders' equity for Leuz Architect Services.

**M3-23.ᴬ Preparing Closing Journal Entries  (LO5)**

The adjusted trial balance at December 31, 2007, for Francis Real Estate Company includes the following selected accounts.

|  | Debits | Credits |
|---|---|---|
| Commissions Earned. . . . . . . . . . . . . . . |  | $84,900 |
| Wages Expense . . . . . . . . . . . . . . . . . . | $36,000 |  |
| Insurance Expense. . . . . . . . . . . . . . . . | 1,900 |  |
| Utilities Expense. . . . . . . . . . . . . . . . . . | 8,200 |  |
| Depreciation Expense . . . . . . . . . . . . . . | 9,800 |  |
| Retained Earnings . . . . . . . . . . . . . . . . . |  | 72,100 |

Assume that the company has not yet closed any accounts to retained earnings. Prepare journal entries to close the temporary accounts above. Set up the needed T-accounts and post the closing entries. After these entries are posted, what is the balance of the Retained Earnings account?

**M3-24. Inferring Transactions from Financial Statements  (LO1, 2)**

Lowe's is the second-largest home improvement retailer in the world with 1,234 stores in 49 states. During its fiscal year ended in 2006, Lowe's purchased merchandise inventory at a cost of $29,238 ($ millions). Assume that all purchases were made on account and that accounts payable is only used for inventory purchases. The following T-accounts reflect information contained in the company's 2006 and 2005 balance sheets.

Lowe's Companies (LOW)

| Merchandise Inventories | | | Accounts Payable | | |
|---|---|---|---|---|---|
| 2005 Bal. | 5,911 | | | 2,695 | 2005 Bal. |
| 2006 Bal. | 6,706 | | | 2,832 | 2006 Bal. |

*a.* Use the financial statement effects template to record Lowe's purchases during fiscal 2006.
*b.* What amount did Lowe's pay in cash to its suppliers during fiscal-year 2006? Explain.
*c.* Use the financial statement effects template to record cost of goods sold for its fiscal year ended in 2006.

**M3-25.ᴬ Closing Journal Entries  (LO5)**

The adjusted trial balance as of December 31, 2007, for Hanlon Consulting contains the following selected accounts.

|  | Debits | Credits |
|---|---|---|
| Service Fees Earned . . . . . . . . . . . . . . . |  | $80,300 |
| Rent Expense. . . . . . . . . . . . . . . . . . . . . | $20,800 |  |
| Salaries Expense . . . . . . . . . . . . . . . . . . | 45,700 |  |
| Supplies Expense. . . . . . . . . . . . . . . . . . | 5,600 |  |
| Depreciation Expense . . . . . . . . . . . . . . | 10,200 |  |
| Retained Earnings . . . . . . . . . . . . . . . . . |  | 67,000 |

Prepare entries to close these accounts in journal entry form. Set up T-accounts for each account and record the adjusted trial balance amount in each account. Then, post the closing entries to the T-accounts. After these entries are posted, what is the balance of the Retained Earnings account?

# EXERCISES

**E3-26.**    **Assessing Financial Statement Effects of Adjustments**    (LO2)

For each of the following separate situations, prepare the necessary accounting adjustments using the financial statement effects template.

*a.*    Unrecorded depreciation on equipment is $610.

*b.*    The Supplies account has an unadjusted balance of $2,990. Supplies still available at the end of the period total $1,100.

*c.*    On the date for preparing financial statements, an estimated utilities expense of $390 has been incurred, but no utility bill has yet been received or paid.

*d.*    On the first day of the current period, rent for four periods was paid and recorded as a $2,800 debit to Prepaid Rent and a $2,800 credit to Cash.

*Allstate Insurance Company (ALL)*

*e.*    Nine months ago, Allstate Insurance Company sold a one-year policy to a customer and recorded the receipt of the premium by debiting Cash for $624. No adjusting entries have been prepared during the nine-month period. Allstate's annual financial statements are now being prepared.

*f.*    At the end of the period, employee wages of $965 have been incurred but not paid or recorded.

*g.*    At the end of the period, $300 of interest has been earned but not yet received or recorded.

**E3-27.**    **Preparing Accounting Adjustments**    (LO2)

Refer to the information in E3-26. Prepare journal entries for each accounting adjustment.

**E3-28.**    **Assessing Financial Statement Effects of Adjustments Across Two Periods**    (LO1, 2)

Engel Company closes its accounts on December 31 each year. The company works a five-day work week and pays its employees every two weeks. On December 31, 2006, Engel accrued $4,700 of salaries payable. On January 9, 2007, the company paid salaries of $12,000 cash to employees. Prepare entries using the financial statement effects template to (a) accrue the salaries payable on December 31; and (b) record the salary payment on January 9.

**E3-29.**[A]    **Preparing Accounting Adjustments**    (LO1, 2)

Refer to the information in E3-28. Prepare journal entries to accrue the salaries in December; close salaries expense for the year; and pay the salaries in January. Assume that there is no change in the pay rate during the year, and no change in the company's work force.

**E3-30.**    **Financial Analysis using Adjusted Account Data**    (LO2)

Selected T-account balances for Bloomfield Company are shown below as of January 31, 2008; accounting adjustments have already been posted. The firm uses a calendar-year accounting period but prepares *monthly* adjustments.

| Supplies | Supplies Expense |
|---|---|
| Jan. 31 Bal.   800 | Jan. 31 Bal.   960 |

| Prepaid Insurance | Insurance Expense |
|---|---|
| Jan. 31 Bal.   574 | Jan. 31 Bal.    82 |

| Wages Payable | Wages Expense |
|---|---|
| Jan. 31 Bal.   500 | Jan. 31 Bal. 3,200 |

| Truck | Accumulated Depreciation-Truck |
|---|---|
| Jan. 31 Bal. 8,700 | Jan. 31 Bal. 2,610 |

*a.*    If the amount in Supplies Expense represents the January 31 adjustment for the supplies used in January, and $620 worth of supplies were purchased during January, what was the January 1 beginning balance of Supplies?

*b.*    The amount in the Insurance Expense account represents the adjustment made at January 31 for January insurance expense. If the original insurance premium was for one year, what was the amount of the premium and on what date did the insurance policy start?

*c.*    If we assume that no beginning balance existed in either Wages Payable or Wages Expense on January 1, how much cash was paid as wages during January?

*d.*    If the truck has a useful life of five years (or 60 months), what is the monthly amount of depreciation expense and how many months has Bloomfield owned the truck?

**E3-31.**   **Assessing Financial Statement Effects of Adjustments**   (LO2)

T. Lys began Thomas Refinishing Service on July 1, 2007. Selected accounts are shown below as of July 31, before any adjusting entries have been made.

|  | Debits | Credits |
|---|---|---|
| Prepaid Rent .................... | $5,700 | |
| Prepaid Advertising ............. | 630 | |
| Supplies ....................... | 3,000 | |
| Unearned Refinishing Fees ........ | | $ 600 |
| Refinishing Fees Revenue .......... | | 2,500 |

Using the following information, prepare the accounting adjustments necessary on July 31 using the financial statement effects template.

*a.*   On July 1, the firm paid one year's rent of $5,700 in cash.

*b.*   On July 1, $630 cash was paid to the local newspaper for an advertisement to run daily for the months of July, August, and September.

*c.*   Supplies still available at July 31 total $1,100.

*d.*   At July 31, refinishing services of $800 have been performed but not yet recorded or billed to customers. The firm uses the account Fees Receivable to reflect amounts due but not yet billed.

*e.*   In early July, a customer paid $600 in advance for a refinishing project. At July 31, the project is one-half complete.

**E3-32.**   **Preparing Accounting Adjustments and Posting**   (LO2)

Refer to the information in E3-31. Prepare adjusting journal entries for each transaction. Set up T-accounts for each of the ledger accounts and post the journal entries to them.

**E3-33.**   **Inferring Transactions from Financial Statements**   (LO1)

Harley-Davidson manufactures and sells motorcycles as well as retail parts and accessories throughout the world. The following information is taken from Harley-Davidson's fiscal 2005 annual report.

Harley-Davidson, Inc. (HOG)

| Selected Balance Sheet Data | 2005 | 2004 |
|---|---|---|
| Inventories ...................... | $221,418 | $226,893 |
| Accounts receivable................ | $121,333 | $122,087 |

*a.*   Harley-Davidson spent $3,296,240 to purchase and manufacture inventories during its 2005 fiscal year. Use the financial statement effects template to record cost of goods sold for Harley-Davidson's fiscal year ended 2005.

*b.*   Assume that Harley-Davidson had $1,003,881 sales on credit during fiscal year 2005. What amount did the company collect from credit customers during the year? Record this with the financial statement effects template.

**E3-34.**   **Inferring Transactions and Preparing Journal Entries**   (LO1)

Refer to the information in E3-33. Prepare journal entries for each transaction.

Harley-Davidson, Inc. (HOG)

**E3-35.**[A]   **Preparing Closing Journal Entries**   (LO5)

The adjusted trial balance of Plumlee Corporation, dated December 31, 2007, contains the following selected accounts.

|  | Debit | Credit |
|---|---|---|
| Service Fees Earned ............... | | $92,500 |
| Interest Income................... | | 2,200 |
| Salaries Expense ................. | $41,800 | |
| Advertising Expense............... | 4,300 | |
| Depreciation Expense ............. | 8,700 | |
| Income Tax Expense .............. | 9,900 | |
| Retained Earnings ................ | | 42,700 |

Prepare entries to close these accounts in journal entry form. Set up T-accounts for each of the ledger accounts and post the entries to them. After these entries are posted, what is the balance of the Retained Earnings account?

**E3-36.**   **Inferring Transactions from Financial Statements   (LO1, 2)**

Costco Wholesale
Corporation (COST)

Costco Wholesale Corporation operates membership warehouses selling food, appliances, consumer electronics, apparel and other household goods at 471 locations across the U.S. as well as in Canada, Mexico and Puerto Rico. As of its fiscal year-end 2005, Costco had approximately 21.2 million members. Selected fiscal-year information from the company's balance sheets follow ($ thousands).

| Selected Balance Sheet Data | 2005 | 2004 |
|---|---|---|
| Merchandise Inventories ........................ | $4,014,699 | $3,643,585 |
| Deferred membership income (liability) ........... | 500,558 | 453,881 |

*a.*   During fiscal 2005, Costco collected $1,119,833 cash for membership fees. Use the financial statement effects template to record the cash collected for membership fees.

*b.*   Calculate the membership fee revenue that Costco recognized during the year. Use the financial statement effects template to record this revenue.

*c.*   Costco recorded merchandise costs (that is, cost of goods sold) of $46,346,961 in 2005. Record this transaction in the financial statements effects template.

*d.*   Determine the value of merchandise that Costco purchased during fiscal-year 2005. Use the financial statement effects template to record these merchandise purchases. Assume all of Costco's purchases are on credit.

**E3-37.**   **Inferring Transactions and Preparing Journal Entries   (LO1, 2)**

Costco Wholesale
Corporation (COST)

Refer to the information in E3-36. Prepare journal entries for transactions in parts *a* through *d*.

**E3-38.**[A]   **Preparing Financial Statements and Closing Entries   (LO4, 5)**

The adjusted trial balance for Beneish Corporation is as follows.

| BENEISH CORPORATION Adjusted Trial Balance December 31, 2008 | | |
|---|---|---|
| | **Debit** | **Credit** |
| Cash............................ | $   4,000 | |
| Accounts Receivable ................ | 6,500 | |
| Equipment ........................ | 78,000 | |
| Accumulated Depreciation............ | | $ 14,000 |
| Notes Payable ..................... | | 10,000 |
| Common Stock ..................... | | 43,000 |
| Retained Earnings .................. | | 20,600 |
| Dividends......................... | 8,000 | |
| Service Fees Earned ................ | | 71,000 |
| Rent Expense...................... | 18,000 | |
| Salaries Expense ................... | 37,100 | |
| Depreciation Expense .............. | 7,000 | |
| Totals .......................... | $158,600 | $158,600 |

*a.*   Prepare Beneish Corporation's income statement and statement of stockholders' equity for year-end December 31, 2008, and its balance sheet as of December 31, 2008. The company paid cash dividends of $8,000 and there were no stock issuances or repurchases during 2008.

*b.*   Prepare journal entries to close Beneish's temporary accounts.

*c.*   Set up T-accounts for each of its accounts and post the closing entries.

# PROBLEMS

**P3-39.** **Assessing Financial Statement Effects of Transactions and Adjustments** (LO2)

The following information relates to December 31 adjustments for Koonce Kwik Print Company. The firm's fiscal year ends on December 31.

1. Weekly salaries for a five-day week total $1,800, payable on Fridays. December 31 of the current year is a Tuesday.
2. Koonce Kwik Print has $20,000 of notes payable outstanding at December 31. Interest of $200 has accrued on these notes by December 31, but will not be paid until the notes mature next year.
3. During December, Koonce Kwik Print provided $900 of printing services to clients who will be billed on January 2. The firm uses the account Fees Receivable to reflect amounts due but not yet billed.
4. Starting December 1, all maintenance work on Koonce Kwik Print's equipment is handled by Richardson Repair Company under an agreement whereby Koonce Kwik Print pays a fixed monthly charge of $400. Koonce Kwik Print paid six months' service charge of $2,400 cash in advance on December 1, and increased its Prepaid Maintenance account by $2,400.
5. The firm paid $900 cash on December 15 for a series of radio commercials to run during December and January. One-third of the commercials have aired by December 31. The $900 payment was recorded in its Prepaid Advertising account.
6. Starting December 16, Koonce Kwik Print rented 400 square feet of storage space from a neighboring business. The monthly rent of $0.80 per square foot is due in advance on the first of each month. Nothing was paid in December, however, because the neighbor agreed to add the rent for one-half of December to the January 1 payment.
7. Koonce Kwik Print invested $5,000 cash in securities on December 1 and earned interest of $38 on these securities by December 31. No interest will be received until January.
8. Annual depreciation on the firm's equipment is $2,175. No depreciation has been recorded during the year.

**Required**

Prepare its accounting adjustments required at December 31 using the financial statement effects template.

**P3-40.** **Preparing Accounting Adjustments** (LO2)

Refer to the information in P3-39. Prepare adjustments required at December 31 using journal entries.

**P3-41.** **Assessing Financial Statement Effects of Adjustments Across Two Periods** (LO1, 2)

The following selected accounts appear in Sloan Company's unadjusted trial balance at December 31, 2008, the end of its fiscal year (all accounts have normal balances).

| | | | |
|---|---|---|---|
| Prepaid Advertising | $ 1,200 | Unearned Service Fees | $ 5,400 |
| Wages Expense | 43,800 | Service Fees Earned | 87,000 |
| Prepaid Insurance | 3,420 | Rental Income | 4,900 |

**Required**

a. Prepare its accounting adjustments at December 31, 2008, using the financial statement effects template and the following additional information.
   1. Prepaid advertising at December 31 is $800.
   2. Unpaid wages earned by employees in December are $1,300.
   3. Prepaid insurance at December 31 is $2,280.
   4. Unearned service fees at December 31 are $3,000.
   5. Rent revenue of $1,000 owed by a tenant is not recorded at December 31.

b. Prepare entries on January 4, 2009, using the financial statement effects template to record (1) payment of $2,400 cash in wages and (2) cash receipt from the tenant of the $1,000 rent revenue.

**P3-42.** **Preparing Accounting Adjustments** (LO1, 2)

Refer to the information in P3-41. Prepare journal entries for parts a and b.

**P3-43.** **Journalizing and Posting Transactions, and Preparing a Trial Balance and Adjustments** (LO1, 2, 3)

D. Roulstone opened Roulstone Roofing Service on April 1, 2008. Transactions for April follow.

Apr. 1 Roulstone contributed $11,500 cash to the business in exchange for common stock.
2 Paid $6,100 cash for the purchase of a used truck.
2 Purchased $3,100 of ladders and other equipment; the company paid $1,000 cash, with the balance due in 30 days.
3 Paid $2,880 cash for two-year (or 24-month) premium toward liability insurance.
5 Purchased $1,200 of supplies on credit.
5 Received an advance of $1,800 cash from a customer for roof repairs to be done during April and May.
12 Billed customers $5,500 for roofing services performed.
18 Collected $4,900 cash from customers toward their accounts billed on April 12.
29 Paid $675 cash for truck fuel used in April.
30 Paid $100 cash for April newspaper advertising.
30 Paid $2,500 cash for assistants' wages earned.
30 Billed customers $4,000 for roofing services performed.

**Required**

a. Set up T-accounts for the following accounts: Cash; Accounts Receivable; Supplies; Prepaid Insurance; Trucks; Accumulated Depreciation–Trucks; Equipment; Accumulated Depreciation–Equipment; Accounts Payable; Unearned Roofing Fees; Common Stock; Roofing Fees Earned; Fuel Expense; Advertising Expense; Wages Expense; Insurance Expense; Supplies Expense; Depreciation Expense–Trucks; and Depreciation Expense–Equipment.
b. Record these transactions for April using journal entries.
c. Post these entries to their T-accounts (key numbers in T-accounts by date).
d. Prepare an unadjusted trial balance at April 30, 2008.
e. Prepare entries to adjust the following accounts: Insurance Expense, Supplies Expense, Depreciation Expense—Trucks, Depreciation Expense—Equipment, and Roofing Fees Earned in journal entry form. Supplies still available on April 30 amount to $400. Depreciation for April was $125 on the truck and $35 on equipment. One-fourth of the roofing fee received in advance was earned by April 30.
f. Post adjusting entries to their T-accounts.

**P3-44.** **Assessing Financial Statement Effects of Transactions and Adjustments** (LO1, 2)

Refer to the information in P3-43.
a. Use the financial statement effects template to record the transactions for April.
b. Use the financial statement effects template to record the adjustments at the end of April (described in part e of P3-43).

**P3-45.** **Preparing an Unadjusted Trial Balance and Accounting Adjustments** (LO2, 3)

Pownall Photomake Company, a commercial photography studio, completed its first year of operations on December 31, 2008. General ledger account balances before year-end adjustments follow; no adjustments have been made to the accounts at any time during the year. Assume that all balances are normal.

| | | | | |
|---|---|---|---|---|
| Cash | $ 2,150 | | Accounts Payable | $ 1,910 |
| Accounts Receivable | 3,800 | | Unearned Photography Fees | 2,600 |
| Prepaid Rent | 12,600 | | Common Stock | 24,000 |
| Prepaid Insurance | 2,970 | | Photography Fees Earned | 34,480 |
| Supplies | 4,250 | | Wages Expense | 11,000 |
| Equipment | 22,800 | | Utilities Expense | 3,420 |

An analysis of the firm's records discloses the following (business began on January 1, 2008).

1. Photography services of $925 have been rendered, but customers have not yet paid or been billed. The company uses the account Fees Receivable to reflect amounts due but not yet billed.
2. Equipment, purchased January 1, 2006, has an estimated life of 10 years.

3. Utilities expense for December is estimated to be $400, but the bill will not arrive or be paid until January of next year. (All prior months' utilities bills have been received and paid.)
4. The balance in Prepaid Rent represents the amount paid on January 1, 2008, for a 2-year lease on the studio it operates from.
5. In November, customers paid $2,600 cash in advance for photos to be taken for the holiday season. When received, these fees were credited to Unearned Photography Fees. By December 31, all of these fees are earned.
6. A 3-year insurance premium paid on January 1, 2008, was debited to Prepaid Insurance.
7. Supplies still available at December 31 are $1,520.
8. At December 31, wages expense of $375 has been incurred but not yet paid or recorded.

**Required**

*a.* Prepare Pownall Photomake's unadjusted trial balance at December 31, 2008.
*b.* Prepare its adjusting entries using the financial statement effects template.

**P3-46.** **Recording Adjustments with Journal Entries and T-Accounts**   **(LO2, 3)**
Refer to the information in P3-45.
*a.* Prepare journal entries to record the accounting adjustments.
*b.* Set up T-accounts for each account and post the journal entries to them.

**P3-47.** **Preparing an Unadjusted Trial Balance and Accounting Adjustments**   **(LO2, 3)**
BensEx, a mailing service, has just completed its first year of operations on December 31, 2008. Its general ledger account balances before year-end adjustments follow; no adjusting entries have been made to the accounts at any time during the year. Assume that all balances are normal.

| | | | |
|---|---|---|---|
| Cash. . . . . . . . . . . . . . . . . . . . . . . . . . . | $ 2,300 | Accounts Payable. . . . . . . . . . . . . . . . | $ 2,700 |
| Accounts Receivable . . . . . . . . . . . . . . | 5,120 | Common Stock. . . . . . . . . . . . . . . . . | 9,530 |
| Prepaid Advertising . . . . . . . . . . . . . . | 1,680 | Mailing Fees Earned . . . . . . . . . . . . . | 86,000 |
| Supplies . . . . . . . . . . . . . . . . . . . . . | 6,270 | Wages Expense . . . . . . . . . . . . . . . . | 38,800 |
| Equipment . . . . . . . . . . . . . . . . . . . . | 42,240 | Rent Expense . . . . . . . . . . . . . . . . . | 6,300 |
| Notes Payable . . . . . . . . . . . . . . . . . | 7,500 | Utilities Expense. . . . . . . . . . . . . . . | 3,020 |

An analysis of the firm's records reveals the following (business began on January 1, 2008).

1. The balance in Prepaid Advertising represents the amount paid for newspaper advertising for one year. The agreement, which calls for the same amount of space each month, covers the period from February 1, 2008, to January 31, 2009. BensEx did not advertise during its first month of operations.
2. Equipment, purchased January 1, has an estimated life of eight years.
3. Utilities expense does not include expense for December, estimated at $325. The bill will not arrive until January 2009.
4. At year-end, employees have earned $1,200 in wages that will not be paid or recorded until January.
5. Supplies available at year-end amount to $1,520.
6. At year-end, unpaid interest of $450 has accrued on the notes payable.
7. The firm's lease calls for rent of $525 per month payable on the first of each month, plus an amount equal to 0.5% of annual mailing fees earned. The rental percentage is payable within 15 days after the end of the year.

**Required**

*a.* Prepare its unadjusted trial balance at December 31, 2008.
*b.* Prepare its adjusting entries using the financial statement effects template.

**P3-48.** **Recording Accounting Adjustments with Journal Entries and T-Accounts**   **(LO2, 3)**
Refer to information in P3-47.
*a.* Prepare journal entries to record the accounting adjustments.
*b.* Set up T-accounts for each account and post the journal entries to them.

**P3-49.**[A]    **Preparing Accounting Adjustments**   **(LO2, 4, 5)**

Wysocki Wheels began operations on March 1, 2008, to provide automotive wheel alignment and balancing services. On March 31, 2008, the unadjusted balances of the firm's accounts follow.

| WYSOCKI WHEELS<br>Unadjusted Trial Balance<br>March 31, 2008 | | |
| --- | --- | --- |
| | **Debit** | **Credit** |
| Cash . . . . . . . . . . . . . . . . . . . . . . . . . . . . | $ 1,900 | |
| Accounts Receivable . . . . . . . . . . . . . . . | 3,820 | |
| Prepaid Rent. . . . . . . . . . . . . . . . . . . . . . | 4,770 | |
| Supplies . . . . . . . . . . . . . . . . . . . . . . . . | 3,700 | |
| Equipment . . . . . . . . . . . . . . . . . . . . . . | 36,180 | |
| Accounts Payable . . . . . . . . . . . . . . . . . . | | $ 2,510 |
| Unearned Service Revenue . . . . . . . . . . . | | 1,000 |
| Common Stock . . . . . . . . . . . . . . . . . . . . | | 38,400 |
| Service Revenue. . . . . . . . . . . . . . . . . . . | | 12,360 |
| Wages Expense . . . . . . . . . . . . . . . . . . . | 3,900 | |
| | $54,270 | $54,270 |

The following information is also available.
1.   The balance in Prepaid Rent was the amount paid on March 1 to cover the first 6 months' rent.
2.   Supplies available on March 31 amounted to $1,720.
3.   Equipment has an estimated life of nine years (or 108 months).
4.   Unpaid and unrecorded wages at March 31 were $560.
5.   Utility services used during March were estimated at $390; a bill is expected early in April.
6.   The balance in Unearned Service Revenue was the amount received on March 1 from a car dealer to cover alignment and balancing services on cars sold by the dealer in March and April. Wysocki Wheels agreed to provide the services at a fixed fee of $500 each month.

**Required**
*a.*   Prepare its accounting adjustments at March 31, 2008 in journal entry form.
*b.*   Set up T-accounts and post the accounting adjustments to them.
*c.*   Prepare its income statement for March and its balance sheet at March 31, 2008.
*d.*   Prepare entries to close its temporary accounts in journal entry form. Post the closing entries to the T-accounts.

# CASES

**C3-50.**   **Preparing Accounting Adjustments and Financial Statements**   **(LO1, 2, 4)**

Stocken Surf Shop began operations on July 1, 2008, with an initial investment of $50,000. During the initial three months of operations, the following cash transactions were recorded in the firm's checking account.

| **Deposits** | |
| --- | --- |
| Initial investment by owner . . . . | $ 50,000 |
| Collected from customers . . . . | 81,000 |
| Borrowings from bank . . . . . . . | 10,000 |
| | $141,000 |

| **Checks drawn** | |
| --- | --- |
| Rent . . . . . . . . . . . . . . . . . . . . . | $ 24,000 |
| Fixtures and equipment . . . . . . . | 25,000 |
| Merchandise inventory. . . . . . . . | 62,000 |
| Salaries . . . . . . . . . . . . . . . . . . | 6,000 |
| Other expenses . . . . . . . . . . . . | 13,000 |
| | $130,000 |

Additional information:

a.  Most sales were for cash, however, the store accepted a limited amount of credit sales; at September 30, 2008, customers owed the store $9,000.

b.  Rent was paid on July 1 for six months.

c.  Salaries of $3,000 per month are paid on the 1st of each month for salaries earned in the month prior.

d.  Inventories are purchased for cash; at September 30, 2008, inventory of $21,000 was still available.

e.  Fixtures and equipment were expected to last five years (or 60 months) with zero salvage value.

f.  The bank charges 12% annual interest (1% per month) on its $10,000 bank loan. Stocken took the loan out July 1.

**Required**

a.  Record all of Stocken's cash transactions and prepare any necessary adjusting entries at September 30, 2008. You may either use the financial statement effects template or journal entries combined with T-accounts.

b.  Prepare the income statement for the three months ended September 30, 2008, and its balance sheet at September 30, 2008.

c.  Analyze the statements from part b and assess the company's performance over its initial three months.

**C3-51.   Analyzing Transactions, Impacts on Financial Ratios, and Loan Covenants (LO2)**

Kadous Consulting, a firm started three years ago by K. Kadous, offers consulting services for material handling and plant layout. Its balance sheet at the close of 2008 follows.

| KADOUS CONSULTING Balance Sheet December 31, 2008 | | | | | |
|---|---|---|---|---|---|
| **Assets** | | | **Liabilities** | | |
| Cash.................. | | $ 3,400 | Notes Payable ................. | | $30,000 |
| Accounts Receivable ..... | | 22,875 | Accounts Payable .............. | | 4,200 |
| Supplies .............. | | 13,200 | Unearned Consulting Fees......... | | 11,300 |
| Prepaid Insurance ....... | | 4,500 | Wages Payable.................. | | 400 |
| Equipment ............ | $68,500 | | Total Liabilities ................. | | 45,900 |
| Less: Accumulated | | | **Equity** | | |
| Depreciation........... | 23,975 | 44,525 | Common Stock ................. | | 8,000 |
| Total Assets ............ | | $88,500 | Retained Earnings .............. | | 34,600 |
| | | | Total liabilities and Equity......... | | $88,500 |

Earlier in the year Kadous obtained a bank loan of $30,000 cash for the firm. One of the provisions of the loan is that the year-end debt-to-equity ratio (ratio of total liabilities to total equity) cannot exceed 1.0. Based on the above balance sheet, the ratio at the end of 2008 is 1.08. Kadous is concerned about being in violation of the loan agreement and requests assistance in reviewing the situation. Kadous believes that she might have overlooked some items at year-end. Discussions with Kadous reveal the following.

1.  On January 1, 2008, the firm paid a $4,500 insurance premium for 2 years of coverage; the amount in Prepaid Insurance has not yet been adjusted.

2.  Depreciation on the equipment should be 10% of cost per year; the company inadvertently recorded 15% for 2008.

3.  Interest on the bank loan has been paid through the end of 2008.

4.  The firm concluded a major consulting engagement in December, doing a plant layout analysis for a new factory. The $6,000 fee has not been billed or recorded in the accounts.

5.  On December 1, 2008, the firm received an $11,300 cash advance payment from Dichev Corporation for consulting services to be rendered over a 2-month period. This payment was credited to the Unearned Consulting Fees account. One-half of this fee was earned but unrecorded by December 31, 2008.

6.  Supplies costing $4,800 were available on December 31; the company has made no adjustment of its Supplies account.

**Required**

a.  What is the correct debt-to-equity ratio at December 31, 2008?

b.  Is the firm in violation of its loan agreement? Prepare computations to support the correct total liabilities and total equity figures at December 31, 2008.

**C3-52.** **Ethics, Accounting Adjustments, and Auditors** (LO1, 2)

It is the end of the accounting year for Anne Beatty, controller of a medium-sized, publicly held corporation specializing in toxic waste cleanup. Within the corporation, only Beatty and the president know that the firm has been negotiating for several months to land a large contract for waste cleanup in Western Europe. The president has hired another firm with excellent contacts in Western Europe to help with negotiations. The outside firm will charge an hourly fee plus expenses, but has agreed not to submit a bill until the negotiations are in their final stages (expected to occur in another 3 to 4 months). Even if the contract falls through, the outside firm is entitled to receive payment for its services. Based upon her discussion with a member of the outside firm, Beatty knows that its charge for services provided to date will be $150,000. This is a material amount for the company.

Beatty knows that the president wants negotiations to remain as secret as possible so that competitors will not learn of the contract the company is pursuing in Europe. In fact, the president recently stated to her, "This is not the time to reveal our actions in Western Europe to other staff members, our auditors, or the readers of our financial statements; securing this contract is crucial to our future growth." No entry has been made in the accounting records for the cost of contract negotiations. Beatty now faces an uncomfortable situation. The company's outside auditor has just asked her if she knows of any year-end adjustments that have not yet been recorded.

**Required**

*a.* What are the ethical considerations that Beatty faces in answering the auditor's question?

*b.* How should Beatty respond to the auditor's question?

**C3-53.** **Inferring Accounting Adjustments from Financial Statements** (LO1, 2)

Coldwater Creek
(CWTR)

Coldwater Creek, Inc., a specialty retailer of women's apparel, markets its products through retail stores and catalogs. Selected information from its 2006 and 2005 balance sheets follows ($ thousands).

| Selected Balance Sheet Data | 2006 | 2005 |
| --- | --- | --- |
| Prepaid and deferred marketing costs asset . . . . . . . . | $10,438 | $6,905 |
| Unearned gift certificate revenue liability . . . . . . . . . . . | 13,719 | 9,329 |

The following excerpt is from Coldwater Creek's fiscal 2006 10-K report.

All direct costs associated with the development, production and circulation of catalogs are accumulated as prepaid marketing costs until such time as the related catalog is mailed. After that, these costs are reclassified as deferred marketing costs and are amortized into selling, general and administrative expenses over the expected sales realization cycle, typically several weeks. The Company's policy regarding gift certificates and gift cards is to record revenue as the gift certificates and gift cards are redeemed for merchandise. Prior to their redemption, amounts under the gift certificates and gift cards are recorded as a liability.

**Required**

*a.* Assume that Coldwater Creek spent $84,933 cash for direct costs associated with catalogs in 2006. Prepare the entry, using the financial statement effects template, to reflect these direct costs.

*81400*

*b.* Use the financial statement effects template to adjust the balance in the prepaid and deferred marketing costs account as of its 2006 year-end.

*c.* Assume that Coldwater Creek sold gift certificates valued at $31,470 in 2006. Use the financial statement effects template to reflect the cash received when customers purchased gift cards.

*27080*

*d.* Use the financial statement effects template to record the 2006 merchandise sales to customers who paid with gift certificates.

**C3-54.** **Preparing Journal Entries and Posting** (LO1, 2)

Refer to the information in C3-53. Prepare journal entries for parts *a* through *d*. Create T-accounts for the Prepaid and Deferred Marketing Costs account and for the Unearned Gift Certificate Revenue account; then post your journal entries to the relevant T-accounts.

Coldwater Creek (CWTR)

# Analyzing and Interpreting Financial Statements

## LEARNING OBJECTIVES

**LO1** Compute return on equity (ROE) and disaggregate it into components of operating and nonoperating returns. (p. 4-4)

**LO2** Disaggregate operating return (RNOA) into its components of profitability and asset turnover. (p. 4-12)

**LO3** Compute and interpret measures of liquidity and solvency. (p. 4-18)

## HOME DEPOT

Home Depot measures its employee activities, everything from gross margin per labor-hour to the number of "greets" at its entry doors. It also applies several measures to assess its overall performance and financial condition. These measures include the debt-to-equity ratio, current ratio, inventory turnover, and return on invested capital. Analysts, too, use a variety of measures to capture different aspects of company performance to answer questions such as: Is it managed efficiently and profitably? Does it use assets effectively? Is performance achieved with a minimum of debt?

One fundamental measure is that which Warren Buffett, CEO of the investment firm Berkshire Hathaway, lists in his acquisition criteria cited in Module 1: "Our preference would be to reach our goal by directly owning a diversified group of businesses that generate cash and consistently earn above-average returns on capital." Buffett is referring to return on invested capital, one of the most powerful metrics in the analyst's toolkit.

All return metrics follow the same basic formula—they divide some measure of profit by some measure of investment. A company's performance is commonly judged by its profitability. Although analysis of profit is important, it is only part of the story. A more meaningful analysis is to compare level of profitability with the amount of investment in operating assets. Home Depot's return on invested capital in the past few years has gone from 18% to over 21%. Is that a good return? Well, the median return on invested capital for the S&P 500 for this past year was 10%. By that token, Home Depot is doing very well.

A variation of the return on invested capital metric is the return on equity (ROE), which focuses on shareholder investment. By focusing on the *equity* investment, ROE measures return from the perspective of the common shareholder rather than the company overall. Home Depot's ROE for 2006 was 22.9%, up from 18.4% four years ago. The 2006 median

ROE for the S&P 500 was 15.9%. Home Depot has consistently out-performed this benchmark as the graph to the side illustrates.

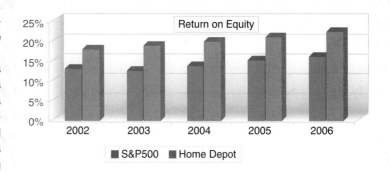

This module focuses on analysis of returns. We put special emphasis on the return on net operating assets (RNOA), computed as net operating profit after tax (NOPAT) divided by average net operating assets (NOA). RNOA focuses on operating activities—operating profit relative to investment in net operating assets. It is important to distinguish operating activities from nonoperating activities because the capital markets value each component differently, placing much greater emphasis on operations. Home Depot's RNOA rose from 16% in 2002 to over 21% in 2006.

RNOA consists of two components: profitability and asset productivity. Increasing either component increases RNOA. These components reflect on the first two questions we posed above. The profitability component of RNOA measures net operating profit after tax for each sales dollar (NOPAT/Sales), and is called the net operating profit margin (NOPM). Over the past five years, Home Depot has increased NOPM from 6% to over 7.2%. As *BusinessWeek* reports "by squeezing more out of each orange box through centralized purchasing and a $1.1 billion investment in technology, such as self-checkout aisles and in-store Web kiosks, profits have more than doubled." Home Depot cannot achieve greater profit margin by simply raising prices because the market is too competitive and there are many substitutes for its products. Instead, it must manage product costs and control overhead costs.

Asset productivity, the second component of RNOA, is reflected in net operating asset turnover (NOAT). NOAT is measured as sales divided by average net operating assets—it captures the notion of how many sales dollars are generated by each dollar of invested assets. Home Depot has increased its NOAT only slightly from 2.8 to 2.9 in the past five years. Increasing the turnover for large asset bases is difficult, and NOAT

*(Continued on next page)*

*(Continued from previous page)*

measures tend to fluctuate in a narrow band. When companies are able to make a meaningful improvement in NOAT, however, it usually has a large impact on RNOA.

RNOA is an important metric in assessing the performance of company management. We can use the RNOA components, NOPM and NOAT, to assess how effectively and efficiently management uses the company's operating assets to produce a return.

The difference between ROE and RNOA is important for our analysis. Specifically, ROE consists of a return on operating activities (RNOA) *plus* a return on nonoperating activities, where the latter reflects how well the company uses borrowed funds. Companies can increase ROE by borrowing money and effectively using those borrowed funds. However, debt can increase the company's risk—where severe consequences can result if debt is not repaid when due. This is why Warren Buffett focuses on "businesses earning good returns on equity while employing little or no debt." For those companies that do employ debt, our analysis seeks to evaluate their ability to repay the amounts owed when due. We cover that aspect of analysis using concepts of liquidity and solvency in the latter part of this module.

Over the years, analysts, creditors and others have developed hundreds of ratios to measure specific aspects of financial performance. Most of these seek answers to the root question: Can the company achieve a high return on its invested capital and, if so, is that return sustainable?

Sources: *BusinessWeek*, 2006; Home Depot 10-K, 2006; Home Depot Annual Report, 2006; Berkshire Hathaway 10-K, 2006.

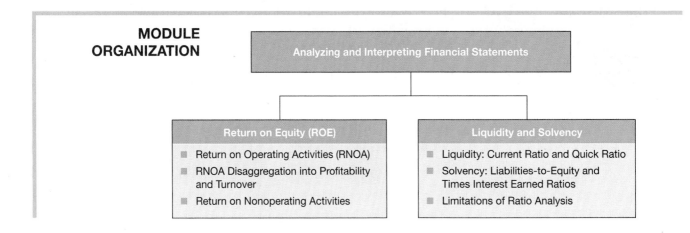

# INTRODUCTION

A key aspect of any analysis is identifying the business activities that drive company success. We pursue an answer to the question: Is the company earning an acceptable rate of return on its invested capital? We also want to know the extent to which the company's return on invested capital results from its operating versus its nonoperating activities. The distinction between returns from operating and nonoperating activities is important and plays a key role in our analysis.

Operating activities are the core activities of a company. They consist of those activities required to deliver a company's products or services to its customers. A company engages in operating activities when it conducts research and development, establishes supply chains, assembles administrative support, produces and markets its products, and follows up with after-sale customer services.

The asset side of a company's balance sheet reflects resources devoted to operating activities with accounts such as cash, receivables, inventories, and property, plant and equipment (PPE). They are reflected in liabilities with accounts such as accounts payable, accrued expenses, and long-term operating liabilities such as pension and health care obligations. The income statement reflects operating activities through accounts such as revenues, costs of goods sold, and operating expenses such as selling, general, and administrative expenses that include wages, advertising, depreciation, occupancy, insurance, and research and development. Operating activities create the most long-lasting (persistent) effects on future profitability and cash flows of the company. Operations provide the primary value drivers for company stakeholders. It is for this reason that operating activities play such a prominent role in assessing profitability.

Nonoperating activities relate to the investing of excess cash in marketable securities and in other nonoperating investments. They also relate to borrowings. Nonoperating activities are reflected in a company's balance sheet though accounts such as investments and short- and long-term debt. These nonoperating assets and liabilities expand and contract to buffer fluctuations in operating asset and liability levels. When operating assets grow faster than operating liabilities, companies typically increase their nonoperating liabilities to fund the deficit. Later, these liabilities decline when operating assets decline. When companies have cash in excess of what is needed for operating activities, they often invest the cash temporarily in marketable securities or other investments to provide some return until those funds are needed for operations.

The income statement reflects nonoperating activities through accounts such as interest and dividend revenue, capital gains or losses relating to investments, and interest expense on borrowed funds. Nonoperating expenses, net of any nonoperating revenues, provide a nonoperating return for a company. Although nonoperating activities are important and must be managed well, they are not the main value drivers for company stakeholders.

We begin this module by explaining the return on equity (ROE). We then discuss in more detail how ROE consists of both an operating return (RNOA) and a nonoperating return. Next, we discuss the two RNOA components that measure profitability and asset turnover. We conclude the first half of this module with a discussion of nonoperating return, focusing on the notion that companies can increase ROE through judicious use of debt.

In the second half of this module, we expand our explanation of nonoperating return by exploring how much debt a company can reasonably manage. For this purpose, we examine a number of liquidity and solvency metrics. As part of that analysis, we identify ratios typically used by bond rating agencies, which are key determinants of bond prices and the cost of debt financing for public companies.

# RETURN ON EQUITY (ROE)

**LO1** Compute return on equity (ROE) and disaggregate it into components of operating and nonoperating returns.

**Return on equity (ROE)** is the principle summary measure of company performance and is defined as follows:

$$\text{ROE} = \frac{\text{Net income}}{\text{Average stockholders' equity}}$$

ROE relates net income to the average investment by shareholders as measured by total stockholders' equity from the balance sheet. Warren Buffett highlights this return as part of his acquisition criteria: "Businesses earning good returns on equity while employing little or no debt." The ROE formula can be rewritten in a way to better see the point Buffett is making (derivation of this ROE formula is in Appendix 4B):

$$\text{ROE} = \text{Operating return} + \text{Nonoperating return}$$

The equation above shows that ROE consists of two returns: (1) the return from the company's operating activities, linked to revenues and expenses from the company's products or services, and (2) the return from the company's use of debt, net of any return from nonoperating investments. Companies can use debt to increase their return on equity, but this increases risk as the failure to make required debt payments can yield many legal consequences, including bankruptcy. This is one reason why Warren Buffett focuses on companies whose return on equity is derived primarily from operating activities.

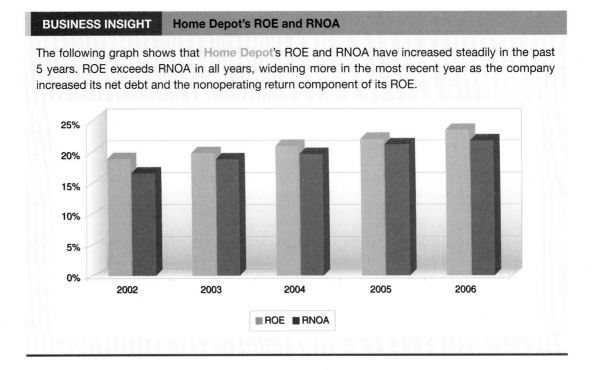

**BUSINESS INSIGHT** | **Home Depot's ROE and RNOA**

The following graph shows that Home Depot's ROE and RNOA have increased steadily in the past 5 years. ROE exceeds RNOA in all years, widening more in the most recent year as the company increased its net debt and the nonoperating return component of its ROE.

## Operating Return (RNOA)

Operating returns are captured by the **return on net operating assets (RNOA),** defined as follows:

$$\text{RNOA} = \frac{\text{Net operating profit after tax (NOPAT)}}{\text{Average net operating assets (NOA)}}$$

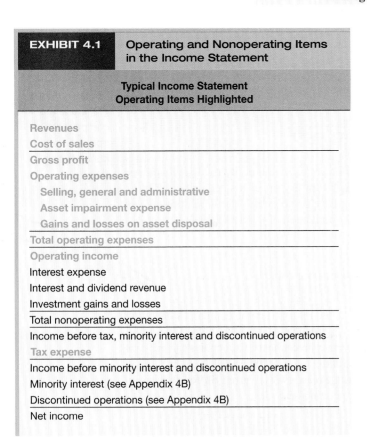

| **EXHIBIT 4.1** | **Operating and Nonoperating Items in the Income Statement** |
|---|---|

**Typical Income Statement Operating Items Highlighted**

Revenues
Cost of sales
Gross profit
Operating expenses
  Selling, general and administrative
  Asset impairment expense
  Gains and losses on asset disposal
Total operating expenses
Operating income
Interest expense
Interest and dividend revenue
Investment gains and losses
Total nonoperating expenses
Income before tax, minority interest and discontinued operations
Tax expense
Income before minority interest and discontinued operations
Minority interest (see Appendix 4B)
Discontinued operations (see Appendix 4B)
Net income

To implement this formula, we must first classify the income statement and balance sheet into operating and nonoperating components so that we can assess each separately. We first consider operating activities on the income statement and explain how to compute NOPAT. Second, we consider operating activities on the balance sheet and explain how to compute NOA.

### Operating Items in the Income Statement—NOPAT Computed

The income statement reports both operating and nonoperating activities. Exhibit 4.1 shows a typical income statement with the operating activities highlighted.

Some companies divide the income statement into operating and nonoperating sections to facilitate analysis (this division is not required by GAAP). Operating activities are those that relate to bringing a company's products or services to market and any after-sales support. The income statement in Exhibit 4.1 reflects operating activities through revenues, costs of goods sold (COGS), and other expenses. Selling, general, and administrative expense (SG&A) includes wages, advertising, occupancy, insurance, research and development, depreciation, and many other operating expenses the company incurs in the ordinary course of business (some of these are often reported as separate line items in the income statement). Companies also dispose of operating assets, and can realize gains or losses from their disposal, or write them off in full or partially when they become impaired. These, too, are operating activities. Finally, the reported tax expense on the income statement reflects both operating and nonoperating activities. Later in this section we use Home Depot's income statement to explain how to separately compute the effect of taxes on NOPAT.

Nonoperating activities relate to borrowed money that creates interest expense. Nonoperating activities also relate to investments such as marketable securities and other investments that yield interest or dividend revenue and capital gains or losses from any sales of nonoperating investments during the period.

Following is Home Depot's 2006 income statement with the operating items highlighted.

| HOME DEPOT<br>Income Statement ($ millions)<br>For Year Ended January 29, 2006 | |
| --- | --- |
| Revenues | $81,511 |
| Cost of sales | 54,191 |
| Gross profit | 27,320 |
| Operating expenses | |
| Selling, general and administrative | 16,485 |
| Depreciation | 1,472 |
| Total operating expenses | 17,957 |
| Operating income | 9,363 |
| Interest revenue | 62 |
| Interest expense | (143) |
| Earnings before taxes | 9,282 |
| Tax expense | 3,444 |
| Net income | $ 5,838 |

Home Depot's operating items include sales, cost of sales, SG&A, and depreciation expense. Home Depot's earned pretax operating income is $9,363 million. Its nonoperating activities relate to its borrowed money (interest expense is $143 million) and its investment in marketable securities (interest revenue is $62 million). These two nonoperating items combined yield net nonoperating expense of $81 million ($143 million − $62 million).

**Computing Tax on Operating Profit—Method 1** Home Depot's income statement reports net operating profit *before* tax of $9,363 million. But, the numerator of the RNOA formula, defined previously, uses net operating profit *after tax* (NOPAT). Thus, we need to subtract taxes to determine NOPAT. The tax expense of $3,444 million that Home Depot reports on its income statement pertains to both operating *and* nonoperating activities. To compute NOPAT, we need to compute the tax expense relating solely to operating profit as follows:

**Tax on operating profit = Tax expense + (Net nonoperating expense × Statutory tax rate)**

$$\boxed{\text{Tax Shield}}$$

The amount in parentheses is called the *tax shield*, which are the taxes that Home Depot saved by having tax-deductible nonoperating expenses (see Tax Shield box on page 4–7 for details). That tax benefit, however, does not apply to operating profit; as such, the tax shield is added back to compute tax on operating profit. (For companies with nonoperating revenue greater than nonoperating expense, so-called *net nonoperating revenue*, the tax on operating profit is computed as: Tax expense − [Net nonoperating revenue × Statutory tax rate]). Next, we subtract the tax on operating profit from the net operating profit before tax to obtain NOPAT.

Applying this method, we see that Home Depot had a tax shield of $31 million; computed as net non-operating expense of $81 million times its statutory tax rate of 38%).[1] Thus, Home Depot's net operating profit after tax is computed as follows ($ millions):

| | | |
|---|---|---|
| Net operating profit before tax . . . . . . . . . . . . . . . . . . . . | | $9,363 |
| Less tax on operating profit | | |
| Tax expense (from income statement) . . . . . . . . . . . | $3,444 | |
| Tax shield ($81 × 38%). . . . . . . . . . . . . . . . . . . . . . . | + 31 | (3,475) |
| Net operating profit after tax (NOPAT) . . . . . . . . . . . . . | | $5,888 |

---

**BUSINESS INSIGHT**    **Tax Shield**

Those of us with a home mortgage understand well the beneficial effects of the "interest tax shield." To see how the interest tax shield works, consider two individuals, each with income of $50,000 and each with only one expense: a home. Assume that one person pays $10,000 per year in rent; the other pays $10,000 in interest on a home mortgage. Rent is not deductible for tax purposes, whereas mortgage interest (but not principal) is deductible. Each person pays taxes at 25%, the personal tax rate for this income level. Their tax payments follow.

| | Renter | Home owner |
|---|---|---|
| Income . . . . . . . . . . . . . . . . . . . . | $50,000 | $50,000 |
| Less interest deduction . . . . . . . . | 0 | (10,000) |
| Taxable income . . . . . . . . . . . . . | $50,000 | $40,000 |
| Taxes paid (25% rate). . . . . . . . . | $12,500 | $10,000 |

The renter reports $50,000 in taxable income and pays $12,500 in taxes. The home owner deducts $10,000 in interest, which lowers taxable income to $40,000 and reduces taxes to $10,000. By deducting mortgage interest, the home owner's tax bill is $2,500 lower. The $2,500 is called the interest tax shield, and we can compute it directly as the $10,000 interest deduction multiplied by the 25% tax rate. Similarly, we can compute the interest tax shield for corporations using the net interest expense and the statutory corporate tax rate (commonly 37% for federal and state taxes). The adjustment made to determine the tax rate on operating income adds back the tax savings from any interest deduction, since this is a nonoperating item.

---

***Computing Tax on Operating Profit—Method 2*** Alternatively, by rearranging terms, we can also compute NOPAT using the following two-step method. First, we compute the tax rate on operating profit as follows.

$$\text{Tax rate on operating profit} = \frac{\text{Tax expense} + (\text{Net nonoperating expense} \times \text{Statutory tax rate})}{\text{Net operating profit before taxes}}$$

---

[1] The statutory federal tax rate for corporations is 35% (per U.S. tax code). Also, each state taxes corporate income, and those state taxes are deductible for federal tax purposes. The *net* state tax rate is the statutory rate less the federal tax deduction. Home Depot's 10-K reports federal taxes of $3,249 million and net state taxes of $279 million. Its *tax rate* is, therefore, 38%, computed as ($3,249 million + $279 million)/$9,282 million [the denominator is pretax profit, which is different from operating income before tax reported on the income statement]. This is the "statutory tax rate" used in computing the tax shield to determine tax on operating profit. Most companies, however, provide both the federal and net state tax *percentages* in the income tax footnote (instead of dollars for tax expense). In this case, the tax rate on operating profit is the sum of the two. Lowe's, for example, identifies its federal rate as 35% and its net state tax rate as 3.5% in its income tax footnote. The tax rate on operating profit for Lowe's is 38.5% (35% + 3.5%). This is the rate we use in the Lowe's NOPAT example in Mid-Module Review 1. (The Business Insight on page 4-8 provides an example of this presentation format and Module 5 has additional discussion of income taxes.)

Second, we use that rate to compute NOPAT.

$$\textbf{NOPAT = Net operating profit before tax} \times \textbf{(1 − Tax rate on operating profit)}$$

Home Depot's tax rate on operating profit is 37.11%, computed as $\left(\dfrac{\$3{,}444 + (\$81 \times 38\%)}{\$9{,}363}\right)$, and its NOPAT is $5,888 million, computed as $9,363 million $\times (1 - 37.11\%)$.

---

| **BUSINESS INSIGHT** | **Tax Rates for computing NOPAT** |
| --- | --- |

Computing NOPAT requires the tax rate on operating profit, which in turn requires the statutory tax rate (sum of federal and state tax rates). These are disclosed in the required income tax footnote to the 10-K. Following is this footnote from General Mills' 10-K.

| Fiscal Year | 2005 |
| --- | --- |
| U.S. statutory rate .................................... | 35.0% |
| State and local income taxes, net of federal tax benefits ....... | 2.0 |
| Divestitures, net ....................................... | 1.8 |
| Other, net .......................................... | (2.2) |
| Effective Income Tax Rate ............................. | 36.6% |

The federal statutory rate is 35.0%, and General Mills pays state and local taxes amounting to an additional 2.0%. It also incurred another 1.8% in tax related to divestitures, and received miscellaneous deductions that lowered its rate by 2.2%. Thus, General Mills effective tax rate for *ALL* its income is the sum of all its taxes paid less benefits received, or 36.6%. However, the interest tax shield that we add back in computing NOPAT only uses *federal and state tax rates*. For General Mills, the tax rate used to compute the tax shield is 37.0% (35.0% + 2.0%).

---

# MID-MODULE REVIEW 1

Following is the income statement of Lowe's Companies, Inc.

| **LOWE'S COMPANIES, INC.**<br>**Income Statement ($ millions)**<br>**For Fiscal Year Ended February 3, 2006** | |
| --- | --- |
| Net sales .......................... | $43,243 |
| Cost of sales......................... | 28,443 |
| Gross margin ....................... | 14,800 |
| Expenses | |
| Selling, general and administrative....... | 9,014 |
| Store opening costs ................. | 142 |
| Depreciation ...................... | 980 |
| Interest .......................... | 158 |
| Total expenses ...................... | 10,294 |
| Pretax earnings ..................... | 4,506 |
| Income tax provision .................. | 1,735 |
| Net earnings........................ | $ 2,771 |

**Required**

Compute Lowe's net operating profit after tax (NOPAT) assuming a 38.5% tax rate on operating profit.

**Solution**

All expenses reported in Lowe's income statement pertain to operating activities except for interest expense. Therefore, its net operating profit after tax (NOPAT) equals $2,868.4 million, computed as ($ millions) [$43,243 − $28,443 − $9,014 − $142 − $980] × [1 − 0.385]. (This computation uses method 2 as described on page 4-7.)

## Operating Items in the Balance Sheet—NOA Computed

RNOA relates NOPAT to the average net operating assets (NOA) of the company. We compute NOA as follows:

$$\text{Net operating assets} = \text{Operating assets} - \text{Operating liabilities}$$

To compute NOA we must partition the balance sheet into operating and nonoperating items. Exhibit 4.2 shows a typical balance sheet and highlights the operating items.

| EXHIBIT 4.2 | Operating and Nonoperating Items in the Balance Sheet |
|---|---|

**Typical Balance Sheet
Operating Items Highlighted**

**Current assets**
Cash and cash equivalents
Short-term investments
Accounts receivable
Inventories
Prepaid expenses
Deferred income tax assets
Other current assets

**Long-term assets**
Long-term investments in securities
Property, plant and equipment, net
Capitalized lease assets
Natural resources
Equity method investments
Goodwill and Intangible assets
Deferred income tax assets
Other long-term assets

**Current liabilities**
Short-term notes and interest payable
Accounts payable
Accrued liabilities
Deferred income tax liabilities
Current maturities of long-term debt

**Long-term liabilities**
Bonds and notes payable
Capitalized lease obligations
Pension and other post-employment liabilities
Deferred income tax liabilities
Minority Interest

**Stockholders' equity**
All equity accounts

Operating assets are those assets directly linked to operating activities, the company's ongoing business operations. They typically include cash, receivables, inventories, prepaid expenses, property, plant and equipment (PPE), and capitalized lease assets, and exclude short-term and long-term investments in marketable securities. Equity investments in affiliated companies and goodwill are considered operating assets if they pertain to the ownership of stock in other firms linked to the company's operating activities (see Module 7). Deferred tax assets (and liabilities) are operating items because they relate to future tax deductions (or payments) arising from operating activities (see Module 5).

Operating liabilities are liabilities that arise from operating revenues and expenses and commonly relate to operating assets. For example, accounts payable and accrued expenses help fund inventories, wages, utilities, and other operating expenses; also, deferred revenue (an operating liability) relates to operating revenue. Similarly, pension and other post-employment obligations relate to long-term obligations for employee retirement and health care, which by definition are operating activities (see Module 10). Operating liabilities exclude bank loans, mortgages or other debt, which are nonoperating. Further, companies often use capitalized leases to finance assets, and these capitalized lease liabilities are also nonoperating (see Module 10).

The following is Home Depot's balance sheets for 2006 and 2005. Its operating assets and operating liabilities are highlighted.

| HOME DEPOT Balance Sheet | | |
|---|---|---|
| **$ millions** | **Jan. 29, 2006** | **Jan. 30, 2005** |
| **Assets** | | |
| Current assets | | |
| Cash and cash equivalents | $ 793 | $ 506 |
| Short-term investments | 14 | 1,659 |
| Receivables, net | 2,396 | 1,499 |
| Inventories | 11,401 | 10,076 |
| Other current assets | 742 | 533 |
| Total current assets | 15,346 | 14,273 |
| Net property and equipment | 24,901 | 22,726 |
| Other long-term assets | 4,235 | 2,021 |
| Total assets | $44,482 | $39,020 |
| **Liabilities and stockholders' equity** | | |
| Current liabilities | | |
| Short-term borrowings | $ 1,413 | $ 11 |
| Accounts payable | 6,032 | 5,766 |
| Accrued expenses and other current liabilities | 5,456 | 4,678 |
| Total current liabilities | 12,901 | 10,455 |
| Long-term debt | 2,672 | 2,148 |
| Other long-term obligations | 2,000 | 2,259 |
| Stockholders' equity | | |
| Common stock | 7,407 | 6,769 |
| Retained earnings | 28,943 | 23,962 |
| Other stockholders' equity | (9,441) | (6,573) |
| Total stockholders' equity | 26,909 | 24,158 |
| Total liabilities and stockholders' equity | $44,482 | $39,020 |

We assume that Home Depot's "other" assets and liabilities are operating. We can sometimes make a finer distinction if footnotes to financial statements provide additional information. For now, assume that these "other" items reported in balance sheets pertain to operations.

Using the highlighted balance sheet above, we compute net operating assets for Home Depot in 2006 and 2005 as follows (we use: Net operating assets (NOA) = Total operating assets − Total operating liabilities).

| $ millions | Jan. 29, 2006 | Jan. 30, 2005 |
|---|---|---|
| **Operating Assets** | | |
| Cash and cash equivalents | $ 793 | $ 506 |
| Receivables, net | 2,396 | 1,499 |
| Inventories | 11,401 | 10,076 |
| Other current assets | 742 | 533 |
| Net property and equipment | 24,901 | 22,726 |
| Other long-term assets | 4,235 | 2,021 |
| Total operating assets | 44,468 | 37,361 |
| **Operating Liabilities** | | |
| Accounts payable | 6,032 | 5,766 |
| Accrued expenses and other current liabilities | 5,456 | 4,678 |
| Other long-term obligations | 2,000 | 2,259 |
| Total operating liabilities | 13,488 | 12,703 |
| Net operating assets (NOA) | $30,980 | $24,658 |

To determine average NOA, we take a simple average of two consecutive years' numbers. Thus, return on net operating assets (RNOA) for Home Depot for 2006 is computed as follows ($ millions).

$$\text{RNOA} = \frac{\text{NOPAT}}{\text{Average NOA}} = \frac{\$5,888}{(\$30,980 + \$24,658)/2} = 21.2\%$$

Home Depot's 2006 RNOA is 21.2%. By comparison, Lowe's Companies' (its main competitor) RNOA is 18%, and the average for all publicly traded companies is about 10%.

Recall that RNOA is related to ROE as follows: ROE = Operating return + Nonoperating return, where RNOA is the operating return. Thus, we can ask how do Home Depot's RNOA and ROE compare? Home Depot's 2006 ROE is computed as follows ($ millions).

$$\text{ROE} = \frac{\text{Net income}}{\text{Average stockholders' equity}} = \frac{\$5,838}{(\$26,909 + \$24,158)/2} = 22.9\%$$

In relative terms, Home Depot's operating return is 93% (21.2%/22.9%) of its total ROE. Its nonoperating return of 1.7% (22.9% − 21.2%) makes up the remaining 7% of ROE. Home Depot's RNOA as a percent of ROE is impressive because the average publicly traded company's RNOA is only 84% of ROE (Nissim and Penman, 2001). Thus, Home Depot appears to satisfy Warren Buffett's criterion of earning good returns on equity while employing little or no debt. Indeed, Home Depot's debt accounts for only 9% of its total assets, computed as [$1,413 + $2,672]/$44,482 ($ millions).

Exhibit 4.3 provides a summary of key terms introduced to this point and their definitions.

| EXHIBIT 4.3 | Key Ratio Definitions |
|---|---|
| **Ratio** | **Definition** |
| **ROE:** Return on equity | Net income/Average stockholders' equity |
| **NOPAT:** Net operating profit after tax | Operating revenues less operating expenses such as cost of sales, selling, general and administrative expense, and taxes; it excludes nonoperating revenues and expenses such as interest revenue, dividend revenue, interest expense, gains and losses on investments, and minority interest. |
| **NOA:** Net operating assets | Operating assets less operating liabilities; it excludes investments in marketable securities and interest-bearing debt. |
| **RNOA:** Return on net operating assets | NOPAT/Average NOA |
| **NNE:** Net nonoperating expense | NOPAT − Net income; NNE consists of nonoperating expenses and revenues, net of tax |

## RNOA Disaggregation into Margin and Turnover

Disaggregating RNOA into its two components, profit margin and asset turnover, yields further insights into a company's performance. This disaggregation follows.

$$\text{RNOA} = \frac{\text{NOPAT}}{\text{Average NOA}} = \frac{\text{NOPAT}}{\text{Sales}} \times \frac{\text{Sales}}{\text{Average NOA}}$$

| Net operating profit margin (NOPM) | Net operating asset turnover (NOAT) |

**LO2** Disaggregate operating return (RNOA) into its components of profitability and asset turnover.

**Net operating profit margin (NOPM)** reveals how much operating profit the company earns from each sales dollar. All things equal, a higher NOPM is preferable. NOPM is affected by the level of gross profit the company earns on its products (revenue minus cost of goods sold), which depends on product prices and manufacturing or purchase costs. NOPM is also affected by the level of operating expenses the company requires to support its products or services. This includes overhead costs such as wages, marketing, occupancy, and research and development. Finally, NOPM is affected by the level of competition (which affects product pricing) and the company's willingness and ability to control costs.

Home Depot's net operating profit margin is computed as follows ($ millions).

$$\text{NOPM} = \frac{\text{NOPAT}}{\text{Revenues}} = \frac{\$5,888}{\$81,511} = 7.22\%$$

This result means that for each dollar of sales at Home Depot, the company earns just over 7.2¢ profit after all operating expenses and tax. As a reference, the median NOPM for all publicly traded firms is 5.5¢ (Nissim and Penman, 2001).

---

**BUSINESS INSIGHT**    Home Depot's NOPM

The following chart shows that Home Depot's net operating profit margin increased from 5.8% of revenues in 2002 to 7.2% in 2006, which is a substantial increase for such a competitive industry.

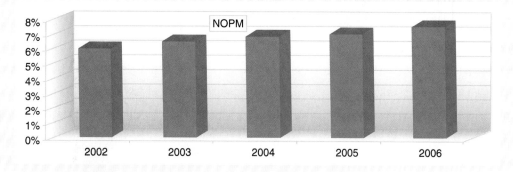

---

**Net operating asset turnover (NOAT)** measures the productivity of the company's net operating assets. This metric reveals the level of sales the company realizes from each dollar invested in net operating assets. All things equal, a higher NOAT is preferable. Home Depot's net operating asset turnover ratio follows ($ millions).

$$\text{NOAT} = \frac{\text{Revenues}}{\text{Average NOA}} = \frac{\$81,511}{(\$30,980 + \$24,658)/2} = 2.93$$

This result means that for each dollar of net operating assets, Home Depot realizes $2.93 in sales. As a reference, the median for all publicly traded companies is $1.97 (Nissim and Penman, 2001).

NOAT can be increased by either increasing sales for a given level of investment in operating assets, or by reducing the amount of operating assets necessary to generate a dollar of sales, or both. Reducing operating working capital (current operating assets less current operating liabilities) is usually easier than

**BUSINESS INSIGHT**    Home Depot's NOAT

The following chart shows Home Depot's net operating asset turnover from 2002 to 2006. Its largest value is 3.05 in 2005 and its lowest is 2.78 in 2002. Home Depot's net operating asset turnover exceeds the 1.97 median for publicly traded firms in each of these years.

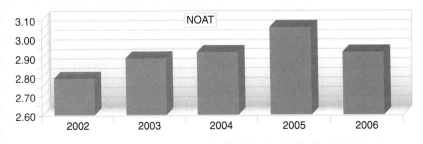

reducing net long-term operating assets. For example, companies can implement strategies to collect their receivables faster, reduce their inventories, and delay payments to their suppliers. All of these actions reduce operating working capital and, thereby, increase NOAT. These strategies must be managed, however, so as not to negatively impact sales or supplier relations. Working capital management is an important part of managing the company effectively.

It is usually more difficult to reduce the level of net long-term operating assets. The level of PPE required by the company is determined more by the demands of the products or services offered than by management action. For example, telecommunications companies require more capital investment than do retail stores. Still, there are several actions that managers can take to reduce capital investment. Some companies pursue novel approaches, such as corporate alliances, outsourcing, and use of special purpose entities; we discuss some of these approaches in Module 10.

**MANAGERIAL DECISION**    **You Are the Entrepreneur**

You are analyzing the performance of your start-up company. Your analysis of RNOA reveals the following (industry benchmarks in parenthesis): RNOA is 16% (10%), NOPM is 18% (17%), and NOAT is 0.89 (0.59). What interpretations do you draw that are useful for managing your company?
[Answer, p. 4-30]

## Trade-Off between Margin and Turnover

Operating profit margin and turnover of operating assets are largely affected by a company's business model. This is an important concept. Specifically, an infinite number of combinations of net operating profit margin and net operating asset turnover will yield a given RNOA. This relation is depicted in Exhibit 4.4 (where the curved line reflects the median RNOA for all publicly traded companies; from Nissim and Penman, 2001).

This exhibit reveals that some industries, like communication and pharmaceuticals, are capital intensive with relatively low operating asset turnover. Accordingly, for such industries to achieve a required RNOA (to be competitive in the overall market), they must obtain a higher profit margin. On the other hand, service companies such as retailers and restaurants hold fewer assets and, therefore, can operate on lower operating profit margins to achieve a sufficient RNOA. This is because their asset turnover is far greater.

This exhibit warns of blindly comparing the performance of companies across different industries. For instance, a higher profit margin in the Communication industry compared with the Apparel industry is not necessarily the result of better management. Instead, the Communication industry is extremely capital intensive and thus, to achieve an equivalent RNOA, Communications firms must earn a higher profit margin to offset their lower asset turnover. Basic economics suggests that all industries must earn an acceptable return on investment if they are to continue to attract investors and survive.

The trade-off between margin and turnover is obvious when comparing firms that operate in sole industries (*pure-play* firms). Analyzing conglomerates that operate in several industries is more challenging. Conglomerates' margins and turnover rates are a weighted-average of the margins and turnover

| EXHIBIT 4.4 | Profitability and Productivity across Industries |
| --- | --- |

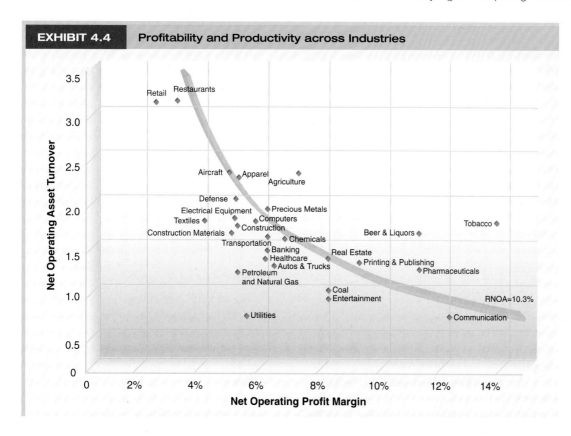

rates for the various industries in which they operate. For example, Ford Motor Company is a blend of a manufacturing company and a financial institution (Ford Motor Credit Company); thus, the margin and turnover benchmarks for Ford on a consolidated basis is a weighted average of the two industries.

To summarize, ROE is the sum of the returns from operating (RNOA) and nonoperating activities. RNOA is the product of NOPM and NOAT.

# MID-MODULE REVIEW 2

Following is the balance sheet of Lowe's Companies, Inc.

## LOWE'S COMPANIES, INC.
### Balance Sheet

| $ millions | February 3, 2006 | January 28, 2005 |
| --- | --- | --- |
| **Assets** | | |
| Cash and cash equivalents . . . . . . . . . . . . . . . . . | $ 423 | $ 530 |
| Short-term investments . . . . . . . . . . . . . . . . . . . . | 453 | 283 |
| Accounts receivable, net . . . . . . . . . . . . . . . . . . | 18 | 9 |
| Merchandise inventory, net . . . . . . . . . . . . . . . . | 6,706 | 5,911 |
| Deferred income taxes, net . . . . . . . . . . . . . . . . | 127 | 95 |
| Other assets. . . . . . . . . . . . . . . . . . . . . . . . . . . . . | 104 | 75 |
| Total current assets . . . . . . . . . . . . . . . . . . . . . . | 7,831 | 6,903 |
| Property, net . . . . . . . . . . . . . . . . . . . . . . . . . . . | 16,354 | 13,911 |
| Long-term investments . . . . . . . . . . . . . . . . . . . . | 294 | 146 |
| Other assets. . . . . . . . . . . . . . . . . . . . . . . . . . . . | 203 | 178 |
| Total assets. . . . . . . . . . . . . . . . . . . . . . . . . . . . . | $24,682 | $21,138 |

*continued*

**LOWE'S COMPANIES, INC.**
**Balance Sheet**

| $ millions | February 3, 2006 | January 28, 2005 |
|---|---|---|
| Liabilities and shareholders' equity | | |
| Current maturities of long-term debt . . . . . . . . . . | $ 32 | $ 630 |
| Accounts payable. . . . . . . . . . . . . . . . . . . . . . . . | 2,832 | 2,695 |
| Accrued salaries and wages . . . . . . . . . . . . . . . | 424 | 386 |
| Self-insurance liabilities . . . . . . . . . . . . . . . . . . . | 571 | 467 |
| Deferred revenue . . . . . . . . . . . . . . . . . . . . . . . | 709 | 539 |
| Other current liabilities . . . . . . . . . . . . . . . . . . . . | 1,264 | 931 |
| Total current liabilities. . . . . . . . . . . . . . . . . . . . . | 5,832 | 5,648 |
| Long-term debt . . . . . . . . . . . . . . . . . . . . . . . . | 3,499 | 3,060 |
| Deferred income taxes. . . . . . . . . . . . . . . . . . . . | 735 | 736 |
| Other long-term liabilities. . . . . . . . . . . . . . . . . . | 277 | 159 |
| Total liabilities. . . . . . . . . . . . . . . . . . . . . . . . . . | 10,343 | 9,603 |
| Shareholders' equity | | |
| Common stock . . . . . . . . . . . . . . . . . . . . . . . . | 392 | 387 |
| Capital in excess of par value . . . . . . . . . . . . . . | 1,712 | 1,514 |
| Retained earnings . . . . . . . . . . . . . . . . . . . . . . . | 12,234 | 9,634 |
| Other . . . . . . . . . . . . . . . . . . . . . . . . . . . . . . . . | 1 | — |
| Total shareholders' equity . . . . . . . . . . . . . . . . . | 14,339 | 11,535 |
| Total liabilities and shareholders' equity. . . . . . . . | $24,682 | $21,138 |

## Required

1. Compute Lowe's net operating assets for 2006 and 2005.
2. Refer to Lowe's income statement and NOPAT from Mid-Module Review 1. Compute Lowe's return on net operating assets (RNOA) for 2006.
3. Compute Lowe's 2006 ROE. What percentage of Lowe's ROE comes from operations?
4. Disaggregate Lowe's 2006 RNOA into net operating profit margin (NOPM) and net operating asset turnover (NOAT).
5. Compare and contrast Lowe's ROE, RNOA, NOPM, and NOAT with those same measures computed in this module for Home Depot. Interpret the results.

## Solution ($ millions)

1.

**LOWE'S COMPANIES, INC.**
**Balance Sheet**

| $ millions | February 3, 2006 | January 28, 2005 |
|---|---|---|
| Cash and cash equivalents . . . . . . . . . . . . . . . . | $ 423 | $ 530 |
| Accounts receivable, net . . . . . . . . . . . . . . . . . . | 18 | 9 |
| Merchandise inventory, net . . . . . . . . . . . . . . . . | 6,706 | 5,911 |
| Deferred income taxes, net . . . . . . . . . . . . . . . . | 127 | 95 |
| Other assets. . . . . . . . . . . . . . . . . . . . . . . . . . . | 104 | 75 |
| Property, net . . . . . . . . . . . . . . . . . . . . . . . . . . | 16,354 | 13,911 |
| Other assets. . . . . . . . . . . . . . . . . . . . . . . . . . . | 203 | 178 |
| Accounts payable. . . . . . . . . . . . . . . . . . . . . . . | (2,832) | (2,695) |
| Accrued salaries and wages . . . . . . . . . . . . . . . | (424) | (386) |
| Self-insurance liabilities . . . . . . . . . . . . . . . . . . . | (571) | (467) |
| Deferred revenue . . . . . . . . . . . . . . . . . . . . . . . | (709) | (539) |
| Other current liabilities . . . . . . . . . . . . . . . . . . . . | (1,264) | (931) |
| Deferred income taxes. . . . . . . . . . . . . . . . . . . . | (735) | (736) |
| Other long-term liabilities. . . . . . . . . . . . . . . . . . | (277) | (159) |
| Net operating assets . . . . . . . . . . . . . . . . . . . . . | $17,123 | $14,796 |

2. $\text{RNOA} = \dfrac{\$2,868.4}{(\$17,123 + \$14,796)/2} = 18.0\%$

3. $\text{ROE} = \dfrac{\$2,771}{(\$14,339 + \$11,535)/2} = 21.4\%$

   Lowe's RNOA makes up 84.1% of its ROE, computed as 18.0%/21.4%.

4. $\text{NOPM} = \dfrac{\$2,868.4}{\$43,243} = 6.63\%$

   $\text{NOAT} = \dfrac{\$43,243}{(\$17,123 + \$14,796)/2} = 2.71$

5. Despite similar business models, Home Depot is superior on the profitability measures of ROE, RNOA, NOPM, and NOAT.

| | ROE | RNOA | NOPM | NOAT |
|---|---|---|---|---|
| Home Depot . . . . . . . . | 22.9% | 21.2% | 7.22% | 2.93% |
| Lowe's . . . . . . . . . . . | 21.4 | 18.0 | 6.63 | 2.71 |

Home Depot's RNOA comprises 92.6% of its ROE (computed as 21.2%/22.9%), while Lowe's is 84.1%. Lowe's is relying on the beneficial effects of borrowing to a greater extent, but its ROE still lags behind Home Depot's. Home Depot's net operating profit margin and net operating asset turnover both exceed those for Lowe's. Additional analysis (in the next section) of gross profit margins and expense management provides further insight into the reasons for Home Depot's superior operating profitability. Further, asset management can be assessed by analyzing the control of receivables and inventories, as well as construction costs and sales per square foot.

## Further RNOA Disaggregation

While disaggregation of RNOA into net operating profit margin (NOPM) and net operating asset turnover (NOAT) yields valuable insight into factors driving company performance, analysts and creditors usually disaggregate those components even further. The purpose is to better identify the specific drivers of both profitability and turnover.

To disaggregate NOPM, we examine the gross profit on products sold and the individual expense accounts that affect operating profit as a percentage of sales (such as Gross profit/Sales and SG&A/Sales). These margin ratios aid comparisons across companies of differing sizes and across different time periods for the same company. We further discuss profit margin disaggregation in Appendix 4A and in other modules that focus on operating results.

To disaggregate NOAT, we examine the individual balance sheet accounts that comprise NOA and compare them to the related income statement activity. Specifically, we compute accounts receivable turnover (ART), inventory turnover (INVT), property, plant and equipment turnover (PPET), as well as turnovers for liability accounts such as accounts payable turnover (APT). Analysts and creditors often compute the net operating working capital turnover (NOWCT) to assess a company's working capital management compared to its competitors and recent trends. These turnover rates are further discussed in other modules that focus on operating assets and liabilities. Exhibit 4.5 provides a broad overview of ratios commonly used for component disaggregation and analysis.

## Nonoperating Return

This section discusses a company's nonoperating return. In simplest form, the return on nonoperating activities measures the extent to which a company is using debt to increase its return on equity. The following example provides the intuition for this return. Assume that a company has $1,000 in average assets for the current year in which it earns a 20% RNOA. It finances those assets entirely with equity investment (no debt). Its ROE is computed as follows:

$$
\begin{aligned}
\text{ROE} &= \text{Operating return} + \text{Nonoperating return} \\
&= \quad\;\; 20\% \quad\;\; + \quad\;\; 0\% \\
&= \quad\quad\quad\quad 20\%
\end{aligned}
$$

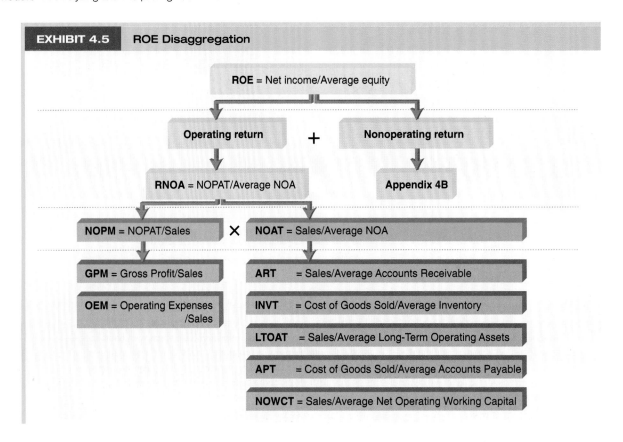

**EXHIBIT 4.5   ROE Disaggregation**

Next, assume that this company borrows $500 at 7% interest and uses those funds to acquire additional assets yielding the same operating return. Its average assets for the year now total $1,500, and its profit is $265, computed as follows:

| | | |
|---|---:|---:|
| Profit from assets financed with equity ($1,000 × 20%) . . . . . | | $200 |
| Profit from assets financed with debt ($500 × 20%) . . . . . . . . | $100 | |
| Less interest expense from debt ($500 × 7%) . . . . . . . . . . . . | (35) | 65 |
| Net profit. . . . . . . . . . . . . . . . . . . . . . . . . . . . . . . . . . . . . . . . . | | $265 |

We see that this company has increased its profit to $265 (up from $200) with the addition of debt, and its ROE is now 26.5% ($265/$1,000). The reason for the increased ROE is that the company borrowed $500 at 7% (and paid $35 of interest expense) and invested those funds in assets earning 20% (which generated $100 of profits). The difference of 13% ($65 profit, computed as 13% × $500) accrues to shareholders. Stated differently, the company's ROE now consists of the following.

$$\text{ROE} = \text{Operating return} + \text{Nonoperating return}$$
$$= \quad 20\% \quad + \quad 6.5\%$$
$$= \quad\quad\quad 26.5\%$$

The company has made effective use of debt to increase its ROE. The nonoperating return is inferred as the difference between ROE and RNOA. This return can be computed directly, and we provide an expanded discussion of this computation in Appendix 4B.

We might further ask: If a higher ROE is desirable, why don't companies use the maximum possible debt? The answer is that increasing levels of debt result in successively higher interest rates charged by creditors (see Module 8). At some point, the cost of debt exceeds the return on assets that a company can acquire from the debt financing. Thereafter, further debt financing does not make economic sense. The market, in essence, places a limit on the level of debt that a company can effectively acquire. In sum, shareholders benefit from increased use of debt provided that the assets financed with the debt earn a return that exceeds the cost of the debt.

**RESEARCH INSIGHT    Ratio Behavior over Time**

How do ROE, RNOA, and NNEP (net nonoperating expense percent, defined later in this module) behave over time? Following is a graph of these ratios over a recent 34-year period (from graph B, p.134, of Nissim and Penman, 2001, *Review of Accounting Studies* 6 (1), pp. 109–154, with permission of Springer Science and Business Media). There is considerable variability in these ratios over time. The proportion of RNOA to ROE is greater for some periods of time than for others. Yet, in all periods, RNOA exceeds the net nonoperating expense percent, NNEP. This is evidence of a positive effect, on average, for ROE from financial leverage.

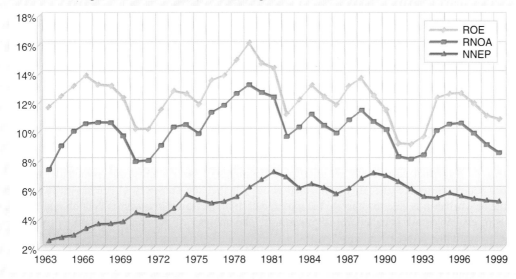

In addition, creditors usually require a company to execute a loan agreement that places varying restrictions on its operating activities. These restrictions, called *covenants*, help safeguard debtholders in the face of increased risk. This is because debtholders do not have a voice on the board of directors like stockholders do. These debt covenants impose a "cost" on the company beyond that of the interest rate, and these covenants are more stringent as a company increases its reliance on debt financing.

# LIQUIDITY AND SOLVENCY

**LO3** Compute and interpret measures of liquidity and solvency.

Companies can effectively use debt to increase ROE with returns from nonoperating activities. The advantage of debt is that it typically is a less costly source of financing; currently the cost of debt is about 4% versus a cost of equity of about 12%, on average. Although it reduces financing costs, debt does carry default risk: the risk that the company will be unable to repay debt when it comes due. Creditors have several legal remedies when companies default, including forcing a company into bankruptcy and possibly liquidating its assets.

The median ratio of total liabilities to stockholders' equity, which measures the relative use of debt versus equity in a company's capital structure, is about 1.0 for all publicly traded companies. This means that the average company is financed with about half debt and half equity. However, the relative use of debt varies considerably across industries as illustrated in Exhibit 4.6.

Companies in the utilities industry have among the highest proportions of debt. Since the utilities industry is regulated, profits and cash flows are relatively certain and stable and, as a result, utility companies can support a higher debt level. The transportation industry also utilizes a relatively high proportion of debt. However, this industry is not regulated, its market is more competitive and volatile and, consequently, its use of debt carries more risk. At the lower end of debt financing are pharmaceuticals and software companies. Historically, these industries have been characterized by relatively uncertain profits and cash flows. Consequently, they use less debt in their capital structures.

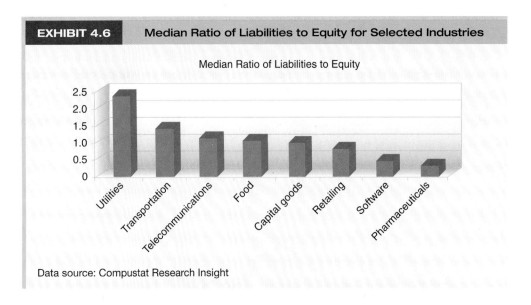

EXHIBIT 4.6    Median Ratio of Liabilities to Equity for Selected Industries

Data source: Compustat Research Insight

The core of our analysis relating to debt is the examination of a company's ability to generate cash to *service* its debt (that is, to make required debt payments of both interest and principal). Analysts, investors and creditors are primarily concerned about whether the company either has sufficient cash available or whether it is able to generate the required cash in the future to cover its debt obligations. The analysis of available cash is called *liquidity analysis*. The analysis of the company's ability to generate sufficient cash in the future is called *solvency analysis* (so named because a bankrupt company is said to be "insolvent").

## Liquidity Analysis

*Liquidity* refers to cash availability: how much cash a company has, and how much it can raise on short notice. Two of the most common ratios used to assess the degree of liquidity are the current ratio and the quick ratio. Both of these ratios link required near-term payments to cash available in the near-term.

### Current Ratio

*Current assets* are those assets that a company expects to convert into cash within the next operating cycle, which is typically a year. *Current liabilities* are those liabilities that come due within the next year. An excess of current assets over current liabilities (Current assets − Current liabilities), is known as *net working capital* or simply *working capital*.[2] Positive working capital implies more expected cash inflows than cash outflows in the short run. The current ratio expresses working capital as a ratio and is computed as follows:

$$\text{Current ratio} = \frac{\text{Current assets}}{\text{Current liabilities}}$$

A current ratio greater than 1.0 implies positive working capital. Both working capital and the current ratio consider existing balance sheet data only and ignore cash inflows from future sales or other sources. The current ratio is more commonly used than working capital because ratios allow comparisons across companies of different size. Generally, companies prefer a higher current ratio; however, an excessively high current ratio indicates inefficient asset use. Furthermore, a current ratio less than 1.0 is not always bad for at least two reasons:

---

[2] Both operating assets and operating liabilities can be either current or long-term. "Current" means that the asset is expected to be used, or the liability paid, within the next operating cycle or one year, whichever is longer, which for most companies means a year. Using the current versus long-term nature of operating assets and liabilities we derive two types of net operating assets: net operating working capital (NOWC), and net long-term operating assets. Net operating working capital is defined as:

**Net operating working capital (NOWC) = Current operating assets − Current operating liabilities**

For Home Depot, NOWC is $3,844 million for 2006 ($15,332 million − $11,488 million).

1. A cash-and-carry company (like a grocery store) can have potentially few current assets (and a low current ratio), but consistently large operating cash inflows ensure the company will be sufficiently liquid.

2. A company can efficiently manage its working capital by minimizing receivables and inventories and maximizing payables. Dell and Wal-Mart, for example, use their buying power to exact extended credit terms from suppliers. Consequently, because both companies are essentially cash-and-carry companies, their current ratios are less than 1.0 and both are sufficiently liquid.

The aim of current ratio analysis is to discern if a company is having, or is likely to have, difficulty meeting its short-term obligations. Home Depot's current ratio for 2006 is 1.19 ($15,346 million/$12,901 million) and for 2005 it is 1.37 ($14,273 million/$10,455 million). Its current ratio has steadily declined over the past five years as shown in the margin graph.

Although, according to this measure, Home Depot's liquidity has declined, it is a cash-and-carry business as it reports only $2.4 billion of accounts receivable on $81.5 billion in sales. We would not expect Home Depot's current ratio to be as high as those companies that carry a high level of receivables. Thus, Home Depot seems sufficiently liquid.

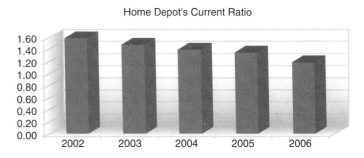

Home Depot's Current Ratio

## Quick Ratio

The quick ratio is a variant of the current ratio. It focuses on quick assets, which are those assets likely to be converted to cash within a relatively short period of time. Specifically, quick assets include cash, marketable securities, and accounts receivable; they exclude inventories and prepaid assets. The quick ratio is defined as follows:

$$\text{Quick ratio} = \frac{\text{Cash} + \text{Marketable securities} + \text{Accounts receivables}}{\text{Current liabilities}}$$

The quick ratio reflects on a company's ability to meet its current liabilities without liquidating inventories that could require markdowns. It is a more stringent test of liquidity than the current ratio.

Home Depot's 2006 quick ratio is 0.25 $\left(\frac{\$793 \text{ million} + \$14 \text{ million} + \$2,396 \text{ million}}{\$12,901 \text{ million}}\right)$, compared with 0.35 $\left(\frac{\$506 \text{ million} + \$1,659 \text{ million} + \$1,499 \text{ million}}{\$10,455 \text{ million}}\right)$ in 2005, and has steadily declined over the past five years—see margin graph. It is not uncommon for a company's quick ratio to be less than 1.0. Home Depot's liquidity has declined according to the quick ratio, which is similar to the pattern of its current ratio over recent years. Although liquidity is not a major concern for Home Depot, the current decline is something financial statement users would want to monitor.

Home Depot's Quick Ratio

## Solvency Analysis

**Solvency** refers to a company's ability to meet its debt obligations, including both periodic interest payments and the repayment of the principal amount borrowed. Solvency is crucial since an insolvent company is a failed company. There are two general approaches to measuring solvency. The first approach uses balance sheet data and assesses the proportion of capital raised from creditors. The second approach uses income statement data and assesses the profit generated relative to debt payment obligations. We discuss each approach in turn.

### Liabilities-to-Equity

The liabilities-to-equity ratio is a useful tool for the first type of solvency analysis. It is defined as follows:

$$\text{Liabilities-to-equity ratio} = \frac{\text{Total liabilities}}{\text{Stockholders' equity}}$$

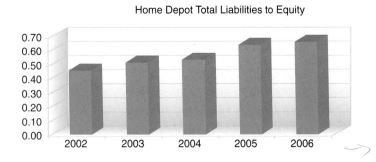

Home Depot Total Liabilities to Equity

This ratio conveys how reliant a company is on creditor financing compared with equity financing. A higher ratio indicates less solvency, and more risk. Home Depot's 2006 liabilities-to-equity ratio is 0.65 $\left(\frac{\$12{,}901\text{ million} + \$2{,}672\text{ million} + \$2{,}000\text{ million}}{\$26{,}909\text{ million}}\right)$, and for 2005 it is 0.62 $\left(\frac{\$10{,}455\text{ million} + \$2{,}148\text{ million} + \$2{,}259\text{ million}}{\$24{,}158\text{ million}}\right)$. This ratio has consistently increased for Home Depot over the past five years—see margin graph. Still, its ratio is lower than 1.0, the average for publicly traded companies.

A variant of this ratio considers a company's *long-term* debt divided by equity. This approach assumes that current liabilities are repaid from current assets (so-called self-liquidating). Thus, it assumes that creditors and stockholders need only focus on the relative proportion of long-term capital.

### Times Interest Earned

The second type of solvency analysis compares profits to liabilities. This approach assesses how much operating profit is available to cover debt obligations. A common measure for this type of solvency analysis is the times interest earned ratio, defined as follows:

$$\textbf{Times interest earned} = \frac{\textbf{Earnings before interest and taxes}}{\textbf{Interest expense}}$$

The times interest earned ratio reflects the operating income available to pay interest expense. The underlying assumption is that only interest needs to be paid because the principal will be refinanced. This ratio is sometimes abbreviated as EBIT/I. The numerator is similar to net operating profits after tax (NOPAT), but it is *pretax* instead of after tax.

Management wants this ratio to be sufficiently high so that there is little risk of default. Although declining over the past five years, Home Depot's 2006 times interest earned ratio is a healthy 66, computed as $\left(\frac{\$9{,}282\text{ million} + \$143\text{ million}}{\$143\text{ million}}\right)$—see margin graph. This result implies that Home Depot could suffer a

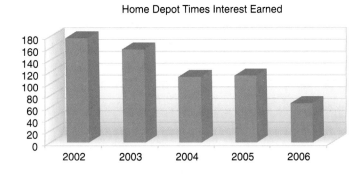

Home Depot Times Interest Earned

large decline in profitability and still be able to service its interest payments when due. Any solvency concerns we might have had relating to Home Depot's lack of liquidity are mitigated by its earning power and its relatively low level of debt in relation to its shareholder investment.

There are many variations of solvency and liquidity analysis and the ratios used. The basic idea is to construct measures that reflect a company's credit risk exposure. There is not one "best" financial leverage ratio. Instead, as financial statement users, we want to use measures that capture the risk we are most concerned with. It is also important to compute the ratios ourselves to ensure we know what is included and excluded from each ratio.

## Limitations of Ratio Analysis

The quality of financial statement analysis depends on the quality of financial information. We ought not blindly analyze numbers; doing so can lead to faulty conclusions and suboptimal decisions. Instead, we need to acknowledge that current accounting rules (GAAP) have limitations, and be fully aware of the company's environment, its competitive pressures, and any structural and strategic changes. This section discusses some of the factors that limit the usefulness of financial accounting information for ratio analysis.

***GAAP Limitations*** Several limitations in GAAP can distort financial ratios. Limitations include:

1. **Measurability.** Financial statements reflect what can be reliably measured. This results in nonrecognition of certain assets, often internally developed assets, the very assets that are most

likely to confer a competitive advantage and create value. Examples are brand name, a superior management team, employee skills, and a reliable supply chain.

2. **Non-capitalized costs.** Related to the concept of measurability is the expensing of costs relating to "assets" that cannot be identified with enough precision to warrant capitalization. Examples are brand equity costs from advertising and other promotional activities, and research and development costs relating to future products.

3. **Historical costs.** Assets and liabilities are usually recorded at original acquisition or issuance costs. Subsequent increases in value are not recorded until realized, and declines in value are only recognized if deemed permanent.

Thus, GAAP balance sheets omit important and valuable assets. Our analysis of ROE, including that of liquidity and solvency, must consider that assets can be underreported and that ratios can be distorted. We discuss many of these limitations in more detail in later modules.

**Company Changes**  Many companies regularly undertake mergers, acquire new companies and divest subsidiaries. Such major operational changes can impair the comparability of company ratios across time. Companies also change strategies, such as product pricing, R&D, and financing. We must understand the effects of such changes on ratios and exercise caution when we compare ratios from one period to the next. Companies also behave differently at different points in their life cycles. For instance, growth companies possess a different profile than do mature companies. Seasonal effects also markedly impact analysis of financial statements at different times of the year. Thus, we must consider life cycle and cyclicality when we compare ratios across companies and over time.

**Conglomerate Effects**  Few companies are pure-play; instead, most companies operate in several businesses or industries. Most publicly traded companies consist of a parent company and multiple subsidiaries, often pursuing different lines of business. Most heavy equipment manufacturers, for example, have finance subsidiaries (Ford Credit Corporation and Cat Financial are subsidiaries of Ford and Caterpillar respectively). Financial statements of such conglomerates are consolidated and include the financial statements of the parent and its subsidiaries. Consequently, such consolidated statements are challenging to analyze. Typically, analysts break the financials apart into their component businesses and separately analyze each component. Fortunately, companies must report financial information (albeit limited) for major business segments in their 10-Ks.

**Means to an End**  Ratios reduce, to a single number, the myriad complexities of a company's operations. No scalar can accurately capture the qualitative aspect of company. Ratios cannot hope to capture the innumerable transactions and events that occur each day between a company and various parties. Ratios cannot meaningfully convey a company's marketing and management philosophies, its human resource activities, its financing activities, its strategic initiatives, and its product management. In our analysis we must learn to look through the numbers and ratios to better understand the operational factors that drive financial results. Successful analysis seeks to gain insight into what a company is really about and what the future portends. Our overriding purpose in analysis is to understand the past and present to better predict the future. Computing and examining ratios is just one step in that process.

## MODULE-END REVIEW

Refer to the income statement and balance sheet of Lowe's Companies, Inc., from Mid-Module Reviews 1 and 2 earlier in this module.

### Required

Compute the following liquidity and solvency ratios for Lowe's. Interpret and assess these ratios for Lowe's relative to those same ratios previously computed for Home Depot in the text.

1. Current ratio
2. Quick ratio
3. Liabilities-to-equity ratio
4. Times interest earned

## Solution ($ millions)

| Ratio | Lowe's Companies | Home Depot |
|---|---|---|
| Current ratio | $7,831/$5,832 = 1.34 | $15,346/$12,901 =1.19 |
| Quick ratio | ($423 + $453 + $18)/$5,832 = 0.15 | ($793 + $14 + $2,396)/$12,901 = 0.25 |
| Liabilities-to-equity ratio | $10,343/$14,339 = 0.72 | ($12,901 + $2,672 + $2,000)/$26,909 = 0.65 |
| Times interest earned | ($4,506 + $158)/$158 = 29.52 | ($9,282 + $143)/$143 = 65.9 |

Interpretation: Home Depot is slightly less liquid than Lowe's. Both its current ratio and quick ratio are lower for Home Depot but the difference is not striking. Home Depot and Lowe's both have fewer liabilities than equity; the ratio is less than 1.0 for both firms. Lowe's liabilities-to-equity ratio indicates that it is slightly less solvent than Home Depot, but again, the difference is not striking. Both companies have extremely high times-interest-earned ratios. In conclusion, each company appears sufficiently liquid and each has strong solvency ratios.

# APPENDIX 4A: Vertical and Horizontal Analysis

Companies come in all sizes, which presents difficulties when making inter-firm comparisons. There are several methods that attempt to overcome this obstacle.

**Vertical analysis** expresses financial statements in ratio form. Specifically, it is common to express income statement items as a percent of net sales, and balance sheet items as a percent of total assets. Such *common-size financial statements* facilitate comparisons *across companies* of different sizes and comparisons of accounts within a set of financial statements.

**Horizontal analysis** is the scrutiny of financial data *across time*. Comparing data across two or more consecutive periods assists in analyzing company performance and in predicting future performance.

Exhibits 4A.1 and 4A.2 present Home Depot's common-size balance sheet and common-size income statement. We also present data for horizontal analysis by showing three years of common-size statements.

Home Depot's total assets in dollars have increased by 29% since 2004. However, we are primarily interested in the *composition* of the balance sheet, or the proportion invested in each asset category. Specifically, liquidity has generally deteriorated as cash, short-term investments, and receivables represent 7.2% of total assets in 2006, down from 11.5% in 2004. Inventories, on the other hand, have remained at about the same percentage of total assets. Home Depot reports in the MD&A section of its 10-K that it has used some of its excess liquidity to repurchase common stock in 2006. Generally, companies repurchase their stock when they feel it is undervalued and wish to send that signal to the market. Despite the depletion of its short-term investment portfolio, Home Depot asserts that its liquidity is sufficient in this excerpt from its 2006 10-K.

> As of January 29, 2006, we had $807 million in Cash and Short-Term Investments. We believe that our current cash position and cash flow generated from operations should be sufficient to enable us to complete our capital expenditure programs and any required long-term debt payments through the next several fiscal years. In addition, we have funds available from the $2.5 billion commercial paper program and the ability to obtain alternative sources of financing for future acquisitions and other requirements.

Home Depot's property and equipment have decreased as a percentage of total assets, from 58.3% to 56%. Still, it remains a capital-intensive company. Other long-term assets have increased as a percentage of the total, from 3% in 2004 to 9.5% in 2006. This category represents goodwill arising from numerous acquisitions that it executed over the past few years.

Home Depot's short-term liabilities have increased as a percentage of total financing. This mainly results from a 1.7% percentage point increase in short-term debt. Accounts payable and accrued liabilities have decreased slightly (from 26.3% to 25.9%) in the past two years. Short-term and long-term debt have been used to fund a recent acquisition, and Home Depot indicated its intent to repay $900 million in short-term debt in fiscal 2007. The proportion of equity in its capital structure has declined from 65.1% in 2004 to 60.5% in 2006 as the company used debt to finance new-store construction and acquire other companies. It is not uncommon for companies to utilize lower-cost debt to finance expansion, especially if they feel that their stock price is not sufficiently high to fund those expenditures.

| EXHIBIT 4A.1 | Common-Size Comparative Balance Sheets |
|---|---|

## HOME DEPOT
### Common-Size Comparative Balance Sheets

| | Amounts ($ millions) | | | Percentages | | |
|---|---|---|---|---|---|---|
| | 2006 | 2005 | 2004 | 2006 | 2005 | 2004 |
| **Assets** | | | | | | |
| Cash and cash equivalents . . . . . . . . . . . . . . . . . . | $ 793 | $ 506 | $ 1,103 | 1.8% | 1.3% | 3.2% |
| Short-term investments . . . . . . . . . . . . . . . . . . . . . | 14 | 1,659 | 1,749 | 0.0 | 4.3 | 5.1 |
| Receivables, net. . . . . . . . . . . . . . . . . . . . . . . . . . | 2,396 | 1,499 | 1,097 | 5.4 | 3.8 | 3.2 |
| Inventories . . . . . . . . . . . . . . . . . . . . . . . . . . . . . | 11,401 | 10,076 | 9,076 | 25.6 | 25.8 | 26.4 |
| Other current assets. . . . . . . . . . . . . . . . . . . . . . . | 742 | 533 | 303 | 1.7 | 1.4 | 0.9 |
| Total current assets . . . . . . . . . . . . . . . . . . . . . . . | 15,346 | 14,273 | 13,328 | 34.5 | 36.6 | 38.7 |
| Net property and equipment, net. . . . . . . . . . . . . | 24,901 | 22,726 | 20,063 | 56.0 | 58.2 | 58.3 |
| Other long-term assets . . . . . . . . . . . . . . . . . . . . | 4,235 | 2,021 | 1,046 | 9.5 | 5.2 | 3.0 |
| Total assets. . . . . . . . . . . . . . . . . . . . . . . . . . . . . | $44,482 | $39,020 | $34,437 | 100.0 | 100.0 | 100.0 |
| **Liabilities and Stockholders' Equity** | | | | | | |
| Short-term borrowings. . . . . . . . . . . . . . . . . . . . . | $ 1,413 | $ 11 | $ 509 | 3.2% | 0.0% | 1.5% |
| Accounts payable. . . . . . . . . . . . . . . . . . . . . . . . | 6,032 | 5,766 | 5,159 | 13.6 | 14.8 | 15.0 |
| Accrued expenses and other current liabilities . . . | 5,456 | 4,678 | 3,886 | 12.3 | 12.0 | 11.3 |
| Total current liabilities. . . . . . . . . . . . . . . . . . . . . | 12,901 | 10,455 | 9,554 | 29.0 | 26.8 | 27.7 |
| Long-term debt . . . . . . . . . . . . . . . . . . . . . . . . . . | 2,672 | 2,148 | 856 | 6.0 | 5.5 | 2.5 |
| Other long-term obligations . . . . . . . . . . . . . . . . . | 2,000 | 2,259 | 1,620 | 4.5 | 5.8 | 4.7 |
| Stockholders' equity | | | | | | |
| Common stock. . . . . . . . . . . . . . . . . . . . . . . . . . | 7,407 | 6,769 | 6,303 | 16.7 | 17.3 | 18.3 |
| Retained earnings . . . . . . . . . . . . . . . . . . . . . . . | 28,943 | 23,962 | 19,694 | 65.1 | 61.4 | 57.2 |
| Other stockholders' equity. . . . . . . . . . . . . . . . . . | (9,441) | (6,573) | (3,590) | (21.2) | (16.8) | (10.4) |
| Total stockholders' equity . . . . . . . . . . . . . . . . . | 26,909 | 24,158 | 22,407 | 60.5 | 61.9 | 65.1 |
| Total liabilities and stockholders' equity. . . . . . . . | $44,482 | $39,020 | $34,437 | 100.0 | 100.0 | 100.0 |

| EXHIBIT 4A.2 | Common-Size Comparative Income Statements |
|---|---|

## HOME DEPOT
### Common-Size Comparative Income Statements

| | Amounts ($ millions) | | | Percentages | | |
|---|---|---|---|---|---|---|
| | 2006 | 2005 | 2004 | 2006 | 2005 | 2004 |
| Revenues . . . . . . . . . . . . . . . . . . . . . . . . . . . . . . | $81,511 | $73,094 | $64,816 | 100.0% | 100.0% | 100.0% |
| Cost of sales . . . . . . . . . . . . . . . . . . . . . . . . . . . | 54,191 | 48,664 | 44,236 | 66.5 | 66.6 | 68.2 |
| Gross profit . . . . . . . . . . . . . . . . . . . . . . . . . . . . | 27,320 | 24,430 | 20,580 | 33.5 | 33.4 | 31.8 |
| Operating expenses | | | | | | |
| Selling, general and administrative . . . . . . . . . . . | 16,485 | 15,256 | 12,713 | 20.2 | 20.9 | 19.6 |
| Depreciation . . . . . . . . . . . . . . . . . . . . . . . . . . . . | 1,472 | 1,248 | 1,021 | 1.8 | 1.7 | 1.6 |
| Total operating expenses . . . . . . . . . . . . . . . . . . | 17,957 | 16,504 | 13,734 | 22.0 | 22.6 | 21.2 |
| Operating income. . . . . . . . . . . . . . . . . . . . . . . . | 9,363 | 7,926 | 6,846 | 11.5 | 10.8 | 10.6 |
| Interest income. . . . . . . . . . . . . . . . . . . . . . . . . . | 62 | 56 | 59 | 0.1 | 0.1 | 0.1 |
| Interest expense. . . . . . . . . . . . . . . . . . . . . . . . . | (143) | (70) | (62) | (0.2) | (0.1) | (0.1) |
| Earnings before taxes. . . . . . . . . . . . . . . . . . . . . | 9,282 | 7,912 | 6,843 | 11.4 | 10.8 | 10.6 |
| Tax expense . . . . . . . . . . . . . . . . . . . . . . . . . . . . | 3,444 | 2,911 | 2,539 | 4.2 | 4.0 | 3.9 |
| Net income. . . . . . . . . . . . . . . . . . . . . . . . . . . . . | $ 5,838 | $ 5,001 | $ 4,304 | 7.2 | 6.8 | 6.6 |

Home Depot's Gross Profit Percentage

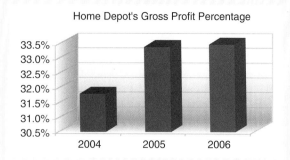

Home Depot's income statement reflects a marked increase in its gross profit percentage, increasing from 31.8% in 2004 to 33.5% in 2006—see margin graph. This is a large increase for a company operating in competitive conditions. Further, Home Depot has successfully reduced its selling, general and administrative expenses as a percentage of revenues, from 20.9% in 2005 to 20.2% in 2006. Finally, its operating income increased from 10.6% of revenues to 11.5% from 2004 to 2006, and its net income from 6.6% to 7.2%. Home Depot's increase in debt is not as threatening if profitability increases, as it has in the past year.

# APPENDIX 4B: Nonoperating Return Component of ROE

In this appendix, we consider the nonoperating return component of ROE in more detail. We also provide a derivation of that nonoperating return and discuss several special topics pertaining to it. We begin by considering three special cases of capital structure financing.

## Nonoperating Return With Debt Only

In the module, we infer the nonoperating return as the difference between ROE and RNOA. The nonoperating return can also be computed directly as FLEV × SPREAD, where FLEV is the degree of financial leverage.

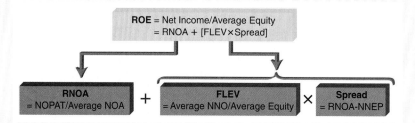

Exhibit 4B.1 provides definitions for each of the terms required in this computation.

| **EXHIBIT 4B.1** | **Nonoperating return definitions** |
|---|---|
| NNO: net nonoperating obligations . . . . . . . . . . . . | Nonoperating obligations less nonoperating assets |
| FLEV: financial leverage . . . . . . . . . . . . . . . . . . . . | Average NNO/Average equity |
| NNE: net nonoperating expense . . . . . . . . . . . . . . | NOPAT – Net income; NNE consists of nonoperating expenses and revenues, net of tax |
| NNEP: net nonoperating expense percent. . . . . . . | NNE/Average NNO |
| Spread . . . . . . . . . . . . . . . . . . . . . . . . . . . . . . . . . | RNOA – NNEP |

To illustrate computation of the nonoperating return when the company has only debt (no investments), let's refer to our example in this module of the company which increases its ROE through use of debt. (For this first illustration, view FLEV as the relative use of debt in the capital structure, and SPREAD as the difference between RNOA and the net nonoperating expense percent). Again, assume that this company has $1,000 of equity and $500 of 7% debt invested in $1,500 of total assets earning a 20% return. The net income of this firm is $265, computed as follows:

| | | |
|---|---:|---:|
| Profit from assets financed with equity ($1,000 × 20%) . . . . . | | $200 |
| Profit from assets financed with debt ($500 × 20%) . . . . . . . . | $100 | |
| Less interest expense from debt ($500 × 7%) . . . . . . . . . . . | (35) | 65 |
| Net profit. . . . . . . . . . . . . . . . . . . . . . . . . . . . . . . . . . . . . . . . . | | $265 |

Its ROE is 26.5%, computed as $265/$1,000 (assuming income received at year-end for simplicity; meaning average equity is $1,000). Its RNOA is 20%, FLEV is 0.50 (computed as $500 of average net nonoperating obligations divided by $1,000 average equity), and its SPREAD is 13% (computed as 20% less 7%). This company's ROE, shown with the nonoperating return being directly computed, is as follows:

$$ROE = RNOA + [FLEV \times SPREAD]$$
$$= 20\% + [0.50 \times 13\%]$$
$$= 26.5\%$$

## Nonoperating Return With Investments Only

When a company's nonoperating activities relate solely to the borrowing of money (no investments in marketable securities), FLEV collapses to the debt-to-equity ratio, a ratio similar to that which we explained in the solvency section of this module. However, many high-tech companies have no debt, and maintain large portfolios of marketable securities. They hold these highly liquid assets so that they can respond quickly to new opportunities or react to competitive pressures. With high levels of nonoperating assets and no nonoperating liabilities, net nonoperating obligations (NNO) has a negative sign (NNO = Nonoperating obligations − Nonoperating assets). Likewise, FLEV is negative: Average NNO (−) / Average Equity (+). Further, net nonoperating expense (NNE = NOPAT − Net income) is negative because investment *income* is a negative nonoperating expense. However, the net nonoperating expense percent (NNEP) is positive because the negative NNE is divided by the negative NNO. This causes ROE to be less than RNOA (see computations below). We use the 2005 10-K of Cisco Systems, Inc to explain this curious result.

| ($ millions, except percentages) | 2005 | 2004 |
|---|---|---|
| NOA | $ 11,871 | $ 10,371 |
| NNO | $(11,303) | $(15,455) |
| Stockholders' equity | $ 23,174 | $ 25,826 |
| Net income | $ 5,741 | |
| NOPAT | $ 4,820 | |
| NNE | $ (921) | |
| FLEV | (54.6)% | |
| RNOA | 43.3% | |
| NNEP | 6.9% | |
| Spread | 36.4% | |

Cisco's NNO is negative because its investment in marketable securities exceeds its debt. Cisco's ROE is 23.4%, and it consists of the following:

$$ROE = RNOA + [FLEV \times SPREAD]$$
$$= 43.3\% + [-54.6\% \times 36.4\%]$$
$$= 43.3\% + [-19.9\%]$$
$$= 23.4\%$$

Cisco's ROE is lower than its RNOA because of its large investment in marketable securities. That is, its excessive liquidity is penalizing in its return on equity. The rationale for this seemingly incongruous result is this: Cisco's ROE derives from operating and nonoperating assets. Cisco's operating assets are providing an outstanding return (43.3%), much higher than the return on its marketable securities (6.9%). Holding liquid assets that are less productive means that Cisco's shareholders are funding a sizeable level of liquidity, and sacrificing returns in the process. Why? Many companies in high-tech industries feel the need to maintain excessive liquidity to gain flexibility—the flexibility to take advantage of opportunities and to react quickly to competitor maneuvers. Cisco's management, evidently, feels that the investment of costly equity capital in this manner will reap future rewards for its shareholders. Its 43.3% RNOA provides some evidence that this strategy is not necessarily misguided.

## Nonoperating Return With Both Debt and Investments

Many companies report both debt and investments on their balance sheets. If that debt markedly exceeds the investment balance, their ROE will look more like our first example (with debt only). Instead, if investments predominate, their ROE will look more like Cisco's. It is important to remember that both the average NNO (and FLEV) and NNE can be either positive (debt) or negative (investments), and it is not always the case that ROE exceeds RNOA. We now compute nonoperating return for Home Depot, a company with both debt and investments.

# Nonoperating Return for Home Depot

Home Depot has both debt and investments. Its debt (with interest expense) exceeds nonoperating investments (with interest income). Recall that nonoperating activities primarily relate to two activities: borrowed money that creates interest expense and nonoperating investments that yield interest revenue or dividend revenue and capital gains or losses. Combining interest expense with nonoperating income and gains or losses yields net nonoperating expense. Exhibit 4B.2 highlights the typical components of net nonoperating expense.

| **EXHIBIT 4B.2**   Simplified Income Statement |
| --- |
| **Nonoperating Items Highlighted** |
| Revenues |
| Cost of sales |
| Gross profit |
| Total operating expenses |
| Operating income |
| Interest expense |
| Interest and dividend revenues |
| Investment gains and losses |
| Total nonoperating expenses |
| Income before tax |
| Tax expense |
| Net income |

The nonoperating items are reported on the income statement before tax. However, nonoperating expenses (net) create a tax shield and thus, we need to consider the after-tax value of net nonoperating expense. This is called the net nonoperating expense (NNE), which we compute as:

$$\text{Net nonoperating expense (NNE)} = \begin{bmatrix} \text{Interest expense} - \text{Interest revenue} \\ - \text{Dividend revenue} - \text{Investment} \\ \text{gains } (+\text{losses}) \end{bmatrix} \times [1 - \text{Tax rate on operating profit}]$$

The simple illustration shown earlier in this appendix ignored taxes and thus, NNE was equal to the $35 interest paid on the debt. Recall from page 4-8 that Home Depot's tax rate on operating profit is 37.11%. Thus, for Home Depot, we can compute NNE as follows ($ millions): [$143 − $62] × [1 − 37.11%] = $51.

To compute operating return (RNOA) we divided NOPAT from the income statement, by NOA from the balance sheet. Similarly, to compute the net nonoperating expense percent (NNEP), we divide NNE from the income statement by net nonoperating items from the balance sheet (called net nonoperating obligations, NNO). Exhibit 4B.3 shows how a balance sheet can be reorganized into operating and nonoperating items.

| **EXHIBIT 4B.3**   Simplified Balance Sheet |
| --- |

|  | **Assets** | **Liabilities** |
| --- | --- | --- |
| Net operating assets (NOA) . . . . . . . . . . . | Current Operating Assets | Current Operating Liabilities |
| (assets − liabilities) | + Long-Term Operating Assets | + Long-Term Operating Liabilities |
|  | = Total Operating Assets | = Total Operating Liabilities |
| Net nonoperating obligations (NNO). . . . . . . | Current Nonoperating Assets | Current Nonoperating Liabilities |
| (liabilities − assets) | + Long-Term Nonoperating Assets | + Long-Term Nonoperating Liabilities |
|  | = Total Nonoperating Assets | = Total Nonoperating Liabilities |
|  |  | **Equity** |
| Equity (NOA − NNO) . . . . . . . . . . . . . . . . . |  | Stockholders' Equity |
|  | Total Assets | Total Liabilities and Equity |

Net nonoperating obligations are total nonoperating liabilities less total nonoperating assets. The accounting equation stipulates that Assets = Liabilities + Equity, so we can adjust the balance sheet to yield the following identity:

**Net operating assets (NOA) = Net nonoperating obligations (NNO) + Stockholders' Equity**

For Home Depot, we compute NNO as follows:

| $ millions | 2006 | 2005 |
|---|---|---|
| Short-term borrowings.................. | $1,413 | $   11 |
| Long-term debt ...................... | 2,672 | 2,148 |
| Total nonoperating liabilities ............ | 4,085 | 2,159 |
| Short-term investments ................ | 14 | 1,659 |
| Long-term investments ................ | 0 | 0 |
| Total nonoperating assets ............. | 14 | 1,659 |
| Net nonoperating obligations (NNO) ...... | $4,071 | $  500 |

Accordingly (drawing on NNE from the income statement and NNO from the balance sheet), we compute the net nonoperating expense percent (NNEP) as follows:

$$\text{Net Nonoperating Expense Percent (NNEP)} = \frac{\text{Net Nonoperating Expense (NNE)}}{\text{Average Net Nonoperating Obligations (NNO)}}$$

The net nonoperating expense percent (NNEP) measures the average rate of return on nonoperating activities. The denominator uses the average NNO similar to the prior return calculations we previously discussed (ROE and RNOA).

In the simple illustration from earlier in this appendix, the company's net nonoperating expense percent is 7%, computed as $35/$500, which is exactly equal to the interest rate on the loan. With real financial statements, such as Home Depot, NNEP is more complicated because NNE includes both interest on borrowed money and nonoperating income, and NNO is the net of operating liabilities less nonoperating assets. Thus NNEP reflects an average return on nonoperating activities. For Home Depot, its 2006 NNEP is 2.2%, computed as $51/[($4,071 + $500)/2], $ millions.

Home Depot's 2006 RNOA is 21.2%, which means that net operating assets generate more return than the 2.2% cost of its net nonoperating obligations. That is, Home Depot earns a SPREAD of 19%, the difference between RNOA (21.2%) and NNEP (2.2%), on each asset financed with borrowed funds compared to other assets. By borrowing funds, Home Depot creates leverage, which can be measured relative to shareholder's equity; that ratio is called financial leverage (FLEV). Total nonoperating return is computed by the following formula:

$$\text{Nonoperating return} = \underbrace{(\text{RNOA} - \text{NNEP})}_{\text{SPREAD}} \times \underbrace{\frac{\text{Average Net Nonoperating Obligations (NNO)}}{\text{Average Stockholders' Equity}}}_{\text{FLEV}}$$

For Home Depot, its 2006 spread between RNOA and NNEP is 19%. It has average NNO of $2,286 [($4,071 + $500)/2] and average equity of $25,534 [($26,909 + $24,158)/2], $ millions. Thus, Home Depot' ROE consists of the following ($ millions):

$$
\begin{aligned}
\text{ROE} &= \text{Operating return} + \quad \text{Nonoperating return} \\
&= \quad 21.2\% \qquad +(21.2\% - 2.2\%) \times (\$2,286/\$25,534) \\
&= \quad 21.2\% \qquad + \qquad\quad 1.7\% \\
&= \qquad\qquad 22.9\%
\end{aligned}
$$

Two points are immediately clear from this equation. First, ROE increases with the spread between RNOA and NNEP. The more profitable the return on operating assets, the higher the return to shareholders. Second, the higher the debt relative to equity, the higher the ROE (assuming, of course, a positive spread).

# Derivation of Nonoperating Return Formula

Following is the algebraic derivation of the nonoperating return formula.

$$
\begin{aligned}
\text{ROE} &= \frac{\text{NI}}{\text{SE}} \\
&= \frac{\text{NOPAT} - \text{NNE}}{\text{SE}} \\
&= \frac{\text{NOPAT}}{\text{SE}} - \frac{\text{NNE}}{\text{SE}} \\
&= \left(\frac{\text{NOA}}{\text{SE}} \times \text{RNOA}\right) - \left(\frac{\text{NNO}}{\text{SE}} \times \text{NNEP}\right) \\
&= \left(\frac{(\text{SE} + \text{NNO})}{\text{SE}} \times \text{RNOA}\right) - \left(\frac{\text{NNO}}{\text{SE}} \times \text{NNEP}\right) \\
&= \left[\text{RNOA} \times \left(1 + \frac{\text{NNO}}{\text{SE}}\right)\right] - \left(\frac{\text{NNO}}{\text{SE}} \times \text{NNEP}\right) \\
&= \text{RNOA} + \left(\frac{\text{NNO}}{\text{SE}} \times \text{RNOA}\right) - \left(\frac{\text{NNO}}{\text{SE}} \times \text{NNEP}\right) \\
&= \text{RNOA} + \left(\frac{\text{NNO}}{\text{SE}}\right)(\text{RNOA} - \text{NNEP}) \\
&= \text{RNOA} + (\text{FLEV} \times \text{SPREAD})
\end{aligned}
$$

where NI is net income, SE is average stockholders' equity, and all other terms are as defined in Exhibit 4B.1.

## Special topics

The return on equity (ROE) computation becomes a bit more complicated in the presence of discontinued operations, preferred stock, and minority (or noncontrolling) equity interest. The first of these apportions ROE between operating and nonoperating returns, and the other two affect the dollar amount included in the denominator (average equity) of the ROE computation. Recall that ROE measures the return on investment for common shareholders. The ROE numerator should include only the income available to pay common dividends, and the denominator should include common equity only, not that relating to preferred or minority shareholders.

*Discontinued operations* Discontinued operations are subsidiaries or business segments that the board of directors has formally decided to divest. Companies must report discontinued operations on a separate line, below income from continuing operations. The separate line item includes the net income or loss from discontinued operations along with any gains or losses on the disposal of discontinued net assets (see Module 5 for details). Although not required, many companies disclose the net assets of discontinued operations on the balance sheet to distinguish them from continuing net assets (if the net assets are not separated on the balance sheet, the footnotes provide details to facilitate a disaggregated analysis). These net assets of discontinued operations should be considered to be nonoperating (they represent an investment once they have been classified as discontinued) and their after-tax profit (loss) should be treated as nonoperating as well. Although the ROE computation is unaffected, the nonoperating portion of that return will include the contribution of discontinued operations.

*Preferred stock* The ROE formula takes the perspective of the common shareholder in that it relates the income available to pay common dividends to the average common shareholder investment. As such, preferred stock should not be included in average stockholders' equity in the denominator of the ROE formula. Similarly, any dividends paid on preferred stock should be subtracted from net income to yield the profit available to pay common dividends. (Dividends are not an expense in computing net income; thus, net income is available to both preferred and common shareholders. To determine net income available to common shareholders, we must subtract preferred dividends.) Thus, the presence of preferred stock requires two adjustments to the ROE formula.

1. Preferred dividends must be subtracted from net income in the numerator.
2. Preferred stock must be subtracted from stockholders' equity in the denominator.

This modified return on equity formula is more accurately labeled return on common equity (ROCE).

$$
\text{ROCE} = \frac{\text{Net income} - \text{Preferred dividends}}{\text{Average stockholders' equity} - \text{Average preferred equity}}
$$

*Minority (non-controlling) Interest* When a company acquires controlling interest of the outstanding voting stock of another company, the parent company must consolidate the new subsidiary in its balance sheet and income statement (see Module 7). This means that the parent company must include 100% of the subsidiary's assets, liabilities, revenues and expenses. Should the parent acquire less than 100% of the subsidiary's voting stock, the remaining claim of minority shareholders is reported on the balance sheet as a liability usually called minority interest (in a proposed amendment to current accounting standards, the FASB will require recognition of minority interest as a component of stockholders' equity, if passed).

On the consolidated income statement, the minority (non-controlling) shareholders' claim to the subsidiary's net income is reported as a separate line item called minority interest expense. This minority interest expense represents the portion of income attributable to minority interests. Reported net income is, therefore, attributable to the parent's shareholders.

If minority interest is excluded from stockholders' equity, no adjustments need be made to the ROE computation (ROE = Net income / Average stockholders' equity) as net income already excludes the income attributable to minority interests (treated as an expense). If minority interest is included in stockholders' equity (which it will be under the proposed amendment to the business combinations accounting standard), it must be subtracted from stockholders' equity before computing ROE.

It is possible to take additional steps to add back the effects of minority interest expense and minority interest equity to distinguish return to common shareholders as follows:

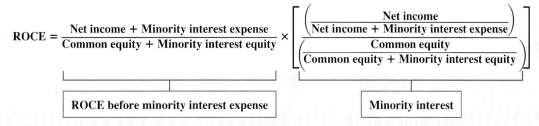

However, as the following equations show, the end result is the same because terms in the equations cancel and we are left with ROE:

$$
\text{ROCE} = \frac{\text{Net income} + \text{Minority interest expense}}{\text{Common equity} + \text{Minority interest equity}} \times \left[ \frac{\left( \dfrac{\text{Net income}}{\text{Net income} + \text{Minority interest expense}} \right)}{\left( \dfrac{\text{Common equity}}{\text{Common equity} + \text{Minority interest equity}} \right)} \right]
$$

$$
= \frac{\text{Net income} + \text{Minority interest expense}}{\text{Common equity} + \text{Minority interest equity}} \times \left[ \frac{\text{Net income}}{\text{Net income} + \text{Minority interest expense}} \times \frac{\text{Common equity} + \text{Minority interest equity}}{\text{Common equity}} \right]
$$

$$
= \text{Net income/Common equity}
$$

(Technically, this ROCE calculation should use comprehensive income rather than net income because the former includes several relevant items, which we explain in Module 5.)

Calculating RNOA involves no modifications because NOPAT is operating income before minority interest, and NOA excludes minority interest on the balance sheet. Similarly, SPREAD is computed as usual. However, we need to adjust FLEV to reflect total equity because a company's operating and nonoperating activities generate returns to both the majority (the common shareholders' equity or CSE) and minority shareholders (labelled MI). Consequently, for companies with minority interest on the balance sheet, we adjust FLEV as follows: FLEV = NNO/ (CSE + MI). An alternative way of describing this relation is:

$$\text{ROCE} = \text{RNOA} + [\text{NNO/(CSE + MI)}] \times [\text{Spread} \times \text{Minority interest sharing ratio}].$$

# GUIDANCE ANSWERS

**MANAGERIAL DECISION**    **You Are the Entrepreneur**

Your company is performing substantially better than its competitors. Namely, your RNOA of 16% is markedly superior to competitors' RNOA of 10%. However, RNOA disaggregation shows that this is mainly attributed to your NOAT of 0.89 versus competitors' NOAT of 0.59. Your NOPM of 18% is essentially identical to competitors' NOPM of 17%. Accordingly, you will want to maintain your NOAT as further improvements are probably difficult to achieve. Importantly, you are likely to achieve the greatest benefit with efforts at improving your NOPM of 18%, which is only marginally better than the industry norm of 17%.

**Superscript ^A(B) denotes assignments based on Appendix 4A (4B).**

# DISCUSSION QUESTIONS

**Q4-1.** Explain in general terms the concept of return on investment. Why is this concept important in the analysis of financial performance?

**Q4-2.^B** (a) Explain how an increase in financial leverage can increase a company's ROE. (b) Given the potentially positive relation between financial leverage and ROE, why don't we see companies with 100% financial leverage (entirely nonowner financed)?

**Q4-3.** Gross profit margin (Gross profit/Sales) is an important determinant of NOPAT. Identify two factors that can cause gross profit margin to decline. Is a reduction in the gross profit margin always bad news? Explain.

**Q4-4.** When might a reduction in operating expenses as a percentage of sales denote a short-term gain at the cost of long-term performance?

**Q4-5.** Describe the concept of asset turnover. What does the concept mean and why it is so important to understanding and interpreting financial performance?

**Q4-6.** Explain what it means when a company's ROE exceeds its RNOA.

**Q4-7.^B** Discontinued operations are typically viewed as a nonoperating activity in the analysis of the balance sheet and the income statement. What is the rationale for this treatment?

**Q4-8.** Describe what is meant by the "tax shield."

**Q4-9.** What is meant by the term "net" in net operating assets (NOA).

**Q4-10.** Why is it important to disaggregate RNOA into operating profit margin (NOPM) and net operating assets turnover (NOAT)?

**Q4-11.** What insights do we gain from the graphical relation between profit margin and asset turnover?

**Q4-12.** Explain the concept of liquidity and why it is crucial to company survival.

**Q4-13.** Identify at least two factors that limit the usefulness of ratio analysis.

**Q4-14.^A** What are common-size financial statements? What role do they play in financial statement analysis?

# MINI EXERCISES

**M4-15. Identify and Compute Net Operating Assets and its Components (LO2)**

Target Corporation (TGT)

Following is the balance sheet for Target Corporation. Identify and compute its fiscal year-end 2006 net operating assets.

| ($ millions) | January 28, 2006 | January 29, 2005 |
|---|---|---|
| **Assets** | | |
| Cash and cash equivalents | $ 1,648 | $ 2,245 |
| Accounts receivable, net | 5,666 | 5,069 |
| Inventory | 5,838 | 5,384 |
| Other curret assets | 1,253 | 1,224 |
| Total current assets | 14,405 | 13,922 |
| Property and equipment | | |
| Land | 4,449 | 3,804 |
| Buildings and improvements | 14,174 | 12,518 |
| Fixtures and equipment | 3,219 | 2,990 |
| Computer hardware and software | 2,214 | 1,998 |
| Construction-in-progress | 1,158 | 962 |
| Accumulated depreciation | (6,176) | (5,412) |
| Property and equipment, net | 19,038 | 16,860 |
| Other noncurrent assets | 1,552 | 1,511 |
| Total assets | $34,995 | $32,293 |

*continued*

| ($ millions) | January 28, 2006 | January 29, 2005 |
| --- | --- | --- |
| **Liabilities and shareholders' investment** | | |
| Accounts payable. | $ 6,268 | $ 5,779 |
| Accrued liabilities. | 2,193 | 1,633 |
| Income taxes payable | 374 | 304 |
| Current portion of long-term debt and notes payable | 753 | 504 |
| Total current liabilities. | 9,588 | 8,220 |
| Long-term debt | 9,119 | 9,034 |
| Deferred income taxes and other. | 851 | 973 |
| Other noncurrent liabilities. | 1,232 | 1,037 |
| Shareholders' investment | | |
| Common stock. | 73 | 74 |
| Additional paid-in-capital. | 2,121 | 1,810 |
| Retained earnings. | 12,013 | 11,148 |
| Accumulated other comprehensive income. | (2) | (3) |
| Total shareholders' investment. | 14,205 | 13,029 |
| Total liabilities and shareholders' investment | $34,995 | $32,293 |

**M4-16. Identify and Compute NOPAT (LO2)**

Following is the income statement for Target Corporation. (*a*) Compute Target's net operating profit *before* tax. (*Hint:* Treat Target's credit card revenues and related expenses as operating.) (*b*) Assume that the combined federal and state statutory tax rate is 38.3%. Compute NOPAT for Target for 2006.

Target Corporation (TGT)

| ($ millions) | 2006 |
| --- | --- |
| Sales. | $51,271 |
| Net credit card revenues | 1,349 |
| Total revenues. | 52,620 |
| Cost of sales. | 34,927 |
| Selling, general and administrative expenses | 11,185 |
| Credit card expenses. | 776 |
| Depreciation and amortization. | 1,409 |
| Earnings from continuing operations before interest expense and income taxes. | 4,323 |
| Net interest expense | 463 |
| Earnings from continuing operations before income taxes. | 3,860 |
| Provision for income taxes. | 1,452 |
| Net earnings. | $ 2,408 |

**M4-17. Compute RNOA, NOPAT Margin, and NOA Turnover (LO2)**

Selected balance sheet and income statement information for Target Corporation, a department store retailer, follows.

Target Corporation (TGT)

| Company ($ millions) | Ticker | 2006 Revenues | 2006 NOPAT | 2006 Net Operating Assets | 2005 Net Operating Assets |
| --- | --- | --- | --- | --- | --- |
| Target Corp. | TGT | $52,620 | $2,693 | $24,077 | $22,567 |

*a.* Compute its 2006 return on net operating assets (RNOA).

*b.* Disaggregate RNOA into net operating profit margin (NOPM) and net operating asset turnover (NOAT). Confirm that RNOA = NOPM × NOAT.

**M4-18.** **Identify and Compute Net Operating Assets** **(LO2)**

Following is the balance sheet for 3M Company. Identify and compute its net operating assets (NOA).

| 3M COMPANY AND SUBSIDIARIES | | |
|---|---|---|
| December 31 ($ millions, except per share amount) | 2005 | 2004 |
| **Assets** | | |
| Cash and cash equivalents . . . . . . . . . . . . . . . . . . . . . . . . . . . . . . . . . . | $ 1,072 | $ 2,757 |
| Accounts receivable—net of allowances of $73 and $83 . . . . . . . . . . . . | 2,838 | 2,792 |
| Inventories | | |
|     Finished goods . . . . . . . . . . . . . . . . . . . . . . . . . . . . . . . . . . . . . . . . | 1,050 | 947 |
|     Work in process . . . . . . . . . . . . . . . . . . . . . . . . . . . . . . . . . . . . . . | 706 | 614 |
|     Raw materials and supplies . . . . . . . . . . . . . . . . . . . . . . . . . . . . . . | 406 | 336 |
| Total inventories . . . . . . . . . . . . . . . . . . . . . . . . . . . . . . . . . . . . . . . . . | 2,162 | 1,897 |
| Other current assets . . . . . . . . . . . . . . . . . . . . . . . . . . . . . . . . . . . . . . | 1,043 | 1,274 |
| Total current assets . . . . . . . . . . . . . . . . . . . . . . . . . . . . . . . . . . . . . . | 7,115 | 8,720 |
| Investments . . . . . . . . . . . . . . . . . . . . . . . . . . . . . . . . . . . . . . . . . . . . | 272 | 227 |
| Property, plant and equipment . . . . . . . . . . . . . . . . . . . . . . . . . . . . . . | 16,127 | 16,290 |
| Less: Accumulated depreciation . . . . . . . . . . . . . . . . . . . . . . . . . . . . . | (10,534) | (10,579) |
| Property, plant and equipment—net . . . . . . . . . . . . . . . . . . . . . . . . . . | 5,593 | 5,711 |
| Goodwill . . . . . . . . . . . . . . . . . . . . . . . . . . . . . . . . . . . . . . . . . . . . . . . | 3,473 | 2,655 |
| Intangible assets—net . . . . . . . . . . . . . . . . . . . . . . . . . . . . . . . . . . . . | 486 | 277 |
| Prepaid pension and postretirement benefits . . . . . . . . . . . . . . . . . . . . | 2,905 | 2,591 |
| Other assets . . . . . . . . . . . . . . . . . . . . . . . . . . . . . . . . . . . . . . . . . . . | 669 | 527 |
| Total assets . . . . . . . . . . . . . . . . . . . . . . . . . . . . . . . . . . . . . . . . . . . | $20,513 | $20,708 |
| **Liabilities and Stockholders' Equity** | | |
| Short-term borrowings and current portion of long-term debt . . . . . . . . | $ 1,072 | $ 2,094 |
| Accounts payable . . . . . . . . . . . . . . . . . . . . . . . . . . . . . . . . . . . . . . . . | 1,256 | 1,168 |
| Accrued payroll . . . . . . . . . . . . . . . . . . . . . . . . . . . . . . . . . . . . . . . . . | 469 | 487 |
| Accrued income taxes . . . . . . . . . . . . . . . . . . . . . . . . . . . . . . . . . . . . | 989 | 867 |
| Other current liabilities . . . . . . . . . . . . . . . . . . . . . . . . . . . . . . . . . . . | 1,452 | 1,455 |
| Total current liabilities . . . . . . . . . . . . . . . . . . . . . . . . . . . . . . . . . . . | 5,238 | 6,071 |
| Long-term debt . . . . . . . . . . . . . . . . . . . . . . . . . . . . . . . . . . . . . . . . . | 1,309 | 727 |
| Other liabilities . . . . . . . . . . . . . . . . . . . . . . . . . . . . . . . . . . . . . . . . . | 3,866 | 3,532 |
| Total liabilities . . . . . . . . . . . . . . . . . . . . . . . . . . . . . . . . . . . . . . . . . | 10,413 | 10,330 |
| Stockholders' equity | | |
|     Common stock, par value $.01 per share . . . . . . . . . . . . . . . . . . . . . | 9 | 9 |
|       Share outstanding—2005: 754,538,387 | | |
|       Share outstanding—2004: 773,518,281 | | |
|     Capital in excess of par value . . . . . . . . . . . . . . . . . . . . . . . . . . . . . | 287 | 287 |
|     Retained earnings . . . . . . . . . . . . . . . . . . . . . . . . . . . . . . . . . . . . . . | 17,358 | 15,649 |
|     Treasury stock . . . . . . . . . . . . . . . . . . . . . . . . . . . . . . . . . . . . . . . . | (6,965) | (5,503) |
|     Unearned compensation . . . . . . . . . . . . . . . . . . . . . . . . . . . . . . . . . | (178) | (196) |
|     Accumulated other comprehensive income (loss) . . . . . . . . . . . . . . . | (411) | 132 |
| Stockholders' equity—net . . . . . . . . . . . . . . . . . . . . . . . . . . . . . . . . . | 10,100 | 10,378 |
| Total liabilities and stockholders' equity . . . . . . . . . . . . . . . . . . . . . . . | $20,513 | $20,708 |

**M4-19.** **Identify and Compute NOPAT** **(LO2)**

Following is the income statement for 3M Company. Compute its 2005 net operating profit after tax (NOPAT) assuming a 36.3% total statutory tax rate.

| 3M COMPANY AND SUBSIDIARIES | | | |
|---|---|---|---|
| Year ended December 31 ($ millions) | 2005 | 2004 | 2003 |
| Net sales. . . . . . . . . . . . . . . . . . . . . . . . . . . . . . . . . . . . . | $21,167 | $20,011 | $18,232 |
| Operating expenses | | | |
| Cost of sales . . . . . . . . . . . . . . . . . . . . . . . . . . . . . . . . | 10,381 | 9,958 | 9,285 |
| Selling, general and administrative expenses . . . . . . . . | 4,535 | 4,281 | 3,994 |
| Research, development and related expenses . . . . . . . | 1,242 | 1,194 | 1,147 |
| Other expense . . . . . . . . . . . . . . . . . . . . . . . . . . . . . | — | — | 93 |
| Total . . . . . . . . . . . . . . . . . . . . . . . . . . . . . . . . . . . | 16,158 | 15,433 | 14,519 |
| Operating income . . . . . . . . . . . . . . . . . . . . . . . . . . . . . | 5,009 | 4,578 | 3,713 |
| Interest expense and income | | | |
| Interest expense . . . . . . . . . . . . . . . . . . . . . . . . . . . . | 82 | 69 | 84 |
| Interest income . . . . . . . . . . . . . . . . . . . . . . . . . . . . . | (56) | (46) | (28) |
| Total . . . . . . . . . . . . . . . . . . . . . . . . . . . . . . . . . . . | 26 | 23 | 56 |
| Income before income taxes, minority interest and cumulative effect of accounting change . . . . . . . . . . . . . | 4,983 | 4,555 | 3,657 |
| Provision for income taxes . . . . . . . . . . . . . . . . . . . . . . . | 1,694 | 1,503 | 1,202 |
| Minority interest . . . . . . . . . . . . . . . . . . . . . . . . . . . . . . . | 55 | 62 | 52 |
| Income before cumulative effect of accounting change . . . | 3,234 | 2,990 | 2,403 |
| Cumulative effect of accounting change . . . . . . . . . . . . . . | (35) | — | — |
| Net income . . . . . . . . . . . . . . . . . . . . . . . . . . . . . . . . . . | $ 3,199 | $ 2,990 | $ 2,403 |

**M4-20. Compute RNOA, NOPAT Margin, and NOA Turnover** (LO2)

Selected balance sheet and income statement information for 3M Company, a manufacturing company, follows.

3M Company (MMM)

| Company ($ millions) | Ticker | 2005 Sales | 2005 NOPAT | 2005 Net Operating Assets | 2004 Net Operating Assets |
|---|---|---|---|---|---|
| 3M Company . . . . . . . . | MMM | $21,167 | $3,306 | $12,209 | $12,972 |

*a.* Compute 3M's 2005 return on net operating assets (RNOA).

*b.* Disaggregate RNOA into net operating profit margin (NOPM) and net operating asset turnover (NOAT). Confirm that RNOA = NOPM × NOAT.

**M4-21. Compute RNOA, NOPAT Margin and NOA Turnover for Competitors** (LO2)

Selected balance sheet and income statement information from Abercrombie & Fitch and TJX Companies, clothing retailers in the high-end and value-priced segments, respectively, follows.

Abercrombie & Fitch (ANF) and TJX Companies (TJX)

| Company ($ millions) | Ticker | 2006 Sales | 2006 NOPAT | 2006 Net Operating Assets | 2005 Net Operating Assets |
|---|---|---|---|---|---|
| Abercrombie & Fitch . . . | ANF | $ 2,784.7 | $324.7 | $ 615.6 | $ 700.5 |
| TJX Companies . . . . . . | TJX | 16,057.9 | 708.5 | 2,701.5 | 2,508.5 |

**Required**

*a.* Compute the 2006 return on net operating assets (RNOA) for both companies.

*b.* Disaggregate RNOA into net operating profit margin (NOPM) and net operating asset turnover (NOAT) for each company. Confirm that RNOA = NOPM × NOAT.

*c.* Discuss differences observed with respect to NOPM and NOAT and interpret these differences in light of each company's business model.

**M4-22. Compute and Interpret Liquidity and Solvency Ratios (LO3)**

Selected balance sheet and income statement information from Verizon follows.

| ($ millions) | 2005 | 2004 |
|---|---|---|
| Current assets . . . . . . . . . . . . . . . . . . . . . . . . | $ 16,448 | $ 19,479 |
| Current liabilities. . . . . . . . . . . . . . . . . . . . . . . | 25,063 | 23,129 |
| Total liabilities . . . . . . . . . . . . . . . . . . . . . . . . . | 101,696 | 103,345 |
| Equity . . . . . . . . . . . . . . . . . . . . . . . . . . . . . . | 66,434 | 62,613 |
| Earnings before interest and taxes. . . . . . . . . . | 12,787 | 12,496 |
| Interest expense. . . . . . . . . . . . . . . . . . . . . . . | 2,180 | 2,384 |
| Net cash flow from operating activities . . . . . . | 22,012 | 21,820 |

a. Compute the current ratio for each year and discuss any trend in liquidity. What additional information about the numbers used to calculate this ratio might be useful in helping us assess liquidity? Explain.

b. Compute times interest earned, the total-liabilities-to-equity, and the net cash from operating activities to total liabilities ratios for each year and discuss any trends for each. (The median total-liabilities-to-equity ratio for the telecommunications industry is 1.13.) Do you have any concerns about the extent of Verizon's financial leverage and the company's ability to meet interest obligations? Explain.

c. Verizon's capital expenditures are expected to increase substantially as it seeks to respond to competitive pressures to upgrade the quality of its communication infrastructure. Assess Verizon's liquidity and solvency in light of this strategic direction.

**M4-23. Compute Tax Rates on Operating Profit and NOPAT (LO2)**

Selected income statement information is presented below for Proctor & Gamble, McDonald's, Valero Energy and Abercrombie and Fitch.

| Company ($ millions) | Ticker | Net Operating Profit Before Tax | Net Nonoperating Expense (Revenue) Before Tax | Tax Expense | Statutory Tax Rate |
|---|---|---|---|---|---|
| Procter & Gamble. . . . . . | PG | $10,927.0 | $488.0 | $3,182.0 | 35.0% |
| McDonald's . . . . . . . . . . | MCD | $4,021.6 | $320.0 | $1,099.4 | 36.8% |
| Valero Energy . . . . . . . . . | VLO | $5,459.0 | $172.0 | $1,697.0 | 35.1% |
| Abercrombie and Fitch  . | ANF | $542.7 | (6.7) | $215.4 | 39.2% |

a. Compute the tax shield for each company: Net nonoperating expense (revenue) × Statutory rate.

b. Use the following equation to compute the tax rate on net operating profit for each company.

$$\text{Tax rate on operating profit} = \frac{\text{Tax expense} + (\text{Net nonoperating expense} \times \text{Statutory tax rate})}{\text{Net operating profit before tax}}$$

c. Compute NOPAT using the tax rates from part b.

# EXERCISES

**E4-24. Compute and Interpret RNOA, Profit Margin, and Asset Turnover of Competitors (LO2)**

Selected balance sheet and income statement information for department store retailers Target Corporation and Wal-Mart Stores follows.

| Company ($ millions) | Ticker | 2006 Sales | 2006 NOPAT | 2006 Net Operating Assets | 2005 Net Operating Assets |
|---|---|---|---|---|---|
| Target . . . . . . . . . . . . . | TGT | $ 52,620 | $ 2,693 | $24,077 | $22,567 |
| Wal-Mart. . . . . . . . . . . | WMT | 312,427 | 12,290 | 93,457 | 81,788 |

*87622,5*

a.  Compute the 2006 return on net operating assets (RNOA) for each company.
b.  Disaggregate RNOA into net operating profit margin (NOPM) and net operating asset turnover (NOAT) for each company.
c.  Discuss any differences in these ratios for each company. Your interpretation should reflect the distinct business strategies of each company.

**E4-25.   Compute, Disaggregate, and Interpret RNOA of Competitors   (LO2)**

Selected balance sheet and income statement information for the clothing retailers, Abercrombie & Fitch and The GAP, Inc., follows.

Abercrombie & Fitch (ANF)

The GAP, Inc. (GPS)

| Company ($ millions) | Ticker | 2006 Sales | 2006 NOPAT | 2006 Net Operating Assets | 2005 Net Operating Assets |
|---|---|---|---|---|---|
| Abercrombie & Fitch. . . | ANF | $ 2,785 | $ 324.7 | $ 615.7 | $ 700.5 |
| The GAP. . . . . . . . . . . | GPS | 16,023 | 1,047.7 | 4,986.0 | 6,005.0 |

a.  Compute the 2006 return on net operating assets (RNOA) for each company.
b.  Disaggregate RNOA into net operating profit margin (NOPM) and net operating asset turnover (NOAT) for each company.
c.  Discuss any differences in these ratios for each company. Your interpretation should reflect the distinct business strategies of each company.

**E4-26.   Compute, Disaggregate, and Interpret RNOA of Competitors   (LO2)**

Selected balance sheet and income statement information for the drug retailers CVS Corporation and Walgreen Company follows.

CVS Corporation (CVS)

Walgreen Company (WAG)

| Company ($ millions) | Ticker | 2006 Sales | 2006 NOPAT | 2006 Net Operating Assets | 2005 Net Operating Assets |
|---|---|---|---|---|---|
| CVS Corp. . . . . . . . . . | CVS | $37,006 | $1,292 | $10,520 | $9,829 |
| Walgreen Company . . . | WAG | 42,202 | 1,539 | 8,395 | 6,888 |

*10175*
*7642*

a.  Compute the 2006 return on net operating assets (RNOA) for each company.
b.  Disaggregate RNOA into net operating profit margin (NOPM) and net operating asset turnover (NOAT) for each company.
c.  Discuss any differences in these ratios for each company. Identify the factor(s) that drives the differences in RNOA observed from your analyses in parts *a* and *b*.

**E4-27.   Compute, Disaggregate, and Interpret ROE and RNOA   (LO1)**

Selected fiscal year balance sheet and income statement information for the computer chip maker, Intel, follows ($ millions).

Intel (INTC)

| Company | Ticker | 2005 Sales | 2005 Net Income | 2005 Net Operating Profit After Tax | 2005 Net Operating Assets | 2004 Net Operating Assets | 2005 Stockholders' Equity | 2004 Stockholders' Equity |
|---|---|---|---|---|---|---|---|---|
| Intel. . . . . . . | INTC | $38,826 | $8,664 | $8,487 | $28,481 | $27,499 | $36,182 | $38,579 |

*27 990*        *37280,5*

a. Compute the 2005 return on equity (ROE) and the 2005 return on net operating assets (RNOA).
b. Disaggregate RNOA into net operating profit margin (NOPM) and net operating asset turnover (NOAT).
c. Compute the percentage of RNOA to ROE, and infer the return from nonoperating activities. How do we interpret this finding?

**E4-28. Compute, Disaggregate and Interpret ROE and RNOA (LO1)**

Staples (SPLS)

Selected balance sheet and income statement information from Staples, Inc. follows ($ millions).

| Company | Ticker | 2006 Sales | 2006 Net Income | 2006 Net Operating Profit After Tax | 2006 Net Operating Assets | 2005 Net Operating Assets | 2006 Stockholders' Equity | 2005 Stockholders' Equity |
|---------|--------|-----------|-----------------|-------------------------------------|---------------------------|---------------------------|---------------------------|---------------------------|
| Staples . . . . | SPLS | $16,079 | $834 | $832 | $4,367 | $4,202 | $4,425 | $4,115 |

a. Compute the 2006 return on equity (ROE) and 2006 return on net operating assets (RNOA)
b. Disaggregate RNOA into net operating profit margin (NOPM) and net operating asset turnover (NOAT).
c. Compute the percentage of RNOA to ROE. What inferences do we draw from NOPM compared to NOAT?

**E4-29. Compute, Disaggregate and Interpret ROE and RNOA (LO2)**

Intuit (INTU)

Selected balance sheet and income statement information from the software company, Intuit, Inc., follows ($ millions).

| Company | Ticker | 2005 Sales | 2005 Net Income | 2005 Net Operating Profit After Tax | 2005 Net Operating Assets | 2004 Net Operating Assets | 2005 Stockholders' Equity | 2004 Stockholders' Equity |
|---------|--------|-----------|-----------------|-------------------------------------|---------------------------|---------------------------|---------------------------|---------------------------|
| Intuit . . . . . . | INTU | $2,038 | $382 | $330 | $651 | $680 | $1,696 | $1,822 |

a. Compute the 2005 return on equity (ROE) and 2005 return on net operating assets (RNOA)
b. Disaggregate the RNOA from part a into net operating profit margin (NOPM) and net operating asset turnover (NOAT).
c. Compute the percentage of RNOA to ROE. What explanation can we offer for the relation between ROE and RNOA observed and for Intuit's use of stockholders' equity?

**E4-30. Compute and Interpret Liquidity and Solvency Ratios (LO3)**

Comcast Corporation (CMCSA)

Selected balance sheet and income statement information from Comcast Corporation for 2003 through 2005 follows ($ millions).

| | Total Current Assets | Total Current Liabilities | Pretax Income | Interest Expense | Total Liabilities | Stockholders' Equity |
|---|---------------------|---------------------------|---------------|------------------|-------------------|----------------------|
| 2003 . . . . | $5,403 | $9,654 | $ (137) | $2,018 | $67,105 | $42,054 |
| 2004 . . . . | 3,535 | 8,635 | 1,810 | 1,807 | 62,804 | 41,890 |
| 2005 . . . . | 2,594 | 6,269 | 1,880 | 1,796 | 62,270 | 40,876 |

a. Compute the current ratio for each year and discuss any trend in liquidity. Do you believe the company is sufficiently liquid? Explain. What additional information about the accounting numbers comprising this ratio might be useful in helping you assess liquidity? Explain.
b. Compute times interest earned and the total-liabilities-to-stockholders' equity ratio for each year and discuss any trends for each.
c. What is your overall assessment of the company's liquidity and solvency from the analyses in (a) and (b)? Explain.

**E4-31.** **Compute and Interpret Liquidity and Solvency Ratios** (LO3)

Selected balance sheet and income statement information from Verizon Communications, Inc., for 2003 through 2005 follows ($ millions).

Verizon Communications, Inc. (VZ)

| | Total Current Assets | Total Current Liabilities | Pretax Income | Interest Expense | Total Liabilities | Stockholders' Equity |
|---|---|---|---|---|---|---|
| 2003 . . . . | $18,293 | $26,570 | $ 6,344 | $2,797 | $108,154 | $57,814 |
| 2004 . . . . | 19,479 | 23,129 | 12,521 | 2,384 | 103,345 | 62,613 |
| 2005 . . . . | 16,448 | 25,063 | 13,652 | 2,180 | 74,942 | 66,434 |

a.  Compute the current ratio for each year and discuss any trend in liquidity. Do you believe the company is sufficiently liquid? Explain. What additional information about the accounting numbers comprising this ratio might be useful in helping you assess liquidity? Explain.

b.  Compute times interest earned and the total-liabilities-to-stockholders' equity ratio for each year and discuss any trends for each.

c.  What is your overall assessment of the company's liquidity and solvency from the analyses in (a) and (b)? Explain.

**E4-32.** **Compute and Interpret Solvency Ratios for Business Segments** (LO2)

Selected balance sheet and income statement information from General Electric Company and its two principle business segments (Industrial and Financial) for 2005 follows.

General Electric (GE)

| ($ millions) | Pretax Income | Interest Expense | Total Liabilities | Stockholders' Equity |
|---|---|---|---|---|
| Industrial segment . . . . . . . . . . . . . . . . | $21,025 | $ 1,432 | $ 74,599 | $109,354 |
| Financial segment . . . . . . . . . . . . . . . . | 10,246 | 14,308 | 487,542 | 50,815 |
| Other. . . . . . . . . . . . . . . . . . . . . . . . . | (9,142)[1] | (553)[2] | (6,207)[2] | |
| General Electric Consolidated . . . . . . . . | 22,129 | 15,187 | 555,934 | 109,354[3] |

[1] Includes unallocated corporate operating activities.

[2] Includes intercompany loans and related interest expense; these are deducted (eliminated) in preparing consolidated financial statements.

[3] The consolidated equity equals the equity of the parent (industrial); this is explained in Module 7.

a.  Compute times interest earned and the total-liabilities-to-stockholders' equity ratio for 2005 for its two business segments (Industrial and Financial) and the company as a whole

b.  What is your overall assessment of the company's solvency? Explain. What differences do you observe between the two business segments? Do these differences correspond to your prior expectations given each company's business model?

c.  Discuss the implications of the analysis of consolidated financial statements and the additional insight that can be gained from a more in-depth analysis of primary business segments.

**E4-33.**[B] **Direct Computation of Nonoperating Return** (LO1)

Refer to the income statement and balance sheet of Lowe's Companies, Inc., from Mid-Module Reviews 1 and 2.

Lowe's Companies, Inc. (LOW)

**Required**

a.  Compute the FLEV and SPREAD for Lowe's for 2006.

b.  Use RNOA from Mid-Module review 2, and the FLEV and SPREAD from part a, to compute ROE. Compare the ROE calculated in this exercise with the ROE we compute in the Mid-Module review 2.

**E4-34.** **Compute Tax Rates on Operating Profit and NOPAT** **(LO1)**

*The TJX Companies, Inc.*

The income statement for The TJX Companies, Inc., follows.

| THE TJX COMPANIES, INC. Consolidated Statements of Income | | | |
|---|---|---|---|
| Fiscal Year Ended ($ Thousands) | January 28, 2006 | January 29, 2005 | January 31, 2004 |
| Net sales. . . . . . . . . . . . . . . . . . . . . . . . . . . . . . . . . . . . | $16,057,935 | $14,913,483 | $13,327,938 |
| Cost of sales, including buying and occupancy costs. . . . | 12,295,016 | 11,398,656 | 10,101,279 |
| Selling, general and administrative expenses . . . . . . . . . . | 2,723,960 | 2,500,119 | 2,212,669 |
| Interest expense, net . . . . . . . . . . . . . . . . . . . . . . . . . . . | 29,632 | 25,757 | 27,252 |
| Income before provision for income taxes. . . . . . . . . . . . . | 1,009,327 | 988,951 | 986,738 |
| Provision for income taxes. . . . . . . . . . . . . . . . . . . . . . . . | 318,904 | 379,252 | 377,326 |
| Net income. . . . . . . . . . . . . . . . . . . . . . . . . . . . . . . . . . . | $ 690,423 | $ 609,699 | $ 609,412 |

*a.* Compute the tax shield for 2006 and 2005. Assume that the combined statutory tax rate is 38% for both years.

*b.* Use the following equation to compute TJX's tax rate on operating profit for both years.

$$\text{Tax rate on operating profit} = \frac{\text{Tax expense} + (\text{Net nonoperating expense} \times \text{Statutory tax rate})}{\text{Operating profit before taxes}}$$

*c.* Compute NOPAT using the tax rate from part *b*, for 2006 and 2005.

# PROBLEMS

**P4-35.** **Analysis and Interpretation of Profitability** **(LO1, 2)**

*Lockheed Martin Corporation (LMT)*

Balance sheets and income statements for Lockheed Martin Corporation (LMT) follow. Refer to these financial statements to answer the requirements.

| Income Statement (In millions) | Year Ended December 31, | | |
|---|---|---|---|
| | 2005 | 2004 | 2003 |
| Net sales | | | |
| Products . . . . . . . . . . . . . . . . . . . . . . | $31,518 | $30,202 | $27,290 |
| Service . . . . . . . . . . . . . . . . . . . . . . | 5,695 | 5,324 | 4,534 |
| | 37,213 | 35,526 | 31,824 |
| Cost of sales | | | |
| Products . . . . . . . . . . . . . . . . . . . . . . | 28,800 | 27,879 | 25,306 |
| Services . . . . . . . . . . . . . . . . . . . . . . | 5,073 | 4,765 | 4,099 |
| Unallocated corporate costs . . . . . . . | 803 | 914 | 443 |
| | 34,676 | 33,558 | 29,848 |
| | 2,537 | 1,968 | 1,976 |
| Other income and exenses, net . . . . . . . | 449 | 121 | 43 |
| Operating profit . . . . . . . . . . . . . . . . . . | 2,986 | 2,089 | 2,019 |
| Interest expense. . . . . . . . . . . . . . . . . . | 370 | 425 | 487 |
| Earnings before taxes. . . . . . . . . . . . . . | 2,616 | 1,664 | 1,532 |
| Income tax expense. . . . . . . . . . . . . . . | 791 | 398 | 479 |
| Net earnings. . . . . . . . . . . . . . . . . . . . . | $ 1,825 | $ 1,266 | $ 1,053 |

| Balance Sheet (In millions) | December 31, 2005 | December 31, 2004 |
|---|---|---|
| **Assets** | | |
| Cash and cash equivalents . . . . . . . . . . . . . . . . . . . | $ 2,244 | $ 1,060 |
| Short-term investments . . . . . . . . . . . . . . . . . . . . . . | 429 | 396 |
| Receivables . . . . . . . . . . . . . . . . . . . . . . . . . . . . . . | 4,579 | 4,094 |
| Inventories . . . . . . . . . . . . . . . . . . . . . . . . . . . . . . . | 1,921 | 1,864 |
| Deferred income taxes . . . . . . . . . . . . . . . . . . . . . . | 861 | 982 |
| Other current assets . . . . . . . . . . . . . . . . . . . . . . . . | 495 | 557 |
| Total current assets . . . . . . . . . . . . . . . . . . . . . . . | 10,529 | 8,953 |
| Property, plant and equipment net . . . . . . . . . . . . . | 3,924 | 3,599 |
| Investments in equity securities . . . . . . . . . . . . . . . | 196 | 812 |
| Goodwill . . . . . . . . . . . . . . . . . . . . . . . . . . . . . . . . . | 8,447 | 7,892 |
| Purchased intangibles, net . . . . . . . . . . . . . . . . . . . | 560 | 672 |
| Prepaid pension asset . . . . . . . . . . . . . . . . . . . . . . | 1,360 | 1,030 |
| Other assets . . . . . . . . . . . . . . . . . . . . . . . . . . . . . . | 2,728 | 2,596 |
| Total assets . . . . . . . . . . . . . . . . . . . . . . . . . . . . . . | $27,744 | $25,554 |
| **Liabilities and stockholders' equity** | | |
| Accounts payable . . . . . . . . . . . . . . . . . . . . . . . . . . | $ 1,998 | $ 1,726 |
| Customer advances and amounts in excess of costs incurred . . . . . . . . . . . . . . . . . . . | 4,331 | 4,028 |
| Salaries, benefits and payroll taxes . . . . . . . . . . . . | 1,475 | 1,346 |
| Current maturities of long-term debt . . . . . . . . . . . | 202 | 15 |
| Other current liabilities . . . . . . . . . . . . . . . . . . . . . . | 1,422 | 1,451 |
| Total current liabilities . . . . . . . . . . . . . . . . . . . . . . | 9,428 | 8,566 |
| Long-term debt . . . . . . . . . . . . . . . . . . . . . . . . . . . | 4,784 | 5,104 |
| Accrued pension liabilities . . . . . . . . . . . . . . . . . . . | 2,097 | 1,660 |
| Other postretirement benefit liabilities . . . . . . . . . . | 1,277 | 1,236 |
| Other liabilities . . . . . . . . . . . . . . . . . . . . . . . . . . . . | 2,291 | 1,967 |
| Stockholders' equity | | |
| Common stock, $1 par value per share . . . . . . . . | 432 | 438 |
| Additional paid-in capital . . . . . . . . . . . . . . . . . . . | 1,724 | 2,223 |
| Retained earnings . . . . . . . . . . . . . . . . . . . . . . . . | 7,278 | 5,915 |
| Accumulated other comprehensive loss . . . . . . . | (1,553) | (1,532) |
| Other . . . . . . . . . . . . . . . . . . . . . . . . . . . . . . . . . . | (14) | (23) |
| Total stockholders' equity . . . . . . . . . . . . . . . . . . . | 7,867 | 7,021 |
| Total liabilities and stockholders' equity . . . . . . . . . | $27,744 | $25,554 |

**Required**

a. Compute net operating profit after tax (NOPAT) for 2005 and 2004. Assume that combined federal and state statutory tax rates are 37.2% for 2005 and 37.9% for 2004.

b. Compute net operating assets (NOA) for 2005 and 2004.

c. Compute and disaggregate Lockheed Martin's RNOA into net operating profit margin (NOPM) and net operating asset turnover (NOAT) for 2005 and 2004; the 2003 NOA is $11,664 million. Has its RNOA improved or worsened? Explain why.

d. Compute net nonoperating obligations (NNO) for 2005 and 2004. Confirm the relation: NOA = NNO + Stockholders' equity.

e. Compute return on equity (ROE) for 2005 and 2004. (Stockholders' equity in 2003 is $6,756 million.)

f. What is Lockheed Martin's nonoperating return component of ROE for 2005 and 2004?

g. Comment on the difference between ROE and RNOA. What inference can we draw from this comparison?

**P4-36.**    **Analysis and Interpretation of Liquidity and Solvency**    **(LO3)**

Refer to the financial information of Lockheed Martin (LMT) in P4-35 to answer the following requirements.

**Required**

a.    Compute Lockheed Martin's current ratio and quick ratio for 2005 and 2004. Comment on any observed trends.

b.    Compute times interest earned and total-liabilities-to-stockholders' equity ratios for 2005 and 2004. Comment on any trends observed.

c.    Summarize your findings in a conclusion about the company's liquidity and solvency. Do you have any concerns about its ability to meet its debt obligations?

**P4-37.**[B]    **Direct Computation of Nonoperating Return**    **(LO1, 2)**

Refer to the financial information of Lockheed Martin (LMT) in P4-35 to answer the following requirements.

a.    Compute Lockheed Martin's financial leverage (FLEV) and Spread for 2005. Recall that NNE = NOPAT − Net income.

b.    Assume that Lockheed Martin's return on equity (ROE) for 2005 is 24.52% and its return on net operating assets (RNOA) is 17.76%. Confirm computations to yield the relation: ROE = RNOA + (FLEV × Spread).

c.    What do your computations of the nonoperating return imply about the company's use of borrowed funds?

**P4-38.**    **Analysis and Interpretation of Profitability**    **(LO1, 2)**

Balance sheets and income statements for Target Corporation (TGT) follow. Refer to these financial statements to answer the requirements.

| Income Statement | | | |
| --- | --- | --- | --- |
| **For Years Ended (In millions)** | **2006** | **2005** | **2004** |
| Sales. . . . . . . . . . . . . . . . . . . . . . . . . . . . . . . . . . . . . . . . . . . . . . . . | $51,271 | $45,682 | $40,928 |
| Net credit card revenues . . . . . . . . . . . . . . . . . . . . . . . . . . . . . . . . . | 1,349 | 1,157 | 1,097 |
| Total revenues. . . . . . . . . . . . . . . . . . . . . . . . . . . . . . . . . . . . . . . | 52,620 | 46,839 | 42,025 |
| Cost of sales. . . . . . . . . . . . . . . . . . . . . . . . . . . . . . . . . . . . . . . . . . | 34,927 | 31,445 | 28,389 |
| Selling, general and administrative expenses . . . . . . . . . . . . . . . . . . . . | 11,185 | 9,797 | 8,657 |
| Credit card expenses . . . . . . . . . . . . . . . . . . . . . . . . . . . . . . . . . . . . . | 776 | 737 | 722 |
| Depreciation and amortization . . . . . . . . . . . . . . . . . . . . . . . . . . . . . . . | 1,409 | 1,259 | 1,098 |
| Earnings from continuing operations before interest expense and income taxes . . . . . . . . . . . . . . . . . . . . . . . . . . . . . . . . . . . . | 4,323 | 3,601 | 3,159 |
| Net interest expense . . . . . . . . . . . . . . . . . . . . . . . . . . . . . . . . . . . . . | 463 | 570 | 556 |
| Earnings from continuing operations before income taxes . . . . . . . . . . . . . . . | 3,860 | 3,031 | 2,603 |
| Provision for income taxes. . . . . . . . . . . . . . . . . . . . . . . . . . . . . . . . . . | 1,452 | 1,146 | 984 |
| Earnings from continuing operations . . . . . . . . . . . . . . . . . . . . . . . . . . . . | 2,408 | 1,885 | 1,619 |
| Earnings from discontinued operations, net of taxes of $6 and $116 . . . . . . . . | — | 75 | 190 |
| Gain on disposal of discontinued operations, net of taxes of $761 . . . . . . . . . | — | 1,238 | — |
| Net earnings. . . . . . . . . . . . . . . . . . . . . . . . . . . . . . . . . . . . . . . . . . . | $ 2,408 | $ 3,198 | $ 1,809 |

| Balance Sheet | | |
|---|---|---|
| **(In millions)** | **January 28, 2006** | **January 28, 2005** |
| **Assets** | | |
| Cash and cash equivalents . . . . . . . . . . . . . . . . . . . | $ 1,648 | $ 2,245 |
| Accountings receivable, net. . . . . . . . . . . . . . . . . . | 5,666 | 5,069 |
| Inventory. . . . . . . . . . . . . . . . . . . . . . . . . . . . . . . | 5,838 | 5,384 |
| Other current assets. . . . . . . . . . . . . . . . . . . . . . . | 1,253 | 1,224 |
| Total current assets . . . . . . . . . . . . . . . . . . . . . . | 14,405 | 13,922 |
| Property and equipment | | |
| Land . . . . . . . . . . . . . . . . . . . . . . . . . . . . . . . . | 4,449 | 3,804 |
| Buildings and improvements . . . . . . . . . . . . . . . | 14,174 | 12,518 |
| Fixtures and equipment . . . . . . . . . . . . . . . . . . | 3,219 | 2,990 |
| Computer hardware and software . . . . . . . . . . . | 2,214 | 1,998 |
| Construction-in-progress . . . . . . . . . . . . . . . . . | 1,158 | 962 |
| Accumulated depreciation . . . . . . . . . . . . . . . . . | (6,176) | (5,412) |
| Property and equipment, net . . . . . . . . . . . . . . | 19,038 | 16,860 |
| Other noncurrent assets. . . . . . . . . . . . . . . . . . . | 1,552 | 1,511 |
| Total assets. . . . . . . . . . . . . . . . . . . . . . . . . . . | $34,995 | $32,293 |
| **Liabilities and shareholders' investment** | | |
| Accounts payable. . . . . . . . . . . . . . . . . . . . . . . . | $ 6,268 | $ 5,779 |
| Accrued liabilities . . . . . . . . . . . . . . . . . . . . . . . . | 2,193 | 1,633 |
| Income taxes payable . . . . . . . . . . . . . . . . . . . . | 374 | 304 |
| Current portion of long-term debt | | |
| and notes payable . . . . . . . . . . . . . . . . . . . . . | 753 | 504 |
| Total current liabilities. . . . . . . . . . . . . . . . . . . . | 9,588 | 8,220 |
| Long-term debt . . . . . . . . . . . . . . . . . . . . . . . . . . | 9,119 | 9,034 |
| Deferred income taxes. . . . . . . . . . . . . . . . . . . . | 851 | 973 |
| Other noncurrent liabilities . . . . . . . . . . . . . . . . . | 1,232 | 1,037 |
| Shareholders' investment | | |
| Common stock. . . . . . . . . . . . . . . . . . . . . . . . . . | 73 | 74 |
| Additional paid-in-capital. . . . . . . . . . . . . . . . . . . | 2,121 | 1,810 |
| Retained earnings . . . . . . . . . . . . . . . . . . . . . . . | 12,013 | 11,148 |
| Accumulated other comprehensive income. . . . . . . | (2) | (3) |
| Total shareholders' investment. . . . . . . . . . . . . . | 14,205 | 13,029 |
| Total liabilities and shareholders' investment. . . . . . | $34,995 | $32,293 |

**Required**

a. Compute net operating profit after tax (NOPAT) for 2006 and 2005. Assume that the combined federal and state statutory tax rates for both 2006 and 2005 are 38.3%.

b. Compute net operating assets (NOA) for 2006 and 2005.

c. Compute and disaggregate Target's RNOA into net operating profit margin (NOPM) and net operating asset turnover (NOAT) for 2006 and 2005; the 2004 NOA is $21,307 million. Comment on the drivers of the improvement in Target's RNOA.

d. Compute net nonoperating obligations (NNO) for 2006 and 2005. Confirm the relation: NOA = NNO + Stockholders' equity.

e. Compute return on equity (ROE) for 2006 and 2005; the 2004 stockholders' equity is $11,132 million.

f. Infer the nonoperating return component of ROE for both 2006 and 2005.

g. Comment on the difference between ROE and RNOA. What does this relation suggest about Target's use of equity capital?

**P4-39. Analysis and Interpretation of Liquidity and Solvency (LO3)**

Refer to the financial information of Target Corporation (TGT) in P4-38 to answer the following requirements.

**Required**

a. Compute Target's current ratio and quick ratio for 2006 and 2005. Comment on any observed trends.
b. Compute Target's times interest earned and its total-liabilities-to-stockholders' equity ratios for 2006 and 2005. Comment on any trends observed.
c. Summarize your findings in a conclusion about the company's liquidity and solvency. Do you have any concerns about Target's ability to meet its debt obligations?

**P4-40.[B] Direct Computation of Nonoperating Return (LO1)**

Refer to the financial information of Target Corporation (TGT) in P4-38 to answer the following requirements.

**Required**

a. Compute Target's financial leverage (FLEV) and Spread for 2006; recall, NNE = NOPAT − Net income.
b. Assume that Target's return on equity (ROE) for 2006 is 17.68% and its return on net operating assets (RNOA) is 11.55%. Confirm computations to yield the relation: ROE = RNOA + (FLEV × Spread).
c. What do your computations of the nonoperating return in parts a and b imply about the company's use of borrowed funds?

**P4-41. Analysis and Interpretation of Profitability (LO1, 2)**

Balance sheets and income statements for Intel Corporation (INTC) follow. Refer to these financial statements to answer the requirements.

| INTEL CORPORATION Consolidated Statements of Income | | | |
| --- | --- | --- | --- |
| Three Years Ended December 31 (In Millions) | 2005 | 2004 | 2003 |
| Net revenue | $38,826 | $34,209 | $30,141 |
| Cost of sales | 15,777 | 14,463 | 13,047 |
| Gross margin | 23,049 | 19,746 | 17,094 |
| Research and development | 5,145 | 4,778 | 4,360 |
| Marketing, general and administrative | 5,688 | 4,659 | 4,278 |
| Impairment of goodwill | — | — | 617 |
| Amortization and impairment of acquisition-related intangibles and costs | 126 | 179 | 301 |
| Purchased in-process research and development | — | — | 5 |
| Operating expenses | 10,959 | 9,616 | 9,561 |
| Operating income | 12,090 | 10,130 | 7,533 |
| Losses on equity securities, net | (45) | (2) | (283) |
| Interest and other, net | 565 | 289 | 192 |
| Income before taxes | 12,610 | 10,417 | 7,442 |
| Provision for taxes | 3,946 | 2,901 | 1,801 |
| Net income | $ 8,664 | $ 7,516 | $ 5,641 |

## INTEL CORPORATION
### Consolidated Balance Sheets

| December 31 (In Millions, except par value) | 2005 | 2004 |
|---|---|---|
| **Assets** | | |
| Cash and cash equivalents | $ 7,324 | $ 8,407 |
| Short-term investments | 3,990 | 5,654 |
| Trading assets | 1,458 | 3,111 |
| Accounts receivable, net of allowance for doubtful accounts of $64 ($43 in 2004) | 3,914 | 2,999 |
| Inventories | 3,126 | 2,621 |
| Deferred tax assets | 1,149 | 979 |
| Other current assets | 233 | 287 |
| Total current assets | 21,194 | 24,058 |
| Property, plant and equipment, net | 17,111 | 15,768 |
| Marketable strategic equity securities | 537 | 656 |
| Other long-term investments | 4,135 | 2,563 |
| Goodwill | 3,873 | 3,719 |
| Deferred taxes and other assets | 1,464 | 1,379 |
| Total assets | $48,314 | $48,143 |
| **Liabilities and stockholders' equity** | | |
| Short-term debt | $ 313 | $ 201 |
| Accounts payable | 2,249 | 1,943 |
| Accrued compensation and benefits | 2,110 | 1,858 |
| Accrued advertising | 1,160 | 894 |
| Deferred income on shipments to distributors | 632 | 592 |
| Other accrued liabilities | 810 | 1,355 |
| Income taxes payable | 1,960 | 1,163 |
| Total current liabilities | 9,234 | 8,006 |
| Long-term debt | 2,106 | 703 |
| Deferred tax liabilities | 703 | 855 |
| Other long-term liabilities | 89 | — |
| Stockholders' equity | | |
| Perferred stock, $0.001 par value, 50 shares authorized; none issued | — | — |
| Common stock, $0.001 par value, 10,000 shares authorized; 5,919 issued and outstanding (6,253 in 2004) and capital in excess of par value | 6,245 | 6,143 |
| Acquisition-related unearned stock compensation | — | (4) |
| Accumulated other comprehensive income | 127 | 152 |
| Retained earnings | 29,810 | 32,288 |
| Total stockholders' equity | 36,182 | 38,579 |
| Total liabilities and stockholders' equity | $48,314 | $48,143 |

**Required**

a.   Compute net operating profit after tax (NOPAT) for 2005 and 2004. Assume that the combined federal and state statutory tax rates are 36.3% for 2005 and 34.6% for 2004.

b.   Compute net operating assets (NOA) for 2005 and 2004. (*Hint:* Assume that trading assets and other long-term investments are investments in marketable securities and are therefore, nonoperating assets. Assume that marketable strategic equity securities are operating investments.)

c.   Compute RNOA and disaggregate it into net operating profit margin (NOPM) and net operating asset turnover (NOAT) for 2005 and 2004; the 2003 NOA is $28,947 million. Comment on the drivers of RNOA.

d.   Compute net nonoperating obligations (NNO) for 2005 and 2004. Confirm the relation: NOA = NNO + Stockholders' equity.

e.   Compute return on equity (ROE) for 2005 and 2004; the 2003 stockholders' equity is $37,846 million.

f.   Infer the nonoperating return component of ROE for both 2005 and 2004.

g.   Comment on the difference between ROE and RNOA. What does this relation suggest about Intel's use of equity capital?

**P4-42.   Analysis and Interpretation of Profitability   (LO1, 2)**

Merck & Co. (MRK)

Balance sheets and income statements for Merck & Co. (MRK) follow. Refer to these financial statements to answer the requirements. (Note: This problem requires computation of ROCE in the presence of minority interest.)

### MERCK & CO., INC. AND SUBSIDIARIES
#### Consolidated Statement of Income

| Years Ended December 31 ($ millions, except per share amounts) | 2005 | 2004 | 2003 |
|---|---|---|---|
| Sales | $22,011.9 | $22,938.6 | $22,485.9 |
| Costs, expenses and other | | | |
| Materials and production | 5,149.6 | 4,959.8 | 4,436.9 |
| Marketing and administrative | 7,155.5 | 7,238.7 | 6,200.3 |
| Research and development | 3,848.0 | 4,010.2 | 3,279.9 |
| Restructuring costs | 322.2 | 107.6 | 194.6 |
| Equity income from affiliates | (1,717.1) | (1,008.2) | (474.2) |
| Other (income) expense, net | (110.2) | (344.0) | (203.2) |
| | 14,648.0 | 14,964.1 | 13,434.3 |
| Income from continuing operations before taxes | 7,363.9 | 7,974.5 | 9,051.6 |
| Taxes on income | 2,732.6 | 2,161.1 | 2,462.0 |
| Income from continuing operations | 4,631.3 | 5,813.4 | 6,589.6 |
| Income from discontinued operations, net of taxes | — | — | 241.3 |
| Net income | $ 4,631.3 | $ 5,813.4 | $ 6.830.9 |

### MERCK & CO., INC. AND SUBSIDIARIES
#### Consolidated Balance Sheet

| December 31 ($ millions) | 2005 | 2004 |
|---|---|---|
| **Assets** | | |
| Cash and cash equivalents | $ 9,585.3 | $ 2,878.8 |
| Short-term investments | 6,052.3 | 4,211.1 |
| Accounts receivable | 2,927.3 | 3,627.7 |
| Inventories (excludes inventories of $753.8 in 2005 and $638.7 in 2004 classified in Other assets) | 1,658.1 | 1,898.7 |
| Prepaid expenses and taxes | 826.3 | 858.9 |
| Total current assets | 21,049.3 | 13,475.2 |

*continued*

**MERCK & CO., INC. AND SUBSIDIARIES**
**Consolidated Balance Sheet**

| December 31 ($ millions) | 2005 | 2004 |
|---|---|---|
| Investments . . . . . . . . . . . . . . . . . . . . . . . . . . . . . . . . . . . . . . . . . . . . . . . . . . . | 1,107.9 | 6,727.1 |
| Property, plant and equipment (at cost) | | |
| Land . . . . . . . . . . . . . . . . . . . . . . . . . . . . . . . . . . . . . . . . . . . . . . . . . . . . . | 433.0 | 366.6 |
| Buildings. . . . . . . . . . . . . . . . . . . . . . . . . . . . . . . . . . . . . . . . . . . . . . . . . . | 9,479.6 | 8,874.3 |
| Machinery, equipment and office furnishings. . . . . . . . . . . . . . . . . . . . . . . . . . | 12,785.2 | 11,926.1 |
| Construction in progress . . . . . . . . . . . . . . . . . . . . . . . . . . . . . . . . . . . . . . | 1,015.5 | 1,641.6 |
| | 23,713.3 | 22,808.6 |
| Less allowance for depreciation. . . . . . . . . . . . . . . . . . . . . . . . . . . . . . . . . . . | 9,315.1 | 8,094.9 |
| | 14,398.2 | 14,713.7 |
| Goodwill . . . . . . . . . . . . . . . . . . . . . . . . . . . . . . . . . . . . . . . . . . . . . . . . . . . | 1,085.7 | 1,085.7 |
| Other intangibles, net . . . . . . . . . . . . . . . . . . . . . . . . . . . . . . . . . . . . . . . . . . | 518.7 | 679.2 |
| Other assets . . . . . . . . . . . . . . . . . . . . . . . . . . . . . . . . . . . . . . . . . . . . . . . | 6,686.0 | 5,891.9 |
| Total assets. . . . . . . . . . . . . . . . . . . . . . . . . . . . . . . . . . . . . . . . . . . . . . . . . | $44,845.8 | $42,572.8 |
| **Liabilities and Stockholders' Equity** | | |
| Loans payable and current portion of long-term debt . . . . . . . . . . . . . . . . . . . . . | $ 2,972.0 | $ 2,181.2 |
| Trade accounts payable . . . . . . . . . . . . . . . . . . . . . . . . . . . . . . . . . . . . . . . . | 471.1 | 421.4 |
| Accrued and other current liabilities. . . . . . . . . . . . . . . . . . . . . . . . . . . . . . . . | 5,381.2 | 5,288.1 |
| Income taxes payable . . . . . . . . . . . . . . . . . . . . . . . . . . . . . . . . . . . . . . . . | 3,649.2 | 3,012.3 |
| Dividends payable . . . . . . . . . . . . . . . . . . . . . . . . . . . . . . . . . . . . . . . . . . . | 830.0 | 841.1 |
| Total current liabilities. . . . . . . . . . . . . . . . . . . . . . . . . . . . . . . . . . . . . . . . . | 13,303.5 | 11,744.1 |
| Long-term debt . . . . . . . . . . . . . . . . . . . . . . . . . . . . . . . . . . . . . . . . . . . . . | 5,125.6 | 4,691.5 |
| Deferred income taxes and noncurrent liabilities. . . . . . . . . . . . . . . . . . . . . . . | 6,092.9 | 6,442.1 |
| Minority interests . . . . . . . . . . . . . . . . . . . . . . . . . . . . . . . . . . . . . . . . . . . | 2,407.2 | 2,406.9 |
| Stockholders' equity | | |
| Common stock, one cent par value | | |
| Authorized—5,400,000,000 shares | | |
| Issued—2,976,223,337 shares—2005 | | |
| —2,976,230,393 shares—2004 . . . . . . . . . . . . . . . . . . . . . . . . . . | 29.8 | 29.8 |
| Other paid-in capital . . . . . . . . . . . . . . . . . . . . . . . . . . . . . . . . . . . . . . . . | 6,900.0 | 6,869 8 |
| Retained earnings. . . . . . . . . . . . . . . . . . . . . . . . . . . . . . . . . . . . . . . . . . | 37,918.9 | 36,626.3 |
| Accumulated other comprehensive income (loss) . . . . . . . . . . . . . . . . . . . . . | 52.3 | (45.9) |
| | 44,901.0 | 43,480.0 |
| Less treasury stock, at cost | | |
| 794,299,347 shares—2005 | | |
| 767,591,491 shares—2004. . . . . . . . . . . . . . . . . . . . . . . . . . . . . . . . | 26,984.4 | 26,191.8 |
| Total stockholders' equity . . . . . . . . . . . . . . . . . . . . . . . . . . . . . . . . . . . . . | 17,916.6 | 17,288.2 |
| Total liabilities and stockholders' equity. . . . . . . . . . . . . . . . . . . . . . . . . . . . . | $44,845.8 | $42,572.8 |

**Required**

a. Compute net operating profit after tax (NOPAT) for 2005 and 2004. Assume that the combined federal and state statutory tax rates are 37.5% for 2005 and 36.3% for 2004. Other income includes net interest expense and minority interest expense of $121.8 million in 2005 and $154.2 million in 2004.

b. Compute net operating assets (NOA) for 2005 and 2004. (*Hint:* Short- and long-term investments are investments in marketable securities.)

c. Compute RNOA and disaggregate it into net operating profit margin (NOPM) and net operating asset turnover (NOAT) for 2005 and 2004; the 2003 NOA is $15,374.4 million. Comment on the drivers of RNOA.

d. Compute net nonoperating obligations (NNO) for 2005 and 2004. Confirm the relation: NOA = NNO + Stockholders' equity + Minority interest.

e. Compute return on equity for the common shareholders (ROCE) for 2005 and 2004; the 2003 stockholders' equity is $15,576.4 million. For 2005 only, show that ROCE = ROCE before minority interest × Minority interest sharing ratio, see Appendix 4B.

f. Compute Merck's R&D as a percentage of sales and its sales growth for 2003 through 2005; its 2003 sales are $21,445.8 million. Comment on your findings.

**P4-43.** **Analysis and Interpretation of Profitability** **(LO1, 2)**

United Parcel Service (UPS)

Balance sheets and income statements for United Parcel Service (UPS) follow. Refer to these financial statements to answer the following requirements.

| UNITED PARCEL SERVICE Income Statement | | | |
| --- | --- | --- | --- |
| Years Ended December 31 ($ millions) | 2005 | 2004 | 2003 |
| Revenue | $42,581 | $36,582 | $33,485 |
| Operating expenses | | | |
| Compensation and benefits | 22,517 | 20,823 | 19,251 |
| Other | 13,921 | 10,770 | 9,789 |
| | 36,438 | 31,593 | 29,040 |
| Operating profit | 6,143 | 4,989 | 4,445 |
| Other income and (expense) | | | |
| Investment income | 104 | 82 | 18 |
| Interest expense | (172) | (149) | (121) |
| Gain on redemption of long-term debt | — | — | 28 |
| | (68) | (67) | (75) |
| Income before income taxes | 6,075 | 4,922 | 4,370 |
| Income taxes | 2,205 | 1,589 | 1,472 |
| Net income | $ 3,870 | $ 3,333 | $ 2,898 |

| UNITED PARCEL SERVICE Balance Sheet | | |
| --- | --- | --- |
| December 31 ($ millions, except per share amounts) | 2005 | 2004 |
| **Assets** | | |
| Cash & cash equivalents | $ 1,369 | $ 739 |
| Marketable securities & short-term investments | 1,672 | 4,458 |
| Accounts receivable, net | 5,950 | 5,156 |
| Finance receivables, net | 411 | 524 |
| Income tax receivable | — | 371 |
| Deferred income taxes | 475 | 392 |
| Other current assets | 1,126 | 965 |
| Total current assets | 11,003 | 12,605 |
| Property, plant & equipment—at cost, net of accumulated depreciation & amortization of $14,268 and $13,505 in 2005 and 2004 | 15,289 | 13,973 |
| Prepaid pension cost | 3,932 | 3,222 |
| Goodwill | 2,549 | 1,255 |
| Intangible assets, net | 684 | 669 |
| Other assets | 1,765 | 1,364 |
| Total assets | $35,222 | $33,088 |

*continued*

**UNITED PARCEL SERVICE**
Balance Sheet

| December 31 ($ millions, except per share amounts) | 2005 | 2004 |
|---|---|---|
| **Liabilities and shareowners' equity** | | |
| Current maturities of long-term debt and commercial paper. . . . . . . . . . . . . . . . . . . . . . . . | $    821 | $  1,187 |
| Accounts payable. . . . . . . . . . . . . . . . . . . . . . . . . . . . . . . . . . . . . . . . . . . . . . . . . . . . . . | 2,352 | 2,312 |
| Accrued wages & withholdings . . . . . . . . . . . . . . . . . . . . . . . . . . . . . . . . . . . . . . . . . . . | 1,324 | 1,197 |
| Dividends payable . . . . . . . . . . . . . . . . . . . . . . . . . . . . . . . . . . . . . . . . . . . . . . . . . . . . . . | 364 | 315 |
| Income taxes payable . . . . . . . . . . . . . . . . . . . . . . . . . . . . . . . . . . . . . . . . . . . . . . . . . . | 180 | 79 |
| Other current liabilities . . . . . . . . . . . . . . . . . . . . . . . . . . . . . . . . . . . . . . . . . . . . . . . . . | 1,752 | 1,439 |
| Total current liabilities. . . . . . . . . . . . . . . . . . . . . . . . . . . . . . . . . . . . . . . . . . . . . . . . . . | 6,793 | 6,529 |
| Long-term debt . . . . . . . . . . . . . . . . . . . . . . . . . . . . . . . . . . . . . . . . . . . . . . . . . . . . . . . | 3,159 | 3,261 |
| Accumulated postretirement benefit obligation, net . . . . . . . . . . . . . . . . . . . . . . . . . . . . | 1,704 | 1,470 |
| Deferred taxes, credits & other liabilities . . . . . . . . . . . . . . . . . . . . . . . . . . . . . . . . . . . | 6,682 | 5,450 |
| Shareowners' equity | | |
| Preferred stock, no par value, authorized 200 shares, none issued. . . . . . . . . . . . . . . . | — | — |
| Class A common stock, par value $.01 per share, authorized 4,600 shares, issued 454 and 515 in 2005 and 2004 . . . . . . . . . . . . . . . . . . . . . . . . . . . . . . . . . . . . . . . . | 5 | 5 |
| Class B common stock, par value $.01 per share, authorized 5,600 shares, issued 646 and 614 in 2005 and 2004 . . . . . . . . . . . . . . . . . . . . . . . . . . . . . . . . . . . . . . . . | 6 | 6 |
| Additional paid-in capital . . . . . . . . . . . . . . . . . . . . . . . . . . . . . . . . . . . . . . . . . . . . . . . . | — | 417 |
| Retained earnings. . . . . . . . . . . . . . . . . . . . . . . . . . . . . . . . . . . . . . . . . . . . . . . . . . . . . | 17,037 | 16,192 |
| Accumulated other comprehensive loss . . . . . . . . . . . . . . . . . . . . . . . . . . . . . . . . . . . . | (164) | (242) |
| Deferred compensation obligations . . . . . . . . . . . . . . . . . . . . . . . . . . . . . . . . . . . . . . . | 161 | 169 |
| | 17,045 | 16,547 |
| Less: Treasury stock (3 shares in 2005 and 2004) . . . . . . . . . . . . . . . . . . . . . . . . . . . | (161) | (169) |
| Total shareowners' equity. . . . . . . . . . . . . . . . . . . . . . . . . . . . . . . . . . . . . . . . . . . . . . | 16,884 | 16,378 |
| Total liabilities and shareowners' equity. . . . . . . . . . . . . . . . . . . . . . . . . . . . . . . . . . . . | $35,222 | $33,088 |

**Required**

a.  Compute net operating profit after tax (NOPAT) for 2005 and 2004. Assume that the combined federal and state statutory tax rates are 37.0% for 2005 and 36.2% for 2004.

b.  Compute net operating assets (NOA) for 2005 and 2004.

c.  Compute RNOA and disaggregate it into net operating profit margin (NOPM) and net operating asset turnover (NOAT) for 2005 and 2004; the 2003 NOA is $15,787 million. Comment on the drivers of the improvement in RNOA.

d.  Compute net nonoperating obligations (NNO) for 2005 and 2004. Confirm the relation: NOA = NNO + Stockholders' equity.

e.  Compute return on equity (ROE) for 2005 and 2004; the 2003 stockholders' equity is $14,852 million.

f.  Infer the nonoperating return component of ROE for both 2005 and 2004.

g.  Comment on the difference between ROE and RNOA. What does this relation suggest about UPS's use of debt?

**P4-44.  Analysis and Interpretation of Liquidity and Solvency  (LO3)**

Refer to the financial information of United Parcel Service in P4-43 to answer the following requirements.

United Parcel Service (UPS)

**Required**

a.  Compute its current ratio and quick ratio for 2005 and 2004. Comment on any observed trends.

b.  Compute its times interest earned and its total-liabilities-to-stockholders' equity ratios for 2005 and 2004. Comment on any trends observed.

c.  Summarize your findings in a conclusion about the company's liquidity and solvency. Do you have any concerns about its ability to meet its debt obligations?

**P4-45.**[B]   **Direct Computation of Nonoperating Return**   (LO1)

Refer to the financial information of United Parcel Service in P4-43 to answer the following requirements.

**Required**

a.   Compute its financial leverage (FLEV) and Spread for 2005; recall, NNE = NOPAT − Net income.

b.   Assume that UPS's NOPAT for 2005 is $3,913 million, its 2005 return on equity (ROE) is 23.27%, and its 2005 return on net operating assets (RNOA) is 22.01%. Confirm computations to yield the relation: ROE = RNOA + (FLEV × Spread). (*Hint:* Compute net nonoperating expense as NOPAT − Net income.)

c.   What do your computations of the nonoperating return in parts *a* and *b* imply about the company's use of borrowed funds?

**P4-46.**   **Analysis and Interpretation of Profit Margin, Asset Turnover, and RNOA for Several Companies**   (LO2)

Net operating profit margin (NOPM) and net operating asset turnover (NOAT) for several selected companies for 2005 follow.

|  | NOPM | NOAT |
|---|---|---|
| Albertsons................ | 1.99% | 2.83 |
| Caterpillar ................ | 8.25% | 1.40 |
| Home Depot .............. | 7.56% | 2.69 |
| McDonald's............... | 13.04% | 0.78 |
| Merck..................... | 19.05% | 0.74 |
| Southwest Airlines .......... | 7.03% | 0.75 |
| Target.................... | 5.31% | 2.07 |
| Verizon................... | 12.59% | 0.52 |

Albertsons, Inc. (ABS)
Caterpillar, Inc. (CAT)
Home Depot, Inc. (HD)
McDonalds Corporation (MCD)
Merck (MRK)
Southwest Airlines (LUV)
Target (TGT)
Verizon (VZ)

**Required**

a.   Graph NOPM and NOAT for each of these companies. Do you see a pattern revealed that is similar to that shown in this module? Explain. (The graph in the module is based on medians for selected industries; the graph for this problem uses fewer companies than in the module and, thus, will not be as smooth.)

b.   Consider the trade-off between profit margin and asset turnover. How can we evaluate companies on the profit margin and asset turnover trade-off? Explain.

# CASES

**C4-47.**   **Management Application: Gross Profit and Strategic Management**   (LO2)

One way to increase overall profitability is to increase gross profit. This can be accomplished by raising prices and/or by reducing manufacturing costs.

**Required**

a.   Will raising prices and/or reducing manufacturing costs unambiguously increase gross profit? Explain.

b.   What strategy might you develop as a manager to (i) yield a price increase for your product, or (ii) reduce product manufacturing cost?

**C4-48.** **Management Application: Asset Turnover and Strategic Management** **(LO2)**

Increasing net operating asset turnover requires some combination of increasing sales and/or decreasing net operating assets. For the latter, many companies consider ways to reduce their investment in working capital (current assets less current liabilities). This can be accomplished by reducing the level of accounts receivable and inventories, or by increasing the level of accounts payable.

**Required**

*a.* Develop a list of suggested actions to achieve all three of these objectives as manager.

*b.* Examine the implications of each. That is, describe the marketing implications of reducing receivables and inventories, and the supplier implications of delaying payment. How can a company achieve working capital reduction without negatively impacting its performance?

**C4-49.** **Ethics and Governance: Earnings Management**

Companies are aware that analysts focus on profitability in evaluating financial performance. Managers have historically utilized a number of methods to improve reported profitability that are cosmetic in nature and do not affect "real" operating performance. These are typically subsumed under the general heading of "earnings management." Justification for such actions typically includes the following arguments:

- Increasing stock price by managing earnings benefits shareholders; thus, no one is hurt by these actions.

- Earnings management is a temporary fix; such actions will be curtailed once "real" profitability improves, as managers expect.

**Required**

*a.* Identify the affected parties in any scheme to manage profits to prop up stock price.

*b.* Do the ends (of earnings management) justify the means? Explain.

*c.* To what extent are the objectives of managers different from those of shareholders?

*d.* What governance structure can you envision that might prohibit earnings management?

# Reporting and Analyzing Operating Income

## LEARNING OBJECTIVES

**LO1** Explain revenue recognition criteria and identify transactions of special concern. (p. 5-5)

**LO2** Describe accounting for operating expenses, including research and development, and restructuring. (p. 5-11)

**LO3** Explain and analyze accounting for income taxes. (p. 5-17)

**LO4** Compute earnings per share and explain the effect of dilutive securities. (p. 5-24)

**LO5** Explain how foreign currency fluctuations affect the income statement. (p. 5-26)

## PFIZER

Pfizer's business is to discover, develop, manufacture and market leading prescription medicines. These endeavors define the company's operating activities and include research and development, manufacturing, advertising, sales, after-sale customer support, and all administrative functions necessary to support Pfizer's various activities.

Accounting for operating activities involves numerous estimates and choices, and GAAP often grants considerable latitude. To illustrate, consider the choice of when to recognize sales revenue. Should Pfizer recognize revenue when it receives a customer order? When it ships the drug order? Or, when the customer pays? GAAP requires that revenues be recognized when *earned*. It is up to the company to decide when that condition is met. This module identifies several revenue-recognition scenarios that are especially troublesome for companies, their auditors, regulators, and outside stakeholders.

Pfizer's key operating activity is its research and development (R&D). To protect its discoveries, Pfizer holds thousands of patents and applies for hundreds more each year. However, patents don't protect Pfizer indefinitely—patents expire or fail legal challenges and, then, Pfizer's drugs face competition from other drug manufacturers. In 2005, Pfizer's sales declined by 2%, in part because patents expired. Indeed, as the company reported in the MD&A section of its 10-K, "revenues of major products with lost exclusivity in the U.S. declined by 44% from 2004." In addition, several Pfizer products have recently come under fire, and the company's 10K reports the bad news: "uncertainty related to Celebrex and the suspension of Bextra sales have resulted in a significant decline in prescription volume in the arthritis and pain market, resulting in a 63% decline in revenues in those products from 2004." Even the company's blockbuster drug, Lipitor, with sales exceeding $12 billion in 2005 (24% of Pfizer's total revenues), is not a panacea for what ails Pfizer—the Lipitor patent expires in 2010.

Getty Images

Wall Street is not optimistic about Pfizer's ability to replace patents that will lapse over the next decade. While Pfizer's revenues have increased by 77% since 2001, its profits have only increased by 4%, and Pfizer's stock price has fallen 40 percent—see stock price chart below. Over that same period the American Stock Exchange Pharmaceutical index (DRG) fell by only 13 percent.

Accounting for R&D costs is controversial. Even though R&D activities generally yield future benefits and, thus, meet the criteria to be recorded as an asset, GAAP requires that companies expense all R&D costs. This creates balance sheets with significant "missing" assets. For example, the only asset that Pfizer has on its books related to Lipitor is the legal cost of filing the patent with the U.S. Patent Office. Clearly this does not capture Lipitor's full value to Pfizer. This module explains R&D accounting and the resulting financial statement implications.

Pfizer has restructured its activities several times in an attempt to maintain operating profit in light of declining sales. Restructurings typically involve two types of costs: severance costs relating to employee terminations and asset write-offs. GAAP grants leeway in how to account for restructuring activities. Should

*(Continued on next page)*

*(Continued from previous page)*

Pfizer expense the severance costs when the board of directors approves the layoffs? Or when the employees are actually paid? Or at some other point? This module discusses accounting for restructurings, including footnote disclosures that can help financial statement readers interpret restructuring activities.

A necessary part of operations is paying income taxes on profits earned. The IRS has its own rules for computing taxes owed. These rules, called the Internal Revenue Code, are different from GAAP. Thus, it is legal (and necessary) for companies to prepare two sets of financial reports, one for shareholders and one for tax authorities. In this module, we will see that tax expense reported on the income statement is not computed as a simple percentage of pretax income. The module also discusses the valuation allowance that is related to deferred tax assets, and explains how the allowance can markedly affect net income.

Earnings per share (EPS) is the most frequently quoted operating number in the financial press. It represents earnings that are available to pay dividends to common shareholders. Companies report two EPS numbers: basic and diluted. The latter represents the lower bound on that year's EPS. It is important that we understand the difference between the two, and this module describes the two EPS computations.

Pfizer does business around the world, transacting in many currencies. Indeed, many of Pfizer's subsidiaries maintain their entire financial records in currencies other than the U.S. dollar. Consequently, to prepare its financial statements in $US, Pfizer must translate each transaction from foreign currencies into $US. This module describes the effects of foreign currency translation. When the dollar strengthens and weakens against other world currencies, a company's foreign revenues and expenses increase or decrease even if unit volumes remain unchanged. It is important to understand this mechanical relation if we are to properly analyze companies with global operations. This module considers these issues.

Sources: Pfizer 2005 10-K, Pfizer 2005 Annual Report; *Fortune*, January 2007; *BusinessWeek*, January 2007.

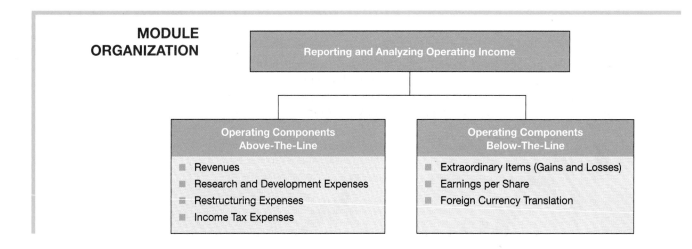

**MODULE ORGANIZATION**

Reporting and Analyzing Operating Income

**Operating Components Above-The-Line**
- Revenues
- Research and Development Expenses
- Restructuring Expenses
- Income Tax Expenses

**Operating Components Below-The-Line**
- Extraordinary Items (Gains and Losses)
- Earnings per Share
- Foreign Currency Translation

# INTRODUCTION

Operating activities refer to a company's primary transactions. These include the purchase of goods from suppliers and, if a manufacturing company, the conversion of goods into finished products, the promotion and distribution of goods, the sale of goods to customers, and post-sale customer support. Operating activities are reported in the income statement under items such as sales, cost of goods sold, and selling, general, and administrative expenses. They represent a company's primary activities, and they must be executed successfully for a company to consistently succeed.

Nonoperating activities relate to the borrowing of money and the securities investment activities of a company. They are not a company's primary activities.[1] These activities are typically reported in the income statement under items such as interest revenues and expenses, dividend revenues, and gains and losses on sales of securities.

---

[1] However, income derived from investments is considered to be operating income for financial-services firms such as banks and insurance companies. Many analysts also consider as operating, the income derived from financing subsidiaries of manufacturing companies, such as Ford Motor Credit and Caterpillar Financial, because these activities can be viewed as extensions of the sales process.

Proper identification of operating and nonoperating components is important for valuation of companies' equity (stock) and debt (note and bond) securities. It is of interest, for example, to know whether company profitability results from operating activities, or whether poor operating performance is being masked by income from nonoperating activities (income from nonoperating activities usually depends on a favorable investment climate, which can be short-lived).

Exhibit 5.1 classifies several common income components as operating and nonoperating.

| **EXHIBIT 5.1** | **Distinguishing Operating and Nonoperating Income Components** |
|---|---|
| **Operating Activities** | **Nonoperating Activities** |
| • Sales | • Interest revenues and expenses |
| • Cost of goods sold | • Dividend revenues |
| • Selling, general and administrative expenses | • Gains and losses on sales of investments |
| • Depreciation expense | • Gains and losses on debt retirement |
| • Research and development expenses | • Gains and losses on discontinued operations |
| • Restructuring expenses | • Minority interest expense |
| • Income tax expenses | • Investment write-downs |
| • Extraordinary gains and losses | |
| • Gains and losses on sales of operating assets | |
| • Foreign currency translation effects | |
| • Operating asset write-downs | |
| • Other income or expenses | |

The list of operating activities above includes all the familiar operating items, as well as gains and losses on transactions relating to operating assets and the write-down of operating assets.[2] The list also includes "other" income statement items. We treat these as operating unless the income statement designates them as nonoperating or footnote information indicates that some or all of these "other" items are nonoperating. Footnotes are usually uninformative about "other" income statement items and "other" balance sheet items. GAAP does not require specific disclosure of such items unless they are deemed *material*.[3]

We build our discussion of operating income around the operating accounts in Pfizer's income statement (Exhibit 5.2), which includes all of the typical operating accounts. We highlight the following topics in this module:

▦ Revenues

▦ Research and development expenses

▦ Restructuring expenses

▦ Income tax expenses

▦ Extraordinary gains and losses

▦ Earnings per share (EPS)

▦ Foreign currency translation effects

---

[2] For example, a loss on the sale of equipment implies that the company did not depreciate the equipment quickly enough. Had the company recorded the "right" amount of depreciation over the years (that is, the amount of depreciation that perfectly matched the equipment's economic devaluation over time), the equipment's book value would have been exactly the same as its market value and no loss would have been recorded. Thus, we treat the loss on disposal in the same manner as depreciation expense—as operating. The same logic applies to write-downs of operating assets.

[3] *Material* is an accounting term that means that the item in question is significant enough to make a difference to someone relying on the financial statements to make a business decision. Investors, for example, might find an item material if it is large enough to change their investment decision (whether to buy or sell the stock). This *materiality* judgment is in the eye of the beholder, and this subjectivity makes materiality an elusive concept.

---

| BUSINESS INSIGHT | Ratios Across Industries |
| --- | --- |

Over time, industries evolve and reach equilibrium levels for operating activities. For example, some industries require a high level of selling, general and administrative (SG&A) expenses, perhaps due to high advertising demands or high occupancy costs. Other industries require intense research and development (R&D) expenditures to remain competitive. To a large extent, these cost structures dictate the prices that firms in the industry charge—each industry prices its product or service to yield a sufficient level of gross profit (Sales less Cost of Goods Sold) to cover the operating expenses and allow the industry to remain viable. Review the following table of selected operating margins for companies in various industries.

| | Gross profit/Sales | SG&A/Sales | R&D/Sales | NOPM |
| --- | --- | --- | --- | --- |
| Pfizer..................... | 88.0% | 47.1% | 17.7% | 14.6% |
| Intel ....................... | 70.9 | 27.9 | 13.3 | 20.2 |
| Cisco Systems .............. | 70.4 | 36.3 | 13.5 | 19.4 |
| Procter & Gamble ........... | 54.3 | 31.7 | 3.4 | 12.5 |
| Home Depot ............... | 33.7 | 20.1 | 0.0 | 7.5 |
| Dell ....................... | 19.1 | 9.8 | 0.8 | 5.6 |
| Target ..................... | 33.6 | 22.8 | 0.0 | 5.3 |

We see that Cisco, Intel, Pfizer, and Proctor & Gamble report high gross profit margins. This does not necessarily suggest they are better managed than Dell. Instead, their industries require higher levels of gross profit to cover their high levels of SG&A and R&D. Dell, on the other hand, is in a highly price competitive segment of the computer industry. To maintain its competitive advantage Dell must control costs. Indeed, Dell reports the lowest SG&A-to-sales ratio of any of the companies listed.

---

# OPERATING INCOME COMPONENTS

Pfizer's 2005 income statement in Exhibit 5.2 highlights the operating income components discussed in this module. We defer discussion of cost of goods sold to Module 6, which focuses on inventories and other operating assets. Modules 2 and 4 discuss items typically included in selling, general and administrative (SG&A) expenses, and Module 7 addresses the accounts related to acquisitions of other companies (such as amortization of intangible assets, merger-related in-process research and development charges, discontinued operations, and minority interest expense).

We begin by discussing revenue, including the criteria for revenue recognition that companies must employ and improper revenue recognition that the SEC has recently challenged. Next, we discuss Pfizer's research and development expenses, restructuring charges, provision for taxes, extraordinary items, and earnings per share (EPS). We finish with a discussion of the effects of foreign currency fluctuations on the income statement.

## Revenues

**LO1** Explain revenue recognition criteria and identify transactions of special concern.

Pfizer reports over $51 billion of revenue. This revenue represents the culmination of a process that includes the manufacture of the drugs, their promotion, the receipt of orders, delivery to the customer, billing for the sale amount, and collection of the amounts owed. At what point in this process should Pfizer recognize its revenue and the related profit? When the drugs are delivered to the customer? When payment is received? And, how should Pfizer treat sales discounts or rights of return?

GAAP specifies two **revenue recognition criteria** that must both be met for revenue to be recognized on the income statement. Revenue must be (1) **realized or realizable**, and (2) **earned**.[4] *Realized or*

---

[4] SEC provides guidance for revenue recognition in *Staff Accounting Bulletin (SAB) 101* (http://www.sec.gov/interps/account/sab101.htm), which states that revenue is realized, or realizable, and earned when *each* of the following criteria are met: (1) there is persuasive evidence that a sales agreement exists; (2) delivery has occurred or services have been rendered; (3) the seller's price to the buyer is fixed or determinable; and (4) collectibility is reasonably assured.

| EXHIBIT 5.2 | Pfizer Income Statement |
|---|---|

| (Millions, Except per Common Share Data) | 2005 |
|---|---|
| Revenues ................................................................. | $51,298 |
| Costs and expenses | |
|    Cost of sales....................................................... | 8,525 |
|    Selling, informational and administative expenses........................... | 16,997 |
|    Research and development expenses ..................................... | 7,442 |
|    Amortization of intangible assets ........................................ | 3,409 |
|    Merger-related in-process research and development charges ................ | 1,652 |
|    Restructuring charges and merger-related costs .......................... | 1,392 |
|    Other (income)/deductions—net....................................... | 347 |
| Income from continuing operations before provision for taxes on income, minority interests and cumulative effect of a change in accounting principles...... | 11,534 |
| Provision for taxes on income......................................... | 3,424 |
| Minority interest...................................................... | 16 |
| Income from continuing operalions ....................................... | 8,094 |
| Discontinued operations | |
|    (Loss)/income from discontinued operations—net of tax .................... | (31) |
|    Gains on sales of discontinued operations—net of tax ...................... | 47 |
| Discontinued operations—net of tax ..................................... | 16 |
| Other income (expense) ............................................... | (25) |
| Net income...................................................... | $ 8,085 |
| Earnings per common share—basic | |
|    Income from continuing operations before cumulative effect of a change in accounting principles............................................ | $   1.10 |
|    Discontinued operations ............................................ | — |
|    Net income....................................................... | $   1.10 |
| Earnings per common share—diluted | |
|    Income from continuing operations before cumulative effect of a change in accounting principles............................................ | $   1.09 |
|    Discontinued operations ............................................ | — |
|    Net income....................................................... | $   1.09 |
| Weighted-average shares—basic........................................ | 7,361 |
| Weighted-average shares—diluted ..................................... | 7,411 |

*realizable* means that the seller's net assets (assets less liabilities) increase. That is, the seller receives an asset, such as cash or accounts receivable, or satisfies a liability, such as deferred revenue, as a result of a transaction. The company does not have to wait to recognize revenue until after it collects the accounts receivable; the increase in the account receivable (asset) means that the revenue is realizable. *Earned* means that the seller has performed its duties under the terms of the sales agreement and that title to the product sold has passed to the buyer with no right of return or other contingencies. As long as Pfizer has delivered the drugs ordered by its customers, and its customers are obligated to make payment, Pfizer can recognize revenue. The following conditions would each argue *against* revenue recognition:

 *Rights of return exist,* other than due to routine product defects covered under product warranty.

 *Consignment sales,* where products are held on consignment until ultimately sold by the consignee.

 *Continuing involvement by seller in product resale,* such as where the seller retains possession of the product until it's resold.

 *Contingency sales,* such as when product sales are contingent on product performance or further approvals by the customer.

Revenue is not recognized in these cases until the factors inhibiting revenue recognition are resolved.

Companies are required to report their revenue recognition policies in footnotes to their 10-K reports. Pfizer recognizes its revenues as follows:

> Revenue Recognition—we record revenue from product sales when the goods are shipped and title passes to the customer. At the time of sale, we also record estimates for a variety of sales deductions, such as sales rebates, discounts and incentives, and product returns.

Pfizer adopts the position that its revenues are *earned* when its products are shipped and title to the merchandise passes to its customers. At that point, Pfizer has done everything required and, thus, recognizes the sale in the income statement. Most companies recognize revenues using these criteria. Pfizer does *not* recognize revenues for the gross selling price. Instead, Pfizer deducts that portion of gross sales that is likely to be refunded to customers through sales rebates, discounts or incentives (including volume purchases). Pfizer estimates the likely cost of those price reductions and deducts that amount from gross sales. Similarly, Pfizer does not recognize revenues for those products that it estimates will be returned, possibly because the drugs hit their expiration date before they are sold by Pfizer's customers. In sum, Pfizer recognizes revenues for products delivered to customers, and for only for the sales price *net* of anticipated discounts and returns. This is why we often see "Revenues, net" on companies' income statements.

---

**BUSINESS INSIGHT**     **Cisco's Revenue Recognition**

Following is an excerpt from Cisco Systems' policies on revenue recognition as reported in footnotes to its recent annual report.

> We recognize product revenue when persuasive evidence of an arrangement exists, delivery has occurred, the fee is fixed or determinable, and collectibility is reasonably assured. In instances where final acceptance of the product, system, or solution is specified by the customer, revenue is deferred until all acceptance criteria have been met . . . Service revenue is generally deferred and, in most cases, recognized ratably over the period during which the services are to be performed . . . Contracts and customer purchase orders are generally used to determine the existence of an arrangement. Shipping documents and customer acceptance, when applicable, are used to verify delivery . . . When a sale involves multiple elements, such as sales of products that include services, the entire fee from the arrangement is allocated to each respective element based on its relative fair value and recognized when revenue recognition criteria for each element are met.

Cisco's criteria for revenue recognition mirror SEC guidance. The key components are that revenue is *earned* and that proceeds are *realized or realizable*. For Cisco, earned means that delivery to and acceptance by the customer occurs, or that Cisco is available to perform service commitments, even if not called upon.

---

## Risks of Revenue Recognition

More than 70% of SEC accounting and auditing enforcement actions involve misstated revenues (Dechow, P., and C. Schrand. 2004. "Earnings quality," The Research Foundation of CFA Institute. Charlottesville, Virginia). The SEC is so concerned about aggressive (premature) revenue recognition that it recently issued a special *Staff Accounting Bulletin (SAB) 101* on the matter. The SEC provides the following examples of problem areas to assist companies in properly recognizing revenue:

- *Case 1: Channel stuffing.* Some sellers use their market power over customers to induce (or even require) them to purchase more goods than they actually need. This practice, called *channel stuffing*, increases period-end sales and net income. If no side agreements exist for product returns, the practice does not violate GAAP revenue recognition guidelines, but the SEC contends that revenues are misrepresented and that the practice is a violation of securities laws.

- *Case 2: Barter transactions.* Some barter transactions are concocted to create the illusion of revenue. Examples include the advertising swaps that dot-com companies engage in, and the excess capacity swaps of fiber optic communications businesses. The advertising swap relates to the simultaneous sale and purchase of advertising. The excess capacity swap relates to a company selling excess capacity to a competitor and, simultaneously, purchasing excess capacity from that competitor. Both types of swaps are equal exchanges and do not provide income or create an expense for either party. Further, these transactions do not represent a culmination of the normal earning process and, thus, the "earned" revenue recognition criterion is not met.

- *Case 3: Mischaracterizing transactions as arm's-length.* Transfers of inventories or other assets to related entities are typically not recognized as revenue until arm's-length sales occur. Sometimes, companies disguise non-arm's length transactions as sales to unrelated entities. This practice is improper when (1) the buyer is related to the seller, (2) the seller is providing financing, or (3) the buyer is a special-purpose entity that fails to meet independence requirements. Revenue should not be recognized unless the sales process is complete, that is, goods have been transferred and an asset has been created (future payment from a solvent, independent party).

- *Case 4: Pending execution of sales agreements.* Sometimes companies boost current period profits by recording revenue for goods delivered for which formal customer approval has yet to be received. The SEC's position is that if the company's practice is to obtain sales authorization, then revenue is *not* earned until such approval is obtained, even though product delivery is made and customer approval is anticipated.

- *Case 5: Gross versus net revenues.* Some companies use their distribution network to sell other companies' goods at a slight markup (i.e. for a commission). There are increasing reports of companies that inflate revenues by reporting such transactions on a gross basis (separately reporting both sales and cost of goods sold) instead of reporting only the commission (typically a percentage of sales price). The incentives for such reporting are high for some dot.com companies and start-ups that believe the market prices of their stocks are based on revenue growth and not on profitability. Reporting revenues at gross rather than net would have enormous impact on the valuations of those companies. The SEC prescribes that such sales be reported on a net basis.

- *Case 6: Sales on consignment.* Some companies deliver goods to other companies with the understanding that these goods will be ultimately sold to third parties. At the time of delivery, title does not pass to the second company, and the second company has no obligation to make payment to the seller until the product is sold. This type of transaction is called a *consignment sale.* The SEC's position is that a sale has not occurred, and revenue is *not* to be recognized by the original company, until the product is sold to a third party. Further, the middleman (consignee) cannot report the gross sale, and can only report its commission revenue.

- *Case 7: Failure to take delivery.* Some customers may not take delivery of the product by period-end. In this case, revenue is *not* yet earned. The earning process is only complete once the product is delivered and accepted. An example is a layaway sale. Even though the product is ordered, and even partially paid for, revenue is not recognized until the product is delivered and final payment is made or agreed to be made.

- *Case 8: Nonrefundable fees.* Sellers sometimes receive fees that are nonrefundable to the customer. An example is a health club initiation fee or a cellular phone activation fee. Some sellers wish to record these cash receipts as revenue to boost current sales and income. However, even though cash is received and nonrefundable, revenue is not recognized until the product is delivered or the service performed. Until that time, the company reports the cash received as a liability (deferred revenue). Once the obligation is settled, the liability is removed and revenue is reported.

In sum, revenue is only recognized when it is earned and when it is realized or realizable. This demands that the seller has performed its obligations (no contingencies exist) and the buyer is an independent party with the financial capacity to pay the amounts owed.

## Percentage-of-Completion Revenue Recognition

Challenges arise in determining the point at which revenue is earned for companies with long-term sales contracts (spanning more than one period), such as construction companies and defense contractors. For these companies, revenue is often recognized using the percentage-of-completion method, which recognizes revenue by determining the costs incurred under the contract relative to its total expected costs.

To illustrate, assume that Abbott Construction signs a $10 million contract to construct a building. Abbott estimates construction will take two years and will cost $7,500,000. This means the contract yields an expected gross profit of $2,500,000 over two years. The following table summarizes construction costs incurred each year and the revenue Abbott recognizes.

| | Construction costs incurred | Percentage complete | Revenue recognized |
|---|---|---|---|
| Year 1 . . . . . . . . . | $4,500,000 | $\frac{\$4,500,000}{\$7,500,000} = 60\%$ | $10,000,000 × 60% = $6,000,000 |
| Year 2 . . . . . . . . . | $3,000,000 | $\frac{\$3,000,000}{\$7,500,000} = 40\%$ | $10,000,000 × 40% = $4,000,000 |

This table reveals that Abbott would report $6 million in revenue and $1.5 million ($6 million − $4.5 million) in gross profit on the construction project in the first year and $4 million in revenue and $1 million ($4 million − $3 million) in gross profit in the second year.

Next, assume that Abbott's client makes a $1 million deposit at the signing of the contract and that Abbott submits bills to the client based on the percentage of completion. The following table reflects the bills sent to, and the cash received from, the client.

| | Revenue recognized | Client billed | Cash received |
|---|---|---|---|
| At signing . . . . . . . . . . . . . . . | $ 0 | $ 0 | $1,000,000 |
| Year 1 . . . . . . . . . . . . . . . . . | 6,000,000 | 5,000,000 | 3,000,000 |
| Year 2 . . . . . . . . . . . . . . . . . | 4,000,000 | 4,000,000 | 6,000,000 |

At the signing of the contract, Abbott recognizes no revenue because construction has not begun and thus, Abbott has not earned any revenue. At the end of the second year, Abbott has recognized all of the contract revenue and the client has paid all monies owed per the accounts receivable.

The following template captures Abbott Construction's transactions over this two-year period (M indicates millions).

| | | Balance Sheet | | | | | | Income Statement | | |
|---|---|---|---|---|---|---|---|---|---|---|
| | Transaction | Cash Asset | + Noncash Assets | = Liabil- ities | + Contrib. Capital | + Earned Capital | | Rev- enues | − Expen- ses | = Net Income |
| Cash 1M<br>UR 1M<br>Cash<br>1M<br>UR<br>1M | Start of year 1: Record $1M deposit received at contract signing | +1M Cash | | = +1M Unearned Revenue | | | | − | | = |
| COGS 4.5M<br>Cash 4.5M<br>COGS<br>4.5M<br>Cash<br>4.5M | Year 1: Record $4.5M construction costs | −4.5M Cash | | = | | −4.5M Retained Earnings | | +4.5M | − Cost of Sales | = −4.5M |
| AR 5M<br>UR 1M<br>REV 6M<br>AR<br>5M<br>UR<br>1M<br>REV<br>6M | Year 1: Recognize $6M revenue on partly completed contract | | +5M Accounts Receivable | = −1M Unearned Revenue | | +6M Retained Earnings | | +6M Revenue | − | = +6M |
| Cash 3M<br>AR 3M<br>Cash<br>3M<br>AR<br>3M | Year 1: Record $3M cash received from client | +3M Cash | −3M Accounts Receivable | = | | | | − | | = |
| COGS 3M<br>Cash 3M<br>COGS<br>3M<br>Cash<br>3M | Year 2: Record $3M construction costs | −3M Cash | | = | | −3M Retained Earnings | | +3M | − Cost of Sales | = −3M |

*continued*

| Transaction | Balance Sheet | | | | | Income Statement | | | |
|---|---|---|---|---|---|---|---|---|---|
| | Cash Asset | + Noncash Assets | = Liabil- ities | + Contrib. Capital | + Earned Capital | Rev- enues | − Expen- ses | = Net Income | |
| Year 2: Recognize $4M revenue for completed contract | | +4M Accounts = Receivable | | | +4M Retained Earnings | +4M Revenue | − | = +4M | AR 4M Rev 4M <br> AR 4M Rev 4M |
| Year 2: Record $6M cash received from client | +6M Cash | −6M Accounts = Receivable | | | | | | = | Cash 6M AR 6M <br> Cash 6M AR 6M |

Revenue recognition policies for these types of contracts are disclosed in a manner typical to the following from the 2005 10-K report footnotes of Raytheon Company:

> Revenue Recognition—Sales under long-term contracts generally are recorded under the percentage of completion method. Incurred costs and estimated gross margins are recorded as sales when work is performed based on the percentage that incurred costs bear to the Company's estimates of total costs and contract value . . . Due to the long-term nature of many of the Company's programs, developing estimates of total costs and contract value often requires significant judgment.

The percentage-of-completion method of revenue recognition requires an estimate of total costs. This estimate is made at the beginning of the contract and is typically the one used to initially bid the contract. However, estimates are inherently inaccurate. If the estimate changes during the construction period, the percentage-of-completion is computed as the total costs incurred to date divided by the *current* estimate of total anticipated costs (costs incurred to date plus total estimated costs to complete).

If total construction costs are underestimated, the percentage-of-completion is overestimated (the denominator is too low) and revenue and gross profit to date are overstated. The estimation process inherent in this method has the potential for inaccurate or, even, improper revenue recognition. In addition, estimates of remaining costs to complete projects are difficult for the auditors to verify. This uncertainty adds additional risk to financial statement analysis.

---

**BUSINESS INSIGHT    Disney's Revenue Recognition**

The Walt Disney Company uses a method similar to percentage-of-completion to determine the amount of production cost to match against film and television revenues. Following is an excerpt from its 10-K.

> Film and television production costs are expensed based on the ratio of the current period's gross revenues to estimated remaining total gross revenues from all sources on an individual production basis. Television network series costs and multi-year sports rights are charged to expense based on the ratio of the current period's gross revenues to estimated remaining total gross revenues from such programs.

As Disney pays production costs, they record those costs on the balance sheet as inventory. Then, as film and television revenues are recognized, the company matches a portion of production costs (from inventory) against revenues in computing income. Each period, the costs recognized are equal to the proportion of total revenues recognized in the period to the total revenues expected over the life of the film or television show. Thus, estimates of both costs and income depend on the quality of its revenue estimates, which are, likely, imprecise.

---

## Recognition of Unearned Revenue

In some industries it is common to receive cash before recording revenue. Customers might pay in advance for special orders, make deposits for future services, or buy concert tickets, subscriptions, or gift cards. In those cases, companies must record unearned revenues, a liability, and only record revenue when those products and services are provided. Specifically, deposits or advance payments are not recorded as revenue until the company performs the services owed or delivers the goods. Until then, the company's balance sheet shows the advance payment as a liability (called unearned revenue or deferred revenue) because the company is obligated to deliver those products and services.

To illustrate, assume that on January 1 a client pays Pfizer $360,000 for a guaranteed one year supply of a rare medicine. Pfizer initially records $360,000 cash and a $360,000 liability (unearned revenue). Pfizer will earn that revenue by delivering the medicine during the coming year. Revenue is computed as a proportion of medicine delivered to the total amount purchased under the contract. For example, if Pfizer prepares quarterly financial statements and it has provided one-fourth of the contracted medicine by first quarter-end, it would record one-fourth of that revenue as earned. As revenue is earned, the unearned revenue account on the balance sheet is reduced and revenue is recorded in the income statement. The following template reflects the cash received for the medicine contract and the subsequent first quarter accounting adjustment.

| | | Balance Sheet | | | | | | Income Statement | | | |
|---|---|---|---|---|---|---|---|---|---|---|---|
| | Transaction | Cash Asset | + Noncash Assets | = Liabil- ities | + Contrib. Capital | + Earned Capital | | Rev- enues | − Expen- ses | = Net Income |
| | Jan 1: Receive $360,000 cash advance for medicine | +360,000 Cash | | +360,000 Unearned Revenue | | | | | | = |
| | Mar 31: Recognize one-fourth of unearned revenue | | | −90,000 Unearned Revenue | | +90,000 Retained Earnings | | +90,000 Revenue | | = +90,000 |

T-account margin notes:
- Cash 360,000 / UR 360,000
- Cash: 360,000 | ; | UR: | 360,000
- UR 90,000 / Rev 90,000
- UR: 90,000 | ; Rev: | 90,000

## Research and Development (R&D) Expenses

**LO2** Describe accounting for operating expenses, including research and development, and restructuring.

R&D activities are a major expenditure for many companies, especially for those in technology and pharmaceutical industries. Pfizer's R&D costs, for example, make up 14.5% of revenues ($7,442 million/$51,298 million). These expenses include employment costs for R&D personnel, R&D related contract services, and R&D fixed-asset costs.

Accounting for R&D activities follows a uniform method: *expense all R&D costs as incurred*. For many companies this creates unrecorded assets because R&D often yields future economic benefits to the company. Because measuring the benefits is difficult, GAAP requires all R&D to be immediately expensed. Even costs related to plant assets are expensed in certain circumstances, and this expensing of R&D fixed assets contrasts sharply with the capitalization-and-depreciation of non-R&D fixed assets. The expensing of R&D fixed assets is mandated *unless those assets have alternative future uses* (in other R&D projects or otherwise). For example, a general research facility housing multi-use lab equipment is capitalized and depreciated like any other depreciable asset. However, project-directed research buildings and equipment with no alternate uses must be expensed.

Following is a footnote excerpt from Pfizer's 2005 annual report related to its research and development expenditures:

> Research and development (R&D) costs are expensed as incurred. These expenses include the costs of our proprietary R&D efforts, as well as costs incurred in connection with our third-party collaboration efforts. Pre-approval milestone payments made by us to third parties under contracted R&D arrangements are expensed when the specific milestone has been achieved. Once the product receives regulatory approval, we record any subsequent milestone payments in *Identifiable intangible assets, less accumulated amortization* and amortize them evenly over the remaining agreement term or the expected product life cycle, whichever is shorter.

Pfizer capitalizes and depreciates general research facilities (those with alternate uses). All other R&D costs are expensed as incurred.

When a company immediately expenses its R&D fixed assets, it lowers current period income, total assets, and stockholders' equity. These effects are mitigated to the extent that a company's R&D purchases are relatively constant from year to year. Specifically, after the average useful life is reached, say in 5 to 10 years, the expensing of current year purchases will approximate the depreciation that would have been reported had the assets been capitalized (thus, the effect on net income is minimal). However, the recorded assets are permanently lower than they would be if the R&D fixed assets had been capitalized and depreciated. This affects asset turnover ratios and, consequently, analysis of RNOA and ROE. In particular the ratios are biased upwards due to unrecorded assets (and equity) in the denominator. More generally, the effects of expensing R&D for financial statements is summarized in Exhibit 5.3.

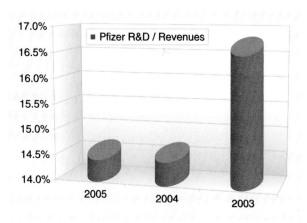

| EXHIBIT 5.3 | Financial Reporting of R&D Expenditures |
|---|---|

| Balance Sheet | Income Statement | Statement of Cash Flows |
|---|---|---|
| • R&D assets with no alternate use are not capitalized<br>• Unrecorded assets increase return ratios (RNOA and ROE) and asset turnover ratios<br>• R&D expensing reduces equity, which can affect ROE | • R&D expensing (versus capitalization-and-depreciation) lowers income; more so when R&D costs are increasing | • R&D expensing (versus capitalization-and-depreciation) has no cash effect |

To illustrate the effect of immediately expensing R&D plant assets, consider the following example. Assume in year 1, that Pfizer purchases equipment designed solely to develop a new drug that it anticipates selling in years 2 and 3. The equipment costs $600,000 and Pfizer realizes sales of $800,000 per year in the two subsequent years. The following template shows the effects of those transactions over these three years ($ 000s).

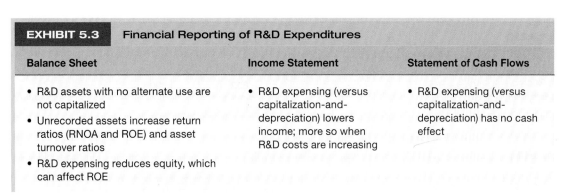

Pfizer charges the entire cost of the plant asset to income in year 1. There are no revenues in year 1 related to the R&D expense. Then, in years 2 and 3, revenue earned from the new drug has no related expenses. This accounting treatment reports no R&D (plant) asset on the balance sheet (see that no transactions affect the Noncash Assets column in the template). Thus, analyzing the financial performance of the drug is complicated because the drug's revenues and expenses impact different years and because there is no asset on the balance sheet. Return metrics such as ROE and RNOA are inaccurate in all three years.

Next, assume that, instead, the equipment has some alternate use to Pfizer. In that case Pfizer can capitalize and depreciate the asset. Also assume that Pfizer's accounting policy is to depreciate plant assets of this nature using the straight-line method over two years and that no depreciation is taken in the acquisition year. With these facts, the template reveals the following financial effects ($ 000s).

| Transaction | Balance Sheet | | | | | | Income Statement | | |
|---|---|---|---|---|---|---|---|---|---|
| | Cash Asset + | Noncash Assets = | Liabil- ities + | Contrib. Capital + | Earned Capital | | Rev- enues − | Expen- ses = | Net Income |
| Year 1: Purchase R&D plant assets | −600 Cash | +600 Equipment = | | | | | | = | |
| Year 2: Record sales from newly developed drug | +800 Cash | = | | | +800 Retained Earnings | | +800 Revenues − | = | +800 |
| Year 2: Depreciate R&D plant assets | | −300 Equipment (Accumulated = Depreciation) | | | −300 Retained Earnings | | | +300 R&D − Expense = | −300 |
| Year 3: Record sales from newly developed drug | +800 Cash | = | | | +800 Retained Earnings | | +800 Revenues − | = | +800 |
| Year 3: Depreciate R&D plant assets | | −300 Equipment (Accumulated = Depreciation) | | | −300 Retained Earnings | | | +300 R&D − Expense = | −300 |

*Margin T-accounts:*

PPE 600
Cash 600
PPE
600
Cash
600

Cash 800
REV 800
Cash
800
REV
800

RDE 300
AD 300
RDE
300
AD
300

Cash 800
REV 800
Cash
800
REV
800

RDE 300
AD 300
RDE
300
AD
300

With this accounting treatment, Pfizer reports no revenue and no expenses in the first year. Then in years 2 and 3, as Pfizer recognizes drug sales, the cost of the R&D equipment is transferred to the income statement and, thus, matched to the related revenues. This enables more accurate analysis of the drug's financial performance and yields a more accurate representation of Pfizer's R&D operations. Nonetheless, if the R&D equipment has no alternate use, then GAAP requires the first treatment (full expensing).

One last effect deserves mention: because expensing R&D assets generally depresses profits and book value of equity, the market-to-book ratios (market price per share divided by equity book value per share) for high-R&D industries tend to be higher than those for less-R&D intensive industries. This difference is driven as much by accounting conservatism as it is by fundamental differences in industry characteristics and market expectations about future performance. This emphasizes the need to compare financial ratios within industries, particularly for industries with substantial R&D activities.

**BUSINESS INSIGHT**   Pfizer R&D

Pfizer spends about $7.4 billion annually for R&D compared with its revenues of $51.3 billion, or about 14.4%. This reflects a high percent of revenues devoted to R&D for the pharmaceutical industry. Following is the R&D-expense-to-sales ratio for Pfizer and some of its competitors.

| | 2005 | 2004 | 2003 |
|---|---|---|---|
| Bristol-Meyers Squibb ......... | 14.3% | 13.2% | 10.9% |
| GlaxoSmithKline ............. | 14.2 | 13.9 | 12.9 |
| Eli Lilly..................... | 20.7 | 22.2 | 18.7 |
| Merck ..................... | 17.5 | 17.1 | 14.6 |
| Pfizer...................... | 14.4 | 14.6 | 16.7 |

# Restructuring Expenses

Restructuring expenses are substantial in many income statements. They tend to be large in magnitude and, as a result, GAAP requires enhanced disclosure, either as a separate line item in the income statement or as a footnote. Restructuring costs typically consists of two components:

1. Employee severance or relocation costs
2. Asset write-downs

The first part, **employee severance or relocation costs**, represent accrued (estimated) costs to terminate or relocate employees as part of a restructuring program. By accruing those costs, we mean:

■ Estimating total costs of terminating or relocating selected employees; costs might include severance pay (typically a number of weeks of pay based on the employee's tenure with the company), outplacement costs, and relocation or retraining costs for remaining employees.

■ Reporting *total* estimated costs as an expense (and a liability) in the period the costs are estimated and the restructuring program announced; subsequent payments reduce this liability.

The second part of restructuring costs is **asset write-downs**, also called *write-offs* or *charge-offs*. Restructuring activities usually involve closure or relocation of manufacturing or administrative facilities. This can require write-down of long-term assets (such as plant assets or goodwill), and the write-down of inventories whose market value is less than book value. Recall that asset cost is first recorded on the balance sheet and is subsequently transferred from the balance sheet to the income statement as expense when the asset is used. The write-down of an asset accelerates this process for a portion, or all, of the asset cost. Write-downs have no cash flow effects unless the write-down has some potential tax benefits.

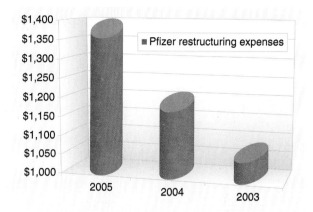

The financial statement effects of restructuring charges can be large. We must remember that management determines the amount of restructuring costs and when to recognize them. As such, it is not uncommon for a company to time recognition of restructuring costs in a period when its income is already depressed. This behavior is referred to as a **big bath**.

---

**RESEARCH INSIGHT** | **Restructuring Costs and Managerial Incentives**

Research has investigated the circumstances and effects of restructuring costs. Some research finds that stock prices increase when a company announces a restructuring as if the market appreciates the company's candor. Research also finds that many companies that reduce income through restructuring costs later reverse a portion of those costs, resulting in a substantial income boost for the period of reversal. These reversals often occur when the company would have otherwise reported an earnings decline. Whether or not the market responds favorably to trimming the fat or simply disregards restructuring costs as transitory and, thus, as uninformative, managers have incentives to exclude such income-decreasing items from operating income. These incentives often derive from contracts such as debt covenants and managerial bonus plans.

---

The FASB has tightened rules relating to restructuring costs in an effort to mitigate abuses. For example, a company is required to have a formal restructuring plan that is approved by its board of directors before any restructuring charges are accrued. Also, a company must identify the relevant employees and notify them of its plan. In each subsequent year, the company must disclose in its footnotes the original amount of the liability (accrual), how much of that liability is settled in the current period (such as employee payments), how much of the original liability has been reversed because of cost overestimation, any new accruals for unforeseen costs, and the current balance of the liability. This creates more transparent financial statements, which presumably deters earnings management.

**BUSINESS INSIGHT**    **Pfizer's Restructuring**

A portion of Pfizer's restructuring activities in 2005 relates to its "Adapting to Scale" (AtS) initiative. The company describes this activity in its footnotes as follows:

> Pfizer management has performed a comprehensive review of our processes, organizations, systems and decision-making procedures, in a company-wide effort to improve performance and efficiency. We expect the costs associated with this multi-year effort to continue through 2008 and to total approximately $4 billion to $5 billion, on a pre-tax basis. The actions associated with the AtS productivity initiative will include restructuring charges, such as asset impairments, exit costs and severance costs. We incurred the following costs in connection with our AtS initiative, which was launched in the first quarter of 2005:

| (Millions of Dollars) | Year Ended Dec. 31, 2005 |
|---|---|
| Implementation costs .................... | $330 |
| Restructuring charges................... | 450 |
| Total AtS costs........................ | $780 |

> Through December 31, 2005, the restructuring charges primarily relate to employee termination costs at our manufacturing facilities in North America and in our U.S. marketing and worldwide research and development operations, and the implementation costs primarily relate to system and process standardization, as well as the expansion of shared services. The components of restructuring charges associated with AtS follow:

| (Millions of Dollars) | Costs Incurred 2005 | Utilization Through Dec. 31, 2005 | Accrual as of Dec. 31, 2005[a] |
|---|---|---|---|
| Employee termination costs .... | $305 | $166 | $139 |
| Asset impairments............ | 131 | 131 | — |
| Other ..................... | 14 | 3 | 11 |
| | $450 | $300 | $150 |

(a) Included in Other current liabilities.

Financial statement effects of Pfizer's accounting for restructuring costs are illustrated in the following template ($ millions).

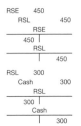

| | Balance Sheet | | | | | | Income Statement | | |
|---|---|---|---|---|---|---|---|---|---|
| Transaction | Cash Asset | + Noncash Assets | = Liabil- ities | + Contrib. Capital | + Earned Capital | | Rev- enues | − Expen- ses | = Net Income |
| Record restructuring expense and liability | | | +450 = Restructuring Liability | | −450 Retained Earnings | | | +450 − Restructuring = Expense | −450 |
| Paid $300 cash toward liability | −300 Cash | | −300 = Restructuring Liability | | | | | | |

When Pfizer estimated restructuring costs of $450 million, it recorded the expense and established a $450 million liability on its balance sheet. As costs are incurred, cash is paid out and the liability is reduced. GAAP requires disclosure of the initial liability, together with subsequent reductions or reversals of amounts not ultimately used. Through 2005, Pfizer spent $300 million for restructuring; the remaining $150 million is reported as a current liability on Pfizer's 2005 balance sheet.

Restructuring costs are typically large and, as such, greatly affect reported profits. Our analysis must consider whether these costs are properly chargeable to the accounting period in which they are recognized. Following are some guidelines relating to the two components of restructuring costs:

1. **Asset write-downs** Asset write-downs accelerate (or catch up) the depreciation process to reflect asset impairment. Impairment implies the loss of cash-generating capability and, likely, occurs over several years. However, the write-down expense is included in a single period's income statement when the impairment is recognized. It can be argued that the loss of cash-generating ability occurred over recent prior periods in addition to the current period. Thus, prior periods' profits are arguably not as high as reported, and the current period's profit is not as low. This measurement error is difficult to estimate and, thus, many analysts do not adjust balance sheets and income statements for write-downs. At a minimum, however, we must recognize informally the implications of restructuring costs for the profitability of recent prior periods and the current period.

2. **Employee severance or relocation costs** GAAP permits recognition of costs relating to employee separation or relocation that are *incremental* and that do not benefit future periods. Thus, accrual of these costs is treated like other liability accruals. We must, however, be aware of over- or understated costs and its effects on current and future profitability. GAAP requires a reconciliation of this restructuring accrual in future years (see Business Insight on page 5-16). Overstatements are followed by a reversal of the restructuring liability, and understatements are followed by further accruals. Should a company develop a reputation for recurring reversals or understatements, its management loses credibility.

---

**MANAGERIAL DECISION**     **You Are the Financial Analyst**

You are analyzing the 10-K of a company that reports a large restructuring expense, involving both employee severance and asset write-downs. How do you interpret and treat this cost in your analysis of the company's current and future profitability? [Answer, p. 5-28]

---

# MID-MODULE REVIEW 1

Merck & Co., Inc., reports the following income statements for 2003 through 2005.

| ($ in millions) | 2005 | 2004 | 2003 |
|---|---|---|---|
| Sales . . . . . . . . . . . . . . . . . . . . . . . . . . . . . . . . . . . . . | $22,011.9 | $22,938.6 | $22,485.9 |
| Costs, expenses and other | | | |
| Materials and production. . . . . . . . . . . . . . . . . . . . . . . | 5,149.6 | 4,959.8 | 4,436.9 |
| Marketing and administrative . . . . . . . . . . . . . . . . . . | 7,155.5 | 7,238.7 | 6,200.3 |
| Research and development. . . . . . . . . . . . . . . . . . . . | 3,848.0 | 4,010.2 | 3,279.9 |
| Restructuring cost . . . . . . . . . . . . . . . . . . . . . . . . . . . | 322.2 | 107.6 | 194.6 |
| Equity income from affiliates . . . . . . . . . . . . . . . . . . . | (1,717.1) | (1,008.2) | (474.2) |
| Other (income) expense, net . . . . . . . . . . . . . . . . . . . | (110.2) | (344.0) | (203.2) |
| | 14,648.0 | 14,964.1 | 13,434.3 |
| Income from continuing operations before taxes. . . . . . | 7,363.9 | 7,974.5 | 9,051.6 |
| Taxes on income . . . . . . . . . . . . . . . . . . . . . . . . . . . . . | 2,732.6 | 2,161.1 | 2,462.0 |
| Income from continuing operations . . . . . . . . . . . . . . . . | 4,631.3 | 5,813.4 | 6,589.6 |
| Income from discontinued operations, net taxes. . . . . . | — | — | 241.3 |
| Net income. . . . . . . . . . . . . . . . . . . . . . . . . . . . . . . . . . | $ 4,631.3 | $ 5,813.4 | $ 6,830.9 |

## Required

1. Merck's revenue recognition policy, as outlined in footnotes to its 10-K, includes the following: "Revenues from sales of products are recognized when title and risk of loss passes to the customer." What is the importance for revenue recognition of 'title and risk of loss passing to the customer'?

2. Merck's research and development (R&D) efforts require specialized equipment and facilities that cannot be used for any other purpose. How does Merck account for costs related to this specialized equipment and facilities? Would Merck account for these costs differently if they were not used for R&D? Explain.

3. Merck reports restructuring cost (expenses) each year. What are the two general categories of restructuring expenses? How do accrual accounting and disclosure requirements prevent companies from intentionally overstating restructuring expenses in one year (referred to as taking a "big bath") and reversing the unused expenses in a future year?

## Solution

1. Revenues are only recognized when the earning process is complete. Merck delivers its product before the customer is obligated to make payment. Passage of title typically constitutes delivery.

2. All R&D related equipment and/or facilities that have no alternative use must be expensed under GAAP. Should the assets have other uses, they are capitalized and depreciated like other plant assets. R&D costs are aggregated into one line item (research and development expense) on Merck's income statement. Other costs are reported under materials and production and/or marketing and administrative expenses.

3. Restructuring expenses generally fall into two categories: severance costs and asset write-offs. Restructuring programs must be approved by the board of directors before they are recognized in financial statements. Further, companies are required to disclose the initial liability accrual together with the portion that was subsequently utilized and reversed, if any. Because the restructuring accrual is an estimate, overestimates and subsequent reversals are possible. Should the company develop a reputation for recurring reversals, it will lose credibility with analysts and other stakeholders.

## Income Tax Expenses

**LO3** Explain and analyze accounting for income taxes.

Companies maintain two sets of accounting records, one for preparing financial statements for external constituents, including current and prospective shareholders, and another for reporting to tax authorities. Two sets of accounting records are necessary because the U.S. tax code is different from GAAP. These two different sets of accounting records can report dramatically different levels of pretax income (in publicly available financial reports) and taxable income (in reports sent to taxing authorities).

One common difference between these two sets of records relates to fixed assets. Companies usually compute depreciation expense using the straight-line method for financial reporting purposes—this means they transfer the same amount of the asset's cost from the balance sheet to the income statement each year. However, for tax reporting, companies (legally) transfer more of the asset's cost from the balance sheet to the income statement in the earlier years of the asset's life (referred to as *accelerated* depreciation). This reduces taxable income and the company's tax liability and, thereby, increases cash flows during the early years of an asset's useful life. However, in the later years of the asset's useful life, the amount of depreciation expense for tax reporting declines and, consequently, taxable income and income taxes paid will be higher than for earlier years. Financial reporting (GAAP) requires that companies recognize this future tax liability. To see this, assume that Pfizer acquires office equipment for $200. The equipment has a four-year life, and zero salvage value. Further assume that Pfizer has $300 income before depreciation and a 40% tax rate. For tax purposes, assume that Pfizer uses an accelerated depreciation method that permits the company to deduct depreciation of $100, $50, $30 and $20 over the four years. Depreciation schedules for GAAP and tax accounting records follow:

|  | Year 1 | Year 2 | Year 3 | Year 4 | Total |
|---|---|---|---|---|---|
| Financial reporting depreciation (computed) .... | $ 50 | $ 50 | $ 50 | $ 50 | $ 200 |
| Financial reporting income (assumed) ......... | 250 | 250 | 250 | 250 | 1,000 |
| Financial reporting tax expense (40%) ......... | 100 | 100 | 100 | 100 | 400 |
| Financial reporting net book value of asset[†] .... | 150 | 100 | 50 | 0 | |
| | | | | | |
| Tax reporting depreciation (given). ........... | 100 | 50 | 30 | 20 | 200 |
| Tax reporting (taxable) income* ............. | 200 | 250 | 270 | 280 | 1,000 |
| Taxes paid (40%) ......................... | 80 | 100 | 108 | 112 | 400 |
| Tax reporting net book value of asset[†] ........ | 100 | 50 | 20 | 0 | |

[†]Cost less accumulated depreciation.
*$250 − Tax depreciation expense.

The table shows that because the financial reporting (GAAP) depreciation expense differs from its tax reporting counterpart, the equipment will have a different net book value for financial and tax reporting purposes. To keep track of the tax consequences arising from the difference between financial and tax reporting net book values, companies record *deferred income taxes* on the balance sheet. In this example, the company records deferred tax liabilities because the book value for tax purposes is less than that for financial reporting purposes (we later discuss deferred tax assets and how they arise).

To illustrate a deferred tax liability, let's use the information from the preceding table. In year 1, the financial reporting net book value of the asset is $150 ($200 − $50 GAAP depreciation expense) whereas the tax reporting net book value is only $100 ($200 − $100 tax depreciation expense). The difference of $50 creates a deferred tax liability of $20 ($50 × 40% tax rate). The intuition for this is that since the two book values must eventually be equal, taxable income will be higher in the future (comparatively less depreciation expense), thus giving rise to higher taxes that must be recognized currently on the balance sheet. The following template captures these effects.

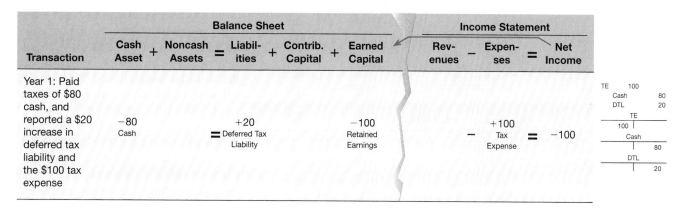

Accounting standards require a company to first compute the taxes it owes (per its tax return), then to compute any changes in deferred tax liabilities and assets, and finally to compute tax expense reported in the income statement (as a residual figure). Tax expense is, thus, not computed as pretax income multiplied by the company's tax rate as we might initially have expected. Instead, tax expense is computed as follows:

**Tax Expense = Taxes Paid − Increase (or + Decrease) in Deferred Tax Assets + Increase (or − Decrease) in Deferred Tax Liabilities**

In year 2, the difference between the financial reporting net book value of the equipment ($100) and its tax reporting net book value ($50) is still $50. Thus, the deferred tax liability is unchanged. Another way of seeing this is that the company pays taxes of $100 and records $100 tax expense on the income statement, because depreciation expense in the company's tax return is the same as the depreciation on the income statement. Net book value decreased by the same amount on both sets of books. The following template shows the year 2 tax expense effects.

| | Balance Sheet | | | | | Income Statement | | |
|---|---|---|---|---|---|---|---|---|
| Transaction | Cash Asset | + Noncash Assets | = Liabil- ities | + Contrib. Capital | + Earned Capital | Rev- enues | − Expen- ses | = Net Income |
| Year 2: Paid taxes of $100 cash and reported $100 tax expense | −100 Cash | | = | | −100 Retained Earnings | | − +100 Tax Expense | = −100 |

TE    100
    Cash    100
TE
100 |
    Cash
    | 100

In year 3, the difference between the financial reporting net book value of the equipment ($50) and its tax reporting net book value ($20) has declined to $30. This means that the deferred tax liability decreases to $12 ($30 × 40%) from the $20 in the prior year. Pfizer must adjust the deferred tax liability account by $8 ($20 − $12) to reflect this lower value. The deferred tax liability decreases in year 3 because financial reporting depreciation expense of $50 exceeds the tax reporting depreciation expense of $30. Following the rule for computing tax expense, Pfizer reports $100 on the income statement ($108 cash paid less the decrease in deferred tax liabilities). The template below captures these effects.

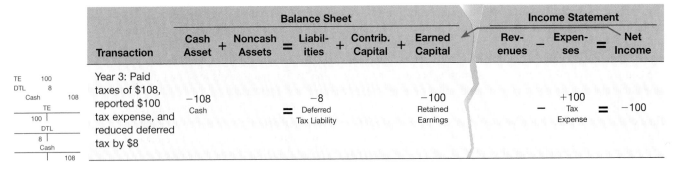

TE      100
DTL       8
     Cash      108
        TE
   100 |
       DTL
     8 |
      Cash
          | 108

| | Balance Sheet | | | | | | Income Statement | | |
|---|---|---|---|---|---|---|---|---|---|
| Transaction | Cash Asset | + Noncash Assets | = Liabil- ities | + Contrib. Capital | + Earned Capital | | Rev- enues | − Expen- ses | = Net Income |
| Year 3: Paid taxes of $108, reported $100 tax expense, and reduced deferred tax by $8 | −108 Cash | | = −8 Deferred Tax Liability | | −100 Retained Earnings | | | − +100 Tax Expense | = −100 |

---

| EXHIBIT 5.4 | Sources of Deferred Tax Assets and Liabilities |
|---|---|

**Net Book Value of Assets**

| Financial reporting net book value | > | Tax reporting net book value | → | Deferred tax liability on balance sheet |
|---|---|---|---|---|
| Financial reporting net book value | < | Tax reporting net book value | → | Deferred tax asset on balance sheet |

**Net Book Value of Liabilities**

| Financial reporting net book value | < | Tax reporting net book value | → | Deferred tax liability on balance sheet |
|---|---|---|---|---|
| Financial reporting net book value | > | Tax reporting net book value | → | Deferred tax asset on balance sheet |

The example above demonstrates how accelerated depreciation for tax purposes and straight-line for financial reporting creates deferred tax liabilities. Other differences between the two sets of books create other types of deferred tax accounts. Exhibit 5.4 shows the relation between the financial reporting and tax-reporting net book values and the resulting deferred taxes on the balance sheet.

*Deferred tax assets* arise when the net book value of liabilities is greater for financial reporting than for tax reporting, or when the net book value of assets is smaller for financial reporting than for tax reporting. A frequent example relates to restructuring. In the year a reorganization plan is approved, the company will accrue restructuring costs (this creates a GAAP liability) and will write down assets to their market values (this reduces the net book value of the assets for financial reporting purposes). However, tax authorities do not recognize these accrual accounting transactions. In particular, for tax purposes, restructuring costs are not deductible until paid in the future and asset write-downs are not deductible until the loss is realized when the asset is sold. As a result, the restructuring accrual is not a liability for tax reporting purposes—it has a tax-reporting net book value of $0. Moreover, the tax-reporting value of the assets remains unchanged. Both of these differences (the liability and the assets) give rise to a deferred tax asset. The deferred tax asset will be transferred to the income statement in the future when the company pays the restructuring costs and sells the assets for a loss.

Another common deferred tax asset relates to tax loss carryforwards. Specifically, when a company reports a loss for tax purposes, it can carry back that loss for up to two years to recoup previous taxes paid. Any unused losses can be carried forward for up to twenty years to reduce future taxes. This creates a benefit (an "asset") on the tax reporting books for which there is no corresponding financial reporting asset and thus the company records a deferred tax asset.

Companies are also required to establish a **deferred tax valuation** allowance for deferred tax assets when the future realization of their benefits is uncertain. The effect on financial statements is to reduce reported assets, increase tax expense, and reduce equity. These effects are reversed if the allowance is reversed in the future when realization of these tax benefits becomes more likely. Pfizer reported an allowance of $177 million in 2004, of which $35 million was then reversed in 2005 when it determined that the realization of the tax benefits was more certain. The effect of a change (increase or decrease) in the deferred tax valuation allowance on net income is dollar-for-dollar (meaning Pfizer's net income increased by $35 million in 2005).

To see how income tax expense is disclosed, Pfizer's tax footnote to its income statement is shown in Exhibit 5.5. Pfizer's $3,424 million tax expense reported in its income statement (called the *provision*) consists of the following two components (organized by federal, state and foreign):

1. *Current tax expense.* Current tax expense is determined from the company's tax returns; it is the amount payable (in cash) to tax authorities (some of these taxes have been paid during the year as the company makes installments). Pfizer labels this "Taxes currently payable."

2. *Deferred tax expense.* Effect on tax expense from changes in deferred tax liabilities and deferred tax assets (in the above example, deferred tax liabilities increase by $20 in year 1, reflecting a future

liability, which yields a higher income tax expense than taxes paid). Pfizer labels this "Deferred income taxes."

| EXHIBIT 5.5 | Income Tax Expense Footnote for Pfizer |
| --- | --- |
| **(Millions of Dollars)** | **2005** |
| United States: | |
| Taxes currently payable | |
| Federal ......................................... | $1,369 |
| State and local ................................ | 122 |
| Deferred income taxes........................... | 12 |
| Total U.S. tax provision ........................... | 1,503 |
| International: | |
| Taxes currently payable.......................... | 3,317 |
| Deferred income taxes........................... | (1,396) |
| Total international tax provision ..................... | 1,921 |
| Total provision for taxes on income ................. | $3,424 |

Companies must disclose the components of deferred tax liabilities and assets. Pfizer's deferred tax footnote to its balance sheet (shown in Exhibit 5.6) reports total deferred tax assets of $7,070 million and total deferred tax liabilities of $15,164. Companies are permitted to net some deferred tax assets and liabilities, and Pfizer reports a net deferred tax liability of $8,094 million on its 2005 balance sheet. Many of Pfizer's deferred tax assets relate to accrued liabilities or asset write-downs arising from expenses included in financial reporting income, but not yet recognized for tax reporting (such as prepaid items, allowance for doubtful accounts, restructuring accruals, employee benefits, inventory allowances, investment provisions, and write-offs of in-process R&D expenditures). Pfizer also has a deferred tax asset from a net operating loss carryforward and has recorded a small valuation allowance. These deferred tax assets represent future reductions of the company's tax liability and are, therefore, classified as assets.

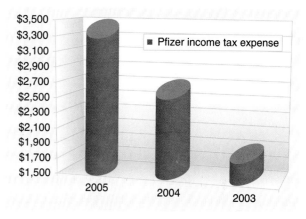

Pfizer's deferred tax liabilities relate to a number of items. Intangible assets and property plant and equipment have different tax and financial reporting net book values because Pfizer uses accelerated depreciation for tax purposes and straight-line for financial reporting. The deferred tax liability relating to employee benefits arises from pension contributions and other payments that are deductible for tax purposes but that Pfizer has not yet accrued for financial reporting purposes (thus there is no GAAP liability). The deferred tax liability relating to unremitted earnings results from consolidation of Pfizer's subsidiaries. The subsidiaries' profits are included in Pfizer's consolidated income statement and reflected in the net book value of the investment on

| EXHIBIT 5.6 | Deferred Taxes Footnote for Pfizer | |
| --- | --- | --- |
| | **2005 Deferred Tax** | |
| **(Millions of Dollars)** | **Assets** | **(Liabilities)** |
| Prepaid/deferred items ........................ | $1,318 | $ (753) |
| Intangibles.................................... | 857 | (8,748) |
| Inventories ................................... | 583 | — |
| Property, plant and equipment.................. | 87 | (1,183) |
| Employee benefits ............................ | 2,282 | (1,376) |
| Restructurings and other charges .............. | 729 | (118) |
| Net operating loss/credit carryforwards.......... | 406 | — |
| Unremitted earnings .......................... | — | (2,651) |
| All other ..................................... | 950 | (335) |
| Subtotal ..................................... | 7,212 | (15,164) |
| Valuation allowance........................... | (142) | — |
| Total deferred taxes........................... | $7,070 | $ (15,164) |
| Net deferred tax liability ...................... | | $ (8,094) |

Pfizer's balance sheet (we discuss accounting for intercompany investments in Module 7). The subsidiaries' profits are not taxable until the subsidiaries actually pay dividends to Pfizer. Thus, the net book value of the investment asset for financial reporting (related to profits from the subsidiary) is greater than its tax reporting book values. Pfizer will pay taxes on the subsidiaries' profits when the subsidiaries pay dividends in the future.

Pfizer's 2005 income before tax is $11,534 million. Its tax expense of $3,424 million represents an effective tax rate of 29.7%. The *effective tax rate* is defined as tax expense divided by pretax income ($3,424 million/$11,534 million = 29.7%).[5] By comparison, the federal *statutory tax rate* for corporations (the rate prescribed in tax regulations) is 35%. Companies must provide a schedule that reconciles the effective tax rate (29.7% for Pfizer) with the Federal statutory rate of 35%. Following is the schedule that Pfizer reports in its 10-K.

Reconciliation of the U.S. statutory income tax rate to our effective tax rate for continuing operations before the cumulative effect of a change in accounting principles follows:

| Year Ended | 2005 | 2004 | 2003[a] |
| --- | --- | --- | --- |
| U.S. statutory income tax rate | 35.0% | 35.0% | 35.0% |
| Earnings taxed at other than U.S. statutory rate | (19.5) | (18.3) | (53.2) |
| U.S. research tax credit | (0.7) | (0.6) | (3.1) |
| Repatriation of foreign earnings | 14.4 | — | — |
| Resolution of certain tax positions | (5.1) | — | — |
| Acquired IPR&D | 5.0 | 2.7 | 54.2 |
| Litigation settlement provisions | — | — | 13.7 |
| All other—net | 0.6 | 0.2 | 3.1 |
| Effective tax rate for income from continuing operations before cumulative effect of a change in accounting principles | 29.7% | 19.0% | 49.7% |

(a) The large component percentages in 2003 reflect lower income from continuing operations in 2003 due to the impact of the Pharmacia acquisition.

In addition to federal taxes (paid to the IRS), companies also pay taxes to state, local, and foreign jurisdictions where they operate. These tax rates are typically lower than the statutory rate of 35%. In 2005, for example, these taxes reduced Pfizer's effective tax rate by 19.5%. In addition, Pfizer received tax credits for research (reducing the effective tax rate by another 0.7%). Repatriation of foreign earnings resulted in additional tax, raising the effective tax rate by 14.4%. (*American Jobs Creation Act of 2004* created a temporary incentive for U.S. corporations to repatriate accumulated income earned abroad by providing a deduction for certain dividends from controlled foreign corporations in 2005. Pfizer chose to repatriate earnings from its foreign subsidiaries, paying additional tax at a much lower rate than it would have otherwise paid.) Favorable settlements of tax disputes with taxing authorities reduced its effective tax rate by 5.1%, and other miscellaneous items added another 0.6% to the effective tax rate.

In sum, Pfizer's effective tax rate for 2005 is 29.7%, 5.3 percentage points below the 35% statutory rate. In 2004, however, the effective tax rate was only 19%, and in 2003 it was 49.7%, due mainly to additional taxes it incurred as a result of the Pharmacia acquisition. Fluctuations, such as these, in the effective tax rate are not uncommon and highlight the difference between income reported under GAAP and that computed using multiple tax codes under which companies operate.

Analysis of deferred taxes can yield useful insights. Generally, income is not taxable until received. Thus, revenue accruals (such as accounts receivable for percentage-of-completion contracts) increase deferred tax liabilities as GAAP assets (accounts receivable) exceeds tax-reporting assets (similar to the effect of using straight-line depreciation for financial reporting purposes and accelerated depreciation for tax returns). An increase in deferred tax liabilities indicates that a company is reporting higher GAAP income relative to taxable income and can indicate the company is managing earnings upwards.

---

[5] This is the effective tax rate for *all* of Pfizer's income. In the previous module we computed the tax rate on operating income by first deducting the taxes related to nonoperating income (or adding back the tax shield related to nonoperating expenses). The effective tax rate on total income, is a weighted average of the two (operating and nonoperating).

The difference between reported corporate profits and taxable income increased substantially in the late 1990s, just prior to huge asset write-offs. *CFO Magazine* (November 2002) implied that such differences are important for analysis and should be monitored:

> Fueling the sense that something [was] amiss [was] the growing gap between the two sets of numbers. In 1992, there was no significant difference between pretax book income and taxable net income . . . By 1996, according to IRS data, a $92.5 billion gap had appeared. By 1998 [prior to the market decline], the gap was $159 billion—a fourth of the total taxable income reported . . . If people had seen numbers showing very significant differences between book numbers for trading and tax numbers, they would have wondered if those [income] numbers were completely real.

Although an increase in deferred tax liabilities can legitimately result, for example, from an increase in depreciable assets and the use of accelerated depreciation for tax purposes, we must be aware of the possibility that such an increase is the result of improper revenue recognition in that the company may not be reporting those revenues to tax authorities.

## Adequacy of Deferred Tax Asset Valuation

Analysis of the deferred tax asset valuation account provides us with additional insight. This analysis involves (1) assessing the adequacy of the valuation allowance and (2) determining how and why the valuation account changed during the period and how that change affects net income.

When a company reports a deferred tax asset, the company implies that it will more likely than not receive a future tax benefit equal to the deferred tax asset. If the company is uncertain about the future tax benefit, it records an allowance to reduce the asset. How can we gauge the adequacy of a valuation allowance account? We might assess the reasons for the valuation account (typically reported in the tax footnote). We might examine other companies in the industry for similar allowances. We might also review the MD&A for any doubt on company prospects for future profitability.

We can quantify our analysis in at least three ways. First, we can examine the allowance as a percentage of the deferred tax assets (most valuation allowances relate to tax loss carryforwards). For Pfizer, this 2005 percentage is 35%; see below. We also want to gather data from other pharmaceutical companies and compare the sizes of their allowance accounts relative to their related deferred tax assets. The important point is that we must be comfortable with the size of the valuation account and remember that management has control over the adequacy and reporting of the allowance account (with audit assurances).

| ($ millions) | 2005 | 2004 | 2003 |
|---|---|---|---|
| Deferred tax asset from net operating loss carryforward . . . . . . . . . . . . . . . | $406 | $353 | $92 |
| Valuation allowance . . . . . . . . . . . . . . . . . . . . . . . . . . . . . . . . . . . . . . . . . . . . | $142 | $177 | $3 |
| Valuation allowance as a percent of net operating loss carryforward . . . . . . | 35.0% | 50.1% | 3.3% |

Second, we can examine changes in the allowance account. During a year, circumstances change and the company might be more or less assured of receiving the tax benefit. In that case, the company might decrease or increase its allowance account. For Pfizer, the allowance markedly declined from the prior year (from 50% in 2004 to 35% in 2005). What does such a decline denote? Perhaps Pfizer's overall economic environment has improved, rendering it more likely that it will be profitable for tax purposes. We want to determine why it reduced the allowance and assess the validity of its claims in light of industry and economy-wide factors.

Third, we can quantify how a change in the valuation allowance affects net income and its effective tax rate (see table on next page). To see this, recall that changes in the valuation allowance affect tax expense in the same direction, dollar for dollar. This is turn, affects net income (in the opposite direction) again, dollar for dollar. For Pfizer, its 2005 valuation allowance decreased by $35 million ($177 million − $142 million), which decreased tax expense and increased net income by $35 million. This is not a large effect on income for Pfizer, or on its effective tax rate (29.7% after the valuation allowance change versus 29.4% before). However, changes in valuation allowances can have (and have had) marked effects on net income for numerous companies. For our analysis, we must remember that a company can increase current period income by deliberately decreasing the valuation allowance. Knowing that such decreases can boost net income, companies might deliberately create too large a valuation allowance in one of more prior years and use it as a *cookie jar reserve*. We want to assess the details of the valuation account and changes therein from the footnotes and from the MD&A.

| ($ millions) | 2005 | 2004 | 2003 |
|---|---|---|---|
| Change in valuation allowance . . . . . . . . . . . . . . . . . . . . . . . . . . . . | $(35) | $ 174 | |
| Impact of valuation allowance change on net income . . . . . . . . . . | $ 35 | $(174) | |
| Income before tax . . . . . . . . . . . . . . . . . . . . . . . . . . . . . . . . . . . . . | $11,534 | $14,007 | $3,246 |
| Tax expense. . . . . . . . . . . . . . . . . . . . . . . . . . . . . . . . . . . . . . . . . . | $ 3,424 | $ 2,665 | $1,614 |
| Effective tax rate . . . . . . . . . . . . . . . . . . . . . . . . . . . . . . . . . . . . . | 29.7% | 19.0% | 49.7% |
| Tax expense before change in valuation account . . . . . . . . . . . . . | $ 3,389 | $ 2,839 | |
| Effective tax rate before change in valuation account . . . . . . . . . . | 29.4% | 20.3% | |

## MID-MODULE REVIEW 2

Refer to the Merck & Co., Inc., 2005 income statement in the Mid-Module Review 1. Merck provides the following additional information in footnotes to its 10-K.

Taxes on income from continuing operations consisted of:

| Years Ended December 31 | 2005 | 2004 | 2003 |
|---|---|---|---|
| Current provision | | | |
| Federal . . . . . . . . . . . . . . . . . . . . . . | $1,688.1 | $1,420.0 | $1,464.2 |
| Foreign . . . . . . . . . . . . . . . . . . . . . . | 739.6 | 530.9 | 611.3 |
| State . . . . . . . . . . . . . . . . . . . . . . . . | 295.9 | 161.3 | 254.8 |
| | 2,723.6 | 2,112.2 | 2,330.3 |
| Deferred provision | | | |
| Federal . . . . . . . . . . . . . . . . . . . . . . | 97.0 | 95.6 | 21.3 |
| Foreign . . . . . . . . . . . . . . . . . . . . . . | (134.0) | (32.3) | 96.5 |
| State . . . . . . . . . . . . . . . . . . . . . . . . | 46.0 | (14.4) | 13.9 |
| | 9.0 | 48.9 | 131.7 |
| | $2,732.6 | $2,161.1 | $2,462.0 |

### Required

1. What is the total income tax expense that Merck reports in its income statement?
2. What amount of its total tax expense did (or will) Merck pay in cash (that is, what amount is currently payable)?
3. Explain how Merck calculates its income tax expense.

### Solution

1. Total income tax expense is $2,732.6 million.
2. Of the total, $2,723.6 million is currently payable.
3. Income tax expense is the sum of current taxes (that is, currently payable as determined from the company's tax returns) plus the change in deferred tax assets and liabilities. It is a calculated figure, not a percentage that is applied to pretax income.

# OPERATING COMPONENTS 'BELOW-THE-LINE'

Pfizer's income statement includes a subtotal labeled "income from continuing operations." Historically, this presentation highlighted the non-recurring (*transitory*) portions of the income statement so that they could be eliminated to facilitate the projection of future profitability. The word "continuing" was meant to imply that income was purged of one-time items, as these were presented "below-the-line," that is, below income from continuing operations. Two categories of items are presented below-the-line:[6]

1. **Discontinued operations**   Net income (loss) from business segments that have been or will be sold, and any gains (losses) on net assets related to those segments sold in the current period.
2. **Extraordinary items**   Gains or losses from events that are both *unusual* and *infrequent*.

Discontinued operations are generally viewed as nonoperating, and we discuss their accounting treatment in Module 7. Explanation of the accounting for extraordinary items follows.

## Extraordinary Items

**Extraordinary items** refer to events that are both unusual *and* infrequent. Their effects are reported following income from continuing operations. Management determines whether an event is unusual and infrequent (with auditor approval) for financial reporting purposes. Further, management often has incentives to classify unfavorable items as extraordinary because they will be reported separately, after income from continuing operations (*below-the-line*). These incentives derive from investors who tend to focus more on items included in income from continuing operations and less on non-recurring items that are not included in continuing operations.

GAAP provides the following guidance in determining whether or not an item is extraordinary:

▪ *Unusual nature.* The underlying event or transaction must possess a high degree of abnormality and be clearly unrelated to, or only incidentally related to, the ordinary activities of the entity, taking into account the entity's operating environment.

▪ *Infrequency of occurrence.* The underlying event or transaction must be of a type that would not reasonably be expected to recur in the foreseeable future, taking into account the entity's operating environment.

The following items are generally *not reported* as extraordinary items:

▪ Gains and losses on retirement of debt
▪ Write-down or write-off of operating or nonoperating assets
▪ Foreign currency gains and losses
▪ Gains and losses from disposal of specific assets or business segment
▪ Effects of a strike
▪ Accrual adjustments related to long-term contracts
▪ Costs of a takeover defense
▪ Costs incurred as a result of the September 11, 2001, events

Extraordinary items are reported separately (net of tax) and below income from continuing operations on the income statement.[7]

## Earnings Per Share

The income statement reports earnings per share (EPS) numbers. At least one, and potentially two, EPS figures are reported: basic and diluted. The difference between the two measures is shown in Exhibit 5.7.

**LO4** Compute earnings per share and explain the effect of dilutive securities.

---

[6] Prior accounting standards included a third category, **changes in accounting principles.** This category included voluntary and mandated changes in accounting policies utilized by a company, such as a change in the depreciation method. Under current GAAP, changes in accounting principles are no longer reported below-the-line. Instead, they are applied retrospectively (unless it is impractical to do so, in which case they are applied at the earliest practical date). No cumulative effect adjustment is made to income as was the case in prior standards. Instead, changes in depreciation methods are now accounted for as changes in estimates, which are applied prospectively.

[7] Until recently, gains and losses on debt retirement were treated as extraordinary items. To explain, understand that debt is accounted for at historical cost, just like the accounting for equipment. The *market price* of debt, however, is determined by fluctuations in interest rates. As a result, if a company retires (pays off) its debt before maturity, the purchase price often differs from the debt amount reported on the balance sheet, resulting in gains and losses on retirement. These gains and losses were formerly treated as extraordinary. Following passage of SFAS 145, these gains and losses are no longer automatically treated as extraordinary, but instead must be unusual and infrequent to be designated as extraordinary.

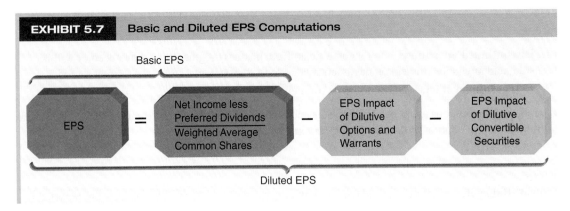

**EXHIBIT 5.7** Basic and Diluted EPS Computations

**Basic EPS** is computed as: (Net income − Dividends on preferred stock)/Weighted average number of common shares outstanding during the year. The subtraction of preferred stock dividends yields the income available for dividend payments to common shareholders. Computation of **diluted EPS** reflects the additional shares that would be issued if all stock options, warrants, and convertible securities had been converted into common shares at the beginning of the year. Diluted EPS never exceeds basic EPS.

Pfizer reports Basic EPS of $1.10 in 2005 and Diluted EPS of $1.09. Given the near identical results for basic and diluted EPS, we know that Pfizer has few dilutive securities. Symantec Corporation's 2005 EPS, however, differs by 7¢ (81¢ compared to 74¢ diluted, a difference of almost 10%) as reported in the following footnote disclosure to its 2005 10-K.

| (in thousands, except per share amounts) | 2005 |
|---|---|
| **Basic net income per share** | |
| Net income. . . . . . . . . . . . . . . . . . . . . . . . . . . . . . . . . . . . . . . . . . . . . . | $536,159 |
| Weighted average number of common shares outstanding during the period. . . . . . . . . . . | 660,631 |
| Basic net income per share. . . . . . . . . . . . . . . . . . . . . . . . . . . . . . . . . . . . . | $ 0.81 |
| **Diluted net income per share** | |
| Net income. . . . . . . . . . . . . . . . . . . . . . . . . . . . . . . . . . . . . . . . . . . . . . . | $536,159 |
| Interest on convertible subordinated notes, net of income tax effect. . . . . . . . . . . . . . . . | 8,380 |
| Net income, as adjusted . . . . . . . . . . . . . . . . . . . . . . . . . . . . . . . . . . . . . . . . | $544,539 |
| Weighted average number of common shares outstanding during the period. . . . . . . . . . . | 660,631 |
| Shares issuable from assumed exercise of options using the treasury stock method. . . . . | 35,745 |
| Shares issuable from assumed conversion of convertible subordinated notes . . . . . . . . . | 41,780 |
| Restricted stock. . . . . . . . . . . . . . . . . . . . . . . . . . . . . . . . . . . . . . . . . . . . . | 89 |
| Total shares for purpose of calculating diluted net income per share. . . . . . . . . . . . . . . | 738,245 |
| Diluted net income per share . . . . . . . . . . . . . . . . . . . . . . . . . . . . . . . . . . . . . | $ 0.74 |

Diluted earnings per share for Symantec is 7¢ lower than basic EPS, mainly due to convertible bonds. If the bonds had been converted to stock, Symantec would have avoided interest expense of $8.4 million (net of tax) and net income would have increased by that amount. In addition, the weighted average number of shares in the denominator would have increased by 77.5 million (35.7 million + 41.8 million), representing the shares issued in the bond conversion. The two effects reduced earnings per share from $0.81 to $0.74.[8]

In addition to convertible bonds such as Symantec's, companies might have potentially dilutive convertible preferred stock and stock options. To compute diluted EPS for convertible preferred stock, the company

---

[8] The effects of dilutive securities are only included if they are, in fact, dilutive. If they are *antidilutive,* inclusion would actually increase EPS, and they are, thus, excluded from the computation. An example of an antidilutive security is employee stock options whose exercise price is greater than the stock's current market price. These *underwater* (or out-of-the-money) options are antidilutive and are, therefore, excluded from the EPS computation. Symantec, for example, excludes 4.2 million of underwater stock options from its 2005 EPS computation. Should the market price of Symantec's common stock increase above the exercise price of the options, their effects will, once again, be included and diluted EPS will decline, all else equal.

---

**BUSINESS INSIGHT**    Pro Forma Income and Managerial Motives

Income from continuing operations per GAAP, once a key measure of company performance, is often supplemented or even supplanted by pro forma income in company financial statements and press releases. **Pro forma income** begins with the GAAP income from continuing operations (that excludes discontinued operations and extraordinary items), and then excludes other one-time items (most notably, restructuring charges), and some additional items such as acquisition expenses (goodwill amortization and other acquisition costs), stock-option compensation expense, and research and development expenditures.

The purported motive for reporting pro forma income is to eliminate transitory (one-time) items to enhance year-to-year comparability. Although this might be justified on the basis that pro forma income has greater predictive ability, important information is lost in the process. One role for accounting is to report how effective management has been in its stewardship of invested capital. Asset write-downs, liability accruals, and other charges that are eliminated in calculating pro forma income often reflect outcomes of poor management decisions. Our analysis must not blindly eliminate information contained in nonrecurring items by focusing solely on pro forma income. Critics of pro forma income also argue that the items excluded by managers from GAAP income are inconsistent across companies and time. They contend that a major motive for pro forma income is to mislead stakeholders. Legendary investor Warren Buffet puts pro forma in context: "When companies or investment professionals use terms such as 'EBITDA' and 'pro forma,' they want you to unthinkingly accept concepts that are dangerously flawed." (Berkshire Hathaway, Annual Report)

---

would add back preferred dividends previously subtracted from net income in the EPS numerator and would increase the denominator by the number of shares that would be issued to the preferred stockholders. The adjustment for stock-option exercise is a bit more complicated. The number of shares issued to the option holder upon exercise is added to the diluted EPS denominator. Then, the number of shares that the company could have repurchased with the exercise proceeds, is subtracted from the denominator.

EPS figures are often used as a method of comparing operating results for companies of different sizes under the assumption that the number of shares outstanding is proportional to the income level (that is, a company twice the size of another will report double the income and will have double the common shares outstanding, leaving EPS approximately equal for the two companies). This assumption is erroneous. Management controls the number of common shares outstanding and there is no relation between firm size and number of shares outstanding. Different companies also have different philosophies regarding share issuance and repurchase. For example, consider that most companies report annual EPS of less than $5, while Berkshire Hathaway reported EPS of $5,538 for 2005! This is because Berkshire Hathaway has so few common shares outstanding, not necessarily because it has stellar profits.

---

**RESEARCH INSIGHT**    "Pro Forma" Income

Transitory items such as discontinued operations, restructuring charges, and extraordinary items make it difficult for investors to predict future income. The past decade has seen more companies reporting pro forma income, which excludes nonrecurring or noncash items that companies feel are unimportant for valuation purposes. Research, however, provides no evidence that pro forma income is a better predictor of future cash flows. More important, investors appear to be misled when firms report pro forma income. Research also finds that companies reporting pro forma income tend to be young companies concentrated in technology and business services. Too often, these companies have below-average sales and income, which might explain why they choose to report pro forma income.

---

## Foreign Currency Translation

Many companies conduct international operations and transact business in currencies other than $US. It is common for companies to purchase assets in foreign currencies, borrow money in foreign currencies, and transact business with their customers in foreign currencies. Increasingly many companies have subsidiaries whose balance sheets and income statements are prepared in foreign currencies.

Financial statements prepared according to U.S. GAAP must be reported in $US. This means that any transactions conducted in foreign currencies must be reported in $US, and the financial statements of any

**L05** Explain how foreign currency fluctuations affect the income statement.

foreign subsidiaries must be translated into $US before consolidation with the U.S. parent company. This translation process can markedly alter both the balance sheet and income statement. We discuss income statement effects of foreign currency translation in this module; we discuss the effects on stockholders' equity in Module 9.

## Effects of Foreign Currency Transactions on Income

A change in the strength of the $US vis-à-vis foreign currencies affects reported income in the following manner: changes in foreign currency exchange rates have a direct effect on the $US equivalent for revenues, expenses, and income of the foreign subsidiary because revenues and expenses are translated at the average exchange rate for the period. Exhibit 5.8 shows those financial effects.

| EXHIBIT 5.8 | Income Statement Effects from Foreign Currency Movements | | |
|---|---|---|---|
| | **Revenues** – | **Expenses** = | **Profit** |
| $US Weakens......... | Increase | Increase | Increase |
| $US Strengthens...... | Decrease | Decrease | Decrease |

Specifically, when the foreign currency strengthens ($US weakens), the subsidiary's revenues, expenses, and income increase. On the other hand, when the $US strengthens, the subsidiary's revenues, expenses, and income decrease. (The profit effect assumes that revenues exceed expenses; if expenses exceed revenues, a loss occurs, which increases if the $US weakens and decreases if the $US strengthens.)

Pfizer discusses how currency fluctuations affect its income statement in the following excerpt from footnotes to the company's 2005 10-K.

> 48% of our 2005 revenues were derived from international operations, including 18% from countries in the Euro zone and 7% from Japan. These international-based revenues expose our revenues and earnings to foreign currency exchange rate changes . . . Depending on the direction of change relative to the U.S. dollar, foreign currency values can increase or decrease the reported dollar value of our results of operations . . . Changes in foreign exchange rates increased total revenues in 2005 by $945 million or 1.8% compared to 2004. The foreign exchange impact on 2005 revenue growth was due to the weakening of the U.S. dollar relative to many foreign currencies, especially the Euro, which accounted for about 35% of the impact in 2005

The $US weakened against many foreign currencies for several years preceding and including 2005. Thus, each unit of foreign currency purchased more $US. Therefore, revenues and expenses denominated in foreign currencies were translated to higher $US equivalents, yielding increased revenues and profits even when unit volumes remained unchanged. Pfizer also discloses that it attempts to dampen the effect that these fluctuations have on reported profit:

> While we cannot predict with certainty future changes in foreign exchange rates or the effect they will have on us, we attempt to mitigate their impact through operational means and by using various financial instruments.

The phrase 'operational means' includes attempts to structure transactions in $US rather than a foreign currency. Foreign currency financial instruments are common and include forward and futures contracts, which lock in future currency values. We explain how these instruments (called derivatives) work in Appendix 7A. In sum, we must be cognizant of the effects of currency fluctuations on reported revenues, expenses, and profits for companies with substantial foreign-currency transactions.

## MODULE-END REVIEW

Refer to the Merck & Co., Inc., 2005 income statement in the Mid-Module Review.

### Required

1. Assume that during 2005 the $US weakened with respect to the currencies in which Merck conducts its business. How would that weakening affect Merck's income statement?
2. What is the difference between basic and diluted earnings per share?

### Solution

1. Income statement accounts that are denominated in foreign currencies must be translated into $US before the financial statements are publicly disclosed. When the $US weakens, each foreign currency unit is worth more $US. Consequently, each account in Merck's income statement is larger because the dollar weakened.

2. Basic earnings per share is equal to net income (less preferred dividends) divided by the weighted average number of common shares outstanding during the period. Diluted EPS considers the effects of dilutive securities. In diluted EPS, the denominator increases by the additional shares that would have been issued assuming exercise of all options and conversion of all convertible securities. The numerator is also adjusted for any preferred dividends and/or interest that would not have been paid upon conversion.

# GUIDANCE ANSWERS

**MANAGERIAL DECISION**     **You Are the Financial Analyst**

Typically, restructuring charges have two components: asset write-downs (such as inventories, property, plant, and goodwill) and severance costs. Write-downs occur when the cash-flow-generating ability of an asset declines, thus reducing its current market value below its book value reported on the balance sheet. Arguably, this decline in cash-flow-generating ability did not occur solely in the current year and, most likely, has developed over several periods. It is not uncommon for companies to delay loss recognition, such as write-downs of assets. Thus, prior period income is, arguably, not as high as reported, and the current period loss is not as great as reported. Turning to severance costs, GAAP permits restructuring expense to include only those costs that are *incremental* and will *not* benefit future periods. The accrual of severance-related expenses can be viewed like other accruals; that is, it might be over- or understated. In future periods, the required reconciliation of the restructuring accrual will provide insight into the adequacy of the accrual in that earlier period.

# DISCUSSION QUESTIONS

**Q5-1.** What are the criteria that guide firms in recognition of revenue? What does each of the criteria mean? How are the criteria met for a company like Abercrombie & Fitch, a clothing retailer? How are the criteria met for a construction company that builds offices under long-term contracts with developers?

Abercrombie & Fitch (ANF)

**Q5-2.** Why are extraordinary items reported separately from continuing operations in the income statement?

**Q5-3.** What are the criteria for categorizing an event as an extraordinary item? Provide an example of an event that would properly be categorized as an extraordinary item and one that would not.

**Q5-4.** What is the difference between basic earnings per share and diluted earnings per share? Are potentially dilutive securities always included in the EPS computation?

**Q5-5.** What effect, if any, does a weakening $US have on reported sales and net income for companies operating outside the United States?

**Q5-6.** Identify the two typical categories of restructuring costs and their effects on the balance sheet and the income statement. Explain the concept of a big bath and why restructuring costs are often identified with this event.

**Q5-7.** What is the proper accounting treatment for research and development costs? Why are R&D costs normally not capitalized under GAAP?

**Q5-8.** Under what circumstances will deferred taxes likely result in a cash outflow?

**Q5-9.** What is the concept of pro forma income and why has this income measure been criticized?

**Q5-10.** What is unearned revenue? Provide three examples of unearned revenue.

# MINI EXERCISES

**M5-11. Computing Percentage-of-Completion Revenues (LO1)**

Bartov Corporation agreed to build a warehouse for a client at an agreed contract price of $2,500,000. Expected (and actual) costs for the warehouse follow: 2005, $400,000; 2006, $1,000,000; and 2007, $500,000. The company completed the warehouse in 2007. Compute revenues, expenses, and income for each year 2005 through 2007 using the percentage-of-completion method.

**M5-12.  Applying the Financial Statement Effects Template.  (LO1)**

Refer to the information for Bartov Corporation in M5-11.

*a.*  Use the financial statement effects template to record contract revenues and expenses for each year 2005 through 2007 using the percentage-of-completion method.

*b.*  Prepare journal entries and T-accounts to record contract revenues and expenses for each year 2005 through 2007 using the percentage-of-completion method.

**M5-13.  Assessing Revenue Recognition of Companies    (LO1)**

Identify and explain when each of the following companies should recognize revenue.

The GAP (GPS)

Merck & Company (MRK)

John Deere (DE)

Bank of America (BAC)

Johnson Controls (JCI)

*a.*  The GAP: The GAP is a retailer of clothing items for all ages.

*b.*  Merck & Company: Merck engages in developing, manufacturing, and marketing of pharmaceutical products. It sells its drugs to retailers like CVS and Walgreen.

*c.*  John Deere: Deere manufactures heavy equipment. It sells equipment to a network of independent distributors, who in turn sell the equipment to customers. Deere provides financing and insurance services both to distributors and customers.

*d.*  Bank of America: Bank of America is a banking institution. It lends money to individuals and corporations and invests excess funds in marketable securities.

*e.*  Johnson Controls: Johnson Controls manufactures products for the government under long-term contracts.

**M5-14.  Assessing Risk Exposure to Revenue Recognition    (LO1)**

BannerAD Corporation manages a Website in which it sells products on consignment from sellers. It pays these sellers a portion of the sales price, absent its commission. Identify at least two potential revenue recognition problems relating to such sales.

**M5-15.  Estimating Revenue Recognition with Right of Return    (LO1)**

The GAP (GPS)

The GAP offers an unconditional return policy. It normally expects 2% of sales at retail selling prices to be returned before the return period expires. Assuming that The GAP records total sales of $5 million for the current period, how much in *net* sales should it record for this period?

**M5-16.  Assessing Research and Development Expenses    (LO2)**

Abbott Laboratories (ABT)

Abbott Laboratories reports the following (summary) income statement.

| Year Ended December 31 ($ 000s) | 2005 |
|---|---|
| Net sales | $22,338 |
| Cost of products sold | 10,641 |
| Research and development | 1,821 |
| Selling, general and administrative | 5,514 |
| Total operating cost and expenses | 17,976 |
| Pretax operating earnings | $ 4,362 |

*a.*  Compute the percent of net sales that Abbott Laboratories spends on research and development (R&D). How would you assess the appropriateness of its R&D expense level?

*b.*  Describe how accounting for R&D expenditures affects Abbott Laboratories' balance sheet and income statement.

**M5-17.  Interpreting Foreign Currency Translation Disclosure    (LO5)**

Bristol-Myers Squibb (BMY)

Bristol-Myers Squibb (BMY) reports the following footnote to its 10-K report relating to the year-over-year change in sales.

| | | Analysis of % Change | | |
|---|---|---|---|---|
| | Total Change | Volume | Price | Foreign Exchange |
| 2005 vs. 2004 | (1)% | (2)% | — | 1% |
| 2004 vs. 2003 | 4% | — | — | 4% |

*a.*  Did sales increase or decrease in 2004 and 2005? By what percentage? What amount of this change was attributable to fluctuations in the value of foreign currencies vis-a-vis the $US?

b.   What can we infer from the table about the relative strength of the $US compared with the currencies in the countries in which BMY does business?

**M5-18.   Analyzing Income Tax Disclosure   (LO3)**

Cisco Systems reports the following footnote disclosure to its 10-K report ($ millions).

Cisco Systems (CSCO)

| Years Ended | July 30, 2005 |
|---|---|
| **Federal** | |
| Current . . . . . . . . . . . . | $1,340 |
| Deferred . . . . . . . . . . | 497 |
| | 1,837 |
| **State** | |
| Current . . . . . . . . . . . | 496 |
| Deferred . . . . . . . . . . | (292) |
| | 204 |
| **Foreign** | |
| Current . . . . . . . . . . . | 404 |
| Deferred . . . . . . . . . . | (150) |
| | 254 |
| Total . . . . . . . . . . . . . . | $2,295 |

a.   What amount of income tax expense does Cisco report in its income statement for 2005?
b.   How much of Cisco's income tax expense is current (as opposed to deferred)?
c.   Why do deferred tax assets and liabilities arise? How do they impact the tax expense that Cisco reports in its 2005 income statement?

**M5-19.   Defining and Computing Earnings per Share   (LO4)**

Lucent Corporation (LU) reports the following basic and diluted earnings per share in its 2005 10-K report. (a) Describe the accounting definitions for basic and diluted earnings per share. (b) Identify the Lucent numbers that make up both EPS computations. (c) Why does Lucent add back $86 million for interest expense on the convertible debt securities in the diluted EPS calculation?

Lucent Corporation (LU)

| (in millions, except per share amounts) | 2005 |
|---|---|
| Net income (loss). . . . . . . . . . . . . . . . . . . . . . . . . . . . . . . . . . . . . . . . . . | $1,185 |
| Conversion and redemption cost—8.00% covertible securities. . . . . . . . | — |
| Preferred stock dividends and accretion . . . . . . . . . . . . . . . . . . . . . . . . . | — |
| Net income (loss) applicable to common shareowners—basic. . . . . . . . . | 1,185 |
| Adjustment for dilutive securities on net income (loss): | |
| Interest expense related to convertible securities . . . . . . . . . . . . . . . . . . | 86 |
| Net income (loss) applicable to common shareowners—diluted . . . . . . . | $1,271 |
| | |
| Weighted average shares outstanding—basic. . . . . . . . . . . . . . . . . . . . . | 4,426 |
| Effect of dilutive securities: | |
| Stock options. . . . . . . . . . . . . . . . . . . . . . . . . . . . . . . . . . . . . . . . . . . . . . | 60 |
| Warrants. . . . . . . . . . . . . . . . . . . . . . . . . . . . . . . . . . . . . . . . . . . . . . . . . . . | 15 |
| 2.75% covertible securities. . . . . . . . . . . . . . . . . . . . . . . . . . . . . . . . . . . . | 542 |
| 8.00% convertible securities. . . . . . . . . . . . . . . . . . . . . . . . . . . . . . . . . . . | 167 |
| 7.75% convertible securities . . . . . . . . . . . . . . . . . . . . . . . . . . . . . . . . . . . | 8 |
| Weighted average shares outstanding—diluted . . . . . . . . . . . . . . . . . . . | 5,218 |
| **EPS:** | |
| Basic . . . . . . . . . . . . . . . . . . . . . . . . . . . . . . . . . . . . . . . . . . . . . . . . . . . . . | $ 0.27 |
| Diluted . . . . . . . . . . . . . . . . . . . . . . . . . . . . . . . . . . . . . . . . . . . . . . . . . . . | 0.24 |

**M5-20.    Assessing Revenue Recognition for Advance Payments    (LO1)**

Koonce Company operates a performing arts center. The company sells tickets for its upcoming season of six Broadway musicals and receives $420,000 cash.  The performances occur monthly over the next six months.

    *a.*    When should Koonce record revenue for the Broadway musical series?

    *b.*    Use the financial statement effects template to show the $420,000 cash receipt and recognition of the first month's revenue.

**M5-21.    Reporting Unearned Revenue and its Recognition    (LO1)**

Target Corporation
(TGT)

Target Corporation sells gift cards that can be used at any of the company's Target or Greatland stores. Target encodes information on the card's magnetic strip about the card's value, the date it expires (typically two years after issuance), and the store where it was purchased.

    *a.*    How will Target's balance sheet reflect the gift card?

    *b.*    When does Target record revenue from the gift card?

# EXERCISES

**E5-22.    Assessing Revenue Recognition Timing    (LO1)**

Explain when each of the following businesses should recognize revenues:

Limited (LTD)
Boeing Corp. (BA)
Supervalu, Inc. (SVU)
MTV(MTV)

    *a.*    A clothing retailer like The Limited.

    *b.*    A contractor like Boeing Corporation that performs work under long-term government contracts.

    *c.*    A grocery store like Supervalu.

    *d.*    A producer of television shows like MTV that syndicates its content to television stations.

    *e.*    A residential real estate developer who constructs only speculative houses and later sells these houses to buyers.

Bank of America (BAC)
Harley-Davidson (HOG)
Time-Warner (TW)

    *f.*    A banking institution like Bank of America that lends money for home mortgages.

    *g.*    A manufacturer like Harley-Davidson.

    *h.*    A publisher of magazines such as Time-Warner.

**E5-23.    Assessing Revenue Recognition Timing and Income Measurement    (LO1)**

Explain when each of the following businesses should recognize revenue and identify any income measurement issues that could arise.

TheStreet.Com
(TSCM)

    *a.*    RealMoney.Com, a division of TheStreet.Com, provides investment advice to customers for an up-front fee. It provides these customers with password-protected access to its Website where customers can download investment reports. RealMoney has an obligation to provide updates on its Website.

Oracle (ORCL)

    *b.*    Oracle develops general ledger and other business application software that it sells to its customers. The customer pays an up-front fee for the right to use the software and a monthly fee for support services.

Intuit (INTU)

    *c.*    Intuit develops tax preparation software that it sells to its customers for a flat fee. No further payment is required and the software cannot be returned, only exchanged if defective.

    *d.*    A developer of computer games sells its software with a 10-day right of return period during which the software can be returned for a full refund. After the 10-day period has expired, the software cannot be returned.

**E5-24.    Constructing and Assessing Income Statements Using Percentage-of-Completion    (LO1)**

General Electric
Company (GE)

Assume that General Electric Company agreed in May 2006 to construct a nuclear generator for NSTAR, a utility company serving the Boston area. The contract price of $500 million is to be paid as follows: $200 million at the time of signing; $100 million on December 31, 2006; and $200 million at completion in May 2007. General Electric incurred the following costs in constructing the generator: $100 million in 2006, and $300 million in 2007.

    *a.*    Compute the amount of General Electric's revenue, expense, and income for both 2006 and 2007 under the percentage-of-completion revenue recognition method.

    *b.*    Discuss whether or not you believe the percentage-of-completion method provides a good measure of General Electric's performance under the contract.

**E5-25.** **Constructing and Assessing Income Statements Using Percentage-of-Completion** (LO1)

On March 15, 2005, Frankel Construction contracted to build a shopping center at a contract price of $120 million. The schedule of expected (which equals actual) cash collections and contract costs follows:

| Year | Cash Collections | Cost Incurred |
|---|---|---|
| 2005 . . . . . | $ 30 million | $15 million |
| 2006 . . . . . | 50 million | 40 million |
| 2007 . . . . . | 40 million | 30 million |
| Total . . . . . | $120 million | $85 million |

a. Calculate the amount of revenue, expense, and net income for each of the three years 2005 through 2007 using the percentage-of-completion revenue recognition method.

b. Discuss whether or not the percentage-of-completion method provides a good measure of this construction company's performance under the contract.

**E5-26.** **Interpreting the Income Tax Expense Footnote Disclosure** (LO3)

The income tax footnote to the financial statements of FedEx follows.      FedEx (FDX)

The components of the provision for income taxes for the years ended May 31 were as follows:

| ($ millions) | 2005 | 2004 | 2003 |
|---|---|---|---|
| Current provision | | | |
| Domestic | | | |
|     Federal . . . . . . . . . . . . . . . . . | $634 | $371 | $112 |
|     State and local . . . . . . . . . . . | 65 | 54 | 28 |
|     Foreign . . . . . . . . . . . . . . . . . . | 103 | 85 | 39 |
| | 802 | 510 | 179 |
| Deferred provision (benefit) | | | |
| Domestic | | | |
|     Federal . . . . . . . . . . . . . . . . . | 67 | (22) | 304 |
|     State and local . . . . . . . . . . . | (4) | (7) | 25 |
|     Foreign . . . . . . . . . . . . . . . . . . | (1) | — | — |
| | 62 | (29) | 329 |
| Provision for income taxes . . . . . . | $864 | $481 | $508 |

a. What is the amount of income tax expense reported in FedEx's 2005, 2004 and 2003 income statements?

b. What percentage of total tax expense is currently payable in each of 2003, 2004, and 2005? Explain why the percentages are different each year.

c. One possible reason for the $67 million federal deferred tax expense in 2005 is that deferred tax liabilities increased during that year. Provide an example that gives rise to an increase in the deferred tax liability.

**E5-27. Identifying Operating and Transitory Income Components** (LO3)

Following is the Bristol-Myers Squibb income statement.

a. Identify the components in its statement that you would consider operating.

b. BMY's net profit increased despite a slight decrease in sales. Identify the main reason for its profit increase and discuss whether that factor is sustainable.

| Dollars in Millions | 2005 | 2004 |
|---|---|---|
| Net sales | $19,207 | $19,380 |
| Cost of products sold | 5,928 | 5,989 |
| Marketing, selling and administrative | 5,106 | 5,016 |
| Advertising and product promotion | 1,476 | 1,411 |
| Research and development | 2,746 | 2,500 |
| Provision for restructuring, net | 32 | 104 |
| Litigation charges, net | 269 | 420 |
| Gain on sale of business | (569) | (320) |
| Equity in net income of affiliates | (334) | (273) |
| Other expense, net | 37 | 115 |
| Total expenses | 14,691 | 14,962 |
| Earnings from continuing operations before minority interest and income taxes | 4,516 | 4,418 |
| Provision for income taxes | 932 | 1,519 |
| Minority interest, net of taxes | 592 | 521 |
| Earnings from continuing operations | 2,992 | 2,378 |
| Discontinued operations | | |
| Net earnings | (5) | 10 |
| Net gain on disposal | 13 | — |
| | 8 | 10 |
| Net earnings | $ 3,000 | $ 2,388 |

Notes:

- **Equity in net income of affiliates** refers to income BMY earned on investments in affiliated (but unconsolidated) companies.

- **Minority interest** expense relates to the claims of outside shareholders of BMY's (consolidated) subsidiaries in the income of those companies.

Excerpt from BMY's income tax footnotes in 2004 and 2005

The effective income tax rate on earnings from continuing operations before minority interest and income taxes was 20.6% in 2005 compared with 34.4% in 2004 and 25.8% in 2003. The lower effective tax rate in 2005 was due primarily to a 2004 charge of approximately $575 million for estimated deferred income taxes related to the repatriation of approximately $9 billion in special dividends from the Company's non-U.S. subsidiaries.

The AJCA, which President Bush signed into law on October 22, 2004, provides for a temporary 85 percent dividends-received deduction for certain cash distributions of the earnings of foreign subsidiaries. The deduction would result in a federal tax rate of approximately 5.25% on the repatriated earnings (assuming a marginal federal tax rate of 35% on those earnings). To qualify for the deduction, the repatriated earnings must be reinvested in the United States pursuant to a domestic reinvestment plan approved by a company's chief executive officer and subsequently by its board of directors.

**E5-28.** **Identifying Operating and Transitory Income Components** **(LO2)**

Following is the Deere & Company income statement for 2005.

Deere & Company (DE)

| ($ millions) | 2005 |
|---|---|
| Net sales and revenues | |
| Net sales .......................................... | $19,401.4 |
| Finance and interest income........................... | 1,439.5 |
| Health care premiums and fees ....................... | 724.9 |
| Other income...................................... | 364.7 |
| Total ......................................... | 21,930.5 |
| Costs and expenses | |
| Cost of sales ..................................... | 15,163.4 |
| Research and development expenses ................... | 677.3 |
| Selling, administrative and general expenses ............ | 2,218.6 |
| Interest expense .................................. | 761.0 |
| Health care claims and costs ......................... | 573.9 |
| Other operating expenses............................ | 380.5 |
| Total ......................................... | 19,774.7 |
| Income of consolidated group before income taxes ........ | 2,155.8 |
| Provision for income taxes ........................... | 715.1 |
| Income of consolidated group ........................ | 1,440.7 |
| Equity in income of unconsolidated affiliates | |
| Credit ........................................ | 0.6 |
| Other......................................... | 5.5 |
| Total ......................................... | 6.1 |
| Net income....................................... | $ 1,446.8 |

Notes:

- Income statement includes John Deere commercial and consumer tractor segment, a finance subsidiary that provides loan and lease financing relating to the sales of those tractors, and a health care segment that provides managed health care services for the company and certain outside customers.
- **Equity in income of unconsolidated affiliates** refers to income John Deere has earned on investments in affiliated (but unconsolidated) companies. These are generally investments made for strategic purposes.

Deere provides the following description of its business segments in footnotes to its 10-K.

> The company's Equipment Operations generate revenues and cash primarily from the sale of equipment to John Deere dealers and distributors. The Equipment Operations manufacture and distribute a full line of agricultural equipment; a variety of commercial and consumer equipment; and a broad range of construction and forestry equipment. The company's Financial Services primarily provide credit services and managed health care plans. The credit operations primarily finance sales and leases of equipment by John Deere dealers and trade receivables purchased from the Equipment Operations. The health care operations provide managed health care services for the company and certain outside customers.

**Required**

*a.* Identify the components in its income statement that you would consider operating.

*b.* Discuss your treatment of Deere's activities relating to the financing of its John Deere lawn and garden, commercial tractors, and its health care business segments.

**E5-29. Assessing the Income Tax Footnote (LO3)**

Dow Chemical reports the following income tax footnote disclosure in its 10-K report.

| Deferred Tax Balances at December 31 (In millions) | 2005 | | 2004 | |
| --- | --- | --- | --- | --- |
| | Deferred Tax Assets | Deferred Tax Liabilities | Deferred Tax Assets | Deferred Tax Liabilities |
| Property............................. | $ 382 | $(2,304) | $ 674 | $(2,998) |
| Tax loss and credit carryforwards ....... | 2,297 | — | 2,514 | — |
| Postretirement benefit obligations ....... | 1,501 | (861) | 2,038 | (594) |
| Other accruals and reserves............ | 1,666 | (437) | 1,839 | (625) |
| Inventory ........................... | 160 | (184) | 152 | (135) |
| Long-term debt ...................... | 216 | (64) | 650 | (71) |
| Investments ......................... | 282 | — | 218 | (4) |
| Other—net........................... | 551 | (643) | 389 | (635) |
| Subtotal ............................ | $7,055 | $(4,493) | $8,474 | $(5,062) |
| Valuation allowance................... | (179) | — | (165) | — |
| Total ............................... | $6,876 | $(4,493) | $8,309 | $(5,062) |

**Required**

a. Dow reports $2,304 million of deferred tax liabilities in 2005 relating to "Property." Explain how such liabilities arise.

b. Describe how a deferred tax asset can arise from postretirement benefit (health care) obligations.

c. Dow reports $2,297 million in deferred tax assets for 2005 relating to tax loss carryforwards. Describe how these loss carryforwards arise and under what conditions these assets will be realized.

d. Dow has established a deferred tax asset valuation allowance of $179 million for 2005. What is the purpose of this allowance? How did the increase in this allowance of $14 million from 2004 to 2005 affect net income?

e. Assuming that cash paid for income tax is $918 million, compute Dow's income tax expense (as reported in its income statement) of $1,782 million for 2005 using the financial statement effects template. (*Hint*: Show the effects of changes in deferred taxes.)

**E5-30. Analyzing and Assessing Research and Development Expenses (LO2)**

Advanced Micro Devices (AMD) and Intel (INTC) are competitors in the high-tech computer processor industry. Following is a table ($ millions) of sales and R&D expenses for both companies.

| AMD | R&D Expense | Sales | INTC | R&D Expense | Sales |
| --- | --- | --- | --- | --- | --- |
| 2003...... | $ 852.1 | $3,519.2 | 2003...... | $4,365.0 | $30,141.0 |
| 2004...... | 934.6 | 5,001.4 | 2004...... | 4,778.0 | 34,209.0 |
| 2005...... | 1,144.0 | 5,847.6 | 2005...... | 5,145.0 | 38,826.0 |

a. What percentage of sales are AMD and INTC spending on research and development?

b. How are AMD and INTC's balance sheets and income statements affected by the accounting for R&D costs?

c. How can one evaluate the effectiveness of R&D spending? Does the difference in R&D as a percentage of sales necessarily imply that one company is more heavily invested in R&D? Why might this not be the case?

**E5-31.    Analyzing and Interpreting Foreign Currency Translation Effects    (LO5)**

Johnson Controls reports the following table and discussion in its 2005 10-K.

Johnson Controls
(JCI)

The company's net sales for the fiscal years ended September 30, 2005 and 2004, were as follows.

| Sales (In millions) | 2005 | 2004 | % Change |
|---|---|---|---|
| Building efficiency.................... | $ 5,717.7 | $ 5,323.7 | 7% |
| Interior experience—North America...... | 8,498.6 | 8,237.4 | 3% |
| Interior experience—Europe........... | 8,935.5 | 7,677.6 | 16% |
| Interior experience—Asia ............. | 1,399.1 | 1,092.6 | 28% |
| Power solutions..................... | 2,928.5 | 2,271.7 | 29% |
| Total............................. | $27,479.4 | $24,603.0 | 12% |

Consolidated net sales in the current fiscal year were $27.5 billion, increasing 12% above the prior year sales of $24.6 billion. Excluding the favorable effects of currency translation, sales increased 9% above the prior year. For fiscal 2006, management anticipates that net sales will grow to $32 billion, an increase of approximately 16% from fiscal 2005 net sales. The growth is expected to be partially offset by unfavorable effects of currency translation, as the company assumes the dollar will strengthen relative to the euro assuming a euro exchange rate of $1.20.

RISK MANAGEMENT—*Foreign Exchange* The Company has manufacturing, sales and distribution facilities around the world and thus makes investments and enters into transactions denominated in various foreign currencies. In order to maintain strict control and achieve the benefits of the Company's global diversification, foreign exchange exposures for each currency are netted internally so that only its net foreign exchange exposures are, as appropriate, hedged with financial instruments. The Company hedges 70 to 90 percent of its known foreign exchange transactional exposures. The Company primarily enters into foreign currency exchange contracts to reduce the earnings and cash flow impact of non-functional currency denominated receivables and payables. Gains and losses resulting from hedging instruments offset the foreign exchange gains or losses on the underlying assets and liabilities being hedged. The maturities of the forward exchange contracts generally coincide with the settlement dates of the related transactions. Realized and unrealized gains and losses on these contracts are recognized in the same period as gains and losses on the hedged items. The Company also selectively hedges anticipated transactions that are subject to foreign exchange exposure, primarily with foreign currency exchange contracts, which are designated as cash flow hedges in accordance with SFAS No. 133, "Accounting for Derivative Instruments and Hedging Activities," as amended by SFAS No. 137, No. 138, and No. 149.

*a.*    How did foreign currency exchange rates affect sales for Johnson Controls in 2005?

*b.*    In what direction does Johnson Controls expect exchange rate fluctuations to affect sales in 2006? Explain. What crucial assumption is JCI making to project 2006 operating results?

*c.*    Describe how the accounting for foreign exchange translation affects reported sales and profits.

*d.*    How does Johnson Controls manage the risk related to its foreign exchange exposure? Describe the financial statement effects of this risk management activity.

**E5-32.    Interpreting Revenue Recognition for Gift Cards    (LO1)**

Footnotes to the 2005 annual report of Barnes & Noble Booksellers disclose the following:

Barnes & Noble
Booksellers (BKS)

The Barnes & Noble Membership Program entitles the customer to receive a 10% discount on all purchases made during the twelve-month membership period. The annual membership fee of $25.00 is nonrefundable after the first 30 days of the membership term. Revenue is being recognized over the twelve-month membership period based upon historical spending patterns for Barnes & Noble customers. Refunds of membership fees due to cancellations within the first 30 days are minimal.

**Required**

*a.*    Explain in layman terms how Barnes & Noble accounts for the cash received for its membership program. When does Barnes & Noble record revenue from this program?

*b.*    How does Barnes & Noble's balance sheet reflect those membership fees?

*c.*    Does the 10% discount affect Barnes & Noble's income statement when memberships fees are received?

# PROBLEMS

**P5-33.   Analyzing and Interpreting Revenue Recognition Policies and Risks   (LO1)**

Amazon.com (AMZN)

Amazon.com, Inc., provides the following explanation of its revenue recognition policies from its 10-K report.

> The Company generally recognizes revenue from product sales or services rendered when the following four revenue recognition criteria are met: persuasive evidence of an arrangement exists, delivery has occurred or services have been rendered, the selling price is fixed or determinable, and collectibility is reasonably assured.
>
> The Company evaluates the criteria outlined in EITF Issue No. 99-19, "Reporting Revenue Gross as a Principal versus Net as an Agent," in determining whether it is appropriate to record the gross amount of product sales and related costs or the net amount earned as commissions. Generally, when the Company is the primary obligor in a transaction, is subject to inventory risk, has latitude in establishing prices and selecting suppliers, or has several but not all of these indicators, revenue is recorded gross as a principal. If the Company is not the primary obligor and amounts earned are determined using a fixed percentage, a fixed-payment schedule, or a combination of the two, the Company generally records the net amounts as commissions earned.
>
> Product sales (including sales of products through the Company's Syndicates Stores program), net of promotional gift certificates and return allowances, are recorded when the products are shipped and title passes to customers. Return allowances are estimated using historical experience.
>
> Commissions received on sales of products from Amazon Marketplace, Auctions and zShops are recorded as a net amount since the Company is acting as an agent in such transactions. Amounts earned are recognized as net sales when the item is sold by the third-party seller and our collectibility is reasonably assured. The Company records an allowance for refunds on such commissions using historical experience.
>
> The Company earns revenues from services, primarily by entering into business-to-business strategic alliances, including providing the Company's technology services such as search, browse and personalization; permitting third parties to offer products or services through the Company's Websites; and powering third-party Websites, providing fulfillment services, or both. These strategic alliances also include miscellaneous marketing and promotional agreements. As compensation for the services the Company provides under these agreements, it receives one or a combination of cash and equity securities. If the Company receives non-refundable, up-front payments, such amounts are deferred until service commences, and are then recognized on a straight-line basis over the estimated corresponding service period. Generally, the fair value of consideration received, whether in cash, equity securities, or a combination thereof, is measured when agreement is reached, and any subsequent appreciation or decline in the fair value of the securities received does not affect the amount of revenue recognized over the term of the agreement. To the extent that equity securities received or modified after March 16, 2000 are subject to forfeiture or vesting provisions and no significant performance commitment exists upon signing of the agreements, the fair value of the securities and corresponding revenue is determined as of the date of the respective forfeiture or as vesting provisions lapse. The Company generally recognizes revenue from these services on a straight-line basis over the period during which the Company performs services under these agreements, commencing at the launch date of the service. Outbound shipping charges to customers are included in net sales.

**Required**

*a.*   Identify and discuss the main revenue recognition policies for its two primary sources of business revenues.

*b.*   Identify and describe at least three potential areas for revenue recognition shams in a business such as Amazon.

**P5-34.   Analyzing and Interpreting Income Tax Disclosures   (LO3)**

Pfizer (PFE)

The 2005 income statement for Pfizer is reproduced in this module. Pfizer also reports the following footnote relating to its income taxes in its 2005 10-K report.

> **Deferred Taxes** Deferred taxes arise because of different treatment between financial statement accounting and tax accounting, known as "temporary differences." We record the tax effect of these temporary differences as "deferred tax assets" (generally items that can be used as a tax deduction or credit in future periods) or "deferred tax liabilities" (generally items for which we received a tax deduction,

but that have not yet been recorded in the consolidated statement of income). The tax effects of the major items recorded as deferred tax assets and liabilities as of December 31 are:

| (Millions of Dollars) | 2005 Deferred Tax | |
|---|---|---|
| | Assets | (Liabilities) |
| Prepaid/deferred items . . . . . . . . . . . . . . . . . . . . . . . | $1,318 | $ (753) |
| Intangibles . . . . . . . . . . . . . . . . . . . . . . . . . . . . . . . . | 857 | (8,748) |
| Inventories . . . . . . . . . . . . . . . . . . . . . . . . . . . . . . . . | 583 | — |
| Property, plant and equipment . . . . . . . . . . . . . . . . . | 87 | (1,183) |
| Employee benefits . . . . . . . . . . . . . . . . . . . . . . . . . . | 2,282 | (1,376) |
| Restructructuring and other charges . . . . . . . . . . . . | 729 | (118) |
| Net operating loss/credit carryforwards . . . . . . . . . . | 406 | — |
| Unremitted earnings . . . . . . . . . . . . . . . . . . . . . . . . . | — | (2,651) |
| All other . . . . . . . . . . . . . . . . . . . . . . . . . . . . . . . . . . | 950 | (335) |
| Subtotal . . . . . . . . . . . . . . . . . . . . . . . . . . . . . . . . . . | 7,212 | (15,164) |
| Valuation allowance . . . . . . . . . . . . . . . . . . . . . . . . . | (142) | — |
| Total deferred taxes . . . . . . . . . . . . . . . . . . . . . . . . . | $7,070 | $ (15,164) |
| Net deferred tax liability . . . . . . . . . . . . . . . . . . . . . . | | $ (8,094) |

The net deferred tax liability position is primarily due to the deferred taxes recorded in connection with our acquisition of Pharmacia. We have carryforwards primarily related to net operating losses which are available to reduce future U.S. federal and state, as well as international income, expiring at various times between 2006 and 2025. Valuation allowances are provided when we believe that our deferred tax asstes are not recoverable based on an assessment of estimated future taxable income that incorporates ongoing, prudent, feasible tax planning strategies.

**Required**

*a.*    Describe the terms "deferred tax liabilities" and "deferred tax assets." Include a description of how these accounts can arise.

*b.*    Intangible assets (other than goodwill) acquired in the purchase of a company are depreciated (amortized) similar to buildings and equipment (see Module 7 for a discussion). Describe how the deferred tax liability of $8,748 million relating to intangibles arose.

*c.*    Pfizer has many employee benefit plans, such as a long-term health plan and a pension plan. Some of these are generating deferred tax assets and others are generating deferred tax liabilities. Explain the timing of the recognition of expenses under these plans that would give rise to these different outcomes.

*d.*    Pfizer is reporting a deferred tax liability that it labels as "unremitted earnings." This relates to an investment in an affiliated company for which Pfizer is recording income, but has not yet received dividends. Generally, investment income is taxed when received. Explain what information the deferred tax liability for unremitted earnings is conveying.

*e.*    Pfizer reports a deferred tax asset relating to net operating loss carryforwards. Explain what loss carryforwards are.

*f.*    Pfizer reports a valuation allowance of $142 million in 2005. Explain why Pfizer has established this allowance and its effect on reported profit. Pfizer's valuation allowance was $177 million in 2004. Compute the change in its allowance during 2005 and explain how that change affected 2005 tax expense and net income.

**P5-35. Analyzing and Interpreting Income Components and Disclosures** (LO2,3)

The income statement for Xerox Corporation follows.

| Year ended December 31 (in millions) | 2005 | 2004 | 2003 |
|---|---|---|---|
| Sales | $ 7,400 | $ 7,259 | $ 6,970 |
| Service, outsourcing and rentals | 7,426 | 7,529 | 7,734 |
| Finance income | 875 | 934 | 997 |
| Total revenues | 15,701 | 15,722 | 15,701 |
| Costs and expenses | | | |
| Cost of sales | 4,695 | 4,545 | 4,346 |
| Cost of service, outsourcing and rentals | 4,207 | 4,295 | 4,307 |
| Equipment financing interest | 326 | 345 | 362 |
| Research, development and engineering expenses | 943 | 914 | 962 |
| Selling, administrative and general expenses | 4,110 | 4,203 | 4,249 |
| Restructuring and asset impairment charges | 366 | 86 | 176 |
| Other expenses, net | 224 | 369 | 863 |
| Total costs and expenses | 14,871 | 14,757 | 15,265 |
| Income from continuing operations before income taxes, equity income and discontinued operations | 830 | 965 | 436 |
| Income tax (benefits) expenses | (5) | 340 | 134 |
| Equity in net income of unconsolidated affiliates | 98 | 151 | 58 |
| Income from continuing operations before discontinued operations | 933 | 776 | 360 |
| Income from discontinued operations, net of tax | 45 | 83 | — |
| Net income | $ 978 | $ 859 | $ 360 |

Notes:

- The income statement includes sales of Xerox copiers and a finance subsidiary that provides loan and lease financing relating to the sales of those copiers.
- **Equity in net income of unconsolidated affiliates** refers to income Xerox has earned on investments in affiliated (but unconsolidated) companies.
- Xerox tax expense was reduced in 2005 as a result of an audit. The company makes the following disclosure in its footnotes: "In June 2005, the 1996–1998 IRS audit was finalized. As a result, we recorded an aggregate second quarter 2005 net income benefit of $343."

**Required**

a. Xerox reports three main sources of income: sales, service, and finance income. How should revenue be recognized for each of these business activities? Explain.

b. Xerox reports research and development (R&D) expenses of $943 million in 2005, which is 12.7% of its sales. (1) How are R&D expenses accounted for under GAAP? (2) Why do you believe GAAP prohibits the capitalization of expenses such as R&D?

c. Xerox reports restructuring costs of $366 million in 2005. It also reports restructuring costs in each of 2004 and 2003. (1) Describe the two typical categories of restructuring costs and the accounting for each. (2) How do you recommend treating these costs for analysis purposes? (3) Should regular recurring restructuring costs be treated differently than isolated occurrences of such costs for analysis purposes?

d. Xerox's tax expense was reduced as a result of a favorable IRS ruling in 2005. How should this benefit be treated in your analysis of the company?

e. Xerox reports $224 million in expenses in 2005 labeled as 'Other expenses, net.' How can a company use such an account to potentially obscure its actual financial performance?

**P5-36. Analyzing and Interpreting Income Tax Footnote** (LO3)

FedEx reports the following footnote for its income taxes in its 2005 10-K report.

The components of the provision for income taxes for the years ended May 31 were as follows.

| (in millions) | 2005 | 2004 | 2003 |
|---|---|---|---|
| Current provision | | | |
| Domestic: | | | |
| Federal . . . . . . . . . . . . . . . | $634 | $371 | $112 |
| State and local . . . . . . . . . | 65 | 54 | 28 |
| Foreign . . . . . . . . . . . . . . . . | 103 | 85 | 39 |
| | 802 | 510 | 179 |
| Deferred provision (benefit) | | | |
| Domestic: | | | |
| Federal . . . . . . . . . . . . . . . | 67 | (22) | 304 |
| State and local . . . . . . . . . | (4) | (7) | 25 |
| Foreign . . . . . . . . . . . . . . . . | (1) | — | — |
| | 62 | (29) | 329 |
| Provision for income taxes . . . | $864 | $481 | $508 |

The significant components of deferred tax assets and liabilities as of May 31 were as follows.

| | 2005 | | 2004 | |
|---|---|---|---|---|
| (in millions) | Deferred Tax Assets | Deferred Tax Liabilities | Deferred Tax Assets | Deferred Tax Liabilities |
| Property, equipment, leases and intangibles . . | $ 301 | $1,455 | $ 310 | $1,372 |
| Employee benefits . . . . . . . . . . . . . . . . . . . . . | 397 | 453 | 386 | 406 |
| Self-insurance accruals. . . . . . . . . . . . . . . . . . | 311 | — | 297 | — |
| Other . . . . . . . . . . . . . . . . . . . . . . . . . . . . . . . | 319 | 128 | 277 | 104 |
| Net operating loss/credit carryforwards. . . . . . | 54 | — | 47 | — |
| Valuation allowance. . . . . . . . . . . . . . . . . . . . . | (42) | — | (52) | — |
| Totals . . . . . . . . . . . . . . . . . . . . . . . . . . . . . . . | $1,340 | $2,036 | $1,265 | $1,882 |

**Required**

*a.* What income tax expense does FedEx report in its 2005 income statement? How much of this expense is currently payable?

*b.* FedEx reports deferred tax liabilities relating to property, equipment, leases and intangibles. Describe how these liabilities arise. How likely is it that these liabilities will be paid? Specifically, describe a scenario that will (i) defer these taxes indefinitely, and (ii) will result in these liabilities requiring payment within the near future.

*c.* FedEx reports a deferred tax asset relating to self-insurance accruals. When a company self-insures, it does not purchase insurance from a third-party insurance company. Instead, it records an expense and related liability to reflect the probable payment of losses that can occur in the future. Explain why this accrual results in a deferred tax asset.

*d.* FedEx reports net loss carryforwards. Explain how these arise and how they will result in a future benefit.

*e.* FedEx reports a valuation allowance related to its deferred tax assets. Why did FedEx set up such an allowance? How did the increase in the allowance from 2004 to 2005 affect net income? How can a company use this allowance to meet its income targets in a particular year?

**P5-37.    Analyzing and Interpreting Tax Footnote (Financial Statement Effects Template)   (LO3)**

Benihana, Inc. (BNHN), reports the following deferred tax information in a footnote to its 10-K filing.    Benihana Inc. (BNHN)

**Income Taxes** Deferred tax assets and liabilities reflect the tax effect of temporary differences between amounts of assets and liabilities for financial reporting purposes and the amounts of such assets and liabilities as measured by income tax law. A valuation allowance is recognized to reduce deferred tax assets to the amounts that are more likely than not to be realized. The income tax effects of temporary differences that give rise to deferred tax assets and liabilities are as follows (in thousands):

| | March 27, 2005 | March 28, 2004 |
|---|---|---|
| Deferred tax assets | | |
| Rent straight-lining........... | $1,483 | $1,422 |
| Tax credit carryforward........ | 1,017 | 1,383 |
| Gift certificate liability........ | 870 | 554 |
| Amortization of gain.......... | 807 | 847 |
| Employee benefit accruals .... | 308 | 366 |
| Tax loss carryforwards ....... | — | 301 |
| Other..................... | 234 | 161 |
| | 4,719 | 5,034 |
| Deferred tax liabilities | | |
| Property and equipment ...... | 2,501 | 3,307 |
| Inventories ................. | 839 | 764 |
| Goodwill ................... | 1,118 | 778 |
| | 4,458 | 4,849 |
| Net deferred tax asset.......... | $ 261 | $ 185 |

The net deferred tax asset is classified on the balance sheet as follows (in thousands):

| | March 27, 2005 | March 28, 2004 |
|---|---|---|
| Current asset................. | $ 417 | $ 185 |
| Long-term liability ............. | 156 | — |
| Net deferred tax asset.......... | $ 261 | $ 185 |

The income tax provision consists of (in thousands):

| Fiscal Year Ended | March 27, 2005 | March 28, 2004 | March 30, 2003 |
|---|---|---|---|
| Current | | | |
| Federal.................... | $3,037 | $1,876 | $2,826 |
| State..................... | 1,559 | 680 | 1,244 |
| Deferred | | | |
| Federal and State............ | (76) | 2,265 | 655 |
| Income tax provision........... | $4,520 | $4,821 | $4,725 |

**Required**

a. Did Benihana's deferred tax assets increase or decrease during the most recent fiscal year? Interpret the change.

b. Did Benihana's deferred tax liabilities increase or decrease during the most recent fiscal year? Explain how the change arose (*Hint:* Look at the individual deferred tax liabilities and the most significant change during the year.)

c. Use the financial statement effects template to record Benihana's income tax expense for 2005 along with the changes in both deferred tax assets and liabilities. Your transaction should have two parts, one for the current portion of tax expense (the cash paid, or payable to the tax authorities) and one for the deferred portion of tax expense.

**P5-38.** **Analyzing and Interpreting Restructuring Costs and Effects** (LO2)

Dow Jones & Company (DJ)

Dow Jones & Company reports the following footnote disclosure in its 2005 10-K relating to its restructuring programs.

Restructuring and other items included in operating expenses were as follows:

| (in thousands) | 2005 | 2004 |
|---|---|---|
| Severance ............................ | $11,367 | $6,813 |
| Other exit costs ......................... | — | (120) |
| Reversal of lease obligation reserve-WFC .... | — | (2,761) |
| Total ................................. | $11,367 | $3,932 |

The following table displays the activity and balances of the restructuring reserve (liability) accounts through December 31, 2005.

| (in thousands) | December 31, 2004 Reserve | 2005 Expense | Cash Payments | December 31, 2005 Reserve |
|---|---|---|---|---|
| Employee severance—2005 ...... | $ — | $11,367 | $ (6,771) | $4,596 |
| Employee severance—2004 ...... | 7,262 | — | (4,408) | 2,854 |
| Total ........................ | $7,262 | $11,367 | $(11,179) | $7,450 |

The workforce reductions related to the restructuring actions are substantially complete. The remaining reserve relates primarily to continuing payments for employees that have already been terminated and is expected to be paid over the next twelve months.

**2005** In the second quarter of 2005, the company recorded a restructuring charge of $11.4 million ($6.9 million, net of taxes) primarily reflecting employee severance related to a workforce reduction of about 120 full-time employees. Most of the charge related to the Company's efforts to reposition its international print and online operations but also included headcount reductions at other parts of the business.

**2004** In the fourth quarter of 2004, the Company recorded a restructuring charge of $6.7 million ($4.0 million, net of taxes) primarily reflecting employee severance related to a workforce reduction of about 100 employees. The majority of this charge was related to employee severance in connection with the Company's decision to publish Far Eastern Economic Review (FEER) as a monthly periodical beginning in December 2004, with the balance of the charge related to headcount reductions in circulation and international operations.

On September 11, 2001, the Company's headquarters at the World Financial Center (WFC) sustained damage from debris and dust as a result of the terrorist attacks on the World Trade Center. Approximately 60% of the floor space, including furniture and related equipment, had been deemed a total loss. In the fourth quarter 2001, the company recorded a charge of $32.2 million as a result of its decision to permanently re-deploy certain personnel and to abandon four of seven floors that were leased at its WFC headquarters. This charge primarily reflected the Company's rent obligation through May 2005 on this vacated space. In the first quarter of 2004, the Company decided to extend the term of its lease for one of the floors that was previously abandoned and reoccupy this floor with personnel from another of its New York locations, whose lease term was expiring. As a result, the Company reversed $2.8 million ($1.7 million, net of taxes) of the remaining lease obligation reserve for the previously abandoned floor at WFC.

**Required**

a.   Why did DJ reverse restructuring charges in 2004? What effect did this reversal have on operating expenses and operating profit for the year? In your analysis of the DJ operating results for 2004, how might you treat this reversal?

b.   Describe the circumstances relating to the 2005 restructuring expense. What were the effects on the income statement and the balance sheet when DJ initially recorded the expense? Explain why the accrual was reduced in 2005.

**P5-39.   Analyzing and Interpreting Restructuring Accruals (Financial Statement Effects Template)   (LO2)**

Consider the footnote information for Dow Jones & Company from P5-38.

Dow Jones & Company (DJ)

**Required**

a.   Use the financial statement effects template to record the activity in the restructuring reserve account for the year ended December 31, 2005. You should record two separate entries in the template, one for the 2005 restructuring expense accrual and one for the cash payments during the year.

b.   Prepare journal entries and T-account entries for the activity in the restructuring reserve account for the year ended December 31, 2005.

**P5-40.   Analyzing and Interpreting Gains and Losses on Asset (Subsidiary) Sales   (LO2)**

Altria Group, Inc., formerly Phillip Morris Companies, sold its Miller Brewing subsidiary. Following is a footnote to its 10-K report, which describes that transaction.

Altria Group, Inc. (MO)

On May 30, 2002, ALG announced an agreement with SAB to merge Miller into SAB. The transaction closed on July 9, 2002, and SAB changed its name to SABMiller plc ("SABMiller"). At closing, ALG received 430 million shares of SABMiller valued at approximately $3.4 billion, based upon a share price of 5.12 British pounds per share, in exchange for Miller, which had $2.0 billion of existing debt. The shares in SABMiller owned by ALG resulted in a 36% economic interest in SABMiller and a 24.9% voting interest. The transaction resulted in a pre-tax gain of approximately $2.6 billion or approximately $1.7 billion after-tax. The gain was recorded in the third quarter of 2002. Beginning with the third quarter of 2002, ALG's ownership interest in SABMiller is being accounted for under the equity method. Accordingly, ALG's investment in SABMiller of approximately $1.9 billion is included in other assets on the consolidated balance sheet at December 31, 2002. In addition, ALG records its share of SABMiller's net earnings, based on its economic ownership percentage, in minority interest in earnings and other, net, on the consolidated statement of earnings.

**Required**

a.  Identify (1) the total value received by Altria in exchange for Miller, (2) the book value of Altria's investment in the Miller Brewing subsidiary, and (3) the pretax and after-tax gains recognized by Altria from the Miller transaction.
b.  How much of the purchase price was received in cash by Altria? Explain.
c.  How should the gain from this transaction be interpreted in an analysis of Altria, especially with respect to projections of Altria's future cash flows?

**P5-41.**    **Analyzing Unearned Revenue Disclosures**    (LO1)

Costco Wholesale (COST)

The following disclosures are from the August 28, 2005, annual report of Costco Wholesale Corporation.

**Summary of Significant Accounting Policies  (excerpt)**

Membership fee revenue represents annual membership fees paid by substantially all of the Company's members. The Company accounts for membership fee revenue on a "unearned basis," whereby membership fee revenue is recognized ratably over the one-year term of the membership.

| Current Liabilities ($ thousands) | 2005 | 2004 |
|---|---|---|
| Short-term borrowings | $    54,356 | $    21,595 |
| Accounts payable | 4,213,724 | 3,600,200 |
| Accrued salaries and benefits | 1,025,181 | 904,209 |
| Accrued sales and other taxes | 263,899 | 223,009 |
| Deferred membership income | 500,558 | 453,881 |
| Current portion long-term debt | 3,225 | 305,594 |
| Other current liabilities | 548,031 | 662,062 |
| Total current liabilities | $6,608,974 | $6,170,550 |

| Revenue ($ thousands) | 2005 | 2004 | 2003 |
|---|---|---|---|
| Net sales | $51,862,072 | $47,145,712 | $41,692,699 |
| Membership fees | 1,073,156 | 961,280 | 852,853 |
| Total revenue | $52,935,228 | $48,106,992 | $42,545,552 |

**Required**

a.  Explain in layman terms how Costco accounts for the cash received for its membership fees.
b.  Use the balance sheet information on Costco's Deferred Membership Income liability account and its income statement revenues related to membership fees earned during 2005 to compute the cash that Costco received during 2005 for membership fees.
c.  Use the financial statement effects template to show the effect of the cash Costco received during 2005 for memberships and the recognition of membership fees revenue for 2005.

**P5-42.**    **Analyzing Unearned Revenue Transactions**    (LO1)

Centex Corp. (CTX)

The annual report of Centex Corporation, a home builder, reveals the following information about new home sales order backlogs by geographic region. Assume that each sales order includes a $1,000 deposit from the customer.

**Sales (Orders) Backlog, at the end of the period (in units):**

Centex Corp. (CTX)

|  | As of March 31, | | | | |
|---|---|---|---|---|---|
|  | **2006** | **2005** | **2004** | **2003** | **2002** |
| Mid-Atlantic . . . . . . . . . . | 3,073 | 3,461 | 2,801 | 2,148 | 1,503 |
| Southeast. . . . . . . . . . . | 4,116 | 5,006 | 3,707 | 2,713 | 2,315 |
| Midwest . . . . . . . . . . . . | 2,755 | 3,273 | 3,392 | 2,920 | 2,093 |
| Southwest . . . . . . . . . . | 4,094 | 3,688 | 2,869 | 2,258 | 2,361 |
| West Coast. . . . . . . . . . | 3,349 | 3,161 | 2,645 | 2,011 | 1,099 |
|  | 17,387 | 18,589 | 15,414 | 12,050 | 9,371 |

We define backlog units as units that have been sold, as evidenced by a signed contract with the customer, but not closed. Substantially all of the orders in sales backlog as of March 31, 2006 are expected to close during fiscal year 2007. For each unit in backlog, we have received a customer deposit, which is refundable under certain circumstances. The backlog units included in the table above are net of cancellations. Cancellations occur for a variety of reasons including: a customer's inability to obtain financing, customer relocations or other customer financial hardships.

**Required**

a.  Explain in layman terms how Centex records a customer deposit when a sale is not yet closed.
b.  How does Centex's balance sheet reflect the deposits on the backlog units at the end of March 2006?
c.  When, if ever, will Centex's income statement reflect the deposits on the backlog units?
d.  Explain how Centex might account for deposits that are refunded to customers.

# CASES

**C5-43.  Management Application: Managing Foreign Currency Risk   (LO5)**

Fluctuations in foreign currency exchange rates can result in increased volatility of revenues, expenses, and profits. Companies generally attempt to reduce this volatility.

a.  Identify two possible solutions to reduce the volatility effect of foreign exchange rate fluctuations. (*Hint*: Examine the risk management discussion for Johnson Controls in Exercise E5-31)
b.  What costs would arise if you implemented each of your solutions?

**C5-44.  Ethics and Governance: Revenue Recognition   (LO1)**

GAAP offers latitude in determining when revenue is earned. Assume that a company that normally required acceptance by its customers prior to recording revenue as earned, delivers a product to a customer near the end of the quarter. The company believes that acceptance is assured, but cannot obtain it prior to quarter-end. Recording the revenue would assure "making its numbers" for the quarter. Although formal acceptance is not obtained, the sales person records the sale, fully intending to obtain written acceptance as soon as possible.

a.  What are the revenue recognition requirements in this case?
b.  What are the ethical issues relating to this sale?
c.  Assume you are on the board of directors of this company. What safeguards can you put in place to provide assurance that the company's revenue recognition policy is followed?

**C5-45.  Ethics and Governance: Earnings Management   (LO2)**

Assume that you are CEO of a company. Your company has reported a loss for the current year. Since it cannot carry back the entire loss to recoup taxes paid in prior years, it records a loss carryforward as a deferred tax asset. Your expectation is that future profitability will be sufficient to realize the tax benefits of the carryforward. Your chief financial officer approaches you with an idea to create a deferred tax valuation allowance that will reduce the deferred tax asset, increase tax expense for the year, and increase your reported loss. He reasons that the company's stock price will not be reduced markedly by the additional reported loss since a loss year has already been factored into the current price. Further, this deferred tax valuation allowance will create a reserve that can be used in future years to increase profit (via reversal of the allowance) if needed to meet analyst expectations.

a.  What stakeholders are potentially affected by the CFO's proposal?
b.  How do you respond to the proposal? Justify your response.

# Reporting and Analyzing Operating Assets

## LEARNING OBJECTIVES

**LO1** Describe accounting for accounts receivable and the importance of the allowance for uncollectible accounts in determining profit. (p. 6-4)

**LO2** Explain accounting for inventories and the effects on the balance sheet and income statement from different inventory costing methods. (p. 6-13)

**LO3** Describe accounting for property, plant and equipment and explain the impacts on profit and cash flows from different depreciation methods. (p. 6-26)

## CISCO SYSTEMS

Cisco Systems, Inc., manufactures and sells networking and communications products for transporting data, voice, and video within buildings, across town and around the world. Cisco's products are everywhere, here are but a few applications:

- Schoolchildren can view a virtual science experiment from a neighborhood center's Cisco-outfitted computer room.
- Airline passengers can check flight information and print boarding passes at convenient Cisco kiosks.
- Hospital nurses check medication levels at patients' bedsides using Cisco handheld devices and wireless networks.
- Auto designers in Japan, assembly technicians in the U.S., and component makers worldwide trade manufacturing data over a Cisco network in real time.
- Police rely on citywide Cisco wireless networks to deliver fingerprint files, mug shots, and voicemail to mobile units.
- Customers call their bank's Cisco Internet Protocol (IP) based center, where account profiles immediately appear to call agents.
- Companies shore up their databases with Cisco network security.

Cisco reported 2005 net income of $5.7 billion on $24.8 billion in sales, and a return on net operating assets (RNOA) of 43%. Four years earlier, Cisco reported a *loss* of $1 billion after recording $2.25 billion of restructuring costs, including costs related to the severance of 6,000 employees and the write-off of obsolete inventory and other assets.

Cisco's turnaround is remarkable. Sales have increased by 31% in the past two years, and its return on net operating assets has nearly doubled. The RNOA improvement cannot be attributed to profit increases alone. It also reflects Cisco's effective asset (balance sheet) management. Recall that RNOA comprises both a profitability component and a productivity

Getty Images

component (see Module 4). The productivity component (reflected in net operating asset turnover, NOAT) is measured as sales divided by average net operating assets. Effective management of operating assets is crucial to achieving a high RNOA. We focus on three important operating assets in this module: accounts receivable, inventories, and property, plant and equipment (PPE).

As part of their overall marketing efforts, companies extend credit to customers. At Cisco, for example, accounts receivable are a significant asset because all sales are on account. While favorable credit terms stimulate sales, the resulting accounts receivables are costly. First, accounts receivable are generally non-interest bearing and tie up a company's working capital in non-earning assets. Second, receivables expose the company to collectibility risk - the risk that some customers won't pay. Third, companies incur the administrative costs associated with billing and collection. These costs must be weighed against the costs of other marketing tools, like advertising, sales incentives, and price discounts. Management of receivables is critical to financial success.

Inventories are significant assets at many companies, particularly for manufacturers such as Cisco, where inventories consist of raw materials (the basic product inputs), work in process (the cost of partially completed products), and finished goods (completed products awaiting sale). Inventories too are costly to maintain. The cost of buying and manufacturing the goods must be financed and inventories must be stored, moved, and insured. Consequently, companies prefer lower inventory levels whenever possible. However, companies must be careful to hold enough inventory. If they reduce inventory quantities too far, they risk inventory stock-outs, that is, not having enough inventory to meet demand. Management of inventories is also a critical activity.

Property, plant and equipment (PPE) is often the largest, and usually the most important, asset on the balance sheet. Companies need administrative offices, IT and R&D facilities, regional sales and customer service offices, manufacturing and distribution facilities, vehicles, computers, and a host of other fixed assets. Fixed asset costs are substantial and are indirectly linked to sales and profits. Consequently, fixed-asset investments are often difficult to justify and, once acquired, fixed assets are often difficult to divest. Effective management of PPE assets usually requires management review of the entire value chain.

John Chambers, CEO of Cisco, recalls a conversation he once had with the legendary Jack Welch, former Chairman of GE. Following Cisco's announced restructuring program in 2001, Welch commented, "John, you'll never have a great company until you go through the really tough times. What builds a company is not just how

*(Continued on next page)*

*(Continued from previous page)*
you handle the successes, but it's the way you handle the real challenges." Cisco survived the tech bubble burst, which is as "real" a challenge as any company is likely to face. Further, Cisco is now reporting impressive financial results. To ensure future financial performance, however, Cisco must effectively manage both its income statement and its operating assets.

Sources: *BusinessWeek,* 2003 and 2006; Cisco Systems 10-K, 2006; Cisco Systems Annual Report, 2006.

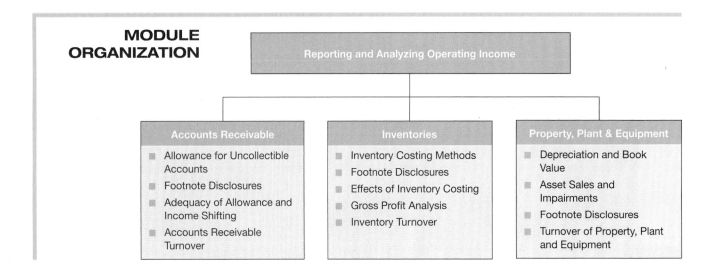

**MODULE ORGANIZATION**

**Reporting and Analyzing Operating Income**

**Accounts Receivable**
- Allowance for Uncollectible Accounts
- Footnote Disclosures
- Adequacy of Allowance and Income Shifting
- Accounts Receivable Turnover

**Inventories**
- Inventory Costing Methods
- Footnote Disclosures
- Effects of Inventory Costing
- Gross Profit Analysis
- Inventory Turnover

**Property, Plant & Equipment**
- Depreciation and Book Value
- Asset Sales and Impairments
- Footnote Disclosures
- Turnover of Property, Plant and Equipment

# INTRODUCTION

Managing net operating assets is crucial to creating shareholder value. To manage and assess net operating assets, we need to understand how they are measured and reported. This module describes the reporting and measuring of operating working capital, mainly receivables and inventories, and of long-term operating assets such as property, plant, and equipment. We do not discuss other long-term operating assets, such as equity investments in affiliated companies, investment in intangible assets, and nonoperating investments in marketable securities, as they are covered in other modules.

Receivables are usually a major part of operating working capital. They must be carefully managed as they represent a substantial asset for most companies and are an important marketing tool. GAAP requires companies to report receivables at the amount they expect to collect. This requires estimation of uncollectible accounts. The receivables reported on the balance sheet, and expenses reported on the income statement, impound management's estimate of uncollectible amounts. Accordingly, it is important that companies accurately assess uncollectible accounts and timely report them. It is also necessary that readers of financial reports understand management's accounting choices and their effects on reported balance sheets and income statements.

Inventory is another major component of operating working capital. Inventories usually constitute one of the three largest assets (along with receivables and long-term operating assets). Also, cost of goods sold, which flows from inventory, is the largest expense category for retailing and manufacturing companies. GAAP allows several methods for inventory accounting, and inventory-costing choices can markedly impact balance sheets and income statements, especially for companies experiencing relatively high inflation, coupled with slowly turning inventories.

Long-term plant assets are often the largest component of operating assets. Indeed, long-term operating assets are typically the largest asset for manufacturing companies, and their related depreciation expense is typically second only in amount to cost of goods sold in the income statement. GAAP allows different accounting methods for computing depreciation that can significantly impact the income statement and the balance sheet. When companies dispose of fixed assets, a gain or loss may result. Understanding these gains and losses on asset sales is important as we assess performance. Further, accounting for asset write-downs not only affects companies' current financial performance, but also future profitability. We must understand these effects when we assess future income statements. This module considers all of these fixed asset accounting choices and consequences.

# ACCOUNTS RECEIVABLE

Our focus on operating assets begins with accounts receivable. To help frame our discussion, we refer to the following graphic as we proceed through the module:

| Income Statement | Balance Sheet | |
| --- | --- | --- |
| Sales | Cash | Current liabilities |
| Cost of goods sold | Accounts receivable, net | Long-term liabilities |
| Selling, general & administrative | Inventory | |
| Income taxes | Property, plant, and equipment, net | Shareholders' equity |
| Net income | Investments | |

**LO1** Describe accounting for accounts receivable and the importance of the allowance for uncollectible accounts in determining profit.

The graphic highlights the balance sheet and income statement effects of accounts receivable. This section explains the accounting, reporting, and analysis of these highlighted items.

Retail companies transact mostly in cash. But other companies, including those that sell to other firms, usually do not expect cash upon delivery. Instead, they offer credit terms and have *credit sales* or *sales on account*.[1] An account receivable on the seller's balance sheet is always matched by a corresponding account payable on the buyer's balance sheet. Accounts receivable are reported on the seller's balance sheet at *net realizable value*, which is the net amount the seller expects to collect.

Sellers do not expect to collect all accounts receivable; they anticipate that some buyers will be unable to pay their accounts when they come due. For example, buyers can suffer business downturns that limit the cash available to meet liabilities. Then, buyers must decide which liabilities to pay. Typically, financially distressed companies decide to pay off liabilities to the IRS, to banks, and to bondholders because those creditors have enforcement powers and can quickly seize assets and disrupt operations, leading to bankruptcy and eventual liquidation. Buyers also try to cover their payroll, as they cannot exist without employees. Then, if there is cash remaining, buyers will pay suppliers to ensure continued flow of goods.

Accounts payable are *unsecured liabilities,* meaning that buyers have not pledged collateral to guarantee payment of amounts owed. As a result, when a company declares bankruptcy, accounts payable are comingled with other unsecured creditors (after the IRS and the secured creditors), and are typically not paid in full. Consequently, there is risk in the collectibility of accounts receivable. This *collectibility risk* is crucial to analysis of accounts receivable.

Cisco reports $2,216 million of accounts receivable in the following current asset section from its 2005 balance sheet:

| $ millions | July 30, 2005 |
| --- | --- |
| Cash and cash equivalents | $ 4,742 |
| Short-term investments | 2,227 |
| Accounts receivable, net of allowance for doubtful accounts of $162 | 2,216 |
| Inventories | 1,297 |
| Deferred tax assets | 1,582 |
| Prepaid expenses and other current assets | 967 |
| Total current assets | $13,031 |

Cisco reports its receivables net of allowances for doubtful (uncollectible) accounts of $162 million. This means the total amount owed to Cisco is $2,378 million ($2,216 million + $162 million), but Cisco *estimates* that $162 million are uncollectible and reports on its balance sheet only the amount it expects to collect.

---

[1] An example of common credit terms are 2/10, net 30. These terms indicate that the seller offers the buyer an early-pay incentive, in this case a 2% discount off the cost if the buyer pays within 10 days of billing. If the buyer does not take advantage of the discount, it must pay 100% of the invoice cost within 30 days of billing. From the seller's standpoint, offering the discount is often warranted because it speeds up cash collections and then the seller can invest the cash to yield a return greater than the early-payment discount. The buyer often wishes to avail itself of attractive discounts even if it has to borrow money to do so. If the discount is not taken, however, the buyer should withhold payment as long as possible (at least for the full net period) so as to maximize its available cash. Meanwhile, the seller will exert whatever pressure it can to collect the amount due as quickly as possible. Thus, it is normal for there to be some tension between sellers and buyers.

We might ask why buyers would sell to companies from whom they do not expect to collect. The answer is they would not have extended credit *if* they knew beforehand which companies would eventually not pay. For example, Cisco probably cannot identify those companies that constitute the $162 million in uncollectible accounts. Yet, it knows from past experience that a certain portion of its receivables will prove uncollectible. GAAP requires companies to estimate the dollar amount of uncollectible accounts (even if it cannot identify specific accounts that are uncollectible), and to report accounts receivable at the resulting *net realizable value* (total receivables less an allowance for uncollectible accounts).

## Allowance for Uncollectible Accounts

Companies typically use an *aging analysis* to estimate the amount of uncollectible accounts. This requires an analysis of receivables as of the balance sheet date. Specifically, customer accounts are categorized by the number of days that the related invoices have been unpaid (outstanding). Based on prior experience, or on other available statistics, uncollectible percentages are applied to each category, with larger percentages applied to older accounts. The result of this analysis is a dollar amount for the allowance for uncollectible accounts (also called allowance for doubtful accounts) at the balance sheet date.

### Aging Analysis

To illustrate, Exhibit 6.1 shows an aging analysis for a seller with $100,000 of accounts receivable at period-end. The current accounts are those that are still within their original credit period. As an example, if a seller's credit terms are 2/10, net 30, all invoices that have been outstanding for 30 days or fewer are current. Accounts listed as 1–60 days past due are those 1 to 60 days past their due date. This would include an account that is 45 days outstanding for a net 30-day invoice. This same logic applies to all categories.

| EXHIBIT 6.1 | Aging of Accounts Receivable | | |
|---|---|---|---|
| **Age of Accounts** | **Receivable Balance** | **Estimated Percent Uncollectible** | **Estimated Uncollectible Accounts** |
| Current................. | $ 50,000 | 2% | $1,000 |
| 1-60 days past due........ | 30,000 | 3 | 900 |
| 61-90 days past due....... | 15,000 | 4 | 600 |
| Over 90 days past due...... | 5,000 | 8 | 400 |
| Total.................. | $100,000 | | $2,900 |

Exhibit 6.1 also reflects the seller's experience with uncollectible accounts, which manifests itself in the uncollectible percentages for each aged category. For example, on average, 3% of buyers' accounts that are 1-60 days past due prove uncollectible for this seller. Hence, the company estimates a potential loss of $900 for the $30,000 in receivables one to sixty days past due.

### Reporting Receivables

The seller represented in Exhibit 6.1 reports its accounts receivable on the balance sheet as follows:

Accounts receivable, net of $2,900 in allowances.........    $97,100

Assume that, as of the end of the *previous* accounting period, the company had estimated total uncollectible accounts of $2,200 based on an aging analysis of the receivables at that time. Also assume that the company did not write off any accounts receivable during the period. The *reconciliation* of its allowance account for the period follows:

| | |
|---|---|
| Beginning allowance for uncollectible accounts.......... | $ 2,200 |
| Add: Provision for uncollectible accounts............... | 700 |
| Less: Write-offs of accounts receivable................. | 0 |
| Ending allowance for uncollectible accounts............ | $ 2,900 |

The aging analysis revealed that the allowance for uncollectible accounts is $700 too low and therefore, the company increased the allowance accordingly. This adjustment affects the financial statements as follows:

1. Accounts receivable are reduced by an additional $700 on the balance sheet (receivables are reported *net* of the allowance account).

2. A $700 expense, called bad debts expense, is reported in the income statement (usually part of SG&A expense). This reduces pretax profit by the same amount.[2]

The allowance for uncollectible accounts increases with new provisions (additional bad debts expense) and decreases as accounts are written off. Individual accounts are written off when the seller identifies them as uncollectible. (A write-off reduces both accounts receivable and the allowance for uncollectible accounts as described below.) As with all permanent accounts on the balance sheet, the ending balance of the allowance account is the beginning balance for next period.

## Writing Off Accounts

To illustrate the write-off of an account receivable, assume that subsequent to the period-end shown above, the seller receives notice that one of its customers, owing $500 at the time, has declared bankruptcy. The seller's attorneys believe that legal costs in attempting to collect this receivable would likely exceed the amount owed. So, the seller decides not to pursue collection and to write off this account. The write-off has the following effects:

1. Gross accounts receivable are reduced from $100,000 to $99,500.
2. Allowance for uncollectible accounts is reduced from $2,900 to $2,400.

After the write-off, the seller's balance sheet appears as follows:

Accounts receivable, net of $2,400 in allowances. . . . . . . . .    $97,100

Exhibit 6.2 shows the effects of this write-off on the individual accounts.

| EXHIBIT 6.2 | Effects of an Accounts Receivable Write-Off | | |
|---|---|---|---|
| **Account** | **Before Write-Off** | **Effects of Write-Off** | **After Write-Off** |
| Accounts receivable. . . . . . . . . . . . . . . . . . . . . . . . . | $100,000 | $(500) | $99,500 |
| Less: Allowance for uncollectible accounts. . . . . . . . . | 2,900 | (500) | 2,400 |
| Accounts receivable, net of allowance. . . . . . . . . . . . | $ 97,100 | | $97,100 |

The balance of net accounts receivable is the same before and after the write-off. This is always the case. The write-off of an account is a non-event from an accounting point of view. That is, total assets do not change, liabilities stay the same, and equity is unaffected as there is no net income effect. The write-off affects individual asset accounts, but not total assets.

Let's next consider what happens when additional information arrives that alters management's expectations of uncollectible accounts. To illustrate, assume that sometime after the write-off above, the seller realizes that it has underestimated uncollectible accounts and that $3,000 (not $2,400) of the remaining $99,500 accounts receivable are uncollectible. The company must increase the allowance for uncollectible accounts by $600. The additional $600 provision has the following financial statement effects:

1. Allowance for uncollectible accounts increases by $600 to the revised estimated balance of $3,000; and accounts receivable (net of the allowance for uncollectible accounts) declines by $600 from $97,100 to $96,500 (or $99,500 − $3,000).

---

[2] Companies can also estimate uncollectible accounts using the *percentage of sales* method. The percentage of sales method computes bad debts expense directly, as a percentage of sales and the allowance for uncollectible accounts is estimated indirectly. In contrast, the aging method computes the allowance balance directly and the bad debts expense is the amount required to bring the allowance account up to (or down to) the amount determined by the aging analysis. To illustrate, if a company reports sales of $100,000 and estimates the provision at 1% of sales, it would report a bad debts expense of $1,000 and an allowance balance of $3,200 instead of the $700 bad debts expense and the $2,900 allowance as determined using the aging analysis. The two methods nearly always report different values for the allowance, net accounts receivable, and bad debts expense.

2. A $600 bad debts expense is added to the income statement, which reduces pretax income. Recall that in the prior period, the seller reported $700 of bad debts expense when the allowance account was increased from $2,200 to $2,900.

## Analyzing Receivable Transactions

To summarize, recording bad debts expense increases the allowance for uncollectible accounts, which affects both the *balance sheet* and *income statement*. Importantly, the financial statement effects occur when the allowance is estimated, and not when accounts are written off. In this way, sales are matched with bad debts expense, and accounts receivable are matched with expected uncollectible accounts. Exhibit 6.3 illustrates each of the transactions discussed in this section using the financial statement effects template:

**EXHIBIT 6.3** — Financial Statement Effects of Key Accounts Receivable Transactions

| Transaction | Cash Asset | + | Noncash Assets | = | Liabil- ities | + | Contrib. Capital | + | Earned Capital | | Rev- enues | – | Expen- ses | = | Net Income |
|---|---|---|---|---|---|---|---|---|---|---|---|---|---|---|---|
| a. Credit sales of $100,000 | | | +100,000 Accounts Receivable | = | | | | | +100,000 Retained Earnings | | +100,000 Sales | | | = | +100,000 |
| b. Increase allowance for uncollectible accounts by $700 | | | −700 Allowance for Uncollectible Accounts | = | | | | | −700 Retained Earnings | | | – | +700 Bad Debts Expense | = | −700 |
| c. Write off $500 in accounts receivable | | | −500 Accounts receivable +500 Allowance for Uncollectible Accounts | = | | | | | | | | | | = | |
| d. Increase allowance for uncollectible accounts by $600 | | | −600 Allowance for Uncollectible Accounts | = | | | | | −600 Retained Earnings | | | – | +600 Bad Debts Expense | = | −600 |

## Footnote Disclosures

To illustrate the typical accounts receivable footnote disclosure, consider Cisco's discussion of its allowance for uncollectible accounts:

> **Allowance for Doubtful Accounts** The allowance for doubtful accounts as of July 30, 2005, was $162 million or 6.8% of the gross accounts receivable balance. This compares with $179 million or 8.9% of the gross accounts receivable balance as of July 31, 2004. The allowance is based on an assessment of the collectibility of customer accounts. Companies regularly review the allowance by considering factors such as historical experience, credit quality, the age of the accounts receivable balances, and current economic conditions that may affect a customer's ability to pay. If a major customer's creditworthiness deteriorates, or if actual defaults are higher than historical experience, or if other circumstances arise, estimates of the recoverability of amounts due could be overstated, and additional allowances are probably required.

Cisco's allowance for uncollectible accounts declined as a percentage of gross receivables from the prior year. As the level of uncollectible accounts decreases, the company recognizes less bad debts expense. The effect is to raise net income. Cisco alludes to the level of estimation required, and cautions the reader that additional allowances (provisions) could be required under certain circumstances, and that would adversely affect profit.

Cisco provides a footnote reconciliation of its allowance for uncollectible (doubtful) accounts for the past three years as shown in Exhibit 6.4.

| **EXHIBIT 6.4** | **Reconciliation of Cisco's Allowance for Uncollectible Accounts** |
|---|---|
| **$ millions** | **Allowance for Doubtful Accounts** |
| **Year ended July 26, 2003** | |
| Balance at beginning of fiscal year | $335 |
| (Credited) to expenses | (59) |
| Deductions for write-offs | (93) |
| Balance at end of fiscal year | $183 |
| **Year ended July 31, 2004** | |
| Balance at beginning of fiscal year | $183 |
| Charged to expenses | 19 |
| Deductions for write-offs | (23) |
| Balance at end of fiscal year | $179 |
| **Year ended July 30, 2005** | |
| Balance at beginning of fiscal year | $179 |
| Charged to expenses | — |
| Deductions for write-offs | (17) |
| Balance at end of fiscal year | $162 |

Reconciling Cisco's allowance account provides insight into the level of the provision (expense) each year relative to the actual write-offs. Cisco wrote off $93 million of accounts receivable in 2003, $23 million in 2004, and $17 million in 2005. This pattern is impressive especially given that gross receivables increased by 30% over this three-year period. Over the same period, Cisco reduced the allowance as a percentage of gross receivables from 10% ($183 million/$1,834 million) in 2003 to 8.9% ($179 million/$2,004 million) in 2004, and to 6.8% ($162 million/$2,378 million) in 2005. Because the allowance account was too high in 2003, Cisco *reversed* the provision by $59 million in 2003 (that is, Cisco recorded a negative bad debts expense in 2003), a minimal provision of $19 million in 2004, and no provision at all in 2005. Since 2002, Cisco as reduced its allowance for uncollectible accounts by $173 million.

## Analysis Implications

This section considers analysis of accounts receivable and the provision for uncollectible accounts.

## Adequacy of Allowance Account

A company makes two representations when reporting accounts receivable (net) in the current asset section of its balance sheet:

1. It expects to collect the amount reported on the balance sheet (remember, accounts receivable are reported net of allowance for uncollectible accounts).
2. It expects to collect the amount within the next year (implied by the classification of accounts receivable as a current asset).

From an analysis viewpoint, we scrutinize the adequacy of a company's provision for its uncollectible accounts. If the provision is inadequate, the cash ultimately collected will be less than the net receivables reported on the balance sheet.

How can an outsider assess the adequacy of the allowance account? One answer is to compare the allowance account to gross accounts receivable. For Cisco, the 2005 percentage is 6.8% (see above), a 24% decline from the prior year. What does such a decline signify? Perhaps the overall economic environment has improved, rendering write-offs less likely. Perhaps the company has improved its credit underwriting or receivables collection efforts. The MD&A section of the 10-K report is likely to discuss such new initiatives. Or perhaps the company's customer mix has changed and it is now selling to more creditworthy customers (or, it eliminated a risky class of customers).

The important point is that we must be comfortable with the percentage of uncollectible accounts reported by the company. We must remember that management controls the size of the allowance account—albeit with audit assurances.

### Income Shifting

We noted that the financial statement effects of uncollectible accounts transpire when the allowance is increased for new bad debts expense and not when the allowance account is decreased for the write-off of uncollectible accounts. It is also important to note that management controls the amount and timing of the uncollectible provision. Although external auditors assess the reasonableness of the allowance for uncollectible accounts, they do not possess management's inside knowledge and experience. This puts the auditors at an information disadvantage, particularly if any dispute arises.

Studies show that many companies use the allowance for uncollectible accounts to shift income from one year into another. For example, a company can increase current-period income by deliberately underestimating bad debts expense. However, in the future it will become apparent that the bad debts expense was too low when the company's write-offs exceed the balance in the allowance account. Then, the company will need to increase the allowance to make up for the earlier period's underestimate. As an example, consider a company that accurately estimates that it has $1,000 of uncollectible accounts at the end of 2007. Assume that the current balance in the allowance for uncollectible accounts is $200. But instead of recording bad debts expense of $800 as needed to have an adequate ($1,000) allowance, the company records only $100 of bad debts expense and reports an allowance of $300 at the end of 2007. Now if the company's original estimate was accurate, in 2008 it will write off accounts totaling $1,000. The write-offs ($1,000) are greater than the allowance balance ($300) and the company will need to increase the allowance by recording an additional $700 in 2008. The effect of this is that the company borrowed $700 of income from 2008 in order to report higher income in 2007. This is called "income shifting."

Why would a company want to shift income from a later period into the current period? Perhaps it is a lean year and the company is in danger of missing income targets. For example, internal targets influence manager bonuses and external targets set by the market influence stock prices. Or, perhaps the company is in danger of defaulting on loan agreements tied to income levels. The reality is that income pressures are great and these pressures can cause managers to bend (or even break) the rules.

Companies can just as easily shift income from the current period to one or more future periods by underestimating the current period bad debts expense and allowance for uncollectible accounts. Why would a company want to shift income to one or more future periods? Perhaps current times are good and the company wants to "bank" some of that income for future periods; sometimes called a *cookie jar reserve*. It can then draw on that reserve, if necessary, to boost income in one or more future lean years. Another reason for a company to shift income from the current period is that it does not wish to unduly inflate market expectations for future period income. Or perhaps the company is experiencing a very bad year and it feels that overestimating the provision will not drive income materially lower than it is. Thus, it decides to take a big bath (a large loss) and create a reserve that can be used in future periods. (Sears provides an interesting case as described in the Business Insight on next page).

Use of the allowance for uncollectible accounts to shift income is a source of concern. This is especially so for banks where the allowance for loan losses is a large component of banks' balance sheets and loan loss expense is a major component of reported income. Our analysis must scrutinize the allowance for uncollectible accounts to identify any changes from past practices or industry norms and, then, to justify those changes before accepting them as valid.

### Accounts Receivable Turnover and Average Collection Period

The net operating asset turnover (NOAT) is sales divided by average net operating assets. An important component of this measure is the **accounts receivables turnover (ART)**, which is defined as:[3]

$$\textbf{Accounts Receivable Turnover = Sales/Average Accounts Receivable}$$

---

[3] Technically, the numerator should be net credit sales because receivables arise from credit sales. Including cash sales in the numerator inflates the ratio. Typically, outsiders do not know the level of cash sales and, therefore, must use total sales to calculate the turnover ratio.

| BUSINESS INSIGHT | Sears' Cookie Jar |
|---|---|

The Heard on the Street column in *The Wall Street Journal* (1996) reported the following: "Analyst David Poneman argues that Sears' earnings growth this year of 24%, or $134 million, has been aided by a 1993 balance-sheet maneuver that softens the impact of soaring levels of bad credit-card debt among its 50 million cardholders. Wall Street got a wake-up call in the second quarter, when Sears increased its provision for bad credit-card debt by $254 million, up 73% from the year earlier. Then in the third quarter, it made another $286 million provision, a 53% increase. Yet the retailer posted a 22% gain in third-quarter net. How so? "Sears is using its superabundant balance sheet to smooth out its earnings," says Mr. Poneman. He says 'Sears has a quality-of-earnings' issue.

Poneman is referring to a $2 billion reserve for credit losses that Sears set up in 1993. As it turned out, the reserve was higher than needed. Three years later, Sears still had a nearly $1 billion reserve on its balance sheet. That was nearly twice the size of reserves at most credit-card companies as a percentage of receivables. The credit-card reserve was part of a big bath that included restructuring charges that Sears took in 1993. Such charges and reserves can be a big help for a new CEO (which Sears had) who wishes to show a pattern of improving results in future years. Poneman says the big addition to reserves "moved income out of 1992 and 1993 and into 1995 and 1996." Why is that bad? The overly large reserve allowed Sears to prop up its earnings at a time when losses in its credit-card unit were soaring. Sears' credit-card delinquencies had risen by $420 million in 1996. Poneman asserts that "Considering that increased delinquencies exceed year-to-date increased earnings, it could be argued that the increase in Sears' year-to-date earnings has depended entirely on its over-reserved condition."

Accounts receivable turnover reveals how many times receivables have turned (been collected) during the period. More turns indicate that receivables are being collected more quickly.

A companion measure to accounts receivable turnover is the **average collection period (ACP)** for accounts receivable, also called *days sales outstanding*, which is defined as:

$$\textbf{Average Collection Period} = \textbf{Accounts Receivable/Average Daily Sales}$$

where average daily sales equals sales divided by 365 days. The average collection period indicates how long, on average, the receivables are outstanding before being collected.[4]

To illustrate, assume that sales are $1,000, ending accounts receivable are $230, and average accounts receivable are $200. The accounts receivable turnover is 5, computed as $1,000/$200, and the average collection period (days sales outstanding) is 84 days, computed as $230/($1,000/365 days).

The accounts receivable turnover and the average collection period yield valuable insights on at least two dimensions:

1. *Receivables quality* Changes in receivable turnover (and collection period) speak to accounts receivable quality. If turnover slows (collection period lengthens), the reason could be deterioration in collectibility. However, there are at least three alternative explanations:

   a. *A seller can extend its credit terms.* If the seller is attempting to enter new markets or take market share from competitors, it may extend credit terms to attract buyers.

   b. *A seller can take on longer-paying customers.* For example, facing increased competition, many computer and automobile companies began leasing their products, thus reducing customers' cash outlays and stimulating sales. Moving away from cash sales and toward leasing reduced receivables turnover and increased the collection period.

---

[4] The average collection period computation in this Module uses *ending* accounts receivable. This focuses the analysis on the most current receivables. Cisco uses a variant of this approach, described in its MD&A section as follows: Accounts receivable/Average annualized 4Q sales (or AR/[(4Q Sales × 4)/365]). Arguably, Cisco's variant focuses even more on the most recent collection period because ending accounts receivable relate more closely to 4Q sales than to reported annual sales. Most analysts use the reported annual sales instead of the annualized 4Q sales because the former are easily accessed in financial statement databases. As an alternative, we could also examine average daily sales in *average* accounts receivable (Average accounts receivable/Average daily sales). The approach we use in the text addresses the average collection period of *current* accounts receivable, and the latter approach examines the average collection period of *average* accounts receivable. The "correct" ratio depends on the issue we wish to investigate. It is important to choose the formula that best answers the question we are asking.

c. *The seller can increase the allowance provision.* Receivables turnover is often computed using net receivables (after the allowance for uncollectible accounts). Overestimating the provision reduces net receivables and increases the turnover ratio.

2. *Asset utilization*  Asset turnover is an important financial performance measure used both by managers for internal performance goals, as well as by the market in evaluating companies. High-performing companies must be both effective (controlling margins and operating expenses) and efficient (getting the most out of their asset base). An increase in receivables ties up cash. As well, slower-turning receivables carry increased risk of loss. One of the first "low-hanging fruits" that companies pursue in efforts to improve overall asset utilization is efficiency in receivables collection.

The following chart shows the average collection period for accounts receivable of Cisco and six peer competitors that Cisco indentifies in its 10-K.

## Average Collection Period for Cisco and Competitors

**Average Collection Period for Receivables**

Cisco's average collection period of 33 days compares favorably with its primary competitors. Only Cisco, 3COM and Dell report collection periods less than 40 days.

To appreciate differences in average collection periods across industries, let's compare the average collection periods across a number of industries as follows:

## Accounts Receivable Turnover for Different Industries

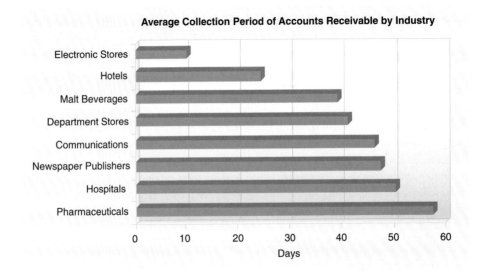

**Average Collection Period of Accounts Receivable by Industry**

Electronic stores and hotels have the shortest collection periods. For those industries, receivables are minimal because sales are made mainly via cash, check or credit card. Most of the other industries in the table have collection periods ranging from 30 to 60 days. This corresponds with typical credit terms offered on commercial transactions. Pharmaceutical companies and hospitals have longer collection periods because they often require payment from third party insurers.

**You Are the Receivables Manager**

You are analyzing your receivables turnover report for the period and you are concerned that the average collection period is lengthening. What specific actions can you take to reduce the average collection period? [Answer, p. 6-36]

# MID-MODULE REVIEW 1

At December 31, 2007, assume that Lucent Technologies had a balance of $770,000 in its Accounts Receivable account and a balance of $7,000 in its Allowance for Uncollectible Accounts. The company then analyzed and aged its accounts receivable as shown below. Assume that Lucent experienced past losses as follows: 1% of current balances, 5% of balances 1-60 days past due, 15% of balances 61-180 days past due, and 40% of balances over 180 days past due. The company bases its provision for credit losses on the aging analysis.

| | |
|---|---|
| Current . . . . . . . . . . . . . . . . . . . . . . . | $468,000 |
| 1-60 days past due . . . . . . . . . . . . . | 244,000 |
| 61-180 days past due . . . . . . . . . . . | 38,000 |
| Over 180 days past due . . . . . . . . . . | 20,000 |
| Total accounts receivable . . . . . . . . . | $770,000 |

## Required

1. What amount of uncollectible accounts (bad debts) expense will Lucent report in its 2007 income statement?
2. Show how Accounts Receivable and the Allowance for Uncollectible Accounts appear in its December 31, 2007, balance sheet.
3. Assume that Lucent's allowance for uncollectible accounts has maintained an historical average of 2% of gross accounts receivable. How do you interpret the current allowance percentage?

## Solution

1. As of December 31, 2007:

| | | | |
|---|---|---|---|
| Current . . . . . . . . . . . . . . . . . . . . . . . | $468,000 × 1% = | $ 4,680 | |
| 1-60 days past due . . . . . . . . . . . . . . . | 244,000 × 5% = | 12,200 | |
| 61-180 days past due . . . . . . . . . . . . | 38,000 × 15% = | 5,700 | |
| Over 180 days past due . . . . . . . . . . . | 20,000 × 40% = | 8,000 | |
| Amount required . . . . . . . . . . . . . . . . . | | $ 30,580 | |
| Unused allowance balance . . . . . . . . . | | 7,000 | |
| Provision . . . . . . . . . . . . . . . . . . . . . . | | $ 23,580 | 2007 bad debts expense |

2. Current assets section of balance sheet:

| | |
|---|---|
| Accounts receivable, net of $30,580 in allowances . . . | $739,420 |

3. The information here reveals that Lucent has markedly increased the percentage of the allowance for uncollectible accounts to gross accounts receivable-from the historical 2% to the current 4% ($30,580/$770,000). There are at least two possible interpretations:

a. The quality of Lucent's receivables has declined. Possible causes include the following: (1) Sales have stagnated and the company is selling to lower quality accounts to maintain sales volume; (2) It may have introduced new products for which average credit losses are higher; and (3) Its administration of accounts receivable has become lax.

b. The company has intentionally increased its allowance account above the level needed for expected future losses so as to reduce current period income and "bank" that income for future periods (income shifting).

# INVENTORY

**LO2** Explain accounting for inventories and the effects on the balance sheet and income statement from different inventory costing methods.

The second major component of operating working capital is inventory. To help frame this discussion, we refer to the following graphic that highlights inventory, a major asset for manufacturers and merchandisers. The graphic also highlights cost of goods sold on the income statement, which reflects the matching of inventory costs to related sales. This section explains the accounting, reporting, and analysis of inventory and related items.

| Income Statement | Balance Sheet | |
|---|---|---|
| Sales | Cash | Current liabilities |
| Cost of goods sold | Accounts receivable, net | Long-term liabilities |
| Selling, general & administrative | Inventory | |
| Income taxes | Property, plant, and equipment, net | Shareholders' equity |
| Net income | Investments | |

Inventory is reported on the balance sheet at its purchase price or the cost to manufacture goods that are internally produced. Inventory costs vary over time with changes in market conditions. Consequently, the cost per unit of the goods available for sale varies from period to period—even if the quantity of goods available remains the same.

When inventory is purchased or produced, it is "capitalized." That is, it is carried on the balance sheet as an asset until it is sold, at which time its cost is transferred from the balance sheet to the income statement as an expense (cost of goods sold). The process by which costs are removed from the balance sheet is important. For example, if higher cost units are transferred from the balance sheet, then cost of goods sold is higher and gross profit (sales less cost of goods sold) is lower. Conversely, if lower cost units are transferred to cost of goods sold, gross profit is higher. The remainder of this section discusses the accounting for inventory including the mechanics, reporting, and analysis of inventory costing.

## Capitalization of Inventory Cost

**Capitalization** means that a cost is recorded on the balance sheet and is not immediately expensed on the income statement. Once costs are capitalized, they remain on the balance sheet as assets until they are used up, at which time they are transferred from the balance sheet to the income statement as expense. If costs are capitalized rather than expensed, then assets, current income, and current equity are all higher.

For purchased inventories (such as merchandise), the amount of cost capitalized is the purchase price. For manufacturers, cost capitalization is more difficult, as **manufacturing costs** consist of three components: cost of direct materials used in the product, cost of direct labor to manufacture the product, and manufacturing overhead. Direct materials cost is relatively easy to compute. Design specifications list the components of each product, and their purchase costs are readily determined. The direct labor cost per unit of inventory is based on how long each unit takes to construct and the rates for each labor class working on that product. Overhead costs are also capitalized into inventory, and include the costs of plant asset depreciation, utilities, supervisory personnel, and other costs that contribute to manufacturing activities—that is, all costs of manufacturing other than direct materials and direct labor. (How these costs are assigned to individual units and across multiple products is a *managerial accounting* topic.)

When inventories are sold, their costs are transferred from the balance sheet to the income statement as cost of goods sold (COGS). COGS is then deducted from sales to yield **gross profit**:

$$\text{Gross Profit} = \text{Sales} - \text{Cost of Goods Sold}$$

The manner in which inventory costs are transferred from the balance sheet to the income statement affects both the level of inventories reported on the balance sheet and the amount of gross profit (and net income) reported on the income statement.

## Inventory Costing Methods

Exhibit 6.5 shows the computation of cost of goods sold.

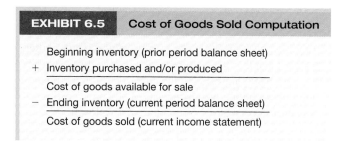

| EXHIBIT 6.5 | Cost of Goods Sold Computation |
| --- | --- |

Beginning inventory (prior period balance sheet)
+ Inventory purchased and/or produced

Cost of goods available for sale
− Ending inventory (current period balance sheet)

Cost of goods sold (current income statement)

The cost of inventory available at the beginning of a period is a carryover from the ending inventory balance of the prior period. Current period inventory purchases (or costs of newly manufactured inventories) are added to the beginning inventory balance, yielding the total cost of goods (inventory) available for sale. Then, the goods available are either sold, and end up in cost of goods sold for the period (reported on the income statement), or the goods available remain unsold and are still in inventory at the end of the period (reported on the balance sheet). Exhibit 6.6 shows this cost flow graphically.

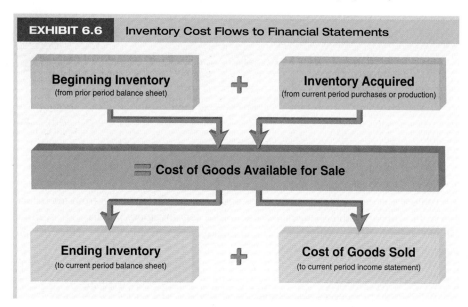

**EXHIBIT 6.6    Inventory Cost Flows to Financial Statements**

**Beginning Inventory**
(from prior period balance sheet)

**+**

**Inventory Acquired**
(from current period purchases or production)

**Cost of Goods Available for Sale**

**Ending Inventory**
(to current period balance sheet)

**+**

**Cost of Goods Sold**
(to current period income statement)

Understanding the flow of inventory costs is important. If all inventory purchased or manufactured during the period is sold, then COGS is equal to the cost of the goods purchased or manufactured. However, when inventory remains at the end of a period, companies must distinguish the cost of the inventories that were sold from the cost of the inventories that remain. GAAP allows for several options.

To illustrate, Exhibit 6.7 illustrates the partial inventory records of a company.

| EXHIBIT 6.7 | Summary Inventory Records | | |
| --- | --- | --- | --- |
| Inventory on January 1, 2007 | 500 units | @ $100 per unit | $ 50,000 |
| Inventory purchased in 2007 | 200 units | @ $150 per unit | 30,000 |
| Total cost of goods available for sale in 2007 | 700 units | | $ 80,000 |
| Inventory sold in 2007 | 450 units | @ $250 per unit | $112,500 |

This company began the period with 500 units of inventory that were purchased or manufactured for $50,000 ($100 each). During the period the company purchased and/or manufactured an additional 200 units costing $30,000. The total cost of goods available for sale for this period equals $80,000.

The company sold 450 units during 2007 for $250 per unit for total sales of $112,500. Accordingly, the company must remove the cost of the 450 units sold from the inventory account on the balance sheet and match this cost against the revenues generated from the sale. An important question is which costs should management remove from the balance sheet and report as cost of goods sold in the income statement? Three inventory costing methods (FIFO, LIFO and average cost) are common and all are acceptable under GAAP.

### First-In, First-Out (FIFO)

The FIFO inventory costing method transfers costs from inventory in the order that they were initially recorded. That is, FIFO assumes that the first costs recorded in inventory (first-in) are the first costs transferred from inventory (first-out). Applying FIFO to the data in Exhibit 6.7 means that the costs of the 450 units sold comes from *beginning* inventory, which consists of 500 units costing $100 each. The company's cost of goods sold and gross profit, using FIFO, is computed as follows:

| | |
|---|---:|
| Sales. . . . . . . . . . . . . . . . . . . . . . . . . . . . . . . . . . . . | $112,500 |
| COGS (450 @ $100 each). . . . . . . . . . . . . . . . . . . . . . | 45,000 |
| Gross profit. . . . . . . . . . . . . . . . . . . . . . . . . . . . . . . | $ 67,500 |

The cost remaining in inventory and reported on the 2007 year-end balance sheet is $35,000 ($80,000 goods available for sale less $45,000 COGS). The following financial statement effects template captures the transaction.

| | Balance Sheet | | | | | | Income Statement | | |
|---|---|---|---|---|---|---|---|---|---|
| **Transaction** | **Cash Asset** + | **Noncash Assets** = | **Liabil- ities** + | **Contrib. Capital** + | **Earned Capital** | | **Rev- enues** − | **Expen- ses** = | **Net Income** |
| Sold 450 units using FIFO costing (450 @ $100 each) | | −45,000 Inventory = | | | −45,000 Retained Earnings | | | +45,000 Cost of Goods Sold | = −45,000 |

COGS 45,000
INV  45,000

| COGS | |
|---|---|
| 45,000 | |
| INV | |
| | 45,000 |

### Last-In, First-Out (LIFO)

The LIFO inventory costing method transfers the most recent inventory costs from the balance sheet to COGS. That is, the LIFO method assumes that the most recent inventory purchases (last-in) are the first costs transferred from inventory (first-out). The company's cost of goods sold and gross profit, using LIFO, is computed as follows:

| | | |
|---|---:|---:|
| Sales. . . . . . . . . . . . . . . . . . . . . . . . . . . . | | $112,500 |
| COGS: 200 @ $150 per unit . . . . . . . . . . . . . | $30,000 | |
| 250 @ $100 per unit . . . . . . . . . . . . | 25,000 | 55,000 |
| Gross profit. . . . . . . . . . . . . . . . . . . . . . . . | | $ 57,500 |

The cost remaining in inventory and reported on the company's 2007 balance sheet is $25,000 (computed as $80,000 − $55,000). This is reflected in our financial statements effects template as follows.

| | Balance Sheet | | | | | | Income Statement | | |
|---|---|---|---|---|---|---|---|---|---|
| **Transaction** | **Cash Asset** + | **Noncash Assets** = | **Liabil- ities** + | **Contrib. Capital** + | **Earned Capital** | | **Rev- enues** − | **Expen- ses** = | **Net Income** |
| Sold 450 units using LIFO costing (200 @ $150) + (250 @ $100) | | −55,000 Inventory = | | | −55,000 Retained Earnings | | | +55,000 Cost of Goods Sold | = −55,000 |

COGS 55,000
INV  55,000

| COGS | |
|---|---|
| 55,000 | |
| INV | |
| | 55,000 |

## Average Cost (AC)

The average cost method computes the cost of goods sold as an average of the cost to purchase or manufacture all of the inventories that were available for sale during the period. To calculate the average cost of $114.286 per unit the company divides the total cost of goods available for sale by the number of units available for sale ($80,000/700 units). The company's sales, cost of sales, and gross profit follow.

| | |
|---|---:|
| Sales. . . . . . . . . . . . . . . . . . . . . . . . . . . . . . . . . . . . . . . . | $112,500 |
| COGS (450 @ $114.286 per unit). . . . . . . . . . . . . . . . . | 51,429 |
| Gross profit. . . . . . . . . . . . . . . . . . . . . . . . . . . . . . . . . . | $ 61,071 |

The cost remaining in inventory and reported on the company's 2007 balance sheet is $28,571 ($80,000 − $51,429). This is reflected in our financial statements effects template as follows.

| | Balance Sheet | | | | | | | | Income Statement | | | | |
|---|---|---|---|---|---|---|---|---|---|---|---|---|---|
| **Transaction** | **Cash Asset** | + | **Noncash Assets** | = | **Liabil-ities** | + | **Contrib. Capital** | + | **Earned Capital** | **Rev-enues** | − | **Expen-ses** | = | **Net Income** |
| Sold 450 units using average cost method (450 @ $114.286) | | | −51,429 Inventory | = | | | | | −51,429 Retained Earnings | | − | +51,429 Cost of Goods Sold | = | −51,429 |

```
COGS  51,429
        INV        51,429
             COGS
   51,429 |
             INV
               | 51,429
```

It is important to understand that the inventory costing method a company chooses is independent of the actual flow of inventory. The method choice determines COGS and ending inventory but not the actual physical inventory sold. For example, many grocery chains use LIFO inventory but certainly do not sell the freshest products first. (Companies do not frequently change inventory costing methods. Companies can adopt a new inventory costing method if doing so enhances the quality of the company's financial reports. Also, IRS regulations prohibit certain inventory costing method changes.)

## Footnote Disclosures

Notes to financial statements describe the inventory accounting method a company uses. To illustrate, Cisco reports $1,297 million in inventory on its 2005 balance sheet as a current asset. Cisco includes a general footnote on inventory along with more specific disclosures in other footnotes. Following is an excerpt from Cisco's general footnote on inventories.

> **Inventories.** Inventories are stated at the lower of cost or market. Cost is computed on a first-in, first-out basis. The Company provides inventory allowances based on excess and obsolete inventories determined primarily by future demand forecasts. The allowance is measured as the difference between the cost of the inventory and market based upon assumptions about future demand and charged to the provision for inventory, which is a component of cost of sales. At the point of the loss recognition, a new, lower-cost basis for that inventory is established, and subsequent changes in facts and circumstances do not result in the restoration or increase in that newly established cost basis.

This footnote includes at least two items of interest for our analysis of inventory:

1. Cisco uses the FIFO method of inventory costing.
2. Inventories are reported at the lower of cost or market (LCM), which means that inventory is written down if its replacement cost, referred to as 'market,' declines below its balance sheet cost (see impairment cost discussion on the following page).

For example, if the current value of Cisco's inventories is less than its reported cost, Cisco would set up an "allowance" for inventories, similar to the allowance for uncollectible accounts. The inventory allowance reduces the reported inventory amount to the current (lower) market value.

Cisco also includes a more detailed inventory footnote as follows:

| $ millions | | July 30, 2005 | July 31, 2004 |
|---|---|---|---|
| Inventories | | | |
| Raw materials | | $ 82 | $ 58 |
| Work in process | | 431 | 416 |
| Finished goods | | | |
| Distributor inventory and deferred cost of sales | $385 | | $316 |
| Manufacturing finished goods | 184 | | 206 |
| Total finished goods | | 569 | 522 |
| Service related spares | | 180 | 177 |
| Demonstration systems | | 35 | 34 |
| Total | | $1,297 | $1,207 |

This disclosure separately reports inventory costs by the following stages in the production cycle:

- *Raw materials and supplies* These are costs of direct materials and inputs into the production process including, for example, chemicals in raw state, plastic and steel for manufacturing, and incidental direct materials such as screws and lubricants.

- *Work in process* These are costs of partly finished products (also called work-in-progress).

- *Finished goods* These are the costs of products that are completed and awaiting sale.

Cisco's raw materials and work-in-process inventories have remained at 2004 levels despite a $2 billion increase in sales. Finished goods inventory increased slightly during the year.

Why do companies disclose such details about inventory? First, investment in inventory is typically large—markedly impacting both balance sheets and income statements. Second, risks of inventory losses are often high, due to technical obsolescence and consumer tastes. This is an important issue for a company such as Cisco that operates in a technology-sensitive industry. Indeed, Cisco reported a loss of over $2 billion in 2001 when the tech bubble burst, demand dried up, and the company had to write down obsolete inventories. Third, inventory details can provide insight into future performance—both good and bad. Fourth, high inventory levels result in substantial costs for the company, such as the following:

- Financing costs to hold inventories (when not purchased on credit)
- Storage costs (such as warehousing and related facilities)
- Handling costs (including wages)
- Insurance costs

Consequently, companies seek to minimize inventory levels provided this does not exceed the cost of holding insufficient inventory, called stock-outs. Stock-outs result in lost sales and production delays if machines and employees must be reconfigured to fill order backlogs.

## Lower of Cost or Market

Cisco's inventory disclosures refer to the cost of its inventories not exceeding market value. Companies must write down the carrying amount of inventories on the balance sheet *if* the reported cost (using FIFO, for example) exceeds market value (determined by current replacement cost). This process is called reporting inventories at the **lower of cost or market** and creates the following financial statement effects:

- Inventory book value is written down to current market value (replacement cost); reducing inventory and total assets.

- Inventory write-down is reflected as an expense (part of cost of goods sold) on the income statement; reducing current period gross profit, income, and equity.

To illustrate, assume that a company has inventory on its balance sheet at a cost of $27,000. Management learns that the inventory's replacement cost is $23,000 and writes inventories down to a balance of $23,000. The following financial statement effects template shows the adjustment.

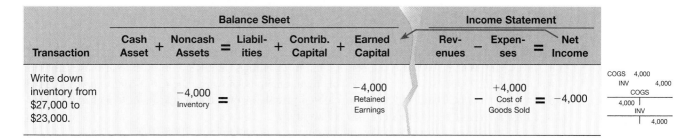

The inventory write-down (a noncash expense) is reflected in cost of goods sold and reduces gross profit by $4,000. Inventory write-downs are included in cost of goods sold. They are *not* reported in selling, general, and administrative expenses, which is common for other asset write-downs. The most common occurrence of inventory write-downs is in connection with restructuring activities.

The write-down of inventories can potentially shift income from one period to another. If, for example, inventories were written down below current replacement cost, future gross profit would be increased via lower future cost of goods sold. GAAP anticipates this possibility by requiring that inventories not be written down below a floor that is equal to net realizable value less a normal markup. Although this still allows some discretion (and the ability to manage income), the auditors must assess net realizable value and markups.

## Financial Statement Effects of Inventory Costing

This section describes the financial statement effects of different inventory costing methods.

### Income Statement Effects

The three inventory costing methods yield differing levels of gross profit as Exhibit 6.8 shows.

| **EXHIBIT 6.8** | Income Effects from Inventory Costing Methods | | |
|---|---|---|---|
| | **Sales** | **Cost of Goods Sold** | **Gross Profit** |
| FIFO . . . . . . . . . . . . . . . . . | $112,500 | $45,000 | $67,500 |
| LIFO . . . . . . . . . . . . . . . . . | 112,500 | 55,000 | 57,500 |
| Average cost . . . . . . . . . . . | 112,500 | 51,429 | 61,071 |

Recall that inventory costs rose during this period from $100 per unit to $150 per unit. The higher gross profit reported under FIFO arises because FIFO matches older, lower cost inventory against current selling prices. To generalize: in an inflationary environment, FIFO yields higher gross profit than LIFO or average cost methods do.

In recent years, the gross profit impact from using the FIFO method has been minimal due to lower rates of inflation and increased management focus on reducing inventory quantities through improved manufacturing processes and better inventory controls. The FIFO gross profit effect can still arise, however, with companies subject to high inflation and slow inventory turnover.

### Balance Sheet Effects

In our illustration above, the ending inventory using LIFO is less than that reported using FIFO. In periods of rising costs, LIFO inventories are markedly lower than under FIFO. As a result, balance sheets using LIFO do not accurately represent the cost that a company would incur to replace its current investment in inventories.

Caterpillar (CAT), for example, reports 2005 inventories under LIFO costing $5,224 million. As disclosed in the footnotes to its 10-K, if CAT valued these inventories using FIFO, the reported amount would be $2,345 million greater, a 45% increase. This suggests that CAT's balance sheet omits over $2,345 million in inventories.

## Cash Flow Effects

Unlike for most other accounting method choices, inventory costing methods affect taxable income and, thus, taxes paid. When a company adopts LIFO in its tax filings, the IRS requires it to also use LIFO for financial reporting purposes (in its 10-K). This requirement is known as the *LIFO conformity rule*. In an inflationary economy, using FIFO results in higher taxable income and, consequently, higher taxes payable. Conversely, using LIFO reduces the tax liability.

Caterpillar, Inc. discloses the following inventory information in its 2005 10-K:

> Inventories are stated at the lower of cost or market. Cost is principally determined using the last-in, first-out (LIFO) method. The value of inventories on the LIFO basis represented about 80% of total inventories at December 31, 2005, 2004 and 2003. If the FIFO (first-in, first-out) method had been in use, inventories would have been $2,345 million, $2,124 million and $1,863 million higher than reported at December 31, 2005, 2004 and 2003, respectively.

CAT uses LIFO for most of its inventories.[5] The use of LIFO has reduced the carrying amount of 2005 inventories by $2,345 million. Had it used FIFO, its inventories would have been reported at $7,569 million ($5,224 million + $2,345 million) rather than the $5,224 million that is reported on its balance sheet as of 2005. This difference, referred to as the **LIFO reserve**, is the amount that must be added to LIFO inventories to adjust them to their FIFO value.

$$\text{FIFO Inventory} = \text{LIFO Inventory} + \text{LIFO Reserve}$$

This relation also impacts cost of goods sold (COGS) as follows:

$$\textbf{FIFO COGS} = \textbf{LIFO COGS} - \textbf{Increase in LIFO Reserve (or } + \textbf{ Decrease)}$$

Use of LIFO reduced CAT's inventories by $2,345 million, resulting in a cumulative increase in cost of goods sold and a cumulative decrease in gross profit and pretax profit of that same amount.[6] Because CAT also uses LIFO for tax purposes, the decrease in pretax profits reduced CAT's cumulative tax bill by about $821 million ($2,345 million × 35% assumed corporate tax rate). This had real cash-flow consequences: CAT's cumulative operating cash flow was $821 million higher because CAT used LIFO instead of FIFO. The increased cash flow from tax savings is often cited as a compelling reason for management to adopt LIFO.

Because companies use different inventory costing methods, their financial statements are often not comparable. The problem is most serious when companies hold large amounts of inventory and when prices markedly rise or fall. To compare companies using different inventory costing methods, say LIFO and FIFO, we need to adjust the LIFO numbers to their FIFO equivalents or vice versa. For example, one way to compare CAT with another company that uses FIFO, is to add CAT's LIFO reserve to its LIFO inventory. As explained above, this $2,345 million increase in 2005 inventories would have increased its cumulative pretax profits by $2,345 million and taxes by $821 million. Thus, to adjust the 2005 balance sheet we increase inventories by $2,345 million, tax liabilities by $821 million (the extra taxes CAT would have had to pay under FIFO), and equity by the difference of $1,524 million (computed as $2,345 − $821).

To adjust CAT's 2005 income statement from LIFO to FIFO, we use the change in LIFO reserve. For CAT, the LIFO reserve increased by $221 million during 2005, from $2,124 million in 2004 to $2,345 million in 2004. This means that had it been using FIFO, its COGS would have been $221 million lower, and 2005 gross profit and pretax income would have been $221 million higher. In 2005, CAT would have paid $77 million more in taxes had it used FIFO ($221 million × 35% assumed tax rate).

---

[5] Neither the IRS nor GAAP requires use of a single inventory costing method. That is, companies are allowed to, and frequently do, use different inventory costing methods for different types of inventory (such as spare parts versus finished goods).

[6] Recall: Cost of Goods Sold = Beginning Inventories + Purchases − Ending Inventories. Thus, as ending inventories decrease, cost of goods sold increases.

**RESEARCH INSIGHT**    **LIFO and Stock Prices**

The value-relevance of inventory disclosures depends at least partly on whether investors rely more on the income statement or the balance sheet to assess future cash flows. Under LIFO, cost of goods sold reflects current costs, whereas FIFO ending inventory reflects current costs. This implies that LIFO enhances the usefulness of the income statement to the detriment of the balance sheet. This trade-off partly motivates the required LIFO reserve disclosure (the adjustment necessary to restate LIFO ending inventory and cost of good sold to FIFO). Research suggests that LIFO-based income statements better reflect stock prices than do FIFO income statements that are restated using the LIFO reserve. Research also shows a negative relation between stock prices and LIFO re-serve—meaning that higher magnitudes of LIFO reserve are associated with lower stock prices. This is consistent with the LIFO reserve being viewed as an inflation indicator (for either current or future inventory costs), which the market views as detrimental to company value.

## Tools of Inventory Analysis

This section describes several useful tools for analysis of inventory and related accounts.

### Gross profit analysis

The **gross profit margin (GPM)** is gross profit divided by sales. This important ratio is closely monitored by management and outsiders. Exhibit 6.9 shows the gross profit margin on Cisco's product sales for the past three years.

| EXHIBIT 6.9 | Gross Profit Margin for Cisco | | |
|---|---|---|---|
| | 2005 | 2004 | 2003 |
| Product sales . . . . . . . . . . . . . . . . . . | $20,853 | $18,550 | $15,565 |
| Product cost of goods sold . . . . . . . . | 6,758 | 5,766 | 4,594 |
| Gross profit. . . . . . . . . . . . . . . . . . . . | $14,095 | $12,784 | $10,971 |
| Gross profit margin. . . . . . . . . . . . . . | 67.6% | 68.9% | 70.5% |

The gross profit margin is commonly used instead of the dollar amount of gross profit as it allows for comparisons across companies and over time. A decline in GPM is usually cause for concern since it indicates that the company has less ability to pass on increased product cost to customers or that the company is not effectively managing product costs. Some possible reasons for a GPM decline follow:

- *Product line is stale.* Perhaps it is out of fashion and the company must resort to markdowns to reduce overstocked inventories. Or, perhaps the product lines have lost their technological edge, yielding reduced demand.
- *New competitors enter the market.* Perhaps substitute products are now available from competitors, yielding increased pressure to reduce selling prices.
- *General decline in economic activity.* Perhaps an economic downturn reduces product demand. The recession of the early 2000s led to reduced gross profits for many companies.
- *Inventory is overstocked.* Perhaps the company overproduced goods and finds itself in an overstock position. This can require reduced selling prices to move inventory.
- *Manufacturing costs have increased.* This could be due to poor planning, production glitches, or unfavorable supply chain reconfiguration.
- *Changes in product mix.* Perhaps the company is selling a higher proportion of low margin goods.

Cisco's gross profit margin on product sales has declined by 3 percentage points over the past two years. Following is Cisco's discussion of its gross profit situation taken from its 2005 10-K:

**Product Gross Margin** Product gross margin percentage decreased by 1.3%. Changes in the mix of products sold decreased product gross margin by approximately 2.5% due to higher sales of certain lower-margin switching products and increased sales of home networking products. Product pricing reductions and sales discounts decreased product gross margin by approximately 2%. In addition, a higher provision for warranty and a higher provision for inventory decreased product gross margin by approximately 0.5%. However, lower overall manufacturing costs related to lower component costs and value engineering and other manufacturing-related costs increased product gross margin by approximately 2%. Value engineering is the process by which the production costs are reduced through component redesign, board configuration, test processes, and transformation processes. Higher shipment volumes also increased product gross margin by approximately 1.5%.

Product gross margin may continue to be adversely affected in the future by: changes in the mix of products sold, including further periods of increased growth of some of our lower-margin products; introduction of new products, including products with price-performance advantages; our ability to reduce production costs; entry into new markets, including markets with different pricing and cost structures; changes in distribution channels; price competition, including competitors from Asia and especially China; changes in geographic mix; sales discounts; increases in material or labor costs; excess inventory and obsolescence charges; warranty costs; changes in shipment volume; loss of cost savings due to changes in component pricing; impact of value engineering; inventory holding charges; and how well we execute on our strategic and operating plans.

Cisco's gross profit margin declined in 2005 because product mix changed toward lower margin products, the company faced increased price competition and increased product warranty expense, and management increased the provision (expense) for inventory obsolescence. The gross profit margin decline was partially offset by reductions in the cost to manufacture and by higher shipment volumes that spread out manufacturing overhead over a greater unit volume. Cisco's report includes a general discussion of factors that can adversely affect gross profit margins: changes in product mix, introduction of new products at lower introductory prices to gain market share, increases in production costs, sales discounts, inventory obsolescence and warranty costs, and changes in production volume.

Competitive pressures mean that companies rarely have the opportunity to affect gross profit with price increases. Improvements in gross profit on existing product lines typically arise from a result of better management of supply chains, production processes, or distribution networks. Companies that succeed typically do so because of better performance on basic business processes. This is one of Cisco's primary objectives.

## Inventory Turnover

**Inventory turnover (INVT)** reflects the management of inventory and is computed as follows:

$$\text{Inventory Turnover} = \text{Cost of Goods Sold/Average Inventory}$$

Cost of goods sold is in the numerator because inventory is reported at cost. Inventory turnover indicates how many times inventory turns (is sold) during a period. More turns indicate that inventory is being sold more quickly, which decreases the risk of obsolete inventory and increases liquidity.

**Average inventory days outstanding (AIDO)**, also called *days inventory outstanding*, is a companion measure to inventory turnover and is computed as follows:

$$\text{Average Inventory Days Outstanding} = \text{Inventory/Average Daily Cost of Goods Sold}$$

where average daily cost of goods sold equals cost of goods sold divided by 365 days.[7]

Average inventory days outstanding indicates how long, on average, inventories are *on the shelves* before being sold. For example, if cost of goods sold is $1,200 and inventories are $300, inventories are on the shelves 91.25 days ($300/[$1,200/365 days]) on average. This performance might be an acceptable turnover for the retail fashion industry where firms need to sell out inventories each retail selling season,

---

[7] Similar to the average receivables collection period, this formula examines the average daily COGS in *ending* inventories to focus analysis on current inventories. One can also examine average daily COGS in *average* inventories (Average inventories/Average daily COGS). These two approaches address different issues: the first addresses the average days outstanding of *current ending* inventories, and the second examines the average days outstanding of *average* inventories. It is important that we first identify the issue under investigation and then choose the formula that best addresses that issue.

but it would not be acceptable for the grocery industry where perishability is a concern, or for Cisco where obsolescence is of concern.

Overall, analysis of inventory turnover and days outstanding is important for at least two reasons:

1. *Inventory quality.* Inventory turnover can be compared over time and across competitors. Higher turnover is viewed favorably, because it implies that products are salable, preferably without undue discounting (we would compare profit margins to assess discounting). Conversely, lower turnover implies that inventory is on the shelves for a longer period of time, perhaps from excessive purchases or production, missed fashion trends or technological advances, increased competition, and so forth. Our conclusions about higher or lower turnover must consider alternative explanations including the following:

   - Product mix can include more (or less) higher margin, slower turning inventories. This can occur from business acquisitions that consolidate different types of inventory.

   - A company can change its promotion policies. Increased, effective advertising is likely to increase inventory turnover. Advertising expense is in SG&A, not COGS. This means the additional advertising cost is in operating expenses, but the benefit is in gross profit and turnover. If the promotion campaign is successful, the positive effects in margin and turnover should offset the promotion cost in SG&A.

   - A company can realize improvements in manufacturing efficiency and lower investments in direct materials and work-in-process inventories. Such improvements reduce inventory and, consequently, increase inventory turnover. Although a good sign, it does not yield any information about the desirability of a company's product line.

2. *Asset utilization.* Companies strive to optimize their inventory investment. Carrying too much inventory is expensive, and too little inventory risks stock-outs and lost sales (current and future). Companies can make the following operational changes to reduce inventory.

   - Improved manufacturing processes can eliminate bottlenecks and the consequent build-up of work-in-process inventories.

   - Just-in-time (JIT) deliveries from suppliers, that provide raw materials to the production line when needed, can reduce the level of raw materials and associated holding costs.

   - Demand-pull production, in which raw materials are released into the production process when final goods are demanded by customers instead of producing for estimated demand, can reduce inventory levels. Dell Computer, for example, does not manufacture a computer until it receives the customer's order; thus, Dell produces for actual, rather than estimated, demand.

Reducing inventories reduces inventory carrying costs, thus improving profitability and increasing cash flows. The reduction in inventory is reflected as an operating cash inflow in the statement of cash flows.

There is normal tension between the sales side of a company, that argues for depth and breadth of inventory, and the finance side that monitors inventory carrying costs and seeks to maximize cash flow. Companies, therefore, seek to *optimize* inventory investment, not minimize it.

Following is a chart comparing Cisco's average inventory days outstanding with its peer companies.

## Average Inventory Days Outstanding for Cisco and Competitors

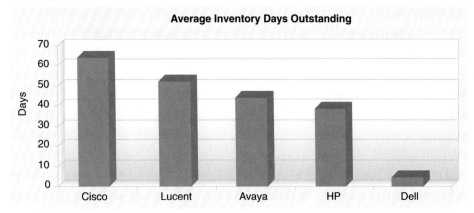

Cisco's average inventory days outstanding of 64 does not compare favorably with its peers. Cisco's 2005 10-K provides the following comments regarding inventory management :

> Inventory management remains an area of focus as we balance the need to maintain strategic inventory levels to ensure competitive lead times against the risk of inventory obsolescence because of rapidly changing technology and customer requirements. We believe the amount of our inventory is appropriate for our current revenue level.

Dell's average inventory days outstanding of 5 is markedly lower than other companies shown in this graph. Dell has traditionally focused on excellence in this area, and views this as a competitive advantage. Dell's 2005 10-K reports the following:

> Dell believes the direct business model is the most effective model for providing solutions that address customer needs. In addition, Dell's flexible, build-to-order manufacturing process enables Dell to reduce inventory levels. This allows Dell to rapidly introduce the latest relevant technology more quickly than companies with slow-moving, indirect distribution channels, and to rapidly pass on component cost savings directly to customers . . . Dell's direct business model allows the company to maintain a leading asset management system in comparison to its major competitors. Dell is capable of minimizing inventory risk while collecting amounts due from customers before paying vendors, thus allowing the company to generate annual cash flows from operating activities that typically exceed net income.

It is also instructive to compare the average inventory days outstanding for selected industries.

## Inventory Turnover for Companies from Different Industries

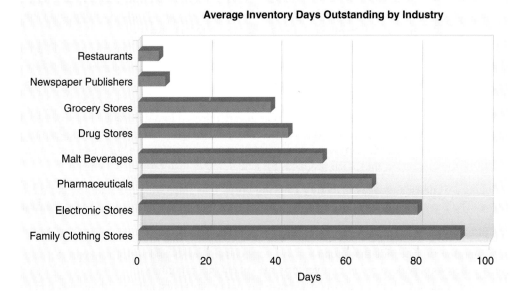

Restaurants and newspaper publishers carry only a few days' inventory at any point in time. Restaurants are mindful of the perishable nature of their food products, and inventories are low in the publishing industry because newspapers are printed and sold daily. On the other hand, pharmaceuticals, electronic stores, and family clothing stores must carry high levels of inventory to support customer demand.

---

**MANAGERIAL DECISION**    **You Are the Plant Manager**

You are analyzing your inventory turnover report for the month and are concerned that the average inventory days outstanding is lengthening. What actions can you take to reduce average inventory days outstanding? [Answer, p. 6-37]

## LIFO Liquidations

When companies acquire inventory at different costs, they are required to maintain each cost level as a separate inventory pool or layer (for example, there are the $100 and $150 units in our Exhibit 6.7 illustration). When companies reduce inventory levels, older inventory costs flow to the income statement. When companies use LIFO, older costs are often markedly different than current replacement costs. Given the usual inflationary environment, sales of older pools often yield a boost to gross profit as older, lower costs are matched against current selling prices on the income statement.

The increase in gross profit resulting from a reduction of inventory quantities in the presence of rising costs is called **LIFO liquidation.** The effect of LIFO liquidation is evident in the following footnote from General Motors Corporation's 2005 10-K:

Inventories are stated generally at cost, which is not in excess of market. The cost of approximately 67% of U.S. inventories is determined by the last-in, first-out (LIFO) method. Generally, the cost of all other inventories is determined by either the first-in, first-out (FIFO) or average cost methods.

During 2005 and 2004, U.S. LIFO eligible inventory quantities were reduced. This reduction resulted in a liquidation of LIFO inventory quantities carried at lower costs prevailing in prior years as compared with the cost of 2005 and 2004 purchases, the effect of which decreased cost of goods sold by approximately $100 million, pre-tax, in both 2005 and 2004.

GM reports that reductions in inventory quantities led to the sale (at current selling prices) of products that carried very low costs from prior years. As a result of these inventory reductions, pretax income increased by $100 million from lower COGS. In this case, the inventory LIFO liquidation yielded a profit increase. We must be aware, however, of potentially different income effects from LIFO liquidations when inventory costs fluctuate.

## MID-MODULE REVIEW 2

At the beginning of the current period, assume that Avaya, Inc., holds 1,000 units of its only product with a unit cost of $18. A summary of purchases during the current period follows:

|  | Units | Unit Cost | Cost |
|---|---|---|---|
| Beginning Inventory | 1,000 | $18.00 | $18,000 |
| Purchases: #1 | 1,800 | 18.25 | 32,850 |
| #2 | 800 | 18.50 | 14,800 |
| #3 | 1,200 | 19.00 | 22,800 |
| Goods available for sale | 4,800 |  | $88,450 |

During the current period, Avaya sells 2,800 units.

### Required
1. Assume that Avaya uses the first-in, first-out (FIFO) method. Compute the cost of goods sold for the current period and the ending inventory balance.
2. Assume that Avaya uses the last-in, first-out (LIFO) method. Compute the cost of goods sold for the current period and the ending inventory balance.
3. Assume that Avaya uses the average cost (AC) method. Compute the cost of goods sold for the current period and the ending inventory balance.
4. As manager, which of these three inventory costing methods would you choose:
   a. To reflect what is probably the physical flow of goods? Explain.
   b. To minimize income taxes for the period? Explain.
5. Assume that Avaya utilizes the LIFO method and both allows its inventory level to decline *and* delays purchasing lot #3 until the next period. Compute cost of goods sold under this scenario and discuss how the LIFO liquidation affects profit.

## Solution

Preliminary computation: Units in ending inventory = 4,800 available − 2,800 sold = 2,000

1. First-in, first-out (FIFO)

| *Cost of goods sold computation:* | Units | | Cost | | Total |
|---|---|---|---|---|---|
| | 1,000 | @ | $18.00 | = | $18,000 |
| | 1,800 | @ | $18.25 | = | 32,850 |
| | 2,800 | | | | **$50,850** |

| | |
|---|---|
| Cost of goods available for sale. . . . . . . . . . . . . . | $88,450 |
| Less: Cost of goods sold . . . . . . . . . . . . . . . . . . | 50,850 |
| Ending inventory ($22,800 + $14,800). . . . . . . . . | **$37,600** |

2. Last-in, first-out (LIFO)

| *Cost of goods sold computation:* | Units | | Cost | | Total |
|---|---|---|---|---|---|
| | 1,200 | @ | $19.00 | = | $22,800 |
| | 800 | @ | $18.50 | = | 14,800 |
| | 800 | @ | $18.25 | = | 14,600 |
| | 2,800 | | | | **$52,200** |

| | |
|---|---|
| Cost of goods available for sale. . . . . . . . . . . . . . | $88,450 |
| Less: Cost of goods sold . . . . . . . . . . . . . . . . . . | 52,200 |
| Ending inventory ($18,000 + [1,000 × $18.25]). . . . | **$36,250** |

3. Average cost (AC)

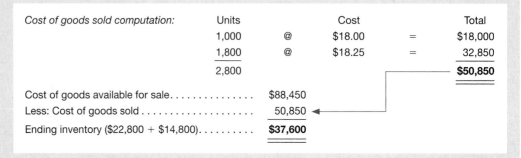

Average unit cost  = $88,450/4,800 units = $18.427
Cost of goods sold = 2,800 × $18.427 = $51,596
Ending inventory  = 2,000 × $18.427 = $36,854

4. a. FIFO is normally the method that most closely reflects physical flow. For example, FIFO would apply to the physical flow of perishable units and to situations where the earlier units acquired are moved out first because of risk of deterioration or obsolescence.

   b. LIFO results in the highest cost of goods sold during periods of rising costs (as in the Avaya case); and, accordingly, LIFO yields the lowest net income and the lowest income taxes.

5. Last-in, first-out with LIFO liquidation

| *Cost of goods sold computation:* | Units | | Cost | | Total |
|---|---|---|---|---|---|
| | 800 | @ | $18.50 | = | $14,800 |
| | 1,800 | @ | $18.25 | = | 32,850 |
| | 200 | @ | $18.00 | = | 3,600 |
| | 2,800 | | | | $51,250 |

| | |
|---|---|
| Cost of goods available for sale. . . . . . . . . . . . . . | $65,650 |
| Less: Cost of goods sold . . . . . . . . . . . . . . . . . . | 51,250 |
| Ending inventory (800 × $18). . . . . . . . . . . . . . . | $14,400 |

The company's LIFO gross profit has increased by $950 ($52,200 − $51,250) because of the LIFO liquidation. The reduction of inventory quantities matched older (lower) cost layers against current selling prices. The company has, in effect, dipped into lower cost layers to boost current period profit—all from a simple delay of inventory purchases.

# PROPERTY, PLANT, AND EQUIPMENT (PPE)

Many companies' largest operating asset is property, plant, and equipment. To frame our PPE discussion, the following graphic highlights long-term operating assets on the balance sheet, and selling, general and administrative expenses on the income statement. The latter includes depreciation and asset write-downs that match the assets' cost against sales derived from the assets. (Depreciation on any manufacturing facilities is included in cost of goods sold.) This section explains the accounting, reporting, and analysis of PPE and related items.

**LO3** Describe accounting for property, plant and equipment and explain the impacts on profit and cash flows from different depreciation methods.

| Income Statement | Balance Sheet | |
| --- | --- | --- |
| Sales | Cash | Current liabilities |
| Cost of goods sold | Accounts receivable, net | Long-term liabilities |
| Selling, general & administrative | Inventory | |
| Income taxes | Property, plant, and equipment, net | Shareholders' equity |
| Net income | Investments | |

## Capitalization of Asset Costs

Companies capitalize costs as an asset on the balance sheet only if that asset possesses both of the following characteristics:

1. The asset is owned or controlled by the company.
2. The asset provides future expected benefits.

Owning the asset means the company has title to the asset as provided in a purchase contract. (Assets acquired under leases are also capitalized if certain conditions are met—see Module 10.) Future expected benefits usually refer to future cash inflows. Companies capitalize the full cost to acquire the asset, including the purchase price, transportation, setup, and all other costs necessary to get the asset into service. This is called the asset's acquisition cost.

Companies can only capitalize asset costs that are *directly linked* to future cash inflows, and the costs capitalized as an asset can be no greater than the related expected future cash inflows. This means that if a company reports a $200 asset, we can reasonably expect that it will derive at least $200 in expected cash inflows from the use and ultimate disposal of the asset.

The *directly linked* condition for capitalization of asset cost is important. When a company acquires a machine, it capitalizes the cost because the company expects the machine's output to yield cash inflows from the sale of product made by the machine and from the cash received when the company eventually disposes of the machine. On the other hand, when it comes to research and development (R&D) activities, it is more difficult to directly link expected cash inflows with the R&D expenditures because R&D activities are often unsuccessful. Further, companies cannot reliably estimate the future cash flows from successful R&D activities. Accordingly, GAAP requires that R&D expenditures be expensed when paid. Similar arguments are applied to advertising, promotion and wages to justify expensing of those costs.

Each of these examples relates to items or activities that we generally think of as intangible assets. That is, we reasonably expect R&D efforts and advertising campaigns to produce results. If not, companies would not pursue them. We also generally view employee activities as generating future benefits. Indeed, we often refer to the *human resources* (asset) of a company. However, the link between these items or activities and their outputs is not as direct as GAAP requires for capitalizing such costs. The nonrecognition of these assets is one reason why it is difficult to analyze and value knowledge-based companies and such companies are less suited to traditional ROE disaggregation analysis. Capitalization and noncapitalization of costs can markedly impact financial statements and, therefore, our analysis inferences and assessment of a company as an investment prospect.

| BUSINESS INSIGHT | WorldCom and Improper Cost Capitalization |

WorldCom's CEO, Bernie Ebbers, and chief financial officer, Scott Sullivan, were convicted in 2005 of *cooking the books* so the company would not show a loss for 2001 and subsequent quarters. Specifically, WorldCom incurred large costs in anticipation of an increase in Internet-related business that did not materialize. Instead of expensing the costs as GAAP requires and reporting a loss in the WorldCom income statement, executives shifted the costs to the balance sheet. By capitalizing these costs (recording them on the balance sheet), WorldCom was able to disguise these costs as assets, thereby inflating current profitability. Although the WorldCom case involved massive fraud, which is difficult for outsiders to detect, an astute analyst would have suspected something was amiss from analysis of WorldCom's long-term asset turnover (Sales/Average long-term assets) as shown below. The obvious decline in turnover reveals that WorldCom's assets constituted an ever increasing percent of total sales during periods leading up to 2002. This finding does not, in itself, imply fraud. It does, however, raise serious questions that analysts should have posed to WorldCom executives in analyst meetings.

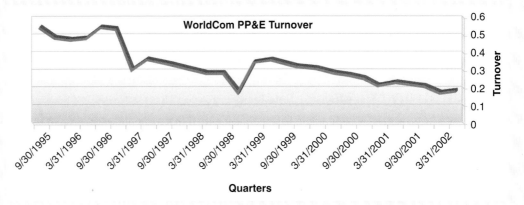

## Depreciation

Once a cost is capitalized on the balance sheet as an asset, it must be systematically transferred from the balance sheet to the income statement as depreciation expense to match the asset's cost to the revenues it generates. The depreciation process requires the following estimates:

1. **Useful life.** Period of time over which the asset is expected to generate cash inflows
2. **Salvage value.** Expected disposal amount at the end of the asset's useful life
3. **Depreciation rate.** An estimate of how the asset will be used up over its useful life

Management must determine each of these factors when the asset is acquired. Depreciation commences immediately upon asset acquisition and use. Management also can revise estimates that determine depreciation during the asset's useful life.

The **depreciation base**, also called *nonrecoverable cost*, is the amount to be depreciated. The depreciation base is the acquisition cost less estimated salvage value. This means that at the end of the asset's useful life, only the salvage value remains on the balance sheet.

**Depreciation rate** refers to the manner in which the asset is used up. Companies make one of the following three assumptions about the depreciation rate:

1. Asset is used up by the same amount each period.
2. Asset is used up more in the early years of its useful life.
3. Asset is used up in proportion to its actual usage.

A company can depreciate different assets using different depreciation rates (and different useful lives). After a depreciation rate is chosen, however, the company must generally stick with that rate throughout the asset's useful life. This is not to say that companies can't change depreciation rates, but changes must be justified as providing more useful financial reports.

The using up of an asset generally relates to physical or technological obsolescence. *Physical obsolescence* relates to an asset's diminished capacity to produce output. *Technological obsolescence* relates to an asset's diminished efficiency in producing output in a competitive manner.

All depreciation methods have the following general formula:

**Depreciation Expense = Depreciation Base × Depreciation Rate**

Remembering this general formula helps us understand the depreciation process. Also, each depreciation method reports the same amount of depreciation expense *over the life of the asset*. The only difference is in the amount of depreciation expense reported *for a given period*. To illustrate, consider a machine with the following details: $100,000 cost, $10,000 salvage value, and a five-year useful life. We look at two of the most common methods of depreciation.

## Straight-Line Method

Under the straight-line (SL) method, depreciation expense is recognized evenly over the estimated useful life of the asset as follows:

| Depreciation Base | Depreciation Rate |
|---|---|
| Cost − Salvage value | 1/Estimated useful life |
| = $100,000 − $10,000 | = 1/5 years |
| = $90,000 | = 20% |

Depreciation expense per year for this asset is $18,000, computed as $90,000 × 20%. For the asset's first full year of usage, $18,000 of depreciation expense is reported in the income statement. (If an asset is purchased midyear, it is typically depreciated only for the portion of the year it is used. For example, had the asset in this illustration been purchased on May 1, the company would report $10,500 of depreciation in the first year, computed as 7/12 × $18,000, assuming the company has a December 31 year-end.) This depreciation is reflected in the company's financial statements as follows:

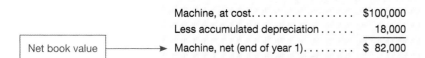

| | | Balance Sheet | | | | | Income Statement | | |
|---|---|---|---|---|---|---|---|---|---|
| Transaction | Cash Asset | + Noncash Assets | = Liabil-ities | + Contrib. Capital | + Earned Capital | | Rev-enues | − Expen-ses | = Net Income |
| Record $18,000 straight-line depreciation | | −18,000 Accumulated Depreciation | = | | −18,000 Retained Earnings | | | +18,000 Depreciation Expense | = −18,000 |

DE 18,000
AD 18,000
DE 18,000
AD 18,000

The accumulated depreciation (contra asset) account increases by $18,000, thus reducing net PPE by the same amount. Also, $18,000 of the asset cost is transferred from the balance sheet to the income statement as depreciation expense. At the end of the first year the asset is reported on the balance sheet as follows:

| | |
|---|---|
| Machine, at cost.................. | $100,000 |
| Less accumulated depreciation...... | 18,000 |
| Machine, net (end of year 1)........ | $ 82,000 |

Net book value → (points to "Machine, net (end of year 1)")

**Accumulated depreciation** is the sum of all depreciation expense that has been recorded to date. The asset **net book value (NBV)**, or *carrying value*, is cost less accumulated depreciation. Although the word value is used here, it does not refer to market value. Depreciation is a cost allocation concept (transfer of costs from the balance sheet to the income statement), not a valuation concept.

In the second year of usage, another $18,000 of depreciation expense is recorded in the income statement and the net book value of the asset on the balance sheet follows:

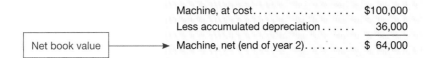

|  | Machine, at cost. | $100,000 |
| --- | --- | --- |
|  | Less accumulated depreciation | 36,000 |
| Net book value → | Machine, net (end of year 2). | $ 64,000 |

Accumulated depreciation of $36,000 now includes the sum of the first and second years' depreciation, and the net book value of the asset is now reduced to $64,000. After the fifth year, a total of $90,000 of accumulated depreciation will be recorded ($18,000 per year × 5 years), yielding a net book value for the machine of $10,000. The net book value at the end of the machine's useful life is exactly equal to the salvage value that management estimated when the asset was acquired.

## Double-Declining-Balance Method

GAAP also allows *accelerated* methods of depreciation, the most common being the double-declining-balance method. This method records more depreciation in the early years of an asset's useful life (hence the term *accelerated*) and less depreciation in later years. At the end of the asset's useful life, the balance sheet will still report a net book value equal to the asset's salvage value. The difference between straight-line and accelerated depreciation methods is not in the total amount of depreciation, but in the rate at which costs are transferred from the balance sheet to the income statement.

For the double-declining-balance (DDB) method, the depreciation base is net book value, which declines over the life of the asset (this is why the method is called "declining balance"). The depreciation rate is twice the straight-line (SL) rate (which explains the word "double"). The depreciation base and rate for the asset in our illustrative example are computed as follows:

| Depreciation Base | Depreciation Rate |
| --- | --- |
| Net Book Value = Cost − Accumulated Depreciation | 2 × SL rate = 2 × 20% = 40% |

The depreciation expense for the first year is $40,000, computed as $100,000 × 40%. This depreciation is reflected in the company's financial statements as follows:

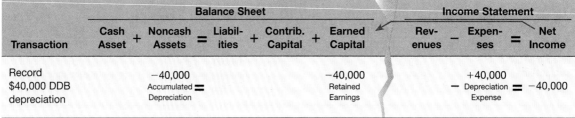

| | | Balance Sheet | | | | | | Income Statement | | |
| --- | --- | --- | --- | --- | --- | --- | --- | --- | --- | --- |
| Transaction | Cash Asset | + Noncash Assets | = Liabil- ities | + Contrib. Capital | + Earned Capital | | Rev- enues | − Expen- ses | = Net Income |
| Record $40,000 DDB depreciation | | −40,000 Accumulated = Depreciation | | | −40,000 Retained Earnings | | | +40,000 − Depreciation = Expense | −40,000 |

The accumulated depreciation (contra asset) account increases by $40,000 which reduces net PPE (compare this to the $18,000 depreciation under straight-line). This means that $40,000 of the asset cost is transferred from the balance sheet to the income statement as depreciation expense. At the end of the first year, the asset is reported on the balance sheet as follows:

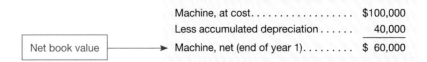

|  | Machine, at cost. | $100,000 |
| --- | --- | --- |
|  | Less accumulated depreciation | 40,000 |
| Net book value → | Machine, net (end of year 1). | $ 60,000 |

In the second year, the net book value of the asset is the new depreciable base, and the company records depreciation of $24,000 ($60,000 × 40%) in the income statement. At the end of the second year, the net book value of the asset on the balance sheet is:

|  |  |
|---|---|
| Machine, at cost.................. | $100,000 |
| Less accumulated depreciation...... | 64,000 |
| Machine, net (end of year 2)........ | $ 36,000 |

Net book value → Machine, net (end of year 2)

Under the double-declining-balance method, a company continues to record depreciation expense in this manner until the salvage value is reached, at which point the depreciation process is discontinued. This leaves a net book value equal to the salvage value, as with the straight-line method.[8] The DDB depreciation schedule for the life of this asset is in Exhibit 6.10.

| **EXHIBIT 6.10** | **Double-Declining-Balance Depreciation Schedule** | | |
|---|---|---|---|
| **Year** | **Book Value at Beginning of Year** | **Depreciation Expense** | **Book Value at End of Year** |
| 1 ........... | $100,000 | $40,000 | $60,000 |
| 2 ........... | 60,000 | 24,000 | 36,000 |
| 3 ........... | 36,000 | 14,400 | 21,600 |
| 4 ........... | 21,600 | 8,640 | 12,960 |
| 5 ........... | 12,960 | 2,960* | 10,000 |

*The formula value of $5,184 ($12,960 × 40%) is *not* reported because it would depreciate the asset below salvage value; only the $2,960 needed to reach salvage value is reported.

Exhibit 6.11 shows the depreciation expense and net book value for both the SL and DDB methods. During the first two years, the DDB method yields a higher depreciation expense compared to the SL method. Beginning in the third year, this pattern reverses and the SL method produces higher depreciation expense. Over the asset's life, the same $90,000 of asset cost is transferred to the income statement as depreciation expense, leaving a salvage value of $10,000 on the balance sheet under both methods.

| **EXHIBIT 6.11** | **Comparison of Straight-Line and Double-Declining-Balance Depreciation** | | | |
|---|---|---|---|---|
|  | **Straight-Line** | | **Double-Declining-Balance** | |
| **Year** | **Depreciation Expense** | **Book Value at End of Year** | **Depreciation Expense** | **Book Value at End of Year** |
| 1 ........... | $18,000 | $82,000 | $40,000 | $60,000 |
| 2 ........... | 18,000 | 64,000 | 24,000 | 36,000 |
| 3 ........... | 18,000 | 46,000 | 14,400 | 21,600 |
| 4 ........... | 18,000 | 28,000 | 8,640 | 12,960 |
| 5 ........... | 18,000 | 10,000 | 2,960 | 10,000 |
|  | $90,000 | | $90,000 | |

All depreciation methods yield the same salvage value

Total depreciation over asset life is identical for all methods

Companies typically use the SL method for financial reporting purposes and an accelerated depreciation method for tax returns.[9] The reason is that in early years the SL depreciation yields higher income on shareholder reports, whereas accelerated depreciation yields lower taxable income. Even though this relation reverses in later years, companies prefer to have the tax savings sooner rather than later so that the cash savings can be invested to produce earnings. Further, the reversal may never occur—if depreciable

---

[8] A variant of DDB allows for a change from DDB to SL at the point when SL depreciation exceeds that for DDB.

[9] The IRS mandates the use of MACRS (Modified Accelerated Cost Recovery System) for tax purposes. This method fixes the useful life for various classes of assets, assumes no salvage value, and generally uses the double-declining-balance method.

assets are growing at a fast enough rate, the additional first year's depreciation on acquired assets more than offsets the lower depreciation expense on older assets, yielding a "permanent" reduction in taxable income and taxes paid.[10]

## Asset Sales and Impairments

This section discusses gains and losses from asset sales, and the computation and disclosure of asset impairments.

### Gains and Losses on Asset Sales

The gain or loss on the sale (disposition) of a long-term asset is computed as follows.

**Gain or Loss on Asset Sale = Proceeds from Sale − Net Book Value of Asset Sold**

An asset's net book value is its acquisition cost less accumulated depreciation. When an asset is sold, its acquisition cost and related accumulated depreciation are both removed from the balance sheet and any gain or loss is reported in income from continuing operations.

Gains and losses on asset sales can be large, and analysts must be aware that these gains are *transitory operating* income components. It is often difficult to uncover gains and losses from asset sales because, if the gain or loss is small (immaterial), companies often include the item in selling, general and administrative expenses. To illustrate, Ford Motor Company provides the following footnote disclosure to its 2005 10-K relating to the sale of its Hertz automotive leasing subsidiary ($ millions):

> **Held-for-Sale Operations** During 2005, management committed to sell Hertz as it is not core to our Automotive business. On September 12, 2005, we entered into a definitive agreement with an investor group of private equity firms under which we agreed to sell Hertz in a transaction valued at approximately $15 billion. On December 21, 2005, we completed, through our wholly-owned subsidiary Ford Holdings LLC, the sale of our 100% ownership interest in Hertz to CCMG Investor, LLC. We received $5.6 billion in cash for the sale of Hertz. As a result of the sale, we recognized in *Gain on sale of Hertz* a pre-tax gain of $1.1 billion.

Ford sold a subsidiary company, carried on its balance sheet at a net book value of $13.9 billion (computed as $15 billion sale less $1.1 billion gain), for $15 billion. The impacts on its financial statements follow:

| | Balance Sheet | | | | | | Income Statement | | |
|---|---|---|---|---|---|---|---|---|---|
| Transaction | Cash Asset | + Noncash Assets | = Liabil-ities | + Contrib. Capital | + Earned Capital | | Rev-enues | − Expen-ses | = Net Income |
| Sale of subsidiary | 15.0 Bil. Cash | −13.9 Bil. Investment in Hertz = | | | 1.1 Bil. Retained Earnings | | 1.1 Bil. Gain on Asset Sale | | = 1.1 Bil. |

Cash   15.0 Bil.
   Hertz   13.9 Bil.
   Gain    1.1 Bil.
Cash
15.0 Bil.
   Hertz
    13.9 Bil.
    Gain
     1.1 Bil.

Ford reported a pretax gain of $1.1 billion from this sale, which was more than half of its total pretax income for that year.

### Asset Impairments

Property, plant, and equipment (PPE) assets are reported at their net book values (original cost less accumulated depreciation). This is the case even if the market values of these assets increase subsequent to acquisition. As a result, there can be unrecognized gains *buried* in the balance sheet.

---

[10] The **units-of-production depreciation** method is also common, which depreciates assets according to use. Specifically, the depreciation base is cost less salvage value, and the depreciation rate is the units produced and sold during the year compared with the total expected units to be produced and sold. For example, if a truck is driven 10,000 miles out of a total expected 100,000 miles, 10% of its nonrecoverable cost is reflected as depreciation expense. This method is common for extractive industries like timber and coal.

On the other hand, if market values of PPE assets subsequently decrease—and the asset value is deemed as permanently impaired—then companies must write off the impaired cost and recognize losses on those assets. **Impairment** of PPE assets is determined by comparing the asset's net book value to the sum of the asset's *expected* future (undiscounted) cash flows. If the sum of expected cash flow is greater than net book value, there is no impairment. However, if the sum of the expected cash flow is less than net book value, the asset is deemed impaired and it is written down to its current market value (generally, the present value of those expected cash flows). Exhibit 6.12 depicts this impairment analysis.

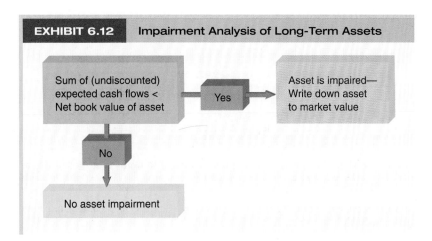

**EXHIBIT 6.12**    Impairment Analysis of Long-Term Assets

When a company takes an impairment charge, assets are reduced by the amount of the write-down and the loss is recognized in the income statement. To illustrate, a footnote to the 2005 10-K of Agilent Technologies, Inc., reports the following about asset impairments:

> **Valuation of long-lived assets.** We have assessed the recoverability of our long-lived assets, by determining whether the carrying value of such assets will be recovered through undiscounted future cash flows. We incurred $26 million of investment and restructuring asset impairment charges in 2005.

Agilent's write-down of impaired assets affected its financial statements as follows:

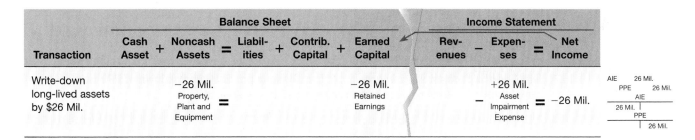

Agilent wrote down the carrying value (net book value) of its long-lived assets by $26 million. This write-down accelerated the transfer of the asset's cost from the balance sheet to the income statement. Consequently, Agilent recognized an expense of $26 million in the current year rather than over time via the depreciation process.

It is important to note that management determines if and when to recognize asset impairments. Thus, there is room for management to opportunistically over- or under-estimate asset impairments. Write-downs of long-term assets are often recognized in connection with a restructuring program.

Analysis of asset write-downs present at least two potential challenges:

1. *Insufficient write-down.* Assets sometimes are impaired but an impairment charge is not recognized. This can arise if management is overly optimistic about future prospects or is reluctant to recognize the full impairment in income.

2. *Aggressive write-down.* This *big bath* scenario can arise if income is already very low in a given year. Management's view is that the market will not penalize the company's stock for an extra

write-off when the year was already bad. Taking a larger impairment charge purges the balance sheet of costs that would otherwise hit future years' income.

GAAP condones neither of these cases. Yet, because management must estimate future cash flows for the impairment test, it has some degree of control over the timing and amount of the asset write-off and can use that discretion to manage reported income.

## Footnote Disclosures

Cisco reports the following PPE asset amounts in its balance sheet:

| At December 31 ($ millions) | 2005 | 2004 |
|---|---|---|
| Property, Plant and Equipment, net . . . . . . . . . . | 3,320 | 3,290 |

In addition to its balance sheet disclosure, Cisco provides two footnotes that more fully describe its PPE assets:

1. *Summary of Significant Accounting Policies.* This footnote describes Cisco's accounting for PPE assets in general terms:

   **Depreciation and Amortization** Property and equipment are stated at cost, less accumulated depreciation and amortization. Depreciation and amortization are computed using the straight-line method over the estimated useful lives of the assets. Estimated useful lives of 25 years are used for buildings. Estimated useful lives of 30 to 36 months are used for computer equipment and related software and five years for furniture and fixtures. Estimated useful lives of up to five years are used for production, engineering, and other equipment. Depreciation of operating lease assets is computed based on the respective lease terms, which generally range up to three years. Depreciation and amortization of leasehold improvements are computed using the shorter of the remaining lease terms or five years.

   There are a two items of interest in this disclosure: (a) Cisco, like most publicly traded companies, depreciates its PPE assets using the straight-line method (for tax purposes it uses an accelerated method). (b) Cisco provides general disclosures on the useful lives of its assets: 30 months to 25 years. We will discuss a method to more accurately estimate the useful lives in the next section.

2. *Supplemental balance sheet information.* This footnote provides a breakdown of PPE assets by category as well as the balance in the accumulated depreciation account:

| Property and equipment, net (millions) | |
|---|---|
| Land, buildings and leasehold improvements . . . . . . . . . . . . | $3,492 |
| Computer equipment and related software . . . . . . . . . . . . . | 1,244 |
| Production, engineering and other equipment. . . . . . . . . . . | 3,095 |
| Operating lease assets. . . . . . . . . . . . . . . . . . . . . . . . . . . | 136 |
| Furniture and fixtures . . . . . . . . . . . . . . . . . . . . . . . . . . . . . | 355 |
| . . . . . . . . . . . . . . . . . . . . . . . . . . . . . . . . . . . . . . . . . . . . . . | 8,322 |
| Less accumulated depreciation and amortization . . . . . . . . | (5,002) |
| Total . . . . . . . . . . . . . . . . . . . . . . . . . . . . . . . . . . . . . . . . . . | $3,320 |

## Analysis Implications

This section explains how to measure long-term asset utilization and asset age.

### PPE Turnover

A crucial issue in analyzing PPE assets is determining their productivity (utilization). For example, what level of plant assets is necessary to generate a dollar of revenues? How capital intensive is the company and its competitors? To address these and similar questions, we use **PPE turnover**, defined as follows:

$$\text{PPE Turnover (PPET)} = \text{Sales/Average PPE Assets}$$

Cisco's 2005 PPE turnover is 7.5 times ($24,801 million/[($3,320 million + $3,290 million)/2]). This turnover places Cisco solidly among its peers (see chart below). Dell's asset utilization is legendary and its PPE turnover of 30 is about four times higher than most of the other companies Cisco identifies as its peers.

### PPE Turnover for Cisco and Its Peer Companies

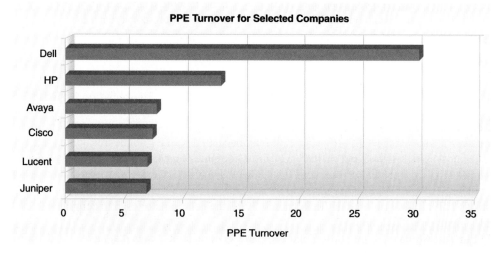

Higher PPE turnover is preferable to lower. A higher PPE turnover implies a lower capital investment for a given level of sales. Higher turnover, therefore, increases profitability because the company avoids asset carrying costs and because the freed-up assets can now generate operating cash flow.

PPE turnover is lower for capital-intensive manufacturing companies than it is for companies in service or knowledge-based industries. To this point, consider the following chart of PPE turnover for selected industries.

### PPE Turnover for Selected Industries

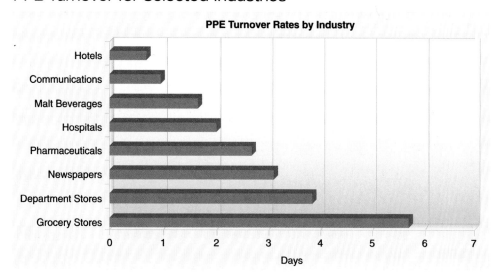

Hotels and communications companies are capital-intensive businesses. Their PPE turnover rates are, correspondingly, lower than for other industries. On the other hand, department stores and grocery stores require comparatively less capital investment. Their PPE turnover rates are much higher.

| MANAGERIAL DECISION | **You Are the Division Manager** |
|---|---|

You are the manager for a main operating division of your company. You are concerned that a declining PPE turnover is adversely affecting your division's return on net operating assets. What specific actions can you take to increase PPE turnover? [Answer, p. 6-37]

## Useful Life and Percent Used Up

Cisco reports that the useful lives of its depreciable assets range from 30 months for computer equipment and up to 25 years for buildings. The longer an asset's useful life, the lower the annual depreciation expense reported in the income statement and the higher the income each year. It might be of interest, therefore, to know whether a company's useful life estimates are more conservative or more aggressive than its competitors.

If we assume straight-line (SL) depreciation and zero salvage value, we can estimate the average useful life for depreciable assets as follows:

**Estimated Average Useful Life = Depreciable Asset Cost/Depreciation Expense**

For Cisco, the estimated useful life for its plant assets is 10.6 years ($8,322 million/$782 million). Land cost is nearly always excluded from gross PPE cost because land is a nondepreciable asset. However, Cisco does not provide a breakout of land cost in its footnotes and Cisco does not report depreciation expense as a separate line item on the income statement. Therefore, we use the depreciation and amortization expense of $1,009 million (reported in the statement of cash flows) and subtract the amortization expense of $227 million disclosed in the footnotes. Thus, the denominator used to compute the useful life of Cisco's assets is $782 million.

We can also estimate the proportion of a company's depreciable assets that have already been transferred to the income statement. This ratio reflects the percent of depreciable assets that are no longer productive—as follows:

**Percent Used Up = Accumulated Depreciation/Depreciable Asset Cost**

Cisco's assets are 60% used up, computed as $5,002 million/$8,322 million. If a company replaced all of its assets evenly each year, the percent used up ratio would be 50%. Cisco's depreciable assets are slightly older than this benchmark. Knowing the degree to which a company's assets are used up is of interest in forecasting future cash flows. If, for example, depreciable assets are 80% used up, we might anticipate a higher level of capital expenditures in the near future. We also expect that older assets are less efficient and will incur higher maintenance costs.

## MODULE-END REVIEW

On January 2, assume that Hewlett-Packard purchases equipment that fabricates a key-product part. The equipment costs $95,000, and its estimated useful life is five years, after which it is expected to be sold for $10,000.

## Required
1. Compute depreciation expense for each year of the equipment's useful life for each of the following depreciation methods:
   a. Straight-line
   b. Double-declining-balance
2. Show how HP reports the equipment on its balance sheet at the end of the third year assuming straight-line depreciation.

3. Assume that this is the only depreciable asset the company owns and that it uses straight-line depreciation. Using the depreciation expense computed in 1a and the balance sheet presentation from 2, estimate the useful life and the percent used up for this asset at the end of the third year.

## Solution

1. *a.* Straight-line depreciation expense = ($95,000 − $10,000)/5 years = $17,000 per year

   *b.* Double-declining-balance (note: twice straight-line rate = 2 × [100%/5 years] = 40%)

| Year | Book Value × Rate | Depreciation Expense |
|------|-------------------|----------------------|
| 1 ......... | $95,000 × 0.40 = | $38,000 |
| 2 ......... | ($95,000 − $38,000) × 0.40 = | 22,800 |
| 3 ......... | ($95,000 − $60,800) × 0.40 = | 13,680 |
| 4 ......... | ($95,000 − $74,480) × 0.40 = | 8,208 |
| 5 ......... | ($95,000 − $82,688) × 0.40 = | 2,312* |

   *The formula value of $4,925 is not reported for year 5 because doing so would depreciate the asset below the estimated salvage value; only the $2,312 needed to reach salvage value is depreciated.

2. HP reports the equipment on its balance sheet at its net book value of $44,000.

| | |
|---|---|
| Equipment, cost...................... | $95,000 |
| Less accumulated depreciation.......... | 51,000 |
| Equipment, net (end of year 3)........... | $44,000 |

3. The estimated useful life is computed as: Depreciable asset cost/Depreciation expense = $95,000/ $17,000 = 5.6 years. Because companies do not usually disclose salvage values (not required disclosure), the useful-life estimate is a bit high for this asset. This estimate is still informative because companies typically only provide a range of useful lives for depreciable assets in the footnotes.

   The percent used up is computed as: Accumulated depreciation/Depreciable asset cost = $51,000/ $95,000 = 53.7%. The equipment is more than one-half used up at the end of the third year. Again, the lack of knowledge of salvage value yields an underestimate of the percent used up. Still, this estimate is useful in that we know that the company's asset is over one-half used up and is likely to require replacement in about 2 years (estimated as less than one-half of its estimated useful life of 5.6 years). This replacement will require a cash outflow or financing when it arises and should be considered in our projections of future cash flows.

# GUIDANCE ANSWERS

**MANAGERIAL DECISION**   **You Are the Receivables Manager**

First, you must realize that extending credit is an important tool in the marketing of your products, often as important as advertising and promotion. Given that receivables are necessary, there are certain ways to speed their collection. (1) We can better screen the customers to whom we extend credit. (2) We can negotiate advance or progress payments from customers. (3) We can use bank letters of credit or other automatic drafting procedures that obviate billing. (4) We can make sure products are sent as ordered to reduce disputes. (5) We can improve administration of past due accounts to provide for more timely notices of delinquencies and better collection procedures.

**MANAGERIAL DECISION**    **You Are the Plant Manager**

Companies need inventories to avoid lost sales opportunities; however, there are several ways to minimize inventory needs. (1) We can reduce product costs by improving product design to eliminate costly features that customers don't value. (2) We can use more cost-efficient suppliers; possibly producing in lower wage-rate parts of the world. (3) We can reduce raw material inventories with just-in-time delivery from suppliers. (4) We can eliminate bottlenecks in the production process that increase work-in-process inventories. (5) We can manufacture for orders rather than for estimated demand to reduce finished goods inventories. (6) We can improve warehousing and distribution to reduce duplicate inventories. (7) We can monitor product sales and adjust product mix as demand changes to reduce finished goods inventories.

**MANAGERIAL DECISION**    **You Are the Division Manager**

PPE is a difficult asset to reduce. Since companies need long-term operating assets, managers usually try to maximize throughput to reduce unit costs. Also, many companies form alliances to share administrative, production, logistics, customer service, IT and other functions. These alliances take many forms (such as joint ventures) and are designed to spread ownership of assets among many users. The goal is to identify underutilized assets and to increase capacity utilization. Another solution might be to reconfigure the value chain from raw material to end user. Examples include the sharing of IT or manufacturing facilities, outsourcing of production or administration such as customer service centers, and the use of variable interest entities for asset securitization (see Module 9).

# DISCUSSION QUESTIONS

**Q6-1.** Explain how management can shift income from one period into another by its estimation of uncollectible accounts.

**Q6-2.** Why do relatively stable inventory costs across periods reduce the importance of management's choice of an inventory costing method?

**Q6-3.** What is one explanation for increased gross profit during periods of rising inventory costs when FIFO is used?

**Q6-4.** If inventory costs are rising, which inventory costing method—first-in, first-out; last-in, first-out; or average cost—yields the (a) lowest ending inventory? (b) lowest net income? (c) largest ending inventory? (d) largest net income? (e) greatest cash flow assuming the same method is used for tax purposes?

**Q6-5.** Even though it may not reflect their physical flow of goods, why might companies adopt last-in, first-out inventory costing in periods when costs are consistently rising?

Kaiser Aluminum Corporation    **Q6-6.** In a recent annual report, Kaiser Aluminum Corporation made the following statement in reference to its inventories: "The Company recorded pretax charges of approximately $19.4 million because of a reduction in the carrying values of its inventories caused principally by prevailing lower prices for alumina, primary aluminum, and fabricated products." What basic accounting principle caused Kaiser Aluminum to record this $19.4 million pretax charge? Briefly describe the rationale for this principle.

**Q6-7.** Why is depreciation expense necessary to properly match revenues and expenses?

**Q6-8.** How might a company treat a revision of depreciation due to a change in an asset's estimated useful life or salvage value?

**Q6-9.** When is a PPE asset considered to be impaired? How is an impairment loss computed?

**Q6-10.** What is the benefit of accelerated depreciation for income tax purposes when the total depreciation taken over the asset's life is identical under any method of depreciation?

**Q6-11.** What factors determine the gain or loss on the sale of a PPE asset?

# MINI EXERCISES

**M6-12.** **Estimating Uncollectible Accounts and Reporting Accounts Receivables** **(LO1)**
Mohan Company estimates its uncollectible accounts by aging its accounts receivable and applying percentages to various aged categories of accounts. Mohan computes a total of $2,100 in estimated

uncollectible accounts as of December 31, 2007. Its Accounts Receivable has a balance of $98,000, and its Allowance for Uncollectible Accounts has an unused balance of $500 before adjustment at December 31, 2007.

a. What amount of bad debts expense will Mohan report in 2007?
b. Determine the net amount of accounts receivable reported in current assets at December 31, 2007.

**M6-13. Interpreting the Allowance Method for Accounts Receivable (LO1)**

At a recent board of directors meeting of Ascot, Inc., one of the directors expressed concern over the allowance for uncollectible accounts appearing in the company's balance sheet. "I don't understand this account," he said. "Why don't we just show accounts receivable at the amount owed to us and get rid of that allowance?" Respond to the director's question, include in your response (a) an explanation of why the company has an allowance account, (b) what the balance sheet presentation of accounts receivable is intended to show, and (c) how the matching principle relates to the analysis and presentation of accounts receivable.

**M6-14. Analyzing the Allowance for Uncollectible Accounts (LO1)**

Following is the current asset section from the Kraft Foods, Inc., balance sheet.

Kraft Foods, Inc.
(KFT)

| $ millions | 2005 | 2004 |
|---|---|---|
| Cash and cash equivalents | $ 316 | $ 282 |
| Receivables (less allowances of $92 in 2005 and $118 in 2004) | 3,385 | 3,541 |
| Inventories: | | |
| Raw materials | 1,363 | 1,367 |
| Finished product | 1,980 | 2,080 |
| | 3,343 | 3,447 |
| Deferred income taxes | 879 | 749 |
| Assets of discontinued operations held for sale | — | 1,458 |
| Other current assets | 230 | 245 |
| Total current assets | $8,153 | $9,722 |

a. Compute the gross amount of accounts receivable for both 2005 and 2004. Compute the percentage of the allowance for uncollectible accounts relative to the gross amount of accounts receivable for each of those years.
b. How do you interpret the change in the percentage computed in part a?

**M6-15. Evaluating Accounts Receivable Turnover for Competitors (LO1)**

Procter & Gamble (PG) and Colgate-Palmolive (CL) report the following sales and accounts receivable balances ($ millions).

Procter & Gamble
(PG)
Colgate-Palmolive
(CL)

| | Procter & Gamble | | Colgate-Palmolive | |
|---|---|---|---|---|
| | Sales | Accounts Receivable | Sales | Accounts Receivable |
| 2004 | $51,407 | $4,062 | $10,584 | $1,320 |
| 2005 | 56,741 | 4,185 | 11,397 | 1,309 |

a. Compute the 2005 accounts receivable turnover for both companies.
b. Identify and discuss a potential explanation for the difference between these competitors' accounts receivable turnover.

**M6-16. Computing Cost of Goods Sold and Ending Inventory under FIFO, LIFO, and Average Cost (LO2)**

Assume that Gode Company reports the following initial balance and subsequent purchase of inventory.

| Beginning inventory, 2007 | 1,000 units @ $100 each | $100,000 |
|---|---|---|
| Inventory purchased in 2007 | 2,000 units @ $150 each | 300,000 |
| Cost of goods available for sale in 2007 | 3,000 units | $400,000 |

Assume that 1,700 units are sold during 2007. Compute the cost of goods sold for 2007 and the balance reported as ending inventory on the 2007 balance sheet under the following inventory costing methods:

a.   FIFO
b.   LIFO
c.   Average Cost

**M6-17.   Computing Cost of Goods Sold and Ending Inventory   (LO2)**

Bartov Corporation reports the following beginning inventory and inventory purchases for 2007.

| | | |
|---|---|---|
| Beginning inventory, 2007 . . . . . . . . . . . . . . . | 400 units @ $10 each | $ 4,000 |
| Inventory purchased in 2007 . . . . . . . . . . . . . | 700 units @ $12 each | 8,400 |
| Cost of goods available for sale in 2007 . . . . | 1,100 units | $12,400 |

Bartov sells 600 of its inventory units in 2007. Compute its cost of goods sold for 2007 and the ending inventory reported on its 2007 balance sheet under the following inventory costing methods:

a.   FIFO
b.   LIFO
c.   Average Cost

**M6-18.   Computing and Evaluating Inventory Turnover for Two Companies   (LO5)**

Abercrombie and
Fitch (ANF)
TJ Maxx (TJX)

Abercrombie and Fitch (ANF) and TJ Maxx (TJX) report the following information in their respective January 2006 10-K reports.

| | Abercrombie & Fitch | | | TJ Maxx | | |
|---|---|---|---|---|---|---|
| $ millions | Sales | Cost of Goods Sold | Inventories | Sales | Cost of Goods Sold | Inventories |
| 2005 . . . . . . . | $2,021 | $680 | $211 | $14,913 | $11,398 | $2,352 |
| 2006 . . . . . . . | 2,785 | 933 | 363 | 16,058 | 12,295 | 2,366 |

a.   Compute the 2006 inventory turnover for each of these two retailers.
b.   Discuss any difference you observe in inventory turnover between these two companies. Does the difference confirm your expectations given their respective business models? Explain. (*Hint:* ANF is a higher-end retailer and TJX sells more value-priced clothing.)
c.   Describe ways that a retailer can improve its inventory turnover.

**M6-19.   Computing Depreciation under Straight-Line and Double-Declining-Balance   (LO3)**

A delivery van costing $18,000 is expected to have a $1,500 salvage value at the end of its useful life of 5 years. Assume that the truck was purchased on January 1, 2007. Compute the depreciation expense for 2007 and 2008 (its second year) under the following depreciation methods:

a.   Straight-line.
b.   Double-declining-balance.

**M6-20.   Computing Depreciation under Straight-Line and Double-Declining-Balance for Partial Years   (LO3)**

A company with a calendar year-end, purchases a machine costing $145,800 on May 1, 2007. The machine is expected to be obsolete after three years (36 months) and, thereafter, no longer useful to the company. The estimated salvage value is $5,400. The company's depreciation policy is to record depreciation for the portion of the year that the asset is in service. Compute depreciation expense for both 2007 and 2008 under the following depreciation methods:

a.   Straight-line.
b.   Double-declining-balance.

**M6-21. Computing and Comparing PPE Turnover for Two Companies** (LO3)

Texas Instruments (TXN) and Intel Corporation (INTC) report the following information.

Texas Instruments
(TXN)

Intel Corporation
(INTC)

| $ millions | Intel Corp | | Texas Instruments | |
|---|---|---|---|---|
| | Sales | Plant, Property and Equipment, net | Sales | Plant, Property and Equipment, net |
| 2004 | $34,209 | $15,768 | $12,580 | $3,918 |
| 2005 | 38,826 | 17,111 | 13,392 | 3,899 |

a.  Compute the 2005 PPE turnover for both companies. Comment on any difference you observe.
b.  Discuss ways in which high-tech manufacturing companies like these can increase their PPE turnover.

# EXERCISES

**E6-22. Estimating Uncollectible Accounts and Reporting Accounts Receivable** (LO1)

LaFond Company analyzes its accounts receivable at December 31, 2007, and arrives at the aged categories below along with the percentages that are estimated as uncollectible.

| Age Group | Accounts Receivable | Estimated Loss % |
|---|---|---|
| 0–30 days past due | $ 90,000 | 1% |
| 31–60 days past due | 20,000 | 2 |
| 61–120 days past due | 11,000 | 5 |
| 121–180 days past due | 6,000 | 10 |
| Over 180 days past due | 4,000 | 25 |
| Total accounts receivable | $131,000 | |

The unused balance of the allowance for uncollectible accounts is $520 on December 31, 2007, before any adjustments.

a.  What amount of bad debts expense will LaFond report for 2007?
b.  Use the financial statement effects template to record LaFond's bad debts expense for 2007.
c.  What is the balance of accounts receivable that it reports on its December 31, 2007, balance sheet?

**E6-23. Analyzing and Reporting Receivable Transactions and Uncollectible Accounts (using percentage of sales method)** (LO1)

At the beginning of 2007, Penman Company had the following account balances in its financial records.

| | |
|---|---|
| Accounts Receivable | $122,000 |
| Allowance for Uncollectible Accounts | 7,900 |

During 2007, Penman's credit sales were $1,173,000 and collections on accounts receivable were $1,150,000. The following additional transactions occurred during the year.

Feb. 17  Wrote off Nissim's account, $3,600.
May 28  Wrote off Weiss's account, $2,400.
Dec. 15  Wrote off Ohlson's account, $900.
Dec. 31  Recorded the bad debts expense assuming that Penman's policy is to record bad debts expense as 0.8% of credit sales. (*Hint*: The allowance account is increased by 0.8% of credit sales regardless of write-offs.)

Compute the ending balances in accounts receivable and the allowance for uncollectible accounts. Show how Penman's December 31, 2007 balance sheet reports the two accounts.

**E6-24. Interpreting the Accounts Receivable Footnote (LO1)**

Hewlett-Packard Company (HP) reports the following trade accounts receivable in its 2005 10-K report.

| October 31 (In millions) | 2005 | 2004 |
|---|---|---|
| Accounts receivable, net of allowance for doubtful accounts of $227 and $286 as of October 31, 2005 and 2004, respectively .......................... | $9,903 | $10,226 |

HP's footnotes to its 10-K provide the following additional information relating to its allowance for doubtful accounts.

| For the fiscal years ended October 31 (In millions) | 2005 | 2004 | 2003 |
|---|---|---|---|
| **Allowance for doubtful accounts—accounts receivable** | | | |
| Balance, beginning of period ........................... | $286 | $347 | $410 |
| Amount acquired through acquisition..................... | — | 9 | — |
| Addition (reversal) of bad debts provision ............... | 17 | (6) | 29 |
| Deductions, net of recoveries......................... | (76) | (64) | (92) |
| Balance, end of period .............................. | $227 | $286 | $347 |

a. What is the gross amount of accounts receivables for HP in fiscal 2005 and 2004?
b. What is the percentage of the allowance for doubtful accounts to gross accounts receivable for 2005 and 2004?
c. What amount of bad debts expense did HP report each year 2003 through 2005? How does bad debts expense compare with the amounts of its accounts receivable actually written off? (Identify the amounts and explain.)
d. Explain the changes in the allowance for doubtful accounts from 2003 through 2005. Does it appear that HP increased or decreased its allowance for doubtful accounts in any particular year beyond what seems reasonable?

**E6-25. Estimating Bad Debts Expense and Reporting Receivables (LO1)**

At December 31, 2007, Sunil Company had a balance of $375,000 in its accounts receivable and an unused balance of $4,200 in its allowance for uncollectible accounts. The company then aged its accounts as follows:

| | |
|---|---|
| Current ....................... | $304,000 |
| 1–60 days past due .............. | 44,000 |
| 61–180 days past due ............ | 18,000 |
| Over 180 days past due........... | 9,000 |
| Total accounts receivable......... | $375,000 |

The company has experienced losses as follows: 1% of current balances, 5% of balances 1–60 days past due, 15% of balances 61–180 days past due, and 40% of balances over 180 days past due. The company continues to base its allowance for uncollectible accounts on this aging analysis and percentages.

a. What amount of bad debts expense does Sunil report on its 2007 income statement?
b. Show how Sunil's December 31, 2007, balance sheet will report the accounts receivable and the allowance for uncollectible accounts.

**E6-26. Estimating Uncollectible Accounts and Reporting Receivables over Multiple Periods (LO1)**

Barth Company, which has been in business for three years, makes all of its sales on credit and does not offer cash discounts. Its credit sales, customer collections, and write-offs of uncollectible accounts for its first three years follow:

| Year | Sales | Collections | Accounts Written Off |
|------|-------|-------------|----------------------|
| 2005 . . . . . | $751,000 | $733,000 | $5,300 |
| 2006 . . . . . | 876,000 | 864,000 | 5,800 |
| 2007 . . . . . | 972,000 | 938,000 | 6,500 |

*a.* Barth recognizes bad debts expense as 1% of sales. (*Hint:* This means the allowance account is increased by 1% of credit sales regardless of any write-offs and unused balances.) What does Barth's 2007 balance sheet report for accounts receivable and the allowance for uncollectible accounts? What total amount of bad debts expense appears on Barth's income statement for each of the three years?

*b.* Comment on the appropriateness of the 1% rate used to provide for bad debts based on your analysis in part *a*.

**E6-27.**   **Applying and Analyzing Inventory Costing Methods**   **(LO2)**

At the beginning of the current period, Chen carried 1,000 units of its product with a unit cost of $20. A summary of purchases during the current period follows:

| | Units | Unit Cost | Cost |
|---|-------|-----------|------|
| Beginning Inventory . . . . . . | 1,000 | $20 | $20,000 |
| Purchases: #1. . . . . . . . . . | 1,800 | 22 | 39,600 |
| #2. . . . . . . . . . | 800 | 26 | 20,800 |
| #3. . . . . . . . . . | 1,200 | 29 | 34,800 |

During the current period, Chen sold 2,800 units.

*a.* Assume that Chen uses the first-in, first-out method. Compute both cost of goods sold for the current period and the ending inventory balance. Use the financial statement effects template to record cost of goods sold for the period.

*b.* Assume that Chen uses the last-in, first-out method. Compute both cost of goods sold for the current period and the ending inventory balance.

*c.* Assume that Chen uses the average cost method. Compute both cost of goods sold for the current period and the ending inventory balance.

*d.* Which of these three inventory costing methods would you choose to:
1. Reflect what is probably the physical flow of goods? Explain.
2. Minimize income taxes for the period? Explain.
3. Report the largest amount of income for the period? Explain.

**E6-28.**   **Analyzing an Inventory Footnote Disclosure**   **(LO2)**

General Electric Company reports the following footnote in its 10-K report.

General Electric
Company (GE)

| December 31 (In millions) | 2005 | 2004 |
|---------------------------|------|------|
| Raw materials and work in process . . . . . | $ 5,527 | $ 5,042 |
| Finished goods. . . . . . . . . . . . . . . . . . . . | 5,152 | 4,806 |
| Unbilled shipments. . . . . . . . . . . . . . . . . | 333 | 402 |
| | 11,012 | 10,250 |
| Less revaluation to LIFO. . . . . . . . . . . . . | (697) | (661) |
| | $10,315 | $ 9,589 |

The company reports its inventories using the LIFO inventory costing method.

*a.* What is the balance in inventories reported on GE's 2005 balance sheet?

*b.* What would GE's 2005 balance sheet have reported for inventories had the company used FIFO inventory costing?

*c.* What *cumulative* effect has GE's choice of LIFO over FIFO had on its pretax income as of year-end 2005? Explain.

  *d.* Assume GE has a 35% income tax rate. As of the 2005 year-end, how much has GE saved in taxes by choosing LIFO over FIFO method for costing inventory? Has the use of LIFO increased or decreased GE's cumulative tax liability?

  *e.* What effect has the use of LIFO inventory costing had on GE's pretax income and tax liability for 2005 only (assume a 35% income tax rate)?

**E6-29.**  **Computing Cost of Sales and Ending Inventory**  **(LO2)**

Stocken Company has the following financial records for the current period.

| | Units | Unit Cost |
|---|---|---|
| Beginning inventory . . . . . . | 100 | $46 |
| Purchases: #1. . . . . . . . . . | 650 | 42 |
| #2. . . . . . . . . . | 550 | 38 |
| #3. . . . . . . . . . | 200 | 36 |

Ending inventory at the end of this period is 350 units. Compute the ending inventory and the cost of goods sold for the current period using (a) first-in, first out, (b) average cost, and (c) last-in, first-out.

**E6-30.**  **Analyzing an Inventory Footnote Disclosure**  **(LO2)**

Deere & Co. (DE)

The inventory footnote from the Deere & Company's 2005 10-K follows ($ millions).

> **Inventories**  Most inventories owned by Deere & Company and its United States equipment subsidiaries are valued at cost, on the "last-in, first-out" (LIFO) basis. Remaining inventories are generally valued at the lower of cost, on the "first-in, first-out" (FIFO) basis, or market. The value of gross inventories on the LIFO basis represented 61 percent of worldwide gross inventories at FIFO value on October 31, 2005 and 2004, respectively. If all inventories had been valued on a FIFO basis, estimated inventories by major classification at October 31 in millions of dollars would have been as follows:

| | 2005 | 2004 |
|---|---|---|
| Raw materials and supplies . . . . . . . . | $ 716 | $ 589 |
| Work-in-process. . . . . . . . . . . . . . . | 425 | 408 |
| Finished machines and parts . . . . . . . | 2,126 | 2,004 |
| Total FIFO value . . . . . . . . . . . . . . | 3,267 | 3,001 |
| Less adjustment to LIFO value. . . . . . | 1,132 | 1,002 |
| Inventories . . . . . . . . . . . . . . . . . . . | $2,135 | $1,999 |

We notice that not all of Deere's inventories are reported using the same inventory costing method (companies can use different inventory costing methods for different inventory pools).

  *a.* What amount does Deere report for inventories on its 2005 balance sheet?

  *b.* What would Deere have reported as inventories on its 2005 balance sheet had the company used FIFO inventory costing for all of its inventories?

  *c.* What *cumulative* effect has the use of LIFO inventory costing had, as of year-end 2005, on Deere's pretax income compared with the pretax income it would have reported had it used FIFO inventory costing for all of its inventories? Explain.

  *d.* Assuming a 35% income tax rate, by what *cumulative* dollar amount has Deere's tax liability been affected by use of LIFO inventory costing as of year-end 2005? Has the use of LIFO inventory costing increased or decreased Deere's cumulative tax liability?

  *e.* What effect has the use of LIFO inventory costing had on Deere's pretax income and tax liability for 2005 only (assume a 35% income tax rate)?

**E6-31.**  **Computing Straight-Line and Double-Declining-Balance Depreciation**  **(LO3)**

On January 2, Haskins Company purchases a laser cutting machine for use in fabrication of a part for one of its key products. The machine cost $80,000, and its estimated useful life is five years, after which the expected salvage value is $5,000. (*a*) Compute depreciation expense for each year of the machine's useful life under each of the following depreciation methods. (*b*) Use the financial statements effects template to show the effect of depreciation on the first year only for both methods.

  *a.* Straight-line

  *b.* Double-declining-balance

**E6-32.** **Computing Depreciation, Asset Book Value, and Gain or Loss on Asset Sale** **(LO3)**

Sloan Company owns an executive plane that originally cost $800,000. It has recorded straight-line depreciation on the plane for six full years, calculated assuming an $80,000 expected salvage value at the end of its estimated 10-year useful life. Sloan disposes of the plane at the end of the sixth year.

a. At the disposal date, what is the (1) cumulative depreciation expense and (2) net book value of the plane?

b. How much gain or loss is reported at disposal if the sales price is:
1. A cash amount equal to the plane's net book value.
2. $195,000 cash.
3. $600,000 cash.

**E6-33.** **Computing Straight-Line and Double-Declining-Balance Depreciation** **(LO3)**

On January 2, 2007, Dechow Company purchases a machine that manufactures a part for one of its key products. The machine cost $218,700 and is estimated to have a useful life of six years, with an expected salvage value of $23,400. Compute depreciation expense for 2007 and 2008 for each of the following depreciation methods.

a. Straight-line.
b. Double-declining-balance.

**E6-34.** **Computing Depreciation, Asset Book Value, and Gain or Loss on Asset Sale** **(LO3)**

Palepu Company owns and operates a delivery van that originally cost $27,200. Palepu has recorded straight-line depreciation on the van for three years, calculated assuming a $2,000 expected salvage value at the end of its estimated six-year useful life. Depreciation was last recorded at the end of the third year, at which time Palepu disposes of this van.

a. Compute the net book value of the van on the sale date.
b. Compute the gain or loss on sale of the van if its sales price is:
1. A cash amount equal to the van's net book value.
2. $15,000 cash.
3. $12,000 cash.

**E6-35.** **Estimating Useful Life and Percent Used Up** **(LO3)**

The property and equipment footnote from the Deere & Company balance sheet follows.     Deere & Co. (DE)

**Property and Depreciation** A summary of property and equipment at October 31 follows:

| ($ millions) | Average Useful Lives (Years) | 2005 | 2004 |
|---|---|---|---|
| **Equipment Operations** | | | |
| Land | | $ 79 | $ 75 |
| Buildings and building equipment | 25 | 1,490 | 1,419 |
| Machinery and equipment | 10 | 2,961 | 2,870 |
| Dies, patterns, tools, etc. | 7 | 1,039 | 987 |
| All other | 5 | 589 | 571 |
| Construction in progress | | 232 | 156 |
| Total at cost | | 6,390 | 6,078 |
| Less accumulated depreciation | | 4,113 | 3,966 |
| Total | | $2,277 | $2,112 |

During 2005, the company reported $636.5 million of depreciation expense (this expense also includes amortization expense relating to computer software that is included with property and equipment).

a. Compute the estimated useful life of Deere's depreciable assets. (*Hint:* Exclude land and construction in progress.) How does this estimate compare with the useful lives reported in Deere's footnote disclosure?

b. Estimate the percent used up of Deere's depreciable assets. How do you interpret this figure?

**E6-36. Computing and Evaluating Receivables, Inventory and PPE Turnovers (LO1, 2, 3)**

3M Company reports the following financial statement amounts in its 2005 10-K report.

| $ millions | Sales | Cost of Goods Sold | Receivables, net | Inventories | Plant, property and equipment, net |
|---|---|---|---|---|---|
| 2003 ........ | $18,232 | $ 9,285 | $2,714 | $1,816 | $5,609 |
| 2004 ........ | 20,011 | 9,958 | 2,792 | 1,897 | 5,711 |
| 2005 ........ | 21,167 | 10,381 | 2,838 | 2,162 | 5,593 |

**Required**

a. Compute the receivables, inventory, and PPE turnover ratios for both 2004 and 2005.

b. What changes are evident in the turnover rates of 3M for these years? Discuss ways in which a company such as 3M can improve receivables, inventory, and PPE turnover ratios.

**E6-37. Computing and Assessing Plant Asset Impairment (LO3)**

On July 1, 2003, Zeibart Company purchases equipment for $225,000. The equipment has an estimated useful life of 10 years and expected salvage value of $25,000. The company uses straight-line depreciation. On July 1, 2007, economic factors cause the market value of the equipment to decline to $90,000. On this date, Zeibart examines the equipment for impairment and estimates $125,000 in undiscounted future cash inflows from this equipment.

a. Is the equipment impaired at July 1, 2007? Explain.

b. If the equipment is impaired at July 1, 2007, compute the impairment loss.

# PROBLEMS

**P6-38. Evaluating Turnover Rates for Different Companies (LO1, 2, 3)**

Following are asset turnover rates for accounts receivable; inventory; and property, plant, and equipment (PPE) for Best Buy (retailer of consumer products), Carnival (vacation cruise line), Caterpillar (manufacturer of heavy equipment), Harley-Davidson (manufacturer of motorcycles), Microsoft (software company), Oracle (software company), and Sharper-Image (retailer of specialty consumer products).

| Company Name | Receivables Turnover | Inventory Turnover | Plant, Property and Equipment Turnover |
|---|---|---|---|
| Best Buy Co ............... | 70.03 | 7.47 | 11.92 |
| Carnival Corp ............. | 27.14 | 25.28 | 0.53 |
| Caterpillar Inc ............. | 2.59 | 5.07 | 4.64 |
| Harley-Davidson Inc......... | 3.67 | 14.28 | 5.57 |
| Microsoft Corp ............. | 6.09 | 11.66 | 17.03 |
| Oracle Corp............... | 4.51 | n.a. | 9.40 |
| Sharper Image Corp......... | 32.46 | 3.35 | 8.91 |

**Required**

a. Interpret and explain differences in receivables turnover for the retailers (Best Buy and Sharper Image) vis-à-vis that for the manufacturers (Caterpillar and Harley-Davidson).

b. Interpret and explain the difference in inventory turnover for Harley-Davidson versus Sharper Image. Why is Oracle's inventory turnover reported as n.a.?

c. Interpret and explain the difference in PPE turnover for Carnival versus Microsoft.

d. What are some general observations you might draw regarding the relative levels of these turnover rates across the different industries?

**P6-39.** **Interpreting Accounts Receivable and its Footnote Disclosure**   (LO1)

Following is the current asset section from the W.W. Grainger, Inc., balance sheet.

W.W. Grainger, Inc.
(GWW)

| As of December 31 ($ 000s) | 2005 | 2004 | 2003 |
|---|---|---|---|
| Cash and cash equivalents . . . . . . . . . . . . . . . . . . . . . | $ 544,894 | $ 429,246 | $ 402,824 |
| Accounts receivable (less allowances for doubtful accounts of $18,401, $23,375 and $24,736, respectively . . . . . . . . . . . . . . . . . . . . . . . . | 518,625 | 480,893 | 431,896 |
| Inventories . . . . . . . . . . . . . . . . . . . . . . . . . . . . . . . . . | 791,212 | 700,559 | 661,247 |
| Prepaid expenses and other assets. . . . . . . . . . . . . . . | 54,334 | 47,086 | 37,947 |
| Deferred income taxes. . . . . . . . . . . . . . . . . . . . . . . . . | 88,803 | 96,929 | 99,499 |
| Total current assets . . . . . . . . . . . . . . . . . . . . . . . . . . | $1,997,868 | $1,754,713 | $1,633,413 |

Grainger reports the following footnote relating to its receivables.

**Allowance for Doubtful Accounts**   The following table shows the activity in the allowance for doubtful accounts.

| For Years Ended December 31 ($ 000s) | 2005 | 2004 | 2003 |
|---|---|---|---|
| Balance at beginning of period . . . . . . . . . . . . . . . . . . | $23,375 | $24,736 | $26,868 |
| Provision for uncollectible accounts . . . . . . . . . . . . . . | 1,326 | 5,159 | 9,263 |
| Write-off of uncollectible accounts, less recoveries. . . . | (6,380) | (6,662) | (11,713) |
| Foreign currency exchange impact . . . . . . . . . . . . . . . | 80 | 142 | 318 |
| Balance at end of period . . . . . . . . . . . . . . . . . . . . . . . | $18,401 | $23,375 | $24,736 |

**Required**

*a.*   What amount do customers owe Grainger at each of the year-ends 2003 through 2005?

*b.*   What percentage of its total accounts receivable does Grainger feel are uncollectible? (*Hint:* Percentage of uncollectible accounts = Allowance for uncollectible accounts/Gross accounts receivable)

*c.*   What amount of bad debts expense did Grainger report in its income statement for each of the years 2003 through 2005?

*d.*   Explain the change in the balance of the allowance for uncollectible accounts since 2003. Specifically, did the allowance increase or decrease as a percentage of gross accounts receivable, and why?

*e.*   If Grainger had kept its 2005 allowance for uncollectible accounts at the same percentage of gross accounts receivable as it was in 2004, by what amount would its profit have changed (ignore taxes)? Explain.

*f.*   Overall, what is your assessment of Grainger's allowance for uncollectible accounts and the related expense provision?

**P6-40.** **Analyzing and Interpreting Receivables and Related Ratios**   (LO1)

Following is the current asset section from Intuit's balance sheet.

Intuit, Inc. (INTU)

| July 31 ($ 000s) | 2005 | 2004 |
|---|---|---|
| Cash and cash equivalents . . . . . . . . . . . . . . . . . . . . . . . . . . . | $ 83,842 | $ 25,992 |
| Investments . . . . . . . . . . . . . . . . . . . . . . . . . . . . . . . . . . . . . | 910,416 | 991,971 |
| Accounts receivable, net of allowance for doubtful accounts of $15,653 and $6,994, respectively. . . . . . . . . . . . . . . . . . . . . | 86,125 | 81,615 |
| Deferred income taxes. . . . . . . . . . . . . . . . . . . . . . . . . . . . . . | 54,854 | 31,094 |
| Prepaid expenses and other current assets. . . . . . . . . . . . . . . | 99,275 | 62,792 |
| Current assets of discontinued operations . . . . . . . . . . . . . . . | 21,989 | 12,279 |
| Current assets before funds held for payroll customers. . . . . . . | 1,256,501 | 1,205,743 |
| Funds held for payroll customers. . . . . . . . . . . . . . . . . . . . . . . | 357,838 | 323,041 |
| Total current assets . . . . . . . . . . . . . . . . . . . . . . . . . . . . . . . . | $1,614,339 | $1,528,784 |

Total revenues were $2,038 million ($1,243 million in product sales and $795 million in service revenues and other) in 2005.

**Required**
a. What are Intuit's gross accounts receivable at the end of 2005 and 2004?
b. For both 2005 and 2004, compute the ratio of the allowance for uncollectible accounts to gross receivables. What trend do you observe?
c. Compute the receivables turnover ratio and the average collection period for 2005 based on gross receivables computed in part a. Does the collection period (days sales in receivables) appear reasonable given Intuit's lines of business (Intuit's products include QuickBooks, TurboTax and Quicken, which it sells to consumers and small businesses)? Explain.
d. Is the percentage of Intuit's allowance for uncollectible accounts to gross accounts receivable consistent with what you expect for Intuit's line of business? Explain.
e. Intuit discloses the following table related to its allowance for uncollectible accounts from its 10-K. Comment on the change in the allowance account during 2003 through 2005.

| (In thousands) | Balance at Beginning of Period | Additions Charged to Expense | Deductions | Balance at End of Period |
|---|---|---|---|---|
| **Year ended July 31, 2005** | | | | |
| Allowance for doubtful accounts ... | $6,994 | $13,815 | $(5,156) | $15,653 |
| **Year ended July 31, 2004** | | | | |
| Allowance for doubtful accounts ... | $5,095 | $5,325 | $(3,426) | $6,994 |
| **Year ended July 31, 2003** | | | | |
| Allowance for doubtful accounts ... | $5,535 | $1,410 | $(1,850) | $5,095 |

**P6-41.** **Analyzing and Interpreting Inventories and Related Ratios and Disclosures** **(LO2)**

Dow Chemical (DOW)

The current asset section from The Dow Chemical Company's 2005 annual report follows.

| December 31 (In millions) | 2005 | 2004 |
|---|---|---|
| Cash and cash equivalents | $ 3,806 | $ 3,108 |
| Marketable securities and interest-bearing deposits | 32 | 84 |
| Accounts and notes receivable | | |
| Trade (net of allowance for doubtful receivables—2005: $169; 2004: $136) | 5,124 | 4,753 |
| Other | 2,802 | 2,604 |
| Inventories | 5,319 | 4,957 |
| Deferred income tax assets—current | 321 | 384 |
| Total current assets | $17,404 | $15,890 |

The Dow Chemical inventory footnote follows.

**Inventories** The following provides a breakdown of inventories at December 31, 2005 and 2004.

| Inventories at December 31 (In millions) | 2005 | 2004 |
|---|---|---|
| Finished goods | $2,941 | $2,989 |
| Work in process | 1,247 | 889 |
| Raw materials | 645 | 605 |
| Supplies | 486 | 474 |
| Total inventories | $5,319 | $4,957 |

Inventory reserves reduce Dow's inventories from the first-in, first-out ("FIFO") basis to the last-in, first-out ("LIFO") basis. These reserves amount to $1,149 million at December 31, 2005 and $807 million at December 31, 2004.

**Required**

*a.* What inventory costing method does Dow Chemical use? As of 2005, what is the effect on cumulative pretax income and cash flow of using this inventory costing method? (Assume a 35% tax rate.) What is the effect on 2005 pretax income and cash flow of using this inventory costing method.

*b.* Compute inventory turnover and days sales in inventory for 2005 (2005 cost of goods sold is $38,276 million). Comment on the level of these two ratios. Is the level what you expect given Dow's industry? Explain.

*c.* Dow provides the following additional disclosure in its inventory footnote: "A reduction of certain inventories resulted in the liquidation of some of the Company's LIFO inventory layers, increasing pretax income $110 million in 2005, $154 million in 2004 and $70 million in 2003." Explain why a reduction of inventory quantities increased income in 2003, 2004 and 2005.

**P6-42.** **Estimating Useful Life and Percent Used Up    (LO3)**

The property and equipment section of the Abbott Laboratories 2005 balance sheet follows.

Abbott Laboratories
(ABT)

| Property and equipment, at cost ($ thousands) | |
| --- | --- |
| Land | $    370,949 |
| Buildings | 2,655,356 |
| Equipment | 8,813,517 |
| Construction in progess | 920,599 |
| | 12,760,421 |
| Less: accumulated depreciation and amortization | 6,757,280 |
| Net property and equipment | $ 6,003,141 |

The company also provides the following disclosure relating to the useful lives of its depreciable assets.

**Property and Equipment**—Depreciation and amortization are provided on a straight-line basis over the estimated useful lives of the assets. The following table shows estimated useful lives of property and equipment.

| Classification | Estimated Useful Lives |
| --- | --- |
| Buildings | 10 to 50 years (average 27 years) |
| Equipment | 3 to 20 years (average 11 years) |

During 2005, the company reported $868,808 ($ 000s) for depreciation expense.

**Required**

*a.* Compute the estimated useful life of Abbott Laboratories' depreciable assets. How does this compare with its useful lives footnote disclosure above?

*b.* Compute the estimated percent used up of Abbott Laboratories' depreciable assets. How do you interpret this figure?

**P6-43.    Interpreting and Applying Disclosures on Property and Equipment    (LO3)**

Following are selected disclosures from the Rohm and Haas Company (a specialty chemical company) 2005 10-K.

**Land, Building and Equipment, Net**

| (in millions) | 2005 | 2004 |
|---|---|---|
| Land . . . . . . . . . . . . . . . . . . . . . . . . . | $ 139 | $ 141 |
| Buildings and improvements . . . . . . . | 1,683 | 1,744 |
| Machinery and equipment . . . . . . . . . | 5,570 | 5,656 |
| Capitalized interest. . . . . . . . . . . . . . | 329 | 320 |
| Construction in progress . . . . . . . . . . | 168 | 166 |
|  | 7,889 | 8,027 |
| Less: Accumulated depreciation . . . . | 5,208 | 5,098 |
| Total . . . . . . . . . . . . . . . . . . . . . . . . | $2,681 | $2,929 |

The principal lives (in years) used in determining depreciation rates of various assets are: buildings and improvement (10–50); machinery and equipment (5–20); automobiles, trucks and tank cars (3–10); furniture and fixtures, laboratory equipment and other assets (5–10); capitalized software (5–7). The principle life used in determining the depreciation rate for leasehold improvements is the years remaining in the lease term or the useful life (in years) of the asset, whichever is shorter.

**IMPAIRMENT OF LONG-LIVED ASSETS**

Long-lived assets, other than investments, goodwill and indefinite-lived intangible assets, are depreciated over their estimated useful lives, and are reviewed for impairment whenever changes in circumstances indicate the carrying value of the asset may not be recoverable. Such circumstances would include items such as a significant decrease in the market price of a long-lived asset, a significant adverse change in the manner the asset is being used or planned to be used or in its physical condition or a history of operating or cash flow losses associated with the use of the asset . . . When such events or changes occur, we assess the recoverability of the asset by comparing the carrying value of the asset to the expected future cash flows associated with the asset's planned future use and eventual disposition of the asset, if applicable . . . We utilize marketplace assumptions to calculate the discounted cash flows used in determining the asset's fair value. In 2005, $81 million of asset impairments were recognized for the impairment of certain finite-lived intangible assets and fixed assets across several of our chemical businesses and our Electronic Materials segment.

**Required**

a.    Compute the PPE (land, buildings and equipment) asset turnover for 2005 (Sales in 2005 are $7,994 million). Does the level of its PPE turnover suggest that Rohm and Haas is capital intensive? (*Hint:* The median PPE turnover for all publicly traded companies is approximately 1.3 in 2005.) Explain. Do you believe that Rohm and Haas' balance sheet reflects all of the company's operating assets? Explain.

b.    Rohm and Haas reported depreciation expense of $422 million in 2005. Assuming that Rohm and Haas uses straight-line depreciation, estimate the useful life, on average, for its depreciable PPE assets.

c.    By what percentage are Rohm and Haas' assets "used up" at year-end 2005? What implication does the assets used up computation have for forecasting cash flows?

d.    Rohm and Haas reports an asset impairment charge in 2005. How do companies determine if assets are impaired? How do asset impairment charges affect Rohm and Haas' cash flows for 2005? How would we treat these charges for analysis purposes?

# CASES

**C6-44.** **Management Application: Managing Operating Asset Reduction** **(LO1, 2, 3)**

Return on net operating assets (RNOA = NOPAT/Average NOA, see Module 4) is commonly used to evaluate financial performance. If managers cannot increase NOPAT, they can still increase this return by reducing the amount of net operating assets (NOA). List specific ways that managers could reduce the following assets:

*a.* Receivables

*b.* Inventories

*c.* Plant, property and equipment

**C6-45.** **Ethics and Governance: Managing the Allowance for Uncollectible Accounts** **(LO1)**

Assume that you are the CEO of a publicly traded company. Your chief financial officer (CFO) informs you that your company will not be able to meet earnings per share targets for the current quarter. In that event, your stock price will likely decline. The CFO proposes reducing the quarterly provision for uncollectible accounts (bad debts expense) to increase your EPS to the level analysts expect. This will result in an allowance account that is less than it should be. The CFO explains that outsiders cannot easily detect a reduction in this allowance and that the allowance can be increased next quarter. The benefit is that your shareholders will not experience a decline in stock price.

*a.* Identify the parties that are likely to be affected by this proposed action.

*b.* How will reducing the provision for uncollectible accounts affect the income statement and the balance sheet?

*c.* How will reducing the provision for uncollectible accounts in the current period affect the income statement and the balance sheet in a future period?

*d.* What argument might the CFO use to convince the company's external auditors that this action is justified?

*e.* How might an analyst detect this earnings management activity?

*f.* How might this action affect the moral compass of your company? What repercussions might this action have?

# Reporting and Analyzing Intercorporate Investments

## LEARNING OBJECTIVES

**LO1** Describe and illustrate accounting for passive investments. (p. 7-5)

**LO2** Explain and illustrate accounting for equity method investments. (p. 7-13)

**LO3** Describe and illustrate accounting for consolidations. (p. 7-18)

## GOOGLE

How does Google make money? A recent *BusinessWeek* article explains: "everybody knows that Google Inc.'s innovations in search technology made it the No. 1 search engine. But Google didn't make money until it started auctioning ads that appear alongside the search results. Advertising today accounts for 99% of the revenue of a company whose market capitalization now tops $100 billion." This seems to suggest that Google is a media company. Indeed, with a market capitalization of $100 billion, (greater even than that of Time Warner), Google is the world's largest media company and among America's top 30 most valuable companies. Since its IPO in 2004, Google's (GOOG) stock price has quadrupled making Google one of the fastest growing companies on any stock exchange.

Google's operations generated nearly $2.5 billion of cash in 2005, over eight times the cash generated two years before. During 2005, Google completed its second public offering, netting $4.3 billion. By fiscal year-end 2005, Google reported nearly $3.9 billion of cash and $4.2 billion of investments in marketable securities.

Google's investments in marketable securities are *passive investments* because Google owns a relatively small percentage of the stock for a variety of companies. Google holds these investments because it has excess cash awaiting deployment in other business activities and expects to earn dividends and potentially capital gains from these securities. The accounting for these marketable securities differs markedly from the accounting for most other assets—Google's balance sheet reports these marketable securities at their current market value. As a result, the assets on Google's balance sheet fluctuate with the stock market. This causes stockholders' equity to fluctuate because, as we know from the accounting equation, assets equal liabilities plus equity.

We might wonder why Google would report these assets at market value when nearly all other assets are reported at historical cost. As well, we might ask how these fluctuations in market value affect Google's reported profit, if at all. This module answers both questions and explains the accounting for, and analysis of, such so-called passive investments in marketable securities.

To expand its business activities beyond its current search-engine and advertising base, Google has strategically invested in the stock of several other companies, which is a second category of investments. Through these strategic investments, Google has acquired substantial ownership of those companies such that Google can significantly influence their operations. The nature and purpose of these investments differs from Google's passive investment in marketable securities and, accordingly, the accounting reflects that difference. In particular, if Google owns enough voting stock to exert significant influence over another company, Google uses the *equity method* to account for those investments. Under the equity method, Google carries the investment on its balance sheet at an amount equal to its proportionate share of the investee company's equity. An equity method investment increases and decreases, not with changes in the stock's market value, but with changes in the investee company's stockholders' equity. That is, Google's share of the investee's net assets (assets less liabilities) appear on Google's balance sheet as a long-term investment

An interesting by-product of the equity method is that Google's balance sheet does not reflect the investee company's individual assets and liabilities, but only its net assets (the stockholders' equity). This is important because Google could be using the investee's assets and be responsible, to some extent, for the investee's liabilities. Yet, these are not detailed on Google's balance sheet. This creates what is called *off-balance-sheet financing*, potentially of great concern to accountants, analysts, creditors and others who rely on financial reports. This module describes the equity method of accounting for investments, including the implications of this type of off-balance-sheet financing.

When an investor company acquires a sufficiently large proportion of the voting stock of another company, it can effectively control the other company. At that point, the acquired company is *consolidated*. Most of the financial statements of public companies are titled "consolidated." Consolidation essentially adds together the financial statements of two or more companies. It is important that we understand what consolidated financial statements tell us and what they do not. This module covers consolidation along with a discussion of its implications for analysis.

*(Continued on next page)*

*(Continued from previous page)*

There was much consternation among investors when Google's stock price passed $100, then $200, then $300, then $400. At each milestone, investors became increasingly concerned that Google's stock was overvalued. That concern still abounds. But, as Google continues to make strategic investments necessary to broaden its revenue base, its share price will likely increase. Google's management believes that investments are a crucial part of the company's strategic plan. Understanding the accounting for all three types of inter-corporate investment is, thus, important to our understanding of Google's (and other companies') ongoing operations.

Sources: *Google Form 10-K*, 2006; *Google Annual Report*, 2006; *BusinessWeek*, 2006; and *Fortune*, 2006.

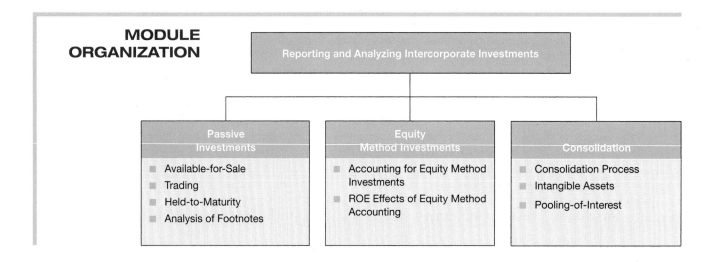

# INTRODUCTION

It is common for one company to purchase the voting stock of another. These purchases, called *intercorporate investments*, have the following strategic aims:

- **Short-term investment of excess cash.** Companies might invest excess cash to use during slow times of the year (after receivables are collected and before seasonal production begins) or to maintain liquidity (such as to counter strategic moves by competitors or to quickly respond to acquisition opportunities).

- **Alliances for strategic purposes.** Companies might acquire an equity interest in other companies for strategic purposes, such as gaining access to their research and development activities, to their supply or distribution markets, or to their production and marketing expertise.

■  **Market penetration or expansion.** Companies might acquire control of other companies to achieve vertical or horizontal integration in existing markets or to penetrate new and growth markets.

Accounting for intercorporate investments follows one of three different methods, each of which affects the balance sheet and the income statement differently. These differences can be quite substantial. To help assimilate the materials in this module, Exhibit 7.1 graphically depicts the accounting for investments.

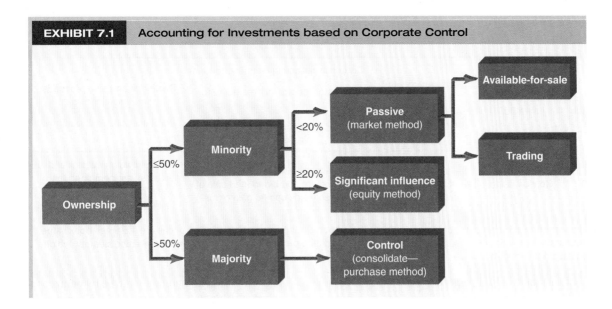

**EXHIBIT 7.1     Accounting for Investments based on Corporate Control**

The degree of influence or control that the investor company (purchaser) can exert over the investee company (the company whose securities are being purchased) determines the accounting method. GAAP identifies three levels of influence/control.

1. **Passive.** A passive investment is one where the purchasing company has a relatively small investment and cannot exert influence over the investee company. The investor's goal is to realize dividends and capital gains. Generally, the investment is considered passive if the investor company owns less than 20% of the outstanding voting stock of the investee.

2. **Significant influence.** A company can sometimes exert significant influence over, but not control, the activities of the investee company. Significant influence can result when the percentage of voting stock owned is more significant than a passive, short-term investment. However, an investment can also exhibit "significant influence" if there exist legal agreements between the investor and investee, such as a license to use technology, a formula, or a trade secret like production know-how. A significant investment also can occur when the investor company is a large supplier or customer of the investee. Generally, significant influence is presumed if the investor company owns 20% to 50% of the voting stock of the investee.

3. **Control.** When a company has control over another, it has the ability to elect a majority of the board of directors and, as a result, the ability to affect the investee company's strategic direction and the hiring of executive management. Control is generally presumed if the investor company owns more than 50% of the outstanding voting stock of the investee company. Control can sometimes occur at less than 50% stock ownership by virtue of legal agreements, technology licensing, or other contractual means.

The level of influence/control determines the specific accounting method applied and its financial statement implications as outlined in Exhibit 7.2.

| EXHIBIT 7.2 | | Investment Type, Accounting Treatment, and Financial Statement Effects | | |
|---|---|---|---|---|
| | **Accounting** | **Balance Sheet Effects** | **Income Statement Effects** | **Cash Flow Effects** |
| Passive | Market method | Investment account is reported at current market value | Dividends and capital gains included in income<br><br>Interim changes in market value may or may not affect income depending on whether the investor actively trades the securities<br><br>Sale of investment yields capital gain or loss | Dividends and sale proceeds are cash inflows<br><br>Purchases are cash outflows |
| Significant influence | Equity method | Investment account equals percent owned of investee company's equity* | Dividends reduce investment account<br><br>Investor reports income equal to percent owned of investee income<br><br>Sale of investment yields capital gain or loss | Dividends and sale proceeds are cash inflows<br><br>Purchases are cash outflows |
| Control | Consolidation | Balance sheets of investor and investee are combined | Income statements of investor and investee are combined (and sale of investee yields capital gain or loss) | Cash flows of investor and investee are combined (and sale/purchase of investee yields cash inflow/outflow) |

*Investments are often acquired at purchase prices in excess of book value (on average, market prices are 1.5 times book value for public companies). In this case the investment account exceeds the proportionate ownership of the investee's equity, which we discuss later in the module.

There are two basic reporting issues with investments: (1) how investment income should be recognized in the income statement and (2) at what amount (cost or fair market value) the investment should be reported on the balance sheet. We next discuss both of these issues as we consider the three investment types.

# PASSIVE INVESTMENTS

**LO1** Describe and illustrate accounting for passive investments.

Short-term investments of excess cash are typically passive investments. Passive investments can involve equity or debt securities. Equity securities involve an ownership interest such as common stock or preferred stock, whereas debt securities have no ownership interest. A voting stock investment is passive when the investor does not possess sufficient ownership to either influence or control the investee company. The *market method* is used to account for passive investments.

## Acquisition and Sale

When a company makes a passive investment, it records the shares acquired on the balance sheet at fair market value, that is, the purchase price. This is the same as accounting for the acquisition of other assets such as inventories or plant assets. Subsequent to acquisition, passive investments are carried on the balance sheet as current or long-term assets, depending on management's expectations about their ultimate holding period.

When investments are sold, any recognized gain or loss on sale is equal to the difference between the proceeds received and the book (carrying) value of the investment on the balance sheet as follows:

**Gain or Loss on Sale = Proceeds from Sale − Book Value of Investment Sold**

To illustrate the acquisition and sale of a passive investment, assume that Microsoft purchases 1,000 shares of Ask.com for $20 cash per share (this includes transaction costs such as brokerage fees). Microsoft, subsequently, sells 400 of the 1,000 shares for $22 cash per share. The following financial statement effects template shows how these transactions affect Microsoft.

| | Balance Sheet | | | | | Income Statement | | |
|---|---|---|---|---|---|---|---|---|
| Transaction | Cash Asset | + Noncash Assets | = Liabil-ities | + Contrib. Capital | + Earned Capital | Rev-enues | − Expen-ses | = Net Income |
| 1. Purchase 1,000 shares of Ask.com common stock for $20 cash per share | −20,000 Cash | +20,000 Marketable Securities | = | | | | | = |
| 2. Sell 400 shares of Ask.com common stock for $22 cash per share | +8,800 Cash | −8,000 Marketable Securities | = | | +800 Retained Earnings | +800 Gain on Sale | | = +800 |

(T-accounts shown at right:)

```
MS    20,000
    Cash   20,000
        MS
20,000 |
   Cash
       |  20,000

Cash   8,800
    MS      8,000
    GN       800
       Cash
8,800 |
       MS
       |  8,000
       GN
       |    800
```

Income statements include the gain or loss on sale of marketable securities as a component of *other income*, which is typically reported separately from operating income and often aggregated with interest and dividend revenue. Accounting for the purchase and sale of passive investments is the same as for any other asset. Further, there is no difference in accounting for purchases and sales across the different types of passive investments discussed in this section. However, there are differences in accounting for different types of passive investments between their purchase and their sale. We next address this issue.

## Mark-to-Market versus Cost

If a passive investment in securities has an active market with published prices, that investment is reported on the balance sheet at market value. **Market value** is the published price (as listed on a stock exchange) multiplied by the number of shares owned. This is one of few assets that are reported at market value instead of historical cost.[1] If there exists no active market with published prices for the stock, the investment is reported at its historical cost.

Why are passive investments recorded at current market value on the balance sheet? The answer lies in understanding the trade-off between the *objectivity* of historical cost and the *relevance* of market value. All things equal, current market values of assets are more relevant in determining the market value of the company. However, for most assets, market values cannot be reliably determined. Adding unreliable "market values" to the balance sheet would introduce subjectivity into financial reports.

In the case of marketable securities, market prices result from numerous transactions between willing buyers and sellers. Market prices in this case provide an unbiased (objective) estimate of value to report on balance sheets. This reliability is the main reason GAAP allows passive investments to be recorded at market value instead of at historical cost.

This market method of accounting for securities causes asset values (the marketable securities) to fluctuate, with a corresponding change in equity (liabilities are unaffected). This is reflected in the following accounting equation:

$$\text{Assets} \uparrow = \text{Liabilities} + \text{Equity} \uparrow \qquad \text{or} \qquad \text{Assets} \downarrow = \text{Liabilities} + \text{Equity} \downarrow$$

An important issue is whether such changes in equity should be reported as income (with a consequent change in retained earnings), or whether they should bypass the income statement and directly impact equity via *other comprehensive income (OCI)*. The answer differs depending on the classification of securities, which we explain next.

---

[1] Other assets reported at market value include (1) derivative securities (such as forward contracts, options, and futures) that are purchased to provide a hedge against price fluctuations or to eliminate other business risks (such as interest or exchange rate fluctuations), and (2) inventories and long-term assets that must be written down to market when their values permanently decline.

# Investments Marked to Market

For accounting purposes, marketable securities are classified into two types, both of which are reported on the balance sheet at current market value (*marked-to-market*):

1. **Available-for-sale (AFS).** These are securities that management intends to hold for capital gains and dividend revenue; although, they can be sold if the price is right.
2. **Trading (T).** These are investments that management intends to actively buy and sell for trading profits as market prices fluctuate.

Management classifies securities depending on the degree of turnover (transaction volume) it expects in the investment portfolio, which reflects management's intent to actively trade the securities or not. Available-for-sale portfolios exhibit less turnover than trading portfolios. (GAAP permits companies to have multiple portfolios, each with a different classification, and management can change portfolio classification provided it adheres to strict disclosure and reporting requirements if its expectations of turnover change.) The classification as either available-for-sale or trading determines the accounting treatment, as Exhibit 7.3 summarizes.

| EXHIBIT 7.3 | Accounting Treatment for Available-for-Sale and for Trading Investments | |
| --- | --- | --- |
| **Investment Classification** | **Reporting of Market Value Changes** | **Reporting of Dividends Received and Gains and Losses on Sale** |
| Available-for-Sale (AFS) | Market value changes bypass the income statement and are reported in accumulated *other comprehensive income* (OCI) as part of equity | Reported as *other income* in income statement |
| Trading (T) | Market value changes are reported in the income statement as unrealized gains or losses; impacting equity via retained earnings | Reported as *other income* in income statement |

The difference between the accounting treatment of available-for-sale and trading investments relates to how market value changes affect equity. Changes in the market value of available-for-sale securities have no income effect; changes in market value of trading securities have an income affect. The impact on total stockholders' equity is identical for both classifications. The only difference is whether the change is reflected in retained earnings or in the accumulated other comprehensive income (AOCI) component of stockholders' equity. Dividends and any gains or losses on security sales are reported in the other income section of the income statement for both classifications.

## Market Adjustments

To illustrate the accounting for changes in market value subsequent to purchase (and before sale), assume that Microsoft's investment in Ask.com (600 remaining shares purchased for $20 per share) increases in value to $25 per share at year-end. The investment must be marked to market to reflect the $3,000 unrealized gain ($5 per share increase for 600 shares). The financial statement effects depend on whether the investment is classified as available-for-sale or as trading as follows:

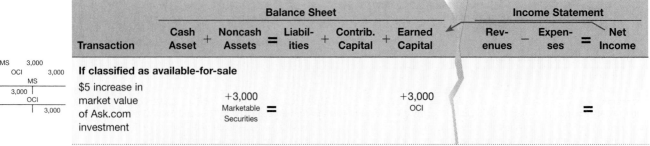

*continued*

| | Balance Sheet | | | | | | Income Statement | | |
|---|---|---|---|---|---|---|---|---|---|
| Transaction | Cash Asset | + Noncash Assets | = Liabil-ities | + Contrib. Capital | + Earned Capital | | Rev-enues | − Expen-ses | = Net Income |
| **If classified as trading** | | | | | | | | | |
| $5 increase in market value of Ask.com investment | | +3,000<br>Marketable **=**<br>Securities | | | +3,000<br>Retained<br>Earnings | | +3,000<br>Unrealized<br>Gain | | **=** +3,000 |

```
MS    3,000
   UG         3,000
         MS
3,000 |
   UG
         |     3,000
```

Under both classifications, the investment account increases by $3,000 to reflect the increase in the stock's market value. If Microsoft classifies these securities as available-for-sale, the unrealized gain increases the accumulated other comprehensive income (AOCI) account (which analysts typically view as a component of earned capital). However, if Microsoft classifies the securities as trading, the unrealized gain is recorded as income, thus increasing both reported income and retained earnings for the period. (Our illustration uses a portfolio with only one security for simplicity. Portfolios usually consist of multiple securities, and the unrealized gain or loss is computed based on the total cost and total market value of the entire portfolio.)

These market adjustments only apply if market prices are available, that is, for publicly traded securities. Thus, this mark-to-market accounting does not apply to investments in start-up companies or privately held corporations. Investments in nonpublicly traded companies are accounted for at cost as we discuss later in this section.

## Financial Statement Disclosures

Companies are required to disclose cost and market values of their investment portfolios in footnotes to financial statements. Google reports the accounting policies for its investments in the following footnote to its 10-K report:

**Cash and Cash Equivalents and Marketable Securities**　All highly liquid investments with stated maturities of three months or less from date of purchase are classified as cash equivalents; all highly liquid investments with stated maturities of greater than three months are classified as marketable securities. Our marketable debt and equity securities have been classified and accounted for as available for sale. These securities are carried at fair value, with the unrealized gains and losses, net of taxes, reported as a component of stockholders' equity

**Non-Marketable Equity Securities**　We have accounted for non-marketable equity security investments at historical cost because we do not have significant influence over the investees. They are subject to a periodic impairment review. To the extent any impairment is considered other-than-temporary, the investment is written down to its fair value and the loss is recorded as interest income and other, net.

Google accounts for its investments in marketable securities at market value. Because Google classifies those investments as "available-for-sale," unrealized gains and losses flow to the other comprehensive income (OCI) component of stockholders' equity. When Google sells the securities, it will record any *realized* gains or losses in income together with dividend and/or interest income. Google uses historical cost to account for investments in non-marketable securities (equity investments where Google cannot exert significant influence over the investee company). Google moniters the value of these invesments and writes them down to market value if they suffer a permanent decline in value.

Following is the current asset section of Google's 2005 balance sheet reflecting these investments.

| December 31 ($ 000s) | 2004 | 2005 |
|---|---|---|
| Cash and cash equivalents | $ 426,873 | $3,877,174 |
| Marketable securities | 1,705,424 | 4,157,073 |
| Accounts receivable, net of allowances of $3,962 and $14,852 | 311,836 | 687,976 |
| Income taxes receivable | 70,509 | — |
| Deferred income taxes, net | 19,463 | 49,341 |
| Prepaid revenue share, expenses and other assets | 159,360 | 229,507 |
| Total current assets | $2,693,465 | $9,001,071 |

Google's investments in marketable securities that are expected to mature within 90 days of the balance sheet date are recorded together with cash as cash equivalents. Its remaining investments are reported as marketable securities.

Footnotes to the Google 10-K provide further information about the composition of its investment portfolio.

| As of December 31 ($ 000s) | 2004 | 2005 |
|---|---|---|
| Cash and cash equivalents | | |
| Cash . . . . . . . . . . . . . . . . . . . . . . . . . . . . . . . . . . . . . . . . . . | $ 394,460 | $1,588,515 |
| Cash equivalents | | |
| Municipal securities. . . . . . . . . . . . . . . . . . . . . . . . . . . . | 2,951 | — |
| U.S. government note and agencies. . . . . . . . . . . . . . . . | 18,997 | 2,281,858 |
| Money market mutual funds . . . . . . . . . . . . . . . . . . . . . . | 10,465 | 6,801 |
| Total cash and cash equivalents. . . . . . . . . . . . . . . . . . . | 426,873 | 3,877,174 |
| Marketable securities | | |
| Municipal securities . . . . . . . . . . . . . . . . . . . . . . . . . . . . . | 1,616,684 | 1,203,209 |
| U.S. governement notes and agencies . . . . . . . . . . . . . . | 5,163 | 2,906,698 |
| U.S. corporate securities . . . . . . . . . . . . . . . . . . . . . . . . . | 83,577 | — |
| Equity security . . . . . . . . . . . . . . . . . . . . . . . . . . . . . . . . . | — | 47,166 |
| Total marketable securities. . . . . . . . . . . . . . . . . . . . . . . | 1,705,424 | 4,157,073 |
| Total cash, equivalents and marketable securities. . . . . . . . . . . | $2,132,297 | $8,034,247 |

The majority of Google's investments are in government debt securities such as bonds and T-bills, with a relatively small portion invested in equity securities. Google accounts for all of these investments as available-for-sale and reports them in the current asset section of the balance sheet because they mature within the coming year or can be readily sold, if necessary.

Google provides additional (required) disclosures on the costs, market values, and unrealized gains and losses for its available-for-sale investments as follows:

| December 31, 2005 ($ 000s) | Adjusted Cost | Gross Unrealized Gains | Gross Unrealized Losses | Fair Value |
|---|---|---|---|---|
| Municipal securities . . . . . . . . . . . . . . . . . | $1,219,078 | $ 28 | $(15,897) | $1,203,209 |
| U.S. government notes and agencies . . . . | 2,911,410 | 418 | (5,130) | 2,906,698 |
| Equity security . . . . . . . . . . . . . . . . . . . . . . | 5,000 | 42,166 | — | 47,166 |
| Total marketable securities. . . . . . . . . . . . | $4,135,488 | $42,612 | $(21,027) | $4,157,073 |

For each type investment, Google reports its cost, fair market value, and gross unrealized gains and losses; the latter reflect differences between cost and market. Google reports that the cost of its investment portfolio is $4,135,488, and that there are unrealized gains (losses) of $42,612 ($21,027) as of December 31, 2005. Google's balance sheet reports the total market value of $4,157,073 at December 31, 2005 ($ 000s).

Google' net unrealized gain of $21,585 ($42,612 − $21,027) is reported net of tax in the accumulated other comprehensive income (AOCI) section of its stockholders' equity as follows ($ 000s):

| December 31 ($ 000s) | 2004 | 2005 |
|---|---|---|
| Class A and Class B common stock . . . . . . . . . . . . . . . . . . . . . . | $ 267 | $ 293 |
| Additional paid-in capital . . . . . . . . . . . . . . . . . . . . . . . . . . . . . . | 2,582,352 | 7,477,792 |
| Deferred stock-based compensation. . . . . . . . . . . . . . . . . . . . . | (249,470) | (119,015) |
| Accumulated other comprehensive income. . . . . . . . . . . . . . . | 5,436 | 4,019 |
| Retained earnings . . . . . . . . . . . . . . . . . . . . . . . . . . . . . . . . . . | 590,471 | 2,055,868 |
| Total stockholders' equity . . . . . . . . . . . . . . . . . . . . . . . . . . . | $2,929,056 | $9,418,957 |

Google does not identify the components of its 2005 accumulated other comprehensive income of $4,019 except to report that the other component, beyond the unrealized gains on available-for-sale investments, is the cumulative translation adjustment relating to subsidiaries whose balance sheets are denominated in currencies other than $US. This lack of information can be confusing because the amount of unrealized gain (loss) reported in the investment footnote and the amount reported in accumulated other comprehensive income differ. Part of this difference relates to taxes: the net unrealized gain of $21,585 reported in the investment footnote is pretax while the amount reported in the accumulated other comprehensive income section of stockholders' equity is after-tax.

## Investments Reported at Cost

Companies often purchase debt securities, including bonds issued by other companies or by the U.S. government. Such debt securities have maturity dates—dates when the security must be repaid by the borrower. If a company buys debt securities, and management intends to hold the securities to maturity (as opposed to selling them early), the securities are classified as **held-to-maturity** (HTM). The cost method applies to held-to-maturity securities. Exhibit 7.4 identifies the reporting of these securities.

| EXHIBIT 7.4 | Accounting Treatment for Held-to-Maturity Investments | |
|---|---|---|
| **Investment Classification** | **Reporting of Market Value Changes** | **Reporting Interest Received and the Gains and Losses on Sale** |
| Held-to-Maturity (HTM) | Market value changes are *not* reported in either the balance sheet or income statement | Reported as *other income* in income statement |

Changes in market value do not affect either the balance sheet or the income statement. The presumption is that these investments will indeed be held to maturity, at which time their market value will be exactly equal to their face value. Fluctuations in market value, as a result, are less relevant for this investment classification. Finally, any interest received, and gains and losses on the sale of these investments, are recorded in current income. Sometimes companies acquire held-to-maturity debt securities for more or less than the security's face value. This can happen if the company acquires the security from the open market (as opposed to buying it directly from the company or government agency that issued it). Because the value of debt securities fluctuates with the prevailing rate of interest, the market value of the security will be greater than its face value if current market interest rates are lower than what the security pays for interest. In that case, the acquirer will pay a premium for the security. Conversely, if current market interest rates exceed what the security pays in interest, the acquirer will purchase the security at a discount. (We cover premiums and discounts on debt securities in more detail in Module 8.) Either way, the company records the investment at its acquisition cost (like any other asset) and amortizes any discount or premium over the remaining life of the held-to-maturity investment. At any point in time, the acquirer's balance sheet carries the investment at "amortized cost," which is never adjusted for subsequent market value changes.

In addition to held-to-maturity investments, companies sometimes acquire equity interests in other companies that are not traded on an organized exchange. These might be start-ups that have never issued stock or established privately held companies. Because there is no market for such securities, they cannot be classified as marketable securities and are carried at historical cost on the balance sheet. Google references one such investment in its 2005 10-K.

> Our investment in this non-marketable equity security will be accounted for at historical cost. In addition, this investment will be subject to a periodic impairment review. To the extent any impairment is considered other-than-temporary, this investment would be written down to its fair value and the loss would be recorded in "interest income and other, net."

If such an investee company ever goes public, Google will change its accounting method. If Google's ownership percentage does not allow it to exert significant influence or control, Google will account for this investment following the procedures described above for marketable securities. However, if Google can exert influence or control, it will apply different accounting methods that we explain in the following sections of this module.

## MID-MODULE REVIEW 1

**Part 1: Available-for-sale securities**
Using the financial statement effects template, enter the effects (amount and account) relating to the following four transactions involving investments in marketable securities classified as available-for-sale.

1. Purchased 1,000 shares of Netscape common stock for $15 cash per share.
2. Received cash dividend of $2 per share on Netscape common stock.
3. Year-end market price of Netscape common stock is $17 per share.
4. Sold all 1,000 shares of Netscape common stock for $17,000 cash in the next period.

## Solution for Part 1:

| | | | Balance Sheet | | | | | Income Statement | | |
|---|---|---|---|---|---|---|---|---|---|---|
| Transaction | Cash Asset | + | Noncash Assets | = | Liabil- ities | + | Contrib. Capital | + | Earned Capital | | Rev- enues | − | Expen- ses | = | Net Income |
| 1. Purchased 1,000 shares of Netscape common stock for $15 cash per share | −15,000 Cash | | +15,000 Marketable Securities | = | | | | | | | | | = | |
| 2. Received cash dividend of $2 per share on Netscape common stock | +2,000 Cash | | | = | | | | | +2,000 Retained Earnings | | +2,000 Dividend Income | | | = +2,000 |
| 3. Year-end market price of Netscape common stock is $17 per share | | | +2,000 Marketable Securities | = | | | | | +2,000 OCI | | | | | = |
| 4. Sold 1,000 shares of Netscape common stock for $17,000 cash | +17,000 Cash | | −17,000 Investments | = | | | | | −2,000 OCI +2,000 Retained Earnings | | +2,000 Gain on Sale | | | = +2,000 |

Margin journal entries:

1.
MS         15,000
  Cash         15,000

MS
15,000 |
  Cash
       | 15,000

2.
Cash       2,000
  DI           2,000

Cash
2,000 |
  DI
       | 2,000

3.
MS         2,000
  OCI          2,000

MS
2,000 |
  OCI
       | 2,000

4.
Cash       17,000
OCI        2,000
  MS           17,000
  GN           2,000

Cash
17,000 |
  OCI
2,000 |
  MS
       | 17,000
  GN
       | 2,000

**Part 2: Trading securities**

Using the financial statement effects template and the transaction information 1 through 4 from part 1, enter the effects (amount and account) relating to these transactions assuming that the investments are classified as trading securities.

## Solution for Part 2:

| | Balance Sheet | | | | | | Income Statement | | | |
|---|---|---|---|---|---|---|---|---|---|---|
| Transaction | Cash Asset | + Noncash Assets | = Liabil- ities | + Contrib. Capital | + Earned Capital | | Rev- enues | − Expen- ses | = Net Income | |
| 1. Purchased 1,000 shares of Netscape common stock for $15 cash per share | −15,000 Cash | +15,000 Marketable Securities | = | | | | | | = | MS 15,000<br>  Cash 15,000<br>MS<br>15,000 \|<br>  Cash<br>   \| 15,000 |
| 2. Received cash dividend of $2 per share on Netscape common stock | +2,000 Cash | | = | | +2,000 Retained Earnings | | +2,000 Dividend Income | | = +2,000 | Cash 2,000<br>  DI 2,000<br>  Cash<br>2,000 \|<br>  DI<br>  \| 2,000 |
| 3. Year-end market price of Netscape common stock is $17 per share | | +2,000 Marketable Securities | = | | +2,000 Retained Earnings | | +2,000 Unrealized Gain | | = +2,000 | MS 2,000<br>  UG 2,000<br>  MS<br>2,000 \|<br>  UG<br>  \| 2,000 |
| 4. Sold all 1,000 shares of Netscape common stock for $17,000 cash | +17,000 Cash | −17,000 Investments | = | | | | | | = | Cash 17,000<br>  MS 17,000<br>  Cash<br>17,000 \|<br>  MS<br>  \| 17,000 |

**Part 3: Footnote Disclosure**

Yahoo! reports the following table in the footnotes to its 2005 10-K ($ millions).

| December 31, 2005 | Gross Amortized Costs | Gross Unrealized Gains | Gross Unrealized Losses | Estimated Fair Value |
|---|---|---|---|---|
| United States Government and agency securities . . . . . . . . . . . . . . . . . . . . . . . . | $1,057,960 | $ 29 | $(13,210) | $1,044,779 |
| Municipal bonds. . . . . . . . . . . . . . . . . . . . . . . . . . | 9,760 | — | (166) | 9,594 |
| Corporate debt securities. . . . . . . . . . . . . . . . . . . | 1,528,282 | 127 | (12,627) | 1,515,782 |
| Corporate equity securities . . . . . . . . . . . . . . . . . | 31,175 | — | (1,168) | 30,007 |
| Total investments in available-for-sale securities. . . . . . . . . . . . . . . . . . . . . . . . . . . . | $2,627,177 | $156 | $(27,171) | $2,600,162 |

## Required

*a.*  What amount does Yahoo! report as investments on its balance sheet? What does this balance represent?

*b.*  How did the net unrealized loss affect reported income in 2005? How do we know?

**Solution for Part 3**

a. Yahoo reports an investment portfolio of $2,600,162. This represents the portfolio's current market value.

b. Yahoo classifies these investments as available-for-sale. Consequently, the net unrealized loss had no effect on Yahoo's reported income. Yahoo will realize gains and losses only when it sells the investments. Then, Yahoo will recognize the gains or losses in current period income.

# INVESTMENTS WITH SIGNIFICANT INFLUENCE

**LO2** Explain and illustrate accounting for equity method investments.

Many companies make equity investments that yield them significant influence over the investee companies. These intercorporate investments are usually made for strategic reasons such as the following:

- **Prelude to acquisition.** Significant ownership can allow the investor company to gain a seat on the board of directors from which it can learn much about the investee company, its products, and its industry.

- **Strategic alliance.** Strategic alliances permit the investor to gain trade secrets, technical know-how, or access to restricted markets. For example, a company might buy an equity share in a company that provides inputs for the investor's production process. This relationship is closer than the usual supplier-buyer relationship and will convey benefits to the investor company.

- **Pursuit of research and development.** Many research activities in the pharmaceutical, software, and oil and gas industries are conducted jointly. The common motivation is to reduce the investor's risk or the amount of capital investment. The investment often carries an option to purchase additional shares, which the investor can exercise if the research activities are fruitful.

A crucial feature in each of these investments is that the investor company has a level of ownership that is sufficient to exert *significant influence* over the investee company. GAAP requires that such investments be accounted for using the *equity method*.

**Significant influence** is the ability of the investor to affect the financing, investing and operating policies of the investee. Ownership levels of 20% to 50% of the outstanding common stock of the investee typically convey significant influence. Significant influence can also exist when ownership is less than 20%. Evidence of such influence can be that the investor company is able to gain a seat on the board of directors of the investee by virtue of its equity investment, or the investor controls technical know-how or patents that are used by the investee, or the investor is able to exert significant influence by virtue of legal contracts with the investee. (There is growing pressure for determining significant influence by the facts and circumstances of the investment instead of a strict ownership percentage rule.)

## Accounting for Investments with Significant Influence

GAAP requires that investors use the **equity method** when significant influence exists. The equity method reports the investment on the balance sheet at an amount equal to the percentage of the investee's equity owned by the investor; hence, the name equity method. (This assumes acquisition at book value. Acquisition at an amount greater than book value is covered later in this section.) Contrary to passive investments whose carrying amounts increase or decrease with the market value of the investee's stock, equity method investments increase (decrease) with increases (decreases) in the investee's stockholders' equity.

Equity method accounting is summarized as follows:

- Investments are recorded at their purchase cost.

- Dividends received are treated as a recovery of the investment and, thus, reduce the investment balance (dividends are not reported as income as with passive investments).

- The investor reports income equal to its percentage share of the investee's reported income; the investment account is increased by the percentage share of the investee's income or decreased by the percentage share of any loss.

- Changes in market value do not affect the investment's carrying value.

To illustrate the equity method, consider the following scenario: Assume that Google acquires a 30% interest in Mitel Networks, a company seeking to develop a new technology. This investment is a strategic alliance for Google. At the acquisition date, Mitel's balance sheet reports $1,000 of stockholders' equity, and Google purchases a 30% stake for $300. At the first year-end, Mitel reports profits of $100 and pays $20 in cash dividends to its shareholders ($6 to Google). Following are the financial statement effects for Google from this investment using the equity method:

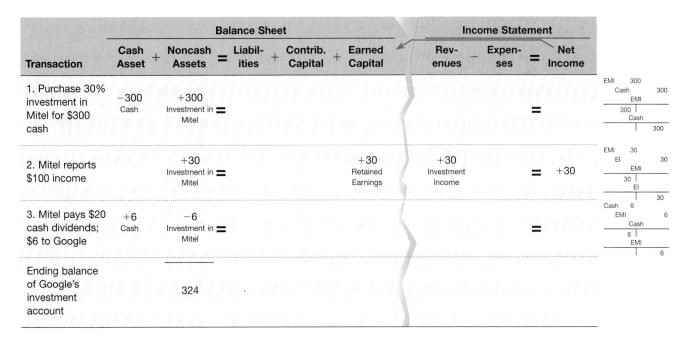

The investment is initially reported on Google's balance sheet at its purchase price of $300, representing a 30% interest in Mitel's total stockholders' equity of $1,000. During the year, Mitel's equity increases to $1,080 ($1,000 plus $100 income and less $20 dividends). Likewise, Google's investment increases by $30 to reflect its 30% share of Mitel's $100 income, and decreases by $6, relating to its share of Mitel's dividends. After these transactions, Google's investment in Mitel is reported on Google's balance sheet at 30% of $1,080, or $324.

Google's investment in Mitel is an asset, just like any other asset. As such, it must be tested annually for impairment. If the investment is found to be permanently impaired, Google must reduce the investment amount on the balance sheet and report a loss in the income statement. If and when Google sells Mitel, any gain or loss on the sale is reported in Google's income statement. The gain or loss is computed as the difference between the sales proceeds and the balance sheet value of the Mitel investment. For example, if Google sold Mitel for $500, Google would report a gain on sale of $176 ($500 proceeds − $324 balance sheet value).

Companies often pay more than book value when they make equity investments. For example, if Google paid $400 for its 30% stake in Mitel, Google would initially report its investment at its $400 purchase price. The $400 investment consists of two parts: the $300 equity investment described above and the $100 additional investment. Google is willing to pay the higher purchase price because it believes that Mitel's reported equity is below its current market value (such as when assets are reported at costs that are below market values or when intangible assets like internally generated goodwill are not recorded on the balance sheet). The $300 portion of the investment is accounted for as described above. Management of the investor company decides on how to allocate the excess of the amount paid over the book value of the investee company's equity and accounts for the excess accordingly. For example, if management decides that the $100 relates to depreciable assets, the $100 is depreciated over the assets' estimated useful lives. Or, if it relates to identifiable intangible assets that have a determinable useful life (like patents), it is amortized over the useful lives of the intangible assets. If it relates to goodwill, however, it is not amortized and remains on the balance sheet at $100 unless and until it is deemed to have become impaired. (See Appendix 7A for an expanded illustration.)

Two final points about equity method accounting: First, there can be a substantial difference between the book value of an equity method investment and its market value. An increase in value is not recognized until the investment is sold. If the market value of the investment has permanently declined, however, the investment is deemed impaired and it is written down to that lower market value. Second, if the investee company reports income, the investor company reports its share. Recognition of equity income by the investor, however, does not mean that it has received that income in cash. Cash is only received if the investee pays a dividend. To highlight this, the investor's statement of cash flows will include a reconciling item (a deduction from net income in computing operating cash flow) for its percentage share of the investee's net income. This is typically reported net of any cash dividends received.

---

**RESEARCH INSIGHT**    **Equity Income and Stock Prices**

Under the equity method of accounting, the investor does not recognize as income any dividends received from the investee, nor any changes in the investee's market value, until the investment is sold. However, research has found a positive relation between investors' and investees' stock prices at the time of investees' earnings and dividend announcements. This suggests that the market includes information regarding investees' earnings and dividends when assessing the stock prices of investor companies, and implies that the market looks beyond the book value of the investment account in determining stock prices of investor companies.

---

## Equity Method Accounting and ROE Effects

The investor company reports equity method investments on the balance sheet at an amount equal to the percentage owned of the investee company's equity when that investment is acquired at book value. To illustrate, consider the case of Abbott Laboratories, Inc., which owns 50% of TAP Pharmaceutical Products Inc. (TAP is a joint venture with Takeda Pharmaceutical Company, Limited of Japan). TAP Pharmaceuticals (TAP) develops and markets pharmaceutical products mainly for the U.S. and Canada. Abbott accounts for its investment in TAP using the equity method as described in the following footnote to its 2005 10-K report:

> **Equity Method Investments ($ millions)** Abbott's 50 percent-owned joint venture, TAP Pharmaceutical Products Inc. (TAP), is accounted for under the equity method of accounting. The investment in TAP was $167, $76 and $340 at December 31, 2005, 2004 and 2003, respectively. Dividends received from TAP were $343, $638 and $606 in 2005, 2004 and 2003, respectively. Abbott performs certain administrative and manufacturing services for TAP at negotiated rates that approximate fair market value.

At the end of 2005, the TAP joint venture reported stockholders' equity of $334.0 million and net income of $882.8 million. (TAP's financial statements are included in an exhibit to Abbott's 2005 10-K; not reproduced here.) In the footnote above, Abbott reports an investment balance at December 31, 2005, of $167 million (TAP equity of $334 million × 50%). In its income statement, Abbott reports income of $441.4 million (TAP net income of $882.8 million × 50%). Provided the investment is originally acquired at book value these relations will always hold.

Let's look a bit closer at TAP. TAP's balance sheet reports assets of $1,470.2 million, liabilities of $1,136.2 million, and stockholders' equity of $334 million. TAP is a highly leveraged company with considerable assets. The $167 million investment balance on Abbott's balance sheet does not provide investors with any clue about the level of TAP's total assets nor about the substantial amount of TAP's financial obligations. It reflects only Abbott's share of TAP's net assets (assets less liabilities, or equity).

Further, although TAP reports net income of $882.8 million, it only paid out $686.2 million in dividends—$343.1 million to Abbott. This means that Abbott reports equity income relating to this investment of $441.4 million, but only receives $343.1 million in cash. Accordingly, Abbott makes the following additional disclosure in its footnotes relating to the cumulative payment of dividends by TAP:

> Undistributed earnings of investments accounted for under the equity method amounted to approximately $151 as of December 31, 2005.

Cumulatively, Abbott has recorded $151 million more of income than it has received in cash dividends from TAP. This shows that equity income does not necessarily equal cash inflow. This is particularly true for equity investments in growth-stage companies that do not pay dividends, or for foreign subsidiaries of U.S. nationals that might not pay dividends for tax reasons or other restrictions.

Another area of concern with equity method accounting relates to unreported liabilities. As described above, TAP reports total liabilities of $1,136.2 million as of 2005, none of which appear on Abbott's balance sheet (Abbott only reports its investment in TAP's equity as an asset). Pharmaceutical companies face large potential liabilities arising from drug sales. (For example, TAP reports a loss of $150 million relating to litigation that it settled in 2004.) Although Abbott might have no direct legal obligation for TAP's liabilities, it might need to fund settlement costs via additional investment or advances to maintain TAP's viability if the company is important to Abbott's strategic plan. Further, companies that routinely fund R&D activities through equity investments in other companies, a common practice in the pharmaceutical and software industries, can find themselves supporting underperforming equity investments to assure continued capital market funding for these entities. One cannot always assume, therefore, that the investee's liabilities will not adversely affect the investor.

To summarize, under equity method accounting, only the net equity owned is reported on the balance sheet (not the underlying assets and liabilities), and only the net equity in earnings is reported in the income statement (not the investee's sales and expenses). From an analysis standpoint, because the assets and liabilities are left off the balance sheet, and because the sales and expenses are omitted from the income statement, the *components* of ROE are markedly affected as follows:

- **Net operating profit margin (NOPM = NOPAT/Sales).** Most analysts include equity income (sales less expenses) in NOPAT since it relates to operating investments. However, investee's sales are not included in the NOPM denominator. The reported NOPM is, thus, *overstated.*

- **Net operating asset turnover (NOAT = Sales/Average NOA).** Investee's sales are excluded from the NOAT denominator. This means that NOAT is *understated.* (When investee assets exceed the investment balance, the impact on NOAT is *indeterminate.*)

- **Financial leverage (FLEV = Net nonoperating obligations/Average equity).** Financial leverage is understated due to the absence of investee liabilities in the numerator.

Although ROE components are affected, ROE is unaffected by equity method accounting because the correct amount of investee net income and equity *is* included in the ROE numerator and denominator, respectively. Still, the evaluation of the quality of ROE is affected. Analysis using reported equity method accounting numbers would use an overstated NOPM and an understated FLEV because the numbers are based on net balance sheet and net income statement numbers. As we discuss in a later module, analysts frequently adjust reported financial statements for these types of items before conducting analysis. One such adjustment might be to consolidate (for analysis purposes) the equity method investee with the investor company.

---

**MANAGERIAL DECISION**   **You Are the Chief Financial Officer**

You are receiving capital expenditure requests for long-term operating asset purchases from various managers. You are concerned that capacity utilization is too low. What potential courses of action can you consider? Explain. [Answer, p. 7-33]

---

# MID-MODULE REVIEW 2

**Part 1:** Using the financial statement effects template, enter the effects (amount and account) relating to the following five transactions involving investments in marketable securities accounted for using the equity method.

1. Purchased 5,000 shares of LookSmart common stock at $10 cash per share; these shares reflect 30% ownership of LookSmart.
2. Received a $2 per share cash dividend on LookSmart common stock.
3. Recorded an accounting adjustment to reflect $100,000 income reported by LookSmart.
4. Year-end market price of LookSmart has increased to $12 per common share.
5. Sold all 5,000 shares of LookSmart common stock for $90,000 cash in the next period.

## Solution to Part 1:

| | | Balance Sheet | | | | | Income Statement | | |
|---|---|---|---|---|---|---|---|---|---|
| Transaction | Cash Asset | + Noncash Assets | = Liabil- ities | + Contrib. Capital | + Earned Capital | | Rev- enues | − Expen- ses | = Net Income |
| 1. Purchased 5,000 shares of LookSmart common stock at $10 cash per share; these shares reflect 30% ownership | −50,000 Cash | +50,000 Investments | = | | | | | | = |
| 2. Received a $2 per share cash dividend on LookSmart stock | 10,000 Cash | −10,000 Investments | = | | | | | | = |
| 3. Made an adjustment to reflect $100,000 income reported by LookSmart | | +30,000 Investments | = | | +30,000 Retained Earnings | | +30,000 Equity Income | | = +30,000 |
| 4. Market value has increased to $12 per share | | NOTHING RECORDED | | | | | | | |
| 5. Sold all 5,000 shares of LookSmart stock for $90,000 | +90,000 Cash | −70,000 Investments | = | | +20,000 Retained Earnings | | +20,000 Gain on Sale | | = +20,000 |

Margin journal entries:

1.
EMI 50,000
 Cash 50,000

EMI
50,000 |

Cash
 | 50,000

2.
Cash 10,000
 EMI 10,000

Cash
10,000 |

EMI
 | 10,000

3.
EMI 30,000
 EI 30,000

EMI
30,000 |

EI
 | 30,000

5.
Cash 90,000
 EMI 70,000
 GN 20,000

CASH
90,000 |

EMI
 | 70,000

GN
 | 20,000

**Part 2:** Yahoo! reports a $349.7 million equity investment in Yahoo! Japan related to its 33.5% ownership interest. Yahoo's footnotes reveal the following financial information about Yahoo! Japan ($ thousands).

| Twelve Months Ended September 30 | 2003 | 2004 | 2005 |
|---|---|---|---|
| Operating data | | | |
| Revenues | $500,091 | $868,281 | $1,367,247 |
| Gross profit | 462,352 | 810,114 | 1,251,599 |
| Income from operations | 262,393 | 470,681 | 656,167 |
| Net income | 145,720 | 290,576 | 382,287 |

| September 30 | 2004 | 2005 |
|---|---|---|
| Balance sheet data | | |
| Current assets | $622,794 | $900,149 |
| Long-term assets | 291,566 | 469,077 |
| Current liabilities | 192,761 | 306,441 |
| Long-term liabilities | 22,803 | 19,663 |

## Required

a. How much income does Yahoo! report in its 2005 income statement related to this equity investment?

b. Show the computations required to yield the $349.7 million balance in the equity investment account on Yahoo!'s balance sheet.

## Solution to Part 2

a. Yahoo! reports $128,066 ($382,287 × 33.5%) of equity income related to this investment in its 2005 income statement.

b. Yahoo! Japan's stockholders' equity is $1,043,519 thousand (computed as $900,149 + $469,077 − $306,044 − $19,663, in $ 000s), and Yahoo!'s investment account equals $349.7 million, computed as $1,043,519 thousand × 33.5% (difference due to rounding).

# INVESTMENTS WITH CONTROL

This section discusses accounting for investments where the investor company "controls" the investee company. For example, in its footnote describing its accounting policies, Google reports the following:

**LO3** Describe and illustrate accounting for consolidations.

> **Basis of Consolidations** The consolidated financial statements include the accounts of Google and wholly-owned subsidiaries. All intercompany balances and transactions have been eliminated.

This means that Google's financial statements are an aggregation (an adding up) of those of the parent company, Google, and all its subsidiary companies, less any intercompany activities.

## Accounting for Investments with Control

Accounting for business combinations (acquiring a controlling interest) goes one step beyond equity method accounting. Under the equity method, the investor's investment balance represents the proportion of the investee's equity owned by the investor, and the investor company's income statement includes its proportionate share of the investee's income. Once "control" over the investee company is achieved, GAAP requires consolidation for financial statements issued to the public (not for the internal financial records of the separate companies). Consolidation accounting includes 100% of the investee's assets and liabilities on the investor's balance sheet and 100% of the investee's sales and expenses on its income statement. Specifically, the consolidated balance sheet includes the gross assets and liabilities of the investee company, and the income statement includes the investee's gross sales and expenses rather than just the investor's share of the investee company's net assets or income. All intercompany sales and expenses are eliminated in the consolidation process to avoid double counting when, for example, goods are sold from the investee (called a subsidiary) to the investor (called the parent company) for resale to the parent's ultimate customers.

To illustrate, consider the following scenario. Penman Company acquires all of the common stock of Nissim Company by exchanging newly issued Penman shares for all of Nissim's common stock. The purchase price is equal to the $3,000 book value of Nissim's stockholders' equity (contributed capital of $2,000 and retained earnings of $1,000). On its balance sheet, Penman accounts for the investment in Nissim Co. using the equity method. This is important. Even if the investor (the parent) owns 100% of the investee, it records the investment on its balance sheet using the equity method described in the previous section. That is, Penman records an initial balance in the investment account of $3,000, equal to the purchase price. The balance sheets for Penman and Nissim immediately after the acquisition, together with the consolidated balance sheet, are shown in Exhibit 7.5.

**EXHIBIT 7.5** Mechanics of Consolidation Accounting (Purchased at Book Value)

| | Penman Company | Nissim Company | Consolidating Adjustments | Consolidated |
|---|---|---|---|---|
| Current assets | $ 5,000 | $1,000 | | $ 6,000 |
| Investment in Nissim | 3,000 | 0 | (3,000) | 0 |
| PPE, net | 10,000 | 4,000 | | 14,000 |
| Total assets | $18,000 | $5,000 | | $20,000 |
| Liabilities | $ 5,000 | $2,000 | | $ 7,000 |
| Contributed capital | 10,000 | 2,000 | (2,000) | 10,000 |
| Retained earnings | 3,000 | 1,000 | (1,000) | 3,000 |
| Total liabilities and equity | $18,000 | $5,000 | | $20,000 |

Since Penman "controls" the activities of Nissim, GAAP requires consolidation of the two balance sheets. This process, shown in Exhibit 7.5, involves summing the individual lines for each balance sheet, after eliminating any intercompany transactions (such as investments and loans, and sales and purchases), within the consolidated group. The consolidated balances for accounts such as current assets, PPE, and liabilities are computed as the sum of those accounts from each balance sheet. The equity investment account, however, represents an intercompany transaction that Penman must eliminate during the consolidation process. This is accomplished by removing the equity investment of $3,000 (from Penman's balance sheet), and removing Nissim's stockholders' equity to which Penman's investment relates.[2]

Exhibit 7.5 shows the consolidated balance sheet in the far right column. It shows total assets of $20,000, total liabilities of $7,000 and stockholders' equity of $13,000. Notice that consolidated equity equals that of the parent company—this is always the case. (Likewise, consolidated net income always equals the parent company's net income as the subsidiary's net income is already reflected in the parent's income statement as equity income from its investment.)

The illustration above assumes that the purchase price of the acquisition equals the book value of the investee company. It is more often the case, however, that the purchase price exceeds the book value. This might arise, for example, if an investor company believes it is acquiring something of value that is not reported on the investee's balance sheet—such as tangible assets whose market values have risen above book value, or unrecorded intangible assets, like patents or corporate synergies. When the acquisition price exceeds book value, all net assets acquired (both tangible and intangible) must be recognized on the consolidated balance sheet.

To illustrate, assume that Penman Company acquires Nissim Company for $4,000 instead of the $3,000 purchase price we used in the previous illustration. Also assume that in determining its purchase price, Penman paid the additional $1,000 because (1) Nissim's PPE is worth $300 more than its book value, and (2) Penman expects to realize $700 in additional value from corporate synergies (these "synergies" are an intangible asset with an unidentifiable useful life; they are classified as an asset called goodwill). The $4,000 investment account reflects two components: the book value acquired of $3,000 (as before) and an additional $1,000 of newly acquired assets. Exhibit 7.6 shows the post-acquisition balance sheets of the two companies, together with the consolidating adjustments and the consolidated balance sheet.

| EXHIBIT 7.6 | Mechanics of Consolidation Accounting (Purchase Price above Book Value) | | | |
|---|---|---|---|---|
| | Penman Company | Nissim Company | Consolidating Adjustments | Consolidated |
| Current assets . . . . . . . . . . . . . . . . . | $ 5,000 | $1,000 | | $ 6,000 |
| Investment in Nissim . . . . . . . . . . . . . . | 4,000 | 0 | (4,000) | 0 |
| PPE, net . . . . . . . . . . . . . . . . . . . . . . | 10,000 | 4,000 | 300 | 14,300 |
| Goodwill . . . . . . . . . . . . . . . . . . . . . | | | 700 | 700 |
| Total assets. . . . . . . . . . . . . . . . . . . | $19,000 | $5,000 | | $21,000 |
| Liabilities. . . . . . . . . . . . . . . . . . . . . | $ 5,000 | $2,000 | | $ 7,000 |
| Contributed capital. . . . . . . . . . . . . . . | 11,000 | 2,000 | (2,000) | 11,000 |
| Retained earnings . . . . . . . . . . . . . . . | 3,000 | 1,000 | (1,000) | 3,000 |
| Total liabilities and equity . . . . . . . . . . | $19,000 | $5,000 | | $21,000 |

The consolidated current assets, PPE, and liabilities are the sum of those accounts on each company's balance sheet. The investment account, however, includes the $1,000 of additional newly acquired assets that

---

[2] In the event that Penman acquires less than 100% of the stock of Nissim, consolidated equity must increase to maintain the accounting equation. This equity account is titled **minority interest**. For example, assume that Penman acquires 80% of Nissim for $2,400 (80% of $3,000). The consolidating adjustments follow. The claim of noncontrolling shareholders is recognized in consolidated stockholders' equity, just like that of the majority shareholders.

| | Balance Sheet | | | | | Income Statement | | |
|---|---|---|---|---|---|---|---|---|
| Transaction | Cash Asset | + Noncash Assets | = Liabil- ities | + Contrib. Capital | + Retained Earnings | Rev- enues | − Expen- ses | = Net Income |
| | | −2,400 Investment in Nissim | | −2,000 Nissim's Common Stock +600 Minority Interest | −1,000 Nissim's Retained Earnings | | | |

must be reported on the consolidated balance sheet. The consolidation process in this case has two steps. First, the $3,000 equity of Nissim Company is eliminated against the investment account as before. Then, the remaining $1,000 of the investment account is eliminated and the newly acquired assets ($300 of PPE and $700 of goodwill not reported on Nissim's balance sheet) are added to the consolidated balance sheet. Thus, the consolidated balance sheet reflects the book value of Penman and the *fair market value* of Nissim (the book value plus the excess of Nissim's market value over its book value).

To illustrate consolidation mechanics with an actual case, consider the consolidated balance sheet (parent company, subsidiary and consolidated balance sheet) that General Electric reports in a supplemental schedule to its 10-K report as shown in Exhibit 7.7.

| **EXHIBIT 7.7** | General Electric's Consolidated Balance Sheet | | |
|---|---|---|---|
| **At December 31, 2005**<br>**(In millions, except share amounts)** | **General Electric Company and Consolidated Affiliates** | **GE (Parent)** | **GECS (Subsidiary)** |
| **ASSETS** | | | |
| Cash and equivalents.......................... | $ 9,011 | $ 2,015 | $ 7,316 |
| Investment securities............................ | 53,144 | 461 | 52,706 |
| Current receivables ............................. | 14,851 | 15,058 | — |
| Inventories...................................... | 10,474 | 10,315 | 159 |
| Financing receivables—net ...................... | 287,639 | — | 287,69 |
| Other GECS receivables.......................... | 14,767 | — | 19,060 |
| Property, plant and equipment—net ................ | 67,528 | 16,504 | 51,024 |
| Investment in GECS............................. | — | 50,815 | — |
| Intangible assets—net ........................... | 81,726 | 57,839 | 23,887 |
| All other assets.................................. | 87,446 | 36,752 | 52,058 |
| Assets of discontinued operations.................. | 46,756 | — | 46,756 |
| Total assets..................................... | $673,342 | $189,759 | $540,605 |
| **LIABILITIES AND EQUITY** | | | |
| Short-term borrowings........................... | $158,156 | $1,127 | $157,672 |
| Accounts payable, principally trade accounts........... | 21,273 | 11,870 | 13,133 |
| Progress collections and price adjustments accrued ..... | 4,456 | 4,456 | — |
| Dividends payable .............................. | 2,623 | 2,623 | — |
| All other current costs and expenses accrued........... | 18,419 | 18,436 | — |
| Long-term borrowings ........................... | 212,281 | 9,081 | 204,397 |
| Investment contracts, insurance liabilities and<br>  insurance annuity benefits ...................... | 45,432 | — | 45,722 |
| All other liabilities.............................. | 40,632 | 23,273 | 17,453 |
| Deferred income taxes........................... | 16,330 | 3,733 | 12,597 |
| Liabilities of and minority interest in<br>  discontinued operations........................ | 36,332 | — | 36,568 |
| Total liabilities ................................. | 555,934 | 74,599 | 487,542 |
| Minority interest in equity of consolidated affiliates....... | 8,054 | 5,806 | 2,248 |
| Common stock (10,484,268,000 and 10,586,358,000<br>  shares outstanding at year-end 2005 and 2004,<br>  respectively) .................................. | 669 | 669 | 1 |
| Accumulated gains (losses)—net | | | |
|   Investment securities .......................... | 1,831 | 1,831 | 1,754 |
|   Currency translation adjustments................... | 2,532 | 2,532 | 2,287 |
|   Cash flow hedges.............................. | (822) | (822) | (813) |
|   Minimum pension liabilities....................... | (874) | (874) | (179) |
| Other capital.................................... | 25,227 | 25,227 | 12,386 |
| Retained earnings .............................. | 98,117 | 98,117 | 35,379 |
| Less common stock held in treasury ................ | (17,326) | (17,326) | — |
| Total shareowners' equity.......................... | 109,354 | 109,354 | 50,815 |
| **Total liabilities and equity** ...................... | $673,342 | $189,759 | $540,605 |

General Electric Company (GE) owns 100% of its financial products subsidiary, General Electric Capital Services (GECS), whose stockholders' equity is $50,815 million as of 2005. The Investment in GECS account is also reported at $50,815 million on GE's (parent company) balance sheet. This investment account is subsequently removed (eliminated) in the consolidation process, together with the equity of GECS to which it relates. Following this elimination, and the elimination of all other intercompany sales and advances, the adjusted balance sheets of the two companies are summed to yield the consolidated balance sheet that is reported in GE's 10-K.

## Reporting of Acquired Intangible Assets

As previously discussed, acquisitions are routinely made at a purchase price in excess of the book value of the investee company's equity. The purchase price is first allocated to the fair market values of tangible assets and liabilities (such as PPE in our example). Then, the remainder is allocated to acquired intangible assets (Goodwill in our example).

As of the acquisition date, the purchasing company values the tangible assets acquired and liabilities assumed in the purchase and records them on the consolidated balance sheet at fair market value. (In the Exhibit 7.6 example, we sum the $4,000 PPE book value of Nissim with the $300 excess of market over book value to yield the $4,300 PPE fair market value that is included among the assets on the consolidated balance sheet.) Any remaining purchase price above book value is allocated to acquired identifiable *intangible* assets, which are also valued at the acquisition date. (In the example, the consolidated balance sheet includes $700 of goodwill, which is one type of intangible asset.) A sampling of the types of intangible assets that are often recognized during acquisitions follows:

- Marketing-related assets like trademarks and Internet domain names
- Customer-related assets like customer lists and customer contracts
- Artistic-related assets like plays, books, and videos
- Contract-based assets like licensing, franchise and royalty agreements, and lease contracts
- Technology-based assets like patents, software, databases, and trade secrets

To illustrate, Hewlett-Packard reported the following allocation of its $24,170 million purchase price for Compaq Computer in the footnotes to its 10-K report ($ millions).

| | | |
|---|---|---:|
| | Cash and cash equivalents | $ 3,615 |
| | Accounts receivable | 4,305 |
| | Financing receivables | 1,241 |
| Tangible assets | Inventory | 1,661 |
| | Current deferred tax assets | 1,475 |
| | Other current assets | 1,146 |
| | Property, plant and equipment | 2,998 |
| | Long-term financing receivables and other assets | 1,914 |
| | Amortizable intangible assets | |
| Acquired intangible assets | Customer contracts and lists, distribution agreements | 1,942 |
| | Developed and core technology, patents | 1,501 |
| | Product trademarks | 74 |
| | Intangible asset with an indefinite life | 1,422 |
| | Goodwill | 14,450 |
| | Accounts payable | (2,804) |
| | Short- and long-term debt | (2,704) |
| Liabilities assumed | Accrued restructuring | (960) |
| | Other current liabilities | (5,933) |
| | Other long-term liabilities | (1,908) |
| IPR&D → | In-process research and development | 735 |
| | Total purchase price | $24,170 |

In its acquisition of Compaq, HP allocated $4,939 million ($1,942 million + $1,501 million + $74 million + $1,422 million) of its purchase price to identifiable intangible assets (before goodwill), as described in the following footnote to its 10-K:

**Amortizable intangible assets**   Of the total purchase price, approximately $3.5 billion [$1,942 million + $1,501 million + $74 million] was allocated to amortizable intangible assets including customer contracts and developed and core technology. . . . HP is amortizing the fair value of these assets on a straight-line basis over a weighted average estimated useful life of approximately 9 years. Developed technology, which consists of products that have reached technological feasibility, includes products in most of Compaq's product lines. . . . Core technology and patents represent a combination of Compaq processes, patents and trade secrets. . . . HP is amortizing the developed and core technology and patents on a straight-line basis over a weighted average estimated useful life of approximately 6 years.

**Intangible asset with an indefinite life**   The estimated fair value of the intangible asset with an indefinite life was $1.4 billion, consisting of the estimated fair value allocated to the Compaq trade name. This intangible asset will not be amortized because it has an indefinite remaining useful life based on many factors and considerations, including the length of time that the Compaq name has been in use, the Compaq brand awareness and market position and the plans for continued use of the Compaq brand.

HP allocated a portion of the purchase price to the following identifiable intangible assets:

- Customer contracts
- Customer lists and distribution agreements
- Developed technology
- Core technology and patents
- Compaq trade name

HP deemed the first four of these identifiable intangible assets as amortizable assets, which are those having a finite useful life. HP will subsequently amortize them over their useful lives (similar to depreciation). The last asset (Compaq trade name) is deemed to have an indefinite useful life. It is not amortized, but is tested annually for impairment like goodwill.

HP also allocated $735 million of the purchase price to *In-Process Research and Development*. This relates to the acquisition-date value of research projects that have not yet reached technological feasibility. HP immediately expensed this R&D asset like all other R&D costs (rather than capitalize the costs on the balance sheet). This treatment was consistent with GAAP when HP acquired Compaq.

The IPR&D write-off has been subject to abuse. Excessive allocation of the purchase price to IPR&D artificially reduces current period income and inflates income in successive periods (by the elimination of future depreciation or amortization expense). The SEC monitors purchase allocations closely and challenges those with which it disagrees. As a result of these reviews, a number of companies have subsequently been forced to restate the amounts of their initial IPR&D write-offs. As well, the FASB monitored the IPR&D write-off issue and, in 2005, proposed an amendment to accounting standards to "prohibit writing-off immediately after the business combination the fair value of in-process research and development assets acquired." Under the new standard, companies will capitalize IPR&D costs on the balance sheet, amortize them, and test the IPR&D asset annually for impairment. The standard will likely come into play in 2007.

Once the purchase price has been allocated to identifiable tangible and intangible assets (net of liabilities assumed), any remaining purchase price is allocated to goodwill. Goodwill, thus, represents the remainder of the purchase price that is not allocated to other assets. HP allocated $14.45 billion (60%) of the Compaq purchase price to goodwill. The SEC is also scrutinizing companies that assign an excessive proportion of the purchase price to goodwill (companies might do this to avoid the future earnings drag from amortization expense).

## Reporting of Goodwill

Goodwill is no longer amortized, as it was prior to 2001. Instead, GAAP requires companies to test the goodwill asset annually for impairment just like any other asset. The impairment test is a two-step process:

1. The market value of the investee company is compared with the book value of the investor's equity investment account.[3]

---

[3] The fair market value of the investee company can be determined using market comparables or other valuation methods (such as the discounted cash flow model, residual operating income model, or P/E multiples—see Module 12).

2. If the market value is less than the investment balance, the *investment* is deemed impaired. Step 2, then, determines if the *goodwill* portion of the investment is impaired rather than other acquired assets. The investor estimates the goodwill value as if the subsidiary were acquired at current market value, and the imputed balance for goodwill becomes the balance in the goodwill account. If this imputed goodwill amount is less than its book value, the company writes goodwill down, resulting in an impairment loss on the consolidated income statement.

To illustrate the impairment computation, assume that an investment, currently reported at $1 million on the investor's balance sheet, has a current fair market value of $900,000 (we know, therefore, that the investment is impaired); also assume the consolidated balance sheet reports goodwill at $300,000. Management review reveals that the current fair market value of the net assets of the investee company (absent goodwill) is $700,000. This indicates that the goodwill component of the investment account is impaired by $100,000, which is computed as follows:

| | |
|---|---:|
| Fair market value of investee company | $ 900,000 |
| Fair market value of net assets (absent goodwill) | (700,000) |
| Implied goodwill | 200,000 |
| Current goodwill balance | (300,000) |
| Impairment loss | $(100,000) |

This analysis implies that goodwill must be written down by $100,000. The impairment loss is reported in the consolidated income statement. The related footnote disclosure would describe the reasons for the write-down and the computations involved.

Corning provides an example of a goodwill impairment disclosure in its 10-K report:

**Impairment Charge** Pursuant to SFAS No 142, "Goodwill and Other Intangible Assets," (SFAS 142) goodwill is required to be tested for impairment annually at the reporting unit level. In addition, goodwill should be tested for impairment between annual tests if an event occurs or circumstances change that would more likely than not reduce the fair value of the reporting unit below its related carrying value. In the third quarter of 2004, we identified certain factors that caused us to lower our estimates and projections for the long-term revenue growth of the Telecommunications segment, which indicated that the fair value of the Telecommunications segment reporting unit was less than its carrying value. We performed an interim impairment test of the Telecommunications segment goodwill in the third quarter of 2004 and, as a result, recorded an impairment charge of $1,420 million to reduce the carrying value of goodwill to its implied fair value at September 30, 2004 of $117 million.

Corning determined that goodwill, reported on its balance sheet at $1,537 million, had a current (implied) market value $117 million. That is, Corning's goodwill was impaired, resulting in a write-down of $1,420 million. Corning reported a pretax operating loss of $1,485 million in 2004, nearly all of this related to its goodwill write-down.

**BUSINESS INSIGHT**  **Pitfalls of Acquired Growth**

One of the greatest destructions of shareholder value occurred during the bull market between 1995 and 2001 when market exuberance fueled a tidal wave of corporate takeovers. Companies often overpaid as a result of overestimating the cost-cutting and synergies their planned takeovers would bring. Then, acquirers failed to quickly integrate operations. The result? Subsequent years' market returns of most acquirers fell below those of their peers and were often negative. Indeed, 61% of corporate buyers saw their shareholders' wealth *decrease* after the acquisition. Who won? The sellers; which are the target-company shareholders who sold their stock within the first week of the takeover and reaped enormous profits at the expense of the acquirers' shareholders.

## Reporting Subsidiary Stock Issuances

After subsidiaries are acquired, they can, and often do, issue stock. If issued to outside investors, the result is an infusion of cash into the subsidiary and a reduction in the parent's percentage ownership. For example, Clear Channel Communications' (CCU) 10-K report discloses the following stock issuance by one of its subsidiaries.

> **Initial Public Offering ("IPO") of Clear Channel Outdoor Holdings, Inc. ("CCO")** The Company completed the IPO on November 11, 2005, which consisted of the sale of 35.0 million shares, for $18.00 per share, of Class A common stock of CCO, its indirect, wholly owned subsidiary prior to the IPO. After completion of the IPO, the Company owns all 315.0 million shares of CCO's outstanding Class B common stock, representing approximately 90% of the outstanding shares of CCO's common stock and approximately 99% of the total voting power of CCO's common stock. The net proceeds from the offering, after deducting underwriting discounts and offering expenses, were approximately $600.6 million. All of the net proceeds of the offering were used to repay a portion of the outstanding balances of intercompany notes owed to the Company by CCO. Under the guidance in SEC Staff Accounting Bulletin Topic 5H, *Accounting for Sales of Stock by a Subsidiary*, the Company has recorded approximately $120.9 million of minority interest and $479.7 million of additional paid in capital on its consolidated balance sheet at December 31, 2005 as a result of this transaction.

While the note is complicated, the gist is that CCO, a Clear Channel Communications' subsidiary, issued stock to the public (an IPO). This increased the amount that Clear Channel reports on its balance sheet for this equity investment. To illustrate, consider Parent Company that acquires 100% of Subsidiary Company at book value, and the latter has a book value for stockholders' equity of $500. The investment account on Parent's balance sheet, using the equity method, is $500. Next, Subsidiary issues shares to outsiders for $100, which reduces Parent's ownership to, say, 90%. Parent now owns 90% of Subsidiary whose book value of equity has increased to $600. The Parent's investment should therefore, have a balance sheet value of $540 (90% × $600). The value of Parent's equity method investment account rose by $40 ($540 vs. $500) because of the Subsidiary's stock sale.

Similarly, Clear Channel's equity method investment account increased by $600.6 million. This increase must be matched with a corresponding increase in Clear Channel's stockholders' equity. The question is, what stockholders' equity account ought to increase? Should Clear Channel record the $600.6 million as income (thereby affecting retained earnings) or as an increase to paid-in capital? Clear Channel did the latter. It recognized a $600.6 million increase in stockholders' equity in two parts. First, Clear Channel added $479.7 million to additional paid-in capital. Second, it recorded minority interest for $120.9 million, which represents the book value of the CCO shares that were sold to the public. Minority interest is the part of CCO not owned by Clear Channel.

Current accounting standards also allow companies the option to record this sort of equity increase as income. For example, Citigroup, Inc., reports the following stock issuance in its 10-K report by one of its subsidiaries:

> Travelers Property Casualty Corp. (an indirect wholly owned subsidiary of Citigroup on December 31, 2001) sold 231 million shares of its class A common stock representing approximately 23.1% of its outstanding equity securities in an initial public offering (the IPO) on March 27, 2002. In 2002, Citigroup recognized an after-tax gain of $1.158 billion as a result of the IPO.

Under proposed changes to the business combinations accounting standard, the effects of stock sales by subsidiaries will be recognized only as additional paid-in capital, and not as gains on the income statement. However, unless and until this standard is enacted, companies will be able to choose to report changes in the equity investment balance either way: as income or as additional paid-in capital. Analysts need to be mindful of this option when assessing profitability and other equity changes that arise from sales of stock by subsidiary companies.

## Reporting the Sale of Subsidiary Companies

Discontinued operations refer to any separately identifiable business unit that the company sells or intends to sell. The income or loss of the discontinued operations (net of tax), and the after-tax gain or loss on sale of the unit, are reported in the income statement below income from continuing operations. The segregation of discontinued operations means that its revenues and expenses are *not* reported with revenues and expenses from continuing operations.

To illustrate, assume that Google's recent periods' results were generated by both continuing and discontinuing operations as follows:

| | Continuing Operations | Discontinued Operations | Total |
|---|---|---|---|
| Revenues . . . . . . . . . . . . . . . . . . . . | $10,000 | $3,000 | $13,000 |
| Expenses . . . . . . . . . . . . . . . . . . . | 7,000 | 2,000 | 9,000 |
| Pretax Income . . . . . . . . . . . . . . . . | 3,000 | 1,000 | 4,000 |
| Tax expense (40%) . . . . . . . . . . . . . | 1,200 | 400 | 1,600 |
| Net Income . . . . . . . . . . . . . . . . . . | $ 1,800 | $ 600 | $ 2,400 |

Its reported income statement would appear as follows—notice the separate disclosure for discontinued operations (as highlighted).

| | |
|---|---|
| Revenues . . . . . . . . . . . . . . . . . . . . . . . . . . . . . . | $10,000 |
| Expenses . . . . . . . . . . . . . . . . . . . . . . . . . . . . . | 7,000 |
| Pretax Income . . . . . . . . . . . . . . . . . . . . . . . . . | 3,000 |
| Tax expense (40%) . . . . . . . . . . . . . . . . . . . . . | 1,200 |
| Income from continuing operations . . . . . . . . . . . | 1,800 |
| Income from discontinued operations, net . . . . | 600 |
| Net income . . . . . . . . . . . . . . . . . . . . . . . . . . . . | $ 2,400 |

Revenues and expenses reflect those of the continuing operations only, and the (persistent) income from continuing operations is reported net of its related tax expense. Results from the (transitory) discontinued operations are collapsed into one line item and reported separately net of its own tax (this includes any gain or loss from sale of the discontinued unit's net assets). The net income figure is unchanged by this presentation.

Importantly, results of the discontinued operations are segregated from those of continuing operations. This presentation facilitates the prediction of results from the (persistent) continuing operations. The segregation of discontinued operations is made in the current year and for the two prior years' comparative results reported in the income statement. To illustrate, Agilent reports the following footnote to its 2005 10-K relating to the decision to divest its semiconductor products business.

**Discontinued Operations** In August 2005, the Board of Directors approved the divestiture of our semiconductor products business. We subsequently signed an Asset Purchase Agreement with Avago Technologies Ltd. (f/k/a Argos Acquisition Pte. Ltd.) ("Avago") providing for the sale of our semiconductor products business for approximately $2.66 billion. The purchase price is subject to adjustment based on a determination of our semiconductor products business' Adjusted EBITDA (as defined in the Asset Purchase Agreement) and working capital at closing. The sale closed in December 2005. Our consolidated financial statements reflect our semiconductor products business, including the camera module business, as a discontinued operation in accordance with SFAS No.144, "Accounting for the Impairment or Disposal of Long-Lived Assets" ("SFAS No.144"). As required under SFAS No.144, we have ceased depreciation and amortization on our assets held for sale as of August 2005. The financial position, results of operations and cash flows of our semiconductor products business have been classified as discontinued operations and prior periods have been restated.

| Years Ended October 31 (Restated, in millions) | 2005 | 2004 | 2003 |
|---|---|---|---|
| Net revenue. . . . . . . . . . . . . . . . . . . . . . . . . . . . . . . . . . . . . . . . | $1,796 | $2,021 | $1,688 |
| Costs and expenses . . . . . . . . . . . . . . . . . . . . . . . . . . . . . . . . . | 1,670 | 1,779 | 1,594 |
| Income (loss) from discontinued operations . . . . . . . . . . . . . . . . . . . . . . | 226 | 242 | (6) |
| Other income (expense), net . . . . . . . . . . . . . . . . . . . . . . . . . . . . . | 6 | — | 3 |
| Income (loss) from discontinued operations before taxes . . . . . . . . . . . . . | 232 | 242 | (3) |
| Provision (benefit) for taxes . . . . . . . . . . . . . . . . . . . . . . . . . . . . | 46 | — | 10 |
| Net income (loss) from discontinued operations . . . . . . . . . . . . . . . . . . | $ 186 | $ 242 | $ (13) |

The revenue and expenses of Agilent's discontinued operation are eliminated from its 2005 income statement, leaving only the revenues and expenses of continuing operations. Restated revenues, for example, are $1,796 million lower. Revenues for the other years reported are, likewise, restated. Only the net income (loss) of the discontinued operations is reported in a separate line below income from continuing operations. Also, assets and liabilities of the discontinued operation are segregated on Agilent's balance sheet as highlighted in the following current asset section of its report.

| October 31 (Restated, in millions) | 2005 | 2004 |
|---|---|---|
| Cash and cash equivalents | $2,226 | $2,315 |
| Short term investments | 25 | — |
| Cash and cash equivalents and short term investments | 2,251 | 2,315 |
| Accounts receivable, net | 753 | 788 |
| Inventory | 722 | 809 |
| Other current assets | 298 | 266 |
| Current assets of discontinued operations | 423 | 485 |
| Total current assets | $4,447 | $4,663 |

The discontinued operation is reported in this manner until it is sold, at which time its assets and liabilities are removed from the balance sheet, and a gain or loss on the sale is reported in the income statement below income from continuing operations, as illustrated in the footnote above. The reported gain or loss on sale is equal to the proceeds received less the balance of the (equity method) investment that is reported on the parent's balance sheet at the sale date.

## Limitations of Consolidation Reporting

Consolidation of financial statements is meant to present a financial picture of the entire set of companies under the control of the parent. Since investors typically purchase stock in the parent company, and not in the subsidiaries, that view is more relevant than the parent company merely reporting subsidiaries as equity investments in its balance sheet. Still, we must be aware of certain limitations that the consolidation process entails:

1. Consolidated income does not imply that the parent company has received any or all of the subsidiaries' net income as cash. The parent can only receive cash from subsidiaries via dividend payments. Conversely, the consolidated cash is not automatically available to the individual subsidiaries. It is quite possible, therefore, for an individual subsidiary to experience cash flow problems even though the consolidated group has strong cash flows. Likewise, unguaranteed debts of a subsidiary are not obligations of the consolidated group. Thus, even if the consolidated balance sheet is strong, creditors of a failing subsidiary are often unable to sue the parent or other subsidiaries to recoup losses.

2. Consolidated balance sheets and income statements are a mix of the various subsidiaries, often from different industries. Comparisons across companies, even if in similar industries, are often complicated by the different mix of subsidiary companies.

3. Segment disclosures on individual subsidiaries are affected by intercorporate transfer pricing policies relating to purchases of products or services that can artificially inflate the profitability of one segment at the expense of another. Companies also have considerable discretion in the allocation of corporate overhead to subsidiaries, which can markedly affect segment profitability.

## Reporting Consolidations under Pooling-of-Interests

Prior to 2001, companies had a choice in their accounting for business combinations. They could use the *purchase method* as described in this module (now required for all acquisitions), or they could use the *pooling-of-interests (pooling) method.* A large number of acquisitions were accounting for under the pooling-of-interest method, and its impact on financial statements will linger for many years.

The main difference between the pooling-of-interest and the purchase method of accounting for acquisitions is this: under the purchase method the investment account is initially recorded at the *fair market*

| BUSINESS INSIGHT | Determining the parent company in an acquisition |
|---|---|

Sensor, Inc. is acquiring Boston Instrument Company through an exchange of stock valued at $500 million. Sensor will survive as the continuing company, and the senior management of Boston Instrument will own 65% of the outstanding stock, reflecting a premium in the exchange ratios paid by Sensor to acquire Boston Instrument. Sensor's Chairman will remain as Chairman of the company, but the purchase agreement specifies that the board of directors will elect a new Chairman within six months of the deal's close. Boston Instrument's President and CFO will assume those same positions in the new entity. Following are the market values of the tangible and intangible net assets of both companies on the date of acquisition: Sensor, $400 million; and Boston Instrument, $200 million. Which of these two companies should be viewed as the acquiring firm (parent company) for purposes of consolidation, and how does this decision affect the amount of goodwill recorded on the consolidated balance sheet? Although Sensor is the larger firm, its name will survive, and its Chairman will serve in that capacity in the combined company, most accountants would likely conclude that Boston Instrument is the parent company for purposes of consolidation. This determination is based on the 65% ownership interest of the Boston Instrument shareholders who control the new entity. Further, these shareholders will be able to elect a new Chairman within six months. The amount of goodwill recorded following the acquisition is equal to the purchase price less the market value of the net tangible and identifiable intangible assets acquired. If Senror is the acquiring firm, $100 million ($500 million − $400 million) of goodwill will be recorded. If Boston Instrument is the acquiring firm, $300 million ($500 million − $200 million) of goodwill will be recorded. This decision will dramatically affect both the balance sheet (relative amounts of goodwill and other assets recorded) as well as the income statement (depreciation of tangible assets and amortization of identifiable intangible assets recognized vs. annual impairment testing for goodwill).

*value* of the acquired company. Under the pooling-of-interest method, the investment account is initially recorded at the *book value* (amount reported on the balance sheet) of stockholders' equity for the acquired company, regardless of the amount actually paid. As a result, the pooling method created no goodwill. Further, since goodwill amortization was required under previous GAAP, subsequent income was larger under pooling. This feature spawned widespread use of pooling-of-interest, especially for high-tech companies.

Acquisitions previously accounted for under pooling-of-interest remain unaffected under current GAAP. We must be aware of at least two points for analysis purposes:

1. Assets were usually understated with the pooling-of-interest method because the investee's assets were recorded at book rather than market value. This implies that consolidated return on net operating assets (RNOA) and asset turnover ratios are overstated.

2. Net income with the pooling-of-interest method was nearly always overstated due to elimination of goodwill amortization. This continues to create difficulties for comparative analysis when looking at companies that previously applied pooling-of-interest accounting.

## MODULE-END REVIEW

On January 1 of the current year, assume that Yahoo!, Inc., purchased all of the common shares of EarthLink for $600,000 cash—this is $200,000 more than the book value of EarthLink's stockholders' equity. Assume that the balance sheets of the two companies immediately after the acquisition follow:

| | Yahoo! (Parent) | EarthLink (Subsidiary) | Consolidating Adjustments | Consolidated |
|---|---|---|---|---|
| Current assets . . . . . . . . . . . . | $1,000,000 | $100,000 | | |
| Investment in EarthLink . . . . . | 600,000 | — | | |
| PPE, net . . . . . . . . . . . . . . . . | 3,000,000 | 400,000 | | |
| Goodwill . . . . . . . . . . . . . . . . | — | — | | |
| Total assets. . . . . . . . . . . . . | $4,600,000 | $500,000 | | |
| Liabilities. . . . . . . . . . . . . . . | $1,000,000 | $100,000 | | |
| Contributed capital. . . . . . . . | 2,000,000 | 200,000 | | |
| Retained earnings . . . . . . . . | 1,600,000 | 200,000 | | |
| Total liabilities and equity . . . . | $4,600,000 | $500,000 | | |

During purchase negotiations, EarthLink's PPE was appraised at $500,000, and all of EarthLink's remaining assets and liabilities were appraised at values approximating their book values. Also, Yahoo! concluded that payment of an additional $100,000 was warranted because of anticipated corporate synergies. Prepare the consolidating adjustments and the consolidated balance sheet at acquisition.

## Solution

| | Yahoo! (Parent) | EarthLink (Subsidiary) | Consolidating Adjustments | Consolidated |
|---|---|---|---|---|
| Current assets . . . . . . . . . . . . | $1,000,000 | $100,000 | | $1,100,000 |
| Investment in EarthLink . . . . . | 600,000 | — | $(600,000) | |
| PPE, net . . . . . . . . . . . . . . . . | 3,000,000 | 400,000 | 100,000 | 3,500,000 |
| Goodwill . . . . . . . . . . . . . . . . | — | — | 100,000 | 100,000 |
| Total assets. . . . . . . . . . . . . | $4,600,000 | $500,000 | | $4,700,000 |
| Liabilities. . . . . . . . . . . . . . . | $1,000,000 | $100,000 | | $1,100,000 |
| Contributed capital. . . . . . . . | 2,000,000 | 200,000 | (200,000) | 2,000,000 |
| Retained earnings . . . . . . . . | 1,600,000 | 200,000 | (200,000) | 1,600,000 |
| Total liabilities and equity . . . . | $4,600,000 | $500,000 | | $4,700,000 |

*Explanation:* The $600,000 investment account is eliminated together with the $400,000 book value of Earth-Link's equity to which Yahoo's investment relates. The remaining $200,000 consists of the additional $100,000 in PPE assets and the $100,000 in goodwill from expected corporate synergies. Following these adjustments, the balance sheet items are summed to yield the consolidated balance sheet.

# APPENDIX 7A: Equity Method Mechanics

The appendix provides a comprehensive example of accounting for an equity method investment. Assume that Petroni Company acquires a 30% interest in the outstanding voting shares of Wahlen Company on January 1, 2005. To obtain these shares, Petroni pays $126,000 cash and issues 6,000 of its $10 par value common stock. On that date, Petroni's stock has a fair market value of $18 per share, and Wahlen's book value of equity is $560,000. Petroni agrees to pay $234,000 ($126,000 plus 6,000 shares at $18 per share) for a company with a book value of equity equivalent to $168,000 ($560,000 × 30%) because it believes that (1) Wahlen's balance sheet is undervalued by $140,000 (Petroni estimates PPE with a remaining useful life of 9 years is undervalued by $50,000 and that Wahlen has unrecorded patents with remaining useful lives of 5 years, valued at $90,000) and (2) the investment will yield intangible benefits valued at $24,000. (The $140,000 by which the balance sheet is undervalued translates into an investment equivalent of $42,000 [$140,000 × 30%]; this, plus the intangible benefits valued at $24,000, comprises the $66,000 difference between the purchase price of $234,000 and the book value equivalent of $168,000.)

To record the investment, Petroni reduces cash and/or increases financing by $234,000 and creates a new asset account for the investment in Wahlen for $234,000. The investment is reported at its fair market value at acquisition, just like all other asset acquisitions, and it is reported as a noncurrent asset because investors typically expect to hold strategic equity method investments more than one year. Subsequent to this purchase there are four main aspects of equity method accounting:

1. Dividends received from the investee are treated as a return *of* the investment rather than a return *on* the investment (investor company records an increase in cash received and a decrease in the investment account). This mirrors the effect of dividends on the investee's equity—dividends decrease stockholders' equity and thus, they also decrease the equity method investment on the investor's balance sheet.
2. When the investee company reports net income for a period, the investor company reports its percentage share, typically as "Other income" in the income statement. Thus, the investor's equity and investment account both increase from equity method income. If the investee company reports a net *loss* for the period, the investor company reduces its own income as well as its investment account by its proportionate share of the loss.
3. When the purchase price exceeds the investor's share of the investee's book value of the equity, the excess is added to the investment account. To the extent it relates to identifiable assets, the excess must be depreciated (for tangible assets) and amortized (for intangibles) over the assets' lives. This reduces both the equity method income reported each year and the investment account.
4. The investment balance is not marked-to-market as with passive investments. Instead, it is recorded at its historical cost and is increased (decreased) by the investor company's proportionate share of investee income (loss) and decreased by any cash dividends received. Unrecognized gains (losses) will occur if the market value of the investment differs from this adjusted cost, but the investor will not change the balance sheet value of the investment (unless the decline in value is deemed permanent, at which time the investment is written down as with any impaired asset).

To illustrate these mechanics, assume that, subsequent to acquisition, Wahlen reports net income of $50,000 and pays $10,000 cash dividends. Petroni calculates extra depreciation of $3,000 on the additional PPE (the excess of $50,000 over the 5-year life × Petroni's 30% share of Wahlen) and extra amortization of $3,000 on the patents (the excess of $90,000 for patents with 9 year lives × 30%). Petroni reduces the equity income it reports on its income statement by a total of $6,000 and reduces its investment account on the balance sheet by $6,000. Petroni's balance sheet and income statement are impacted as follows:

| Transaction | Change in Investment Account on Petroni's Balance Sheet | Equity Income on Petroni's Income Statement |
|---|---|---|
| Acquisition balance . . . . . . . . . . . . . . . . . . . . . . . . . . . . | $234,000 | |
| Wahlen reports income of $50,000 (30% for Petroni). . . . . . . . . . . . . . . . . . . . . . . . . . | 15,000 | $15,000 |
| Depreciation and amortization of excess of purchase price over book value of identifiable assets. . . . . . . . . . . . . . . . . . . . . . . . . . . | (6,000) | (6,000) |
| Wahlen pays a $10,000 cash dividend ($3,000 to Petroni) . . . . . . . . . . . . . . . . . . . . . . . . . | (3,000)* | |
| Total . . . . . . . . . . . . . . . . . . . . . . . . . . . . . . . . . . . . . | $240,000 | $ 9,000 |

* Accompanied by an increase in cash.

Petroni's ending investment balance is $240,000, an increase of $6,000 and its cash balance increased by the $3,000 dividend received. Corresponding to the $9,000 increase in assets from Wahlen's income (adjusted by Petroni for the depreciation and amortization of the excess paid over book value) is a $9,000 increase in Petroni's retained earnings because Petroni reports $9,000 ($15,000 − $6,000) as investment income. Cash dividends received are treated as a return of the capital that Petroni invested in Wahlen and, thus, the investment account is reduced.

There is symmetry between Petroni's investment account and Wahlen's stockholders' equity as follows:

| Investment Account on Petroni's Balance Sheet | | Wahlen's Stockholders' Equity | |
|---|---|---|---|
| Acquisition balance . . . . . . . . . . . | $234,000 | Acquisition balance . . . . . . . . . . . . | $560,000 |
| Income . . . . . . . . . . . . . . . . . . . . . | 9,000 | Income . . . . . . . . . . . . . . . . . . . . . | 50,000 |
| Dividends . . . . . . . . . . . . . . . . . . | (3,000) | Dividends . . . . . . . . . . . . . . . . . . | (10,000) |
| Ending balance. . . . . . . . . . . . . . . | $240,000 | Ending balance. . . . . . . . . . . . . . . | $600,000 |

Petroni's ending investment balance of $240,000 is 30% of Wahlen's $600,000 stockholders' equity plus the original $66,000 excess less the depreciation/amortization of the excess of $6,000. The balance of the excess is therefore $60,000 at the end of the period, and it will shrink over time as Petroni continues to depreciate and amortize it. This excess explains why the equity investment balance we see reported on a balance sheet does not always equal the percentage owned of the investee company.

# APPENDIX 7B: Consolidation Accounting Mechanics

This appendix extends the example we introduced in Appendix 7A, to include the consolidation of a parent company and one wholly owned subsidiary. Assume that Petroni Company acquires 100 percent (rather than 30% as in Appendix 7A) of the outstanding voting shares of Wahlen Company on January 1, 2005. To obtain these shares, Petroni pays $420,000 cash and issues 20,000 shares of its $10 par value common stock. On this date, Petroni's stock has a fair market value of $18 per share, and Wahlen's book value of equity is $560,000. Petroni is willing to pay $780,000 ($420,000 plus 20,000 shares at $18 per share) for this company with a book value of equity of $560,000 because it believes Wahlen's balance sheet is understated by $140,000 (PPE with 5 years of remaining useful life is undervalued by $50,000 and it has unrecorded patents that expire in 9 years, valued at $90,000). The remaining $80,000 of the purchase price excess over book value is ascribed to corporate synergies and other unidentifiable intangible assets (goodwill). Thus, the purchase price consists of the following three components:

Investment
($780,000)
{
Book value of Wahlen ($560,000)

Excess fair market value over book value ($140,000)

Goodwill ($80,000)
}

On its own (unconsolidated) balance sheet, Petroni uses the equity method of accounting to account for the Wahlen acquisition.[4] This means that, at acquisition, Petroni's assets (investments) increase by $780,000, cash decreases by $420,000, and contributed capital increases by $360,000 (20,000 shares $\times$ $18). The balance sheets of Petroni and Wahlen at acquisition follow, including the adjustments that occur in the consolidation process and the ultimate consolidated balance sheet.

| Accounts | Petroni Company | Wahlen Company | Consolidation Adjustments* | | Consolidated Balance Sheet |
|---|---|---|---|---|---|
| Cash. . . . . . . . . . . . . . . . . . . | $ 168,000 | $ 80,000 | | | $ 248,000 |
| Receivables, net. . . . . . . . . . | 320,000 | 180,000 | | | 500,000 |
| Inventory. . . . . . . . . . . . . . . . | 440,000 | 260,000 | | | 700,000 |
| Investment in Wahlen. . . . . . | 780,000 | 0 | [S] | (560,000) | 0 |
| | | | [A] | (220,000) | |
| Land . . . . . . . . . . . . . . . . . . . | 200,000 | 120,000 | | | 320,000 |
| PPE, net . . . . . . . . . . . . . . . . | 1,040,000 | 320,000 | [A] | 50,000 | 1,410,000 |
| Patent. . . . . . . . . . . . . . . . . . | 0 | 0 | [A] | 90,000 | 90,000 |
| Goodwill . . . . . . . . . . . . . . . . | 0 | 0 | [A] | 80,000 | 80,000 |
| Totals . . . . . . . . . . . . . . . . . | $2,948,000 | $960,000 | | | $3,348,000 |
| Accounts payable. . . . . . . . . | $ 320,000 | $ 60,000 | | | $ 380,000 |
| Long-term liabilities . . . . . . . | 760,000 | 340,000 | | | 1,100,000 |
| Contributed capital. . . . . . . . | 1,148,000 | 80,000 | [S] | (80,000) | 1,148,000 |
| Retained earnings . . . . . . . . | 720,000 | 480,000 | [S] | (480,000) | 720,000 |
| Totals . . . . . . . . . . . . . . . . . | $2,948,000 | $960,000 | | | $3,348,000 |

*[S] refers to elimination of stockholders' equity and [A] refers to recognition of assets acquired.

---

[4] The equity method is used for all investments other than passive investments. Once "control" is achieved, the investor company is required to consolidate its financial statements. The investment account remains unchanged on the parent's books, it is merely replaced with the assets and liabilities of the subsidiaries to which it relates during the consolidation process.

The initial balance of the investment account at acquisition ($780,000) reflects the $700,000 market value of Wahlen's net tangible and intangible (patent) assets ($560,000 book value and the $140,000 undervaluation of the net assets) plus the goodwill ($80,000) acquired. Goodwill is the excess of the purchase price over the fair market of the net assets acquired. Neither the patent nor the goodwill appear on Petroni's balance sheet as explicit assets. They are, however, included in the investment balance, and will emerge as a separate asset during consolidation.

The process of completing the initial consolidated balance sheet involves eliminating the investment account and replacing it with the assets and liabilities of Wahlen Company to which it relates. Recall the investment account consists of three items: the book value of Wahlen ($560,000), the excess of market price over book value ($140,000), and goodwill ($80,000). The consolidation process eliminates each item as follows:

[S]   Elimination of Wahlen's book value of equity: Investment account is reduced by the $560,000 book value of Wahlen, and each of the components of Wahlen's equity ($80,000 common stock and $480,000 retained earnings) are eliminated.

[A]   Elimination of the excess of purchase price over book value: Investment account is reduced by $220,000. The remaining adjustments increase assets (A) by the additional purchase price paid. PPE is written up by $50,000, and a $90,000 patent asset and an $80,000 goodwill asset are reported.

Consolidation is similar in successive periods. To the extent that the excess purchase price has been assigned to depreciable assets, or identifiable intangible assets that are amortized over their useful lives, the new assets recognized initially are depreciated. For example, if the PPE has an estimated life of 10 years with no salvage value, Petroni would add $10,000 to depreciation expense on the consolidated income statement. This would reduce the consolidated PPE. Likewise, the $90,000 patent is amortized over its remaining life of nine years and thus, consolidated amortization expense is increased by $10,000 a year. Recall from Appendix 7A, above, that Petroni reduces its investment in Wahlen for its share of the extra depreciation and amortization each year. Here, that would be for the entire amount because Petroni owns 100% of Wahlen. Finally, since goodwill is not amortized under GAAP, it remains at its carrying amount of $80,000 on the consolidated balance sheet unless and until it is impaired and written down.

As the excess of the purchase price over book value acquired is depreciated/amortized, the investment account on Petroni's balance sheet gradually declines. Assuming goodwill is not impaired, the investment reaches a balance equal to the percentage of the investee's equity owned (100% in this case) plus the balance of goodwill. Generally, the investment account equals the percentage of the equity owned plus any remaining undepreciated/unamortized excess over purchase price.

# APPENDIX 7C: Accounting for Derivatives

**Derivatives** refer to financial instruments that companies use to reduce various kinds of risks. Some examples follow:

- A company expects to purchase raw materials for its production process and wants to reduce the risk that the purchase price increases prior to the purchase.
- A company has an accounts receivable on its books that is payable in a foreign currency and wants to reduce the risk that exchange rates move unfavorably prior to collection.
- A company borrows funds on a floating rate of interest (such as linked to the prime rate) and wants to convert the loan to a fixed interest rate.

Companies are routinely exposed to these and many other risks. Although companies are generally willing to assume the normal market risks that are inherent in their business, financial-type risks can add variability to income because they are uncontrollable. Fortunately, commodities, currencies, and interest rates are all traded on various markets and, further, securities have been developed to manage all of these risks. These securities, called derivatives, include forward contracts, futures contracts, option contracts, and swap agreements.

Companies use derivatives to manage (hedge) financial risks. But risk reduction comes at a price: another party (called the counterparty) charges a fee to assume the company's financial risk. Most counterparties are financial institutions, and managing financial risk is their business and is a source of their profits. Although derivatives can be used effectively to manage financial risk, they can also be used for speculation with potentially disastrous results. It is for this reason that regulators passed standards regarding derivative disclosure in financial statements.

## Reporting of Derivatives

Derivatives work by offsetting gains or losses on the related (hedged) assets or liabilities. Derivatives shelter the company from fluctuations in the value of the related assets or liabilities that are hedged. For example, if a company has a receivable denominated in a foreign currency, which later declines in value (due to a strengthening of the $US), the company will incur a foreign currency loss. To avoid this situation, the company can hedge the receivable with a foreign-currency derivative. When the $US strengthens, the derivative will increase in value by an amount that exactly offsets the decrease in the value of the receivable. As a result, the company's net asset position (receivable less derivative) remains unaffected and no gain or loss arises.[5]

Although accounting for derivatives is complex, it essentially boils down to this: the derivative contract, and the asset or liability to being hedged, are both reported on the balance sheet at market value. If the market value of the hedged asset or liability changes, the value of the derivative changes in the opposite direction *if* the hedge is effective and, thus, net assets and liabilities are unaffected. Likewise, the related gains and losses are largely offsetting, leaving income unaffected. Income is impacted only to the extent that the hedging activities are ineffective or result from speculative activities. It is this latter activity, in particular, that prompted regulators to formulate newer, tougher accounting standards for derivatives.

## Disclosure of Derivatives

Companies must disclose both qualitative and quantitative information about derivatives in notes to their financial statements and elsewhere (usually in Management's Discussion and Analysis section). The aim of these disclosures is to inform outsiders about potential risks associated with derivative use.

Following is Southwest Airlines's disclosures from its 2005 10-K report relating to its use of derivatives:

> **Financial Derivative Instruments** The Company utilizes financial derivative instruments primarily to manage its risk associated with changing jet fuel prices, and accounts for them under Statement of Financial Accounting Standards No. 133, "Accounting for Derivative Instruments and Hedging Activities", as amended (SFAS 133) . . . SFAS 133 requires that all derivatives be marked to market (fair value) and recorded on the Consolidated Balance Sheet. At December 31, 2005, the Company was a party to over 400 financial derivative instruments, related to fuel hedging, for year 2006 and beyond. The fair value of the Company's fuel hedging financial derivative instruments recorded on the Company's Consolidated Balance Sheet as of December 31, 2005, was $1.7 billion, compared to $796 million at December 31, 2004. The large increase in fair value primarily was due to the dramatic increase in energy prices throughout 2005, and the Company's addition of derivative instruments to increase its hedge positions in future years. Changes in the fair values of these instruments can vary dramatically, as was evident during 2005, based on changes in the underlying commodity prices . . . The Company enters into financial derivative instruments with third party institutions in "over-the-counter" markets. Since the majority of the Company's financial derivative instruments are not traded on a market exchange, the Company estimates their fair values . . . To the extent that the total change in the estimated fair value of a fuel hedging instrument differs from the change in the estimated price of the associated jet fuel to be purchased, both on a cumulative and a period-to-period basis, ineffectiveness of the fuel hedge can result, as defined by SFAS 133. This could result in the immediate recording of noncash charges or income, even though the derivative instrument may not expire until a future period . . . Ineffectiveness is inherent in hedging jet fuel with derivative positions based in other crude oil-related commodities, especially considering the recent volatility in the prices of refined products. In addition, given the magnitude of the Company's fuel hedge portfolio total market value, ineffectiveness can be highly material to financial results . . . This may result in increased volatility in the Company's results.

Southwest Airlines uses derivatives mainly to hedge fuel costs. Those hedges place a ceiling on fuel cost and are used for 30% to 60% of Southwest Airlines' fuel purchases.

These derivatives are cash flow hedges. Thus, unrealized gains and losses on these derivative contracts are added to the Accumulated Other Comprehensive Income (AOCI) (part of stockholders' equity) until the fuel is purchased. Once that fuel is purchased, any unrealized gains and losses are removed from AOCI to income. The gain (loss) on the derivative contract offsets the increased (decreased) cost of fuel. In 2005, $900 million of hedging gains were used to offset fuel expense for Southwest Airlines. This use of fuel derivatives is the prime reason that soaring oil prices in that year did not affect Southwest Airlines as harshly as at other large carriers.

Although the market value of derivatives and their related assets or liabilities can be large, the net effect on stockholders' equity is usually minor. This is because companies use derivatives mainly to hedge and not to speculate. The FASB enacted SFAS 133, 'Accounting for derivative instruments and hedging activities,' to respond to concerns that speculative activities were not adequately disclosed. However, subsequent to the passage of SFAS 133, the financial effects have been minimal. Either companies were not speculating to the extent suspected, or they have since reduced their level of speculation in response to increased scrutiny from better disclosures.

---

[5] Unrealized gains and losses on derivatives classified as *cash flow hedges* (such as those relating to planned purchases of commodities) are included in accumulated other comprehensive income (OCI) and are not recognized in income until the planned transaction is complete (such as when the purchase of inventory occurs). Unrealized gains and losses on derivatives classified as *fair value hedges* (including those relating to existing assets or liabilities such as inventory or debt) are recorded in current income along with the changes in value of the hedged asset or liability.

# GUIDANCE ANSWERS

Capacity utilization is important. If long-term operating assets are used inefficiently, cost per unit produced is too high. Cost per unit does not relate solely to manufacturing products, but also applies to the cost of providing services and many other operating activities. However, if we purchase assets with little productive slack, our costs of production at peak levels can be excessive. Further, the company may be unable to service peak demand and risks losing customers. In response, the company might explore strategic alliances. These take many forms. Some require a simple contract to use another company's manufacturing, service, or administrative capability for a fee (note: these executory contracts are not recorded under GAAP). Another type of alliance is that of a joint venture to share ownership of manufacturing or IT facilities. In this case, if demand can be coordinated with that of a partner, perhaps operating assets can be more effectively used. Finally, a variable interest entity (VIE) can be formed to acquire the asset for use by the company and its partner—explained in Module 10.

---

Superscript $^{A(B,C)}$ denotes assignments based on Appendix 7A (7B, 7C).

# DISCUSSION QUESTIONS

**Q7-1.** What measure (fair market value or amortized cost) is on the balance sheet for (a) trading securities, (b) available-for-sale securities, and (c) held-to-maturity securities?

**Q7-2.** What is an unrealized holding gain (loss)? Explain.

**Q7-3.** Where are unrealized holding gains and losses related to trading securities reported in the financial statements? Where are unrealized holding gains and losses related to available-for-sale securities reported in the financial statements?

**Q7-4.** What does *significant influence* imply regarding intercorporate investments? Describe the accounting procedures used for such investments.

**Q7-5.** On January 1 of the current year, Yetman Company purchases 40% of the common stock of Livnat Company for $250,000 cash. This 40% ownership allows Yetman to exert significant influence over Livnat. During the year, Livnat reports $80,000 of net income and pays $60,000 in cash dividends. At year-end, what amount should appear in Yetman's balance sheet for its investment in Livnat?

**Q7-6.** What accounting method is used when a stock investment represents more than 50% of the investee company's voting stock and allows the investor company to "control" the investee company? Explain.

**Q7-7.** What is the underlying objective of consolidated financial statements?

**Q7-8.** Finn Company purchases all of the common stock of Murray Company for $750,000 when Murray Company has $300,000 of common stock and $450,000 of retained earnings. If a consolidated balance sheet is prepared immediately after the acquisition, what amounts are eliminated in consolidation? Explain.

**Q7-9.** Bradshaw Company owns 100% of Dee Company. At year-end, Dee owes Bradshaw $75,000 arising from a loan made during the year. If a consolidated balance sheet is prepared at year-end, how is the $75,000 handled? Explain.

**Q7-10.** What are some limitations of consolidated financial statements?

# MINI EXERCISES

**M7-11.** **Interpreting Disclosures of Available-for-Sale Securities** **(LO1)**

Pfizer Inc. (PFE)

Use the following year-end footnote disclosure from Pfizer's 10-K report to answer parts *a* and *b*.

| (Millions of Dollars) | 2005 |
| --- | --- |
| Cost of available-for-sale equity securities . . . . . . . . . | $270 |
| Gross unrealized gains. . . . . . . . . . . . . . . . . . . . . . . . | 189 |
| Gross unrealized losses . . . . . . . . . . . . . . . . . . . . . . . | (12) |
| Fair value of available-for-sale equity securities . . . . . | $447 |

a. What amount does Pfizer report on its 2005 balance sheet as available-for-sale equity securities? Explain.

b. How does Pfizer report the net unrealized gain of $177 million ($189 million − $12 million) in its financial statements?

**M7-12. Accounting for Available-for-Sale and Trading Securities** (LO1)
Assume that Wasley Company purchases 6,000 common shares of Pincus Company for $12 cash per share. During the year, Wasley receives a cash dividend of $1.10 per common share from Pincus, and the year-end market price of Pincus common stock is $13 per share. How much income does Wasley report relating to this investment for the year if it accounts for the investment as:

a. Available-for-sale investment

b. Trading investment

**M7-13. Interpreting Disclosures of Investment Securities** (LO1)
Abbott Laboratories reports the following disclosure relating to its December 31 comprehensive income. How is Abbott accounting for its investment in marketable equity securities? How do you know? Explain how its 2005 financial statements are impacted by its investment in marketable equity securities.

Abbott Laboratories (ABT)

| Comprehensive Income, net of tax ($ 000s) | 2005 |
|---|---|
| Foreign currency translation adjustments | $ (953,726) |
| Minimum pension liability adjustments, net of taxes of $57,219 | 346,172 |
| Unrealized (losses) gains on marketable equity securities | (9,219) |
| Net (losses) gains on derivative instruments designated as cash flow hedges | 38,574 |
| Reclassification adjustments for realized (gains) | (35) |
| Other comprehensive income | (578,234) |
| Net earnings | 3,372,065 |
| Comprehensive income | $2,793,831 |

**M7-14. Analyzing and Interpreting Equity Method Investments** (LO2)
Stober Company purchases an investment in Lang Company at a purchase price of $1 million cash, representing 30% of the book value of Lang. During the year, Lang reports net income of $100,000 and pays cash dividends of $40,000. At the end of the year, the market value of Stober's investment is $1.2 million.

a. What amount does Stober report on its balance sheet for its investment in Lang?

b. What amount of income from investments does Stober report? Explain.

c. Stober's $200,000 unrealized gain in the market value of the Lang investment (choose one and explain):
   (1) Is not reflected on either its income statement or balance sheet.
   (2) Is reported in its current income.
   (3) Is reported on its balance sheet only.
   (4) Is reported in its other comprehensive income.

**M7-15. Computing Income for Equity Method Investments** (LO2)
Kross Company purchases an equity investment in Penno Company at a purchase price of $5 million, representing 40% of the book value of Penno. During the current year, Penno reports net income of $600,000 and pays cash dividends of $200,000. At the end of the year, the market value of Kross's investment is $5.3 million. What amount of income does Kross report relating to this investment in Penno for the year? Explain.

**M7-16. Interpreting Disclosures on Investments in Affiliates** (LO2)
Merck's 10-K report included the following footnote disclosure:

Merck & Co., Inc. (MRK)

> **Joint Ventures and Other Equity Method Affiliates** Investments in affiliates accounted for using the equity method . . . totaled $3 billion at December 31, 2005. These amounts are reported in Other assets. Dividends and distributions received from these affiliates were $1.1 billion in 2005.

a. At what amount are the equity method investments reported on Merck's balance sheet? Does this amount represent Merck's adjusted cost or market value?

b. How does Merck account for the dividends received on these investments?

**M7-17. Computing Consolidating Adjustments and Minority Interest** (LO3)

Philipich Company purchases 80% of Hirst Company's common stock for $600,000 cash when Hirst Company has $300,000 of common stock and $450,000 of retained earnings. If a consolidated balance sheet is prepared immediately after the acquisition, what amounts are eliminated when preparing that statement? What amount of minority interest appears in the consolidated balance sheet?

**M7-18. Computing Consolidated Net Income** (LO3)

Benartzi Company purchased a 90% interest in Liang Company on January 1 of the current year and the purchase price reflected 90% of Liang's net book value of equity. Benartzi Company had $600,000 net income for the current year *before* recognizing its share of Liang Company's net income. If Liang Company had net income of $150,000 for the year, what is the consolidated net income for the year?

**M7-19. Computing Earnings under Pooling-of-Interest Method** (LO3)

DeFond Company acquired 100% of Verduzco Company on September 1 of the current year. Why might the consolidated earnings of the two companies for the current year be higher if DeFond had treated the transaction as a pooling-of-interest (which is no longer accepted under GAAP for new acquisitions, but is allowed for acquisitions made prior to the effective date of the new business combinations standard) rather than as a purchase?

# EXERCISES

**E7-20. Assessing Financial Statement Effects of Trading and Available-for-Sale Securities** (LO1)

a. Use the financial statement effects template to record the following four transactions involving investments in marketable securities classified as trading.
  (1) Purchased 6,000 common shares of Liu, Inc., for $12 cash per share.
  (2) Received a cash dividend of $1.10 per common share from Liu.
  (3) Year-end market price of Liu common stock was $11.25 per share.
  (4) Sold all 6,000 common shares of Liu for $66,900.

b. Using the same transaction information as above, complete the financial statement effects template (with amounts and accounts) assuming the investments in marketable securities are classified as available-for-sale.

**E7-21. Assessing Financial Statement Effects of Trading and Available-for-Sale Securities** (LO1)

Use the financial statement effects template to record the accounts and amounts for the following four transactions involving investments in marketable securities:
  (1) Ohlson Co. purchases 5,000 common shares of Freeman Co. at $16 cash per share.
  (2) Ohlson Co. receives a cash dividend of $1.25 per common share from Freeman.
  (3) Year-end market price of Freeman common stock is $17.50 per share.
  (4) Ohlson Co. sells all 5,000 common shares of Freeman for $86,400 cash.

a. Assume the investments are classified as trading.
b. Assume the investments are classified as available-for-sale.

**E7-22. Interpreting Footnotes on Security Investments** (LO1)

Berkshire Hathaway
(BRKA)

Berkshire Hathaway reports the following footnotes with its 10-K report ($ millions).

| Years Ended December 31 | 2005 | 2004 | 2003 |
|---|---|---|---|
| **Accumulated Other Comprehensive Income** | | | |
| Unrealized appreciation of investments............................ | $ 2,081 | $ 2,599 | $10,842 |
|    Applicable income taxes..................................... | (728) | (905) | (3,802) |
| Reclassification adjustment for appreciation | | | |
|    included in net earnings.................................... | (6,261) | (1,569) | (2,922) |
|    Applicable income taxes..................................... | 2,191 | 549 | 1,023 |
| Foreign currency translation adjustments ...................... | (359) | 140 | 267 |
|    Applicable income taxes..................................... | (26) | 134 | (127) |
| Minimum pension liability adjustment ......................... | (62) | (38) | 1 |
|    Applicable income taxes..................................... | 38 | 3 | (3) |
| Other, including minority interests ........................... | 51 | (34) | 6 |
| Other comprehensive income ............................... | (3,075) | 879 | 5,285 |
| Accumulated other comprehensive income at beginning of year .... | 20,435 | 19,556 | 14,271 |
| Accumulated other comprehensive income at end of year ......... | $17,360 | $20,435 | $19,556 |

Data with respect to investments in equity securities are shown below. Amounts are in millions.

| December 31, 2005 | Cost | Unrealized Gains/losses | Fair Value |
|---|---|---|---|
| American Express Company.......... | $ 1,287 | $ 6,515 | $ 7,802 |
| The Coca-Cola Company ............. | 1,299 | 6,763 | 8,062 |
| The Proctor & Gamble Company ....... | 5,963 | (175) | 5,788 |
| Wells Fargo & Company............... | 2,754 | 3,221 | 5,975 |
| Other............................ | 10,036 | 9,058 | 19,094 |
| | $21,339 | $25,382 | $46,721 |

American Express Company (AXP)

The Coca-Cola Company (KO)

Proctor & Gamble Company (PG)

Wells Fargo & Company (WFC)

*a.* At what amount does Berkshire Hathaway report its equity securities investment portfolio on its balance sheet? Does that amount include any unrealized gains or losses? Explain.

*b.* How is Berkshire Hathaway accounting for its equity securities investment portfolio—as an available-for-sale or trading portfolio? How do you know?

*c.* What does the number $2,081 represent in the Accumulated Other Comprehensive Income footnote? Is this number pretax or after-tax? Explain.

**E7-23.** **Interpreting Footnote Disclosures for Investments** **(LO1)**

CNA Financial Corporation provides the following footnote to its 2005 10-K report.

CNA Financial Corporation (CNA)

**Valuation of investments:** CNA classifies its fixed maturity securities (bonds and redeemable preferred stocks) and its equity securities as available-for-sale, and as such, they are carried at fair value. The amortized cost of fixed maturity securities is adjusted for amortization of premiums and accretion of discounts to maturity, which are included in net investment income. Changes in fair value are reported as a component of other comprehensive income. Investments are written down to fair value and losses are recognized in income when a decline in value is determined to be other-than-temporary.

## Summary of Fixed Maturity and Equity Securities

| December 31, 2005 (In millions) | Cost or Amortized Cost | Gross Unrealized Gains | Gross Unrealized Losses Less than 12 Months | Gross Unrealized Losses Greater than 12 Months | Estimated Fair Value |
|---|---|---|---|---|---|
| Fixed maturity securities available-for-sale | | | | | |
| U.S. Treasury securities and obligations of government agencies ................... | $ 1,355 | $ 119 | $ 4 | $ 1 | $ 1,469 |
| Asset-backed securities ......... | 12,986 | 43 | 137 | 33 | 12,859 |
| States, municipalities and political subdivisions—tax-exempt ..... | 9,054 | 193 | 31 | 7 | 9,209 |
| Corporate securities ............ | 5,906 | 322 | 52 | 11 | 6,165 |
| Other debt securities ........... | 2,830 | 234 | 18 | 2 | 3,044 |
| Redeemable preferred stock ..... | 213 | 4 | — | 1 | 216 |
| Options embedded in convertible debt securities.............. | 1 | — | — | — | 1 |
| Total fixed maturity securities..... | 32,345 | 915 | 242 | 55 | 32,963 |
| Total fixed maturity securities trading ..................... | 271 | — | — | — | 271 |
| Equity securities available-for-sale | | | | | |
| Common stock................ | 140 | 150 | 1 | — | 289 |
| Preferred stock............... | 322 | 22 | 1 | — | 343 |
| Total equity securities available-for-sale............. | 462 | 172 | 2 | — | 632 |
| Total equity securities trading....... | 49 | — | — | — | 49 |
| Total ........................ | $33,127 | $1,087 | $244 | $55 | $33,915 |

    *a.*  At what amount does CNA report its investment portfolio on its balance sheet? In your answer identify the portfolio's market value, cost, and any unrealized gains and losses.

    *b.*  How do CNA's balance sheet and income statement reflect any unrealized gains and/or losses on the investment portfolio?

    *c.*  How do CNA's balance sheet and income statement reflect gains and losses realized from the sale of available-for-sale securities?

**E7-24.** **Assessing Financial Statement Effects of Equity Method Securities** **(LO2)**

Use the financial statement effects template (with amounts and accounts) to record the following transactions involving investments in marketable securities accounted for using the equity method:

    *a.*  Purchased 12,000 common shares of Barth Co. at $9 per share; the shares represent 30% ownership in Barth.

    *b.*  Received a cash dividend of $1.25 per common share from Barth.

    *c.*  Barth reported annual net income of $80,000.

    *d.*  Sold all 12,000 common shares of Barth for $120,500.

**E7-25.** **Assessing Financial Statement Effects of Equity Method Securities** **(LO2)**

Use the financial statement effects template (with amounts and accounts) to record the following transactions involving investments in marketable securities accounted for using the equity method:

    *a.*  Healy Co. purchases 15,000 common shares of Palepu Co. at $8 per share; the shares represent 25% ownership of Palepu.

    *b.*  Healy receives a cash dividend of $0.80 per common share from Palepu.

    *c.*  Palepu reports annual net income of $120,000.

    *d.*  Healy sells all 15,000 common shares of Palepu for $140,000.

**E7-26.** **Assessing Financial Statement Effects of Passive and Equity Method Investments** **(LO1, 2)**

On January 1, 2007, Ball Corporation purchased shares of Leftwich Company common stock.

    *a.*  Assume that the stock acquired by Ball represents 15% of Leftwich's voting stock and that Ball classifies the investment as available-for-sale. Use the financial statement effects template (with amounts and accounts) to record the following transactions:

        (1)  Ball purchased 10,000 common shares of Leftwich at $15 cash per share; the shares represent a 15% ownership in Leftwich.

        (2)  Leftwich reported annual net income of $80,000.

        (3)  Ball received a cash dividend of $1.10 per common share from Leftwich.

        (4)  Year-end market price of Leftwich common stock is $19 per share.

    *b.*  Assume that the stock acquired by Ball represents 30% of Leftwich's voting stock and that Ball accounts for this investment using the equity method since it is able to exert significant influence. Use the financial statement effects template (with amounts and accounts) to record the following transactions:

        (1)  Ball purchased 10,000 common shares of Leftwich at $15 cash per share; the shares represent a 30% ownership in Leftwich.

        (2)  Leftwich reported annual net income of $80,000.

        (3)  Ball received a cash dividend of $1.10 per common share from Leftwich.

        (4)  Year-end market price of Leftwich common stock is $19 per share.

**E7-27.** **Interpreting Equity Method Investment Footnotes** **(LO2)**

DuPont (DD)

DuPont's 2005 10-K report includes information relating to the company's equity method investments ($ millions). The following footnote reports summary balance sheets for affiliated companies for which DuPont uses the equity method of accounting. The information below is shown on a 100 percent basis followed by the carrying value of DuPont's investment in these affiliates.

| Financial Position at December 31 (in millions) | 2005 | 2004 |
|---|---|---|
| Current assets | $1,292 | $1,972 |
| Noncurrent assets | 1,780 | 2,811 |
|     Total assets | $3,072 | $4,783 |
| Short-term borrowings | $606 | $734 |
| Other current liabilities | 621 | 932 |
| Long-term borrowings | 259 | 716 |
| Other long-term liabilities | 111 | 305 |
|     Total liabilities | $1,597 | $2,687 |
| DuPont's investment in affiliates (includes advances of $55 and $84, respectively) | $ 844 | $1,034 |

a.   DuPont reports its investment in equity method affiliates on its balance sheet at $844 million. Does this reflect the adjusted cost or market value of DuPont's interest in these companies?

b.   What is the total stockholders' equity of the affiliates at the end of 2005? What is the carrying (book value) of DuPont's investment without the advances, at the end of 2005? Approximately what percentage does DuPont own, on average, of these affiliates? Explain.

c.   DuPont reports that its equity interest in reported profits of these affiliates is approximately $108 million in 2005, and that it received $107 million in dividends from these affiliates in 2005. It also reports the sale of an affiliate with an equity investment balance of $162. Use this information, and the footnote above, to explain the change in the investment account from $950 million in 2004 to $789 million (net of advances) in 2005.

d.   How does use of the equity method impact DuPont's ROE and its RNOA components (net operating asset turnover and net operating profit margin)?

**E7-28.  Analyzing and Interpreting Disclosures on Equity Method Investments   (LO2)**

Caterpillar, Inc. (CAT) reports investments in affiliated companies, consisting mainly of its 50% ownership of Shin Caterpillar Mitsubishi, Ltd. Caterpillar reports those investments on its balance sheet at $565 million, and provides the following footnote in its 10-K report.

**Caterpillar, Inc. (CAT)**
**Shin Caterpillar Mitsubishi, Ltd.**

**Investment in unconsolidated affiliated companies** Our investment in affiliated companies accounted for by the equity method consists primarily of a 50% interest in Shin Caterpillar Mitsubishi Ltd. (SCM) located in Japan. Combined financial information of the unconsolidated affiliated companies accounted for by the equity method (generally on a three-month lag, e.g., SCM results reflect the periods ending September 30) was as follows:

| Years Ended December 31 (Millions of Dollars) | 2005 | 2004 | 2003 |
|---|---|---|---|
| Results of operations | | | |
| Sales. | $4,140 | $3,628 | $2,946 |
| Cost of sales. | 3,257 | 2,788 | 2,283 |
| Gross profit. | 883 | 840 | 663 |
| Profit. | $ 161 | $ 129 | $ 48 |
| Caterpillar's profit. | $ 73 | $ 59 | $ 20 |

| December 31 (Millions of Dollars) | 2005 | 2004 | 2003 |
|---|---|---|---|
| Financial position | | | |
| Assets | | | |
| Current assets. | $1,714 | $1,540 | $1,494 |
| Property, plant and equipment—net. | 1,121 | 1,097 | 961 |
| Other assets | 193 | 145 | 202 |
| | 3,028 | 2,782 | 2,657 |
| Liabilities | | | |
| Current liabilities | 1,351 | 1,345 | 1,247 |
| Long-term debt due after one year. | 336 | 276 | 343 |
| Other liabilities. | 188 | 214 | 257 |
| | 1,875 | 1,835 | 1,847 |
| Ownership. | $1,153 | $ 947 | $ 810 |

| Caterpillar's investment in unconsolidated affiliated companies (Millions of Dollars) | | | |
|---|---|---|---|
| Investment in equity method companies | $ 540 | $ 487 | $ 432 |
| Plus: Investment in cost method companies | 25 | 30 | 368 |
| Investment in unconsolidated affiliated companies | $ 565 | $ 517 | $ 800 |

Certain investments in unconsolidated affiliated companies are accounted for using the cost method.

a. What assets and liabilities of unconsolidated affiliates are omitted from CAT's balance sheet as a result of the equity method of accounting for those investments?

b. Do the liabilities of the unconsolidated affiliates affect CAT directly? Explain.

c. How does the equity method impact CAT's ROE and its RNOA components (net operating asset turnover and net operating profit margin)?

**E7-29.** **Reporting and Interpreting Stock Investment Performance** (LO1)

Kasznik Company began operations in 2007 and, by year-end (December 31), had made six stock investments. Year-end information on these stock investments follows.

| December 31, 2007 | Cost or Equity Basis (as appropriate) | Year-End Market Value | Market Classification |
|---|---|---|---|
| Barth, Inc. ............... | $ 68,000 | $ 65,300 | Trading |
| Foster, Inc. ............... | 162,500 | 160,000 | Trading |
| McNichols, Inc. ........... | 197,000 | 192,000 | Available-for-sale |
| Patell, Inc. ............... | 157,000 | 154,700 | Available-for-sale |
| Ertimur, Inc. .............. | 100,000 | 102,400 | Equity method |
| Soliman, Inc. ............. | 136,000 | 133,200 | Equity method |

a. What does Kaznik's balance sheet report for trading stock investments at December 31, 2007?

b. What does Kaznik's balance sheet report for available-for-sale stock investments at December 31, 2007?

c. What does Kaznik's balance sheet report for equity method stock investments at December 31, 2007?

d. What total amount of unrealized holding gains or unrealized holding losses related to stock investments appear in Kasnik's 2007 income statement?

e. What total amount of unrealized holding gains or unrealized holding losses related to stock investments appear in the stockholders' equity section of Kasnik's December 31, 2007, balance sheet?

f. What total amount of market value adjustment to stock investments appears in the December 31, 2007, balance sheet? Which category of stock investments does the market value adjustment relate to? Does the market value adjustment increase or decrease the carrying value of these stock investments?

**E7-30.** **Interpreting Equity Method Investment Footnotes** (LO2)

AT&T, Inc. (T)

AT&T reports the following footnote to its 2005 10-K report.

**Equity Method Investments** We account for our nationwide wireless joint venture, Cingular, and our investments in equity affiliates under the equity method of accounting. The following table is a reconciliation of our investments in and advances to Cingular as presented on our Consolidated Balance Sheets.

| | 2005 | 2004 |
|---|---|---|
| Beginning of year ........ | $33,687 | $11,003 |
| Contributions ........... | — | 21,688 |
| Equity in net income...... | 200 | 30 |
| Other adjustments ....... | (2,483) | 966 |
| End of year ............ | $31,404 | $33,687 |

Undistributed earnings from Cingular were $2,711 and $2,511 at December 31, 2005 and 2004. "Other adjustments" in 2005 included the net activity of $2,442 under our revolving credit agreement with Cingular, consisting of a reduction of $1,747 (reflecting Cingular's repayment of their shareholder loan during 2005) and a decrease of $695 (reflecting Cingular's net repayment of their revolving credit balance during 2005). During 2004, we made an equity contribution to Cingular in connection with its acquisition of AT&T Wireless. "Other adjustments" in 2004 included the net activity of $972 under our revolving credit agreement with Cingular, consisting of a reduction of $30 (reflecting Cingular's repayment of advances during 2004) and an increase of $1,002 (reflecting the December 31, 2004 balance of advances to Cingular under this revolving credit agreement).

We account for our 60% economic interest in Cingular under the equity method of accounting in our consolidated financial statements since we share control equally (i.e., 50/50) with our 40% economic partner in the joint venture. We have equal voting rights and representation on the Board of Directors that controls Cingular. The following table presents summarized financial information for Cingular at December 31, or for the year then ended.

| | 2005 | 2004 | 2003 |
|---|---|---|---|
| Income Statements | | | |
| Operating revenues . . . | $34,433 | $19,565 | $15,577 |
| Operating income . . . . . | 1,824 | 1,528 | 2,254 |
| Net income . . . . . . . . . | 333 | 201 | 977 |
| Balance Sheets | | | |
| Current assets . . . . . . . | $ 6,049 | $ 5,570 | |
| Noncurrent assets . . . . . | 73,270 | 76,668 | |
| Current liabilities . . . . . . | 10,008 | 7,983 | |
| Noncurrent liabilities . . . | 24,333 | 29,719 | |

We have made a subordinated loan to Cingular that totaled $4,108 and $5,855 at December 31, 2005 and 2004, which matures in June 2008. This loan bears interest at an annual rate of 6.0%. During 2005, Cingular repaid $1,747 to reduce the balance of this loan in accordance with the terms of a revolving credit agreement. We earned interest income on this loan of $311 during 2005, $354 in 2004 and $397 in 2003. This interest income does not have a material impact on our net income as it is mostly offset when we record our share of equity income in Cingular.

a. At what amount is the equity investment in Cingular reported on AT&T's balance sheet? (*Hint:* the table in the footnote reports AT&T's equity investment plus its "advances" of $4,108 to Cingular plus $311 of interest accrued on the advances.) Confirm that this amount is equal to its proportionate share of Cingular's equity.
b. Did Cingular pay out any of its earnings as dividends in 2005? How do you know?
c. How much income did AT&T report in 2005 relating to this investment in Cingular?
d. Interpret the AT&T statement that "undistributed earnings from Cingular were $2,711 and $2,511 at December 31, 2005 and 2004."
e. How does use of the equity method impact AT&T's ROE and its RNOA components (net operating asset turnover and net operating profit margin)?
f. AT&T accounts for its investment in Cingular under the equity method, despite its 60% economic ownership position. Why?
g. In 2006, AT&T merged with Bell South, its joint venture partner in Cingular. What impact will this merger have on the way AT&T accounts for its investment in Cingular?

**E7-31. Constructing the Consolidated Balance Sheet at Acquisition (LO3)**
On January 1 of the current year, Healy Company purchased all of the common shares of Miller Company for $500,000 cash. Balance sheets of the two firms at acquisition follow:

| | Healy Company | Miller Company | Consolidating Adjustments | Consolidated |
|---|---|---|---|---|
| Current assets . . . . . . . . . . . | $1,700,000 | $120,000 | | |
| Investment in Miller . . . . . . . . | 500,000 | — | | |
| Plant assets, net . . . . . . . . . . | 3,000,000 | 410,000 | | |
| Goodwill . . . . . . . . . . . . . . . . . | — | — | | |
| Total assets . . . . . . . . . . . . . . | $5,200,000 | $530,000 | | |
| Liabilities . . . . . . . . . . . . . . . . | $ 700,000 | $ 90,000 | | |
| Contributed capital . . . . . . . . . | 3,500,000 | 400,000 | | |
| Retained earnings . . . . . . . . . | 1,000,000 | 40,000 | | |
| Total liabilities and equity . . . . | $5,200,000 | $530,000 | | |

During purchase negotiations, Miller's plant assets were appraised at $425,000 and all of its remaining assets and liabilities were appraised at values approximating their book values. Healy also concluded that an additional $45,000 (in goodwill) demanded by Miller's shareholders was warranted because Miller's earning power was better than the industry average. Prepare the consolidating adjustments and the consolidated balance sheet at acquisition.

**E7-32.** **Constructing the Consolidated Balance Sheet at Acquisition** **(LO3)**
Rayburn Company purchased all of Kanodia Company's common stock for cash on January 1, at which time the separate balance sheets of the two corporations appeared as follows:

|  | Rayburn Company | Kanodia Company | Consolidating Adjustments | Consolidated |
|---|---|---|---|---|
| Investment in Kanodia . . . . . . | $ 600,000 | — | | |
| Other assets . . . . . . . . . . . . . | 2,300,000 | $700,000 | | |
| Goodwill . . . . . . . . . . . . . . . . | — | — | | _____ |
| Total assets. . . . . . . . . . . . . | $2,900,000 | $700,000 | | |
| | | | | |
| Liabilities. . . . . . . . . . . . . . . | $ 900,000 | $160,000 | | |
| Contributed capital. . . . . . . . | 1,400,000 | 300,000 | | |
| Retained earnings . . . . . . . . | 600,000 | 240,000 | | _____ |
| Total liabilities and equity . . . . | $2,900,000 | $700,000 | | |

During purchase negotiations, Rayburn determined that the appraised value of Kanodia's Other Assets was $720,000; and, all of its remaining assets and liabilities were appraised at values approximating their book values. The remaining $40,000 of the purchase price was ascribed to goodwill. Prepare the consolidating adjustments and the consolidated balance sheet at acquisition.

**E7-33.** **Assessing Financial Statement Effects from a Subsidiary Stock Issuance** **(LO3)**
Ryan Company owns 80% of Lev Company. Information reported by Ryan Company and Lev Company as of January 1, 2007, follows:

**Ryan Company**
Shares owned of Lev . . . . . . . . . . . . . 40,000
Book value of investment in Lev. . . . . $320,000

**Lev Company**
Shares outstanding. . . . . . . . . . . . . . 50,000
Book value of equity . . . . . . . . . . . . . $400,000
Book value per share . . . . . . . . . . . . $8

Assume Lev Company issues 30,000 additional shares of previously authorized but unissued common stock solely to outside investors (none to Ryan Company) for $12 cash per share. Indicate the financial statement effects of this stock issuance on Ryan Company using the financial statement effect template for both of the reporting options available under GAAP. Identify and explain both options.

**Ryan Company's Financial Statements**

| | Balance Sheet | | | | | | Income Statement | | |
|---|---|---|---|---|---|---|---|---|---|
| Transaction | Cash Asset | + Noncash Assets | = Liabil- ities | + Contrib. Capital | + Earned Capital | | Rev- enues | − Expen- ses | = Net Income |
| Lev Co. issues 30,000 shares (Option A) | | | = | | | | | | = |
| Lev Co. issues 30,000 shares (Option B) | | | = | | | | | | = |

**E7-34.    Estimating Goodwill Impairment    (LO3)**

On January 1, 2007, Engel Company purchases 100% of Ball Company for $16.8 million. At the time of acquisition, the fair market value of Ball's tangible net assets (excluding goodwill) is $16.2 million. Engel ascribes the excess of $600,000 to goodwill. Assume that the market value of Ball declines to $12.5 million and that the fair market value of Ball's tangible net assets is estimated at $12.3 million as of December 31, 2007.

a.    Determine if the goodwill has become impaired and, if so, the amount of the impairment.

b.    What impact does the impairment of goodwill have on Engel's financial statements?

**E7-35.    Allocating Purchase Price including In-Process R&D    (LO3)**

Amgen, Inc., reports the following footnote to its 10-K report.                                      Amgen Inc. (AMGN)

**Immunex acquisition.** On July 15, 2002, the Company acquired all of the outstanding common stock of Immunex in a transaction accounted for as a business combination. Immunex was a leading biotechnology company dedicated to developing immune system science to protect human health. The acquisition enhanced Amgen's strategic position within the biotechnology industry by strengthening and diversifying its (1) product base and product pipeline in key therapeutic areas, and (2) discovery research capabilities in proteins and antibodies. The purchase price was allocated to the tangible and identifiable intangible assets acquired and liabilities assumed based on their estimated fair values at the acquisition date. The following table summarizes the estimated fair values of the assets acquired and liabilities assumed as of the acquisition date (in millions):

| | |
|---|---:|
| Current assets, principally cash and marketable securities | $ 1,619.1 |
| Deferred tax assets | 200.2 |
| Property, plant, and equipment | 571.6 |
| In-process research and development | 2,991.8 |
| Identifiable intangible assets, principally developed product technology and core technology | 4,803.2 |
| Goodwill | 9,774.2 |
| Other assets | 26.2 |
| Current liabilities | (579.0) |
| Deferred tax liabilities | (1,635.5) |
| Net assets | $17,771.8 |

The allocation of the purchase price was based, in part, on a third-party valuation of the fair values of in-process research and development, identifiable intangible assets, and certain property, plant, and equipment. The estimated fair value of the in-process R&D projects was determined based on the use of a discounted cash flow model. For each project, the estimated after-tax cash flows were probability weighted to take into account the stage of completion and the risks surrounding the successful development and commercialization. These cash flows were then discounted to a present value using discount rates ranging from 12% to 14%.

a.    Of the total assets acquired, what portion is allocated to tangible assets and what portion to intangible assets?

b.    Are the assets (both tangible and intangible) of Immunex reported on the consolidated balance sheet at the book value or at the fair market value on the date of the acquisition? Explain.

c.    How are the tangible and intangible assets accounted for subsequent to the acquisition?

d.    Comment on the valuation of the in-process R&D. How is IPR&D accounted for under current GAAP?

e.    If the amount allocated to in-process R&D was decreased, what effect would this have on the allocation of the purchase price to the remaining acquired assets? What effect would this have on current and future earnings?

**E7-36.ᴮ    Constructing the Consolidated Balance Sheet at Acquisition    (LO3)**

Easton Company acquires 100 percent of the outstanding voting shares of Harris Company. To obtain these shares, Easton pays $210,000 in cash and issues 5,000 of its $10 par value common stock. On this date, Easton's stock has a fair market value of $36 per share, and Harris's book value of stockholders' equity is $280,000. Easton is willing to pay $390,000 for a company with a book value for equity of $280,000 because it believes that (1) Harris's buildings are undervalued by $40,000, and (2) Harris has an unrecorded patent that Easton values at $30,000. Easton considers the remaining balance sheet items to be fairly valued (no book-to-market difference). The remaining $40,000 of the purchase price is ascribed to corporate synergies and other general unidentifiable intangible assets (goodwill). The balance sheets at the acquisition date follow:

| | Easton Company | Harris Company | Consolidating Adjustments | Consolidated |
|---|---|---|---|---|
| Cash..................... | $ 84,000 | $ 40,000 | | |
| Receivables .............. | 160,000 | 90,000 | | |
| Inventory................. | 220,000 | 130,000 | | |
| Investment in Harris........ | 390,000 | — | | |
| Land..................... | 100,000 | 60,000 | | |
| Buildings, net ............. | 400,000 | 110,000 | | |
| Equipment, net............ | 120,000 | 50,000 | | |
| Total assets............... | $1,474,000 | $480,000 | | |
| | | | | |
| Accounts payable.......... | $ 160,000 | $ 30,000 | | |
| Long-term liabilities ........ | 380,000 | 170,000 | | |
| Common stock............ | 500,000 | 40,000 | | |
| Additional paid-in capital .... | 74,000 | — | | |
| Retained earnings ......... | 360,000 | 240,000 | | |
| Total liabilities & equity...... | $1,474,000 | $480,000 | | |

a. Show the breakdown of the investment into the book value acquired, the excess of fair value over book value, and the portion of the investment representing goodwill.

b. Prepare the consolidating adjustments and the consolidated balance sheet on the date of acquisition. Identify the adjustments by whether they relate to the elimination of stockholders' equity [S] or the excess of purchase price over book value [A].

c. How will the excess of the purchase price over book value acquired be treated in years subsequent to the acquisition?

**E7-37.**^C **Reporting and Analyzing Derivatives   (LO1)**

Hewlett Packard (HPQ)

Hewlett Packard reports the following schedule of comprehensive income (net income plus other comprehensive income) in its 2005 10-K report ($ millions):

| 2005 Comprehensive income (millions) | |
|---|---|
| Net earnings..................................... | $2,398 |
| Net unrealized loss on available-for-sale securities.... | (1) |
| Net unrealized gain on cash flow hedges ........... | 69 |
| Minimum pension liability, net of taxes ............. | 171 |
| Cumulative translation adjustment ................ | (17) |
| Comprehensive income ......................... | $2,620 |

a. Describe how firms like Hewlett Packard typically use derivatives.

b. How does HP report its derivatives and the hedged assets (and/or liabilities) on its balance sheet?

c. By what amount has the unrealized gain of $69 million on the cash flow hedges affected its current income? What are the analysis implications?

# PROBLEMS

**P7-38.** **Analyzing and Interpreting Available-for-Sale Securities Disclosures** **(LO1)**

Following is a portion of the investments footnote from MetLife's 2005 10-K report. Investment earnings are a crucial component of the financial performance of insurance companies such as MetLife, and investments comprise a large part of Metlife's assets. MetLife accounts for its bond investments as available-for-sale securities.

MetLife, Inc. (MET)

| December 31, 2005 (in millions) | Cost or Amortized Cost | Gross Unrealized | | Estimated Fair Value |
|---|---|---|---|---|
| | | Gain | Loss | |
| U.S. corporate securities . . . . . . . . . . . . . . . | $ 72,339 | $2,814 | $ 835 | $ 74,318 |
| Residential mortgaged-backed securities . . . . | 47,365 | 353 | 472 | 47,246 |
| Foreign corporate securities. . . . . . . . . . . . . . | 33,578 | 1,842 | 439 | 34,981 |
| U.S. treasury/agency securities . . . . . . . . . . . | 25,643 | 1,401 | 86 | 26,958 |
| Commercial mortgaged-backed securities . . . | 17,682 | 223 | 207 | 17,698 |
| Asset-backed securities. . . . . . . . . . . . . . . . . | 11,533 | 91 | 51 | 11,573 |
| Foreign government securities. . . . . . . . . . . . . | 10,080 | 1,401 | 35 | 11,446 |
| State and political subdivision securities . . . . . | 4,601 | 185 | 36 | 4,750 |
| Other fixed maturity securities . . . . . . . . . . . . . | 912 | 17 | 41 | 888 |
| Total bonds. . . . . . . . . . . . . . . . . . . . . . . . | 223,733 | 8,327 | 2,202 | 229,858 |
| Redeemable preferred stocks . . . . . . . . . . . . | 193 | 2 | 3 | 192 |
| Total fixed maturities. . . . . . . . . . . . . . . . . | $223,926 | $8,329 | $2,205 | $230,050 |

| December 31, 2004 (in millions) | Cost or Amortized Cost | Gross Unrealized | | Estimated Fair Value |
|---|---|---|---|---|
| | | Gain | Loss | |
| U.S. corporate securities . . . . . . . . . . . . . . . | $ 58,022 | $ 3,870 | $172 | $ 61,720 |
| Residential mortgaged-backed securities . . . . | 31,683 | 612 | 65 | 32,230 |
| Foreign corporate securities. . . . . . . . . . . . . . | 24,972 | 2,582 | 85 | 27,469 |
| U.S. treasury/agency securities . . . . . . . . . . . | 16,534 | 1,314 | 22 | 17,826 |
| Commercial mortgaged-backed securities . . . | 12,099 | 440 | 38 | 12,501 |
| Asset-backed securities. . . . . . . . . . . . . . . . . | 10,784 | 125 | 33 | 10,876 |
| Foreign government securities. . . . . . . . . . . . . | 7,621 | 973 | 26 | 8,568 |
| State and political subdivision securities . . . . . | 3,683 | 220 | 4 | 3,899 |
| Other fixed maturity securities . . . . . . . . . . . . . | 887 | 131 | 33 | 985 |
| Total bonds. . . . . . . . . . . . . . . . . . . . . . . . | 166,285 | 10,267 | 478 | 176,074 |
| Redeemable preferred stocks . . . . . . . . . . . . | 326 | — | 23 | 303 |
| Total fixed maturities. . . . . . . . . . . . . . . . . | $166,611 | $10,267 | $501 | $176,377 |

**Required**

a.   At what amount does MetLife report its bond investments on its balance sheets for 2005 and 2004?

b.   What are the net unrealized gains (losses) for 2005 and 2004? How did these unrealized gains (losses) affect the company's reported income in 2005 and 2004?

c.   What is the difference between *realized* and *unrealized* gains and losses? Are realized gains and losses treated differently in the income statement than unrealized gains and losses?

d.   MetLife reports a balance for unrealized gains (losses) on fixed maturities investments of approximately $4 billion in the equity section of its 2005 balance sheet. Explain the difference between this amount and the amount computed in part *b*.

**P7-39.** **Analyzing and Interpreting Disclosures on Equity Method Investments** (LO2)

General Mills invests in a number of joint ventures to manufacture and distribute its food products as discussed in the following footnote to its fiscal year 2005 10-K report:

> **Investments in Joint Ventrues** We have a 50 percent equity interest in Cereal Partners Worldwide (CPW), a joint venture with Nestlé that manufactures and markets ready-to-eat cereals outside the United States and Canada. We have guaranteed 50 percent of CPW's debt. We have a 50 percent equity interest in 8th Continent, LLC, a domestic joint venture with DuPont to develop and market soy foods and beverages. We have 50 percent interests in the following joint ventures for the manufacture, distribution and marketing of Häagen-Dazs frozen ice cream products and novelties: Häagen-Dazs Japan K.K., Häagen-Dazs Korea Company Limited, Häagen-Dazs Distributors (Thailand) Company Limited, and Häagen-Dazs Marketing & Distribution (Philippines) Inc. We also have a 50 percent interest in Seretram, a joint venture with Co-op de Pau for the production of Green Giant canned corn in France.
>
> On February 28, 2005, our 40.5 percent ownership interest in the Snack Ventures Europe (SVE) joint venture was redeemed for $750 million. The redemption ended the European snack joint venture between General Mills and PepsiCo, Inc.
>
> The joint ventures are reflected in our consolidated financial statements on the equity basis of accounting. We record our share of the earnings or losses of these joint ventures. We also receive royalty income from certain joint ventures, incur various expenses (primarily research and development) and record the tax impact of certain joint venture operations that are structured as partnerships.
>
> Our cumulative investment in these joint ventures (including our share of earnings and losses) was $223 million, $434 million and $372 million at the end of fiscal 2005, 2004 and 2003, respectively. We made aggregate investments in the joint ventures of $15 million, $31 million and $17 million in fiscal 2005, 2004 and 2003, respectively. We received aggregate dividends from the joint ventures of $83 million, $60 million and $95 million in fiscal 2005, 2004 and 2003, respectively.
>
> Summary combined financial information for the joint ventures on a 100 percent basis follows:

Combined Financial Information—Joint Ventures—100 Percent Basis

| In Millions, Fiscal Year | 2005 | 2004 |
| --- | --- | --- |
| Net sales. . . . . . . . . . . . . . . . . . . . . . . | $2,652 | $2,625 |
| Net Sales less Cost of Sales . . . . . . . . . | 1,184 | 1,180 |
| Earnings before Income Taxes. . . . . . . . | 231 | 205 |
| Earnings after Income Taxes . . . . . . . . . | 184 | 153 |

| In Millions, Fiscal Year Ended | 2005 | 2004 |
| --- | --- | --- |
| Current assets . . . . . . . . . . . . . . . . . . . | $604 | $852 |
| Noncurrent assets . . . . . . . . . . . . . . . . | 612 | 972 |
| Current liabilities. . . . . . . . . . . . . . . . . . | 695 | 865 |
| Noncurrent liabilities. . . . . . . . . . . . . . . | 7 | 14 |

**Required**

a. How does General Mills account for its investments in joint ventures? How are these investments reflected on General Mills' balance sheet, and how generally is income recognized on these investments?

b. General Mills reports the total of all of these investments on its May 29, 2005, balance sheet at $223 million. Approximately what percent of these joint ventures does it own, on average?

c. Does the $223 million investment reported on General Mills' balance sheet sufficiently reflect the assets and liabilities required to conduct these operations? Explain.

d. Do you believe that the liabilities of these joint venture entities represent actual obligations of General Mills? Explain.

e. What potential problem(s) does equity method accounting present for analysis purposes?

**P7-40.    Analyzing and Interpreting Disclosures on Consolidations    (LO3)**

Caterpillar Inc. consists of two business units: the manufacturing company (parent corporation) and a wholly owned finance subsidiary. These two units are consolidated in Caterpillar's 10-K report. Following is a supplemental disclosure that Caterpillar includes in its 10-K report that shows the separate balance sheets of the parent and its subsidiary, as well as consolidating adjustments and the consolidated balance sheet presented to shareholders. This supplemental disclosure is not mandated under GAAP, but is voluntarily reported by Caterpillar as useful information for investors and creditors. Using this disclosure, answer the following questions:

**Required**

a. Does each individual company (unit) maintain its own financial statements? Explain. Why does GAAP require consolidation instead of separate financial statements of individual companies (units)?

b. What is the balance of Investments in Financial Products Subsidiaries as of December 31, 2005, on the parent's balance sheet? What is the equity balance of the financial products subsidiary to which this relates as of December 31, 2005? Do you see a relation? Will this relation always exist?

c. Refer to your answer for (a). How does the equity method of accounting for the investment in the subsidiary company obscure the actual financial condition of the parent company that is revealed in the consolidated financial statements?

d. Refer to the Consolidating Adjustments column reported—it is used to prepare the consolidated balance sheet. Generally, what do these adjustments accomplish?

e. Compare the consolidated balance of stockholders' equity with the stockholders' equity of the parent company (Machinery and Engines). Will the relation that is evident always hold? Explain.

f. Recall that the parent company uses the equity method of accounting for its investment in the subsidiary, and that this account is eliminated in the consolidation process. What is the relation between consolidated net income and the net income of the parent company? Explain.

g. What do you believe is the implication for the consolidated balance sheet if the market value of the Financial Products subsidiary is greater than the book value of its stockholders' equity?

| December 31, 2005 (Millions of Dollars) | Consolidated | Supplemental Consolidating Data | | |
| --- | --- | --- | --- | --- |
| | | Machinery and Engines | Financial Products | Consolidating Adjustments |
| Cash and short-term investments . . . . . . . . . . . . . . . | $ 1,108 | $ 951 | $ 157 | $ — |
| Receivables—trade and other . . . . . . . . . . . . . . . . . | 7,526 | 2,833 | 419 | 4,274 |
| Receivables—finance. . . . . . . . . . . . . . . . . . . . . . . | 6,442 | — | 11,058 | (4,616) |
| Deferred and refundable income taxes . . . . . . . . . . . | 344 | 276 | 68 | — |
| Prepaid expenses. . . . . . . . . . . . . . . . . . . . . . . . . . | 2,146 | 2,139 | 26 | (19) |
| Inventories . . . . . . . . . . . . . . . . . . . . . . . . . . . . . . . | 5,224 | 5,224 | — | — |
| Total current assets . . . . . . . . . . . . . . . . . . . . . . . . | 22,790 | 11,423 | 11,728 | (361) |
| Property, plant and equipment—net . . . . . . . . . . . . . | 7,988 | 5,067 | 2,921 | — |
| Long-term receivables—trade and other . . . . . . . . . . | 1,037 | 301 | 36 | 700 |
| Long-term receivables—finance . . . . . . . . . . . . . . . . | 10,301 | — | 11,036 | (735) |
| Investments in unconsolidated affiliated companies . . . . . . . . . . . . . . . . . . . . . . . | 565 | 526 | 39 | — |
| Investments in Financial Products subsidiaries . . . . . | — | 3,253 | — | (3,253) |
| Deferred income taxes . . . . . . . . . . . . . . . . . . . . . . . | 768 | 1,057 | 32 | (321) |
| Intangible assets . . . . . . . . . . . . . . . . . . . . . . . . . . . | 424 | 418 | 6 | — |
| Goodwill . . . . . . . . . . . . . . . . . . . . . . . . . . . . . . . . . | 1,451 | 1,451 | — | — |
| Other assets . . . . . . . . . . . . . . . . . . . . . . . . . . . . . . | 1,745 | 491 | 1,254 | — |
| Total assets. . . . . . . . . . . . . . . . . . . . . . . . . . . . . . . | $47,069 | $23,987 | $27,052 | $(3,970) |

*(Continued on next page)*

*(Continued from previous page)*

| December 31, 2005 (Millions of Dollars) | Consolidated | Supplemental Consolidating Data | | |
| --- | --- | --- | --- | --- |
| | | Machinery and Engines | Financial Products | Consolidating Adjustments |
| **Liabilities** | | | | |
| Short-term borrowings. . . . . . . . . . . . . . . . . . . . . . . | $ 5,569 | $ 871 | $ 4,897 | $ (199) |
| Accounts payable. . . . . . . . . . . . . . . . . . . . . . . . . . | 3,471 | 3,347 | 261 | (137) |
| Accrued expenses . . . . . . . . . . . . . . . . . . . . . . . . . | 2,617 | 1,605 | 1,038 | (26) |
| Accrued wages, salaries and employee benefits. . . . | 1,845 | 1,826 | 19 | — |
| Customer Advances. . . . . . . . . . . . . . . . . . . . . . . . | 395 | 395 | — | — |
| Dividends payable . . . . . . . . . . . . . . . . . . . . . . . . . | 168 | 168 | — | — |
| Deferred and current income taxes payable . . . . . . . | 528 | 448 | 84 | (4) |
| Long-term debt due within one year . . . . . . . . . . . . . | 4,499 | 340 | 4,159 | — |
| Total current liabilities. . . . . . . . . . . . . . . . . . . . . . . | 19,092 | 9,000 | 10,458 | (366) |
| Long-term debt due after one year . . . . . . . . . . . . . . | 15,677 | 2,752 | 12,960 | 35 |
| Liability for postemployment benefits . . . . . . . . . . . . | 2,991 | 2,991 | — | — |
| Deferred income taxes and other liabilities . . . . . . . . | 877 | 812 | 381 | (316) |
| Total liabilities. . . . . . . . . . . . . . . . . . . . . . . . . . . . . | 38,637 | 15,555 | 23,799 | (717) |
| **Stockholders' equity** | | | | |
| Common stock. . . . . . . . . . . . . . . . . . . . . . . . . . . . | 1,859 | 1,859 | 875 | (875) |
| Treasury stock . . . . . . . . . . . . . . . . . . . . . . . . . . . . | (4,637) | (4,637) | — | — |
| Profit employed in the business. . . . . . . . . . . . . . . . | 11,808 | 11,808 | 2,197 | (2,197) |
| Accumulated other comprehensive income. . . . . . . . | (598) | (598) | 181 | (181) |
| Total stockholders' equity . . . . . . . . . . . . . . . . . . . . | 8,432 | 8,432 | 3,253 | (3,253) |
| Total liabilities and stockholders' equity. . . . . . . . . . . | $47,069 | $23,987 | $27,052 | $(3,970) |

# CASES

**C7-41.    Management Application:  Determining the Reporting of an Investment    (LO1, 2, 3)**

Assume that your company acquires 20% of the outstanding common stock of APEX Software as an investment. You also have an option to purchase the remaining 80%. APEX is developing software (its only activity) that it hopes to eventually package and sell to customers. You do not intend to exercise your option unless its software product reaches commercial feasibility. APEX has employed your software engineers to assist in the development efforts and you are integrally involved in its software design. Your ownership interest is significant enough to give you influence over APEX' software design specifications.

**Required**

*a.*    Describe the financial statement effects of the three possible methods to accounting for this investment (market, equity, or consolidation).

*b.*    What method of accounting is appropriate for this investment (market, equity, or consolidation)? Explain.

**C7-42.    Ethics and Governance:  Establishing Corporate Governance    (LO2, 3)**

Effective corporate governance policies are a crucial component of contemporary corporate management.

**Required**

What provisions do you believe should be incorporated into such a policy? How do such policies impact financial accounting?

# Reporting and Analyzing Nonowner Financing

## LEARNING OBJECTIVES

**LO1** Describe the accounting for current operating liabilities, including accounts payable and accrued liabilities. (p. 8-4)

**LO2** Describe the accounting for current and long-term nonoperating liabilities. (p. 8-10)

**LO3** Explain how credit ratings are determined and identify their effect on the cost of debt. (p. 8-21)

## VERIZON COMMUNICATIONS

**Verizon Communications, Inc.**, began doing business in 2000, when **Bell Atlantic Corporation** merged with **GTE Corporation**. Verizon is one of the world's leading providers of communications services. It is the largest provider of wireline and wireless communications in the U.S., and is the largest of the 'Baby Bells' as of 2005 with $75 billion in revenues and $168 billion in assets.

When Ivan Seidenberg became sole CEO of Verizon in mid-2002 (and its chairman in late 2003), the Internet frenzy had cooled and Verizon's stock price had plunged, falling from an all-time high of $70 in late 1999 to $27 in mid-2002. Since then, the stock has rebounded somewhat, but continues to trade below $40 per share in late 2006.

Verizon survived the Internet and telecom downturn. Now it faces a formidable new challenger: cable. Cable companies spent an estimated $75 billion in recent years upgrading their infrastructure to offer customers discounted bundled packages of local voice, high-speed Internet connec-

tions, and video. Market analysts estimate that cable companies could capture a quarter of the local voice market over the next decade as they deploy new voice over Internet protocol (VOIP) technology.

While Verizon and the other traditional phone companies see their market positions erode, they also struggle to retain their image as innovators. They face creative pressures from researchers and from companies (including Intel) who continue to develop new wireless technologies. BusinessWeek (2006) explains:

> AT&T and Verizon are rushing to build networks to deliver TV service and high-speed broadband access . . . Verizon is spending billions to roll out a next-generation phone, data, and video network called FiOS (as in "fiber optic") to give its customers faster Internet service and an alternative to cable. Indeed, over the past three years, Verizon has spent $40 billion on capital expenditures in addition to its 2006 acquisition of MCI. The demand for new capital spending is coming at an inopportune time for Verizon. Saddled with a debt load of over $36 billion as of 2005, a third of which matures over the next five years, Verizon must also pay over $4 billion in stock dividends annually plus nearly $20 billion in accumulated employee pensions and health-care costs. Verizon is concerned. Faced with a question from a stockholder about why Verizon isn't repurchasing its stock given its decline in value, Seidenberg said "our number-one priority for using free cash flow over the last two years has been reducing debt.

This module focuses on liabilities; that is, short-term and long-term obligations. Liabilities are one of two financing sources for a company. The other is shareholder financing. Bonds and notes are a major part of most companies' liabilities. In this module, we show how to price liabilities and how the issuance and subsequent payment of the principal and interest affect financial statements. We also discuss the required disclosures that enable us to effectively analyze a company's ability to pay its debts as they come due.

Verizon's current slogan is "we never stop working for you." The company is now working harder than ever to transform itself in an era of fiber optics and wireless communication. The dilemma facing Silverberg is how to allocate available cash flow between strategic investment and debt payments.

Sources: *BusinessWeek* 2003, 2004 and 2006; *TheStreet.Com* 2003; *Verizon* 2005 and 2004 Annual Reports; *Verizon* 2004 and 2005 10-Ks.

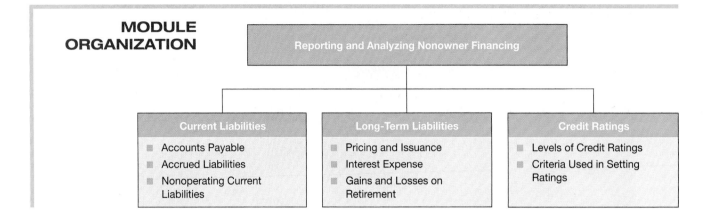

## INTRODUCTION

The accounting equation (Assets = Liabilities + Equity) is a useful tool in helping us think about how the balance sheet and income statement are constructed, the linkages among the financial statements, and the effects of transactions on financial statements. The accounting equation is also useful in helping us think about the statements from another perspective, namely, how the business is financed. Consider the following representation of the accounting equation:

$$\underbrace{\text{Assets}}_{\text{Uses}} = \underbrace{\text{Liabilities} + \text{Equity}}_{\text{Sources}}$$

Assets represent investments (uses of funds) that management has made. It includes current operating assets such as cash, accounts receivable, and inventories. It also includes long-term operating assets such as manufacturing and administrative facilities. Most companies also invest a portion of funds in nonoperating assets (marketable securities) that provide the liquidity a company needs to conduct transactions and to react to market opportunities and changes.

Just as asset disclosures provide us with information on where a company invests its funds, liability and equity disclosures inform us as to how those assets are financed. These are the sources of funds. To be successful, a company must not only invest funds wisely, but must also be astute in the manner in which it raises funds.

Companies strive to finance their assets at the lowest possible cost. Current liabilities (such as accounts payable and accrued liabilities) are generally non-interest-bearing. As a result, companies try to maximize the financing of their assets with these sources of funds.

Current liabilities, as the name implies, are short-term in nature, generally requiring payment within the coming year. As a result, they are not a suitable source of funding for long-term assets that generate cash flows over several years. Instead, companies often finance long-term assets with long-term liabilities that require payments over several years. Generally, companies try to link the cash outflows of the financing source with the cash inflows of the related asset. As such, long-term financing is usually in the form of bonds, notes, and stock issuances.

When a company acquires assets, and finances them with liabilities, its financial leverage increases. Also, the required liability payments increase proportionally with the level of liabilities, and those larger payments imply a higher probability of default should a downturn in business occur. Increasing levels of liabilities, then, make the company riskier to investors who, consequently, demand a higher return. Assessing the appropriate level of liabilities is part of liquidity and solvency analysis.

This module describes and assesses *on-balance-sheet financing,* namely current and noncurrent liabilities that are reported on financial statements. If companies can find a way to purchase assets and have neither the asset, nor its related financing, appear on the balance sheet, they can report higher levels of asset turnover and appear less risky. This creates off-balance-sheet financing, which is the focus of Module 10.

# CURRENT LIABILITIES

Current liabilities consist of both operating and nonoperating liabilities. Most *current operating liabilities* such as those related to inventory (accounts payable) or to utilities, wages, insurance, rent, and taxes (accrued liabilities), impact operating expenses such as cost of goods sold or selling, general and administrative expenses. *Current nonoperating liabilities* typically relate to short-term bank notes or the current portion of long-term debt. **Verizon**'s balance sheet reports the following current liabilities:

**LO1** Describe the accounting for current operating liabilities, including accounts payable and accrued liabilities.

| At December 31 ($ millions) | 2005 | 2004 |
|---|---|---|
| Debt maturing within one year . . . . . . . . . . . . . . . . . . . . | $ 7,141 | $ 3,593 |
| Accounts payable and accrued liabilities . . . . . . . . . . . | 12,351 | 13,177 |
| Liabilities of discontinued operations . . . . . . . . . . . . . . | — | 525 |
| Other . . . . . . . . . . . . . . . . . . . . . . . . . . . . . . . . . . . . . . . | 5,571 | 5,834 |
| Total current liabilities . . . . . . . . . . . . . . . . . . . . . . . . . | $25,063 | $23,129 |

Verizon reports four categories of current liabilities: (1) long-term obligations that are scheduled for payment in the upcoming year, (2) accounts payable and accrued liabilities, (3) current liabilities from discontinued operations (these operations were sold in 2005, hence they are no longer reported on Verizon's balance sheet), and (4) other current liabilities, which consist mainly of customer deposits, dividends payable, and miscellaneous obligations.

Analysis and interpretation of the return on net operating assets (RNOA) requires that we separate current liabilities into operating and nonoperating components. In general, these two components consist of the following:

1. **Current operating liabilities**
   - **Accounts payable** Obligations to others for amounts owed on purchases of goods and services; these are usually non-interest-bearing.
   - **Accrued liabilities** Obligations for which there is no related external transaction in the current period. These include, for example, accruals for employee wages earned but yet unpaid, accruals for taxes (usually quarterly) on payroll and current period profits, and accruals for other liabilities such as rent, utilities, and insurance. Companies make accruals to properly reflect the liabilities owed as of the statement date and the expenses incurred for the period reported.
   - **Unearned revenue** Obligations to provide goods or services in the coming year; these arise from customers' deposits, subscriptions, or prepayments.
2. **Current nonoperating liabilities**
   - **Short-term interest-bearing debt** Short-term bank borrowings and notes expected to mature in whole or in part during the upcoming year; this item can include any accrued interest payable.
   - **Current maturities of long-term debt** Long-term borrowings that are scheduled to mature in whole or in part during the upcoming year; this current portion of long-term debt includes maturing principal payments only.

The remainder of this section describes current operating liabilities followed by a discussion of current nonoperating liabilities.

## Accounts Payable

Accounts payable arise from the purchase of goods and services from others. Accounts payable are normally non-interest-bearing and are, thus, an inexpensive financing source. Verizon does not break out accounts payable on its balance sheet but, instead, reports them with other accruals. It reports $12,351 million in accounts payable and accrued liabilities. The footnotes reveal that accounts payable represent $2,827 million, or 23%, of this total amount.

The following financial statement effects template shows the accounting for a typical purchase of goods on credit and the ultimate sale of those goods. A series of four connected transactions illustrate the revenue and cost cycle.

| | | Balance Sheet | | | | | | | Income Statement | | | | |
|---|---|---|---|---|---|---|---|---|---|---|---|---|---|
| | Transaction | Cash Asset | + | Noncash Assets | = | Liabil- ities | + | Contrib. Capital | + | Earned Capital | Rev- enues | − | Expen- ses | = | Net Income |
| INV 100<br>  AP 100<br>― INV<br>100 \|<br>  AP<br>  \| 100 | 1. Purchase $100 inventory on credit | | | +100 Inventory | = | +100 Accounts Payable | | | | | | | | = |
| AR 140<br>  Sales 140<br>― AR<br>140 \|<br>  Sales<br>  \| 140 | 2a. Sell inventory on credit for $140 | | | +140 Accounts Receivable | = | | | | | +140 Retained Earnings | +140 Sales | | | = +140 |
| COGS 100<br>  INV 100<br>― COGS<br>100 \|<br>  INV<br>  \| 100 | 2b. Record $100 cost of inventory sold in 2a | | | −100 Inventory | = | | | | | −100 Retained Earnings | | − | +100 Cost of Goods Sold | = −100 |
| Cash 140<br>  AR 140<br>― Cash<br>140 \|<br>  AR<br>  \| 140 | 3. Receive $140 cash from accounts receivable | +140 Cash | | −140 Accounts Receivable | = | | | | | | | | | = |
| AP 100<br>  Cash 100<br>― AP<br>100 \|<br>  Cash<br>  \| 100 | 4. Pay $100 cash for accounts payable | −100 Cash | | | = | −100 Accounts Payable | | | | | | | | = |

The financial statement effects template reveals several impacts related to the purchase of goods on credit and their ultimate sale.

- Purchase of inventory is reflected on the balance sheet as an increase in inventory and an increase in accounts payable.

- Sale of inventory involves two components—revenue and cost. The revenue part reflects the increase in sales and the increase in accounts receivable (revenue is recognized when earned, even though cash is not yet received).

- The cost part of the sales transaction reflects the decrease in inventory and the increase in cost of goods sold (COGS). COGS is reported in the income statement and matched against revenues (this expense is recognized because the inventory asset is sold, even though inventory-related payables may not yet be paid).

- Collection of the receivable reduces accounts receivable and increases cash. It is solely a balance sheet transaction and does not impact the income statement.

- Cash payment of accounts payable is solely a balance sheet transaction and does not impact income statement accounts (expense relating to inventories is recognized when the inventory is sold or used up, not when the liability is paid).

## Accounts Payable Turnover (APT)

Inventories are financed, in large part, by accounts payable (also called *trade credit* or *trade payables*). Such payables usually represent interest-free financing and are, therefore, less expensive than using available cash or borrowed money to finance purchases or production. Accordingly, companies use trade credit whenever possible. This is called *leaning on the trade*.

The **accounts payable turnover** reflects management's success in using trade credit to finance purchases of goods and services. It is computed as:

**Accounts Payable Turnover (APT) = Cost of Goods Sold/Average Accounts Payable**

Payables reflect the cost of inventory, not its retail value. Thus, to be consistent with the denominator, the ratio uses cost of goods sold (and not sales) in the numerator. Management desires to use trade credit to the greatest extent possible for financing. This means that a lower accounts payable turnover is preferable. Verizon's accounts payable turnover rate has increased from 6.67 times per year in 2004 to 9.01 times per year in 2005. (Its APT for 2005 is computed as $25,469 million/[$2,827 million + $2,827 million/2]; by coincidence, it reports the same accounts payable balance in 2005 and 2004.) This increase in accounts payable turnover indicates that Verizon is paying its obligations more quickly, which is *not* a positive development (unless the prior year is excessively low).

A metric analogous to accounts payable turnover is the **accounts payable days outstanding**, which is defined as follows:

**Accounts Payable Days Outstanding (APDO) = Accounts Payable/Average Daily Cost of Goods Sold**

Since accounts payable are a source of low cost financing, management desires to extend the accounts payable days outstanding as long as possible, provided that this action does not harm supply channel relations. Verizon's accounts payable remain unpaid for 40.51 days in 2005, down from 44.54 days in the prior year. (Its 2005 APDO is computed as $2,827 million/[$25,469 million/365 days].) Verizon is, therefore, leaning on the trade less than it has in the recent past. As with APT, this is generally not a positive development.

Accounts payable reflect a source of interest-free financing. Increased payables reduce the amount of net operating working capital as payables (along with other current operating liabilities) are deducted from current operating assets in the computation of net operating working capital. Also, increased payables mean increased cash flow (as increased liabilities increase net cash from operating activities) and increased profitability (as the level of interest-bearing debt that is required to finance operating assets declines). RNOA increases when companies make use of this low-cost financing source. Yet, companies must be careful to avoid excessive 'leaning on the trade' as short-term income gains can yield long-term costs such as damaged supply channels.[1,2]

## MID-MODULE REVIEW 1

Verizon's accounts payable turnover (cost of goods sold/average accounts payable) increased from 6.67 in 2004 to 9.01 in 2005.

 a. Does this change indicate that accounts payable have increased or decreased relative to cost of goods sold? Explain.
 b. What effect does this change have on net cash flows from operating activities?
 c. What management concerns, if any, might this change in accounts payable turnover pose?

## Solution

 a. We know that accounts payable turnover is computed as cost of goods sold divided by average accounts payable. Thus, an increase in accounts payable turnover indicates that accounts payable have decreased relative to cost of goods sold (all else equal).
 b. A decrease in accounts payable results in a decrease in net cash flows from operating activities because Verizon is using cash to pay bills more quickly.
 c. Decreased accounts payable yield an increase net operating working capital (all else equal), with a consequent decline in profitability and cash flow. While detrimental to profitability and cash flow, the more timely payment of accounts payable can improve supplier relations. Analysts must be aware of the potentially damaging consequences of leaning on the trade too heavily.

---

[1] Excessive delays in payment of payables can result in suppliers charging a higher price for their goods or, ultimately, refusing to sell to certain buyers. Although a hidden "financing" cost is not interest, it is still a real cost.

[2] Accounts payable often carry credit terms such as 2/10, net 30. These terms give the buyer, for example, 2% off the invoice price of goods purchased if paid within 10 days. Otherwise the entire invoice is payable within 30 days. By failing to take a discount, the buyer is effectively paying 2% interest charge to keep its funds for an additional 20 days. Since there are approximately 18 such 20-day periods in a year (365/20), this equates to an annual rate of interest of about 36%. Thus, borrowing funds at less than 36% to pay this liability within the discount period would be cost effective.

## Accrued Liabilities

Accrued liabilities reflect expenses that have been incurred during the period but not yet paid in cash. (Accruals can also be used to recognize revenue and a corresponding receivable; an example might be revenue recognition on a long-term contract that has reached a particular milestone, or for interest earned on an investment in bonds but not yet received by period-end. Accruals can also reflect unearned revenue as explained in Module 5.) Verizon reports details of its accrued liabilities (along with accounts payable) in the following footnote to its 2005 10-K report.

| At December 31 (dollars in millions) | 2005 | 2004 |
|---|---|---|
| Accounts payable. . . . . . . . . . . . . . . . . . . . . . . . . . . . . . . | $ 2,827 | $ 2,827 |
| Accrued expenses . . . . . . . . . . . . . . . . . . . . . . . . . . . . . | 3,036 | 3,071 |
| Accrued vacation pay. . . . . . . . . . . . . . . . . . . . . . . . . . | 914 | 842 |
| Accrued salaries and wages . . . . . . . . . . . . . . . . . . . . | 2,390 | 2,526 |
| Interest payable . . . . . . . . . . . . . . . . . . . . . . . . . . . . . . | 579 | 585 |
| Accrued taxes . . . . . . . . . . . . . . . . . . . . . . . . . . . . . . . | 2,605 | 3,326 |
| Total accounts payable and accrued liabilities. . . . . . . . | $12,351 | $13,177 |

Verizon reports one nonoperating accrual: interest payable. Its other accrued liabilities are operating accruals that include miscellaneous accrued expenses, accrued vacation pay, accrued salaries and wages, and accrued taxes. Verizon's accruals are typical. To record accruals, companies recognize a liability on the balance sheet and a corresponding expense on the income statement. This means that liabilities increase, current income decreases, and equity decreases. When an accrued liability is ultimately paid, both cash and the liability decrease (but no expense is recorded because it was recognized previously).

### Accounting for Accrued Liabilities

Accounting for a typical accrued liability such as accrued wages, for two consecutive periods, follows:

| | Balance Sheet | | | | | | Income Statement | | |
|---|---|---|---|---|---|---|---|---|---|
| Transaction | Cash Asset | + Noncash Assets | = Liabil- ities | + Contrib. Capital | + Earned Capital | | Rev- enues | − Expen- ses | = Net Income |
| 1. Period 1: Accrued $75 for employee wages earned at period-end | | = | +75 Wages Payable | | −75 Retained Earnings | | | − +75 Wages Expense | = −75 |
| 2. Period 2: Paid $75 for wages earned in prior period | −75 Cash | = | −75 Wages Payable | | | | | | = |

WE 75
 WP 75
 WE
75
 WP
 75

WP 75
 Cash 75
 WP
75
 Cash
 75

The following financial statement effects result from this accrual of employee wages:

- Employees have worked during a period and have not yet been paid. The effect of this accrual is to increase wages payable on the balance sheet and to recognize wages expense on the income statement. Failure to recognize this liability and associated expense would understate liabilities on the balance sheet and overstate income in the current period.

- When the company pays employees in the following period, cash and wages payable both decrease. This payment does not result in expense because the expense was recognized in the prior period when incurred.

The accrued wages illustration relates to events that are fairly certain. We know, for example, when wages are incurred but not paid. Other examples of such accruals are rental costs, insurance premiums, and taxes owed.

**Contingent Accrued Liabilities** Some accrued liabilities are less certain than others. Consider a company facing a lawsuit. Should it record the possible liability and related expense? The answer depends on the likelihood of occurrence and the ability to estimate the obligation. Specifically, if the obligation is *probable* and the amount *estimable* with reasonable certainty, then a company will recognize this obligation, called a **contingent liability**. If an obligation is only *reasonably possible* (or cannot be reliably estimated), the contingent liability is not reported on the balance sheet and is merely disclosed in the footnotes. All other contingent liabilities that are less than reasonably possible are not disclosed.

**Management of Accrued Liabilities** Management has some latitude in determining the amount and timing of accruals. This latitude can lead to misreporting of income and liabilities (unintentional or otherwise). Here's how: If accruals are underestimated, then expenses are underestimated, income is overestimated, and retained earnings are overestimated. In subsequent periods when an understated accrued liability is reversed, reported income is lower than it should be; this is because prior period income was higher than it should have been. (The reverse holds for overestimated accruals.) The misreporting of accruals, therefore, shifts income from one period into another. We must be keenly aware of this potential for income shifting as we analyze the financial condition of a company.

Experience tells us that accrued liabilities related to restructuring programs (including severance accruals and accruals for asset write-downs), or to legal and environmental liabilities, or business acquisitions are somewhat problematic. These accruals too often represent early recognition of expenses. Sometimes companies aggressively overestimate one-time accruals and record an even larger expense. This is called taking a *big bath*. The effect of a big bath is to depress current period income, which relieves future periods of these expenses (thus, shifting income forward in time). Accordingly, we must monitor any change or unusual activity with accrued liabilities and view large one-time charges with skepticism.

## Estimating Accruals

Some accrued liabilities require more estimation than others. Warranty liabilities are an example of an accrual that requires managerial assumptions and estimates. Warranties are commitments that manufacturers make to their customers to repair or replace defective products within a specified period of time. The expected cost of this commitment can be reasonably estimated at the time of sale based on past experience. As a result, GAAP requires manufacturers to record the expected cost of warranties as a liability, and to record the related expected warranty expense in the income statement in the same period that the sales revenue is reported.

To illustrate, assume that a company estimates that its defective units amount to 1% of sales and that each unit costs $10 to replace. If sales during the period are $10,000, the estimated warranty cost is $1,000 ($10,000 × 1% × $10). The entries to accrue this liability and its ultimate payment follow.

| Transaction | Balance Sheet | | | | | | Income Statement | | |
|---|---|---|---|---|---|---|---|---|---|
| | Cash Asset | + Noncash Assets | = Liabil- ities | + Contrib. Capital | + Earned Capital | | Rev- enues | − Expen- ses | = Net Income |
| 1. Period 1: Accrued $1,000 of expected warranty costs on units sold during the period | | | +1,000 = Warranty Payable | | −1,000 Retained Earnings | | | − +1,000 Warranty Expense | = −1,000 |
| 2. Period 2: Delivered $1,000 in replacement products to cover warranty claims | | −1,000 Inventory | −1,000 = Warranty Payable | | | | | | = |

WRE   1,000
    WRP    1,000
        WRE
1,000 |
        WRP
    |   1,000

WRP   1,000
    INV    1,000
        WRP
1,000 |
        INV
    |   1,000

Accruing warranty liabilities has the same effect on financial statements as accruing wages expense in the previous section. That is, a liability is recorded on the balance sheet and an expense is reported in the income statement. When the defective product is later replaced (or repaired), the liability is reduced together with the cost of the inventory or the cash paid for other costs that were necessary to satisfy the claim. (Only a portion of the products estimated to fail does so in the current period; we expect other product failures in future periods. Management monitors this estimate and adjusts it if failure is higher or lower than expected.) As in the accrual of wages, the expense and the liability are reported when incurred and not when paid.

To illustrate, Ford Motor Company reports $6,158 million of warranty liability on its 2005 balance sheet. Its footnotes reveal the following additional information:

*Warranty.* Estimated warranty costs and additional service actions are accrued for at the time the vehicle is sold to a dealer. Included in the warranty cost accruals are costs for basic warranty coverages on vehicles sold. Additional service actions such as product recalls and other customer service actions are not included in the warranty reconciliation below, but are also accrued for at the time of sale. Estimates for warranty costs are made based primarily on historical warranty claim experience. The following is a tabular reconciliation of the product warranty accrual.

| (in millions) | 2005 | 2004 |
|---|---|---|
| Beginning balance | $ 5,751 | $ 5,443 |
| Payments made during the year | (3,986) | (3,694) |
| Changes in accrual related to warranties issued during the year | 3,949 | 3,611 |
| Changes in accrual related to pre-existing warranties | 593 | 161 |
| Foreign currency translation and other | (149) | 230 |
| Ending balance | $ 6,158 | $ 5,751 |

Of the $5,751 million balance at the beginning of 2005, Ford incurred costs of $3,986 million to replace or repair defective automobiles during 2005. This reduced Ford's liability by that amount. These costs include cash paid to customers, or to employees as wages, and the cost of parts used for repairs. Ford accrued an additional $4,542 ($3,949 + $593) million in new warranty liabilities in 2005, and recorded additional miscellaneous adjustments amounting to a net decrease in the liability of $149 million. It is important to understand that only the increase in the liability resulting from additional accruals impacts the income statement, reducing income through additional warranty expense. Payments made to settle warranty claims do not affect current period income; they merely reduce the pre-existing liability.

GAAP requires that the warranty liability reflects the estimated amount of cost that the company expects to incur as a result of warranty claims. This is often a difficult estimate to make and is prone to error. There is also the possibility that a company might underestimate its warranty liability to report higher current income, or overestimate it so as to depress current income and create an additional liability on the balance sheet (*cookie jar reserve*) that can be used to absorb future warranty costs and, thus, to reduce future expenses. The overestimation would shift income from the current period to one or more future periods. Warranty liabilities must, therefore, be examined closely and compared with sales levels. Any deviations from the historical relation of the warranty liability to sales, or from levels reported by competitors, should be scrutinized.

## MID-MODULE REVIEW 2

Assume that Verizon's employees worked during the current month and earned $10,000 in wages that Verizon will not pay until the first of next month. Must Verizon recognize any wages liability and expense for the current month? Explain with reference to the financial statement effects template.

### Solution

Yes. Verizon must recognize liabilities and expenses when incurred, regardless of when payment is made. Accruing expenses as incurred will match the expenses to the revenues they helped generate. Failure to recognize the wages owed to employees for the period would understate liabilities and overstate income. Verizon must reflect the wages earned and the related expense in its financial statements as follows:

| | Balance Sheet | | | | | | Income Statement | | |
|---|---|---|---|---|---|---|---|---|---|
| Transaction | Cash Asset | + Noncash Assets | = Liabil-ities | + Contrib. Capital | + Earned Capital | | Rev-enues | − Expen-ses | = Net Income |
| Accrue $10,000 in wages expense | | | +10,000 Wages Payable | | −10,000 Retained Earnings | | | − +10,000 Wages Expense | = −10,000 |

WE    10,000
   WP        10,000
         WE
10,000 |
       WP
       | 10,000

# Current Nonoperating Liabilities

Current nonoperating liabilities include short-term bank loans, accrued interest on those loans, and the current maturities of long-term debt. Companies generally try to structure their financing so that debt service requirements (payments) coincide with the cash inflows from the assets financed. This means that current assets are usually financed with current liabilities, and that long-term assets are financed with long-term liabilities (and equity).

**LO2** Describe the accounting for current and long-term nonoperating liabilities.

To illustrate, a seasonal company's investment in current assets tends to fluctuate during the year as depicted in the graphic below:

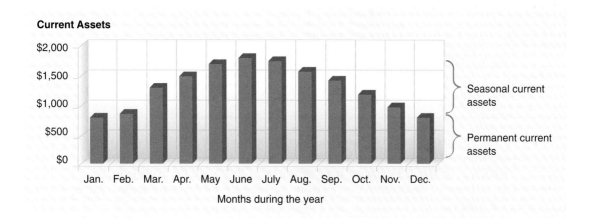

This company does most of its selling in the summer months. More inventory is purchased and manufactured in the early spring than at any other time of the year. High summer sales give rise to accounts receivable that are higher than normal during the fall. The company's working capital peaks at the height of the selling season and is lowest as the business slows in the off-season. There is a permanent level of working capital required for this business (about $750), and a seasonal component (maximum of about $1,000). Different businesses exhibit different patterns in their working capital requirements, but many have both permanent and seasonal components.

The existence of permanent and seasonal current operating assets often require that financing sources also have permanent and seasonal components. Consider again the company depicted in the graphic above. A portion of the company's assets is in inventories that are financed, in part, with accounts payable and accruals. Thus, we expect that current operating liabilities also exhibit a seasonal component that fluctuates with the level of operations. These payables are generally non-interest-bearing and, thus, provide low-cost financing that should be used to the greatest extent possible. Additional financing needs are covered by short-term interest-bearing debt.

This section focuses on current nonoperating liabilities, which include short-term debt, current maturities of long-term liabilities, and accrued interest expenses.

## Short-Term Interest-Bearing Debt

Seasonal swings in working capital are often financed with a bank line of credit (short-term debt). In this case the bank provides a commitment to lend up to a maximum amount with the understanding that the amounts borrowed will be repaid in full sometime during the year. An interest-bearing note evidences any such borrowing.

When the company borrows these short-term funds, it reports the cash received on the balance sheet together with an increase in liabilities (notes payable). The note is reported as a current liability since the expectation is that it will be repaid within a year. This borrowing has no effect on income or equity. The borrower incurs (and the lender earns) interest on the note as time passes. GAAP requires the borrower to accrue the interest liability and the related interest expense each time financial statements are issued.

To illustrate, assume that Verizon borrows $1,000 cash on January 1. The note bears interest at a 12% annual rate, and the interest (3% per quarter) is payable on the first of each subsequent quarter (April 1, July 1, October 1, January 1). Assuming that Verizon issues calendar-quarter financial statements, this borrowing results in the following financial statement effects for January 1 through April 1.

| | | Balance Sheet | | | | | | Income Statement | | |
|---|---|---|---|---|---|---|---|---|---|---|
| Transaction | Cash Asset | + Noncash Assets | = Liabil-ities | + Contrib. Capital | + Earned Capital | | Rev-enues | − Expen-ses | = Net Income |
| Jan 1: Borrow $1,000 cash and issue note payable | +1,000 Cash | | = +1,000 Note Payable | | | | | | = |
| Mar 31: Accrue quarterly interest on 12%, $1,000 note payable | | | = +30 Interest Payable | | −30 Retained Earnings | | | − +30 Interest Expense | = −30 |
| Apr 1: Pay $30 cash for interest due | −30 Cash | | = −30 Interest Payable | | | | | | = |

Cash   1,000
NP     1,000
Cash
1,000 |
    NP
    | 1,000

IE   30
IP     30
IE
30 |
  IP
  | 30

IP   30
Cash   30
IP
30 |
  Cash
  | 30

The January 1 borrowing increases both cash and notes payable. On March 31, Verizon issues its quarterly financial statements. Although interest is not paid until April 1, the company has incurred three months' interest obligation as of March 31. Failure to recognize this liability and the expense incurred would not fairly present the financial condition of the company. Accordingly, the quarterly accrued interest payable is computed as follows:

$$\text{Interest Expense} = \text{Principal} \times \text{Annual Rate} \times \text{Portion of Year Outstanding}$$
$$\$30 \quad = \quad \$1,000 \quad \times \quad 12\% \quad \times \quad 3/12$$

The subsequent interest payment on April 1 reduces both cash and the interest payable that Verizon accrued on March 31. There is no expense reported on April 1, as it was recorded the previous day (March 31) when Verizon prepared its financial statements. (For fixed-maturity borrowings specified in days, such as a 90-day note, we use a 365-day year for interest accrual computations, see Mid-Module Review 3.)

### Current Maturities of Long-Term Debt

Principal payments that must be made during the upcoming 12 months on long-term debt (such as for a mortgage), or on bonds and notes that mature within the next year, are reported as current liabilities called *current maturities of long-term debt*. All companies must provide a schedule of the maturities of their long-term debt in the footnotes to the financial statements. To illustrate, Verizon reports $7,141 million in long-term debt due within one year in the the current liability section of the balance sheet shown on page 8-4.

### MID-MODULE REVIEW 3

On January 15, assume that Verizon borrowed $10,000 on a 90-day, 6% note payable. The bank accrues interest daily based on a 365-day year. Use the financial statement effects template to show the January 31 interest accrual.

## Solution

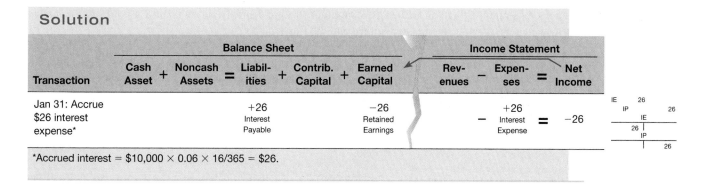

| | Balance Sheet | | | | | | Income Statement | | |
|---|---|---|---|---|---|---|---|---|---|
| Transaction | Cash Asset | + Noncash Assets | = Liabil- ities | + Contrib. Capital | + Earned Capital | | Rev- enues | − Expen- ses | = Net Income |
| Jan 31: Accrue $26 interest expense* | | | +26 Interest Payable | | −26 Retained Earnings | | | − +26 Interest Expense | = −26 |

*Accrued interest = $10,000 × 0.06 × 16/365 = $26.

# LONG-TERM NONOPERATING LIABILITIES

Companies often include long-term nonoperating liabilities in their capital structure to fund long-term assets. Long-term debt in smaller amounts can be readily obtained from banks, private placements with insurance companies, and other credit sources. However, when a large amount of financing is required, the issuance of bonds (and notes) in capital markets is a cost-efficient way to raise capital. The following discussion uses bonds for illustration, but the concepts also apply to long-term notes.

Bonds are structured like any other borrowing. The borrower receives cash and agrees to pay it back with interest. Generally, the entire **face amount** (principal) of the bond is repaid at maturity (at the end of the bond's life) and interest payments are made in the interim (usually semiannually).

Companies that raise funds in the bond market normally work with an underwriter (like Merrill Lynch) to set the terms of the bond issue. The underwriter then sells individual bonds (usually in $1,000 denominations) from this general bond issue to its retail clients and professional portfolio managers (like The Vanguard Group), and receives a fee for underwriting the bond issue. These bonds are investments for individual investors, other companies, retirement plans and insurance companies.

After they are issued, the bonds can trade in the secondary market just like stocks. Market prices of bonds fluctuate daily despite the fact that the company's obligation for payment of principal and interest normally remains fixed throughout the life of the bond. Then, why do bond prices change? The answer is that the bond's fixed-rate of interest can be higher or lower than the interest rates offered on other securities of similar risk. Because bonds compete with other possible investments, bond prices are set relative to the prices of other investments. In a competitive investment market, a particular bond will become more or less desirable depending on the general level of interest rates offered by competing securities. Just as for any item, competitive pressures will cause bond prices to rise and fall.

This section analyzes and interprets the reporting for bonds. We also examine the mechanics of bond pricing and describe the accounting for and reporting of bonds.

## Pricing of Debt

The following two different interest rates are crucial for pricing debt.

- **Coupon (contract or stated) rate**  The coupon rate of interest is stated in the bond contract; it is used to compute the dollar amount of (semiannual) interest payments that are paid to bondholders during the life of the bond issue.

- **Market (yield or effective) rate**  This is the interest rate that investors expect to earn on the investment for this debt security; this rate is used to price the bond.

*The coupon (contract) rate is used to compute interest payments and the market (yield) rate is used to price the bond.* The coupon rate and the market rate are nearly always different. This is because the coupon rate is fixed prior to issuance of the bond and normally remains fixed throughout its life. Market rates of interest, on the other hand, fluctuate continually with the supply and demand for bonds in the market place, general macroeconomic conditions, and the financial condition of borrowers.

The bond price, both its initial sales price and the price it trades at in the secondary market subsequent to issuance, equals the present value of the expected cash flows to the bondholder. Specifically, bondholders normally expect to receive two different types of cash flows:

1. **Periodic interest payments** (usually semiannual) during the bond's life; these payments are called an **annuity** because they are equal in amount and made at regular intervals.
2. **Single payment** of the face (principal) amount of the bond at maturity; this is called a *lump sum payment* because it occurs only once.

The bond price equals the present value of the periodic interest payments plus the present value of the single payment. If the present value of the two cash flows is equal to the bond's face value, the bond is sold at par. If the present value is less than or greater than the bond's face value, the bond sells at a discount or premium, respectively. We next illustrate the issuance of bonds at three different prices: at par, at a discount, and at a premium.

### Bonds Issued at Par

To illustrate a bond sold at par, assume that a bond with a face amount of $10 million, has a 6% annual coupon rate payable semiannually (3% semiannual rate), and a maturity of 10 years. (Semiannual interest payments are typical for bonds. This means that the issuer pays bondholders two interest payments per year. Each semiannual interest payment is equal to the bond's face value times the annual rate divided by two.) Investors purchasing this issue receive the following cash flows.

| | Number of Payments | Dollars per Payment | Total Cash Flows |
|---|---|---|---|
| Semiannual interest payments..... | 10 years × 2 = 20 | $10,000,000 × 3% = $300,000 | $ 6,000,000 |
| Principal payment at maturity...... | 1 | $10,000,000 | 10,000,000 |
| | | | $16,000,000 |

Specifically, the bond agreement dictates that the borrower must make 20 semiannual payments of $300,000 each, computed as $10,000,000 × (6%/2). At maturity, the borrower must repay the $10,000,000 face amount. To price bonds, investors identify the *number* of interest payments and use that number when computing the present value of *both* the interest payments and the principal (face) payment at maturity.

The bond price is the present value of the periodic interest payments (the annuity) plus the present value of the principal payment (the lump sum). In our example, assuming that investors desire a 3% semiannual market rate (yield), the bond sells for $10,000,000, which is computed as follows:

Present value factors are from Appendix A

| | Payment | Present Value Factor[a] | Present Value |
|---|---|---|---|
| Interest................. | $    300,000 | 14.87747[b] | $ 4,463,200[d] |
| Principal.............. | $10,000,000 | 0.55368[c] | 5,536,800 |
| | | | $10,000,000 |

[a] Mechanics of using tables to compute present values are explained in Appendix 8A; present value factors come from Appendix A near the end of the book.

[b] Present value of an ordinary annuity for 20 periods discounted at 3% per period.

[c] Present value of a single payment in 20 periods discounted at 3% per period.

[d] Rounded.

Since the bond contract pays investors a 3% semiannual rate when investors demand a 3% semiannual market rate, given the borrower's credit rating and the time to maturity, the investors purchase those bonds at the **par (face) value** of $10 million.

## Discount Bonds

As a second illustration, assume investors demand a 4% semiannual return for the 3% semiannual coupon bond, while all other details remain the same. The bond now sells for $8,640,999, computed as follows:

| | Payment | Present Value Factor | Present Value |
|---|---|---|---|
| Interest . . . . . . . . . . . . . . . . | $ 300,000 | 13.59033[a] | $ 4,077,099 |
| Principal . . . . . . . . . . . . . . . | $10,000,000 | 0.45639[b] | 4,563,900 |
| | | | $ 8,640,999 |

[a] Present value of an ordinary annuity for 20 periods discounted at 4% per period.
[b] Present value of a single payment in 20 periods discounted at 4% per period.

Since the bond carries a coupon rate *lower* than what investors demand, the bond is less desirable and sells at a **discount**. More generally, bonds sell at a discount whenever the coupon rate is less than the market rate.

## Premium Bonds

As a third illustration, assume that investors demand a 2% semiannual return for the 3% semiannual coupon bonds, while all other details remain the same. The bond now sells for $11,635,129, computed as follows:

| | Payment | Present Value Factor | Present Value |
|---|---|---|---|
| Interest . . . . . . . . . . . . . . . . | $ 300,000 | 16.35143[a] | $ 4,905,429 |
| Principal . . . . . . . . . . . . . . . | $10,000,000 | 0.67297[b] | 6,729,700 |
| | | | $11,635,129 |

[a] Present value of an ordinary annuity for 20 periods discounted at 2% per period.
[b] Present value of a single payment in 20 periods discounted at 2% per period.

Since the bond carries a coupon rate *higher* than what investors demand, the bond is more desirable and sells at a **premium**. More generally, bonds sell at a premium whenever the coupon rate is greater than the market rate.[3] Exhibit 8.1 summarizes this relation for bond pricing.

| **EXHIBIT 8.1** | **Coupon Rate, Market Rate, and Bond Pricing** |
|---|---|
| Coupon rate > market rate → | Bond sells at a **premium** (above face amount) |
| Coupon rate = market rate → | Bond sells at **par** (at face amount) |
| Coupon rate < market rate → | Bond sells at a **discount** (below face amount) |

Exhibit 8.2 shows an announcement (called a *tombstone*) of a recent General Electric $5 billion debt issuance. It has a 5% coupon rate paying 2.5% semiannual interest, maturing in 2013, with an issue price of 99.626 (sold at a discount). GE's underwriters took 0.425 in fees (more than $21 million) for underwriting and selling this debt issue.[4]

---

[3] Bond prices are often stated in percent form. For example, a bond sold at par is said to be sold at 100 (that is, 100% of par). The bond sold at $8,640,999 is said to be sold at 86.41 (86.41% of par, computed as $8,640,999/$10,000,000). The bond sold for a premium is said to be sold at 116.35 (116.35% of the bond's face value).

[4] The tombstone makes clear that if we purchase any of these notes (in denominations of $1,000) after the semiannual interest date, we must pay accrued interest in addition to the purchase price. This interest is returned to us in the regular interest payment. (This procedure makes the bookkeeping easier for the issuer/underwriter because all interest payments are equal regardless of when GE actually sold the bond.)

**EXHIBIT 8.2**    Announcement (Tombstone) of Debt Offering to Public

# General Electric Company

### $5,000,000,000
### 5% Notes due 2013

### Issue price: 99.626%

We will pay interest on the notes semiannually on February 1 and August 1 of each year, beginning August 1, 2003. The notes will mature on February 1, 2013. We may not redeem the notes prior to maturity.

The notes will be unsecured obligations and rank equally with our other unsecured debt securities that are not subordinated obligations. The notes will be issued in registered form in denominations of $1,000.

Neither the Securities and Exchange Commission nor any state securities commission has approved or disapproved of the notes or determined if this prospectus supplement or the accompanying prospectus is truthful or complete. Any representation to the contrary is a criminal offense.

|  | Per Note | Total |
|---|---|---|
| Public Offering Price(1) | 99.626% | $4,981,300,000 |
| Underwriting Discounts | .425% | $    21,250,000 |
| Proceeds to General Electric Company (before expenses) | 99.201% | $4,960,050,000 |

(1)   Plus accrued interest from January 28, 2003, if settlement occurs after that date.

The underwriters expect to deliver the notes in book-entry form only through the facilities of The Depository Trust Company, Clearstream, Luxembourg or the Euroclear System, as the case may be, on or about January 28, 2003.

*Joint Bookrunners*

**Lehman Brothers**    **Morgan Stanley**    **Salomon Smith Barney**

*Senior Co-Managers*

| Banc of America Securities LLC | Credit Suisse First Boston | Deutsche Bank Securities |
|---|---|---|
| Goldman. Sachs & Co. | JPMorgan | Merrill Lynch & Co. |
|  | UBS Warburg |  |

*Co-Managers*

| Banc One Capital Markets, Inc. | Barclays Capital | Blaylock & Partners, L.P. |
|---|---|---|
| BNP PARIBAN | Dresdner Kleinwort Wasserstein | Guzman & Company |
| HSBC | Loop Capital Markets | Ormes Capital Markets, Inc. |
| Utendahl Capital Partners, L.P. | The Williams Capital Group, L.P. |  |

## Effective Cost of Debt

When a bond sells for par, the cost to the issuing company is the cash interest paid. In our first illustration above, the *effective cost* of the bond is the 6% interest paid by the issuer.

When a bond sells at a discount, the issuer must repay more (the face value when the bond matures) than the cash received at issuance (the discounted bond proceeds). This means that the effective cost of a discount bond is greater than if the bond had sold at par. A discount is a cost and, like any other cost, must eventually be transferred from the balance sheet to the income statement as an expense.

When a bond sells at a premium, the borrower received more cash at issuance than it must repay. The difference, the premium, is a benefit that must eventually find its way into the income statement as a *reduction* of interest expense. As a result of the premium, the effective cost of a premium bond is less than if the bond had sold at par.

Bonds are priced to yield the return (market rate) demanded by investors. Consequently, the effective rate of a bond *always* equals the yield (market) rate demanded by investors, regardless of the coupon rate of the bond. This means that companies cannot influence the effective cost of debt by raising or lowering the coupon rate. Doing so will only result in a bond premium or discount. We discuss the factors affecting the yield demanded by investors later in the module.

The effective cost of debt is reflected in the amount of interest expense reported in the issuer's income statement. Because of bond discounts and premiums, interest expense is usually different from the cash interest paid. The next section discusses how management reports bonds on the balance sheet and interest expense on the income statement.

# REPORTING OF DEBT FINANCING

This section identifies and describes the financial statement effects of bond transactions.

## Financial Statement Effects of Debt Issuance

### Bonds Issued at Par

When a bond sells at par, the issuing company receives the cash proceeds and accepts an obligation to make payments per the bond contract. Specifically, cash is increased and a long-term liability (bonds payable) is increased by the same amount. There is no revenue or expense at bond issuance. Using the facts from our $10 million bond illustration above, the issuance of bonds at par has the following financial statement effects:

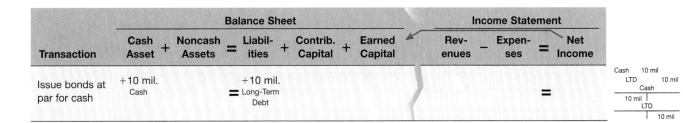

### Discount Bonds

When a bond is sold at a discount, the cash proceeds and net bond liability are recorded at the amount of the proceeds received (not the face amount of the bond). Again, using the facts above from our bond discount illustration, the financial statement effects follow:

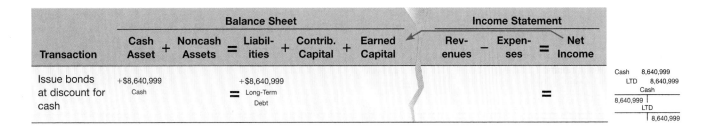

The net bond liability reported on the balance sheet consists of two components as follows:

| | |
|---|---:|
| Bonds payable, face......... | $10,000,000 |
| Less bond discount ......... | (1,359,001) |
| Bonds payable, net ......... | $ 8,640,999 |

Bonds are reported on the balance sheet net of any discount (or premium). When the bond matures, however, the company is obligated to repay $10 million. Accordingly, at maturity, the bond liability needs to read $10 million, the amount that is owed. This means that between the bond issuance and its maturity, the discount must decline to zero. This reduction of the discount over the life of the bond is called **amortization**. The next section shows how discount amortization results in additional interest expense in the income statement. This amortization causes the effective interest expense to be greater than the periodic cash interest payments.

| BUSINESS INSIGHT | Verizon's Zero Coupon Debt |
|---|---|

Zero coupon bonds and notes, called *zeros,* do not carry a coupon rate. Pricing of these bonds and notes is done in the same manner as those with coupon rates—the exception is the absence of an interest annuity. This means that the price is the present value of the principal payment at maturity; hence the bond is sold at a *deep discount.* Following is an example from Verizon's 2005 10-K report:

> **Zero-Coupon Convertible Notes** In May 2001, Verizon . . . issued approximately $5.4 billion in principal amount at maturity of zero-coupon convertible notes due 2021, resulting in gross proceeds of approximately $3 billion. The notes are convertible into shares of our common stock at an initial price of $69.50 per share if the closing price of Verizon common stock on the NYSE exceeds specified levels or in other specified circumstances. The conversion price increases by at least 3% a year. The initial conversion price represents a 25% premium over the May 8, 2001, closing price of $55.60 per share. There are no scheduled cash interest payments associated with the notes. The zero-coupon convertible notes are callable by Verizon . . . on or after May 15, 2006. In addition, the notes are redeemable at the option of the holders on May 15th in each of the years 2004, 2006, 2011 and 2016. On May 15, 2004, $3,292 million of principal amount of the notes ($1,984 million after unamortized discount) were redeemed by Verizon. As of December 31, 2005, the remaining zero-coupon convertible notes were classified as debt maturing within one year since they are redeemable at the option of the holders on May 15, 2006.

When Verizon issued its zero-coupon convertible notes in 2001, they had a maturity value of $5.4 billion and were slated to mature in 2021. No interest is paid in the interim. The notes sold for $3 billion. The difference between the $3 billion sales proceeds and the $5.4 billion maturity value represents Verizon's interest costs, which is the return to the investor. The effective cost of the debt is the interest rate that equates the issue price and maturity value, or approximately 3%. In May 2004, Verizon redeemed almost $3.3 billion of the bonds—this constituted an early repayment.

## Premium Bonds

When a bond is sold at a premium, the cash proceeds and net bond liability are recorded at the amount of the proceeds received (not the face amount of the bond). Again, using the facts above from our premium bond illustration, the financial statement effects follow:

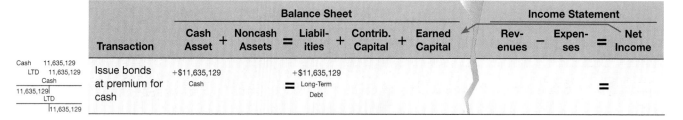

| | | Balance Sheet | | | | | | Income Statement | | |
|---|---|---|---|---|---|---|---|---|---|---|
| Transaction | Cash Asset | + Noncash Assets | = Liabil-ities | + Contrib. Capital | + Earned Capital | | Rev-enues | − Expen-ses | = Net Income |
| Issue bonds at premium for cash | +$11,635,129 Cash | | +$11,635,129 Long-Term Debt | | | | | | = |

Cash 11,635,129
LTD 11,635,129

Cash
11,635,129 |
LTD
|11,635,129

The bond liability amount reported on the balance sheet, again, consists of two parts:

| | |
|---|---|
| Bonds payable, face. . . . . . . . | $10,000,000 |
| Add bond premium . . . . . . . . . | 1,635,129 |
| Bonds payable, net . . . . . . . . | $11,635,129 |

The $10 million must be repaid at maturity, and the premium is amortized to zero over the life of the bond. The premium represents a *benefit,* which *reduces* interest expense on the income statement.

## Effects of Discount and Premium Amortization

For bonds issued at par, interest expense reported on the income statement equals the cash interest payment. However, for bonds issued at a discount or premium, interest expense reported on the income statement also includes any amortization of the bond discount or premium as follows:

| Cash interest paid | | Cash interest paid |
| + Amortization of discount | or | − Amortization of premium |
| Interest expense | | Interest expense |

Specifically, periodic amortization of a discount is added to the cash interest paid to get interest expense. Amortization of the discount reflects the additional cost the issuer incurs from issuing the bonds at a discount. Over the bond's life, the discount is transferred from the balance sheet to the income statement via amortization, as an increase to interest expense. For a premium bond, the premium is a benefit the issuer receives at issuance. Amortization of the premium reduces interest expense over the bond's life. In both cases, interest expense on the income statement represents the *effective cost* of debt (the *nominal cost* of debt is the cash interest paid).

Companies amortize discounts and premiums using the effective interest method. To illustrate, recall the assumptions of the discount bond above—face amount of $10 million, a 6% annual coupon rate payable semiannually (3% semiannual rate), a maturity of 10 years, and a market (yield) rate of 8% annual (4% semiannual). These facts resulted in a bond issue price of $8,640,999. Exhibit 8.3 shows the first two and final two periods of a bond discount amortization table for this bond.

| **EXHIBIT 8.3** | Bond Discount Amortization Table | | | | |
|---|---|---|---|---|---|
| Period | **[A]**<br>*([E] × market%)*<br>Interest<br>Expense | **[B]**<br>*(Face × coupon%)*<br>Cash<br>Interest Paid | **[C]**<br>*([A] − [B])*<br>Discount<br>Amortization | **[D]**<br>*(Prior bal − [C])*<br>Discount<br>Balance | **[E]**<br>*(Face − [D])*<br>Bond<br>Payable, Net |
| 0 | | | | $1,359,001 | $ 8,640,999 |
| 1 | $345,640 | $300,000 | $45,640 | 1,313,361 | 8,686,639 |
| 2 | 347,466 | 300,000 | 47,466 | 1,265,895 | 8,734,105 |
| ⋮ | ⋮ | ⋮ | ⋮ | ⋮ | ⋮ |
| 19 | 392,458 | 300,000 | 92,458 | 96,087 | 9,903,913 |
| 20 | 396,157* | 300,000 | 96,157* | 0 | 10,000,000 |

\* Due to rounding, we must subtract $70 from both [A] and [C] in period 20 to yield the $10,000,000 face value.

The interest period is denoted in the left-most column. Period 0 is the point at which the bond is issued, and period 1 and following are successive six-month periods (recall, interest is paid semiannually). Column [A] is interest expense, which is reported in the income statement. Interest expense is computed as the bond's net balance sheet value (the carrying amount of the bond) at the beginning of the period (column [E]) multiplied by the 4% semiannual rate used to compute the bond issue price. Column [B] is cash interest paid, which is a constant $300,000 per the bond contract (face amount × coupon rate). Column [C] is discount amortization, which is the difference between interest expense and cash interest paid. Column [D] is the discount balance, which is the previous balance of the discount less the discount amortization in column [C]. Column [E] is the net bond payable, which is the $10 million face amount less the unamortized discount from column [D].

The table shows amounts for interest in periods 0, 1, 2, 19, and 20. The amortization process continues until period 20, at which time the discount balance is 0 and the net bond payable is $10 million (the maturity value). Each semiannual period, interest expense is recorded at 4%, the market rate of interest at the bond's issuance. This rate does not change over the life of the bond, even if the prevailing market interest rates change. An amortization table reveals the financial statement effects of the bond for its duration. Specifically, we see the income statement effects in column [A], the cash effects in column [B], and the balance sheet effects in columns [D] and [E]. (A fully completed amortization table is shown in Appendix 8B.)

To illustrate amortization of a premium bond, we use the assumptions of the premium bond above— $10 million face value, a 6% annual coupon rate payable semiannually (3% semiannual rate), a maturity of 10 years, and a 2% semiannual market interest rate. These parameters resulted in a bond issue price of $11,635,129. Exhibit 8.4 shows the first and last two periods of a bond premium amortization table for this bond.

| | **[A]** | **[B]** | **[C]** | **[D]** | **[E]** |
|---|---|---|---|---|---|
| | *([E] × market%)* | *(Face × coupon%)* | *([B] − [A])* | *(Prior bal − [C])* | *(Face + [D])* |
| | **Interest** | **Cash** | **Premium** | **Premium** | **Bond** |
| **Period** | **Expense** | **Interest Paid** | **Amortization** | **Balance** | **Payable, Net** |
| 0 | | | | $1,635,129 | $11,635,129 |
| 1 | $232,703 | $300,000 | $67,297 | 1,567,832 | 11,567,832 |
| 2 | 231,357 | 300,000 | 68,643 | 1,499,188 | 11,499,188 |
| ⋮ | ⋮ | ⋮ | ⋮ | ⋮ | ⋮ |
| 19 | 203,883 | 300,000 | 96,117 | 98,018 | 10,098,018 |
| 20 | 201,960* | 300,000 | 98,040* | 0 | 10,000,000 |

**EXHIBIT 8.4** Bond Premium Amortization Table

* Due to rounding, we must add $22 to [A] and subtract $22 from [C] in period 20 to yield the $10,000,000 face value.

Interest expense is computed using the same process that we used for discount bonds. The difference is that the yield rate is 2% semiannual in the premium case. Also, cash interest paid follows from the bond contract (face amount × coupon rate), and the other columns' computations reflect the premium amortization. After period 20, the premium is fully amortized (equals zero) and the net bond payable balance is $10 million, the amount owed at maturity. Again, an amortization table reveals the financial statement effects of the bond—the income statement effects in column [A], the cash effects in column [B], and the balance sheet effects in columns [D] and [E].

## Financial Statement Effects of Bond Repurchase

Companies report bonds payable at *historical (adjusted) cost.* Specifically, net bonds payable amounts follow from the amortization table, as do the related cash flows and income statement numbers. All financial statement relations are set when the bond is issued and do not subsequently change.

Once issued, however, bonds trade in secondary markets. The yield rate used to compute bond prices for these subsequent transactions is the market interest rate prevailing at the time. These rates change daily based on the level of interest rates in the economy and the perceived creditworthiness of the bond issuer.

Companies can and sometimes do repurchase (or *redeem*) their bonds prior to maturity. The bond indenture (contract agreement) can include provisions giving the company the right to repurchase its bonds. Or, the company can repurchase bonds in the open market. To illustrate, Verizon's 2005 10-K includes the following footnote relating to its repurchase of MCI debt in connection with the MCI acquisition:

> **Redemption of MCI Debt**   On January 17, 2006, Verizon announced offers to purchase two series of MCI senior notes, MCI $1,983 million aggregate principal amount of 6.688% Senior Notes Due 2009 and MCI $1,699 million aggregate principal amount of 7.735% Senior Notes Due 2014, at 101% of their par value. Due to the change in control of MCI that occurred in connection with the merger with Verizon on January 6, 2006, Verizon is required to make this offer to noteholders within 30 days of the closing of the merger of MCI and Verizon. Separately, Verizon notified noteholders that MCI is exercising its right to redeem both series of Senior Notes prior to maturity under the optional redemption procedures provided in the indentures. The 6.688% Notes were redeemed on March 1, 2006, and the 7.735% Notes were redeemed on February 16, 2006. In addition, on January 20, 2006, Verizon announced an offer to repurchase MCI $1,983 million aggregate principal amount of 5.908% Senior Notes Due 2007 at 101% of their par value. On February 21, 2006, $1,804 million of these notes were redeemed by Verizon. Verizon satisfied and discharged the indenture governing this series of notes shortly after the close of the offer for those noteholders who did not accept this offer.

When a bond repurchase occurs, a gain or loss usually results, and is computed as follows:

**Gain or Loss on Bond Repurchase = Net Bonds Payable − Repurchase Payment**

The net bonds payable, also referred to as the *book value,* is the net amount reported on the balance sheet. If the issuer pays more to retire the bonds than the amount carried on its balance sheet, it reports a loss on its income statement, usually called *loss on bond retirement*. The issuer reports a *gain on bond retirement* if the repurchase price is less than the net bonds payable.

GAAP dictates that any gains or losses on bond repurchases be reported as part of ordinary income unless they meet the criteria for treatment as an extraordinary item (unusual and infrequent, see Module 5). Relatively few debt retirements meet these criteria and, hence, most gains and losses on bond repurchases are reported as part of income from continuing operations.

How should we treat these gains and losses for analysis purposes? That is, do they carry economic effects? The answer is no—the gain or loss on repurchase is exactly offset by the present value of the future cash flow implications of the repurchase (Appendix 8B demonstrates this).

Another analysis issue involves assessing the market value of bonds and other long-term liabilities. This information is relevant for some investors and creditors in revealing unrealized gains and losses (similar to that reported for marketable securities). GAAP requires companies to provide information about current market values of their long-term liabilities in footnotes (see Verizon's fair value of debt disclosure in the next section). However, these market values are *not* reported on the balance sheet and changes in these market values are not reflected in net income. We must make our own adjustments to the balance sheet and income statement if we want to include changes in market values of liabilities.

## Financial Statement Footnotes

Companies are required to disclose details about their long-term liabilities, including the amounts borrowed under each debt issuance, the interest rates, maturity dates, and other key provisions. Following is Verizon's disclosure for its long-term debt.

**Long-Term Debt**  Outstanding long-term obligations are as follows:

| At December 31 ($ millions) | Interest Rates % | Maturities | 2005 | 2004 |
|---|---|---|---|---|
| Notes payable | 4.00–8.61 | 2006–2035 | $16,310 | $17,481 |
| Telephone subsidiaries—debentures | | | | |
| and first/refunding mortgage bonds | 4.63–7.00 | 2006–2042 | 11,869 | 12,958 |
| | 7.15–7.65 | 2007–2032 | 1,725 | 1,825 |
| | 7.85–9.67 | 2010–2031 | 1,926 | 1,930 |
| Other subsidiaries—debentures and other | 4.25–8.75 | 2006–2028 | 3,410 | 3,480 |
| Zero-coupon convertible notes, net of | | | | |
| unamortized discount of $790 and $830 | 3.18 | 2021 | 1,360 | 1,320 |
| Employee stock ownership plan loans: | | | | |
| NYNEX debentures | 9.55 | 2010 | 113 | 145 |
| Capital lease obligations (average rate | | | | |
| 11.9% and 9.4%) | | | 112 | 138 |
| Property sale holdbacks held in escrow, | | | | |
| vendor financing and other | 3.00–3.25 | 2006–2009 | 13 | 21 |
| Unamortized discount, net of premium | | | (43) | (55) |
| Total long-term debt, including | | | | |
| current maturities | | | 36,795 | 39,243 |
| Less: debt maturing within one year | | | (4,926) | (3,569) |
| Total long-term debt | | | $31,869 | $35,674 |

Verizon reports a book value for long-term debt of $36,795 million at year-end 2005. Of this amount, $4,926 million matures in the next year and is classified as a current liability (current maturities of long-term debt). The remainder of $31,869 matures after 2006. Verizon also reports $43 million in unamortized discount (net of premium) on this debt.

In addition to long-term debt amounts, rates, and due dates, and as required under GAAP, Verizon reports aggregate maturities for the five years subsequent to the balance sheet date as follows:

**Maturities of Long-Term Debt**  Maturities of long-term debt outstanding at December 31, 2005 are $4.9 billion in 2006, $4.7 billion in 2007, $2.5 billion in 2008, $1.7 billion in 2009, $2.8 billion in 2010 and $20.2 billion thereafter.

This reveals that Verizon is required to make principal payments of $16.6 billion in the next five years, with $9.6 billion of that coming due in the next two years. Such maturities are important information as a company must meet its required payments, negotiate a rescheduling of the indebtedness, or refinance the debt to avoid default. Failing to repay debts (defaulting) usually has severe consequences as debtholders have legal remedies available to them that can bankrupt the company.

Verizon's disclosure on the market value of its total debt follows:

| December 31, 2005 ($ millions) | Carrying Amount | Fair Value |
|---|---|---|
| Short- and long-term debt . . . . . . . . . . . | $38,898 | $40,313 |

As of 2005, indebtedness with a book value of $38,898 million had a market value of $40,313 million, resulting in an unrecognized liability (which would be realized if Verizon redeemed the debt) of $1,415 million. The increase in market value is due mainly to a decline in interest rates subsequent to the bonds' issuance. The justification for not recognizing unrealized gains and losses on the balance sheet and income statement is that such amounts can reverse with future fluctuations in interest rates. Further, since only the face amount of debt is repaid at maturity, unrealized gains and losses that arise during intervening years are not necessarily relevant. This is the same logic for nonrecognition of gains and losses on held-to-maturity debt investments (see Module 7).

# CREDIT RATINGS AND THE COST OF DEBT

**LO3** Explain how credit ratings are determined and identify their effect on the cost of debt.

Earlier in the module we explained that the effective cost of debt to the issuing company is the market (yield) rate of interest used to price the bond, regardless of the bond coupon rate. The market rate of interest is usually defined as the yield on U.S. Government borrowings such as treasury bills, notes, and bonds, called the *risk-free rate*, plus a *spread* (also called a risk premium).

$$\textbf{Yield Rate} = \textbf{Risk-Free Rate} + \textbf{Spread}$$

Both treasury yields (the so-called risk-free rates) and corporate yields vary over time as illustrated in the following graphic.

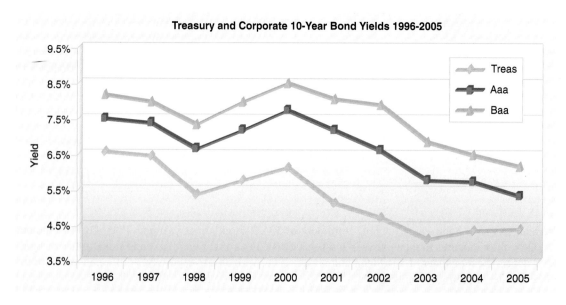

The rate of interest that investors expect for a particular bond is a function of the risk-free rate and the spread that depends on the creditworthiness of the issuing entity.

The yield increases (shifts upward) as debt quality moves from Treasury securities (generally considered to be risk free), which is the highest quality debt reflected in the line nearest to zero, to the AAA (highest) rated corporates and, finally, to the Baa (lower-rated) corporates shown in this graph. That is, higher credit-rated issuers warrant a lower rate than lower credit-rated issuers. This difference is substantial. For example, in 2005, the average 10-year treasury bond yield is 4.29%, while the AAA corporate bond yield is 5.23% and the average Baa (the lowest investment grade corporate) yield is 6.06%.

---

**RESEARCH INSIGHT**    **Accounting Conservatism and Cost of Debt**

Research indicates that companies that use more conservative accounting policies incur a lower cost of debt. Research also suggests that while accounting conservatism can lead to lower-quality accounting income (because such income does not fully reflect economic reality), creditors are more confident in the numbers and view them as more credible. Evidence also implies that companies can lower the required return demanded by creditors (the spread) by issuing high-quality financial reports that include enhanced footnote disclosures and detailed supplemental reports.

---

A company's credit rating, also referred to as debt rating, credit quality or creditworthiness, is related to default risk. **Default** refers to the nonpayment of interest and principal and/or the failure to adhere to the various terms and conditions (covenants) of the bond indenture. Companies seeking to obtain bond financing from the capital markets, normally first seek a rating on their proposed debt issuance from one of several rating agencies such as Standard & Poor's, Moody's Investors Service, or Fitch. The aim of rating agencies is to rate debt so that its default risk is more accurately conveyed to and priced by the market. Each rating agency uses its own rating system, as Exhibit 8.5 shows. This exhibit includes the general description for each rating class—for example, AAA is assigned to debt of prime maximum safety (maximum creditworthiness).

| ▸ EXHIBIT 8.5 | Corporate Debt Ratings and Descriptions | | |
|---|---|---|---|
| **Moody's** | **S&P** | **Fitch** | **Description** |
| Aaa | AAA | AAA | Prime Maximum Safety |
| Aa1 | AA+ | AA+ | High Grade, High Quality |
| Aa2 | AA | AA | |
| Aa3 | AA− | AA− | |
| A1 | A+ | A+ | Upper-Medium Grade |
| A2 | A | A | |
| A3 | A− | A− | |
| Baa1 | BBB+ | BBB+ | Lower-Medium Grade |
| Baa2 | BBB | BBB | |
| Baa3 | BBB− | BBB− | |
| Ba1 | BB+ | BB+ | Non-Investment Grade |
| Ba2 | BB | BB | Speculative |
| Ba3 | BB− | BB− | |
| B1 | B+ | B+ | Highly Speculative |
| B2 | B | B | |
| B3 | B− | B− | |
| Caa1 | CCC+ | CCC | Substantial Risk |
| Caa2 | CCC | | In Poor Standing |
| Caa3 | CCC− | | |
| Ca | | | Extremely Speculative |
| C | | | May be in Default |
| | | DDD | Default |
| | | DD | |
| | D | D | |

| MANAGERIAL DECISION | You Are the Vice President of Finance |
|---|---|

Your company is currently rated B1/B+ by the Moody's and S&P credit rating agencies, respectively. You are considering possible financial and other restructurings to increase your company's credit rating. What types of restructurings might you consider? What benefits will your company receive from those restructurings? What costs will your company incur to implement such restructurings? [Answer, p. 8-30]

Verizon bonds are rated A3/A by Moody's and S&P, respectively, as of 2006. It is this rating, in conjunction with the maturity of Verizon's bonds, that establishes the market interest rate and the bonds' selling price. There are a number of considerations that affect the rating of a bond. Standard & Poor's lists the following factors, categorized by business risk and financial risk, among its credit rating criteria:

| **Business Risk** | **Financial Risk** |
|---|---|
| Industry characteristics | Financial characteristics |
| Competitive position (marketing, technology, efficiency, regulation) | Financial policy |
| | Profitability |
| | Capital structure |
| Management | Cash flow protection |
| | Financial flexibility |

Debt ratings are set to convey information primarily to debt investors who are mainly interested in assessing the probability that the borrower will make interest and principal payments on time. If a company defaults on its debt, debtholders seek legal remedies, including forcing the borrower to liquidate its assets to settle obligations. However, in forced liquidations, debtholders rarely realize the entire amounts owed to them.

Standard and Poor's uses several financial ratios to assess default risk. A list of these ratios, together with median averages for various risk classes, is in Exhibit 8.6. In examining the ratios, recall that debt is increasingly more risky as we move from the first column, AAA, to the last, CCC.[5]

---

[5] Definitions for the key ratios in Exhibit 8.6 follow:

$$\text{EBIT interest coverage} = \frac{\text{Earnings from continuing operations before interest and taxes}}{\text{Gross interest incurred before subtracting (1) capitalized interest and (2) interest income}}$$

$$\text{EBITDA interest coverage} = \frac{\text{Earnings from continuing operations before interest and taxes, depreciation, and amortization}}{\text{Gross interest incurred before subtracting (1) capitalized interest and (2) interest income}}$$

$$\text{Funds from operations/total debt} = \frac{\text{Net income from continuing operations plus depreciation, amortization, deferred income taxes, and other noncash items}}{\text{Long-term debt plus current maturities, commercial paper, and other short-term borrowings}}$$

$$\text{Free operating cash flow/total debt} = \frac{\text{Funds from operations minus capital expenditures, minus (plus) the increase (decrease) in working capital (excluding changes in cash, marketable securities, and short-term debt)}}{\text{Long-term debt plus current maturities, commercial paper, and other short-term borrowings}}$$

$$\text{Return on capital} = \frac{\text{Earnings from continuing operations before interest and taxes}}{\text{Average of beginning of year and end of year capital, including short-term debt, current maturities, long-term debt, noncurrent deferred taxes, and equity}}$$

$$\text{Operating income/sales} = \frac{\text{Sales minus cost of goods manufactured (before depreciation and amortization), selling, general and administrative, and research and development costs}}{\text{Sales}}$$

$$\text{Long-term debt/capital} = \frac{\text{Long-term debt}}{\text{Long-term debt plus shareholders' equity (including preferred stock) plus minority interest}}$$

$$\text{Total debt/capital} = \frac{\text{Long-term debt plus current maturities, commercial paper, and other short-term borrowings}}{\text{Long-term debt plus current maturities, commercial paper, and other short-term borrowings plus shareholders' equity (including preferred stock) plus minority interest}}$$

| EXHIBIT 8.6 | Ratio Values for Different Risk Classes of Corporate Debt* | | | | | | |
|---|---|---|---|---|---|---|---|
| **Three-Year Medians** | **AAA** | **AA** | **A** | **BBB** | **BB** | **B** | **CCC** |
| EBIT interest coverage (×)............ | 21.4 | 10.1 | 6.1 | 3.7 | 2.1 | 0.8 | 0.1 |
| EBITDA interest coverage (×) ........ | 26.5 | 12.9 | 9.1 | 5.8 | 3.4 | 1.8 | 1.3 |
| FFO/Total debt (%)................. | 128.8 | 55.4 | 43.2 | 30.8 | 18.8 | 7.8 | 1.6 |
| Free oper. cash flow/Total debt (%) .... | 84.2 | 25.2 | 15.0 | 8.5 | 2.6 | (3.2) | (12.9) |
| Return on capital (%) .............. | 34.9 | 21.7 | 19.4 | 13.6 | 11.6 | 6.6 | 1.0 |
| Operating income/Sales (%) ......... | 27.0 | 22.1 | 18.6 | 15.4 | 15.9 | 11.9 | 11.9 |
| Long-term debt/Capital (%) .......... | 13.3 | 28.2 | 33.9 | 42.5 | 57.2 | 69.7 | 68.8 |
| Total debt/Capital (incl. STD) (%) ...... | 22.9 | 37.7 | 42.5 | 48.2 | 62.6 | 74.8 | 87.7 |

*Corporate Ratings Criteria—Adjusted Key Financial Ratios, Standard & Poor's Ratings, Standard & Poor's, a division of The McGraw-Hill Companies (reproduced with permission).

A review of these ratios indicates that S&P considers the following factors relevant in evaluating a company's ability to meet its debt service requirements:

1. Liquidity (ratios 1 through 4)
2. Profitability (ratios 5 and 6)
3. Solvency (ratios 7 and 8)

Further, these ratios are variants of many of the ratios we describe in Module 4.
   Other relevant debt-rating factors include the following:

- **Collateral**   Companies can provide security for debt by pledging certain assets against the bond. This is like mortgages on assets. To the extent debt is secured, the debtholder is in a preferred position vis-à-vis other creditors.

- **Covenants**   Debt agreements (indentures) can restrict the behavior of the issuing company so as to protect debtholders. For example, covenants commonly prohibit excessive dividend payment, mergers and acquisitions, further borrowing, and commonly prescribe minimum levels for key liquidity and solvency ratios. These covenants provide debtholders an element of control over the issuer's operations since, unlike equity investors, debtholders have no voting rights.

- **Options**   Options are sometimes written into debt contracts. Examples are options to convert debt into stock (so that debtholders have a stake in value creation) and options allowing the issuing company to repurchase its debt before maturity (usually at a premium).

---

**RESEARCH INSIGHT**    **Valuation of Debt Options**

Debt instruments can include features such as conversion options, under which the debt can be converted to common stock. Such conversion features are not accounted for separately under GAAP. Instead, convertible debt is accounted for just like debt with no conversion features (unless the conversion option can be separately traded). However, option-pricing models can be used to estimate the value of such debt features even when no market for those features exist. Empirical results suggest that those debt features represent a substantial part of debt value. These findings contribute to the current debate regarding the separation of compound financial instruments into debt and equity portions for financial statement presentation and analysis.

## MODULE-END REVIEW

On January 1, assume that Sprint Nextel Corporation issues $300,000 of 15-year, 10% bonds payable for $351,876, yielding an effective semiannual interest rate of 4%. Interest is payable semiannually on June 30 and December 31. (1) Show computations to confirm the issue price of $351,876, and (2) complete Sprint's financial statement effects template for (a) bond issuance, (b) semiannual interest payment and premium amortization on June 30 of the first year, and (c) semiannual interest payment and premium amortization on December 31 of the first year.

### Solution

1.

| | |
|---|---|
| Issue price for $300,000, 15-year bonds that pay, 10% interest semiannually discounted at 8%: | |
| Present value of principal payment ($300,000 × 0.30832) . . . . . . . . . . . . . . . . . . . . . . . . . | $ 92,496 |
| Present value of semiannual interest payments ($15,000 × 17.29203). . . . . . . . . . . . . . . . | 259,380 |
| Issue price of bonds. . . . . . . . . . . . . . . . . . . . . . . . . . . . . . . . . . . . . . . . . . . . . . . . . . . . . . | $351,876 |

2.

Cash 351,876
LTD 351,876
Cash
351,876 |
LTD
| 351,876

IE 14,075
LTD 925
Cash 15,000
IE
14,075 |
LTD
925 |
Cash
| 15,000

IE 14,038
LTD 962
Cash 15,000
IE
14,038 |
LTD
962 |
Cash
| 15,000

| | Balance Sheet | | | | | | Income Statement | | |
|---|---|---|---|---|---|---|---|---|---|
| Transaction | Cash Asset | + Noncash Assets | = Liabil- ities | + Contrib. Capital | + Earned Capital | | Rev- enues | − Expen- ses | = Net Income |
| January 1: Issue 10% bonds | +351,876 Cash | | +351,876 = Long-Term Debt | | | | | | = |
| June 30: Pay interest and amortize bond premium[1] | −15,000 Cash | | −925 = Long-Term Debt | | −14,075 Retained Earnings | | | +14,075 − Interest Expense | = −14,075 |
| December 31: Pay interest and amortize bond premium[2] | −15,000 Cash | | −962 = Long-Term Debt | | −14,038 Retained Earnings | | | +14,038 − Interest Expense | = −14,038 |

[1] $300,000 × 0.10 × 6/12 = $15,000 cash payment; 0.04 × $351,876 = $14,075 interest expense; the difference is the bond premium amortization, which reduces the net bond carrying amount.

[2] 0.04 × ($351,876 − $925) = $14,038 interest expense. The difference between this amount and the $15,000 cash payment is the premium amortization, which reduces the net bond carrying amount.

# APPENDIX 8A: Compound Interest

This appendix explains the concepts of present and future value.

## Present Value Concepts

Would you rather receive a dollar now or a dollar one year from now? Most people would answer, a dollar now. Intuition tells us that a dollar received now is more valuable than the same amount received sometime in the future. Sound reasons exist for choosing the dollar now, the most obvious of which concerns risk. Since the future is uncertain, any number of events can prevent us from receiving the dollar a year from now. To avoid this risk, we choose the earlier date. Another reason is that the dollar received now could be invested. That is, one year from now, we would have the dollar and the interest earned on that dollar.

## Present Value of a Single Amount

Risk and interest factors yield the following generalizations: (1) the right to receive an amount of money now, its **present value,** is worth more than the right to receive the same amount later, its **future value;** (2) the longer we must wait to receive an amount, the less attractive the receipt is; (3) the greater the interest rate the greater the amount we will receive in the future. (Putting 2 and 3 together we see that difference between the present value of an amount and its future value is a function of both interest rate and time, that is, Principal × Interest Rate × Time); and (4) the more risk associated with any situation, the higher the interest rate.

To illustrate, let's compute the amount we would need to receive today (the present value) that would be equivalent to receiving $100 one year from now if money can be invested at 10%. We recognize intuitively that, with a 10% interest rate, the present value (the equivalent amount today) will be less than $100. The $100 received in the future must include 10% interest earned for the year. Thus, the $100 received in one year (the future value) must be 1.10 times the amount received today (the present value). Dividing $100/1.10, we obtain a present value of $90.91 (rounded). This means that we would do as well to accept $90.91 today as to wait one year and receive $100. To confirm the equality of the $90.91 receipt now to a $100 receipt one year later, we calculate the future value of $90.91 at 10% for one year as follows:

$$\textbf{\$90.91} \times \textbf{1.10} \times \textbf{1 year} = \textbf{\$100 (rounded)}$$

To generalize, we compute the present value of a future receipt by *discounting* the future receipt back to the present at an appropriate interest rate (also called the *discount rate*). We present this schematically below:

$$\textbf{Present Value} \longleftarrow \boxed{\begin{array}{c}\textbf{Discounted for} \\ \textbf{1 year at 10\%}\end{array}} \longleftarrow \textbf{Future Value}$$
$$\textbf{\$90.91} \qquad\qquad\qquad\qquad\qquad \textbf{\$100}$$

If either the time period or the interest rate were increased, the resulting present value would decrease. If more than one time period is involved, our future receipts include interest on interest. This is called *compounding*.

## Time Value of Money Tables

Appendix A near the end of the book includes time value of money tables. Table 1 is a present value table that we can use to compute the present value of future amounts. A present value table provides present value factors (multipliers) for many combinations of time periods and interest rates that determine the present value of $1.

Present value tables are used as follows. First, determine the number of interest compounding periods involved (three years compounded annually are 3 periods, and three years compounded semiannually are 6 periods). The extreme left-hand column indicates the number of periods. It is important to distinguish between years and compounding periods. The table is for compounding periods (years × number of compounding periods per year).

Next, determine the interest rate per compounding period. Interest rates are usually quoted on a *per year* (annual) basis. The rate per compounding period is the annual rate divided by the number of compounding periods per year. For example, an interest rate of 10% *per year* would be 10% per period if compounded annually, and 5% *per period* if compounded semiannually.

Finally, locate the present value factor, which is at the intersection of the row of the appropriate number of compounding periods and the column of the appropriate interest rate per compounding period. Multiply this factor by the dollars that will be paid or received in the future.

All values in Table 1 are less than 1.0 because the present value of $1 received in the future is always smaller than $1. As the interest rate increases (moving from left to right in the table) or the number of periods increases (moving from top to bottom), the present value factors decline. This illustrates two important facts: (1) present values decline as interest rates increase, and (2) present values decline as the time to receipt lengthens. Consider the following two cases:

**Case 1.** Compute the present value of $100 to be received one year from today, discounted at 10% compounded semiannually:

        Number of periods (one year, semiannually) = 2
        Rate per period (10%/2) = 5%
        Multiplier = 0.90703
        Present value = $100.00 × 0.90703 = $90.70 (rounded)

**Case 2.** Compute the present value of $100 to be received two years from today, discounted at 10% compounded semiannually:

        Number of periods (two years, semiannually) = 4
        Rate per period (10%/2) = 5%
        Multiplier = 0.82270
        Present value = $100 × 0.82270 = $82.27 (rounded)

**Case 3.** Compute the present value of $100 to be received two years from today, discounted at 12% compounded semiannually:

Number of periods (two years, semiannually) = 4
Rate per period (12%/2) = 6%
Multiplier = 0.79209
Present value = $100 = 0.79209 = $79.21 (rounded)

In Case 2, the present value of $82.27 is less than for Case 1 ($90.70) because the time increased from one to two years—the longer we must wait for money, the lower its value to us today. Then in Case 3, the present value of $79.21 was lower than in Case 2 because, while there were still four compounding periods, the interest rate per year was higher (12% annually instead of 10%)—the higher the interest rate the more interest that could have been earned on the money and therefore the lower the value today.

## Present Value of an Annuity

In the examples above, we computed the present value of a single amount (also called a lump sum) made or received in the future. Often, future cash flows involve the same amount being paid or received each period. Examples include semiannual interest payments on bonds, quarterly dividend receipts, or monthly insurance premiums. If the payment or the receipt (the cash flow) is equally spaced over time and each cash flow is the same dollar amount, we have an *annuity*. One way to calculate the present value of the annuity would be to calculate the present value of each future cash flow separately. However, there is a more convenient method.

To illustrate, assume $100 is to be received at the end of each of the next three years as an annuity. When annuity amounts occur at the *end of each period*, the annuity is called an *ordinary annuity*. As shown below, the present value of this ordinary annuity can be computed from Table 1 by computing the present value of each of the three individual receipts and summing them (assume a 5% annual rate).

| Future Receipts (ordinary annuity) | | | PV Multiplier (Table 1) | | Present Value |
|---|---|---|---|---|---|
| Year 1 | Year 2 | Year 3 | | | |
| $100 | | | × 0.95238 | = | $ 95.24 |
| | $100 | | × 0.90703 | = | 90.70 |
| | | $100 | × 0.86384 | = | 86.38 |
| | | | 2.72325 | | $272.32 |

Table 2 in Appendix A provides a single multiplier for computing the present value of an ordinary annuity. Referring to Table 2 in the row for three periods and the column for 5%, we see that the multiplier is 2.72325. When applied to the $100 annuity amount, the multiplier gives a present value of $272.33. As shown above, the same present value (with 1 cent rounding error) is derived by summing the three separate multipliers from Table 1. Considerable computations are avoided by using annuity tables.

## Bond Valuation

Recall that (1) a bond agreement specifies a pattern of future cash flows—usually a series of interest payments and a single payment of the face amount at maturity, and (2) bonds are priced using the prevailing market rate on the day the bond is sold. This is the case for the original bond issuance and for subsequent open-market sales. The market rate on the date of the sale is the rate we use to determine the bond's market value (its price). That rate is the bond's *yield*. The selling price of a bond is determined as follows:

1. Use Table 1 to compute the present value of the future principal payment at the prevailing market rate.
2. Use Table 2 to compute the present value of the future series of interest payments (the annuity) at the prevailing market rate.
3. Add the present values from steps 1 and 2.

We illustrate in Exhibit 8A.1 the price of $100,000, 8%, 4-year bonds paying interest semiannually and sold when the prevailing market rate was (1) 8%, (2) 10% or (3) 6%. Note that the price of 8% bonds sold to yield 8% is the face (or par) value of the bonds. A bond issue price of $93,537 (discount bond) yields 10%. A bond issue price of $107,019 (premium bond) yields 6%.

| EXHIBIT 8A.1 | Calculation of Bond Price Using Present Value Tables |
|---|---|

| Future Cash Flows | Multiplier (Table 1) | Multiplier (Table 2) | Present Values at 4% Semiannually |
|---|---|---|---|
| (1) $100,000 of 8%, 4-year bonds with interest payable semiannually priced to yield 8%. | | | |
| Principal payment, $100,000 (a single amount received after 8 semiannual periods)................ | 0.73069 | | $ 73,069 |
| Interest payments, $4,000 at end of each of 8 semiannual periods.......... | | 6.73274 | 26,931 |
| Present value (issue price) of bonds ........ | | | $100,000 |

| Future Cash Flows | Multiplier (Table 1) | Multiplier (Table 2) | Present Values at 5% Semiannually |
|---|---|---|---|
| (2) $100,000 of 8%, 4-year bonds with interest payable semiannually priced to yield 10%. | | | |
| Principal payment, $100,000 (a single amount received after 8 semiannual periods)................ | 0.67684 | | $ 67,684 |
| Interest payments, $4,000 at end of each of 8 semiannual periods.......... | | 6.46321 | 25,853 |
| Present value (issue price) of bonds ........ | | | $ 93,537 |

| Future Cash Flows | Multiplier (Table 1) | Multiplier (Table 2) | Present Values at 3% Semiannually |
|---|---|---|---|
| (3) $100,000 of 8%, 4-year bonds with interest payable semiannually priced to yield 6%. | | | |
| Principal repayment, $100,000 (a single amount received after 8 semiannual periods)................ | 0.78941 | | $ 78,941 |
| Interest payments, $4,000 at end of each of 8 semiannual periods.......... | | 7.01969 | 28,079 |
| Present value (issue price) of bonds ........ | | | $107,020 |

# Future Value Concepts

## Future Value of a Single Amount

The **future value** of a single sum is the amount that a specific investment is worth at a future date if invested at a given rate of compound interest. To illustrate, suppose that we decide to invest $6,000 in a savings account that pays 6% annual interest and we intend to leave the principal and interest in the account for five years. We assume that interest is credited to the account at the end of each year. The balance in the account at the end of five years is determined using Table 3 in Appendix A, which gives the future value of a dollar, as follows:

$$\textbf{Principal} \times \textbf{Factor} = \textbf{Future Value}$$
$$\textbf{\$6,000} \times \textbf{1.33823} = \textbf{\$8,029}$$

The factor 1.33823 is at the intersection of the row for five periods and the column for 6%.

Next, suppose that the interest is credited to the account semiannually rather than annually. In this situation, there are 10 compounding periods, and we use a 3% semiannual rate (one-half the annual rate since there are two compounding periods per year). The future value calculation follows:

$$\textbf{Principal} \times \textbf{Factor} = \textbf{Future Value}$$
$$\textbf{\$6,000} \times \textbf{1.34392} = \textbf{\$8,064}$$

## Future Value of an Annuity

If, instead of investing a single amount at the beginning of a series of periods, we invest a specified amount *each period,* then we have an annuity. To illustrate, assume that we decide to invest $2,000 at the end of each year for five years at an 8% annual rate of return. To determine the accumulated amount of principal and interest at the end of five years, we refer to Table 4 in Appendix A, which furnishes the future value of a dollar invested at the end of each period. The factor 5.86660 is in the row for five periods and the column for 8%, and the calculation is as follows:

$$\text{Periodic Payment} \times \text{Factor} = \text{Future Value}$$
$$\$2,000 \times 5.86660 = \$11,733$$

If we decide to invest $1,000 at the end of each six months for five years at an 8% annual rate of return, we would use the factor for 10 periods at 4%, as follows:

$$\text{Periodic Payment} \times \text{Factor} = \text{Future Value}$$
$$\$1,000 \times 12.00611 = \$12,006$$

# APPENDIX 8B: Economics of Gains and Losses on Bond Repurchases

Is a reported gain or loss on bond repurchases before maturity of economic substance? The short answer is no. To illustrate, assume that on January 1, a company issues $50 million face value bonds with an 8% annual coupon rate. The interest is to be paid semiannually (4% each semiannual period) for a term of five years (10 semiannual periods), at which time the principal will be repaid. If investors demand a 10% annual return (5% semiannually) on their investment, the bond price is computed as follows:

| | | |
|---|---|---|
| Present value of semiannual interest ($2,000,000 × 7.72173) | = | $15,443,460 |
| Present value of principal ($50,000,000 × 0.61391) | = | 30,695,500 |
| Present value of bond | = | $46,138,960 |

This bond's amortization table follows:

| | [A]<br>([E] × market%)<br>Interest<br>Expense | [B]<br>(Face × coupon%)<br>Cash<br>Interest Paid | [C]<br>([A] − [B])<br>Discount<br>Amortization | [D]<br>(Prior bal − [C])<br>Discount<br>Balance | [E]<br>(Face − [D])<br>Bond<br>Payable, Net |
|---|---|---|---|---|---|
| **Period** | | | | | |
| 0 | | | | $3,861,040 | $46,138,960 |
| 1 | $2,306,948 | $2,000,000 | $306,948 | 3,554,092 | 46,445,908 |
| 2 | 2,322,295 | 2,000,000 | 322,295 | 3,231,797 | 46,768,203 |
| 3 | 2,338,410 | 2,000,000 | 338,410 | 2,893,387 | 47,106,613 |
| 4 | 2,355,331 | 2,000,000 | 355,331 | 2,538,056 | 47,461,944 |
| 5 | 2,373,097 | 2,000,000 | 373,097 | 2,164,959 | 47,835,041 |
| 6 | 2,391,752 | 2,000,000 | 391,752 | 1,773,207 | 48,226,793 |
| 7 | 2,411,340 | 2,000,000 | 411,340 | 1,361,867 | 48,638,133 |
| 8 | 2,431,907 | 2,000,000 | 431,907 | 929,960 | 49,070,040 |
| 9 | 2,453,502 | 2,000,000 | 453,502 | 476,458 | 49,523,542 |
| 10 | 2,476,458 | 2,000,000 | 476,458 | 0 | 50,000,000 |

**EXHIBIT 8B.4  Bond Premium Amortization Table**

Next, assume we are at period 6 (three years after issuance) and the market rate of interest for this bond has risen from 10% to 12%. The firm decides to retire (redeem) the outstanding bond issue and finances the retirement by issuing new bonds. That is, it issues bonds with a face amount equal to the market value of the old bonds and uses the proceeds to retire the existing (old) bonds. The new bond issue will have a term of two years (four semiannual periods), the remaining life of the existing bond issue.

At the end of the third year, there are four $2,000,000 semiannual interest payments remaining on the old bonds, plus the repayment of the face amount of the bond due at the end of the fourth semiannual period. The present value of this cash flow stream, discounted at the current 12% annual rate (6% semiannual rate) is:

| | | |
|---|---|---|
| Present value of semiannual interest ($2,000,000 × 3.46511) | = | $ 6,930,220 |
| Present value of principal ($50,000,000 × 0.79209) | = | 39,604,500 |
| Present value of bond | = | $46,534,720 |

This means the company pays $46,534,720 to redeem a bond that is on its books at a carrying amount of $48,226,793. The difference of $1,692,073 is reported as a gain on repurchase (also called *redemption*). GAAP requires this gain be reported in income from continuing operations unless it meets the tests for treatment as an extraordinary item (the item is both unusual and infrequent).

Although the company reports a gain in its income statement, has it actually realized an economic gain? Consider that this company issues new bonds that carry a coupon rate of 12% (6% semiannually) for $46,534,720. Since we assume that those bonds are sold with a coupon rate equal to the market rate, they will sell at par (no discount or premium). The interest expense per six-month period, therefore, equals the interest paid in cash, or $2,792,083 ($46,534,720 × 6%). Total expense for the four-period life of the bond is $11,168,333 ($2,792,083 × 4). That amount, plus the $46,534,720 face amount of bonds due at maturity, results in total bond payments of $57,703,053. Had this company not redeemed the bonds, it would have paid four additional interest payments of $2,000,000 each plus the face amount of $50,000,000 at maturity, for total bond payments of $58,000,000. On the surface, it appears that the firm is able to save $296,947 by redeeming the bonds and, therefore, reports a gain. (Also, total interest expense on the new bond issue is $3,168,333 [$11,168,333 − $8,000,000] more than it would have recorded under the old issue; so, although it is recording a present gain, it also incurs future higher interest costs which are not recognized under GAAP.)

However, this gain is misleading. Specifically, this gain has two components. First, interest payments increase by $792,083 per year ($2,792,083 − $2,000,000). Second, the face amount of the bond that must be repaid in four years decreases by $3,465,280 ($50,000,000 − $46,534,720). To evaluate whether a real gain has been realized, we must consider the present value of these cash outflows and savings. The present value of the increased interest outflow, a four-period annuity of $792,083 discounted at 6% per period, is **$2,744,655** ($792,083 × 3.46511). The present value of the reduced maturity amount, $3,465,280 in four periods hence, is **$2,744,814** ($3,465,280 × 0.79209)—note: the two amounts differ by $159, which is due to rounding. The conclusion is that the two amounts are the same.

This analysis shows there is no real economic gain from early redemption of debt. The present value of the increased interest payments exactly offsets the present value of the decreased amount due at maturity. Why, then, does GAAP yield a gain? The answer lies in use of historical costing. Bonds are reported at amortized cost, that is, the face amount less any applicable discount or plus any premium. These amounts are a function of the bond issue price and its yield rate at issuance, which are both fixed for the bond duration. Market prices for bonds, however, vary continually with changes in market interest rates. Companies do not adjust bond liabilities for these changes in market value. As a result, when companies redeem bonds, their carrying amount differs from market value and GAAP reports a gain or loss equal to this difference.

# GUIDANCE ANSWERS

**MANAGERIAL DECISION**    **You Are the Vice President of Finance**

You might consider the types of restructuring that would strengthen financial ratios typically used to assess liquidity and solvency by the rating agencies. Such restructuring includes generating cash by reducing inventory, reallocating cash outflows from investing activities (PPE) to debt reduction, and issuing stock for cash and using the proceeds to reduce debt (an equity for debt recapitalization). These actions increase liquidity or reduce financial leverage and, thus, should improve debt rating. An improved debt rating will attract more debtholders because your current debt rating is below investment grade and is not a suitable investment for many professionally managed portfolios. An improved debt rating will also lower the interest rate on your debt. Offsetting these benefits are costs such as the following: (1) potential loss of sales from inventory stock-outs; (2) potential future cash flow reductions and loss of market power from reduced PPE investments; and (3) costs of equity issuances (equity costs more than debt because investors demand a higher return to compensate for added risk and the lack of tax deductibility of dividends vis-à-vis interest payments), which can yield a net increase in the total cost of capital. All cost and benefits must be assessed before you pursue any restructuring.

Superscript ^A(^B) denotes assignments based on Appendix 8A (8B).

# DISCUSSION QUESTIONS

**Q8-1.**   What does the term *current liabilities* mean? What assets are usually used to settle current liabilities?

**Q8-2.**   What is an accrual? How do accruals impact the balance sheet and the income statement?

**Q8-3.**   What is the difference between a bond's coupon rate and its market interest rate (yield)?

**Q8-4.**   Why do companies report a gain or loss when they repurchase their bonds? Is this a real economic gain or loss.

**Q8-5.**   How do credit (debt) ratings affect the cost of borrowing for a company?

**Q8-6.**   How would you interpret a company's reported gain or loss on the repurchase of its bonds?

# MINI EXERCISES

**M 8-7.    Interpreting a Contingency Footnote    (LO1)**

Altria Group, Inc.
(MO)

Altria Group, Inc., reports the following footnote to its 2005 10-K related to pending smoking-related litigation.

> **Contingencies:** Legal proceedings covering a wide range of matters are pending or threatened in various United States and foreign jurisdictions against ALG, its subsidiaries and affiliates, including PM USA and PMI, as well as their respective indemnitees. Various types of claims are raised in these proceedings, including product liability, consumer protection, antitrust, tax, contraband shipments, patent infringement, employment matters, claims for contribution and claims of competitors and distributors . . . It is not possible to predict the outcome of the litigation pending against ALG and its subsidiaries . . .
>
> *Contingencies:* (i) management has not concluded that it is probable that a loss has been incurred in any of the pending tobacco-related litigation; [and] (ii) management is unable to make a meaningful estimate of the amount or range of loss that could result from an unfavorable outcome of pending tobacco-related litigation . . .
>
> The present legislative and litigation environment is substantially uncertain, and it is possible that the business and volume of ALG's subsidiaries, as well as Altria Group, Inc.'s consolidated results of operations, cash flows or financial position could be materially affected by an unfavorable outcome or settlement of certain pending litigation or by the enactment of federal or state tobacco legislation.

*a.*   Review the content of this footnote. In what manner do you believe Altria is reporting this potential liability on its balance sheet?

*b.*   Altria discloses over 10 pages of discussion relating to pending litigation in its footnotes (an abnormally large disclosure). Irrespective of your answer to part *a*, what do you believe is Altria's motivation for this extended disclosure?

**M8-8.    Analyzing and Computing Financial Statement Effects of Interest    (LO1)**

DeFond Company signed a 90-day, 8% note payable for $7,200 on December 16. Use the financial statement effects template to illustrate the year-end December 31 accounting adjustment DeFond must make.

**M8-9.    Analyzing and Determining Liability Amounts    (LO1)**

For each of the following situations, indicate the liability amount, if any, that is reported on the balance sheet of Basu, Inc., at December 31, 2007.

*a.*   Basu owes $110,000 at year-end 2007 for its inventory purchases.

*b.*   Basu agreed to purchase a $28,000 drill press in January 2008.

*c.*   During November and December of 2007, Basu sold products to a customer and warranted them against product failure for 90 days. Estimated costs of honoring this 90-day warranty during 2008 are $2,200.

*d.*   Basu provides a profit-sharing bonus for its executives equal to 5% of reported pretax annual income. The estimated pretax income for 2007 is $600,000. Bonuses are not paid until January of the following year.

**M8-10.    Interpreting Relations among Bond Price, Coupon, Yield, and Credit Rating    (LO2, 3)**

Boston Scientific
(BSX)

The following notice appeared in *The Wall Street Journal* regarding a bond issuance by Boston Scientific.

> **Boston Scientific Corp.**—$500 million of notes was priced with the following terms in two parts via joint lead managers Merrill Lynch & Co., UBS Securities and Wachovia:
>
> (1) Amount: $250 million; Maturity: Jan. 12, 2011; Coupon: 4.25%; Price: 99.476; Yield: 4.349%; Ratings: Baa1 (Moody's), A2 (S&P).
>
> (2) Amount: $250 million; Maturity: Jan. 12, 2017; Coupon: 5.125%; Price: 99.926; Yield: 5.134%; Ratings: Baa1 (Moody's), A2 (S&P).

a. Discuss the relation among the coupon rate, issuance price, and yield for the 2011 issuance.

b. Compare the yields on the two parts of the bond issuances. Why are the yields different when the credit ratings are the same?

**M8-11.** **Determining Gain or Loss on Bond Redemption** **(LO2)**
On April 30, one year before maturity, Easton Company retired $200,000 of its 9% bonds payable at the current market price of 101 (101% of the bond face amount, or $200,000 × 1.01 = $202,000). The bond book value on April 30 is $197,600, reflecting an unamortized discount of $2,400. Bond interest is currently fully paid and recorded up to the date of retirement. What is the gain or loss on retirement of these bonds? Is this gain or loss a real economic gain or loss? Explain.

**M8-12.** **Interpreting Bond Footnote Disclosures** **(LO2)**
Bristol-Myers Squibb (BMY) reports the following in the long-term debt footnote to its 2005 10-K.

> The aggregate maturities of long-term debt for each of the next five years are as follows: 2006, $522.0 million; 2007, $351.7 million; 2008, $1.4 billion; 2009, $306.5 million; 2010, $5.4 million.

a. What does the $ 1.4 billion in 2008 indicate about BMY's future payment obligations?

b. What implications does this payment schedule have for our evaluation of BMY's liquidity and solvency?

**Bristol-Myers Squibb (BMY)**

**M8-13.** **Classifying Liability-Related Accounts into Balance Sheet or Income Statement** **(LO2)**
Indicate the proper financial statement classification (balance sheet or income statement) for each of the following liability-related accounts.

a. Gain on Bond Retirement     e. Bond Interest Expense
b. Discount on Bonds Payable     f. Bond Interest Payable (due next period)
c. Mortgage Notes Payable     g. Premium on Bonds Payable
d. Bonds Payable     h. Loss on Bond Retirement

**M8-14.** **Interpreting Bond Footnote Disclosures** **(LO2)**
Comcast Corporation reports the following footnote to the long-term debt section of its 2005 10-K.

> **Debt Covenants** Some of our subsidiaries' loan agreements require that we maintain financial ratios based on debt, interest and operating income before depreciation and amortization, as defined in the agreements. We were in compliance with all financial covenants for all periods presented.

a. The financial ratios to which Comcast refers are similar to those discussed in the section on credit ratings and the cost of debt. What effects might these ratios have on the degree of freedom that management has in running Comcast?

b. Violation of debt covenants is a serious event that typically triggers an 'immediately due and payable' provision in the debt contract. What pressures might management face if the company's ratios are near covenant limits?

**Comcast Corporation (CMCSA)**

**M8-15.** **Analyzing Financial Statement Effects of Bond Redemption** **(LO2)**
Holthausen Corporation issued $400,000 of 11%, 20-year bonds at 108 on January 1, 2003. Interest is payable semiannually on June 30 and December 31. Through January 1, 2008, Holthausen amortized $5,000 of the bond premium. On January 1, 2008, Holthausen retires the bonds at 103. Use the financial statement effects template to illustrate the bond retirement at January 1, 2008.

**M8-16.** **Analyzing Financial Statement Effects of Bond Redemption** **(LO2)**
Dechow, Inc., issued $250,000 of 8%, 15-year bonds at 96 on July 1, 2003. Interest is payable semiannually on December 31 and June 30. Through June 30, 2008, Dechow amortized $3,000 of the bond discount. On July 1, 2008, Dechow retired the bonds at 101. Use the financial statement effects template to illustrate the bond retirement at June 30, 2008.

**M8-17.** **Analyzing and Computing Accrued Interest on Notes** **(LO1)**
Compute any interest accrued for each of the following notes payable owed by Penman, Inc., as of December 31, 2007 (use a 365-day year).

| Lender | Issuance Date | Principal | Coupon Rate (%) | Term |
|---|---|---|---|---|
| Nissim......... | 11/21/07 | $18,000 | 10% | 120 days |
| Klein.......... | 12/13/07 | 14,000 | 9 | 90 days |
| Bildersee....... | 12/19/07 | 16,000 | 12 | 60 days |

**M8-18.    Interpreting Credit Ratings    (LO3)**

**General Mills** reports the following information in the Management Discussion & Analysis section of its 2005 10-K report.

> We believe that two important measures of financial strength are the ratios of fixed charge coverage and cash flows from operations to adjusted debt plus certain minority interests. Our fixed charge coverage in fiscal 2005 was 4.7 times compared to 3.8 times in fiscal 2004, and cash flows from operations to adjusted debt plus certain minority interests increased to 26 percent. We expect to pay down between $100 and $200 million of adjusted debt plus certain minority interests in fiscal 2006. Our goal is to return to a mid single-A rating for our long-term debt, and to the top tier short-term rating, that we held prior to our announcement of the Pillsbury acquisition. Currently, Standard and Poor's Corporation has ratings of BBB+ on our publicly held long-term debt and A-2 on our commercial paper. Moody's Investors Services, Inc. has ratings of Baa2 for our long-term debt and P-2 for our commercial paper. Fitch Ratings, Inc. rates our long-term debt BBB+ and our commercial paper F-2.

   *a.*   Why will debt reduction result in a higher credit rating for General Mills' bonds?

   *b.*   What effect will a higher credit rating have on General Mills' borrowing costs? Explain.

**M8-19.    Computing Bond Issue Price    (LO2)**

Bushman, Inc., issues $500,000 of 9% bonds that pay interest semiannually and mature in 10 years. Compute the bond issue price assuming that the prevailing market rate of interest is:

   *a.*   8% per year compounded semiannually.

   *b.*   10% per year compounded semiannually.

**M8-20.    Computing Issue Price for Zero Coupon Bonds    (LO2)**

Bushman, Inc., issues $500,000 of zero coupon bonds that mature in 10 years. Compute the bond issue price assuming that the bonds' market rate is:

   *a.*   8% per year compounded semiannually.

   *b.*   10% per year compounded semiannually.

**M8-21.    Determining the Financial Statement Effects of Accounts Payable Transactions    (LO1)**

Petroni Company had the following transactions relating to its accounts payable.

   *a.*   Purchases $300 of inventory on credit.

   *b.*   Sells inventory for $420 on credit.

   *c.*   Records $300 cost of sales for transaction *b*.

   *d.*   Receives $420 cash toward accounts receivable.

   *e.*   Pays $300 cash to settle accounts payable.

Use the financial statement effects template to identify the effects (both amounts and accounts) for these transactions.

**M8-22.    Computing Bond Issue Price and Preparing an Amortization Table in Excel    (LO2)**

On January 1, 2007, Bushman, Inc., issues $500,000 of 9% bonds that pay interest semiannually and mature in 10 years (December 31, 2016).

   *a.*   Using the Excel PRICE function, compute the issue price assuming that the bonds' market rate is 8% per year compounded semiannually. (Use 100 for the redemption value to get a price as a percentage of the face amount, and use 1 for the basis.)

   *b.*   Prepare an amortization table in Excel to demonstrate the amortization of the book (carrying) value to the $500,000 maturity value at the end of the 20th semiannual period.

# EXERCISES

**E8-23.    Analyzing and Computing Accrued Warranty Liability and Expense    (LO1)**

Waymire Company sells a motor that carries a 60-day unconditional warranty against product failure. From prior years' experience, Waymire estimates that 2% of units sold each period will require repair at an average cost of $100 per unit. During the current period, Waymire sold 69,000 units and repaired 1,000 units.

   *a.*   How much warranty expense must Waymire report in its current period income statement?

   *b.*   What amount of warranty liability related to current period sales will Waymire report on its current period-end balance sheet? (*Hint:* Remember that some units were repaired in the current period.)

   *c.*   What analysis issues must we consider with respect to the amount of reported warranty liability?

**E8-24.** **Analyzing Contingencies and Assessing Liabilities**　(LO1)

The following independent situations represent various types of liabilities. Analyze each situation and indicate which of the following is the proper accounting treatment for the company: (a) record a liability on the balance sheet, (b) disclose the liability in a financial statement footnote, or (c) neither record nor disclose any liability.

1. A stockholder has filed a lawsuit against **Clinch Corporation**. Clinch's attorneys have reviewed the facts of the case. Their review revealed that similar lawsuits have never resulted in a cash award and it is highly unlikely that this lawsuit will either.

2. **Foster Company** signed a 60-day, 10% note when it purchased items from another company.

3. The Environmental Protection Agency notifies **Shevlin Company** that a state where it has a plant is filing a lawsuit for groundwater pollution against Shevlin and another company that has a plant adjacent to Shevlin's plant. Test results have not identified the exact source of the pollution. Shevlin's manufacturing process often produces by-products that can pollute ground water.

4. **Sloan Company** manufactured and sold products to a retailer that sold the products to consumers. The Sloan Company will replace the product if it is found to be defective within 90 days of the sale to the consumer. Historically, 1.2% of the products are returned for replacement.

**E8-25.** **Recording and Analyzing Warranty Accrual and Payment**　(LO1)

Refer to the discussion of and excerpt from the Ford Motor Company warranty reserve on page 8-9 to answer the following questions.

Ford Motor Company (F)

*a.* Using the financial statement effects template, record the accrual of warranty liability relating only to the "Changes in accrual related to warranties issued during the year" and to the "Payments made during the year."

*b.* Does the level of Ford's warranty accrual appear to be reasonable?

*c.* General Motors reports the following table relating to its warranty accrual.

| December 31 ($ millions) | 2005 | 2004 |
|---|---:|---:|
| Beginning balance | $9,315 | $8,832 |
| Payments | (4,696) | (4,669) |
| Increase in liability (warranties issued during period) | 5,159 | 5,065 |
| Adjustments to liability (pre-existing warranties) | (381) | (85) |
| Effect of foreign currency translation | (269) | 172 |
| Ending balance | $9,128 | $9,315 |

For both companies, compare the size of the warranty liability with the claims made. What insight does this comparison give us regarding the adequacy of the warranty accruals for both companies.

**E8-26.** **Analyzing and Computing Accrued Wages Liability and Expense**　(LO1)

Demski Company pays its employees on the 1st and 15th of each month. It is March 31 and Demski is preparing financial statements for this quarter. Its employees have earned $25,000 since the 15th of March and have not yet been paid. How will Demski's balance sheet and income statement reflect the accrual of wages on March 31? What balance sheet and income statement accounts would be incorrectly reported if Demski failed to make this accrual (for each account indicate whether it would be overstated or understated)?

**E8-27.** **Analyzing and Reporting Financial Statement Effects of Bond Transactions**　(LO2)

On January 1, Hutton Corp. issued $300,000 of 15-year, 10% bonds payable for $351,876, yielding an effective interest rate of 8%. Interest is payable semiannually on June 30 and December 31. (a) Show computations to confirm the issue price of $351,876. (b) Indicate the financial statement effects using the template for (1) bond issuance, (2) semiannual interest payment and premium amortization on June 30 of the first year, and (3) semiannual interest payment and premium amortization on December 31 of the first year.

**E8-28.** **Analyzing and Reporting Financial Statement Effects of Mortgages**　(LO2)

On January 1, Piotroski, Inc., borrowed $700,000 on a 12%, 15-year mortgage note payable. The note is to be repaid in equal semiannual installments of $50,854 (payable on June 30 and December 31). Each mortgage payment includes principal and interest. Interest is computed using the effective interest method. Indicate the financial statement effects using the template for (a) issuance of the mortgage note payable, (b) payment of the first installment on June 30, and (c) payment of the second installment on December 31.

**E8-29.** **Assessing the Effects of Bond Credit Rating Changes** (LO3)

Ford (F)      Ford reports the following footnote to its 2005 10-K report.

*Credit Ratings.* Our short- and long-term debt is rated by four credit rating agencies designated as nationally recognized statistical rating organizations ("NRSROs") by the Securities and Exchange Commission:

- Dominion Bond Rating Service Limited ("DBRS");
- Fitch. Inc. ("Fitch");
- Moody's Investors Service, Inc. ("Moody's"); and
- Standard & Poor's Rating Services, a division of McGraw-Hill Companies, Inc. ("S&P").

In several markets, locally recognized rating agencies also rate us. A credit rating reflects an assessment by the rating agency of the credit risk associated with particular securities we issue, based on information provided by us and other sources. Credit ratings are not recommendations to buy, sell or hold securities and are subject to revision or withdrawal at any time by the assigning rating agency. Each rating agency may have different criteria for evaluating company risk, and therefore ratings should be evaluated independently for each rating agency. Lower credit ratings generally result in higher borrowing costs and reduced access to capital markets. The NRSROs have indicated that our lower ratings are primarily a reflection of the rating agencies' concerns regarding our automotive cash flow and profitability, declining market share, excess industry capacity, industry pricing pressure and rising health care costs.

*Ford.* In December 2005, Fitch lowered Ford's long-term raring to BB+ from BBB−, lowered our short-term rating to B from F2 and maintained our outlook at Negative. In January 2006, S&P lowered our long-term rating to BB− from BB+, lowered our short-term rating to B-2 from B-1 and maintained our outlook at Negative. In January 2006, Moody's lowered our long-term rating to Ba3 from Ba1 and maintained our outlook at Negative. In January 2006, DBRS lowered our long-term rating to BB (low) from BB (high), affirmed our short-term rating at R-3 (high) and maintained our trend at Negative.

*Ford Credit.* In December 2005, Fitch lowered Ford Credit's long-term rating to BB+ from BBB−, lowered Ford Credit's short-term rating to B from F2 and maintained Ford Credit's outlook at Negative. In January 2006, S&P lowered Ford Credit's long-term rating to BB− from BB+, lowered Ford Credit's short-term debt rating to B-2 from B-1 and maintained Ford Credit's outlook at Negative. In January 2006, Moody's lowered Ford Credit's long-term rating to Ba2 from Baa3, lowered Ford Credit's short-term rating to Not Prime ("NP") from P3 and maintained Ford Credit's outlook at Negative. In January 2006, DBRS lowered Ford Credit's long-term rating to BB from BBB (low), lowered Ford Credit's short-term rating to R-3 (high) from R-2 (low) and maintained Ford Credit's trend at Negative.

*a.* What financial ratios do credit rating companies such as the four NRSROs listed above, use to evaluate the relative riskiness of borrowers?

*b.* Why might a reduction in credit ratings result in higher interest costs and restrict Ford's access to credit markets?

*c.* What type of actions can Ford take to improve its credit ratings?

**E8-30.** **Analyzing and Reporting Financial Statement Effects of Bond Transactions** (LO2)

Lundholm, Inc., reports financial statements each December 31 and issues $500,000, 9%, 15-year bonds dated May 1, 2007, with interest payments on October 31 and April 30. Assuming the bonds are sold at par on May 1, 2007, complete the financial statement effects template to reflect the following events: (a) bond issuance, (b) the first semiannual interest payment, and (c) retirement of $300,000 of the bonds at 101 on November 1, 2007.

**E8-31.** **Analyzing and Reporting Financial Statement Effects of Bond Transactions** (LO2)

On January 1, 2007, McKeown, Inc., issued $250,000 of 8%, 9-year bonds for $220,776, which implies a market (yield) rate of 10%. Semiannual interest is payable on June 30 and December 31 of each year. (a) Show computations to confirm the bond issue price. (b) Indicate the financial statement effects using the template for (1) bond issuance, (2) semiannual interest payment and discount amortization on June 30, 2007, and (3) semiannual interest payment and discount amortization on December 31, 2007.

**E8-32.** **Analyzing and Reporting Financial Statement Effects of Bond Transactions** (LO2)

On January 1, 2007, Shields, Inc., issued $800,000 of 9%, 20-year bonds for $879,172, yielding a market (yield) rate of 8%. Semiannual interest is payable on June 30 and December 31 of each year. (a) Show computations to confirm the bond issue price. (b) Indicate the financial statement effects using the template for (1) bond issuance, (2) semiannual interest payment and premium amortization on June 30, 2007, and (3) semiannual interest payment and premium amortization on December 31, 2007.

**E8-33.** **Determining Bond Prices, Interest Rates, and Financial Statement Effects** (LO2)

Deere & Company's 2005 10-K reports the following footnote relating to long-term debt. Deere's    Deere & Co (DE)
borrowings include $200 million, 6.55% debentures (unsecured bonds), due in 2028 (highlighted below).

Long-term borrowings at October 31 consisted of the following in millions of dollars:

| Notes and debentures | 2005 | 2004 |
|---|---|---|
| Medium-term notes: | | |
| Average interest rate of 9.2%—2004 . . . . . . . . . . . . . . . . . . . . . . . . | | $ 20 |
| 5-7/8% U.S. dollar notes due 2006: ($250 principal) | | |
| Swapped $170 to Euro at average variable interest rates of 3.1%—2004 . . . . . . . . . . . . . . . . . . . . . . . . . . . | | 250 |
| 7.85% debentures due 2010 . . . . . . . . . . . . . . . . . . . . . . . . . . . | $ 500 | 500 |
| 6.95% notes due 2014: ($700 principal) | | |
| Swapped to variable interest rates of 5.2%—2005, 3.1%—2004 . . . . . . . . . . . . . . . . . . . . . . . . . . | 744 | 786 |
| 8.95% debentures due 2019 . . . . . . . . . . . . . . . . . . . . . . . . . . . | 200 | 200 |
| 8-1/2% debentures due 2022 . . . . . . . . . . . . . . . . . . . . . . . . . | 200 | 200 |
| 6.55% debentures due 2028 . . . . . . . . . . . . . . . . . . . . . . . . . . | 200 | 200 |
| 8.10% debentures due 2030 . . . . . . . . . . . . . . . . . . . . . . . . . . | 250 | 250 |
| 7.125% notes due 2031 . . . . . . . . . . . . . . . . . . . . . . . . . . . . . | 300 | 300 |
| Other notes . . . . . . . . . . . . . . . . . . . . . . . . . . . . . . . . . . . . | 29 | 22 |
| Total . . . . . . . . . . . . . . . . . . . . . . . . . . . . . . . . . . . . . . . . | $2,423 | $2,728 |

A recent price quote (from www.BondPage.com) on Deere's 6.55% debentures follows.

| Credit ratings | Issuer name | Issue | Coupon rate | Maturity | Price quote | Yield |
|---|---|---|---|
| A3/A-<br>Industrial | Deere & Co<br>Non Callable, NYBE, DE | 6.550<br>10-01-2028 | 108.104<br>5.890 |

This price quote indicates that Deere's bonds have a market price of 108.104 (108.104% of face value), resulting in a yield to maturity of 5.89%.

*a.* Assuming that these bonds were originally issued at par value, what does the market price reveal about interest rate changes since Deere issued its bonds? (Assume that Deere's credit rating has remained the same.)

*b.* Does the change in interest rates since the issuance of these bonds affect the amount of interest expense that Deere reports in its income statement? Explain.

*c.* How much cash would Deere have to pay to repurchase the 6.55% debentures at the quoted market price of 108.104. (Assume no interest is owed when Deere repurchases the debentures.) How would the repurchase affect Deere's current income?

*d.* Assuming that the bonds remain outstanding until their maturity, at what market price will the bonds sell on their due date in 2028?

**E8-34.ᴬ** **Computing Present Values of Single Amounts and Annuities** (LO2)

Refer to Tables 1 and 2 in Appendix A near the end of the book to compute the present value for each of the following amounts:

*a.* $90,000 received 10 years hence if the annual interest rate is:
1. 8% compounded annually.
2. 8% compounded semiannually.

*b.* $1,000 received at the end of each year for the next eight years discounted at 10% compounded annually.

*c.* $600 received at the end of each six months for the next 15 years if the interest rate is 8% per year compounded semiannually.

*d.* $500,000 received 10 years hence discounted at 10% per year compounded annually.

**E8-35.** **Analyzing and Reporting Financial Statement Effects of Bond Transactions** **(LO2)**

On January 1, 2007, Trueman Corporation issued $600,000 of 20-year, 11% bonds for $554,860, yielding a market (yield) rate of 12%. Interest is payable semiannually on June 30 and December 31. (a) Confirm the bond issue price. (b) Indicate the financial statement effects using the template for (1) bond issuance, (2) semiannual interest payment and discount amortization on June 30, 2007, and (3) semiannual interest payment and discount amortization on December 31, 2007.

**E8-36.** **Analyzing and Reporting Financial Statement Effects of Bond Transactions** **(LO2)**

On January 1, 2007, Verrecchia Company issued $400,000 of 5-year, 13% bonds for $446,329, yielding a market (yield) rate of 10%. Interest is payable semiannually on June 30 and December 31. (a) Confirm the bond issue price. (b) Indicate the financial statement effects using the template for (1) bond issuance, (2) semiannual interest payment and premium amortization on June 30, 2007, and (3) semiannual interest payment and premium amortization on December 31, 2007.

# PROBLEMS

**P8-37.** **Interpreting Term Structures of Coupon Rates and Yield Rates** **(LO2)**

The Pepsi Bottling
Group (PBG)

The Pepsi Bottling Group reports $4,561 million of long-term debt outstanding as of December 2005 in the following schedule to its 10-K report.

| Short-term Borrowings and Long-term Debt ($ millions) | 2005 | 2004 |
|---|---|---|
| **Short-term borrowings** | | |
| Current maturities of long-term debt | $ 594 | $ 53 |
| SFAS No. 133 adjustment | (4) | — |
| Unamortized discount, net | (1) | — |
| Current maturities of long-term debt, net | 589 | 53 |
| Other short-term borrowings | 426 | 155 |
| | $1,015 | $ 208 |

| ($ millions) | 2005 | 2004 |
|---|---|---|
| **Long-term debt** | | |
| 2.45% senior notes due 2006 | $ 500 | $ 500 |
| 5.63% senior notes due 2009 | 1,300 | 1,300 |
| 4.63% senior notes due 2012 | 1,000 | 1,000 |
| 5.00% senior notes due 2013 | 400 | 400 |
| 4.13% senior notes due 2015 | 250 | 250 |
| 7.00% senior notes due 2029 | 1,000 | 1,000 |
| Other | 111 | 109 |
| | 4,561 | 4,559 |
| Unamortized discount, net and other | (33) | (17) |
| Current maturities of long-term debt, net | (589) | (53) |
| | $3,939 | $4,489 |

Certain of our credit facilities and senior notes have financial covenants consisting of the following:

- Our debt to capitalization ratio should not be greater than .75 on the last day of a fiscal quarter when PepsiCo Inc.'s ratings are A by S&P and A3 by Moody's or higher. Debt is defined as total long-term and short-term debt plus accrued interest plus total standby letters of credit and other guarantees less cash and cash equivalents not in excess of $500 million. Capitalization is defined as debt plus shareholders' equity plus minority interest excluding the impact of the cumulative translation adjustment.

- Our debt to EBITDA ratio should not be greater than five on the last day of a fiscal quarter when PepsiCo Inc.'s ratings are less than A− by S&P or A3 by Moody's. EBITDA is defined as the last four quarters of earnings before depreciation, amortization, net interest expense, income taxes, minority interest, net other non-operating expenses and extraordinary items.
- New secured debt should not be greater than 10 percent of Bottling Group, LLC's net tangible assets. Net tangible assets are defined as total assets less current liabilities and net intangible assets.

We are in compliance with all debt covenants.

The price of the $1,000 million 7% senior notes due 2029 as of August 2006 is as follows (from Yahoo! Finance Bond Center; Finance.yahoo.com/Bonds):

| Issue | Price | Coupon (%) | Maturity | YTM (%) | Fitch Ratings |
|---|---|---|---|---|---|
| Pepsi Bottling Group Inc..... | 114.05 | 7.000 | 1-Mar-2029 | 5.869 | A |

**Required**

a. PBG reports current maturities of long-term debt of $589 million as part of short-term debt. Why is this amount reported that way? PBG reports $1,300 million of long-term debt maturing in 2009. What does this mean? Is this amount important to our analysis of Pepsi Bottling Group? Explain.

b. The $1,000 million 7% senior notes maturing in 2029 are priced at 114.05 (114.05% of face value, or $1,140.5 million) as of August 2006, resulting in a yield to maturity of 5.869%. Assuming that the credit rating of PBG has not changed, what does the pricing of this 7% coupon bond imply about interest rate changes since PBG issued the bond?

c. PBG identifies a number of financial covenants relating to its long-term debt. Describe each of these covenants and how they affect our financial analysis.

d. PBG reports an unamortized discount of $14 million in another disclosure to its financial statements. How does a discount arise and what effect will its amortization have on reported interest expense?

**P8-38. Interpreting Debt Footnotes on Interest Rates and Interest Expense  (LO2)**

CVS Corporation discloses the following footnote in its 10-K relating to its debt.

CVS Corporation (CVS)

**BORROWING AND CREDIT AGREEMENTS**

Following is a summary of the Company's borrowings as of the respective balance sheet dates.

| In millions | Dec. 31, 2005 | Jan. 1, 2005 |
|---|---|---|
| Commercial paper .............................. | $ 253.4 | $ 885.6 |
| 5.625% senior notes due 2006 .................. | 300.0 | 300.0 |
| 3.875% senior notes due 2007 .................. | 300.0 | 300.0 |
| 4.0% senior notes due 2009 ..................... | 650.0 | 650.0 |
| 4.875% senior notes due 2014 .................. | 550.0 | 550.0 |
| 8.52% ESOP notes due 2008 ................... | 114.0 | 140.9 |
| Mortgage notes payable ....................... | 21.0 | 14.8 |
| Capital lease obligations ...................... | 0.7 | 0.8 |
| | 2,189.1 | 2,842.1 |
| Less: | | |
| Short-term debt ............................. | (253.4) | (885.6) |
| Current portion of long-term debt .............. | (341.6) | (30.6) |
| | $1,594.1 | $1,925.9 |

CVS also discloses the following information.

**Interest expense, net**—Interest expense was $117.0 million, $64.4 million and $53.9 million, and interest income was $6.5 million, $5.7 million and $5.8 million, in 2005, 2004 and 2003, respectively. Interest paid totaled $135.9 million in 2005, $70.4 million in 2004 and $64.9 million in 2003.

**Required**

a. What is the average coupon rate (interest paid) and the average effective rate (interest expense) on CVS' long-term debt? (*Hint:* Use the disclosure for interest expense, net.)

b. Does your computation of the coupon rate in part *a* seem reasonable given the footnote disclosure relating to specific bond issues? Explain.

c. Explain how the amount of interest paid can differ from the amount of interest expense recorded in the income statement.

**P8-39.** **Analyzing Bond Rates, Yields, Prices, and Credit Ratings** (LO2, 3)

Southwest Airlines (LUV)

Reproduced below is the long-term debt footnote from the 10-K report of Southwest Airlines.

| Long-Term Debt (In millions) | 2005 | 2004 |
|---|---|---|
| 8% Notes due 2005 . . . . . . . . . . . . . . . . . . . . . . | $ — | $ 100 |
| Zero Coupon Notes due 2006 . . . . . . . . . . . . . | 58 | 58 |
| Pass Through Certificates . . . . . . . . . . . . . . . . | 523 | 544 |
| 7⅞% Notes due 2007 . . . . . . . . . . . . . . . . . . . | 100 | 100 |
| French Credit Agreements due 2012 . . . . . . . . | 41 | 44 |
| 6½% Notes due 2012 . . . . . . . . . . . . . . . . . . . | 370 | 377 |
| 5¼% Notes due 2014 . . . . . . . . . . . . . . . . . . . | 340 | 348 |
| 5⅛% Notes due 2017 . . . . . . . . . . . . . . . . . . . | 300 | — |
| French Credit Agreements due 2017 . . . . . . . . | 106 | 111 |
| 7⅜% Debentures due 2027 . . . . . . . . . . . . . . . | 100 | 100 |
| Capital leases (Note 8) . . . . . . . . . . . . . . . . . . . | 74 | 80 |
| | 2,012 | 1,862 |
| Less current maturities . . . . . . . . . . . . . . . . . . . | 601 | 146 |
| Less debt discount and issue costs . . . . . . . . . | 17 | 16 |
| | $1,394 | $1,700 |

During February 2005, the Company issued $300 million senior unsecured Notes due 2017. The Notes bear interest at 5.125 percent, payable semi-annually in arrears, with the first payment made on September 1, 2005. Southwest used the net proceeds from the issuance of the notes, approximately $296 million, for general corporate purposes.

In fourth quarter 2004, the Company entered into four identical 13-year floating-rate financing arrangements, whereby it borrowed a total of $112 million from French banking partnerships. Although the interest on the borrowings is at floating rates, the Company estimates that, considering the full effect of the "net present value benefits" included in the transactions, the effective economic yield over the 13-year term of the loans will be approximately LIBOR minus 45 basis points. Principal and interest are payable semi-annually on June 30 and December 31 for each of the loans, and the Company may terminate the arrangements in any year on either of those dates, with certain conditions. The Company pledged four aircraft as collateral for the transactions.

In September 2004, the Company issued $350 million senior unsecured Notes due 2014. The notes bear interest at 5.25 percent, payable semi-annually in arrears, on April 1 and October 1. Concurrently, the Company entered into an interest-rate swap agreement to convert this fixed-rate debt to a floating rate. See Note 10 for more information on the interest-rate swap agreement. Southwest used the net proceeds from the issuance of the notes, approximately $346 million, for general corporate purposes.

In February 2004 and April 2004, the Company issued two separate $29 million two-year notes, each secured by one new 737-700 aircraft. Both of the notes are non-interest bearing and accrete to face value at maturity at annual rates of 2.9 percent and 3.4 percent, respectively. The proceeds of these borrowings were used to fund the individual aircraft purchases.

On March 1, 2002, the Company issued $385 million senior unsecured Notes due March 1, 2012. The notes bear interest at 6.5 percent, payable semi-annually on March 1 and September 1. Southwest used the net proceeds from the issuance of the notes, approximately $380 million, for general corporate purposes. During 2003, the Company entered into an interest rate swap agreement relating to these notes. See Note 10 for further information.

As of December 31, 2005, aggregate annual principal maturities for the five-year period ending December 31, 2010, were $612 million in 2006, $127 million in 2007, $28 million in 2008, $29 million in 2009, $30 million in 2010, and $1.186 billion thereafter.

Reproduced below is a summary of the market values of the Southwest Airlines' bonds maturing from 2012 to 2017 from the Yahoo! Finance bond center (Finance.yahoo.com/bonds).

| Issue | Price | Coupon (%) | Maturity | YTM (%) | Current Yield (%) | Fitch Ratings |
|-------|-------|------------|----------|---------|-------------------|---------------|
| SW Air...... | 105.28 | 6.500 | 1-Mar-2012 | 5.389 | 6.174 | A |
| SW Air...... | 97.00 | 5.250 | 1-Oct-2014 | 5.715 | 5.413 | A |
| SW Air...... | 95.64 | 5.125 | 1-Mar-2017 | 5.678 | 5.358 | A |

**Required**

a. What is the amount of long-term debt reported on Southwest's 2005 balance sheet? What are the scheduled maturities for this indebtedness? Why is information relating to a company's scheduled maturities of debt useful in an analysis of its financial condition?

b. Southwest reported $122 million in interest expense in its 2005 income statement. In the note to its statement of cash flows, Southwest indicates that the cash portion of this expense is $71 million. What could account for the difference between interest expense and interest paid? Explain.

c. Southwest's long-term debt is rated "A" by Fitch and similarly by other credit rating agencies. What factors would be important to consider in attempting to quantify the relative riskiness of Southwest compared with other borrowers? Explain.

d. Southwest's $370 million 6.5% notes traded at 105.28, or 105.28% of par, as of August 2006. What is the dollar value of these notes? How is the difference between this market value and the $370 million face value reflected in Southwest's financial statements? What effect would the repurchase of this entire note issue have on Southwest's financial statements? What does the 105.28 price tell you about the general trend in interest rates since Southwest sold this bond issue? Explain.

e. Southwest's 5.25% bonds are trading at 97.00 as of August 2006. What is the market value of these bonds? Why does trading at a discount result in a yield to maturity of 5.715%, which is higher than the coupon rate of 5.25%?

f. Examine the yields to maturity of the three bonds in the table above. What relation do we observe between these yields and the maturities of the bonds? Also, explain why this relation applies in general.

**P8-40**  **Analyzing Notes, Bonds, and Credit Ratings**  (LO2, LO3)

Comcast Corporation reports long-term senior notes totaling over $21 billion in its 2005 10-K. A selected listing of the market values for these notes as of August 2006 follows:

Comcast Corp. (CMCSA)

| Borrower | Price | Coupon (%) | Maturity | YTM (%) | Fitch Ratings |
|----------|-------|------------|----------|---------|---------------|
| COMCAST CORP....... | 99.67 | 6.45 | 3/15/37 | 6.474 | BBB |
| COMCAST CORP....... | 105.55 | 6.50 | 1/15/17 | 5.784 | BBB |
| COMCAST CORP....... | 92.77 | 4.95 | 6/15/16 | 5.928 | BBB |
| COMCAST CORP....... | 99.67 | 5.90 | 3/15/16 | 5.945 | BBB |
| COMCAST CORP....... | 99.31 | 5.85 | 11/15/15 | 5.947 | BBB |
| COMCAST CORP....... | 104.04 | 6.50 | 1/15/15 | 5.885 | BBB |
| COMCAST CORP....... | 97.07 | 5.30 | 1/15/14 | 5.790 | BBB |
| COMCAST CABLE COMMUNICATIONS... | 107.41 | 7.125 | 6/15/13 | 5.799 | BBB |
| COMCAST CORP....... | 100.99 | 5.50 | 3/15/11 | 5.255 | BBB |
| COMCAST CABLE COMMUNICATIONS... | 105.97 | 6.75 | 1/30/11 | 5.237 | BBB |
| COMCAST CORP....... | 101.16 | 5.45 | 11/15/10 | 5.142 | BBB |
| COMCAST CORP....... | 102.79 | 5.85 | 1/15/10 | 4.956 | BBB |
| COMCAST CABLE COMMUNICATIONS... | 105.32 | 6.875 | 6/15/09 | 4.853 | BBB |
| COMCAST CABLE COMMUNICATIONS... | 103.36 | 6.20 | 11/15/08 | 4.621 | BBB |
| COMCAST CABLE COMMUNICATIONS... | 104.04 | 8.375 | 5/1/07 | 2.763 | BBB |

These notes have been issued by Comcast Corporation (the parent company) and its wholly-owned subsidiary, Comcast Cable Communications.

Following are selected ratios from Exhibit 8.6 computed for Comcast Corp. utilizing its 2005 data.

EBIT interest coverage . . . . . . . . . . . . $3,690/$1,796 = 2.05

EBITDA interest coverage . . . . . . . . . ($3,690 + $3,630 + $1,173)/$1,796 = 4.73

FFO/Total debt . . . . . . . . . . . . . . . . . . ($947 + $3,630 + $1,173 + $183)/($21,682 + $1,689) = 0.25

Free operating cash flow/Total debt. . . ($4,922 − $3,621 + $97 + $65 + $860)/($21,682 + $1,689) = 0.10

Return on capital . . . . . . . . . . . . . . . . $1,880/[($1,689 + $3,499 + $21,682 + $20,093 + $27,370 +
$26,815 + $40,219 + $41,422)/2] = .021

Operating income/Sales . . . . . . . . . . . $3,690/$22,255 = 16.6%

Long-term debt/Capital . . . . . . . . . . . . $2,1682/($21,682 + $657 + $40,219) = 0.35

Total debt/Capital . . . . . . . . . . . . . . . . ($1,689 + $21,682)/($1,689 + $21,682 + $657 + $40,219) = 0.36

**Required**

*a.* Graph the yield to maturity (YTM) on the Y-axis and the maturity on the X-axis. What pattern do we observe? Explain this pattern.

*b.* Comcast's credit ratings for all of these bonds are BBB, which is a low medium grade. Examine Comcast's 2005 10-K (download from EDGAR or the Comcast Website) as well as the ratios provided above. What factors do you believe contribute to Comcast's credit rating being less than stellar?

*c.* Some of Comcast's bonds are trading at a premium and others at a discount. Why is this the case?

# CASES

**C8-41.  Management Application: Coupon Rate versus Effective Rate   LO2**

Assume that you are the CFO of a company that intends to issue bonds to finance a new manufacturing facility. A subordinate suggests lowering the coupon rate on the bond to lower interest expense and to increase the profitability of your company. Is the rationale for this suggestion a good one? Explain.

**C8-42.  Ethics and Governance: Bond Covenants   (LO2)**

Since lenders do not have voting rights like shareholders do, they often reduce their risk by invoking various bond covenants that restrict the company's operating, financing and investing activities. For example, debt covenants often restrict the amount of debt that the company can issue (in relation to its equity) and can impose operating restrictions (such as the ability to acquire other companies or to pay dividends). Failure to abide by these restrictions can have serious consequences, including forcing the company into bankruptcy and potential liquidation. Assume that you are on the board of directors of a company that issues bonds with such restrictions. What safeguards can you identify to ensure compliance with those restrictions?

# Reporting and Analyzing Owner Financing

## LEARNING OBJECTIVES

**LO1** Describe and illustrate accounting for contributed capital, including stock sales and repurchases. (p. 9-5)

**LO2** Explain and illustrate accounting for earned capital, including cash dividends, stock dividends, and comprehensive income. (p. 9-12)

**LO3** Describe accounting for equity carve outs and convertible debt. (p. 9-20)

## ACCENTURE

Accenture is one of the world's leading management consulting, technology services, and outsourcing companies. With more than 120,000 employees based in 48 countries, Accenture's 2005 revenues exceeded $15 billion. Accenture explains its business model as follows:

> We use our industry and business-process knowledge, our service offering expertise and our insight into and deep understanding of emerging technologies to identify new business and technology trends and formulate and implement solutions for clients . . . We help clients identify and enter new markets, increase revenues in existing markets, improve operational performance and deliver their products and services more effectively and efficiently.

Accenture is organized into three key service areas:

- Consulting. Clients draw on Accenture's expertise in strategy, business transformation, and specialty and functional consulting.
- Technology. Accenture helps clients manage their information technology needs; it develops and deploys software to streamline and integrate business processes and systems.
- Outsourcing. Accenture's outsourcing services include business process outsourcing (BPO), application outsourcing, and infrastructure outsourcing.

Following is a listing of several clients of Accenture and the types of services they purchased from Accenture:

- Vodafone Accenture defined and executed a program to improve key functions for Vodafone Germany including its IT customer service, network development, rollout and operations, and overall technology governance.
- Staples Accenture refined Staples' "big box" retail model, helping the company to focus on operational excellence to simplify customers'

shopping experience; Accenture focused on Staples' supply chain, inventory management, retail operations, merchandising, and marketing.

- **Royal & SunAlliance** Accenture provided several outsourcing and business solutions including R&SA's UK and Ireland IT application and maintenance functions as well as UK sales and service calls.

- **KeySpan Corporation** Accenture helped KeySpan deliver a scalable operating model, build leading capabilities, optimize its cost structure, and create a performance-based culture for all employees.

*The Wall Street Journal* explains that:

> Accenture has no operational headquarters and no formal branches. Its chief financial officer lives in Silicon Valley. Its chief technologist is based in Germany. The head of human resources is in Chicago. And the firm's thousands of management and technology consultants are constantly on the go, often reviewing projects and negotiating new contracts in clients' offices or working temporarily in offices that Accenture leases in more than 100 locations around the world.

Accenture's value lies not in plant assets, such as land and buildings, but in the knowledge capital of its employees, most of whom are Accenture shareholders. This module considers how shareholders' investment is accounted for on the balance sheet. We consider capital stock, stock options, share issuances, share repurchases, and dividend payments.

Accenture initially operated as a collection of related partnerships located throughout the world. Then, in 2001, the partnership converted to a corporation and the partners became shareholders. Accenture's capital structure provides liquidity and incentives to its employee/owners as well as a vehicle to raise additional funds.

Accenture has three classes of stock: preferred, which has been authorized, but has yet to be issued, and two classes of common, one voting (Class A) and the other nonvoting (Class X). Only the Class A shares are entitled to dividends and Accenture issues these shares to raise new capital. The company is currently in the process of redeeming its Class X shares.

Accenture also has restricted shares. These shares are awarded to employees under the company's deferred compensation plan, which entitles the employees to convert their restricted shares into Class A common shares. Employees cannot immediately convert their restricted shares. Instead, they must wait until the shares vest in the future. In the meantime, restricted shares are included as deferred compensation in

*(Continued on next page)*

*(Continued from previous page)*

shareholders' equity. Over time, as the restricted shares vest, Accenture issues Class A shares and records compensation expense. Vesting and conversion do not increase stockholders' equity because the increase in capital stock is exactly offset by a reduction in retained earnings. Restricted stock has become a popular way to compensate employees following recent changes in accounting for employee stock options. This module covers both employee stock options and restricted stock.

Accenture has repurchased over $760 million of its common stock. Many companies routinely repurchase their common stock as it is the best use of excess cash when a company has no better outside investment opportunities. Another reason for repurchasing stock is to offset the dilutive effect of stock-based compensation programs. This module explains stock repurchases. The module also discusses a variety of equity transactions under the general heading of equity carve outs and convertibles. These transactions include a number of methods by which companies seek to unlock hidden value for the benefit of their shareholders.

Sources: Accenture 2005 Form 10-K; Accenture 2005 Annual Report; *Fortune*, January 2007; *The Wall Street Journal*, June 2006.

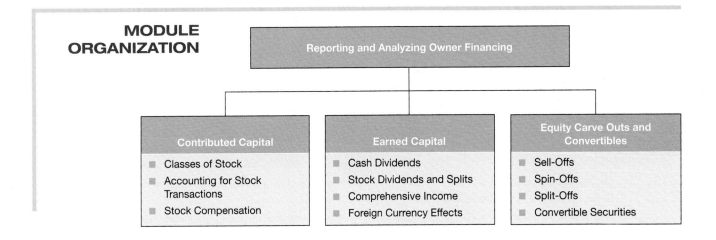

## INTRODUCTION

A company finances its assets through operating cash flows or it taps one or both of the following sources: either it borrows funds or it sells stock to shareholders. On average, companies obtain about half of their external financing from borrowed sources and the other half from shareholders. This module describes the issues relating to stockholders' equity, including the accounting for stock transactions (sales and repurchases of stock, dividends, stock-based compensation, and convertible securities). We also discuss equity carve outs, a process by which companies can unlock substantial shareholder value via spin-offs and split-offs of business units into separate companies. Finally, we discuss the accumulated other comprehensive income component of stockholders' equity.

When a company issues stock to the public, it records the receipt of cash (or other assets) and an increase in stockholders' equity, representing the shareholders' investment in the company. The increase in cash and equity is equal to the market price of the stock on the issue date multiplied by the number of shares sold.

Like bonds, stockholders' equity is accounted for at *historical cost.* Consequently, the company's financial statements do not reflect fluctuations in the market price of the stock subsequent to the initial public offering. This is because these market transactions involve outside parties and not the company. However, if the company repurchases and/or resells shares of its own stock, the balance sheet will be affected because those transactions involve the company.

There is an important difference between accounting for stockholders' equity and accounting for transactions involving assets and liabilities: *there is never any gain or loss reported on the purchase and sale of a company's own stock or the payment of dividends to its shareholders.* Instead, these "gains and losses" are reflected as increases and decreases in the contributed capital component of stockholders' equity.

The typical balance sheet has two broad categories of stockholders' equity:

1. **Contributed capital** These accounts report the proceeds received by the issuing company from original stock issuances. It often includes common stock, preferred stock, and additional paid-in capital. Netted against these contributed capital accounts is treasury stock, the amounts paid to repurchase shares of the issuer's stock from its investors, less the proceeds from the resale of such shares. Collectively, these accounts are referred to as contributed capital (or *paid-in capital*).

2. **Earned capital** This section consists of (a) retained earnings, which represent the cumulative income and losses of the company, less any dividends to shareholders, and (b) accumulated other comprehensive income (AOCI), which includes changes to equity that have not yet impacted income and are, therefore, not reflected in retained earnings.

Exhibit 9.1 illustrates the stockholders' equity section of Accenture's balance sheet (both contributed capital and earned capital). Accenture's balance sheet reports eight equity accounts that make up contributed capital: preferred stock, two classes of common stock, restricted share units, deferred compensation, additional paid-in capital, and two types of treasury (repurchased) stock. Accenture's balance sheet also reports two earned capital accounts: retained earnings and accumulated other comprehensive income (loss).

| EXHIBIT 9.1 | Stockholders' Equity from Accenture's Balance Sheet | | |
|---|---|---|---|
| | ($ 000) | 2005 | 2004 |
| | Preferred shares, 2,000,000,000 shares authorized, zero shares issued and outstanding | $ — | $ — |
| | Class A common shares, par value $0.0000225 per share, 20,000,000,000 shares authorized, 602,705,936 and 591,496,780 shares issued as of August 31, 2005 and 2004, respectively | 13 | 13 |
| | Class X common shares, par value $0.0000225 per share, 1,000,000,000 shares authorized, 321,088,062 and 365,324,882 shares issued and outstanding as of August 31, 2005 and 2004, respectively | 7 | 9 |
| Contributed Capital | Restricted share units (related to Class A common shares) 32,180,787 and 28,278,704 units issued and outstanding as of August 31, 2005 and 2004, respectively | 606,623 | 475,240 |
| | Deferred compensation | (240,915) | (150,777) |
| | Additional paid-in capital | 1,365,013 | 1,643,652 |
| | Treasury shares, at cost, 32,265,976 and 6,098,122 shares at August 31, 2005 and 2004, respectively | (763,682) | (132,313) |
| | Treasury shares owned by Accenture Ltd. Share Employee Compensation Trust, at cost, zero and 13,120,050 shares at August 31, 2005 and 2004, respectively | — | (296,894) |
| Earned Capital | Retained earnings | 962,339 | 46,636 |
| | Accumulated other comprehensive loss | (232,484) | (113,760) |
| | Total shareholders' equity | $1,696,914 | $1,471,806 |

We discuss contributed capital and earned capital in turn. For each section, we provide a graphic that displays the part of stockholders' equity in the balance sheet impacted by the discussion of that section.

# CONTRIBUTED CAPITAL

Contributed capital represents the cumulative cash inflow that the company has received from the sale of various classes of stock, less the net cash that it has paid out to repurchase its stock from the market. The contributed capital of Accenture is highlighted in the following graphic:

| Shareholders' Equity ($ 000) | 2005 | 2004 |
|---|---|---|
| Preferred shares, 2,000,000,000 shares authorized, zero shares issued and outstanding . . . . . . . . . . . . . . . . . . . . . . . . . . . . . . . . . . . . . . . . . . . . | $ — | $ — |
| Class A common shares, par value $0.0000225 per share, 20,000,000,000 shares authorized, 602,705,936 and 591,496,780 shares issued as of August 31, 2005 and 2004, respectively . . . . . . . . . . . . . . . . . . . . . . . . . . | 13 | 13 |
| Class X common shares, par value $0.0000225 per share, 1,000,000,000 shares authorized, 321,088,062 and 365,324,882 shares issued and outstanding as of August 31, 2005 and 2004, respectively . . . . . . . . . . . . . | 7 | 9 |
| Restricted share units (related to Class A common shares) 32,180,787 and 28,278,704 units issued and outstanding as of August 31, 2005 and 2004, respectively . . . . . . . . . . . . . . . . . . . . . . . . . . . . . . . . . . . . . | 606,623 | 475,240 |
| Deferred compensation . . . . . . . . . . . . . . . . . . . . . . . . . . . . . . . . . . . . . . | (240,915) | (150,777) |
| Additional paid-in capital . . . . . . . . . . . . . . . . . . . . . . . . . . . . . . . . . . . . | 1,365,013 | 1,643,652 |
| Treasury shares, at cost, 32,265,976 and 6,098,122 shares at August 31, 2005 and 2004, respectively . . . . . . . . . . . . . . . . . . . . . . . . . | (763,682) | (132,313) |
| Treasury shares owned by Accenture Ltd. Share Employee Compensation Trust, at cost, zero and 13,120,050 shares at August 31, 2005 and 2004, respectively . . . . . . . . . . . . . . . . . . . . . . . . . . . . . . . . . . . . . . . . . . . | — | (296,894) |
| Retained earnings . . . . . . . . . . . . . . . . . . . . . . . . . . . . . . . . . . . . . . . . . | 962,339 | 46,636 |
| Accumulated other comprehensive loss . . . . . . . . . . . . . . . . . . . . . . . . . . | (232,484) | (113,760) |
| Total shareholders' equity . . . . . . . . . . . . . . . . . . . . . . . . . . . . . . . . . . . | $1,696,914 | $1,471,806 |

For Accenture, contributed capital consists of par value and additional paid-in capital for its preferred stock (if issued), common stock, and restricted share units (its stock compensation plan). Its contributed capital is reduced by the cost of shares awarded to employees as deferred compensation and by the cost of Accenture's treasury stock (repurchased shares).

## Classes of Stock

**LO1** Describe and illustrate accounting for contributed capital, including stock sales and repurchases.

There are two general classes of stock: preferred and common. The difference between the two lies in the legal rights conferred upon each class.

### Preferred Stock

**Preferred stock** generally has preference, or priority, with respect to common stock. Two usual preferences are:

1. **Dividend preference** Preferred shareholders receive dividends on their shares before common shareholders do. If dividends are not paid in a given year, those dividends are normally forgone. However, some preferred stock contracts include a *cumulative provision* stipulating that any forgone dividends (dividends in *arrears*) must first be paid to preferred shareholders, together with the current year's dividends, before any dividends are paid to common shareholders.

2. **Liquidation preference** If a company fails, its assets are sold (liquidated) and the proceeds are paid to the creditors and shareholders, in that order. Shareholders, therefore, have a greater risk of loss than creditors. Among shareholders, the preferred shareholders receive payment in full before common shareholders. This liquidation preference makes preferred shares less risky than common shares. Any liquidation payment to preferred shares is normally at par value, although sometimes the liquidation is specified in excess of par; called a *liquidating value*.

To illustrate the typical provisions contained in preferred stock agreements, consider the following footnote disclosure from Chesapeake Energy Corporation (2005 10-K).

In April 2005, we issued 4,600,000 shares of 5.00% (Series 2005) cumulative convertible preferred stock, par value $0.01 per share and liquidation preference $100 per share, in a private offering, all of which were outstanding as of December 31, 2005. The net proceeds from the offering were $447.2 million. Each share of preferred stock is convertible, at the holder's option at any time, initially into approximately 3.8811 shares of our common stock based on an initial conversion price of $25.766 per share, subject to specified adjustments. At December 31, 2005, 17,853,060 shares of our common stock were reserved for issuance upon conversion. The preferred stock is subject to mandatory conversion, at our option, on or after April 15, 2010 . . . Annual cumulative cash dividends of $5.00 per share are payable quarterly on the fifteenth day of each January, April, July and October.

Following are several important features of Chesapeake's preferred stock:

- Each share of preferred stock is convertible into 3.8811 shares of common shares at the option of the preferred shareholder. After April 15, 2010, the company has the option of converting the preferred stock to common.

- The preferred stock pays an annual dividend of $5 per share, payable quarterly.

- The preferred stock is *cumulative*. This feature protects preferred shareholders in that unpaid dividends (called *dividends in arrears*) must be paid before any dividends are paid to common shareholders.

Chesapeake's cumulative preferred shares carry a dividend yield of 5%. This preferred dividend yield compares favorably with the $0.20 of dividends per share (1.09% yield on a $18.31 share price) paid to its common shareholders in 2005. Generally, preferred stock can be an attractive investment for shareholders seeking higher dividend yields, especially when tax laws wholly or partially exempt such dividends from taxation. (In comparison, interest payments received by debtholders are not tax exempt.)

In addition to the sorts of conversion features outlined above, preferred shares sometimes carry a *participation feature* that allows preferred shareholders to share ratably with common stockholders in dividends. The dividend preference over common shares can be a benefit when dividend payments are meager, but a fixed dividend yield limits upside potential if the company performs exceptionally well. A participation feature can overcome this limitation.

## Common Stock

Accenture has two classes of common stock, Class A and Class X. The Accenture common stock has the following important characteristics:

- Both classes of common stock have a par value of $0.0000225 per share. **Par value** is an arbitrary amount set by company organizers at the time of formation and has no relation to or impact on the stock's market value. Generally, par value has no substance from a financial reporting or financial statement analysis perspective (there are some legal implications, which are usually minor). Its main impact is in specifying the allocation of proceeds from stock issuances between the two contributed capital accounts on the balance sheet: common stock and additional paid-in capital, as we describe below.

- Accenture has authorized the issuance of 20 billion class A common shares. Shareholders control the number of shares that can be issued—called *authorized shares*. The articles of incorporation set the number of shares authorized for issuance. Once that limit is reached, shareholders must approve any increase in authorized shares. As of 2005, over 602.7 million shares are issued. When shares are first issued the number of shares outstanding equals the number issued. Any shares subsequently repurchased as treasury stock are no longer "outstanding" and the number of treasury shares are deducted from issued shares to derive *outstanding shares*. Because Accenture has repurchased some Class A shares, the number outstanding is fewer than the 602.7 million issued.[1]

---

[1] Accenture has a second class of common shares (Class X) issued and outstanding. These shares have a par value $0.0000225. Footnotes reveal that Class X shares are entitled to vote but are not entitled to dividends, do not have any preference in liquidation, and cannot be sold without the company's consent. Accenture's Class X shares are not publicly traded. Accenture has issued about 321 million Class X shares and has not repurchased any (the issued and outstanding number of shares are the same).

## Accounting for Stock Transactions

We cover the accounting for stock transactions in this section, including the accounting for stock issuances and repurchases.

### Stock Issuance

Companies issue stock to obtain cash and other assets for use in their business. Stock issuances increase assets (cash) by the issue proceeds: the number of shares sold multiplied by the price of the stock on the issue date. Equity increases by the same amount, which is reflected in contributed capital accounts. If the stock has a par value, the common stock account increases by the number of shares sold multiplied by its par value and the additional paid-in capital account increases for the remainder. If the stock is no-par, the common stock account increases by the total cash received. (Stock can also be issued as "no-par" or as "no-par with a stated value." For no-par stock, the common stock account is increased by the entire proceeds of the sale and no amount is assigned to additional paid-in capital. For no-par stock with a stated value, the stated value is treated just like par value, that is, common stock is increased by the number of shares multiplied by the stated value, and the remainder is assigned to the additional paid-in capital account.)

To illustrate, assume that Accenture issues 100,000 shares of its $0.0000225 par value common stock at a market price of $43 cash per share. This stock issuance has the following financial statement effects:

| | Balance Sheet | | | | | | | Income Statement | | |
|---|---|---|---|---|---|---|---|---|---|---|
| Transaction | Cash Asset | + Noncash Assets | = Liabil- ities | + Contrib. Capital | + Earned Capital | | | Rev- enues | − Expen- ses | = Net Income |
| Issue 100,000 common shares with $0.0000225 par value for $43 cash per share | +4,300,000 Cash | | = | +2 Common Stock +4,299,998 Additional Paid-In Capital | | | | | | = |

Cash 4,300,000
CS  2
APIC 4,299.998
　Cash
4,300,000 |
　CS
| 2
APIC
| 4,299,998

Specifically, the stock issuance affects the financial statements as follows:

1. Cash increases by $4,300,000 (100,000 shares × $43 per share)
2. Common stock increases by the par value of shares sold (100,000 shares × $0.0000225 par value = $2.25, rounded to $2 here)
3. Additional paid-in capital increases by the $4,299,998 difference between the issue proceeds and par value ($4,300,000 − $2)

Once shares are issued, they are traded in the open market among investors. The proceeds of those sales and their associated gains and losses, as well as fluctuations in the company's stock price subsequent to issuance, do not affect the issuing company and are not recorded in its accounting records.

Refer again to the following report of common stock on Accenture's balance sheet:

| ($ 000) | 2005 | 2004 |
|---|---|---|
| Class A common shares, par value $0.0000225 per share, 20,000,000,000 shares authorized, 602,705,936 and 591,496,780 shares issued as of August 31, 2005 and 2004, respectively | $ 13 | $ 13 |
| Additional paid-in capital | 1,365,013 | 1,643,652 |

Accenture's Class A common stock, in the amount of $13 million, equals the number of shares issued multiplied by the common stock's par value: 602,705,936 × $0.0000225 = $13,561 (rounded to $13 thousand). Total proceeds from its stock issuances are $1,365,026,000, the sum of the par value and additional paid-in capital. This implies that Class A shares were sold, on average, for $2.26 per share ($1,365,026,000/602,705,936 shares).

| RESEARCH INSIGHT | Stock Issuance and Stock Returns |
|---|---|

Research shows that, historically, companies issuing equity securities experience unusually low stock returns for several years following those offerings. Evidence suggests that this poor performance is partly due to overly optimistic estimates of long-term growth for these companies by equity analysts. That optimism causes offering prices to be too high. This over-optimism is most pronounced when the analyst is employed by the brokerage firm that underwrites the stock issue. There is also evidence that companies manage earnings upward prior to an equity offering. This means the observed decrease in returns following an issuance likely reflects the market's negative reaction, on average, to earnings management.

## Stock Repurchase

Accenture provides the following description of its stock repurchase program in notes to its 10-K report:

> **Share Purchase Activity** Since April 2002, the Board of Directors of Accenture Ltd has authorized funding for its publicly announced open-market share purchase program for acquiring Accenture Ltd Class A common shares . . . Effective as of October 15, 2004, the Board of Directors of Accenture Ltd has authorized the purchase, redemption and exchange from time to time of up to an additional $3 billion of Accenture shares.

This footnote goes on to say that Accenture has repurchased over $2.9 billion of its common stock since the share repurchase program was approved by its board of directors. One reason a company repurchases shares is because it believes that the market undervalues them. The logic is that the repurchase sends a favorable signal to the market about the company's financial condition that positively impacts its share price and, thus, allows it to resell those shares for a "gain." Any such gain on resale is *never* reflected in the income statement. Instead, any excess of the resale price over the repurchase price is added to additional paid-in capital. GAAP prohibits companies from reporting gains and losses from stock transactions with their own shareholders.

Another reason companies repurchase shares is to offset the dilutive effects of an employee stock option program. When an employee exercises stock options, the number of shares outstanding increases. These additional shares reduce earnings per share and are, therefore, viewed as *dilutive*. In response, many companies repurchase an equivalent number of shares in a desire to keep outstanding shares constant. Of the $2.9 billion in share repurchases, $2.1 billion has been purchased from Accenture executives. Those shares were originally issued under Accenture's incentive compensation program (disclosed in footnotes not reproduced here).

A stock repurchase reduces the size of the company (cash declines and, thus, total assets decline). A repurchase has the opposite financial statement effects from a stock issuance. That is, cash is reduced by the price of the shares repurchased (number of shares repurchased multiplied by the purchase price per share), and stockholders' equity is reduced by the same amount. The reduction in equity is achieved by increasing a contra equity (negative equity) account called **treasury stock,** which reduces stockholders' equity. Thus, when the treasury stock contra equity account increases, total equity decreases.

When the company subsequently reissues treasury stock there is no accounting gain or loss. Instead, the difference between the proceeds received and the original purchase price of the treasury stock is reflected as an increase or decease to additional paid-in capital.

To illustrate, assume that 3,000 common shares of Accenture previously issued for $43 are repurchased for $40. This repurchase has the following financial statement effects:

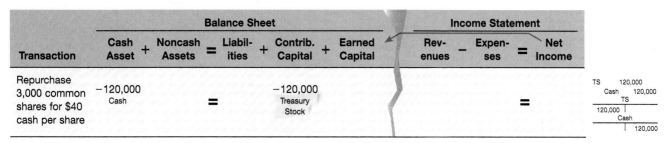

| | Balance Sheet | | | | | | Income Statement | | | |
|---|---|---|---|---|---|---|---|---|---|---|
| Transaction | Cash Asset | + Noncash Assets | = Liabil- ities | + Contrib. Capital | + Earned Capital | | Rev- enues | − Expen- ses | = Net Income | |
| Repurchase 3,000 common shares for $40 cash per share | −120,000 Cash | | = | −120,000 Treasury Stock | | | | | = | |

Assets (cash) and equity both decrease. Treasury stock (a contra equity account) increases by $120,000, which reduces stockholders' equity by that amount.

Assume that these 3,000 shares are subsequently resold for $42 cash per share. This resale of treasury stock has the following financial statement effects:

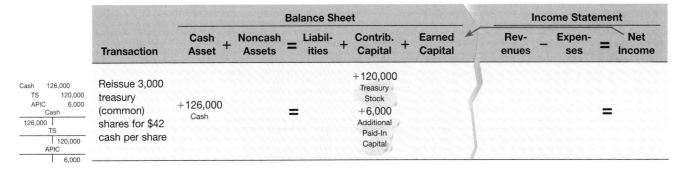

| | Balance Sheet | | | | | Income Statement | | |
|---|---|---|---|---|---|---|---|---|
| Transaction | Cash Asset | + Noncash Assets | = Liabil- ities | + Contrib. Capital | + Earned Capital | Rev- enues | − Expen- ses | = Net Income |
| Reissue 3,000 treasury (common) shares for $42 cash per share | +126,000 Cash | | = | +120,000 Treasury Stock +6,000 Additional Paid-In Capital | | | | = |

Cash 126,000
  TS 120,000
  APIC 6,000
    Cash
126,000 |
    TS
      | 120,000
    APIC
      | 6,000

Cash assets increase by $126,000 (3,000 shares × $42 per share), the treasury stock account is reduced by the $120,000 cost of the treasury shares issued, and the $6,000 excess (3,000 shares × $2 per share) is reported as an increase in additional paid-in capital. (If the reissue price is below the repurchase price, then additional paid-in capital is reduced until it reaches a zero balance, after which retained earnings are reduced.) Again, there is no effect on the income statement as companies are prohibited from reporting gains and losses from repurchases and reissuances of their own stock.

The treasury stock section of Accenture's balance sheet is reproduced below:

| ($ 000s) | 2005 | 2004 |
|---|---|---|
| Treasury shares, at cost, 32,265,976 and 6,098,122 shares at August 31, 2005 and 2004, respectively . . . . . . . . . . . . . . . . . . . . . . . . . . . . . . . . . . . . . . . . . . . . | $(763,682) | $(132,313) |

Accenture has repurchased a cumulative total of 32,265,976 shares of its common stock for $763,682,000, an average repurchase price of $23.67 per share. This compares with total contributed capital of $1,730,741 ($13 + $7 + $606,623 − $240,915 + 1,365,013; all $ in 000s, see page 9-5). Thus, Accenture has repurchased about 44% of its original contributed capital. Although some of Accenture's treasury purchases were to meet stock option exercises, it appears that most of these purchases are motivated by a perceived low stock price by Accenture management.

---

**MANAGERIAL DECISION**    **You Are the Chief Financial Officer**

As CFO, you believe that your company's stock price is lower than its real value. You are considering various alternatives to increase that price, including the repurchase of company stock in the market. What are some factors you should consider before making your decision? [Answer, p. 9-25]

---

## Stock Compensation Plans

Common stock has been an important component of executive compensation for decades. The general idea follows: If the company executives own stock they will have an incentive to increase its value. This aligns the executives' interests with those of other shareholders. Although the strength of this alignment is the subject of much debate, its logic compels boards of directors of most American companies to use stock-based compensation.

Common stock can be used as a performance incentive in several possible ways. One popular form is to give an employee the right to purchase common stock at a pre-specified price for a given period of time. This is called a stock option plan. Options allow employees to purchase stock at a fixed price (called the exercise price) and resell it at the prevailing (expectedly higher) market price, thus realizing an immediate gain. Because there is a good chance of future stock price increases, options are valuable to employees when they receive them, even if the exercise price is exactly equal to the stock's market price the day the options are awarded. (The fair value of the stock option to the employee can be determined using a formula developed by professors Fisher Black and Myron Scholes. The "Black-Scholes" formula is widely used to value a wide variety of options although other fair-value formulae exist.)

Under prior GAAP, companies could avoid recognizing the fair value of options in the income statement as compensation expense, and only needed to disclose that fair value in footnotes. Accounting standards were changed in 2005 and now income statements must include as compensation expense, the fair value of the options granted during the period. This eliminated one key financial reporting benefit for companies of this form of compensation.

Many companies, including Accenture, then began compensating employees with **restricted stock** instead of with stock options. Under a restricted stock plan, the company transfers shares to the employee, but the shares are restricted in that they cannot be sold until the end of a "vesting" period. (Vesting is the period of time over which an employee gains ownership of the shares, usually 5-7 years; employees commonly acquire ownership ratably over time, such as 1/5 each year over 5 years, or acquire full (100%) vesting after the vesting period ends—called *cliff vesting*.) Accounting for restricted stock is illustrated in the following template:

| | Balance Sheet | | | | | | Income Statement | | |
|---|---|---|---|---|---|---|---|---|---|
| Transaction | Cash Asset | + Noncash Assets | = Liabil- ities | + Contrib. Capital | + Earned Capital | | Rev- enues | − Expen- ses | = Net Income |
| Company issues 100 shares of $10 par restricted stock with a market value of $30 per share, vesting ratably over 6 years | | = | | +1,000 Common Stock +2,000 Additional Paid-In Capital -3,000 Deferred Compensation | | | | = | |
| Record compensation expense for first year (same entry for the next 5 years) | | = | | +500 Deferred Compensation | -500 Retained Earnings | | | +500 Wage Expense = -500 | |

DC   3,000
  CS       1,000
  APIC    2,000
      DC
3,000 |
      CS
      | 1,000
      APIC
      | 2,000

WE   500
  DC       500
      WE
500 |
      DC
      | 500

The company records the restricted stock grants as a share issuance exactly as if the shares were sold. That is, the common stock account increases by the par value of the shares and additional paid-in capital increases for the remainder of the share value. However, instead of cash received, the company records a deferred compensation (contra equity) account for the value of the shares that have not yet been issued. This reduces equity. Thus, granting restricted shares leaves the total dollar amount of equity unaffected.

Subsequently, the value of shares given to employees is treated as compensation expense and recorded over the vesting period. Each year, the deferred compensation account is reduced by the vested shares and wage expense is recorded, thus reducing retained earnings. Total equity is unaffected by this transaction as the reduction of the deferred compensation contra equity account (thereby increasing stockholders' equity) is exactly offset by the decrease in retained earnings. The remaining deferred compensation account decreases total stockholders' equity until the end of the vesting period when the total restricted stock grant has been recognized as wage expense. Equity is, therefore, never increased when restricted stock is issued.

Accenture's restricted stock compensation program is reflected in stockholders' equity as follows:

| ($ 000s) | 2005 | 2004 |
|---|---|---|
| Restricted share units (related to Class A common shares) 32,180,787 and 28,278,704 units issued and outstanding as of August 31, 2005 and 2004, respectively. . . . . . . . . . . . . . . . . . . . . . . . . . . . . . . . . . . . . . . . . . . . . . . . . . | $606,623 | $475,240 |
| Deferred compensation . . . . . . . . . . . . . . . . . . . . . . . . . . . . . . . . . . . . . . . . . . . . | (240,915) | (150,777) |

As of 2005, Accenture had granted employees $606,623,000 in restricted stock, $365,708,000 of which has been reflected as compensation expense, leaving a balance in deferred compensation of $240,915,000. These restricted share units (RSU) entitle the employee to receive one share of Accenture Class A common stock under the company's vesting schedule as described in the following excerpt from its 10-K.

> **Restricted Share Units** Under the [Share Incentive Plan], participants may be granted restricted share units without cost to the participant. Each restricted share unit awarded to a participant represents an unfunded, unsecured right, which is nontransferable except in the event of death of the participant, to receive an Accenture Ltd Class A common share on the date specified in the participant's award agreement. The restricted share units granted under this plan vest at various times, generally ranging from immediate vesting to vesting over a ten year period. For awards with graded vesting, compensation expense is recognized over the vesting term of each separately vesting portion. Compensation expense is recognized on a straight-line basis for awards with cliff vesting. A summary of information with respect to restricted share units is as follows:

| | 2005 | 2004 | 2003 |
|---|---|---|---|
| Shares granted.............................. | 7,335,407 | 4,715,894 | 6,908,328 |
| Weighted average fair value of shares............. | $ 25.78 | $ 22.62 | $ 16.13 |
| Pretax compensation expense charged to earnings, net of cancellations......................... | $88,341,000 | $60,486,000 | $51,615,000 |

During 2005, Accenture issued 7,335,407 RSUs, valued at $25.78 per share (the value of the Class A common traded on the NYSE: ACN), for a total value of $189,106,792. During 2005, Accenture recognized $88,341,000 as compensation expense relating to the vesting of the 2005 RSUs and previously issued RSUs. Upon exchange of the RSUs for the Class A common stock, Accenture records issuance of common stock as if it had sold the stock for the cost of the RSU. (If employees forfeit shares, perhaps as a result of employment termination, the compensation recognized to date, and the remaining deferred compensation balance is reversed and offset against the related common stock and paid-in capital accounts. Income increases by the reversal of the compensation expense recognized to date.)

To summarize, restricted stock plans do not affect the total dollar amount of equity. Retained earnings decrease over time as the company recognizes compensation when the restricted shares vest, and paid-in capital increases by the same amount. The effect is a transfer of equity from earned capital to paid-in capital.

## MID-MODULE REVIEW 1

Assume that BearingPoint reported the following transactions relating to its stock accounts in 2005.

Jan. 15 Issued 10,000 shares of $5 par value common stock at $17 cash per share

Mar. 31 Purchased 2,000 shares of its own common stock at $15 cash per share.

June 25 Reissued 1,000 shares of its treasury stock at $20 cash per share.

Use the financial statement effects template to identify the effects of these stock transactions.

### Solution

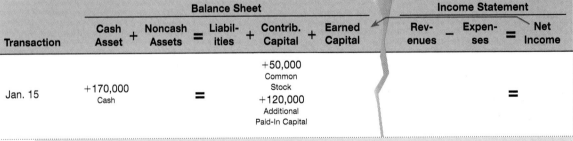

| | | Balance Sheet | | | | | Income Statement | | |
|---|---|---|---|---|---|---|---|---|---|
| Transaction | Cash Asset | + Noncash Assets | = Liabil- ities | + Contrib. Capital | + Earned Capital | | Rev- enues | − Expen- ses | = Net Income |
| Jan. 15 | +170,000 Cash | | = | +50,000 Common Stock +120,000 Additional Paid-In Capital | | | | | = |

Cash 170,000
  CS 50,000
  APIC 120,000

Cash
170,000 |
  CS
  | 50,000
  APIC
  | 120,000

*continued*

| | Balance Sheet | | | | | Income Statement | | |
|---|---|---|---|---|---|---|---|---|
| Transaction | Cash Asset | + Noncash Assets | = Liabil- ities | + Contrib. Capital | + Earned Capital | Rev- enues | − Expen- ses | = Net Income |
| Mar. 31 | −30,000 Cash | = | | −30,000 Treasury Stock | | | | |
| June 25 | +20,000 Cash | | | +15,000 Treasury Stock +5,000 Additional Paid-In Capital | | | | |

```
TS      30,000
    Cash      30,000
        TS
30,000 |
        Cash
            |      30,000
Cash    20,000
        TS          15,000
        APIC         5,000
            Cash
20,000 |
        TS
            |      15,000
        APIC
            |       5,000
```

# EARNED CAPITAL

We now turn attention to the earned capital portion of stockholders' equity. Earned capital represents the cumulative profit that the company has retained. Recall that earned capital increases each period by income earned and decreases by any losses incurred. Earned capital also decreases by dividends paid to shareholders. Not all dividends are paid in the form of cash. Companies can pay dividends in many forms, including property (land, for example) or additional shares of stock. We cover both cash and stock dividends in this section. Earned capital also includes the positive or negative effects of ac- cumulated other comprehensive income (AOCI). The earned capital of Accenture is highlighted in the following graphic:

**LO2** Explain and illustrate accounting for earned capital, including cash dividends, stock dividends, and comprehensive income.

| Shareholders' Equity ($ 000) | 2005 | 2004 |
|---|---|---|
| Preferred shares, 2,000,000,000 shares authorized, zero shares issued and outstanding . . . . . . . . . . . . . . . . . . . . . . . . . . . . . . . . . . . . . . . . . . | $ — | $ — |
| Class A common shares, par value $0.0000225 per share, 20,000,000,000 shares authorized, 602,705,936 and 591,496,780 shares issued as of August 31, 2005 and 2004, respectively . . . . . . . . . . . . . . . . . . . . . . . . . . | 13 | 13 |
| Class X common shares, par value $0.0000225 per share, 1,000,000,000 shares authorized, 321,088,062 and 365,324,882 shares issued and outstanding as of August 31, 2005 and 2004, respectively . . . . . . . . . . . . . . . | 7 | 9 |
| Restricted share units (related to Class A common shares) 32,180,787 and 28,278,704 units issued and outstanding as of August 31, 2005 and 2004, respectively . . . . . . . . . . . . . . . . . . . . . . . . . . . . . . . . . . . . . . . . . | 606,623 | 475,240 |
| Deferred compensation . . . . . . . . . . . . . . . . . . . . . . . . . . . . . . . . . . . . . . . | (240,915) | (150,777) |
| Additional paid-in capital . . . . . . . . . . . . . . . . . . . . . . . . . . . . . . . . . . . . . . | 1,365,013 | 1,643,652 |
| Treasury shares, at cost, 32,265,976 and 6,098,122 shares at August 31, 2005 and 2004, respectively . . . . . . . . . . . . . . . . . . . . . . . . . . . | (763,682) | (132,313) |
| Treasury shares owned by Accenture Ltd. Share Employee Compensation Trust, at cost, zero and 13,120,050 shares at August 31, 2005 and 2004, respectively. . . . . . . . . . . . . . . . . . . . . . . . . . . . . . . . . . . . . . . . . . . . | — | (296,894) |
| Retained earnings . . . . . . . . . . . . . . . . . . . . . . . . . . . . . . . . . . . . . . . . . . . | 962,339 | 46,636 |
| Accumulated other comprehensive loss . . . . . . . . . . . . . . . . . . . . . . . . . . | (232,484) | (113,760) |
| Total shareholders' equity . . . . . . . . . . . . . . . . . . . . . . . . . . . . . . . . . . . . | $1,696,914 | $1,471,806 |

## Cash Dividends

Many companies, but not all, pay dividends. Their reasons for dividend payments are varied. Most divi- dends are paid in cash on a quarterly basis. The following is a description of Accenture's dividend policy from its 10-K.

**Dividend Policy** From our incorporation in 2001 through the end of fiscal 2005, Accenture Ltd did not declare or pay any cash dividends on any class of equity. On October 6, 2005, Accenture Ltd declared a cash dividend of $0.30 per share on its Class A common shares for shareholders of record at the close of business on October 17, 2005. Dividends are to be payable on November 15, 2005. Future dividends on the Accenture Ltd Class A common shares, if any, will be at the discretion of the Board of Directors of Accenture Ltd and will depend on, among other things, our results of operations, cash requirements and surplus, financial condition, contractual restrictions and other factors that the Board of Directors may deem relevant.

Outsiders closely monitor dividend payments. It is generally perceived that the level of dividend payments is related to the company's expected long-term recurring income. Accordingly, dividend increases are usually viewed as positive signals about future performance and are accompanied by stock price increases. By that logic, companies rarely reduce their dividends unless absolutely necessary because dividend reductions are often met with substantial stock price declines.

## Financial Effects of Cash Dividends

Cash dividends reduce both cash and retained earnings by the amount of the cash dividends paid. To illustrate, Accenture's Board of Directors authorized cash dividends of approximately $181 million to be paid in fiscal 2006 to Class A common stockholders (602,705,936 shares × $0.30 per share). The financial statement effects of this cash dividend payment are as follows:

| | Balance Sheet | | | | | | Income Statement | | |
|---|---|---|---|---|---|---|---|---|---|
| Transaction | Cash Asset | + Noncash Assets | = Liabil- ities | + Contrib. Capital | + Earned Capital | | Rev- enues | − Expen- ses | = Net Income |
| Payment of $181 million in cash dividends | −181 mil. Cash | | = | | −181 mil. Retained Earnings | | | | = |

RE       181 mil.
　Cash       181 mil.
　　　RE
181 mil. |
　　Cash
　　　| 181 mil.

Dividend payments do not affect net income. They directly reduce retained earnings and bypass the income statement.

Dividends on preferred stock have priority over those on common stock, including unpaid prior years' preferred dividends (dividends in arrears) when preferred stock is cumulative. To illustrate, assume that a company has 15,000 shares of $50 par value, 8% preferred stock outstanding and 50,000 shares of $5 par value common stock outstanding. During its first three years in business, assume that the company declares $20,000 dividends in the first year, $260,000 of dividends in the second year, and $60,000 of dividends in the third year. If the preferred stock is cumulative, the total amount of cash dividends paid to each class of stock in each of the three years follows:

| | Preferred Stock | Common Stock |
|---|---|---|
| Year 1—$20,000 cash dividends paid | | |
| Current year dividend ($750,000 × 8%; but only $20,000 paid, leaving $40,000 in arrears) . . . . . . . . . . . . . . . . . . . . . . . . . . . . . . . . . . . . . . . . . | $20,000 | |
| Balance to common . . . . . . . . . . . . . . . . . . . . . . . . . . . . . . . . . . . . . . . . . . . . . | | $      0 |
| Year 2—$260,000 cash dividends paid | | |
| Dividends in arrears from Year 1 ([$750,000 × 8%] − $20,000) . . . . . . . . . . | 40,000 | |
| Current year dividend ($750,000 × 8%). . . . . . . . . . . . . . . . . . . . . . . . . . . . . | 60,000 | |
| Balance to common . . . . . . . . . . . . . . . . . . . . . . . . . . . . . . . . . . . . . . . . . . . . . | | 160,000 |
| Year 3—$60,000 cash dividends paid | | |
| Current year dividend ($750,000 × 8%). . . . . . . . . . . . . . . . . . . . . . . . . . . . . | 60,000 | |
| Balance to common . . . . . . . . . . . . . . . . . . . . . . . . . . . . . . . . . . . . . . . . . . . . . | | 0 |

## MID-MODULE REVIEW 2

Assume that Electronic Data Systems (EDS) has outstanding 10,000 shares of $100 par value, 5% preferred stock and 50,000 shares of $5 par value common stock. During its first three years in business, assume that EDS declared no dividends in the first year, $300,000 of cash dividends in the second year, and $80,000 of cash dividends in the third year.

a.  If preferred stock is cumulative, determine the dividends paid to each class of stock for each of the three years.
b.  If preferred stock is noncumulative, determine the dividends paid to each class of stock for each of the three years.

## Solution

a.

| Cumulative Preferred Stock | Preferred Stock | Common Stock |
|---|---|---|
| Year 1—$0 cash dividends paid. . . . . . . . . . . . . . . . . . . . . . . . | $ 0 | $ 0 |
| Year 2—$300,000 cash dividends paid | | |
| Dividends in arrears from Year 1 ($1,000,000 × 5%). . . . . . . . | 50,000 | |
| Current year dividend ($1,000,000 × 5%) . . . . . . . . . . . . . . . | 50,000 | |
| Balance to common . . . . . . . . . . . . . . . . . . . . . . . . . . . . . . . . | | 200,000 |
| Year 3—$80,000 cash dividends paid | | |
| Current year dividend ($1,000,000 × 5%) . . . . . . . . . . . . . . . | 50,000 | |
| Balance to common . . . . . . . . . . . . . . . . . . . . . . . . . . . . . . . . | | 30,000 |

b.

| Noncumulative Preferred Stock | Preferred Stock | Common Stock |
|---|---|---|
| Year 1—$0 cash dividends paid. . . . . . . . . . . . . . . . . . . . . . . . | $ 0 | $ 0 |
| Year 2—$300,000 cash dividends paid | | |
| Current year dividend ($1,000,000 × 5%) . . . . . . . . . . . . . . . | 50,000 | |
| Balance to common . . . . . . . . . . . . . . . . . . . . . . . . . . . . . . . . | | 250,000 |
| Year 3—$80,000 cash dividends paid | | |
| Current year dividend ($1,000,000 × 5%) . . . . . . . . . . . . . . . | 50,000 | |
| Balance to common . . . . . . . . . . . . . . . . . . . . . . . . . . . . . . . . | | 30,000 |

# Stock Dividends and Splits

Dividends need not be paid in cash. Many companies pay dividends in the form of additional shares of stock. Companies can also distribute additional shares to their stockholders with a stock split. We cover both of these distributions in this section.

## Stock Dividends

When dividends are paid in the form of the company's stock, retained earnings are reduced and contributed capital is increased. However, the amount by which retained earnings are reduced depends on the proportion of the outstanding shares distributed to the total outstanding shares on the dividend distribution date. Exhibit 9.2 illustrates two possibilities depending on whether stock dividends are classified as either small stock dividends or large stock dividends. The break point between small and large is 20–25% of the outstanding shares. (When the number of additional shares issued as a stock dividend is so great that it could materially reduce share price, the transaction is akin to a stock split. The 20–25% guideline is used as a rule of thumb to distinguish material stock price effects.)

For *small stock dividends,* retained earnings are reduced by the *market* value of the shares distributed (dividend shares × market price per share), and par value and contributed capital together are increased by the same amount. For *large stock dividends,* retained earnings are reduced by the *par* value of the shares distributed (dividend shares × par value per share), and common stock is increased by the same amount (no change to additional paid-in capital).

| EXHIBIT 9.2 | Analysis of Stock Dividend Effects | | |
|---|---|---|---|
| **Percentage of Outstanding Shares Distributed** | | **Retained Earnings** | **Contributed Capital** |
| Less than 20-25% *(small stock dividend treated as a dividend)* | | Reduce by **market value** of shares distributed | Common stock increased by: Dividend shares × Par value per share; Additional paid-in capital increased for the balance |
| More than 20-25% *(large stock dividend treated as a stock split)* | | Reduce by **par value** of shares distributed | Common stock increased by: Dividend shares × Par value per share |

To illustrate the financial statement effects of stock dividends, assume that **BearingPoint** has 1 million shares of $5 par common stock outstanding. It then declares a small stock dividend of 15% of the outstanding shares (1,000,000 shares × 15% = 150,000 shares) when the market price of the stock is $30 per share. This small stock dividend has the following financial statement effects:

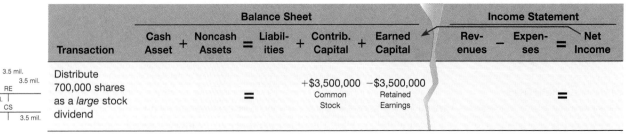

The company reduces retained earnings by $4,500,000, which equals the market value of the small stock dividend (150,000 shares × $30 market price per share). The increase in contributed capital is split between the par value of $750,000 (150,000 shares × $5 par value) and additional paid-in capital ($3,750,000). Similar to cash dividend payments, stock dividends, whether large or small, never impact income.

Next, assume that instead, **BearingPoint** declares a large stock dividend of 70% of the 1 million outstanding common ($5 par) shares when the market price of the stock is $30 per share. This large stock dividend is treated like a stock split and has the following financial statement effects:

| | Balance Sheet | | | | | | Income Statement | | |
|---|---|---|---|---|---|---|---|---|---|
| Transaction | Cash Asset | + Noncash Assets | = Liabil- ities | + Contrib. Capital | + Earned Capital | | Rev- enues | − Expen- ses | = Net Income |
| Distribute 700,000 shares as a *large* stock dividend | | | = | +$3,500,000 Common Stock | −$3,500,000 Retained Earnings | | | | = |

RE 3.5 mil.
CS 3.5 mil.
RE
3.5 mil. |
CS
| 3.5 mil.

The company's retained earnings declines by $3,500,000, which equals the par value of the large stock dividend (700,000 shares × $5 par value per share). Common stock is increased by the par value of $3,500,000. There is no effect on additional paid-in capital since large stock dividends are reported at par value.

For both large and small stock dividends, companies are required to show comparable shares outstanding for all prior periods for which earnings per share (EPS) is reported in the statements. The reasoning is that a stock dividend has no effect on the ownership percentage of each common stockholder. As such, to show a dilution in reported EPS would erroneously suggest a decline in profitability when it is simply due to an increase in shares outstanding.

## Stock Splits

A stock split is a proportionate distribution of shares and, as such, is similar in substance to a stock dividend. A typical stock split is 2-for-1, which means that the company distributes one additional share for each share owned by a shareholder. Following the distribution, each investor owns twice as many shares, so that their percentage ownership in the company is unchanged.

A stock split is not a monetary transaction and, as such, there are no financial statement effects. However, companies must disclose the new number of shares outstanding for all periods presented in the financial statements. Further, many states require that the par value of shares be proportionately adjusted as well (for example, halved for a 2-for-1 split).

If state law requires that par value not be reduced for a stock dividend, this event should be described as a *stock split affected in the form of a dividend*. The following disclosure from Adobe Systems' 2005 annual report provides such an example:

> **Stock Dividend** On March 16, 2005, our Board of Directors approved a two-for-one stock split, in the form of a stock dividend, of our common stock payable on May 23, 2005, to stockholders of record as of May 2, 2005. Share and per share data, for all periods presented, have been adjusted to give effect to this stock split.

## MID-MODULE REVIEW 3

Assume that the stockholders' equity of Ceridian Corporation at December 31, 2007, follows.

| | |
|---|---|
| 5% preferred stock, $100 par value, 10,000 shares authorized; 4,000 shares issued and outstanding. . . . . . . . . . . . . . . . . . . . . . . . | $ 400,000 |
| Common stock, $5 par value, 200,000 shares authorized; 50,000 shares issued and outstanding . . . . . . . . . . . . . . . . . . . . . . . | 250,000 |
| Paid-in capital in excess of par value-Preferred stock. . . . . . . . . . . . . . | 40,000 |
| Paid-in capital in excess of par value-Common stock. . . . . . . . . . . . . . | 300,000 |
| Retained earnings . . . . . . . . . . . . . . . . . . . . . . . . . . . . . . . . . . . . . . . | 656,000 |
| Total stockholders' equity . . . . . . . . . . . . . . . . . . . . . . . . . . . . . . . . . | $1,646,000 |

Use the template to identify the financial statement effects for each of the following transactions that occurred during 2008:

Apr. 1 Declared and issued a 100% stock dividend on all outstanding shares of common stock when the market value of the stock was $11 per share.

Dec. 7 Declared and issued a 3% stock dividend on all outstanding shares of common stock when the market value of the stock was $7 per share.

Dec. 31 Declared and paid a cash dividend of $1.20 per share on all outstanding shares.

## Solution

| | Balance Sheet | | | | | | Income Statement | | | |
|---|---|---|---|---|---|---|---|---|---|---|
| **Transaction** | Cash Asset | + Noncash Assets | = Liabil- ities | + Contrib. Capital | + Earned Capital | | Rev- enues | – Expen- ses | = Net Income | |
| Apr. 1 | | = | | +250,000 Common Stock | −250,000[1] Retained Earnings | | | = | | RE 250,000<br>  CS 250,000<br>RE<br>250,000<br>  CS<br>  250,000 |
| Dec. 7 | | = | | +15,000 Common Stock +6,000 Additional Paid-In Capital | −21,000[2] Retained Earnings | | | = | | RE 21,000<br>  CS 15,000<br>  APIC 6,000<br>RE<br>21,000<br>  CS<br>  15,000<br>  APIC<br>  6,000 |
| Dec. 31 | −123,600 Cash | = | | | −123,600[3] Retained Earnings | | | = | | RE 123,600<br>  Cash 123,600<br>RE<br>123,600<br>  Cash<br>  123,600 |

[1] This large stock dividend reduces retained earnings at the par value of shares distributed (50,000 shares × 100% × $5 par value = $250,000). Contributed capital (common stock) increases by the same amount.

[2] This small stock dividend reduces retained earnings at the market value of shares distributed (3% × 100,000 shares × $7 per share = $21,000). Contributed capital increases by the same amount ($15,000 to common stock and $6,000 to paid-in capital).

[3] At the time of the cash dividend, there are 103,000 shares outstanding. The cash paid is, therefore, 103,000 shares × $1.20 per share = $123,600.

## Accumulated Other Comprehensive Income

Comprehensive income is a more inclusive notion of company performance than net income. It includes all recognized changes in equity that occur during a period except those resulting from contributions by and distributions to owners. It's important to note that comprehensive income includes both net income and other items.

Specifically, comprehensive income includes (and net income excludes) foreign currency translation adjustments, unrealized changes in market values of available-for-sale securities, pension liability adjustments, and changes in market values of certain derivative investments. Comprehensive income, therefore, includes the effects of economic events that are often outside of management's control. Accordingly, some assert that net income measures management's performance, while comprehensive income measures company performance. Each period, net income or loss is added to retained earnings so that the balance sheet maintains a running total of the company's cumulative net income and losses (less any dividends paid out). In the same way, each period, comprehensive income items that are not included in net income are added to a balance sheet account called Accumulated Other Comprehensive Income (or loss if the comprehensive items are losses). This account maintains a running balance of the cumulative differences between net income and comprehensive income.

Accenture reports the following components of its accumulated other comprehensive loss from its 10-K report:

| ($ 000s) | 2005 | 2004 |
|---|---|---|
| Foreign currency translation adjustments . . . . . . . . . . . . . . . | $ (43,036) | $ (22,752) |
| Unrealized (losses) gains on marketable securities, net of reclassification adjustments . . . . . . . . . . . . . . . . . . . . . . . . . | (2,219) | 524 |
| Minimum pension liability adjustments, net of taxes . . . . . . . . | (187,229) | (91,532) |
| Accumulated other comprehensive loss . . . . . . . . . . . . . . . . | $(232,484) | $(113,760) |

Accenture's accumulated other comprehensive loss includes the three following items that affect stockholders' equity and are not reflected in net income:

1. **Foreign currency translation adjustment** ($43,036,000). This is the unrecognized loss on assets and liabilities denominated in foreign currencies. A loss implies that the $US has strengthened relative to foreign currencies; such as when assets denominated in foreign currencies translate to fewer $US. We discuss the effects of foreign currency translation adjustments on accumulated other comprehensive income in more detail below.

2. **Unrealized gains (losses) on available-for-sale securities** ($2,219,000). Unrealized gains and losses on available-for-sale securities are not reflected in net income. Instead, they are accumulated in a separate equity account until the securities are sold.

3. **Minimum pension liability** ($187,229,000). This is the additional pension liability that must be recorded under GAAP because some of Accenture's pension plans are underfunded.

We discuss accounting for available-for-sale securities and pensions in Modules 7 and 10, respectively, and the income statement effects of foreign currency translation adjustments in Module 5. In the next section, we discuss the balance sheet effects of foreign currency translation adjustments, specifically their impact on accumulated other comprehensive income.

### Foreign Currency Translation Effects on Accumulated Other Comprehensive Income

Many companies have international transactions denominated in foreign currencies. They might purchase assets in foreign currencies, borrow money in foreign currencies, and transact business with their customers and suppliers in foreign currencies. Other companies might have subsidiaries whose entire balance sheets and income statements are stated in foreign currencies. Financial statements prepared according to U.S. GAAP must be reported in $US. This means that financial statements of foreign subsidiaries must be translated into $US before they are consolidated with those of the U.S. parent company. This translation process can markedly alter both the balance sheet and income statement. We discuss the income statement effects of foreign currency translation in Module 5 and the balance sheet effects in this section.

Consider a U.S. company with a foreign subsidiary that conducts its business in Euros. The subsidiary prepares its financial statements in Euros. Assume that the $US weakens vis-à-vis the Euro during the current period—that is, each Euro can now purchase more $US. When the balance sheet is translated into $US, the assets and liabilities are reported at higher $US than before the $US weakened. This result is shown in accounting equation format in Exhibit 9.3.[2]

| EXHIBIT 9.3 | Balance Sheet Effects of Euro Strengthening versus the Dollar | | | | | |
|---|---|---|---|---|---|---|
| Currency | Assets | = | Liabilities | + | Equity | |
| $US weakens............. | Increase | = | Increase | + | Increase | |
| $US strengthens........... | Decrease | = | Decrease | + | Decrease | |

The amount necessary to balance the accounting equation is reported in equity and is called a **foreign currency translation adjustment**. The *cumulative* foreign currency translation adjustment is included in accumulated other comprehensive income (or loss) as illustrated above for Accenture. Foreign currency translation adjustments are direct adjustments to stockholders' equity; they do not impact reported net income. Since assets are greater than liabilities for solvent companies, the cumulative translation adjustment is positive when the $US weakens and negative when the dollar strengthens.

Referring to Accenture's accumulated other comprehensive income table on p 9-17, the cumulative foreign currency translation is a loss of $22,752,000 at the beginning of 2005, which grows to a loss of $43,036,000 by year-end. The $20,284,000 increase in the loss (decrease in Accenture's equity) reflects a strengthening of the $US vis-à-vis the foreign currencies that Accenture dealt with in 2005. That is, as the $US strengthened, Accenture's foreign assets and liabilities translated into fewer $US at year-end (the opposite effect from that described above). This decreased Accenture's equity. In general, unrealized losses (or gains) remain in other accumulated comprehensive income as long as the company owns the foreign subsidiaries to which the losses relate. The translation adjustments fluctuate between positive and negative amounts as the value of the $US fluctuates. However, when a subsidiary is sold, any remaining foreign currency translation adjustment (positive or negative) is immediately recognized in current income along with other gains or losses arising from sale of the subsidiary.

## Summary of Stockholders' Equity

The statement of shareholders' equity summarizes the transactions that affect stockholders' equity during the period. This statement reconciles the beginning and ending balances of important stockholders' equity accounts. Accenture's statement of stockholders' equity is in Exhibit 9.4.

---

[2] We assume that the company translates the subsidiary's financial statements using the more common **current rate method**, which is required for subsidiaries operating independently from the parent. Under the current rate method, most items in the balance sheet are translated using exchange rates in effect at the period-end consolidation date and the income statement is translated using the average exchange rate for the period. An alternative procedure is the *temporal method,* which is covered in advanced accounting courses.

## EXHIBIT 9.4 — Accenture's Statement of Stockholders' Equity

| Line No. | ($ and shares in 000s) | Class A Shares $ 000s | Shares | Restricted Share Units $ 000s | Shares | Deferred Compensation Expense | Additional Paid-In Capital | Treasury Stock $ 000s | Shares | Retained Earnings | Accumulated Other Comprehensive Income | Other | Total |
|---|---|---|---|---|---|---|---|---|---|---|---|---|---|
| 1 | Balance, August 31, 2004 | $13 | 591,497 | $475,240 | 28,279 | $(150,777) | $1,643,652 | $(429,207) | (19,218) | $ 46,636 | $(113,760) | $9 | $1,471,806 |
| 2 | Net income | | | | | | | | | 940,474 | | | 940,474 |
| 3 | Unrealized loss on available-for-sale securities | | | | | | | | | | (2,743) | | (2,743) |
| 4 | Foreign currency translation adjustment | | | | | | | | | | (20,284) | | (20,284) |
| 5 | Minimum pension liability adjustment | | | | | | | | | | (95,697) | | (95,697) |
| 6 | Stock-based compensation | | | | | | 84,378 | | | | | | 84,378 |
| 7 | Contract termination | | | | | | | | | 134 | | | 134 |
| 8 | Purchase of Class A shares | | (562) | | | | (13,286) | (503,088) | (21,497) | | | | (516,374) |
| 9 | Grant of Restricted Share Units | | | 177,778 | 6,745 | (177,778) | | | | | | | 0 |
| 10 | Stock compensation expense | | | | | 87,640 | 701 | | | | | | 88,341 |
| 11 | Redemption of SCA shares | | | | | | (1,095,155) | | | | | (2) | (1,095,157) |
| 12 | Employee share purchases | | 4,955 | | | | 99,678 | 72,916 | 3,831 | (4,270) | | | 168,324 |
| 13 | Employee stock options | | 5,008 | | | | 69,193 | 75,538 | 3,582 | (17,775) | | | 126,956 |
| 14 | Restricted Share Units | | 1,808 | (46,395) | (2,843) | | 29,096 | 20,159 | 1,036 | (2,860) | | | 0 |
| 15 | Transaction fees | | | | | | 3,427 | | | | | | 3,427 |
| 16 | Minority interest | | | | | | 543,329 | | | | | | 543,329 |
| 17 | Balance, August 31, 2005 | $13 | 602,706 | $606,623 | 32,181 | $(240,915) | $1,365,013 | $(763,682) | (32,266) | $962,339 | $(232,484) | $7 | $1,696,914 |

Accenture's statement of shareholders' equity reveals the following key transactions for 2005:

- Line 2: Accenture's retained earnings increased by $940,474,000 from net income (the company paid no dividends in 2005).

- Lines 3–5: Accumulated other comprehensive income began the year with a loss balance of $113,760,000. Other comprehensive income recorded during the year included an unrecognized loss on available-for-sale securities of $2,743,000, a foreign currency translation adjustment loss of $20,284,000, and an increase in the minimum pension liability adjustment of $95,697,000. Together, these three items increased the accumulated other comprehensive loss to $232,484 by year-end.

- Line 6: Tax benefits arising from employee exercise of stock options are recorded as an increase in additional paid-in capital (rather than as a reduction of tax expense).

▧ Line 8: Repurchase of Class A common shares increased treasury stock by $503,088,000 with a small balance also reducing additional paid-in capital (reducing equity by that amount). The column for Class A shares includes both dollars and number of shares.

▧ Line 9: Accenture granted its employees an additional 6,745,000 restricted share units under its deferred compensation plan; market value of the shares was $177,778,000. The restricted share unit capital account increased by $177,778,000 with an offsetting increase in the deferred compensation contra equity account. There is no net increase in equity from this grant.

▧ Line 10: Accenture recorded $87,640,000 of stock compensation expense in 2005 relating to the restricted stock units in line 9; this represents the 2005 amortization of the deferred compensation over the vesting period.

▧ Line 11: Redemption of SCA shares relates to the purchase of restricted shares held by Accenture executives. In 2005, Accenture repurchased and retired $1,095,155,000 of these shares. Because Accenture retired these shares, they were not treated as treasury stock. Instead, Accenture reduced additional paid-in capital because the shares cannot be resold.

▧ Line 12–13: Employees purchased Accenture Class A common stock in 2005, either newly issued or from the company's treasury stock. These purchases are related to employee share purchases and to the exercise of employee stock options. These purchases increased equity by $295,280,000 ($168,324,000 + $126,956,000).

▧ Line 14: Employees exchanged restricted share units for Class A common stock in 2005; the exchange had no effect on total equity.

▧ Line 16: Accenture repurchased shares from minority shareholders at less than book value in 2005. This is similar to the effect from the sale of shares by a subsidiary (an IPO) at a price in excess of book value (see Module 7).

One final point: the financial press sometimes refers to a measure called **book value per share**. This is the net book value of the company that is available to common shareholders, defined as: stockholders' equity less preferred stock (and preferred additional paid-in capital) divided by the number of common shares outstanding (issued common shares less treasury shares). Accenture's book value per share of the Class A stock at the end of 2005 (assuming that all additional paid-in capital is related to that class of stock) is computed as: ($1,696,914,000 − $7,000)/( 602,705,936 − 32,265,976) = $2.97 book value per share. In contrast, Accenture's **market price per share** ranged from $22.20 to $25.70 in the 4th quarter of 2005.

# EQUITY CARVE OUTS AND CONVERTIBLES

Corporate divestitures, or **equity carve outs**, are increasingly common as companies seek to increase shareholder value through partial or total divestiture of operating units. Generally, equity carve outs are motivated by the notion that consolidated financial statements often obscure the performance of individual business units, thus complicating their evaluation by outsiders. Corporate managers are concerned that this difficulty in assessing the performance of individual business units limits their ability to reach full valuation. Shareholder value is, therefore, not maximized. In response, conglomerates have divested subsidiaries so that the market can individually price them.

**LO3** Describe accounting for equity carve outs and convertible debt.

## Sell-Offs

Equity carve outs take many forms. The first and simplest form of divestiture is the outright sale of a business unit, called a **sell-off**. In this case, the company sells its equity interest to an unrelated party. The sale is accounted for just like the sale of any other asset. Specifically, any excess (deficit) of cash received over the book value of the business unit sold is recorded as a gain (loss) on the sale.

To illustrate, in 2005, Accenture purchased the North American Health practice from The Capgemini Group for $175 million (€143 million). Capgemini recorded a gain on the sale of €123 million as disclosed in the following excerpt from its 2005 annual report:

> On June 16, 2005, the Group sold its US healthcare business to the Accenture Group for €143 million, generating a capital gain of €123 million.

The financial statement effects of this transaction follow:

- Capgemini received €143 million in cash.

- The North American Health practice was carried on Capgemini's balance sheet as an investment with a book value of €20 million (inferred from the proceeds less gain).

- Capgemini's gain on sale equaled the sale proceeds less the book value: €143 million − €20 million = €123 million gain on sale.

- The gain on sale is reported in Capgemini's 2005 income from continuing operations.

- Capgemini subtracts the gain from net income in its statement of cash flows to compute net cash flows from operations since the transaction generated a noncash operating gain. Instead, the €143 million cash proceeds are reported as a cash inflow from investing activities.

## Spin-Offs

A **spin-off** is a second form of divestiture. In this case, the parent company distributes the subsidiary shares that it owns as a dividend to its shareholders who, then, own shares in the subsidiary directly rather than through the parent company. In recording this dividend, retained earnings are reduced by the book value of the equity method investment, and the subsidiary's investment account is removed from the parent's balance sheet.

The spin-off of the Medco Health subsidiary by its parent company, Merck & Co., Inc., is an example of this form of equity carve out. Merck described this spin-off as follows:

> On August 19, 2003, Merck completed the spin-off of Medco Health. The spin-off was effected by way of a pro rata dividend to Merck stockholders. Holders of Merck common stock at the close of business on August 12, 2003, received a dividend of .1206 shares of Medco Health common stock for every one share of Merck common stock held on that date. No fractional shares of Medco Health common stock were issued. Shareholders entitled to a fractional share of Medco Health common stock in the distribution received the cash value instead. Based on a letter ruling Merck received from the U.S. Internal Revenue Service, receipt of Medco Health shares in the distribution was tax-free for U.S. federal income tax purposes, but any cash received in lieu of fractional shares was taxable . . . The following is a summary of the assets and liabilities of discontinued operations that were spun off:

| August 19, 2003 ($ millions) | |
|---|---:|
| **Assets** | |
| Cash and cash equivalents | $ 247.4 |
| Other current assets | 2,728.4 |
| Property, plant and equipment, net | 816.3 |
| Goodwill | 3,310.2 |
| Other intangibles, net | 2,351.9 |
| Other assets | 138.4 |
| | $9,592.6 |
| **Liabilities** | |
| Current liabilities | $2,176.2 |
| Long-term debt | 1,362.3 |
| Deferred income taxes | 1,195.0 |
| | $4,733.5 |
| Net Assets Transferred | $4,859.1 |

This distribution was reflected in Merck's statement of retained earnings as follows:

| MERCK & CO., INC. AND SUBSIDIARIES Consolidated Statement of Retained Earnings | | |
| --- | --- | --- |
| Years Ended December 31 ($ millions) | 2003 | 2002 |
| Balance January 1 . . . . . . . . . . . . . . . . . . . | $35,434.9 | $31,489.6 |
| Net Income. . . . . . . . . . . . . . . . . . . . . . . . | 6,830.9 | 7,149.5 |
| Common Stock Dividends Declared . . . . . | (3,264.7) | (3,204.2) |
| Spin-off of Medco Health. . . . . . . . . . . . . | (4,859.1) | — |
| Balance, December 31. . . . . . . . . . . . . . | $34,142.0 | $35,434.9 |

The spin-off is treated as a dividend distribution of 100% of the subsidiary's stock to Merck shareholders. Merck reduced retained earnings by the book value of the Medco Health shares distributed, or $4,859.1 million in this case. Merck also removes the investment in Medco Health account (for the same amount) from its balance sheet.

## Split-Offs

The **split-off** is a third form of equity carve out. In this case, the parent company buys back its own stock using the shares of the subsidiary company instead of cash. After completing this transaction, the subsidiary is an independent publicly traded company.

The parent treats the split-off like any other purchase of treasury stock. As such, the treasury stock account is increased and the equity method investment account is reduced, reflecting the distribution of that asset. The dollar amount recorded for this treasury stock depends on how the distribution is set up. There are two possibilities:

1. **Pro rata distribution.** Shares are distributed to stockholders on a pro rata basis. Namely, a shareholder owning 10% of the outstanding stock of the parent company receives 10% of the shares of the subsidiary. The treasury stock account is increased by the *book value* of the investment in the subsidiary. The accounting is similar to the purchase of treasury stock for cash, except that shares of the subsidiary are paid to shareholders instead of cash.

2. **Non pro rata distribution.** This case is like a tender offer where individual stockholders can accept or reject the distribution. The treasury stock account is recorded at the *market value* of the shares of the subsidiary distributed. Since the investment account can only be reduced by its book value, a gain or loss on distribution is recorded in the income statement for the difference. (The SEC also allows companies to record the difference as an adjustment to additional paid-in capital; the usual practice, as might be expected, is for companies to report any gain as part of income.)

AT&T's split-off of its subsidiary, AT&T Wireless (AWE), provides an example. This transaction is described in the following excerpt from footnotes to AT&T's 10-K:

> On July 9, 2001, AT&T completed the split-off of AT&T Wireless as a separate, independently traded company . . . Shares of AT&T Wireless common stock held by AT&T were [exchanged for] AT&T common. AT&T common shareowners received whole shares of AT&T Wireless and cash payments for fractional shares. The IRS ruled that the transaction qualified as tax-free for AT&T and its shareowners for U.S. federal income tax purposes, with the exception of cash received for fractional shares . . . The split-off of AT&T Wireless resulted in a noncash tax-free gain of $13.5 billion, which represented the difference between the fair value of the AT&T Wireless tracking stock at the date of the split-off and AT&T's book value in AT&T Wireless. This gain was recorded in the third quarter of 2001 as a "Gain on disposition of discontinued operations."

Key financial statement facts and effects of this transaction follow:

▪ AT&T Wireless was a wholly owned subsidiary of AT&T Corporation.

▪ The split-off resulted in a separate, publicly traded company

▒ AT&T received shares of its common stock from participating shareholders in exchange for shares of AT&T Wireless.

▒ Since the exchange was made via a tender offer, it is non pro rata as only those shareholders wishing to exchange their AT&T common stock accepted the offer.

▒ AT&T realized a gain on the exchange in the amount of $13.5 billion.

Three years later, as a separately traded company, AT&T Wireless was acquired by Cingular Wireless.

## Analysis of Equity Carve Outs

Sell-offs, spin-offs, and split-offs all involve the divestiture of an operating segment. They are usually stock transactions and, as a result, do not involve cash. Although they are one-time occurrences, they can result in substantial gains that can markedly alter the income statement and balance sheet. Consequently, we need to interpret them carefully. This involves learning as many details about the carve out as possible from the annual report, the Management Discussion and Analysis, and other publicly available information.

Following an equity carve out, the parent company loses the cash flows (positive or negative) of the divested business unit. As such, the divestiture should be treated like any other discontinued operation. Any recognized gain or loss from divestiture is treated as a nonoperating activity. The sale price of the divested unit reflects the valuation of *future expected* cash flows by the purchaser and is best viewed as a nonoperating activity by the seller. Income (and cash flows) of the divested unit up to the date of sale, however, is part of operations, although discontinued operations are typically segregated.

---

### MID-MODULE REVIEW 4

Assume that BearingPoint announced the split-off of its Canadian subsidiary. BearingPoint reported a gain from the split-off. (1) Describe the accounting for a split-off. (2) Why was BearingPoint able to report a gain on this transaction?

#### Solution

1. In a split-off, shares of the parent company owned by the shareholders are exchanged for shares of the subsidiary owned by the parent. If the distribution is non pro rata, the parent can report a gain equal to the difference between the fair market value of the subsidiary and its book value on the parent's balance sheet.
2. BearingPoint met the conditions for a split-off as described in part 1, which enabled it to report a gain.

---

## Convertible Securities

**Convertible securities** are debt and equity securities that provide the holder with an option to convert those securities into other securities. Convertible debentures, for example, are debt securities that give the holder the option to convert the debt into common stock at a predetermined conversion price.

### Convertible Debt Securities

Symantec Corporation had convertible debt transactions in 2005, as explained in the following excerpt from footnotes to its 10-K report:

> **Convertible Subordinated Notes** On October 24, 2001, we completed a private offering of $600 million of 3% convertible subordinated notes due November 1, 2006, the net proceeds of which were $585 million. The notes are convertible into shares of our common stock by the holders at any time before maturity at a conversion price of $17.07 per share, subject to certain adjustments. We had the right to redeem the remaining notes on or after November 5, 2004, at a redemption price of 100.75% of stated principal during the period November 5, 2004 through October 31, 2005. Interest was paid semiannually and we commenced making these payments on May 1, 2002. Debt issuance costs of $16 million related to the notes were being amortized on a straight-line basis through November 1, 2006. We had reserved 70.3 million shares of common stock for issuance upon conversion of the notes. On July 20, 2004, our Board of Directors approved the redemption of all of the outstanding

convertible subordinated notes and in September 2004 we sent notice to registered holders that all notes would be redeemed November 5, 2004. As of November 4, 2004 (the day prior to the redemption date), substantially all of the outstanding convertible subordinated notes were converted into 70.3 million shares of our common stock. The remainder was redeemed for cash. Unamortized debt issuance costs of $6 million relative to the converted notes were charged to Capital in excess of par value on the Consolidated Balance Sheet during fiscal 2005.

To summarize, in 2001, Symantec issued $600 million of 3% convertible notes. The noteholders (Symantec's creditors) could convert the notes into 34,271,000 common shares at the initial conversion price of $17.07 ($585,000,000/$17.07 per share = 34,271,000 shares). At any time before October 2005, Symantec could redeem the notes (repay them before maturity and without conversion). In July 2004, Symantec announced that it would exercise its redemption option in November that year. In response, all of the noteholders converted their notes to Symantec common stock. Symantec's statement of stockholders' equity records the effects of the conversion as follows.

| (In thousands) | Common Stock | | Capital In Excess of Par Value | Accumulated Other Comprehensive Income (Loss) | Retained Earnings | Total Stockholders' Equity |
| --- | --- | --- | --- | --- | --- | --- |
| | Shares | Amount | | | | |
| Conversion of convertible debt . . . | 35,142 | $352 | $593,182 | — | — | $593,534 |

On the conversion date, Symantec's balance sheet carried the notes at $593,534,000. The notes were retired and Symantec issued 35,142,000 shares to the noteholders. This represented a conversion price for the stock of $16.89 a share ($593,534,000/35,142,000). The market price of Symantec common stock on November 4, 2005, (the date of conversion) was $18.63. The conversion, therefore, made economic sense for the noteholders.

　　When Symantec originally issued the convertible notes, the balance sheet reported their issue price without consideration of the conversion feature, because a conversion option is *not* valued on the balance sheet unless it is detachable from the security (and can be separately sold). Instead, the convertible debt was recorded just like debt that does not have a conversion feature. Accounting for the conversion of the Symantec bonds is illustrated in the following financial statement effects template.

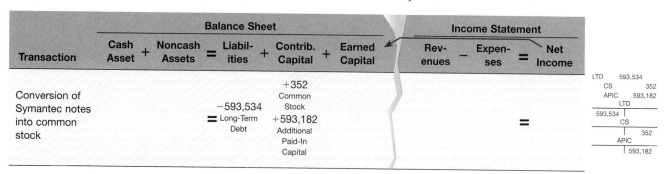

| | Balance Sheet | | | | | | Income Statement | | |
| --- | --- | --- | --- | --- | --- | --- | --- | --- | --- |
| Transaction | Cash Asset | + Noncash Assets | = Liabil- ities | + Contrib. Capital | + Earned Capital | | Rev- enues | − Expen- ses | = Net Income |
| Conversion of Symantec notes into common stock | | | −593,534 = Long-Term Debt | +352 Common Stock +593,182 Additional Paid-In Capital | | | | | = |

Accounting for the Symantec conversion is straightforward and yields the following effects:

▪ The debt's carrying amount is removed from the balance sheet because the debt is retired.

▪ Symantec issues 35,142,000 shares of $0.01 par value common stock for an "issue" price of $593,534,000 (book value of bonds); common stock, therefore, increases by $352 million (35,142,000 × $0.01, rounded up), and capital in excess of par value (additional paid-in capital) increases by the amount of $593,182,000.

▪ No gain or loss (or cash inflow or outflow) is recorded from the conversion.

## Convertible Preferred Stock

Preferred stock can also contain a conversion privilege. **Pfizer** provides an example of the latter in its description of the Pharmacia acquisition:

　　**Preferred Stock** In connection with our acquisition of Pharmacia in 2003, we issued a newly created class of Series A convertible perpetual preferred stock . . . Each share is convertible, at the holder's option, into 2,574.87 shares of our common stock with equal voting rights. The conversion option is indexed to our common stock and requires share settlement, and therefore, is reported at the fair value at the date of issuance. The Company may redeem the preferred stock, at any time, at its option, in cash, in shares of common stock or a combination of both at a price of $40,300 per share.

Accounting for the conversion of preferred stock is essentially the same as that for debt that we describe above: the preferred stock account is removed from the balance sheet and common stock is issued for the dollar amount of the preferred.

Conversion privileges offer an additional benefit to the holder of a security. That is, debtholders and preferred stockholders carry senior positions as claimants in bankruptcy, and also carry a fixed or dividend yield. Thus, they are somewhat protected from losses and their annual return is guaranteed. With a conversion privilege, debtholders or preferred stockholders can enjoy the residual benefits of common shareholders should the company perform well.

A conversion option is valuable and yields a higher price for the securities than they would otherwise command. However, conversion privileges impose a cost on common shareholders. That is, the higher market price received for convertible securities is offset by the cost imposed on the subordinate (common) securities.

One final note, diluted earnings per share (EPS) takes into account the potentially dilutive effect of convertible securities. Specifically, the diluted EPS computation assumes conversion at the beginning of the year (or when the security is issued if during the year). The earnings available to common shares in the numerator are increased by any forgone after-tax interest expense or preferred dividends, and the additional shares that would have been issued in the conversion increase the shares outstanding in the denominator (see Module 5).

## MODULE-END REVIEW

Assume that IBM has issued the following convertible debentures: each $1,000 bond is convertible into 200 shares of $1 par common. Assume that the bonds were sold at a discount, and that each bond has a current unamortized discount equal to $150. Using the financial statements effect template, illustrate the effects on the financial statements of the conversion of one of these convertible debentures.

### Solution

| | Balance Sheet | | | | | | Income Statement | | |
|---|---|---|---|---|---|---|---|---|---|
| Transaction | Cash Asset | + Noncash Assets | = Liabil- ities | + Contrib. Capital | + Earned Capital | | Rev- enues | − Expen- ses | = Net Income |
| Convert a bond with $850 book value into 200 common shares with $1 par value | | | −850 = Long-Term Debt | +200 Common Stock +650 Additional Paid-In Capital | | | | | = |

## GUIDANCE ANSWERS

**You Are the Chief Financial Officer**

Several points must be considered. (1) Treasury shares are likely to prop up earnings per share (EPS). While the EPS numerator (earnings) is likely dampened by the use of cash for the stock repurchase, EPS is likely to increase because of the reduced shares in the denominator. (2) Another motivation is that, if the shares are sufficiently undervalued (in management's opinion), the stock repurchase and subsequent resale can provide a better return than alternative investments. (3) Stock repurchases send a strong signal to the market that management feels its stock is undervalued. This is more credible than merely making that argument with analysts. On the other hand, company cash is diverted from other investments. This is bothersome if such investments are mutually exclusive either now or in the future.

# DISCUSSION QUESTIONS

**Q9-1.** Define *par value stock*. What is the significance of a stock's par value from an accounting and analysis perspective?

**Q9-2.** What are the basic differences between preferred stock and common stock? What are the typical features of preferred stock?

**Q9-3.** What features make preferred stock similar to debt? Similar to common stock?

**Q9-4.** What is meant by preferred dividends in arrears? If dividends are two years in arrears on $500,000 of 6% preferred stock, and dividends are declared at the end of this year, what amount of total dividends must the company pay to preferred shareholders before paying any dividends to common shareholders?

**Q9-5.** Distinguish between authorized shares and issued shares. Why might the number of shares issued be more than the number of shares outstanding?

**Q9-6.** Describe the difference between contributed capital and earned capital. Specifically, how can earned capital be considered as an investment by the company's shareholders?

**Q9-7.** How does the account "additional paid-in capital" (APIC) arise? Does the amount of APIC reported on the balance sheet relative to the common stock amount provide any information about the financial condition of the company?

**Q9-8.** Define *stock split*. What are the major reasons for a stock split?

**Q9-9.** Define *treasury stock*. Why might a corporation acquire treasury stock? How is treasury stock reported in the balance sheet?

**Q9-10.** If a corporation purchases 600 shares of its own common stock at $10 per share and resells them at $14 per share, where would the $2,400 increase in capital be reported in the financial statements? Why is no gain reported?

**Q9-11.** A corporation has total stockholders' equity of $4,628,000 and one class of $2 par value common stock. The corporation has 500,000 shares authorized; 300,000 shares issued; 260,000 shares outstanding; and 40,000 shares as treasury stock. What is its book value per share?

**Q9-12.** What is a stock dividend? How does a common stock dividend distributed to common shareholders affect their respective ownership interests?

**Q9-13.** What is the difference between the accounting for a small stock dividend and the accounting for a large stock dividend?

**Q9-14.** Employee stock options potentially dilute earnings per share (EPS). What can companies do to offset these dilutive effects and how might this action affect the balance sheet?

**Q9-15.** What information is reported in a statement of stockholders' equity?

**Q9-16.** What items are typically reported under the stockholders' equity category of other comprehensive income (OCI)?

**Q9-17.** What is the difference between a spin-off and a split-off? Under what circumstances can either result in the recognition of a gain in the income statement?

**Q9-18.** Describe the accounting for a convertible bond. Can the conversion ever result in the recognition of a gain in the income statement?

# MINI EXERCISES

**M9-19. Analyzing and Identifying Financial Statement Effects of Stock Issuances  (LO1)**
On June 1, 2007, Beatty Company, (*a*) issues 8,000 shares of $50 par value preferred stock at $68 cash per share and (*b*) issues 12,000 shares of $1 par value common stock at $10 cash per share. Indicate the financial statement effects of these two issuances using the financial statement effects template.

**M9-20. Analyzing and Identifying Financial Statement Effects of Stock Issuances  (LO1)**
On September 1, 2007, Magliolo, Inc., (*a*) issues 18,000 shares of $10 par value preferred stock at $48 cash per share and (*b*) issues 120,000 shares of $2 par value common stock at $37 cash per share. Indicate the financial statement effects of these two issuances using the financial statement effects template.

**M9-21. Distinguishing between Common Stock and Additional Paid-in Capital  (LO1)**
Following is the 2005 stockholders' equity section from the Cisco Systems, Inc., balance sheet.

Cisco Systems, Inc.
(CSCO)

| Shareholders' Equity (in millions, except par value) | July 30, 2005 |
|---|---|
| Preferred stock, no par value: 5 shares authorized; none issued and outstanding....... | $  — |
| Common stock and additional paid-in capital, $0.001 par value: 20,000 shares authorized; 6,331 shares issued and outstanding at July 30, 2005................ | 22,394 |
| Retained earnings ........................................................ | 506 |
| Accumulated other comprehensive income...................................... | 274 |
| Total shareholders' equity ............................................... | $23,174 |

a.  For the $22,394 million reported as "common stock and additional paid-in capital," what portion is common stock and what portion is additional paid-in capital?

b.  Explain why Cisco does not report the two components described in part a separately.

**M9-22. Identifying Financial Statement Effects of Stock Issuance and Repurchase  (LO1)**

On January 1, 2007, Bartov Company issues 5,000 shares of $100 par value preferred stock at $250 cash per share. On March 1, the company repurchases 5,000 shares of previously issued $1 par value common stock at $83 cash per share. Use the financial statement effects template to record these two transactions.

**M9-23. Assessing the Financial Statement Effects of a Stock Split  (LO2)**

Procter & Gamble
Company (PG)

Procter & Gamble Company discloses the following footnote to its 10-K report:

> **Stock Split** In March 2004, the Company's Board of Directors approved a two-for-one stock split effective for common and preferred shareholders of record as of May 21, 2004. The financial statements, notes and other references to share and per share data have been restated to reflect the stock split for all periods presented.

What restatements has P&G made to its balance sheet as a result of the stock split?

**M9-24. Reconciling Common Stock and Treasury Stock Balances  (LO1)**

Abercrombie & Fitch
(ANF)

Following is the stockholders' equity section from the Abercrombie & Fitch balance sheet.

| Shareholders' Equity ($ thousands) | January 28, 2006 | January 29, 2005 |
|---|---|---|
| Class A common stock—$.01 par value: 150,000,000 shares authorized and 103,300,000 shares issued at January 28, 2006 and January 29, 2005, respectively.... | $     1,033 | $     1,033 |
| Paid-in capital ..................................... | 161,678 | 140,251 |
| Retained earnings ................................ | 1,357,791 | 1,076,023 |
| Accumulated other comprehensive income............. | (796) | — |
| Deferred compensation ........................... | 26,206 | 15,048 |
| Treasury stock at average cost: 15,573,789 and 17,262,943 shares at January 28, 2006 and January 29, 2005, respectively..................... | (550,795) | (563,029) |
| Total shareholders' equity ......................... | $  995,117 | $  669,326 |

a.  Show the computation to yield the $1,033 balance reported for common stock.

b.  How many shares are outstanding at its 2006 fiscal year-end?

c.  Use the common stock and paid-in capital accounts to determine the average price at which Abercrombie & Fitch issued its common stock.

d.  Use the treasury stock account to determine the average price Abercrombie & Fitch paid when it repurchased its common shares.

**M9-25. Identifying and Analyzing Financial Statement Effects of Cash Dividends  (LO2)**

Freid Company has outstanding 6,000 shares of $50 par value, 6% preferred stock, and 40,000 shares of $1 par value common stock. The company has $328,000 of retained earnings. At year-end, the company declares and pays the regular $3 per share cash dividend on preferred stock and a $2.20 per share cash dividend on common stock. Use the financial statement effects template to indicate the effects of these two dividend payments.

**M9-26.    Analyzing and Identifying Financial Statement Effects of Stock Dividends    (LO2)**

Dutta Corp. has outstanding 70,000 shares of $5 par value common stock. At year-end, the company declares and issues a 4% common stock dividend when the market price of the stock is $21 per share. Use the financial statement effects template to indicate the effects of this stock dividend declaration and payment.

**M9-27.    Analyzing, Identifying and Explaining the Effects of a Stock Split    (LO2)**

On September 1, 2007, Weiss Company has 250,000 shares of $15 par value ($165 market value) common stock that are issued and outstanding. Its balance sheet on that date shows the following account balances relating to its common stock:

| | |
|---|---|
| Common stock. . . . . . . . . . . . . . . . . . . . . . . . | $3,750,000 |
| Paid-in capital in excess of par value. . . . . . . | 2,250,000 |

On September 2, 2007 Weiss splits its stock 3-for-2 and reduces the par value to $10 per share.
*a.*    How many shares of common stock are issued and outstanding immediately after the stock split?
*b.*    What is the dollar balance of the common stock account immediately after the stock split?
*c.*    What is the likely reason that Weiss Company split its stock?

**M9-28.    Determining Cash Dividends to Preferred and Common Shareholders    (LO2)**

Dechow Company has outstanding 20,000 shares of $50 par value, 6% cumulative preferred stock and 80,000 shares of $10 par value common stock. The company declares and pays cash dividends amounting to $160,000.
*a.*    If there are no preferred dividends in arrears, how much in total dividends, and in dividends per share, does Dechow pay to each class of stock?
*b.*    If there are one year's dividends in arrears on the preferred stock, how much in total dividends, and in dividends per share, does Dechow pay to each class of stock?

**M9-29.    Reconciling Retained Earnings    (LO2)**

Use the following data to reconcile the 2007 retained earnings (that is, explain the change in retained earnings during the year) for Bamber Company.

| | |
|---|---|
| Total retained earnings, December 31, 2006 . . . . | $347,000 |
| Stock dividends declared and paid in 2007. . . . . | 28,000 |
| Cash dividends declared and paid in 2007 . . . . . | 35,000 |
| Net income for 2007. . . . . . . . . . . . . . . . . . . . . . | 94,000 |

**M9-30.    Interpreting a Spin-Off Disclosure    (LO3)**

Bristol-Myers Squibb discloses the following in notes to its 2003 10-K report.

Bristol-Myers Squibb (BMY)

> The Company spun off Zimmer Holdings, Inc. (Zimmer), in a tax-free distribution, resulting in a common stock dividend of $156 million.

*a.*    Describe the difference between a spin-off and a split-off.
*b.*    What effects did BMY's spin-off have on its balance sheet and its income statement?

**M9-31.    Interpreting a Proposed Split-Off Disclosure    (LO3)**

Viacom, Inc., reports the following footnote in its 2005 10-K.

Viacom, Inc. (VIA)

> **DISCONTINUED OPERATIONS** In 2004, Viacom completed the exchange offer for the split-off of Blockbuster Inc. ("Blockbuster") (NYSE: BBI and BBI.B). Under the terms of the offer, Viacom accepted 27,961,165 shares of Viacom common stock in exchange for the 144 million common shares of Blockbuster that Viacom owned. Each share of Viacom Class A or Class B common stock accepted for exchange by Viacom was exchanged for 5.15 shares of Blockbuster common stock, consisting of 2.575 shares of Blockbuster class A common stock and 2.575 shares of Blockbuster class B common stock.

*a.*    Describe the accounting for a split-off.
*b.*    How will the proposed split-off affect the number of Viacom shares outstanding?
*c.*    Under what circumstances will Viacom be able to report a gain for this proposed split-off?

AT&T (T)

**M9-32.** **Interpreting Disclosure Related to the Split-Off of AT&T Wireless** **(LO3)**

AT&T reports the following footnote to its 2003 10-K.

> In 2001, we realized a tax-free noncash gain on the disposition of discontinued operations of $13.5 billion, representing the difference between the fair value of the AT&T Wireless tracking stock at the date of the split-off and our book value of AT&T Wireless.

*a.* Describe the accounting for a split-off.

*b.* Describe the circumstances that allowed AT&T to recognize a gain on this split-off.

*c.* How should you interpret the gain from this split-off in your analysis of AT&T for 2003?

JetBlue Airways
Corporation (JBLU)

**M9-33.** **Analyzing Financial Statement Effects of Convertible Securities** **(LO3)**

JetBlue Airways Corporation reports the following footnote to its 2005 10-K.

> In March 2005, we completed a public offering of $250 million aggregate principal amount of 3¾% convertible unsecured debentures due 2035, which are currently convertible into 14.6 million shares of our common stock at a price of approximately $17.10 per share.

*a.* Describe the effects on JetBlue's balance sheet if the convertible bonds are converted.

*b.* Would the conversion affect earnings? Explain.

# EXERCISES

**E9-34.** **Identifying and Analyzing Financial Statement Effects of Stock Transactions** **(LO1)**

Lipe Company reports the following transactions relating to its stock accounts.

| | |
|---|---|
| Feb 20 | Issued 10,000 shares of $1 par value common stock at $25 cash per share |
| Feb 21 | Issued 15,000 shares of $100 par value, 8% preferred stock at $275 cash per share. |
| Jun 30 | Purchased 2,000 shares of its own common stock at $15 cash per share. |
| Sep 25 | Sold 1,000 shares of its treasury stock at $21 cash per share. |

Use the financial statement effects template to indicate the effects from each of these transactions.

**E9-35.** **Analyzing and Identifying Financial Statement Effects of Stock Transactions** **(LO1)**

McNichols Corp. reports the following transactions relating to its stock accounts in 2007.

| | |
|---|---|
| Jan 15 | Issued 25,000 shares of $5 par value common stock at $17 cash per share |
| Jan 20 | Issued 6,000 shares of $50 par value, 8% preferred stock at $78 cash per share. |
| Mar 31 | Purchased 3,000 shares of its own common stock at $20 cash per share. |
| June 25 | Sold 2,000 shares of its treasury stock at $26 cash per share. |
| July 15 | Sold the remaining 1,000 shares of treasury stock at $19 cash per share. |

Use the financial statement effects template to indicate the effects from each of these transactions.

**E9-36.** **Analyzing and Computing Average Issue Price and Treasury Stock Cost** **(LO1)**

Best Buy (BBY)

Following is the stockholders' equity section from the Best Buy balance sheet.

| Shareholders' Equity ($ millions) | February 25, 2006 | February 26, 2005 |
|---|---|---|
| Preferred stock, $1.00 par value: Authorized—400,000 shares; Issued and outstanding—none | $ — | $ — |
| Common stock, $.10 par value: Authorized—1 billion shares; Issued and outstanding—485,098,000 and 492,512,000 shares, respectively | 49 | 49 |
| Additional paid-in capital | 643 | 936 |
| Retained earnings | 4,304 | 3,315 |
| Accumulated other comprehensive income | 261 | 149 |
| Total shareholders' equity | $5,257 | $4,449 |

Best Buy also reports the following statement of stockholders' equity.

| ($ and shares in millions) | Common Shares | Common Stock | Additional Paid-in Capital | Retained Earnings | Accumulated Other Comprehensive Income | Total |
|---|---|---|---|---|---|---|
| Balances at February 26, 2005 .... | 493 | $49 | $936 | $3,315 | $149 | $4,449 |
| Net earnings................. | — | — | — | 1,140 | — | 1,140 |
| Other comprehensive income, net of tax: | | | | | | |
|   Foreign currency translation adjustments............... | — | — | — | — | 101 | 101 |
|   Other...................... | — | — | — | — | 11 | 11 |
| Total comprehensive income ...... | | | | | | 1,252 |
| Stock options exercised.......... | 9 | 1 | 256 | — | — | 257 |
| Tax benefit from stock options exercised and employee stock purchase plan ........... | — | — | 55 | — | — | 55 |
| Issuance of common stock under employee stock purchase plan... | 1 | — | 35 | — | — | 35 |
| Stock-based compensation....... | — | — | 132 | — | — | 132 |
| Common stock dividends, $0.31 per share.............. | — | — | — | (151) | — | (151) |
| Repurchase of common stock..... | (18) | (1) | (771) | — | — | (772) |
| **Balances at February 25, 2006** ... | **485** | **$49** | **$643** | **$4,304** | **$261** | **$5,257** |

   *a.* Show the computation to arrive at the $49 million in the common stock account.
   *b.* At what average price were the Best Buy shares issued?
   *c.* Reconcile the beginning and ending balances of retained earnings.
   *d.* Best Buy reports $101 million in an account labeled foreign currency translation adjustments. Explain what this account represents. What effect has this account had on net earnings for the year?
   *e.* Best Buy reports an increase in stockholders' equity relating to the exercise of stock options. This transaction involves the purchase of common stock by employees at a pre-set price. Describe how this transaction affects stockholders' equity.
   *f.* Describe the transaction relating to the "repurchase of common stock" line in the statement of stockholders' equity.

**E9-37.** **Analyzing Cash Dividends on Preferred and Common Stock**   (LO2)
Moser Company began business on March 1, 2005. At that time, it issued 20,000 shares of $60 par value, 7% cumulative preferred stock and 100,000 shares of $5 par value common stock. Through the end of 2007, there has been no change in the number of preferred and common shares outstanding.
   *a.* Assume that Moser declared and paid cash dividends of $0 in 2005, another $183,000 in 2006, and $200,000 in 2007. Compute the total cash dividends and the dividends per share paid to each class of stock in 2005, 2006, and 2007.
   *b.* Assume that Moser declared and paid cash dividends of $0 in 2005, another $84,000 in 2006, and $150,000 in 2007. Compute the total cash dividends and the dividends per share paid to each class of stock in 2005, 2006, and 2007.

**E9-38.** **Analyzing Cash Dividends on Preferred and Common Stocks**   (LO2)
Potter Company has outstanding 15,000 shares of $50 par value, 8% preferred stock and 50,000 shares of $5 par value common stock. During its first three years in business, it declared and paid no cash dividends in the first year, $280,000 in the second year, and $60,000 in the third year.
   *a.* If the preferred stock is cumulative, determine the total amount of cash dividends paid to each class of stock in each of the three years.
   *b.* If the preferred stock is noncumulative, determine the total amount of cash dividends paid to each class of stock in each of the three years.

**E9-39.** **Analyzing and Computing Issue Price, Treasury Stock Cost, and Shares Outstanding**   **(LO1)**

Altria (MO)

Following is the stockholders' equity section from Altria's 2005 balance sheet.

| December 31 ($ million) | 2005 |
| --- | --- |
| Common stock, par value $0.33^1/_3$ per share (2,805,961,317 shares issued) . . . . . . . . . . . . . . | $ 935 |
| Additional paid-in capital . . . . . . . . . . . . . . . . . . . . . . . . . . . . . . . . . . . . . . . . . . . . . . . | 6,061 |
| Earnings reinvested in the business. . . . . . . . . . . . . . . . . . . . . . . . . . . . . . . . . . . . . . . . . | 54,666 |
| Accumulated other comprehensive losses (including currency translation of $1,317 in 2005) . . | (1,853) |
| Cost of repurchased stock (721,696,918 shares in 2005) . . . . . . . . . . . . . . . . . . . . . . . . . . | (24,102) |
| Total stockholders' equity . . . . . . . . . . . . . . . . . . . . . . . . . . . . . . . . . . . . . . . . . . . . . . . . | $35,707 |

*a.*   Show the computation to derive the $935 million for common stock.
*b.*   At what average price has Altria issued its common stock?
*c.*   How many shares of Altria common stock are outstanding as of December 31, 2005?
*d.*   At what average cost has Altria repurchased its treasury stock as of December 31, 2005?
*e.*   Why would a company such as Altria want to repurchase $24,102 million of its common stock?

**E9-40.** **Analyzing Cash Dividends on Preferred and Common Stock**   **(LO2)**

Skinner Company began business on June 30, 2005. At that time, it issued 18,000 shares of $50 par value, 6% cumulative preferred stock and 90,000 shares of $10 par value common stock. Through the end of 2007, there has been no change in the number of preferred and common shares outstanding.

*a.*   Assume that Skinner declared and paid cash dividends of $63,000 in 2005, $0 in 2006, and $378,000 in 2007. Compute the total cash dividends and the dividends per share paid to each class of stock in 2005, 2006, and 2007.

*b.*   Assume that Skinner declared and paid cash dividends of $0 in 2005, $108,000 in 2006, and $189,000 in 2007. Compute the total cash dividends and the dividends per share paid to each class of stock in 2005, 2006, and 2007.

**E9-41.** **Analyzing and Identifying Financial Statement Effects of Dividends**   **(LO2)**

Chaney Company has outstanding 25,000 shares of $10 par value common stock. It also has $405,000 of retained earnings. Near the current year-end, the company declares and pays a cash dividend of $1.90 per share and declares and issues a 4% stock dividend. The market price of the stock the day the dividends are declared is $35 per share. Use the financial statement effects template to indicate the effects of these two separate dividend transactions.

**E9-42.** **Identifying and Analyzing Financial Statement Effects of Dividends**   **(LO2)**

The stockholders' equity of Revsine Company at December 31, 2006, appears below.

| | |
| --- | --- |
| Common stock, $10 par value, 200,000 shares authorized; 80,000 shares issued and outstanding. . . . . . . . . . . . . . . . . . . . . . | $800,000 |
| Paid-in capital in excess of par value. . . . . . . . . . . . . . . . . . . . . . . . . . | 480,000 |
| Retained earnings . . . . . . . . . . . . . . . . . . . . . . . . . . . . . . . . . . . . . . . | 305,000 |

During 2007, the following transactions occurred:

May 12   Declared and issued a 7% stock dividend; the common stock market value was $18 per share.

Dec. 31   Declared and paid a cash dividend of 75 cents per share.

*a.*   Use the financial statement effects template to indicate the effects of these transactions.
*b.*   Reconcile retained earnings for 2007 assuming that the company reports 2007 net income of $283,000.

**E9-43.** **Analyzing and Identifying Financial Statement Effects of Dividends** (LO2)

The stockholders' equity of Kinney Company at December 31, 2006, is shown below.

| | |
|---|---:|
| 5% preferred stock, $100 par value, 10,000 shares authorized; 4,000 shares issued and outstanding. . . . . . . . . . . . . . . . . . . . . . . . . . | $ 400,000 |
| Common stock, $5 par value, 200,000 shares authorized; 50,000 shares issued and outstanding. . . . . . . . . . . . . . . . . . . . . . . . | 250,000 |
| Paid-in capital in excess of par value—preferred stock. . . . . . . . . . . . . | 40,000 |
| Paid-in capital in excess of par value—common stock. . . . . . . . . . . . . | 300,000 |
| Retained earnings . . . . . . . . . . . . . . . . . . . . . . . . . . . . . . . . . . . . . | 656,000 |
| Total stockholders' equity . . . . . . . . . . . . . . . . . . . . . . . . . . . . . . . . | $1,646,000 |

The following transactions, among others, occurred during 2007:

Apr. 1    Declared and issued a 100% stock dividend on all outstanding shares of common stock. The market value of the stock was $11 per share.

Dec. 7    Declared and issued a 3% stock dividend on all outstanding shares of common stock. The market value of the stock was $14 per share.

Dec. 20    Declared and paid (1) the annual cash dividend on the preferred stock and (2) a cash dividend of 80 cents per common share.

*a.*    Use the financial statement effects template to indicate the effects of these separate transactions.

*b.*    Compute retained earnings for 2007 assuming that the company reports 2007 net income of $253,000.

**E9-44.** **Analyzing, Identifying and Explaining the Effects of a Stock Split** (LO2)

On March 1 of the current year, Xie Company has 400,000 shares of $20 par value common stock that are issued and outstanding. Its balance sheet shows the following account balances relating to common stock.

| | |
|---|---:|
| Common stock. . . . . . . . . . . . . . . . . . . . . . . . | $8,000,000 |
| Paid-in capital in excess of par value. . . . . . . . | 3,400,000 |

On March 2, Xie Company splits its common stock 2-for-1 and reduces the par value to $10 per share.

*a.*    How many shares of common stock are issued and outstanding immediately after the stock split?

*b.*    What is the dollar balance in its common stock account immediately after the stock split?

*c.*    What is the dollar balance in its paid-in capital in excess of par value account immediately after the stock split?

**E9-45.** **Analyzing and Computing Issue Price, Treasury Stock Cost, and Shares Outstanding** (LO1)

Following is the stockholders' equity section of the 2005 Caterpillar, Inc., balance sheet.

Caterpillar, Inc. (CAT)

| Stockholders' Equity ($ millions) | 2005 | 2004 | 2003 |
|---|---:|---:|---:|
| Common stock of $1.00 par value; Authorized shares: 900,000,000; Issued shares (2005, 2004 and 2003—814,894,624) at paid-in amount . . . . . . . . . . . . . . . . . . . . . . . . . . . . . . . . | $1,859 | $1,231 | $1,059 |
| Treasury stock (2005—144,027,405 shares; 2004—129,020,726 shares; 2003—127,370,544 shares) at cost . . . . . . . . . . . . . . . . . . | (4,637) | (3,277) | (2,914) |
| Profit employed in the business. . . . . . . . . . . . . . . . . . . . . . . . . . . . | 11,808 | 9,937 | 8,450 |
| Accumulated other comprehensive income. . . . . . . . . . . . . . . . . . . . | (598) | (424) | (517) |
| Total stockholders' equity . . . . . . . . . . . . . . . . . . . . . . . . . . . . . . . . | $8,432 | $7,467 | $6,078 |

CAT also provides the following schedule in its statement of stockholders' equity:

| ($ millions) | 2005 | 2004 | 2003 |
|---|---|---|---|
| **Common stock** | | | |
| Balance at beginning of year ............................ | **$1,231** | $1,059 | $1,034 |
| Common shares issued from treasury stock ................. | 290 | 172 | 25 |
| Impact of 2-for-1 stock split ........................... | 338 | — | — |
| Balance at year-end ................................... | **$1,859** | $1,231 | $1,059 |
| **Treasury stock** | | | |
| Balance at beginning of year ............................ | **$(3,277)** | $(2,914) | $(2,669) |
| Shares issued: 2005—18,912,521; 2004—12,216,618; 2003—9,913,946 ..................................... | 324 | 176 | 160 |
| Shares repurchased: 2005—33,919,200; 2004—13,866,800; 2003—10,900,000 ..................................... | **(1,684)** | (539) | (405) |
| Balance at year-end ................................... | **$(4,637)** | $(3,277) | $(2,914) |

**Stock Split**  On June 8, 2005, Caterpillar's Board of Directors approved a 2-for-1 stock split in the form of a 100 percent stock dividend. The stock split shares were distributed on July 13, 2005, to stockholders of record at the close of business on June 22, 2005. Capital accounts, share data and profit per share data reflect the stock split, applied retroactively, to all periods presented.

a. How many shares of Caterpillar common stock are outstanding at year-end 2005?

b. What does the phrase "at paid-in amount" in the stockholders' equity section mean?

c. At what average cost has Caterpillar repurchased its stock as of year-end 2005?

d. Why would a company such as Caterpillar want to repurchase its common stock?

e. Explain how CAT's "issued shares" remains constant over the three-year period while the dollar amount of its common stock account increases.

f. Show the computation of the $338 million addition to capital as a result of the 2-for-1 stock split.

**E9-46.**   **Analyzing Equity Changes from Convertible Preferred and Employee Stock Options**   **(LO3)**

JetBlue Airways Corporation (JBLU)

Following is the 2002 statement of stockholders' equity for JetBlue Airways Corporation.

| ($ thousands) | Convertible Redeemable Preferred Stock | Stockholders' Equity (Deficit) | | | | | Total |
|---|---|---|---|---|---|---|---|
| | | Common Stock | Additional Paid-in Capital | Accumulated Deficit/ Retained Earnings | Unearned Compensation | Accumulated Other Comprehensive Income | |
| Balance at December 31, 2001 .... | $210,441 | $ 65 | $ 3,868 | $(33,117) | $(2,983) | $ — | $ (32,167) |
| Net income ................. | — | — | — | 54,908 | — | — | 54,908 |
| Other comprehensive income.... | — | — | — | — | — | 187 | 187 |
| Total comprehensive income ...... | | | | | | | 55,095 |
| Accrued undeclared dividends on preferred stock ........... | 5,955 | — | — | (5,955) | — | — | (5,955) |
| Proceeds from initial public offering, net of offering expenses ........ | — | 101 | 168,177 | — | — | — | 168,278 |
| Conversion of redeemable preferred stock .............. | (216,394) | 461 | 215,933 | — | — | — | 216,394 |
| Exercise of common stock options..................... | — | 8 | 1,058 | — | — | — | 1,066 |
| Tax benefit of stock options exercised .................. | — | — | 6,568 | — | — | — | 6,568 |

*continued*

*continued*

| ($ thousands) | Convertible Redeemable Preferred Stock | Stockholders' Equity (Deficit) | | | | | |
|---|---|---|---|---|---|---|---|
| | | Common Stock | Additional Paid-in Capital | Accumulated Deficit/ Retained Earnings | Unearned Compensation | Accumulated Other Comprehensive Income | Total |
| Unearned compensation on common stock options, net of forfeitures . . . . . . . . . . . . . . . . . | — | — | 8,144 | — | (8,144) | — | — |
| Amortization of unearned compensation. . . . . . . . . . . . . . . | — | — | — | — | 1,713 | — | 1,713 |
| Stock issued under crew member stock purchase plan . . . . | — | 3 | 3,711 | — | — | — | 3,714 |
| Other. . . . . . . . . . . . . . . . . . . . . . . . | (2) | — | 12 | (45) | — | — | (33) |
| Balance at December 31, 2002 . . . | $    — | $638 | $407,471 | $ 15,791 | $(9,414) | $187 | $414,673 |

a. Identify the line labeled, "Conversion of redeemable preferred stock." Discuss the linkage among the convertible redeemable preferred stock, common stock, and additional paid-in capital accounts for 2002.

b. During 2002, JetBlue issued 811,623 shares to employees who exercised stock options. How did these option exercises affect stockholders' equity in 2002? JetBlue's stock traded in the $20 per share range during that same period. How does this compare to per share price employees paid for the stock at exercise?

**E9-47. Analyzing and Computing Issue Price, Treasury Stock Cost, and Shares Outstanding    (LO1)**

Following is the stockholders' equity and minority interest sections of the 2005 Merck & Co., Inc., balance sheet.

Merck & Co., Inc. (MRK)

| Stockholders' Equity ($ millions) | 2005 |
|---|---|
| Common stock, one cent par value; Authorized—5,400,000,000 shares; Issued—2,976,223,337 shares—2005 . . . . . . . . . . . . . . . . . . . . . . . . . . . | $    29.8 |
| Other paid-in capital. . . . . . . . . . . . . . . . . . . . . . . . . . . . . . . . . . . . . | 6,900.0 |
| Retained earnings . . . . . . . . . . . . . . . . . . . . . . . . . . . . . . . . . . . . . . . | 37,918.9 |
| Accumulated other comprehensive income. . . . . . . . . . . . . . . . . . . . . | 52.3 |
| | 44,901.0 |
| Less treasury stock, at cost; 794,299,347 shares—2005 . . . . . . . . . . . . . . | 26,984.4 |
| Total stockholders' equity . . . . . . . . . . . . . . . . . . . . . . . . . . . . . . . . . . | $17,916.6 |

a. Explain the derivation of the $29.8 million in the common stock account.
b. At what average price were the Merck common shares issued?
c. At what average cost was the Merck treasury stock purchased?
d. How many common shares are outstanding as of December 31, 2005?

**E9-48. Interpreting a Split-Off Disclosure    (LO3)**

IMS Health reports the following footnote to its 2003 10-K related to the split-off of its CTS subsidiary.

IMS Health (RX)

**CTS Split-OFF**  On February 6, 2003, the Company completed an exchange offer to distribute its majority interest in CTS. The Company exchanged 0.309 shares of CTS class B common shares for each share of the Company that was tendered. Under terms of the offer, the Company accepted 36,540 IMS common shares tendered in exchange for all 11,291 CTS common shares that the Company owned. As the offer was oversubscribed, the Company accepted tendered IMS shares on a pro-rata basis in proportion to the number of shares tendered. The proration factor was 21.115717%. As a result of this exchange offer, during 2003, the Company recorded a net gain from discontinued operations of $496,887. This gain was based on the Company's closing market price on February 6, 2003 multiplied by the 36,540 shares of IMS common shares accepted in the offer, net of the Company's carrying value of CTS and after deducting direct and incremental expenses related to the exchange offer.

    *a.*  Describe the accounting procedures for a split-off.

    *b.*  Describe the circumstances that allowed IMS to recognize a gain from this split-off.

    *c.*  How should we interpret this gain in our analysis of the company for 2003?

# PROBLEMS

**P9-49.**  **Analyzing and Identifying Financial Statement Effects of Stock Transactions**  **(LO1)**

The stockholders' equity section of Gupta Company at December 31, 2006, follows:

| | |
|---|---:|
| 8% preferred stock, $25 par value, 50,000 shares authorized; | |
|   6,800 shares issued and outstanding. . . . . . . . . . . . . . . . . . . . . . . . | $170,000 |
| Common stock, $10 par value, 200,000 shares authorized; | |
|   50,000 shares issued and outstanding. . . . . . . . . . . . . . . . . . . . . . . | 500,000 |
| Paid-in capital in excess of par value—preferred stock. . . . . . . . . . . . . | 68,000 |
| Paid-in capital in excess of par value—common stock. . . . . . . . . . . . . . | 200,000 |
| Retained earnings . . . . . . . . . . . . . . . . . . . . . . . . . . . . . . . . . . . . . . . . | 270,000 |

During 2007, the following transactions occurred:

    Jan.  10  Issued 28,000 shares of common stock for $17 cash per share.

    Jan.  23  Repurchased 8,000 shares of common stock at $19 cash per share.

    Mar.  14  Sold one-half of the treasury shares acquired January 23 for $21 cash per share.

    July  15  Issued 3,200 shares of preferred stock for $128,000 cash.

    Nov.  15  Sold 1,000 of the treasury shares acquired January 23 for $24 cash per share.

**Required**

    *a.*  Use the financial statement effects template to indicate the effects from each of these transactions.

    *b.*  Prepare the December 31, 2007, stockholders' equity section of the balance sheet assuming the company reports 2007 net income of $59,000.

**P9-50.**  **Analyzing and Identifying Financial Statement Effects of Stock Transactions**  **(LO1)**

The stockholders' equity of Sougiannis Company at December 31, 2006, follows:

| | |
|---|---:|
| 7% Preferred stock, $100 par value, 20,000 shares authorized; | |
|   5,000 shares issued and outstanding. . . . . . . . . . . . . . . . . . . . . . . | $ 500,000 |
| Common stock, $15 par value, 100,000 shares authorized; | |
|   40,000 shares issued and outstanding. . . . . . . . . . . . . . . . . . . . . . | 600,000 |
| Paid-in capital in excess of par value—preferred stock. . . . . . . . . . . . . | 24,000 |
| Paid-in capital in excess of par value—common stock. . . . . . . . . . . . . . | 360,000 |
| Retained earnings . . . . . . . . . . . . . . . . . . . . . . . . . . . . . . . . . . . . . . . . | 325,000 |
| Total stockholders' equity . . . . . . . . . . . . . . . . . . . . . . . . . . . . . . . . . . | $1,809,000 |

The following transactions, among others, occurred during the year:

    Jan.  12  Announced a 3-for-1 common stock split, reducing the par value of the common stock to $5 per share. The authorized shares were increased to 300,000 shares.

    Sept.  1  Repurchased 10,000 shares of common stock at $10 cash per share.

    Oct.  12  Sold 1,500 treasury shares acquired September 1 at $12 cash per share.

    Nov.  21  Issued 5,000 shares of common stock at $11 cash per share.

    Dec.  28  Sold 1,200 treasury shares acquired September 1 at $9 cash per share.

**Required**

    *a.*  Use the financial statement effects template to indicate the effects from each of these transactions.

    *b.*  Prepare the December 31, 2007, stockholders' equity section of the balance sheet assuming that the company reports 2007 net income of $83,000.

**P9-51.** **Identifying and Analyzing Financial Statement Effects of Stock Transactions** (LO1)

The stockholders' equity of Verrecchia Company at December 31, 2006, follows:

| | |
|---|---|
| Common stock, $5 par value, 350,000 shares authorized; 150,000 shares issued and outstanding. . . . . . . . . . . . . . . . . . . . . . . | $750,000 |
| Paid-in capital in excess of par value. . . . . . . . . . . . . . . . . . . . . . . . | 600,000 |
| Retained earnings . . . . . . . . . . . . . . . . . . . . . . . . . . . . . . . . . . . . . | 346,000 |

During 2007, the following transactions occurred:

Jan.  5   Issued 10,000 shares of common stock for $12 cash per share.

Jan.  18   Repurchased 4,000 shares of common stock at $14 cash per share.

Mar  12   Sold one-fourth of the treasury shares acquired January 18 for $17 cash per share.

July  17   Sold 500 shares of the remaining treasury stock for $13 cash per share.

Oct.  1   Issued 5,000 shares of 8%, $25 par value preferred stock for $35 cash per share. This is the first issuance of preferred shares from the 50,000 authorized preferred shares.

**Required**

*a.*   Use the financial statement effects template to indicate the effects of each transaction.

*b.*   Prepare the December 31, 2007, stockholders' equity section of the balance sheet assuming that the company reports net income of $72,500 for the year.

**P9-52.** **Identifying and Analyzing Financial Statement Effects of Stock Transactions** (LO1)

Following is the stockholders' equity of Dennis Corporation at December 31, 2006:

| | |
|---|---|
| 8% preferred stock, $50 par value, 10,000 shares authorized; 7,000 shares issued and outstanding. . . . . . . . . . . . . . . . . . . . . . . | $  350,000 |
| Common stock, $20 par value, 50,000 shares authorized; 25,000 shares issued and outstanding. . . . . . . . . . . . . . . . . . . . . . . | 500,000 |
| Paid-in capital in excess of par value—preferred stock. . . . . . . . . . . . . | 70,000 |
| Paid-in capital in excess of par value—common stock. . . . . . . . . . . . . | 385,000 |
| Retained earnings . . . . . . . . . . . . . . . . . . . . . . . . . . . . . . . . . . . . . | 238,000 |
| Total stockholders' equity . . . . . . . . . . . . . . . . . . . . . . . . . . . . . . . | $1,543,000 |

The following transactions, among others, occurred during the year:

Jan.  15   Issued 1,000 shares of preferred stock for $62 cash per share.

Jan.  20   Issued 4,000 shares of common stock at $36 cash per share.

May  18   Announced a 2-for-1 common stock split, reducing the par value of the common stock to $10 per share. The authorization was increased to 100,000 shares.

June  1   Issued 2,000 shares of common stock for $60,000 cash.

Sept. 1   Repurchased 2,500 shares of common stock at $18 cash per share.

Oct.  12   Sold 900 treasury shares at $21 cash per share.

Dec. 22   Issued 500 shares of preferred stock for $59 cash per share.

**Required**

Use the financial statement effects template to indicate the effects of each transaction.

**P9-53.** **Analyzing and Interpreting Equity Accounts and Comprehensive Income** (LO2)

Following is the stockholders' equity section of the 2006 balance sheet for Procter & Gamble Company and its statement of stockholders' equity.

Procter & Gamble Company (PG)

| Amounts in millions; June 30 | 2006 | 2005 |
|---|---|---|
| **Shareholders' Equity** | | |
| Convertible Class A preferred stock, stated value $1 per share (600 shares authorized)............................................. | $ 1,451 | $ 1,483 |
| Non-Voting Class B preferred stock, stated value $1 per share (200 shares authorized)............................................. | — | — |
| Common stock, stated value $1 per share (10,000 shares authorized; shares outstanding: 2006—3,975.8, 2005—2,976.6)................. | 3,976 | 2,977 |
| Additional paid-in capital ........................................ | 57,856 | 3,030 |
| Reserve for ESOP debt retirement................................. | (1,288) | (1,259) |
| Accumulated other comprehensive income........................... | (518) | (1,566) |
| Treasury stock, at cost (shares held: 2006—797.0, 2005—503.7)........... | (34,235) | (17,194) |
| Retained earnings ............................................... | 35,666 | 31,004 |
| Total shareholders' equity ....................................... | $62,908 | $18,475 |

### Consolidated Statement of Shareholders' Equity

| Dollars in millions/ Shares in thousands | Common Shares Outstanding | Common Stock | Preferred Stock | Additional Paid-in Capital | Reserve for ESOP Debt Retirement | Accumulated Other Comprehensive Income | Treasury Stock | Retained Earnings | Total | Total Comprehensive Income |
|---|---|---|---|---|---|---|---|---|---|---|
| **Bal. June 30, 2005....** | 2,472,934 | $2,977 | $1,483 | $3,030 | $(1,259) | $(1,566) | $(17,194) | $31,004 | $18,475 | |
| Net earnings......... | | | | | | | | 8,684 | 8,684 | $8,684 |
| Other comprehensive income: | | | | | | | | | | |
| Financial statement translation....... | | | | | | 1,316 | | | 1,316 | 1,316 |
| Net investment hedges, net of $472 tax............. | | | | | | (786) | | | (786) | (786) |
| Other, net of tax benefits...... | | | | | | 518 | | | 518 | 518 |
| Total comprehensive income......... | | | | | | | | | | $9,732 |
| Dividends to shareholders: | | | | | | | | | | |
| Common.......... | | | | | | | | (3,555) | (3,555) | |
| Preferred, net of tax benefits...... | | | | | | | | (148) | (148) | |
| Treasury purchases ... | (297,132) | | | (9) | | | (16,821) | | (16,830) | |
| Employee plan issuances......... | 36,763 | 16 | | 1,308 | | | 887 | (319) | 1,892 | |
| Preferred stock conversions........ | 3,788 | | (32) | 5 | | | 27 | | — | |
| Gillette acquisition .... | 962,488 | 983 | | 53,522 | | | (1,134) | | 53,371 | |
| Change in ESOP debt reserve....... | | | | | (29) | | | | (29) | |
| **Bal. June 30, 2006....** | 3,178,841 | $3,976 | $1,451 | $57,856 | $(1,288) | $ (518) | $(34,235) | $35,666 | $62,908 | |

**Required**

a. What does the term *convertible* mean?

b. How many shares of common stock did Procter & Gamble issue when convertible class A preferred stock was converted during fiscal 2006?

c. Assuming that the convertible class A preferred stock was sold at par value, at what average price were the common shares issued as of year-end 2006?

d. What is the accumulated other comprehensive income account? Explain.

e. What items are included in the $9,732 million 'total comprehensive income' for the year ended June 30, 2006? How do these items affect stockholders' equity? How do these items affect net income?

f. What cash dividends did Procter & Gamble pay in 2006 for each class of stock?

**P9-54.** **Analyzing and Interpreting Equity Accounts and Comprehensive Income** (LO2)

Following is the stockholders' equity section of Fortune Brands balance sheet and its statement of stockholders' equity.

Fortune Brands (FO)

| December 31 (In millions, except per share amounts) | 2005 | 2004 |
|---|---|---|
| $2.67 Convertible preferred stock | $ 6.6 | $ 7.1 |
| Common stock, par value $3.125 per share, 229.6 shares issued | 717.4 | 717.4 |
| Paid-in capital | 182.8 | 155.8 |
| Accumulated other comprehensive (loss) income | (22.2) | 6.4 |
| Retained earnings | 5,890.2 | 5,447.2 |
| Treasury stock, at cost | (3,129.2) | (3,203.2) |
| Total stockholders' equity | $3,645.6 | $3,130.7 |

| (In millions, except per share amounts) | $2.67 Convertible Preferred Stock | Common Stock | Paid-in Capital | Accumulated Other Comprehensive Income (Loss) | Retained Earnings | Treasury Stock At Cost | Total |
|---|---|---|---|---|---|---|---|
| Balance at December 31, 2004 | $ 7.1 | $717.4 | $155.8 | $ 6.4 | $5,447.2 | $(3,203.2) | $3,130.7 |
| Comprehensive income | | | | | | | |
| Net income | — | — | — | — | 621.1 | — | 621.1 |
| Foreign exchange adjustments, net of effect of hedging activities | — | — | — | 1.7 | — | — | 1.7 |
| Minimum pension liability adjustments | — | — | — | (30.3) | — | — | (30.3) |
| Total comprehensive Income | — | — | — | (28.6) | 621.1 | — | 592.5 |
| Dividends ($1.38 per share) | — | — | — | — | (201.6) | — | (201.6) |
| Tax benefit on exercise of stock options | — | — | 26.0 | — | — | — | 26.0 |
| Conversion of preferred stock (0.1 shares) and delivery of stock plan shares (1.9 shares) | (0.5) | — | 1.0 | — | — | 74.0 | 74.5 |
| Spin-off of ACCO World Corporation | — | — | — | — | 23.5 | — | 23.5 |
| Balance at December 31, 2005 | $ 6.6 | $717.4 | $182.8 | $(22.2) | $5,890.2 | $(3,129.2) | $3,645.6 |

**Discontinued Operation** On August 16, 2005, the Company completed the spin-off of the Office products business, ACCO World Corporation (ACCO), to the Company's shareholders. In addition to retaining their shareholdings in Fortune Brands, each Fortune Brands shareholder received one share of ACCO World Corporation for each 4.255 shares of Fortune Brands stock held. Fortune Brands did not record a gain or loss on the transaction as a result of the spin-off. As a part of the spin-off, ACCO paid a cash dividend of $625 million, of which Fortune Brands received $613.3 million and the minority shareholder received $11.7 million. The statements of income and consolidated balance sheets for all prior periods have been adjusted to reflect the presentation of the spin-off of ACCO as a discontinued operation.

**Required**

a. Explain the "$2.67" component of the convertible preferred stock account title.

b. Show (confirm) the computation that yields the $717.4 million common stock at year-end 2005.

c. Assuming that the convertible preferred stock was sold at par value, at what average price were its common shares issued as of year-end 2005?

    *d.* What accounts are included in Fortune Brands' accumulated other comprehensive income and loss adjustments for 2005? What other accounts are typically included in accumulated other comprehensive income?

    *e.* Consider the "Discontinued Operation" note reproduced above from Fortune Brands footnotes. Assuming that the investment in ACCO World Corporation was carried on Fortune Brands' balance sheet at $589.8 million on the date of the spin-off, explain why the spin-off increased Fortune Brands' retained earnings by $23.5 million.

**E9-55. Interpreting Footnote Disclosure on Convertible Debentures** **(LO3)**

Lucent Technologies reports the following footnote to its 2005 10-K related to its convertible debentures.

> **2.75% series A and B debentures** During the third quarter of fiscal 2003, we sold 2.75% Series A Convertible Senior Debentures and 2.75% Series B Convertible Senior Debentures for an aggregate amount of $1.6 billion, net of the underwriters' discount and related fees and expenses of $46 million. The debentures were issued at a price of $1,000 per debenture and were issued under our universal shelf. The debentures rank equal in priority with all of the existing and future unsecured and unsubordinated indebtedness and senior in right of payment to all of the existing and future subordinated indebtedness. The terms governing the debentures limit our ability to create liens, secure certain indebtedness and merge with or sell substantially all of our assets to another entity. The debentures are convertible into shares of common stock only if (1) the average sale price of our common stock is at least equal to 120% of the applicable conversion price, (2) the average trading price of the debentures is less than 97% of the product of the sale price of the common stock and the conversion rate, (3) the debentures have been called for redemption by us or (4) certain specified corporate actions occur.

**Required**

    *a.* How did Lucent initially account for the issuance of the 2.75% debentures, assuming that the conversion option cannot be detached and sold separately?

    *b.* How will Lucent account for the conversion of the 2.75% debentures, if and when conversion occurs? Specifically, will Lucent recognize any gain or loss related to conversion? Explain.

    *c.* How are the convertible debentures treated in the computation of basic and diluted earnings per share (EPS)?

    *d.* How should we treat the convertible debentures in our analysis of Lucent?

**P9-56. Interpreting Disclosure on Convertible Preferred Securities** **(LO3)**

Lucent Technologies reports the following footnote to its 2003 10-K related to its convertible preferred stock.

> **Mandatorily Redeemable Convertible Preferred Stock** We have 250,000,000 shares of authorized preferred stock. During fiscal 2001, we designated and sold 1,885,000 shares of non-cumulative 8% redeemable convertible preferred stock having an initial liquidation preference of $1,000 per share, subject to accretion. The net proceeds were $1.8 billion, including fees of $54 million. . . . Holders of the preferred stock have no voting rights, except as required by law, and rank junior to our debt obligations. In addition, upon our dissolution or liquidation, holders are entitled to the liquidation preference plus any accrued and unpaid dividends prior to any distribution of net assets to common shareowners . . . Each trust preferred security is convertible at the option of the holder into 206.6116 shares of our common stock.

**Required**

    *a.* Explain the terms and phrases: *noncumulative, 8%, convertible,* and *liquidation preference.*

    *b.* Describe the general impact on Lucent's balance sheet when it issued the preferred shares. (*Hint:* Aggregate all equity into the contributed capital account, that is, do not break out par value and additional paid-in capital.)

    *c.* Describe the general impact on Lucent's balance sheet for the following transactions related to the mandatorily redeemable convertible preferred stock:

       1. The preferred stock is redeemed for cash.

       2. The preferred stock is converted into common stock

    (*Hint:* Aggregate all equity into the contributed capital account, that is, do not break out par value and additional paid-in capital).

    *d.* How should we treat the convertible stock for our analysis of Lucent?

# CASES

**C9-57.** **Management Application: Convertible Debt**  (LO3)

When convertible debt is issued, the conversion option is not valued, unless it can be detached and sold separately from the debt security. Since many conversion options cannot be separately sold, convertible debt is priced like any other debt (see Module 8). Explain why the accounting for convertible debt with nondetachable options can result in interest expense that is lower if the conversion option had been accounted for separately.

**C9-58.** **Ethics and Governance: Equity Carve Outs**  (LO3)

Many companies use split-offs as a means to unlock shareholder value. The split-off effectively splits the company into two pieces, each of which can then be valued separately by the stock market. If managers are compensated based on reported profit, how might they strategically structure the split-off? What corporate governance issues does this present?

# Reporting and Analyzing Off-Balance-Sheet Financing

## LEARNING OBJECTIVES

**LO1** Describe and illustrate the accounting for capitalized leases. (p. 10-4)

**LO2** Describe and illustrate the accounting for pensions. (p. 10-12)

**LO3** Explain the accounting for special purpose entities (SPEs). (p. 10-22)

## SOUTHWEST AIRLINES

Southwest Airlines is one of the few air carriers to have successfully performed in the past five years. Its management makes the following claim:

> As a result of our discipline and financial conservatism, we have strengthened our balance sheet during the most difficult period in aviation history . . . our unmortgaged assets have a value of nearly $7 billion, and our debt to total capital is approximately 35 percent, including aircraft leases as debt.

Southwest Airline's debt to total capital ratio of 35%, *including aircraft leases as debt*, comes as a surprise to many. Not the ratio part, but the reference to aircraft leases. Many airlines do not own most of the planes that they fly. To a large extent, those planes are owned by commercial leasing companies like General Electric Commercial Credit (GE's financial subsidiary), and are leased to the airlines for periods of one to five years, at which time the airline can extend the leases for an additional period of time.

If structured in a specific way, neither the leased planes (the assets) nor the lease obligation (the liability) appear on Southwest's balance sheet. That non-disclosure can substantially alter investors' perceptions of the capital investment Southwest needs to operate as well as the amount of debt it carries. Including aircraft leases as debt (as Southwest did in computing its 35% ratio quoted above) is an analytical procedure that provides a more complete view of the company's investing and financing activities.

The analytical adjustment adds a huge liability to Southwest's balance sheet: lease payment obligations on aircrafts totaling $1.8 billion, which is a large amount when compared to its net operating assets of $8.4 billion. This module discusses the accounting for leases and explains this analytical adjustment and how to apply it.

Pensions and long-term health care plans are another large obligation for many large companies, including Southwest. Pension and health care liabilities can be enormous. Until recently, information about these obligations was buried in footnotes. Recent accounting rule changes now require companies to report that information on the balance sheet. In particular, the balance sheet now reports the net pension and health care liabilities (the total liability less related investments that fund the liabilities).

For Southwest, the net pension liability is not huge (about $94 million) in comparison with its $14 billion in reported liabilities and equity. However, for American Airlines, a Southwest competitor, the net pension and health care liability exceeds $6.4 billion. That amount is staggering considering American Airlines' total assets are $30 billion. This module walks through the accounting for both pensions and health care obligations. The discussion includes footnote disclosures that convey a wealth of information relating to assumptions underlying estimates of these obligations.

As the market has increased its scrutiny of balance sheets and footnotes, some companies have begun to utilize increasingly sophisticated techniques to shift liabilities (and expenses) to outside entities. This is called *off-balance-sheet financing*. Although the idea of off-balance-sheet financing has been around for decades, the techniques companies use to achieve it have become increasingly complex. One of the more popular techniques is to use special purpose entities (SPEs). Companies use SPEs to finance a wide range of activities from manufacturing facilities to consumer loans. This module discusses SPEs as a financing tool, and explains the accounting for these entities and the required footnote disclosures.

Sources: Southwest Airlines 2005 annual report; Southwest Airlines 2005 Form 10-K; American Airlines 2005 Form 10-K; *Fortune*, January 2007.

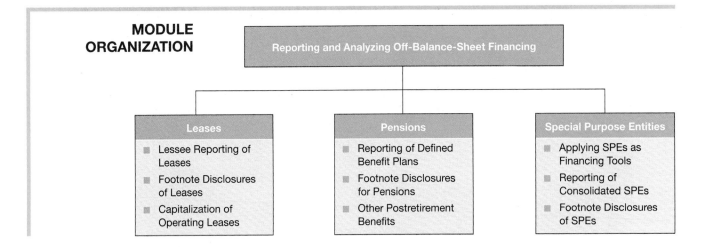

## INTRODUCTION

Company stakeholders pay attention to the composition of the balance sheet and its relation to the income statement. This attention extends to their analysis and valuation of both equity and debt securities. Of particular importance in this valuation process is the analysis of return on equity (ROE) and its components: return on net operating assets (RNOA)—including its components of net operating profit margin (NOPM) and net operating asset turnover (NOAT)—and the degree of financial leverage (FLEV), which is a component of nonoperating return. (Module 4 and its appendix explain these measures.)

To value debt securities such as bonds and notes, one must consider a company's financial leverage (claims against assets) and the level of debt service (interest and principal payments), and compare them with expected cash flows. If analysis reveals that ROE and cash flows are inadequate, companies' credit ratings could decline. The resulting higher cost of debt capital could limit the number of investment projects that yield a return greater than their financing cost. This restricts the company's growth and profitability.

Financial managers are aware of the importance of how financial markets perceive their companies. They also recognize the market attention directed at the quality of their balance sheets and income statements. This reality can pressure managers to *window dress* financial statements to present the company's financial condition and performance in the best possible light. Consider the following cases:

- **Case 1.** A company is concerned that its liquidity is perceived as insufficient. Prior to the end of the current financial reporting period, it takes out a short-term bank loan and delays payment of accounts payable. The company's cash and current assets increase, yielding a balance sheet that appears more liquid.

- **Case 2.** A company's level of accounts receivable is perceived as too high, suggesting possible collection problems and reduced liquidity. Prior to the statement date, the company sells receivables to a financial institution or other third party entity. The sale of receivables increases the company's reported cash balance and presents a healthier current financial picture. Further, if inventory is too high, the company can reduce its available quantities and increase its liquidity position by delaying purchases or by inflating sales via steep price markdowns.

- **Case 3.** A company faces the maturity of a long-term liability, such as the maturity of a bond or note. The amount coming due is reported as a current liability (current maturities of long-term debt), thus reducing net working capital. Prior to the end of its accounting period, the company renegotiates the debt to extend the maturity date of the payment or refinances the indebtedness with longer-term debt. The company reports the indebtedness as a long-term liability thereby increasing net working capital.

- **Case 4.** The company's financial leverage is deemed excessive, resulting in lower credit ratings and increased borrowing costs. To remedy the problem, the company issues new common equity and utilizes the proceeds to reduce its indebtedness.

To increase reported solvency and decrease risk metrics, companies generally wish to present a balance sheet with low levels of debt. Companies that are more liquid and less financially leveraged are viewed as less likely to go bankrupt. As a result, the risk of default on their debt is less, resulting in a better credit rating and a lower interest rate.

Companies also generally wish to present a balance sheet with fewer assets. This is driven by return considerations. ROE has two components: operating return and nonoperating return. The latter is a function of the company's effective use of debt. We generally prefer a company's ROE to be derived from operations (RNOA) rather than from its use of debt. So, if a company can maintain a given level of profitability with fewer assets, the related increase in ROE is perceived to be driven by higher RNOA (asset turnover), and not by increased financial leverage.

**Off-balance-sheet** financing means that assets or liabilities, or both, are not reported on the balance sheet. Even though GAAP requires detailed footnote disclosures, managers generally believe that keeping such assets and liabilities off the balance sheet improves market perception of their operating performance and financial condition. This belief presumes that the market is somewhat inefficient, a notion that persists despite empirical evidence suggesting that analysts adjust balance sheets to include assets and liabilities that managers exclude.

This module explains and illustrates several types of off-balance-sheet financing. Major topics we discuss are leases, pensions, health care liabilities, and special purpose entities (SPEs). This is not an exhaustive list of the techniques that managers have invented to achieve off-balance-sheet financing, but it includes the most common methods. We must keep one point in mind: the relevant information to assess off-balance-sheet financing is mainly in footnotes. While GAAP footnote disclosures on such financing are fairly good, we must have the analytic tools to interpret them and to understand the nature and the magnitude of assets and liabilities that managers have moved off of the balance sheet. This module provides those tools.

# LEASES

We begin the discussion of off-balance-sheet financing with leases. The following graphic shows that leasing impacts both sides of the balance sheet (liabilities and assets) and the income statement (leasing expenses are often reported in selling, general and administrative).

**LO1** Describe and illustrate the accounting for capitalized leases.

| Income Statement | Balance Sheet | |
|---|---|---|
| Sales | Cash | Current liabilities |
| Cost of goods sold | Accounts receivable | **Long-term liabilities** |
| **Selling, general & administrative** | Inventory | |
| Income taxes | **Long-term operating assets** | Shareholders' equity |
| Net income | Investments | |

| Footnote Disclosures—Off-Balance-Sheet Financing | | |
|---|---|---|
| Leases | Pensions | SPEs |

A lease is a contract between the owner of an asset (the **lessor**) and the party desiring to use that asset (the **lessee**). Since this is a private contract between two willing parties, it is governed only by applicable commercial law, and can include whatever provisions the parties negotiate.

Leases generally provide for the following terms:

- Lessor allows the lessee the unrestricted right to use the asset during the lease term.
- Lessee agrees to make periodic payments to the lessor and to maintain the asset.
- Title to the asset remains with the lessor, who usually takes physical possession of the asset at lease-end unless the lessee negotiates the right to purchase the asset at its market value or other predetermined price.

From the lessor's standpoint, lease payments are set at an amount that yields an acceptable return on investment, commensurate with the lessee's credit rating. The lessor has an investment, and the lessee gains use of the asset.

The lease serves as a financing vehicle, similar to a secured bank loan. However, there are several advantages to leasing over bank financing:

■ Leases often require less equity investment by the lessee (borrower) compared with bank financing. Leases usually require the first lease payment be made at the inception of the lease. For a 60-month lease, this amounts to a 1/60 (1.7%) investment by the lessee, compared with a typical bank loan of 70-80% of the asset cost (thus requiring 20-30% equity by the borrower).

■ Since leases are contracts between two parties, their terms can be structured to meet both parties' needs. For example, a lease can allow variable payments to match the lessee's seasonal cash inflows or have graduated payments for start-up companies.

■ If the lease is properly structured, neither the lease asset nor the lease liability is reported on the balance sheet. Accordingly, leasing can be a form of off-balance-sheet financing.

## Lessee Reporting of Leases

GAAP identifies two different approaches for the reporting of leases by the lessee:

■ **Capital lease method.** This method requires that both the lease asset and the lease liability be reported on the balance sheet. The lease asset is depreciated like any other long-term asset. The lease liability is amortized like debt, where lease payments are separated into interest expense and principal repayment.

■ **Operating lease method.** Under this method, neither the lease asset nor the lease liability is reported on the balance sheet. Lease payments are recorded as rent expense by the lessee when paid.

The financial statement effects for the lessee of these methods are summarized in Exhibit 10.1

| **EXHIBIT 10.1** | Financial Statement Effects of Lease Type for the Lessee | | | |
|---|---|---|---|---|
| **Lease Type** | **Assets** | **Liabilities** | **Expenses** | **Cash Flows** |
| **Capital** . . . . . . . . . . | Lease asset reported | Lease liability reported | Depreciation and interest expense | Payments per lease contract |
| **Operating** . . . . . . . | Lease asset **not** reported | Lease liability **not** reported | Rent expense | Payments per lease contract |

GAAP defines criteria to determine whether a lease is capital or operating.[1] Managers seeking off-balance-sheet financing structure their leases around the GAAP rules so as to fail the "capitalization tests."

Under the operating method, lease assets and lease liabilities are *not* recorded on the balance sheet. The company merely discloses key details of the transaction in the lease footnote. The income statement reports the lease payment as rent expense. And, the cash outflows (payments to lessor) per the lease contract are included in the operating section of the statement of cash flows.

For capital leases, both the lease asset and lease liability are reported on the balance sheet. In the income statement, depreciation and interest expense are reported instead of rent expense. (Since only depreciation is an operating expense, NOPAT is higher when a lease is classified as a capital lease.) Further, although the cash payments to the lessor are identical whether or not the lease is capitalized on the balance sheet, the cash flows are classified differently for capital leases—that is, each payment is part interest (operating cash flow) and part principal (financing cash flow). Operating cash flows are, therefore, greater when a lease is classified as a capital lease.

Classifying leases as "operating" has four important benefits for the lessee:

1. The lease asset is not reported on the balance sheet. This means that net operating asset turnover (NOAT) is higher because reported operating assets are lower and revenues are unaffected.

2. The lease liability is not reported on the balance sheet. This means that balance sheet measures of financial leverage (like the total liabilities-to-equity ratio) are improved; many managers believe the

---

[1] Leases must be capitalized when one or more of the following four criteria are met: (1) The lease automatically transfers ownership of the lease asset from the lessor to the lessee at termination of the lease. (2) The lease provides that the lessee can purchase the lease asset for a nominal amount (a bargain purchase) at termination of the lease. (3) The lease term is at least 75% of the economic useful life of the lease asset. (4) The present value of the lease payments is at least 90% of the fair market value of the lease asset at inception of the lease.

reduced financial leverage will result in a better credit rating and, consequently, a lower interest rate on borrowed funds.

3. Without analytical adjustments (see later section on capitalization of operating leases), the portion of ROE derived from operating activities (RNOA) appears higher, which improves the perceived quality of the company's ROE.

4. During the early years of the lease term, rent expense reported for an operating lease is less than the depreciation and interest expense reported for a capital lease.[2] This means that net income is higher in those early years with an operating lease.[3] Further, if the company is growing and continually adding operating lease assets, the level of profits will continue to remain higher during the growth period.

The benefits of applying the operating method for leases are obvious to managers, thus leading them to avoid lease capitalization. Furthermore, the lease accounting standard includes rigid requirements relating to capitalization. Whenever accounting standards are rigidly defined, managers can structure transactions to meet the letter of the standard to achieve a desired accounting result when the essence of the transaction would suggest a different accounting treatment. This is *form over substance*.

## Footnote Disclosures of Leases

Disclosures of expected payments for leases are required under both operating and capital lease methods. Southwest Airlines provides a typical disclosure from its 2005 annual report:

**Leases** The Company had nine aircraft classified as capital leases at December 31, 2005. The amounts applicable to these aircraft included in property and equipment were:

| (In millions) | 2005 | 2004 |
|---|---|---|
| Flight equipment................. | $164 | $173 |
| Less accumulated depreciation..... | 113 | 126 |
| | $ 51 | $ 47 |

Total rental expense for operating leases, both aircraft and other, charged to operations in 2005, 2004, and 2003 was $409 million, $403 million, and $386 million, respectively. The majority of the Company's terminal operations space, as well as 84 aircraft, were under operating leases at December 31, 2005. Future minimum lease payments under capital leases and noncancelable operating leases with initial or remaining terms in excess of one year at December 31, 2005, were:

| (In millions) | Capital Leases | Operating Leases |
|---|---|---|
| 2006....................................... | $16 | $ 332 |
| 2007....................................... | 16 | 309 |
| 2008....................................... | 16 | 274 |
| 2009....................................... | 16 | 235 |
| 2010....................................... | 15 | 219 |
| After 2010................................ | 12 | 1,164 |
| Total minimum lease payments ................... | 91 | $2,533 |
| Less amount representing interest................. | 17 | |
| Present value of minimum leases payments ......... | 74 | |
| Less current portion........................... | 11 | |
| Long-term portion ........................... | $63 | |

The aircraft leases generally can be renewed at rates based on fair market value at the end of the lease term for one to five years. Most aircraft leases have purchase options at or near the end of the lease term at fair market value, generally limited to a stated percentage of the lessor's defined cost of the aircraft.

---

[2] This is true even if the company employs straight-line depreciation for the lease asset since interest expense accrues on the outstanding balance of the lease liability, which is higher in the early years of the lease life. Total expense is the same *over the life of the lease*, regardless of whether the lease is capitalized or not. That is: Total rent expense (from operating lease) = Total depreciation expense (from capital lease) + Total interest expense (from capital lease).

[3] However, NOPAT is *lower* for an operating lease because rent expense is an operating expense whereas only depreciation expense (and not interest expense) is an operating expense for a capital lease.

Lease disclosures such as this provide information concerning current and future payment obligations. These contractual obligations are similar to debt payments and must be factored into our evaluation of the company's financial condition.

Southwest Airlines' footnote disclosure reports minimum (base) contractual lease payment obligations for each of the next five years and the total lease payment obligations that come due in year six and beyond. This is similar to disclosures of future maturities for long-term debt. The company also must provide separate disclosures for operating leases and capital leases (Southwest Airlines has both operating and capital leases outstanding).

---

**MANAGERIAL DECISION**     **You Are the Division President**

You are the president of an operating division. Your CFO recommends operating lease treatment for asset acquisitions to reduce reported assets and liabilities on your balance sheet. To achieve this classification, you must negotiate leases with shorter base terms and lease renewal options that you feel are not advantageous to your company. What is your response? [Answer, p. 10-28]

---

## Capitalization of Operating Leases

Although not recognized on-balance-sheet, leased properties represent assets (and create liabilities) as defined under GAAP. That is, the company controls the assets and will profit from their future benefits. Also, lease liabilities represent real contractual obligations. Although the financial statements are prepared in conformity with GAAP, the failure to capitalize operating lease assets and lease liabilities for analysis purposes distorts ROE analysis—specifically:

▪ Net operating profit margin (NOPM) is understated; although, over the life of the lease, rent expense under operating leases equals depreciation plus interest expense under capital leases, only depreciation expense is included in net operating profit (NOPAT) as interest is a nonoperating expense. Operating expense is, therefore, overstated, and NOPM is understated. (While cash payments are the same whether the lease is classified as operating or capital, *operating cash flow* is higher with capital leases since depreciation is an add-back, and the reduction of the capital lease obligation is classified as a *financing* outflow. Operating cash flows are, therefore, lower with operating leases than with capital leases.)

▪ Net operating asset turnover (NOAT) is overstated due to nonreporting of lease assets.

▪ Financial leverage (FLEV) is understated by the omitted lease liabilities—recall that lease liabilities are nonoperating.

Although aggregate ROE is relatively unaffected (assuming that the leases are at their midpoint on average so that rent expense is approximately equal to depreciation plus interest) failure to capitalize an operating lease results in a balance sheet that, arguably, neither reflects all of the assets that are used in the business, nor the nonoperating obligations for which the company is liable. Such noncapitalization of leases makes ROE appear to be of higher quality since it derives from higher RNOA (due to higher NOA turnover) and not from higher financial leverage. This is, of course, the main reason why managers want to exclude leases from the balance sheet.

Lease disclosures that are required under GAAP allow us to capitalize operating leases for analysis purposes. This capitalization process involves three steps (this is the same basic process that managers would have used if the leases had been classified as capital leases):

1. Determine the discount rate.[4]

---

[4] There are at least two approaches to determine the appropriate discount rate for our analysis: (1) If the company discloses capital leases, we can infer a rate equal to the rate that yields the present value computed by the company given the future capital leases payments (see Business Insight box later in this section). (2) Use the rate that corresponds to the company's credit rating or the rate from any recent borrowings involving intermediate term secured obligations. Companies typically disclose these details in their long-term debt footnote.

2. Compute the present value of future operating lease payments.

3. Adjust the financials to include the present value from step 2 as both a lease asset and a lease liability.

To illustrate the capitalization of operating leases, we use Southwest Airline's footnote. We determine the implicit rate on its capital leases (step 1) to be 7% (see Business Insight box on page 10-9). We then use this 7% discount rate to compute the present value of its operating leases in Exhibit 10.2.

| EXHIBIT 10.2 | Present Value of Operating Lease Payments ($ millions) | | |
| --- | --- | --- | --- |
| **Year** | **Operating Lease Payment** | **Discount Factor (i = 0.07)** | **Present Value** |
| 1 . . . . . . . . . . . . . . . . . | $ 332 | 0.93458 | $ 310 |
| 2 . . . . . . . . . . . . . . . . | 309 | 0.87344 | 270 |
| 3 . . . . . . . . . . . . . . . | 274 | 0.81630 | 224 |
| 4 . . . . . . . . . . . . . . . | 235 | 0.76290 | 179 |
| 5 . . . . . . . . . . . . . . . | 219 | 0.71299 | 156 |
| >5 . . . . . . . . . . . . . . . | 1,164 [$219 for ~5 years] | 4.10020 × 0.71299 | 640 |
| | | | $1,779 |
| Remaining life . . . . . . . . | $1,164/$219 = 5.315 years | | |

Step 2, determining the present value of future operating lease payments, has four parts:

1. Discount each of the first five lease payments using the present value factor for that number of years.

2. Compute the number of annual payments beyond year 5. To do this we assume that the company continues to pay the same amount each year as it paid in year 5 (an annuity) and continues to do so until it exhausts the remaining payments disclosed in the lease footnote. For Southwest Airlines, if the company continues to pay $219 per year, it will take 5.315 years to exhaust the remaining payments of $1,164, computed as $1,164/$219.

3. Compute the present value of the remaining lease payment annuity. There are three ways to arrive at this present value. One way is to use the factor from the time value of money tables in the appendix near the end of the book. To do this, we first round the number of years computed (5.315) to the nearest whole year (5). The tables show an annuity factor of 4.10020 for 5 years at 7%. A second way is to include the exact number of years in the annuity formula $\frac{1 - (1 + 0.07)^{-5.315}}{0.07}$, which yields an annuity factor of 4.31498. Third, we can compute the present value of the annuity using a financial calculator with inputs: N = 5.315, I = 7%, PMT = 219, FV = 0. This also yields the present value of 4.31498. Regardless of the method used, the computed amount is the present value of the annuity at the end of year 5. We must discount that amount to the present (year 0) by multiplying it by the year 5 present value factor of a single sum (0.71299). Thus, the present value is $640 under the first computational method and $674 under methods 2 and 3. Methods 2 and 3 are more exact, but may or may not yield a material difference as compared to method 1. Exhibit 10.2 shows the results using method 1. For simplicity, we use method 1 hereafter.

4. Sum the present values for the first five years and that for years after year 5. For Southwest, this totals $1,779, computed as $310 + $270 + $224 + $179 + $156 + $640 (or $1,813 under the alternate computational methods).

## Balance Sheet Effects

These steps yield the adjusted figures in Exhibit 10.3 for Southwest Airlines at year-end 2005.

| EXHIBIT 10.3 | Adjustments to Balance Sheet from Capitalization of Operating Leases | | |
|---|---|---|---|
| ($ millions) | Reported Figures | Adjustments | Adjusted Figures |
| Net operating assets ................. | $8,419 | $1,779 | $10,198 |
| Net nonoperating liabilities............. | 1,744 | 1,779 | 3,523 |
| Equity............................ | 6,675 | | 6,675 |

The capitalization of its operating leases has a marked impact on Southwest Airline's balance sheet. For the airline and retailing industries, in particular, lease assets (airplanes and real estate) comprise a large portion of net operating assets, which are typically accounted for using the operating lease method. Thus, companies in these industries usually have sizeable off-balance-sheet assets and liabilities.

## Income Statement Effects

Capital leases also affect the income statement via depreciation of the leased equipment and interest on the lease liability. Operating lease payments are reported as rent expense, typically included in selling, general and administrative expenses. The income statement adjustments relating to the capitalization of operating leases involve two steps:

1. Remove rent expense from operating expense (for simplicity, we assume that the current year rent expense is approximated by the year 1 projected lease payment of $332 million).
2. Add depreciation expense from the lease assets to operating expense and add interest expense from the lease obligation as a nonoperating expense. Lease assets are estimated at $1,779 million (see Exhibit 10.3). GAAP requires companies to depreciate capital lease assets over their useful lives or the lease terms, whichever is less. For this example, we assume that the remaining lease term is 10 years (5 years reported in the lease schedule plus 5 years after the fifth year). Using this term and zero salvage value results in estimated straight-line depreciation for lease assets of $178 million ($1,779 million/10 years). Interest expense on the $1,779 million lease liability at the 7% capitalization rate is $125 million ($1,779 million $\times$ 7%) for the first year.[5]

Southwest Airlines reports operating income of $820 million, nonoperating income of $54 million, income tax expense of $326 million, and a federal and state statutory tax rate of 36.8% in 2005. Thus, its tax rate on operating income is 37.3%, computed as ($326 million − [$54 million $\times$ 36.8%])/$820 million. The net adjustment to NOPAT, reflecting the elimination of rent expense and the addition of depreciation expense, is $97 million, computed as ($332 million − $178 million) $\times$ (1 − 37.3%). The after-tax increase in nonoperating expense is $79 million, computed as $125 million $\times$ (1 − 36.8%). Exhibit 10.4 summarizes these adjustments to some of Southwest's profitability measures.

| EXHIBIT 10.4 | Adjustments to Income Statement from Capitalization of Operating Leases | | |
|---|---|---|---|
| ($ millions) | Reported Figures | Adjustments | Adjusted Figures |
| NOPAT ............................ | $571 | $97 | $668 |
| Nonoperating expense................. | 23 | 79 | 102 |
| Net income........................ | $548 | $18 | $566 |

[5] This approach uses the operating lease payments from year 1 of the projected payments to approximate the rent expense for operating leases and the depreciation and interest expense for capital leases. An alternative approach is to use *actual* rent expense for the year (disclosed in the leasing footnote) together with depreciation and interest computed based on capitalization of the *prior* year forecast lease payments. Although, arguably more exact, most analysts use the simplified approach illustrated here given the extent of other estimates involved (such as discount rates, depreciation lives, and salvage values).

## ROE and Disaggregation Effects

Adjustments to capitalize operating leases can alter our assessment of ROE components. The impact for ROE and its components, defined in Module 4, is summarized in Exhibit 10.5 for Southwest Airlines.

| **EXHIBIT 10.5** | Ratio Effects of Adjustments from Capitalization of Operating Leases | | |
|---|---|---|---|
| **($ millions)** | **Reported** | **Adjusted** | **Computations for Adjustments** |
| NOPM. . . . . . . . . . . . . . . . . . . . . . . . . . . . . . . . . . . | 7.5% | 8.8% | $668/$7,584 |
| NOAT . . . . . . . . . . . . . . . . . . . . . . . . . . . . . . . . . . | 0.90 | 0.74 | $7,584/$10,198 |
| RNOA . . . . . . . . . . . . . . . . . . . . . . . . . . . . . . . . . . | 6.8% | 6.6% | $668/$10,198 |
| Nonoperating return . . . . . . . . . . . . . . . . . . . . . . | 1.4% | 1.9% | (residual number) |
| ROE . . . . . . . . . . . . . . . . . . . . . . . . . . . . . . . . . . . | 8.2% | 8.5% | $566/$6,693* |

* Reported equity of $6,675 + $18.

Using year-end (reported and adjusted) data, and Southwest Airlines total revenues of $7,584 million, its adjusted RNOA is 6.6% (down from 6.8% reported). The increase in net operating profit margin (from 7.5% to 8.8% reflecting the increased operating income resulting from elimination of rent expense that is only partially offset by the increase in depreciation expense) is more than offset by a reduction of net operating asset turnover (from 0.90 to 0.74; reflecting the increase in operating lease assets).

Although Southwest's ROE increases only by 0.3%, this analysis reveals that 22% (1.9%/8.5%) of its ROE results from nonoperating activities, up from 17% (1.4%/8.2%) using reported figures. The adjusted figures reveal a greater financial leverage in the form of capital lease obligations. Specifically, its liabilities-to-equity ratio is 0.53 times equity using adjusted figures ($3,523/$6,693) versus 0.26 times using reported figures ($1,744/$6,675). Financial leverage is, therefore, revealed to play a greater role in ROE.

Adjusted assets and liabilities arguably present a more realistic picture of the invested capital required to operate Southwest Airlines and of the amount of leverage represented by its leases. Similarly, operating profitability is revealed to be higher than reported, since a portion of Southwest's rent payments represent repayment of the lease liability (a nonoperating cash outflow) rather than operating expense.

| **BUSINESS INSIGHT** | Imputed Discount Rate for Leases |
|---|---|

When companies report both operating and capital leases, the average rate used to discount capital leases can be imputed from disclosures in the leasing footnote. Southwest Airlines reports total undiscounted minimum capital lease payments of $91 million and a discounted value for those lease payments of $75 million in its footnote disclosure below. Using Excel, we can estimate by trial and error the discount rate that yields the present value—which is about 7% (see chart below). We used this 7% discount rate to capitalize the operating lease payments for Southwest.

| Year | Capital Lease Payment | Discount Factor (i = 0.07) | Present Value |
|---|---|---|---|
| 1 . . . . . . . . . . . . . . | $16 | 0.93458 | $15 |
| 2 . . . . . . . . . . . . . . | 16 | 0.87344 | 14 |
| 3 . . . . . . . . . . . . . . | 16 | 0.81630 | 13 |
| 4 . . . . . . . . . . . . . . | 16 | 0.76290 | 12 |
| 5 . . . . . . . . . . . . . . | 15 | 0.71299 | 11 |
| >5 . . . . . . . . . . . . . | 12 [$15 for ~1 year] | 0.93458* × 0.71299 | 10† |
| | | | $75 |

Remaining life . . . . . . $12/$15 = 0.8 years, rounded to 1 year

*The annuity factor from the tables for 1 year at 7% is 0.93458.
†$15 × 0.93458 × 0.71299 = $9.995 (or approximately $10).

# MID-MODULE REVIEW 1

Following is the leasing footnote disclosure from American Airlines's 2005 10-K report.

**Leases** AMR's subsidiaries lease various types of equipment and property, primarily aircraft and airport facilities. The future minimum lease payments required under capital leases, together with the present value of such payments, and future minimum lease payments required under operating leases that have initial or remaining non-cancelable lease terms in excess of one year as of December 31, 2005, were (in millions):

| Year Ending December 31 | Capital Leases | Operating Leases |
|---|---|---|
| 2006 | $ 263 | $ 1,065 |
| 2007 | 196 | 1,039 |
| 2008 | 236 | 973 |
| 2009 | 175 | 872 |
| 2010 | 140 | 815 |
| 2011 and thereafter | 794 | 7,453 |
| | 1,804 | $12,217 |
| Less amount representing interest | 716 | |
| Present value of net minimum lease payments | $1,088 | |

At December 31, 2005, the Company was operating 213 aircraft and 27 turboprop aircraft under operating leases and 91 jet aircraft and three turboprop aircraft under capital leases. The aircraft leases can generally be renewed at rates based on fair market value at the end of the lease term for one to five years. Some aircraft leases have purchase options at or near the end of the lease term at fair market value, but generally not to exceed a stated percentage of the defined lessor's cost of the aircraft or a predetermined fixed amount.

1. What adjustments would you make to American Airline's balance sheet to capitalize the operating leases at the end of 2005? (*Hint:* The implicit rate on AMR's capital leases is approximately 11%.)
2. Assuming the same facts as in part 1, what income statement adjustments might you consider?

## Solution

1. Using an 11% discount rate, the present value of American Airline's operating leases follows ($ millions):

| Year | Operating Lease Payment | Discount Factor (i = 0.11) | Present Value |
|---|---|---|---|
| 1 | $ 1,065 | 0.90090 | $ 959 |
| 2 | 1,039 | 0.81162 | 843 |
| 3 | 973 | 0.73119 | 711 |
| 4 | 872 | 0.65873 | 574 |
| 5 | 815 | 0.59345 | 484 |
| >5 | 7,453  [$815 for ~9 years] | 5.53705* × 0.59345 | 2,678† |
| | | | $6,249 |

Remaining life...... $7,453/$815 = 9.145 years, rounded to 9 years

*The annuity factor for 9 years at 11% is 5.53705.
†$815 × 5.53705 × 0.59345 = $2,678. (Under the alternate method the present value is $815 × 5.59034 × 0.59345 = $2,704.)

AMR's operating leases represent $6,249 million in both unreported operating assets and unreported non-operating liabilities. These amounts should be added to the balance sheet for analysis purposes.

2. Income statement adjustments relating to capitalization of operating leases involve two steps:
   a. Remove rent expense of $1,065 million from operating expense.
   b. Add depreciation expense from lease assets to operating expense and also reflect interest expense on the lease obligation as a nonoperating expense. We assume that the remaining lease term is 14 years (5 years reported in the lease schedule plus 9 years after year 5). Using this term and zero salvage value results in estimated straight-line depreciation for lease assets of $446 million ($6,249 million/14 years). Interest expense on the $6,249 million lease liability at the 11% capitalization rate is $687 million ($6,249 million × 11%).

# PENSIONS

Companies frequently offer pension plans as a benefit for their employees. There are two general types of pension plans:

**LO2** Describe and illustrate the accounting for pensions.

1. **Defined contribution plan.** This plan requires the company to make periodic contributions to an employee's account (usually with a third party trustee like a bank), and many plans require an employee matching contribution. Following retirement, the employee makes periodic withdrawals from that account. A tax-advantaged 401(k) account is a typical example. Under a 401(k) plan, the employee makes contributions that are exempt from federal taxes until they are withdrawn after retirement.

2. **Defined benefit plan.** This plan also requires the company to make periodic payments to a third party, which then makes payments to an employee after retirement. Payments are usually based on years of service and the employee's salary. The company may or may not set aside sufficient funds to cover these obligations (federal law does set minimum funding requirements). As a result, defined benefit plans can be overfunded or underfunded. All pension investments are retained by the third party until paid to the employee. In the event of bankruptcy, employees have the standing of a general creditor, but usually have additional protection in the form of government pension benefit insurance.

For a defined contribution plan, the company contribution is recorded as an expense in the income statement when the cash is paid or the liability accrued. For a defined benefit plan, it is not so simple. This is because while the company contributes cash or securities to the pension investment account, the pension obligation is not satisfied until the employee receives pension benefits, which may be many years into the future. This section focuses on how a defined benefit plan impacts financial statements, and how we assess company performance and financial condition when such a plan exists.

## Reporting of Defined Benefit Pension Plans

There are two accounting issues concerning the reporting of defined benefit pension plans.

1. How are pension plans (assets and liabilities) reported in the balance sheet (if at all)?
2. How are pension costs and returns from pension plan assets reported in the income statement?

The following graphic shows where pensions appear on the balance sheet (liabilities and assets) and the income statement (pension expense is usually reported in SG&A).

| Income Statement | Balance Sheet | |
| --- | --- | --- |
| Sales | Cash | Current liabilities |
| Cost of goods sold | Accounts receivable | Long-term liabilities |
| Selling, general & administrative | Inventory | |
| Income taxes | Long-term operating assets | Shareholders' equity |
| Net income | Investments | |

| Footnote Disclosures—Off-Balance-Sheet Financing | | |
| --- | --- | --- |
| Leases | Pensions | SPEs |

## Balance Sheet Effects

**Pension plan assets** are primarily investments in stocks and bonds (mostly of other companies, but it is not uncommon for companies to invest pension funds in their own stock). Pension liabilities (called the **projected benefit obligation** or **PBO**) are the company's obligations to pay current and former employees. The difference between the market value of the pension plan assets and the projected benefit obligation is called the **funded status** of the pension plan. If the PBO exceeds the pension plan assets, the pension is **underfunded**. Conversely, if pension plan assets exceed the PBO, the pension plan is **overfunded**. Under current GAAP, companies are required to record only the funded status on their balance sheets (namely, the *net* amount, not the pension plan assets and PBO separately), either as an asset if the plan is overfunded, or as a liability if it is underfunded.

Pension plan assets consist of stocks and bonds whose value changes each period in three ways. First, the value of the investments increases or decreases as a result of interest, dividends, and gains or losses on the stocks and bonds held. Second, the pension plan assets increase when the company contributes additional cash or stock to the investment account. Third, the pension plan assets decrease by the amount of benefits paid to retirees during the period. These three changes in the pension plan assets are articulated below.

| Pension Plan Assets |
| --- |
| Pension plan assets, beginning balance |
| + Actual returns on investments (interest, dividends, gains and losses) |
| + Company contributions to pension plan |
| − Benefits paid to retirees |
| = Pension plan assets, ending balance |

The pension liability, or PBO (projected benefit obligation), is computed as the present value of the expected future benefit payments to employees. The present value of these future payments depend on the number of years the employee is expected to work (years of service) and the employee's salary level at retirement. Consequently, companies must estimate future wage increases, as well as the number of employees expected to reach retirement age with the company and how long they are likely to receive pension benefits following retirement. Once the future retiree pool is determined, the expected future payments under the plan are discounted to arrive at the present value of the pension obligation. This is the PBO. A reconciliation of the PBO from beginning balance to year-end balance follows.

| Pension Obligation |
| --- |
| Projected benefit obligation, beginning balance |
| + Service cost |
| + Interest cost |
| +/− Actuarial losses (gains) |
| − Benefits paid to retirees |
| = Projected benefit obligation, ending balance |

As this reconciliation shows, the balance in the PBO changes during the period for four reasons.

- First, as employees continue to work for the company, their pension benefits increase. The annual **service cost** represents the additional (future) pension benefits earned by employees during the current year.

- Second, **interest cost** accrues on the outstanding pension liability, just as it would with any other long-term liability (see the accounting for bond liabilities in Module 8). Because there are no scheduled interest payments on the PBO, the interest cost accrues each year, that is, interest is added to the existing liability.

- Third, the PBO can increase (or decrease) due to actuarial losses (and gains), which arise when companies make changes in their pension plans or make *changes in actuarial assumptions* (including assumptions that are used to estimate the PBO, such as the rate of wage inflation, termination and mortality rates, and the discount rate used to compute the present value of future obligations). For example, if a company increases the discount rate used to compute the present value of future pension plan payments from, say, 8% to 9%, the present value of future benefit payments declines (just like bond prices.) Conversely, if the discount rate is reduced to 7%, the present value of the PBO increases. Other actuarial assumptions used to estimate the pension liability (such as the expected wage inflation rate or the expected life span of current and former employees) can also create similar actuarial losses or gains.

■ Fourth, pension benefit payments to retirees reduce the PBO (just as the payments reduce the pension plan assets).

Finally, the net pension liability (or asset) that is reported in a company's balance sheet, then, is computed as follows:

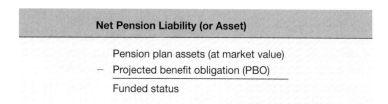

|  | **Net Pension Liability (or Asset)** |
|---|---|
|  | Pension plan assets (at market value) |
| − | Projected benefit obligation (PBO) |
|  | Funded status |

If the funded status is positive (assets exceed liabilities such that the plan is overfunded), the overfunded pension plan is reported on the balance sheet as an asset, typically called prepaid pension cost. If the funded status is negative (liabilities exceed assets and the plan is underfunded), it is reported as a liability.[6,7] During the early 2000s, long-term interest rates declined drastically and many companies lowered their discount rate for computing the present value of future pension payments. Lower discount rates meant higher PBO values. This period also witnessed a bear market and pension plan assets declined in value. The combined effect of the increase in PBO and the decrease in asset values caused many pension funds to become severely underfunded. Of the 1,912 U.S. publicly traded companies reporting pension plans in 2005, a total of 1,721 (90%) were underfunded. (American Airlines, for example, reports an underfunded pension plan of $3.2 billion in 2005.)

## Income Statement Effects

A company's net pension expense is computed as follows.

|  | **Net Pension Expense** |
|---|---|
|  | Service cost |
| + | Interest cost |
| − | *Expected* return on pension plan assets |
| ± | Amortization of deferred amounts |
|  | Net pension expense |

The net pension expense is rarely reported separately on the income statement. Instead, it is included with other forms of compensation expense in selling, general and administrative (SG&A) expenses. However, pension expense is disclosed separately in footnotes.

The net pension expense has four components. The previous PBO section described the first two components: service costs and interest costs. The third component of pension expense relates to the return on pension plan assets, which *reduces* total pension expense. To compute this component, companies use

---

[6] Balance sheet recognition of the funded status is a new requirement. In 2006, the FASB issued new rules entitled "Employers' Accounting for Defined Benefit Pension and Other Postretirement Plans an amendment of FASB Statements No. 87, 88, 106, and 132(R)." Previously, companies' balance sheets did not recognize certain types of pension obligations. Instead, these were reported only in the footnotes. Recognizing the funded status will increase total liabilities for most companies. To balance the accounting equation, the FASB allowed companies to recognize the offsetting amount in stockholders' equity, using the Accumulated Other Comprehensive Income (OCI) account.

[7] Companies typically maintain many pension plans. Some are overfunded and others are underfunded. Current GAAP requires companies to group all of the overfunded and underfunded plans together, and to present a net asset for the overfunded plans and a net liability for the underfunded plans.

the long-term *expected* rate of return on the pension plan assets, rather than the *actual* return, and multiply that expected rate by the prior year's balance in pension plan assets account (usually the average balance in the prior year). Use of the expected return rather than actual return is an important distinction. Company CEOs and CFOs dislike income variability because they believe that stockholders react negatively to it, and so company executives intensely (and successfully) lobbied the FASB to use the more stable expected long-term investment return, rather than the actual return, in computing pension expense. Thus, the pension plan assets' expected return is deducted to compute net pension expense.[8]

Any difference between the expected and the actual return is accumulated, together with other deferred amounts, off-balance-sheet and reported in the footnotes. (Other deferred amounts include changes in PBO resulting from changes in estimates used to compute the PBO and from amendments to the pension plans made by the company.) However, if the deferred amount exceeds certain limits, the excess is recognized on-balance-sheet with a corresponding amount recognized (as amortization of deferred amounts) in the income statement.[9] This amortization is the fourth component of pension expense and can be either a positive or negative amount depending on the sign of the difference between expected and actual return on plan assets. (We discuss the amortization component of pension expense further in Appendix 10A.)

Most analysts consider the service cost portion of pension expense to be an operating expense, similar to salaries and other benefits. However, the interest cost component is generally viewed as a nonoperating (financing) cost. Similarly, the expected return on plan assets is considered nonoperating. Consequently, proper analysis of the income statement requires the parsing of pension expense into these operating and nonoperating components.

## Footnote Disclosures—Components of Plan Assets and PBO

GAAP requires extensive footnote disclosures for pensions (and other postretirement benefits which we discuss later). These notes provide details relating to the net pension liability reported in the balance sheet and the components of pension expense are reported as part of SG&A expense in the income statement.

American Airlines' pension footnote indicates that the funded status of its pension plan is $(3,225) million on December 31, 2005. (Southwest Airlines has not yet funded its pension liability of $94 million, a relatively small amount compared with its total liabilities and equity of $14 billion; consequently, Southwest's pension footnote does not provide all of the information necessary for a complete illustration.) This means American's plan is underfunded. Following are the disclosures American Airlines makes in its pension footnote, $ millions.

| | |
|---|---:|
| Pension obligation at January 1, 2005 | $10,022 |
| Service cost | 372 |
| Interest cost | 611 |
| Actuarial loss | 649 |
| Benefit payments | (651) |
| Obligation at December 31, 2005 | $11,003 |
| | |
| Fair value of plan assets at January 1, 2005 | $ 7,335 |
| Actual return on plan assets | 779 |
| Employer contributions | 315 |
| Benefit payments | (651) |
| Fair value of plan assets at December 31, 2005 | $ 7,778 |
| | |
| Funded status at December 31, 2005 | $ (3,225) |

---

[8] The FASB has issued an exposure draft containing a proposal to further amend the pension accounting standard to eliminate the use of the expected return. If passed, this amendment will result in increased earnings volatility as changes in the market value of the pension investments will impact net pension expense (and operating profits before tax) directly.

[9] To avoid amortization, the deferred amounts must be less than 10% of the PBO or pension investments, whichever is less. The excess, if any, is amortized until no further excess remains. When the excess is eliminated (by investment returns or company contributions, for example), the amortization ceases.

American Airlines' PBO began the year with a balance of $10,022 million. It increased by the accrual of $372 million in service cost and $611 million in interest cost. During the year, American also realized an actuarial loss of $649 million, which increased the pension liability. The PBO decreased as a result of $651 million in benefits paid to retirees, leaving a balance of $11,003 million at year-end.

Pension plan assets began the year with at a fair market value of $7,335 million, which increased by $779 million from investment returns and by $315 million from company contributions. The company drew down its investments to make pension payments of $651 million to retirees. Notice that the $651 million payment reduced the PBO by the same amount, as discussed above, leaving the pension plan assets with a year-end balance of $7,778 million. The funded status of American Airlines' pension plan at year-end is $(3,225) million ($11,003 million − $7,778 million) at year-end. The negative balance indicates that its pension plan is underfunded.[10] The PBO and pension plan assets accounts cannot be separated into operating and nonoperating components; thus, most analysts treat the entire funded status as an operating item (either asset or liability).

American Airlines incurred $392 million of pension expense in 2005. This is not broken out separately in its income statement. Instead, it is included in SG&A expense. Details of this expense are found in its pension footnote, which follows ($ millions):

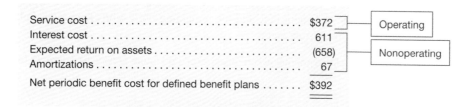

| | |
|---|---|
| Service cost . . . . . . . . . . . . . . . . . . . . . . . . . . . . . . . . . | $372 |
| Interest cost . . . . . . . . . . . . . . . . . . . . . . . . . . . . . . . . . | 611 |
| Expected return on assets . . . . . . . . . . . . . . . . . . . . . . . | (658) |
| Amortizations . . . . . . . . . . . . . . . . . . . . . . . . . . . . . . . . | 67 |
| Net periodic benefit cost for defined benefit plans . . . . . . . | $392 |

Using the information in American Airlines' footnote, we can parse the pension expense into operating and nonoperating components. Most analysts treat service cost as operating, and interest costs and expected return as nonoperating. The amortization expense of $67 million indicates that the deferred amounts have exceeded the maximum limit prescribed under GAAP, and the excess is now amortized gradually to expense so long as the deferred amount still exceeds those limits. The amortization is partly operating (pension plan changes) and partly nonoperating (changes in actuarial assumptions and discount rates). For our analysis, we will treat the entire amortization of $67 as nonoperating. Thus, the pension expense comprises $372 operating expense and $20 nonoperating expense.

---

**RESEARCH INSIGHT**    **Valuation of Pension Footnote Disclosures**

The FASB requires footnote disclosure of the major components of pension cost presumably because it is useful for investors. Pension-related research has examined whether investors assign different valuation multiples to the components of pension cost when assessing company market value. Research finds that the market does, indeed, attach different interpretation to pension components, reflecting differences in information about perceived permanent earnings.

---

## Footnote Disclosures and Future Cash Flows

Companies use their pension plan assets to pay pension benefits to retirees. When markets are booming, as during the 1990s, pension plan assets can grow rapidly. However, when markets reverse, as in the bear market of the early 2000s, the value of pension plan assets can decline. The company's annual pension plan contribution is an investment decision influenced, in part, by market conditions and minimum

---

[10] American Airlines also reports deferred amounts of $2,343 million. This represents components of the PBO that were not required to be recognized on-balance-sheet under prior GAAP. Consequently, it only reported $(882) million ($3,225 million − $2,343 million) on its balance sheet as a liability in 2005. The nonrecognition of pension obligations, of concern to many financial-report users, prompted the FASB to amend the pension accounting standard in 2006 to require recognition on-balance-sheet of the *entire* funded status.

| RESEARCH INSIGHT | Why do Companies offer Pensions? |
|---|---|

Research examines why companies choose to offer pension benefits. It finds that deferred compensation plans and pensions help align the long-term interests of owners and emloyees. Research also examines the composition of pension investments. It finds that a large portion of pension fund assets are invested in fixed-income securities, which are of lower risk than other investment securities. This implies that pension assets are less risky than nonpension assets.

required contributions specified by law.[11] Companies' cash contributions come from borrowed funds or operating cash flows.

American Airlines paid $651 million in pension benefits to retirees in 2005, yet it contributed only $315 million to pension assets that year. The remaining amount was paid out of available funds in the investment account. Cash contributions to the pension plan assets are the relevant amounts for an analysis of projected cash flows. Benefits paid in relation to the pension liability balance can provide a clue about the need for *future* cash contributions. Companies are required to disclose the expected benefit payments for five years after the statement date and the remaining obligations thereafter. Following is American Airlines' benefit disclosure statement:

The following benefit payments, which reflect expected future service as appropriate, are expected to be paid:

| ($ millions) | Pension |
|---|---|
| 2006 . . . . . . . . . . . . . . . . . . . . | $  494 |
| 2007 . . . . . . . . . . . . . . . . . . . | 561 |
| 2008 . . . . . . . . . . . . . . . . . . . | 595 |
| 2009 . . . . . . . . . . . . . . . . . . . | 698 |
| 2010 . . . . . . . . . . . . . . . . . . . | 682 |
| 2011–2015 . . . . . . . . . . . . . . | 3,660 |

As of 2005, American Airlines pension plan assets account reports a balance of $7,778 million, as discussed above, and during the year, the plan assets generated actual returns of $779 million. The pension plan asset account is currently generating investment returns sufficient to cover the $500 million to $700 million in projected benefit payments outlined in the schedule above. Were investment returns not sufficient, the company would have to use operating cash flow or borrow money to fund the deficit.

One application of the pension footnote is to assess the likelihood that the company will be required to increase its cash contributions to the pension plan. This estimate is made by examining the funded status of the pension plan and the projected payments to retirees. For severely underfunded plans, the projected payments to retirees ($500 to $700 million per year in American's footnote disclosure) will not be covered by existing pension assets and projected investment returns. In this case, the company might need to divert operating cash flow from other prospective projects to cover its pension plan. Alternatively, if operating cash flows are not available, it might need to borrow to fund those payments. This can be especially troublesome as the debt service payments include interest, thus, effectively increasing the required pension contribution. GM's situation illustrates the problems associated with underfunded plans, as shown in the following Business Insight.

---

[11] The Pension Protection Act of 2006 mandates that companies fully fund pension obligations by 2013. The bipartisan act also shields taxpayers from assuming airline pension plan obligations, tightens funding requirements so employers make greater cash contributions to pension funds, closes loopholes that allow companies with underfunded plans to skip cash pension payments, prohibits employers and union leaders from promising extra benefits if pension plans are markedly underfunded, and strengthens disclosure rules to give workers and retirees more information about the status of their pension plan.

**BUSINESS INSIGHT**   **Why GM's Bonds Were Rated Junk**

Analysts have long been concerned with General Motors' mounting obligations to its employees stemming from generous pension and health care packages. The following graphic tracks the funded status of GM's pension and health care obligations since 1997. The unfunded obligation has exceeded $40 billion in eight out of nine years, reaching a peak of over $70 billion in 2002, and has only declined slightly since then.

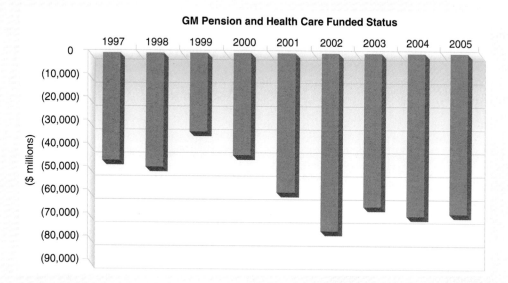

**GM Pension and Health Care Funded Status**

Companies can only look to two sources of funds to pay pension and health-care liabilities. Either plan investments must increase in value or the company must make additional cash contributions to the plan. The latter, of course, uses borrowed money or operating cash flows, potentially at the expense of needed capital investment, R&D, or employee wages, resulting in long-term damage to the company's market position. The bond markets also became increasingly concerned about GM's ability to generate sufficient cash flow to pay its bonds when they mature and to make the payments promised to employees. That is why GM's bonds were eventually downgraded to junk status.

## Footnote Disclosures and Profit Implications

Recall the following earlier breakdown for pension expense:

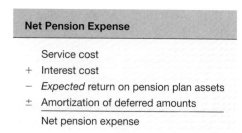

|  | **Net Pension Expense** |
|---|---|
|  | Service cost |
| + | Interest cost |
| − | *Expected* return on pension plan assets |
| ± | Amortization of deferred amounts |
|  | Net pension expense |

Interest cost is the product of the PBO and the discount rate. This discount rate is set by the company. The expected dollar return on pension assets is the product of the pension plan asset balance and the expected long-run rate of return on the investment portfolio. This rate is also set by the company. Further, PBO is affected by the expected rate of wage inflation, termination and mortality rates, all of which are estimated by the company.

GAAP requires disclosure of several rates used by the company in its estimation of PBO and the related pension expense. American Airlines discloses the following table in its pension footnote:

| Pension Benefits | 2005 | 2004 |
|---|---|---|
| Weighted-average assumptions used to determine net periodic benefit cost for the years ended December 31 | | |
| Discount rate . . . . . . . . . . . . . . . . . . . . . . . . . . . . . . . . . . . . . . . . . . . . . . . . . . . | 6.00% | 6.25% |
| Salary scale (ultimate). . . . . . . . . . . . . . . . . . . . . . . . . . . . . . . . . . . . . . . . | 3.78 | 3.78 |
| Expected return on plan assets . . . . . . . . . . . . . . . . . . . . . . . . . . . . . . . . | 9.00 | 9.00 |

During 2005, American Airlines reduced its discount rate (used to compute the present value of its pension obligations, or PBO) by 0.25%, while leaving unchanged its estimates of the rate of wage inflation and the expected return on plan assets.

Changes in these assumptions have the following general effects on pension expense and, thus, profitability. This table summarizes the effects of increases in the various rates. Decreases have the exact opposite effects.

| Estimate change | Probable effect on pension expense | Reason for effect |
|---|---|---|
| Discount rate increase . . . . . . . . . | Increase | While the higher discount rate reduces the PBO, the lower PBO is multiplied by a higher rate. The rate effect is larger than the discount effect, resulting in increased pension expense.* |
| Investment return increase . . . . . . . . . | Decreases | The dollar amount of expected return on plan assets is the product of the plan assets balance and the expected long-term rate of return. Increasing the return increases the expected return on plan assets, thus reducing pension expense. |
| Wage inflation increase . . . . . . . . . | Increases | The expected rate of wage inflation affects future wage levels that determine expected pension payments. An increase, thus, increases PBO, which increases both the service and interest cost components of pension expense. |

* The effect on the PBO and interest cost is seen in the following table of the present values of an annuity of $1 for 10 and 40 years, respectively (dollar amounts are the present value factors from Appendix A; present value of an ordinary annuity, rounded to 2 decimal places).

| | Discount rate | 10 Years | 40 Years |
|---|---|---|---|
| PBO | 5% | $7.72 | $17.16 |
| | 8% | 6.71 | 11.92 |

As the discount rate increases, the PBO decreases. This is the discount effect. Second, the interest cost component of pension expense is computed as the PBO × Discount rate. For the four PBO amounts and related discount rates above, interest cost is computed as follows:

| | Discount rate | 10 Years | 40 Years |
|---|---|---|---|
| Interest cost | 5% | $0.39 | $0.86 |
| | 8% | 0.54 | 0.95 |

See that interest cost increases with increases in the discount rate, regardless of the length of the liability. This is the rate effect.

In the case of American Airlines, reduction of the discount rate, coupled with no change in the expected rate of wage inflation and return on investments, served to reduce pension costs and increase profitability in that year. It is often the case that companies reduce the expected investment returns with a lag, but increase them without a lag, to favorably impact profitability. We must be aware of the impact of these changes in assumptions in our evaluation of company profitability.

**BUSINESS INSIGHT**     How Pensions Confound Income Analysis

Overfunded pension plans and boom markets can inflate income. Specifically, when the stock market is booming, pension investments realize large gains that flow to income (via reduced pension expense). Although pension plan assets do not belong to shareholders (as they are the legal entitlement of current and future retirees), the gains and losses from those plan assets are reported in income. The following graph plots the funded status of General Electric's pension plan together with pension expense (revenue) that GE reported from 1996 to 2005.

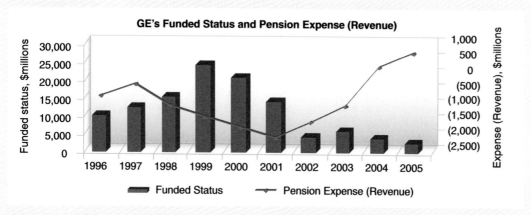

GE's funded status has consistently been positive (indicating an overfunded plan). The degree of overfunding peaked in 1999 at the height of the stock market, and began to decline during the bear market of the early 2000s. GE reported pension *revenue* (not expense) during this period. In 2001, GE's reported pension *revenue* was $2,095 million (10.6% of its pretax income). Because of the plan's overfunded status, the expected return and amortization of deferred gains components of pension expense amounted to $5,288 million, far in excess of the service and interest costs of $3,193 million. In 2004 and 2005, GE recorded pension expense (rather than revenue) as the pension plan's overfunding and expected long-term rates of return declined.

## Other Post-Employment Benefits

In addition to pension benefits, many companies provide health care and insurance benefits to retired employees. These benefits are referred to as **other post-employment benefits (OPEB)**. These benefits present reporting challenges similar to pension accounting. However, companies most often provide these benefits on a "pay-as-you-go" basis and it is rare for companies to make contributions in advance for OPEB. As a result, this liability, known as the **accumulated post-employment benefit obligation (APBO)**, is largely, if not totally, unfunded. GAAP requires that the unfunded APBO liability, net of any unrecognized amounts, be reported in the balance sheet and the annual service costs and interest costs be accrued as expenses each year. This requirement is controversial for two reasons. First, future health care costs are especially difficult to estimate, so the value of the resulting APBO (the present value of the future benefits) is fraught with error. Second, these benefits are provided at the discretion of the employer and can be altered or terminated at any time. Consequently, employers argue that without a legal obligation to pay these benefits, the liability should not be reported in the balance sheet.

Other post-employment benefits can produce large liabilities. For example, American Airlines' footnotes report a funded status for the company's health care obligation of $3,223 million, consisting of an APBO liability of $3,384 million less health care plan investments with a market value of $161 million. General Motors provides an extreme OPEB example (as described in the following Business Insight box). Our analysis of cash flows related to pension obligations can be extended to other post-employment benefit obligations. For example, in addition to its pension payments, American Airlines also discloses that it is obligated to make health care payments to retirees totaling $200 million per year. Because health care obligations are rarely funded until payment is required (federal minimum funding standards do not apply to OPEB and there is no tax benefit to pre-funding), there are no investment returns to fund the payments. Our analysis of projected cash flows must consider this potential cash outflow.

**RESEARCH INSIGHT** **Valuation of Nonpension Post-Employment Benefits**

The FASB requires employers to accrue the costs of all nonpension post-employment benefits; known as *accumulated post-employment benefit obligation* (APBO). These benefits consist primarily of health care and insurance. This requirement is controversial due to concerns about the reliability of the liability estimate. Research finds that the APBO (alone) is associated with company value. However, when other pension-related variables are included in the research, the APBO liability is no longer useful in explaining company value. Research concludes that the pension-related variables do a better job at conveying value-relevant information than the APBO number alone, which implies that the APBO number is less reliable.

# MID-MODULE REVIEW 2

Following is the pension disclosure footnote from Midwest Airlines' 10-K report. All questions relate only to its U.S. plan.

| (in $000) | 2005 | 2004 |
|---|---|---|
| **Change in Benefit Obligation** | | |
| Net benefit obligation at beginning of year . . . . . . . . . . . | $ 20,770 | $ 17,743 |
| Service cost . . . . . . . . . . . . . . . . . . . . . . . . . . . . . . . . . . . | 1,355 | 1,167 |
| Interest cost . . . . . . . . . . . . . . . . . . . . . . . . . . . . . . . . . . . | 1,132 | 986 |
| Actuarial (gain) loss . . . . . . . . . . . . . . . . . . . . . . . . . . . . | (917) | 915 |
| Gross benefits paid . . . . . . . . . . . . . . . . . . . . . . . . . . . . . | (78) | (41) |
| Net benefit obligation at end of year . . . . . . . . . . . . . . . | $ 22,262 | $ 20,770 |
| **Change in Plan Assets** | | |
| Fair value of assets at beginning of year . . . . . . . . . . . . . | $ 4,077 | $ 3,383 |
| Actual return on plan assets. . . . . . . . . . . . . . . . . . . . . . . | 97 | 299 |
| Employer contributions . . . . . . . . . . . . . . . . . . . . . . . . . . | 1,472 | 436 |
| Gross benefits paid . . . . . . . . . . . . . . . . . . . . . . . . . . . . . | (78) | (41) |
| Fair value of plan assets at end of year . . . . . . . . . . . . . . | $ 5,568 | $ 4,077 |
| Funded status at end of year . . . . . . . . . . . . . . . . . . . . . . | $(16,694) | $(16,693) |

Following is Midwest Airlines' footnote for its pension cost as reported in its income statement.

| Components of Net Periodic Benefit Cost (in $000) | 2005 | 2004 | 2003 |
|---|---|---|---|
| Service cost . . . . . . . . . . . . . . . . . . . . . . . . . . . . . . . . . . . | $1,355 | $1,167 | $924 |
| Interest cost . . . . . . . . . . . . . . . . . . . . . . . . . . . . . . . . . . . | 1,132 | 986 | 838 |
| Expected return on assets . . . . . . . . . . . . . . . . . . . . . . . . | (372) | (319) | (233) |
| Amortization of: | | | |
| Prior service cost . . . . . . . . . . . . . . . . . . . . . . . . . . . . . | 310 | 310 | 310 |
| Actuarial loss (gain). . . . . . . . . . . . . . . . . . . . . . . . . . . . | 353 | 329 | 199 |
| Total net periodic benefit cost . . . . . . . . . . . . . . . . . . . . . | $2,778 | $2,473 | $2,038 |

## Required

1. In general, what factors impact a company's pension benefit obligation during a period?
2. In general, what factors impact a company's pension plan investments during a period?
3. What amount is reported on the balance sheet relating to the Midwest Airlines pension plan?
4. How does the expected return on plan assets affect pension cost?
5. How does Midwest Airlines' expected return on plan assets compare with its actual return (in $s) for 2005?

6. How much net pension cost is reflected in Midwest Airlines' 2005 income statement?
7. Assess Midwest Airlines' ability to meet payment obligations to retirees.

## Solution

1. A pension benefit obligation increases primarily by service cost, interest cost, and actuarial losses (which are increases in the pension liability as a result of changes in actuarial assumptions). It is decreased by the payment of benefits to retirees and by any actuarial gains.
2. Pension investments increase by positive investment returns for the period and cash contributions made by the company. Investments decrease by benefits paid to retirees and by investment losses.
3. Midwest Airlines' funded status is $(16,694,000) as of 2005. The negative amount indicates that the plan is underfunded. Consequently, this amount is reflected as a liability on its balance sheet.
4. Expected return on plan assets acts as an offset to service cost and interest cost in computing net pension cost. As the expected return increases, net pension cost decreases.
5. Midwest Airlines' expected return of $372,000 is greater than its actual return of $97,000 in 2005.
6. Midwest Airlines reports a net pension cost of $2,778,000 in its 2005 income statement.
7. Midwest Airlines' funded status is negative, indicating a severely underfunded plan. In 2005, the company contributed $1,472,000 to the pension plan, up from $436,000 in the prior year. It is likely that the company will need to increase its future funding levels to cover the plan's requirements. This might have negative repercussions for its ability to fund other operating needs, and can eventually damage its competitive position.

# SPECIAL PURPOSE ENTITIES (SPEs)

**Special purpose entities** (SPEs) allow companies to structure projects or transactions with a number of financial advantages. SPEs have long been used and are an integral part of corporate finance. The SPE concept is illustrated by the following graphic that summarizes information taken from Ford's 2005 10-K relating to the SPE structure it uses to securitize the receivables of Ford Credit (its financing subsidiary):

**LO3** Explain the accounting for special purpose entities (SPEs).

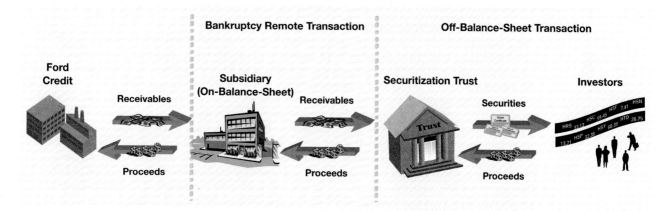

This graph is typical of many SPEs and has the following characteristics of all SPEs:

- A sponsoring company (here, Ford Credit) forms a subsidiary that is capitalized entirely with equity; this creates a *bankruptcy remote transaction*, which reduces the likelihood of bankruptcy for subsequent investors).

- The subsidiary purchases assets from the sponsoring company and sells them to a securitization (off-balance-sheet) trust (the SPE), which purchases the assets using borrowed funds (here, the SPE purchases receivables from Ford Credit's subsidiary).

- Cash flows from the acquired assets are used by the SPE to repay its debt (here, the SPE collects receivables and uses the funds to repay any borrowings).

The sponsoring company benefits in two ways. First, SPEs create direct economic benefits by improving the company's operating cash flows and by mitigating certain types of risk. Second, SPEs create indirect economic benefits by providing financial reporting benefits and alternatives. These indirect benefits derive from having assets, and their related debt, moved off-balance-sheet. The SPE owns the sponsoring company's former assets. Thus, the sponsoring company enjoys an improved asset turnover ratio (assets are less in the denominator of the turnover ratio) and an improved financial leverage ratio (liabilities are less in the numerator of the liabilities-to-equity ratio).

The following graphic shows that SPEs impact both the balance sheet (liabilities and assets) and the income statement of the sponsoring company.

| Income Statement | Balance Sheet | |
| --- | --- | --- |
| Sales | Cash | Current liabilities |
| Cost of goods sold | Accounts receivable | Long-term liabilities |
| Selling, general & administrative | Inventory | |
| Income taxes | Long-term operating assets | Shareholders' equity |
| Net income | Investments | |

| Footnote Disclosures—Off-Balance-Sheet Financing | | |
| --- | --- | --- |
| Leases | Pensions | SPEs |

## Applying SPEs as Financing Tools

This section describes two common means of using SPEs as financing tools.

### Asset Securitization

Consumer finance companies, retailers, and financial subsidiaries of manufacturing companies commonly use SPEs to securitize (sell) their financial assets. Ford Credit, the finance subsidiary of Ford Motor Company, provides a common example as illustrated in the footnotes to Ford's 2005 10-K report:

**Sales of Receivables by Ford Credit**

*Securitization.* Ford Credit sells receivables in securitizations and other structured financings and in whole-loan sale transactions. Some of these arrangements satisfy accounting sale treatment and are not reflected on Ford Credit's balance sheet in the same way as debt funding. Securitization involves the sale of a pool of receivables to a special purpose entity ("SPE"), typically a trust. The SPE issues interest-bearing securities, commonly called asset-backed securities, that are backed by the sold receivables. The SPE uses proceeds from the sale of these securities to pay the purchase price for the sold receivables. The SPE may only purchase the receivables, issue asset-backed securities and make payments on the securities. The SPE has a limited duration and generally is dissolved when investors holding the asset-backed securities have been paid all amounts owed to them. Ford Credit's use of SPEs in securitizations is consistent with conventional practices in the securitization industry. The sale to the SPE achieves isolation of the sold receivables for the benefit of securitization investors and protects them from the claims of Ford Credit's creditors. The use of SPEs combined with the structure of these transactions means that the payment of the asset-backed securities is based on the creditworthiness of the underlying finance receivables . . . and not Ford Credit's creditworthiness. As a result, the senior asset-backed securities issued by the SPEs generally receive the highest short-term credit ratings and among the highest long term credit ratings from the credit rating agencies that rate them and are sold to securitization investors at cost-effective pricing.

Ford Credit's typical U.S. retail securitization is a two-step transaction. Ford Credit sells a pool of its retail installment sale contracts to a wholly owned, bankruptcy-remote special purpose subsidiary that establishes a separate SPE, usually a trust, and transfers the receivables to the SPE in exchange for the proceeds from securities issued by the SPE. The securities issued by the trust, usually notes of various maturities and interest rates, are paid by the SPE from collections on the pool of receivables it owns. These securities are usually structured into senior and subordinated classes. The senior classes have priority over the subordinated classes in receiving collections from the sold receivables. The receivables acquired by the SPE and the asset-backed securities issued by the SPE are assets and obligations of the SPE.

Ford Credit's use of SPEs is typical. As Ford Credit finances the purchases of autos by customers of Ford Motor Company, it accumulates the receivables on its balance sheet. Periodically, through a subsidiary, it packages certain receivables and sells them to its SPE, which funds the purchase by selling certificates entitling the holder to a portion of the cash receipts from eventual collection of receivables. Ford Credit does not provide any other form of protection to the outside certificate holders (its footnote indicates that the receivables are sold "without recourse," meaning without collection rights against Ford Credit or its parent, Ford Motor Company). Nonrecourse is required if Ford Credit wants to account for the sale of receivables as a sale. If Ford Credit has ongoing responsibilities for the receivables, the transfer is not deemed a sale and the transferred assets would remain on Ford Credit's balance sheet.

Ford Motor Company's credit ratings have declined in recent years, thus making its unsecured borrowings more costly and limiting its availability to borrowed funds. In response, it has increased its use of SPEs as a financing source. This funding mechanism is now an important source of liquidity for the company, as highlighted in the following excerpt from the liquidity analysis section of its 10-K.

> Ford Credit's funding strategy is to maintain liquidity and access to diverse funding sources that are cost effective. As a result of lower credit ratings, Ford Credit's unsecured borrowing costs have increased, its access to the unsecured debt market has become more restricted, and its outstanding short- and long-term unsecured debt balances have declined. In response, Ford Credit has increased its use of securitization and other asset-related sources of liquidity, and will continue to expand and diversify its asset-backed funding by asset class, region and channel . . . During 2005, Ford Credit continued to meet a significant portion of its funding requirements through securitizations because of their lower relative costs given our credit ratings (as described below), the stability of the market for asset-backed securities, and the diversity of funding sources that they provide. Securitized funding (both on- and off-balance sheet, net of retained interests) as a percent of total managed receivables was as follows at the end of each of the last three years: 2005–38%, 2004–26%, 2003–25% . . .
>
> The cost of both debt and funding in securitizations is based on a margin or spread over a benchmark interest rate, such as interest rates paid on U.S. Treasury securities of similar maturities. Ford Credit's unsecured spreads have been very volatile over the last three years, as a result of market perception and its lower credit ratings, whereas its securitized funding spreads (which are based on the underlying finance receivables and credit enhancements) have not. In 2005, Ford Credit's unsecured long-term debt funding spreads fluctuated between 165 and 660 basis points above comparable U.S. Treasury securities, while its spreads on securitized funding fluctuated between 42 and 58 basis points above comparable U.S. Treasury securities.

Ford's use of SPEs as a funding source provides necessary liquidity and also provides capital at a substantially lower interest rate. Due to the SPEs limited scope of operations, and its isolation from the general business risk of the parent company, lenders to the SPE face lower risk of default and can, therefore, charge a comparatively lower rate of interest on its borrowings.

## Project and Real Estate Financing

Another common use of SPEs is to finance construction projects. For example, a sponsoring company desires to construct a manufacturing plant. It establishes a SPE and executes a contract with the SPE to build the plant and to later purchase output from the plant. The SPE uses the contract, and the newly constructed manufacturing plant assets, to collateralize debt that it issues to finance the plant's construction. The sponsoring company obtains the benefits of the plant, but does not recognize either the PPE asset or the related liability on its balance sheet. The sponsoring company has commitments with the SPE, labeled executory contracts, but GAAP currently does not require such contracts be recognized in the balance sheet, nor does it even require footnote disclosure of these contracts.

Clothing retailers such as Gap and Abercrombie & Fitch use these types of executory contracts involving outside manufacturers. The manufacturing assets, and related liabilities, of these SPEs are consequently kept off the balance sheet.

A slight variation is to add leasing to this transaction. To illustrate, assume a company desires to construct an office building. It establishes a SPE to construct and finance the building and then lease it back to the company under an operating lease. As we explained earlier in this module, if the lease is structured as an operating lease, neither the lease asset nor the lease obligation is reported on the company's balance sheet. Thus, the company obtains the use and benefit of the building without recording either the building or the related debt on its balance sheet.

## Rationale for SPE Financing

Each of the cases in this section demonstrates the financing capabilities of SPEs. There are two main reasons for the popularity of SPEs.

1. **Lower cost of capital.** SPEs can provide lower cost financing for a company. Since the SPE is not burdened with the myriad of business risks that can affect a company (for example, in Ford's case, the SPE only has the risk of uncollectibility), its investors do not need to be compensated for additional risk. Further, because the SPEs are formed by an all-equity (no debt) subsidiary of the parent company, it is generally perceived that SPEs are protected from the bankruptcy of the sponsoring company, thus further reducing investment risk.

2. **Nonconsolidation.** SPEs can provide a mechanism for off-balance-sheet financing if unconsolidated with the sponsoring company. As we discuss in the next section, however, recent accounting standards have made it more difficult to avoid consolidation.

## Reporting of Consolidated SPEs

Nonconsolidation of SPEs allows assets and liabilities related to the business to be reported off-balance-sheet. This improves the sponsoring company's net operating asset turnover (Sales/NOA), which in turn improves return on net operating assets (RNOA), an important metric of financial performance.[12]

In recent years, regulators have passed legislation making it difficult to conduct SPE-related transactions off-balance-sheet. For instance, in 2001 the FASB published *SFAS 140,* that prescribed the conditions for asset securitization to be treated as a sale; that is, conditions under which the company can consider the securitized assets as sold and remove them from the balance sheet. To account for a securitization as a sale, the SPE must be an independent entity with sufficient equity capital to finance its ongoing operations without the support of the sponsoring company. These SPEs are called Qualifying Special Purpose Entities (QSPEs). Many previously existing SPEs did not meet these independence and capitalization conditions and, as a result, the sponsoring companies were forced to consolidate the SPE balance sheets. By consolidating the SPE, the sponsoring company includes the SPE's assets and liabilities on-balance-sheet, thus negating any financial reporting benefits of the off-balance-sheet financing. Since the passage of this standard, companies have been careful to structure their SPEs as QSPEs to avoid consolidation, and to be able to treat the transfer of securitized assets as sales and to remove the asset from the balance sheet. (Ford Credit's SPEs are structured as QSPEs to avoid consolidation.)

Subsequent to passage of *SFAS 140,* the FASB issued Interpretation Number 46R (FIN 46R), *Consolidation of Variable Interest Entities, an Interpretation of ARB No. 51* in 2003. (FASB issues Interpretations, FINS, periodically to modify or extend existing accounting standards.) This interpretation identified a new class of SPEs, called Variable Interest Entities (VIEs) and the characteristics of VIEs that require consolidation. Generally, any SPE that lacks independence from the sponsoring company (that is, does not qualify as a QSPE) and lacks sufficient capital to conduct its operations apart from the sponsoring company, must be consolidated with the entity that bears the greatest risk of loss and stands to reap the greatest rewards from the SPE's activities. That entity is called the *primary beneficiary*. VIEs can only be consolidated with the primary beneficiary, defined as the entity that bears most of the risk and enjoys most of the potential return. In a joint venture, entities typically share risks and rewards equally. As a result, no primary beneficiary exists. These joint ventures are accounted for under the equity method (see Module 7). As such, the investor company's balance sheet shows only the net investment in the VIE, thereby moving substantial assets and liabilities off-balance-sheet. This structure presents a different set of analysis issues as we discuss in Module 7.

We have witnessed a marked increase in the use of QSPEs in recent years. These entities are structured with the degree of independence and capital investment necessary to avoid consolidation. Ford discloses that the securitization of its consumer loans is a substantial source of liquidity. This is true for many companies that utilize this method of financing.

---

[12] RNOA is improved so long as the increase in asset turnover (NOAT) is not offset by a reduction in operating profit margin (NOPM) due to the increased cost of using the SPE structure (such as from purchasing goods in a finished state from wholesalers rather than manufacturing those goods, selling receivables at a discount, or leasing property from outside investors). This is a reasonable assumption; because, otherwise, the sponsoring company would likely not have created the SPE and transferred assets.

Unfortunately, GAAP does not mandate disclosure of summary balance sheets and income statements of QSPEs. Therefore, consolidation of these entities for analysis purposes is not possible. Nevertheless, in our analysis of companies, we must be aware of this financing source and assess its continued viability, just as we must assess a company's access to other sources of capital to meet liquidity needs.

Following are two analysis implications related to SPEs.

- **Cost of capital.** As discussed, SPEs reduce business risk and bankruptcy risk for their lenders. Consequently, the sponsoring company is able to obtain capital at a lower cost. Ford Motor Company (the manufacturer), for example, has witnessed a reduction in its credit ratings and a consequent increase in its cost of borrowed funds. Ordinarily, its negative credit rating would be ascribed to its subsidiaries as well, including its finance subsidiary. Using SPEs, however, the finance subsidiary, Ford Credit, is able to obtain financing at lower interest rates, which allows it to pass along that lower cost in the form of lower interest rates on auto and other loans to its customers. Without that financing source, Ford Credit would be less competitive in the market place vis-à-vis other, financially stronger, financial institutions.

- **Liquidity.** Financial institutions, and finance subsidiaries of manufacturing companies, rely on a business model of generating a high volume of loans, each of which carries a relatively small profit (spread of the interest rate over the cost of the funds). If they were forced to hold all of those loans on their own balance sheets, they would eventually need to raise costly equity capital to balance the increase in debt financing. That would also serve to reduce their competitiveness in the marketplace. These companies must, therefore, be able to package loans for sale, a crucial source of liquidity.

Given the importance of the cash flows to Ford Motor Company contributed by its Ford Credit financing subsidiary, analysts would become concerned about the welfare of the overall entity were there indications that its SPE financing sources would no longer be available (say, if further accounting standards limited Ford's ability to remove these loans from its consolidated balance sheet and record their transfer to the SPE as a sale). Analysts would also become concerned if the credit markets no longer favored this SPE structure as a financing mechanism (say, if the presumed bankruptcy protection of the SPEs was ultimately proven to be false following the bankruptcy of the sponsoring company and the consequent bankruptcy of an SPE that it sponsored). Neither of these events has occurred, and lenders rely on legal opinions that SPEs are "bankruptcy remote." Analysts must always assess these risks when assessing the financial strength of companies that rely on the SPE financial structure.

## MODULE-END REVIEW

Following is the footnote disclosure relating to General Motors' receivable securitization program from its 2005 10-K report.

> GM and GMAC use off-balance sheet arrangements where the economics and sound business principles warrant their use. GM's principal use of off-balance sheet arrangements occurs in connection with the securitization and sale of financial assets generated or acquired in the ordinary course of business by GMAC and its subsidiaries and, to a lesser extent, by GM . . . The Corporation securitizes automotive and mortgage financial assets as a funding source. GMAC sells retail finance receivables, wholesale loans, residential mortgage loans, commercial mortgage loans and commercial mortgage securities.

1. Why does GM securitize its receivables?
2. What are the requirements for the transfer of these receivables to be recorded as a sale with consequent removal from the balance sheet?
3. What are the financial reporting implications if GM does not structure the transaction as a sale?

### Solution

1. Companies in the financial sector typically securitize receivables as a source of liquidity. Their business model is to realize comparatively low margins on a high volume of assets. As receivables are sold, the proceeds are reinvested into new loans that are, likewise, sold. GM realizes a small interest spread on each of these loans.
2. To account for the transfer as a sale, GM must sell the assets without recourse. That means that GM must "surrender control" of the assets transferred. On that point, "the transferee has the right to pledge

or exchange the assets" and GM has "surrendered control over the rights and obligations of the receivables."

3. If GM does not structure the transaction as a sale, the transferred assets remain on GM's balance sheet and no gain on sale is reported on GM's income statement. Such a transaction, thus, amounts to a secured borrowing. This would potentially compromise the liquidity goals of GM's securitization program.

# APPENDIX 10A: Amortization Component of Pension Expense

One of the more difficult aspects of pension accounting relates to the issue of what is recognized on-balance-sheet and what is disclosed in the footnotes off-balance-sheet. This is an important distinction, and the FASB is moving toward more on-balance-sheet recognition and less off-balance-sheet disclosure in two important initiatives that will result in new pension accounting rules. The first of these is to recognize on-balance-sheet the funded status of pension plans as described in the text. This first initiative has been enacted. The second initiative, which we discuss below, is to eliminate deferred gains and losses, and to require recognition in the income statement of *all* changes to pension assets and liabilities. This second initiative is still under discussion. Until this standard is enacted, deferred gains and losses will only impact reported pension expense via their amortization (the fourth component of pension expense described on page 10-14).

There are three sources of *unrecognized gains and losses*:

1. The difference between actual and expected return on pension investments.

2. Changes in actuarial assumptions such as expected wage inflation, termination and mortality rates, and the discount rate used to compute the present value of the projected benefit obligation.

3. Amendments to the pension plan to provide employees with additional benefits (called **prior service costs**).

Accounting for gains and losses resulting from these three sources is the same; specifically:

- Balance sheets report the net pension asset (overfunded status) or liability (underfunded status) irrespective of the magnitude of deferred gains and losses; that is, based solely on the relative balances of the pension assets and PBO accounts.

- Cumulative unrecognized gains and losses from all sources are recorded in one account, called deferred gains and losses, which is only disclosed in the footnotes, not on-balance-sheet.

- When the balance in the deferred gains and losses account exceeds prescribed levels, companies transfer a portion of the deferred gain or loss onto the balance sheet, with a matching expense on the income statement. This is the amortization process described in the text.

Recall that a company reports the *estimated* return on pension investments as a component (reduction) of pension expense. The pension assets, however, increase (decrease) by the *actual* return (loss). The difference between the two returns is referred to as a deferred (unrecognized) gain or loss. To illustrate, let's assume that the pension plan is underfunded at the beginning of the year by $200, with pension assets of $800, a PBO of $1,000, and no deferred gains or losses. Now, let's assume that actual returns for the year of, say, $100 exceed the long-term expected return of $70. We can illustrate the accounting for the deferred gain as follows:

| Year 1 | On-Balance-Sheet | | | Off-Balance-Sheet (Footnotes) | | |
| | Liabilities | Earned Capital | Income Statement | Pension Assets | PBO | Deferred Gains (Losses) |
| --- | --- | --- | --- | --- | --- | --- |
| Balance, Jan. 1 | $200 | | $ 0 | $800 | $1,000 | $ 0 |
| Return | (100) | $70 (Retained Earnings) 30 (AOCI) | 70 | 100 | | 30 |
| Balance, Dec. 31 | $100 | $70 (Retained Earnings) 30 (AOCI) | $70 | $900 | $1,000 | $30 |

The balance sheet at the beginning of the year reports the funded status of the pension plan as a $200 liability, reflecting the underfunded status of the pension plan. Neither the $800 pension asset account, nor the $1,000 PBO appear on-balance-sheet. Instead, their balances are only disclosed in a pension footnote.

During the year, pension assets (off-balance-sheet) increase by the actual return of $100 with no change in the PBO, thus decreasing the pension liability (negative funded status) by $100. The pension expense on the income statement, however, only reflects the expected return of $70, and retained earnings increase by that amount. The remaining $30 is recognized in accumulated other comprehensive income (AOCI), a component of earned capital.

These deferred gains and losses do not affect reported profit until they exceed prescribed limits, after which the excess is gradually recognized in income.[13] For example, assume that in the following year, $5 of the $30 deferred gain is amortized (recognized on-balance-sheet). This amortization would result in the following effects:

| Year 2 | On-Balance-Sheet | | | Off-Balance-Sheet (Footnotes) | | |
| | Liabilities | Earned Capital | Income Statement | Pension Assets | PBO | Deferred Gains (Losses) |
| --- | --- | --- | --- | --- | --- | --- |
| Balance, Jan. 1....... | $100 | $70 (Retained Earnings) 30 (AOCI) | $ 0 | $900 | $1,000 | $30 |
| Amortization......... | | $ 5 (Retained Earnings) | 5 | | | (5) |
| Balance, Dec. 31 ..... | $100 | $ 75 (Retained Earnings) 25 (AOCI) | $ 5 | $900 | $1,000 | $25 |

The deferred gain is reduced by $5 and is now recognized in reported income as a reduction of pension expense. (This amortization is the fourth line of the Net Pension Expense computation table from page 10-18.) This is the only change, as the pension assets still report a balance of $900 and the PBO reports a balance of $1,000, for a funded status of $(100) that is reported as a liability on the balance sheet.

In addition to the difference between actual and expected gains (losses) on pension assets, the deferred gains (losses) account includes increases or decreases in the PBO balance that result from changes in assumptions used to compute it, namely, the expected rate of wage inflation, termination and mortality rates for employees, and changes in the discount rate used to compute the present value of the pension obligations. Some of these can be offsetting, and all accumulate in the same deferred gains (losses) account. Justification for off-balance-sheet treatment of these items was the expectation that their offsetting nature would combine to keep the magnitude of deferred gains (losses) small. It is only in relatively extreme circumstances that this account becomes large enough to warrant amortization and, consequently, on-balance-sheet recognition. Further, the amortization effect on reported pension expense is usually small.

# GUIDANCE ANSWERS

**MANAGERIAL DECISION**    **You are the Division President**

Lease terms that are not advantageous to your company but are structured merely to achieve off-balance-sheet financing can destroy shareholder value. Long-term shareholder value is created by managing your operation well, including negotiating leases with acceptable terms. Lease footnote disclosures also provide sufficient information for skilled analysts to undo the operating lease treatment. This means that you can end up with effective capitalization of a lease with lease terms that are not in the best interests of your company and with few benefits from off-balance-sheet financing. There is also the potential for lost credibility with stakeholders.

---

[13] The upper (lower) bound on the deferred gains (losses) account is 10% of the PBO or Plan Asset account balance, whichever is greater, at the beginning of the year. Once this limit is exceeded, the excess is amortized until the account balance is below that threshold, irrespective of whether such reduction results from amortization, or changes in the PBO or Pension Asset accounts (from changes in actuarial assumptions, company contributions, or positive investment returns).

# DISCUSSION QUESTIONS

**Q10-1.** What are the financial reporting differences between an operating lease and a capital lease? Explain.

**Q10-2.** Are footnote disclosures sufficient to overcome nonrecognition on the balance sheet of assets and related liabilities for operating leases? Explain.

**Q10-3.** Is the expense of a lease over its entire life the same whether or not it is capitalized? Explain.

**Q10-4.** What are the economic and accounting differences between a defined contribution plan and a defined benefit plan?

**Q10-5.** Under what circumstances will a company report a net pension asset? A net pension liability?

**Q10-6.** What are the components of pension expense that are reported in the income statement?

**Q10-7.** What effect does the use of expected returns on pension investments and the deferral of unexpected gains and losses on those investments have on income?

**Q10-8.** What is a special purpose entity (SPE)? Provide an example of the use of a SPE as a financing vehicle.

**Q10-9.** What effect does FIN 46R have on both accounting for SPEs and the balance sheets of companies that sponsor them?

# MINI EXERCISES

**M10-10. Analyzing and Interpreting Lease Footnote Disclosures** **(LO1)**

YUM! Brands, Inc.
(YUM)

YUM! Brands, Inc., discloses the following schedule to its 2005 10-K report relating to its leasing activities.

Future minimum commitments and amounts to be received as lessor or sublessor under non-cancelable leases are set forth below:

| Commitments ($ millions) | Capital | Operating |
|---|---|---|
| 2006 | $ 16 | $ 362 |
| 2007 | 15 | 326 |
| 2008 | 14 | 286 |
| 2009 | 14 | 258 |
| 2010 | 13 | 230 |
| Thereafter | 91 | 1,218 |
| | $163 | $2,680 |

a. Yum reports both capital and operating leases. In general, what effects does each of these lease types have on Yum's balance sheet and its income statement?

b. What types of adjustments might we consider to Yum's balance sheet and income statement for analysis purposes?

**M10-11. Analyzing and Capitalizing Operating Lease Payments Disclosed in Footnotes** **(LO1)**

Continental Airlines,
Inc. (CAL)

Continental discloses the following in the footnotes to its 10-K report relating to its leasing activities.

| Year ending December 31 ($ millions) | Capital Leases | Aircraft Operating Leases |
|---|---|---|
| 2006 | $ 39 | $ 1,003 |
| 2007 | 40 | 966 |
| 2008 | 46 | 955 |
| 2009 | 16 | 910 |
| 2010 | 16 | 924 |
| Later years | 457 | 6,310 |
| Total minimum lease payments | 614 | $11,068 |
| Less: amount representing interest | 341 | |
| Present value of capital leases | 273 | |
| Less: current maturities of capital leases | 22 | |
| Long-term capital leases | $251 | |

Operating leases are not reflected on-balance-sheet. In our analysis of a company, we often desire to capitalize these operating leases, that is, add the present value of the future operating lease payments to both the reported assets and liabilities. (*a*) Compute the present value of Continental's operating lease payments assuming a 7% discount rate (the approximate implicit rate on the capitalized leases). (*b*) What effect does capitalization of operating leases have on Continental's total liabilities (it reported total liabilities of $10,303 million for 2005).

**M10-12. Analyzing and Interpreting Pension Disclosures—Expenses and Returns** (LO2)

American Express discloses the following pension footnote in its 10-K report.

American Express (AXP)

| (Millions) | 2005 |
| --- | --- |
| Service cost | $104 |
| Interest cost | 117 |
| Expected return on plan assets | (141) |
| Other | 32 |
| Net periodic pension benefit cost | $112 |

a. How much pension expense does American Express report in its 2005 income statement?
b. Explain, in general, how expected return on plan assets affects reported pension expense. How did expected return affect American Express' 2005 pension expense?
c. Explain use of the word 'expected' as it relates to pension plan investments.

**M10-13. Analyzing and Interpreting Pension Disclosures—Expenses and Returns** (LO2)

YUM! Brands, Inc., discloses the following pension footnote in its 10-K report.

YUM! Brands, Inc. (YUM)

| Pension Benefits ($ millions) | 2005 | 2004 |
| --- | --- | --- |
| Benefit obligation at beginning of year | $700 | $629 |
| Service cost | 33 | 32 |
| Interest cost | 43 | 39 |
| Plan amendments | — | 1 |
| Curtailment gain | (2) | (2) |
| Settlement loss | 1 | — |
| Benefits and expenses paid | (33) | (26) |
| Actuarial (gain) loss | 73 | 27 |
| Benefit obligation end of year | $815 | $700 |

a. Explain the terms "service cost" and "interest cost."
b. How do actuarial losses arise?
c. The fair market value of YUM!'s plan assets is $610 million as of 2005. What is the funded status of the plan, and how will this be reflected on YUM!'s balance sheet?

**M10-14. Analyzing and Interpreting Pension Plan Benefit Footnote** (LO2)

YUM! Brands, Inc. discloses the following pension footnote in its 10-K report.

YUM! Brands, Inc. (YUM)

| Pension Benefits ($ millions) | 2005 | 2004 |
| --- | --- | --- |
| **Change in plan assets** | | |
| Fair value of plan assets at beginning of year | $518 | $438 |
| Actual return on plan assets | 63 | 53 |
| Employer contributions | 64 | 54 |
| Benefits paid | (33) | (26) |
| Administrative expenses | (2) | (1) |
| Fair value of plan assets end of year | $610 | $518 |

   *a.* How does the "actual return on plan assets" of $63 million affect YUM!'s reported profits for 2005?
   *b.* What are the cash flow implications of the pension plan for YUM! in 2005?
   *c.* YUM!'s pension plan paid out $33 million in benefits during 2005. Where else is this payment reflected?

**M10-15. Analyzing and Interpreting Retirement Benefit Footnote   (LO2)**

Abercrombie and Fitch (ANF)

Abercrombie and Fitch discloses the following footnote relating to its retirement plans in its 2005 10-K report.

> **RETIREMENT BENEFITS**  The Company maintains a qualified defined contribution retirement plan and a nonqualified retirement plan. Participation in the qualified plan is available to all associates who have completed 1,000 or more hours of service with the Company during certain 12-month periods and attained the age of 21. Participation in the nonqualified plan is subject to service and compensation requirements. The Company's contributions to these plans are based on a percentage of associates' eligible annual compensation. The cost of these plans was $10.5 million in Fiscal 2005, $9.9 million in Fiscal 2004 and $7.0 million in Fiscal 2003.

   *a.* Does Abercrombie have a defined contribution or defined benefit pension plan? Explain.
   *b.* How does Abercrombie account for its contributions to its retirement plan?
   *c.* How does Abercrombie report its obligation for its retirement plan on the balance sheet?

**M10-16. Analyzing and Interpreting Disclosure on Variable Interest Entities (VIEs)   (LO3)**

Dow Chemical Company (DOW)

Dow Chemical Company provided the following footnote in its 2002 10-K report relating to special purpose entities, which would now be classified as variable interest entities (VIEs).

> Dow has operating leases with various special purpose entities. Nine of these entities qualify as variable interest entities ("VIEs") under *FIN No. 46*, "Consolidation of Variable Interest Entities." Based on the current terms of the lease agreements and the residual value guarantees Dow provides to the lessors, the Company expects to be the primary beneficiary of the VIEs. As a result, if the facts and circumstances remain the same, Dow would be required to consolidate the assets and liabilities held by these VIEs in the third quarter of 2003.

Three years later, in its 2005 10-K report, Dow Chemical provided the following update.

> In the second quarter of 2003, Dow terminated its lease of an ethylene facility in The Netherlands with a variable interest entity ("VIE") and entered into a lease with a new owner trust, which is also a VIE. However, Dow is not the primary beneficiary of the owner trust and, therefore, is not required to consolidate the owner trust. Based on the valuation completed in mid-2003, the facility was valued at $394 million. Upon expiration of the lease, which matures in 2014, Dow may purchase the facility for an amount based upon a fair market value determination. At December 31, 2005, Dow had provided to the owner trust a residual value guarantee of $363 million, which represents Dow's maximum exposure to loss under the lease. Given the productive nature of the facility, it is probable that the facility will have continuing value to Dow or the owner trust in excess of the residual value guarantee.

   *a.* In general, what business reason(s) prompted Dow to establish these VIEs?
   *b.* How does Dow account for these VIEs in 2002? In 2005?
   *c.* What would have been the effect on Dow's balance sheet had consolidation of its VIEs been required under FIN 46R?
   *d.* Why do you suppose Dow restructured its lease of an ethylene facility as reported in 2005?

**M10-17. Analyzing and Interpreting Disclosure on Contract Manufacturers   (LO3)**

Nike, Inc. (NKE)

Nike reports the following information relating to its manufacturing activities in footnotes to its 2005 10-K report.

> **Manufacturing**  Virtually all of our footwear is produced outside of the United States. In fiscal 2005, contract suppliers in China, Vietnam, Indonesia and Thailand manufactured 36 percent, 26 percent, 22 percent and 15 percent of total NIKE brand footwear, respectively. We also have manufacturing agreements with independent factories in Argentina, Brazil, India, Italy, Mexico and South Africa to manufacture footwear for sale primarily within those countries. Our largest single footwear supplier accounted for approximately 7 percent of total fiscal 2005 footwear production.

   *a.* What effect does the use of contract manufacturers have on Nike's balance sheet?
   *b.* How does Nike's use of contract manufacturers affect Nike's return on net operating assets (RNOA) and its components? Explain.
   *c.* Nike executes agreements with its contract manufacturers to purchase their output. How are such "executory contracts" reported under GAAP? Does your answer suggest a possible motivation for the use of contract manufacturing?

**M10-18. Analyzing and Interpreting Pension Plan Benefit Footnotes (LO2)**

Lockheed Martin Corporation discloses the following funded status for its defined benefit pension plans in its 10-K report.

Lockheed Martin Corp. (LMT)

| Defined Benefit Pension Plans (In millions) | 2005 | 2004 |
|---|---|---|
| Unfunded status of the plans....... | $(4,989) | $(4,876) |

The company also reports that it is obligated for the following expected payments to retirees in the next five years.

| (In millions) | Pension Benefits |
|---|---|
| 2006 ........................ | $1,380 |
| 2007 ........................ | 1,430 |
| 2008 ........................ | 1,490 |
| 2009 ........................ | 1,550 |
| 2010 ........................ | 1,610 |

Lockheed contributed $1,054 million to its pension plan assets in 2005, up from $505 million in the prior year.

a. How is this funded status reported in Lockheed's balance sheet under current GAAP?
b. How should we interpret this funded status in our analysis of the company?
c. Lockheed reports total assets of $27.7 billion and stockholders' equity of $7.9 billion. How does this funded status, and the projected benefit payments, impact our evaluation of Lockheed's financial condition?
d. Lockheed reports $3.2 billion of net cash inflows from operating activities and $900 million in capital expenditures for 2005. How does this information impact our evaluation of Lockheed's financial condition?

# EXERCISES

**E10-19. Analyzing and Interpreting Leasing Footnote (LO1)**

Fortune Brands, Inc., reports the following footnote relating to its leased facilities in its 2005 10-K report.

Fortune Brands, Inc. (FO)

Future minimum rental payments under noncancelable operating leases as of December 31, 2005 are as follows:

| (In millions) | |
|---|---|
| 2006 ........................... | $ 45.6 |
| 2007 ........................... | 33.5 |
| 2008 ........................... | 26.9 |
| 2009 ........................... | 20.2 |
| 2010 ........................... | 15.7 |
| Remainder ...................... | 37.3 |
| Total minimum rental payments ....... | $179.2 |

a. Assuming that this is the only information available about its leasing activities, does Fortune Brands classify its leases as operating or capital? Explain.
b. What effect has its lease classification had on Fortune Brands' balance sheet? Over the life of the lease, what effect does this classification have on net income?
c. Compute the present value of these operating leases using a discount rate of 7%. How might we use this information in our analysis of the company?

E10-20. **Analyzing and Interpreting Footnote on Operating and Capital Leases** (LO1)

Verizon Communications, Inc., provides the following footnote relating to its leasing activities in its 10-K report.

The aggregate minimum rental commitments under noncancelable leases for the periods shown at December 31, 2005, are as follows:

| Years (dollars in millions) | Capital Leases | Operating Leases |
|---|---|---|
| 2006 . . . . . . . . . . . . . . . . . . . . . . . . . . . . . . . . . . . . . . | $ 37 | $1,184 |
| 2007 . . . . . . . . . . . . . . . . . . . . . . . . . . . . . . . . . . . . . . | 28 | 791 |
| 2008 . . . . . . . . . . . . . . . . . . . . . . . . . . . . . . . . . . . . . . | 21 | 652 |
| 2009 . . . . . . . . . . . . . . . . . . . . . . . . . . . . . . . . . . . . . . | 13 | 504 |
| 2010 . . . . . . . . . . . . . . . . . . . . . . . . . . . . . . . . . . . . . . | 12 | 316 |
| Thereafter . . . . . . . . . . . . . . . . . . . . . . . . . . . . . . . . | 55 | 1,050 |
| Total minimum rental commitments . . . . . . . . . . . . . . | 166 | $4,497 |
| Less interest and executory costs . . . . . . . . . . . . . . . | (54) | |
| Present value of minimum lease payments . . . . . . . . . | 112 | |
| Less current installments . . . . . . . . . . . . . . . . . . . . . . | (17) | |
| Long-term obligation at December 31, 2005 . . . . . . . . | $ 95 | |

a. Assuming that this is the only available information relating to its leasing activities, what amount does Verizon report on its balance sheet for its lease obligations? Does this amount represent its total obligation to lessors? How do you know?

b. What effect has its lease classification as capital or operating had on Verizon's balance sheet? Over the life of its leases, what effect does this lease classification have on its net income?

c. Compute the present value of Verizon's operating leases, assuming a 10% discount rate (the approximate implicit rate on the capitalized leases). How might we use this additional information in our analysis of the company?

E10-21. **Analyzing, Interpreting and Capitalizing Operating Leases** (LO1)

Staples, Inc., reports the following footnote relating to its capital and operating leases in its 2005 10-K report ($ thousands).

Future minimum lease commitments due for retail and support facilities (including lease commitments for 54 retail stores not yet opened at January 28, 2006) and equipment leases under non-cancelable operating leases are as follows (in thousands):

| Fiscal Year | Total |
|---|---|
| 2006 . . . . . . . . . . . . . . . | $ 617,021 |
| 2007 . . . . . . . . . . . . . . . | 593,176 |
| 2008 . . . . . . . . . . . . . . . | 558,355 |
| 2009 . . . . . . . . . . . . . . . | 526,981 |
| 2010 . . . . . . . . . . . . . . . | 491,310 |
| Thereafter . . . . . . . . . . . | 2,460,031 |
| | $5,246,874 |

a. What dollar adjustment(s) might we consider to Staples' balance sheet and income statement given this information and assuming that Staples intermediate-term borrowing rate is 7%? Explain.

b. Would the adjustment from part a make a substantial difference to Staples' total liabilities? (Staples reported total liabilities of $3,251,118 ($ 000s) for 2005.)

**E10-22.** **Analyzing, Interpreting and Capitalizing Operating Leases** **(LO1)**

YUM! Brands, Inc., reports the following footnote relating to its capital and operating leases in its 2005 10-K report ($ millions).

YUM! Brands, Inc. (YUM)

Future minimum commitments under non-cancelable leases are set forth below:

| Commitments | Capital | Operating |
|---|---|---|
| 2006 . . . . . . . . . . . . . . . | $ 16 | $ 362 |
| 2007 . . . . . . . . . . . . . . | 15 | 326 |
| 2008 . . . . . . . . . . . . . . | 14 | 286 |
| 2009 . . . . . . . . . . . . . . | 14 | 258 |
| 2010 . . . . . . . . . . . . . . | 13 | 230 |
| Thereafter . . . . . . . . . . | 91 | 1,218 |
| | $163 | $2,680 |

a.  What adjustment(s), assuming a discount rate of 7%, might we consider making to Yum's balance sheet and income statement given this information? Explain.

b.  Would the adjustment from part *a* make a sizeable difference to Yum's total liabilities? Yum reported total liabilities of $4,249 million for 2005.

**E10-23.** **Analyzing, Interpreting and Capitalizing Operating Leases** **(LO1)**

Nordstrom reports the following footnote relating to its capital and operating leases in its fiscal 2005 10-K report.

Nordstrom (JWN)

**Leases**   Future minimum lease payments as of January 28, 2006 are as follows:

| Fiscal Year ($000) | Capital Leases | Operating Leases |
|---|---|---|
| 2006 . . . . . . . . . . . . . . . . . . . . . . . . . . . . . . . . . . . . . . | $ 1,946 | $ 73,389 |
| 2007 . . . . . . . . . . . . . . . . . . . . . . . . . . . . . . . . . . . . . | 1,946 | 73,296 |
| 2008 . . . . . . . . . . . . . . . . . . . . . . . . . . . . . . . . . . . . . | 1,946 | 70,525 |
| 2009 . . . . . . . . . . . . . . . . . . . . . . . . . . . . . . . . . . . . . | 1,376 | 67,892 |
| 2010 . . . . . . . . . . . . . . . . . . . . . . . . . . . . . . . . . . . . . | 1,270 | 63,524 |
| Thereafter . . . . . . . . . . . . . . . . . . . . . . . . . . . . . . . | 6,990 | 332,016 |
| Total minimum lease payments . . . . . . . . . . . . . . . . | 15,474 | $680,642 |
| Less amount representing interest . . . . . . . . . . . . . . | (6,137) | |
| Present value of net minimum lease payments . . . . . | $ 9,337 | |

What adjustment(s) might we consider to Nordstrom's balance sheet and income statement given this information and assuming that Nordstrom's discount rate is 12% (the approximate implicit rate in its capital leases)? Explain.

**E10-24. Analyzing and Interpreting Pension Disclosures** (LO2)

Ford Motor Company (F)

Ford Motor Company reports the following pension footnote in its 10-K report.

| | Pension Benefits | |
| --- | --- | --- |
| ($ millions) | U.S. Plans 2005 | Non-U.S. Plans 2005 |
| **Change in Benefit Obligation** | | |
| Benefit obligation at January 1............ | $43,077 | $29,452 |
| Service cost.......................... | 734 | 630 |
| Interest cost........................ | 2,398 | 1,408 |
| Amendments........................ | — | 218 |
| Separation programs................... | 179 | 422 |
| Plan participant contributions............ | 41 | 146 |
| Benefits paid....................... | (2,856) | (1,355) |
| Foreign exchange translation............. | — | (2,936) |
| Divestiture........................... | (400) | (163) |
| Actuarial (gain) loss.................. | 722 | 2,878 |
| Benefit obligation at December 31......... | $43,895 | $30,700 |
| **Change in Plan Assets** | | |
| Fair value of plan assets at January 1...... | $39,628 | $20,595 |
| Actual return on plan assets............. | 3,922 | 3,239 |
| Company contributions................. | 1,432 | 1,355 |
| Plan participant contributions............ | 41 | 150 |
| Benefits paid....................... | (2,856) | (1,355) |
| Foreign exchange translation............. | — | (1,924) |
| Divestiture........................... | (309) | (95) |
| Other................................ | (1) | (38) |
| Fair value of plan assets at December 31 ... | $41,857 | $21,927 |

Ford also discloses the following expected payments to its retirees.

| | Pension Benefits | |
| --- | --- | --- |
| | U.S. Plans Benefit Payments | Non-U.S. Plans Benefit Payments |
| 2006.................. | $ 2,870 | $1,370 |
| 2007.................. | 2,940 | 1,230 |
| 2008.................. | 3,010 | 1,250 |
| 2009.................. | 3,050 | 1,290 |
| 2010.................. | 3,070 | 1,330 |
| 2011–2015............. | 15,410 | 7,340 |

a. Describe what is meant by *service cost* and *interest cost*.
b. What is the total amount paid to retirees during fiscal 2005 for its U.S. and non-U.S. plans? What is the source of funds to make these payments to retirees?
c. Compute the 2005 funded status for Ford's pension plan.
d. What are actuarial gains and losses? What are the plan amendment adjustments, and how do they differ from the actuarial gains and losses?
e. In 2005, Ford contributed $2,787 million ($1,432 million + $1,355 million) to its pension plan in 2005. Ford reports $21.7 billion of net cash inflows from operating activities and $7.5 billion in capital expenditures for 2005. How does this information impact our evaluation of Ford's financial condition given the pension disclosures discussed above?

**E10-25.** **Analyzing and Interpreting Pension and Health Care Footnote** (LO2)

Xerox reports the following pension footnote as part of its 2005 10-K report.

Xerox Corporation
(XRX)

| (in millions) | Pension Benefits | | Other Benefits | |
|---|---|---|---|---|
| | 2005 | 2004 | 2005 | 2004 |
| **Change in Benefit Obligation** | | | | |
| Benefit obligation, January 1 . . . . . . . . . . . . . . | $10,028 | $8,971 | $1,662 | $1,579 |
| Service cost . . . . . . . . . . . . . . . . . . . . . . . . . . | 234 | 222 | 19 | 22 |
| Interest cost . . . . . . . . . . . . . . . . . . . . . . . . . | 581 | 660 | 90 | 89 |
| Plan participants' contributions . . . . . . . . . . | 11 | 14 | 15 | 18 |
| Plan amendments . . . . . . . . . . . . . . . . . . . . | 30 | 232 | 44 | — |
| Actuarial loss (gain) . . . . . . . . . . . . . . . . . . . | 527 | 272 | (54) | 70 |
| Currency exchange rate changes . . . . . . . . . | (486) | 356 | 4 | 6 |
| Curtailments. . . . . . . . . . . . . . . . . . . . . . . . . . | (5) | (2) | — | — |
| Special termination benefits. . . . . . . . . . . . . | — | 2 | — | — |
| Benefits paid/settlements. . . . . . . . . . . . . . . | (618) | (699) | (127) | (122) |
| Benefit obligation, December 31 . . . . . . . . . | $10,302 | $10,028 | $1,653 | $1,662 |
| **Change in Plan Assets** | | | | |
| Fair value of plan assets, January 1. . . . . . . . | $ 8,110 | $ 7,301 | $ — | $ — |
| Actual return on plan assets. . . . . . . . . . . . . | 933 | 772 | — | — |
| Employer contribution . . . . . . . . . . . . . . . . . | 388 | 409 | 112 | 104 |
| Plan participants' contributions . . . . . . . . . . | 11 | 14 | 15 | 18 |
| Currency exchange rate changes . . . . . . . . . | (418) | 311 | — | — |
| Transfers/divestitures . . . . . . . . . . . . . . . . . . | 38 | 2 | — | — |
| Benefits paid/settlements. . . . . . . . . . . . . . . | (618) | (699) | (127) | (122) |
| Fair value of plan assets, December 31. . . . . | $ 8,444 | $ 8,110 | $ — | $ — |

| (in millions) | Pension Benefits | | | Other Benefits | | |
|---|---|---|---|---|---|---|
| | 2005 | 2004 | 2003 | 2005 | 2004 | 2003 |
| **Components of Net Periodic Benefit Cost** | | | | | | |
| Defined benefit plans | | | | | | |
| Service cost . . . . . . . . . . . . . . . . . . . . . . . . . . | $234 | $222 | $197 | $ 20 | $ 22 | $ 26 |
| Interest cost . . . . . . . . . . . . . . . . . . . . . . . . . | 581 | 660 | 934 | 90 | 89 | 91 |
| Expected return on plan assets . . . . . . . . . . . | (622) | (678) | (940) | — | — | — |
| Recognized net actuarial loss . . . . . . . . . . . . | 98 | 104 | 53 | 31 | 24 | 13 |
| Amortization of prior service cost . . . . . . . . . | (3) | (1) | — | (24) | (24) | (18) |
| Recognized net transition (asset) obligation . . . | 1 | (1) | — | — | — | — |
| Recognized curtailment/settlement loss (gain) . . | 54 | 44 | 120 | — | — | (4) |
| Net periodic benefit cost . . . . . . . . . . . . . . . | 343 | 350 | 364 | 117 | 111 | 108 |
| Special termination benefits. . . . . . . . . . . . . | — | 2 | — | — | — | — |
| Defined contribution plans . . . . . . . . . . . . . . | 71 | 69 | 62 | — | — | — |
| Total . . . . . . . . . . . . . . . . . . . . . . . . . . . . . . . | $414 | $421 | $426 | $117 | $111 | $108 |

a. Describe what is meant by *service cost* and *interest cost* (the service and interest costs appear both in the reconciliation of the PBO and in the computation of pension expense).

b. What is the actual return on pension and health care plan investments in 2005? Was Xerox's profitability impacted by this amount?

c. Provide an example under which an "actuarial loss," such as the $527 million charge in 2005 that Xerox reports, might arise.

    *d.* What is the source of funds to make payments to retirees?
    *e.* How much cash did Xerox contribute to its pension and health care plans in 2005?
    *f.* How much cash did retirees receive in 2005? How much cash did Xerox pay retirees?
    *g.* Show the computation of its 2005 funded status for the pension and health care plans.

**E10-26. Analyzing and Interpreting Pension and Health Care Disclosures** (LO2)

Verizon (VZ)

Verizon reports the following pension and health care benefits footnote as part of its 10-K report.

| Obligations At December 31 (dollars in millions) | Pension 2005 | Pension 2004 | Health Care and Life 2005 | Health Care and Life 2004 |
|---|---|---|---|---|
| **Change in Benefit Obligation** | | | | |
| Beginning of year | $37,395 | $40,968 | $27,077 | $24,581 |
| Service cost | 721 | 712 | 373 | 282 |
| Interest cost | 2,070 | 2,289 | 1,519 | 1,479 |
| Plan amendments | 181 | (65) | 59 | 248 |
| Actuarial loss, net | 390 | 2,467 | 520 | 2,017 |
| Benefits paid | (2,977) | (2,884) | (1,706) | (1,532) |
| Termination benefits | 11 | 4 | 1 | 2 |
| Settlements | (35) | (6,105) | — | — |
| Acquisitions and divestitures, net | (194) | — | (34) | — |
| Other | (1) | 9 | — | — |
| End of year | $37,561 | $37,395 | $27,809 | $27,077 |
| **Change in Plan Assets** | | | | |
| Beginning of year | $39,106 | $42,776 | $ 4,549 | $ 4,467 |
| Actual return on plan assets | 4,246 | 4,874 | 348 | 471 |
| Company contributions | 852 | 443 | 1,085 | 1,143 |
| Benefits paid | (2,977) | (2,884) | (1,706) | (1,532) |
| Settlements | (35) | (6,105) | — | — |
| Acquisitions and divestitures, net | (202) | 2 | — | — |
| End of year | $40,990 | $39,106 | $ 4,276 | $ 4,549 |

| Net Periodic Cost Years Ended December 31 (dollars in millions) | Pension 2005 | Pension 2004 | Pension 2003 | Health Care and Life 2005 | Health Care and Life 2004 | Health Care and Life 2003 |
|---|---|---|---|---|---|---|
| Service cost | $ 721 | $ 712 | $ 785 | $ 373 | $ 282 | $ 176 |
| Interest cost | 2,070 | 2,289 | 2,436 | 1,519 | 1,479 | 1,203 |
| Expected return on plan assets | (3,348) | (3,709) | (4,150) | (353) | (414) | (430) |
| Amortization of transition asset | — | (4) | (41) | 2 | 2 | 2 |
| Amortization of prior service cost | 45 | 60 | 23 | 285 | 234 | (9) |
| Actuarial loss (gain), net | 146 | 57 | (337) | 278 | 187 | 130 |
| Net periodic benefit (income) cost | $ (366) | $ (595) | $(1,284) | $2,104 | $1,770 | $1,072 |

    *a.* Describe what is meant by *service cost* and *interest cost*.
    *b.* What payments did retirees receive during fiscal 2005 from the pension and from the health care plans? What is the source of funds to make payments to retirees?
    *c.* Show the computation of Verizon's 2005 funded status for both the pension and health care plans.
    *d.* What expense does Verizon's income statement report for both its pension and health care plans?
    *e.* Explain the difference between the actuarial loss of $390 million that Verizon reported in its reconciliation of the PBO, and the loss relating to plan amendments of $181 million.

**E10-27. Analyzing and Interpreting Disclosure on Off-Balance-Sheet Financing (LO3)**

Harley-Davidson provides the following footnote in its 10-K report relating to the securitization of receivables by its finance subsidiary, Harley-Davidson Financial Services (HDFS).

Harley-Davidson, Inc. (HOG)

> **OFF-BALANCE-SHEET ARRANGEMENTS:** As part of its securitization program, HDFS transfers retail motorcycle loans to a special purpose bankruptcy-remote wholly-owned subsidiary. The subsidiary sells the retail loans to a securitization trust in exchange for the proceeds from asset-backed securities issued by the securitization trust. The asset-backed securities, usually notes with various maturities and interest rates, are secured by future collections of the purchased retail installment loans. Activities of the securitization trust are limited to acquiring retail loans, issuing asset-backed securities and making payments on securities to investors. Due to the nature of the assets held by the securitization trust and the limited nature of its activities, the securitization trusts are considered QSPEs as defined by SFAS No. 140. In accordance with SFAS No. 140, assets and liabilities of the QSPEs are not consolidated in the financial statements of the Company.
>
> HDFS does not guarantee payments on the securities issued by the securitization trusts or the projected cash flows from the related loans purchased from HDFS. Investors also do not have recourse to assets of HDFS for failure of the obligors on the retail loans to pay when due.

a. Describe in your own words, the securitization process employed by HDFS.
b. What is the importance of the characterization of its SPE as a Qualifying Special Purpose Entity (QSPE)?
c. What is the importance of the statement that HDFS does not guarantee obligations of its QSPE?
d. What is the importance of "bankruptcy remote." How is this achieved?
e. What are the analysis implications of the use of QSPEs?

# PROBLEMS

**P10-28. Analyzing, Interpreting and Capitalizing Operating Leases (LO1)**

The Abercrombie & Fitch 10-K report contains the following footnote relating to its leasing activities. This is the only information it discloses relating to its leasing activity.

Abercrombie & Fitch (ANF)

> At January 28, 2006, the Company was committed to non-cancelable leases with remaining terms of one to 15 years. A summary of operating lease commitments under non-cancelable leases follows (thousands):

| | |
|---|---|
| 2006 . . . . . . . . . . . . . . | $187,674 |
| 2007 . . . . . . . . . . . . . . | $187,397 |
| 2008 . . . . . . . . . . . . . . | $178,595 |
| 2009 . . . . . . . . . . . . . . | $169,856 |
| 2010 . . . . . . . . . . . . . . | $155,670 |
| Thereafter . . . . . . . . . . | $538,635 |

**Required**

a. What lease assets and lease liabilities does Abercrombie report on its balance sheet? How do we know?
b. What effect has the operating lease classification have on A&F's balance sheet? Over the life of the lease, what effect does this classification have on its net income?
c. Using a 7% discount rate, estimate the assets and liabilities that A&F fails to report as a result of its off-balance-sheet lease financing.
d. Assuming that its operating leases relate to real estate, and that A&F depreciated such assets on a straight-line basis with no salvage value and useful life of 8 years, estimate the effect on the company's operating profit before tax of capitalizing these operating leases.
e. How are the financial ratios from the ROE disaggregation (such as margin, turnover, and leverage) affected and in what direction (increased or decreased) if A&F's operating leases are capitalized?

**P10-29.** **Analyzing, Interpreting and Capitalizing Operating Leases** (LO1)

The Best Buy 10-K report has the following footnote related to its leasing activities.

The future minimum lease payments under our capital and operating leases by fiscal year at February 25, 2006, are as follows ($ millions):

| Fiscal Year | Capital Leases | Operating Leases |
|---|---|---|
| 2007 | $ 5 | $ 602 |
| 2008 | 4 | 605 |
| 2009 | 4 | 582 |
| 2010 | 3 | 546 |
| 2011 | 3 | 513 |
| Thereafter | 20 | 3,080 |
| Subtotal | 39 | $5,928 |
| Less: imputed interest | (12) | |
| Present value of lease obligations | $27 | |

**Required**

a. What is the balance of the lease liabilities reported on Best Buy's balance sheet?
b. What effect has the operating lease classification had on its balance sheet? Over the life of the lease, what effect does this classification have on its net income?
c. Compute the imputed rate on Best Buy's capital leases.
d. Use a 7% discount rate to estimate the assets and liabilities that Best Buy fails to report as a result of its off-balance-sheet lease financing.
e. Assuming that the operating leases relate to real estate, and that Best Buy depreciated such assets on a straight-line basis with no salvage value and a useful life of 11 years, estimate the effect on the company's operating profit before tax of capitalizing these operating leases.
f. How are financial ratios from the ROE disaggregation (such as margins, turnover, and leverage) affected and in what direction (increased or decreased) if Best Buy's operating leases are capitalized?

**P10-30.** **Analyzing, Interpreting and Capitalizing Operating Leases** (LO1)

FedEx reports total assets of $20,404 and total liabilities of $10,816 for 2005 ($ millions). Its 10-K report has the following footnote related to its leasing activities.

A summary of future minimum lease payments under capital leases at May 31, 2005 is as follows (in millions):

| | |
|---|---|
| 2006 | $121 |
| 2007 | 22 |
| 2008 | 99 |
| 2009 | 11 |
| 2010 | 96 |
| Thereafter | 130 |
| | 479 |
| Less amount representing interest | 78 |
| Present value of net minimum lease payments | $401 |

A summary of future minimum lease payments under non-cancelable operating leases (principally aircraft, retail locations and facilities) with an initial or remaining term in excess of one year at May 31, 2005 is as follows (in millions):

| | Aircraft and Related Equipment | Facilities and Other | Total |
|---|---|---|---|
| 2006 . . . . . . . . . . . . . . . . . . . | $   607 | $1,039 | $  1,646 |
| 2007 . . . . . . . . . . . . . . . . . . | 606 | 912 | 1,518 |
| 2008 . . . . . . . . . . . . . . . . . . | 585 | 771 | 1,356 |
| 2009 . . . . . . . . . . . . . . . . . . | 555 | 636 | 1,191 |
| 2010 . . . . . . . . . . . . . . . . . | 544 | 501 | 1,045 |
| Thereafter . . . . . . . . . . . . . . | 4,460 | 2,789 | 7,249 |
| | $7,357 | $6,648 | $14,005 |

**Required**

a.  What is the balance of lease assets and lease liabilities as reported on FedEx's balance sheet? Explain.

b.  Impute the discount rate that FedEx is using to compute the present value of its capital leases.

c.  Assuming a 3% discount rate, estimate the amount of assets and liabilities that FedEx fails to report as a result of its off-balance-sheet lease financing.

d.  Assuming that the operating leases relate to real estate, and that FedEx depreciated such assets on a straight-line basis with no salvage value and a useful life of 12 years, estimate the effect on the company's operating profit before tax of capitalizing these operating leases.

e.  How are financial ratios from the ROE disaggregation (such as margin, turnover, and leverage) affected and in what direction (increased or decreased) if FedEx's operating leases are capitalized?

f.  What portion of total lease liabilities did FedEx report on-balance-sheet and what portion is off-balance-sheet?

g.  Based on your analysis, do you believe that FedEx's balance sheet adequately reports its aircraft and facilities assets and related obligations? Explain.

**P10-31.  Analyzing and Interpreting Pension Disclosures   (LO2)**

DuPont's 10-K report has the following disclosures related to its retirement plans ($ millions).                DuPont (DD)

| ($ millions) | Pension Benefits | |
|---|---|---|
| | 2005 | 2004 |
| **Change in benefit obligation** | | |
| Benefit obligation at beginning of year . . . . . . | $21,757 | $21,196 |
| Service cost . . . . . . . . . . . . . . . . . . . . . . . . | 349 | 351 |
| Interest cost . . . . . . . . . . . . . . . . . . . . . . . . | 1,160 | 1,198 |
| Plan participants' contributions . . . . . . . . . . . | 11 | 12 |
| Actuarial loss (gain) . . . . . . . . . . . . . . . . . . | 1,537 | 1,409 |
| Foreign currency exchange rate changes . . . | (402) | 275 |
| Benefits paid . . . . . . . . . . . . . . . . . . . . . . . | (1,503) | (1,528) |
| Amendments . . . . . . . . . . . . . . . . . . . . . . . | 3 | 6 |
| Net effects of acquisitions/divestitures . . . . . | 23 | (1,162) |
| Benefit obligation at end of year . . . . . . . . . | $22,935 | $21,757 |
| **Change in plan assets** | | |
| Fair value of plan assets at beginning of year | $18,250 | $17,967 |
| Actual gain on plan assets . . . . . . . . . . . . . . | 2,038 | 2,182 |
| Foreign currency exchange rate changes . . . | (261) | 187 |
| Employer contributions . . . . . . . . . . . . . . . . | 1,253 | 709 |
| Plan participants' contributions . . . . . . . . . . | 11 | 12 |
| Benefits paid . . . . . . . . . . . . . . . . . . . . . . . | (1,503) | (1,528) |
| Net effects of acquisitions/divestitures . . . . . | 4 | (1,279) |
| Fair value of plan assets at end of year . . . . . | $19,792 | $18,250 |

| | Pension Benefits | | |
|---|---|---|---|
| **Components of net periodic benefit cost (credit)** | **2005** | **2004** | **2003** |
| Service cost . . . . . . . . . . . . . . . . . . . . . . . . . . . . . . . . . . . . . . . . . | $ 349 | $ 351 | $ 342 |
| Interest cost . . . . . . . . . . . . . . . . . . . . . . . . . . . . . . . . . . . . . . . . | 1,160 | 1,198 | 1,223 |
| Expected return on plan assets . . . . . . . . . . . . . . . . . . . . . . . | (1,416) | (1,343) | (1,368) |
| Amortization of transition asset . . . . . . . . . . . . . . . . . . . . . . . | (1) | (5) | (8) |
| Amortization of unrecognized loss. . . . . . . . . . . . . . . . . . . . . | 304 | 306 | 237 |
| Amortization of prior service cost . . . . . . . . . . . . . . . . . . . . | 37 | 42 | 51 |
| Curtailment/settlement (gain) loss . . . . . . . . . . . . . . . . . . . | (1) | 448 | 77 |
| Net periodic benefit cost . . . . . . . . . . . . . . . . . . . . . . . . . . | $ 432 | $ 997 | $ 554 |

| **Weighted-average assumptions used to determine net periodic benefit cost for years ended December 31** | Pension Benefits | |
|---|---|---|
| | **2005** | **2004** |
| Discount rate . . . . . . . . . . . . . . . . . . . . . . . . . . . . . . . . . . . . . . . . . . . . . . . . . . . . . . . . | 5.58% | 6.06% |
| Expected return on plan assets . . . . . . . . . . . . . . . . . . . . . . . . . . . . . . . . . . . . . . . . | 8.74% | 8.85% |
| Rate of compensation increase . . . . . . . . . . . . . . . . . . . . . . . . . . . . . . . . . . . . . . . | 4.29% | 4.29% |

The following benefit payments, which reflect future service, as appropriate, are expected to be paid:

| (In millions) | Pension Benefits |
|---|---|
| 2006 . . . . . . . . . . . . . . . . . . . . . . . | $1,449 |
| 2007 . . . . . . . . . . . . . . . . . . . . . . . | 1,432 |
| 2008 . . . . . . . . . . . . . . . . . . . . . . . | 1,420 |
| 2009 . . . . . . . . . . . . . . . . . . . . . . . | 1,417 |
| 2010 . . . . . . . . . . . . . . . . . . . . . . . | 1,417 |
| Years 2011–2015 . . . . . . . . . . . . . | 7,360 |

**Required**

a. How much pension expense (revenue) does DuPont report in its 2005 income statement? *432*

b. DuPont reports a $1,416 million expected return on pension plan assets as an offset to 2005 pension expense. Approximately, how is this amount computed? What is DuPont's actual gain or loss realized on its 2005 pension plan assets? What is the purpose of using this estimated amount instead of the actual gain or loss?

c. What factors affected DuPont's pension liability during 2005? What factors affected its pension plan assets during 2005?

d. What does the term *funded status* mean? What is the funded status of the 2005 DuPont pension plans?

e. DuPont reduced its discount rate from 6.06% to 5.58% in 2005. What effect(s) does this reduction have on its balance sheet and its income statement?

f. How did DuPont's pension plan affect the company's cash flow in 2005?

g. In 2005, DuPont contributed $1.253 billion to its pension plan.
  (1) DuPont reports total assets of $33.3 billon and stockholders' equity of $8.9 billion. How does this funded status, and the projected benefit payments, impact our evaluation of DuPont's financial condition.
  (2) DuPont reports $2.5 billion of net cash inflows from operating activities and $1.3 billion in capital expenditures for 2005. How does this information impact our evaluation of DuPont's financial condition.

**P10-32.** **Analyzing and Interpreting Pension Disclosures** (LO2)

Dow Chemical provides the following footnote disclosures in its 10-K report relating to its defined benefit pension plans and its other postretirement benefits.

Dow Chemical (DOW)

| Net Periodic Benefit Cost (Credit) for All Significant Plans | | | | | | |
|---|---|---|---|---|---|---|
| | Defined Benefit Pension Plans | | | Other Postretirement Benefits | | |
| In millions | 2005 | 2004 | 2003 | 2005 | 2004 | 2003 |
| Service cost | $ 279 | $ 260 | $ 242 | $ 24 | $ 24 | $ 31 |
| Interest cost | 815 | 804 | 773 | 124 | 125 | 134 |
| Expected return on plan assets | (1,056) | (1,092) | (1,082) | (27) | (23) | (19) |
| Amortization of prior service cost (credit) | 24 | 8 | 21 | (7) | (11) | (9) |
| Amortization of unrecognized loss | 123 | 39 | 13 | 10 | 8 | 8 |
| Special termination/curtailment cost | 2 | 42 | 5 | 6 | 37 | — |
| Net periodic benefit cost (credit) | $ 187 | $ 61 | $ (28) | $130 | $160 | $145 |

| Change in Projected Benefit Obligation, Plan Assets and Funded Status of All Significant Plans | | | | |
|---|---|---|---|---|
| | Defined Benefit Pension Plans | | Other Postretirement Benefits | |
| In millions | 2005 | 2004 | 2005 | 2004 |
| **Change in projected benefit obligation** | | | | |
| Benefit obligation at beginning of year | $15,004 | $13,443 | $2,167 | $2,134 |
| Service cost | 279 | 260 | 24 | 24 |
| Interest cost | 815 | 804 | 124 | 125 |
| Plan participants' contributions | 18 | 18 | — | — |
| Amendments | 26 | 6 | — | 21 |
| Actuarial changes in assumptions and experience | 698 | 917 | 28 | 37 |
| Acquisition/divestiture activity | — | 7 | — | (5) |
| Benefits paid | (808) | (779) | (179) | (208) |
| Currency impact | (401) | 303 | 4 | 6 |
| Special termination/curtailment cost (credit) | (14) | 25 | — | 33 |
| Benefit obligation at end of year | $15,617 | $15,004 | $2,168 | $2,167 |
| **Change in plan assets** | | | | |
| Market value of plan assets at beginning of year | $12,206 | $11,139 | $ 368 | $ 343 |
| Actual return on plan assets | 877 | 1,428 | 25 | 32 |
| Employer contributions | 1,031 | 399 | — | 33 |
| Plan participants' contributions | 18 | 19 | — | — |
| Acquisition/divestiture activity | — | — | — | (6) |
| Benefits paid | (808) | (779) | (16) | (34) |
| Market value of plan assets at end of year | $13,324 | $12,206 | $ 377 | $ 368 |

| U.S. Plan Assumptions for Other Postretirement Benefits | Net Periodic Costs for the Year | |
|---|---|---|
| | 2005 | 2004 |
| Discount rate | 5.875% | 6.25% |
| Expected long-term rate of return on plan assets | 8.75% | 9.00% |
| Initial health care cost trend rate | 10.16% | 6.70% |
| Ultimate health care cost trend rate, assumed to be reached in 2011 | 6.00% | 6.70% |

**Required**

a.  How much pension expense does Dow Chemical report in its 2005 income statement?

b.  Dow reports a $1,056 million expected return on pension plan assets as an offset to 2005 pension expense. Approximately, how is this amount computed? What is the actual gain or loss realized on Dow's 2005 pension plan assets? What is the purpose of using this estimated amount instead of the actual gain or loss?

c.  What factors affected Dow's pension liability during 2005? What factors affected its pension plan assets during 2005?

d.  What does the term *funded status* mean? What is the funded status of the 2005 Dow pension plans and postretirement benefit plans?

e.  Dow reduced its discount rate from 6.25% to 5.875% in 2005. What effect(s) does this reduction have on its balance sheet and its income statement?

f.  Dow decreased its estimate of expected returns on plan assets from 9% to 8.75% in 2005. What effect(s) does this decrease have on its income statement? Explain.

g.  How did Dow's pension plan affect the company's cash flow in 2005?

# CASES

**C10-33. Management Application and Ethics: Structuring Leases**  (L01)

You are the CEO of a company. Your CFO is concerned about certain covenants in your debt agreement that specify a maximum ratio of liabilities to stockholders' equity. He proposes to structure your leases as "operating" so as to avoid capitalization. In order to do so, he proposes to structure the lease with an initial term of 5 years, and with three 5-year renewal options instead of a flat 20-year lease. That way, the lease term will not exceed 75% of the useful life of the leased assets, and the present value of the lease payments will not exceed 90% of the fair market value of the leased assets. The CFO explains that these two requirements usually trigger lease capitalization. He asks for your input into this decision.

a.  What are the management issues that you feel are relevant for this decision? That is, how might this lease structure impact your company?

b.  What are the ethical issues that are raised by the CFO's proposal? Explain.

# Adjusting and Forecasting Financial Statements

## LEARNING OBJECTIVES

**LO1** Describe and illustrate adjustments to financial statements. (p. 11-4)

**LO2** Explain and illustrate the forecasting of financial statements. (p. 11-11)

**LO3** Describe and illustrate a parsimonious method for multiyear forecasting of net operating profit and net operating assets. (p. 11-24)

## PROCTER & GAMBLE

Procter & Gamble (P&G) has successfully reinvented itself . . . again. It has shed its image as the "lumbering giant" of its industry with new products and directed marketing. Its annual sales now exceed $68 billion, following its acquisition of Gillette. P&G has also focused on its higher margin products such as those in beauty care. This has improved its profit margin and provided much needed dollars for marketing activities. Its advertising budget is nearly 10% of sales, which is nearly double the budget of some of its key competitors. P&G also spends over $2 billion per year (3% of sales) on R&D. *BusinessWeek* (2006) reported that "P&G had to tear apart and re-stitch much of its research organization. It created new job classifications, such as 70 worldwide 'technology entrepreneurs,' or TEs, who act as scouts, looking for the latest breakthroughs from places such as university labs." P&G's goal is for 50% of its new products to come from outside of the company.

P&G's financial performance has been impressive. In 2006, it generated over $11 billion of operating cash flow, and the company has only begun to fully exploit the resources acquired in the Gillette acquisition. Its abundant cash flow allows it to fund the level of advertising and R&D necessary to remain a dominant force in the consumer products industry as well as to pay over $3.5 billion in dividends to shareholders. *Business-Week* (2006) asserts that "P&G long has been the largest household-

Getty Images

products company in the world, and under (CEO) Lafley's six-year tenure, it may have become the best operator in its group."

P&G's product list is impressive. It consists of numerous well-recognized household brands. Total sales of Procter & Gamble products are distributed across its three business segments as illustrated in the chart to the side. A partial listing of its brands follows:

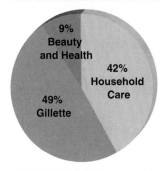

- **Beauty and Health.** Always, Head & Shoulders, Olay, Pantene, Wella, Cover Girl, Herbal Essences, Hugo Boss, Nice 'n Easy, Old Spice, Safeguard, Secret, Tampax, Crest, Oral-B, Fixodent, Metamucil, Pepto-Bismol, Prilosec OTC, PUR, Scope, ThermaCare, Vicks
- **Household Care.** Ariel, Dawn, Downy, Tide, Bold, Bounce, Cascade, Cheer, Dash, Febreze, Gain, Mr. Clean, Swiffer, Bounty, Charmin, Pampers, Luvs, Puffs, Folgers, Iams, Pringles
- **Gillette.** MACH3, Fusion, Gillette, Duracell, Braun

P&G's recent successes have coincided with strong leadership. A.G. Lafley's innovations and market savvy have consistently propelled P&G. *BusinessWeek* (2004) explains: "From its Swiffer mop to battery-powered Crest SpinBrush toothbrushes and Whitestrip tooth whiteners, P&G has simply done a better job than rivals." Since assuming the top job, Lafley has guided P&G to successive increases in sales, income, and cash flows. Such increases have driven impressive gains in its stock price as follows.

*(Continued on next page)*

*(Continued from previous page)*

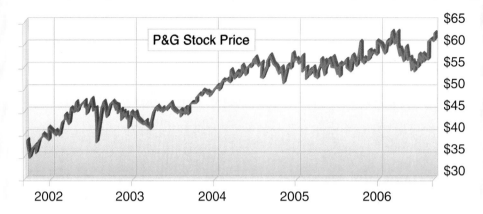

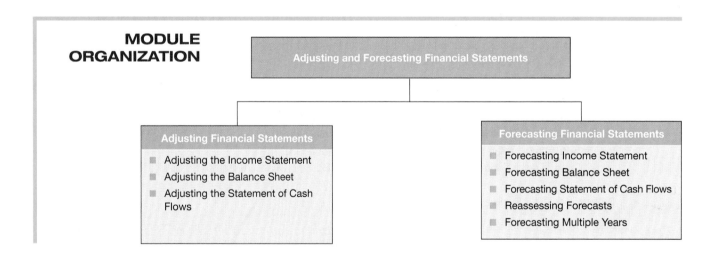

Forecasts of financial performance drive stock price. Historical financial statements are relevant to the extent that they provide information useful to forecast financial performance. Accordingly, considerable emphasis is placed on generating reliable forecasts.

This module explains the forecasting process, which typically involves two steps: (1) Historical financial statements are adjusted, if needed, to yield an income statement and statement of cash flows that identifies recurring operating income and cash flows, and an adjusted balance sheet that reflects all of the assets used in the business and the total amounts for which the company is liable. (2) Future financial performance is forecasted using the adjusted financial statements. The steady increase in P&G's stock price reflects increased optimism about its future financial performance and condition.

Sources: *Procter & Gamble* 2005–2006 10-K and Annual Reports; *BusinessWeek,* April 2006; *Barron's,* November 2006; *The Wall Street Journal,* January 2005.

## MODULE ORGANIZATION

**Adjusting and Forecasting Financial Statements**

**Adjusting Financial Statements**
- Adjusting the Income Statement
- Adjusting the Balance Sheet
- Adjusting the Statement of Cash Flows

**Forecasting Financial Statements**
- Forecasting Income Statement
- Forecasting Balance Sheet
- Forecasting Statement of Cash Flows
- Reassessing Forecasts
- Forecasting Multiple Years

## INTRODUCTION

Forecasting financial performance is integral to a variety of business decisions ranging from investing to managing a company effectively. We might, for example, wish to value a company's common stock before purchasing its shares. To that end, we might use one of the valuation models we discuss in Module 12. Or, we might be interested in evaluating the creditworthiness of a prospective borrower. In that case, we forecast the borrower's cash flows to estimate its ability to repay its obligations. We might also be interested in evaluating alternative strategic investment decisions. In this case, we can use our forecasts to evaluate the shareholder value that the investment will create.

The forecasting process begins with a retrospective analysis. That is, we analyze current and prior years' statements to be sure that they accurately reflect the company's financial condition and performance. If we believe that they do not, we adjust those statements to better reflect economic reality. Once we've adjusted the historical results, we are ready to forecast future results.

Why would we need to adjust historical results? The answer resides in the fact that financial statements prepared in conformity with GAAP do not always accurately reflect the "true" financial condition and performance of the company. This situation can arise for several reasons including the following:

▨ The income statement might include transitory items, such as an asset write-down or the accrual of expected restructuring costs; thus, current period income does not provide an accurate forecast of future income as we expect one-time (transitory) items to not recur.

▨ The balance sheet might include nonoperating assets and liabilities such as those from discontinued operations; by definition, such assets do not generate future profits. Conversely, the balance sheet might exclude operating assets and liabilities such as those from operating leases or from investments accounted for using the equity method. Forecasts would be less accurate if they failed to take these excluded assets and liabilities into account.

▨ The statement of cash flows might include operating cash inflows from excessive inventory reductions, from securitization of accounts receivable, or from tax benefits on the exercise of employee stock options. Adjustments to the current statement of cash flows might be necessary before projecting future cash flows.

These are just a few examples of how GAAP financial statements might not accurately reflect a company's true economic performance and condition. Consequently, we want to adjust GAAP financial statements before using them to forecast future financial statements.

# ADJUSTING FINANCIAL STATEMENTS

We begin by discussing how to adjust financial statements for purposes of forecasting. This *adjusting process,* also referred to as recasting or reformulating, is not "black and white." It requires judgment and estimation. Our discussion of adjusting (and forecasting) financial statements is meant to introduce a reasonable and reliable, but not the only, process for these tasks. It is important to distinguish between the purposes of GAAP-based financial statements and the adjusting process of this module for purposes of forecasting. Specifically, GAAP-based statements provide more than just information for forecasting. For example, financial statements are key inputs into contracts among business parties. This means that historical results, including any transitory activities, must be reported to meet management's fiduciary responsibilities. On the other hand, to forecast future performance, we need to create a set of financial statements that focus on those items that we expect to persist, with a special emphasis on persistent operating activities.

**LO1** Describe and illustrate adjustments to financial statements.

## Adjusting the Income Statement

This section describes how to adjust the income statement for forecasting purposes. Adjustments generally consist of the following three steps:

1. **Separate persistent and transitory items.** The aim of forecasting is to project financial results. Since transitory items are, by definition, nonrecurring, we exclude them from current operating results. Common transitory items include gains and losses from asset sales, the results of discontinued operations, and one-time legal judgments. The purpose of these adjustments is to determine persistent earnings, that is, earnings we expect to recur in the future. Restructuring costs are often considered transitory. Alternatively, we might consider allocating restructuring costs to past and/or future income statements. Assume that a loss on an asset disposal in the current period arises because depreciation in prior periods was too low; that is, depreciation expense failed to match the asset's economic depreciation. Rather than exclude from the income statement the (transitory) loss on disposal, we might adjust prior years' depreciation expense upward. Some other restructuring costs might be better viewed as expenses for future periods. Assume that a firm incurs restructuring costs in the current period with the expectation of increasing future profit via streamlined productions or more efficient work force. Since the benefits of restructuring accrue in the future, we might allocate the restructuring charge to future periods (say, the next three to five). The implications of these adjustments are: current period's profit is usually not as low, and prior

and future periods' profits are typically not as high, because absent these adjustments, the costs are recorded in one period rather than spread over all affected periods. As we see, adjusting earnings requires in-depth knowledge of a company's competitive strategy and how its accounting data reflect its underlying economics. For simplicity only, we simply exclude restructuring costs rather than allocate them (in some ad hoc manner) over past or future periods.

2. **Separate operating and nonoperating items.** Operating activities have the most long-lasting (persistent) effects on future profitability and cash flows and, thus, are the primary value drivers for company stakeholders. It is important to separate operating items from nonoperating items for effective profitability analysis.

3. **Include (or exclude) expenses that GAAP-based income excludes (or includes).** We review the types and levels of operating expenses to determine their reasonableness. To the extent a company fails to recognize expenses, whether due to underaccrual of reserves or liabilities, or due to reduced expenditures for key operating activities, reported income is overstated for forecasting purposes. On the other hand, certain expenses can be temporarily high, at levels that the company does not plan to sustain. Our adjustment process includes assessment of both understated and overstated expenses.

Exhibit 11.1 lists some typical adjustments. The list is not exhaustive, it only indicates the types of adjustments that are commonly made.

| EXHIBIT 11.1 | Common Income Statement Adjustments |
| --- | --- |

1. Separate persistent and transitory items; examples of items to exclude:
   a. Gains and losses relating to
      - Asset sales of long-term assets and investments
      - Asset write-downs of long-term assets and inventories
      - Stock issuances by subsidiaries
      - Debt retirements
   b. Transitory items reported after income from continued operations
      - Discontinued operations
      - Extraordinary items
   c. Restructuring expenses
   d. Merger costs
   e. LIFO liquidation gains
   f. Liability accruals deemed excessive
   g. Lawsuit gains and losses
   h. Revenue or expense from short-term fluctuations in tax rates and from changes in deferred tax valuation allowance
2. Separate operating and nonoperating items; examples:
   a. Treating interest revenue and expense, and investment gains and losses, as nonoperating
   b. Treating pension service cost as operating, and pension interest costs and expected returns as nonoperating
   c. Treating debt retirement gains and losses as nonoperating
   d. Treating income and losses from discontinued operations as nonoperating
3. Include expenses not reflected in net income; examples:
   a. Inadequate (or excessive) reserves for bad debts or asset impairment
   b. Reductions in R&D, advertising, and other discretionary expenses that were made to achieve short-term income targets; conversely, exclude excessive expenses related to product or market development
   c. Employee stock option expense (for financial statements issued before 2006)

The first category in Exhibit 11.1 includes gains and losses from asset sales and asset write-downs, and the financial gains and losses from debt retirements and subsidiary stock sales. To the extent that these items are transitory, they should be excluded when forecasting operating results. GAAP-based income statements help by identifying two types of transitory items that are reported net of tax and below income from continuing operations: discontinued operations and extraordinary items. We exclude other transitory items including restructuring expenses, merger and acquisition costs, LIFO liquidation gains and losses, excessive liability accruals, lawsuit gains or losses, and increases and decreases in tax expense from changes in the deferred tax asset valuation account. Another adjustment relates to tax expense. If the current period's expense is too high or too low because of one-time events such as short-lived tax law changes, the resulting tax rate will not persist. Such temporary swings in tax expense should be excluded.

The second step in the adjustment process is to separate operating and nonoperating items. Common nonoperating items are interest revenue and expense, the gains and losses from sales of investments, and pension interest costs and expected returns. Nonoperating components also include gains and losses on debt retirements and income or losses related to discontinued operations.

The third category of adjustments commonly involves adding expenses excluded from current income. Some omitted expenses arise because GAAP does not require their inclusion (such as employee stock option expenses before 2006). Other omitted expenses reflect management's accounting choices, estimates and predictions, which may not coincide with our conclusions about the company's true economic condition. This might include inadequate reserves for uncollectible accounts receivable or contingent liabilities such as warranties, and unrecognized asset impairment costs. We also might adjust income to include additional amounts for R&D, advertising, and other operating expenses that undo discretionary reductions of operating activities to achieve short-term income targets, or exclude those expenses incurred to help achieve the target such as new product development or other discretionary increases.

---

**MANAGERIAL DECISION**     **You Are a Corporate Analyst**

You are a corporate analyst working in the finance department for a company that is preparing its financial statements. You must make a decision regarding the format of its income statement. Specifically, should you subtotal to *pretax operating profit* and segregate nonoperating items? Or, should you subtotal to *pretax profit* and include operating and nonoperating items together? GAAP permits you to report either way. [Answer, p. 11-25]

---

## Adjusting the Balance Sheet

There are two reasons to adjust the balance sheet for forecasting purposes. First, we must separate (exclude) nonoperating assets and liabilities that are reported on the balance sheet. Second, we must include operating assets and liabilities that are *not* reported on the balance sheet. Both types of adjustments typically require use of footnote disclosures to properly assess the nature of the company's assets and liabilities and to determine the nature and size of any excluded assets and liabilities.

Exhibit 11.2 lists several common balance sheet adjustments, but this listing is not exhaustive.

---

**EXHIBIT 11.2     Common Balance Sheet Adjustments**

1. Exclude nonoperating assets and liabilities
   a. Eliminate assets and liabilities from discontinued operations
   b. Write-down of assets, including goodwill, that is judged to be impaired
2. Include operating assets and liabilities not reflected in balance sheet; examples:
   a. Capitalize operating assets from operating leases; nonoperating capitalized lease liabilities are also increased
   b. Consolidate off-balance-sheet investments:
      • Equity method investments
      • Special purpose entities (SPEs)
   c. Accrue understated liabilities and assets

---

The first category in Exhibit 11.2 involves separating (excluding) nonoperating assets and liabilities on the balance sheet. The income statement segregates the gains and losses from discontinued operations (see Exhibit 11.1). Likewise, the assets and liabilities related to discontinued operations are excluded since, by definition, neither those assets and liabilities, nor the sales and expenses of discontinued operations, remain in continuing operations. Other adjustments to the balance sheet include the write-down of impaired assets. Adjustments to reduce assets are difficult judgment calls that benefit from information outside of the financial statements such as financial reports of competitors and analyst reports of the state of the industry. Seeking additional information can refine our opinion about such potential asset impairments.

The second category of adjustments seeks to include operating assets and liabilities not reported in the balance sheet per GAAP. One example is operating leases that are prevalent in several industries, including the retailing and airline industries. Lease disclosures mandated under GAAP provide sufficient information for us to effectively capitalize these operating leases for forecasting purposes (by including both the operating lease assets and the nonoperating lease liabilities, as detailed in Module 10). We also need to consider whether to adjust the balance sheet for unconsolidated investments. When a company exerts significant influence over an investee company (but not control), the equity method of accounting is used. (The equity method of accounting is used for investments in partnerships, joint ventures, and trusts in addition to minority interest in corporations.) Under the equity method, the company's balance sheet has a single investment (asset) account equal to the percentage of the equity in the investee company that the company owns, rather than the full amount of the assets and liabilities of the investee company that would be recognized on-balance-sheet if the entity were consolidated. This means that many unconsolidated assets and liabilities are unreported. Unfortunately, footnote disclosures about equity method investments are insufficient to estimate the full value of the assets and liabilities (and risk) of the investee companies. To the extent that sufficient information is provided in the footnotes, the adjustment process replaces the investment account with the related assets and liabilities using the consolidation mechanics discussed in Module 7.

Other adjustments to the balance sheet include the accrual of understated liabilities. Common accruals such as those relating to operating activities like warranties, premiums, and coupons are somewhat easier to assess and estimate from prior balance sheet data. Accruals for contingent liabilities such as environmental and litigation exposure are more difficult and require use of information outside of the financial statements.

---

**RESEARCH INSIGHT**     **Earnings Quality and Accounting Conservatism**

Accounting researchers commonly measure *earnings quality* in terms of sustainability, meaning that the income items persist in future periods. Sustainability is important because persistent income items are better indicators of future earnings than are transitory items. One factor that affects earnings quality is accounting conservatism. Research finds that conservative accounting leads to transitory earnings changes when the levels of investment within the firm changes. Researchers have constructed a conservatism index to study the effect conservatism and growth have on earnings changes. The index is defined as the level of estimated reserves created by conservative accounting (such as LIFO versus FIFO, and expensing of R&D and advertising) divided by the level of net operating assets. Earnings quality is then a function of changes in the conservatism index for each firm, and it is a function of the difference between the firm-specific and industry-specific conservatism index. Poor earnings quality occurs when the firm's and accounting accruals grow more quickly or more slowly than net operating assets. A firm-specific conservatism index that substantially differs from that of the firm's industry is one sign of poor earnings quality. This is because a firm's profitability reverts toward the industry mean. While the conservatism index appears to indicate whether or not a firm's earnings are sustainable, market participants do not appear to fully consider the information contained in this index when determining stock prices.

---

## Adjusting the Statement of Cash Flows

The focus of cash flow adjustments is threefold: (1) to adjust operating cash flows for any transitory (abnormal) items, (2) to adjust (exclude) transitory items from investing cash flows, and (3) to reclassify cash flows into their proper sections—investing, investing, or financing. These adjustments typically require use of the other financial statements, including footnote disclosures, and sometimes information from outside the financial statements. It's important to remember why we are adjusting GAAP-based financial statements. It is not because the financials are wrong; the auditor's report provides some assurance that those statements are free of material misstatement. Instead, we are adjusting the cash flow statement to better forecast future cash flows. By including all cash expenditures that we expect to persist, and by excluding transitory items, we obtain cash flows that better reflect the company's future cash flows than the cash flows reported in GAAP-based financial statements.

Exhibit 11.3 lists several common statement of cash flow adjustments, but this listing is not exhaustive. The first category in Exhibit 11.3 involves adjusting operating cash flows for transitory items. These transitory items commonly involve discretionary activities whose amounts are determined by management and sometimes are not in line with reasonable norms. To better understand, recall that operating cash flows increase with an increase in operating income and/or a decrease in net operating working capital (the

| EXHIBIT 11.3 | Common Statement of Cash Flow Adjustments |
|---|---|

1. Adjust operating cash flows for transitory items; examples of adjustments that potentially impact operating cash flows:
   a. Adjust discretionary costs (advertising, R&D, maintenance) to normal, expected levels
   b. Adjust current operating assets (receivables, inventory) to normal, expected levels
   c. Adjust current operating liabilities (payables, accruals) to normal, expected levels
2. Adjust investing cash flows for transitory items, such as cash proceeds from asset disposals (including disposals of discontinued operations) and from tax benefits due to exercise of stock options
3. Review cash flows and reassign them, if necessary, to operating, investing, or financing sections; examples:
   a. Reclassify operating cash inflows from asset securitization to the financing section
   b. Reclassify interest payments from the operating to the financing section

latter occurs from either or both a decrease in current operating assets or an increase in current operating liabilities). Although higher operating cash flows are generally viewed favorably, it is necessary to understand the drivers of that increase to discern whether or not future cash flows are expected to exhibit similar behavior. Following are several common adjustments to operating cash flows for nonoperating items:

- **Cost decreases.** Transitory, abnormal reductions of necessary, expected operating costs related to discretionary expenditures on advertising, promotion, R&D, and maintenance. Such reductions increase income and operating cash flows, which usually yield short-term benefits at long-term costs.

- **Current asset decreases.** Transitory, abnormal reductions in current operating assets, such as accounts receivable and inventory, increase net cash flows from operations. Such reductions are generally desirable. However, if such reductions are the result of overly restrictive credit policies or depressed inventories below what is necessary to conduct operations, then increased (short-term) operating cash flows likely result in long-term costs as customers leave or face stock-outs causing the company's image to deteriorate.

- **Current liability increases.** Transitory, abnormal increases in current operating liabilities such as accounts payable and other accrued liabilities increase operating cash flows. After some point, however, the cash inflows from extending the payment of accounts payable or other liabilities come at the cost of supplier and creditor relations.

The second category involves adjusting investing cash flows for transitory items. One example is cash proceeds from asset disposals that are greater than normal levels. To determine the normal level of operating cash flows from asset disposals, we must look at trends over time and asset growth patterns.

| BUSINESS INSIGHT | What is eBay's Operating Cash Flow? |
|---|---|

Steve Milunovich of Merrill Lynch believes that operating cash flow should exclude what companies spend to buy back stock to offset employee stock option-related dilution. This gets tricky in eBay's case because it, unlike many others, hasn't bought back any stock to offset the dilutive effects of additional stock issuances following the exercise of stock options. This means that, even if you're a stockholder who never sold a share, you own less of eBay now than you did five years ago. It is estimated that had eBay bought back shares to enable stockholders to maintain their ownership stake rather than seeing it decline, the cash outflow would have been $1.2 billion, which is huge relative to eBay's five-year cumulative operating cash flow of $1.8 billion. (*Fortune* 2004)

The third category involves the proper categorization of cash flows into operating, investing, and financing sections. One example is cash inflows from asset securitizations, which are reported as operating cash flows per GAAP. However, companies commonly sell accounts receivable to a special purpose entity (see Module 10). The cash flow from the sale is categorized as an operating cash inflow in the year of sale, but is better viewed as a financing cash inflow (similar to borrowing against the receivables). Another example is cash flows from discontinued operations that should be reclassified from operating to investing.

| BUSINESS INSIGHT | Tyco Buys Operating Cash Flow |

Corporate management is aware of the market's focus on operating cash flow, which is a main driver of free cash flow and is used in many stock valuation models. In 2001, Tyco touted its free cash flows in a press release: *Free Cash Flow Reaches $1.7 Billion for the Fourth Quarter and $4.75 Billion for the Fiscal Year.* Said L. Dennis Kozlowski, then chairman and CEO of Tyco, "Strong cash flow generation throughout all of our businesses funds further investment in these businesses and provides the means to opportunistically expand them as circumstances allow." Tyco eventually admitted to spending $830 million to purchase roughly 800,000 individual customer contracts for its security-alarm business from a network of independent dealers. Cash outflows relating to this purchase were reported in the *investing* section of its statement of cash flows. However, fees paid by these new customers were reported in net income and immediately added to its *operating* cash flow. *The Wall Street Journal* (March 2002) declared that Tyco effectively bought earnings and operating cash flow with its contract purchases.

## MID-MODULE REVIEW 1

Part 1 Income Statement Adjustments.

Following is the income statement of Time Warner, Inc.

| Years ended December 31 ($ millions) | 2005 | 2004 | 2003 |
|---|---|---|---|
| Revenues | | | |
| Subscriptions | $22,222 | $21,605 | $20,448 |
| Advertising | 7,612 | 6,955 | 6,180 |
| Content | 12,615 | 12,350 | 11,446 |
| Other | 1,203 | 1,179 | 1,489 |
| Total revenues | 43,652 | 42,089 | 39,563 |
| Costs of revenues | (25,075) | (24,449) | (23,422) |
| Selling, general and administrative | (10,478) | (10,274) | (9,778) |
| Amortization of intangible assets | (597) | (626) | (640) |
| Amounts related to securities litigation and government investigations | (2,865) | (536) | (56) |
| Merger-related and restructuring costs | (117) | (50) | (109) |
| Asset impairments | (24) | (10) | (318) |
| Gains on disposal of assets, net | 23 | 21 | 14 |
| Operating income | 4,519 | 6,165 | 5,254 |
| Interest expense, net | (1,266) | (1,533) | (1,734) |
| Other income, net | 1,124 | 521 | 1,210 |
| Minority interest expense, net | (285) | (246) | (214) |
| Income before income taxes, discontinued operations and cumulative effect of accounting change | 4,092 | 4,907 | 4,516 |
| Income tax provision | (1,187) | (1,698) | (1,370) |
| Income before discontinued operations and cumulative effect of accounting change | 2,905 | 3,209 | 3,146 |
| Discontinued operations, net of tax | — | 121 | (495) |
| Other revenues (expenses) | — | 34 | (12) |
| Net income | $ 2,905 | $ 3,364 | $ 2,639 |

### Required
Identify and discuss any items that you would adjust in the income statement of Time Warner to forecast its future earnings.

### Solution
Time Warner's income statement should be adjusted in several ways to forecast future earnings. Consider the following potential adjustments:

1. *Separate persistent and transitory items*
    a. Time Warner faces litigation every year; so, while the $2,865 million line item relating to securities litigation is a persistent item, the amount has increased substantially over this three year period. We want to know the reasons for this litigation and whether the trend will continue. The portion of the expense that is deemed to be transitory should be eliminated for forecasting purposes.
    b. Although Time Warner has reported merger and restructuring costs, each year over this period, these costs are considered transitory for our purposes. Further, Time Warner is not a typical *roll-up company* (achieving growth via acquisitions). Thus, we treat these costs as nonrecurring and we want to know more details about these costs. The portion of the expense that is deemed to be transitory should be eliminated for forecasting purposes.
    c. Asset impairments have been recurring, but declining as a proportion of revenue; we want to know if this trend will continue. The portion of the expense that is deemed to be transitory should be eliminated for forecasting purposes.
    d. Its net gain on disposal of assets, although a minor amount in this case, warrants attention. We must watch for recognition of gains and losses on asset sales, especially when the gain allows a company to achieve earnings targets or the loss is taken in a year of excessive income (or losses). This gain should be eliminated in our forecasts as it is likely transitory.
    e. Its income (loss) from discontinued operations is, by definition, eliminated from the income statement once the operations are disposed of; thus, this item is transitory and we exclude it.
2. *Separate operating and nonoperating items*
    a. Time Warner classifies $1,124 million of income as nonoperating, which is 23% of its pretax income. We would read the financial statement footnotes and the MD&A from the 10-K to learn more about this nonoperating income. We will use the Time Warner classification, unless further information in the footnotes or otherwise leads us to consider it as operating.
3. *Include expenses not reflected in net income*
    a. Time Warner has written off a substantial amount of goodwill since its merger with AOL. Yet, goodwill remains a third of its total assets at 2005 year-end. We want to know if further impairment will be recognized. If so, we should recognize the goodwill impairment before commencing our projections.

## Part 2 Balance Sheet Adjustments.

DuPont's 2005 10-K report includes information relating to the company's equity method investments. The following footnote reports summary balance sheet amounts for its affiliated companies for which DuPont uses the equity method of accounting. The information below is shown on a 100 percent basis followed by the carrying value of DuPont's investment in these affiliates.

| Financial Position at December 31 (in millions) | 2005 | 2004 |
|---|---|---|
| Current assets | $1,292 | $1,972 |
| Noncurrent assets | 1,780 | 2,811 |
| Total assets | $3,072 | $4,783 |
| Short-term borrowings | $ 606 | $ 734 |
| Other current liabilities | 621 | 932 |
| Long-term borrowings | 259 | 716 |
| Other long-term liabilities | 111 | 305 |
| Total liabilities | $1,597 | $2,687 |
| DuPont's investment in affiliates (includes advances of $55 and $84, respectively) | $ 844 | $1,034 |

## Required

What adjustments to DuPont's net operating assets are necessary to incorporate the footnote information above assuming that we conclude these equity method investments are integral to DuPont's operating activities (each of the investee companies' assets are operating, as are "other" liabilities)?

## Solution

The equity of the investee companies is $1,475 million ($3,072 million − $1,597 million). These investments must have been acquired at an amount greater than book value since the investment balance represents 53% of the equity ([$844 million − $55 million] / $1,475 million). Assuming that these investments are 50% owned, the required adjustments to DuPont's NOA follow ($ millions):

| | |
|---|---:|
| Elimination of equity method investment from DuPont's NOA ($844 million − $55 million) .. | $ (789) |
| Add NOA of equity method investees ($3,072 million − $621 million − $111 million) . . . . . . | 2,340 |
| Net increase in DuPont's NOA . . . . . . . . . . . . . . . . . . . . . . . . . . . . . . . . . . . . . . . . . . . . . . . . . . | $1,551 |

DuPont's NOA, therefore, increased by $1,551 million. (*Note:* The minority interest of outside investors is accounted for as a Minority Interest account, a nonoperating liability.)

# FORECASTING FINANCIAL STATEMENTS

**LO2** Explain and illustrate the forecasting of financial statements.

Stock valuation models typically use forecasted financial information to estimate stock price. Creditors also utilize forecasted financial information to evaluate the cash flows available to repay indebtedness. Knowing how to forecast financial information is, therefore, an important skill to master. In this section, we introduce the most common method to forecast the income statement, balance sheet, and statement of cash flows. It is important to forecast the income statement first, then the balance sheet, and then the statement of cash flows in that order since each succeeding statement uses forecast information from the previous forecasted statement(s). Our description, therefore, proceeds in that same order.

We use Procter & Gamble's fiscal 2006 financial statements for illustration. In practice, the forecasting process begins with the adjusted financial statements resulting from the adjusting process explained in the prior section. P&G is generally free from needed adjustments with one exception. Comparing P&G sales for 2005 and 2006, we see a 20.2% increase ([$68,222/$56,741] − 1). This sales growth is high and we question its persistence. Further analysis reveals P&G's 2006 sales include eight months of sales from Gillette after its acquisition by P&G during 2006. P&G's 2005 sales do not include those from Gillette. Thus, comparing 2005 to 2006 is not a valid comparison. Footnotes reveal pro forma sales that show what the income statement would have reported had Gillette's full-year sales been included in both 2005 and 2006, P&G's sales growth would have been 4.4%, which is more realistic and is the forecasted sales growth we use. Although this item does not require us to actually adjust P&G's income statement, it does necessitate an adjustment to our assumptions before we can forecast future income.

## Forecasting the Income Statement

Procter & Gamble's fiscal year income statement is shown in Exhibit 11.4.

| EXHIBIT 11.4 | Procter & Gamble Income Statement | | |
|---|---:|---:|---:|
| **Years ended June 30 (in millions)** | **2006** | **2005** | **2004** |
| Net sales. . . . . . . . . . . . . . . . . . . . . . . . . . . . . . . . . . . . . | $68,222 | $56,741 | $51,407 |
| Cost of products sold. . . . . . . . . . . . . . . . . . . . . . . . . . . | 33,125 | 27,872 | 25,143 |
| Selling, general and administrative expense . . . . . . . . . . | 21,848 | 18,400 | 16,882 |
| Operating income. . . . . . . . . . . . . . . . . . . . . . . . . . . . . . | 13,249 | 10,469 | 9,382 |
| Interest expense. . . . . . . . . . . . . . . . . . . . . . . . . . . . . . . | 1,119 | 834 | 629 |
| Other nonoperating income, net . . . . . . . . . . . . . . . . . . | 283 | 346 | 152 |
| Earnings before income taxes . . . . . . . . . . . . . . . . . . . . | 12,413 | 9,981 | 8,905 |
| Income taxes . . . . . . . . . . . . . . . . . . . . . . . . . . . . . . . . . | 3,729 | 3,058 | 2,749 |
| Net earnings. . . . . . . . . . . . . . . . . . . . . . . . . . . . . . . . . . | $ 8,684 | $ 6,923 | $ 6,156 |

Assuming that we have made all necessary adjustments (see prior section), we can use the adjusted (persistent) income statement numbers to forecast future earnings.

The first step is to forecast sales.[1] As explained, we expect P&G's sales growth rate to be 4.4%. The second step in the forecasting process is to identify several key relations among the income statement line items. These key relations capture associations between specific income statement items; associations that we *assume* will persist at the same level in the future. Exhibit 11.5 lists these key relations using the Procter & Gamble income statement from Exhibit 11.4.

| **EXHIBIT 11.5**    **Procter & Gamble Key Income Statement Relations** | |
| --- | --- |
| **$ millions** | **2006** |
| Net sales growth (see text explanation using pro forma numbers) . . . . . . . . . . . . . . . . . . . . . . . . . | 4.4% |
| Cost of products sold margin ($33,125/$68,222). . . . . . . . . . . . . . . . . . . . . . . . . . . . . . . . . . . . . . | 48.6% |
| Selling, general and administrative expense/Net sales ($21,848/$68,222) . . . . . . . . . . . . . . . . . . . | 32.0% |
| Interest expense. . . . . . . . . . . . . . . . . . . . . . . . . . . . . . . . . . . . . . . . . . . . . . . . . . . . . . . . . . . . . . | no change |
| Other nonoperating income, net . . . . . . . . . . . . . . . . . . . . . . . . . . . . . . . . . . . . . . . . . . . . . . . . . . | no change |
| Income taxes/Earnings before income taxes ($3,729/$12,413)* . . . . . . . . . . . . . . . . . . . . . . . . . . | 30.0% |

* Exhibit 11.5 uses P&G's average tax rate of 30%, computed as total tax expense divided by total pretax income. This is a simplification that usually works well, yields reasonable forecasts, and is used throughout Module 11. A refinement uses the tax rate on operating profit as discussed in Module 4. Under that method, we compute tax expense on net nonoperating expense using the firm's statutory rate (which averages 36.5% for U.S. companies), and then determine the tax rate on operating profit:

$$\text{Tax rate on operating profit} = \frac{\text{Tax expense} + (\text{Net nonoperating expense} \times \text{Statutory tax rate})}{\text{Net operating profit before taxes}}$$

In this case, income statement forecasts use both rates—the statutory rate for nonoperating items and the computed rate for operating items. With a statutory tax rate of 36.5% on P&G's net nonoperating expense of $836 ($1,119 − $283), we find a tax rate on nonoperating profit of 30.49%, slightly higher than the 30% used here. Thus, the simplification works well for P&G and, in general, works well when we do not expect marked changes over time in the proportions of operating and nonoperating profits.

We use these key income statement relations to forecast future amounts. In practice, we would also review the MD&A section, footnotes, and nonfinancial information to assess whether these historical income statement relations represent persistent operating performance and, if not, adjust these income statement relations accordingly. Following are examples of how we can use additional information to enhance our income statement relations and measures.

| **Company Scenario** | **Forecasting Implications** |
| --- | --- |
| McDonalds reports an 8% increase in 2005 sales; its MD&A reports that sales increased by 2% from a weakened $US | We might forecast a less than 8% future sales growth if we do not expect the $US to further weaken (or strengthen) |
| Target reports a 2005 sales increase of 12%; most of this is from new store openings as comparable store growth is 5% | Growth via acquisition or construction requires capital outlays, and is different from *organic growth;* if we forecast continuation of a 12% growth, we also must forecast the required capital outlays |
| Ford reports a $1.1 billion gain on sale of its Hertz subsidiary | This is a transitory item and we do not want to forecast its recurrence; we also do not want to include any operating results from this discontinued subsidiary in our forecasting process |
| CBS Corp. reports a 2005 goodwill impairment charge of $9.5 billion reducing the carrying values of its television and radio investments | This is a transitory item that we should not forecast as it is nonrecurring (assuming remaining goodwill is not further impaired) |

---

[1] A key to financial statement forecasting is the sales forecast. Although there is no perfect method, the more information we can gather and assimilate, the more accurate the forecast will be. Using the current sales growth rate to forecast future sales is simple, and usually reasonable, and is the approach we typically take in this module and its assignments. Many other forecasting methods are employed, with varying success. For example, we could use a time series of sales and fit a trend line using statistical modeling techniques. We also could use additional company, industry, and economic variables and build a multivariate forecast model. There is no guarantee, however, that the benefits of such forecasts are worth the costs.

The forecasting mechanics in this module assume that key financial statement relations will continue to hold in the future. In practice, analysts and investors carefully review these relations and modify them as necessary. This is the *art* of forecasting. We use the income statement relations from Exhibit 11.5, to derive P&G's forecasted income statement, shown in Exhibit 11.6. We assume that the nonoperating items remain constant as we do not forecast any changes to the investing and financing activities of the company (at this point).

| EXHIBIT 11.6 | Procter & Gamble Forecasted Income Statement | |
|---|---|---|
| **Year ended June 30 (in millions)** | | **2007 Est.** |
| Net sales ($68,222 × 1.044)........................................ | | **$71,224** |
| Cost of products sold ($71,224 × 48.6%)............................ | | **34,615** |
| Gross profit (subtotal) ........................................... | | **36,609** |
| Selling, general and administrative expense ($71,224 × 32.0%) ........... | | **22,792** |
| Operating income (subtotal)....................................... | | **13,817** |
| Interest expense (no change assumed) .............................. | | **1,119** |
| Other nonoperating income, net (no change assumed).................. | | **283** |
| Earnings before income taxes (subtotal) ............................ | | **12,981** |
| Income taxes ($12,981 x 30.0%)................................... | | **3,894** |
| Net earnings (total)............................................. | | **$ 9,087** |

## Forecasting the Balance Sheet

Forecasting the balance sheet requires information from our forecasted income statement as well as historical financial and nonfinancial information. Therefore, we forecast the balance sheet *after* forecasting the income statement. P&G's historical balance sheet is reproduced in Exhibit 11.7.

Forecasting of the balance sheet proceeds in two steps:

1. Forecast each asset account (*other than cash*) and each liability and equity account
2. Compute the cash amount needed to balance the forecasted accounting equation
   (Assets = Liabilities + Equity)

There are several ways to obtain forecasts of specific asset, liability, and equity accounts:

▪ Assume no change in balance sheet amounts.

▪ Use computed relations, such as capital expenditures to sales, and predicted events for accounts with more complex relations, such as scheduled payments of long-term debt and dividend policies drawn from information gleaned from MD&A and footnote disclosures.

▪ Use turnover rates and simple assumptions to forecast balance sheet amounts.

The first method is straightforward, but unlikely to yield accurate forecasts. The second method requires estimates and assumptions beyond the scope of this book. The third method is the one we use. It relies on plausible assumptions and typically yields reasonable forecasts. This method also uses key turnover rates. To illustrate use of turnover rates to forecast balance sheet amounts, recall the following definition of a generic turnover rate *based on year-end account balances:*

**Turnover Rate = Sales (or Cost of Goods Sold)/Year-End Account Balance**

Rearranging terms, we get the forecasted *year-end* account balance as

$$\text{Forecasted Year-End Account Balance} = \frac{\text{Forecasted Sales (or Cost of Goods Sold)}}{\text{Estimated Turnover Rate}}$$

We use year-end amounts in the denominator of the turnover rate because we are trying to estimate year-end account balances (and not the average balance). While this form of the turnover ratio can seem inconsistent with the turnover definitions in Module 4, it is because the purpose here is to forecast a year-end account balance, and not an average account balance. The forecasted year-end balance is, thus,

## EXHIBIT 11.7   Procter & Gamble Balance Sheet

| June 30 (in millions) | 2006 | 2005 |
|---|---|---|
| **Assets** | | |
| Cash and cash equivalents | $ 6,693 | $ 6,389 |
| Investment securities | 1,133 | 1,744 |
| Accounts receivable | 5,725 | 4,185 |
| Inventories | | |
| Materials and supplies | 1,537 | 1,424 |
| Work in process | 623 | 350 |
| Finished goods | 4,131 | 3,232 |
| Total inventories | 6,291 | 5,006 |
| Deferred income taxes | 1,611 | 1,081 |
| Prepaid expenses and other receivables | 2,876 | 11,924 |
| Total current assets | 24,329 | 20,329 |
| Property, plant and equipment | | |
| Buildings | 5,871 | 5,292 |
| Machinery and equipment | 25,140 | 20,397 |
| Land | 870 | 636 |
| | 31,881 | 26,325 |
| Accumulated depreciation | (13,111) | (11,993) |
| Net property, plant and equipment | 18,770 | 14,332 |
| Goodwill and other intangible assets | | |
| Goodwill | 55,306 | 19,816 |
| Trademarks and other intangible assets, net | 33,721 | 4,347 |
| Net goodwill and other intangible assets | 89,027 | 24,163 |
| Other noncurrent assets | 3,569 | 2,703 |
| Total assets | $135,695 | $61,527 |
| **Liabilities and Shareholders' Equity** | | |
| Accounts payable | $ 4,910 | $ 3,802 |
| Accrued and other liabilities | 9,587 | 7,531 |
| Taxes payable | 3,360 | 2,265 |
| Debt due within one year | 2,128 | 11,441 |
| Total current liabilities | 19,985 | 25,039 |
| Long-term debt | 35,976 | 12,887 |
| Deferred income taxes | 12,354 | 1,896 |
| Other noncurrent liabilities | 4,472 | 3,230 |
| Total liabilities | 72,787 | 43,052 |
| Shareholders' equity | | |
| Convertible Class A preferred stock, stated value $1 per share (600 shares authorized) | 1,451 | 1,483 |
| Non-Voting Class B preferred stock, stated value $1 per share (200 shares authorized) | — | — |
| Common stock, stated value $1 per share (10,000 shares authorized; shares issued: 2006—3,975.8, 2005—2,976.6) | 3,976 | 2,977 |
| Additional paid-in capital | 57,856 | 3,030 |
| Reserve for ESOP debt retirement | (1,288) | (1,259) |
| Accumulated other comprehensive income | (518) | (1,566) |
| Treasury stock, at cost (shares held: 2006—797.0, 2005—503.7) | (34,235) | (17,194) |
| Retained earnings | 35,666 | 31,004 |
| Total shareholders' equity | 62,908 | 18,475 |
| Total liabilities and shareholders' equity | $135,695 | $61,527 |

forecasted sales (or forecasted cost of goods sold) divided by the turnover rate estimated from prior year-end balances.

Assuming that we have made all necessary adjustments (see adjusting section), we identify and estimate several key turnover relations and other measures from information in the P&G balance sheet and income statement. We use these relations and measures (reported in Exhibit 11.8) to forecast the balance sheet.

| EXHIBIT 11.8 | P&G Key Relations using Income Statement and Balance Sheet[†] | |
|---|---|---|
| **$ millions** | | **2006** |
| Net sales/Year-end accounts receivable ($68,222/$5,725) . . . . . . . . . . . . . . . . . . . . . . . . . . . . . . . . . . . . . . . | | 11.92 |
| Cost of products sold/Year-end inventories ($33,125/$6,291). . . . . . . . . . . . . . . . . . . . . . . . . . . . . . . . . . . . | | 5.27 |
| Cost of products sold/Year-end accounts payable ($33,125/$4,910) . . . . . . . . . . . . . . . . . . . . . . . . . . . . . . | | 6.75 |
| Net sales/Year-end net PPE ($68,222/$18,770). . . . . . . . . . . . . . . . . . . . . . . . . . . . . . . . . . . . . . . . . . . . . . . | | 3.64 |
| Net sales/Year-end accrued and other liabilities ($68,222/$9,587) . . . . . . . . . . . . . . . . . . . . . . . . . . . . . . . | | 7.12 |
| Taxes payable/Income taxes ($3,360/$3,729) . . . . . . . . . . . . . . . . . . . . . . . . . . . . . . . . . . . . . . . . . . . . . . . . | | 90.1% |
| Dividends to shareholders (from statement of cash flows in Exhibit 11.11) . . . . . . . . . . . . . . . . . . . . . . . . . . | | $3,703 |
| Dividends/Net earnings ($3,703/$8,684) . . . . . . . . . . . . . . . . . . . . . . . . . . . . . . . . . . . . . . . . . . . . . . . . . . . . | | 42.6% |
| Depreciation and amortization expense/SG&A expense (from footnotes not reproduced in book)* . . . . . . . . . | | 9.3% |
| Forecasted long-term debt = Long-term debt − Current maturities ($35,976 − $2,128). . . . . . . . . . . . . . . | | $33,848 |

* For use in the statement of cash flows, not the balance sheet

[†] No change is assumed for the following accounts: investment securities, deferred income taxes, prepaid expenses and other receivables, net goodwill and other intangible assets, other noncurrent assets, debt due within one year, deferred income taxes, other noncurrent liabilities, and all shareholders' equity accounts with the exception of retained earnings.

The relations and amounts in Exhibit 11.8 are intuitively appealing. For example, accounts receivable and accrued liabilities are typically related to sales levels (because receivables are at selling prices and accruals typically include operating costs that relate to sales volume). Also, inventories and accounts payable are both logically related to cost of goods sold (because payables typically relate to inventory volume). Capital expenditures and dividends are taken from the statement of cash flows (see Exhibit 11.11). We assume no change in P&G capital expenditures from the prior year.

Using the income statement and balance sheet relations from Exhibit 11.8, the P&G forecasted balance sheet is shown in Exhibit 11.9; detailed computations are shown in parentheses. We should confirm each of the computations to understand the forecasted balance sheet.

The final step in forecasting the balance sheet is computing the cash balance, which equals total assets less all noncash assets. Since this is computed as a residual amount, it can be unusually high, low, or even negative. The residual cash balance is an indicator of whether the company is accumulating too much or too little cash from its operating activities less its capital expenditures (we are holding financing activities constant at this point). The following table presents two possible adjustments to the cash balance that we would consider at this point in the forecasting process.

| Forecasted Cash | Possible Adjustments to Forecasted Balance Sheet and Income Statement |
|---|---|
| Too low | • Liquidate marketable securities (then adjust forecasted investment income)<br>• Raise cash by increasing long-term debt and/or equity (then adjust forecasted interest expense and/or expected dividends) |
| Too high | • Invest excess cash in marketable securities (then adjust investment income)<br>• Repay debt or pay out to shareholders as repurchased (treasury) stock or dividends (then adjust forecasted interest expense and/or expected dividends) |

Determining whether the resulting cash balance is too high or too low is a judgment call. We choose to use the historical cash balance as a percentage of total assets as a benchmark (computed for the company under analysis or the industry). When adjusting the final cash balance, we must take care to not inadvertently change the financial leverage of the company. Financial leverage is an important consideration in both the

| EXHIBIT 11.9 | Procter & Gamble Forecasted Balance Sheet |
|---|---|

| June 30 (in millions) | 2007 Est. |
|---|---|
| **Assets** | |
| Cash and cash equivalents (total forecasted liabilities and equity less all noncash assets) . . . . . . . | $ 9,240 |
| Investment securities (no change assumed) . . . . . . . . . . . . . . . . . . . . . . . . . . . . . . . . . . . . . . . | 1,133 |
| Accounts receivable ($71,224/11.92). . . . . . . . . . . . . . . . . . . . . . . . . . . . . . . . . . . . . . . . . . | 5,975 |
| Inventories ($34,615/5.27) . . . . . . . . . . . . . . . . . . . . . . . . . . . . . . . . . . . . . . . . . . . . . . . . . | 6,568 |
| Deferred income taxes (no change assumed) . . . . . . . . . . . . . . . . . . . . . . . . . . . . . . . . . . . . | 1,611 |
| Prepaid expenses and other receivables (no change assumed) . . . . . . . . . . . . . . . . . . . . . . . . | 2,876 |
| Total current assets (subtotal) . . . . . . . . . . . . . . . . . . . . . . . . . . . . . . . . . . . . . . . . . . . . . . . | 27,403 |
| Net property, plant and equipment ($71,224/3.64) . . . . . . . . . . . . . . . . . . . . . . . . . . . . . . . . | 19,567 |
| Net goodwill and other intangible assets (no change assumed) . . . . . . . . . . . . . . . . . . . . . . . . | 89,027 |
| Other noncurrent assets (no change assumed) . . . . . . . . . . . . . . . . . . . . . . . . . . . . . . . . . . . | 3,569 |
| Total assets (subtotal). . . . . . . . . . . . . . . . . . . . . . . . . . . . . . . . . . . . . . . . . . . . . . . . . . . . | $139,566 |
| **Liabilities and Shareholders' Equity** | |
| Accounts payable ($34,615/6.75). . . . . . . . . . . . . . . . . . . . . . . . . . . . . . . . . . . . . . . . . . . . | $ 5,128 |
| Accrued and other liabilities ($71,224/7.12). . . . . . . . . . . . . . . . . . . . . . . . . . . . . . . . . . . . | 10,003 |
| Taxes payable ($3,894 × 90.1%). . . . . . . . . . . . . . . . . . . . . . . . . . . . . . . . . . . . . . . . . . . . | 3,509 |
| Debt due within one year (no change assumed) . . . . . . . . . . . . . . . . . . . . . . . . . . . . . . . . . | 2,128 |
| Total current liabilities (subtotal). . . . . . . . . . . . . . . . . . . . . . . . . . . . . . . . . . . . . . . . . . . . | 20,768 |
| Long-term debt ($35,976 − $2,128) . . . . . . . . . . . . . . . . . . . . . . . . . . . . . . . . . . . . . . . . . | 33,848 |
| Deferred income taxes (no change assumed) . . . . . . . . . . . . . . . . . . . . . . . . . . . . . . . . . . . | 12,354 |
| Other noncurrent liabilities (no change assumed) . . . . . . . . . . . . . . . . . . . . . . . . . . . . . . . . | 4,472 |
| Total liabilities (subtotal) . . . . . . . . . . . . . . . . . . . . . . . . . . . . . . . . . . . . . . . . . . . . . . . . . | 71,442 |
| Preferred stock (no change assumed) . . . . . . . . . . . . . . . . . . . . . . . . . . . . . . . . . . . . . . . . | 1,451 |
| Common stock (no change assumed) . . . . . . . . . . . . . . . . . . . . . . . . . . . . . . . . . . . . . . . . | 3,976 |
| Additional paid-in capital (no change assumed) . . . . . . . . . . . . . . . . . . . . . . . . . . . . . . . . . | 57,856 |
| Reserve for ESOP debt retirement (no change assumed) . . . . . . . . . . . . . . . . . . . . . . . . . . . | (1,288) |
| Accumulated other comprehensive income (no change assumed) . . . . . . . . . . . . . . . . . . . . . . | (518) |
| Treasury stock (no change assumed). . . . . . . . . . . . . . . . . . . . . . . . . . . . . . . . . . . . . . . . . | (34,235) |
| Retained earnings (computed*) . . . . . . . . . . . . . . . . . . . . . . . . . . . . . . . . . . . . . . . . . . . . . | 40,882 |
| Total shareholders' equity (subtotal). . . . . . . . . . . . . . . . . . . . . . . . . . . . . . . . . . . . . . . . . | 68,124 |
| Total liabilities and shareholders' equity (subtotal). . . . . . . . . . . . . . . . . . . . . . . . . . . . . . . . | $139,566 |

* Estimated retained earnings = Prior year retained earnings of $35,666 + Forecasted net income of $9,087 − Dividends of $3,871, where Dividends = Forecasted net income of $9,087 × Dividend payout rate (Dividends/Net income) of 42.6%.

analysis and forecasting of company financials (see Module 4 for a discussion). Accordingly, we must adjust the proportion of debt and equity, if necessary, to avoid an inadvertent shift in financial leverage.

To illustrate, the projected cash balance for P&G of $9,240 million is 6.62% of total assets. In 2005, PG's cash level was approximately 5% of total assets. This suggests that P&G will accumulate excess cash in 2006 and will not require additional financing. In our forecasted balance sheet, we can take the computed excess cash and (1) invest it in securities, in which case we must adjust the forecasted investment returns, or (2) assume that P&G repays some of its debt and/or repurchases some of its stock to maintain the existing total liabilities-to-equity ratio. (At December 31, 2005, P&G's liabilities-to-equity ratio was 1.16, computed as $72,787/$62,908.)

How we determine the adjustment to cash depends on whether we will adjust marketable securities or adjust a liability or equity account such as long-term debt or treasury stock. Adjusting the marketable securities account is straightforward and is the approach we take. We first compute the desired level of cash as: Prior year cash-to-total assets ratio × Forecasted total assets. This amount is then subtracted from the forecasted cash and the difference added to or subtracted from marketable securities. Adjusting a liability or equity account involves an additional calculation so that the final cash balance yields the same proportionate [common size] balances as the prior year given that total assets will be reduced by the excess cash. Specifically, we use the following equation:

$$\text{Cash adjustment} = \frac{\text{Forecasted cash balance} - (\text{Prior year cash-to-total-assets ratio} \times \text{Forecasted total assets})}{1 - \text{Prior year cash-to-total-assets ratio}}$$

P&G's cash-to-total-assets in 2006 is 5%. Using the initial forecasted cash balance of $9,240 million and the forecasted total assets of $139,566 million from our forecasted balance sheet (Exhibit 11.9), we determine that reducing cash by $2,262 million (and increasing investment securities by a like amount) yields a 5% ratio of cash-to-total-assets ratio. (If we had instead decided to adjust either long-term debt or an equity account, we would have reduced the cash balance by $2,380; computed as $\frac{\$9,240 - (5\% \times \$139,566)}{1 - 5\%}$.)

Exhibit 11.10 shows the new projected balances after the cash reduction of $2,262 million. Again, this approach assumes that P&G invests any excess cash in marketable securities. (Low-risk marketable securities presently yield about 2%; the excess cash of $2,262 will yield about $45 of additional investment income for P&G's fiscal 2008.) Exhibit 11.10 shows the revised balance sheet that invests the excess cash in marketable securities. (Alternatively, using the excess cash to retire long-term debt would reduce the cash level to 5% of forecasted total assets, and the total liabilities-to-equity ratio to 1.01; a leverage ratio of 1.01 is markedly different from 1.16 and so this alternative is problematic.)

| EXHIBIT 11.10 | P&G Forecasted Balance Sheet with Excess Cash Invested in Securities | | |
|---|---|---|---|
| **June 30, 2007 (in millions)** | **Initial Est.** | **Adjustment** | **Final Est.** |
| **Assets** | | | |
| Cash and cash equivalents . . . . . . . . . . . . . . . . . . . . . | $ 9,240 | $(2,262) | $ 6,978 |
| Investment securities . . . . . . . . . . . . . . . . . . . . . . . . . | 1,133 | 2,262 | 3,395 |
| Accounts receivable. . . . . . . . . . . . . . . . . . . . . . . . . . | 5,975 | | 5,975 |
| Inventories . . . . . . . . . . . . . . . . . . . . . . . . . . . . . . . . | 6,568 | | 6,568 |
| Deferred income taxes . . . . . . . . . . . . . . . . . . . . . . . . | 1,611 | | 1,611 |
| Prepaid expenses and other receivables . . . . . . . . . . . | 2,876 | | 2,876 |
| Total current assets . . . . . . . . . . . . . . . . . . . . . . . . . . | 27,403 | | 27,403 |
| Net property, plant and equipment . . . . . . . . . . . . . . . | 19,567 | | 19,567 |
| Net goodwill and other intangible assets. . . . . . . . . . . | 89,027 | | 89,027 |
| Other noncurrent assets. . . . . . . . . . . . . . . . . . . . . . . | 3,569 | | 3,569 |
| Total assets. . . . . . . . . . . . . . . . . . . . . . . . . . . . . . . . | $139,566 | | $139,566 |
| **Liabilities and Shareholders' Equity** | | | |
| Accounts payable. . . . . . . . . . . . . . . . . . . . . . . . . . . . | $ 5,128 | | $ 5,128 |
| Accrued and other liabilities. . . . . . . . . . . . . . . . . . . . | 10,003 | | 10,003 |
| Taxes payable. . . . . . . . . . . . . . . . . . . . . . . . . . . . . . | 3,509 | | 3,509 |
| Debt due within one year . . . . . . . . . . . . . . . . . . . . . . | 2,128 | | 2,128 |
| Total current liabilities. . . . . . . . . . . . . . . . . . . . . . . . | 20,768 | | 20,768 |
| Long-term debt . . . . . . . . . . . . . . . . . . . . . . . . . . . . . | 33,848 | | 33,848 |
| Deferred income taxes . . . . . . . . . . . . . . . . . . . . . . . . | 12,354 | | 12,354 |
| Other noncurrent liabilities . . . . . . . . . . . . . . . . . . . . . | 4,472 | | 4,472 |
| Total liabilities . . . . . . . . . . . . . . . . . . . . . . . . . . . . . . | 71,442 | | 71,442 |
| Preferred stock. . . . . . . . . . . . . . . . . . . . . . . . . . . . . | 1,451 | | 1,451 |
| Common stock. . . . . . . . . . . . . . . . . . . . . . . . . . . . . . | 3,976 | | 3,976 |
| Additional paid-in capital . . . . . . . . . . . . . . . . . . . . . . | 57,856 | | 57,856 |
| Reserve for ESOP debt retirement. . . . . . . . . . . . . . . . | (1,288) | | (1,288) |
| Accumulated other comprehensive income. . . . . . . . . | (518) | | (518) |
| Treasury stock . . . . . . . . . . . . . . . . . . . . . . . . . . . . . | (34,235) | | (34,235) |
| Retained earnings . . . . . . . . . . . . . . . . . . . . . . . . . . . | 40,882 | | 40,882 |
| Total shareholders' equity . . . . . . . . . . . . . . . . . . . . . | 68,124 | | 68,124 |
| Total liabilities and shareholders' equity. . . . . . . . . . . | $139,566 | | $139,566 |

# Forecasting the Statement of Cash Flows

Procter & Gamble's 2006 statement of cash flows is shown in Exhibit 11.11. We forecast the statement of cash flows using the forecasted income statement and cash-adjusted forecasted balance sheet (in Exhibit 11.10). We refer to the historical statement of cash flows primarily to check the reasonableness of our forecasts. We draw on the mechanics behind the preparation of the statement of cash flows, which we discuss in Module 3 and Appendix B. Specifically, once we have forecasts of the balance sheet and income statement, we can compute the forecasted statement of cash flows just as we would its historical counterpart. In particular, we compute changes in each of the balance sheet accounts and determine what type of cash flow arises from the change (operating, investing, or financing). The forecasted statement of cash flows for P&G, and its related computations, is in Exhibit 11.12.

| **EXHIBIT 11.11** | **Procter & Gamble Statement of Cash Flows** | | |
|---|---|---|---|
| **Years ended June 30 (in millions)** | **2006** | **2005** | **2004** |
| Cash and cash equivalents, beginning of year | $ 6,389 | $ 4,232 | $ 5,428 |
| Operating activities | | | |
| Net earnings | 8,684 | 6,923 | 6,156 |
| Depreciation and amortization | 2,627 | 1,884 | 1,733 |
| Share-based compensation expense | 585 | 524 | 491 |
| Deferred income taxes | (112) | 564 | 342 |
| Change in accounts receivable | (524) | (86) | (159) |
| Change in inventories | 383 | (644) | 56 |
| Change in accounts payable, accrued and other liabilities | 230 | (101) | 597 |
| Change in other operating assets and liabilities | (508) | (498) | (88) |
| Other | 10 | 113 | 227 |
| Total operating activities | 11,375 | 8,679 | 9,355 |
| Investing activities | | | |
| Capital expenditures | (2,667) | (2,181) | (2,024) |
| Proceeds from asset sales | 882 | 517 | 230 |
| Acquisitions, net of cash acquired | 171 | (572) | (7,476) |
| Change in investment securities | 884 | (100) | (874) |
| Total investing activities | (730) | (2,336) | (10,144) |
| Financing activities | | | |
| Dividends to shareholders | (3,703) | (2,731) | (2,539) |
| Change in short-term debt | (8,627) | 2,016 | 4,911 |
| Additions to long-term debt | 22,545 | 3,108 | 1,963 |
| Reductions of long-term debt | (5,282) | (2,013) | (1,188) |
| Impact of stock options and other | 1,319 | 521 | 562 |
| Treasury purchases | (16,830) | (5,026) | (4,070) |
| Total financing activities | (10,578) | (4,125) | (361) |
| Effect of exchange rate changes on cash and cash equivalents | 237 | (61) | (46) |
| Change in cash and cash equivalents | 304 | 2,157 | (1,196) |
| Cash and cash equivalents, end of year | $ 6,693 | $ 6,389 | $ 4,232 |

# Reassessing the Forecasts

After preparing the forecasted financial statements, it is useful to reassess whether they are reasonable in light of current economic and company conditions. This task is subjective and benefits from your knowledge of company, industry, and economic factors.

Many analysts and managers prepare "what-if" forecasted financial statements. Specifically, they change key assumptions, such as the forecasted sales growth or key cost ratios and then recompute the forecasted financial statements. These alternative forecasting scenarios indicate the sensitivity of a set of predicted outcomes to different assumptions about future economic conditions. Such sensitivity estimates can be useful for setting contingency plans and in identifying areas of vulnerability for future company performance and condition.

| EXHIBIT 11.12 | Procter & Gamble Forecasted Statement of Cash Flows |
|---|---|

| Year ended June 30 (in millions) | 2007 Est. |
|---|---:|
| Cash and cash equivalents, beginning of year (from prior year balance sheet)............ | $ 6,693 |
| Operating activities | |
| Net earnings...................................................... | 9,087 |
| Depreciation ($22,792 × 9.3%)*.......................................... | 2,120 |
| Share-based compensation expense (assumed to be zero)......................... | 0 |
| Change in deferred income taxes (assumed to be zero)........................... | 0 |
| Change in accounts receivable ($5,725 − $5,975)............................... | (250) |
| Change in inventories ($6,291 − $6,568)..................................... | (277) |
| Change in accounts payable ($4,910 − $5,128)................................ | 218 |
| Change in accrued and other liabilities ($9,587 − $10,003)....................... | 416 |
| Change in taxes payable ($3,360 − $3,509).................................. | 149 |
| Total operating activities (subtotal)........................................ | 11,463 |
| Investing activities | |
| Increase in marketable securities (from excess cash)............................ | (2,262) |
| Capital expenditures, net of proceeds from asset sales ($18,770 − $19,567 − $2,120)..... | (2,917) |
| Acquisitions, net of cash acquired (assumed to be zero).......................... | 0 |
| Change in investment securities (assumed to be zero)............................ | 0 |
| Total investing activities (subtotal)........................................ | (5,179) |
| Financing activities | |
| Dividends to shareholders (Est. net income $9,087 × Dividend payout rate 42.6%)........ | (3,871) |
| Change in short-term debt (assumed to be zero)................................ | 0 |
| Additions to long-term debt (assumed to be zero)............................... | 0 |
| Reductions of long-term debt ($35,976 − $33,848).............................. | (2,128) |
| Total financing activities (subtotal)........................................ | (5,999) |
| Change in cash and cash equivalents (subtotal)................................ | 285 |
| Cash and cash equivalents, end of year (total)................................ | $ 6,978 |

* For simplicity in this case, amortization is assumed to be zero.

## Forecasting Multiple Years

Many business decisions require forecasted financial statements for more than one year ahead. For example, managerial and capital budgeting, security valuation, and strategic analyses all benefit from reliable multiyear forecasts. Module 12 uses multiyear forecasts of financial results to estimate stock price for investment decisions.

Although there are different methods to achieve multiyear forecasts, we apply a straightforward approach: we repeat the forecasting procedure we used to forecast one-year ahead numbers. To illustrate, using the same forecasting assumptions we use to forecast 2007 results (shown in Exhibit 11.6), we can forecast P&G's 2008 sales as $74,358 million, computed as $71,224 million × 1.044. The remainder of the income statement can be forecasted from this sales level using the methodology we discuss above for one-year-ahead forecasts. Similarly for the balance sheet, and assuming a continuation of the current asset (and liability) turnover rates, we can forecast current assets and liabilities using the same methodology for one-year-ahead forecast. For example, 2008 accounts receivable are forecasted as $6,238 million, computed as $74,358 million/11.92.

Exhibit 11.13 illustrates two-year-ahead (2008) forecasting for P&G's income statement, balance sheet, and statement of cash flows; the 2007 forecasts are shown in the first column for reference. To reiterate, the two-year-ahead forecast is prepared using the same forecast assumptions we employed previously. As with the one-year-ahead forecast, we must adjust the final cash balance because residual cash will build up during the 2008 fiscal year. The projected cash of $9,758 million represents 6.8% of total assets whereas the historical relation (from 2005) is 5%. We adjust the cash for the residual amount by reducing cash by $2,570 million to $7,188 million, the latter computed as $143,759 million × 5%. The excess cash causes marketable securities to increase from $3,395 million to $5,965 million.

Any forecast assumptions (such as cost percentages and turnover rates) can be changed in future years as necessary. For example, we might reduce expected sales growth if we feel that the market is becoming saturated or reduce the accounts receivable turnover rate if we expect the economy to slow. We can replicate the process for any desired forecast horizon.

| EXHIBIT 11.13 | Procter & Gamble Two-Year-Ahead Forecasted Income Statement | |
| --- | --- | --- |
| **2007 Est.** | **($ millions)** | **2008 Est.** |
| $ 71,224 | Net sales ($71,224 × 1.044) .................................. | $ 74,358 |
| 34,615 | Cost of products sold ($74,358 × 48.6%)........................ | 36,138 |
| 36,609 | Gross profit ($74,358 × 51.4%)................................ | 38,220 |
| 22,792 | Selling, general and administrative expense ($74,358 × 32.0%) ....... | 23,795 |
| 13,817 | Operating income (subtotal)................................. | 14,425 |
| 1,119 | Interest expense (no change assumed).......................... | 1,119 |
| 283 | Other nonoperating income, net ($283 + $45)*................... | 328 |
| 12,981 | Earnings before income taxes (subtotal) ........................ | 13,634 |
| 3,894 | Income taxes ($13,634 × 30.0%) .............................. | 4,090 |
| $ 9,087 | Net earnings (total)........................................ | $ 9,544 |

*Includes $45 interest income from excess cash invested in 2% marketable securities, computed as $2,262 × 2%.

| | Procter & Gamble Two-Year-Ahead Forecasted Balance Sheet | |
| --- | --- | --- |
| **2007 Est.** | **($ millions)** | **2008 Est.** |
| $ 6,978 | Cash and cash equivalents (total liabilities and equity less all noncash assets) ..................................... | $ 7,188 |
| 3,395 | Investment securities (adjusted for excess cash) .................. | 5,965 |
| 5,975 | Accounts receivable ($74,358/11.92)........................... | 6,238 |
| 6,568 | Inventories ($36,138/5.27) ................................... | 6,857 |
| 1,611 | Deferred income taxes (no change assumed) .................... | 1,611 |
| 2,876 | Prepaid expenses and other receivables (no change assumed) ........ | 2,876 |
| 27,403 | Total current assets (subtotal) ................................ | 30,735 |
| 19,567 | Net property, plant and equipment ($74,358/3.64) ................. | 20,428 |
| 89,027 | Net goodwill and other intangible assets (no change assumed)........ | 89,027 |
| 3,569 | Other noncurrent assets (no change assumed)................... | 3,569 |
| $139,566 | Total assets (total) ........................................ | $143,759 |
| $ 5,128 | Accounts payable ($36,138/6.75) ............................. | $ 5,354 |
| 10,003 | Accrued and other liabilities ($74,358/7.12)..................... | 10,444 |
| 3,509 | Taxes payable ($4,090 × 90.1%)............................... | 3,685 |
| 2,128 | Debt due within one year (no change assumed) .................. | 2,128 |
| 20,768 | Total current liabilities (subtotal)............................. | 21,611 |
| 33,848 | Long-term debt ($38,848 − $2,128) ........................... | 31,720 |
| 12,354 | Deferred income taxes (no change assumed) .................... | 12,354 |
| 4,472 | Other noncurrent liabilities (no change assumed) ................. | 4,472 |
| 71,442 | Total liabilities (subtotal)..................................... | 70,157 |
| 1,451 | Preferred stock (no change assumed)........................... | 1,451 |
| 3,976 | Common stock (no change assumed)............................ | 3,976 |
| 57,856 | Additional paid-in capital (no change assumed) ................... | 57,856 |
| (1,288) | Reserve for ESOP debt retirement (no change assumed)............. | (1,288) |
| (518) | Accumulated other comprehensive income (no change assumed)...... | (518) |
| (34,235) | Treasury stock (no change assumed) ........................... | (34,235) |
| 40,882 | Retained earnings ($40,882 + $9,544 − [$9,544 × 42.6%])........... | 46,360 |
| 68,124 | Total shareholders' equity (subtotal) ........................... | 73,602 |
| $139,566 | Total liabilities and shareholders' equity (total) ................... | $143,759 |

| | Procter & Gamble Two-Year-Ahead Forecasted Statement of Cash Flows | |
|---:|:---|---:|
| **2007 Est.** | **($ millions)** | **2008 Est.** |
| $ 6,693 | Cash and cash equivalents, beginning of year . . . . . . . . . . . . . . . . . . . . | $ 6,978 |
| | Operating activities | |
| 9,087 | Net earnings. . . . . . . . . . . . . . . . . . . . . . . . . . . . . . . . . . . . . . . . . . . . . . | 9,544 |
| 2,120 | Depreciation and amortization ($23,795 × 9.3%) . . . . . . . . . . . . . . . . . | 2,213 |
| 0 | Share-based compensation expense (assumed to be zero) . . . . . . . . . . | 0 |
| 0 | Deferred income taxes (assumed to be zero) . . . . . . . . . . . . . . . . . . . . | 0 |
| (250) | Change in accounts receivable ($5,975 − $6,238) . . . . . . . . . . . . . . . . | (263) |
| (277) | Change in inventories ($6,568 − $6,857). . . . . . . . . . . . . . . . . . . . . . . | (289) |
| 218 | Change in accounts payable ($5,354 − $5,128) . . . . . . . . . . . . . . . . . . | 226 |
| 416 | Change in accrued and other liabilities ($10,444 − $10,003) . . . . . . . . . | 441 |
| 149 | Change in taxes payable ($3,685 − $3,509) . . . . . . . . . . . . . . . . . . . . . | 176 |
| 11,463 | Total operating activities (subtotal) . . . . . . . . . . . . . . . . . . . . . . . . . . . . | 12,048 |
| | Investing activities | |
| (2,262) | Increase in marketable securities (excess cash) . . . . . . . . . . . . . . . . . . | (2,570) |
| (2,917) | Capital expenditures, net of proceeds from asset sales ($19,567 − $20,428 − $2,213) . . . . . . . . . . . . . . . . . . . . . . . . . . . . . . . | (3,074) |
| 0 | Acquisitions, net of cash acquired (assumed to be zero) . . . . . . . . . . . . | 0 |
| (5,179) | Total investing activities (subtotal) . . . . . . . . . . . . . . . . . . . . . . . . . . . . . | (5,644) |
| | Financing activities | |
| (3,871) | Dividends to shareholders ($9,544 × 42.6%) . . . . . . . . . . . . . . . . . . . . | (4,066) |
| | Change in short-term debt (assumed to be zero) . . . . . . . . . . . . . . . . . . | 0 |
| | Additions to long-term debt (assumed to be zero) . . . . . . . . . . . . . . . . . | 0 |
| (2,128) | Reductions of long-term debt ($35,976 − $31,348 ). . . . . . . . . . . . . . . . | (2,128) |
| (5,999) | Total financing activities (subtotal). . . . . . . . . . . . . . . . . . . . . . . . . . . . . | (6,194) |
| 285 | Change in cash and cash equivalents (subtotal) . . . . . . . . . . . . . . . . . . | 210 |
| $ 6,978 | Cash and cash equivalents, end of year (total) . . . . . . . . . . . . . . . . . . . | $ 7,188 |

The two-year-ahead forecasts in Exhibit 11.13 illustrate the technique used to forecast an additional year. To simplify exposition, we have not altered any of the forecast assumptions, and focus solely on the forecasting mechanics. However, it is often appropriate to modify these assumptions. For example, we might wish to increase the forecasted depreciation expense due to the forecasted acquisition of depreciable long-term operating assets in 2007, and to reduce the forecasted interest expense for 2007 in consideration of the repayment of long-term debt.

## MID-MODULE REVIEW 2

Following is financial statement information from Colgate-Palmolive Company.

| Income Statement For years ended December 31 ($ millions) | 2005 | 2004 |
|:---|---:|---:|
| Net sales. . . . . . . . . . . . . . . . . . . . . . . . . . . . . . . . . . . . | $11,396.9 | $10,584.2 |
| Cost of sales. . . . . . . . . . . . . . . . . . . . . . . . . . . . . . . . . | 5,191.9 | 4,747.2 |
| Gross profit. . . . . . . . . . . . . . . . . . . . . . . . . . . . . . . . . . | 6,205.0 | 5,837.0 |
| Selling, general and administrative expenses . . . . . . . . | 3,990.0 | 3,714.9 |
| Operating profit . . . . . . . . . . . . . . . . . . . . . . . . . . . . . . | 2,215.0 | 2,122.1 |
| Interest expense, net . . . . . . . . . . . . . . . . . . . . . . . . . . | 136.0 | 119.7 |
| Income before income taxes . . . . . . . . . . . . . . . . . . . . | 2,079.0 | 2,002.4 |
| Provision for income taxes. . . . . . . . . . . . . . . . . . . . . . | 727.6 | 675.3 |
| Net income. . . . . . . . . . . . . . . . . . . . . . . . . . . . . . . . . . | $ 1,351.4 | $ 1,327.1 |

| Balance Sheet As of December 31 ($ millions) | 2005 | 2004 |
|---|---|---|
| **Assets** | | |
| Cash and cash equivalents | $ 340.7 | $ 319.6 |
| Receivables (less allowances of $41.7 and $47.2, respectively) | 1,309.4 | 1,319.9 |
| Inventories | 855.8 | 845.5 |
| Other current assets | 251.2 | 254.9 |
| Total current assets | 2,757.1 | 2,739.9 |
| Property, plant, and equipment, net | 2,544.1 | 2,647.7 |
| Goodwill | 1,845.7 | 1,891.7 |
| Other intangible assets, net | 783.2 | 832.4 |
| Other assets | 577.0 | 561.2 |
| Total assets | $8,507.1 | $8,672.9 |
| **Liabilities and Shareholders' Equity** | | |
| Notes and loans payable | $ 171.5 | $ 134.3 |
| Current portion of long-term debt | 356.7 | 451.3 |
| Accounts payable | 876.1 | 864.4 |
| Accrued income taxes | 215.5 | 153.1 |
| Other accruals | 1,123.2 | 1,127.6 |
| Total current liabilities | 2,743.0 | 2,730.7 |
| Long-term debt | 2,918.0 | 3,089.5 |
| Deferred income taxes | 554.7 | 509.6 |
| Other liabilities | 941.3 | 1,097.7 |
| Shareholders' equity | | |
| Preference stock | 253.7 | 274.0 |
| Common stock, $1 par value (1,000,000,000 shares authorized, 732,853,180 shares issued) | 732.9 | 732.9 |
| Additional paid-in capital | 1,064.4 | 1,093.8 |
| Retained earnings | 8,968.1 | 8,223.9 |
| Accumulated other comprehensive income | (1,804.7) | (1,806.2) |
| | 9,214.4 | 8,518.4 |
| Unearned compensation | (283.3) | (307.6) |
| Treasury stock, at cost | (7,581.0) | (6,965.4) |
| Total shareholders' equity | 1,350.1 | 1,245.4 |
| Total liabilities and shareholders' equity | $8,507.1 | $8,672.9 |

Forecast the Colgate-Palmolive balance sheet and income statement for 2006 using the following additional information (cost of goods sold margin can be inferred as sales minus gross profit margin; assume no change for all other accounts not listed below).

| Key Financial Relations and Measures ($ millions) | 2005 |
|---|---|
| Net sales growth ([$11,396.9/$10,584.2] − 1) | 7.7% |
| Gross profit margin ($6,205.0/$11,396.9) | 54.4% |
| Selling, general and administrative expenses/ Net sales ($3,990.0/$11,396.9) | 35.0% |
| Depreciation / Selling, general and administrative expenses* ($329.3/$3,990.0) | 8.3% |
| Provision for income taxes/ Income before income taxes ($727.6/$2,079.0)) | 35.0% |
| Net sales/ Year-end receivables ($11,396.9/$1,309.4) | 8.70 |
| Cost of sales/ Year-end inventories ($5,191.9/$855.8) | 6.07 |
| Cost of sales/ Year-end accounts payable ($5,191.9/$876.1) | 5.93 |
| Net sales/ Year-end property, plant and equipment, net ($11,396.9/$2,544.1) | 4.48 |
| Net sales/ Year-end other accruals ($11,396.9/$1,123.2) | 10.15 |
| Accrued income taxes/ Provision for income taxes ($215.5/$727.6) | 29.6% |
| Dividends paid (provided in statement of cash flows; not reproduced here) | $607.2 |
| Current maturities of long-term debt | $356.7 |

*Depreciation expense of $329 is reported in the statement of cash flows (not reproduced here) and is included in selling, general and administrative expenses. All other accounts are assumed to remain constant.

## Solution

Forecasted 2006 financial statements for Colgate-Palmolive follow.

| Forecasted Income Statement | |
|---|---|
| ($ millions) | 2006 Est. |
| Net sales ($11,396.9 × 1.077) | $12,274.5 |
| Cost of sales ($12,274.5 × 45.6%) | 5,597.2 |
| Gross profit ($12,274.5 × 54.4%) | 6,677.3 |
| Selling, general, administrative, and other expenses ($12,274.5 × 35.0%) | 4,296.1 |
| Operating profit (subtotal) | 2,381.2 |
| Interest expense, net (no change assumed) | 136.0 |
| Income before income taxes (subtotal) | 2,245.2 |
| Provision for income taxes ($2,245.2 × 35%) | 785.8 |
| Net income (total) | $ 1,459.4 |

| Forecasted Balance Sheet | |
|---|---|
| ($ millions) | 2006 Est. |
| **Assets** | |
| Cash and cash equivalents (total forecasted liabilities and equity less all noncash assets) | $ 643.7 |
| Receivables ($12,274.5/8.70) | 1,410.9 |
| Inventories ($5,597.2/6.07) | 922.1 |
| Other current assets (no change assumed) | 251.2 |
| Total current assets (subtotal) | 3,227.9 |
| Property, plant and equipment, net ($12,274.5/4.48) | 2,739.8 |
| Goodwill and other intangible assets, net (no change assumed) | 2,628.9 |
| Other assets (no change assumed) | 577.0 |
| Total assets (total) | $9,173.6 |
| **Liabilities and Shareholders' Equity** | |
| Notes and loans payable (no change assumed) | $ 171.5 |
| Current portion of long-term debt (no change assumed) | 356.7 |
| Accounts payable ($5,597.2/5.93) | 943.9 |
| Accrued income taxes ($785.8 x 29.6%) | 232.6 |
| Other accruals ($12,274.5/10.15) | 1,209.3 |
| Total current liabilities (subtotal) | 2,914.0 |
| Long-term debt (Prior year long-term debt of $2,918 − Prior year debt due within one year $356.7) | 2,561.3 |
| Deferred income taxes (no change assumed) | 554.7 |
| Other liabilities (no change assumed) | 941.3 |
| Total liabilities (subtotal) | 6,971.3 |
| Preference stock (no change assumed) | 253.7 |
| Common stock (no change assumed) | 732.9 |
| Additional paid-in capital (no change assumed) | 1,064.4 |
| Retained earnings (Prior year retained earnings, $8,968.1 + Forecasted net income, $1,459.4 − Dividends, $607.2) | 9,820.3 |
| Accumulated other comprehensive income (no change assumed) | (1,804.7) |
| Unearned compensation (no change assumed) | (283.3) |
| Treasury stock (no change assumed) | (7,581.0) |
| Total shareholders' equity (subtotal) | 2,202.3 |
| Total liabilities and shareholders' equity (total) | $9,173.6 |

*Note:* To compute the residual cash balance, we initially assume no change in the capital accounts and the level of debt (other than repayment of $356.7 in current maturities of long-term debt). This yields a forecasted cash balance of $643.7 million, which is 7% of projected total assets. In 2005, Colgate-Palmolive reported cash at 4% of total assets. The forecasting process suggests an accumulation of excess cash; that is, more cash than necessary to efficiently operate. One additional forecasting adjustment would be to assume either the investment of the excess cash in securities or the use of it to retire long-term debt and equity (in a manner to maintain the historic leverage ratio).

## Parsimonious Method to Multiyear Forecasting

**LO3** Describe and illustrate a parsimonious method for multiyear forecasting of net operating profit and net operating assets.

The forecasting process described above uses a considerable amount of available information to derive accurate forecasts. We can, however, simplify the process by using less information without seriously impairing accuracy. Stock valuation models commonly use more parsimonious methods to compute multiyear forecasts for an initial screening of prospective securities. For example, in Module 12 we introduce two stock valuation models that use parsimonious methods. One model utilizes forecasted free cash flows and the other uses forecasted net operating profits after tax (NOPAT) and net operating assets (NOA); see Module 4 for descriptions of these variables. Since free cash flows are equal to net operating profits after tax (NOPAT) less the change in net operating assets (NOA), we can accommodate both stock valuation models with forecasts of NOPAT and NOA.

One approach is to forecast NOPAT and NOA using the methodology outlined in this Module. A second approach is to use a more parsimonious method that requires three crucial inputs:

1. Sales growth
2. Net operating profit margin (NOPM); defined in Module 4 as NOPAT divided by sales
3. Net operating asset turnover (NOAT); defined in Module 4 as sales divided by average NOA, but using year-end NOA rather than average NOA to forecast year-end amounts.

To illustrate, we use P&G's 2006 income statement, from Exhibit 11.4, and its 2006 balance sheet, from Exhibit 11.7, to determine the following measures (assuming a statutory tax rate of 36.5% on nonoperating revenues and expenses):

| | |
|---|---:|
| Sales. . . . . . . . . . . . . . . . . . . . . . . . . . . . . . . . . . . . . . . . . . . . . . . . . . . . . . . | $68,222 |
| Sales growth rate . . . . . . . . . . . . . . . . . . . . . . . . . . . . . . . . . . . . . . . . . . . . . | 4.4% |
| Net operating profit *before* tax . . . . . . . . . . . . . . . . . . . . . . . . . . . . . . . . . . . | $13,249 |
| Tax rate on operating profit* {$3,729 + [($1,119 − $283) × 0.365)]}/$13,249 . . . . . . . . . . . . | 30.4% |
| NOPAT ($13,249 × [1 − 0.304]) . . . . . . . . . . . . . . . . . . . . . . . . . . . . . . . . . . . . . . | $9,221 |
| NOA ($135,695 − $1,133) − ($4,910 + $9,587 + $3,360 + $12,354 + $4,472) . . . . . . . . . | $99,879 |
| NOPM ($9,221/$68,222). . . . . . . . . . . . . . . . . . . . . . . . . . . . . . . . . . . . . . . . . . . | 13.5% |
| NOAT ($68,222/$99,879) . . . . . . . . . . . . . . . . . . . . . . . . . . . . . . . . . . . . . . . . . . | 0.68 |

\* See Exhibit 11.5 for an explanation.

Using these inputs, we forecast P&G's sales, NOPAT and NOA. Each year's forecasted sales is the prior year sales multiplied successively by (1+ Growth rate), or 1.044 in this case, and then rounded to whole digits. NOPAT is computed using forecasted (and rounded) sales each year times the 2006 NOPM of 13.5%; and NOA is computed using forecasted (and rounded) sales divided by the 2006 NOAT of 0.68. Forecasted numbers for 2007 through 2010 are in Exhibit 11.14; supporting computations are in parentheses.

| EXHIBIT 11.14 | Procter & Gamble Multiyear Forecasts of Sales, NOPAT and NOA | | | | |
|---|---|---|---|---|---|
| **($ millions)** | **2006** | **2007 Est.** | **2008 Est.** | **2009 Est.** | **2010 Est.** |
| Net sales. . . . . | $68,222 | **$71,224** | **$74,358** | **$77,629** | **$81,045** |
| | | ($68,222 × 1.044) | ($71,224 × 1.044) | ($74,358 × 1.044) | ($77,629 × 1.044) |
| NOPAT . . . . . . | $9,221 | **$9,615** | **$10,038** | **$10,480** | **$10,941** |
| | ($13,249 × [1 − 0.304]) | ($71,224 × 13.5%) | ($74,358 × 13.5%) | ($77,629 × 13.5%) | ($81,045 × 13.5%) |
| NOA . . . . . . . . | $99,879 | **$104,741** | **$109,350** | **$114,160** | **$119,184** |
| | | ($71,224/0.68) | ($74,358/0.68) | ($77,629/0.68) | ($81,045/0.68) |

This forecasting process can be continued for any desired forecast horizon. Also, the forecast assumptions such as sales growth, NOPM, and NOAT can be varied by year, if desired. This alternative, parsimonious method is much simpler than the primary method illustrated in this module. However, its simplicity does forgo information that can impact forecast accuracy.

## MODULE-END REVIEW

Johnson & Johnson (J&J) reports 2005 sales of $50,514 million, net operating profit after tax (NOPAT) of $10,134 million, and net operating assets (NOA) of $40,453 million. J&J's NOPM is computed as 20% ($10,134 million/$50,514 million). In a review of J&J's 10-K, we see in its tax footnote that its effective tax rate for 2005 is 23.8%, compared with 33.7% in 2004 and 30.2% in 2003. Analysis reveals that its 2005 effective tax rate is lower due to foreign tax credits and a reversal of a tax liability tied to a technical correction with the American Jobs Creation Act of 2004. We view the tax credits and technical correction as transitory. As a result, we view J&J's NOPM as abnormally high. Accordingly, in our projection of its financial information, we decide to use 32% as J&J's effective tax rate, an average of its 2004 and 2003 effective tax rates.

### Required

1. Assume that J&J's pretax GAAP income for 2005 is $13,656 million, and its reported tax expense is $3,245 million. Compute J&J's adjusted NOPAT and NOPM using the adjusted 32% tax rate.
2. Compute J&J's NOAT for 2005.
3. Use the parsimonious forecast model to project J&J's sales, NOPAT and NOA for 2006 through 2009. Use the NOPAT and NOAT computed in parts *1* and *2*, and assume a sales growth rate of 6.5%.

### Solution

1. If we apply 32% to J&J's $13,656 million pretax GAAP income for 2005 we get tax expense of $4,370 million, an increase of $1,125 million. J&J's adjusted 2005 NOPAT is, therefore, reduced by that amount to $9,009 million ($10,134 million − $1,125 million). The adjusted NOPM is, therefore, 18% ($9,009/$50,514), a reduction of 2 percentage points from the reported NOPM. This adjusted NOPM is the one we use in our projections.
2. NOAT = Sales/NOA = $50,514/$40,453 = 1.25
3. Projections for 2006 through 2009 using the parsimonious model follow.

| | 2005 | 2006 | 2007 | 2008 | 2009 |
|---|---|---|---|---|---|
| Sales...... | $50,514 | $53,797 | $57,294 | $61,018 | $64,985 |
| | | ($50,514 × 1.065) | ($53,797 × 1.065) | ($57,294 × 1.065) | ($61,018 × 1.065) |
| NOPAT .... | $9,009 | $9,683 | $10,313 | $10,983 | $11,697 |
| | (given) | ($53,797 × 0.18) | ($57,294 × 0.18) | ($61,018 × 0.18) | ($64,985 × 0.18) |
| NOA ...... | $40,453 | $43,038 | $45,835 | $48,814 | $51,988 |
| | (given) | ($53,797/1.25) | ($57,294/1.25) | ($61,018/1.25) | ($64,985/1.25) |

## GUIDANCE ANSWERS

**MANAGERIAL DECISION** **You Are a Corporate Analyst**

GAAP allows considerable flexibility in the format of the income statement, as long as all of the required elements are present. Although combining operating and nonoperating items and subtotaling to pretax profit is common in practice, many companies subtotal to pretax operating profit, which segregates nonoperating items. The argument to break with tradition and subtotal to pretax operating profit rests on the concept of *transparency*. Transparency in financial reporting means that the financial statements are clear and understandable to the reader. Many believe that greater transparency results in more trust and credibility by users of financial information. Empirical evidence supports the positive benefits of financial statement transparency. Since analysts are concerned with operating profits, your company might reap intangible benefits by being up-front in its presentation. Conversely, seeking to mask operating results, especially if misleading to outsiders, can damage management credibility.

# DISCUSSION QUESTIONS

**Q11-1.** Describe the process of *adjusting* financial statements in preparation for forecasting them.

**Q11-2.** Identify three types of adjustments (for forecasting purposes) that relate to the income statement and provide two examples of each.

**Q11-3.** What is the objective of the adjusting process as it relates to forecasting of the balance sheet?

**Q11-4.** What are the main types of adjustments (for forecasting purposes) that relate to the statement of cash flows? Provide two examples of each.

**Q11-5.** Identify at least two applications that use forecasted financial statements.

**Q11-6.** What procedures must normally take place before the forecasting process begins?

**Q11-7.** In addition to recent trends, what other types and sources of information can be brought to bear in the forecasting of sales?

**Q11-8.** Describe the rationale for use of year-end balances in the computation of turnover rates that are used to forecast selected balance sheet accounts.

**Q11-9.** Identify and describe the steps in forecasting the income statement.

**Q11-10.** Describe the two-step process of forecasting and adjusting the residual cash balance when forecasting the balance sheet.

# MINI EXERCISES

**M11-11. Forecasting an Income Statement (LO2)**

Abercrombie & Fitch reports the following fiscal year income statements.

Abercrombie & Fitch (ANF)

| Income Statement ($ thousands) | 2006 | 2005 | 2004 |
|---|---|---|---|
| Net sales | $2,784,711 | $2,021,253 | $1,707,810 |
| Cost of goods sold | 933,295 | 680,029 | 624,640 |
| Gross profit | 1,851,416 | 1,341,224 | 1,083,170 |
| Stores and distribution expense | 1,000,755 | 738,244 | 597,416 |
| Marketing, general and administrative expense | 313,457 | 259,835 | 155,553 |
| Other operating income, net | (5,534) | (4,490) | (979) |
| Operating income | 542,738 | 347,635 | 331,180 |
| Interest income, net | (6,674) | (5,218) | (3,708) |
| Income before income taxes | 549,412 | 352,853 | 334,888 |
| Provision for income taxes | 215,426 | 136,477 | 130,058 |
| Net Income | $ 333,986 | $ 216,376 | $ 204,830 |

Forecast Abercrombie & Fitch's 2007 income statement assuming the following income statement relations ($ 000s); cost of goods sold can be inferred as sales minus gross profit, and assume no change for all other accounts not listed below.

| | |
|---|---|
| Net sales | 37.8% |
| Gross profit margin | 66.5% |
| Stores and distribution expense/Net sales | 35.9% |
| Marketing, general and administrative expense/Net sales | 11.3% |
| Other operating income, net/Net sales | −0.2% |
| Provision for income taxes/Income before income taxes | 39.2% |
| Interest income, net | no change |

**M11-12. Forecasting an Income Statement (LO2)**

Best Buy reports the following fiscal year income statements.

| Income Statement<br>For the Fiscal Years Ended ($ millions) | February 25,<br>2006 | February 26,<br>2005 | February 28,<br>2004 |
|---|---|---|---|
| Revenue | $30,848 | $27,433 | $24,548 |
| Cost of goods sold | 23,122 | 20,938 | 18,677 |
| Gross profit | 7,726 | 6,495 | 5,871 |
| Selling, general and administrative expenses | 6,082 | 5,053 | 4,567 |
| Operating income | 1,644 | 1,442 | 1,304 |
| Net interest income (expense) | 77 | 1 | (8) |
| Earnings from continuing operations before<br>  income tax expense | 1,721 | 1,443 | 1,296 |
| Income tax expense | 581 | 509 | 496 |
| Earnings from continuing operations | 1,140 | 934 | 800 |
| Loss from discontinued operations, net of tax | — | — | (29) |
| Gain (loss) on disposal of discontinued operations,<br>  net of tax | — | 50 | (66) |
| Net earnings | $ 1,140 | $ 984 | $ 705 |

Forecast Best Buy's fiscal year 2007 income statement assuming the following income statement relations; cost of goods sold can be inferred as sales minus gross profit, and assume no change for all other accounts not listed below.

| | |
|---|---|
| Revenue growth | 12.4% |
| Gross profit margin | 25.0% |
| Selling, general and administrative expense/Revenue | 19.7% |
| Income tax expense/Earnings from continuing operations before income tax | 33.8% |

**M11-13. Forecasting an Income Statement (LO2)**

General Mills reports the following fiscal year income statements.

| Income Statement<br>Fiscal year ended (in millions, except per share data) | May 28, 2006 | May 29, 2005 | May 30, 2004 |
|---|---|---|---|
| Net sales | $11,640 | $11,244 | $11,070 |
| Costs and expenses | | | |
| Cost of sales | 6,966 | 6,834 | 6,584 |
| Selling, general and administrative | 2,678 | 2,418 | 2,443 |
| Interest, net | 399 | 455 | 508 |
| Restructuring and other exit costs | 30 | 84 | 26 |
| Divestitures (gain) | — | (499) | — |
| Debt repurchase costs | — | 137 | — |
| Total costs and expenses | 10,073 | 9,429 | 9,561 |
| Earnings before income taxes and after-tax earnings<br>  from joint ventures | 1,567 | 1,815 | 1,509 |
| Income taxes | 541 | 664 | 528 |
| After-tax earnings from joint ventures | 64 | 89 | 74 |
| Net earnings | $ 1,090 | $ 1,240 | $ 1,055 |
| Earnings per share—basic | $ 3.05 | $ 3.34 | $ 2.82 |
| Earnings per share—diluted | $ 2.90 | $ 3.08 | $ 2.60 |
| Dividends per share | $ 1.34 | $ 1.24 | $ 1.10 |

Forecast General Mill's fiscal year 2007 income statement assuming the following income statement relations (assume no change for Interest, net).

| | |
|---|---:|
| Net sales growth. . . . . . . . . . . . . . . . . . . . . . . . . . . . . . . . . . . . . . . . . . . . . . . . . . . . . | 3.5% |
| Cost of sales margin. . . . . . . . . . . . . . . . . . . . . . . . . . . . . . . . . . . . . . . . . . . . . . . . . . | 59.8% |
| Selling, general and administrative/Net sales . . . . . . . . . . . . . . . . . . . . . . . . . . . . . . | 23.0% |
| Restructuring and other exit costs/Net sales. . . . . . . . . . . . . . . . . . . . . . . . . . . . . . . | 0.3% |
| After-tax earnings from joint ventures/Net sales . . . . . . . . . . . . . . . . . . . . . . . . . . . . | −0.5% |
| Income taxes/Earnings before income taxes and after-tax earnings from joint ventures . . . . | 33.2% |

**M11-14. Analyzing, Forecasting, and Interpreting Working Capital  (LO2)**

Harley-Davidson reports 2005 net operating working capital of $2,384 million and 2005 long-term operating assets of $812 million.

Harley-Davidson (HOG)

*a.* Forecast Harley-Davidson's 2006 net operating working capital assuming forecasted revenues of $6,051 million, net operating working capital turnover of 2.38 times, and long-term operating asset turnover of 6.99 times. (Both turnover rates are computed here using year-end balances. Finance receivables and related debt are considered operating under the assumption that they are an integral part of Harley's operating activities).

*b.* Most of Harley's receivables arise from its financing activities relating to purchases of motorcycles by consumers and dealers. What effect will these receivables have on Harley's operating working capital turnover rate?

**M11-15. Analyzing, Forecasting, and Interpreting Working Capital  (LO2)**

Nike reports 2005 net operating working capital of $3,992 million and 2005 long-term operating assets of $1,980 million.

Nike (NKE)

*a.* Forecast Nike's 2006 net operating working capital assuming forecasted sales of $15,389 million, net operating working capital turnover of 3.44 times, and long-term operating asset turnover of 6.94 times. (Both turnover rates are computed here using year-end balances.)

*b.* Does it seem reasonable that Nike's operating working capital turnover is less than its long-term operating asset turnover? Explain.

**M11-16. Interpreting and Adjusting Balance Sheet Forecasts for a Negative Cash Balance  (LO2)**

Assume that your initial forecast of a balance sheet yields a negative cash balance.

*a.* What does a forecasted negative cash balance imply?

*b.* Given a negative cash balance, what would be your next step in forecasting the balance sheet? Explain.

**M11-17. Forecasting the Balance Sheet and Operating Cash Flows  (LO2)**

Refer to the General Mills information in M11-13. General Mills reports the following current assets and current liabilities from its 2006 fiscal year-end balance sheet.

General Mills (GIS)

| (In millions) | May 28, 2006 | May 29, 2005 |
|---|---:|---:|
| **Current assets** | | |
| Cash and cash equivalents. . . . . . . . . . . . . . . . . . . . . | $ 647 | $ 573 |
| Receivables . . . . . . . . . . . . . . . . . . . . . . . . . . . . . . . . | 1,076 | 1,034 |
| Inventories . . . . . . . . . . . . . . . . . . . . . . . . . . . . . . . . . | 1,055 | 1,037 |
| Prepaid expenses and other current assets. . . . . . . . . | 216 | 203 |
| Deferred income taxes . . . . . . . . . . . . . . . . . . . . . . . . | 182 | 208 |
| Total current assets. . . . . . . . . . . . . . . . . . . . . . . . . . | $3,176 | $3,055 |
| **Current liabilities** | | |
| Accounts payable. . . . . . . . . . . . . . . . . . . . . . . . . . . . | $1,151 | $1,136 |
| Current portion of long-term debt . . . . . . . . . . . . . . . . | 2,131 | 1,638 |
| Notes payable. . . . . . . . . . . . . . . . . . . . . . . . . . . . . . . | 1,503 | 299 |
| Other current liabilities . . . . . . . . . . . . . . . . . . . . . . . . | 1,353 | 1,111 |
| Total current liabilities . . . . . . . . . . . . . . . . . . . . . . . . | $6,138 | $4,184 |

Using your forecasted income statement from M11-13, and the following information on General Mills' financial statement relations, forecast General Mill's accounts receivable, inventories, and accounts payable as of the end of May 2007.

| Year-end turnover rates | 2006 |
|---|---|
| Net sales/Year-end receivables . . . . . . . . . . . . . . . . . | 10.82 |
| Cost of sales/Year-end inventories. . . . . . . . . . . . . . . | 6.60 |
| Cost of sales/Year-end accounts payable . . . . . . . . . | 6.05 |

**M11-18. Adjusting the Balance Sheet (LO1)**

Prizer, Inc. (PFE)

Prizer, Inc. (PFE) reports the following footnote to its 2005 10-K:

> In the third quarter of 2005, we sold the last of three European generic pharmaceutical businesses which we had included in our Human Health segment and had become a part of Pfizer in April 2003 in connection with our acquisition of Pharmacia, for 4.7 million euro (approximately $5.6 million) and recorded a loss of $3 million ($2 million, net of tax) in *Gains on sales of discontinued operations—net of tax* in the consolidated statement of income for 2005.

What adjustment(s) might we consider before we forecast Pfizer's income for 2006? How would we treat the cash proceeds that Pfizer realized on such a sale?

# EXERCISES

**E11-19. Analyzing, Forecasting, and Interpreting both Income Statement and Balance Sheet (LO2)**

Whole Foods Market, Inc. (WFMI)

Following are the fiscal year income statement and balance sheet of Whole Foods Market, Inc.

| Income Statement (in $ 000s) | 2005 | 2004 | 2003 |
|---|---|---|---|
| Sales. . . . . . . . . . . . . . . . . . . . . . . . . . . . . . . . . . . | $4,701,289 | $3,864,950 | $3,148,593 |
| Cost of goods sold and occupancy costs . . . . . . | 3,052,184 | 2,523,816 | 2,070,334 |
| Gross profit. . . . . . . . . . . . . . . . . . . . . . . . . . . . . . | 1,649,105 | 1,341,134 | 1,078,259 |
| Direct store expenses. . . . . . . . . . . . . . . . . . . . . | 1,223,473 | 986,040 | 794,422 |
| General and administrative expenses . . . . . . . . . | 158,864 | 119,800 | 100,693 |
| Pre-opening and relocation costs . . . . . . . . . . . . | 37,035 | 18,648 | 15,765 |
| Operating income. . . . . . . . . . . . . . . . . . . . . . . . | 229,733 | 216,646 | 167,379 |
| Other income expense | | | |
| Interest expense. . . . . . . . . . . . . . . . . . . . . . . . . | (2,223) | (7,249) | (8,114) |
| Investment and other income. . . . . . . . . . . . . . . | 9,623 | 6,456 | 5,593 |
| Income before income taxes . . . . . . . . . . . . . . . | 237,133 | 215,853 | 164,858 |
| Provision for income taxes. . . . . . . . . . . . . . . . . | 100,782 | 86,341 | 65,943 |
| Net income. . . . . . . . . . . . . . . . . . . . . . . . . . . . . | $ 136,351 | $ 129,512 | $ 98,915 |

| Balance Sheet (in $000s) | 2005 | 2004 |
|---|---|---|
| **Assets** | | |
| Cash and cash equivalents . . . . . . . . . . . . . . . . . . . . . . . . . . . . . . . . . . . | $308,524 | $194,747 |
| Restricted cash . . . . . . . . . . . . . . . . . . . . . . . . . . . . . . . . . . . . . . . . . . . | 36,922 | 26,790 |
| Trade accounts receivable . . . . . . . . . . . . . . . . . . . . . . . . . . . . . . . . . . . | 66,682 | 64,972 |
| Merchandise inventories . . . . . . . . . . . . . . . . . . . . . . . . . . . . . . . . . . . . | 174,848 | 152,912 |
| Prepaid expenses and other current assets. . . . . . . . . . . . . . . . . . . . . . . | 45,965 | 16,702 |
| Deferred income taxes . . . . . . . . . . . . . . . . . . . . . . . . . . . . . . . . . . . . . . | 39,588 | 29,974 |
| Total current assets . . . . . . . . . . . . . . . . . . . . . . . . . . . . . . . . . . . . . . . | 672,529 | 486,097 |

*continued*

| Balance Sheet (in $000s) | 2005 | 2004 |
|---|---|---|
| Property and equipment, net of accumulated depreciation and amortization. . . . . . . . . . . . . . . . . . . . . . . . . . . . . . . . . . . . . . | 1,054,605 | 873,397 |
| Goodwill . . . . . . . . . . . . . . . . . . . . . . . . . . . . . . . . . . . . . . . . . . | 112,476 | 112,186 |
| Intangible assets, net of accumulated amortization. . . . . . . . . . . . . . . | 21,990 | 24,831 |
| Deferred income taxes . . . . . . . . . . . . . . . . . . . . . . . . . . . . . . . . . . | 22,452 | 4,193 |
| Other assets . . . . . . . . . . . . . . . . . . . . . . . . . . . . . . . . . . . . . . . . . | 5,244 | 20,302 |
| Total assets. . . . . . . . . . . . . . . . . . . . . . . . . . . . . . . . . . . . . . . . . | $1,889,296 | $1,521,006 |
| **Liabilities and shareholders' equity** | | |
| Current installment of long-term debt . . . . . . . . . . . . . . . . . . . . . . . . | $ 5,932 | $ 5,973 |
| Trade accounts payable. . . . . . . . . . . . . . . . . . . . . . . . . . . . . . . . . | 103,348 | 90,751 |
| Accrued payroll, bonus and other benefits due to team members . . . . | 126,981 | 100,536 |
| Dividends payable . . . . . . . . . . . . . . . . . . . . . . . . . . . . . . . . . . . . . | 17,208 | 9,361 |
| Other current liabilities . . . . . . . . . . . . . . . . . . . . . . . . . . . . . . . . . . | 164,914 | 128,329 |
| Total current liabilities . . . . . . . . . . . . . . . . . . . . . . . . . . . . . . . . | 418,383 | 334,950 |
| Long-term debt, less current installments . . . . . . . . . . . . . . . . . . . . . | 12,932 | 164,770 |
| Deferred rent liabilities . . . . . . . . . . . . . . . . . . . . . . . . . . . . . . . . . . | 91,775 | 70,067 |
| Other long-term liabilities . . . . . . . . . . . . . . . . . . . . . . . . . . . . . . . . | 530 | 1,581 |
| Total liabilities . . . . . . . . . . . . . . . . . . . . . . . . . . . . . . . . . . . . . . . | 523,620 | 571,368 |
| Shareholders' equity | | |
| Common stock, no par value, 300,000 and 150,000 shares authorized, 68,009 and 62,771 shares issued, 67,954 and 62,407 shares outstanding in 2005 and 2004, respectively. . . . . . . . . . . . . . . . . . . . . | 874,972 | 535,107 |
| Accumulated other comprehensive income. . . . . . . . . . . . . . . . . . . . . | 4,405 | 2,053 |
| Retained earnings . . . . . . . . . . . . . . . . . . . . . . . . . . . . . . . . . . . . . | 486,299 | 412,478 |
| Total shareholders' equity . . . . . . . . . . . . . . . . . . . . . . . . . . . . . . | 1,365,676 | 949,638 |
| Total liabilities and shareholders' equity. . . . . . . . . . . . . . . . . . . . . . | $1,889,296 | $1,521,006 |

a.  Forecast Whole Food Market's 2006 income statement and year-end balance sheet using the following relations (cost of goods sold and occupancy costs can be inferred as sales minus gross profit; and assume no change for all other accounts not listed below).

| | |
|---|---|
| Sales growth. . . . . . . . . . . . . . . . . . . . . . . . . . . . . . . . . . . . . . . . . . . . . . . . . . . | 21.6% |
| Gross profit margin. . . . . . . . . . . . . . . . . . . . . . . . . . . . . . . . . . . . . . . . . . . . . . . | 35.1% |
| Direct store expenses. . . . . . . . . . . . . . . . . . . . . . . . . . . . . . . . . . . . . . . . . . . . . | 26.0% |
| General and administrative expenses . . . . . . . . . . . . . . . . . . . . . . . . . . . . . . . . . | 3.4% |
| Pre-opening and relocation costs . . . . . . . . . . . . . . . . . . . . . . . . . . . . . . . . . . . | 0.8% |
| Depreciation/Prior year property and equipment, net . . . . . . . . . . . . . . . . . . . . . . | 15.3% |
| Provision for income taxes/Income before income taxes . . . . . . . . . . . . . . . . . . . . | 42.6% |
| Sales/Year-end trade accounts receivable. . . . . . . . . . . . . . . . . . . . . . . . . . . . . . | 70.16 |
| Cost of goods sold and occupancy costs/Year-end merchandise inventories . . . . . . | 17.54 |
| Sales/Year-end property and equipment, net. . . . . . . . . . . . . . . . . . . . . . . . . . . . . | 4.46 |
| Cost of goods sold and occupancy costs/Year-end trade accounts payable. . . . . . . | 29.63 |
| Sales/Year-end accrued payroll, bonus and other benefits due team members. . . . . | 37.02 |
| Dividends/Net income . . . . . . . . . . . . . . . . . . . . . . . . . . . . . . . . . . . . . . . . . . . . | 40.2% |
| Dividends/Dividends payable. . . . . . . . . . . . . . . . . . . . . . . . . . . . . . . . . . . . . . . | 3.22 |

b.  What does the forecasted cash balance from part a reveal to us about the forecasted financing needs of the company? Explain.

Whole Foods Market, Inc. (WFMI)

**E11-20** **Forecasting the Statement of Cash flows** **(LO2)**

Refer to the Whole Foods Market, Inc., financial information from Exercise 11-19. Prepare a forecast of its fiscal year 2006 statement of cash flows.

Abercrombie & Fitch (ANF)

**E11-21.** **Analyzing, Forecasting, and Interpreting both Income Statement and Balance Sheet** **(LO2)**

Following are the fiscal year income statements and balance sheets of Abercrombie & Fitch.

| Consolidated Statements of Net Income | | | |
| --- | --- | --- | --- |
| For Fiscal Year Ended (Thousands) | 2006 | 2005 | 2004 |
| Net sales. . . . . | $2,784,711 | $2,021,253 | $1,707,810 |
| Cost of goods sold. . . . . | 933,295 | 680,029 | 624,640 |
| Gross profit. . . . . | 1,851,416 | 1,341,224 | 1,083,170 |
| Stores and distribution expense. . . . . | 1,000,755 | 738,244 | 597,416 |
| Marketing, general and administrative expense. . . . . | 313,457 | 259,835 | 155,553 |
| Other operating income, net . . . . . | (5,534) | (4,490) | (979) |
| Operating income. . . . . | 542,738 | 347,635 | 331,180 |
| Interest income, net . . . . . | (6,674) | (5,218) | (3,708) |
| Income before income taxes . . . . . | 549,412 | 352,853 | 334,888 |
| Provision for income taxes. . . . . | 215,426 | 136,477 | 130,058 |
| Net income. . . . . | $ 333,986 | $ 216,376 | $ 204,830 |

| Consolidated Balance Sheets | | |
| --- | --- | --- |
| (Thousands, except per share amounts) | January 28, 2006 | January 29, 2005 |
| **Assets** | | |
| Cash and equivalents. . . . . | $ 50,687 | $ 338,735 |
| Marketable securities . . . . . | 411,167 | — |
| Receivables . . . . . | 41,855 | 37,760 |
| Inventories . . . . . | 362,536 | 211,198 |
| Deferred income taxes . . . . . | 29,654 | 39,090 |
| Other current assets. . . . . | 51,185 | 44,001 |
| Total current assets . . . . . | 947,084 | 670,784 |
| Property and equipment, net . . . . . | 813,603 | 687,011 |
| Other assets. . . . . | 29,031 | 28,996 |
| Total assets. . . . . | $1,789,718 | $1,386,791 |
| **Liabilities and shareholders' equity** | | |
| Accounts payable. . . . . | $ 86,572 | $ 83,760 |
| Outstanding checks . . . . . | 58,741 | 53,577 |
| Accrued expenses . . . . . | 215,034 | 205,153 |
| Deferred lease credits . . . . . | 31,727 | 31,135 |
| Income taxes payable . . . . . | 99,480 | 55,587 |
| Total current liabilities. . . . . | 491,554 | 429,212 |
| Deferred income taxes. . . . . | 38,496 | 50,032 |
| Deferred lease credits . . . . . | 191,225 | 177,923 |
| Other liabilities . . . . . | 73,326 | 60,298 |
| Total long-term liabilities. . . . . | 303,047 | 288,253 |

*continued*

| Consolidated Balance Sheets | | |
|---|---|---|
| (Thousands, except per share amounts) | January 28, 2006 | January 29, 2005 |

Shareholders' equity

| | | |
|---|---|---|
| Class A common stock—$.01 par value: 150,000,000 shares authorized and 103,300,000 shares issued at January 28, 2006 and January 29, 2005, respectively . . . . . . . . . . . . . . . . . . . . . | 1,033 | 1,033 |
| Paid-in capital . . . . . . . . . . . . . . . . . . . . . . . . . . . . . . . . . . . . | 161,678 | 140,251 |
| Retained earnings . . . . . . . . . . . . . . . . . . . . . . . . . . . . . . . . . | 1,357,791 | 1,076,023 |
| Accumulated other comprehensive income. . . . . . . . . . . . . . . | (796) | — |
| Deferred compensation . . . . . . . . . . . . . . . . . . . . . . . . . . . . . | 26,206 | 15,048 |
| Treasury stock, at average cost 15,573,789 and 17,262,943 shares at January 28, 2006 and January 29, 2005, respectively. . . . . . . . . . . . . . . . . . . . . . . . . . . . . . . . . . . . . | (550,795) | (563,029) |
| Total shareholders' equity . . . . . . . . . . . . . . . . . . . . . . . . . . . | 995,117 | 669,326 |
| Total liabilities and shareholders' equity. . . . . . . . . . . . . . . . . | $1,789,718 | $1,386,791 |

a.  Forecast its fiscal year 2007 income statement and its 2007 fiscal year-end balance sheet using the following relations (cost of goods sold can be inferred as sales minus gross profit; assume no change for all other accounts not listed on next page).

| | |
|---|---|
| Net sales growth. . . . . . . . . . . . . . . . . . . . . . . . . . . . . . . . . . . . . . . . | 37.8% |
| Gross profit margin. . . . . . . . . . . . . . . . . . . . . . . . . . . . . . . . . . . . . . . | 66.5% |
| Stores and Distribution expense/Net sales . . . . . . . . . . . . . . . . . . . . . | 35.9% |
| Marketing, general and administrative expense/Net sales . . . . . . . . . . . | 11.3% |
| Other operating income, net/Net sales . . . . . . . . . . . . . . . . . . . . . . . . . | −0.2% |
| Depreciation/Prior year property and equipment, net . . . . . . . . . . . . . . . | 18.1% |
| Provision for income taxes/Income before income taxes . . . . . . . . . . . . | 39.2% |
| Interest income, net . . . . . . . . . . . . . . . . . . . . . . . . . . . . . . . . . . . . . . | no change |
| Net sales/Year-end receivable . . . . . . . . . . . . . . . . . . . . . . . . . . . . . . . | 66.53 |
| Cost of goods sold/Year-end inventories. . . . . . . . . . . . . . . . . . . . . . . . | 2.57 |
| Cost of goods sold/Year-end accounts payable . . . . . . . . . . . . . . . . . . | 10.78 |
| Net sales/Year-end property and equipment, net . . . . . . . . . . . . . . . . . | 3.42 |
| Net sales/Year-end accrued expenses. . . . . . . . . . . . . . . . . . . . . . . . . | 12.95 |
| Income taxes payable/Provision for income taxes. . . . . . . . . . . . . . . . . | 46.2% |
| Dividends . . . . . . . . . . . . . . . . . . . . . . . . . . . . . . . . . . . . . . . . . . . . . | $52,218 |

b.  What does the forecasted cash balance from part *a* reveal to us about the forecasted financing needs of the company? Explain.

**E11-22. Forecasting the Statement of Cash flows   (LO2)**

Refer to the Abercrombie & Fitch financial information in Exercise 11-21. Prepare a forecast of its fiscal year 2007 statement of cash flows.

Abercrombie & Fitch (ANF)

**E11-23. Analyzing, Forecasting, and Interpreting both Income Statement and Balance Sheet (LO2)**

Following are the fiscal year income statements and balance sheets of Best Buy, Co., Inc.

| Balance Sheet<br>($ millions, except per share amounts) | February 25, 2006 | February 26, 2005 |
|---|---|---|
| **Assets** | | |
| Cash and cash equivalents | $ 681 | $ 354 |
| Short-term investments | 3,051 | 2,994 |
| Receivables | 506 | 375 |
| Merchandise inventories | 3,338 | 2,851 |
| Other current assets | 409 | 329 |
| Total current assets | 7,985 | 6,903 |
| Property and equipment | | |
| Land and buildings | 580 | 506 |
| Leasehold improvements | 1,325 | 1,139 |
| Fixtures and equipment | 2,898 | 2,458 |
| Property under master and capital lease | 33 | 89 |
| | 4,836 | 4,192 |
| Less accumulated depreciation | 2,124 | 1,728 |
| Net property and equipment | 2,712 | 2,464 |
| Goodwill | 557 | 513 |
| Tradename | 44 | 40 |
| Long-term investments | 218 | 148 |
| Other assets | 348 | 226 |
| Total assets | $11,864 | $10,294 |
| **Liabilities and shareholders' equity** | | |
| Accounts payable | $ 3,234 | $ 2,824 |
| Unredeemed gift card liabilities | 469 | 410 |
| Accrued compensation and related expenses | 354 | 234 |
| Accrued liabilities | 878 | 844 |
| Accrued income taxes | 703 | 575 |
| Current portion of long-term debt | 418 | 72 |
| Total current liabilities | 6,056 | 4,959 |
| Long-term liabilities | 373 | 358 |
| Long-term debt | 178 | 528 |
| Shareholders' equity | | |
| Preferred stock, $1.00 par value: Authorized—400,000 shares; Issued and outstanding-none | — | — |
| Common stock, $.10 par value: Authorized—1 billion shares; Issued and outstanding—485,098,000 and 492,512,000 shares, respectively | 49 | 49 |
| Additional paid-in capital | 643 | 936 |
| Retained earnings | 4,304 | 3,315 |
| Accumulated other comprehensive income | 261 | 149 |
| Total shareholders' equity | 5,257 | 4,449 |
| Total liabilities and shareholders' equity | $11,864 | $10,294 |

| Income Statement<br>Fiscal years ended ($ millions) | February 25,<br>2006 | February 26,<br>2005 | February 28,<br>2004 |
|---|---|---|---|
| Revenue . . . . . . . . . . . . . . . . . . . . . . . . . . . . . . . | $30,848 | $27,433 | $24,548 |
| Cost of goods sold. . . . . . . . . . . . . . . . . . . . . | 23,122 | 20,938 | 18,677 |
| Gross profit. . . . . . . . . . . . . . . . . . . . . . . . . . | 7,726 | 6,495 | 5,871 |
| Selling, general and administrative expenses . . . | 6,082 | 5,053 | 4,567 |
| Operating income. . . . . . . . . . . . . . . . . . . . . . . | 1,644 | 1,442 | 1,304 |
| Net interest income (expense) . . . . . . . . . . . . . . | 77 | 1 | (8) |
| Earnings from continuing operations before<br>income tax expense . . . . . . . . . . . . . . . . . . . . | 1,721 | 1,443 | 1,296 |
| Income tax expense. . . . . . . . . . . . . . . . . . . . . | 581 | 509 | 496 |
| Earnings from continuing operations . . . . . . . . . . | 1,140 | 934 | 800 |
| Loss from discontinued operations, net of tax. . . | — | — | (29) |
| Gain (loss) on disposal of discontinued<br>operations, net of tax . . . . . . . . . . . . . . . . . . . | — | 50 | (66) |
| Net earnings. . . . . . . . . . . . . . . . . . . . . . . . . . . | $ 1,140 | $ 984 | $ 705 |

a.    Forecast Best Buy's fiscal year 2007 income statement and its 2007 fiscal year-end balance sheet
      using the following relations (cost of goods sold can be inferred as revenue minus gross profit; and
      assume no change for all other accounts not listed below).

| | |
|---|---|
| Revenue growth . . . . . . . . . . . . . . . . . . . . . . . . . . . . . . . . . . . . . . . . . . . . . | 12.4% |
| Gross profit margin. . . . . . . . . . . . . . . . . . . . . . . . . . . . . . . . . . . . . . . . . . | 25.0% |
| Selling, general and administrative expenses/Revenue. . . . . . . . . . . . . . . . . . . . . . . | 19.7% |
| Depreciation (included in SG&A expense)/Prior year net property and equipment . . . . . . . . . | 18.5% |
| Income tax expense/Earnings from continuing operations before income taxes . . . . . . . . . . . | 33.8% |
| Revenue/Year-end receivables. . . . . . . . . . . . . . . . . . . . . . . . . . . . . . . . . . . . . . | 60.96 |
| Cost of goods sold/Year-end merchandise inventories . . . . . . . . . . . . . . . . . . . . . . . . . | 6.93 |
| Cost of goods sold/Year-end accounts payable . . . . . . . . . . . . . . . . . . . . . . . . . . . . . | 7.15 |
| Revenue/Year-end net property and equipment . . . . . . . . . . . . . . . . . . . . . . . . . . . . . | 11.38 |
| Revenue/Year-end accrued compensation and related expenses and accrued liabilities. . . . . . | 25.04 |
| Accrued income taxes/Income taxes expense . . . . . . . . . . . . . . . . . . . . . . . . . . . . . . | 121.0% |
| Dividends/Net earnings . . . . . . . . . . . . . . . . . . . . . . . . . . . . . . . . . . . . . . . . . | 13.2% |
| Long term debt due in next fiscal year (February 2007). . . . . . . . . . . . . . . . . . . . . . . . | $16 |

b.    What does the forecasted cash balance from part a reveal to us about the forecasted financing needs
      of the company? Explain.

**E11-24.**  **Forecasting the Statement of Cash flows**   **(LO2)**
      Refer to the Best Buy Co. , Inc., financial information from Exercise 11-23. Prepare a forecast of its fiscal       Best Buy Co., Inc.
      year 2007 statement of cash flows.                                                                                  (BBY)

General Mills, Inc.
(GIS)

**E11-25. Analyzing, Forecasting, and Interpreting Both Income Statement and Balance Sheet (LO2)**

Following are the fiscal year income statements and balance sheets of General Mills, Inc..

| Income Statement<br>Fiscal year ended (In millions) | May 28, 2006 | May 29, 2005 | May 30, 2004 |
|---|---|---|---|
| Net sales. | $11,640 | $11,244 | $11,070 |
| Costs and expenses | | | |
| Cost of sales. | 6,966 | 6,834 | 6,584 |
| Selling, general and administrative. | 2,678 | 2,418 | 2,443 |
| Interest, net. | 399 | 455 | 508 |
| Restructuring and other exit costs | 30 | 84 | 26 |
| Divestitures (gain) | — | (499) | — |
| Debt repurchase costs | — | 137 | — |
| Total costs and expenses. | 10,073 | 9,429 | 9,561 |
| Earnings before income taxes and after-tax earnings from joint ventures | 1,567 | 1,815 | 1,509 |
| Income taxes | 541 | 664 | 528 |
| After-tax earnings from joint ventures | 64 | 89 | 74 |
| Net earnings. | $ 1,090 | $ 1,240 | $ 1,055 |

| Balance Sheet<br>(In millions) | May 28, 2006 | May 29, 2005 |
|---|---|---|
| **Assets** | | |
| Cash and cash equivalents | $ 647 | $ 573 |
| Receivables | 1,076 | 1,034 |
| Inventories | 1,055 | 1,037 |
| Prepaid expenses and other current assets. | 216 | 203 |
| Deferred income taxes | 182 | 208 |
| Total current assets | 3,176 | 3,055 |
| Land, buildings and equipment | 2,997 | 3,111 |
| Goodwill. | 6,652 | 6,684 |
| Other intangible assets. | 3,607 | 3,532 |
| Other assets. | 1,775 | 1,684 |
| Total assets. | $18,207 | $18,066 |
| **Liabilities and equity** | | |
| Accounts payable. | $ 1,151 | $ 1,136 |
| Current portion of long-term debt | 2,131 | 1,638 |
| Notes payable | 1,503 | 299 |
| Other current liabilities | 1,353 | 1,111 |
| Total current liabilities. | 6,138 | 4,184 |
| Long-term debt | 2,415 | 4,255 |
| Deferred income taxes | 1,822 | 1,851 |
| Other liabilities | 924 | 967 |
| Total liabilities. | 11,299 | 11,257 |
| Minority interests | 1,136 | 1,133 |

*continued*

| Balance Sheet (In millions) | May 28, 2006 | May 29, 2005 |
|---|---|---|
| Stockholders' equity | | |
| Cumulative preference stock, none issued. . . . . . . . . . . | — | — |
| Common stock, 502 shares issued . . . . . . . . . . . . . . . . | 50 | 50 |
| Additional paid-in capital . . . . . . . . . . . . . . . . . . . . . . . | 5,737 | 5,691 |
| Retained earnings. . . . . . . . . . . . . . . . . . . . . . . . . . . . . | 5,107 | 4,501 |
| Common stock in treasury, at cost, shares of 146 in 2006 and 133 in 2005 . . . . . . . . . . . . . . . . . . . . . . . . | (5,163) | (4,460) |
| Unearned compensation . . . . . . . . . . . . . . . . . . . . . . . | (84) | (114) |
| Accumulated other comprehensive income. . . . . . . . . . | 125 | 8 |
| Total stockholders' equity . . . . . . . . . . . . . . . . . . . . . . | 5,772 | 5,676 |
| Total liabilities and equity . . . . . . . . . . . . . . . . . . . . . . . | $18,207 | $18,066 |

a.  Forecast General Mill's fiscal year 2007 income statement and its 2007 fiscal year-end balance sheet using the following relations (cost of goods sold can be inferred as sales minus gross profit; assume no change for all other accounts not listed below).

| | |
|---|---|
| Net sales growth. . . . . . . . . . . . . . . . . . . . . . . . . . . . . . . . . . . . . . . . . . . . . . . . . . . . . . . . . . . . . | 3.5% |
| Cost of sales / Net sales . . . . . . . . . . . . . . . . . . . . . . . . . . . . . . . . . . . . . . . . . . . . . . . . . . . . . . | 59.8% |
| Selling, general and administrative / Net sales . . . . . . . . . . . . . . . . . . . . . . . . . . . . . . . . . . . | 23.0% |
| Restructuring and other exit costs / Net sales. . . . . . . . . . . . . . . . . . . . . . . . . . . . . . . . . . . . | 0.3% |
| Other revenues (expenses) / Net sales. . . . . . . . . . . . . . . . . . . . . . . . . . . . . . . . . . . . . . . . . . | −0.5% |
| Depreciation (included in SG&A expense) / Prior year land, buildings and equipment . . . . . . . | 14.1% |
| Income taxes/ Earnings before income taxes . . . . . . . . . . . . . . . . . . . . . . . . . . . . . . . . . . . . | 34.5% |
| Net sales/Year-end receivables . . . . . . . . . . . . . . . . . . . . . . . . . . . . . . . . . . . . . . . . . . . . . . . | 10.82 |
| Cost of sales/ Year-end inventories . . . . . . . . . . . . . . . . . . . . . . . . . . . . . . . . . . . . . . . . . . . . | 6.60 |
| Cost of sales/ Year-end accounts payable. . . . . . . . . . . . . . . . . . . . . . . . . . . . . . . . . . . . . . . | 6.05 |
| Net sales/ Year-end land, buildings and equipment. . . . . . . . . . . . . . . . . . . . . . . . . . . . . . . | 3.88 |
| Net sales/ Year-end other current liabilities . . . . . . . . . . . . . . . . . . . . . . . . . . . . . . . . . . . . . | 8.60 |
| Dividends / Net earnings . . . . . . . . . . . . . . . . . . . . . . . . . . . . . . . . . . . . . . . . . . . . . . . . . . . . | 44.5% |
| Current maturities of long-term debt for year-end May 2007 . . . . . . . . . . . . . . . . . . . . . . . . | $854 |

b.  What does the forecasted cash balance from part *a* reveal to us about the forecasted financing needs of the company? Explain.

**E11-26.   Forecasting the Statement of Cash flows   (LO2)**

Refer to the General Mills, Inc. financial information from Exercise 11-25. Prepare a forecast of its fiscal year 2007 statement of cash flows.

General Mills, Inc. (GIS)

**E11-27.   Adjusting the Balance Sheet for Operating Leases   (LO1)**

Southwest Airlines reports total net operating assets of $8,419 million, liabilities of $1,744 million, and equity of $6,675 in its 2005 10-K. Footnotes reveal the existence of operating leases that have a present value of $1,779 million (see Module 10 for computations). (a) What balance sheet adjustment(s) might we consider relating to those leases in anticipation of forecasting its financial statements? (*Hint:* Consider the distinction between operating and nonoperating assets and liabilities.) (b) What income statement adjustment(s) might we consider? (*Hint:* Reflect on the operating and nonoperating distinction for lease-related expenses.)

Southwest Airlines (LUV)

**E11-28.   Adjusting the Balance Sheet for Equity Method Investments   (LO1)**

Abbott Laboratories, Inc., reports its 50% joint venture investment in TAP Pharmaceutical Products Inc. using the equity method of accounting. The Abbott balance sheet reports an investment balance of $167 million. TAP has total assets of $1,470.2 million, liabilities of $1,136.2 million, and equity of $334 million. Abbott's investment balance is, thus, equal to its 50% interest in TAP's equity ($334 million × 50% = $167 million). What adjustment(s) might we consider to Abbott's balance sheet in anticipation of forecasting its financial statements? (*Hint:* Consider the distinction between operating and nonoperating assets and liabilities.) What risks might Abbott Laboratories face that are not revealed on the face of its balance sheet?

**E11-29.   Projecting NOPAT and NOA using Parsimonious Forecasting Model   (LO3)**

Following are Intel's sales, net operating profit after tax (NOPAT), and net operating assets (NOA) for its year ended December 31, 2005 ($ millions).

| | |
|---|---:|
| Sales. . . . . . . . . . . . . . . . . . . . . . . . . . . . . . . . . . . . . . . . . . . . . . . . . . . . . | $38,826 |
| Net operating profit after tax (NOPAT) . . . . . . . . . . . . . . . . . . . . . . . . . . . . . . | 8,333 |
| Net operating assets (NOA) . . . . . . . . . . . . . . . . . . . . . . . . . . . . . . . . . . . . . . | 29,018 |

Forecast Intel's sales, NOPAT and NOA for years 2006 through 2009 using the following assumptions:

| | |
|---|---:|
| Sales growth per year. . . . . . . . . . . . . . . . . . . . . . . . . . . . . . . . . . . . . . . . . . . | 13.50% |
| Net operating profit margin (NOPM). . . . . . . . . . . . . . . . . . . . . . . . . . . . . . . . . | 21.46% |
| Net operating asset turnover (NOAT), based on NOA at December 31, 2005 . . . | 1.34 |

**E11-30.   Projecting NOPAT and NOA using Parsimonious Forecasting Model   (LO3)**

Following are Oracle's sales, net operating profit after tax (NOPAT), and net operating assets (NOA) for its fiscal year ended May 31, 2006 ($ millions).

| | |
|---|---:|
| Sales. . . . . . . . . . . . . . . . . . . . . . . . . . . . . . . . . . . . . . . . . . . . . . . . . . . . . | $14,380 |
| Net operating profit after tax (NOPAT) . . . . . . . . . . . . . . . . . . . . . . . . . . . . . . | 3,245 |
| Net operating assets (NOA) . . . . . . . . . . . . . . . . . . . . . . . . . . . . . . . . . . . . . . | 19,960 |

Forecast Oracle's sales, NOPAT and NOA for fiscal years 2007 through 2010 using the following assumptions:

| | |
|---|---:|
| Sales growth per year. . . . . . . . . . . . . . . . . . . . . . . . . . . . . . . . . . . . . . . . . . . | 21.90% |
| Net operating profit margin (NOPM). . . . . . . . . . . . . . . . . . . . . . . . . . . . . . . . . | 22.57% |
| Net operating asset turnover (NOAT), based on NOA at May 31, 2006. . . . . . . . | 0.72 |

# PROBLEMS

**P11-31.** **Forecasting the Income Statement, Balance Sheet, and Statement of Cash Flows**   (LO2)

Following are fiscal year financial statements of Oracle Corporation.

Oracle Corporation
(ORCL)

| Consolidated Balance Sheets | | |
|---|---|---|
| May 31 (in millions, except per share data) | 2006 | 2005 |
| **Assets** | | |
| Cash and cash equivalent | $ 6,659 | $ 3,894 |
| Marketable securities | 946 | 877 |
| Trade receivables, net of allowances of $329 and $269 | 3,022 | 2,570 |
| Other receivables | 398 | 330 |
| Deferred tax assets | 714 | 486 |
| Prepaid expenses and other current assets | 235 | 291 |
| Total current assets | 11,974 | 8,448 |
| Non-current assets | | |
| Property, net | 1,391 | 1,442 |
| Intangible assets, net | 4,528 | 3,373 |
| Goodwill | 9,809 | 7,003 |
| Other assets | 1,327 | 421 |
| Total non-current assets | 17,055 | 12,239 |
| Total assets | $29,029 | $20,687 |
| **Liabilities and stockholders' equity** | | |
| Short-term borrowings and current portion of long-term debt | $    159 | $ 2,693 |
| Accounts payable | 268 | 230 |
| Income taxes payable | 810 | 904 |
| Accrued compensation and related benefits | 1,172 | 923 |
| Accrued restructuring | 412 | 156 |
| Deferred revenues | 2,830 | 2,289 |
| Other current liabilities | 1,279 | 868 |
| Total current liabilities | 6,930 | 8,063 |
| Non-current liabilities | | |
| Notes payable and long-term debt, net of current portion | 5,735 | 159 |
| Deferred tax liabilities | 564 | 1,010 |
| Accrued restructuring | 273 | 120 |
| Deferred revenues | 114 | 126 |
| Other long-term liabilities | 401 | 372 |
| Total non-current liabilities | 7,087 | 1,787 |
| Stockholders' equity | | |
| Preferred stock, $0.01 par value-authorized: 1.0 shares; outstanding: none | — | — |
| Common stock, $0.01 par value and additional paid in capital— authorized: 11,000 shares; outstanding: 5,232 shares at May 31, 2006 and 5,145 shares at May 31, 2005 | 9,246 | 6,596 |
| Retained earnings | 5,538 | 4,043 |
| Deferred compensation | (30) | (45) |
| Accumulated other comprehensive income | 258 | 243 |
| Total stockholders' equity | 15,012 | 10,837 |
| Total liabilities and stockholders' equity | $29,029 | $20,687 |

| Consolidated Statements of Operations | | | |
|---|---|---|---|
| **Year ended May 31 (in millions)** | **2006** | **2005** | **2004** |
| Revenues | | | |
| New software licenses . . . . . . . . . . . . . . . . . . . . . . . . | $ 4,905 | $ 4,091 | $ 3,541 |
| Software license updates and product support . . . . . | 6,636 | 5,330 | 4,529 |
| Software revenues . . . . . . . . . . . . . . . . . . . . . . . . . | 11,541 | 9,421 | 8,070 |
| Services . . . . . . . . . . . . . . . . . . . . . . . . . . . . . . . | 2,839 | 2,378 | 2,086 |
| Total revenues . . . . . . . . . . . . . . . . . . . . . . . . . . . . | 14,380 | 11,799 | 10,156 |
| Operating expenses | | | |
| Sales and marketing . . . . . . . . . . . . . . . . . . . . . . . . | 3,177 | 2,511 | 2,123 |
| Software license updates and product support . . . . . | 719 | 618 | 547 |
| Cost of services . . . . . . . . . . . . . . . . . . . . . . . . . . | 2,516 | 2,033 | 1,770 |
| Research and development . . . . . . . . . . . . . . . . . . . | 1,872 | 1,491 | 1,254 |
| General and administrative. . . . . . . . . . . . . . . . . . . . | 555 | 550 | 508 |
| Amortization of intangible assets . . . . . . . . . . . . . . . | 583 | 219 | 36 |
| Acquisition related . . . . . . . . . . . . . . . . . . . . . . . . . | 137 | 208 | 54 |
| Restructuring . . . . . . . . . . . . . . . . . . . . . . . . . . . . | 85 | 147 | — |
| Total operating expenses . . . . . . . . . . . . . . . . . . . . . | 9,644 | 7,777 | 6,292 |
| Operating income. . . . . . . . . . . . . . . . . . . . . . . . . . . | 4,736 | 4,022 | 3,864 |
| Interest expense. . . . . . . . . . . . . . . . . . . . . . . . . . . | (169) | (135) | (21) |
| Nonoperating income, net | | | |
| Interest income. . . . . . . . . . . . . . . . . . . . . . . . . . . | 170 | 185 | 118 |
| Net investment gains . . . . . . . . . . . . . . . . . . . . . . . | 25 | 2 | 29 |
| Other. . . . . . . . . . . . . . . . . . . . . . . . . . . . . . . . . . | 48 | (23) | (45) |
| Total nonoperating income, net . . . . . . . . . . . . . . . | 243 | 164 | 102 |
| Income before provision for income taxes. . . . . . . . . . | 4,810 | 4,051 | 3,945 |
| Provision for income taxes. . . . . . . . . . . . . . . . . . . . | 1,429 | 1,165 | 1,264 |
| Net income. . . . . . . . . . . . . . . . . . . . . . . . . . . . . . . | $ 3,381 | $ 2,886 | $ 2,681 |

**Required**

Forecast its fiscal year 2007 income statement, balance sheet, and statement of cash flows. (*Note*: Oracle's long-term debt footnote reports that current maturities of long-term debt are $159 million and $4 million for May 2006 and 2007, respectively; Oracle includes the current portion due with short-term borrowings on its balance sheet.) Identify all financial statement relations estimated and assumptions made. What do the forecasts imply about the financing needs of Oracle?

**P11-32.** **Forecasting the Income Statement, Balance Sheet, and Statement of Cash Flows** (LO2)

Intuit, Inc. (INTU)

Following are the fiscal year financial statements of Intuit, Inc.

| Consolidated Statements of Operations | | | |
|---|---|---|---|
| **Twelve months ended July 31 (in thousands)** | **2006** | **2005** | **2004** |
| Net revenue | | | |
| Product. . . . . . . . . . . . . . . . . . . . . . . . . . . . . . . . . | $1,351,636 | $1,242,693 | $1,179,101 |
| Service . . . . . . . . . . . . . . . . . . . . . . . . . . . . . . . . | 910,506 | 724,049 | 555,496 |
| Other. . . . . . . . . . . . . . . . . . . . . . . . . . . . . . . . . . | 80,161 | 70,961 | 67,627 |
| Total net revenue . . . . . . . . . . . . . . . . . . . . . . . . . | 2,342,303 | 2,037,703 | 1,802,224 |
| | | | *continued* |

| Consolidated Statements of Operations | | | |
|---|---|---|---|
| **Twelve months ended July 31 (in thousands)** | **2006** | **2005** | **2004** |
| Costs and expenses | | | |
| Cost of revenue | | | |
| Cost of product revenue . . . . . . . . . . . . . . . . . . | 176,188 | 164,551 | 170,769 |
| Cost of service revenue. . . . . . . . . . . . . . . . . . . | 229,435 | 183,969 | 158,083 |
| Cost of other revenue . . . . . . . . . . . . . . . . . . . . | 20,566 | 24,133 | 24,179 |
| Amortization of purchased intangible assets . . . | 9,902 | 10,251 | 10,186 |
| Selling and marketing . . . . . . . . . . . . . . . . . . . . . | 664,056 | 583,408 | 541,387 |
| Research and development . . . . . . . . . . . . . . . . | 398,983 | 305,241 | 276,049 |
| General and administrative. . . . . . . . . . . . . . . . | 270,292 | 225,507 | 178,653 |
| Acquisition-related charges . . . . . . . . . . . . . . . . | 13,337 | 16,545 | 23,435 |
| Total costs and expenses . . . . . . . . . . . . . . . . . . | 1,782,759 | 1,513,605 | 1,382,741 |
| Operating income from continuing operations. . . . . . | 559,544 | 524,098 | 419,483 |
| Interest and other income . . . . . . . . . . . . . . . . . . . | 43,038 | 26,636 | 30,400 |
| Gains on marketable equity securities and other investments, net . . . . . . . . . . . . . . . . . . . . . . . . | 7,629 | 5,225 | 1,729 |
| Income from continuing operations before taxes. . . . | 610,211 | 555,959 | 451,612 |
| Income tax provision . . . . . . . . . . . . . . . . . . . . . . . | 232,090 | 181,074 | 128,290 |
| Minority interest, net of tax. . . . . . . . . . . . . . . . . . | 691 | (98) | — |
| Net income from continuing operations. . . . . . . . . . | 377,430 | 374,983 | 323,322 |
| Net income (loss) from discontinued operations . . . . | 39,533 | 6,644 | (6,292) |
| Net income . . . . . . . . . . . . . . . . . . . . . . . . . . . . . . | $ 416,963 | $ 381,627 | $ 317,030 |

| Consolidated Balance Sheets | | |
|---|---|---|
| **July 31 (in thousands, except par value)** | **2006** | **2005** |
| **Assets** | | |
| Cash and cash equivalents . . . . . . . . . . . . . . . . . . . . . . . . . . . . . . . | $ 179,601 | $ 83,842 |
| Investments . . . . . . . . . . . . . . . . . . . . . . . . . . . . . . . . . . . . . . . . . . | 1,017,599 | 910,416 |
| Accounts receivable, net of allowance for doubtful accounts of $12,328 and $15,653 . . . . . . . . . . . . . . . . . . . . . . . | 97,797 | 86,125 |
| Income taxes receivable. . . . . . . . . . . . . . . . . . . . . . . . . . . . . . . . . | 64,178 | 38,665 |
| Deferred income taxes . . . . . . . . . . . . . . . . . . . . . . . . . . . . . . . . . . | 47,199 | 54,854 |
| Prepaid expenses and other current assets. . . . . . . . . . . . . . . . . . . | 53,357 | 60,610 |
| Current assets of discontinued operations . . . . . . . . . . . . . . . . . . . . | — | 21,989 |
| Current assets before funds held for payroll customers. . . . . . . . . . | 1,459,731 | 1,256,501 |
| Funds held for payroll customers. . . . . . . . . . . . . . . . . . . . . . . . . . . | 357,299 | 357,838 |
| Total current assets. . . . . . . . . . . . . . . . . . . . . . . . . . . . . . . . . . | 1,817,030 | 1,614,339 |
| Property and equipment, net . . . . . . . . . . . . . . . . . . . . . . . . . . . . . . | 194,434 | 208,548 |
| Goodwill, net . . . . . . . . . . . . . . . . . . . . . . . . . . . . . . . . . . . . . . . . . | 504,991 | 509,499 |
| Purchased intangible assets, net . . . . . . . . . . . . . . . . . . . . . . . . . . | 59,521 | 69,678 |
| Long-term deferred income taxes . . . . . . . . . . . . . . . . . . . . . . . . . . | 144,697 | 118,475 |
| Loans to executive officers and other employees . . . . . . . . . . . . . . . | 8,865 | 9,245 |
| Other assets . . . . . . . . . . . . . . . . . . . . . . . . . . . . . . . . . . . . . . . . . | 40,489 | 30,078 |
| Long-term assets of discontinued operations . . . . . . . . . . . . . . . . . . | — | 156,589 |
| Total assets. . . . . . . . . . . . . . . . . . . . . . . . . . . . . . . . . . . . . . . . . | $2,770,027 | $2,716,451 |

*continued*

| Consolidated Balance Sheets | | |
|---|---|---|
| July 31 (in thousands, except par value) | 2005 | 2005 |
| **Liabilities and stockholders' equity** | | |
| Accounts payable.......................................... | $ 70,808 | $ 65,812 |
| Accrued compensation and related liabilities ................... | 171,903 | 144,823 |
| Deferred revenue ........................................ | 293,113 | 279,382 |
| Income taxes payable ..................................... | 33,560 | 30,423 |
| Other current liabilities ................................... | 89,291 | 103,131 |
| Current liabilities of discontinued operations.................... | — | 21,995 |
| Current liabilities before payroll customer fund deposits......... | 658,675 | 645,566 |
| Payroll customer fund deposits ............................. | 357,299 | 357,838 |
| Total current liabilities.................................... | 1,015,974 | 1,003,404 |
| Long-term obligations ..................................... | 15,399 | 17,308 |
| Long-term obligations of discontinued operations ............... | — | 240 |
| Total long-term obligations................................. | 15,399 | 17,548 |
| Commitments and contingencies | | |
| Minority interest ......................................... | 568 | — |
| Stockholders' equity | | |
| Preferred stock, $0.01 par value ............................ | — | — |
| Authorized - 1,345 shares total; 145 shares designated Series A; 250 shares designated Series B Junior Participating Issued and outstanding-None | | |
| Common stock, $0.01 par value ............................ | 3,442 | 1,793 |
| Authorized - 750,000 shares Issued and outstanding - 344,171 post-split shares at July 31, 2006 and 179,270 pre-split shares at July 31, 2005 | | |
| Additional paid-in capital .................................. | 2,089,472 | 1,976,161 |
| Treasury stock, at cost.................................... | (1,944,036) | (1,557,833) |
| Deferred compensation .................................... | — | (16,283) |
| Accumulated other comprehensive income.................... | 1,084 | 174 |
| Retained earnings ....................................... | 1,588,124 | 1,291,487 |
| Total stockholders' equity ................................. | 1,738,086 | 1,695,499 |
| Total liabilities and stockholders' equity...................... | $2,770,027 | $2,716,451 |

**Required**

Forecast Intuit's fiscal year 2007 income statement, balance sheet, and statement of cash flows. Identify all financial statement relations estimated and assumptions made. (*Note*: Intuit's PPE footnote reveals that depreciation for 2006 was $94 million.) What do the forecasts imply about Intuit's financing needs for the upcoming year?

P11-33. **Adjusting the Income Statement Prior to Forecasting** (LO1)

CBS Corporation (CBS)

Following is the income statement of CBS Corporation, along with an excerpt from its MD&A section.

| Income Statement Year ended December 31 ($ millions) | 2005 | 2004 | 2003 |
|---|---|---|---|
| Revenues .................................... | $14,536.4 | $14,547.3 | $13,554.5 |
| Expenses | | | |
| Operating ................................ | 8,671.8 | 8,643.6 | 8,165.4 |
| Selling, general and administrative............. | 2,699.4 | 2,552.5 | 2,376.1 |
| Impairment charges ....................... | 9,484.4 | 17,997.1 | — |
| Depreciation and amortization ............... | 498.7 | 508.6 | 501.7 |
| Total expenses .......................... | 21,354.3 | 29,701.8 | 11,043.2 |
| Operating income (loss)...................... | $ (6,817.9) | $(15,154.5) | $ 2,511.3 |

**Operating Expenses:** Table below presents consolidated operating expenses by type

| Operating expenses by type, Year ended December 31 | 2005 | 2004 | Increase (Decrease) 2005 vs. 2004 | | 2003 | Increase (Decrease) 2004 vs. 2003 | |
|---|---|---|---|---|---|---|---|
| Programming . . . . . . . . . . . . . . . | $3,453.2 | $3,441.8 | $ 11.4 | —% | $3,080.3 | $361.5 | 12% |
| Production . . . . . . . . . . . . . . . . . | 2,453.5 | 2,584.7 | (131.2) | (5) | 2,661.9 | (77.2) | (3) |
| Outdoor operations . . . . . . . . . . | 1,134.2 | 1,102.7 | 31.5 | 3 | 1,012.6 | 90.1 | 9 |
| Publishing operations. . . . . . . . . | 525.0 | 517.6 | 7.4 | 1 | 486.3 | 31.3 | 6 |
| Parks operations . . . . . . . . . . . . . | 243.8 | 232.7 | 11.1 | 5 | 212.2 | 20.5 | 10 |
| Other. . . . . . . . . . . . . . . . . . . . . . | 862.1 | 764.1 | 98.0 | 13 | 712.1 | 52.0 | 7 |
| Total operating expenses . . . . . . . | $8,671.8 | $8,643.6 | $ 28.2 | —% | $8,165.4 | $478.2 | 6% |

For 2005, operating expenses of $8.67 billion increased slightly over $8.64 billion in 2004. For 2004, operating expenses of $8.64 billion increased 6% over $8.17 billion in 2003. The major components and changes in operating expenses were as follows:

- Programming expenses represented approximately 40% of total operating expenses in 2005 and 2004 and 38% in 2003, and reflect the amortization of acquired rights of programs exhibited on the broadcast and cable networks, and television and radio stations. Programming expenses increased slightly to $3.45 billion in 2005 from $3.44 billion in 2004 principally reflecting higher costs for Showtime Networks theatrical titles. Programming expenses increased 12% to $3.44 billion in 2004 from $3.08 billion in 2003 reflecting higher program rights expenses for sports events and primetime series at the broadcast networks.

- Production expenses represented approximately 28% of total operating expenses in 2005, 30% in 2004 and 33% in 2003, and reflect the cost and amortization of internally developed television programs, including direct production costs, residuals and participation expenses, and production overhead, as well as television and radio costs including on-air talent and other production costs. Production expenses decreased 5% to $2.45 billion in 2005 from $2.58 billion in 2004 principally reflecting lower network costs due to the absence of *Frasier* partially offset by increased costs for new network series. Production expenses decreased 3% to $2.58 billion in 2004 from $2.66 billion in 2003 reflecting fewer network series produced in 2004 partially offset by higher news costs for political campaign coverage.

- Outdoor operations costs represented approximately 13% of total operating expenses n 2005 and 2004, and 12% in 2003, and reflect transit and billboard lease, maintenance, posting and rotation expenses. Outdoor operations expenses increased 3% to $1.13 billion in 2005 from $1.10 billion in 2004 principally reflecting higher billboard lease costs and maintenance costs associated with the impact of hurricanes in 2005. Outdoor operations costs increased 9% to $1.10 billion in 2004 from $1.01 billion in 2003 primarily reflecting higher transit and billboard lease costs.

- Publishing operations costs, which represented approximately 6% of total operating expenses in each of the years 2005, 2004 and 2003, reflect cost of book sales, royalties and other costs incurred with respect to publishing operations. Publishing operations expenses for 2005 increased 1% to $525.0 million and increased 6% to $617.6 million in 2004 from $486.3 million in 2003 primarily due to higher revenues.

- Parks operations costs, which represented approximately 3% of total operating expenses in each of the years 2005, 2004 and 2003, increased 5% to $243.8 million in 2005 from $232.7 million in 2004 principally reflecting the cost of fourth quarter 2005 winter events held at the parks and the impact of foreign currency translation. In 2004, Parks operations costs increased 10% to $232.7 million from $212.2 million in 2003 primarily from the impact of foreign currency translation.

- Other operating expenses, which represented approximately 10% of total operating expenses in 2005 and 9% in 2004 and 2003, primarily include distribution costs incurred with respect to television product, costs associated with digital media and compensation. Other operating expenses increased 13% to $862.1 million in 2005 from $764.1 million in 2004 primarily reflecting a 10% increase in distribution costs due to the DVD release of *Charmed* and increased costs associated with digital media from the inclusion of SportsLine.com, Inc. ("SportsLine.com") since its acquisition in December 2004. Other operating expenses for 2004 increased 7% to $764.1 million in 2004 from $712.1 million in 2003 principally reflecting 15% higher distribution costs due to additional volume of DVD releases of the *Star Trek* series and higher compensation.

**Impairment Charges**   SFAS 142 requires the Company to perform an annual fair value-based impairment test of goodwill. The Company performed its annual impairment test as of October 31, 2005 concurrently with its annual budgeting process which begins in the fourth quarter each year. The first step of the test examines whether or not the book value of each of the Company's reporting units exceeds its fair value. If the book value for a reporting unit exceeds its fair value, the second step of the test is required to compare the implied fair value of that reporting unit's goodwill with the book value of the goodwill. The Company's reporting units are generally consistent with or one level below the operating segments underlying the reportable segments. As a result of the 2005 annual impairment test, the Company recorded an impairment charge of $9.48 billion in the fourth quarter of 2005. The $9.48 billion reflects charges to reduce the carrying value of goodwill at the CBS Television reporting unit of $6.44 billion and the Radio reporting unit of $3.05 billion. As a result of the annual impairment test performed for 2004, the Company recorded an impairment charge of $18.0 billion in the fourth quarter of 2004. The $18.0 billion reflects charges to reduce the carrying value of goodwill at the Radio reporting unit of $10.94 billion and the Outdoor reporting unit of $7.06 billion as well as the reduction of the carrying value of intangible assets of $27.8 million related to the FCC licenses at the Radio segment. Several factors led to a reduction in forecasted cash flows and long-term growth rates for both the Radio and Outdoor reporting units. Radio and Outdoor both fell short of budgeted revenue and operating income growth targets in 2004. Competition from other advertising media, including Internet advertising and cable and broadcast television reduced Radio and Outdoor growth rates. Also, the emergence of new competitors and technologies necessitated a shift in management's strategy for the Radio and Outdoor businesses, including changes in composition of the sales force and operating management as well as increased levels of investment in marketing and promotion.

**Required**

Identify and explain any income statement line items over the past three years that you believe should be considered for potential adjustment in preparation for forecasting the income statement of CBS.

**P11-34. Adjusting the Income Statement Prior to Forecasting (LO1)**

Xerox Corporation
(XRX)

Following are the income statements of Xerox Corporation.

| Income Statement<br>Year ended December 31 (in millions) | 2005 | 2004 | 2003 |
|---|---|---|---|
| **Revenues** | | | |
| Sales. . . . . . . . . . . . . . . . . . . . . . . . . . . . . . . . . . . . . . . . . . . . . . . . . . | $ 7,400 | $ 7,259 | $ 6,970 |
| Service, outsourcing and rentals . . . . . . . . . . . . . . . . . . . . . . . . . . . | 7,426 | 7,529 | 7,734 |
| Financial income . . . . . . . . . . . . . . . . . . . . . . . . . . . . . . . . . . . . . . | 875 | 934 | 997 |
| Total revenues. . . . . . . . . . . . . . . . . . . . . . . . . . . . . . . . . . . | 15,701 | 15,722 | 15,701 |
| **Costs and expenses** | | | |
| Cost of sales. . . . . . . . . . . . . . . . . . . . . . . . . . . . . . . . . . . . . . . . | 4,695 | 4,545 | 4,346 |
| Cost of service, outsourcing and rentals . . . . . . . . . . . . . . . . . . . . | 4,207 | 4,295 | 4,307 |
| Equipment financing and interest. . . . . . . . . . . . . . . . . . . . . . . . . | 326 | 345 | 362 |
| Research, development and engineering expenses . . . . . . . . . . . . . | 943 | 914 | 962 |
| Selling, administrative and general expenses . . . . . . . . . . . . . . . . . | 4,110 | 4,203 | 4,249 |
| Restructuring and asset impairment charges . . . . . . . . . . . . . . . . . | 366 | 86 | 176 |
| Gain on affiliate's sale of stock. . . . . . . . . . . . . . . . . . . . . . . . . . . | — | — | (13) |
| Other expenses, net. . . . . . . . . . . . . . . . . . . . . . . . . . . . . . . . . . | 224 | 369 | 876 |
| Total costs and expenses. . . . . . . . . . . . . . . . . . . . . . . . . . . | 14,871 | 14,757 | 15,265 |
| Income from continuing operations before<br>income taxes, equity income, discontinued operations<br>and cumulative effect of change in accounting principal. . . . . . . . | 830 | 965 | 436 |
| Income tax (benefits) expenses . . . . . . . . . . . . . . . . . . . . . . . . . . | (5) | 340 | 134 |
| Equity in net income of unconsolidated affiliates. . . . . . . . . . . . . . | 98 | 151 | 58 |
| Income from continuing operations before discontinued<br>operations and cumulative effect of change in<br>accounting principal. . . . . . . . . . . . . . . . . . . . . . . . . . . . . . . . . . | 933 | 776 | 360 |
| Income from discontinued operations, net of tax . . . . . . . . . . . . . . | 53 | 83 | — |
| Cumulative effect of change in accounting principal, net of tax . . . . | (8) | — | — |
| Net income. . . . . . . . . . . . . . . . . . . . . . . . . . . . . . . . . . . . . . . . . | $ 978 | $ 859 | $ 360 |

**Required**

Identify and explain any income statement line items over the past three years that you believe should be considered for potential adjustment in preparation for forecasting the income statement of Xerox.

# CASES

C11-35. **Adjusting the Income Statement and Forecasting the Income Statement, Balance Sheet, and Statement of Cash Flows    (LO1, 2)**

Following are the income statements and balance sheets of Cisco Systems, Inc.

Cisco Systems, Inc. (CSCO)

| Income Statement<br>Years ended ($ millions) | July 29, 2006 | July 30, 2005 | July 31, 2004 |
|---|---|---|---|
| Net sales | | | |
| Product | $23,917 | $20,853 | $18,550 |
| Service | 4,567 | 3,948 | 3,495 |
| Total net sales | 28,484 | 24,801 | 22,045 |
| Cost of sales | | | |
| Product | 8,114 | 6,758 | 5,766 |
| Service | 1,623 | 1,372 | 1,153 |
| Total cost of sales | 9,737 | 8,130 | 6,919 |
| Gross margin | 18,747 | 16,671 | 15,126 |
| Operating expenses | | | |
| Research and development | 4,067 | 3,322 | 3,192 |
| Sales and marketing | 6,031 | 4,721 | 4,530 |
| General and administrative | 1,169 | 959 | 867 |
| Amortization of purchased intangible assets | 393 | 227 | 242 |
| In-process research and development | 91 | 26 | 3 |
| Total operating expenses | 11,751 | 9,255 | 8,834 |
| Operating income | 6,996 | 7,416 | 6,292 |
| Interest income, net | 607 | 552 | 512 |
| Other income, net | 30 | 68 | 188 |
| Interest and other income, net | 637 | 620 | 700 |
| Income before provision for income taxes and cumulative effect of accounting change | 7,633 | 8,036 | 6,992 |
| Provision for income taxes | 2,053 | 2,295 | 2,024 |
| Income before cumulative effect of accounting change | 5,580 | 5,741 | 4,968 |
| Cumulative effect of accounting change, net of tax | — | — | (567) |
| Net income | $ 5,580 | $ 5,741 | $ 4,401 |

| Balance sheet ($ millions) | July 29, 2006 | July 30, 2005 |
| --- | --- | --- |
| **Assets** | | |
| Cash and cash equivalents | $3,297 | $4,742 |
| Investments | 14,517 | 11,313 |
| Accounts receivable, net of allowance for doubtful accounts of $175 at July 29, 2006 and $162 at July 30, 2005 | 3,303 | 2,216 |
| Inventories | 1,371 | 1,297 |
| Deferred tax assets | 1,604 | 1,475 |
| Prepaid expenses and other current assets | 1,584 | 967 |
| Total current assets | 25,676 | 22,010 |
| Property and equipment, net | 3,440 | 3,320 |
| Goodwill | 9,227 | 5,295 |
| Purchased intangible assets, net | 2,161 | 549 |
| Other assets | 2,811 | 2,709 |
| Total assets | $43,315 | $33,883 |
| **Liabilities and shareholders' equity** | | |
| Accounts payable | $ 880 | $ 735 |
| Income taxes payable | 1,744 | 1,511 |
| Accrued compensation | 1,516 | 1,317 |
| Deferred revenue | 4,408 | 3,854 |
| Other accrued liabilities | 2,765 | 2,094 |
| Total current liabilities | 11,313 | 9,511 |
| Long-term debt | 6,332 | — |
| Deferred revenue | 1,241 | 1,188 |
| Other long-term liabilities | 511 | — |
| Total liabilities | 19,397 | 10,699 |
| Commitments and contingencies | | |
| Minority interest | **6** | 10 |
| Shareholders' equity | | |
| Preferred stock, no par value: 5 shares authorized; none issued and outstanding | — | — |
| Common stock and additional paid-in capital, $0.001 par value: 20,000 shares authorized; 6,059 and 6,331 shares issued and outstanding at July 29, 2006 and July 30, 2005, respectively | 24,257 | 22,394 |
| Retained earnings (Accumulated deficit) | (617) | 506 |
| Accumulated other comprehensive income | 272 | 274 |
| Total shareholders' equity | 23,912 | 23,174 |
| Total liabilities and shareholders' equity | $43,315 | $33,883 |

Excerpts from the Cisco Systems MD&A follow:

**Acquisition of Scientific-Atlanta, Inc.** On February 24, 2006, Cisco completed the acquisition of Scientific-Atlanta, Inc., a provider of set-top boxes, end-to-end video distribution networks, and video system integration. Cisco believes video is emerging as the key strategic application in the service provider "triple play" bundle of consumer entertainment, communications, and online services. Cisco believes the combined entity creates an end-to-end solution for carrier networks and the digital home and delivers large-scale video systems to extend Cisco's commitment to and leadership in the service provider market.

**Stock-Based Compensation Expense**   On July 31, 2005, we adopted SFAS 123(R), which requires the measurement and recognition of compensation expense for all share-based payment awards made to employees and directors including employee stock options and employee stock purchases based on estimated fair values. Stock-based compensation expense related to employee stock options and employee stock purchases under SFAS 123(R) for fiscal 2006 was allocated as follows (in millions):

| | Amount |
|---|---|
| Cost of sales-product. . . . . . . . . . . . . . . . . . . . . . . . . . . . . . . . . . . . . . . . . . . . . . . . . | $    50 |
| Cost of sales-service . . . . . . . . . . . . . . . . . . . . . . . . . . . . . . . . . . . . . . . . . . . . . . . . | 112 |
| Stock-based compensation expense included in cost of sale . . . . . . . . . . . . . . . . | 162 |
| Research and development . . . . . . . . . . . . . . . . . . . . . . . . . . . . . . . . . . . . . . . . . . . | 346 |
| Sales and marketing. . . . . . . . . . . . . . . . . . . . . . . . . . . . . . . . . . . . . . . . . . . . . . . . | 427 |
| General and administrative. . . . . . . . . . . . . . . . . . . . . . . . . . . . . . . . . . . . . . . . . . . | 115 |
| Stock-based compensation expense included in operating expense. . . . . . . . . . . . | 888 |
| Total stock-based compensation expense related to employee stock options and employee stock purchases . . . . . . . . . . . . . . . . . . . . . . . . . . . . . . . . . . . . . | 1,050 |
| Tax benefit . . . . . . . . . . . . . . . . . . . . . . . . . . . . . . . . . . . . . . . . . . . . . . . . . . . . . . . . | (294) |
| Stock-based compensation expense related to employee stock options and employee stock purchases, net of tax. . . . . . . . . . . . . . . . . . . . . . . . . . . . . . | $  756 |

**Gross Margin**   The decrease in gross margin percentage compared to fiscal 2005 was primarily related to the acquisition of Scientific-Atlanta. Other factors contributing to the decrease in gross margin percentage were the sales mix of certain switching and routing products, and the effect of stock-based compensation expense under SFAS 123(R). These factors were partially offset by lower manufacturing costs related to lower component costs and value engineering, and other manufacturing-related costs and higher volume.

**Research and Development, Sales and Marketing, and General and Administrative Expenses**   R&D expenses increased for fiscal 2006 compared to fiscal 2005 primarily due to higher headcount-related expenses reflecting our continued investment in R&D efforts in routers, switches, advanced technologies, and other product technologies; the effect of stock-based compensation expense related to employee stock options and employee stock purchases under SFAS 123(R); and the acquisition of Scientific-Atlanta.

Sales and marketing expenses for fiscal 2006 increased compared to fiscal 2005 primarily due to an increase in sales expenses of approximately $1.1 billion. Sales expenses increased primarily due to an increase in headcount-related expenses, an increase in sales program expenses, and the acquisition of Scientific-Atlanta, which added approximately $30 million of sales expenses. Sales expenses also include stock-based compensation expense related to employee stock options and employee stock purchases under SFAS 123(R) of $337 million during fiscal 2006. Marketing expenses include $90 million of stock-based compensation expense related to employee stock options and employee stock purchases under SFAS 123(R) during fiscal 2006. Scientific-Atlanta added approximately $20 million of marketing expenses.

G&A expenses for fiscal 2006 increased compared to fiscal 2005 primarily because of stock-based compensation expense related to employee stock options and employee stock purchases under SFAS 123(R), and the acquisition of Scientific-Atlanta. G&A expenses include $115 million of stock-based compensation expense related to employee stock options and employee stock purchases under SFAS 123(R) and Scientific-Atlanta contributed approximately $40 million of G&A expenses.

**Accounts Receivable, Net**   The increase in accounts receivable was due to increased sales and the addition of approximately $240 million of accounts receivable related to Scientific-Atlanta. Days sales outstanding in accounts receivable (DSO) as of July 29, 2006 and July 30, 2005 was 38 days and 31 days, respectively. Our DSO is primarily impacted by shipment linearity and collections performance. A steady level of shipments and good collections performance will result in reduced DSO compared with a higher level of shipments toward the end of a quarter, which will result in a shorter amount of time to collect the related accounts receivable and increased DSO.

**Inventories**   Annualized inventory turns were 8.5 in the fourth quarter of fiscal 2006 compared to 6.6 in the fourth quarter of fiscal 2005...In the third quarter of fiscal 2006, we began the initial implementation of the lean manufacturing model. Lean manufacturing is an industry-standard model that seeks to drive efficiency and flexibility in manufacturing processes and in the broader supply chain. Over time, consistent with what we have experienced thus far, we expect this process will result in incremental increases in purchase commitments with contract manufacturers and suppliers and corresponding decreases in manufacturing inventory. Inventory management remains an area of focus as we balance the need to maintain strategic inventory levels to ensure competitive lead times with the risk of inventory obsolescence because of rapidly changing technology and customer requirements. We believe the amount of our inventory is appropriate for our revenue levels.

**Required**

a. Compute the ratios in the following table for fiscal years 2005 and 2006 using the financial statements provided and the following additional information:
   1. Total net sales for 2004 is $22,045 million
   2. 2006 depreciation expense is $900 (included in G&A expense); and 2005 depreciation divided by prior year property and equipment (net) equals 23.3%
   3. Dividends are $0 in 2005 and 2006

   (Ratios should reveal a marked decline in gross profit margin and marked increases in operating expense items from 2005 to 2006.)

b. For the following table, compute and enter assumptions for the forecasting of Cisco's financial statements. Do you believe that margins and operating expenses will continue at 2006 percentages? Or, are they likely to revert to 2005 levels? Explain.

| | Projected | 2006 Actual | 2005 Actual |
|---|---|---|---|
| Gross margin/Total net sales . . . . . . . . . . . . . . . . . . . . . . . . . . | | | |
| Research and development/Total net sales . . . . . . . . . . . . . . . | | | |
| Sales and marketing/Total net sales. . . . . . . . . . . . . . . . . . . . . | | | |
| General and administrative/Total net sales . . . . . . . . . . . . . . | | | |
| (Amortization of purchased intangibles + In-process research and development)/Total net sales . . . . . . . . . . . . . | | | |
| Depreciation (in G&A)/Prior year property and equipment, net . . . . . . . . . . . . . . . . . . . . . . . . . . . . . . . . . . | | | |
| Provision for income taxes/Income before provision for income taxes . . . . . . . . . . . . . . . . . . . . . . . . . . . . . . . . | | | |
| Total net sales/Year-end accounts receivable, net . . . . . . . . . | | | |
| Total cost of sales/Year-end inventories. . . . . . . . . . . . . . . . . | | | |
| Total net sales/Year-end property and equipment, net . . . . . . | | | |
| Total cost of sales/Year-end property and equipment, net . . . | | | |
| Total net sales/Year-end accrued compensation . . . . . . . . . . . | | | |
| Income taxes payable/Provision for income taxes. . . . . . . . . . | | | |
| Total net sales/Year-end deferred revenue. . . . . . . . . . . . . . . | | | |
| Dividends/Net income . . . . . . . . . . . . . . . . . . . . . . . . . . . . . . | | | |

c. Prepare one-year-ahead forecasts of Cisco's income statement, balance sheet, and statement of cash flows using your assumptions from part *b* and the information provided.

d. What does the projected cash balance reveal about Cisco's need for external financing in 2007?

# Analyzing and Valuing Equity Securities

## LEARNING OBJECTIVES

**LO1** Describe and illustrate the discounted free cash flow model to value equity securities. (p. 12-4)

**LO2** Describe and illustrate the residual operating income model to value equity securities. (p. 12-8)

**LO3** Explain how equity valuation models can aid managerial decisions. (p. 12-10)

## JOHNSON & JOHNSON

Pharmaceutical companies have long been the growth stocks of choice for many investors. Their income was steady and climbing, their stocks grew in value, and their growth appeared limitless as the population aged. Stockholders pushed them to grow by acquiring competitors, and encouraged them to further market existing drugs and pursue new product development. All looked rosy. The high profit margins from successful drug products fueled further expansion. Meanwhile, many pharmaceutical companies sold off their lower-growth business segments such as those manufacturing and distributing medical instruments and devices. For example, Pfizer sold off segments that manufactured surgical devices, heart valves, and orthopedic implants, while Eli Lilly sold off many of its medical device segments, including Guidant.

A few pharmaceutical companies bucked the trend to reorganize and consolidate. One of those was Johnson & Johnson (J&J). In contrast with the operating strategies of other pharmaceutical companies, and anticipating a gradual decline in pharmaceutical operating profits, J&J has been steadily increasing its investment in its medical devices and instruments segment. That segment now accounts for 40% of J&J's operating profit, up from 31% in 2004.

As expected, the pharmaceutical segment's proportion of J&J's operating profit has decreased from 58% to 48% in the past two years, while pharmaceutical sales have declined by only 2% to 44.1% of total sales. The following graphics, using data from J&J's 10-K report, reflect these trends.

Getty Images

**Sales by Segment**
($ billions)

**Operating Profit by Segment**
($ billions)

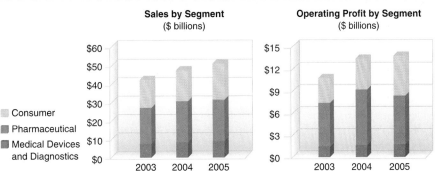

- Consumer
- Pharmaceutical
- Medical Devices and Diagnostics

J&J is currently riding high while many other pharmaceutical companies are struggling. A drug-industry consultant asserts that J&J is ". . . casting a broader net for innovation, it's not just blockbuster drugs. They've held their value or grown, and the pure pharma plays that everyone thought could grow forever are the companies that have lost their luster."

Supported by its more diversified operations and fueled by a steady increase in operating profits, J&J's stock price has climbed since late 2004, as shown here.

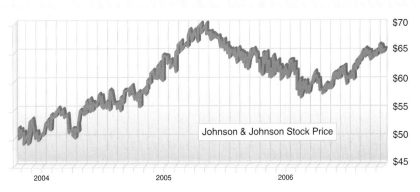

Johnson & Johnson Stock Price

*(Continued on next page)*

Despite the run-up in stock price, analysts remain bullish, continuing to rate the J&J stock a "BUY."

This raises several questions. What factors drive the J&J stock price? Why do analysts expect its price to continue to rise? How do accounting measures of performance and financial condition impact stock price? This module provides insights and answers to these questions. It explains how we can use forecasts of operating profits and cash flows to price equity securities such as J&J's stock.

Sources: *Johnson & Johnson* 2003-2005 10-K and Annual Reports; *The Wall Street Journal*, December 2004; Fortune, January 2007.

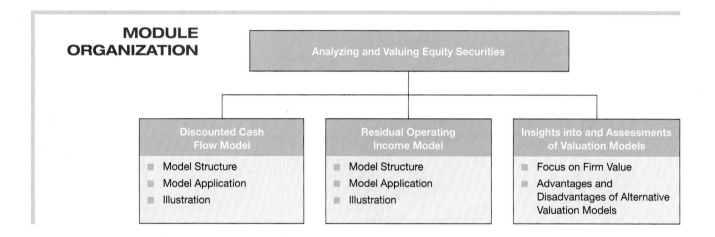

# INTRODUCTION TO SECURITY VALUATION

This module focuses on valuing equity securities (we explain the valuation of debt securities in Module 8). We describe two approaches: the discounted free cash flow model (DCF) and residual operating income model (ROPI). We then conclude by discussing the management implications from an increased understanding of the factors that impact values of equity securities. It is important that we understand the determinants of equity value to make informed decisions. Employees at all levels of an organization, whether public or private, should understand the factors that create shareholder value so that they can work effectively toward that objective. For many senior managers, stock value serves as a scorecard. Successful managers are those who better understand the factors affecting that scorecard.

## Equity Valuation Models

Module 8 explains that the value of a debt security is the present value of the interest and principal payments that the investor *expects* to receive in the future. The valuation of equity securities is similar in that it is also based on expectations. The difference lies in the increased uncertainty surrounding the payments from equity securities.

There are many equity valuation models in use today. Each of them defines the value of an equity security in terms of the present value of future forecasted amounts. They differ primarily in terms of what is forecasted.

The basis of equity valuation is the premise that the value of an equity security is determined by the payments that the investor can expect to receive from the investment. Equity investments involve two types of payoffs: (1) dividends received during the holding period and (2) capital gains when the security is sold.[1] The value of an equity security is, then, based on the present value of expected dividends plus the value of the security at the end of the forecasted holding period. This **dividend discount model** is appealing in its simplicity and its intuitive focus on dividend distribution. As a practical matter, however, the model is not useful because many companies that have a positive stock price have never paid a dividend, and are not expected to pay a dividend in the foreseeable future.

---

[1] The future stock price is, itself, also assumed to be related to the expected dividends that the new investor expects to receive; as a result, the expected receipt of dividends is the sole driver of stock price under this type of valuation model.

A more practical approach to valuing equity securities focuses, instead, on the company's operating and investing activities; that is, on the *generation* of cash rather than the *distribution* of cash. This approach is called the **discounted cash flow (DCF)** model. The focus of the forecasting process for this model is the company's expected *free cash flows to the firm*, which are defined as operating cash flows net of the expected new investments in net operating assets that are required to support the business.

A second practical approach to equity valuation also focuses on operating and investing activities. It is known as the **residual operating income (ROPI)** model. This model uses both net operating profits after tax (NOPAT) and the net operating assets (NOA) to determine equity value; see Module 4 for complete descriptions of the NOPAT and NOA measures. This approach highlights the importance of return on net operating assets (RNOA), and the disaggregation of RNOA into net operating profit margin and NOA turnover. We discuss the implications of this insight for managers later in this module.

# DISCOUNTED CASH FLOW (DCF) MODEL

The discounted cash flow (DCF) model defines firm value as follows:

**LO1** Describe and illustrate the discounted free cash flow model to value equity securities.

**Firm Value = Present Value of Expected Free Cash Flows to Firm**

The expected free cash flows to the firm include cash flows arising from the operating side of the firm; that is, cash generated from the firm's operating activities (but not from nonoperating activities such as interest paid on debt or dividends received on investments), and do not include the cash flows from financing activities. More specifically, **free cash flows to the firm** (FCFF) equal net operating profit after tax that is not used to grow net operating assets.[2] Using the terminology of Module 4

**FCFF = NOPAT − Increase in NOA**

where

> **NOPAT = Net operating profit after tax**
> **NOA = Net operating assets**

Net operating profit after tax is normally positive and net cash flows from increases in net operating assets are normally negative. The sum of the two (positive or negative) represents the net cash flows available to creditors and shareholders. Positive FCFF imply that there are funds available for distribution to creditors and shareholders, either in the form of debt repayments, dividends, or stock repurchases (treasury stock). Negative FCFF imply that the firm requires additional funds from creditors and/or shareholders, in the form of new loans or equity investments, to support its business activities.

The DCF valuation model requires forecasts of *all* future free cash flows; that is, free cash flows for the remainder of the company's life. Generating such forecasts is not realistic. Consequently, analysts typically estimate FCFF over a horizon period, often 4 to 10 years, and then make simplifying assumptions about the FCFF subsequent to that horizon period.

Application of the DCF model to equity valuation involves five steps:

1. Forecast and discount FCFF for the **horizon period**.[3]
2. Forecast and discount FCFF for the post-horizon period, called **terminal period**.[4]

---

[2] FCFF is sometimes approximated by net cash flows from operating activities less capital expenditures. This is not exact because operating cash flows from the statement of cash flows include interest paid and received, which are not part of NOPAT. However, for most companies, the approximation is fairly accurate.

[3] When discounting FCFF, the appropriate discount rate ($r_w$) is the **weighted average cost of capital (WACC)**, where the weights are the relative percentages of debt (*d*) and equity (*e*) in the capital structure applied to the expected returns on debt ($r_d$) and equity ($r_e$), respectively: WACC = $r_w$ = ($r_d$ × % of debt) + ($r_e$ × % of equity).

[4] For an assumed growth, *g*, the terminal period (*T*) present value of FCFF in perpetuity (beyond the horizon period) is given by, $\frac{FCFF_T}{r_w - g}$, where $FCFF_T$ is the free cash flow to the firm for the terminal period, $r_w$ is WACC, and *g* is the assumed long-term growth rate of those cash flows. The resulting amount is then discounted back to the present using the horizon-end period discount factor.

3. Sum the present values of the horizon and terminal periods to yield firm (enterprise) value.
4. Subtract net nonoperating obligations (NNO) from firm value to yield firm equity value. NNO can be either positive or negative; either way, we subtract NNO in step 4. (For most companies, NNO is a positive number because nonoperating liabilities exceed nonoperating assets.)
5. Divide firm equity value by the number of shares outstanding to yield stock value per share.

To illustrate, we apply the DCF model to Johnson & Johnson. J&J's recent financial statements are reproduced in Appendix 12A. Forecasted financials for J&J (forecast horizon of 2006–2009 and terminal period of 2010) are in Exhibit 12.1.[5] The forecasts (in bold) are for sales, NOPAT, and NOA. These forecasts assume an annual 6.5% sales growth during the horizon period, a terminal period sales growth of 1%, net operating profit margin (NOPM) of 18%, and a year-end net operating asset turnover (NOAT) of 1.25 (which is the 2005 turnover rate based on year-end NOA; year-end amounts are used because we are forecasting year-end account balances, not average balances).[6,7]

| EXHIBIT 12.1 | | Application of Discounted Cash Flow Model | | | | |
|---|---|---|---|---|---|---|
| **(In millions, except per share values and discount factors)** | **2005** | **Horizon Period** | | | | **Terminal Period** |
| | | **2006** | **2007** | **2008** | **2009** | |
| Sales. . . . . . . . . . . . . . . . . . . . . . . . . | $ 50,514 | **$53,797** | **$57,294** | **$61,018** | **$64,985** | **$65,634** |
| NOPAT*. . . . . . . . . . . . . . . . . . . . . . . | 10,134 | **9,683** | **10,313** | **10,983** | **11,697** | **11,814** |
| NOA**. . . . . . . . . . . . . . . . . . . . . . . . | 40,453 | **43,038** | **45,835** | **48,814** | **51,988** | **52,507** |
| Increase in NOA . . . . . . . . . . . . . . . . . | | 2,585 | 2,797 | 2,979 | 3,174 | 519 |
| FCFF (NOPAT − Increase in NOA) . . . . | | 7,098 | 7,516 | 8,004 | 8,523 | 11,295 |
| Discount factor [1/(1 + $r_w$)$^t$] . . . . . . . . | | 0.94340 | 0.89000 | 0.83962 | 0.79209 | |
| Present value of horizon FCFF . . . . . . . | | 6,696 | 6,689 | 6,720 | 6,751 | |
| Cum present value of horizon FCFF . . . | 26,856 | | | | | |
| Present value of terminal FCFF . . . . . . | 178,933 | | | | | |
| Total firm value . . . . . . . . . . . . . . . . . . | 205,789 | | | | | |
| Less (plus) NNO† . . . . . . . . . . . . . . . . | 2,582 | | | | | |
| Firm equity value . . . . . . . . . . . . . . . . | $203,207 | | | | | |
| Shares outstanding . . . . . . . . . . . . . . | 2,975 | | | | | |
| Stock value per share. . . . . . . . . . . . . | $ 68.30 | | | | | |

*Given its combined federal and state statutory tax rate of 36%, NOPAT for 2005 is computed as follows ($ mil.): $50,514 − $13,954 − $16,877 − $6,312 − $362 + $214 − ($3,245 − 0.36 × [$487 − $54]) = $10,134, which is 20% of sales ($10,134 million/$50,514 million). Footnotes to J&J's 10-K reveal that its effective tax rate for 2005 is 23.8%, compared with 33.7% in 2004 and 30.2% in 2003. Analysis reveals that its 2005 effective tax rate is lower due to foreign tax credits and a reversal of a tax liability tied to a technical correction with the American Jobs Creation Act of 2004. The credits and reversal are *transitory* and should not be included in our projections. Accordingly, we *project* its tax rate to be 32%, the average of its 2004 and 2003 rates. If we apply 32% to its $13,656 million pretax GAAP income for 2005 we get an adjusted NOPAT of $9,009 million, computed as ($ mil.): $50,514 − $13,954 − $16,877 − $6,312 − $362 + 214 − ([$13,656 × 32%] − [0.36 × {$487 − $54}]). This adjusted NOPAT yields a NOPM of 18% ($9,009 million/$50,514 million) and is the rate we use in forecasts of NOPAT. A note on rounding: Sales are forecasted using current period sales multiplied successively by (1 + Growth rate), without rounding; next, NOPAT and NOA are computed from each period's sales forecast rounded to the whole unit.

**NOA computations for 2005 follow ($ mil.): ($58,025 − $83 − $20) − ($4,315 − $3,529 − $2,017 − $1,166 − $940 − $211 − $3,065 − $2,226) = $40,453.

†NNO is the difference between NOA and total shareholders' equity, which is NNO ($ mil.) = $40,453 − $37,871 = $2,582.

[5] We use a four-period horizon in the text and assignments to simplify the exposition and to reduce the computational burden. In practice, analysts use spreadsheets to forecast future cash flows and value the equity security, and typically have a forecast horizon of seven to ten periods.

[6] **NOPAT** equals revenues less operating expenses such as cost of goods sold, selling, general, and administrative expenses, and taxes. NOPAT excludes any interest revenue and interest expense and any gains or losses from financial investments. NOPAT reflects the operating side of the firm as opposed to nonoperating activities such as borrowing and security investment activities. **NOA** equals operating assets less operating liabilities. (See Module 4.)

[7] NOPAT and NOA are typically forecasted using the detailed forecasting procedures discussed in Module 11. In this module we use the parsimonious method to multiyear forecasting (see Module 11) to focus attention on the valuation process.

The bottom line of Exhibit 12.1 is the estimated J&J equity value of $203,207 million, or a per share stock value of $68.30. The present value computations use a 6% WACC($r_w$) as the discount rate.[8] Specifically, we obtain this stock valuation as follows:

1. **Compute present value of horizon period FCFF.** We compute the forecasted 2006 FCFF of $7,098 million from the forecasted 2006 NOPAT less the forecasted increase in 2006 NOA. The present value of this $7,098 million as of 2005 is $6,696 million, computed as $7,098 million $\times$ 0.94340 (the present value factor for one year discounted at 6%).[9] Similarly, the present value of 2007 FCFF (2 years from the current date) is $6,689 million, computed as $7,516 million $\times$ 0.89000, and so on through 2009. The sum of these present values (*cumulative present value*) is $26,856 million.

2. **Compute present value of terminal period FCFF.** The present value of the terminal period FCFF is $178,933 million, computed as $\dfrac{\left(\dfrac{\$11{,}295 \text{ million}}{0.06-0.01}\right)}{(1.06)^4}$, or ($11,295/0.05) $\times$ 0.79209.

3. **Compute firm equity value.** Sum present values from the horizon and terminal period FCFF to get firm (enterprise) value of $205,789 million. Subtract the value of J&J's net nonoperating obligations of $2,582 million to get firm equity value of $203,207. Dividing firm equity value by the 2,975 million shares outstanding yields the estimated per share valuation of $68.30.

This valuation would be performed in early 2006 (because J&J's 10-K was released in mid-March 2006). J&J's stock closed at $60.25 at year-end 2005. Our valuation estimate of $68.30 indicates that its stock is undervalued. In December 2006 (roughly one year later) J&J stock traded at near $67, and analysts continued to recommend it as a BUY with a target share price in the high $60s.

---

**BUSINESS INSIGHT**  **Analysts' Earnings Forecasts**

Estimates of earnings and cash flows are key to security valuation. Following are earnings estimates at the beginning of 2006 for Johnson & Johnson by Thomson First Call analysts' reports, a division of Thomson Financial™:

| Period | Ending | Mean EPS | High EPS | Low EPS | Median EPS |
|---|---|---|---|---|---|
| Fiscal Year | Dec. 2006 | $3.69 | $3.72 | $3.65 | $3.69 |
| Fiscal Year | Dec. 2007 | $4.01 | $4.11 | $3.88 | $4.01 |
| Long-term growth (%) | — | 10.06% | 13.00% | 7.00% | 10.07% |

The mean (consensus) EPS estimate for 2006 (one year ahead) is $3.69 per share, with a high of $3.72 and a low of $3.65. For 2007, the mean (consensus) EPS estimate is $4.01, with a high of $4.11 and a low of $3.88. The estimated long-term growth rate for EPS (similar to our terminal year growth rate) ranges from 7% to 13%, with a mean (consensus) estimate of 10.06%. Since the terminal year valuation is such a large proportion of total firm valuation, especially for the DCF model, the variability in stock price estimates across analysts covering Johnson & Johnson is due more to variation in estimates for long-term growth rates than to one- and two-year-ahead earnings forecasts.

---

[8] The weighted average cost of capital (WACC) for J&J is computed using the following three-step process:

1. The cost of equity capital is given by the capital asset pricing model (CAPM): $r_e = r_f + \beta\,(r_m - r_f)$, where $\beta$ is the beta of the stock (an estimate of stock price variability that is reported by several services such as Standard and Poors), $r_f$ is the risk free rate (commonly assumed as the 10-year government bond rate), and $r_m$ is the expected return to the entire market. The expression $(r_m - r_f)$ is the "spread" of equities over the risk free rate, often assumed to be around 5%. For J&J, given its beta of 0.24 and a 10-year treasury bond rate of 4.42% ($r_f$) as of January 2006, $r_e$ is estimated as 5.62%, computed as 4.42% + (0.24 $\times$ 5%).

2. Given J&J's AAA bond rating, its cost of debt capital is its after-tax rate on AAA bonds as of January 1, 2006 (5.29%) multiplied by 1-36%, the federal and state statutory tax rate from its tax footnote, yielding 3.39% (its after-tax cost of debt).

3. WACC is the weighted average of the cost of equity capital and the cost of debt capital. J&J capital structure is 95% equity and 5% debt. Thus, J&J's weighted average cost of capital is (95% $\times$ 5.62%) + (5% $\times$ 3.39%) = 5.51%. We have rounded this WACC up to 6% to facilitate use of the present value tables from Appendix A.

[9] Horizon period discount factors follow: $1/(1.06)^1 = 0.94340$; $1/(1.06)^2 = 0.89000$; $1/(1.06)^3 = 0.83962$; $1/(1.06)^4 = 0.79209$.

**You Are the Division Manager**

Assume that you are managing a division of a company that has a large investment in plant assets and sells its products on credit. Identify steps you can take to increase your company's cash flow and hence, your company's firm value. [Answer p. 12-15]

## MID-MODULE REVIEW

Following are forecasts of Procter & Gamble's sales, net operating profit after tax (NOPAT), and net operating assets (NOA). These are taken from our forecasting process in Module 11 and now include a terminal period forecast that reflects a long-term growth rate of 2%.

| (In millions) | 2006 | Horizon Period 2007 | 2008 | 2009 | 2010 | Terminal Period |
|---|---|---|---|---|---|---|
| Sales............ | $68,222 | $ 71,224 | $ 74,358 | $ 77,629 | $ 81,045 | $ 82,666 |
| NOPAT .......... | 9,221 | 9,615 | 10,038 | 10,480 | 10,941 | 11,160 |
| NOA ............ | 99,879 | 104,741 | 109,350 | 114,160 | 119,184 | 121,568 |

Drawing on these forecasts, compute P&G's free cash flows to the firm (FCFF) and an estimate of its stock value using the DCF model. Make the following assumptions: discount rate (WACC) of 5%, shares outstanding of 3,178.8 million, and net nonoperating obligations (NNO) of $35,816 million.

## Solution

The following DCF results yield a P&G stock value estimate of $70.49 as of June 30, 2006. P&G's stock closed at $55.60 on that date. This estimate suggests that P&G's stock is undervalued on that date. P&G stock traded at around $63 in December 2006.

| (In millions, except per share values and discount factors) | 2006 | Horizon Period 2007 | 2008 | 2009 | 2010 | Terminal Period |
|---|---|---|---|---|---|---|
| Increase in NOA[a] ................. | | $ 4,862 | $ 4,609 | $ 4,810 | $ 5,024 | $ 2,384 |
| FCFF (NOPAT − Increase in NOA) ..... | | 4,753 | 5,429 | 5,670 | 5,917 | 8,776 |
| Discount factor $[1/(1 + r_w)^t]$ .......... | | 0.95238 | 0.90703 | 0.86384 | 0.82270 | |
| Present value of horizon FCFF........ | | 4,527 | 4,924 | 4,898 | 4,868 | |
| Cum present value of horizon FCFF.... | $ 19,217 | | | | | |
| Present value of terminal FCFF ....... | 240,667[b] | | | | | |
| Total firm value..................... | 259,884 | | | | | |
| Less NNO........................ | 35,816 | | | | | |
| Firm equity value ................. | $224,068 | | | | | |
| Shares outstanding ................ | 3,178.8 | | | | | |
| Stock value per share.............. | $ 70.49 | | | | | |

[a] NOA increases are viewed as a cash outflow.

[b] Computed as $\dfrac{\left(\dfrac{\$8,776 \text{ million}}{0.05 - 0.02}\right)}{(1.05)^4}$, or ($8,776/0.03) × 0.82270, where 5% is WACC and 2% is the long-term growth rate subsequent to the horizon period that is used to estimate terminal period FCFF.

# RESIDUAL OPERATING INCOME (ROPI) MODEL

The residual operating income (ROPI) model focuses on net operating profit after tax (NOPAT) and net operating assets (NOA). This means it uses key measures from both the income statement and balance sheet in determining firm value. The ROPI model defines firm value as the sum of two components:

**LO2** Describe and illustrate the residual operating income model to value equity securities.

$$\textbf{Firm Value = NOA + Present Value of Expected ROPI}$$

where

> **NOA = Net operating assets**
> **ROPI = Residual operating income**

Net operating assets (NOA) are the foundation of firm value under the ROPI model. This is potentially problematic because we measure NOA using the balance sheet, which is unlikely to fully and contemporaneously capture the true (or intrinsic) value of all of a firm's operating assets.[10] However, the ROPI model adds an adjustment that corrects for the undervaluation or overvaluation of NOA. This adjustment is the present value of expected residual operating income, and is defined as follows:

$$\textbf{ROPI = NOPAT} - \underbrace{\textbf{(NOA}_{\textbf{Beg}} \times r_w)}_{\textbf{Expected NOPAT}}$$

where

> $\text{NOA}_{\text{Beg}}$ = **Net operating assets at beginning (*Beg*) of period**
> $r_w$ = **Weighted average cost of capital (WACC)**

Residual operating income (ROPI) is the net operating profit a firm earns over and above the return that the operating assets are expected to earn given the firm's WACC.

Understanding the ROPI model helps us reap the benefits from the disaggregation of return on net operating assets (RNOA) in Module 4. In addition, the ROPI model is the foundation for many internal and external performance evaluation and compensation systems marketed by management consulting and accounting services firms.[11]

Application of the ROPI model to equity valuation involves five steps:

1. Forecast and discount ROPI for the horizon period.[12]

2. Forecast and discount ROPI for the terminal period.[13]

3. Sum the present values from both the horizon and terminal periods; then add this sum to current NOA to get firm (enterprise) value.

---

[10] If the assets earn more than expected, it could be because NOA does not capture all of the firms' assets. For example, R&D and advertising are not fully and contemporaneously reflected on the balance sheet as assets though they likely produce future cash inflows. Likewise, internally generated goodwill is not fully reflected on the balance sheet as an asset. Similarly, assets are generally not written up to reflect unrealized gains. Conversely, sometimes the balance sheet overstates the true value of NOA. For example, companies can delay the write-down of impaired assets and, thus, overstate their book values. These examples, and a host of others, can yield reported values of NOA that differs from the market value of the operating assets.

[11] Examples are economic value added (EVA™) from Stern Stewart & Company, the economic profit model from McKinsey & Co., the cash flow return on investment (CFROI™) from Holt Value Associates, the economic value management from KPMG, and the value builder from PricewaterhouseCoopers (PwC).

[12] The present value of expected ROPI uses the weighted average cost of capital (WACC) as its discount rate; same as with the DCF model.

[13] As with the DCF model, for an assumed growth, *g*, the present value of the perpetuity of ROPI beyond the horizon period is given by $\frac{\text{ROPI}_T}{r_w - g}$, where $\text{ROPI}_T$ is the residual operating income for the terminal period, $r_w$ is WACC for the firm, and *g* is the assumed growth rate of $\text{ROPI}_T$ following the horizon period. The resulting amount is then discounted back to the present using the WACC computed over the length of the horizon period.

4. Subtract net nonoperating obligations (NNO) from firm value to yield firm equity value.

5. Divide firm equity value by the number of shares outstanding to yield stock value per share.

To illustrate application of the ROPI model, we again use Johnson & Johnson. Forecasted financials for J&J (forecast horizon of 2006–2009 and terminal period of 2010) are in Exhibit 12.2. The forecasts (in bold) are for sales, NOPAT, and NOA, and are the same forecasts from the illustration of the DCF model. Recall that forecasts assume an annual 6.5% sales growth for the horizon period, a terminal period sales growth of 1%, net operating profit margin (NOPM) of 18%, and a year-end net operating asset turnover (NOAT) of 1.25.

| **EXHIBIT 12.2**    Application of Residual Operating Income Model | | | | | | |
|---|---|---|---|---|---|---|
| **(In millions, except per share values and discount factors)** | **2005** | **Horizon Period** | | | | **Terminal Period** |
| | | **2006** | **2007** | **2008** | **2009** | |
| Sales........................ | $ 50,514 | **$53,797** | **$57,294** | **$61,018** | **$64,985** | **$65,634** |
| NOPAT*....................... | 10,134 | **9,683** | **10,313** | **10,983** | **11,697** | **11,814** |
| NOA**........................ | 40,453 | **43,038** | **45,835** | **48,814** | **51,988** | **52,507** |
| ROPI (NOPAT − [NOA$_{Beg}$ × $r_w$]) ...... | | 7,256 | 7,731 | 8,233 | 8,768 | 8,695 |
| Discount factor [1/(1 + $r_w$)$^t$] ........ | | 0.94340 | 0.89000 | 0.83962 | 0.79209 | |
| Present value of horizon ROPI....... | | 6,845 | 6,881 | 6,913 | 6,945 | |
| Cum present value of horizon ROPI... | 27,584 | | | | | |
| Present value of terminal ROPI ...... | 137,744 | | | | | |
| NOA ........................ | 40,453 | | | | | |
| Total firm value.................. | 205,781 | | | | | |
| Less NNO..................... | 2,582 | | | | | |
| Firm equity value ............... | $203,199 | | | | | |
| Shares outstanding ............. | 2,975 | | | | | |
| Stock value per share............ | $ 68.30 | | | | | |

*Given its combined federal and state statutory tax rate of 36%, NOPAT for 2005 is computed as follows ($ mil.): $50,514 − $13,954 − $16,877 − $6,312 − $362 + $214 − ($3,245 − 0.36 × [$487 − $54]) = $10,134, which is 20% of sales ($10,134 million/$50,514 million). Footnotes to J&J's 10-K reveal that its effective tax rate for 2005 is 23.8%, compared with 33.7% in 2004 and 30.2% in 2003. Analysis reveals that its 2005 effective tax rate is lower due to foreign tax credits and a reversal of a tax liability tied to a technical correction with the American Jobs Creation Act of 2004. The credits and reversal are *transitory* and should not be included in our projections. Accordingly, we *project* its tax rate to be 32%, the average of its 2004 and 2003 rates. If we apply 32% to its $13,656 million pretax GAAP income for 2005 we get an adjusted NOPAT of $9,009 million, computed as ($ mil.): $50,514 − $13,954 − $16,877 − $6,312 − $362 + 214 − ([$13,656 × 32%] − [0.36 × {$487 − $54}]). This adjusted NOPAT yields a NOPM of 18% ($9,009 million/$50,514 million) and is the rate we use in forecasts of NOPAT. A note on rounding: Sales are forecasted using current period sales multiplied successively by (1 + Growth rate), without rounding; next, NOPAT and NOA are computed from each period's sales forecast rounded to the whole unit.

**NOA computations for 2005 follow ($ mil.): ($58,025 − $83 − $20) − ($4,315 − $3,529 − $2,017 − $1,166 − $940 − $211 − $3,065 − $2,226) = $40,453.

†NNO is the difference between NOA and total shareholders' equity, which is NNO ($ mil.) = $40,453 − $37,871 = $2,582.

The bottom line of Exhibit 12.2 is the estimated J&J equity value of $203,199 million, or a per share stock value of $68.30. As before, present value computations use a 6% WACC as the discount rate. Specifically, we obtain this stock valuation as follows:

1. **Compute present value of horizon period ROPI.** The forecasted 2006 ROPI of $7,256 million is computed from the forecasted 2006 NOPAT ($9,683) less the product of beginning period NOA ($40,453) and WACC (0.06). The present value of this ROPI as of 2005 is $6,845 million, computed as $7,256 million × 0.94340 (the present value 1 year hence discounted at 6%). Similarly, the present value of 2007 ROPI (2 years hence) is $6,881 million, computed as $7,731 million × 0.89000, and so on through 2009. The sum of these present values (cumulative present value) is $27,584 million.

2. **Compute present value of terminal period ROPI.** The present value of the terminal period ROPI is $137,744 million, computed as $\dfrac{\left(\dfrac{\$8{,}695 \text{ million}}{0.06 - 0.01}\right)}{(1.06)^4}$, or ($8,695/0.05) × 0.79209.

3. **Compute firm equity value.** We must sum the present values from the horizon period ($27,584 million) and terminal period ($137,744 million), plus NOA ($40,453 million), to get firm (enterprise) value of $205,781 million. We then subtract the value of its net nonoperating obligations of $2,582 million to get firm equity value of $203,199 (the small difference from the DCF value is due to rounding). Dividing firm equity value by the 2,975 million shares outstanding yields the estimated per share valuation of $68.30.

J&J's stock closed at $60.25 at year-end 2005. The ROPI model estimate of $68.30 indicates that its stock is undervalued. In December 2006 (roughly one year later) J&J stock traded at near $67.

The ROPI model estimate is equal to that computed using the DCF model. This is the case so long as the firm is in a steady state, that is, NOPAT and NOA are growing at the same rate (for example, when RNOA is constant).

---

**RESEARCH INSIGHT**    **Power of NOPAT Forecasts**

Discounted cash flow (DCF) and residual operating income (ROPI) models yield identical estimates when the expected payoffs are forecasted for an infinite horizon. For practical reasons, we must use horizon period forecasts and a terminal period forecast. This truncation of the forecast horizon is a main cause of any difference in value estimates for these models. Importantly, if we can forecast (GAAP-based) NOPAT and NOA more accurately than forecasts of cash inflows and outflows, we will obtain more accurate estimates of firm value given a finite horizon.

---

# MANAGERIAL INSIGHTS FROM THE ROPI MODEL

The ROPI model defines firm value as the sum of NOA and the present value of expected residual operating income as follows:

$$\text{Firm Value} = \text{NOA} + \text{Present Value of } \underbrace{[\text{NOPAT} - (\text{NOA}_{\text{Beg}} \times r_w)]}_{\textbf{ROPI}}$$

**LO3** Explain how equity valuation models can aid managerial decisions.

Increasing ROPI, therefore, increases firm value. Managers can increase ROPI in two ways:

1. Decrease the NOA required to generate a given level of NOPAT (improve efficiency)
2. Increase NOPAT with the same level of NOA investment (improve profitability)

These are two very important observations. It means that achieving better performance requires effective management of *both* the balance sheet and the income statement. Most operating managers are accustomed to working with income statements. Further, they are often evaluated on profitability measures, such as achieving desired levels of sales and gross profit or efficiently managing operating expenses. The ROPI model focuses management attention on the balance sheet as well.

The two points above highlight two paths to increase ROPI and, accordingly, firm value. First, let's consider how management can reduce the level of NOA while maintaining a given level of NOPAT. Many managers begin by implementing procedures that reduce net operating working capital, such as:

■ Reducing receivables through:
  ● Better assessment of customers' credit quality
  ● Better controls to identify delinquencies and automated payment notices
  ● More accurate and timely invoicing
■ Reducing inventories through:
  ● Use of less costly components (of equal quality) and production with lower wage rates
  ● Elimination of product features not valued by customers
  ● Outsourcing to reduce product cost
  ● Just-in-time deliveries of raw materials
  ● Elimination of manufacturing bottlenecks to reduce work-in-process inventories
  ● Producing to order rather than to estimated demand

▩ Increasing payables through:

● Extending the payment of low or no-cost payables (so long as the supplier relationship is unharmed)

Management would next look at its operating long-term assets for opportunities to reduce unnecessary operating assets, such as the:

▩ Sale of unnecessary long-term assets

▩ Acquisition of production and administrative assets in partnership with other entities for greater throughput

▩ Acquisition of finished or semifinished goods from suppliers to reduce manufacturing assets

The second path to increase ROPI and, accordingly, firm value is to increase NOPAT with the same level of NOA investment. Management would look to strategies that maximize NOPAT, such as:

▩ Increasing gross profit dollars through:

● Better pricing and mix of products sold

● Reduction of raw material and labor cost without sacrificing product quality, perhaps by outsourcing, better design, or better manufacturing

● Increase of throughput to minimize overhead costs per unit (provided inventory does not build up)

▩ Reducing selling, general, and administrative expenses through:

● Better management of personnel

● Reduction of overhead

● Use of derivatives to hedge commodity and interest costs

● Minimization of tax expense

Before undertaking any of these actions, managers must consider both short- and long-run implications for the company. The ROPI model helps managers assess company performance (income statement) relative to the net operating assets committed (balance sheet).

| MANAGERIAL DECISION | **You Are the Operations Manager** |
|---|---|

The residual operating income (ROPI) model highlights the importance of increasing NOPAT and reducing net operating assets, which are the two major components of the return on net operating assets (RNOA). What specific steps can you take to improve RNOA through improvement of its components: net operating profit margin and net operating asset turnover? [Answer, p. 12-16]

# ASSESSMENT OF VALUATION MODELS

Exhibit 12.3 provides a brief summary of the advantages and disadvantages of the DCF and ROPI models. Neither model dominates the other, and both are theoretically equivalent. Instead, professionals must choose the model that performs best under practical circumstances.

There are numerous other equity valuation models in practice. Many require forecasting, but several others do not. A quick review of selected models follows:

The **method of comparables** (often called *multiples*) **model** predicts equity valuation or stock value using price multiples. Price multiples are defined as stock price divided by some key financial statement number. That financial number varies across investors but is usually one of the following: net income, net sales, book value of equity, total assets, or cash flow. The method then compares companies' multiples to those of their competitors to assign value.

The **net asset valuation model** draws on the financial reporting system to assign value. That is, equity is valued as reported assets less reported liabilities. Some investors adjust reported assets and liabilities for several perceived shortcomings in GAAP prior to computing net asset value. This method is commonly applied when valuing privately held companies.

The **dividend discount model** predicts that equity valuation or stock values equal the present value of expected cash dividends. This model is founded on the dividend discount formula and depends on the reliability of forecasted cash dividends.

| EXHIBIT 12.3 | Advantages and Disadvantages of DCF and ROPI Valuation Models | | |
|---|---|---|---|
| **Model** | **Advantages** | **Disadvantages** | **Performs Best** |
| DCF | • Popular and widely accepted model<br>• Cash flows are unaffected by accrual accounting<br>• FCFF is intuitive | • Cash investments in plant assets are treated as cash outflows, even though they create shareholder value<br>• Value not recognized unless evidenced by cash flows<br>• Computing FCFF can be difficult as operating cash flows are affected by<br>  – Cutbacks on investments (receivables, inventories, plant assets); can yield short-run benefits at long-run cost<br>  – Securitization, which GAAP treats as an operating cash flow when many view it as a financing activity | • When the firm reports positive FCFF<br>• When FCFF grows at a relatively constant rate |
| ROPI | • Focuses on value drivers such as profit margins and asset turnovers<br>• Uses both balance sheet and income statement, including accrual accounting information<br>• Reduces weight placed on terminal period value | • Financial statements do not reflect all company assets, especially for knowledge-based industries (for example, R&D assets and goodwill)<br>• Requires some knowledge of accrual accounting | • When financial statements reflect all assets and liabilities; including those items often reported off-balance-sheet |

There are additional models applied in practice that involve dividends, cash flows, research and development outlays, accounting rates of return, cash recovery rates, and real option models. Further, some practitioners, called *chartists* and *technicians,* chart price behavior over time and use it to predict equity value.

### RESEARCH INSIGHT    Using Models to Identify Mispriced Stocks

Implementation of the ROPI model can include parameters to capture differences in growth opportunities, persistence of ROPI, and the conservatism in accounting measures. Research finds differences in how such factors, across firms and over time, affect ROPI and changes in NOA. This research also hints that investors do not entirely understand the properties underlying these factors and, consequently, individual stocks can be mispriced for short periods of time. Other research contends that the apparent mispricing is due to an omitted valuation variable related to riskiness of the firm.

## MODULE-END REVIEW

Following are forecasts of Procter & Gamble's sales, net operating profit after tax (NOPAT), and net operating assets (NOA). These are taken from our forecasting process in Module 11 and now include a terminal period forecast that reflects a long-term growth rate of 2%.

| (In millions) | 2006 | Horizon Period | | | | Terminal Period |
|---|---|---|---|---|---|---|
| | | 2007 | 2008 | 2009 | 2010 | |
| Sales............ | $68,222 | $ 71,224 | $ 74,358 | $ 77,629 | $ 81,045 | $ 82,666 |
| NOPAT ........... | 9,221 | 9,615 | 10,038 | 10,480 | 10,941 | 11,160 |
| NOA ............ | 99,879 | 104,741 | 109,350 | 114,160 | 119,184 | 121,568 |

Drawing on these forecasts, compute P&G's residual operating income (ROPI) and an estimate of its stock value using the ROPI model. Assume the following: discount rate (WACC) of 5%, shares outstanding of 3,178.8 million, and net nonoperating obligations (NNO) of $35,816 million.

## Solution

Results from the ROPI model below yield a P&G stock value estimate of $70.49 as of December 31, 2005 (small difference from DCF estimate due to rounding). P&G's stock closed at a split-adjusted price of $55.60 on that date. This estimate suggests that P&G's stock is undervalued on that date. P&G stock traded at around $63 in December 2006 as shown in the stock price chart below.

| (In millions, except per share values and discount factors) | 2006 | Horizon Period | | | | Terminal Period |
| --- | --- | --- | --- | --- | --- | --- |
| | | 2007 | 2008 | 2009 | 2010 | |
| ROPI (NOPAT − [NOA$_{Beg}$ × $r_w$]) . . . . . . . | | $4,621 | $4,801 | $5,013 | $5,233 | $5,201 |
| Discount factor [1/(1 + $r_w$)$^t$] . . . . . . . . . | | 0.95238 | 0.90703 | 0.86384 | 0.82270 | |
| Present value of horizon ROPI . . . . . . . | | 4,401 | 4,355 | 4,330 | 4,305 | |
| Cum present value of horizon ROPI . . . . | $ 17,391 | | | | | |
| Present value of terminal ROPI . . . . . . . | 142,629[a] | | | | | |
| NOA . . . . . . . . . . . . . . . . . . . . . . . . . . . | 99,879 | | | | | |
| Total firm value . . . . . . . . . . . . . . . . . . . | 259,899 | | | | | |
| Less NNO . . . . . . . . . . . . . . . . . . . . . . . | 35,816 | | | | | |
| Firm equity value . . . . . . . . . . . . . . . . . | $224,083 | | | | | |
| Shares outstanding . . . . . . . . . . . . . . . | 3,178.8 | | | | | |
| Stock value per share . . . . . . . . . . . . . . | $ 70.49 | | | | | |

[a] Computed as $\dfrac{\left(\dfrac{\$5{,}201 \text{ million}}{0.05 - 0.02}\right)}{(1.05^4)}$, or ($5,201/0.03) × 0.82270.

The P&G stock price chart, extending from late 2004 through late 2006, follows.

## APPENDIX 12A: Johnson & Johnson Financial Statements

| Balance Sheet At Fiscal Year End ($ millions, except share and per share data) | 2005 | 2004 |
| --- | --- | --- |
| **Assets** | | |
| Cash and cash equivalents . . . . . . . . . . . . . . . . . . . . . . . . . . . . . . . . . | $16,055 | $ 9,203 |
| Marketable securities . . . . . . . . . . . . . . . . . . . . . . . . . . . . . . . . . . . . . | 83 | 3,681 |
| Accounts receivable trade, less allowances for doubtful accounts $164 (2004, $206) . . . . . . . . . . . . . . . . . . . . . . | 7,010 | 6,831 |
| Inventories . . . . . . . . . . . . . . . . . . . . . . . . . . . . . . . . . . . . . . . . . . . . . | 3,959 | 3,744 |
| Deferred taxes on income . . . . . . . . . . . . . . . . . . . . . . . . . . . . . . . . . | 1,845 | 1,737 |
| Prepaid expenses and other receivables . . . . . . . . . . . . . . . . . . . . . . | 2,442 | 2,124 |
| Total current assets . . . . . . . . . . . . . . . . . . . . . . . . . . . . . . . . . . . . . . | 31,394 | 27,320 |

continued

| Balance Sheet At Fiscal Year End ($ millions, except share and per share data) | 2005 | 2004 |
|---|---|---|
| Market securities, noncurrent. | $ 20 | $ 46 |
| Property, plant and equipment, net | 10,830 | 10,436 |
| Intangible assets, net | 6,185 | 5,979 |
| Goodwill, net | 5,990 | 5,863 |
| Deferred taxes on income | 385 | 551 |
| Other assets | 3,221 | 3,122 |
| Total assets. | $58,025 | $53,317 |
| **Liabilities and Shareholders' Equity** | | |
| Loans and notes payable | $ 668 | $ 280 |
| Accounts payable. | 4,315 | 5,227 |
| Accrued liabilities | 3,529 | 3,523 |
| Accrued rebates, returns and promotions | 2,017 | 2,297 |
| Accrued salaries, wages and commissions | 1,166 | 1,094 |
| Accrued taxes on income. | 940 | 1,506 |
| Total current liabilities. | 12,635 | 13,927 |
| Long-term debt | 2,017 | 2,565 |
| Deferred taxes on income | 211 | 403 |
| Employee related obligations. | 3,065 | 2,631 |
| Other liabilities | 2,226 | 1,978 |
| Total liabilities. | 20,154 | 21,504 |
| Shareholders equity | | |
| Preferred stock—without par value (authorized and unissued 2,000,000 shares) | — | — |
| Common stock—par value $1.00 per share (authorized 4,320,000,000 shares; issued 3,119,842,000 shares) | 3,120 | 3,120 |
| Note receivable from employee stock ownership plan | — | (11) |
| Accumulated other comprehensive income. | (755) | (515) |
| Retained earnings | 41,471 | 35,223 |
| | 43,836 | 37,817 |
| Less: common stock held in treasury, at cost (145,364,000 shares and 148,819,000 shares). | 5,965 | 6,004 |
| Total shareholders' equity | 37,871 | 31,813 |
| Total liabilities and shareholders' equity. | $58,025 | $53,317 |

| Income Statement ($ millions, except per share figures) | 2005 | 2004 | 2003 |
|---|---|---|---|
| Sales to customers. | $50,514 | $47,348 | $41,862 |
| Cost of products sold. | 13,954 | 13,422 | 12,176 |
| Gross profit. | 36,560 | 33,926 | 29,686 |
| Selling, marketing and administrative expenses | 16,877 | 15,860 | 14,131 |
| Research expense | 6,312 | 5,203 | 4,684 |
| Purchased in-process research and development. | 362 | 18 | 918 |
| Interest income. | (487) | (195) | (177) |
| Interest expense, net of portion capitalized. | 54 | 187 | 207 |
| Other (income) expense, net | (214) | 15 | (385) |
| | 22,904 | 21,088 | 19,378 |
| Earnings before provision for taxes on income | 13,656 | 12,838 | 10,308 |
| Provision for taxes on income | 3,245 | 4,329 | 3,111 |
| Net earnings. | $10,411 | $ 8,509 | $ 7,197 |
| Basic net earnings per share | $3.50 | $2.87 | $2.42 |
| Diluted net earnings per share | $3.46 | $2.84 | $2.40 |

| Statement of Cash Flows ($ millions) | 2005 | 2004 | 2003 |
|---|---|---|---|
| **Cash flows from operating activities** | | | |
| Net earnings. . . . . . . . . . . . . . . . . . . . . . . . . . . . . . . . . . . . . . . . . | $10,411 | $ 8,509 | $ 7,197 |
| Adjustments to reconcile net earnings to cash flows: | | | |
| Depreciation and amortization of property and intangibles . . . . . . . . . . | 2,093 | 2,124 | 1,869 |
| Purchased in-process research and development. . . . . . . . . . . . . . . . | 362 | 18 | 918 |
| Deferred tax provision. . . . . . . . . . . . . . . . . . . . . . . . . . . . . . . . . . . | (46) | (498) | (720) |
| Accounts receivable allowances. . . . . . . . . . . . . . . . . . . . . . . . . . . . | (31) | 3 | 6 |
| Changes in assets and liabilities, net of effects from acquisitions: | | | |
| Increase in accounts receivable . . . . . . . . . . . . . . . . . . . . . . . . . . . . | (568) | (111) | (691) |
| (Increase) decrease in inventories. . . . . . . . . . . . . . . . . . . . . . . . . . | (396) | 11 | 39 |
| (Decrease) increase in accounts payable and accrued liabilities . . . . . . | (911) | 607 | 2,192 |
| Decrease (increase) in other current and non-current assets. . . . . . . . | 620 | (395) | (746) |
| Increase in other current and non-current liabilities . . . . . . . . . . . . . . | 343 | 863 | 531 |
| Net cash flows from operating activities . . . . . . . . . . . . . . . . . . . . . . . | 11,877 | 11,131 | 10,595 |
| **Cash flows from investing activities** | | | |
| Addition to property, plant and equipment. . . . . . . . . . . . . . . . . . . . . . . | (2,632) | (2,175) | (2,262) |
| Proceeds from the disposal of assets . . . . . . . . . . . . . . . . . . . . . . . . . | 154 | 237 | 335 |
| Acquisitions, net of cash acquired. . . . . . . . . . . . . . . . . . . . . . . . . . . . | (987) | (580) | (2,812) |
| Purchases of investments . . . . . . . . . . . . . . . . . . . . . . . . . . . . . . . . . | (5,660) | (11,617) | (7,590) |
| Sales of investments . . . . . . . . . . . . . . . . . . . . . . . . . . . . . . . . . . . . | 9,187 | 12,061 | 8,062 |
| Other (primarily intangibles) . . . . . . . . . . . . . . . . . . . . . . . . . . . . . . . | (341) | (273) | (259) |
| Net cash used by investing activities. . . . . . . . . . . . . . . . . . . . . . . . . . | (279) | (2,347) | (4,526) |
| **Cash flows from financing activities** | | | |
| Dividends to shareholders . . . . . . . . . . . . . . . . . . . . . . . . . . . . . . . . . | (3,793) | (3,251) | (2,746) |
| Repurchase of common stock. . . . . . . . . . . . . . . . . . . . . . . . . . . . . . . | (1,717) | (1,384) | (1,183) |
| Proceeds from short-term debt . . . . . . . . . . . . . . . . . . . . . . . . . . . . . . | 1,215 | 514 | 3,062 |
| Retirement of short-term debt . . . . . . . . . . . . . . . . . . . . . . . . . . . . . . . | (732) | (1,291) | (4,134) |
| Proceeds from long-term debt. . . . . . . . . . . . . . . . . . . . . . . . . . . . . . . | 6 | 17 | 1,023 |
| Retirement of long-term debt. . . . . . . . . . . . . . . . . . . . . . . . . . . . . . . . | (196) | (395) | (196) |
| Proceeds from the exercise of stock options. . . . . . . . . . . . . . . . . . . . . | 696 | 642 | 311 |
| Net cash used by financing activities. . . . . . . . . . . . . . . . . . . . . . . . . . | (4,521) | (5,148) | (3,863) |
| Effect of exchange rate changes on cash and cash equivalents. . . . . . . . | (225) | 190 | 277 |
| Increase in cash and cash equivalents. . . . . . . . . . . . . . . . . . . . . . . . . | 6,852 | 3,826 | 2,483 |
| Cash and cash equivalents, beginning of year . . . . . . . . . . . . . . . . . . . | 9,203 | 5,377 | 2,894 |
| Cash and cash equivalents, end of year . . . . . . . . . . . . . . . . . . . . . . . . | $16,055 | $ 9,203 | $ 5,377 |

# GUIDANCE ANSWERS

**MANAGERIAL DECISION** **You Are the Division Manager**

Cash flow can be increased by reducing assets. For example, receivables can be reduced by the following:

- Encouraging up-front payments or progress billings on long-term contracts
- Increasing credit standards to avoid slow-paying accounts before sales are made
- Monitoring account age and sending reminders to past due customers
- Selling accounts receivable to a financial institution or special purpose entity

As another example, plant assets can be reduced by the following:

- Selling unused or excess plant assets
- Forming alliances with other companies to share specialized plant assets
- Owning assets in a special purpose entity with other companies
- Selling production facilities to a contract manufacturer and purchasing the output

| MANAGERIAL DECISION | You Are the Operations Manager |
|---|---|

RNOA can be disaggregated into its two key drivers: NOPAT margin and net operating asset turnover. NOPAT margin can be increased by improving gross profit margins (better product pricing, lower cost manufacturing, etc.) and closely monitoring and controlling operating expenses. Net operating asset turnover can be increased by reducing net operating working capital (better monitoring of receivables, better management of inventories, extending payables, etc.) and making more effective use of plant assets (disposing of unused assets, forming corporate alliances to increase plant asset capacity, selling productive assets to contract producers and purchasing the output, etc). The ROPI model effectively focuses managers on the balance sheet *and* income statement.

# DISCUSSION QUESTIONS

**Q12-1.** Explain how information contained in financial statements is useful in pricing securities. Are there some components of earnings that are more useful than others in this regard? What nonfinancial information might also be useful?

**Q12-2.** In general, what role do expectations play in pricing equity securities? What is the relation between security prices and expected returns (the discount rate, or WACC, in this case)?

**Q12-3.** What are free cash flows to the firm (FCFF) and how are they used in the pricing of equity securities?

**Q12-4.** Define the weighted average cost of capital (WACC).

**Q12-5.** Define net operating profit after tax (NOPAT).

**Q12-6.** Define net operating assets (NOA).

**Q12-7.** Define the concept of residual operating income. How is residual operating income used in pricing equity securities?

**Q12-8.** What insight does disaggregation of RNOA into profit margin and asset turnover provide for managing a company?

# MINI EXERCISES

**M12-9.** **Interpreting Earnings Announcement Effects on Stock Prices** **(LO2)**

Starbucks (SBUX)

In a recent quarterly earnings announcement, Starbucks announced that its earnings had markedly increased (up 7 cents per share over the prior year) and were 1 cent higher than analyst expectations. Starbucks' stock "edged higher," according to *The Wall Street Journal*, but did not markedly increase. Why do you believe that Starbucks' stock price did not markedly increase given the good news?

**M12-10.** **Computing Residual Operating Income (ROPI)** **(LO2)**

3M Company (MMM)

3M Company reports net operating profit after tax (NOPAT) of $3,305 million in 2005. Its net operating assets at the beginning of 2005 are $12,972 million. Assuming a 6.66% weighted average cost of capital (WACC), what is 3M's residual operating income for 2005? Show computations.

**M12-11.** **Computing Free Cash Flows to the Firm (FCFF)** **(LO1)**

3M Company (MMM)

3M Company reports net operating profit after tax (NOPAT) of $3,305 million in 2005. Its net operating assets at the beginning of 2005 are $12,972 million and are $12,209 million at the end of 2005. What are 3M's free cash flows to the firm (FCFF) for 2005? Show computations.

**M12-12.** **Computing, Analyzing and Interpreting Residual Operating Income (ROPI)** **(LO2)**

PepsiCo (PEP)

In its 2005 fiscal year annual report, PepsiCo reports 2005 net operating income after tax (NOPAT) of $4,140 million. As of the beginning of fiscal year 2005 it reports net operating assets of $18,908 million.

   *a.* Did PepsiCo earn positive residual operating income (ROPI) in 2005 if its weighted average cost of capital (WACC) is 5.78%? Explain.

   *b.* At what level of WACC would PepsiCo not report positive residual operating income for 2005? Explain.

# EXERCISES

**E12-13.** **Estimating Share Value using the DCF and ROPI Models** **(LO1, 2)**

Target Corporation (TGT)

Following are forecasts of Target Corporation's sales, net operating profit after tax (NOPAT), and net operating assets (NOA) as of January 31, 2006.

| (In millions) | Reported 2006 | Horizon Period | | | | Terminal Period |
|---|---|---|---|---|---|---|
| | | 2007 | 2008 | 2009 | 2010 | |
| Sales............. | $51,271 | $57,526 | $64,544 | $72,418 | $81,253 | $82,878 |
| NOPAT .......... | 2,694 | 2,876 | 3,227 | 3,621 | 4,063 | 4,144 |
| NOA ............. | 24,077 | 27,008 | 30,302 | 33,999 | 38,147 | 38,910 |

Answer the following requirements assuming a terminal period growth rate of 2%, discount rate (WACC) of 7%, shares outstanding of 874.1 million, and net nonoperating obligations (NNO) of $9,872 million.

a.  Estimate the value of a share of Target common stock using the (1) discounted cash flow (DCF) model and (2) residual operating income (ROPI) model as of January 31, 2006.

b.  Target Corporation (TGT) stock closed at $54.75 on January 31, 2006. How does your valuation estimate compare with this closing price? What do you believe are some reasons for the difference?

**E12-14. Estimating Share Value using the DCF and ROPI Models  (LO1, 2)**

Abercrombie & Fitch (ANF)

Following are forecasts of Abercrombie & Fitch's sales, net operating profit after tax (NOPAT), and net operating assets (NOA) as of January 31, 2006.

| (In millions) | Reported 2006 | Horizon Period | | | | Terminal Period |
|---|---|---|---|---|---|---|
| | | 2007 | 2008 | 2009 | 2010 | |
| Sales............. | $2,785 | $3,838 | $5,289 | $7,288 | $10,043 | $10,244 |
| NOPAT .......... | 325 | 448 | 617 | 850 | 1,172 | 1,195 |
| NOA ............. | 616 | 849 | 1,170 | 1,612 | 2,221 | 2,266 |

Answer the following requirements assuming a discount rate (WACC) of 13%, common shares outstanding of 103.3 million, and net nonoperating obligations (NNO) of $(379) million (negative NNO reflects net investments rather than net obligations).

a.  Estimate the value of a share of Abercrombie & Fitch common stock using the (1) discounted cash flow (DCF) model and (2) residual operating income (ROPI) model as of January 31, 2006.

b.  Abercrombie & Fitch (ANF) stock closed at $66.39 on January 31, 2006. How does your valuation estimate compare with this closing price? What do you believe are some reasons for the difference?

**E12-15. Estimating Share Value using the DCF and ROPI Models  (LO1, 2)**

CVS Corp. (CVS)

Following are forecasts of sales, net operating profit after tax (NOPAT), and net operating assets (NOA) as of December 31, 2005 for CVS Pharmacy.

| (In millions) | Reported 2005 | Horizon Period | | | | Terminal Period |
|---|---|---|---|---|---|---|
| | | 2006 | 2007 | 2008 | 2009 | |
| Sales............. | $37,006 | $44,777 | $54,180 | $65,558 | $79,325 | $80,912 |
| NOPAT .......... | 1,292 | 1,563 | 1,891 | 2,288 | 2,768 | 2,824 |
| NOA ............. | 10,520 | 12,721 | 15,392 | 18,624 | 22,536 | 22,986 |

Answer the following requirements assuming a discount rate (WACC) of 8%, common shares outstanding of 814.3 million, and net nonoperating obligations (NNO) of $2,189 million.

a.  Estimate the value of a share of CVS' common stock using the (1) discounted cash flow (DCF) model and (2) residual operating income (ROPI) model as of December 31, 2005.

b.  CVS Corp. (CVS) stock closed at $26.58 on December 29, 2005. How does your valuation estimate compare with this closing price? What do you believe are some reasons for the difference?

**E12-16.  Identifying and Computing Net Operating Assets (NOA) and Net Nonoperating Obligations (NNO)**  (LO1, 2)

Following is the balance sheet for 3M Company.

3M Company (MMM)

| Balance Sheet<br>At December 31 ($ millions, except per share amount) | 2005 | 2004 |
|---|---|---|
| **Assets** | | |
| Cash and cash equivalents | $ 1,072 | $ 2,757 |
| Accounts receivable—net of allowances of $73 and $83 | 2,838 | 2,792 |
| Inventories | | |
| Finished goods | 1,050 | 947 |
| Work in process | 706 | 614 |
| Raw materials and supplies | 406 | 336 |
| Total inventories | 2,162 | 1,897 |
| Other current assets | 1,043 | 1,274 |
| Total current assets | 7,115 | 8,720 |
| Investments | 272 | 227 |
| Property, plant and equipment | 16,127 | 16,290 |
| Less: Accumulated depreciation | (10,534) | (10,579) |
| Property, plant and equipment—net | 5,593 | 5,711 |
| Goodwill | 3,473 | 2,655 |
| Intangible assets—net | 486 | 277 |
| Prepaid pension and postretirement benefits | 2,905 | 2,591 |
| Other assets | 669 | 527 |
| Total assets | $20,513 | $20,708 |
| **Liabilities and Stockholders' Equity** | | |
| Short-term borrowings and current portion of long-term debt | $ 1,072 | $ 2,094 |
| Accounts payable | 1,256 | 1,168 |
| Accrued payroll | 469 | 487 |
| Accrued income taxes | 989 | 867 |
| Other current liabilities | 1,452 | 1,455 |
| Total current liabilities | 5,238 | 6,071 |
| Long-term debt | 1,309 | 727 |
| Other liabilities | 3,866 | 3,532 |
| Total liabilities | 10,413 | 10,330 |
| Stockholders' equity | | |
| Common stock, par value $.01 per share:<br>  Shares outstanding—2005: 754,538,387;<br>  Shares outstanding—2004: 773,518,281 | 9 | 9 |
| Capital in excess of par value | 287 | 287 |
| Retained earnings | 17,358 | 15,649 |
| Treasury stock | (6,965) | (5,503) |
| Unearned compensation | (178) | (196) |
| Accumulated other comprehensive income (loss) | (411) | 132 |
| Stockholders' equity—net | 10,100 | 10,378 |
| Total liabilities and stockholders' equity | $20,513 | $20,708 |

*a.*  Compute net operating assets (NOA) and net nonoperating obligations (NNO) for 2005.

*b.*  For 2005, show that: NOA = NNO + Stockholders' equity.

**E12-17. Identifying and Computing Net Operating Profit after Tax (NOPAT) and Net Nonoperating Expense (NNE) (LO1, 2)**

3M Company (MMM)

Following is the income statement for 3M Company.

| Income Statement Year Ended December 31 (millions) | 2005 | 2004 | 2003 |
|---|---|---|---|
| Net sales. | $21,167 | $20,011 | $18,232 |
| Operating expenses | | | |
| Cost of sales. | 10,381 | 9,958 | 9,285 |
| Selling, general and administrative expenses | 4,535 | 4,281 | 3,994 |
| Research, development and related expenses | 1,242 | 1,194 | 1,147 |
| Other expense | — | — | 93 |
| Total | 16,158 | 15,433 | 14,519 |
| Operating income. | 5,009 | 4,578 | 3,713 |
| Interest expense and income | | | |
| Interest expense | 82 | 69 | 84 |
| Interest income | (56) | (46) | (28) |
| Total | 26 | 23 | 56 |
| Income before income taxes, minority interest and cumulative effect of accounting change | 4,983 | 4,555 | 3,657 |
| Provision for income taxes. | 1,694 | 1,503 | 1,202 |
| Minority interest | 55 | 62 | 52 |
| Income before cumulative effect of accounting change | 3,234 | 2,990 | 2,403 |
| Cumulative effect of accounting change | (35) | — | — |
| Net income. | $ 3,199 | $ 2,990 | $ 2,403 |

Compute net operating profit after tax (NOPAT) for 2005, assuming a federal and state statutory tax rate of 36.3%. (*Hint:* Other expense is an operating item for 3M.)

**E12-18. Estimating Share Value Using the DCF and ROPI Models (LO1, 2)**

3M Company (MMM)

Following are forecasts of 3M Company's sales, net operating profit after tax (NOPAT), and net operating assets (NOA) as of December 31, 2005.

| (In millions) | Reported 2005 | Horizon Period | | | | Terminal Period |
|---|---|---|---|---|---|---|
| | | 2006 | 2007 | 2008 | 2009 | |
| Sales. | $21,167 | $22,395 | $23,694 | $25,068 | $26,522 | $26,787 |
| NOPAT | 3,306 | 3,498 | 3,701 | 3,916 | 4,143 | 4,184 |
| NOA | 12,209 | 12,945 | 13,696 | 14,490 | 15,331 | 15,484 |

Answer the following requirements assuming a discount rate (WACC) of 7%, common shares outstanding of 754.5 million, and net nonoperating obligations (NNO) of $2,109 million.

a. Estimate the value of a share of 3M's common stock using the (1) discounted cash flow (DCF) model and (2) residual operating income (ROPI) model as of December 31, 2005.

b. 3M (MMM) stock closed at $78.29 on December 31, 2005. How does your valuation estimate compare with this closing price? What do you believe are some reasons for the difference?

**E12-19. Explaining the Equivalence of Valuation Models and the Relevance of Earnings (LO1, 2)**

This module focused on two different valuation models: the discounted cash flow (DCF) model and the residual operating income (ROPI) model. The models focus on free cash flows to the firm and on residual operating income, respectively. We stressed that these two models are theoretically equivalent.

a. What is the *intuition* for why these models are equivalent?

b. Some analysts focus on cash flows as they believe that companies manage earnings, which presumably makes earnings less relevant. Are earnings relevant? Explain.

**E12-20.** **Applying and Interpreting Value Driver Components of RNOA** **(LO3)**

The net operating profit margin and the asset turnover components of net operating assets are often termed *value drivers,* which refers to their positive influence on stock value by virtue of their role as components of return on net operating assets (RNOA).

*a.* How do profit margins and asset turnover ratios influence stock values?

*b.* Assuming that profit margins and asset turnover ratios are value drivers, what insight does this give us about managing companies if the goal is to create shareholder value?

# PROBLEMS

**P12-21.** **Forecasting and Estimating Share Value Using the DCF and ROPI Models** **(LO1, 2)**

Following are the income statement and balance sheet for Intel Corporation.

Intel Corporation
(INTC)

| Income Statement<br>Year Ended December 31 (In millions) | 2005 | 2004 | 2003 |
|---|---|---|---|
| Net revenue | $38,826 | $34,209 | $30,141 |
| Cost of sales | 15,777 | 14,463 | 13,047 |
| Gross margin | 23,049 | 19,746 | 17,094 |
| Research and development | 5,145 | 4,778 | 4,360 |
| Marketing, general and administrative | 5,688 | 4,659 | 4,278 |
| Impairment of goodwill | — | — | 617 |
| Amortization and impairment of acquisition-<br>related intangibles and costs | 126 | 179 | 301 |
| Purchased in-process research and development | — | — | 5 |
| Operating expenses | 10,959 | 9,616 | 9,561 |
| Operating income | 12,090 | 10,130 | 7,533 |
| Losses on equity securities, net | (45) | (2) | (283) |
| Interest and other, net | 565 | 289 | 192 |
| Income before taxes | 12,610 | 10,417 | 7,442 |
| Provision for taxes | 3,946 | 2,901 | 1,801 |
| Net income | $ 8,664 | $ 7,516 | $ 5,641 |

| Balance Sheet<br>December 31 (In millions, except par value) | 2005 | 2004 |
|---|---|---|
| **Assets** | | |
| Cash and cash equivalents | $ 7,324 | $ 8,407 |
| Short-term investments | 3,990 | 5,654 |
| Trading assets | 1,458 | 3,111 |
| Accounts receivable, net of allowance for doubtful<br>accounts of $64 ($43 in 2004) | 3,914 | 2,999 |
| Inventories | 3,126 | 2,621 |
| Deferred tax assets | 1,149 | 979 |
| Other current assets | 233 | 287 |
| Total current assets | 21,194 | 24,058 |

*continued*

| Balance Sheet<br>December 31 (In millions, except par value) | 2005 | 2004 |
|---|---|---|
| Property, plant and equipment, net . . . . . . . . . . . . . . . . . . . . . . . . . . . | 17,111 | 15,768 |
| Marketable strategic equity securities . . . . . . . . . . . . . . . . . . . . . . . | 537 | 656 |
| Other long-term investments . . . . . . . . . . . . . . . . . . . . . . . . . . . . . . . | 4,135 | 2,563 |
| Goodwill . . . . . . . . . . . . . . . . . . . . . . . . . . . . . . . . . . . . . . . . . . . . . . | 3,873 | 3,719 |
| Deferred taxes and other assets . . . . . . . . . . . . . . . . . . . . . . . . . . . . | 1,464 | 1,379 |
| Total assets. . . . . . . . . . . . . . . . . . . . . . . . . . . . . . . . . . . . . . . . . . . | $48,314 | $48,143 |
| **Liabilities and stockholders' equity** | | |
| Short-term debt . . . . . . . . . . . . . . . . . . . . . . . . . . . . . . . . . . . . . . . . | $     313 | $     201 |
| Accounts payable. . . . . . . . . . . . . . . . . . . . . . . . . . . . . . . . . . . . . . . | 2,249 | 1,943 |
| Accrued compensation and benefits . . . . . . . . . . . . . . . . . . . . . . . . . | 2,110 | 1,858 |
| Accrued advertising . . . . . . . . . . . . . . . . . . . . . . . . . . . . . . . . . . . . . | 1,160 | 894 |
| Deferred income on shipments to distributors. . . . . . . . . . . . . . . . . | 632 | 592 |
| Other accrued liabilities . . . . . . . . . . . . . . . . . . . . . . . . . . . . . . . . . . | 810 | 1,355 |
| Income taxes payable . . . . . . . . . . . . . . . . . . . . . . . . . . . . . . . . . . . | 1,960 | 1,163 |
| Total current liabilities. . . . . . . . . . . . . . . . . . . . . . . . . . . . . . . . . . . | 9,234 | 8,006 |
| Long-term debt . . . . . . . . . . . . . . . . . . . . . . . . . . . . . . . . . . . . . . . . | 2,106 | 703 |
| Deferred tax liabilities. . . . . . . . . . . . . . . . . . . . . . . . . . . . . . . . . . . . | 703 | 855 |
| Other long-term liabilities . . . . . . . . . . . . . . . . . . . . . . . . . . . . . . . . | 89 | — |
| Stockholders' equity | | |
| Preferred stock, $0.001 par value, 50 shares authorized;<br>    none issued . . . . . . . . . . . . . . . . . . . . . . . . . . . . . . . . . . . . . . . . | — | — |
| Common stock, $0.001 par value, 10,000 shares authorized;<br>    5,919 issued and outstanding (6,253 in 2004) and capital<br>    in excess of par value. . . . . . . . . . . . . . . . . . . . . . . . . . . . . . . . | 6,245 | 6,143 |
| Acquisition-related unearned stock compensation . . . . . . . . . . . . . . | — | (4) |
| Accumulated other comprehensive income. . . . . . . . . . . . . . . . . . . | 127 | 152 |
| Retained earnings . . . . . . . . . . . . . . . . . . . . . . . . . . . . . . . . . . . . . | 29,810 | 32,288 |
| Total stockholders' equity . . . . . . . . . . . . . . . . . . . . . . . . . . . . . . . | 36,182 | 38,579 |
| Total liabilities and stockholders' equity. . . . . . . . . . . . . . . . . . . . . | $48,314 | $48,143 |

**Required**

*a.* Compute Intel's net operating assets (NOA) for year end 2005.

*b.* Compute net operating profit after tax (NOPAT) for 2005, assuming a federal and state statutory tax rate of 36.3%.

*c.* Forecast Intel's sales, NOPAT, and NOA for years 2006 through 2009 using the following assumptions:

| | |
|---|---|
| Sales growth. . . . . . . . . . . . . . . . . . . . . . . . . . . . . . . . . . . . . . | 13.5% |
| Net operating profit margin (NOPM). . . . . . . . . . . . . . . . . . . | 21.46% |
| Net operating asset turnover (NOAT) at year end . . . . . . . . | 1.34 |

Forecast the terminal period (2010) values assuming a 2% terminal year growth and using the NOPM and NOAT assumptions above.

*d.* Estimate the value of a share of Intel common stock using the (1) discounted cash flow (DCF) model, and (2) residual operating income (ROPI) model as of December 31, 2005; assume a discount rate (WACC) of 12%, common shares outstanding of 5,919 million, and net nonoperating obligations (NNO) of $(7,164) million (NNO is negative which means that Intel has net nonoperating investments).

*e.* Intel (INTC) stock closed at $25.07 on December 29, 2005. How does your valuation estimate compare with this closing price? What do you believe are some reasons for the difference? What investment position is suggested from your results?

**P12-22.** **Forecasting and Estimating Share Value Using the DCF and ROPI Models**  (LO1, 2)

Following are the income statement and balance sheet for Oracle Corporation.

Oracle Corporation
(ORCL)

| Balance Sheet<br>May 31 (in millions, except per share data) | 2006 | 2005 |
|---|---|---|
| **Assets** | | |
| Cash and cash equivalents | $ 6,659 | $ 3,894 |
| Marketable securities | 946 | 877 |
| Trade receivables, net of allowances of $325 and $269 | 3,022 | 2,570 |
| Other receivables | 398 | 330 |
| Deferred tax assets | 714 | 486 |
| Prepaid expenses and other current assets | 235 | 291 |
| Total current assets | 11,974 | 8,448 |
| Property, net | 1,391 | 1,442 |
| Intangible assets, net | 4,528 | 3,373 |
| Goodwill | 9,809 | 7,003 |
| Other assets | 1,327 | 421 |
| Total non-current assets | 17,055 | 12,239 |
| Total assets | $29,029 | $20,687 |
| **Liabilities and stockholders' equity** | | |
| Short-term borrowings and current portion of long-term debt | $ 159 | $ 2,693 |
| Accounts payable | 268 | 230 |
| Income taxes payable | 810 | 904 |
| Accrued compensation and related benefits | 1,172 | 923 |
| Accrued restructuring | 412 | 156 |
| Deferred revenues | 2,830 | 2,289 |
| Other current liabilities | 1,279 | 868 |
| Total current liabilities | 6,930 | 8,063 |
| Notes payable and long-term debt, net of current portion | 5,735 | 159 |
| Deferred tax liabilities | 564 | 1,010 |
| Accrued restructuring | 273 | 120 |
| Deferred revenues | 114 | 126 |
| Other long-term liabilities | 401 | 372 |
| Total non-current liabilities | 7,087 | 1,787 |
| Stockholders' equity | | |
| Preferred stock, $0.01 par value-authorized: 1.0 shares; outstanding: none | — | — |
| Common stock, $0.01 par value and additional paid in capital-authorized: 11,000 shares; outstanding: 5,232 shares at May 31, 2006 and 5,145 shares at May 31, 2005 | 9,246 | 6,596 |
| Retained earnings | 5,538 | 4,043 |
| Deferred compensation | (30) | (45) |
| Accumulated other comprehensive income | 258 | 243 |
| Total stockholders' equity | 15,012 | 10,837 |
| Total liabilities and stockholders' equity | $29,029 | $20,687 |

| Income Statement<br>Year Ended May 31 (in millions) | 2006 | 2005 | 2004 |
|---|---|---|---|
| Revenues | | | |
| New software licenses . . . . . . . . . . . . . . . . . . . . . . . . . . . . | $ 4,905 | $ 4,091 | $ 3,541 |
| Software license updates and product support. . . . . . . . . | 6,636 | 5,330 | 4,529 |
| Software revenues . . . . . . . . . . . . . . . . . . . . . . . . . . . . . . | 11,541 | 9,421 | 8,070 |
| Services . . . . . . . . . . . . . . . . . . . . . . . . . . . . . . . . . . . . . . | 2,839 | 2,378 | 2,086 |
| Total revenues . . . . . . . . . . . . . . . . . . . . . . . . . . . . . . | 14,380 | 11,799 | 10,156 |
| Operating expenses | | | |
| Sales and marketing. . . . . . . . . . . . . . . . . . . . . . . . . . . | 3,177 | 2,511 | 2,123 |
| Software license updates and product support . . . . . . . | 719 | 618 | 547 |
| Cost of services . . . . . . . . . . . . . . . . . . . . . . . . . . . . . | 2,516 | 2,033 | 1,770 |
| Research and development . . . . . . . . . . . . . . . . . . . . . | 1,872 | 1,491 | 1,254 |
| General and administrative. . . . . . . . . . . . . . . . . . . . . . | 555 | 550 | 508 |
| Amortization of intangible assets . . . . . . . . . . . . . . . . | 583 | 219 | 36 |
| Acquisition related . . . . . . . . . . . . . . . . . . . . . . . . . . . | 137 | 208 | 54 |
| Restructuring . . . . . . . . . . . . . . . . . . . . . . . . . . . . . . . | 85 | 147 | — |
| Total operating expenses . . . . . . . . . . . . . . . . . . . . . | 9,644 | 7,777 | 6,292 |
| Operating income. . . . . . . . . . . . . . . . . . . . . . . . . . . . . . | 4,736 | 4,022 | 3,864 |
| Interest expense. . . . . . . . . . . . . . . . . . . . . . . . . . . . . . . | (169) | (135) | (21) |
| Nonoperating income, net | | | |
| Interest income. . . . . . . . . . . . . . . . . . . . . . . . . . . . . . | 170 | 185 | 118 |
| Net investment gains . . . . . . . . . . . . . . . . . . . . . . . . . | 25 | 2 | 29 |
| Other. . . . . . . . . . . . . . . . . . . . . . . . . . . . . . . . . . . . . | 48 | (23) | (45) |
| Total nonoperating income, net . . . . . . . . . . . . . . . . . | 243 | 164 | 102 |
| Income before provision for income taxes. . . . . . . . . . . . | 4,810 | 4,051 | 3,945 |
| Provision for income taxes. . . . . . . . . . . . . . . . . . . . . . . | 1,429 | 1,165 | 1,264 |
| Net income. . . . . . . . . . . . . . . . . . . . . . . . . . . . . . . . . . . | $ 3,381 | $ 2,886 | $ 2,681 |

**Required**

a. Compute net operating assets (NOA) for fiscal year end 2006.

b. Compute net operating profit after tax (NOPAT) for fiscal year 2006, assuming a federal and state statutory tax rate of 36.4%.

c. Forecast Oracle's sales, NOPAT, and NOA for fiscal years 2007 through 2010 using the following assumptions:

| | |
|---|---|
| Sales growth. . . . . . . . . . . . . . . . . . . . . . . . . . . . . . . . . | 21.9% |
| Net operating profit margin (NOPM). . . . . . . . . . . . . . . . | 23.19% |
| Net operating asset turnover (NOAT) at fiscal year-end. . . . | 0.72 |

Forecast the terminal period (fiscal year 2011) values assuming a 2% terminal year growth and using the NOPM and NOAT assumptions above.

d. Estimate the value of a share of Oracle common stock using the (1) discounted cash flow (DCF) model and (2) residual operating income (ROPI) model as of May 31, 2006; assume a discount rate (WACC) of 8%, common shares outstanding of 5,232 million, and net nonoperating obligations (NNO) of $4,948 million.

e. Oracle Corp. (ORCL) stock closed at $14.22 on May 31, 2006. How does your valuation estimate compare with this closing price? What do you believe are some reasons for the difference?

**P12-23.** **Forecasting and Estimating Share Value Using the DCF and ROPI Models** **(LO1, 2)**

Following are the income statement and balance sheet for Abbott Laboratories (ABT).

Abbott Laboratories
(ABT)

| Income Statement<br>Year Ended December 31 ($ 000s) | 2005 | 2004 | 2003 |
|---|---|---|---|
| Net sales. | $22,337,808 | $19,680,016 | $17,280,333 |
| Cost of products sold. | 10,641,111 | 8,884,157 | 7,774,239 |
| Research and development | 1,821,175 | 1,696,753 | 1,623,752 |
| Acquired in-process research and development | 17,131 | 279,006 | 100,240 |
| Selling, general, and administrative | 5,496,123 | 4,921,780 | 4,808,090 |
| Total operating cost and expenses | 17,975,540 | 15,781,696 | 14,306,321 |
| Operating earnings. | 4,362,268 | 3,898,320 | 2,974,012 |
| Net interest expense | 153,662 | 149,087 | 146,365 |
| (Income) from TAP Pharmaceutical Products<br>      joint venture | (441,388) | (374,984) | (580,950) |
| Net foreign exchange (gain) loss | 21,804 | 29,059 | 57,048 |
| Other (income) expense, net | 8,270 | (30,442) | (35,602) |
| Earnings from continuing operations before taxes | 4,619,920 | 4,125,600 | 3,387,151 |
| Taxes on earnings from continuing operations | 1,247,855 | 949,764 | 882,426 |
| Earnings from continuing operations | 3,372,065 | 3,175,836 | 2,504,725 |
| Earnings from discontinued operations, net of taxes. | — | 60,015 | 248,508 |
| Net earnings. | $ 3,372,065 | $ 3,235,851 | $ 2,753,233 |

| Balance Sheet<br>December 31 ($ 000s) | 2005 | 2004 | 2003 |
|---|---|---|---|
| **Assets** | | | |
| Cash and cash equivalents | $ 2,893,687 | $ 1,225,628 | $   995,124 |
| Investment securities, primarily time deposits and<br>    certificates of deposit | 62,406 | 833,334 | 291,297 |
| Trade receivables, less allowances of—2005: $203,683;<br>    2004: $231,704; 2003: $259,514 | 3,576,794 | 3,696,115 | 3,313,377 |
| Inventories | | | |
| Finished products. | 1,203,557 | 1,488,939 | 1,467,441 |
| Work in process | 630,267 | 582,787 | 545,977 |
| Materials. | 708,155 | 548,737 | 725,021 |
| Total inventories | 2,541,979 | 2,620,463 | 2,738,439 |
| Deferred income taxes | 1,248,569 | 1,031,746 | 1,165,259 |
| Other prepaid expenses and receivables. | 932,691 | 1,080,143 | 1,110,885 |
| Assets held for sale | 129,902 | 247,056 | — |
| Total current assets | 11,386,028 | 10,734,485 | 9,614,381 |
| Investment securities, primarily equity securities. | 134,013 | 145,849 | 406,357 |
| Property and equipment, at cost: | | | |
| Land | 370,949 | 338,428 | 356,757 |
| Buildings. | 2,655,356 | 2,519,492 | 2,662,023 |
| Equipment | 8,813,517 | 8,681,655 | 9,479,044 |
| Construction in progress | 920,599 | 962,114 | 792,923 |
| | 12,760,421 | 12,501,689 | 13,290,747 |
| Less: accumulated depreciation and amortization | 6,757,280 | 6,493,815 | 7,008,941 |
| Net property and equipment | 6,003,141 | 6,007,874 | 6,281,806 |

*continued*

| Balance Sheet December 31 ($ 000s) | 2005 | 2004 | 2003 |
|---|---|---|---|
| Intangible assets, net of amortization | 4,741,647 | 5,171,594 | 4,089,882 |
| Goodwill | 5,219,247 | 5,685,124 | 4,449,408 |
| Other long-term assets and investments in joint ventures | 1,624,201 | 952,929 | 1,197,474 |
| Assets held for sale | 32,926 | 69,639 | — |
| Total assets | $29,141,203 | $28,767,494 | $26,039,308 |
| **Liabilities and Shareholders' Investment** | | | |
| Short-term borrowings | $  212,447 | $ 1,836,649 | $  828,092 |
| Trade accounts payable | 1,032,516 | 1,054,464 | 1,078,333 |
| Salaries, wages and commissions | 625,254 | 637,333 | 625,525 |
| Other accrued liabilities | 2,722,685 | 2,491,956 | 2,180,098 |
| Dividends payable | 423,335 | 405,730 | 383,352 |
| Income taxes payable | 488,926 | 156,417 | 158,836 |
| Current portion of long-term debt | 1,849,563 | 156,034 | 1,709,265 |
| Liabilities of operations held for sale | 60,788 | 87,061 | — |
| Total current liabilities | 7,415,514 | 6,825,644 | 6,963,501 |
| Long-term debt | 4,571,504 | 4,787,934 | 3,452,329 |
| Post-employment obligations and other long-term liabilities | 2,154,775 | 2,606,410 | 2,551,220 |
| Liabilities of operations held for sale | 1,062 | 1,644 | — |
| Deferred income taxes | 583,077 | 220,079 | — |
| Shareholders' investment | | | |
| Preferred shares, one dollar par value, Authorized—1,000,000 shares, none issued | — | — | — |
| Common shares, without par value, Authorized— 2,400,000,000 shares; Issued at stated capital amount— Shares: 2005: 1,553,769,958; 2004: 1,575,147,418; 2003: 1,580,247,227 | 3,523,766 | 3,239,575 | 3,034,054 |
| Common shares held in treasury, at cost—Shares: 2005: 14,534,979; 2004: 15,123,800; 2003: 15,729,296 | (212,255) | (220,854) | (229,696) |
| Unearned compensation—restricted stock awards | (46,306) | (50,110) | (56,336) |
| Earnings employed in the business | 10,404,568 | 10,033,440 | 9,691,484 |
| Accumulated other comprehensive income (loss) | 745,498 | 1,323,732 | 632,752 |
| Total shareholders' investment | 14,415,271 | 14,325,783 | 13,072,258 |
| Total liabilities and shareholders' investment | $29,141,203 | $28,767,494 | $26,039,308 |

**Required**

a.　Compute net operating assets (NOA) for year end 2005.

b.　Compute net operating profit after tax (NOPAT) for 2005 assuming a federal and state statutory tax rate of 36.2%.

c.　Forecast Abbott Laboratories' sales, NOPAT, and NOA for 2006 through 2009 using the following assumptions:

| | |
|---|---|
| Sales growth | 13.5% |
| Net operating profit margin (NOPM) | 15.53% |
| Net operating asset turnover (NOAT), year-end | 1.05 |

Forecast the terminal period (2010) values assuming a 2% terminal year growth and using the NOPM and NOAT assumptions above.

d.　Estimate the value of a share of Abbott Laboratories' common stock using the (1) discounted cash flow (DCF) model, and (2) residual operating income (ROPI) model as of December 31, 2005; assume a discount rate (WACC) of 7%, common shares outstanding of 1,539 million, and net nonoperating obligations (NNO) of $6,759 million.

e.  Abbott Laboratories (ABT) stock closed at $39.43 on December 30, 2005. How does your valuation
    estimate compare with this closing price? What do you believe are some reasons for the difference?
    What investment position is suggested from your results?

**P12-24.** **Forecasting and Estimating Share Value Using the DCF and ROPI Models   (LO1, 2)**

Following are the income statement and balance sheet for Harley-Davidson, Inc..

Harley-Davidson, Inc.
(HOG)

| Income Statement<br>Year Ended December 31 (in thousands) | 2005 | 2004 | 2003 |
|---|---|---|---|
| Net revenue | $5,342,214 | $5,015,190 | $4,624,274 |
| Cost of goods sold | 3,301,715 | 3,115,655 | 2,958,708 |
| Gross profit | 2,040,499 | 1,899,535 | 1,665,566 |
| Financial services income | 331,618 | 305,262 | 279,459 |
| Financial services expense | 139,998 | 116,662 | 111,586 |
| Operating income from financial services | 191,620 | 188,600 | 167,873 |
| Selling, administrative and engineering expense | 762,108 | 726,644 | 684,175 |
| Income from operations | 1,470,011 | 1,361,491 | 1,149,264 |
| Investment income, net | 22,797 | 23,101 | 23,088 |
| Other, net | (5,049) | (5,106) | (6,317) |
| Income before provision for income taxes | 1,487,759 | 1,379,486 | 1,166,035 |
| Provision for income taxes | 528,155 | 489,720 | 405,107 |
| Net income | $ 959,604 | $ 889,766 | $ 760,928 |

| Balance Sheet<br>December 31 (In thousands, except share amounts) | 2005 | 2004 |
|---|---|---|
| **Assets** | | |
| Cash and cash equivalents | $ 140,975 | $ 275,159 |
| Marketable securities | 905,197 | 1,336,909 |
| Accounts receivable, net | 122,087 | 121,333 |
| Finance receivables held for sale | 299,373 | 456,516 |
| Finance receivables held for investment, net | 1,342,393 | 1,167,522 |
| Inventories | 221,418 | 226,893 |
| Deferred income taxes | 61,285 | 60,517 |
| Prepaid expenses and other current assets | 52,509 | 38,337 |
| Total current assets | 3,145,237 | 3,683,186 |
| Finance receivables held for investment, net | 600,831 | 488,262 |
| Property, plant and equipment, net | 1,011,612 | 1,024,665 |
| Prepaid pension costs | 368,165 | 133,322 |
| Goodwill | 56,563 | 59,456 |
| Other assets | 72,801 | 94,402 |
| Total assets | $5,255,209 | $5,483,293 |

*continued*

| Balance Sheet<br>December 31 (In thousands, except share amounts) | 2005 | 2004 |
|---|---|---|
| **Liabilities and Shareholders' Equity** | | |
| Accounts payable. | $ 270,614 | $ 244,202 |
| Accrued expenses and other liabilities. | 397,525 | 433,053 |
| Current portion of finance debt | 204,973 | 495,441 |
| Total current liabilities. | 873,112 | 1,172,696 |
| Finance debt. | 1,000,000 | 800,000 |
| Deferred income taxes | 155,236 | 51,432 |
| Postretirement healthcare benefits. | 60,975 | 149,848 |
| Other long-term liabilities. | 82,281 | 90,846 |
| Shareholders' equity | | |
| Series A Junior participating preferred stock, none issued | — | — |
| Common stock, 330,961,869 and 329,908,165 shares<br>issued in 2005 and 2004, respectively | 3,310 | 3,300 |
| Additional paid-in capital | 596,239 | 533,068 |
| Retained earnings | 4,630,390 | 3,844,571 |
| Accumulated other comprehensive income (loss) | 58,653 | (12,096) |
| | 5,288,592 | 4,368,843 |
| Less: Treasury stock (56,960,213 and 35,597,360 shares in<br>2005 and 2004, respectively) at cost | (2,204,987) | (1,150,372) |
| Total shareholders' equity | 3,083,605 | 3,218,471 |
| Total liabilities and shareholders' equity. | $5,255,209 | $5,483,293 |

**Required**

a. Compute net operating assets (NOA) for year end 2005. (*Hint:* Treat Harley-Davidson's financial services assets, revenues, and expenses as operating under the assumption that these are directly related to its sales activities; however, its finance debt, both long-term and current maturities, is nonoperating.)

b. Compute net operating profit after tax (NOPAT) for 2005, assuming a federal and state statutory tax rate of 37.3%. (*Hint:* Treat financial services revenue and expense as well as "other expense" as operating.)

c. Forecast Harley-Davidson's sales, NOPAT, and NOA for 2006 through 2009 using the following assumptions:

| | |
|---|---|
| Sales growth. | 6.5% |
| Net operating profit margin (NOPM). | 17.7% |
| Net operating asset turnover (NOAT), year-end | 1.58 |

Forecast the terminal period (2010) values assuming a 2% terminal year growth and using the NOPM and NOAT assumptions above.

d. Estimate the value of a share of Harley-Davidson common stock using the (1) discounted cash flow (DCF) model, and (2) residual operating income (ROPI) model; assume a discount rate (WACC) of 7%, common shares outstanding of 274 million, and net nonoperating obligations (NNO) of $299 million.

e. Harley-Davidson (HOG) stock closed at $51.49 on December 30, 2005. How does your valuation estimate compare with this closing price? What do you believe are some reasons for the difference?

# CASES

**C12-25. Management Application: Operating Improvement versus Financial Engineering (LO3)**

Assume that you are the CEO of a small publicly traded company. The operating performance of your company has fallen below market expectations, which is reflected in a depressed stock price. At your direction, your CFO provides you with the following recommendations that are designed to increase your company's return on net operating assets (RNOA) and its operating cash flows, both of which will, presumably, result in improved financial performance and an increased stock price.

1. To improve net cash flow from operating activities, the CFO recommends that your company reduce inventories (raw material, work-in-progress, and finished goods) and receivables (through selective credit granting and increased emphasis on collection of past due accounts)

2. The CFO recommends that your company sell and lease back its office building. The lease will be structured so as to be classified as an operating lease under GAAP. The assets will, therefore, not be included in the computation of net operating assets (NOA), thus increasing RNOA.

3. The CFO recommends that your company lengthen the time taken to pay accounts payable (lean on the trade) to increase net cash flows from operating activities.

4. Since your company's operating performance is already depressed, the CFO recommends that you take a "big bath;" that is, write off all assets deemed to be impaired and accrue excessive liabilities for future contingencies. The higher current period expense will, then, result in higher future period income as the assets written off will not be depreciated and your company will have a liability account available to absorb future cash payments rather than recording them as expenses.

5. The CFO recommends that your company increase its expected return on pension investments. This will reduce pension expense and increase operating profit, a component of net operating profit after tax (NOPAT) and, thus, of RNOA.

6. The CFO recommends that your company share ownership of its outbound logistics (trucking division) with another company in a joint venture. This would have the effect of increasing throughput, thus spreading overhead over a larger volume base, and would remove the assets from your company's balance sheet since the joint venture would be accounted for as an equity method investment.

Evaluate each of the CFO's recommendations. In your evaluation, consider whether each recommendation will positively impact the operating performance of your company or whether it is cosmetic in nature.

# Comprehensive Case

## LEARNING OBJECTIVES

**L01** Explain and illustrate a review of financial statements and their components. (p. 13-4)

**L02** Assess company profitability and creditworthiness. (p. 13-27)

**L03** Adjust and forecast financial statements. (p. 13-29)

**L04** Describe and illustrate the valuation of firm equity and stock. (p. 13-31)

## KIMBERLY-CLARK

The past decade has seen a shift in the competitive landscape for consumer products companies. Gone are numerous competitors. Many were gobbled up in the industry's consolidation trend. Also gone is media control. Now, hundreds of different media outlets and venues compete for promotion space and scarce consumer time.

Another development is in-store branding. Companies such as Costco, with its Kirkland Signature brand on everything from candy to apparel, threaten the powerhouse brands from Kimberly-Clark, Procter & Gamble, Colgate-Palmolive, and other consumer products companies.

Five years ago, when Thomas J. Falk assumed the top spot at Kimberly-Clark, the nation's largest disposable diaper producer, he inherited some extra baggage: a company in the throes of an identity crisis, a decades-long rivalry with consumer-products behemoth Procter & Gamble, and a group of investors short on patience following a series of earnings misses.

In a move aimed at boosting its stock price and its return on equity, Kimberly-Clark spun off its paper and pulp businesses in 2004, and began a strategic investment and streamlining initiative in 2005. Under Falk's leadership, the company has steadily improved its focus on its health and hygiene segments.

Kimberly-Clark has also moved to shore up its brand images across its immense product line. With sales of $16 billion, the company manufactures such well-recognized brands as Huggies and Pull-Ups disposable diapers, Kotex and Lightdays feminine products, Kleenex facial tissue, Viva paper towels, and Scott bathroom tissue.

The rocky ride that Kimberly-Clark investors have endured over the past few years is unlikely to subside—see the following stock price chart.

Competition is fierce and well-armed, and the purchase of Gillette by Procter & Gamble further muddies the future of the industry.

On the positive side, Kimberly-Clark's earnings performance is consistent, and its financial position is solid. Kimberly-Clark's RNOA for 2005 was 17.6%, and its nonoperating return increased RNOA to yield a robust 25.7% in return on equity. It also reported $16.3 billion in assets, nearly 46% of which is concentrated in plant, property, and equipment, and another 16.5% in intangible assets.

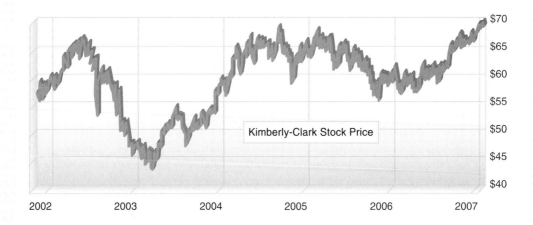

This module presents a financial accounting analysis and interpretation of Kimberly-Clark. It is intended to illustrate the key financial reporting topics covered in the book. We begin with a detailed review of Kimberly-Clark's financial statements and notes, followed by the forecasting of key accounts that we use to value its common stock.

Sources: *Kimberly-Clark* 2003 through 2005 10-K Reports; *BusinessWeek*, 2004; *The Wall Street Journal*, 2002.

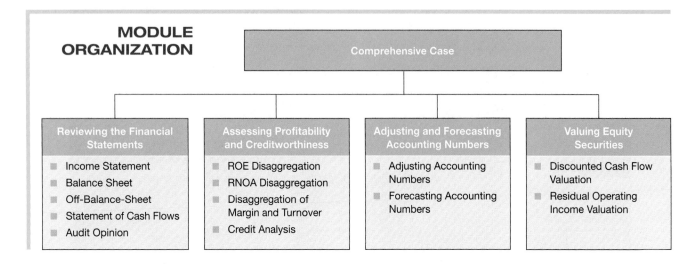

## MODULE ORGANIZATION

**Comprehensive Case**

**Reviewing the Financial Statements**
- Income Statement
- Balance Sheet
- Off-Balance-Sheet
- Statement of Cash Flows
- Audit Opinion

**Assessing Profitability and Creditworthiness**
- ROE Disaggregation
- RNOA Disaggregation
- Disaggregation of Margin and Turnover
- Credit Analysis

**Adjusting and Forecasting Accounting Numbers**
- Adjusting Accounting Numbers
- Forecasting Accounting Numbers

**Valuing Equity Securities**
- Discounted Cash Flow Valuation
- Residual Operating Income Valuation

# INTRODUCTION

Kimberly-Clark is one of the largest consumer products companies in the world. It is organized into three general business segments (percentages are for 2005):

- **Personal Care (40% of sales)**—manufactures and markets disposable diapers, training and youth pants and swim pants, feminine and incontinence care products, and other related products. Products in this segment are primarily for household use and are sold under a variety of brand names, including Huggies, Pull-Ups, GoodNites, Kotex, Lightdays, Depend, and Poise.

- **Consumer Tissue (36% of sales)**—manufactures and markets facial and bathroom tissue, paper towels and napkins for household use, wet wipes, and related products. Products in this segment are sold under the Kleenex, Scott, Cottonelle, Viva, Andrex, Scottex, Hakle, Page, and other brand names.

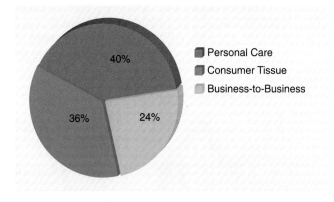

- **Business-to-Business (24% of sales)**—manufactures and markets (1) facial and bathroom tissue, paper towels, wipes and napkins for away-from-home use; (2) health care products such as surgical gowns, drapes, infection control products, sterilization wraps, disposable face masks and exam gloves, respiratory products, and other disposable medical products; (3) printing, premium business and correspondence papers; (4) specialty and technical papers; and other products. Products in this segment are sold under the Kimberly-Clark, Kleenex, Scott, Kimwipes, WypAll, Surpass, Safeskin, Tecnol, Ballard, and other brand names.

Approximately 59% of Kimberly-Clark's sales are in North America, 18% in Europe and 23% in Asia, Latin America, and other areas. Shown below are its U.S. market shares for key categories for each of the years 2003 through 2005:

| Product Category | 2005 | 2004 | 2003 |
| --- | --- | --- | --- |
| Personal care | 39.6% | 39.1% | 39.9% |
| Consumer tissue | 36.4% | 35.0% | 35.6% |
| Business-to-business | 24.1% | 25.9% | 24.5% |

In addition, approximately 13% of Kimberly-Clark's sales are made to Wal-Mart, primarily in the personal care and consumer tissue businesses (source: Kimberly-Clark 2005 10-K).

In the MD&A section of its 10-K, Kimberly-Clark describes its competitive environment as follows:

> The Corporation competes for customers in intensely competitive markets against well-known, branded products and private label products both domestically and internationally. Inherent risks in the Corporation's competitive strategy include uncertainties concerning trade and consumer acceptance, the effects of recent consolidations of retailers and distribution channels, and competitive reaction. Some of the Corporation's major competitors have undergone consolidation, which could result in increased competition and alter the dynamics of the industry. Such consolidation may give competitors greater financial resources and greater market penetration and enable competitors to offer a wider variety of products and services at more competitive prices, which could adversely affect the Corporation's financial results. In addition, the Corporation incurs substantial development and marketing costs in introducing new and improved products and technologies. There is no guarantee that the Corporation will be successful in developing new and improved products and technologies necessary to compete successfully in the industry or that the Corporation will be successful in advertising, marketing and selling its products.

Beyond the competitive business risks described above, Kimberly-Clark faces fluctuating prices for cellulose fiber, the company's principle raw material, uncertain energy costs for manufacturing operations, foreign currency translation risks, and risks resulting from fluctuating interest rates.

Given this background, we begin the accounting analysis of Kimberly-Clark with a discussion of its financial statements.

# REVIEWING THE FINANCIAL STATEMENTS

This section reviews and analyzes the financial statements of Kimberly-Clark.

**LO1** Explain and illustrate a review of financial statements and their components.

## Income Statement Reporting and Analysis

Kimberly-Clark's income statement is reproduced in Exhibit 13.1. The remainder of this section provides a brief review and analysis for Kimberly-Clark's income statement line items.

### Net Sales

Exhibit 13.1 reveals that sales increased 5.43% in 2005 to $15,903 million, following a 7.54% sales increase in the prior year. In its MD&A report, management attributes 37% of the 2003 increase (2% of the 5.43%) to favorable currency effects resulting from the weak $US (foreign currency denominated sales were translated into a higher $US equivalent than in previous years). In addition, volume increases amounted to approximately 3% of this 5.43% increase. Price increases of approximately 1% accounted for the remainder of the sales growth (source: Kimberly-Clark 2005 10-K).

Kimberly-Clark describes its revenue recognition policy as follows:

> Sales revenue for the Corporation and its reportable business segments is recognized at the time of product shipment or delivery, depending on when title passes, to unaffiliated customers, and when all of the following have occurred: a firm sales agreement is in place, pricing is fixed or determinable, and collection is reasonably assured. Sales are reported net of estimated returns, consumer and trade promotions, rebates and freight allowed.

Its revenue recognition conditions are taken directly from GAAP and SEC guidelines, which recognize revenues when "earned and realizable." For Kimberly-Clark, *earned* means when title to the goods passes to the customer, and *realizable* means an account receivable whose collection is reasonably assured.

Sales for retailers and manufacturers are straight forward: revenue is recognized when the product is transferred to the buyer, an obligation for payment exists and collection of that payment is reasonable assured. In that case, the revenue is deemed to have been "earned." The primary issue for retailers and manufacturers relates to sales return allowances. These allowances pertain to product return or sales discounts (sometimes called *mark-downs*). Companies can only report sales when earned, that is, past the return allowance period. Further, companies can only report *net* sales as revenue (i.e., gross sales less any

## EXHIBIT 13.1 Kimberly-Clark Income Statement

**KIMBERLY-CLARK CORPORATION AND SUBSIDIARIES**
**Consolidated Income Statement**

| Year Ended December 31 (Millions of dollars, except per share amounts) | 2005 | 2004 | 2003 |
|---|---|---|---|
| Net sales. . . . . . . . . . . . . . . . . . . . . . . . . . . . . . . . . . . . . . . . . . | $15,902.6 | $15,083.2 | $14,026.3 |
| Cost of products sold. . . . . . . . . . . . . . . . . . . . . . . . . . . . . . . . | 10,827.4 | 10,014.7 | 9,231.9 |
| Gross profit. . . . . . . . . . . . . . . . . . . . . . . . . . . . . . . . . . . . . . . | 5,075.2 | 5,068.5 | 4,794.4 |
| Marketing, research and general expenses . . . . . . . . . . . . . . . . . . | 2,737.4 | 2,510.9 | 2,350.3 |
| Other (income) expense, net . . . . . . . . . . . . . . . . . . . . . . . . . . . | 27.2 | 51.2 | 112.5 |
| Operating profit . . . . . . . . . . . . . . . . . . . . . . . . . . . . . . . . . . . . | 2,310.6 | 2,506.4 | 2,331.6 |
| Nonoperating expense. . . . . . . . . . . . . . . . . . . . . . . . . . . . . . . . | (179.0) | (158.4) | (105.5) |
| Interest . . . . . . . . . . . . . . . . . . . . . . . . . . . . . . . . . . . . . . . . . . | 27.5 | 17.9 | 18.0 |
| Interest expense. . . . . . . . . . . . . . . . . . . . . . . . . . . . . . . . . . . . | (190.2) | (162.5) | (167.8) |
| Income before income taxes, equity interests, discontinued operations and cumulative effect of accounting change . . . . . . . . | 1,968.9 | 2,203.4 | 2,076.3 |
| Provision for income taxes. . . . . . . . . . . . . . . . . . . . . . . . . . . . . | (438.4) | (483.9) | (484.1) |
| Share of net income of equity companies . . . . . . . . . . . . . . . . . . . | 136.6 | 124.8 | 107.0 |
| Minority owners' share of subsidiaries' net income. . . . . . . . . . . . . | (86.5) | (73.9) | (55.6) |
| Income from continuing operations . . . . . . . . . . . . . . . . . . . . . . . | 1,580.6 | 1,770.4 | 1,643.6 |
| Income from discontinued operations, net of income taxes . . . . . . . | — | 29.8 | 50.6 |
| Income before cumulative effect of accounting change . . . . . . . . . . | 1,580.6 | 1,800.2 | 1,694.2 |
| Cumulative effect of accounting change, net of income taxes . . . . . | (12.3) | — | — |
| Net income. . . . . . . . . . . . . . . . . . . . . . . . . . . . . . . . . . . . . . . . | $ 1,568.3 | $ 1,800.2 | $ 1,694.2 |
| Per share basis | | | |
| Basic | | | |
| Continued operations . . . . . . . . . . . . . . . . . . . . . . . . . . . . . . . | $ 3.33 | $ 3.58 | $ 3.24 |
| Discontinued operations. . . . . . . . . . . . . . . . . . . . . . . . . . . . . | — | .06 | .10 |
| Cumulative effect of accounting change . . . . . . . . . . . . . . . . . . | (.03) | — | — |
| Net income . . . . . . . . . . . . . . . . . . . . . . . . . . . . . . . . . . . . . . | $ 3.30 | $ 3.64 | $ 3.34 |
| Diluted | | | |
| Continuing operations . . . . . . . . . . . . . . . . . . . . . . . . . . . . . . | $ 3.31 | $ 3.55 | $ 3.23 |
| Discontinued operations. . . . . . . . . . . . . . . . . . . . . . . . . . . . . | — | .06 | .10 |
| Cumulative effect of accounting change . . . . . . . . . . . . . . . . . . | (.03) | — | — |
| Net income . . . . . . . . . . . . . . . . . . . . . . . . . . . . . . . . . . . . . . | $ 3.28 | $ 3.61 | $ 3.33 |

sales discounts, including volume discounts). K-C's footnotes provide the following table relating to sales allowances:

| December 31, 2005 ($ millions) | Balance at Beginning of Period | Additions | | Deductions | Balance at End of Period |
|---|---|---|---|---|---|
| | | Charged to Costs and Expenses | Charged to Other Accounts | Write-offs and Reclassifications | |
| Allowances for sales discounts . . . . . . . . | 20.1 | 249.5 | (.7) | 247.3 | 21.6 |

K-C's balance sheet includes a contra-asset related to sales discounts. The table indicates that the company had $20.1 million in sales discounts at the start of the year that came from sales in the prior year. During 2005, K-C granted its customers $249.5 million in additional sales discounts, $247.3 million of which had been taken by the customers by the end of the year. The remaining amount of $21.6 million, relates to discounts granted, but not yet taken, and is held over to the following year. These year-end amounts typically relate to discounts given toward the end of the year that are ultimately taken in the first quarter of the following year.

The sales discount process affects net sales and, thus, profit. This allowance works just like any other allowance. If K-C underestimated the sales discount allowance, net sales and profit in the current year would be increased. Overestimation of the sales discount allowance would have the opposite effect: current sales and profit would be depressed. K-C's allowance has not changed appreciably in 2005 and is, therefore, not of concern.

Revenue recognition in service industries and those industries that use the percentage-of-completion method can be problematic. Often, determining when a service contract has been "earned" can be difficult and revenue can easily be mis-estimated, either intentionally or not. Sanjay Kumar, former CEO of Computer Associates, was sentenced to 12 years in jail for his role in an accounting scandal relating primarily to misrepresentation of revenues and profit for the computer services company he headed up. The percentage-of-completion method is difficult to implement because it requires estimates of total costs or revenues of the project. Underestimation of costs results in overestimation of revenues. These estimation errors are often hidden from view because details in footnote disclosures are often vague or completely missing.

## Cost of Products Sold and Gross Profit

Kimberly-Clark's 2005 gross profit margin is 31.9% ($5,075.2/$15,902.6), which is about 2.3 percentage points below what it was in 2003 (34.2%). As a benchmark, Proctor & Gamble, the company's principle competitor, recently reported sales of $68.2 billion, over four times the level of K-C's sales, and a gross profit margin of 51.4%, up from 50.9% in the prior year. This comparison highlights the intense competition that K-C faces from its much larger rival.

The choice of inventory costing method affects cost of goods sold. K-C uses the LIFO method to cost its inventory. In 2005, the company's LIFO reserve increased by $17 million (see inventory discussion later in this Module). This increased cost of goods sold and reduced gross profit by $17 million. COGS can also be increased by inventory write-downs, typically related to restructuring efforts. For example, Cicso Systems, Inc. reported a $2.1 billion inventory write-down in 2001 when the tech bubble burst. This write-down increased COGS and reduced gross profit by that amount.

## Marketing, Research and General Expenses

Kimberly-Clark's marketing, research and general expenses have increased to 17.2% of sales from 16.7% in the prior year. This increase resulted from general cost inflation as well as from the company's restructuring efforts designed to improve long-run manufacturing and operating costs. K-C reports 2005 net operating profit after taxes (NOPAT) of $1,949.9 million [($2,310.6 + $136.6) − ($438.4 + ($190.2 − $27.5) × 36.2%)] and a net operating profit margin (NOPM) of 12.3% ($1,949.9 million/$15,902.6 million) of sales.[1] P&G, by contrast, is able to use its higher gross profit margin to fund a higher level of advertising and other SGA expenditures, resulting in a NOPM of 13.4%.

***Pension Costs.*** Kimberly-Clark's marketing, research and general expenses include $157 million of pension expense. This is reported in the following table in the pension footnote:

| | **Components of Net Periodic Benefit Cost** | | | | | |
| | **Pension Benefits** | | | **Other Benefits** | | |
| **Year Ended December 31**<br>**(Millions of dollars)** | **2005** | **2004** | **2003** | **2005** | **2004** | **2003** |
| --- | --- | --- | --- | --- | --- | --- |
| Service cost . . . . . . . . . . . . . . . . . . . . . . . . . | $ 81.4 | $ 87.4 | $ 76.1 | **$17.4** | $17.8 | $16.2 |
| Interest cost . . . . . . . . . . . . . . . . . . . . . . . . | 294.6 | 296.2 | 288.0 | **47.1** | 48.2 | 48.9 |
| Expected return on plan assets . . . . . . . . . . . . | (322.6) | (324.0) | (286.3) | — | — | — |
| Amortization of prior service cost (benefit)<br>and transition amount. . . . . . . . . . . . . . . . . | 6.3 | 7.3 | 8.7 | **(.2)** | (.7) | (1.5) |
| Recognized net actuarial loss . . . . . . . . . . . . . | 92.7 | 83.3 | 74.0 | **3.9** | 4.0 | 1.9 |
| Other. . . . . . . . . . . . . . . . . . . . . . . . . . . . . . . | 4.4 | 4.6 | 5.4 | — | (1.5) | — |
| Net periodic benefit cost . . . . . . . . . . . . . . . . | $156.8 | $154.8 | $165.9 | **$68.2** | $67.8 | $65.5 |

----

[1] We include equity income of $136.6 million (labeled as "share of net income of equity companies" in K-C's income statement) as operating because it relates to investments in paper-related companies and it, therefore, aligns with K-C's primary operating activities. This amount is reported by K-C net of tax, and therefore, no tax adjustment is necessary when computing NOPAT. We consider K-C's Minority owners' share of subsidiaries' net income, as a non-operating expense.

For 2005, the expected return on pension investments ($322.6 million) provides an offset to the company's pension service and interest costs ($81.4 million and $294.6 million, respectively). Footnotes reveal that Kimberly-Clark's pension investments realized an *actual* return of $359.5 million in 2005 (from the pension footnote in its 10-K report). So, for 2005, use of the expected return results in an unrecognized *gain* that is deferred, along with other unrecognized gains and losses, in the computation of reported profit.

Kimberly-Clark describes how it determines the expected return in its footnotes. It is instructive to review the company's rationale and, thus, the footnote follows:

> The expected long-term rate of return on pension fund assets was determined based on several factors, including input from pension investment consultants and projected long-term returns of broad equity and bond indices. The Corporation also considered the U.S. plan's historical 10-year and 15-year compounded annual returns of 9.36 percent and 10.28 percent, respectively, which have been in excess of these broad equity and bond benchmark indices. The Corporation anticipates that on average the investment managers for each of the plans comprising the Principal Plans will generate annual long-term rates of return of at least 8.5 percent. The Corporation's expected long-term rate of return on the assets in the Principal Plans is based on an asset allocation assumption of about 70 percent with equity managers, with expected long-term rates of return of approximately 10 percent, and 30 percent with fixed income managers, with an expected long-term rate of return of about 6 percent. The Corporation regularly reviews its actual asset allocation and periodically rebalances its investments to the targeted allocation when considered appropriate. Also, when deemed appropriate, the Corporation executes hedging strategies using index options and futures to limit the downside exposure of certain investments by trading off upside potential above an acceptable level. The Corporation last executed this hedging strategy for 2003. No hedging instruments are currently in place. The Corporation will continue to evaluate its long-term rate of return assumptions at least annually and will adjust them as necessary.

The expected return on pension assets offsets service and interest costs, and serves to reduce pension expense. In general, increasing (decreasing) the expected return on pension assets, increases (decreases) profit. In 2005, K-C reduced its expected return from 8.32% to 8.29%. The discount rate (used to compute the PBO and the interest cost component of pension expense) declined by 24 basis points (5.92% to 5.68%). It is not uncommon for the expected return rate to be "stickier" on the downside (thus propping up profits) and more quickly adjusted on the upside (to take advantage of increasing returns). We need to be mindful of these effects when assessing operating profits.

## Transitory versus Persistent Line Items

Expenses relating to restructuring activities have become increasingly common in the past two decades. Kimberly-Clark pursued its own restructuring activities in 2005 and recorded charges of $228.6 million relating to Competitive Improvement Initiatives. These initiatives are designed to further improve the company's competitive position by accelerating investments in targeted growth opportunities and strategic cost reductions to streamline manufacturing and administrative operations, primarily in North America and Europe.

Classification of these charges as transitory or persistent is a judgment call. In K-C's case, these charges relate to a multi-year program that is expected to continue through 2008. Therefore, we classify these expenses as persistent. Our review of the financial statements did not identify any other transitory items and thus, we classified all other activity as persistent.

## Earnings per Share

Net income for Kimberly-Clark has decreased from $1,694.2 million in 2003 to $1,568.3 million in 2005. Basic (diluted) earnings per share, however, has only declined from $3.34 ($3.33) to $3.30 ($3.28). The small relative decline in EPS is a result of K-C's share repurchase program (see the financing section in Exhibit 13.5). Following is Kimberly-Clark's computation of earnings per share:

> **Earnings Per Share** A reconciliation of the average number of common shares outstanding used in the basic and diluted EPS computations follows:

| Average Common Shares Outstanding (Millions) | 2005 | 2004 | 2003 |
|---|---|---|---|
| Basic.......................................... | 474.0 | 495.2 | 507.0 |
| Dilutive effect of stock options..................... | 2.6 | 3.4 | 1.2 |
| Dilutive effect of restricted share awards............. | .8 | .6 | .4 |
| Diluted ........................................ | 477.4 | 499.2 | 508.6 |

Options outstanding that were not included in the computation of diluted EPS because their exercise price was greater than the average market price of the common shares are summarized below:

| Description | 2005 | 2004 | 2003 |
|---|---|---|---|
| Average number of share equivalents (millions)..... | 9.1 | 5.4 | 20.5 |
| Weighted-average exercise price............... | $66.58 | $70.13 | $60.19 |
| Expiration date of options .................... | 2007 to 2015 | 2007 to 2012 | 2006 to 2013 |
| Options outstanding at year-end ............... | 8.8 | 5.4 | 20.2 |

The number of common shares outstanding as of December 31, 2005, 2004 and 2003 was 461.5 million, 482.9 million and 501.6 million, respectively.

Most of the difference between basic and diluted earnings per share usually arises from the dilutive effects of employee stock options. For K-C, such effects were absent in 2005 as its stock options were *under water,* meaning that K-C's stock price was lower than the exercise price of the options. The stock options, therefore, are considered *antidilutive,* meaning that including them would increase EPS. Accordingly, they are excluded in the diluted EPS computation, but remain potentially dilutive if K-C's stock price subsequently rises above the exercise price of the options. (Although not present for Kimberly-Clark, convertible debt and preferred shares are also potentially dilutive for many companies.)

## Income Taxes

Kimberly-Clark's net income was positively affected by a reduction of its effective tax rate. K-C describes this tax effect in the following footnote:

> The Corporation's effective income tax rate was 22.3 percent in 2005 compared with 22.0 percent in 2004. The most significant factors causing the increase were the taxes on the dividends received under the American Jobs Creation Act partially offset by increased synthetic fuel credits.

The American Jobs Creation Act taxed funds repatriated from foreign subsidiaries at a lower tax rate to stimulate investment. Although the tax *rate* was lower, the *dollar amount* of taxes paid increased, resulting in an increase in the effective tax rate (provision for income taxes/income before income taxes). This is a transitory increase and should not be factored into our projections. We discuss this synthetic fuel partnership in our discussion of variable interest entities (VIEs) later in this Module.

## Common-Size Income Statement

It is useful for analysis purposes to prepare common-size statements. Exhibit 13.2 shows Kimberly-Clark's common-size income statement covering the three most recent years.

The gross profit margin declined in 2005; specifically, from 34.2% in 2003 to 31.9%. This reflects the very competitive environment in which K-C operates. Companies typically offset a declining gross profit margin with reductions in SG&A expense. K-C has been unable to do that, however, as its marketing, research and general (SG&A) expense in 2005 actually exceeds its 2003 level as a percentage of sales. Accordingly, 2005 income before taxes declined by 2.4 percentage points relative to 2003. Further, income from equity companies (reported net of tax) increased only slightly as a percentage of sales from 0.8% to 0.9% from 2003 to 2005. Yet, despite the 2.4 percentage point reduction in pretax profit, income from continuing operations declined by only 1.8 percentage points, from 11.7% in 2003 to 9.9% in 2005. This is due to reduced tax expense as a percent of taxable income (lower tax rate).

| EXHIBIT 13.2 | Kimberly-Clark Common-Size Income Statement | | |
|---|---|---|---|
| **Year Ended December 31** | **2005** | **2004** | **2003** |
| Net sales. . . . . . . . . . . . . . . . . . . . . . . . . . . . . . . . . . . . . . . . . . . . . . . . . . . . . . . . | 100.0% | 100.0% | 100.0% |
| Cost of products sold. . . . . . . . . . . . . . . . . . . . . . . . . . . . . . . . . . . . . . . . . . . . . . | 68.1 | 66.4 | 65.8 |
| Gross profit. . . . . . . . . . . . . . . . . . . . . . . . . . . . . . . . . . . . . . . . . . . . . . . . . . . . . . | 31.9 | 33.6 | 34.2 |
| Marketing, research, and general expenses . . . . . . . . . . . . . . . . . . . . . . . . | 17.2 | 16.6 | 16.8 |
| Other (income) expense, net . . . . . . . . . . . . . . . . . . . . . . . . . . . . . . . . . . . . . | 0.2 | 0.3 | 0.8 |
| Operating profit . . . . . . . . . . . . . . . . . . . . . . . . . . . . . . . . . . . . . . . . . . . . . . . . | 14.5 | 16.6 | 16.6 |
| Nonoperating expense. . . . . . . . . . . . . . . . . . . . . . . . . . . . . . . . . . . . . . . . . . . | (1.1) | (1.1) | (0.8) |
| Interest income. . . . . . . . . . . . . . . . . . . . . . . . . . . . . . . . . . . . . . . . . . . . . . . . | 0.2 | 0.1 | 0.1 |
| Interest expense. . . . . . . . . . . . . . . . . . . . . . . . . . . . . . . . . . . . . . . . . . . . . . . | (1.2) | (1.1) | (1.2) |
| Income before income taxes, equity interests, discontinued operations and cumulative effect of accounting change . . . . . . . . . . | 12.4 | 14.6 | 14.8 |
| Provision for income taxes. . . . . . . . . . . . . . . . . . . . . . . . . . . . . . . . . . . . . . . | (2.8) | (3.2) | (3.5) |
| Share of net income of equity companies . . . . . . . . . . . . . . . . . . . . . . . . . | 0.9 | 0.8 | 0.8 |
| Minority owners' share of subsidiaries' net income. . . . . . . . . . . . . . . . . . | (0.5) | (0.5) | (0.4) |
| Income from continuing operations . . . . . . . . . . . . . . . . . . . . . . . . . . . . . . . | 9.9 | 11.7 | 11.7 |
| Income from discontinued operations, net of income taxes . . . . . . . . . . | 0.0 | 0.2 | 0.4 |
| Income before cumulative effect of accounting change . . . . . . . . . . . . . | 9.9 | 11.9 | 12.1 |
| Cumulative effect of accounting change, net of income taxes . . . . . . . . | (0.1) | 0.0 | 0.0 |
| Net income. . . . . . . . . . . . . . . . . . . . . . . . . . . . . . . . . . . . . . . . . . . . . . . . . . . | 9.9% | 11.9% | 12.1% |

Note: All percentages are computed by dividing each income statement line item by that year's net sales.

## Management Discussion and Analysis

The Management Discussion and Analysis section of a 10-K is usually informative for interpreting company financial statements and for additional insights into company operations. To illustrate, Kimberly-Clark provides the following analysis of its operating results in the MD&A section of its 2005 10-K:

> Consolidated net sales increased 5.4 percent from 2004. Sales volumes rose more than 3 percent with each of the business segments contributing to the increase. Currency effects added nearly 2 percent to the increase primarily due to strengthening of the South Korean won, the Brazilian real, the Canadian dollar and the Australian dollar. Net selling prices increased 1 percent offset by a reduction in net sales due to the divestiture of the pulp operations as part of the spin-off of Neenah Paper on November 30, 2004.
>
> Consolidated operating profit decreased 7.8 percent. Significant factors that negatively affected operating profit were approximately $229 million of charges related to the Competitive Improvement Initiatives that are not included in the business segments (as discussed later in this MD&A and in Item 8, Note 3 to the Consolidated Financial Statement), cost inflation of about $400 million and higher marketing, research and general expenses. Those factors were partially offset by gross cost savings of nearly $210 million, increased sales volumes and higher net selling prices. Operating profit as a percent of net sales declined to 14.5 percent from 16.6 percent for 2004.
>
> - Operating profit for personal care products decreased .9 percent. Cost savings, higher sales volumes and favorable currency effects were offset by materials cost inflation—particularly for polymer resins and superabsorbants, lower net selling prices and increased costs for marketing and research activities. The year-over-year change in operating profit was also affected by about $37 million of costs in 2004 to improve the efficiency of the Corporation's diaper operations.
>
>   Operating profit in North America declined about 3 percent as materials cost inflation, lower net selling prices and higher distribution costs more than offset savings and the higher sales volumes. In Europe, operating profit decreased primarily due to the lower net selling prices. Operating profit in the developing and emerging markets increased nearly 16 percent due to the higher sales volumes, higher net selling prices and favorable currency effects, tempered by higher marketing and administrative costs.
>
> - Operating profit for consumer tissue products was essentially even with last year, an increase of .3 percent. The higher net selling prices, higher sales volumes and cost savings were offset by cost inflation for materials, energy and distribution, and higher marketing and research expenses.
>
>   In North America, operating profit grew almost 8 percent because the higher net selling prices and increased sales volumes more than offset the cost inflation. Operating profit in Europe

decreased principally due to the effects of the competitive lower net selling prices. In the developing and emerging markets, operating profit advanced approximately 19 percent on the strength of the higher sales volumes and a favorable product mix.

- Operating profit for business-to-business products increased 2.5 percent. The higher sales volumes and higher net selling prices combined with cost savings and the absence of operating losses related to the divested pulp operations allowed the segment to overcome materials and energy related cost inflation.

## Business Segments

Generally accepted accounting principals require that companies disclose the composition of their operating profit by business segment. Segments are investment centers (those having both income statement and balance sheet data) that the company routinely evaluates at the chief executive level.

We outlined and discussed Kimberly-Clark's business segments at the beginning of the module: personal care, consumer tissue, and business-to-business. Following are its GAAP disclosures for each of its business segments:

**Consolidated Operations by Business Segment**

| (Millions of dollars) | Personal Care | Consumer Tissue | Business-to-Business | Intersegment Sales | Corporate & Other | Consolidated Total |
|---|---|---|---|---|---|---|
| **Net Sales** | | | | | | |
| 2005 | $6,287.4 | $5,781.3 | $3,821.8 | $ (19.3) | $ 31.4 | $15,902.6 |
| 2004 | 5,975.1 | 5,343.0 | 3,957.9 | (217.1) | 24.3 | 15,083.2 |
| 2003 | 5,652.9 | 5,046.7 | 3,477.7 | (154.7) | 3.7 | 14,026.3 |
| **Operating Profit** | | | | | | |
| 2005 | 1,242.2 | 805.8 | 673.2 | — | (410.6) | 2,310.6 |
| 2004 | 1,253.2 | 803.1 | 656.6 | — | (206.5) | 2,506.4 |
| 2003 | 1,221.0 | 728.2 | 602.8 | — | (220.4) | 2,331.6 |
| **Depreciation and Amortization** | | | | | | |
| 2005 | 267.4 | 301.0 | 188.1 | — | 88.0 | 844.5 |
| 2004 | 286.9 | 310.7 | 194.0 | — | 8.7 | 800.3 |
| 2003 | 264.4 | 300.2 | 178.2 | — | 2.5 | 745.3 |
| **Assets** | | | | | | |
| 2005 | 4,650.7 | 5,672.9 | 4,578.9 | — | 1,400.7 | 16,303.2 |
| 2004 | 4,813.3 | 5,881.5 | 4,745.2 | — | 1,578.0 | 17,018.0 |
| 2003 | 4,781.9 | 5,796.5 | 4,850.1 | — | 1,351.4 | 16,779.9 |
| **Capital Spending** | | | | | | |
| 2005 | 297.9 | 296.6 | 115.0 | — | 0.1 | 709.6 |
| 2004 | 242.5 | 202.3 | 89.4 | — | 0.8 | 535.0 |
| 2003 | 344.4 | 366.6 | 141.0 | — | 20.9 | 872.9 |

Given these data, it is possible for us to perform a rudimentary return analysis for each segment. This analysis provides insight into a company's dependence on any one segment. Following is a brief summary analysis of K-C's segment return disaggregation for 2005:

| Segment ($ millions) | Net Sales | Operating Profit | Assets | Operating Profit Margin | Year-End Asset Turnover | Operating Profit Divided by Year-End Assets |
|---|---|---|---|---|---|---|
| Personal care | $6,287.4 | $1,242.2 | $4,650.7 | 19.8% | 1.35 | 26.7% |
| Consumer tissue | 5,781.3 | 805.8 | 5,672.9 | 13.9% | 1.02 | 14.2% |
| Business-to-business | 3,821.8 | 673.2 | 4,578.9 | 17.6% | 0.83 | 14.7% |

The intensely competitive nature of the consumer tissue market is evident in its low profit margin (13.9%) and low return on ending operating assets (14.2%). K-C relies, to a great extent, on its personal care segment to generate income. Many analysts cite the pricing pressure in the consumer tissue segment as a negative factor in their valuations of K-C.

# Balance Sheet Reporting and Analysis

Kimberly-Clark's balance sheet is reproduced in Exhibit 13.3.

| EXHIBIT 13.3 | Kimberly-Clark Balance Sheet | | |
|---|---|---|---|
| **KIMBERLY-CLARK CORPORATION AND SUBSIDIARIES** Consolidated Balance Sheet | | | |
| December 31 (Millions of dollars) | | 2005 | 2004 |
| **Assets** | | | |
| Cash and cash equivalents | | $   364.0 | $   594.0 |
| Accounts receivable, net | | 2,101.9 | 2,038.3 |
| Inventories | | 1,752.1 | 1,670.9 |
| Deferred income taxes | | 223.4 | 278.2 |
| Other current assets | | 341.7 | 380.5 |
| Total current assets | | 4,783.1 | 4,961.9 |
| Property, plant and equipment, net | | 7,494.7 | 7,990.5 |
| Investments in equity companies | | 457.8 | 444.4 |
| Goodwill | | 2,685.6 | 2,702.9 |
| Other assets | | 882.0 | 918.3 |
| Total assets | | $16,303.2 | $17,018.0 |
| **Liabilities and Stockholders' Equity** | | | |
| Debt payable within one year | | $ 1,222.5 | $ 1,214.7 |
| Trade accounts payable | | 1,055.5 | 983.2 |
| Other payables | | 298.8 | 265.5 |
| Accrued expenses | | 1,399.6 | 1,431.6 |
| Accrued income taxes | | 457.9 | 448.0 |
| Dividends payable | | 208.6 | 194.2 |
| Total current liabilities | | 4,642.9 | 4,537.2 |
| Long-term debt | | 2,594.7 | 2,298.0 |
| Noncurrent employee benefit and other obligations | | 1,782.6 | 1,621.7 |
| Deferred income taxes | | 572.9 | 840.3 |
| Minority owners' interests in subsidiaries | | 394.5 | 368.4 |
| Preferred securities of subsidiary | | 757.4 | 722.9 |
| Stockholders' equity | | | |
| Preferred stock—no par value—authorized 20.0 million shares, none issued | | — | — |
| Common stock—$1.25 par value—authorized 1.2 billion shares; issued 568.6 million shares at December 31, 2005 and 2004 | | 710.8 | 710.8 |
| Additional paid-in capital | | 324.6 | 348.6 |
| Common stock held in treasury, at cost—107.1 million and 85.7 million shares at December 31, 2005 and 2004 | | (6,376.1) | (5,047.5) |
| Accumulated other comprehensive income (loss) | | (1,669.4) | (1,226.0) |
| Retained earnings | | 12,581.4 | 11,865.9 |
| Unearned compensation on restricted stock | | (13.1) | (22.3) |
| Total stockholders' equity | | 5,558.2 | 6,629.5 |
| Total liabilities and stockholders' equity | | $16,303.2 | $17,018.0 |

Kimberly-Clark reports total assets of $16,303.2 million in 2005. Its net working capital is relatively illiquid because a large proportion of current assets is tied up in accounts receivable and inventories, and its cash is only 2.2% ($364 million/$16,303.2 million) of total assets at year-end 2005, down from 3.5% in 2004. It also reports no marketable securities that can serve as another source of liquidity, if needed. The lack of liquidity is usually worrisome, but is not a serious concern in this case given Kimberly-Clark's moderate financial leverage and high level of free cash flow (see later discussion in this section).

Following is a brief review and analysis for each of Kimberly-Clark's balance sheet line items.

## Accounts Receivable

Kimberly-Clark reports $2,101.9 million in net accounts receivable at year-end 2005. This represents 12.9% ($2,101.9 million/$16,303.2 million) of total assets, up from 12% in the previous year. Footnotes reveal the following additional information:

| Summary of Accounts Receivable ($ millions), December 31 | 2005 | 2004 |
| --- | --- | --- |
| Accounts Receivable | | |
| From customers . . . . . . . . . . . . . . . . . . . . . . . . . . . . . . . . . . . . . . . . . . . . . . . | $1,930.6 | $1,905.4 |
| Other. . . . . . . . . . . . . . . . . . . . . . . . . . . . . . . . . . . . . . . . . . . . . . . . . . . . . . . . | 228.8 | 195.5 |
| Less allowance for doubtful accounts and sales discounts . . . . . . . . . | (57.5) | (62.6) |
| Accounts receivable, net . . . . . . . . . . . . . . . . . . . . . . . . . . . . . . . . . . . . . . | $2,101.9 | $2,038.3 |

Most accounts receivables are from customers. This means we must consider the following two issues:

1. **Magnitude**—Receivables are generally non-interest-bearing and, therefore, do not earn a return. Further, the company incurs costs to finance them. Accordingly, a company wants to optimize its level of investment in receivables—that is, keep them as low as possible while still meeting industry specific credit policies to meet customer demands.

2. **Collectibility**—Receivables represent unsecured loans to customers. It is critical therefore, to understand the creditworthiness of these borrowers. Receivables are reported at net realizable value, that is, net of the allowance for doubtful accounts. Kimberly-Clark reports an allowance of $35.8 million. In addition, the footnotes reveal the following history of the company's allowance versus its write-offs:

| | | Additions | | Deductions | |
| --- | --- | --- | --- | --- | --- |
| Description (December 31, 2005) | Balance at Beginning of Period | Charged to Costs and Expenses | Charged to Other Accounts | Write-Offs and Reclassifications | Balance at End of Period |
| Allowance for doubtful accounts . . . . . . | $42.5 | $8.9 | $(.6) | $15.0 | $35.8 |

The company reported a balance in the allowance for doubtful accounts of $42.5 million at the beginning of 2005, which is 2.4% of receivables [$42.5/($2,038.3 million + $42.5 million)]. During 2005 it increased this allowance account by $8.9 million. This is the amount of bad debt expense that is reported in the income statement. The company also decreased the allowance by $0.6 million (see table above) by reallocating reserves to other accounts. Write-offs and reclassifications of uncollectible accounts amounted to $15 million during the year, yielding a $35.8 million balance at year-end, which is 1.7% of receivables [$35.8 million/($2,101.9 million + $35.8 million)]. It appears, therefore, that the company's receivables were less adequately reserved at year-end relative to the beginning of the year.

Following is Kimberly-Clark's explanation of its allowance policy:

**Allowance for Doubtful Accounts**  The allowance for doubtful accounts represents the Corporation's best estimate of the accounts receivable that will not be collected. The estimate is based on, among other things, historical collection experience, a review of the current aging status of customer receivables, and a review of specific information for those customers that are deemed to be higher risk. At the time the Corporation becomes aware of a customer whose continued operating success is questionable, collection of their receivable balance is closely monitored and the customer may be required to prepay for shipments. If a customer enters a bankruptcy action, the progress of that action is monitored to determine when and if an additional provision for non-collectibility is warranted. The adequacy of the allowance for doubtful accounts at December 31, 2005 and 2004 was $35.8 million and $42.5 million, respectively, and the write-off of uncollectible accounts was $15.0 million and $13.6 million in 2005 and 2004, respectively.

The allowance for doubtful accounts should always reflect the company's best estimate of the potential loss in its accounts receivable. This amount should not be overly conservative (which would understate profit), and it should not be inadequate (which would overstate profit). K-C's estimate of its potential losses results from its own (unaudited) review of the age of its receivables (older receivables are at greater risk of uncollectibility).

## Inventories

Kimberly-Clark reports $1,752.1 million in inventories as of 2005. Footnote disclosures reveal the following inventory costing policy:

> **Inventories and Distribution Costs**   For financial reporting purposes, most U.S. inventories are valued at the lower of cost, using the Last-In, First-Out (LIFO) method or market. The balance of the U.S. inventories and inventories of consolidated operations outside the U.S. are valued at the lower of cost, using either the First-In, First-Out (FIFO) or weighted-average cost methods, or market. Distribution costs are classified as Cost of Products Sold.

Most of its U.S. inventories are reported on a LIFO basis. Some of its U.S. inventories, as well as those outside of the U.S., are valued at FIFO or weighted-average. The use of multiple inventory costing methods for different pools of inventories is common and acceptable under GAAP.

Kimberly-Clark provides the following footnote disclosure relating to the composition of its inventories:

| Summary of Inventories ($ millions), December 31 | 2005 | 2004 |
|---|---|---|
| Inventories by major class | | |
| At the lower of cost on the FIFO or weighted-average cost methods or market | | |
| Raw materials | $    338.9 | $    332.7 |
| Work in process | 236.7 | 225.9 |
| Finished goods | 1,128.9 | 1,044.6 |
| Supplies and other | 232.3 | 235.4 |
| | 1,936.8 | 1,838.6 |
| Excess of FIFO or weighted-average cost over LIFO cost | (184.7) | (167.7) |
| Total | $1,752.1 | $1,670.9 |

Companies aim to optimize their investment in inventories because inventory is a non-income-producing asset until sold. Inventories must also be financed, stored, moved, and insured at some cost. Kimberly-Clark reports $338.9 million of raw materials, which is 17.5% of the total of $1,936.8 million inventories (see table above). Work-in-process inventories amount to another $236.7 million, and supplies and other amount to $232.3 million. The bulk of its inventories, or $1,128.9 million (58.3% of total inventories), is in finished goods.

Kimberly-Clark reports its total inventory cost *at FIFO* is $1,936.8 million then subtracts $184.7 million from this amount (the *LIFO reserve*) to yield the inventories balance of $1,752.1 million at LIFO as reported on the balance sheet. This means that, over time, Kimberly-Clark has reduced gross profit and pretax operating profit by $184.7 million. This has also reduced pretax income and saved federal income tax, and generated cash flow, of approximately $64.6 million (assuming a 35% statutory federal tax rate and computed as $184.7 million $\times$ 35%). During 2005, its LIFO reserve increased by $17 million, resulting in a $17 million decrease in gross profit and pretax operating profit, and a $5.95 million ($17 million $\times$ 35%) reduction in cash flow from decreased federal income taxes.

## Property, Plant, and Equipment

Kimberly Clark reports Property, Plant, and Equipment, net, of $7,494.7 million at year-end 2005; PPE makes up 45.9% of total assets and is the largest single asset category. Given the cost of depreciable assets of $14,616 million and accumulated depreciation of $7,121.5 million (not reported here), PPE is 48.7% depreciated assuming straight-line depreciation ($7,121.5 million/ $14,616 million) as of 2005. This suggests these assets are about the average age that we would expect assuming a regular replacement policy. Footnotes reveal a useful life range of 40 years for buildings and 16 to 20 years for machinery as follows:

> **Property and Depreciation**   For financial reporting purposes, property, plant and equipment are stated at cost and are depreciated principally on the straight-line method. Buildings are depreciated over their estimated useful lives, primarily 40 years. Machinery and equipment are depreciated over

their estimated useful lives, primarily ranging from 16 to 20 years. For income tax purposes, accelerated methods of depreciation are used. Purchases of computer software are capitalized. External costs and certain internal costs (including payroll and payroll-related costs of employees) directly associated with developing significant computer software applications for internal use are capitalized. Training and data conversion costs are expensed as incurred. Computer software costs are amortized on the straight-line method over the estimated useful life of the software, which generally does not exceed five years.

Again, assuming straight-line depreciation, Kimberly-Clark's 2005 depreciation expense of $818.5 million ($844.5 depreciation and amortization expense reported in its statement of cash flows, Exhibit 13.5, less $26 million reported as amortization expense in footnotes not reproduced in the text) reveals that its long-term depreciable assets, as a whole, are being depreciated over an average useful life of about 17.1 years, computed as $14,616.2 million − $257.4 million of nondepreciable land and $391.3 million of construction in progress divided by $818.5 million depreciation expense.

Each year, Kimberly-Clark tests PPE for impairment and records a write down to net realizable value if the PPE is deemed to be impaired. Following is Kimberly-Clark's discussion relating to its impairment testing:

Estimated useful lives are periodically reviewed and, when warranted, changes are made to them. Long-lived assets, including computer software, are reviewed for impairment whenever events or changes in circumstances indicate that their cost may not be recoverable. An impairment loss would be recognized when estimated undiscounted future cash flows from the use and eventual disposition of an asset group, which are identifiable and largely independent of other asset groups, are less than the carrying amount of the asset over its fair value. Fair value is measured using discounted cash flows or independent appraisals, as appropriate. When property is sold or retired, the cost of the property and the related accumulated depreciation are removed from the balance sheet and any gain or loss on the transaction is included in income.

The company did not report any impairment losses in the periods covered by its recent 10-K.

If present, impairment losses should be treated as a transitory item. Further, we must consider the effects of such losses on current and future income statements. An impairment loss depresses current period income. Further, depreciation expense in future years is decreased because it is computed based on the asset's lower net book value (cost less accumulated depreciation) following the write-down. This will increase future period profitability. The net effect of an impairment charge, therefore, is to shift profit from the current period into future periods.

## Investments in Equity Companies

K-C's balance sheet reports equity investments of $457.8 million at year-end 2005. This amount represents the book value of its investments in affiliated companies over which Kimberly-Clark can exert significant influence, but not control. Footnotes reveal investments in the following companies:

At December 31, 2005, the Corporation's equity companies and ownership interest were as follows: Kimberly-Clark Lever, Ltd. (India) (50%), Kimberly-Clark de Mexico S.A. de C.V. and subsidiaries (47.9%), Olayan Kimberly-Clark Arabia (49%), Olayan Kimberly-Clark (Bahrain) WLL (49%), PT Kimsari Paper Indonesia (50%) and Tecnosur S.A. (34%).

Consolidation is not required unless the affiliate is "controlled." Generally, control is presumed at an ownership level of more than 50%. By this rule, Kimberly-Clark does not control any of these companies. Thus, the company uses the equity method to account for these investments. This means that only the net equity owned of these companies is reported on the balance sheet. We further discuss these investments in the section on off-balance-sheet financing.

## Goodwill

Kimberly-Clark reports $2,685.6 million of goodwill at year-end 2005. This amount represents the excess of the purchase price for acquired companies over the fair market value of the acquired tangible and identifiable intangible assets (net of liabilities assumed). Under GAAP, goodwill is not systematically amortized, but is annually tested for impairment.

Prior to 2001, GAAP required goodwill amortization. Accordingly, Kimberly-Clark last reported goodwill amortization in 2001. Since that time its annual net income is higher by approximately $94 million per year as a result of this mandated accounting change that eliminated goodwill amortization.

## Other Assets

Kimberly-Clark reports $882 million as "other assets." There is no table detailing what assets are included in this total, but footnotes reveal the following: $2 million of long-term marketable securities, $45.7 million of assets related to discontinued operations, $276.8 million of acquired patents and trademarks that are being amortized, and $228.1 million of noncurrent deferred income tax assets. No information is given on the remaining $329.4 million of other assets, most likely because this amount represents several assets each of which is not determined to be material and, therefore, subject to disclosure.

Concerning the deferred income tax assets, Kimberly-Clark provides the following disclosure relating to its composition ($ millions):

| December 31 (Millions of dollars) | 2005 | 2004 |
|---|---|---|
| Net current deferred income tax asset attributable to: | | |
| Other accrued expenses. | $145.5 | $162.0 |
| Pension, postretirement and other employee benefits. | 94.8 | 86.9 |
| Inventory. | (27.5) | (14.6) |
| Prepaid royalties. | — | 27.2 |
| Other. | 19.0 | 24.1 |
| Valuation allowances | (8.4) | (7.4) |
| Net current deferred income tax asset. | (223.4) | (278.2) |
| Net noncurrent deferred income tax asset attributable to: | | |
| Income tax loss carryforwards. | $235.8 | $304.1 |
| State tax credits. | 96.0 | 67.6 |
| Pension and other postretirement benefits. | 22.2 | 37.3 |
| Accumulated depreciation. | 3.7 | 32.6 |
| Other. | 94.8 | 71.5 |
| Valuation allowances | (224.4) | (219.7) |
| Net noncurrent deferred income tax asset included in other assets | $228.1 | $293.4 |

Most of this deferred tax asset (benefit) results from tax loss carryforwards. The IRS allows companies to carry forward losses to offset future taxable income, thereby reducing future tax expense. This benefit can only be realized if the company expects taxable income in the specific entity that generated the tax losses before the carryforwards expire. If the company deems it more likely than not that the carryforwards will *not* be realized, a valuation allowance for the unrealizable portion is required (this is similar to establishing an allowance for uncollectible accounts receivable). As of 2005, Kimberly-Clark has such a valuation allowance (of $224.4 million). Following is its discussion relating to this allowance:

Valuation allowances increased $221.6 million and $4.5 million in 2005 and 2004, respectively. the increase in 2005 was related to an increase in excess foreign tax credits that are potentially not usable in the U.S. during the 2006 through 2015 carryover period. Valuation allowances at the end of 2005 primarily relate to excess foreign tax credits in the U.S. and income tax loss carryforwards of $916.7 million, that potentially are not usable primarily in jurisdictions outside the U.S. If not utilized against taxable income, $425.7 million of the loss carryforwards will expire from 2006 through 2025. The remaining $491.0 million has no expiration date.

Realization of income tax loss carryforwards is dependent on generating sufficient taxable income prior to expiration of these carryforwards. Although realization is not assured, management believes it is more likely than not that all of the deferred tax assets, net of applicable valuation allowances, will be realized. The amount of the deferred tax assets considered realizable could be reduced or increased if estimates of future taxable income change during the carryforward period.

Tax loss carryforwards reduce income tax expense in the year they are recognized, similar to tax loss carry-backs. However, companies often establish a deferred tax asset valuation allowance which increases tax expense. It is common that companies establish both the loss carryforward and the valuation allowance concurrently. The net effect is to leave tax expense (and net income) unchanged. In future years, however, a reduction of the deferred tax asset valuation account, in anticipation of utilization of the tax carry-forwards (and not as a result of their expiration), reduces tax expense and increases net income. This is a transitory increase in profit and should not be factored into projections.

## Current Liabilities

Kimberly-Clark reports current liabilities of $4,642.9 million at year-end 2005. Accrued expenses make up the largest single amount at $1,399.6 million. Footnotes reveal that accrued expenses consist of the following:

| Summary of Accrued Expenses ($ millions), December 31 | 2005 | 2004 |
| --- | --- | --- |
| Accrued advertising and promotion.......................... | $ 260.3 | $ 286.3 |
| Accrued salaries and wages .............................. | 377.1 | 389.6 |
| Other................................................... | 762.2 | 755.7 |
| Total .................................................. | $1,399.6 | $1,431.6 |

Footnotes reveal that the "other" includes accrued benefit costs from the company's pension plans.

The remaining items in current liabilities arise from common external transactions, such as trade accounts payable and taxes payable. These transactions are less prone to management reporting bias. We must, however, determine the presence of excessive "leaning on the trade" as a means to boost operating cash flow. K-C's trade accounts payable have increased as a percentage of total liabilities and equity from 5.8% ($983.2 million/$17,018.0 million) in 2004 to 6.5% ($1,055.5 million/ $16,303.2 million) in 2005. While this change is not drastic, and the level is not excessive, we need to monitor K-C's balance sheet for a continuation of this trend.

The possibility of management reporting bias is typically greater for accrued liabilities, which are often estimated (and difficult to audit), involve no external transaction, and can markedly impact reported balance sheet and income statement amounts. One of Kimberly-Clark's accrued liabilities involves promotions and rebates, estimated at $395.5 million ($235.3 million + $160.2 million) as of 2005. Following is the description of its accrual policy in this area:

**Promotion and Rebate Accruals**  Among those factors affecting the accruals for promotions are estimates of the number of consumer coupons that will be redeemed and the type and number of activities within promotional programs between the Corporation and its trade customers. Rebate accruals are based on estimates of the quantity of products distributors have sold to specific customers. Generally, the estimates for consumer coupon costs are based on historical patterns of coupon redemption, influenced by judgments about current market conditions such as competitive activity in specific product categories. Estimates of trade promotion liabilities for promotional program costs incurred, but unpaid, are generally based on estimates of the quantity of customer sales, timing of promotional activities and forecasted costs for activities within the promotional programs. Settlement of these liabilities sometimes occurs in periods subsequent to the date of the promotion activity. Trade promotion programs include introductory marketing funds such as slotting fees, cooperative marketing programs, temporary price reductions, favorable end of aisle or in-store product displays and other activities conducted by the customers to promote the Corporation's products. Promotion accruals as of December 31, 2005 and 2004 were $235.3 million and $263.3 million, respectively. Rebate accruals as of December 31, 2005 and 2004 were $160.2 million and $163.0 million, respectively.

The company also reports accruals relating to its insurance risks, obsolete inventories, and environmental risks as described in the following footnote:

**Retained Insurable Risks**  Selected insurable risks are retained, primarily those related to property damage, workers' compensation, and product, automobile and premises liability based upon historical loss patterns and management's judgment of cost effective risk retention. Accrued liabilities for incurred but not reported events, principally related to workers' compensation and automobile liability, are based upon loss development factors provided to the Corporation by external insurance brokers and are not discounted.

**Excess and Obsolete Inventory**  All excess, obsolete, damaged or off-quality inventories including raw materials, in-process, finished goods, and spare parts are required to be adequately reserved for or to be disposed of. This process requires an ongoing tracking of the aging of inventories to be reviewed in conjunction with current marketing plans to ensure that any excess or obsolete inventories are identified on a timely basis. This process also requires judgments be made about the salability of existing stock in relation to sales projections. The evaluation of the adequacy of provision for obsolete and excess inventories is performed on at least a quarterly basis. No provisions for future obsolescence, damage or off-quality inventories are made.

**Environmental Expenditures** Environmental expenditures related to current operations that qualify as property, plant, and equipment or which substantially increase the economic value or extend the useful life of an asset are capitalized, and all other such expenditures are expensed as incurred. Environmental expenditures that relate to an existing condition caused by past operations are expensed as incurred. Liabilities are recorded when environmental assessments and/or remedial efforts are probable and the costs can be reasonably estimated. Generally, the timing of these accruals coincides with completion of a feasibility study or a commitment to a formal plan of action. At environmental sites in which more than one potentially responsible party has been identified, a liability is recorded for the estimated allocable share of costs related to the Corporation's involvement with the site as well as an estimated allocable share of costs related to the involvement of insolvent or unidentified parties. At environmental sites in which the Corporation is the only responsible party, a liability for the total estimated costs of remediation is recorded. Liabilities for future expenditures for environmental remediation obligations are not discounted and do not reflect any anticipated recoveries from insurers.

All of these accruals have similar effects on the financial statements: when the accrual is established the company recognizes both an expense in the income statement and a liability on the balance sheet. The company subsequently reduces the liability as payments are made. Companies can (and do) use accruals to shift income from one period to another, say by over-accruing in one period to intentionally depress current period profits, and later reducing the liability account, rather than recording an expense, to increase future period profits. Accruals are sometimes referred to as "pads." They represent a cost that has previously been charged to the income statement. They also represent an account that can absorb future costs. We need to monitor accrual accounts carefully for evidence of earnings management.

## Long-Term Debt

Kimberly-Clark reports $2,661.9 million of long-term debt as of 2005. Footnotes reveal the following:

Long-term debt is composed of the following:

| ($ millions) | Weighted-Average Interest Rate | Maturities | December 31 | |
|---|---|---|---|---|
| | | | 2005 | 2004 |
| Notes and debentures . . . . . . . . . . . . . . . . . . . . . . . . . . . . . . | 5.78% | 2007–2038 | **$2,149.5** | $2,309.8 |
| Industrial development revenue bonds . . . . . . . . . . . . . . . . | 3.74% | 2006–2037 | **299.8** | 300.7 |
| Bank loans and other financing in various currencies . . . . . . | 8.97% | 2006–2031 | **212.6** | 272.9 |
| Total long-term debt. . . . . . . . . . . . . . . . . . . . . . . . . . . . . . | | | **2,661.9** | 2,883.4 |
| Less current portion . . . . . . . . . . . . . . . . . . . . . . . . . . . . . | | | **67.2** | 585.4 |
| Long-term portion . . . . . . . . . . . . . . . . . . . . . . . . . . . . . . . | | | **$2,594.7** | $2,298.0 |

Most of its long-term financing is in the form of notes and debentures, $2,149.5 million in 2005, which mature over the next 25 years. GAAP requires disclosure of scheduled maturities for each of the five years subsequent to the balance sheet date. Kimberly-Clark's five-year maturity schedule follows:

Scheduled maturities of long-term debt for the next five years are $67.2 million in 2006, $337.5 million in 2007, $49.1 million in 2008, $8.0 million in 2009 and $33.1 million in 2010.

Our concern with debt maturity dates is whether or not a company is able to repay debt as it comes due. Alternatively, a company can refinance the debt. If a company is unable or unwilling to repay or refinance its debt, it must approach creditors for a modification of debt terms for those issuances coming due. Creditors are often willing to oblige but will likely increase interest rates or impose additional debt covenants and restrictions. However, if creditors deny default waivers, the company might face the prospect of bankruptcy. This highlights the importance of long-term debt maturity disclosures.

We have little concern about Kimberly-Clark's debt maturity schedule as the company has strong cash flows. Still, it is worth noting that Standard & Poor's (S&P) lowered K-C's debt rating from AA to AA−. This rating is still strong (described as lower "high grade" debt), but lower nonetheless. Following is Kimberly-Clark's explanation of this downgrade disclosed in its 2003 10-K:

In July 2003, Standard & Poor's ("S&P") revised the Corporation's credit rating for long-term debt from AA to AA−. Moody's Investor Service maintained its short- and long-term ratings but changed the Corporation's outlook to negative from stable, indicating that a ratings downgrade could be possible within the next 12 months. These changes were primarily based on the Corporation's business performance in the heightened competitive environment and because S&P changed the way in which it evaluates liabilities for pensions and other postretirement benefits. Management believes that these actions will not have a material adverse effect on the Corporation's access to credit or its borrowing costs since these credit ratings remain strong and are in the top eight percent of companies listed in S&P's ranking of the 500 largest companies. The Corporation's commercial paper continues to be rated in the top category.

## Noncurrent Employee Benefit and Other Obligations

Kimberly-Clark reports a (negative) funded status of its pension plan of $(1,383.0) million at year-end 2005 (disclosed in footnotes). This means that the company's pension plans are underfunded by that amount. This underfunding is computed as the difference between the pension benefit obligation (PBO) of $5,509.2 million and the fair market value of the company's pension assets of $4,126.2 million (these amounts are also reported in the pension footnote not reproduced here).

The central issue with respect to pensions and other post-retirement obligations is the potential demand they present on operating cash flows. Companies can tap cash from two sources to pay pension and other post-retirement obligations: from the returns on plan assets (i.e., the cumulative contributions and investment returns that have not yet been paid out to beneficiaries) and/or from operating cash flow. To the extent that plan assets are insufficient to meet retirement obligations, companies must divert operating cash flows from other investment activities, potentially reducing the dollar amount of capital projects that can be funded.

We can gain insight into potential cash flow issues by comparing expected future benefit payments to the funds available to make those payments. Companies must provide these disclosures in a schedule to the pension footnotes. K-C provides the following schedule of expected payments in the footnotes to its 10-K:

**Estimated Future Benefit Payments**   The following benefit payments, which reflect expected future service, as appropriate, are anticipated to be paid:

| (Millions of dollars) | Pension Benefits | Other Benefits |
|---|---|---|
| 2006 | $ 317 | $ 84 |
| 2007 | 305 | 86 |
| 2008 | 308 | 87 |
| 2009 | 310 | 89 |
| 2010 | 315 | 92 |
| Years 2011–2015 | $1,719 | $485 |

The schedule shows that K-C expects to pay out $317 million in benefits to pension beneficiaries and $84 million in health care and other post-retirement benefits (OPEB) to its former employees in 2006. The schedule also reveals that the company expects these amounts to remain fairly constant over the next five years.

K-C also reports the following table relating to its pension and other post-retirement benefit plans' assets:

| Change in Plan Assets Year Ended December 31 (Millions of dollars) | Pension Benefits | | Other Benefits | |
|---|---|---|---|---|
| | 2005 | 2004 | 2005 | 2004 |
| Fair value of plan assets at beginning of year | $4,044.2 | $4,027.9 | — | — |
| Actual gain on plan assets | 359.5 | 332.8 | — | — |
| Employer contributions | 116.5 | 200.0 | 66.5 | 59.4 |
| Currency and other | (97.2) | 103.1 | 8.5 | 8.4 |
| Benefit payments | (296.8) | (296.3) | (75.0) | (67.8) |
| Spin-off Neenah Paper | — | (323.3) | — | — |
| Fair value of plan assets at end of year | $4,126.2 | $4,044.2 | — | — |

In 2005, K-C contributed $116.5 million to its pension plan. That amount, when combined with investment returns of $359.5 million, was more than sufficient to cover 2005 benefit payments of $296.8 million (K-C expects this amount to be $317 million in 2006). Should pension assets decline markedly as a result of severe underfunding or investment losses, K-C will need to divert operating cash flows from other investment activities into pension contributions, or to borrow funds to meet its pension obligations. Although K-C's pension obligations are under-funded (as represented by the negative funded status), its current contribution levels and investment returns are sufficient to meet its anticipated pension obligations, at least in the near future.

Other post-retirement benefit obligations (future health care payments) present a different picture. Because federal law does not require minimum funding of these plans, and companies do not receive a tax deduction for such contributions, companies rarely fund OPEB plans. All of the OPEB payments to beneficiaries, therefore, must be funded by concurrent company contributions. These payments amounted to $75 million in 2005. Given K-C's $2.3 billion in operating cash flow for 2005, the $75 million cash requirement is not material. However, OPEB funding requirements have been a burden for many companies, most notably General-Motors (see Business Insight in Module 10).

## Deferred Income Taxes

Kimberly-Clark reports a net noncurrent deferred tax liability of $572.9 million at year-end 2005. Footnote disclosures reveal this amount consists of the following ($ millions):

| Year Ended December 31 (Millions of dollars) | 2005 | 2004 |
|---|---|---|
| Net noncurrent deferred income tax liability attributable to: | | |
| Accumulated depreciation | $(1,103.1) | $(1,312.7) |
| Pension, postretirement and other employee benefits | 548.1 | 521.9 |
| Foreign tax credits and loss carryforwards | 484.1 | 160.1 |
| Installment sales | (192.0) | (188.1) |
| Other | (70.2) | 3.8 |
| Valuation allowances | (239.8) | (25.3) |
| Net noncurrent deferred income tax liability | $ (572.9) | $ (840.3) |

Most of the noncurrent deferred tax liability ($1,103.1 million) arises from K-C's use of straight-line depreciation for GAAP reporting and accelerated depreciation for tax reporting. As a result, tax depreciation expense is higher in the early years of the assets' lives. This will reverse in later years for individual assets, resulting in higher taxable income and tax liability. The deferred tax liability account reflects this future expected tax.

Although depreciation expense for an individual asset declines over time, thus increasing taxable income and tax liability, if K-C adds new assets at a sufficient rate, the additional first-year depreciation on those assets will more than offset the reduction of depreciation expense on older assets, resulting in a long-term reduction of tax liability. That is, the deferred tax liability is unlikely to reverse in the aggregate. For this reason, many analysts treat the deferred tax liability as a "quasi-equity" account.

Still, while deferred taxes can be postponed, they cannot be eliminated. If the company's asset growth slows markedly, it will realize higher taxable income and tax liability. We need to be mindful of the potential for a "real" tax liability (requiring cash payment) when companies begin to downsize.

K-C also reports a long-term deferred tax asset valuation allowance of $239.8 million for 2005, an increase of $214.5 million over the prior year. This valuation allowance is related to deferred tax assets that arise from the company's tax loss carry-forwards. The valuation allowance indicates that the company does not expect to fully realize tax loss carry-forwards before their scheduled expiration. Changes in the deferred tax asset valuation allowance impact tax expense, and, thus, net income, dollar for dollar. K-C's net income (and net operating income after tax or NOPAT) was, reduced by $214.5 million in 2005 as a result of the increase in this valuation allowance. This increased tax expense more than likely offset a reduction of tax expense when the loss carryforwards were recorded, leaving net income unaffected in this year. In future years, we need to be aware that profit can increase if and when the allowance account is reversed with no offsetting expense.

## Minority Owner's Interests in Subsidiaries

K-C's reports $394.5 million for the equity interests of minority shareholders in subsidiaries. Minority interests are shareholder claims against the net assets and cash flows of the company (after all senior claims are settled). Consequently, we treat minority interest as a component of stockholders' equity (a current FASB proposal will result in formal classification of minority interest liability as a component of stockholders' equity).

## Preferred Securities of Subsidiary

The preferred securities represent the sale of preferred stock by a subsidiary of Kimberly-Clark to outside interests. This account is treated like all other contributed capital accounts.

## Stockholders' Equity

Kimberly-Clark reports the following statement of stockholders' equity for 2005:

| (Dollars in millions, shares in thousands) | Common Stock Issued Shares | Amount | Additional Paid-in Capital | Treasury Stock Shares | Amount | Unearned Compensation on Restricted Stock | Retained Earnings | Accumulated Other Comprehensive Income (Loss) | Comprehensive Income |
|---|---|---|---|---|---|---|---|---|---|
| Balance at Dec. 31, 2004..... | 568,597 | $710.8 | $348.6 | 85,694 | $(5,047.5) | $(22.3) | $11,865.9 | $(1,226.0) | |
| Net income......... | — | — | — | — | — | — | 1,568.3 | — | $1,568.3 |
| Other comprehensive income: | | | | | | | | | |
| Unrealized translation loss.... | — | — | — | — | — | — | — | (412.6) | (412.6) |
| Minimum pension liability .......... | — | — | — | — | — | — | — | (58.6) | (58.6) |
| Other........... | — | — | — | — | — | — | — | 27.8 | 27.8 |
| Total comprehensive income.......... | | | | | | | | | $1,124.9 |
| Options exercised and other awards.......... | — | — | (39.2) | (3,040) | 181.9 | — | — | — | |
| Option and restricted share income tax benefits ......... | — | — | 15.1 | — | — | — | — | — | |
| Shares repurchased.. | — | — | — | 24,463 | (1,511.2) | — | — | — | |
| Net issuance of restricted stock, less amortization .. | — | — | 0.1 | (9) | 0.7 | 9.2 | — | — | |
| Dividends declared... | — | — | — | — | — | — | (852.8) | — | |
| Balance at Dec. 31, 2005..... | 568,597 | $710.8 | $324.6 | 107,108 | $(6,376.1) | $(13.1) | $12,581.4 | $(1,669.4) | |

K-C has issued 568.597 million shares of its $1.25 par value common stock. The common stock account is, therefore, equal to $710.746 million (rounded to $710.8 million), computed as 568,597 million shares × $1.25. The additional paid-in capital (APIC) represents the excess of proceeds from stock issuance over par value. It also includes three other components for 2005: (1) the difference between the cash K-C received per share of treasury stock and its original purchase cost is added or deducted from APIC; in this case APIC was reduced by $39.2 million when K-C issued shares to option holders and other employees and the cash received was less than the cost of the shares issued, and (2) the tax benefits received by K-C relating to the value of stock options exercised by employees is reported as an increase in APIC; it is not reflected as a component of net income, and (3) APIC is increased by $0.1 million related to the issuance of restricted stock (see below).

Kimberly-Clark's stockholders' equity is reduced by $6,376.1 million relating to repurchases of common stock, less the reissuance of those securities. These treasury shares are the result of a stock purchase plan approved by K-C's board of directors, and evidences K-C's conviction that its stock is undervalued by the marketplace. The repurchased shares are held in treasury and reduce stockholders' equity by the purchase price until such time as they are reissued, perhaps to fund an acquisition or to compensate employees under a stock purchase or stock option plan (treasury shares can also be retired).

K-C compensates employees via restricted stock in addition to other forms of compensation. Under its restricted stock plan, eligible employees are issued stock, which is restricted as to sale until fully vested (owned). When issued, the market value of the restricted stock is deducted from stockholders' equity. As the employees gain ownership of the shares (that is, the restricted stock vests), a portion of this account is transferred to the income statement as compensation expense. The consequent reduction in retained earnings offsets the reduction (and increase in equity) of the restricted stock account. Stockholders' equity is, therefore, unaffected in total, although its components change.

Retained earnings reflect a $1,568.3 million increase relating to net income and a $852.8 million decrease from declaration of dividends. Accumulated other comprehensive income (AOCI), which is often aggregated with retained earnings for analysis purposes, began 2005 with a balance of $(1,226.0) million; this negative balance reduces stockholders' equity. During the period, this AOCI account was further reduced by $412.6 million relating to the decrease in the $US value of net assets of foreign subsidiaries. This decrease in net asset value resulted from a strengthened $US vis-à-vis other currencies in which the company conducts its operations in 2005. In addition, the AOCI account was reduced by $58.6 million relating to the recognition of a minimum pension liability and increased (made less negative) by $27.8 million for activities designated as "other." Finally, K-C's comprehensive income equals net income plus (minus) the components of other comprehensive income.

## Common-Size Balance Sheet

Similar to our analysis of the income statement, it is useful to compute common-size balance sheets. Such statements can reveal changes or relations masked by other analyses. Kimberly-Clark's common-size balance sheet covering its recent two years is shown in Exhibit 13.4.

K-C is somewhat less liquid in 2005 than in 2004 as evidenced by the decreased level of cash to 2.23% of total assets in 2005 from 3.49% in 2004. (Later in the module the statement of cash flows reveals that this is the result of reduced profitability and the repurchase of common stock.) Aside from receivables and inventories, which both increased by approximately one percentage point, the remaining assets and liabilities exhibit little variation from the prior year. There is a marked increase in retained earnings, from 69.73% of assets to 77.17%, but it is more than offset by the increase in treasury stock as K-C continues to draw on its operating cash flow to repurchase its common stock. At year-end 2005, stockholders provide 34.09% of its total capital, down from 38.96% in 2004.

## Off-Balance-Sheet Reporting and Analysis

There are numerous assets and liabilities that do not appear on the balance sheet. Some are excluded because managers and accounting professionals only report what they can reliably measure. Others are excluded because of the rigidity of accounting standards. Following are some areas we might consider in our evaluation and adjustment of the Kimberly-Clark balance sheet.

### Internally Developed Intangible Assets

Many brands and their corresponding values are excluded from the balance sheet. For example, consider the brand "Kleenex." Many individuals actually refer to facial tissues as Kleenex-that is successful branding! So, is the Kleenex brand reported and valued on Kimberly-Clark's balance sheet? No. That brand value cannot be reliably measured and, hence, is not included on K-C's balance sheet.

Likewise, other valuable assets are excluded from the company's balance sheet. Examples are the value of a competent management team, high employee morale, innovative production know-how, a superior supply chain, customer satisfaction, and a host of other assets.

R&D activities often create internally generated intangible assets that are mostly excluded from the balance sheet. Footnotes reveal that Kimberly-Clark spends over $319.5 million (2% of sales) on R&D to remain competitive—and, this is for an admittedly non-high-tech company. Further, K-C reveals that it spends $451 million (nearly 3% of sales) on advertising. Both R&D and advertising costs are expensed under GAAP as opposed to being capitalized on the balance sheet as tangible assets. These unrecognized intangible assets often represent a substantial part of a company's market value.

| EXHIBIT 13.4 | Kimberly-Clark Common-Size Balance Sheet | | |
|---|---|---|---|
| **December 31** | | **2005** | **2004** |
| **Assets** | | | |
| Current assets | | | |
| Cash and cash equivalents . . . . . . . . . . . . . . . . . . . . . . . . . . . . . . . . . . . . . . . . | | 2.23% | 3.49% |
| Accounts receivable, net . . . . . . . . . . . . . . . . . . . . . . . . . . . . . . . . . . . . . . . . . | | 12.89 | 11.98 |
| Inventories . . . . . . . . . . . . . . . . . . . . . . . . . . . . . . . . . . . . . . . . . . . . . . . . . . . . | | 10.75 | 9.82 |
| Deferred income taxes . . . . . . . . . . . . . . . . . . . . . . . . . . . . . . . . . . . . . . . . . . . | | 1.37 | 1.63 |
| Other current assets . . . . . . . . . . . . . . . . . . . . . . . . . . . . . . . . . . . . . . . . . . . . | | 2.10 | 2.24 |
| Total current assets . . . . . . . . . . . . . . . . . . . . . . . . . . . . . . . . . . . . . . . . . . . . | | 29.34 | 29.16 |
| Property, plant and equipment, net . . . . . . . . . . . . . . . . . . . . . . . . . . . . . . . . . . | | 45.97 | 46.95 |
| Investments in equity companies . . . . . . . . . . . . . . . . . . . . . . . . . . . . . . . . . . . | | 2.81 | 2.61 |
| Goodwill . . . . . . . . . . . . . . . . . . . . . . . . . . . . . . . . . . . . . . . . . . . . . . . . . . . . . . | | 16.47 | 15.88 |
| Other assets . . . . . . . . . . . . . . . . . . . . . . . . . . . . . . . . . . . . . . . . . . . . . . . . . . | | 5.41 | 5.40 |
| Total assets . . . . . . . . . . . . . . . . . . . . . . . . . . . . . . . . . . . . . . . . . . . . . . . . . . . | | 100.00% | 100.00% |
| **Liabilities and stockholders' equity** | | | |
| Current liabilities | | | |
| Debt payable within one year . . . . . . . . . . . . . . . . . . . . . . . . . . . . . . . . . . . . . | | 7.50% | 7.14% |
| Trade accounts payable . . . . . . . . . . . . . . . . . . . . . . . . . . . . . . . . . . . . . . . . . | | 6.47 | 5.78 |
| Other payables . . . . . . . . . . . . . . . . . . . . . . . . . . . . . . . . . . . . . . . . . . . . . . . . | | 1.83 | 1.56 |
| Accrued expenses . . . . . . . . . . . . . . . . . . . . . . . . . . . . . . . . . . . . . . . . . . . . . | | 8.58 | 8.41 |
| Accrued income taxes . . . . . . . . . . . . . . . . . . . . . . . . . . . . . . . . . . . . . . . . . . | | 2.81 | 2.63 |
| Dividends payable . . . . . . . . . . . . . . . . . . . . . . . . . . . . . . . . . . . . . . . . . . . . . | | 1.28 | 1.14 |
| Total current liabilities . . . . . . . . . . . . . . . . . . . . . . . . . . . . . . . . . . . . . . . . . . | | 28.48 | 26.66 |
| Long-term debt . . . . . . . . . . . . . . . . . . . . . . . . . . . . . . . . . . . . . . . . . . . . . . . . | | 15.92 | 13.50 |
| Noncurrent employee benefit and other obligations . . . . . . . . . . . . . . . . . . . . . . | | 10.93 | 9.53 |
| Deferred income taxes . . . . . . . . . . . . . . . . . . . . . . . . . . . . . . . . . . . . . . . . . . | | 3.51 | 4.94 |
| Minority owners interests in subsidiaries . . . . . . . . . . . . . . . . . . . . . . . . . . . . . | | 2.42 | 2.16 |
| Preferred securities of subsidiary . . . . . . . . . . . . . . . . . . . . . . . . . . . . . . . . . . | | 4.65 | 4.25 |
| Stockholders equity | | | |
| Preferred stock—no par value—authorized 20.0 million shares, none issued . . . . | | 0.00 | 0.00 |
| Common stock—$1.25 par value—authorized 1.2 billion shares; issued | | | |
| 568.6 million shares at December 31, 2005 and 2004 . . . . . . . . . . . . . . . . . . . | | 4.36 | 4.18 |
| Additional paid-in capital . . . . . . . . . . . . . . . . . . . . . . . . . . . . . . . . . . . . . . . . | | 1.99 | 2.05 |
| Common stock held in treasury, at cost—107.1 million and 85.7 million | | | |
| shares at December 31, 2005 and 2004 . . . . . . . . . . . . . . . . . . . . . . . . . . . . | | (39.11) | (29.66) |
| Accumulated other comprehensive income (loss) . . . . . . . . . . . . . . . . . . . . . . . | | (10.24) | (7.20) |
| Retained earnings . . . . . . . . . . . . . . . . . . . . . . . . . . . . . . . . . . . . . . . . . . . . . | | 77.17 | 69.73 |
| Unearned compensation on restricted stock . . . . . . . . . . . . . . . . . . . . . . . . . . . | | (0.08) | (0.13) |
| Total stockholders' equity . . . . . . . . . . . . . . . . . . . . . . . . . . . . . . . . . . . . . . . | | 34.09 | 38.96 |
| Total liabilities and stockholders' equity . . . . . . . . . . . . . . . . . . . . . . . . . . . . . | | 100.00% | 100.00% |

Note: All percentages are computed by dividing each balance sheet line item by that year's total assets.

## Equity Method Investments

Kimberly-Clark reports equity investments of $457.8 million at year-end 2005. These are unconsolidated affiliates over which K-C can exert significant influence (but not control) and, hence, are accounted for using the equity method. The amount reported on the balance sheet represents the initial cost of the investment, plus (minus) the percentage share of investee earnings and losses, and minus any cash dividends received. Consequently, the investment balance equals the percentage owned of the affiliates' stockholders' equity (plus any unamortized excess purchase price).

Footnotes reveal that, in sum, these K-C affiliates have total assets of $1,861.8 million, liabilities of $1,078.0 million, and stockholders' equity of $783.8 million. K-C's reported investment balance of $457.8 in the balance sheet does not reveal the extent of the investment (assets) required to manage these companies, nor the level of potential liability exposure. For instance, if one of these affiliates falters financially, K-C might have to invest additional cash to support it rather than let it fail. Failure of an important affiliate might affect K-C's ability to finance another such venture in the future.

These investments are reported at cost, not at fair market value as are passive investments. This means that unrecognized gains and losses can be buried in such investment accounts. For example, K-C footnotes reveal the following:

> Kimberly-Clark de Mexico, S.A. de C.V. is partially owned by the public and its stock is publicly traded in Mexico. At December 31, 2005, the Corporation's investment in this equity company was $396.3 million, and the estimated fair value of the investment was $2.0 billion based on the market price of publicly traded shares.

Thus, for at least one of its investments, there is an unrecognized gain of $1,603.7 million.

## Operating Leases

Kimberly-Clark has leases classified as "operating" for financial reporting purposes. As a result, neither the lease asset nor the lease obligation are reported on its balance sheet. For example, K-C reports the following disclosure relating to its operating leases:

> The Corporation has entered into operating leases for certain warehouse facilities, automobiles and equipment. The future minimum obligations under operating leases having a noncancelable term in excess of one year as of December 31, 2005, are as follows:

| Year Ending December 31 (Millions of dollars): | Amount |
|---|---|
| 2006 | $ 85.7 |
| 2007 | 47.4 |
| 2008 | 34.1 |
| 2009 | 26.4 |
| 2010 | 17.1 |
| Thereafter | 47.0 |
| Future minimum obligations | $257.7 |

These leases represent an unreported asset and an unreported liability; both amounting to $220 million. This amount is computed as follows and assumes a 6% discount rate ($ millions):

| Year | Operating Lease Payment | Discount Factor (i = 0.06) | Present Value |
|---|---|---|---|
| 1 | $86 | 0.94340 | $ 81 |
| 2 | 47 | 0.89000 | 42 |
| 3 | 34 | 0.83962 | 29 |
| 4 | 26 | 0.79209 | 21 |
| 5 | 17 | 0.74726 | 13 |
| >5 | 47  [$17 for ~3 years] | 2.67301* × 0.74726 | 34** |
| | | | $220 |

Remaining life = $47/$17 = 2.749 years rounded to 3 years

*The annuity factor for 3 years at 6% is 2.67301.

**2.67301 × 0.74726 × $17 = $34.

The classification of leases as operating for financial reporting purposes often involves a rigid application of accounting rules that depend solely on the structure of the lease. A large amount of assets and liabilities is excluded from many companies' balance sheets because leases are structured as operating leases. For K-C, these excluded assets amount to $220 million. The valuation of K-C common stock (shown later) uses net operating assets (NOA) as one of its inputs. Our adjustment to the K-C balance sheet, then, would entail the addition of these assets to NOA and the inclusion of $220 million in *non*operating liabilities.

## Pensions

Kimberly-Clark's pension plan is underfunded as described earlier in the module. Total pension obligations amount to $5,509.2 million and pension assets have a market value of $4,126.2 million at year-end

2005. Neither of these amounts appears on the balance sheet, but are reported in the footnotes. In fact, neither does the $1,383.0 million ($5,509.2 million − $4,126.2 million) shortfall because in 2005 GAAP permitted the deferment (nonrecognition) of $1,018.4 million of increased pension liabilities resulting from the reduction in the discount rate in 2005 and the consequent increase in the present value of the pension obligation.

In 2006, the Financial Accounting Standards Board amended the pension accounting standard. Companies now must recognize the funded status on the face of the balance sheet with no deferral (off-balance sheet recognition). Under the new standard, K-C would have recognized a liability of $1,383.0 (the negative funded status), resulting in an increase in liabilities of $364.6 million and a reduction of pension-related assets of $442.3 million, with a consequent reduction in stockholders' equity (AOCI) of $806.9 million. These adjustments affect only the balance sheet and not the income statement.

## Variable Interest Entities

Footnotes reveal that Kimberly-Clark has two categories of special purpose entities (SPEs) that have been classified as variable interest entities (VIEs). The first relates to two entities that the company established to securitize (sell) $617 million of notes receivable relating to asset sales. K-C sold the notes to the VIEs, which financed the purchase with debt sold to the public. K-C maintains an equity interest in these entities, but their voting control rests with an independent party (bank) that provides credit guarantees for a fee. The bank is deemed to be the primary beneficiary for financial reporting purposes. As a result, K-C can continue to account for the investment under the equity method and is not required to consolidate the VIE.

The second entity is a synthetic fuel partnership in which K-C has a 49.5% interest. This partnership provides tax credits to K-C, amounting to $234.3 million in 2005 (from its 10-K footnote 12). Since K-C is not the primary beneficiary of the partnership's cash flows, it is not required to consolidate its financial statements as of 2005. K-C asserts that consolidation, if required, will not have a material effect on its consolidated financial statements. As a result, it does not provide detailed disclosures of the financial statements of the VIE.

## Derivatives

Kimberly-Clark is exposed to a number of market risks as outlined in the following footnote to its 10-K:

> As a multinational enterprise, the Corporation is exposed to risks such as changes in foreign currency exchange rates, interest rates and commodity prices. The Corporation employs a variety of practices to manage these risks, including operating and financing activities and, where deemed appropriate, the use of derivative instruments. These derivative instruments, including some that are not designated as either fair value or cash flow hedges, are used only for risk management purposes and not for speculation or trading. Foreign currency derivative instruments are either exchange traded or are entered into with major financial institutions. The Corporation's credit exposure under these arrangements is limited to those agreements with a positive fair value at the reporting date. Credit risk with respect to the counterparties is considered minimal in view of the financial strength of the counterparties.

The company hedges these risks using derivatives, including forwards, options, and swap contracts. This hedging process transfers risk from K-C to another entity (called the counterparty), which assumes that risk for a fee.

The accounting for derivatives is summarized in an appendix to Module 7. In brief, the derivative contracts, and the assets or liabilities to which they relate, are reported on the balance sheet at fair market value. Any unrealized gains and losses are ultimately reflected in net income, although they can be accumulated in AOICI for a short time. To the extent that a company's hedging activities are effective, the market values of the derivatives and the assets or liabilities to which they relate are largely offsetting, as are the net gains or losses on the hedging activities. As a result, the effect of derivative activities is generally minimal on both income and equity.[2]

---

[2] It is generally only when companies use derivatives for speculative purposes that these investments markedly affect income and equity. The aim of the derivatives standard was to highlight these speculative activities and we need to read risk footnotes carefully to assess whether companies are hedging or speculating with derivatives.

# Statement of Cash Flows Reporting and Analysis

The statement of cash flows for Kimberly-Clark is shown in Exhibit 13.5.

| EXHIBIT 13.5 | Kimberly-Clark Statement of Cash Flows | | |
|---|---|---|---|

**KIMBERLY-CLARK CORPORATION AND SUBSIDIARIES**
**Consolidated Cash Flow Statement**

| Year Ended December 31 (Millions of dollars) | 2005 | 2004 | 2003 |
|---|---|---|---|
| **Operating Activities** | | | |
| Income from continuing operations | $1,580.6 | $1,770.4 | $ 1,643.6 |
| Depreciation and amortization | 844.5 | 800.3 | 745.3 |
| Asset impairments | 80.1 | — | — |
| Deferred income taxes | (142.7) | (19.4) | (50.8) |
| Net losses on asset dispositions | 45.8 | 45.5 | 35.0 |
| Equity companies' earnings in excess of dividends paid | (23.8) | (30.1) | (9.6) |
| Minority owners' share of subsidiaries' net income | 86.5 | 73.9 | 55.6 |
| (Increase) decrease in operating working capital | (156.0) | 103.6 | 111.8 |
| Postretirement benefits | 40.9 | (54.4) | (59.9) |
| Other | (44.1) | 36.4 | 81.2 |
| Cash provided by operations | 2,311.8 | 2,726.2 | 2,552.2 |
| **Investing Activities** | | | |
| Capital spending | (709.6) | (535.0) | (872.9) |
| Acquisitions of businesses, net of cash acquired | (17.4) | — | (258.5) |
| Investments in marketable securities | (2.0) | (11.5) | (10.8) |
| Proceeds from sales of investments | 27.3 | 38.0 | 29.4 |
| Net decrease (increase) in time deposits | 75.5 | (22.9) | (149.0) |
| Proceeds from dispositions of property | 46.8 | 30.7 | 7.6 |
| Other | (16.8) | 5.3 | (5.9) |
| Cash used for investing | (596.2) | (495.4) | (1,260.1) |
| **Financing Activities** | | | |
| Cash dividends paid | (838.4) | (767.9) | (671.9) |
| Net increase (decrease) in short-term debt | 524.3 | (54.7) | 424.2 |
| Proceeds from issuance of long-term debt | 397.7 | 38.7 | 540.8 |
| Repayments of long-term debt | (599.7) | (199.0) | (481.6) |
| Issuance of preferred securities of subsidiary | — | 125.0 | — |
| Proceeds from exercise of stock options | 142.7 | 290.0 | 31.0 |
| Acquisitions of common stock for the treasury | (1,519.5) | (1,598.0) | (546.7) |
| Other | (36.8) | (9.0) | (18.3) |
| Cash used for financing | (1,929.7) | (2,174.9) | (1,570.9) |
| Effect of exchange rate changes on cash and cash equivalents | (15.9) | 4.1 | 18.6 |
| Cash (used for) provided by continuing operations | (230.0) | 60.0 | (260.2) |
| **Discontinued operations** | | | |
| Cash provided by discontinued operations | — | 30.0 | 56.3 |
| Cash payment from Neenah Paper,Inc. | — | 213.4 | — |
| Cash provided by discontinued operations | — | 243.4 | 56.3 |
| (Decrease) increase in cash and cash equivalents | (203.0) | 303.4 | (203.9) |
| Cash and cash equivalents, beginning of year | 594.0 | 290.6 | 494.5 |
| Cash and cash equivalents, end of year | $ 364.0 | $ 594.0 | $ 290.6 |

In 2005, K-C generated $2,311.8 million of operating cash flow, primarily from income (net income plus the depreciation add-back amounts to $2,425.1 million). This amount is well in excess of K-C's capital expenditures and business acquisitions of $727.0 million ($709.6 million + $17.4 million). K-C used this excess cash to pay dividends to shareholders ($838.4 million), and to repurchase stock ($1,519.5 million).

Kimberly-Clark offers the following commentary regarding its 2005 operating cash flow:

Cash provided by operations decreased $414.4 million, or 15.2 percent, primarily due to an increased investment in working capital and higher income tax payments, partially offset by lower cash contributions to the U.S. defined benefit pension plan.

Overall, the cash flow picture for Kimberly-Clark is strong: operating cash flows are more than sufficient to cover capital expenditures and acquisitions, leaving excess cash that is being returned to the shareholders in the form of dividends and share repurchases. The strength of its operating cash flows mitigates any concerns we might have regarding its relative lack of liquidity on the balance sheet.

## Independent Audit Opinion

Kimberly-Clark is subject to various audit requirements. Its independent auditor is Deloitte & Touche LLP, which issued the following clean opinion on K-C's 2005 financial statements:

---

### REPORT OF INDEPENDENT REGISTERED PUBLIC ACCOUNTING FIRM

To the Board of Directors and Stockholders of Kimberly-Clark Corporation:

We have audited the accompanying consolidated balance sheets of Kimberly-Clark Corporation and subsidiaries as of December 31, 2005 and 2004, and the related consolidated statements of income, stockholders' equity, and cash flows for each of the three years in the period ended December 31, 2005. Our audits also included the financial statement schedule listed in the Index at Item 15. These financial statements and financial statement schedule are the responsibility of the Corporation's management. Our responsibility is to express an opinion on the financial statements and the financial statement schedule based on our audits.

We conducted our audits in accordance with standards of the Public Company Accounting Oversight Board (United States). Those standards require that we plan and perform the audit to obtain reasonable assurance about whether the financial statements are free of material misstatement. An audit includes examining, on a test basis, evidence supporting the amounts and disclosures in the financial statements. An audit includes examining, on a test basis, evidence supporting the amounts and disclosures in the financial statements. An audit also includes assessing the accounting principles used and significant estimates made by management, as well as evaluating the overall financial statement presentation. We believe that our audits provide a reasonable basis for our opinion.

In our opinion, such consolidated financial statements present fairly, in all material respects, the financial position of Kimberly-Clark Corporation and subsidiaries at December 31, 2005 and 2004, and the results of their operations and their cash flows for each of the three years in the period ended December 31, 2005, in conformity with accounting principles generally accepted in the United States of America. Also, in our opinion, the financial statement schedule, when considered in relation to the basic consolidated financial statements taken as a whole, presents fairly, in all material respects, the information set forth therein.

As discussed in Note 1 to the consolidated financial statements, on December 31, 2005, the Corporation changed its method of determining conditional asset retirement obligations.

We have also audited, in accordance with the standards of the Public Company Accounting Oversight Board (United States), the effectiveness of the Corporation's internal control over financial reporting as of December 31, 2005, based on the criteria established in *Internal Control-Integrated Framework* issued by the Committee of Sponsoring Organizations of the Treadway Commission and our report dated February 21, 2006 expressed an unqualified opinion on management's assessment of the effectiveness of the Corporation's internal control over financial reporting and an unqualified opinion on the effectiveness of the Corporation's internal control over financial reporting.

Deloitte & Touche LLP

---

Although this report is a routine disclosure, it should not be taken for granted. Exceptions to a clean audit report must be scrutinized. Also, any disagreements between management and the independent auditor must be documented in an SEC filing. If this occurs, it is a "red flag" that must be investigated. Management activities and reports that cannot meet usual audit standards raise serious concerns about integrity and credibility. At a minimum, the riskiness of investments and relationships with such a company markedly increases.

# ASSESSING PROFITABILITY AND CREDITWORTHINESS

**L02** Assess company profitability and creditworthiness.

This section reports a profitability analysis of Kimberly-Clark. We begin by computing several key measures that are used in the ROE disaggregation, which is the overriding focus of this section. The ROE disaggregation process is defined in Module 4, and a listing of the ratio acronyms and definitions is in the review section at the end of the book.)

K-C's 2005 net operating profit after-tax (NOPAT) is $1,949.9 million, computed as $2,310.6 million + $136.6 million − ($438.4 million + [($190.2 million − $27.5 million) × 36.2%]), where 36.2% is the combined federal and state statutory income tax rate as disclosed in its tax footnote. In 2005, K-C's net operating assets (NOA) are $10,735.9 million, computed as $(16,303.2 −1,055.5 − 298.8 − 1,399.6 − 457.9 − 1,782.6 − 572.9) million.

## ROE Disaggregation

Our first step is to compute the ROE and, then, disaggregate it into its operating (return on net operating assets or RNOA) and nonoperating components. Using the computations in the previous section, the 2005 disaggregation analysis of ROE for Kimberly-Clark follows:[3]

$$\textbf{ROE} = \textbf{RNOA} + \textbf{Nonoperating return}$$
$$\textbf{25.74\%} = \textbf{17.60\%} + \textbf{8.14\%}$$

where

**ROE = $1,568.3 million/[($5,558.2 million + $6,629.5 million)/2]**

**RNOA = $1,949.9 million/[($10,735.9 million + $11,427.7 million)/2]**

RNOA accounts for 68% (17.60%/25.74%) of K-C's ROE. K-C successfully uses its nonoperating activities to increase its 17.60% RNOA to a 25.74% ROE.

## Disaggregation of RNOA—Margin and Turnover

The next level analysis of ROE focuses on RNOA disaggregation. Kimberly-Clark's net operating profit margin (NOPM) and net operating asset turnover (NOAT) are as follows:

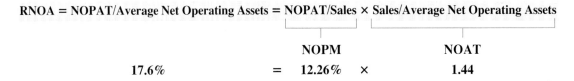

| | | NOPM | | NOAT |
|---|---|---|---|---|
| 17.6% | = | 12.26% | × | 1.44 |

where

**NOPM = $1,949.9 million/$15,902.6 million**

**NOAT = $15,902.6 million/([$10,735.9 million + $11,427.7 million]/2)**

Kimberly-Clark's RNOA of 17.6% consists of a net operating profit margin of 12.26% and a net operating asset turnover of 1.44 times.

## Disaggregation of Margin and Turnover

This section focuses on the disaggregation of profit margin and asset turnover to better understand the drivers of RNOA. Again, understanding the drivers of financial performance (RNOA) is key to predicting

---

[3] Many of these ratios require computation of averages, such as average assets. If we wanted to compute ratios for years prior to 2005, then we would obtain information from prior 10-Ks to compute the necessary averages for these ratios.

future company performance. Our analysis of the drivers of operating profit margin and asset turnover for Kimberly-Clark follows:

**Disaggregation of NOPM**

Gross profit margin (GPM) ($5,075.2 mil./$15,902.6 mil.) ..................................... 31.9%

Marketing, research and general expense margin [($2,737.4 mil)/$15,902.6 mil] ................... 17.2%

**Disaggregation of NOAT**

Accounts receivable turnover (ART) { $15,902.6 mil./[($2,101.9 mil. + $2,038.3 mil.)/2]} .............. 7.68

Inventory turnover (INVT) { $10,827.4 mil./[($1,752.1 mil. + $1,670.9 mil.)/2]} ..................... 6.33

Long-term operating asset turnover (LTOAT) { $15,902.6 mil./[($11,520.1 mil. + $12,056.1 mil.)/2]} ..... 1.35

Accounts payable turnover (APT) {$10,827.4 mil./[($1,055.5 mil. + $983.2 mil.)/2]} ................ 10.62

**Related turnover measures**

Average collection period [$2,101.9 mil./($15,902.6 mil./365)] ............................ 48.24 days

Average inventory days outstanding [$1,752.1 mil./($10,827.4 mil./365)] .................... 59.06 days

Average payable days outstanding [$1,055.5 mil./($10,827.4 mil./365)] ..................... 35.58 days

First, let's look at the disaggregation of NOPM. K-C reports a gross profit margin of 31.9%. A schedule to its 2005 10-K indicates that this important measure has declined by 2 percentage points in the past four years, a marked decline. K-C provides the following explanation in its MD&A:

> **Competitive Environment**  The Corporation experiences intense competition for sales of its principal products in its major markets, both domestically and internationally. The Corporation's products compete with widely advertised, well-known, branded products, as well as private label products, which are typically sold at lower prices. The Corporation has several major competitors in most of its markets, some of which are larger and more diversified than the Corporation.

Declines in gross profit margin are usually countered with reductions in operating expenses to maintain a company's operating profit margin. K-C's marketing, research, and general expenses for 2005 increased by $228.6 million as a result of the company's restructuring efforts. Absent these additional costs, marketing, research and general expense would have been 15.8% of sales, compared with 16.7% and 16.8% of sales in the previous two years, respectively. The company appears to be focusing on future cost reduction (obtained via current restructuring charges) as a way to remain competitive.

Bottom line, K-C's NOPM has not fully reflected the intense competitive environment of its markets because of the decline in its effective tax rate over the past three years. This tax rate decline is mainly due to its synthetic fuel partnership. Although a laudable activity, we prefer to see cost reductions from improvements in operating activities. In addition, tax benefits are often transitory.

Next, we consider the disaggregation of NOAT. K-C's receivables turnover rate of 7.68 times corresponds to an average collection period of 48.2 days, which is reasonable considering normal credit terms. However, the more important issue here is asset productivity (turnover) instead of credit quality. This is because most of K-C's sales are to large retailers; for example, 13% of Kimberly-Clark's sales are to Wal-Mart.

Inventories turn over 6.33 times a year, resulting in an average inventory days outstanding of 59.1 days in 2005. Inventories are an important (and large) asset for companies like Kimberly-Clark. Improved turnover is always a goal so long as the company maintains sufficient inventories to meet market demand.

K-C's long-term operating assets are turning over 1.35 times a year, which is about average for publicly traded companies. The issue with respect to LTOAT is throughput, and K-C does not discuss this aspect of its business in its financial filings.

K-C's trade accounts payable turnover is 10.62, resulting in an average payable days outstanding of 35.6 days. Since payables represent a low cost source of financing, we would prefer to see its days payable lengthened so long as K-C is not endangering its relationships with suppliers.

## Credit Analysis

Credit analysis is an important part of a complete company analysis. Following is a selected set of measures for 2005 that can help us gauge the relative credit standing of Kimberly-Clark ($ millions):

| | |
|---|---|
| Current ratio ($4,783.1/$4,642.9) . . . . . . . . . . . . . . . . . . . . . . . . . . . . . . . . . . . . . . . . . . . . . . . . . . . . . . . | 1.03 |
| Quick ratio ([$364 + $2,101.9]/$4,642.9) . . . . . . . . . . . . . . . . . . . . . . . . . . . . . . . . . . . . . . . . . . . . . . . . | 0.53 |
| Total liabilities/Equity* ([$4,642.9 + $2,594.7 + $1,782.6 + $572.9]/[$394.5 + $757.4 + $5,558.2]) . . . . | 1.43 |
| Long-term debt/Equity ($2,594.7/[$394.5 + $757.4 + $5,558.2]) . . . . . . . . . . . . . . . . . . . . . . . . . . . . . . . | 0.39 |
| Earnings before interest and taxes/Interest expense ($2,310.6 − $179.0 + $190.2)/$190.2 . . . . . . . . . | 12.21 |
| Net operating cash flows/Total liabilities ($2,311.8/[$4,642.9 + $2,594.7 + $1,782.6 + $572.9]) . . . . . . | 0.24 |

* Minority interest and preferred securities of subsidiary treated as equity.

K-C's current and quick ratios are not particularly high, and both have decreased slightly over the past two years (not shown here). These ratios do not imply any excess liquidity, and probably do not suggest any room for a further decrease in liquidity.

K-C's financial leverage, as reflected in both the liability-to-equity and long-term-debt-to-equity ratios, is slightly above the median for all publicly traded companies. Normally, this is cause for some concern. However, Kimberly-Clark has strong operating and free cash flows that mitigate this concern.

K-C's times interest earned ratio of 12.21 is healthy, indicating a sufficient buffer to protect creditors if earnings decline. It also has relatively little off-balance-sheet exposure. Thus, we do not have any serious concerns about K-C's ability to repay its maturing debt obligations.

### Summarizing Profitability and Creditworthiness

An increasingly competitive environment has diminished Kimberly-Clark's gross profit margin. Operating expense reductions have not offset this decline. However, the company has been able to maintain its NOPAT as a result of a decline in its effective tax rate (which is not likely to be persistent). Its level of net operating asset turnover is acceptable, although not stellar. K-C does not provide sufficient information for us to further assess the throughput performance of its operating assets. Finally, its leverage, although higher than average, is not of great concern given K-C's strong cash flows.

# ADJUSTING AND FORECASTING FINANCIAL STATEMENT NUMBERS

**L03** Adjust and forecast financial statements.

The valuation of K-C's common stock requires forecasts of NOPAT and NOA over a forecast horizon period and a forecast terminal period. One possible approach is to project individual income statement and balance sheet items using the methodology we discuss in Module 11. However, in this section, we employ the parsimonious method of forecasting NOPAT and NOA using only sales forecasts, profit margins, and asset turnover rates-described in a latter section of Module 11. We first consider some possible adjustments to the financial statements before commencing the forecasting process.

### Adjusting Accounting Numbers

The two main targets of our parsimonious forecasting process are NOPAT and NOA. This means that we are primarily concerned with income statement and balance sheet adjustments that affect these two financial statements. Some adjustments we might consider for this purpose are shown in Exhibit 13.6 for Kimberly-Clark.

1. K-C reduced its allowance for uncollectible accounts from 2.4% to 1.7% of gross receivables. In 2005, bad debt expense was $8.9 million, compared with write-offs of uncollectible accounts amounting to $15 million. Our adjustment recognizes an additional $6.1 million so that the allowance for uncollectible accounts will not be further eroded.[4]

2. K-C recognized $20.7 million of expense relating to stock options under prior GAAP. Footnotes reveal that new accounting standards related to stock options will require K-C to recognize an additional $36.4 million.

---

[4] Technically, the increase in the projected bad debt expense will result in an increase in the allowance for uncollectible accounts and a consequent reduction in accounts receivable, net. We have not made this adjustment to the balance sheet so as not to overcomplicate the exposition.

3. Capitalization of operating leases will remove rent expense and substitute depreciation expense (an operating item that affects NOPAT) and interest expense (a nonoperating item that does not affect NOPAT). The $220 million leased asset will be depreciated over the remaining 8 years of the lease life, resulting in depreciation expense of $27.5 million. The operating lease adjustment removes the company's $85.7 million of projected minimum rent payments, and substitutes the $27.5 million of depreciation expense. This increases NOPAT by $58.2 million.

| EXHIBIT 13.6 | Kimberly-Clark Adjustments for NOPAT and NOA | |
|---|---|---|
| **Adj.** | **($ millions)** | |
| | Reported NOPAT ............................... | $ 1,949.9 |
| 1 | Bad debt expense ............................... | (6.1) |
| 2 | Stock option expense............................ | (36.4) |
| 3 | Rent expense, net of depreciation expense............ | 58.2 |
| 4 | AJCA tax adjustment ............................. | 53.2 |
| 5 | Synthetic fuel partnerships........................ | (55.3) |
| | Adjusted NOPAT................................. | $ 1,963.5 |
| | Reported NOA .................................. | $10,735.9 |
| 6 | Capitalization of operating leases .................. | 220.0 |
| 7 | Funded status of pension.......................... | (806.9) |
| 8 | Equity method investments ........................ | 539.4 |
| | Adjusted NOA.................................. | $10,688.4 |

4. The American Jobs Creation Act (AJCA) increases income taxes by 2.8 percentage points (as a percent of pre-tax income). This is a transitory item. NOPAT has been increased by 2.7% of pre-tax income for 2005, which amounts to $53.2 million ($1,968.9 million × .027 = $53.2).

5. The synthetic fuel partnerships increase NOPAT by $55.3 million. The company discloses that, due to the expected rise in oil prices, K-C does not expect these benefits to continue. Our adjustment reduces NOPAT by that amount.

6. The capitalization of operating leases adds $220 million to net operating assets (the lease obligation is a nonoperating liability).

7. Recognition of the funded status of K-C's pension plan will decrease NOA by $806.9 million (consisting of a $364.6 increase in pension liability and a $442.3 million decrease in pension assets). Pension obligations are an operating liability.

8. K-C reports $457.8 million relating to equity investments in companies that have assets of $1,561.8 million and current liabilities of $564.6 million (we assume that the long-term liabilities of these companies are nonoperating such as long-term notes and bonds). Upon consolidation, these companies would add $539.4 million ($1,561.8 million − $564.6 million − $457.8 million) of net operating assets (NOPAT will be unaffected as these investments are already accounted for using the equity method and this income is included in our NOPAT calculation).

## Forecasting Accounting Numbers

The adjusted NOPAT and NOA amounts become the starting point for our forecasts that are used to estimate the value of K-C common stock. The simplified forecast process uses three inputs: sales growth, NOPAT margin, and NOA turnover. Our adjusted net operating profit margin (NOPM) is 12.35% ($1,963.5 million/$15,902.6 million) and the adjusted net operating asset turnover based on year-end NOA (NOAT) is 1.49 ($15,902.6 million/$10,688.4 million). (Note: For forecasting, turnover metrics use year-end figures; see Module 11.)

The sales growth forecast is complicated by the foreign currency exchange effects that we discussed earlier. K-C's sales increased by 5.4% in 2005, down from 7.5% the previous year, but 2% of this increase resulted from the weaker $US. The "real" increase was just over 3% in 2005, which is the growth rate we use in our sales projections during the horizon period. We assume a 1% growth rate in the terminal period. Both of these rates are on the conservative side. We also use a NOPM of 12.35% and a NOAT of 1.49 consistent with actual 2005 rates (as adjusted).

Exhibit 13.7 shows forecasts of Kimberly-Clark's sales, net operating profit after tax (NOPAT), and net operating assets (NOA)-these follow from our forecasting process explained in Module 11 and include the terminal year forecast assuming a terminal growth rate of 1%.

| EXHIBIT 13.7 | Kimberly-Clark Forecasts of Sales, NOPAT, and NOA | | | | | |
|---|---|---|---|---|---|---|
| | Current | Horizon Period | | | | Terminal |
| (In millions) | 2005 | 2006 | 2007 | 2008 | 2009 | Year |
| Sales.......... | $15,902.6 | $16,380 | $16,871 | $17,377 | $17,899 | $18,078 |
| NOPAT ........ | 1,963.5 | 2,023 | 2,084 | 2,146 | 2,210 | 2,233 |
| NOA .......... | 10,688.4 | 10,993 | 11,323 | 11,662 | 12,013 | 12,133 |

# VALUING EQUITY SECURITIES

**L04** Describe and illustrate the valuation of firm equity and stock.

This section estimates the values of Kimberly-Clark's equity and common stock per share.

## Discounted Cash Flow Valuation

Exhibit 13.8 shows the discounted cash flow (DCF) model results. In addition to the forecast assumptions from the prior section, these results assume a discount (WACC) rate of 6.5%, a terminal growth rate of 1%, shares outstanding of 461.5 million, and net nonoperating obligations (NNO) of $4,327.4 million.[5]

| EXHIBIT 13.8 | Kimberly-Clark Discounted Cash Flow (DCF) Valuation | | | | | |
|---|---|---|---|---|---|---|
| (In millions, except per share values and discount factors) | Current 2005 | Horizon Period | | | | Terminal Period |
| | | 2006 | 2007 | 2008 | 2009 | |
| Increase in NOA.................... | | $ 304.6 | $ 330.0 | $ 339.0 | $ 351.0 | $ 120.0 |
| FCFF (NOPAT − Increase in NOA)..... | | 1,718.4 | 1,754.0 | 1,807.0 | 1,860.0 | 2,113.0 |
| Discount factor [1/(1 + $r_w$)$^t$] ......... | | 0.93897 | 0.88166 | 0.82785 | 0.77732 | |
| Present value of horizon FCFF........ | | 1,613.5 | 1,546.4 | 1,495.9 | 1,445.8 | |
| Cum. present value of horizon FCFF ... | $ 6,101.7 | | | | | |
| Present value of terminal FCFF ....... | 29,863.2[a] | | | | | |
| Total firm value.................... | 35,964.9 | | | | | |
| Less NNO....................... | 4,327.4 | | | | | |
| Firm equity value ................. | $31,637.5 | | | | | |
| Shares outstanding ............... | 461.5 | | | | | |
| Stock value per share.............. | $ 68.55 | | | | | |

[a] Computed as $\dfrac{\left(\dfrac{\$2{,}113.0 \text{ million}}{0.065 - 0.01}\right)}{(1.065)^4}$

## Residual Operating Income Valuation

Exhibit 13.9 reports estimates of the values of Kimberly-Clark's equity and common stock per share using the residual operating income (ROPI) model.

---

[5] NNO can be inferred from NOA minus equity. Kimberly-Clark's reported and adjusted balance sheet (reflecting the adjustments from Exhibit 13.6) is shown below. The consolidation of equity method investee companies (EMI) requires recognition of the minority interest, $457.8 million, relating to the proportion of the EMI net assets not owned by K-C; and equity is reduced by the $806.9 million reduction of AOCI resulting from recognition of the pension liability ($ millions).

| | Reported | Adjustments | Adjusted |
|---|---|---|---|
| NOA ....... | $10,735.9 | − $47.5 (net)** | $10,688.4 |
| Equity* ..... | 6,710.1 | +$457.8 (EMI) − $806.9 (Pension) | 6,361.0 |
| NNO ....... | $ 4,025.8 | | $ 4,327.4 |

* Includes stockholders' equity, minority interest and preferred stock of subsidiary.

** From Exhibit 13.6.

| EXHIBIT 13.9 | Kimberly-Clark Residual Operating Income (ROPI) Valuation | | | | | |
|---|---|---|---|---|---|---|
| **(In millions, except per share values and discount factors)** | **Current 2005** | **Horizon Period** | | | | **Terminal Period** |
| | | **2006** | **2007** | **2008** | **2009** | |
| ROPI [NOPAT − (NOA$_{Beg}$ × $r_w$)] . . . . . . . | | $ 1,328.3 | $ 1,369.5 | $ 1,410.0 | $ 1,453.0 | $1,452.0 |
| Discount factor [1/(1 + $r_w$)$^t$] . . . . . . . . . . | | 0.93897 | 0.88166 | 0.82785 | 0.77732 | |
| Present value of horizon ROPI . . . . . . . | | 1,247.2 | 1,207.4 | 1,167.3 | 1,129.4 | |
| Cum. present value of horizon ROPI . . . | $ 4,751.3 | | | | | |
| Present value of terminal ROPI[a] . . . . . . . | 20,521.2 | | | | | |
| NOA . . . . . . . . . . . . . . . . . . . . . . . . . . . | 10,688.4 | | | | | |
| Total firm value . . . . . . . . . . . . . . . . . . . | 35,960.9 | | | | | |
| Less NNO . . . . . . . . . . . . . . . . . . . . . . . | 4,327.4 | | | | | |
| Firm equity value . . . . . . . . . . . . . . . . . | $ 31,633.5 | | | | | |
| Shares outstanding . . . . . . . . . . . . . . . | 461.5 | | | | | |
| Stock value per share. . . . . . . . . . . . . . | $    68.55 | | | | | |

[a] Computed as $\dfrac{\left(\dfrac{\$1{,}452.0\ \text{million}}{0.065 - 0.01}\right)}{(1.065)^4}$.

We estimate Kimberly-Clark's equity value at $31,633.5 million as of December 2005, which is equivalent to a per share value estimate of $69.55. As expected, equity value estimates are identical (difference due to rounding) for both models (because K-C is assumed to be in a steady state, that is, NOPAT and NOA growing at the same rate and, therefore, RNOA is constant).

The closing stock price on December 31, 2005, for Kimberly-Clark (KMB) was $59.65 per share. Our model's estimates, therefore, suggest that K-C stock is undervalued as of that date. As it turns out, this valuation proved prophetic as its stock price increased to the mid- to upper-$60s subsequent to that date as shown in the following graph:

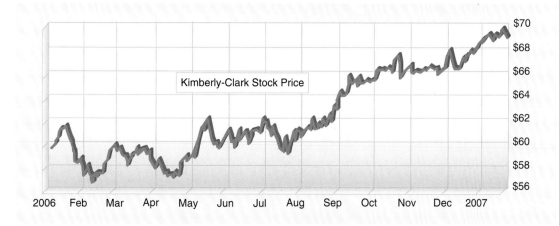

Overall, this module presents a financial accounting analysis and interpretation of Kimberly-Clark's performance and position. It illustrates many of the key financial reporting topics covered in the book. We review the company's financial statements and notes, forecast key accounts, and conclude with estimates of K-C's equity value.

The Kimberly-Clark case provides an opportunity for us to apply many of the procedures conveyed in the book in a comprehensive manner. With analyses of additional companies, we become more comfortable with, and knowledgeable of, variations in financial reporting, which enhances our analysis and business decision-making skills. Our analysis of a company must go beyond the accounting numbers to include competitor and economic factors, and we must appreciate that estimation and judgment are key ingredients in financial accounting. This comprehensive case, textbook, and course provide us with skills necessary to effectively use financial accounting and to advance our business and career opportunities.

# Compound Interest Tables

## TABLE 1 — Present Value of Single Amount

$$p = 1/(1 + i)^t$$

| Period | 0.01 | 0.02 | 0.03 | 0.04 | 0.05 | 0.06 | 0.07 | 0.08 | 0.09 | 0.10 | 0.11 | 0.12 |
|---|---|---|---|---|---|---|---|---|---|---|---|---|
| 1 | 0.99010 | 0.98039 | 0.97087 | 0.96154 | 0.95238 | 0.94340 | 0.93458 | 0.92593 | 0.91743 | 0.90909 | 0.90090 | 0.89286 |
| 2 | 0.98030 | 0.96117 | 0.94260 | 0.92456 | 0.90703 | 0.89000 | 0.87344 | 0.85734 | 0.84168 | 0.82645 | 0.81162 | 0.79719 |
| 3 | 0.97059 | 0.94232 | 0.91514 | 0.88900 | 0.86384 | 0.83962 | 0.81630 | 0.79383 | 0.77218 | 0.75131 | 0.73119 | 0.71178 |
| 4 | 0.96098 | 0.92385 | 0.88849 | 0.85480 | 0.82270 | 0.79209 | 0.76290 | 0.73503 | 0.70843 | 0.68301 | 0.65873 | 0.63552 |
| 5 | 0.95147 | 0.90573 | 0.86261 | 0.82193 | 0.78353 | 0.74726 | 0.71299 | 0.68058 | 0.64993 | 0.62092 | 0.59345 | 0.56743 |
| 6 | 0.94205 | 0.88797 | 0.83748 | 0.79031 | 0.74622 | 0.70496 | 0.66634 | 0.63017 | 0.59627 | 0.56447 | 0.53464 | 0.50663 |
| 7 | 0.93272 | 0.87056 | 0.81309 | 0.75992 | 0.71068 | 0.66506 | 0.62275 | 0.58349 | 0.54703 | 0.51316 | 0.48166 | 0.45235 |
| 8 | 0.92348 | 0.85349 | 0.78941 | 0.73069 | 0.67684 | 0.62741 | 0.58201 | 0.54027 | 0.50187 | 0.46651 | 0.43393 | 0.40388 |
| 9 | 0.91434 | 0.83676 | 0.76642 | 0.70259 | 0.64461 | 0.59190 | 0.54393 | 0.50025 | 0.46043 | 0.42410 | 0.39092 | 0.36061 |
| 10 | 0.90529 | 0.82035 | 0.74409 | 0.67556 | 0.61391 | 0.55839 | 0.50835 | 0.46319 | 0.42241 | 0.38554 | 0.35218 | 0.32197 |
| 11 | 0.89632 | 0.80426 | 0.72242 | 0.64958 | 0.58468 | 0.52679 | 0.47509 | 0.42888 | 0.38753 | 0.35049 | 0.31728 | 0.28748 |
| 12 | 0.88745 | 0.78849 | 0.70138 | 0.62460 | 0.55684 | 0.49697 | 0.44401 | 0.39711 | 0.35553 | 0.31863 | 0.28584 | 0.25668 |
| 13 | 0.87866 | 0.77303 | 0.68095 | 0.60057 | 0.53032 | 0.46884 | 0.41496 | 0.36770 | 0.32618 | 0.28966 | 0.25751 | 0.22917 |
| 14 | 0.86996 | 0.75788 | 0.66112 | 0.57748 | 0.50507 | 0.44230 | 0.38782 | 0.34046 | 0.29925 | 0.26333 | 0.23199 | 0.20462 |
| 15 | 0.86135 | 0.74301 | 0.64186 | 0.55526 | 0.48102 | 0.41727 | 0.36245 | 0.31524 | 0.27454 | 0.23939 | 0.20900 | 0.18270 |
| 16 | 0.85282 | 0.72845 | 0.62317 | 0.53391 | 0.45811 | 0.39365 | 0.33873 | 0.29189 | 0.25187 | 0.21763 | 0.18829 | 0.16312 |
| 17 | 0.84438 | 0.71416 | 0.60502 | 0.51337 | 0.43630 | 0.37136 | 0.31657 | 0.27027 | 0.23107 | 0.19784 | 0.16963 | 0.14564 |
| 18 | 0.83602 | 0.70016 | 0.58739 | 0.49363 | 0.41552 | 0.35034 | 0.29586 | 0.25025 | 0.21199 | 0.17986 | 0.15282 | 0.13004 |
| 19 | 0.82774 | 0.68643 | 0.57029 | 0.47464 | 0.39573 | 0.33051 | 0.27651 | 0.23171 | 0.19449 | 0.16351 | 0.13768 | 0.11611 |
| 20 | 0.81954 | 0.67297 | 0.55368 | 0.45639 | 0.37689 | 0.31180 | 0.25842 | 0.21455 | 0.17843 | 0.14864 | 0.12403 | 0.10367 |
| 21 | 0.81143 | 0.65978 | 0.53755 | 0.43883 | 0.35894 | 0.29416 | 0.24151 | 0.19866 | 0.16370 | 0.13513 | 0.11174 | 0.09256 |
| 22 | 0.80340 | 0.64684 | 0.52189 | 0.42196 | 0.34185 | 0.27751 | 0.22571 | 0.18394 | 0.15018 | 0.12285 | 0.10067 | 0.08264 |
| 23 | 0.79544 | 0.63416 | 0.50669 | 0.40573 | 0.32557 | 0.26180 | 0.21095 | 0.17032 | 0.13778 | 0.11168 | 0.09069 | 0.07379 |
| 24 | 0.78757 | 0.62172 | 0.49193 | 0.39012 | 0.31007 | 0.24698 | 0.19715 | 0.15770 | 0.12640 | 0.10153 | 0.08170 | 0.06588 |
| 25 | 0.77977 | 0.60953 | 0.47761 | 0.37512 | 0.29530 | 0.23300 | 0.18425 | 0.14602 | 0.11597 | 0.09230 | 0.07361 | 0.05882 |
| 30 | 0.74192 | 0.55207 | 0.41199 | 0.30832 | 0.23138 | 0.17411 | 0.13137 | 0.09938 | 0.07537 | 0.05731 | 0.04368 | 0.03338 |
| 35 | 0.70591 | 0.50003 | 0.35538 | 0.25342 | 0.18129 | 0.13011 | 0.09366 | 0.06763 | 0.04899 | 0.03558 | 0.02592 | 0.01894 |
| 40 | 0.67165 | 0.45289 | 0.30656 | 0.20829 | 0.14205 | 0.09722 | 0.06678 | 0.04603 | 0.03184 | 0.02209 | 0.01538 | 0.01075 |

## TABLE 2 — Present Value of Ordinary Annuity

$$p = \{1 - [1/(1 + i)^t]\}/i$$

| Period | 0.01 | 0.02 | 0.03 | 0.04 | 0.05 | 0.06 | 0.07 | 0.08 | 0.09 | 0.10 | 0.11 | 0.12 |
|---|---|---|---|---|---|---|---|---|---|---|---|---|
| 1 | 0.99010 | 0.98039 | 0.97087 | 0.96154 | 0.95238 | 0.94340 | 0.93458 | 0.92593 | 0.91743 | 0.90909 | 0.90090 | 0.89286 |
| 2 | 1.97040 | 1.94156 | 1.91347 | 1.88609 | 1.85941 | 1.83339 | 1.80802 | 1.78326 | 1.75911 | 1.73554 | 1.71252 | 1.69005 |
| 3 | 2.94099 | 2.88388 | 2.82861 | 2.77509 | 2.72325 | 2.67301 | 2.62432 | 2.57710 | 2.53129 | 2.48685 | 2.44371 | 2.40183 |
| 4 | 3.90197 | 3.80773 | 3.71710 | 3.62990 | 3.54595 | 3.46511 | 3.38721 | 3.31213 | 3.23972 | 3.16987 | 3.10245 | 3.03735 |
| 5 | 4.85343 | 4.71346 | 4.57971 | 4.45182 | 4.32948 | 4.21236 | 4.10020 | 3.99271 | 3.88965 | 3.79079 | 3.69590 | 3.60478 |
| 6 | 5.79548 | 5.60143 | 5.41719 | 5.24214 | 5.07569 | 4.91732 | 4.76654 | 4.62288 | 4.48592 | 4.35526 | 4.23054 | 4.11141 |
| 7 | 6.72819 | 6.47199 | 6.23028 | 6.00205 | 5.78637 | 5.58238 | 5.38929 | 5.20637 | 5.03295 | 4.86842 | 4.71220 | 4.56376 |
| 8 | 7.65168 | 7.32548 | 7.01969 | 6.73274 | 6.46321 | 6.20979 | 5.97130 | 5.74664 | 5.53482 | 5.33493 | 5.14612 | 4.96764 |
| 9 | 8.56602 | 8.16224 | 7.78611 | 7.43533 | 7.10782 | 6.80169 | 6.51523 | 6.24689 | 5.99525 | 5.75902 | 5.53705 | 5.32825 |
| 10 | 9.47130 | 8.98259 | 8.53020 | 8.11090 | 7.72173 | 7.36009 | 7.02358 | 6.71008 | 6.41766 | 6.14457 | 5.88923 | 5.65022 |
| 11 | 10.36763 | 9.78685 | 9.25262 | 8.76048 | 8.30641 | 7.88687 | 7.49867 | 7.13896 | 6.80519 | 6.49506 | 6.20652 | 5.93770 |
| 12 | 11.25508 | 10.57534 | 9.95400 | 9.38507 | 8.86325 | 8.38384 | 7.94269 | 7.53608 | 7.16073 | 6.81369 | 6.49236 | 6.19437 |
| 13 | 12.13374 | 11.34837 | 10.63496 | 9.98565 | 9.39357 | 8.85268 | 8.35765 | 7.90378 | 7.48690 | 7.10336 | 6.74987 | 6.42355 |
| 14 | 13.00370 | 12.10625 | 11.29607 | 10.56312 | 9.89864 | 9.29498 | 8.74547 | 8.24424 | 7.78615 | 7.36669 | 6.98187 | 6.62817 |
| 15 | 13.86505 | 12.84926 | 11.93794 | 11.11839 | 10.37966 | 9.71225 | 9.10791 | 8.55948 | 8.06069 | 7.60608 | 7.19087 | 6.81086 |
| 16 | 14.71787 | 13.57771 | 12.56110 | 11.65230 | 10.83777 | 10.10590 | 9.44665 | 8.85137 | 8.31256 | 7.82371 | 7.37916 | 6.97399 |
| 17 | 15.56225 | 14.29187 | 13.16612 | 12.16567 | 11.27407 | 10.47726 | 9.76322 | 9.12164 | 8.54363 | 8.02155 | 7.54879 | 7.11963 |
| 18 | 16.39827 | 14.99203 | 13.75351 | 12.65930 | 11.68959 | 10.82760 | 10.05909 | 9.37189 | 8.75563 | 8.20141 | 7.70162 | 7.24967 |
| 19 | 17.22601 | 15.67846 | 14.32380 | 13.13394 | 12.08532 | 11.15812 | 10.33560 | 9.60360 | 8.95011 | 8.36492 | 7.83929 | 7.36578 |
| 20 | 18.04555 | 16.35143 | 14.87747 | 13.59033 | 12.46221 | 11.46992 | 10.59401 | 9.81815 | 9.12855 | 8.51356 | 7.96333 | 7.46944 |
| 21 | 18.85698 | 17.01121 | 15.41502 | 14.02916 | 12.82115 | 11.76408 | 10.83553 | 10.01680 | 9.29224 | 8.64869 | 8.07507 | 7.56200 |
| 22 | 19.66038 | 17.65805 | 15.93692 | 14.45112 | 13.16300 | 12.04158 | 11.06124 | 10.20074 | 9.44243 | 8.77154 | 8.17574 | 7.64465 |
| 23 | 20.45582 | 18.29220 | 16.44361 | 14.85684 | 13.48857 | 12.30338 | 11.27219 | 10.37106 | 9.58021 | 8.88322 | 8.26643 | 7.71843 |
| 24 | 21.24339 | 18.91393 | 16.93554 | 15.24696 | 13.79864 | 12.55036 | 11.46933 | 10.52876 | 9.70661 | 8.98474 | 8.34814 | 7.78432 |
| 25 | 22.02316 | 19.52346 | 17.41315 | 15.62208 | 14.09394 | 12.78336 | 11.65358 | 10.67478 | 9.82258 | 9.07704 | 8.42174 | 7.84314 |
| 30 | 25.80771 | 22.39646 | 19.60044 | 17.29203 | 15.37245 | 13.76483 | 12.40904 | 11.25778 | 10.27365 | 9.42691 | 8.69379 | 8.05518 |
| 35 | 29.40858 | 24.99862 | 21.48722 | 18.66461 | 16.37419 | 14.49825 | 12.94767 | 11.65457 | 10.56682 | 9.64416 | 8.85524 | 8.17550 |
| 40 | 32.83469 | 27.35548 | 23.11477 | 19.79277 | 17.15909 | 15.04630 | 13.33171 | 11.92461 | 10.75736 | 9.77905 | 8.95105 | 8.24378 |

| TABLE 3 | Future Value of Single Amount | | | | | | | | | | $f = (1 + i)^t$ |

### Interest Rate

| Period | 0.01 | 0.02 | 0.03 | 0.04 | 0.05 | 0.06 | 0.07 | 0.08 | 0.09 | 0.10 | 0.11 | 0.12 |
|---|---|---|---|---|---|---|---|---|---|---|---|---|
| 1 | 1.01000 | 1.02000 | 1.03000 | 1.04000 | 1.05000 | 1.06000 | 1.07000 | 1.08000 | 1.09000 | 1.10000 | 1.11000 | 1.12000 |
| 2 | 1.02010 | 1.04040 | 1.06090 | 1.08160 | 1.10250 | 1.12360 | 1.14490 | 1.16640 | 1.18810 | 1.21000 | 1.23210 | 1.25440 |
| 3 | 1.03030 | 1.06121 | 1.09273 | 1.12486 | 1.15763 | 1.19102 | 1.22504 | 1.25971 | 1.29503 | 1.33100 | 1.36763 | 1.40493 |
| 4 | 1.04060 | 1.08243 | 1.12551 | 1.16986 | 1.21551 | 1.26248 | 1.31080 | 1.36049 | 1.41158 | 1.46410 | 1.51807 | 1.57352 |
| 5 | 1.05101 | 1.10408 | 1.15927 | 1.21665 | 1.27628 | 1.33823 | 1.40255 | 1.46933 | 1.53862 | 1.61051 | 1.68506 | 1.76234 |
| 6 | 1.06152 | 1.12616 | 1.19405 | 1.26532 | 1.34010 | 1.41852 | 1.50073 | 1.58687 | 1.67710 | 1.77156 | 1.87041 | 1.97382 |
| 7 | 1.07214 | 1.14869 | 1.22987 | 1.31593 | 1.40710 | 1.50363 | 1.60578 | 1.71382 | 1.82804 | 1.94872 | 2.07616 | 2.21068 |
| 8 | 1.08286 | 1.17166 | 1.26677 | 1.36857 | 1.47746 | 1.59385 | 1.71819 | 1.85093 | 1.99256 | 2.14359 | 2.30454 | 2.47596 |
| 9 | 1.09369 | 1.19509 | 1.30477 | 1.42331 | 1.55133 | 1.68948 | 1.83846 | 1.99900 | 2.17189 | 2.35795 | 2.55804 | 2.77308 |
| 10 | 1.10462 | 1.21899 | 1.34392 | 1.48024 | 1.62889 | 1.79085 | 1.96715 | 2.15892 | 2.36736 | 2.59374 | 2.83942 | 3.10585 |
| 11 | 1.11567 | 1.24337 | 1.38423 | 1.53945 | 1.71034 | 1.89830 | 2.10485 | 2.33164 | 2.58043 | 2.85312 | 3.15176 | 3.47855 |
| 12 | 1.12683 | 1.26824 | 1.42576 | 1.60103 | 1.79586 | 2.01220 | 2.25219 | 2.51817 | 2.81266 | 3.13843 | 3.49845 | 3.89598 |
| 13 | 1.13809 | 1.29361 | 1.46853 | 1.66507 | 1.88565 | 2.13293 | 2.40985 | 2.71962 | 3.06580 | 3.45227 | 3.88328 | 4.36349 |
| 14 | 1.14947 | 1.31948 | 1.51259 | 1.73168 | 1.97993 | 2.26090 | 2.57853 | 2.93719 | 3.34173 | 3.79750 | 4.31044 | 4.88711 |
| 15 | 1.16097 | 1.34587 | 1.55797 | 1.80094 | 2.07893 | 2.39656 | 2.75903 | 3.17217 | 3.64248 | 4.17725 | 4.78459 | 5.47357 |
| 16 | 1.17258 | 1.37279 | 1.60471 | 1.87298 | 2.18287 | 2.54035 | 2.95216 | 3.42594 | 3.97031 | 4.59497 | 5.31089 | 6.13039 |
| 17 | 1.18430 | 1.40024 | 1.65285 | 1.94790 | 2.29202 | 2.69277 | 3.15882 | 3.70002 | 4.32763 | 5.05447 | 5.89509 | 6.86604 |
| 18 | 1.19615 | 1.42825 | 1.70243 | 2.02582 | 2.40662 | 2.85434 | 3.37993 | 3.99602 | 4.71712 | 5.55992 | 6.54355 | 7.68997 |
| 19 | 1.20811 | 1.45681 | 1.75351 | 2.10685 | 2.52695 | 3.02560 | 3.61653 | 4.31570 | 5.14166 | 6.11591 | 7.26334 | 8.61276 |
| 20 | 1.22019 | 1.48595 | 1.80611 | 2.19112 | 2.65330 | 3.20714 | 3.86968 | 4.66096 | 5.60441 | 6.72750 | 8.06231 | 9.64629 |
| 21 | 1.23239 | 1.51567 | 1.86029 | 2.27877 | 2.78596 | 3.39956 | 4.14056 | 5.03383 | 6.10881 | 7.40025 | 8.94917 | 10.80385 |
| 22 | 1.24472 | 1.54598 | 1.91610 | 2.36992 | 2.92526 | 3.60354 | 4.43040 | 5.43654 | 6.65860 | 8.14027 | 9.93357 | 12.10031 |
| 23 | 1.25716 | 1.57690 | 1.97359 | 2.46472 | 3.07152 | 3.81975 | 4.74053 | 5.87146 | 7.25787 | 8.95430 | 11.02627 | 13.55235 |
| 24 | 1.26973 | 1.60844 | 2.03279 | 2.56330 | 3.22510 | 4.04893 | 5.07237 | 6.34118 | 7.91108 | 9.84973 | 12.23916 | 15.17863 |
| 25 | 1.28243 | 1.64061 | 2.09378 | 2.66584 | 3.38635 | 4.29187 | 5.42743 | 6.84848 | 8.62308 | 10.83471 | 13.58546 | 17.00006 |
| 30 | 1.34785 | 1.81136 | 2.42726 | 3.24340 | 4.32194 | 5.74349 | 7.61226 | 10.06266 | 13.26768 | 17.44940 | 22.89230 | 29.95992 |
| 35 | 1.41660 | 1.99989 | 2.81386 | 3.94609 | 5.51602 | 7.68609 | 10.67658 | 14.78534 | 20.41397 | 28.10244 | 38.57485 | 52.79962 |
| 40 | 1.48886 | 2.20804 | 3.26204 | 4.80102 | 7.03999 | 10.28572 | 14.97446 | 21.72452 | 31.40942 | 45.25926 | 65.00087 | 93.05097 |

| TABLE 4 | Future Value of an Ordinary Annuity | | | | | | | | | | $f = [(1 + i)^t - 1]/i$ |

### Interest Rate

| Period | 0.01 | 0.02 | 0.03 | 0.04 | 0.05 | 0.06 | 0.07 | 0.08 | 0.09 | 0.10 | 0.11 | 0.12 |
|---|---|---|---|---|---|---|---|---|---|---|---|---|
| 1 | 1.00000 | 1.00000 | 1.00000 | 1.00000 | 1.00000 | 1.00000 | 1.00000 | 1.00000 | 1.00000 | 1.00000 | 1.00000 | 1.00000 |
| 2 | 2.01000 | 2.02000 | 2.03000 | 2.04000 | 2.05000 | 2.06000 | 2.07000 | 2.08000 | 2.09000 | 2.10000 | 2.11000 | 2.12000 |
| 3 | 3.03010 | 3.06040 | 3.09090 | 3.12160 | 3.15250 | 3.18360 | 3.21490 | 3.24640 | 3.27810 | 3.31000 | 3.34210 | 3.37440 |
| 4 | 4.06040 | 4.12161 | 4.18363 | 4.24646 | 4.31013 | 4.37462 | 4.43994 | 4.50611 | 4.57313 | 4.64100 | 4.70973 | 4.77933 |
| 5 | 5.10101 | 5.20404 | 5.30914 | 5.41632 | 5.52563 | 5.63709 | 5.75074 | 5.86660 | 5.98471 | 6.10510 | 6.22780 | 6.35285 |
| 6 | 6.15202 | 6.30812 | 6.46841 | 6.63298 | 6.80191 | 6.97532 | 7.15329 | 7.33593 | 7.52333 | 7.71561 | 7.91286 | 8.11519 |
| 7 | 7.21354 | 7.43428 | 7.66246 | 7.89829 | 8.14201 | 8.39384 | 8.65402 | 8.92280 | 9.20043 | 9.48717 | 9.78327 | 10.08901 |
| 8 | 8.28567 | 8.58297 | 8.89234 | 9.21423 | 9.54911 | 9.89747 | 10.25980 | 10.63663 | 11.02847 | 11.43589 | 11.85943 | 12.29969 |
| 9 | 9.36853 | 9.75463 | 10.15911 | 10.58280 | 11.02656 | 11.49132 | 11.97799 | 12.48756 | 13.02104 | 13.57948 | 14.16397 | 14.77566 |
| 10 | 10.46221 | 10.94972 | 11.46388 | 12.00611 | 12.57789 | 13.18079 | 13.81645 | 14.48656 | 15.19293 | 15.93742 | 16.72201 | 17.54874 |
| 11 | 11.56683 | 12.16872 | 12.80780 | 13.48635 | 14.20679 | 14.97164 | 15.78360 | 16.64549 | 17.56029 | 18.53117 | 19.56143 | 20.65458 |
| 12 | 12.68250 | 13.41209 | 14.19203 | 15.02581 | 15.91713 | 16.86994 | 17.88845 | 18.97713 | 20.14072 | 21.38428 | 22.71319 | 24.13313 |
| 13 | 13.80933 | 14.68033 | 15.61779 | 16.62684 | 17.71298 | 18.88214 | 20.14064 | 21.49530 | 22.95338 | 24.52271 | 26.21164 | 28.02911 |
| 14 | 14.94742 | 15.97394 | 17.08632 | 18.29191 | 19.59863 | 21.01507 | 22.55049 | 24.21492 | 26.01919 | 27.97498 | 30.09492 | 32.39260 |
| 15 | 16.09690 | 17.29342 | 18.59891 | 20.02359 | 21.57856 | 23.27597 | 25.12902 | 27.15211 | 29.36092 | 31.77248 | 34.40536 | 37.27971 |
| 16 | 17.25786 | 18.63929 | 20.15688 | 21.82453 | 23.65749 | 25.67253 | 27.88805 | 30.32428 | 33.00340 | 35.94973 | 39.18995 | 42.75328 |
| 17 | 18.43044 | 20.01207 | 21.76159 | 23.69751 | 25.84037 | 28.21288 | 30.84022 | 33.75023 | 36.97370 | 40.54470 | 44.50084 | 48.88367 |
| 18 | 19.61475 | 21.41231 | 23.41444 | 25.64541 | 28.13238 | 30.90565 | 33.99903 | 37.45024 | 41.30134 | 45.59917 | 50.39594 | 55.74971 |
| 19 | 20.81090 | 22.84056 | 25.11687 | 27.67123 | 30.53900 | 33.75999 | 37.37896 | 41.44626 | 46.01846 | 51.15909 | 56.93949 | 63.43968 |
| 20 | 22.01900 | 24.29737 | 26.87037 | 29.77808 | 33.06595 | 36.78559 | 40.99549 | 45.76196 | 51.16012 | 57.27500 | 64.20283 | 72.05244 |
| 21 | 23.23919 | 25.78332 | 28.67649 | 31.96920 | 35.71925 | 39.99273 | 44.86518 | 50.42292 | 56.76453 | 64.00250 | 72.26514 | 81.69874 |
| 22 | 24.47159 | 27.29898 | 30.53678 | 34.24797 | 38.50521 | 43.39229 | 49.00574 | 55.45676 | 62.87334 | 71.40275 | 81.21431 | 92.50258 |
| 23 | 25.71630 | 28.84496 | 32.45288 | 36.61789 | 41.43048 | 46.99583 | 53.43614 | 60.89330 | 69.53194 | 79.54302 | 91.14788 | 104.60289 |
| 24 | 26.97346 | 30.42186 | 34.42647 | 39.08260 | 44.50200 | 50.81558 | 58.17667 | 66.76476 | 76.78981 | 88.49733 | 102.17415 | 118.15524 |
| 25 | 28.24320 | 32.03030 | 36.45926 | 41.64591 | 47.72710 | 54.86451 | 63.24904 | 73.10594 | 84.70090 | 98.34706 | 114.41331 | 133.33387 |
| 30 | 34.78489 | 40.56808 | 47.57542 | 56.08494 | 66.43885 | 79.05819 | 94.46079 | 113.28321 | 136.30754 | 164.49402 | 199.02088 | 241.33268 |
| 35 | 41.66028 | 49.99448 | 60.46208 | 73.65222 | 90.32031 | 111.43478 | 138.23688 | 172.31680 | 215.71075 | 271.02437 | 341.58955 | 431.66350 |
| 40 | 48.88637 | 60.40198 | 75.40126 | 95.02552 | 120.79977 | 154.76197 | 199.63511 | 259.05652 | 337.88245 | 442.59256 | 581.82607 | 767.09142 |

# Constructing the Statement of Cash Flows

## LEARNING OBJECTIVES

**LO1** Define and describe the framework for the statement of cash flows. (p. B-3)

**LO2** Define and explain net cash flows from operating activities. (p. B-7)

**LO3** Define and explain net cash flows from investing activities. (p. B-13)

**LO4** Define and explain net cash flows from financing activities. (p. B-14)

**LO5** Describe and apply ratios based on operating cash flows. (p. B-17)

## STARBUCKS

Starbucks Corporation is the leading retailer, roaster, and brander of specialty coffee in the world. It has more than 7,100 company-owned retail locations in North America, Latin America, Europe, the Middle East, and the Pacific Rim. Starbucks sells high quality coffee and the "Starbucks Experience." It also produces and sells bottled Frappuccino® coffee drinks, Starbucks DoubleShot™ coffee drink, and a line of superpremium ice creams through its joint venture partnerships. Its Tazo Tea line of premium teas and Hear Music compact discs further add to its product offerings. Seattle's Best Coffee® and Torrefazione Italia® Coffee brands also help Starbucks appeal to a broader consumer base.

Starbucks' fiscal year 2006 resulted in $7.8 billion in total net revenues, a 22% year-over-year growth, and $564 million in net income, a 14% year-over-year growth. It also reported a 7% comparable store sales growth, which represents the 15th consecutive year of 5% or greater growth. This past year, Starbucks was recognized by *Fortune* magazine as number 5 on its list of America's Most Admired Companies and number 16 in its ranking of 100 Best Companies to Work For. Starbucks was also listed among *Business Ethics* magazine's 100 Best Corporate Citizens.

Product lines of the major U.S. brewed coffee sellers are well defined. On the high end there is Starbucks, with 7,728 U.S. locations. It has made its expensive cappuccinos, frappuccinos, espressos, and lattes part of the common lexicon. On the other end, there is Dunkin' Donuts, which has 4,400 stores. Dunkin' Donuts is the largest seller of regular, nonflavored brewed coffee in the U.S. fast-food outlets. It has an 18% market share, compared with 15% for McDonald's Corporation and 6% for Starbucks.

*The Wall Street Journal* recently reported that "there's a new brewhaha in Latte-land . . . Starbucks increasingly is looking for growth by opening stores in blue-collar communities where Dunkin' Donuts would typically dominate . . . At the same time, Dunkin' Donuts, a unit of United

Kingdom spirits group Allied Domecq PLC, wants to lure Starbucks' well-heeled customers with a new line of Italian brews that it claims it can deliver faster, cheaper and simpler."

Although competition exists, Starbucks' recent performance is difficult to top. In the last 13 years, Starbucks' sales have increased from $285 million to over nearly $8 billion and its income has increased from $29 million to $564 million. An investor purchasing its stock 10 years ago at a split-adjusted price of $3.76 would have seen its value grow to nearly $35 today.

During this same decade, Starbucks' net income and operating cash flows have increased by 10 times and 11 times, respectively. This is graphically portrayed as follows:

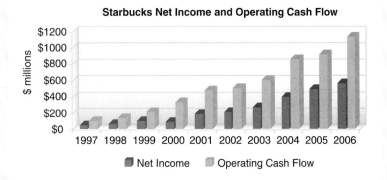

Both net income and operating cash flows are important in assessing the financial health of a company and its value. Starbucks is generating much more cash than it is reporting in income. Why is this? What does it mean? In this module, we describe the process of constructing the statement of cash flows. We also describe how we can use and interpret the statement of cash flows to aid both internal and external decisions.

Sources: Ball and Leung, "Latte Versus Latte—Starbucks, Dunkin' Donuts Seek Growth by Capturing Each Other's Customers," *The Wall Street Journal,* 10 February 2004; Starbucks 2003 through 2006 *Annual Reports* and *10-K Reports.*

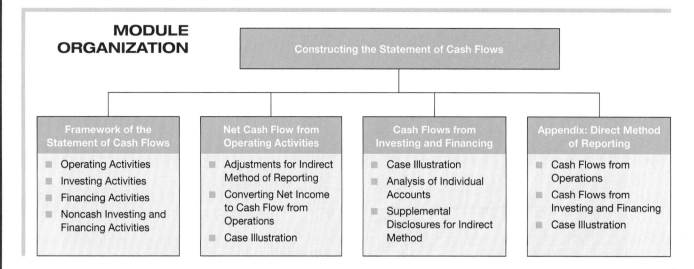

## INTRODUCTION

The **statement of cash flows** is a financial statement that summarizes information about the flow of cash into and out of a company. In this appendix, we discuss the preparation, analysis, and interpretation of the statement of cash flows.

The statement of cash flows complements the balance sheet and the income statement. The balance sheet reports the company's financial position at a point in time (the end of each period) whereas the statement of cash flows explains the change in one of its components—cash—from one balance sheet date to the next. The income statement reveals the results of the company's operating activities for the period, and these operating activities are a major contributor to the change in cash as reported in the statement of cash flows.

The statement of cash flows explains the change in a firm's cash *and* cash equivalents. **Cash equivalents** are short-term, highly liquid investments that are (1) easily convertible into a known cash amount and (2) close enough to maturity so that their market value is not sensitive to interest rate changes (generally, investments with initial maturities of three months or less). Treasury bills, commercial paper (short-term notes issued by corporations), and money market funds are typical examples of cash equivalents.

When preparing a statement of cash flows, the cash and cash equivalents are added together and treated as a single sum. This is done because the purchase and sale of investments in cash equivalents are considered to be part of a firm's overall management of cash rather than a source or use of cash. As statement users evaluate and project cash flows, for example, it should not matter whether the cash is readily available, deposited in a bank account, or invested in cash equivalents. Transfers back and forth between a firm's cash account and its investments in cash equivalents, therefore, are not treated as cash inflows and cash outflows in its statement of cash flows.

When discussing the statement of cash flows, managers generally use the word *cash* rather than the term *cash and cash equivalents*. We will follow the same practice in this appendix.

## FRAMEWORK FOR THE STATEMENT OF CASH FLOWS

**LO1** Define and describe the framework for the statement of cash flows.

In analyzing the statement of cash flows, we must not necessarily conclude that the company is better off if cash increases and worse off if cash decreases. It is not the cash change that is most important, but the sources for that change. For example, what are the sources of cash inflows? Are these sources transitory? Are these sources mainly from operating activities?

We must also review the uses of cash. Has the company invested its cash in operating areas to strengthen its competitive position? Is it able to comfortably meet its debt obligations? Has it diverted cash to creditors or investors at the expense of the other? Such questions and answers are key to properly interpreting the statement of cash flows for business decisions.

The statement of cash flows classifies cash receipts and payments into one of three categories: operating activities, investing activities, or financing activities. Classifying cash flows into these categories identifies the effects on cash of each of the major activities of a firm. The combined effects on cash of all three categories explain the net change in cash for the period. The period's net change in cash is then reconciled with the beginning and ending amounts of cash.

Exhibit B.1 reproduces Starbucks' statement of cash flows ($ thousands). During 2006, Starbucks reported net income of $564.259 million and generated $1,131.633 million of cash from operating activities. The company used $841.040 million of cash for investing activities and $155.326 million of cash for financing activities. In sum, Starbucks increased its cash reserves by $138.797 million (including foreign exchange effects), from $173.809 million at the beginning of fiscal 2006 to $312.606 million at the end of fiscal 2006.

| EXHIBIT B.1 | Statement of Cash Flows for Starbucks | | |
| --- | --- | --- | --- |

| Consolidated Statements of Cash Flows Fiscal Year Ended ($ thousands) | Oct 1, 2006 | Oct 2, 2005 | Oct 3, 2004 |
| --- | --- | --- | --- |
| **Operating activities** | | | |
| Net earnings. . . . . . . . . . . . . . . . . . . . . . . . . . . . . . . . . . . . . . | $ 564,259 | $ 494,370 | $ 388,880 |
| Adjustments to reconcile net earnings to net cash provided by operating activities | | | |
| Cumulative effect accounting change for FIN 47, net of taxes . . | 17,214 | — | — |
| Depreciation and amortization . . . . . . . . . . . . . . . . . . . . . . . . . | 412,625 | 367,207 | 314,047 |
| Provision for impairments and asset disposals . . . . . . . . . . . . . | 19,622 | 19,464 | 17,948 |
| Deferred income taxes, net. . . . . . . . . . . . . . . . . . . . . . . . . . . . | (84,324) | (31,253) | (3,770) |
| Equity in income of investees. . . . . . . . . . . . . . . . . . . . . . . . . . | (60,570) | (49,537) | (31,707) |
| Distributions of income from equity investees . . . . . . . . . . . . . . | 49,238 | 30,919 | 38,328 |
| Stock-based compensation . . . . . . . . . . . . . . . . . . . . . . . . . . . | 105,664 | — | — |
| Tax benefit from exercise of stock options. . . . . . . . . . . . . . . . . | 1,318 | 109,978 | 63,405 |
| Excess tax benefit from exercise of stock options. . . . . . . . . . . | (117,368) | — | — |
| Net amortization of premium on securities. . . . . . . . . . . . . . . . . | 2,013 | 10,097 | 11,603 |
| Cash provided (used) by changes in operating assets and liabilities | | | |
| Inventories. . . . . . . . . . . . . . . . . . . . . . . . . . . . . . . . . . . . . . | (85,527) | (121,618) | (77,662) |
| Accounts payable . . . . . . . . . . . . . . . . . . . . . . . . . . . . . . . . . | 104,966 | 9,717 | 27,948 |
| Accrued compensation and related costs . . . . . . . . . . . . . . . | 54,424 | 22,711 | 54,929 |
| Accrued taxes . . . . . . . . . . . . . . . . . . . . . . . . . . . . . . . . . . . | 132,725 | 14,435 | 7,677 |
| Deferred revenue. . . . . . . . . . . . . . . . . . . . . . . . . . . . . . . . . | 56,547 | 53,276 | 47,590 |
| Other operating assets and liabilities . . . . . . . . . . . . . . . . . . | (41,193) | (6,851) | 3,702 |
| Net cash provided by operating activities . . . . . . . . . . . . . . . . . | 1,131,633 | 922,915 | 862,918 |
| **Investing activities** | | | |
| Purchase of available-for-sale securities . . . . . . . . . . . . . . . . . | (639,192) | (643,488) | (887,969) |
| Maturity of available-for-sale securities . . . . . . . . . . . . . . . . . . | 269,134 | 469,554 | 170,789 |
| Sale of available-for-sale securities . . . . . . . . . . . . . . . . . . . . . | 431,181 | 626,113 | 452,467 |
| Acquisitions, net of cash acquired . . . . . . . . . . . . . . . . . . . . . . | (91,734) | (21,583) | (7,515) |
| Net purchases of equity, other investments and other assets . . . | (39,199) | (7,915) | (64,747) |
| Net additions to property, plant, and equipment . . . . . . . . . . . . | (771,230) | (643,296) | (416,917) |
| Net cash used by investing activities. . . . . . . . . . . . . . . . . . . . . | (841,040) | (220,615) | (753,892) |
| **Financing activities** | | | |
| Proceeds from issuance of common stock . . . . . . . . . . . . . . . . | 159,249 | 163,555 | 137,590 |
| Excess tax benefit from exercise of stock options. . . . . . . . . . . | 117,368 | — | — |
| Net borrowing under revolving credit facility . . . . . . . . . . . . . . . | 423,000 | 277,000 | — |
| Principal payments on long-term debt. . . . . . . . . . . . . . . . . . . . | (898) | (735) | (722) |
| Repurchase of common stock . . . . . . . . . . . . . . . . . . . . . . . . . | (854,045) | (1,113,647) | (203,413) |
| Net cash used by financing activities. . . . . . . . . . . . . . . . . . . . . | (155,326) | (673,827) | (66,545) |
| Effect of exchange rate changes on cash and cash equivalents. . . | 3,530 | 283 | 3,110 |
| Net increase in cash and cash equivalents . . . . . . . . . . . . . . . . | 138,797 | 28,756 | 45,591 |
| **Cash and cash equivalents** | | | |
| Beginning of period . . . . . . . . . . . . . . . . . . . . . . . . . . . . . . . . . | 173,809 | 145,053 | 99,462 |
| End of period . . . . . . . . . . . . . . . . . . . . . . . . . . . . . . . . . . . . . . | $ 312,606 | $ 173,809 | $ 145,053 |

## Operating Activities

A company's income statement reflects primarily the transactions and events that constitute its operating activities. Generally, the cash effects of these operating transactions and events determine the net cash flow from operating activities. The usual focus of a firm's **operating activities** is on selling goods or rendering services, but the activities are defined broadly enough to include any cash receipts or payments that are not classified as investing or financing activities. For example, cash received from collection of receivables and cash payments to purchase inventories are treated as cash flows from operating activities. The following are examples of cash inflows and outflows relating to operating activities.

**Operating Activities**

| **Cash Inflows** | **Cash Outflows** |
| --- | --- |
| 1. Receipts from customers for sales made or services rendered. | 1. Payments to employees or suppliers. |
| 2. Receipts of interest and dividends. | 2. Payments to purchase inventories. |
| 3. Other receipts that are not related to investing or financing activities, such as lawsuit settlements and refunds received from suppliers. | 3. Payments of interest to creditors. |
| | 4. Payments of taxes to government. |
| | 5. Other payments that are not related to investing or financing activities, such as contributions to charity. |

## Investing Activities

A firm's transactions involving (1) the acquisition and disposal of property, plant, and equipment (PPE) assets and intangible assets, (2) the purchase and sale of stocks, bonds, and other securities (that are not cash equivalents), and (3) the lending and subsequent collection of money constitute the basic components of its **investing activities**. The related cash receipts and payments appear in the investing activities section of the statement of cash flows. Examples of these cash flows follow.

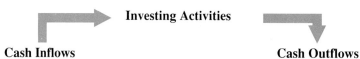

**Investing Activities**

| **Cash Inflows** | **Cash Outflows** |
| --- | --- |
| 1. Receipts from sales of property, plant, and equipment (PPE) assets and intangible assets. | 1. Payments to purchase property, plant, and equipment (PPE) assets and intangible assets. |
| 2. Receipts from sales of investments in stocks, bonds, and other securities (other than cash equivalents). | 2. Payments to purchase stocks, bonds, and-other securities (other than cash equivalents). |
| 3. Receipts from repayments of loans by borrowers. | 3. Payments made to lend money to borrowers. |

## Financing Activities

A firm engages in **financing activities** when it obtains resources from owners, returns resources to owners, borrows resources from creditors, and repays amounts borrowed. Cash flows related to these transactions are reported in the financing activities section of the statement of cash flows. Examples of these cash flows follow.

**Financing Activities**

| **Cash Inflows** | **Cash Outflows** |
| --- | --- |
| 1. Receipts from issuances of common stock and preferred stock and from sales of treasury stock. | 1. Payments to acquire treasury stock. |
| 2. Receipts from issuances of bonds payable, mortgage notes payable, and other notes payable. | 2. Payments of dividends. |
| | 3. Payments to settle outstanding bonds payable, mortgage notes payable, and other notes payable. |

Paying cash to settle such obligations as accounts payable, wages payable, interest payable, and income tax payable are operating activities, not financing activities. Also, cash received as interest and dividends and cash paid as interest (but not as dividends) are classified as cash flows from operating activities.

## Usefulness of Classifications

The classification of cash flows into three categories of activities helps financial statement users interpret cash flow data. To illustrate, assume that companies D, E, and F are similar companies operating in the same industry. Each company reports a $100,000 cash increase during the current year. Information from their statements of cash flows is summarized below.

| | Company D | Company E | Company F |
|---|---|---|---|
| Net cash provided by operating activities . . . . . . . . . . | $100,000 | $ 0 | $ 0 |
| Cash flows from investing activities | | | |
| Sale of property, plant, and equipment (PPE). . . . . . | 0 | 100,000 | 0 |
| Cash flows from financing activities | | | |
| Issuance of notes payable . . . . . . . . . . . . . . . . . . | 0 | 0 | 100,000 |
| Net increase in cash. . . . . . . . . . . . . . . . . . . . . . . . | $100,000 | $100,000 | $100,000 |

Although each company's net cash increase was the same, the source of the increase varied by company. This variation affects the analysis of the cash flow data, particularly for potential short-term creditors who must evaluate the likelihood of obtaining repayment in the future for any funds loaned to the company. Based only on these cash flow data, a potential creditor would feel more comfortable lending money to D than to either E or F. This is because D's cash increase came from its operating activities, whereas both E and F could only break even on their cash flows from operations. Also, E's cash increase came from the sale of property, plant, and equipment (PPE) assets, a source that is not likely to recur regularly. F's cash increase came entirely from borrowed funds. This means F faces additional cash burdens in the future when the interest and principal payments on the note payable become due.

## Noncash Investing and Financing Activities

Another objective of cash flow reporting is to present summary information about a firm's investing and financing activities. Of course, many of these activities affect cash and are therefore already included in the investing and financing sections of the statement of cash flows. Some significant investing and financing events, however, do not affect current cash flows. Examples of **noncash investing and financing activities** are the issuance of stocks, bonds, or leases in exchange for property, plant, and equipment (PPE) assets or intangible assets; the exchange of long-term assets for other long-term assets; and the conversion of long-term debt into common stock. Information about these events must be reported as a supplement to the statement of cash flows.

Noncash investing and financing transactions generally do affect *future* cash flows. Issuing bonds payable to acquire equipment, for example, requires future cash payments for interest and principal on the bonds. On the other hand, converting bonds payable into common stock eliminates future cash payments related to the bonds. Knowledge of these types of events, therefore, is helpful to users of cash flow data who wish to assess a firm's future cash flows.

Information on noncash investing and financing transactions is disclosed in a schedule that is separate from the statement of cash flows. The separate schedule either is reported immediately below the statement of cash flows, or is reported among the notes to the financial statements.

| **BUSINESS INSIGHT** | **Objectivity of Cash** |
|---|---|

Usefulness of financial statements is enhanced when the underlying data are objective and verifiable. Measuring cash and the changes in cash are among the most objective measurements that accountants make. Thus, the statement of cash flows is arguably the most objective financial statement. This characteristic of the statement of cash flows is welcomed by those investors and creditors interested in evaluating the quality of a firm's income.

## Usefulness of the Statement of Cash Flows

A statement of cash flows shows the periodic cash effects of a firm's operating, investing, and financing activities. Distinguishing among these different categories of cash flows helps users compare, evaluate, and predict cash flows. With cash flow information, creditors and investors are better able to assess a firm's ability to settle its liabilities and pay its dividends. A firm's need for outside financing is also better evaluated when using cash flow data. Over time, the statement of cash flows permits users to observe and access management's investing and financing policies.

A statement of cash flows also provides information useful in evaluating a firm's financial flexibility. *Financial flexibility* is a firm's ability to generate sufficient amounts of cash to respond to unanticipated needs and opportunities. Information about past cash flows, particularly cash flows from operations, helps in assessing financial flexibility. An evaluation of a firm's ability to survive an unexpected drop in demand, for example, should include a review of its past cash flows from operations. The larger these cash flows, the greater is the firm's ability to withstand adverse changes in economic conditions. Other financial statements, particularly the balance sheet and its notes, also contain information useful for judging financial flexibility.

Some investors and creditors find the statement of cash flows useful in evaluating the quality of a firm's income. As we know, determining income under accrual accounting procedures requires many accruals, deferrals, allocations, and valuations. These adjustment and measurement procedures introduce more subjectivity into income determination than some financial statement users prefer. These users relate a more objective performance measure—cash flow from operations—to net income. To these users, the higher this ratio is, the higher is the quality of income.

# NET CASH FLOW FROM OPERATING ACTIVITIES

**LO2** Define and explain net cash flows from operating activities.

The first section of a statement of cash flows presents a firm's net cash flow from operating activities. Two alternative formats are used to report the net cash flow from operating activities: the *indirect method* and the *direct method. Both methods report the same amount of net cash flow from operating activities.* (Net cash flows from investing and financing activities are prepared in the same manner under both the indirect and direct methods; only the format for cash flows from operating activities differs.)

## Indirect Method of Reporting

The *indirect method* starts with net income and applies a series of adjustments to net income to convert it to a cash-basis income number, which is the net cash flow from operating activities. The adjustments to net income do not represent specific cash flows, however, so the indirect method does not report any detail concerning individual operating cash inflows and outflows. In contrast, the *direct method* shows individual amounts of cash inflows and cash outflows for the major operating activities. The net difference between these inflows and outflows is the net cash flow from operating activities.

| **BUSINESS INSIGHT** | **Comparison of Accrual and Cash-Basis Amounts** |
|---|---|

Accountants compute net income, shown on the income statement, using accrual accounting procedures. The net cash flow from operating activities may be larger, smaller, or about the same amount. Financial data from recent annual reports of three companies bear this out.

| | Net Income or (Loss) | Net Cash Provided (Used) by Operating Activities |
|---|---|---|
| Ford Motor Company.... | $(7,091) million | $21,728 million |
| Lucent ............... | 527 million | (478) million |
| Home Depot ........... | 6,169 million | 6,494 million |

Accountants estimate that *more than 98% of companies preparing the statement of cash flows use the indirect method.* The indirect method is popular because (1) it is easier and less expensive to prepare than the direct method and (2) the direct method requires a supplemental disclosure showing the indirect method (thus, essentially reporting both methods).

The remainder of this appendix discusses the preparation of the statement of cash flows. The indirect method is presented in this section, and the direct method is presented in Appendix B1. (These discussions are independent of each other; both provide complete coverage of the preparation of the statement of cash flows.)

To prepare a statement of cash flows, we need a firm's income statement, comparative balance sheets, and some additional data taken from the accounting records. Exhibit B.2 presents this information for **Java House**. We use these data to prepare Java's 2007 statement of cash flows using the indirect method. Java's statement of cash flows explains the $25,000 increase in cash that occurred during 2007 (from $10,000 to $35,000) by classifying the firm's cash flows into operating, investing, and financing categories. To get the information to construct the statement we do the following:

1. **Use the indirect method to determine the net cash flow from operating activities.** We apply a series of adjustments to the firm's net income. The adjustments include changes in various current asset and current liability accounts.
2. **Determine cash flows from investing activities.** We do this by analyzing changes in noncurrent asset accounts.
3. **Determine cash flows from financing activities.** We do this by analyzing changes in liability and equity accounts.

| **EXHIBIT B.2** | Financial Data of Java House |
|---|---|

| JAVA HOUSE Income Statement For Year Ended December 31, 2007 | | | JAVA HOUSE Balance Sheet | Dec. 31, 2007 | Dec. 31, 2006 |
|---|---|---|---|---|---|
| Sales. . . . . . . . . . . . . . | | $250,000 | **Assets** | | |
| Cost of goods sold. . . . | $148,000 | | Cash . . . . . . . . . . . . . . . . . . | $ 35,000 | $ 10,000 |
| Wages expense . . . . . . | 52,000 | | Accounts receivable. . . . . . . . | 39,000 | 34,000 |
| Insurance expense. . . . | 5,000 | | Inventory. . . . . . . . . . . . . . . . | 54,000 | 60,000 |
| Depreciation expense. . | 10,000 | | Prepaid insurance. . . . . . . . . . | 17,000 | 4,000 |
| Income tax expense. . . | 11,000 | | Long-term investments . . . . . | 15,000 | — |
| Gain on sale of land . . . | (8,000) | 218,000 | PPE assets . . . . . . . . . . . . . . | 180,000 | 200,000 |
| Net income. . . . . . . . . . | | $ 32,000 | Accumulated depreciation . . . | (50,000) | (40,000) |
| | | | Patent. . . . . . . . . . . . . . . . . . | 60,000 | — |
| | | | Total assets. . . . . . . . . . . . . . | $350,000 | $268,000 |
| **Additional Data for 2007** | | | **Liabilities and Equity** | | |
| 1. Purchased all long-term stock investments for cash at year-end. | | | Accounts payable. . . . . . . . . . | $ 10,000 | $ 19,000 |
| 2. Sold land costing $20,000 for $28,000 cash. | | | Income tax payable . . . . . . . . | 5,000 | 3,000 |
| 3. Acquired $60,000 patent at year-end by issuing common stock at par. | | | Common stock. . . . . . . . . . . | 260,000 | 190,000 |
| | | | Retained earnings . . . . . . . . . | 75,000 | 56,000 |
| 4. All accounts payable relate to merchandise purchases. | | | Total liabilities and equity . . . . | $350,000 | $268,000 |
| 5. Issued common stock at par for $10,000 cash. | | | | | |
| 6. Declared and paid cash dividends of $13,000. | | | | | |

The **indirect method** presents the net cash flow from operating activities by applying a series of adjustments to net income to convert it to a cash-basis amount. The adjustment amounts represent differences between revenues, expenses, gains, and losses recorded under accrual accounting and the related operating cash inflows and outflows. The adjustments are added to or subtracted from net income, depending on whether the related cash flow is more or less than the accrual amount. Exhibit B.3 portrays this process.

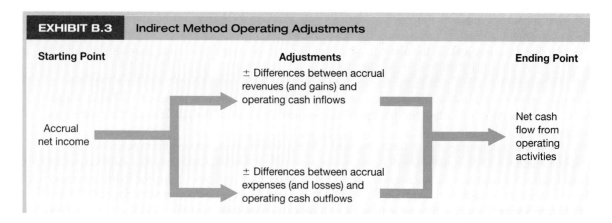

**EXHIBIT B.3**   Indirect Method Operating Adjustments

Starting Point

Accrual net income

Adjustments

± Differences between accrual revenues (and gains) and operating cash inflows

± Differences between accrual expenses (and losses) and operating cash outflows

Ending Point

Net cash flow from operating activities

## Converting Net Income to Net Cash Flow from Operating Activities

Exhibit B.4 summarizes the adjustments to net income in determining operating cash flows. These are the adjustments applied under the indirect method of computing cash flow from operations.

| **EXHIBIT B.4** | **Converting Net Income to Net Cash Flow from Operating Activities** | **Add (+) or Subtract (−) from Net Income** |
|---|---|---|
| Net income | | $ # |
| Add depreciation | | + |
| Add (subtract): Losses (gains) on asset and liability dispositions | | ± |
| Adjust for changes in current assets | | |
|   Subtract increases in current assets | | − |
|   Add decreases in current assets | | + |
| Adjust for changes in current liabilities | | |
|   Add increases in current liabilities | | + |
|   Subtract decreases in current liabilities | | − |
| Net cash flow from operating activities | | $ # |

Net income is first adjusted for noncash expenses such as depreciation, amortization, and gains (losses) from asset and liability dispositions and is then adjusted for changes in current assets and current liabilities to yield net cash flow from operating activities, or cash profit. The depreciation adjustment merely zeros out depreciation expense, a noncash expense, which is deducted in computing net income. The following table provides brief explanations of adjustments for receivables, inventories, payables and accruals:

| | Change in account balance . . . | Means that . . . | Which requires this adjustment to net income to yield cash profit . . . |
|---|---|---|---|
| **Receivables** | Increase | Sales and net income increase, but cash is not yet received | Deduct increase in receivables from net income |
| | Decrease | More cash is received than is reported in sales and net income | Add decrease in receivables to net income |
| **Inventories** | Increase | Cash is paid for inventories that are not yet reflected in cost of goods sold | Deduct increase in inventories from net income |
| | Decrease | Cost of goods sold includes inventory costs that were paid for in a prior period | Add decrease in inventories to net income |

*Continued*

*continued*

| | Change in account balance . . . | Means that . . . | Which requires this adjustment to net income to yield cash profit . . . |
|---|---|---|---|
| Payables and accruals | Increase | More goods and services are acquired on credit, delaying cash payment | Add increase in payables and accruals to net income |
| | Decrease | More cash is paid than that reflected in cost of goods sold or operating expenses | Deduct decrease in payables and accruals from net income |

It is also helpful to use the following decision guide, involving changes in assets, liabilities, and equity, to understand increases and decreases in cash flows.

| | Cash flow increases from | Cash flow decreases from |
|---|---|---|
| Assets. . . . . . . . . . . . . . . . . . . . . | Account decreases | Account increases |
| Liabilities and equity. . . . . . . . . . . | Account increases | Account decreases |

Using this decision guide we can determine the cash flow effects of the income statement and balance sheet information and categorize them into operating, investing or financing.

## Java House Case Illustration

We next explain these adjustments and illustrate them with Java House's data from Exhibit B.2.

### Depreciation, Amortization, and Depletion Expenses

Depreciation, amortization, and depletion expenses represent write-offs of previously recorded assets; so-called noncash expenses. Because depreciation, amortization, and depletion expenses are subtracted in computing net income, we add these expenses to net income as we convert it to a related net operating cash flow. Adding these expenses to net income eliminates them from the income statement and is a necessary adjustment to obtain cash income. Java House had $10,000 of 2007 depreciation expense, so this amount is added to Java's net income of $32,000.

| | |
|---|---|
| Net income. . . . . . . . . . . . . . . . . . . . . . . . . . . . . . . . . . . . . . . . . . . . . . | $32,000 |
| **Add: Depreciation**. . . . . . . . . . . . . . . . . . . . . . . . . . . . . . . . . . . . . . . | **10,000** |

### Gains and Losses Related to Investing or Financing Activities

The income statement may contain gains and losses that relate to investing or financing activities. Gains and losses from the sale of investments, PPE assets, or intangible assets illustrate gains and losses from investing (not operating) activities. A gain or loss from the retirement of bonds payable is an example of a financing gain or loss. The full cash flow effect from these types of events is reported in the investing or financing sections of the statement of cash flows. Therefore, the related gains or losses must be eliminated as we convert net income to net cash flow from operating activities. To eliminate their impact on net income, gains are subtracted and losses are added to net income. Java House had an $8,000 gain from the sale of land in 2007. This gain relates to an investing activity, so it is subtracted from Java's net income.

| | |
|---|---|
| Net income. . . . . . . . . . . . . . . . . . . . . . . . . . . . . . . . . . . . . . . . . . . . . . | $32,000 |
| Add: Depreciation. . . . . . . . . . . . . . . . . . . . . . . . . . . . . . . . . . . . . . . . . | 10,000 |
| **Deduct: Gain on sale of land** . . . . . . . . . . . . . . . . . . . . . . . . . . . . | **(8,000)** |

### Accounts Receivable Change

Credit sales increase accounts receivable; cash collections on account decrease accounts receivable. If, overall, accounts receivable decrease during a year, then cash collections from customers exceed credit sales revenue by the amount of the decrease. Because sales are added in computing net income, the decrease in accounts receivable is added to net income. In essence, this adjustment replaces the sales amount with the larger amount of cash collections from customers. If accounts receivable increase during a year, then sales revenue exceeds the cash collections from customers by the amount of the increase. Because sales are added in computing net income, the increase in accounts receivable is subtracted from net income as we convert it to a net cash flow from operating activities. In essence, this adjustment replaces the sales amount with the smaller amount of cash collections from customers. Java's accounts receivable increased $5,000 during 2007, so this increase is subtracted from net income under the indirect method.

| | |
|---|---:|
| Net income. . . . . . . . . . . . . . . . . . . . . . . . . . . . . . . . . . . . . . . . . . . | $32,000 |
| Add: Depreciation. . . . . . . . . . . . . . . . . . . . . . . . . . . . . . . . . . . . . | 10,000 |
| Deduct: Gain on sale of land . . . . . . . . . . . . . . . . . . . . . . . . . . . | (8,000) |
| **Deduct: Accounts receivable increase**. . . . . . . . . . . . . . . . . . | **(5,000)** |

## Inventory Change

The adjustment for an inventory change is one of two adjustments to net income that together cause the cost of goods sold expense to be replaced by an amount representing the cash paid during the period for merchandise purchased. The second adjustment, which we examine shortly, is for the change in accounts payable. The effect of the inventory adjustment alone is to adjust net income for the difference between the cost of goods sold and the cost of merchandise purchased during the period. The cost of merchandise purchased increases inventory; the cost of goods sold decreases inventory. An overall decrease in inventory during a period must mean, therefore, that the cost of merchandise purchased was less than the cost of goods sold by the amount of the decrease. Because cost of goods sold was subtracted in computing net income, the inventory decrease is added to net income. After this adjustment, the effect of the cost of goods sold on net income has been replaced by the smaller cost of merchandise purchased. Similarly, if inventory increased during a period, the cost of merchandise purchased is larger than the cost of goods sold by the amount of the increase. To replace the cost of goods sold with the cost of merchandise purchased, the inventory increase is subtracted from net income. Java's inventory decreased $6,000 during 2007, so this decrease is added to net income.

| | |
|---|---:|
| Net income. . . . . . . . . . . . . . . . . . . . . . . . . . . . . . . . . . . . . . . . . . . | $32,000 |
| Add: Depreciation. . . . . . . . . . . . . . . . . . . . . . . . . . . . . . . . . . . . . | 10,000 |
| Deduct: Gain on sale of land . . . . . . . . . . . . . . . . . . . . . . . . . . . | (8,000) |
| Deduct: Accounts receivable increase. . . . . . . . . . . . . . . . . . . | (5,000) |
| **Add: Inventory decrease** . . . . . . . . . . . . . . . . . . . . . . . . . . . . . | **6,000** |

## Prepaid Expenses Change

Cash prepayments of various expenses increase a firm's prepaid expenses. When the related expenses for the period are subsequently recorded, the prepaid expenses decrease. An overall decrease in prepaid expenses for a period means that the cash prepayments were less than the related expenses. Because the expenses were subtracted in determining net income, the indirect method adds the decrease in prepaid expenses to net income as it is converted to a cash flow amount. The effect of the addition is to replace the expense amount with the smaller cash payment amount. Similarly, an increase in prepaid expenses is subtracted from net income because an increase means that the cash prepayments during the year were more than the related expenses. Java's prepaid insurance increased $13,000 during 2007, so this increase is deducted from net income.

| | |
|---|---:|
| Net income. . . . . . . . . . . . . . . . . . . . . . . . . . . . . . . . . . . . . . . . . . . | $32,000 |
| Add: Depreciation. . . . . . . . . . . . . . . . . . . . . . . . . . . . . . . . . . . . . | 10,000 |
| Deduct: Gain on sale of land . . . . . . . . . . . . . . . . . . . . . . . . . . . | (8,000) |
| Deduct: Accounts receivable increase. . . . . . . . . . . . . . . . . . . | (5,000) |
| Add: Inventory decrease . . . . . . . . . . . . . . . . . . . . . . . . . . . . . | 6,000 |
| **Deduct: Prepaid insurance increase**. . . . . . . . . . . . . . . . . . . | **(13,000)** |

## Accounts Payable Change

When merchandise is purchased on account, accounts payable increase by the amount of the goods' cost. Accounts payable decrease when cash payments are made to settle the accounts. An overall decrease in accounts payable during a year means that cash payments for purchases were more than the cost of the purchases. An accounts payable decrease, therefore, is subtracted from net income under the indirect method. The deduction, in effect, replaces the cost of merchandise purchased with the larger cash payments for merchandise purchased. (Recall that the earlier inventory adjustment replaced the cost of goods sold with the cost of merchandise purchased.) In contrast, an increase in accounts payable means that cash payments for purchases were less than the cost of purchases for the period. Thus, an accounts payable increase is added to net income as it is converted to a cash flow amount. Java House shows a $9,000 decrease in accounts payable during 2007. This decrease is subtracted from net income.

| | |
|---|---:|
| Net income | $32,000 |
| Add: Depreciation | 10,000 |
| Deduct: Gain on sale of land | (8,000) |
| Deduct: Accounts receivable increase | (5,000) |
| Add: Inventory decrease | 6,000 |
| Deduct: Prepaid insurance increase | (13,000) |
| **Deduct: Accounts payable decrease** | **(9,000)** |

## Accrued Liabilities Change

Changes in accrued liabilities are interpreted the same way as changes in accounts payable. A decrease means that cash payments exceeded the related expense amounts; an increase means that cash payments were less than the related expenses. Decreases are subtracted from net income; increases are added to net income. Java has one accrued liability, income tax payable, and it increased by $2,000 during 2007. The $2,000 increase is added to net income.

| | |
|---|---:|
| Net income | $32,000 |
| Add: Depreciation | 10,000 |
| Deduct: Gain on sale of land | (8,000) |
| Deduct: Accounts receivable increase | (5,000) |
| Add: Inventory decrease | 6,000 |
| Deduct: Prepaid insurance increase | (13,000) |
| Deduct: Accounts payable decrease | (9,000) |
| **Add: Income tax payable increase** | **2,000** |

We have now identified the adjustments to convert Java's net income to its net cash flow from operating activities. The operating activities section of the statement of cash flows appears as follows under the indirect method:

| | |
|---|---:|
| Net income | $32,000 |
| Add (deduct) items to convert net income to cash basis: | |
|     Depreciation | 10,000 |
|     Gain on sale of land | (8,000) |
|     Accounts receivable increase | (5,000) |
|     Inventory decrease | 6,000 |
|     Prepaid insurance increase | (13,000) |
|     Accounts payable decrease | (9,000) |
|     Income tax payable increase | 2,000 |
| Net cash provided by operating activities | $15,000 |

To summarize, net cash flows from operating activities begins with net income (loss) and eliminates non-cash expenses (such as depreciation) and any gains and losses that are properly reported in the investing and financing sections. Next, cash inflows (outflows) relating to changes in the level of current operating assets and liabilities are added (subtracted) to yield net cash flows from operating activities. During the period, Java earned cash operating profits of $34,000 ($32,000 + $10,000 − $8,000), but used $19,000 of cash (−$5,000 + $6,000 − $13,000 − $9,000 + $2,000) to increase net working capital. Cash outflows relating to the increase in net working capital are a common occurrence for growing companies, and this net asset increase must be financed just like the increase in PPE assets.

---

**BUSINESS INSIGHT**     **Starbucks' Add-Backs for Operating Cash Flow**

Starbucks reports $564.259 million of net income for 2006 and $1,131.633 million of operating cash inflows. The difference between these numbers is mainly due to $412.625 million of depreciation expense that is included in net income. Depreciation is a noncash charge; an expense not requiring cash payment. It is added back to income in computing operating cash flows. Starbucks also reports a $19.622 million asset impairment (write-down). This, too, is a noncash charge and is an addback in computing operating cash flows. Starbucks subtracts $84.324 million for deferred taxes, indicating that cash payments of taxes are greater than tax expense reported in income (this is due to increased deferred tax assets). It also subtracts $60.570 million for equity in income of investees, meaning that it reported equity income that it did not receive in cash in the form of dividends (see Module 7). Starbucks also adds back its $105.664 million of stock option expense since that compensation is paid in stock, not in cash, and reclassifies the $117.368 million of tax benefits it receives for the exercise of these options from operating activities to financing activities as required under current GAAP.

---

**MANAGERIAL DECISION**     **You Are the Securities Analyst**

You are analyzing a company's statement of cash flows. The company has two items relating to its accounts receivable. First, the company finances the sale of its products to some customers; the increase to notes receivable is classified as an investing activity. Second, the company sells its accounts receivable to a separate entity, such as a trust. As a result, sale of receivables is reported as an asset sale; this reduces receivables and yields a gain or loss on sale (in this case, the company is not required to consolidate the trust as a Primary Beneficiary of a Variable Interest Entity—see Module 9). This action increases its operating cash flows. How should you interpret this cash flow increase? [Answer, p. B-26]

---

# CASH FLOWS FROM INVESTING ACTIVITIES

## Analyze Remaining Noncash Assets

**LO3** Define and explain net cash flows from investing activities.

Investing activities cause changes in asset accounts. Usually the accounts affected (other than cash) are noncurrent asset accounts such as property, plant and equipment assets and long-term investments, although short-term investment accounts can also be affected. To determine the cash flows from investing activities, *we analyze changes in all noncash asset accounts not used in computing net cash flow from operating activities.* Our objective is to identify any investing cash flows related to these changes.

## Java House Case Illustration

### Analyze Change in Long-Term Investments

Java's comparative balance sheets show that long-term investments increased $15,000 during 2007. The increase means that investments must have been purchased, and the additional data reported indicates that cash was spent to purchase long-term stock investments. Purchasing stock is an investing activity. Thus, a $15,000 purchase of stock investments is reported as a cash outflow from investing activities in the statement of cash flows.

### Analyze Change in Property, Plant and Equipment Assets

Java's PPE assets decreased $20,000 during 2007. PPE assets decrease as the result of disposals, and the additional data for Java House indicate that land was sold for cash in 2007. Selling land is an investing activity. Thus, the sale of land for $28,000 is reported as a cash inflow from investing activities in the statement of cash flows. (Recall that the $8,000 gain on sale of land was deducted as a reconciling item in the operating section; see above)

### Analyze Change in Accumulated Depreciation

Java's accumulated depreciation increased $10,000 during 2007. Accumulated depreciation increases when depreciation expense is recorded. Java's 2007 depreciation expense was $10,000, so the total change in accumulated depreciation is the result of the recording of depreciation expense. As previously discussed, there is no cash flow related to the recording of depreciation expense, and we have previously adjusted for this expense in our computation of net cash flows from operating activities.

### Analyze Change in Patent

We see from the comparative balance sheets that Java had an increase of $60,000 in a patent. The increase means that a patent was acquired, and the additional data indicate that common stock was issued to obtain a patent. This event is a noncash investing (acquiring a patent) and financing (issuing common stock) transaction that must be disclosed as supplementary information to the statement of cash flows.

---

**BUSINESS INSIGHT**    **Starbucks' Investing Activities**

Starbucks used $841.040 million cash for investing activities in 2006. Of this, $61.123 million ($431.181 million + $269.134 million − $639.192 million) is related to the purchase of securities. Investing activities are not necessarily related to operating activities (such as purchases of PPE assets). Starbucks also spent $91.734 million on acquisitions of other companies; which is the cash portion of the acquisition cost. It might also have issued debt and stock to finance this acquisition, which would be excluded from this statement and would be identified as noncash financing and investing activities in a footnote. Starbucks invested $771.230 million in property, plant, and equipment (PPE). These expenditures might have been for owned property or for leasehold improvements on leased property. It also spent $39.199 million on other investments.

---

# CASH FLOWS FROM FINANCING ACTIVITIES

## Analyze Remaining Liabilities and Equity

Financing activities cause changes in liability and stockholders' equity accounts. Usually the accounts affected are noncurrent accounts such as bonds payable and common stock, although a current liability such as short-term notes payable can also be affected. To determine the cash flows from financing activities, *we analyze changes in all liability and stockholders' equity accounts that were not used in computing net cash flow from operating activities.* Our objective is to identify any financing cash flows related to these changes.

**LO4** Define and explain net cash flows from financing activities.

## Java House Case Illustration

### Analyze Change in Common Stock

Java's common stock increased $70,000 during 2007. Common stock increases when shares of stock are issued. As noted in discussing the patent increase, common stock with a $60,000 par value was issued in exchange for a patent. This event is disclosed as a noncash investing and financing transaction. The other $10,000 increase in common stock, as noted in the additional data, resulted from an issuance of stock for cash. Issuing common stock is a financing activity, so a $10,000 cash inflow from a stock issuance appears as a financing activity in the statement of cash flows.

### Analyze Change in Retained Earnings

Retained earnings grew from $56,000 to $75,000 during 2007—a $19,000 increase. This increase is the net result of Java's $32,000 of net income (which increased retained earnings) and a $13,000 cash dividend (which decreased retained earnings). Because every item in Java's income statement was considered in computing the net cash provided by operating activities, only the cash dividend remains to be considered. Paying a cash dividend is a financing activity. Thus, a $13,000 cash dividend appears as a cash outflow from financing activities in the statement of cash flows. We have now completed the analysis of all of Java's noncash balance sheet accounts and can prepare the 2007 statement of cash flows. Exhibit B.5 shows this statement.

If there are cash inflows and outflows from similar types of investing and financing activities, the inflows and outflows are reported separately (rather than reporting only the net difference). For example, proceeds from the sale of plant assets are reported separately from outlays made to acquire plant assets. Similarly, funds borrowed are reported separately from debt repayments, and proceeds from issuing stock are reported separately from outlays to acquire treasury stock.

---

**BUSINESS INSIGHT** | **Starbucks' Financing Activities**

Starbucks realized cash *outflows* of $694.796 million ($159.249 million − $854.045 million) from issuance of common stock, net of repurchases. Only stock issued for cash is reflected in the statement of cash flows. Stock issued in connection with acquisitions is not reflected because it does not involve cash. Issuance of stock is often related to the exercise of employee stock options, and companies frequently repurchase stock to offset the dilution. Starbucks also reports a cash inflow of $423 million from borrowings during the year and a cash outflow of approximately $0.9 million relating to the repayment of long-term debt. The net effect is a decrease in cash of $155.326 million from financing activities.

---

# SUMMARY OF NET CASH FLOW REPORTING

Preparation of the statement of cash flows draws mainly on information from the income statement and the balance sheet. Each of its three sections uses different portions of these two statements as highlighted in bold font as follows:

| | Information from income statement | Information from balance sheet | |
|---|---|---|---|
| Net cash flows from operating activities. . . . | Revenues<br>− Expenses<br>= Net income | Current assets<br>Long-term assets | Current liabilities<br>Long-term liabilities<br>Equity |
| Net cash flows from investing activities . . . . | Revenues<br>− Expenses<br>= Net income | Current assets<br>Long-term assets | Current liabilities<br>Long-term liabilities<br>Equity |
| Net cash flows from financing activities . . . . | Revenues<br>− Expenses<br>= Net income | Current assets<br>Long-term assets | Current liabilities<br>Long-term liabilities<br>Equity |

Specifically, the three sections draw generally on the following information:

- **Net cash flows from operating activities** draws on the income statement and the current asset and current liabilities sections of the balance sheet
- **Net cash flows from investing activities** draws on the long-term assets section of the balance sheet
- **Net cash flows from financing activities** draws on the long-term liabilities and stockholders' equity sections of the balance sheet.

These relations do not hold exactly, but they provide us a useful way to visualize the construction of the statement of cash flows.

We now summarize the cash flow effects of the income statement and balance sheet information we developed on previous pages, and categorize them into the operating, investing and financing classifications in the following table:

| Account | Change | Source or Use | Cash flow effect | Classification on SCF |
|---|---|---|---|---|
| Current assets | | | | |
| Accounts receivable . . . . . . . . . . | +5,000 | Use | −5,000 | Operating |
| Inventories . . . . . . . . . . . . . . . . | −6,000 | Source | +6,000 | Operating |
| Prepaid insurance. . . . . . . . . . . | +13,000 | Use | −13,000 | Operating |
| Noncurrent assets | | | | |
| PPE related. . . . . . . . . . . . . . . . | | | | Investing |
| Accumulated depreciation . . . | +10,000 | Neither | +10,000 | Operating |
| Sale of land | | | | |
| Proceeds . . . . . . . . . . . . . . | +28,000 | Source | +28,000 | Investing |
| Gain . . . . . . . . . . . . . . . . . . | −8,000 | Neither | −8,000 | Operating |
| Investments . . . . . . . . . . . . . . . | +15,000 | Use | −15,000 | Investing |
| Current liabilities | | | | |
| Accounts payable. . . . . . . . . . . . | −9,000 | Use | −9,000 | Operating |
| Income tax payable . . . . . . . . . . | +2,000 | Source | +2,000 | Operating |
| Long-term liabilities . . . . . . . . . . . | | | | Financing |
| Stockholders' equity | | | | |
| Common stock . . . . . . . . . . . . . . | +10,000 | Source | +10,000 | Financing |
| Retained earnings. . . . . . . . . . . | | | | |
| Net income . . . . . . . . . . . . . . | +32,000 | Source | +32,000 | Operating |
| Dividends . . . . . . . . . . . . . . . | +13,000 | Use | −13,000 | Financing |
| Total (net cash flow) . . . . . . . . . . . | | | +25,000 | |

The current year's cash balance increases by $25,000, from $10,000 to $35,000. Formal preparation of the statement of cash flows can proceed once we have addressed one final issue: required supplemental disclosures. We discuss that topic in the next section.

## Supplemental Disclosures for Indirect Method

When the indirect method is used in the statement of cash flows, three separate disclosures are required: (1) two specific operating cash outflows—cash paid for interest and cash paid for income taxes, (2) a schedule or description of all noncash investing and financing transactions, and (3) the firm's policy for determining which highly liquid, short-term investments are treated as cash equivalents. A firm's policy regarding cash equivalents is placed in the financial statement notes. The other two separate disclosures are reported either in the notes or at the bottom of the statement of cash flows.

## Java House Case Illustration

Java House incurred no interest cost during 2007. It did pay income taxes. Our discussion of the $2,000 change in income tax payable during 2007 revealed that the increase meant that cash tax payments were less than income tax expense by the amount of the increase. Income tax expense was $11,000, so the cash paid for income taxes was $2,000 less than $11,000, or $9,000.

Java House did have one noncash investing and financing event during 2007: the issuance of common stock to acquire a patent. This event, as well as the cash paid for income taxes, is disclosed as supplemental information to the statement of cash flows in Exhibit B.5.

| EXHIBIT B.5 | Statement of Cash Flows for Indirect Method with Supplemental Disclosures |
|---|---|

**JAVA HOUSE**
**Statement of Cash Flows**
**For Year Ended December 31, 2007**

| | | |
|---|---:|---:|
| **Net cash flow from operating activities** | | |
| Net income | $32,000 | |
| Add (deduct) items to convert net income to cash basis | | |
| Depreciation | 10,000 | |
| Gain on sale of land | (8,000) | |
| Accounts receivable increase | (5,000) | |
| Inventory decrease | 6,000 | |
| Prepaid insurance increase | (13,000) | |
| Accounts payable decrease | (9,000) | |
| Income tax payable increase | 2,000 | |
| Net cash provided by operating activities | | $15,000 |
| **Cash flows from investing activities** | | |
| Purchase of stock investments | (15,000) | |
| Sale of land | 28,000 | |
| Net cash provided by investing activities | | 13,000 |
| **Cash flows from financing activities** | | |
| Issuance of common stock | 10,000 | |
| Payment of dividends | (13,000) | |
| Net cash used by financing activities | | (3,000) |
| Net increase in cash | | 25,000 |
| Cash at beginning of year | | 10,000 |
| Cash at end of year | | $35,000 |
| | | |
| **Supplemental cash flow disclosures** | | |
| Cash paid for income taxes | | $ 9,000 |
| Schedule of noncash investing and financing activities | | |
| Issuance of common stock to acquire patent | | $60,000 |

## Ratio Analyses of Cash Flows

**LO5** Describe and apply ratios based on operating cash flows.

Data from the statement of cash flows enter into various financial ratios. Two such ratios are the operating cash flow to current liabilities ratio and the operating cash flow to capital expenditures ratio.

### Operating Cash Flow to Current Liabilities Ratio

Two measures previously introduced—the current ratio and the quick ratio—emphasize the relation of current assets to current liabilities in an attempt to measure the ability of the firm to liquidate current liabilities when they become due. The **operating cash flow to current liabilities ratio** is another measure of the ability to liquidate current liabilities and is calculated as follows:

**Operating Cash Flow to Current Liabilities = Net Cash Flow from Operating Activities/Average Current Liabilities**

Net cash flow from operating activities is obtained from the statement of cash flows; it represents the excess amount of cash derived from operations during the year after deducting working capital needs and payments required on current liabilities. The denominator is the average of the beginning and ending current liabilities for the year.

To illustrate, the following amounts are taken from the 2006 financial statements for Cisco Systems, Inc.

| | |
|---|---:|
| Net cash flow from operating activities | $ 7,899 million |
| Current liabilities at beginning of the year | 9,511 million |
| Current liabilities at end of the year | 11,313 million |

Its operating cash flow to current liabilities ratio of 0.76 is computed as follows:

$$\$7,899 \text{ million } ([\$9,511 \text{ million } + \$11,313 \text{ million}]/2) = 0.76$$

Cisco's operating cash flow to current liabilities ratio for the preceding year was 0.83. The higher this ratio, the stronger is a firm's ability to settle current liabilities as they come due. The decrease in Cisco's ratio from 0.83 to 0.76 is unfavorable, although relatively minor. A ratio of 0.5 is considered a good ratio, so, Cisco's ratio of 0.76 is above average.

## Operating Cash Flow to Capital Expenditures Ratio

To remain competitive, an entity must be able to replace, and expand when appropriate, its property, plant, and equipment. A ratio that helps assess a firm's ability to do this from internally generated cash flow is the **operating cash flow to capital expenditures ratio**, which is computed as follows:

**Operating Cash Flow to Capital Expenditures = Net Cash Flow from Operating Activities/Annual Capital Expenditures**

The numerator in this ratio comes from the first section of the statement of cash flows—the section reporting the net cash flow from operating activities. Information for the denominator can be found in one or more places in the financial statements and related disclosures. Data on capital expenditures are part of the required industry segment disclosures in notes to the financial statements. Capital expenditures are often also shown in the investing activities section of the statement of cash flows. Also, capital expenditures often appear in the comparative selected financial data presented as supplementary information to the financial statements. Finally, management's discussion and analysis of the statements commonly identify the annual capital expenditures.

A ratio in excess of 1.0 means that the firm's current operating activities are providing cash in excess of the amount needed to provide the desired level of plant capacity and would normally be considered a sign of financial strength. This ratio is also viewed as an indicator of long-term solvency—a ratio exceeding 1.0 means that there is operating cash flow in excess of capital needs that can then be used to repay outstanding long-term debt.

The interpretation of this ratio for a firm is influenced by its trend in recent years, the ratio size being achieved by other firms in the same industry, and the stage of the firm's life cycle. A firm in the early stages of its life cycle, when periods of rapid expansion occur, is expected to experience a lower ratio than a firm in the mature stage of its life cycle, when maintenance of plant capacity is more likely than expansion of capacity.

To illustrate the ratio's computation, Cicso Systems reported capital expenditures in 2006 of $772 million. Cisco's operating cash flow to capital expenditures ratio for that same year is 10.23, computed as $7,899 million/$772 million. Following are recent operating cash flow to capital expenditures ratios for several companies:

| | |
|---|---|
| Colgate-Palmolive (consumer grocery products) | 4.59 |
| Lockheed Martin (aerospace) | 3.69 |
| Verizon Communications (telecommunications) | 1.44 |
| Harley-Davidson (motorcycle manufacturer) | 4.84 |
| Home Depot (home products) | 1.67 |

## APPENDIX-END REVIEW

**Part A**

1. Which of the following is not disclosed in a statement of cash flows?
   a. A transfer of cash to a cash equivalent investment
   b. The amount of cash at year-end
   c. Cash outflows from investing activities during the period
   d. Cash inflows from financing activities during the period
2. Which of the following events appears in the cash flows from investing activities section of the statement of cash flows?
   a. Cash received as interest
   b. Cash received from issuance of common stock
   c. Cash purchase of equipment
   d. Cash payment of dividends

3. Which of the following events appears in the cash flows from financing activities section of the statement of cash flows?
   a. Cash purchase of equipment
   b. Cash purchase of bonds issued by another company
   c. Cash received as repayment for funds loaned
   d. Cash purchase of treasury stock

4. Tyler Company has a net income of $49,000 and the following related items:

| | |
|---|---:|
| Depreciation expense. . . . . . . . . . . . . . . . . . . . . . . . . . . . | $ 5,000 |
| Accounts receivable increase. . . . . . . . . . . . . . . . . . . . . . | 2,000 |
| Inventory decrease. . . . . . . . . . . . . . . . . . . . . . . . . . . . . | 10,000 |
| Accounts payable decrease. . . . . . . . . . . . . . . . . . . . . | 4,000 |

Using the indirect method, what is Tyler's net cash flow from operations?

a. $42,000         b. $46,000         c. $58,000         d. $38,000

## Solution

1. a                2. c                3. d                4. c

### Part B

Expresso Royale's income statement and comparative balance sheets follow:

**EXPRESSO ROYALE**
**Income Statement**
**For Year Ended December 31, 2007**

| | | |
|---|---:|---:|
| Sales. . . . . . . . . . . . . . . . . . . . . . . . . . . . . . . . . . . | | $385,000 |
| Dividend income. . . . . . . . . . . . . . . . . . . . . . | | 5,000 |
| | | 390,000 |
| Cost of goods sold. . . . . . . . . . . . . . . . . . . . | $233,000 | |
| Wages expense . . . . . . . . . . . . . . . . . . . . . . | 82,000 | |
| Advertising expense. . . . . . . . . . . . . . . . . . . | 10,000 | |
| Depreciation expense. . . . . . . . . . . . . . . . . . | 11,000 | |
| Income tax expense. . . . . . . . . . . . . . . . . . . | 17,000 | |
| Loss on sale of investments. . . . . . . . . . . . . | 2,000 | 355,000 |
| Net income. . . . . . . . . . . . . . . . . . . . . . . . . . | | $ 35,000 |

**EXPRESSO ROYALE**
**Balance Sheets**

| | Dec. 31, 2007 | Dec. 31, 2006 |
|---|---:|---:|
| **Assets** | | |
| Cash. . . . . . . . . . . . . . . . . . . . . . . . . . . . . . . . . . | $ 8,000 | $ 12,000 |
| Accounts receivable. . . . . . . . . . . . . . . . . . . . . . . | 22,000 | 28,000 |
| Inventory. . . . . . . . . . . . . . . . . . . . . . . . . . . . . . . | 94,000 | 66,000 |
| Prepaid advertising. . . . . . . . . . . . . . . . . . . . . . | 12,000 | 9,000 |
| Long-term investments—Available-for-sale. . . . . . . . | 30,000 | 41,000 |
| Fair value adjustment to investments. . . . . . . . . . . . | — | (1,000) |
| Plant assets . . . . . . . . . . . . . . . . . . . . . . . . . . . | 178,000 | 130,000 |
| Accumulated depreciation . . . . . . . . . . . . . . . . . . | (72,000) | (61,000) |
| Total assets. . . . . . . . . . . . . . . . . . . . . . . . . . . | $272,000 | $224,000 |

*Continued*

| EXPRESSO ROYALE Balance Sheets | | |
| --- | --- | --- |
| | **Dec. 31, 2007** | **Dec. 31, 2006** |
| **Liabilities and Equity** | | |
| Accounts payable. . . . . . . . . . . . . . . . . . . . . . . . . . . . | $ 27,000 | $ 14,000 |
| Wages payable. . . . . . . . . . . . . . . . . . . . . . . . . . . . . . | 6,000 | 2,500 |
| Income tax payable . . . . . . . . . . . . . . . . . . . . . . . . . | 3,000 | 4,500 |
| Common stock. . . . . . . . . . . . . . . . . . . . . . . . . . . . . . | 139,000 | 125,000 |
| Retained earnings . . . . . . . . . . . . . . . . . . . . . . . . . . | 97,000 | 79,000 |
| Unrealized loss on investments . . . . . . . . . . . . . . . . | — | (1,000) |
| Total liabilities and equity . . . . . . . . . . . . . . . . . . . . . | $272,000 | $224,000 |

Cash dividends of $17,000 were declared and paid during 2007. Plant assets were purchased for cash in 2007, and, later in the year, additional common stock was issued for cash. Investments costing $11,000 were sold for cash at a $2,000 loss in 2007; an unrealized loss of $1,000 on these investments had been recorded in 2006 (at December 31, 2007, the cost and fair value of unsold investments are equal).

## Required
a. Compute the change in cash that occurred during 2007.
b. Prepare a 2007 statement of cash flows using the indirect method.

## Solution
a. $8,000 ending balance − $12,000 beginning balance = $4,000 decrease in cash
b. (1) Use the indirect method to determine the net cash flow from operating activities.
   • Adjustments to convert Expresso Royale's net income of $35,000 to a net cash provided by operating activities of $38,000 are shown in the following statement of cash flows.
   (2) Analyze changes in remaining noncash asset (and contra asset) accounts to determine cash flows from investing activities.
   • Long-Term Investments: $11,000 decrease resulted from sale of investments for cash at a $2,000 loss. Cash received from sale of investments = $9,000 ($11,000 cost − $2,000 loss).
   • Fair Value Adjustment to Investments: $1,000 decrease resulted from the elimination of this account balance (and the Unrealized Loss of Investments) at the end of 2007. No cash flow effect.
   • Plant Assets: $48,000 increase resulted from purchase of plant assets for cash. Cash paid to purchase plant assets = $48,000.
   • Accumulated Depreciation: $11,000 increase resulted from the recording of 2007 depreciation. No cash flow effect.
   (3) Analyze changes in remaining liability and stockholders' equity accounts to determine cash flows from financing activities.
   • Common Stock: $14,000 increase resulted from the issuance of stock for cash. Cash received from issuance of common stock = $14,000.
   • Retained Earnings: $18,000 increase resulted from net income of $35,000 and dividend declaration of $17,000. Cash dividends paid = $17,000.
   • Unrealized Loss on Investments: $1,000 decrease resulted from the elimination of this account balance (and the Fair Value Adjustment to Investments) at the end of 2007. No cash flow effect.

The statement of cash flows follows:

**EXPRESSO ROYALE**
**Statement of Cash Flows**
**For Year Ended December 31, 2007**

**Net cash flow from operating activities**

| | | |
|---|---:|---:|
| Net income. . . . . . . . . . . . . . . . . . . . . . . . . . . . . . . . . | $35,000 | |
| Add (deduct) items to convert net income to cash basis | | |
| Depreciation . . . . . . . . . . . . . . . . . . . . . . . . . . . . . . . | 11,000 | |
| Loss on sale of investments. . . . . . . . . . . . . . . . . | 2,000 | |
| Accounts receivable decrease . . . . . . . . . . . . . . . | 6,000 | |
| Inventory increase. . . . . . . . . . . . . . . . . . . . . . . . . | (28,000) | |
| Prepaid advertising increase. . . . . . . . . . . . . . . . . | (3,000) | |
| Accounts payable increase. . . . . . . . . . . . . . . . . . | 13,000 | |
| Wages payable increase. . . . . . . . . . . . . . . . . . . . | 3,500 | |
| Income tax payable decrease. . . . . . . . . . . . . . . . | (1,500) | |
| Net cash provided by operating activities . . . . . . . . . | | $38,000 |
| **Cash flows from investing activities** | | |
| Sale of investments . . . . . . . . . . . . . . . . . . . . . . . | 9,000 | |
| Purchase of plant assets . . . . . . . . . . . . . . . . . . . | (48,000) | |
| Net cash used by investing activities. . . . . . . . . . . . . | | (39,000) |
| **Cash flows from financing activities** | | |
| Issuance of common stock. . . . . . . . . . . . . . . . . . | 14,000 | |
| Payment of dividends. . . . . . . . . . . . . . . . . . . . . . | (17,000) | |
| Net cash used by financing activities. . . . . . . . . . . . | | (3,000) |
| Net decrease in cash . . . . . . . . . . . . . . . . . . . . . . . . | | (4,000) |
| Cash at beginning of year . . . . . . . . . . . . . . . . . . . . | | 12,000 |
| Cash at end of year . . . . . . . . . . . . . . . . . . . . . . . . . | | $ 8,000 |

# APPENDIX B1: Direct Method Reporting for the Statement of Cash Flows

To prepare a statement of cash flows, we need a firm's income statement, comparative balance sheets, and some additional data taken from the accounting records. Exhibit B.2 presents this information for Java House. We use these data to prepare Java's 2007 statement of cash flows using the direct method. Java's statement of cash flows explains the $25,000 increase in cash that occurred during 2007 (from $10,000 to $35,000) by classifying the firm's cash flows into operating, investing, and financing categories. To get the information to construct the statement, we do the following:

1. **Use the direct method to determine individual cash flows from operating activities.** We use changes that occurred during 2007 in various current asset and current liability accounts.
2. **Determine cash flows from investing activities.** We do this by analyzing changes in noncurrent asset accounts.
3. **Determine cash flows from financing activities.** We do this by analyzing changes in liability and stockholders' equity accounts.

The net cash flows from investing and financing are identical to those prepared using the indirect method. Only the format of the net cash flows from operating activities differs between the two methods, not the total amount of cash generated from operating activities.

## Cash Flows from Operating Activities

The **direct method** presents net cash flow from operating activities by showing the major categories of operating cash receipts and payments. The operating cash receipts and payments are usually determined by converting the accrual revenues and expenses to corresponding cash amounts. It is efficient to do it this way because the accrual revenues and expenses are readily available in the income statement.

# Converting Revenues and Expenses to Cash Flows

Exhibit B.6 summarizes the procedures for converting individual income statement items to corresponding cash flows from operating activities.

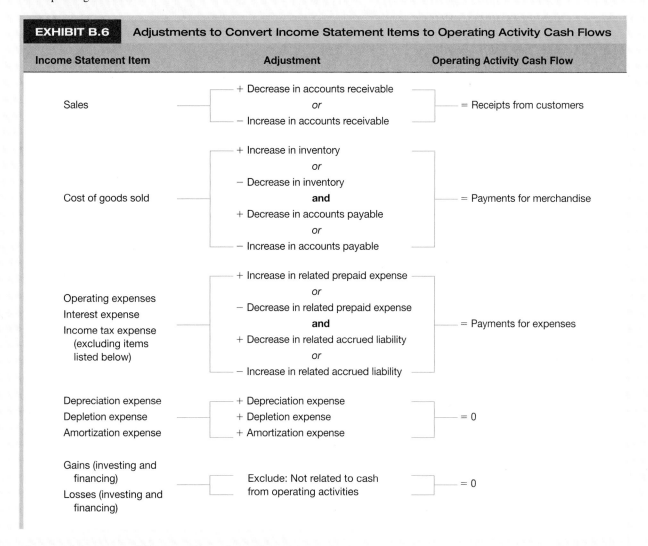

**EXHIBIT B.6    Adjustments to Convert Income Statement Items to Operating Activity Cash Flows**

| Income Statement Item | Adjustment | Operating Activity Cash Flow |
|---|---|---|
| Sales | + Decrease in accounts receivable *or* − Increase in accounts receivable | = Receipts from customers |
| Cost of goods sold | + Increase in inventory *or* − Decrease in inventory **and** + Decrease in accounts payable *or* − Increase in accounts payable | = Payments for merchandise |
| Operating expenses Interest expense Income tax expense (excluding items listed below) | + Increase in related prepaid expense *or* − Decrease in related prepaid expense **and** + Decrease in related accrued liability *or* − Increase in related accrued liability | = Payments for expenses |
| Depreciation expense Depletion expense Amortization expense | + Depreciation expense + Depletion expense + Amortization expense | = 0 |
| Gains (investing and financing) Losses (investing and financing) | Exclude: Not related to cash from operating activities | = 0 |

# Java House Case Illustration

We next explain and illustrate the process of converting Java House's 2007 revenues and expenses to corresponding cash flows from operating activities under the direct method.

## Convert Sales to Cash Received from Customers

During 2007, accounts receivable increased $5,000. This increase means that during 2007, cash collections on account (which decrease accounts receivable) were less than credit sales (which increase accounts receivable). We compute cash received from customers as follows (this computation assumes that no accounts were written off as uncollectible during the period):

|   | Sales | $250,000 |
|---|---|---|
| − | Increase in accounts receivable | (5,000) |
| = | Cash received from customers | $245,000 |

## Convert Cost of Goods Sold to Cash Paid for Merchandise Purchased

The conversion of cost of goods sold to cash paid for merchandise purchased is a two-step process. First, cost of goods sold is adjusted for the change in inventory to determine the amount of purchases during the year. Then the purchases amount is adjusted for the change in accounts payable to derive the cash paid for merchandise purchased. Inventory decreased from $60,000 to $54,000 during 2007. This $6,000 decrease indicates that the cost of goods sold exceeded the cost of goods purchased during the year. The year's purchases amount is computed as follows:

| | |
|---|---|
| Cost of goods sold . . . . . . . . . . . . . . . . . . . | $148,000 |
| − Decrease in inventory . . . . . . . . . . . . . . . . | (6,000) |
| = Purchases . . . . . . . . . . . . . . . . . . . . . . . . . | $142,000 |

During 2007, accounts payable decreased $9,000. This decrease reflects the fact that cash payments for merchandise purchased on account (which decrease accounts payable) exceeded purchases on account (which increase accounts payable). The cash paid for merchandise purchased, therefore, is computed as follows:

| | |
|---|---|
| Purchases . . . . . . . . . . . . . . . . . . . . . . . . . | $142,000 |
| + Decrease in accounts payable . . . . . . . . . | 9,000 |
| = Cash paid for merchandise purchased . . . . | $151,000 |

### Convert Wages Expense to Cash Paid to Employees

No adjustment to wages expense is needed. The absence of any beginning or ending accrued liability for wages payable means that wages expense and cash paid to employees as wages are the same amount: $52,000.

### Convert Insurance Expense to Cash Paid for Insurance

Prepaid insurance increased $13,000 during 2007. The $13,000 increase reflects the excess of cash paid for insurance during 2007 (which increases prepaid insurance) over the year's insurance expense (which decreases prepaid insurance). Starting with insurance expense the cash paid for insurance is computed as follows:

| | |
|---|---|
| Insurance expense . . . . . . . . . . . . . . . . . . . | $ 5,000 |
| + Increase in prepaid insurance . . . . . . . . . . | 13,000 |
| = Cash paid for insurance . . . . . . . . . . . . . . | $18,000 |

### Eliminate Depreciation Expense and Other Noncash Operating Expenses

Depreciation expense is a noncash expense. Because it does not represent a cash payment, depreciation expense is eliminated (by adding it back) as we convert accrual expense amounts to the corresponding amounts of cash payments. If Java House had any amortization expense or depletion expense, it would eliminate them for the same reason. The amortization of an intangible asset and the depletion of a natural resource are noncash expenses.

### Convert Income Tax Expense to Cash Paid for Income Taxes

The increase in income tax payable from $3,000 at December 31, 2006, to $5,000 at December 31, 2007, means that 2007's income tax expense (which increases income tax payable) was $2,000 more than 2007's tax payments (which decrease income tax payable). If we start with income tax expense, then we calculate cash paid for income taxes as follows:

| | |
|---|---|
| Income tax expense . . . . . . . . . . . . . . . . . . | $11,000 |
| − Increase in income tax payable. . . . . . . . . | (2,000) |
| = Cash paid for income taxes . . . . . . . . . . . | $ 9,000 |

### Omit Gains and Losses Related to Investing and Financing Activities

The income statement may contain gains and losses related to investing or financing activities. Examples include gains and losses from the sale of plant assets and gains and losses from the retirement of bonds payable. Because these gains and losses are not related to operating activities, we omit them as we convert income statement items to various cash flows from operating activities. The cash flows relating to these gains and losses are reported in the investing activities or financing activities sections of the statement of cash flows. Java House had an $8,000 gain from the sale of land in 2007. This gain is excluded; no related cash flow appears within the operating activities category.

We have now applied the adjustments to convert each accrual revenue and expense to the corresponding operating cash flow. We use these individual cash flows to prepare the operating activities section of the statement of cash flows; see Exhibit B.7

| EXHIBIT B.7 | Direct Method Operating Section of Statement of Cash Flows | | |
|---|---|---|---|
| Cash received from customers | | | $245,000 |
| Cash paid for merchandise purchased | | $151,000 | |
| Cash paid to employees | | 52,000 | |
| Cash paid for insurance | | 18,000 | |
| Cash paid for income taxes | | 9,000 | 230,000 |
| Net cash provided by operating activities | | | $ 15,000 |

# Cash Flows from Investing and Financing

The reporting of investing and financing activities in the statement of cash flows is identical under the indirect and direct methods. Thus, we simply refer to the previous sections in Appendix B for explanations.

## Supplemental Disclosures

When the direct method is used for the statement of cash flows, three separate disclosures are required: (1) a reconciliation of net income to the net cash flow from operating activities, (2) a schedule or description of all noncash investing and financing transactions, and (3) the firm's policy for determining which highly liquid, short-term investments are treated as cash equivalents. The firm's policy regarding cash equivalents is placed in the financial statement notes. The other two separate disclosures are reported either in the notes or at the bottom of the statement of cash flows.

The required reconciliation is essentially the indirect method of computing cash flow from operating activities. *Thus, when the direct method is used in the statement of cash flows, the indirect method is a required separate disclosure.* We discussed the indirect method earlier in this appendix.

Java House did have one noncash investing and financing event during 2007: the issuance of common stock to acquire a patent. This event is disclosed as supplemental information to the statement of cash flows in Exhibit B.5.

## APPENDIX-END REVIEW

Expresso Royale's income statement and comparative balance sheets follow:

**EXPRESSO ROYALE**
**Income Statement**
**For Year Ended December 31, 2007**

| | | |
|---|---|---|
| Sales | | $385,000 |
| Dividend income | | 5,000 |
| | | 390,000 |
| Cost of goods sold | $233,000 | |
| Wages expense | 82,000 | |
| Advertising expense | 10,000 | |
| Depreciation expense | 11,000 | |
| Income tax expense | 17,000 | |
| Loss on sale of investments | 2,000 | 355,000 |
| Net income | | $ 35,000 |

**EXPRESSO ROYALE**
**Balance Sheets**

|  | Dec. 31, 2007 | Dec. 31, 2006 |
|---|---|---|
| **Assets** | | |
| Cash. . . . . . . . . . . . . . . . . . . . . . . . . . . . . . . . . . | $ 8,000 | $ 12,000 |
| Accounts receivable. . . . . . . . . . . . . . . . . . . . . . . . | 22,000 | 28,000 |
| Inventory. . . . . . . . . . . . . . . . . . . . . . . . . . . . . . . . | 94,000 | 66,000 |
| Prepaid advertising. . . . . . . . . . . . . . . . . . . . . . . . | 12,000 | 9,000 |
| Long-term investments—Available-for-sale. . . . . . . . | 30,000 | 41,000 |
| Fair value adjustment to investments. . . . . . . . . . . . | — | (1,000) |
| Plant assets . . . . . . . . . . . . . . . . . . . . . . . . . . . . . | 178,000 | 130,000 |
| Accumulated depreciation . . . . . . . . . . . . . . . . . . . | (72,000) | (61,000) |
| Total assets. . . . . . . . . . . . . . . . . . . . . . . . . . . . . | $272,000 | $224,000 |
| **Liabilities and Equity** | | |
| Accounts payable. . . . . . . . . . . . . . . . . . . . . . . . . | $ 27,000 | $ 14,000 |
| Wages payable. . . . . . . . . . . . . . . . . . . . . . . . . . . | 6,000 | 2,500 |
| Income tax payable . . . . . . . . . . . . . . . . . . . . . . . | 3,000 | 4,500 |
| Common stock. . . . . . . . . . . . . . . . . . . . . . . . . . . | 139,000 | 125,000 |
| Retained earnings . . . . . . . . . . . . . . . . . . . . . . . . | 97,000 | 79,000 |
| Unrealized loss on investments . . . . . . . . . . . . . . . | — | (1,000) |
| Total liabilities and equity . . . . . . . . . . . . . . . . . . . | $272,000 | $224,000 |

Cash dividends of $17,000 were declared and paid during 2007. Plant assets were purchased for cash in 2007, and later in the year, additional common stock was issued for cash. Investments costing $11,000 were sold for cash at a $2,000 loss in 2007; an unrealized loss of $1,000 on these investments had been recorded in 2006 (at December 31, 2007, the cost and fair value of unsold investments are equal).

## Required

a. Compute the change in cash that occurred during 2007.
b. Prepare a 2007 statement of cash flows using the direct method.

## Solution

a. $8,000 ending balance − $12,000 beginning balance = $4,000 decrease in cash
b. (1) Use the direct method to determine the individual cash flows from operating activities.
  • $385,000 sales + $6,000 accounts receivable decrease = $391,000 cash received from customers
  • $5,000 dividend income = $5,000 cash received as dividends
  • $233,000 cost of goods sold + $28,000 inventory increase − $13,000 accounts payable increase = $248,000 cash paid for merchandise purchased
  • $82,000 wages expense − $3,500 wages payable increase = $78,500 cash paid to employees
  • $10,000 advertising expense + $3,000 prepaid advertising increase = $13,000 cash paid for advertising
  • $17,000 income tax expense + $1,500 income tax payable decrease = $18,500 cash paid for income taxes
  (2) Analyze changes in remaining noncash asset (and contra asset) accounts to determine cash flows from investing activities.
  • Long-term investments: $11,000 decrease resulted from sale of investments for cash at a $2,000 loss. Cash received from sale of investments = $9,000 ($11,000 cost − $2,000 loss).
  • Fair value adjustment to investments: $1,000 decrease resulted from the elimination of this account balance (and the unrealized loss on investments) at the end of 2007. No cash flow effect.
  • Plant assets: $48,000 increase resulted from purchase of plant assets for cash. Cash paid to purchase plant assets = $48,000.
  • Accumulated depreciation: $11,000 increase resulted from the recording of 2007 depreciation. No cash flow effect.

(3) Analyze changes in remaining liability and stockholders' equity accounts to determine cash flows from financing activities.
- Common stock: $14,000 increase resulted from the issuance of stock for cash. Cash received from issuance of common stock = $14,000.
- Retained earnings: $18,000 increase resulted from net income of $35,000 and dividend declaration of $17,000. Cash dividends paid = $17,000.
- Unrealized loss on investments: $1,000 decrease resulted from the elimination of this account balance (and the fair value adjustment to investments) at the end of 2007. No cash flow effect.

The statement of cash flows under the direct method follows:

**EXPRESSO ROYALE**
**Statement of Cash Flows**
**For Year Ended December 31, 2007**

| | | |
|---|---:|---:|
| **Cash flows from operating activities** | | |
| Cash received from customers. . . . . . . . . . . . . . | $391,000 | |
| Cash received as dividends . . . . . . . . . . . . . . . . | 5,000 | |
| Cash paid for merchandise purchased. . . . . . . . . | (248,000) | |
| Cash paid to employees. . . . . . . . . . . . . . . . . . . | (78,500) | |
| Cash paid for advertising . . . . . . . . . . . . . . . . . . | (13,000) | |
| Cash paid for income taxes . . . . . . . . . . . . . . . . | (18,500) | |
| Net cash provided by operating activities . . . . . . . | | $ 38,000 |
| **Cash flows from investing activities** | | |
| Sale of investments . . . . . . . . . . . . . . . . . . . . . . | 9,000 | |
| Purchase of plant assets . . . . . . . . . . . . . . . . . . | (48,000) | |
| Net cash used by investing activities . . . . . . . . . . | | (39,000) |
| **Cash flows from financing activities** | | |
| Issuance of common stock. . . . . . . . . . . . . . . . . | 14,000 | |
| Payment of dividends. . . . . . . . . . . . . . . . . . . . . | (17,000) | |
| Net cash used by financing activities . . . . . . . . . . | | (3,000) |
| Net decrease in cash . . . . . . . . . . . . . . . . . . . . . . | | (4,000) |
| Cash at beginning of year . . . . . . . . . . . . . . . . . . | | 12,000 |
| Cash at end of year . . . . . . . . . . . . . . . . . . . . . . | | $ 8,000 |

# GUIDANCE ANSWERS

**MANAGERIAL DECISION**    **You Are the Securities Analyst**

Many companies, but not all, treat customers' notes receivable as an investing activity. In 2005, the SEC became concerned with this practice and issued letters to a number of companies objecting to this accounting classification. "Presenting cash receipts from receivables generated by the sale of inventory as investing activities in the company's consolidated statements of cash flows is not in accordance with GAAP," wrote the chief accountant for the SEC's division of corporation finance, in her letter to the companies ("Little Campus Lab Shakes Big Firms—Georgia Tech Crew's Report Spurs Change in Accounting for Operating Cash Flow," March 1, 2005, *The Wall Street Journal*). The SEC's position is that these notes receivable are an operating activity and analysts are certainly justified in treating them likewise. Concerning the sale of receivables, so long as the separate entity (a Trust in this case) is properly structured, the transaction can be treated as a sale (rather than require consolidation) with a consequent reduction in receivables and a gain or loss on the sale recorded in the income statement. Many analysts treat this as a financing activity and argue that the cash inflow should not be regarded as an increase in operating cash flows. Bottom line: many argue that operating cash flows do not increase as a result of these two transactions and analysts should adjust the statement of cash flows to properly classify the financing of receivables as an operating activity and the sale of receivables as a financing activity.

**Superscript $^{B1}$ denotes assignments based on Appendix B1.**

# DISCUSSION QUESTIONS

**Q B-1.**    What is the definition of *cash equivalents?* Give three examples of cash equivalents.

**Q B-2.**    Why are cash equivalents included with cash in a statement of cash flows?

**Q B-3.**    What are the three major types of activities classified on a statement of cash flows? Give an example of a cash inflow and a cash outflow in each classification.

**Q B-4.**    In which of the three activity categories of a statement of cash flows would each of the following items appear? Indicate for each item whether it represents a cash inflow or a cash outflow:

    *a.*   Cash purchase of equipment.

    *b.*   Cash collection on loans.

    *c.*   Cash dividends paid.

    *d.*   Cash dividends received.

    *e.*   Cash proceeds from issuing stock.

    *f.*   Cash receipts from customers.

    *g.*   Cash interest paid.

    *h.*   Cash interest received.

**Q B-5.**    Traverse Company acquired a $3,000,000 building by issuing $3,000,000 worth of bonds payable. In terms of cash flow reporting, what type of transaction is this? What special disclosure requirements apply to a transaction of this type?

**Q B-6.**    Why are noncash investing and financing transactions disclosed as supplemental information to a statement of cash flows?

**Q B-7.**    Why is a statement of cash flows a useful financial statement?

**Q B-8.**    What is the difference between the direct method and the indirect method of presenting net cash flow from operating activities?

**Q B-9.**    In determining net cash flow from operating activities using the indirect method, why must we add depreciation back to net income? Give an example of another item that is added back to net income under the indirect method.

**Q B-10.**    Vista Company sold for $98,000 cash land originally costing $70,000. The company recorded a gain on the sale of $28,000. How is this event reported in a statement of cash flows using the indirect method?

**Q B-11.**    A firm uses the indirect method. Using the following information, what is its net cash flow from operating activities?

| | |
|---|---:|
| Net income. . . . . . . . . . . . . . . . . . . . . . . . . . . | $88,000 |
| Accounts receivable decrease . . . . . . . . . . . . . | 13,000 |
| Inventory increase . . . . . . . . . . . . . . . . . . . . . . | 9,000 |
| Accounts payable decrease. . . . . . . . . . . . . . . | 3,500 |
| Income tax payable increase . . . . . . . . . . . . . . | 1,500 |
| Depreciation expense. . . . . . . . . . . . . . . . . . . . | 6,000 |

**Q B-12.**    What separate disclosures are required for a company that reports a statement of cash flows using the indirect method?

**Q B-13.**    If a business had a net loss for the year, under what circumstances would the statement of cash flows show a positive net cash flow from operating activities?

**Q B-14.**$^{B1}$    A firm is converting its accrual revenues to corresponding cash amounts using the direct method. Sales on the income statement are $925,000. Beginning and ending accounts receivable on the balance sheet are $58,000 and $44,000, respectively. What is the amount of cash received from customers?

**Q B-15.**$^{B1}$    A firm reports $86,000 wages expense in its income statement. If beginning and ending wages payable are $3,900 and $2,800, respectively, what is the amount of cash paid to employees?

**Q B-16.**$^{B1}$    A firm reports $43,000 advertising expense in its income statement. If beginning and ending prepaid advertising are $6,000 and $7,600, respectively, what is the amount of cash paid for advertising?

**Q B-17.**$^{B1}$    Rusk Company sold equipment for $5,100 cash that had cost $35,000 and had $29,000 of accumulated depreciation. How is this event reported in a statement of cash flows using the direct method?

**Q B-18.**[B1] What separate disclosures are required for a company that reports a statement of cash flows using the direct method?

**Q B-19.** How is the operating cash flow to current liabilities ratio calculated? Explain its use.

**Q B-20.** How is the operating cash flow to capital expenditures ratio calculated? Explain its use.

**Q B-21.** The statement of cash flows provides information that may be useful in predicting future cash flows, evaluating financial flexibility, assessing liquidity, and identifying financing needs. It is not, however, the best financial statement for learning about a firm's financial performance during a period; information about periodic financial performance is provided by the income statement. Two basic principles—the revenue recognition principle and the matching concept—work to distinguish the income statement from the statement of cash flows. (a) Define the revenue recognition principle and the matching concept. (b) Briefly explain how these two principles work to make the income statement a better report on periodic financial performance than the statement of cash flows.

# MINI EXERCISES

**M B-22. Classification of Cash Flows (LO1)**
For each of the items below, indicate whether the cash flow relates to an operating activity, an investing activity, or a financing activity.
a. Cash receipts from customers for services rendered.
b. Sale of long-term investments for cash.
c. Acquisition of plant assets for cash.
d. Payment of income taxes.
e. Bonds payable issued for cash.
f. Payment of cash dividends declared in previous year.
g. Purchase of short-term investments (not cash equivalents) for cash.

**M B-23. Classification of Cash Flows (LO1)**
For each of the items below, indicate whether it is (1) a cash flow from an operating activity, (2) a cash flow from an investing activity, (3) a cash flow from a financing activity, (4) a noncash investing and financing activity, or (5) none of the above.
a. Paid cash to retire bonds payable at a loss.
b. Received cash as settlement of a lawsuit.
c. Acquired a patent in exchange for common stock.
d. Received advance payments from customers on orders for custom-made goods.
e. Gave large cash contribution to local university.
f. Invested cash in 60-day commercial paper (a cash equivalent).

**M B-24. Net Cash Flow from Operating Activities (Indirect Method) (LO2)**
The following information was obtained from Galena Company's comparative balance sheets. Assume that Galena Company's 2007 income statement showed depreciation expense of $8,000, a gain on sale of investments of $9,000, and a net income of $45,000. Calculate the net cash flow from operating activities using the indirect method.

| | Dec. 31, 2007 | Dec. 31, 2006 |
|---|---|---|
| Cash | $ 19,000 | $ 9,000 |
| Accounts receivable | 44,000 | 35,000 |
| Inventory | 55,000 | 49,000 |
| Prepaid rent | 6,000 | 8,000 |
| Long-term investments | 21,000 | 34,000 |
| Plant assets | 150,000 | 106,000 |
| Accumulated depreciation | 40,000 | 32,000 |
| Accounts payable | 24,000 | 20,000 |
| Income tax payable | 4,000 | 6,000 |
| Common stock | 121,000 | 92,000 |
| Retained earnings | 106,000 | 91,000 |

**M B-25. Net Cash Flow from Operating Activities (Indirect Method)    (LO2)**

Cairo Company had a $21,000 net loss from operations for 2007. Depreciation expense for 2007 was $8,600 and a 2007 cash dividend of $6,000 was declared and paid. Balances of the current asset and current liability accounts at the beginning and end-of 2007 follow. Did Cairo Company's 2007 operating activities provide or use cash? Use the indirect method to determine your answer.

|  | Ending | Beginning |
|---|---|---|
| Cash. . . . . . . . . . . . . . . . . . . . . | $ 3,500 | $ 7,000 |
| Accounts receivable. . . . . . . . . . | 16,000 | 25,000 |
| Inventory. . . . . . . . . . . . . . . . . . | 50,000 | 53,000 |
| Prepaid expenses. . . . . . . . . . . . | 6,000 | 9,000 |
| Accounts payable. . . . . . . . . . . . | 12,000 | 8,000 |
| Accrued liabilities . . . . . . . . . . . . | 5,000 | 7,600 |

**M B-26.[B1] Operating Cash Flows (Direct Method)    (LO2)**

Calculate the cash flow for each of the following cases.

*a.* Cash paid for rent:

| | |
|---|---|
| Rent expense . . . . . . . . . . . . . . . . . . . . | $60,000 |
| Prepaid rent, beginning year . . . . . . . . | 10,000 |
| Prepaid rent, end of year . . . . . . . . . . . | 8,000 |

*b.* Cash received as interest:

| | |
|---|---|
| Interest income. . . . . . . . . . . . . . . . . . | $16,000 |
| Interest receivable, beginning year. . . . | 3,000 |
| Interest receivable, end of year . . . . . . | 3,700 |

*c.* Cash paid for merchandise purchased:

| | |
|---|---|
| Cost of goods sold. . . . . . . . . . . . . . . | $98,000 |
| Inventory, beginning year . . . . . . . . . . . | 19,000 |
| Inventory, end of year. . . . . . . . . . . . . . | 22,000 |
| Accounts payable, beginning year. . . . | 11,000 |
| Accounts payable, end of year. . . . . . . | 7,000 |

**M B-27.[B1] Operating Cash Flows (Direct Method)    (LO2)**

Howell Company's current year income statement reports the following:

| | |
|---|---|
| Sales. . . . . . . . . . . . . . . . . . . . . . . . . | $825,000 |
| Cost of goods sold. . . . . . . . . . . . . . . | 550,000 |
| Gross profit. . . . . . . . . . . . . . . . . . . . . | $275,000 |

Howell's comparative balance sheets show the following (accounts payable relate to merchandise purchases):

| | End of Year | Beginning of Year |
|---|---|---|
| Accounts receivable......... | $ 71,000 | $60,000 |
| Inventory.................. | 109,000 | 96,000 |
| Prepaid expenses........... | 3,000 | 8,000 |
| Accounts payable........... | 31,000 | 37,000 |

Compute Howell's current-year cash received from customers and cash paid for merchandise purchased.

# EXERCISES

**E B-28.  Net Cash Flow from Operating Activities (Indirect Method)   (LO2)**

Lincoln Company owns no plant assets and reported the following income statement for the current year:

| | | |
|---|---|---|
| Sales......................... | | $750,000 |
| Cost of goods sold.............. | $470,000 | |
| Wages expense ................. | 110,000 | |
| Rent expense.................. | 42,000 | |
| Insurance expense.............. | 15,000 | 637,000 |
| Net income.................... | | $113,000 |

Additional balance sheet information about the company follows:

| | End of Year | Beginning of Year |
|---|---|---|
| Accounts receivable......... | $54,000 | $49,000 |
| Inventory.................. | 60,000 | 66,000 |
| Prepaid insurance........... | 8,000 | 7,000 |
| Accounts payable........... | 22,000 | 18,000 |
| Wages payable............. | 9,000 | 11,000 |

Use the information to calculate the net cash flow from operating activities under the indirect method.

**E B-29.  Statement of Cash Flows (Indirect Method)   (LO2, 3, 4)**

Use the following information about Lund Corporation for 2007 to prepare a statement of cash flows under the indirect method.

| | |
|---|---|
| Accounts payable increase ........................ | $ 9,000 |
| Accounts receivable increase....................... | 4,000 |
| Accrued liabilities decrease ....................... | 3,000 |
| Amortization expense............................ | 6,000 |
| Cash balance, beginning of 2007.................... | 22,000 |
| Cash balance, end of 2007 ........................ | 15,000 |
| Cash paid as dividends ........................... | 29,000 |
| Cash paid to purchase land........................ | 90,000 |
| Cash paid to retire bonds payable at par.............. | 60,000 |
| Cash received from issuance of common stock ......... | 35,000 |
| Cash received from sale of equipment................ | 17,000 |
| Depreciation expense............................. | 29,000 |
| Gain on sale of equipment......................... | 4,000 |
| Inventory decrease............................... | 13,000 |
| Net income..................................... | 76,000 |
| Prepaid expenses increase ........................ | 2,000 |

**E B-30.**[B1] **Operating Cash Flows (Direct Method)   (LO2)**
Calculate the cash flow for each of the following cases.
a.   Cash paid for advertising:

| | |
|---|---:|
| Advertising expense.................... | $62,000 |
| Prepaid advertising, beginning of year...... | 11,000 |
| Prepaid advertising, end of year........... | 15,000 |

b.   Cash paid for income taxes:

| | |
|---|---:|
| Income tax expense.................... | $29,000 |
| Income tax payable, beginning of year ..... | 7,100 |
| Income tax payable, end of year .......... | 4,900 |

c.   Cash paid for merchandise purchased:

| | |
|---|---:|
| Cost of goods sold.................... | $180,000 |
| Inventory, beginning of year.............. | 30,000 |
| Inventory, end of year.................. | 25,000 |
| Accounts payable, beginning of year....... | 10,000 |
| Accounts payable, end of year........... | 12,000 |

**E B-31.**[B1] **Statement of Cash Flows (Direct Method)   (LO2, 3, 4)**
Use the following information about the 2007 cash flows of Mason Corporation to prepare a statement of cash flows under the direct method.

| | |
|---|---:|
| Cash balance, end of 2007 .............. | $ 12,000 |
| Cash paid to employees and suppliers ..... | 148,000 |
| Cash received from sale of land........... | 40,000 |
| Cash paid to acquire treasury stock ....... | 10,000 |
| Cash balance, beginning of 2007.......... | 16,000 |
| Cash received as interest................ | 6,000 |
| Cash paid as income taxes .............. | 11,000 |
| Cash paid to purchase equipment......... | 89,000 |
| Cash received from customers ........... | 194,000 |
| Cash received from issuing bonds payable .. | 30,000 |
| Cash paid as dividends ................. | 16,000 |

**E B-32.**[B1] **Operating Cash Flows (Direct Method)**
Refer to the information in Exercise B-28. Calculate the net cash flow from operating activities using the direct method. Show a related cash flow for each revenue and expense.

**E B-33.   Investing and Financing Cash Flows   (LO3, 4)**
During 2007, Paxon Corporation's long-term investments account (at cost) increased $15,000, which was the net result of purchasing stocks costing $80,000 and selling stocks costing $65,000 at a $6,000 loss. Also, its bonds payable account decreased $40,000, the net result of issuing $100,000 of bonds at $103,000 and retiring bonds with a face value (and book value) of $140,000 at a $9,000 gain. What items and amounts appear in the (a) cash flows from investing activities and (b) cash flows from financing activities sections of its 2007 statement of cash flows?

# PROBLEMS

**P B-34.  Statement of Cash Flows (Indirect Method)   (LO2, 3, 4)**

Wolff Company's income statement and comparative balance sheets follow.

| WOLFF COMPANY | | |
| :--- | ---: | ---: |
| **Income Statement** | | |
| **For Year Ended December 31, 2007** | | |
| Sales. . . . . . . . . . . . . . . . . . . . . . . . . . . . . . . . . . . . . | | $635,000 |
| Cost of goods sold. . . . . . . . . . . . . . . . . . . . . . . . . | $430,000 | |
| Wages expense . . . . . . . . . . . . . . . . . . . . . . . . . . | 86,000 | |
| Insurance expense. . . . . . . . . . . . . . . . . . . . . . . . | 8,000 | |
| Depreciation expense. . . . . . . . . . . . . . . . . . . . . | 17,000 | |
| Interest expense. . . . . . . . . . . . . . . . . . . . . . . . . . | 9,000 | |
| Income tax expense. . . . . . . . . . . . . . . . . . . . . . . | 29,000 | 579,000 |
| Net income. . . . . . . . . . . . . . . . . . . . . . . . . . . . . . | | $ 56,000 |

| WOLFF COMPANY | | |
| :--- | ---: | ---: |
| **Balance Sheets** | | |
| | **Dec. 31, 2007** | **Dec. 31, 2006** |
| **Assets** | | |
| Cash. . . . . . . . . . . . . . . . . . . . . . . . . . . | $ 11,000 | $ 5,000 |
| Accounts receivable. . . . . . . . . . . . . . . . | 41,000 | 32,000 |
| Inventory. . . . . . . . . . . . . . . . . . . . . . . . | 90,000 | 60,000 |
| Prepaid insurance. . . . . . . . . . . . . . . . . | 5,000 | 7,000 |
| Plant assets . . . . . . . . . . . . . . . . . . . . . | 250,000 | 195,000 |
| Accumulated depreciation . . . . . . . . . . . | (68,000) | (51,000) |
| Total assets. . . . . . . . . . . . . . . . . . . . . . | $329,000 | $248,000 |
| **Liabilities and Stockholders' Equity** | | |
| Accounts payable. . . . . . . . . . . . . . . . . . | $ 7,000 | $ 10,000 |
| Wages payable. . . . . . . . . . . . . . . . . . . . | 9,000 | 6,000 |
| Income tax payable . . . . . . . . . . . . . . . . | 7,000 | 8,000 |
| Bonds payable . . . . . . . . . . . . . . . . . . . . | 130,000 | 75,000 |
| Common stock. . . . . . . . . . . . . . . . . . . . | 90,000 | 90,000 |
| Retained earnings . . . . . . . . . . . . . . . . . | 86,000 | 59,000 |
| Total liabilities and equity . . . . . . . . . . . . | $329,000 | $248,000 |

Cash dividends of $29,000 were declared and paid during 2007. Also in 2007, plant assets were purchased for cash, and bonds payable were issued for cash. Bond interest is paid semiannually on June 30 and December 31. Accounts payable relate to merchandise purchases.

**Required**

*a.*   Compute the change in cash that occurred during 2007.

*b.*   Prepare a 2007 statement of cash flows using the indirect method.

**P B-35.** **Statement of Cash Flows (Indirect Method)** **(LO2, 3, 4)**

Arctic Company's income statement and comparative balance sheets follow.

**ARCTIC COMPANY**
**Income Statement**
**For Year Ended December 31, 2007**

| | | |
|---|---:|---:|
| Sales. . . . . . . . . . . . . . . . . . . . . . . . . . . . . . . . . . . . . . | | $ 728,000 |
| Cost of goods sold. . . . . . . . . . . . . . . . . . . . . . . . . | $534,000 | |
| Wages expense . . . . . . . . . . . . . . . . . . . . . . . . . . . | 190,000 | |
| Advertising expense. . . . . . . . . . . . . . . . . . . . . . . . | 31,000 | |
| Depreciation expense. . . . . . . . . . . . . . . . . . . . . . . | 22,000 | |
| Interest expense. . . . . . . . . . . . . . . . . . . . . . . . . . . | 18,000 | |
| Gain on sale of land . . . . . . . . . . . . . . . . . . . . . . . . | (25,000) | 770,000 |
| Net loss . . . . . . . . . . . . . . . . . . . . . . . . . . . . . . . . . . | | $( 42,000) |

**ARCTIC COMPANY**
**Balance Sheets**

| | Dec. 31, 2007 | Dec. 31, 2006 |
|---|---:|---:|
| **Assets** | | |
| Cash. . . . . . . . . . . . . . . . . . . . . . . . . . . . | $ 49,000 | $ 28,000 |
| Accounts receivable. . . . . . . . . . . . . . . . | 42,000 | 50,000 |
| Inventory. . . . . . . . . . . . . . . . . . . . . . . . . | 107,000 | 113,000 |
| Prepaid advertising. . . . . . . . . . . . . . . . . | 10,000 | 13,000 |
| Plant assets . . . . . . . . . . . . . . . . . . . . . . | 360,000 | 222,000 |
| Accumulated depreciation . . . . . . . . . . . | (78,000) | (56,000) |
| Total assets. . . . . . . . . . . . . . . . . . . . . . | $490,000 | $370,000 |
| **Liabilities and Stockholders' Equity** | | |
| Accounts payable. . . . . . . . . . . . . . . . . . | $ 17,000 | $ 31,000 |
| Interest payable . . . . . . . . . . . . . . . . . . . | 6,000 | — |
| Bonds payable . . . . . . . . . . . . . . . . . . . . | 200,000 | — |
| Common stock. . . . . . . . . . . . . . . . . . . . | 245,000 | 245,000 |
| Retained earnings . . . . . . . . . . . . . . . . . | 52,000 | 94,000 |
| Treasury stock . . . . . . . . . . . . . . . . . . . . | (30,000) | — |
| Total liabilities and equity . . . . . . . . . . . | $490,000 | $370,000 |

During 2007, Arctic sold land for $70,000 cash that had originally cost $45,000. Arctic also purchased equipment for cash, acquired treasury stock for cash, and issued bonds payable for cash in 2007. Accounts payable relate to merchandise purchases.

**Required**

*a.* Compute the change in cash that occurred during 2007.

*b.* Prepare a 2007 statement of cash flows using the indirect method.

**P B-36.  Statement of Cash Flows (Indirect Method)   (LO2, 3, 4)**

Dair Company's income statement and comparative balance sheets follow.

| DAIR COMPANY<br>Income Statement<br>For Year Ended December 31, 2007 | | |
| --- | ---: | ---: |
| Sales. . . . . . . . . . . . . . . . . . . . . . . . . . . . . . . . . . . . |  | $700,000 |
| Cost of goods sold. . . . . . . . . . . . . . . . . . . . . . . . . | $440,000 |  |
| Wages and other operating expenses . . . . . . . . . . . | 95,000 |  |
| Depreciation expense. . . . . . . . . . . . . . . . . . . . . . . | 22,000 |  |
| Amortization expense. . . . . . . . . . . . . . . . . . . . . . . | 7,000 |  |
| Interest expense. . . . . . . . . . . . . . . . . . . . . . . . . . . | 10,000 |  |
| Income tax expense. . . . . . . . . . . . . . . . . . . . . . . . | 36,000 |  |
| Loss on bond retirement . . . . . . . . . . . . . . . . . . . . | 5,000 | 615,000 |
| Net income. . . . . . . . . . . . . . . . . . . . . . . . . . . . . . . |  | $ 85,000 |

| DAIR COMPANY<br>Balance Sheets | | |
| --- | ---: | ---: |
|  | **Dec. 31, 2007** | **Dec. 31, 2006** |
| **Assets** |  |  |
| Cash. . . . . . . . . . . . . . . . . . . . . . . . . . . | $ 27,000 | $ 18,000 |
| Accounts receivable. . . . . . . . . . . . . . . | 53,000 | 48,000 |
| Inventory. . . . . . . . . . . . . . . . . . . . . . . | 103,000 | 109,000 |
| Prepaid expenses. . . . . . . . . . . . . . . . . | 12,000 | 10,000 |
| Plant assets . . . . . . . . . . . . . . . . . . . . . | 360,000 | 336,000 |
| Accumulated depreciation . . . . . . . . . . . | (87,000) | (84,000) |
| Intangible assets . . . . . . . . . . . . . . . . . | 43,000 | 50,000 |
| Total assets. . . . . . . . . . . . . . . . . . . . . | $511,000 | $487,000 |
| **Liabilities and Stockholders' Equity** |  |  |
| Accounts payable. . . . . . . . . . . . . . . . . | $ 32,000 | $ 26,000 |
| Interest payable . . . . . . . . . . . . . . . . . . | 4,000 | 7,000 |
| Income tax payable . . . . . . . . . . . . . . . | 6,000 | 8,000 |
| Bonds payable . . . . . . . . . . . . . . . . . . . | 60,000 | 120,000 |
| Common stock. . . . . . . . . . . . . . . . . . . | 252,000 | 228,000 |
| Retained earnings . . . . . . . . . . . . . . . . | 157,000 | 98,000 |
| Total liabilities and equity . . . . . . . . . . . | $511,000 | $487,000 |

During 2007, the company sold for $17,000 cash old equipment that had cost $36,000 and had $19,000 accumulated depreciation. Also in 2007, new equipment worth $60,000 was acquired in exchange for $60,000 of bonds payable, and bonds payable of $120,000 were retired for cash at a loss. A $26,000 cash dividend was declared and paid in 2007. Any stock issuances were for cash.

**Required**

a.  Compute the change in cash that occurred in 2007.

b.  Prepare a 2007 statement of cash flows using the indirect method.

c.  Prepare separate schedules showing (1) cash paid for interest and for income taxes and (2) noncash investing and financing transactions.

**P B-37.    Statement of Cash Flows (Indirect Method)    (LO2, 3, 4)**

Rainbow Company's income statement and comparative balance sheets follow.

**RAINBOW COMPANY**
**Income Statement**
**For Year Ended December 31, 2007**

| | | |
|---|---:|---:|
| Sales. . . . . . . . . . . . . . . . . . . . . . . . . . . . . . . . . . . . . | | $750,000 |
| Dividend income. . . . . . . . . . . . . . . . . . . . . . . . . . . | | 15,000 |
| | | 765,000 |
| Cost of goods sold. . . . . . . . . . . . . . . . . . . . . . . . | $440,000 | |
| Wages and other operating expenses . . . . . . . . . . . . | 130,000 | |
| Depreciation expense. . . . . . . . . . . . . . . . . . . . . . | 39,000 | |
| Patent amortization expense . . . . . . . . . . . . . . . . . | 7,000 | |
| Interest expense. . . . . . . . . . . . . . . . . . . . . . . . . . | 13,000 | |
| Income tax expense. . . . . . . . . . . . . . . . . . . . . . . | 44,000 | |
| Loss on sale of equipment. . . . . . . . . . . . . . . . . . . | 5,000 | |
| Gain on sale of investments. . . . . . . . . . . . . . . . . . | (10,000) | 668,000 |
| Net income. . . . . . . . . . . . . . . . . . . . . . . . . . . . . | | $ 97,000 |

**RAINBOW COMPANY**
**Balance Sheets**

| | Dec. 31, 2007 | Dec. 31, 2006 |
|---|---:|---:|
| **Assets** | | |
| Cash and cash equivalents . . . . . . . . . . . . . . . . . . . . . . . . . | $ 19,000 | $ 25,000 |
| Accounts receivable. . . . . . . . . . . . . . . . . . . . . . . . . . . . . . | 40,000 | 30,000 |
| Inventory. . . . . . . . . . . . . . . . . . . . . . . . . . . . . . . . . . . . . . | 103,000 | 77,000 |
| Prepaid expenses. . . . . . . . . . . . . . . . . . . . . . . . . . . . . . . | 10,000 | 6,000 |
| Long-term investments—Available-for-sale. . . . . . . . . . . . . . | — | 50,000 |
| Fair value adjustment to investments. . . . . . . . . . . . . . . . . . | — | 7,000 |
| Land . . . . . . . . . . . . . . . . . . . . . . . . . . . . . . . . . . . . . . . . | 190,000 | 100,000 |
| Buildings. . . . . . . . . . . . . . . . . . . . . . . . . . . . . . . . . . . . . | 445,000 | 350,000 |
| Accumulated depreciation—Buildings. . . . . . . . . . . . . . . . . | (91,000) | (75,000) |
| Equipment . . . . . . . . . . . . . . . . . . . . . . . . . . . . . . . . . . . . | 179,000 | 225,000 |
| Accumulated depreciation—Equipment . . . . . . . . . . . . . . . . | (42,000) | (46,000) |
| Patents. . . . . . . . . . . . . . . . . . . . . . . . . . . . . . . . . . . . . . | 50,000 | 32,000 |
| Total assets. . . . . . . . . . . . . . . . . . . . . . . . . . . . . . . . . . | $903,000 | $781,000 |
| **Liabilities and Stockholders' Equity** | | |
| Accounts payable. . . . . . . . . . . . . . . . . . . . . . . . . . . . . . . | $ 20,000 | $ 16,000 |
| Interest payable . . . . . . . . . . . . . . . . . . . . . . . . . . . . . . . | 6,000 | 5,000 |
| Income tax payable . . . . . . . . . . . . . . . . . . . . . . . . . . . . . | 8,000 | 10,000 |
| Bonds payable. . . . . . . . . . . . . . . . . . . . . . . . . . . . . . . . . | 155,000 | 125,000 |
| Preferred stock ($100 par value) . . . . . . . . . . . . . . . . . . . . | 100,000 | 75,000 |
| Common stock ($5 par value) . . . . . . . . . . . . . . . . . . . . . . | 379,000 | 364,000 |
| Paid-in capital in excess of par value—Common . . . . . . . . . . | 133,000 | 124,000 |
| Retained earnings . . . . . . . . . . . . . . . . . . . . . . . . . . . . . . | 102,000 | 55,000 |
| Unrealized gain on investments. . . . . . . . . . . . . . . . . . . . . . | — | 7,000 |
| Total liabilities and equity . . . . . . . . . . . . . . . . . . . . . . . . . | $903,000 | $781,000 |

During 2007, the following transactions and events occurred:

1. Sold long-term investments costing $50,000 for $60,000 cash. Unrealized gains totaling $7,000 related to these investments had been recorded in earlier years. At year-end, the fair value adjustment and unrealized gain account balances were eliminated.
2. Purchased land for cash.
3. Capitalized an expenditure made to improve the building.
4. Sold equipment for $14,000 cash that originally cost $46,000 and had $27,000 accumulated depreciation.
5. Issued bonds payable at face value for cash.
6. Acquired a patent with a fair value of $25,000 by issuing 250 shares of preferred stock at par value.
7. Declared and paid a $50,000 cash dividend.
8. Issued 3,000 shares of common stock for cash at $8 per share.
9. Recorded depreciation of $16,000 on buildings and $23,000 on equipment.

**Required**

a. Compute the change in cash and cash equivalents that occurred during 2007.
b. Prepare a 2007 statement of cash flows using the indirect method.
c. Prepare separate schedules showing (1) cash paid for interest and for income taxes and (2) noncash investing and financing transactions.

**P B-38.**[B1]  **Statement of Cash Flows (Direct Method)**   **(LO2, 3, 4)**
Refer to the data for Wolff Company in Problem B-34.

**Required**

a. Compute the change in cash that occurred during 2007.
b. Prepare a 2007 statement of cash flows using the direct method.

**P B-39.**[B1]  **Statement of Cash Flows (Direct Method)**   **(LO2, 3, 4)**
Refer to the data for Arctic Company in Problem B-35.

**Required**

a. Compute the change in cash that occurred during 2007.
b. Prepare a 2007 statement of cash flows using the direct method.

**P B-40.**[B1]  **Statement of Cash Flows (Direct Method)**   **(LO2, 3, 4)**
Refer to the data for Dair Company in Problem B-36.

**Required**

a. Compute the change in cash that occurred in 2007.
b. Prepare a 2007 statement of cash flows using the direct method. Use one cash outflow for "cash paid for wages and other operating expenses." Accounts payable relate to inventory purchases only.
c. Prepare separate schedules showing (1) a reconciliation of net income to net cash flow from operating activities (see Exhibit B.4) and (2) noncash investing and financing transactions.

**P B-41.**[B1]  **Statement of Cash Flows (Direct Method)**   **(LO2, 3, 4)**
Refer to the data for Rainbow Company in Problem B-37.

**Required**

a. Compute the change in cash that occurred in 2007.
b. Prepare a 2007 statement of cash flows using the direct method. Use one cash outflow for "cash paid for wages and other operating expenses." Accounts payable relate to inventory purchases only.
c. Prepare separate schedules showing (1) a reconciliation of net income to net cash flow from operating activities (see Exhibit B.4) and (2) noncash investing and financing transactions.

**P B-42.**   **Interpreting the Statement of Cash Flows**   **(LO1, 5)**
Following is the statement of cash flows of Amgen, Inc.                    Amgen, Inc. (AMGN)

| Year Ended December 31 (In millions) | 2003 | 2002 |
|---|---|---|
| **Cash flows from operating activities** | | |
| Net income (loss)- | $ 2,259.5 | $(1,391.9) |
| Write-off of acquired in-process R&D. | — | 2,991.8 |
| Depreciation and amortization | 686.5 | 447.3 |
| Tax benefits related to employee stock options. | 268.6 | 251.6 |
| Deferred income taxes | (189.6) | 174.7 |
| Other noncash expenses | 99.0 | 24.9 |
| Cash provided by (used in) changes in operating assets and liabilities, net of acquisitions | | |
| Trade receivables, net | (255.5) | (121.9) |
| Inventories. | (167.7) | (101.7) |
| Other current assets | (32.8) | (5.2) |
| Accounts payable | 74.0 | 11.0 |
| Accrued liabilities | 824.6 | (31.8) |
| Net cash provided by operating activities | 3,566.6 | 2,248.8 |
| **Cash flows from investing activities** | | |
| Purchases of property, plant, and equipment. | (1,356.8) | (658.5) |
| Purchases of marketable securities | (5,320.3) | (2,952.8) |
| Proceeds from sales of marketable securities | 3,338.6 | 1,621.5 |
| Proceeds from maturities of marketable securities | 370.8 | 778.2 |
| Cash paid for Immunex, net of cash acquired | — | (1,899.0) |
| Proceeds from sale of Leukine® business. | — | 389.9 |
| Purchase of certain rights from Roche. | — | (137.5) |
| Other. | (242.5) | (5.6) |
| Net cash used in investing activities | (3,210.2) | (2,863.8) |
| **Cash flows from financing activities** | | |
| Issuance of zero-coupon convertible notes, net of issuance costs | — | 2,764.7 |
| Repayment of debt. | (123.0) | — |
| Net proceeds from issuance of common stock upon exercise of employee stock options and in connection with employee stock purchase plan | 529.0 | 427.8 |
| Repurchases of common stock | (1,801.0) | (1,420.4) |
| Other. | 23.5 | 5.5 |
| Net cash (used in) provided by financing activities | (1,371.5) | 1,777.6 |
| (Decrease) increase in cash and cash equivalents. | (1,015.1) | 1,162.6 |
| Cash and cash equivalents at beginning of period | 1,851.7 | 689.1 |
| Cash and cash equivalents at end of period | $ 836.6 | $ 1,851.7 |

**Required**

a.  Amgen reports that it generated $3,566.6 million in net cash from operating activities in 2003. Yet, its net income for the year amounted to only $2,259.5 million. Much of this difference is the result of depreciation. Why is Amgen adding depreciation to net income in the computation of operating cash flows?

b.  Amgen reports net cash inflows of $268.6 million in tax benefits arising from employee stock options. These relate to tax benefits the company realizes when employees exercise stock options. Since employees will only exercise stock options when the market price of the stock is above the exercise price, do you feel that this is a reliable source of cash for the company? Explain.

c.  Amgen is reporting $(255.5) million relating to trade receivables. What does the sign on this amount signify about the change in receivables during the year?

d.  Amgen reports $824.6 million relating to accrued liabilities. Describe what this relates to and its implications for Amgen's future cash flows.

e.  Does the composition of Amgen's cash flow present a "healthy" picture for 2003? Explain.

**P B-43.** **Interpreting the Statement of Cash Flows    (LO1, 5)**

Following is the statement of cash flows of Staples, Inc.

Staples, Inc. (SPLS)

| In thousands | Year Ended January 31, 2004 |
|---|---|
| **Operating activities** | |
| Net income. . . . . . . . . . . . . . . . . . . . . . . . . . . . . . . . . . . . . . . . . . . . . . | $   490,211 |
| Adjustments to reconcile net income to net cash provided by operating activities: | |
| Depreciation and amortization . . . . . . . . . . . . . . . . . . . . . . . . . . . . . . . . . | 282,811 |
| Asset impairment and other charges . . . . . . . . . . . . . . . . . . . . . . . . . . . . . | — |
| Store closure charge. . . . . . . . . . . . . . . . . . . . . . . . . . . . . . . . . . . . . . | — |
| Deferred income taxes (benefit) expense. . . . . . . . . . . . . . . . . . . . . . . . . . . | (13,725) |
| Other. . . . . . . . . . . . . . . . . . . . . . . . . . . . . . . . . . . . . . . . . . . . . . . . | 36,434 |
| Change in assets and liabilities, net of companies acquired | |
| (Increase) decrease in receivables . . . . . . . . . . . . . . . . . . . . . . . . . . . . | (4,218) |
| Decrease (increase) in merchandise inventories. . . . . . . . . . . . . . . . . . . . . . | 147,130 |
| Increase in prepaid expenses and other assets . . . . . . . . . . . . . . . . . . . . . . | (34) |
| (Decrease) increase in accounts payable . . . . . . . . . . . . . . . . . . . . . . . . . . | (27,266) |
| Increase in accrued expenses and other current liabilities. . . . . . . . . . . . . . . | 95,549 |
| Increase in other long-term obligations . . . . . . . . . . . . . . . . . . . . . . . . . . | 12,840 |
| **Net cash provided by operating activities** . . . . . . . . . . . . . . . . . . . . . . . . . | 1,019,732 |
| **Investing activities** | |
| Acquisition of property and equipment . . . . . . . . . . . . . . . . . . . . . . . . . . . . | (277,793) |
| Acquisition of businesses, net of cash acquired . . . . . . . . . . . . . . . . . . . . . . | (2,910) |
| Proceeds from sales and maturities of short-term investments. . . . . . . . . . . . . . | — |
| Purchase of short-term investments . . . . . . . . . . . . . . . . . . . . . . . . . . . . . | (834,100) |
| Proceeds from sales and maturities of long-term investments . . . . . . . . . . . . . . | — |
| Purchase of long-term investments . . . . . . . . . . . . . . . . . . . . . . . . . . . . . . | — |
| Acquisition of lease rights. . . . . . . . . . . . . . . . . . . . . . . . . . . . . . . . . . . | — |
| **Net cash used in investing activities** . . . . . . . . . . . . . . . . . . . . . . . . . . . . | (1,114,803) |
| **Financing activities** | |
| Proceeds from sale of capital stock. . . . . . . . . . . . . . . . . . . . . . . . . . . . . . | 389,793 |
| Proceeds from borrowings . . . . . . . . . . . . . . . . . . . . . . . . . . . . . . . . . . . | — |
| Payments on borrowings . . . . . . . . . . . . . . . . . . . . . . . . . . . . . . . . . . . . | (325,235) |
| Repayments under receivables securitization agreement . . . . . . . . . . . . . . . . | (25,000) |
| Termination of interest rate swap agreement . . . . . . . . . . . . . . . . . . . . . . . . | — |
| Purchase of treasury stock. . . . . . . . . . . . . . . . . . . . . . . . . . . . . . . . . . . | (4,287) |
| **Net cash provided by (used in) financing activities.** . . . . . . . . . . . . . . . . . . | 35,271 |
| Effect of exchange rate changes on cash . . . . . . . . . . . . . . . . . . . . . . . . . . | 21,376 |
| **Net (decrease) increase in cash and cash equivalents.** . . . . . . . . . . . . . . . . | (38,424) |
| Cash and cash equivalents at beginning of period . . . . . . . . . . . . . . . . . . . . | 495,889 |
| **Cash and cash equivalents at end of period** . . . . . . . . . . . . . . . . . . . . . . . | $   457,465 |

**Required**

a.    Staples reports net income of $490.211 million and net cash inflows from operating activities of $1,019.732 million. Part of the difference relates to depreciation of $282.811 million. Why does Staples add this amount in the computation of operating cash flows?

b.    Staples reports a positive amount of $147.130 million relating to merchandise inventories. What does this signify about the change in the dollar amount of inventories during the year? Might this positive cash inflow be of some concern? Explain.

c.    Staples reports a cash outflow of $1,114.803 million relating to investing activities. Is this cash outflow a cause for concern? Explain.

d.    Staples net cash flows from financing activities is $35.271 million. Does this relatively small amount imply that there is no informational value in this category for the year? Explain.

e.    Staples cash balance decreased by $38.424 million during the year. Is this a cause for concern? Explain. Does Staples present a "healthy" cash flow picture for the year? Explain.

# Appendix C

# Chart of Accounts with Acronyms

## Assets

| | |
|---|---|
| Cash | Cash |
| MS | Marketable securities |
| EMI | Equity method investments |
| AR | Accounts receivable |
| AU | Allowance for uncollectible accounts |
| INV | Inventory (or Inventories) |
| SUP | Supplies |
| PPD | Prepaid expenses |
| PPDA | Prepaid advertising |
| PPRNT | Prepaid rent |
| PPI | Prepaid insurance |
| PPE | Property, plant and equipment (PPE) |
| AD | Accumulated depreciation |
| INT | Intangible assets |
| DTA | Deferred tax assets |
| OA | Other assets |

## Liabilities

| | |
|---|---|
| NP | Notes payable |
| AP | Accounts payable |
| ACC | Accrued expenses |
| WP | Wages payable |
| RNTP | Rent payable |
| RSL | Restructuring liability |
| WRP | Warranty payable |
| IP | Interest payable |
| CMLTD | Current maturities of long-term debt |
| UR | Unearned (or deferred) revenues |
| LTD | Long-term debt |
| CLO | Capital lease obligations |
| DTL | Deferred tax liabilities |

## Equity

| | |
|---|---|
| CC | Contributed capital |
| CS | Common stock |
| APIC | Additional paid-in capital |
| RE | Retained earnings |
| DIV | Dividends |
| TS | Treasury stock |
| (A)OCI | (Accumulated) other comprehensive income |
| DC | Deferred compensation expense |

## Revenues and Expenses

| | |
|---|---|
| Sales | Sales |
| REV | Revenues |
| COGS | Cost of goods sold (or Cost of sales) |
| OE | Operating expenses |
| WE | Wages expense |
| AE | Advertising expense |
| BDE | Bad debts expense |
| UTE | Utilities expense |
| DE | Depreciation expense |
| RDE | Research and development expense |
| RNTE | Rent expense |
| RSE | Restructuring expense |
| WRE | Warranty expense |
| AIE | Asset impairment expense |
| INSE | Insurance expense |
| SUPE | Supplies expense |
| GN (LS) | Gain (loss)–operating |
| TE | Tax expense |
| OI (OE) | Other nonoperating income (expense) |
| IE | Interest expense |
| UG (UL) | Unrealized gain (loss) |
| DI | Dividend income (or revenue) |
| EI | Equity income (or revenue) |
| GN (LS) | Gain (loss)–nonoperating |

## Closing Account

| | |
|---|---|
| IS | Income summary |

# Quick Review

## Module 1

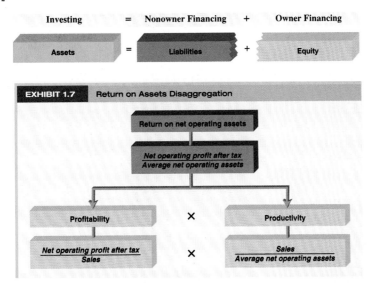

## Module 2

$$\text{Net Working Capital} = \text{Current Assets} - \text{Current Liabilities}$$

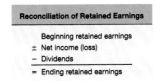

## Module 3

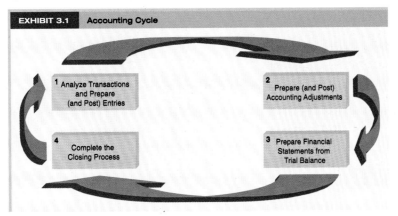

# T-Account Framework

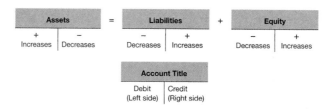

| Assets | = | Liabilities | + | Equity |
|---|---|---|---|---|
| + Increases \| − Decreases | | − Decreases \| + Increases | | − Decreases \| + Increases |

**Account Title**

| Debit (Left side) | Credit (Right side) |
|---|---|

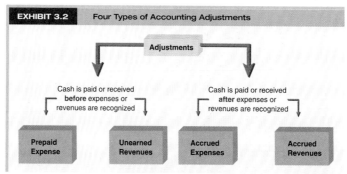

**EXHIBIT 3.2** Four Types of Accounting Adjustments

Adjustments

Cash is paid or received **before** expenses or revenues are recognized

Cash is paid or received **after** expenses or revenues are recognized

| Prepaid Expense | Unearned Revenues | Accrued Expenses | Accrued Revenues |

## Adjustments to Net Income to Yield Operating Cash Flows

| | Change in account balance . . . | Means that . . . | Which requires this adjustment to net income to yield cash profit . . . |
|---|---|---|---|
| Receivables | Increase | Sales and net income increase, but cash is not yet received | Deduct increase in receivables from net income |
| | Decrease | More cash is received than is reported in sales and net income | Add decrease in receivables to net income |
| Inventories | Increase | Cash is paid for inventories that are not yet reflected in cost of goods sold | Deduct increase in inventories from net income |
| | Decrease | Cost of goods sold includes inventory costs that were paid for in a prior period | Add decrease in inventories to net income |
| Payables and accruals | Increase | More goods and services are acquired on credit, delaying cash payment | Add increase in payables and accruals to net income |
| | Decrease | More cash is paid than that reflected in cost of goods sold or operating expenses | Deduct decrease in payables and accruals from net income |

| | Cash flow increases from | Cash flow decreases from |
|---|---|---|
| Assets. . . . . . . . . . . . . . . . . . . . . | Account decreases | Account increases |
| Liabilities and equity. . . . . . . . . . . | Account increases | Account decreases |

# Module 4

$$ROE = \frac{\text{Net income}}{\text{Average stockholders' equity}}$$

$$ROE = \text{Operating return} + \text{Nonoperating return}$$

$$\text{Tax on operating profit} = \text{Tax expense} + (\text{Net nonoperating expense} \times \text{Statutory tax rate})$$

Tax Shield

$$\frac{\text{Tax rate on}}{\text{operating profit}} = \frac{\text{Tax expense} + (\text{Net nonoperating expense} \times \text{Statutory tax rate})}{\text{Net operating profit before taxes}}$$

$$\text{NOPAT} = \text{Net operating profit before tax} \times (1 - \text{Tax rate on operating profit})$$

$$\text{Net operating assets} = \text{Operating assets} - \text{Operating liabilities}$$

$$RNOA = \frac{NOPAT}{Average\ NOA}$$

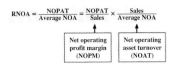

---

**EXHIBIT 4.1**  Operating and Nonoperating Items in the Income Statement

**Typical Income Statement**
**Operating Items Highlighted**

Revenues
Cost of sales
Gross profit
Operating expenses
  Selling, general and administrative
  Asset impairment expense
  Gains and losses on asset disposal
Total operating expenses
Operating income
Interest expense
Interest and dividend revenue
Investment gains and losses
Total nonoperating expenses
Income before tax, minority interest and discontinued operations
Tax expense
Income before minority interest and discontinued operations
Minority interest (see Appendix 4B)
Discontinued operations (see Appendix 4B)
Net income

---

**EXHIBIT 4.2**  Operating and Nonoperating Items in the Balance Sheet

**Typical Balance Sheet**
**Operating Items Highlighted**

**Current assets**
Cash and cash equivalents
Short-term investments
Accounts receivable
Inventories
Prepaid expenses
Deferred income tax assets
Other current assets

**Long-term assets**
Long-term investments in securities
Property, plant and equipment, net
Capitalized lease assets
Natural resources
Equity method investments
Goodwill and Intangible assets
Deferred income tax assets
Other long-term assets

**Current liabilities**
Short-term notes and interest payable
Accounts payable
Accrued liabilities
Deferred income tax liabilities
Current maturities of long-term debt

**Long-term liabilities**
Bonds and notes payable
Capitalized lease obligations
Pension and other post-employment liabilities
Deferred income tax liabilities
Minority Interest

**Stockholders' equity**
All equity accounts

---

**EXHIBIT 4.3**  Key Ratio Definitions

| Ratio | Definition |
|---|---|
| **ROE:** Return on equity . . . . . . . . . . . . . . | Net income/Average stockholders' equity |
| **NOPAT:** Net operating profit after tax . . . . . | Operating revenues less operating expenses such as cost of sales, selling, general and administrative expense, and taxes; it excludes nonoperating revenues and expenses such as interest revenue, dividend revenue, interest expense, gains and losses on investments, and minority interest. |
| **NOA:** Net operating assets . . . . . . . . . . | Operating assets less operating liabilities; it excludes investments in marketable securities and interest-bearing debt. |
| **RNOA:** Return on net operating assets . . . | NOPAT/Average NOA |
| **NNE:** Net nonoperating expense . . . . . . . | NOPAT − Net income; NNE consists of nonoperating expenses and revenues, net of tax |

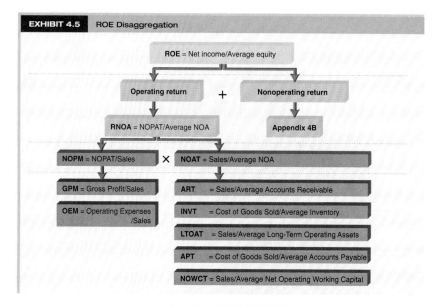

$$\text{Current ratio} = \frac{\text{Current assets}}{\text{Current liabilities}}$$

$$\text{Quick ratio} = \frac{\text{Cash} + \text{Marketable securities} + \text{Accounts receivables}}{\text{Current liabilities}}$$

$$\text{Liabilities-to-equity ratio} = \frac{\text{Total liabilities}}{\text{Stockholders' equity}}$$

# Module 5

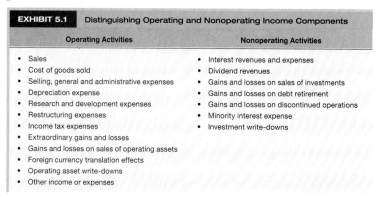

Tax Expense = Taxes Paid − Increase (or + Decrease) in Deferred Tax Assets + Increase (or − Decrease) in Deferred Tax Liabilities

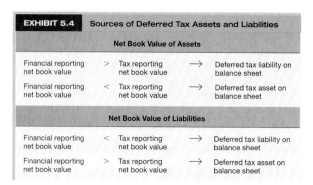

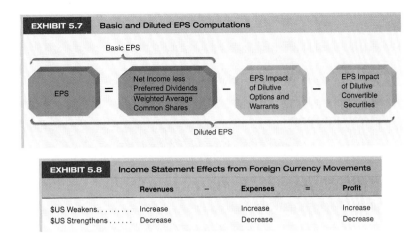

**EXHIBIT 5.7** Basic and Diluted EPS Computations

**EXHIBIT 5.8** Income Statement Effects from Foreign Currency Movements

| | Revenues | − | Expenses | = | Profit |
|---|---|---|---|---|---|
| $US Weakens......... | Increase | | Increase | | Increase |
| $US Strengthens...... | Decrease | | Decrease | | Decrease |

# Module 6

| Allowance for Uncollectible Accounts Determination | |
|---|---|
| Beginning allowance for uncollectible accounts.......... | $ 2,200 |
| Add: Provision for uncollectible accounts.............. | 700 |
| Less: Write-offs of accounts receivable................. | 0 |
| Ending allowance for uncollectible accounts............ | $ 2,900 |

**EXHIBIT 6.2** Effects of an Accounts Receivable Write-Off

| Account | Before Write-Off | Effects of Write-Off | After Write-Off |
|---|---|---|---|
| Accounts receivable.......................... | $100,000 | $(500) | $99,500 |
| Less: Allowance for uncollectible accounts......... | 2,900 | (500) | 2,400 |
| Accounts receivable, net of allowance............. | $ 97,100 | | $97,100 |

**Accounts Receivable Turnover = Sales/Average Accounts Receivable**

*↑ turns Rec. collected quick*

**Average Collection Period = Accounts Receivable/Average Daily Sales**

*↓*

**EXHIBIT 6.5** Cost of Goods Sold Computation

Beginning inventory (prior period balance sheet)
+ Inventory purchased and/or produced
Cost of goods available for sale
− Ending inventory (current period balance sheet)
Cost of goods sold (current income statement)

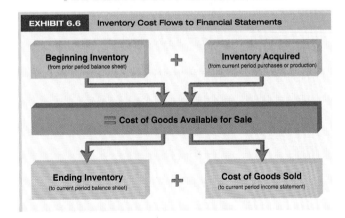

**EXHIBIT 6.6** Inventory Cost Flows to Financial Statements

**Beginning Inventory** (from prior period balance sheet) **+** **Inventory Acquired** (from current period purchases or production)

**Cost of Goods Available for Sale**

**Ending Inventory** (to current period balance sheet) **+** **Cost of Goods Sold** (to current period income statement)

**FIFO Inventory = LIFO Inventory + LIFO Reserve**

**FIFO COGS = LIFO COGS − Increase in LIFO Reserve (or + Decrease)**

*Turns, quick sales*

$$\text{Inventory Turnover} = \text{Cost of Goods Sold/Average Inventory}$$

$$\text{Average Inventory Days Outstanding} = \text{Inventory/Average Daily Cost of Goods Sold}$$

$$\text{Depreciation Expense} = \text{Depreciation Base} \times \text{Depreciation Rate}$$

## Straight-Line Depreciation

| Depreciation Base | Depreciation Rate |
|---|---|
| Cost − Salvage value | 1/Estimated useful life |

## Double-Declining Depreciation

| Depreciation Base | Depreciation Rate |
|---|---|
| Net Book Value = Cost − Accumulated Depreciation | 2 × SL rate |

| EXHIBIT 6.11 | Comparison of Straight-Line and Double-Declining-Balance Depreciation | | | |
|---|---|---|---|---|
| | Straight-Line | | Double-Declining-Balance | |
| Year | Depreciation Expense | Book Value at End of Year | Depreciation Expense | Book Value at End of Year |
| 1 | $18,000 | $82,000 | $40,000 | $60,000 |
| 2 | 18,000 | 64,000 | 24,000 | 36,000 |
| 3 | 18,000 | 46,000 | 14,400 | 21,600 |
| 4 | 18,000 | 28,000 | 8,640 | 12,960 |
| 5 | 18,000 | 10,000 | 2,960 | 10,000 |
| | $90,000 | | $90,000 | |

All depreciation methods yield the same salvage value

Total depreciation over asset life is identical for all methods

$$\text{Gain or Loss on Asset Sale} = \text{Proceeds from Sale} - \text{Net Book Value of Asset Sold}$$

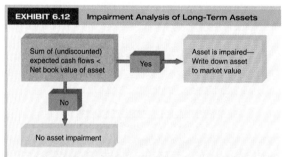

EXHIBIT 6.12   Impairment Analysis of Long-Term Assets

$$\text{PPE Turnover (PPET)} = \text{Sales/Average PPE Assets}$$

$$\text{Estimated Average Useful Life} = \text{Depreciable Asset Cost/Depreciation Expense}$$

$$\text{Percent Used Up} = \text{Accumulated Depreciation/Depreciable Asset Cost}$$

# Module 7

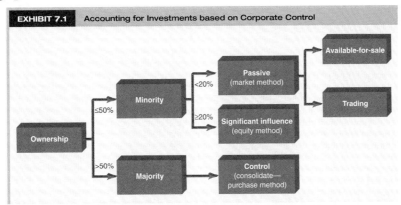

**EXHIBIT 7.1    Accounting for Investments based on Corporate Control**

**EXHIBIT 7.2    Investment Type, Accounting Treatment, and Financial Statement Effects**

| | Accounting | Balance Sheet Effects | Income Statement Effects | Cash Flow Effects |
|---|---|---|---|---|
| Passive | Market method | Investment account is reported at current market value | Dividends and capital gains included in income<br><br>Interim changes in market value may or may not affect income depending on whether the investor actively trades the securities<br><br>Sale of investment yields capital gain or loss | Dividends and sale proceeds are cash inflows<br><br>Purchases are cash outflows |
| Significant influence | Equity method | Investment account equals percent owned of investee company's equity* | Dividends reduce investment account<br><br>Investor reports income equal to percent owned of investee income<br><br>Sale of investment yields capital gain or loss | Dividends and sale proceeds are cash inflows<br><br>Purchases are cash outflows |
| Control | Consolidation | Balance sheets of investor and investee are combined | Income statements of investor and investee are combined (and sale of investee yields capital gain or loss) | Cash flows of investor and investee are combined (and sale/purchase of investee yields cash inflow/outflow) |

*Investments are often acquired at purchase prices in excess of book value (on average, market prices are 1.5 times book value for public companies). In this case the investment account exceeds the proportionate ownership of the investee's equity.

**EXHIBIT 7.3    Accounting Treatment for Available-for-Sale and for Trading Investments**

| Investment Classification | Reporting of Market Value Changes | Reporting of Dividends Received and Gains and Losses on Sale |
|---|---|---|
| Available-for-Sale (AFS) | Market value changes bypass the income statement and are reported in accumulated *other comprehensive income* (OCI) as part of equity | Reported as *other income* in income statement |
| Trading (T) | Market value changes are reported in the income statement as unrealized gains or losses; impacting equity via retained earnings | Reported as *other income* in income statement |

### Summary of Equity Method Accounting

▦ Investments are recorded at their purchase cost.

▦ Dividends received are treated as a recovery of the investment and, thus, reduce the investment balance (dividends are not reported as income as with passive investments).

▦ The investor reports income equal to its percentage share of the investee's reported income; the investment account is increased by the percentage share of the investee's income or decreased by the percentage share of any loss.

▦ Changes in market value do not affect the investment's carrying value.

### Effects of Equity Method Investments on ROE Components

▦ **Net operating profit margin (NOPM = NOPAT/Sales).** Most analysts include equity income (sales less expenses) in NOPAT since it relates to operating investments. However, investee's sales are not included in the NOPM denominator. The reported NOPM is, thus, *overstated*.

▦ **Net operating asset turnover (NOAT = Sales/Average NOA).** Investee's sales are excluded from the NOAT denominator. This means that NOAT is *understated*. (When investee assets exceed the investment balance, the impact on NOAT is *indeterminate*.)

▦ **Financial leverage (FLEV = Net nonoperating obligations/Average equity).** Financial leverage is understated due to the absence of investee liabilities in the numerator.

| EXHIBIT 7.6 | Mechanics of Consolidation Accounting (Purchase Price above Book Value) | | | |
|---|---|---|---|---|
| | Penman Company | Nissim Company | Consolidating Adjustments | Consolidated |
| Current assets . . . . . . . . . . . . . . . . . | $ 5,000 | $1,000 | | $ 6,000 |
| Investment in Nissim . . . . . . . . . . . . . | 4,000 | 0 | (4,000) | 0 |
| PPE, net . . . . . . . . . . . . . . . . . . . . . | 10,000 | 4,000 | 300 | 14,300 |
| Goodwill . . . . . . . . . . . . . . . . . . . . . | | | 700 | 700 |
| Total assets. . . . . . . . . . . . . . . . . . . | $19,000 | $5,000 | | $21,000 |
| | | | | |
| Liabilities. . . . . . . . . . . . . . . . . . . . . | $ 5,000 | $2,000 | | $ 7,000 |
| Contributed capital. . . . . . . . . . . . . . | 11,000 | 2,000 | (2,000) | 11,000 |
| Retained earnings . . . . . . . . . . . . . . | 3,000 | 1,000 | (1,000) | 3,000 |
| Total liabilities and equity . . . . . . . . . | $19,000 | $5,000 | | $21,000 |

# Module 8

$$\text{Accounts Payable Turnover (APT)} = \text{Cost of Goods Sold/Average Accounts Payable}$$

$$\text{Accounts Payable Days Outstanding (APDO)} = \text{Accounts Payable/Average Daily Cost of Goods Sold}$$

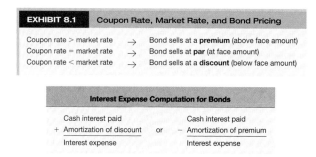

| EXHIBIT 8.1 | Coupon Rate, Market Rate, and Bond Pricing |
|---|---|
| Coupon rate > market rate → | Bond sells at a **premium** (above face amount) |
| Coupon rate = market rate → | Bond sells at **par** (at face amount) |
| Coupon rate < market rate → | Bond sells at a **discount** (below face amount) |

| Interest Expense Computation for Bonds | | |
|---|---|---|
| Cash interest paid | | Cash interest paid |
| + Amortization of discount | or | − Amortization of premium |
| Interest expense | | Interest expense |

$$\text{Gain or Loss on Bond Repurchase} = \text{Net Bonds Payable} - \text{Repurchase Payment}$$

# Module 9

**Components of Stockholders' Equity:**
- Contributed capital: common stock, preferred stock, additional paid-in capital, treasury stock, minority interest
- Earned capital: retained earnings, accumulated other comprehensive income (AOCI)

**Stock Issuance:**
- Common stock is increased by number of shares issued × par value
- Additional paid-in capital is increased for the balance of the issue price

**Treasury Stock:**
- Record at purchase cost
- When reissued, treasury stock is reduced by the cost of the shares reissued and the balance is reflected as an increase in additional paid-in capital

**Dividends and Splits:**
- Cash: reduce retained earnings by the cash dividends paid
- Stock (small): reduce retained earnings by the market value of the shared distributed and increase common stock and additional paid-in capital by the market value of the shares issued
- Stock (large): reduce retained earnings by the par value of the shares issued and increase common stock by the same amount (no increase in additional paid-in capital)
- Split: no accounting entry (adjust number of shares outstanding and their par value, if any)

**Components of Comprehensive Income:**
- Currency translation adjustment
- Unrealized gains and losses on available-for-sale securities
- Minimum pension liability adjustment
- Unrealized gains and losses on certain derivatives

| EXHIBIT 9.3 | Balance Sheet Effects of Euro Strengthening versus the Dollar | | | | | |
|---|---|---|---|---|---|---|
| Currency | | Assets | = | Liabilities | + | Equity |
| $US weakens . . . . . . . . . . . . . | | Increase | = | Increase | + | Increase |
| $US strengthens . . . . . . . . . . . | | Decrease | = | Decrease | + | Decrease |

# Module 10

| EXHIBIT 10.1 | Financial Statement Effects of Lease Type for the Lessee | | | |
|---|---|---|---|---|
| Lease Type | Assets | Liabilities | Expenses | Cash Flows |
| Capital . . . . . . . . . | Lease asset reported | Lease liability reported | Depreciation and interest expense | Payments per lease contract |
| Operating . . . . . . . | Lease asset **not** reported | Lease liability **not** reported | Rent expense | Payments per lease contract |

### Pension Plan Assets

Pension plan assets, beginning balance
+ Actual returns on investments (interest, dividends, gains and losses)
+ Company contributions to pension plan
− Benefits paid to retirees
= Pension plan assets, ending balance

### Pension Obligation

Projected benefit obligation, beginning balance
+ Service cost
+ Interest cost
+/− Actuarial losses (gains)
− Benefits paid to retirees
= Projected benefit obligation, ending balance

### Net Pension Liability (or Asset)

Pension plan assets (at market value)
− Projected benefit obligation (PBO)
Funded status

### Net Pension Expense

Service cost
+ Interest cost
− *Expected* return on pension plan assets
± Amortization of deferred amounts
Net pension expense

| Effects from Changes in Pension Assumptions | | |
|---|---|---|
| Estimate change | Probable effect on pension expense | Reason for effect |
| Discount rate increase . . . . . . . . . . | Increase | While the higher discount rate reduces the PBO, the lower PBO is multiplied by a higher rate. The rate effect is larger than the discount effect, resulting in increased pension expense.* |
| Investment return increase . . . . . . . . . . | Decreases | The dollar amount of expected return on plan assets is the product of the plan assets balance and the expected long-term rate of return. Increasing the return increases the expected return on plan assets, thus reducing pension expense. |
| Wage inflation increase . . . . . . . . . . | Increases | The expected rate of wage inflation affects future wage levels that determine expected pension payments. An increase, thus, increases PBO, which increases both the service and interest cost components of pension expense. |

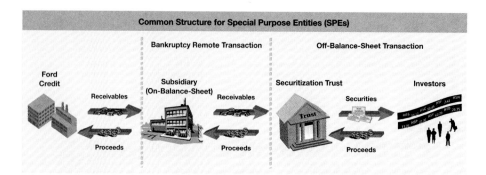

# Module 11

1. Separate persistent and transitory items; examples of items to exclude:
   a. Gains and losses relating to
      • Asset sales of long-term assets and investments
      • Asset write-downs of long-term assets and inventories
      • Stock issuances by subsidiaries
      • Debt retirements
   b. Transitory items reported after income from continued operations
      • Discontinued operations
      • Extraordinary items
   c. Restructuring expenses
   d. Merger costs
   e. LIFO liquidation gains
   f. Liability accruals deemed excessive
   g. Lawsuit gains and losses
   h. Revenue or expense from short-term fluctuations in tax rates and from changes in deferred tax valuation allowance
2. Separate operating and nonoperating items; examples:
   a. Treating interest revenue and expense, and investment gains and losses, as nonoperating
   b. Treating pension service cost as operating, and pension interest costs and expected returns as nonoperating
   c. Treating debt retirement gains and losses as nonoperating
   d. Treating income and losses from discontinued operations as nonoperating
3. Include expenses not reflected in net income; examples:
   a. Inadequate (or excessive) reserves for bad debts or asset impairment
   b. Reductions in R&D, advertising, and other discretionary expenses that were made to achieve short-term income targets; conversely, exclude excessive expenses related to product or market development
   c. Employee stock option expense (for financial statements issued before 2006)

**EXHIBIT 11.2    Common Balance Sheet Adjustments**

1. Exclude nonoperating assets and liabilities
   a. Eliminate assets and liabilities from discontinued operations
   b. Write-down of assets, including goodwill, that is judged to be impaired
2. Include operating assets and liabilities not reflected in balance sheet; examples:
   a. Capitalize operating assets from operating leases; nonoperating capitalized lease liabilities are also increased
   b. Consolidate off-balance-sheet investments:
      • Equity method investments
      • Special purpose entities (SPEs)
   c. Accrue understated liabilities and assets

**EXHIBIT 11.3    Common Statement of Cash Flow Adjustments**

1. Adjust operating cash flows for transitory items; examples of adjustments that potentially impact operating cash flows:
   a. Adjust discretionary costs (advertising, R&D, maintenance) to normal, expected levels
   b. Adjust current operating assets (receivables, inventory) to normal, expected levels
   c. Adjust current operating liabilities (payables, accruals) to normal, expected levels
2. Adjust investing cash flows for transitory items, such as cash proceeds from asset disposals (including disposals of discontinued operations) and from tax benefits due to exercise of stock options
3. Review cash flows and reassign them, if necessary, to operating, investing, or financing sections; examples:
   a. Reclassify operating cash inflows from asset securitization to the financing section
   b. Reclassify interest payments from the operating to the financing section

$$\text{Forecasted Year-End Account Balance} = \frac{\text{Forecasted Sales (or Cost of Goods Sold)}}{\text{Estimated Turnover Rate}}$$

| Forecasted Cash | Possible Adjustments to Forecasted Balance Sheet and Income Statement |
|---|---|
| Too low | • Liquidate marketable securities (then adjust forecasted investment income)<br>• Raise cash by increasing long-term debt and/or equity (then adjust forecasted interest expense and/or expected dividends) |
| Too high | • Invest excess cash in marketable securities (then adjust investment income)<br>• Repay debt or pay out to shareholders as repurchased (treasury) stock or dividends (then adjust forecasted interest expense and/or expected dividends) |

# Module 12

## DCF Valuation Model

$$\text{Firm Value} = \text{Present Value of Expected Free Cash Flows to Firm (FCFF)}$$

$$\text{FCFF} = \text{NOPAT} - \text{Increase in NOA}$$

where

$$\text{NOPAT} = \text{Net operating profit after tax}$$
$$\text{NOA} = \text{Net operating assets}$$

## ROPI Valuation Model

$$\text{Firm Value} = \text{NOA} + \text{Present Value of Expected ROPI}$$

$$\text{ROPI} = \text{NOPAT} - \underbrace{(\text{NOA}_{Beg} \times r_w)}_{\text{Expected NOPAT}}$$

where

$$\text{NOA}_{Beg} = \text{Net operating assets at beginning (\textit{Beg}) of period}$$
$$r_w = \text{Weighted average cost of capital (WACC)}$$

# Glossary

## A

**accelerated cost recovery system (ACRS, MACRS)** A system of accelerated depreciation for tax purposes introduced in 1981 (ACRS) and modified starting in 1987 (MACRS); it prescribes depreciation rates by asset classification for assets acquired after 1980

**accelerated depreciation method** Any depreciation method under which the amounts of depreciation expense taken in the early years of an asset's life are larger than the amounts expensed in the later years; includes the double-declining balance method

**access control matrix** A computerized file that lists the type of access that each computer user is entitled to have to each file and program in the computer system

**account** A record of the additions, deductions, and balances of individual assets, liabilities, permanent owners' equity, revenues, and expenses

**accounting cycle** A series of basic steps followed to process accounting information during a fiscal year

**accounting entity** An economic unit that has identifiable boundaries and that is the focus for the accumulation and reporting of financial information

**accounting equation** An expression of the equivalency of the economic resources and the claims upon those resources of a specific entity; often stated as Assets = Liabilities + Owners' Equity

**accounting period** The time period, typically one year (or quarter), to which periodic accounting reports are related

**accounting system** The structured collection of people, policies, procedures, equipment, files, and records that a company uses to collect, record, classify, process, store, report, and interpret financial data

**accounting** The process of measuring the economic activity of an entity in money terms and communicating the results to interested parties; the purpose is to provide financial information that is useful in making economic decisions

**accounts payable turnover** The ratio obtained by dividing cost of goods sold by average accounts payable

**accounts receivable** A current asset that is created by a sale on a credit basis; it represents the amount owed the company by the customer

**accounts receivable aging method** A procedure that uses an aging schedule to determine the year-end balance needed in the allowance for uncollectible accounts account

**accounts receivable turnover** Annual net sales divided by average accounts receivable (net)

**accrual accounting** Accounting procedures whereby revenues are recorded when they are earned and realized and expenses are recorded in the period in which they help to generate revenues

**accruals** Adjustments that reflect revenues earned but not received or recorded and expenses incurred but not paid or recorded

**accrued expense** An expense incurred but not yet paid; recognized with an adjusting entry

**accrued revenue** Revenue earned but not yet billed or received; recognized with an adjusting entry

**accumulated depreciation** The sum of all depreciation expense recorded to date; it is subtracted from the cost of the asset in order to derive the asset's net book value

**adjusted trial balance** A list of general ledger accounts and their balances taken after adjustments have been made

**adjusting** The process of adjusting the historical financial statements prior to the projection of future results; also called recasting and reformulating

**adjusting entries** Entries made at the end of an accounting period under accrual accounting to ensure the proper matching of expenses incurred with revenues earned for the period

**aging schedule** An analysis that shows how long customers' accounts receivable balances have remained unpaid

**allowance for uncollectible accounts** A contra asset account with a normal credit balance shown on the balance sheet as a deduction from accounts receivable to reflect the expected realizable amount of accounts receivable

**allowance method** An accounting procedure whereby the amount of uncollectible accounts expense is estimated and recorded in the period in which the related credit sales occur

**Altman's Z-score** A predictor of potential bankruptcy based on multiple ratios

**amortization** The periodic writing off of an account balance to expense; similar to depreciation and usually refers to the periodic writing off of an intangible asset

**annuity** A pattern of cash flows in which equal amounts are spaced equally over a number of periods

**articles of incorporation** A document prepared by persons organizing a corporation in the United States that sets forth the structure and purpose of the corporation and specifics regarding the stock to be issued

**articulation** The linkage of financial statements within and across time

**asset turnover** Net income divided by average total assets

**asset write-downs** Adjustment of carrying value of assets down to their current salable value

**assets** The economic resources of an entity that are owned, will provide future benefits and can be reliably measured

**audit** An examination of a company's financial statements by a firm of independent certified public accountants

**audit report** A report issued by independent auditors that includes the final version of the financial statements, accompanying notes, and the auditor's opinion on the financial statements

**authorized stock** The maximum number of shares in a class of stock that a corporation may issue

**available-for-sale securities** Investments in securities that management intends to hold for capital gains and dividend income; although it may sell them if the price is right

**average cash cycle** Average collection period + modified average inventory days outstanding − modified average payable days outstanding

**average collection period** Determined by dividing accounts receivable by average daily sales, sometimes referred to as days sales outstanding or DSO

**average inventory days outstanding (AIDO)** An indication of how long, on average, inventories are on the shelves, computed as inventory divided by average daily cost of goods sold

## B

**balance sheet** A financial statement showing an entity's assets, liabilities, and owners' equity at a specific date; sometimes called a statement of financial position

**bearer** One of the terms that may be used to designate the payee on a promissory note; means the note is payable to whoever holds the note

**bond** A long-term debt instrument that promises to pay interest periodically and a principal amount at maturity, usually issued by the borrower to a group of lenders; bonds may incorporate a wide variety of provisions relating to security for the debt involved, methods of paying the periodic interest, retirement provisions, and conversion options

**book value per share** The dollar amount of net assets represented by one share of stock; computed by dividing the amount of stockholders' equity associated with a class of stock by the outstanding shares of that class of stock

**book value** The dollar amount carried in the accounts for a particular item; the book value of a depreciable asset is derived by deducting the contra account accumulated depreciation from the cost of the depreciable asset

**borrows at a discount** When the face amount of the note is reduced by a calculated cash discount to determine the cash proceeds

## C

**calendar year** A fiscal year that ends on December 31

**call provision** A bond feature that allows the borrower to retire (call in) the bonds after a stated date

**capital expenditures** Expenditures that increase the book value of long-term assets; sometimes abbreviated as CAPEX

**capital lease** A lease that transfers to the lessee substantially all of the benefits and risks related to ownership of the property; the lessee records the leased property as an asset and establishes a liability for the lease obligation

**capital markets** Financing sources, which are formalized when companies issue securities that are traded on organized exchanges; they are informal when companies are funded by private sources

**capitalization** The recording of a cost as an asset on the balance sheet rather than as an expense on the income statement; these costs are transferred to expense as the asset is used up

**capitalization of interest** A process that adds interest to an asset's initial cost if a period of time is required to prepare the asset for use

**cash** An asset category representing the amount of a firm's available cash and funds on deposit at a bank in checking accounts and savings accounts

**cash and cash equivalents** The sum of cash plus short-term, highly liquid investments such as treasury bills and money market funds; includes marketable securities maturing within 90 days of the financial statement date

**cash discount** An amount that a purchaser of merchandise may deduct from the purchase price for paying within the discount period

**cash-basis accounting** Accounting procedures whereby revenues are recorded when cash is received from operating activities and expenses are recorded when cash payments related to operating activities are made

**cash (operating) cycle** The period of time from when cash is invested in inventories until inventory is sold and receivables are collected

**certificate of deposit (CD)** An investment security available at financial institutions generally offering a fixed rate of return for a specified period of time

**change in accounting estimate** Modification to a previous estimate of an uncertain future event, such as the useful life of a depreciable asset, uncollectible accounts receivable, and warranty expenses; applied currently and prospectively only

**changes in accounting principles** Cumulative income or loss from changes in accounting methods (such as depreciation or inventory costing methods)

**chart of accounts** A list of all the general ledger account titles and their numerical code

**clean surplus accounting** Income that explains successive equity balances

**closing procedures** A step in the accounting cycle in which the balances of all temporary accounts are transferred to the retained earnings account, leaving the temporary accounts with zero balances

**commitments** A contractual arrangement by which both parties to the contract still have acts to perform

**common stock** The basic ownership class of corporate capital stock, carrying the rights to vote, share in earnings, participate in future stock issues, and share in any liquidation proceeds after prior claims have been settled

**common-size financial statement** A financial statement in which each item is presented as a percentage of a key figure such as sales or total assets

**comparative financial statements** A form of horizontal analysis involving comparison of two or more periods' financial statements showing dollar and/or percentage changes

**compensating balance** A minimum amount that a financial institution requires a firm to maintain in its account as part of a borrowing arrangement complex capital structure

**comprehensive income** The total income reported by the company, including net profit and all other changes to stockholders' equity other than those arising from capital (stock) transactions; typical components of other comprehensive income (OCI) are unrealized gains (losses) on available-for-sale securities and derivatives, minimum pension liability adjustment, and foreign currency translation adjustments

**conceptual framework** A cohesive set of interrelated objectives and fundamentals for external financial reporting developed by the FASB

**conservatism** An accounting principle stating that judgmental determinations should tend toward understatement rather than overstatement of net assets and income

**consistency** An accounting principle stating that, unless otherwise disclosed, accounting reports should be prepared on a basis consistent with the preceding period

**consolidated financial statements** Financial statements reflecting a parent company and one or more subsidiary companies and/or a variable interest entity (VIE) and its primary beneficiary

**contingency** A possible future event; significant contingent liabilities must be disclosed in the notes to the financial statements

**contingent liabilities** A potential obligation, the eventual occurrence of which usually depends on some future event beyond the control of the firm; contingent liabilities may originate with such events as lawsuits, credit guarantees, and environmental damages

**contra account** An account related to, and deducted from, another account when financial statements are prepared or when book values are computed

**contract rate** The rate of interest stated on a bond certificate

**contributed capital** The net funding that a company receives from issuing and acquiring its equity shares

**convertible bond** A bond incorporating the holder's right to convert the bond to capital stock under prescribed terms

**convertible securities** Debt and equity securities that provide the holder with an option to convert those securities into other securities

**copyright** An exclusive right that protects an owner against the unauthorized reproduction of a specific written work or artwork

**core income** A company's income from its usual business activities that is expected to continue (persist) into the future

**corporation** A legal entity created by the granting of a charter from an appropriate governmental authority and owned by stockholders who have limited liability for corporate debt

**cost of goods sold percentage** The ratio of cost of goods sold divided by net sales

**cost of goods sold** The total cost of merchandise sold to customers during the accounting period

**cost method** An investment is reported at its historical cost, and any cash dividends and interest received are recognized in current income

**cost principle** An accounting principle stating that asset measures are based on the prices paid to acquire the assets

**coupon bond** A bond with coupons for interest payable to bearer attached to the bond for each interest period; whenever interest is due, the bondholder detaches a coupon and deposits it with his or her bank for collection

**coupon (contract or stated) rate** The coupon rate of interest is stated in the bond contract; it is used to compute the dollar amount of (semiannual) interest payments that are paid to bondholder during the life of the bond issue

**covenants** Contractual requirements put into loan or bond agreements by lenders

**credit (entry)** An entry on the right side (or in the credit column) of any account

**credit card fee** A fee charged retailers for credit card services provided by financial institutions; the fee is usually stated as a percentage of credit card sales

**credit guarantee** A guarantee of another company's debt by cosigning a note payable; a guarantor's contingent liability that is usually disclosed in a balance sheet footnote

**credit memo** A document prepared by a seller to inform the purchaser that the seller has reduced the amount owed by the purchaser due to a return or an allowance

**credit period** The maximum amount of time, usually stated in days, that the purchaser of merchandise has to pay the seller

**credit terms** The prescribed payment period for purchases on credit with discount specified for early payment

**cumulative (preferred stock)** A feature associated with preferred stock whereby any dividends in arrears must be paid before dividends may be paid on common stock

**cumulative effect of a change in principle** The cumulative effect on net income to the date of a change in accounting principle

**cumulative translation adjustment** The amount recorded in the equity section as necessary to balance the accounting equation when assets and liabilities of foreign subsidiaries are translated into $US at the rate of exchange prevailing at the statement date

**current assets** Cash and other assets that will be converted to cash or used up during the normal operating cycle of the business or one year, whichever is longer

**current liabilities** Obligations that will require within the coming year or operating cycle, whichever is longer, (1) the use of existing current assets or (2) the creation of other current liabilities

**current rate method** Method of translating foreign currency transactions under which balance sheet amounts are translated using exchange rates in effect at the period-end consolidation date and income statement amounts using the average exchange rate for the period

**current ratio** A firm's current assets divided by its current liabilities

## D

**days' sales in inventory** Inventories divided by average cost of goods sold

**debenture bond** A bond that has no specific property pledged as security for the repayment of funds borrowed

**debit (entry)** An entry on the left side (or in the debit column) of any account

**debt-to-equity ratio** A firm's total liabilities divided by its total owners' equity

**declining-balance method** An accelerated depreciation method that allocates depreciation expense to each year by applying a constant percentage to the declining book value of the asset

**default** The nonpayment of interest and principal and/or the failure to adhere to the various terms and conditions of the bond indenture

**deferrals** Adjustments that allocate various assets and revenues received in advance to the proper accounting periods as expenses and revenues

**deferred revenue** A liability representing revenues received in advance; also called unearned revenue

**deferred tax liability** A liability representing the estimated future income taxes payable resulting from an existing temporary difference between an asset's book value and its tax basis

**deferred tax valuation allowance** Reduction in a reported deferred tax asset to adjust for the amount that is not likely to be realized

**defined benefit plan** A type of retirement plan under which the company promises to make periodic payments to the employee after retirement

**defined contribution plan** A retirement plan under which the company makes cash contribution into an employee's account (usually with a third-party trustee like a bank) either solely or as a matching contribution

**depletion** The allocation of the cost of natural resources to the units extracted and sold or, in the case of timberland, the board feet of timber cut

**depreciation** The decline in economic potential (using up) of plant assets originating from wear, deterioration, and obsolescence

**depreciation accounting** The process of allocating the cost of equipment, vehicles, and buildings (not land) to expense over the time period benefiting from their use

**depreciation base** The acquisition cost of an asset less estimated salvage value

**depreciation rate** An estimate of how the asset will be used up over its useful life-evenly over its useful life, more heavily in the early years, or in proportion to its actual usage

**derivatives** Financial instruments such as futures, options, and swaps that are commonly used to hedge (mitigate) some external risk, such as commodity price risk, interest rate risk, or risks relating to foreign currency fluctuations

**diluted earnings per share** The earnings per share computation taking into consideration the effects of dilutive securities

**dilutive securities** Securities that can be exchanged for shares of common stock and, thereby, increase the number of common shares outstanding

**discontinued operations** Net income or loss from business segments that are up for sale or have been sold in the current period

**discount bond** A bond that is sold for less than its par (face) value

**discount on notes payable** A contra account that is subtracted from the Notes Payable amount on the balance sheet; as the life of the note elapses, the discount is reduced and charged to interest expense

**discount period** The maximum amount of time, usually stated in days, that the purchaser of merchandise has to pay the seller if the purchaser wants to claim the cash discount

**discounting** The exchanging of notes receivable for cash at a financial institution at an amount that is less than the face value of the notes

**discounted cash flow (DCF) model** The value of a security is equal to the present value of the expected free cash flows to the firm, discounted at the weighted average cost of capital (WACC)

**dividends account** A temporary equity account used to accumulate owner dividends from the business

**dividend discount model** The value of a security today is equal to the present value of that security's expected dividends, discounted at the weighted average cost of capital

**dividend payout ratio** Annual dividends per share divided by the earnings per share

**dividend yield** Annual dividends per share divided by the market price per share

**double-entry accounting system** A method of accounting that recognizes the duality of a transaction such that the analysis results in a recording of equal amounts of debits and credits

## E

**earned** When referring to revenue, the seller's execution of its duties under the terms of the agreement, with the resultant passing of title to the buyer with no right of return or other contingencies

**earned capital** The cumulative net income (losses) retained by the company (not paid out to shareholders as dividends)

**earnings per share (EPS)** Net income less preferred stock dividends divided by the weighted average common shares outstanding for the period

**earnings quality** The degree to which reported earnings represent how well the firm has performed from an economic standpoint

**earnings smoothing** Earnings management with a goal to provide an earnings stream with less variability

**economic profit** The number of inventory units sold multiplied by the difference between the sales price and the replacement cost of the inventories (approximated by the cost of the most recently purchased inventories)

**economic value added (EVA)** Net operating profits after tax less a charge for the use of capital equal to beginning capital utilized in the business multiplied by the weighted average cost of capital (EVA = $NOPAT - r_w \times$ Net Operating Assets)

**effective interest method** A method of amortizing bond premium or discount that results in a constant rate of interest each period and varying amounts of premium or discount amortized each period

**effective interest rate** The rate determined by dividing the total discount amount by the cash proceeds on a note payable when the borrower borrowed at a discount

**effective rate** The current rate of interest in the market for a bond or other debt instrument; when issued, a bond is priced to yield the market (effective) rate of interest at the date of issuance

**efficient markets hypothesis** Capital markets are said to be efficient if at any given time, current equity (stock) prices reflect all relevant information that determines those equity prices

**employee severance costs** Accrued (estimated) costs for termination of employees as part of a restructuring program

**employee stock options** A form of compensation that grants a select group of employees the right to purchase a fixed number of company shares at a fixed price for a predetermined time period

**equity carve out** A corporate divestiture of operating units

**equity method** The prescribed method of accounting for investments in which the investor company has a significant influence over the investee company (usually taken to be ownership between 20-50% of the outstanding common stock of the investee company)

**ethics** An area of inquiry dealing with the values, rules, and justifications that governs one's way of life

**expenses** Decreases in owners' equity incurred by a firm in the process of earning revenues

**extraordinary items** Revenues and expenses that are both unusual and infrequent and are, therefore, excluded from income from continuing operations

## F

**face amount** The principal amount of a bond or note to be repaid at maturity

**factoring** Selling an account receivable to another company, typically a finance company or a financial institution, for less than its face value

**financial accounting** The area of accounting activities dealing with the preparation of financial statements showing an entity's results of operations, financial position, and cash flows

**Financial Accounting Standards Board (FASB)** The organization currently responsible for setting accounting standards for reporting financial information

**financial assets** Normally consist of excess resources held for future expansion or unexpected needs; they are usually invested in the form of other companies' stock, corporate or government bonds, and real estate

**financial leverage** The proportionate use of borrowed funds in the capital structure, computed as net financial obligations (NFO) divided by average equity

**financial reporting objectives** A component of the conceptual framework that specifies that financial statements should provide information (1) useful for investment and credit decisions, (2) helpful in assessing an entity's ability to generate future cash flows, and (3) about an entity's resources, claims to those resources, and the effects of events causing changes in these items

**financial statement elements** A part of the conceptual framework that identifies the significant components-such as assets, liabilities, owners' equity, revenues, and expenses-used to put financial statements together

**financing activities** Methods that companies use to raise the funds to pay for resources such as land, buildings, and equipment

**finished goods inventory** The dollar amount of inventory that has completed the production process and is awaiting sale

**first-in, first-out (FIFO) method** One of the prescribed methods of inventory costing; FIFO assumes that the first costs incurred for the purchase or production of inventory are the first costs relieved from inventory when goods are sold

**fiscal year** The annual accounting period used by a business firm

**five forces of competitive intensity** Industry competition, bargaining power of buyers, bargaining power of suppliers, threat of substitution, threat of entry

**fixed assets** An alternate label for long-term assets; may also be called property, plant, and equipment (PPE)

**fixed costs** Costs that do not change with changes in sales volume (over a reasonable range)

**forecast** The projection of financial results over the forecast horizon and terminal periods

**foreign currency transaction** The $US equivalent of an asset or liability denominated in a foreign currency

**foreign exchange gain or loss** The gain (loss) recognized in the income statement relating to the change in the $US equivalent of an asset or liability denominated in a foreign currency

**franchise** Generally, an exclusive right to operate or sell a specific brand of products in a given geographic area

**free cash flow** This excess cash flow (above that required to manage its growth and development) from which dividends can be paid; computed as NOPAT − Increase in NOA

**full disclosure principle** An accounting principle stipulating the disclosure of all facts necessary to make financial statements useful to readers

**fully diluted earnings per share** See diluted earnings per share

**functional currency** The currency representing the primary currency in which a business unit conducts its operations

**fundamental analysis** Uses financial information to predict future valuation and, hence, buy-sell stock strategies

**funded status** The difference between the pension obligation and the fair market value of the pension investments

**future value** The amount a specified investment (or series of investments) will be worth at a future date if invested at a given rate of compound interest

# G

**general journal** A journal with enough flexibility so that any type of business transaction can be recorded in it

**general ledger** A grouping of all of an entity's accounts that are used to prepare the basic financial statements

**generally accepted accounting principles (GAAP)** A set of standards and procedures that guide the preparation of financial statements

**going concern concept** An accounting principle that assumes that, in the absence of evidence to the contrary, a business entity will have an indefinite life

**goodwill** The value that derives from a firm's ability to earn more than a normal rate of return on the fair market value of its specific, identifiable net assets; computed as the residual of the purchase price less the fair market value of the net tangible and intangible assets acquired

**gross margin** The difference between net sales and cost of goods sold: also called gross profit

**gross profit on sales** The difference between net sales and cost of goods sold; also called gross margin

**gross profit margin (GPM) (percentage)** The ratio of gross profit on sales divided by net sales

# H

**held-to-maturity securities** The designation given to a portfolio of bond investments that are expected to be held until they mature

**historical cost** Original acquisition or issuance costs

**holding company** The parent company of a subsidiary

**holding gain** The increase in replacement cost since the inventories were acquired, which equals the number of units sold multiplied by the difference between the current replacement cost and the original acquisition cost

**horizon period** The forecast period for which detailed estimates are made, typically 5-10 years

**horizontal analysis** Analysis of a firm's financial statements that covers two or more years

# I

**impairment** A reduction in value from that presently recorded

**impairment loss** A loss recognized on an impaired asset equal to the difference between its book value and current fair value

**income statement** A financial statement reporting an entity's revenues and expenses for a period of time

**indirect method** A presentation format for the statement of cash flows that refers to the operating section only; that section begins with net income and converts it to cash flows from operations

**intangible assets** A term applied to a group of long-term assets, including patents, copyrights, franchises, trademarks, and goodwill, that benefit an entity but do not have physical substance

**interest cost (pensions)** The increase in the pension obligation due to the accrual of an additional year of interest

**internal auditing** A company function that provides independent appraisals of the company's financial statements, its internal controls, and its operations

**internal controls** The measures undertaken by a company to ensure the reliability of its accounting data, protect its assets from theft or unauthorized use, make sure that employees are following the company's policies and procedures, and evaluate the performance of employees, departments, divisions, and the company as a whole

**inventory carrying costs** Costs of holding inventories, including warehousing, logistics, insurance, financing, and the risk of loss due to theft, damage, or technological or fashion change

**inventory shrinkage** The cost associated with an inventory shortage; the amount by which the perpetual inventory exceeds the physical inventory

**inventory turnover** Cost of goods sold divided by average inventory

**investing activities** The acquiring and disposing of resources (assets) that a company uses to acquire and sell its products and services

**investing creditors** Those who primarily finance investing activities

**investment returns** The increase in pension investments resulting from interest, dividends, and capital gains on the investment portfolio

**invoice** A document that the seller sends to the purchaser to request payment for items that the seller shipped to the purchaser

**invoice price** The price that a seller charges the purchaser for merchandise

**IOU** A slang term for a receivable

**issued stock** Shares of stock that have been sold and issued to stockholders; issued stock may be either outstanding or in the treasury

## J

**journal** A tabular record in which business transactions are analyzed in debit and credit terms and recorded in chronological order

**just-in-time (JIT) inventory philosophy** Receive inventory from suppliers into the production process just at the point it is needed

## L

**land improvements** Improvements with limited lives made to land sites, such as paved parking lots and driveways

**last-in, first-out (LIFO) method** One of the prescribed methods of inventory costing; LIFO assumes that the last costs incurred for the purchase or production of inventory are the first costs relieved form inventory when goods are sold

**lease** A contract between a lessor (owner) and lessee (tenant) for the rental of property

**leasehold improvements** Expenditures made by a lessee to alter or improve leased property

**leasehold** The rights transferred from the lessor to the lessee by a lease

**lessee** The party acquiring the right to the use of property by a lease

**lessor** The owner of property who transfers the right to use the property to another party by a lease

**leveraging** The use of borrowed funds in the capital structure of a firm; the expectation is that the funds will earn a return higher than the rate of interest on the borrowed funds

**liabilities** The obligations, or debts, that an entity must pay in money or services at some time in the future because of past transactions or events

**LIFO conformity rule** IRS requirement to cost inventories using LIFO for tax purposes if they are costed using LIFO for financial reporting purposes

**LIFO liquidation** The reduction in inventory quantities when LIFO costing is used; LIFO liquidation yields an increase in gross profit and income when prices are rising

**LIFO reserve** The difference between the cost of inventories using FIFO and the cost using LIFO

**liquidation value per share** The amount that would be received by a holder of a share of stock if the corporation liquidated

**liquidity** How much cash the company has, how much is expected, and how much can be raised on short notice

**list price** The suggested price or reference price of merchandise in a catalog or price list

**long-term liabilities** Debt obligations not due to be settled within the normal operating cycle or one year, whichever is longer

**lower of cost or market (LCM)** GAAP requirement to write down the carrying amount of inventories on the balance sheet if the reported cost (using FIFO, for example) exceeds market value (determined by current replacement cost)

## M

**maker** The signer of a promissory note

**management discussion and anaysis (MD&A)** The section of the 10-K report in which a company provides a detailed discussion of its business activities

**managerial accounting** The accounting activities carried out by a firm's accounting staff primarily to furnish management with accounting data for decisions related to the firm's operations

**manufacturers** Companies that convert raw materials and components into finished products through the application of skilled labor and machine operations

**manufacturing costs** The costs of direct materials, direct labor, and manufacturing overhead incurred in the manufacture of a product

**market method accounting** Securities are reported at current market values (marked-to-market) on the statement date

**market (yield) rate** This is the interest rate that investors expect to earn on the investment in this debt security; this rate is used to price the bond issue

**market value** The published price (as listed on a stock exchange) multiplied by the number of shares owned

**market value per share** The current price at which shares of stock may be bought or sold

**matching principle** An accounting guideline that states that income is determined by relating expenses, to the extent feasible, with revenues that have been recorded

**materiality** An accounting guideline that states that transactions so insignificant that they would not affect a user's actions or perception of the company may be recorded in the most expedient manner

**materials inventory** The physical component of inventory; the other components of manufactured inventory are labor costs and overhead costs

**maturity date** The date on which a note or bond matures

**measuring unit concept** An accounting guideline noting that the accounting unit of measure is the basic unit of money

**merchandise inventory** A stock of products that a company buys from another company and makes available for sale to its customers

**merchandising firm** A company that buys finished products, stores the products for varying periods of time, and then resells the products

**method of comparables model** Equity valuation or stock values are predicted using price multiples, which are defined as stock price divided by some key financial statement number such as net income, net sales, book value of equity, total assets, or cash flow; companies are then compared with their competitors

**minority interest** The equity claim of a shareholder owning less than a majority or controlling interest in the company

**modified accelerated cost recovery system (MACRS)** See accelerated cost recovery system

## N

**natural resources** Assets occurring in a natural state, such as timber, petroleum, natural gas, coal, and other mineral deposits

**net assets** The difference between an entity's assets and liabilities; net assets are equal to owners' equity

**net asset based valuation model** Equity is valued as reported assets less reported liabilities

**net book value (NBV)** The cost of the asset less accumulated depreciation; also called carrying value

**net financial obligations (NFO)** net total of all financial (nonoperating) obligations less financial (nonoperating) assets

**net income** The excess of a firm's revenues over its expenses

**net loss** The excess of a firm's expenses over its revenues

**net operating assets (NOA)** Current and long-term operating assets less current and long-term operating liabilities; or net operating working capital plus long-term net operating assets

**net operating profit after tax (NOPAT)** Sales less operating expenses (including taxes)

**net realizable value** The value at which an asset can be sold, net of any costs of disposition

**net sales** The total revenue generated by a company through merchandise sales less the revenue given up through sales returns and allowances and sales discounts

**net working capital** Current assets less current liabilities

**nominal rate** The rate of interest stated on a bond certificate or other debt instrument

**noncash investing and financing activities** Significant business activities during the period that do not impact cash inflows or cash outflows

**noncurrent liabilities** Obligations not due to be paid within one year or the operating cycle, whichever is longer

**nonoperating expenses** Expenses that relate to the company's financing activities and include interest income and interest expense, gains and losses on sales of securities, and income or loss on discontinued operations

**no-par stock** Stock that does not have a par value

**NOPAT** Net operating profit after tax

**normal operating cycle** For a particular business, the average period of time between the use of cash in its typical operating activity and the subsequent collection of cash from customers

**note receivable** A promissory note held by the note's payee

**notes to financial statements** Footnotes in which companies discuss their accounting policies and estimates used in preparing the statements

**not-sufficient-funds check** A check from an individual or company that had an insufficient cash balance in the bank when the holder of the check presented it to the bank for payment

## O

**objectivity principle** An accounting principle requiring that, whenever possible, accounting entries are based on objectively determined evidence

**off-balance-sheet financing** The structuring of a financing arrangement so that no liability shows on the borrower's balance sheet

**operating activities** Using resources to research, develop, produce, purchase, market, and distribute company products and services

**operating asset turnover** The ratio obtained by dividing sales by average net operating assets

**operating cash flow to capital expenditures ratio** A firm's net cash flow from operating activities divided by its annual capital expenditures

**operating cash flow to current liabilities ratio** A firm's net cash flow from operating activities divided by its average current liabilities

**operating creditors** Those who primarily finance operating activities

**operating cycle** The time between paying cash for goods or employee services and receiving cash from customers

**operating expense margin (OEM)** The ratio obtained by dividing any operating expense category by sales

**operating expenses** The usual and customary costs that a company incurs to support its main business activities; these include cost of goods sold, selling expenses, depreciation expense, amortization expense, research and development expense, and taxes on operating profits

**operating lease** A lease by which the lessor retains the usual risks and rewards of owning the property

**operating profit margin** The ratio obtained by dividing NOPAT by sales

**operational audit** An evaluation of activities, systems, and internal controls within a company to determine their efficiency, effectiveness, and economy

**organization costs** Expenditures incurred in launching a business (usually a corporation), including attorney's fees and various fees paid to the state

**outstanding checks** Checks issued by a firm that have not yet been presented to its bank for payment

**outstanding stock** Shares of stock that are currently owned by stockholders (excludes treasury stock)

**owners' equity** The interest of owners in the assets of an entity; equal to the difference between the entity's assets and liabilities

# P

**packing list** A document that lists the items of merchandise contained in a carton and the quantity of each item; the packing list is usually attached to the outside of the carton

**paid-in capital** The amount of capital contributed to a corporation by various transactions; the primary source of paid-in capital is from the issuance of shares of stock

**par (bonds)** Face value of the bond

**par value (stock)** An amount specified in the corporate charter for each share of stock and imprinted on the face of each stock certificate, often determines the legal capital of the corporation

**parent company** A company owning one or more subsidiary companies

**parsimonious method to multiyear forecasting** Forecasting multiple years using only sales growth, net operating profit margin (NOPM), and the turnover of net operating assets (NOAT)

**partnership** A voluntary association of two or more persons for the purpose of conducting a business

**password** A string of characters that a computer user enters into a computer terminal to prove to the computer that the person using the computer is truly the person named in the user identification code

**patent** An exclusive privilege granted for 20 years to an inventor that gives the patent holder the right to exclude others from making, using, or selling the invention

**payee** The company or individual to whom a promissory note is made payable

**payment approval form** A document that authorizes the payment of an invoice

**pension plan** A plan to pay benefits to employees after they retire from the company; the plan may be a defined contribution plan or a defined benefit plan

**percentage-of-completion method** Recognition of revenue by determining the costs incurred per the contract as compared to its total expected costs

**percentage of net sales method** A procedure that determines the uncollectible accounts expense for the year by multiplying net credit sales by the estimated uncollectible percentage

**period statement** A financial statement accumulating information for a specific period of time; examples are the income statement, the statement of owners' equity, and the statement of cash flows

**permanent account** An account used to prepare the balance sheet; that is, asset, liability, and equity capital (capital stock and retained earnings) accounts; any balance in a permanent account at the end of an accounting period is carried forward to the next period

**physical inventory** A year-end procedure that involves counting the quantity of each inventory item, determining the unit cost of each item, multiplying the unit cost times quantity, and summing the costs of all the items to determine the total inventory at cost

**plant assets** Land, buildings, equipment, vehicles, furniture, and fixtures that a firm uses in its operations; sometimes referred to by the acronym PPE

**pooling of interests method** A method of accounting for business combinations under which the acquired company is recorded on the acquirer's balance sheet at its book value, rather than market value; this method is no longer acceptable under GAAP for acquisitions occurring after 2001

**position statement** A financial statement, such as the balance sheet, that presents information as of a particular date

**post-closing trial balance** A list of general ledger accounts and their balances after closing entries have been recorded and posted

**postdated check** A check from another person or company with a date that is later than the current date; a postdated check does not become cash until the date of the check

**preemptive right** The right of a stockholder to maintain his or her proportionate interest in a corporation by having the right to purchase an appropriate share of any new stock issue

**preferred stock** A class of corporate capital stock typically receiving priority over common stock in dividend payments and distribution of assets should the corporation be liquidated

**premium bond** A bond that is sold for more than its par (face) value

**present value** The current worth of amounts to be paid (or received) in the future; computed by discounting the future payments (or receipts) at a specified interest rate

**price-earnings ratio** Current market price per common share divided by earnings per share

**pro forma income** A computation of income that begins with the GAAP income from continuing operations (that excludes discontinued operations, extraordinary items and changes in accounting principle), but then excludes other transitory items (most notably, restructuring charges), and some additional items such as expenses arising from acquisitions (goodwill amortization and other acquisition costs), compensation expense in the form of stock options, and research and development expenditures; pro forma income is not GAAP

**promissory note** A written promise to pay a certain sum of money on demand or at a determinable future time

**purchase method** The prescribed method of accounting for business combinations; under the purchase method, assets and liabilities of the acquired company are recorded at fair market value, together with identifiable intangible assets; the balance is ascribed to goodwill

**purchase order** A document that formally requests a supplier to sell and deliver specific quantities of particular items of merchandise at specified prices

**purchase requisition** An internal document that requests that the purchasing department order particular items of merchandise

# Q

**qualitative characteristics of accounting information** The characteristics of accounting information that contribute to decision usefulness; the primary qualities are relevance and reliability

**quarterly data** Selected quarterly financial information that is reported in annual reports to stockholders

**quick ratio** Quick assets (that is, cash and cash equivalents, short-term investments, and current receivables) divided by current liabilities

# R

**realized (or realizable)** When referring to revenue, the receipt of an asset or satisfaction of a liability as a result of a transaction or event

**recognition criteria** The criteria that must be met before a financial statement element may be recorded in the accounts; essentially, the item must meet the definition of an element and must be measurable

**registered bond** A bond for which the issuer (or the trustee) maintains a record of owners and, at the appropriate times, mails out interest payments

**relevance** A qualitative characteristic of accounting information; relevant information contributes to the predictive and evaluative decisions made by financial statement users

**reliability** A qualitative characteristic of accounting information; reliable information contains no bias or error and faithfully portrays what it intends to represent

**remeasurement** The computation of gain or loss in the translation of subsidiaries denominated in a foreign currency into $US when the temporal method is used

**residual operating income** Net operating profits after tax (NOPAT) less the product of net operating assets (NOA) at the beginning of the period multiplied by the weighted average cost of capital (WACC)

**residual net operating income (ROPI) model** An equity valuation approach that equates the firm's value to the sum of its net operating assets (NOA) and the present value of its residual operating income (ROPI)

**retailers** Companies that buy products from wholesale distributors and sell the products to individual customers, the general public

**retained earnings** Earned capital, the cumulative net income and loss, of the company (from its inception) that has not been paid to shareholders as dividends

**retained earnings reconciliation** The reconciliation of retained earnings from the beginning to the end of the year; the change in retained earnings includes, at a minimum, the net income (loss) for the period and dividends paid, if any, but may include other components as well; also called statement of retained earnings

**return** The amount earned on an investment; also called yield

**return on assets** A financial ratio computed as net income divided by average total assets; sometimes referred to by the acronym ROA

**return on common stockholders' equity** A financial ratio computed as net income less preferred stock dividends divided by average common stockholders' equity; sometimes referred to by the acronym ROCE

**return on equity** The ultimate measure of performance from the shareholders' perspective; computed as net income divided by average equity; sometimes referred to by the acronym ROE

**return on investment** The ratio obtained by dividing income by average investment; sometimes referred to by the acronym ROI

**return on net operating assets (RNOA)** The ratio obtained by dividing NOPAT by average net operating assets

**return on sales** The ratio obtained by dividing net income by net sales; sometimes referred to by the acronym ROS

**revenue recognition principle** An accounting principle requiring that revenue be recognized when earned and realized (or realizable)

**revenues** Increases in owners' equity a firm earns by providing goods or services for its customers

## S

**sale on account** A sale of merchandise made on a credit basis

**salvage value** The expected net recovery when a plant asset is sold or removed from service; also called residual value

**secured bond** A bond that pledges specific property as security for meeting the terms of the bond agreement

**Securities and Exchange Commission (SEC)** The commission, created by the 1934 Securities Act, that has broad powers to regulate the issuance and trading of securities, and the financial reporting of companies issuing securities to the public

**segments** Subdivisions of a firm for which supplemental financial information is disclosed

**serial bond** A bond issue that staggers the bond maturity dates over a series of years

**service cost (pensions)** The increase in the pension obligation due to employees working another year for the employer

**significant influence** The ability of the investor to affect the financing or operating policies of the investee

**sinking fund provision** A bond feature that requires the borrower to retire a portion of the bonds each year or, in some cases, to make payments each year to a trustee who is responsible for managing the resources needed to retire the bonds at maturity

**solvency** The ability to meet obligations, especially to creditors

**source document** Any written document or computer record evidencing an accounting transaction, such as a bank check or deposit slip, sales invoice, or cash register tape

**special purpose entity** (See variable interest entity)

**spin-off** A form of equity carve out in which divestiture is accomplished by distribution of a company's shares in a subsidiary to the company's shareholders who then own the shares in the subsidiary directly rather than through the parent company

**split-off** A form of equity carve out in which divestiture is accomplished by the parent company's exchange of stock in the subsidiary in return for shares in the parent owned by its shareholders

**spread** The difference between the net financial return (NFR) and the return on net operating activities (RNOA)

**stated value** A nominal amount that may be assigned to each share of no-par stock and accounted for much as if it were a par value

**statement of cash flows** A financial statement showing a firm's cash inflows and outflows for a specific period, classified into operating, investing, and financing categories

**statement of equity** See statement of stockholders' equity

**statement of financial position** A financial statement showing a firm's assets, liabilities, and owners' equity at a specific date; also called a balance sheet

**statement of owners' equity** A financial statement presenting information on the events causing a change in owners' equity during a period; the statement presents the beginning balance, additions to, deductions from, and the ending balance of owners' equity for the period

**statement of retained earnings** See retained earnings reconciliation

**statement of stockholders' equity** The financial statement that reconciles all of the components of stockholders' equity

**stock dividends** The payment of dividends in shares of stock

**stock split** Additional shares of its own stock issued by a corporation to its current stockholders in proportion to their current ownership interests without changing the balances in the related stockholders' equity accounts; a formal stock split increases the number of shares outstanding and reduces proportionately the stock's per share par value

**straight-line depreciation** A depreciation procedure that allocates uniform amounts of depreciation expense to each full period of a depreciable asset's useful life

**subsequent events** Events occurring shortly after a fiscal year-end that will be reported as supplemental information to the financial statements of the year just ended

**subsidiaries** Companies that are owned by the parent company

**subsidiary ledger** A set of accounts or records that contains detailed information about the items included in the balance of one general ledger account

**summary of significant accounting policies** A financial statement disclosure, usually the initial note to the statements, which identifies the major accounting policies and procedures used by the firm

**sum-of-the-years'-digits method** An accelerated depreciation method that allocates depreciation expense to each year in a fractional proportion, the denominator of which is the sum of the years' digits in the useful life of the asset and the numerator of which is the remaining useful life of the asset at the beginning of the current depreciation period

## T

**T account** An abbreviated form of the formal account in the shape of a T; use is usually limited to illustrations of accounting techniques and analysis

**temporary account** An account used to gather information for an accounting period; at the end of the period, the balance is transferred to a permanent owners' equity account; revenue, expense, and dividends accounts are temporary accounts

**term loan** A long-term borrowing, evidenced by a note payable, which is contracted with a single lender

**terminal period** The forecast period following the horizon period

**times interest earned ratio** Income before interest expense and income taxes divided by interest expense

**total compensation cost** The sum of gross pay, payroll taxes, and fringe benefits paid by the employer

**trade credit** Inventories purchased on credit from other companies

**trade discount** An amount, usually based on quantity of merchandise purchased, that the seller subtracts from the list price of merchandise to determine the invoice price

**trade name** An exclusive and continuing right to use a certain term or name to identify a brand or family of products

**trademark** An exclusive and continuing right to use a certain symbol to identify a brand or family of products

**trading on the equity** The use of borrowed funds in the capital structure of a firm; the expectation is that the funds will earn a return higher than the rate of interest on the borrowed funds

**trading securities** Investments in securities that management intends to actively trade (buy and sell) for trading profits as market prices fluctuate

**transitory items** Transactions or events that are not likely to recur

**translation adjustment** The change in the value of the net assets of a subsidiary whose assets and liabilities are denominated in a foreign currency

**treasury stock** Shares of outstanding stock that have been acquired (and not retired) by the issuing corporation; treasury stock is recorded at cost and deducted from stockholders' equity in the balance sheet

**trend percentages** A comparison of the same financial item over two or more years stated as a percentage of a base-year amount

**trial balance** A list of the account titles in the general ledger, their respective debit or credit balances, and the totals of the debit and credit amounts

## U

**unadjusted trial balance** A list of general ledger accounts and their balances taken before adjustments have been made

**uncollectible accounts expense** The expense stemming from the inability of a business to collect an amount previously recorded as a receivable; sometimes called bad debts expense; normally classified as a selling or administrative expense

**unearned revenue** A liability representing revenues received in advance; also called deferred revenue

**units-of-production method** A depreciation method that allocates depreciation expense to each operating period in proportion to the amount of the asset's expected total production capacity used each period

**useful life** The period of time an asset is used by an entity in its operating activities, running from date of acquisition to date of disposal (or removal from service)

## V

**variable costs** Those costs that change in proportion to changes in sales volume

**variable interest entity (VIE)** Any form of business organization (such as corporation, partnership, trust) that is established by a sponsoring company and provides benefits to that company in the form of asset securitization or project financing; VIEs were formerly known as special purpose entities (SPEs)

**vertical analysis** Analysis of a firm's financial statements that focuses on the statements of a single year

**voucher** Another name for the payment approval form

## W

**warranties** Guarantees against product defects for a designated period of time after sale

**wasting assets** Another name for natural resources; see natural resources

**weighted average cost of capital (WACC)** The discount rate where the weights are the relative percentages of debt and equity in the capital structure and are applied to the expected returns on debt and equity respectively

**work in process inventory** The cost of inventories that are in the manufacturing process and have not yet reached completion

**working capital** The difference between current assets and current liabilities

## Z

**z-score** The outcome of the Altman Z-score bankruptcy prediction model

**zero coupon bond** A bond that offers no periodic interest payments but that is issued at a substantial discount from its face value

# Index

# Financial Accounting for MBAs

"This is a fantastic book. It strikes the right balance between accounting details and user-oriented analysis. The students are going to love it."

"A very refreshing way of presenting the materials and up-to-date on the topics."

"A breath of fresh air—it is a text with a format and structure that breaks, a bit, from the traditional path followed by other financial accounting textbooks."

"There is a strong and consistent emphasis on managerial decision making. The use of actual financial statement data and detailed company profiles allows students to think concretely about the concepts being presented."

"This book uses real world examples to illustrate major accounting concepts; the illustrations are concise yet comprehensive."